Cases and Controversies

Cases and Controversies

Civil Rights and Liberties in Context

Peter Irons
University of California–San Diego

Upper Saddle River, New Jersey 07458

Library of Congress Cataloging-in-Publication Data

Irons, Peter H.
    Cases and controversies: civil rights and liberties in context/
Peter Irons.
        p. cm.
    ISBN 0-13-045624-1
    1. Civil rights—United States.   I. Title.

KF4749.I76 2005
342.7308'5—dc22

                                                    2004009572

Acquisitions Editor: Glenn Johnston
Director of Production and Manufacturing: Barbara Kittle
Project Management and Interior Design: Interactive Composition Corp.
Manufacturing Manager: Nick Sklitsis
Prepress and Manufacturing Buyer: Sherry Lewis
Cover Design: Bruce Kenselaar
Director of Marketing: Beth Mejia
Marketing Manager: Kara Kindstrom
Cover Image Specialist: Karen Sanatar
Cover Art: Stephan Daigle/Stock Illustration Source
Composition: Interactive Composition Corp.
Printer/Binder: Courier Companies, Inc.
Cover Printer: The Lehigh Press, Inc.
Text: 9.5/11 Palatino

Credits and acknowledgments borrowed from other sources and reproduced, with
permission, in this textbook appear on page 493, which constitutes an extension of
this copyright page.

Pearson Education LTD.
Pearson Education Singapore, Pte. Ltd
Pearson Education, Canada, Ltd
Pearson Education—Japan
Pearson Education Australia PTY, Limited
Pearson Education North Asia Ltd
Pearson Educación de Mexico, S.A. de C.V.
Pearson Education Malaysia, Pte. Ltd
Pearson Education, Upper Saddle River, New Jersey

10 9 8 7 6 5 4 3 2 1
ISBN 0-13-045624-1

Contents

CHAPTER 15: THE RIGHT TO DIE   465

APPENDIX A: UNITED STATES CONSTITUTION   481

APPENDIX B: JUSTICES OF THE SUPREME COURT   490

Acknowledgments

I WISH TO THANK THE FOLLOWING REVIEWERS FOR THEIR suggestions: Francis Carleton, University of Wisconsin–Green; Michael J. Horan, University of Wyoming; Dorothy B. James, Connecticut College; and Alex Landi, Spring Hill College.

Cases and Controversies

PART I

The Constitution, the Bill of Rights, and Judicial Review

CHAPTER 1

"To Form a More Perfect Union"

INTRODUCTION

Any study of constitutional law must begin with the Constitution. Many people, including some eminent legal scholars, approach the Constitution simply as a self-contained document, whose interpretation and application should be based solely on its text. Such constitutional "literalists" take an exceedingly narrow view of the Constitution and of the judicial function. One Supreme Court literalist, Justice Owen Roberts, wrote in a 1936 opinion that the only duty of a judge, in deciding whether a law violates the Constitution, was "to lay the article of the Constitution which is invoked beside the statute which is challenged and to decide whether the latter squares with the former." This mechanistic approach, which has been labeled the "T-square rule," begs the question of how judges can make these constitutional measurements with any precision and accuracy. Without any elaboration, Justice Roberts simply asserted that judges should provide their "considered judgment" to the issues raised by each case.

Fifty years after Justice Roberts wrote these words, another member of the Court, Justice William Brennan, advocated a very different approach to the judicial function. Brennan argued in 1986 that judges, in reading provisions of the Constitution, "must accept the ambiguity inherent in the effort to apply them to modern circumstances." He added: "We look to the history of the time of framing and to the intervening history of interpretation. But the ultimate question must be: What do the words of the text mean in our times? For the genius of the Constitution rests not in any static meaning it may have had in a world that is dead and gone but the adaptability of its great principles to cope with current problems and current needs."

The major difference between these divergent approaches to the Constitution lies in their view of that document as one whose interpretation is fixed and unchanging, as Roberts asserted, or whether its meaning is fluid and evolving, as Brennan argued. These perspectives, in turn, rest on contrasting views of history. For Roberts and those who share his literalist approach, the history of every constitutional provision ends with its ratification. Brennan and other advocates of a "living Constitution" see history more fully, as stretching from the time of the Framers until the present. The former view focuses on the "original intent" of those who framed each provision, whether of the original Constitution or its amendments. Those Framers, of course, lived in a country that was considerably different—in population, diversity, technology, and culture—from the United States in the twenty-first century. Justice Brennan and those who share his approach do not ignore the intent of the Framers, but they recognize that these men were products of very different times. Proponents of a "living Constitution" pay heed to the prophetic words of Chief Justice John Marshall, who wrote in 1819 that the Constitution was "intended to endure for ages to come, and to be adapted to the various crises of human affairs."

Some of the crises to which Marshall referred were evident at the time he wrote. The institution of human slavery, the nation's expansion in area and population, conflicts between the rich and poor—all divided the country and gave rise to landmark Supreme Court decisions. Over the succeeding years, such crises as wartime protest and hysteria, the Great Depression, and conflicts over issues such as abortion have presented the Court with new challenges and have produced more landmark decisions.

How the Constitution has been adapted to the American crises that raise issues of civil right and liberties, through Supreme Court decisions in these areas, is the subject of this book. My approach, as editor, is to locate each landmark case within a broader historical, social, and cultural context. In the task of selecting both the cases and supplementary material, I have looked at constitutional law as a story, one with many chapters, fascinating characters, and fundamental divisions of interest and values. Much of the material in this book is designed to introduce readers to the people involved in the cases, people such as Dred Scott, Homer Plessy, Lillian Gobitis, Gordon Hirabayashi, Mary Beth Tinker, and Michael Hardwick. Their stories add human faces and voices to the Supreme Court opinions that often treat them simply as names. I have also selected material that offers the divergent views of commentators and partisans on both sides of the issues raised in the cases. This approach, I hope, will allow readers to see the cases as chapters in the sprawling, and often contradictory, story of American constitutional law.

I begin this story at the beginning, with the framing and ratification of the original Constitution and the Bill of Rights. The following sections of this chapter include excerpts of my book, *A People's History of the Supreme Court,* that offer detail and flavor to a period in American history that is "dead and gone" but whose conflicts—over such crises as slavery and free speech and press—are very much alive in our society today.

Appended to this chapter are excerpts from "Federalist No. 78," in which Alexander Hamilton discusses the role of the Supreme Court in the federal system proposed in the Constitution. He argues both that the Court would have the power to interpret and apply the Constitution, which has "the superior obligation" over legislative acts, and that the Court would be "the least dangerous branch" of government. Hamilton's defense of judicial power has proven the accuracy of his first observation, while critics of the Court have decried the eagerness of unelected judges to thwart the legislative will.

SECTION 1

FRAMING THE CONSTITUTION

On May 14, 1787, a dozen men gathered at the red-brick State House in Philadelphia, Pennsylvania. This was the same building in which another group of men assembled in 1776 and signed a Declaration of Independence that set in motion the revolution against English rule. Seven years of war had sapped the strength and resolve of British troops and their military and political leaders, and the rebellious American colonies won their independence in 1783. But the victorious revolutionaries, united in their rejection of English "tyranny," had not united to replace the thirteen colonies with a new nation. All they had accomplished was to form a "confederation" of thirteen sovereign states, each one jealous of its prerogatives and unwilling to relinquish any of its powers to a national government.

The men who gathered at the State House in 1787 were keenly aware of the failure of the Articles of Confederation, which had been ratified in 1781, to bind the thirteen states into a workable union. The "United States" of the Confederation were anything but united. The Articles did nothing more than establish "a firm league of friendship" among the states. But in the six years since they formed this league, the states had acted in decidedly unfriendly ways toward one another. They fought over trade and commerce, over recognition of their separate currencies, over boundaries between the states, over the creation of new states in the burgeoning western territories. In short, they acted more like quarreling European principalities than like "united states" with common purposes. The Confederation had been created in reaction to the arbitrary rule of a powerful government, but the men who drafted and ratified the Articles of Confederation erred in the opposite direction: the government they designed was weak, divided, and unable to resolve conflicts between warring interests and regions.

The flaws in the Articles were built into the governmental structure they created. Each state retained "its sovereignty, freedom and independence, and every power, jurisdiction, and right, which is not by this Confederation expressly delegated to the United States, in Congress assembled." The only powers that the drafters had delegated to the Confederation Congress were those to conduct foreign affairs, make treaties, and declare war. These were powers that no individual state could exercise by itself, although political leaders in each state continued to squabble over the ways in which Congress conducted the nation's foreign affairs. Congress itself was an ineffective governing body. Members did not vote by themselves; each state had one vote, and nine of the thirteen states had to agree on each piece of legislation. The drafters of the Articles, determined to avoid lodging power in a single executive, created instead a president of Congress, who had no power to enforce the laws passed by its members. No state, in fact, was required to abide by the decisions of Congress; they were, in effect, merely advisory, and states often rejected that advice. The Articles also did not provide for a national judiciary; there was no body to adjudicate conflicts between states or citizens of different states. The drafters, in understandable reaction to the tyrannical rule against which they revolted, had replaced one of the strongest governments in the Western world with one of the weakest.

Well before the 1787 meeting in Philadelphia, leaders of the emerging "Federalist" bloc in politics began to criticize the ineffective Confederation and to call for revision of the Articles. Noah Webster, who had served in the revolutionary army and who was a lawyer as well as a lexicographer, wrote in 1785: "So long as any individual state has power to defeat the measures of the other twelve, our pretended union is but a name, and our confederation, a cobweb." John Jay, who later served as the first Chief Justice of the United States, expressed his fears of disunion to George Washington: "Our affairs seem to lead to some crisis, some revolution—something I cannot see or conjecture. I am uneasy and apprehensive; moreso than during the war." Whatever their concerns about the deficiencies of the Confederation, however, few men of stature wanted to scrap the Articles entirely; most agreed with Benjamin Franklin, widely admired for his wit and wisdom, that "we discover some errors in our general and particular constitutions; which it is no wonder they should have, the time in which they were formed being considered. But these we shall mend."

Despite Franklin's optimism, "mending" the Articles would not be an easy task. First, all thirteen states had to agree on any amendment of the Articles. The prospects for unanimous agreement on any proposal to expand the powers of Congress or to create executive or judicial branches of government were slim. Second, the interests of the separate states, divided by geography along northern and southern lines and by population into larger and smaller, had diverged so rapidly since the Articles were ratified that further division seemed more likely than unification. Few men, however, saw much harm in meeting to discuss possible revisions of the Articles; unanimity might be forged on proposals to "mend" those parts that most leaders thought amenable to minor revision. There were, to be sure, men in various states who desired a strong "federal" government, but they were by no means a majority in numbers or influence. Between 1785 and 1787, those who advocated a convention to revise the Articles of Confederation assured skeptics that they had no larger agenda than tinkering and talk.

As the weaknesses of the Articles became more evident, and as pressure built for a convention to revise them, one of the oldest laws of politics began to operate. Those who are most satisfied with the status quo, which in the Confederation era meant those who felt that the states should remain "sovereign" and only loosely federated, generally sit back and let the "hotheads" blow off steam. Conversely, those who desire rapid and radical change often conceal their designs behind clouds of soothing rhetoric, until they feel confident that they can control events. This law operated perfectly in 1787. James Madison, the scholarly young Virginian whose designs would powerfully shape both the new Constitution and the Bill of Rights that followed its ratification, shared his real views with his friend and fellow Virginian George Washington: "Temporizing applications will dishonor the Councils which propose them, and may foment the internal malignity of the disease. . . . Radical attempts, though unsuccessful, will at least justify the authors of them." But Madison wrote in disarming words to Edmund Randolph, Virginia's governor and an opponent of any major alteration of the Articles: "I think with you that it will be well to retain as much as possible of the old Confederation, though I doubt whether it may not be best to work the valuable articles into the new system, instead of engrafting the latter on the former."

James Madison had begun hatching plans for a new constitution long before he arrived in Philadelphia in May 1787. Born in 1751, the eldest of ten children, Madison grew up on a Virginia plantation whose fields were plowed and planted by slaves. From early childhood, he buried himself in books and relished talk of philosophy and public affairs. Madison's father sent him north for an education at the College of New Jersey, later known as Princeton. Here the young scholar came under the tutelage of John Witherspoon, a Presbyterian minister who drilled his students in the writings of David Hume, the Scottish philosopher who argued for the "utilitarian" principle of promoting "the greatest good for the greatest number." Witherspoon also preached against slavery in passionate sermons; Madison later echoed his teacher in the Philadelphia convention when he denounced slavery as "the most oppressive dominion ever exercised by man over man." He also told the delegates that he "thought

it wrong to admit in the Constitution the idea that there could be property in men." But the "utility" of the Constitution outweighed his personal moral views, and Madison signed a document that recognized slavery as a lawful institution.

* * *

Madison was the first delegate to arrive in Philadelphia for the meeting to "devise" alterations to the Articles of Confederation. During the preceding months, he had buried himself in books, reading widely in political philosophy and histories of republics and confederacies from ancient Greece to the current states of Europe, with special attention to the Swiss Confederation of independent cantons and the United Provinces of the Netherlands. Madison filled one notebook with his gleanings on the topic "Of Ancient and Modern Confederacies" and another with a list of the "Vices of the Political System of the United States." Not a single delegate arrived in Philadelphia after Madison who matched him in knowledge of the world's governments and constitutions or with equal determination to frame a new system that would forge the disunited states of America into a real federal union, one with powers "adequate to the exigencies of the Union."

Madison not only had ideas about the new system he envisioned, but he had a plan. While delegates from other states were trickling into Philadelphia, Madison shared his plan with Washington, who arrived a few days later. Determined to create a strong national government, but also aware that the states would not willingly cede their cherished "sovereignty" over their own affairs, Madison wrote to Washington: "I have sought for some middle ground, which may at once support a due supremacy of the national authority, and not exclude the local authorities wherever they can be subordinately useful." Both the sentence structure and choice of words left no doubt of Madison's views on the primacy of federal power. He underscored this position in telling Washington that his plan would invest the federal government "with positive and complete authority in all cases which require uniformity; such as the regulation of trade, including the right of taxing both exports and imports." Madison then confided to Washington that his plan would place, "over and above this positive power, a negative in all cases whatsoever on the legislative acts of the states. . . . Without this defensive power, every positive power that can be given on paper will be evaded and defeated." This was a radical—even revolutionary—proposal that would in effect reduce the "sovereign" states to a subordinate role in the new federal system.

The convention resolution of the Virginia legislature had set a quorum of seven states to begin deliberations. Eleven days passed between the opening session on May 14 and the first official session on May 25, when the quorum was finally met with twenty-nine delegates from seven states in attendance. During this time, Madison met almost daily with his fellow Virginians, whose seven members formed the largest delegation. He circulated among them copies of the fourteen points in his plan for a new government. His first, and most delicate, task was to convince Edmund Randolph, the powerful and persuasive Virginia governor, to set aside his objections to a new constitution. Madison won Randolph over with a brilliant strategem, allowing him to add to the "Virginia Plan" a fifteenth resolution, elevated to first place above Madison's fourteen. Randolph proposed, and Madison accepted, a resolution that "the Articles of Confederation ought to be so corrected and enlarged as to accomplish the objects proposed by their institution, namely, 'common defense, security of liberty and general welfare.'" This was decidedly *not* what Madison had in mind, but he viewed Randolph's resolution as harmless and his support of the other fourteen as essential.

With that strategic concession in hand, Madison prevailed on Randolph to introduce the Virginia Plan as soon as the convention elected officers and adopted rules. On May 25, the delegates unanimously elected George Washington as the presiding officer, and he took his seat in a high-backed mahogany chair behind a table covered in green baize. Washington assumed a tone of humility in telling the delegates that he "lamented his want of better qualifications, and claimed the indulgence of the House towards the involuntary errors which his inexperience might occasion."

Edmund Randolph's opening speech on the Virginia Plan, delivered with the gestures and flourishes of the practiced orator, first enumerated "the defects of the confederation" and of its Articles; he later played an active role in drafting what he described as a "fundamental constitution" to replace the Articles; and he finally refused to sign the document that emerged from the convention's four months of deliberation.

The Virginia Plan that Randolph presented to the convention drew upon Madison's exhaustive study of other governments, and his conviction that a strong federal system required a dispersal of power among several branches, to avoid both the "monarchical" tendencies of unchecked executive power and the "instability" of governments based on legislative supremacy. Madison proposed, and Randolph presented, a system that included a "National Legislature" of two houses, one "elected by the people of the several states," the other chosen by the elected members of the first house from "persons nominated by the individual legislatures" of each state. The Virginia Plan also called for a "National Executive" with "a general authority to execute the national laws," and a "National Judiciary" to consist of "one or more supreme tribunals, and of inferior tribunals to be chosen by the National Legislature," with a jurisdiction that included "piracies and felonies on the high seas, captures from an enemy; cases in which foreigners or citizens of other states applying to such jurisdictions may be interested, or which respect the collection of the National revenue; impeachments of any National officers, and questions which may involve the national peace and harmony." The Virginia Plan included many features of the Constitution that the delegates later adopted and the states ratified, including a two-house legislature, a "national executive," and a federal judiciary. The principle of "checks and balances" among the branches of the national government reflected Madison's studies of the deficiencies of governments that lodged power in either legislative bodies or executive officers.

* * *

Debates in the Philadelphia convention did not proceed in any orderly or logical fashion, such as beginning with the structure and powers of the Congress, moving to the executive branch, and finally to the federal judiciary. The delegates instead jumped back and forth, debating motions as they were made, setting up committees to refine proposals and report back when they were ready, voting for motions one day and against them the next. The convention lacked a steering committee, or anything like the Rules Committee in the House of Representatives. There were no formal "parties" or party leaders. Delegates asked for the floor to introduce motions or to speak whenever they wished, on whatever subject they pleased. Because of this formless structure, the convention discussed the powers of Congress well before it decided on election procedures, the size of each house, or methods of representation.

The first debate on the powers of Congress took place on May 31, near the end of a long day of long speeches on how members of each house should be chosen. The delegates then moved to Edmund Randolph's proposal in the Virginia Plan—which was really Madison's plan—that Congress should have power "to legislate in all cases to which the separate states were incompetent." The debate on this proposal was surprisingly brief. It was also surprising—to those delegates who did not know of Madison's hand in the Virginia Plan—that Randolph spoke vigorously against his own proposal. He "disclaimed any intention to give indefinite powers to the national legislature, declaring that he was entirely opposed to such an inroad on the state jurisdictions, and that he did not think any considerations whatever could ever change his determination." Madison recorded Randolph's emphatic conclusion: "His opinion was fixed on this point."

As soon as Randolph took his seat, Madison put down his pen and took the floor to answer his fellow Virginian. He told the delegates that "he had brought with him into the convention a strong bias in favor of an enumeration and definition of the powers necessary to be exercised by the national legislature; but also brought doubts concerning its practicability. His wishes remained unaltered; but his doubts had become stronger. What his opinion might ultimately be he could not tell. But he should shrink from nothing which should be found essential to such a form of government as would provide for the safety, liberty and happiness of the community. This being the end of all our deliberations, all the necessary means for attaining it must, however reluctantly, be submitted to." After these heartfelt words, all but one state delegation—Connecticut was divided on the question—voted for the proposal Randolph had made and then opposed. On this issue, Randolph could not sway even his own delegation.

Madison's admission of "doubts" that the Constitution should include an enumeration of congressional powers may have been sincere, but he later gave in to his "wishes" and pressed the convention for a detailed listing of these powers. The delegates spent several steamy days in August debating proposals on congressional powers from the Committee on Detail—whose name aptly described its function—and motions by individual delegates. Many of these motions were to add or delete just one word or phrase, although sometimes adding or deleting a few words made a considerable change in the meaning of a constitutional provision. For example, when the delegates considered the provision of the Virginia Plan that limited the grounds for impeaching the president to "treason and bribery," George

Mason of Virginia proposed adding the word "maladministration" after "bribery." Madison promptly objected. "So vague a term will be equivalent to a tenure during pleasure of the Senate," he complained. Mason thought for a moment, and then suggested the phrase "other high crimes and misdemeanors" as a substitute. By a vote of eight to three, with no recorded discussion, the state delegations agreed. Almost two centuries later, Richard Nixon resigned as president in 1974 to avoid certain impeachment, and Bill Clinton survived an impeachment trial in 1999 for "high crimes and misdemeanors" whose definition the Framers never discussed. The brief colloquy between Mason and Madison is the entirety of the Framers' "original intent" on this crucial provision.

When the delegates finally agreed to an "enumeration" of congressional powers, they debated for several days before agreeing on a listing, which became Section 8 of Article I in the Constitution. Many of the eighteen grants of power were narrow and specific: Congress was authorized to "establish post offices and post roads," to "fix the standards of weights and measures," and to "grant letters of marque and reprisal" for the arming of ships to capture enemy cargo in wartime. Others were broad and momentous: Congress was empowered to "lay and collect taxes" in order to "provide for the common defense and general welfare of the United States," to "borrow money on the credit of the United States," to "regulate commerce with foreign nations, and among the several states," and—after much debate over the respective powers of Congress and the president—to "declare war." On this last point, Madison and Elbridge Gerry—who differed on almost everything else, including support for the final Constitution—joined in a motion to change the wording of the Committee on Detail, which had proposed granting Congress the power to "make war," to the more limited power to "declare war." Gerry spoke for both men in stating that he "never expected to hear in a republic a motion to empower the Executive alone to declare war."

*   *   *

The most divisive issue in the convention, even more than the powers of Congress, arose from the great disparities in population between the large and the small states. The question resolved around representation in the two houses of Congress. One group of delegates pressed for proportional representation in both houses, based on the total population of each state. Another faction argued strenuously that representation in both houses should be based on a combination of population and "wealth," which became a euphemism in convention debates for slaves. A third group, largely but not exclusively from the smaller states, agreed with representation by population in the lower houses, but insisted that each state deserved equal representation in the Senate. Over the course of the summer, the heat of debate on these issues often matched the broiling temperatures in the convention chamber.

The question of representation in Congress, or any legislative body, can be argued from differing principles of political philosophy. Radical democrats are generally loath to allow any deviation from the "one person, one vote" standard in every lawmaking body. Those of more "aristocratic" or elitist leanings are suspicious of popular government and advocate the allocation of legislative seats on such bases as geographic area—counting acres rather than voters—or interests such as farming, logging, or mining. Other issues often lurk in the background when these conflicting positions are debated. During the Philadelphia convention of 1787, the real division was not between democrats and aristocrats, between delegates from rural or urban areas, or even between those from large or small states. The real issue was slavery.

James Madison, perhaps more than any other delegate, understood the positions of each group and worked diligently to forge a workable compromise. His political philosophy, shaped by John Witherspoon at Princeton, and his own temperament as a compassionate person, combined to make Madison an advocate of radical democracy. On the other hand, as the son of a planter and slave owner from Virginia, he knew that delegates from states large in the "wealth" of slaves would insist that their interests be protected in Congress. Madison was also determined that the Philadelphia convention not end without agreement on a Constitution that established and empowered a strong national government. From these differing perspectives, and with his ultimate goal in mind, he sensed—from one day to the next—the shifting coalitions on the question of congressional representation and tried to maneuver each side toward the "Great Compromise" that finally broke the impasse on this issue.

Madison first urged compromise on July 9, after William Paterson of New Jersey had urged that each state have just one vote in the Senate. Paterson had earlier introduced a plan for a national government that called for modest revisions in the Articles of Confederation and the retention of sovereignty in each state. Madison considered the New Jersey Plan, as it came to be called, as the most serious threat to his Virginia Plan, and he considered Paterson a formidable rival in the convention. Both men were Princeton graduates, but Paterson epitomized the elitism that Madison deplored; he wrote favorably of the "good breeding" that produced the "true gentlemen" who were best fitted to govern the masses. Paterson had no deep-rooted objection to slavery, but he appealed to its opponents in seeking to maintain the powers of the smaller states. Madison recorded Paterson as stating that "he could regard negro slaves in no light but as property. They have no free agents, have no personal liberty, no faculty of acquiring property, but on the contrary are themselves property, and like other property entirely at the will of the master."

Paterson made these remarks as matters of fact, with no moral judgment attached. He went on to pose a rhetorical question about representation in state legislatures: "Has a man in Virginia a number of votes in proportion to the number of his slaves?" The answer was obvious: he did not. "And if Negroes are not represented in the states to which they belong," Paterson continued, "why should they be represented in the general government?" His point was clear, but his purpose was devious. Paterson sounded like a true democrat when he asked another rhetorical question: "What is the true principle of representation?" He answered that it was based on "the expedient" of choosing a small number of representatives "in place of the inconvenient meeting of the people themselves." Paterson had only disdain for "the people" themselves—at least those without property—but he wanted to prevent states with small white populations but large numbers of slaves, such as Georgia and South Carolina, from outvoting states like New Jersey and New Hampshire in the federal Congress.

Sensing the dangerous appeal of Paterson's words, Madison felt compelled to respond on the spot. His purpose—keeping the large and small states together in the Congress—was clear, but his words were devious. Madison first "reminded Mr. Paterson that his doctrine of representation which was in its principle the genuine one, must forever silence the pretensions of the small states to an equality of votes with the larger ones." He turned Paterson's democratic pretensions against him. The states should vote in Congress "in the same proportion in which their citizens would do, if the people of all the states were collectively met." But principle gave way to practicality as Madison "suggested as a proper ground of compromise, that in the first branch the states should be represented according to their number of free inhabitants; and in the second, which had for one of its primary objects the guardianship of property, according to the whole number, including slaves."

This first effort at compromise did not succeed, for Madison had misjudged the determination of Paterson and his allies in the small northern states to prevent the southern states—with equally small white populations—from outvoting them in Congress. Following Madison's speech, the delegates voted to refer the question of representation to a committee on which each state had a member. This group, called the Committee of Eleven, replaced the Committee of Five, which the delegates had earlier set up to propose a representation plan. The numbers game on this question illustrated the intransigence on both sides: no committee—however small or large—could fashion a compromise that would satisfy a majority of the state delegations. When the Committee of Eleven reported back on July 10, the delegates spent most of the day haggling over whether New Hampshire should have two or three representatives in the House.

After this contentious session, Hugh Williamson of South Carolina—who had spoken very little on any issue—presented his own compromise, offering a choice between those who wanted to count all inhabitants in apportioning House seats and those who wanted to count only whites. Williamson was a man of moderation, drawn to compromise rather than confrontation. He moved that, "a census shall be taken of the free white inhabitants and three fifths of those of other descriptions" and that "representation be regulated accordingly."

Williamson's proposal had the advantage of seeming a reasonable position between two extremes. Pierce Butler and Charles Cotesworth Pinckney of South Carolina, adamant defenders of slavery, promptly "insisted that blacks be included in the rule of representation, equally with the whites," and moved to strike the words "three fifths" from Williamson's motion. Butler argued that "the labor of a slave in South Carolina was as productive and valuable as that of a freeman in Massachusetts" and that "an equal representation ought to be allowed for them in a government which was instituted principally for the protection of property, and was itself to be supported by property." But only two other states voted with the South Carolinians on this motion.

On the other side, those who argued against proposals to count slaves did so not on moral grounds but simply from expedience. Roger Sherman of Connecticut "thought the number of people alone the best rule" for representation, but he opened the door for compromise by endorsing Edmund Randolph's proposal that some ratio between all or none "ought to be fixed by the Constitution." Rufus King of Massachusetts voiced the sentiments of many delegates who simply wanted to settle the issue and move on to other questions. He found "great force" in the objections of Gouverneur Morris of Pennsylvania, the most insistent opponent of compromise on slavery, but he would vote for Williamson's motion "for the sake of doing something." The debate on representation became complicated by disputes over the number of years between each census; Madison's motion to add the words "at least" after "15 years" was defeated on a tie vote. By the day's end the delegates were so testy that Williamson's "three fifths" motion, weighted down with amendments, was rejected by every state.

What seemed to many weary delegates as the death knell for compromise spurred others to redouble their efforts. After a weekend of private meetings and caucuses, the delegates returned to the State House on Monday, July 16, ready to vote on what soon came to be called the Great Compromise. Over the previous week, debate on the representation issue made clear that the small states would rather bolt from the convention than agree to proportional representation in the Senate. The southern states were also adamant that slaves be counted, either equally with whites or in some substantial ratio, in apportioning House seats. Pierce Butler of South Carolina told the convention that "the security the southern states want is that their Negroes may not be taken from them, which some gentlemen within or without doors, have a very good mind to do." He was answered by James Wilson of Pennsylvania, who proclaimed that "all men wherever placed have equal rights" and that "he could not agree that property was the sole or the primary object of government and society."

James Madison made one last appeal for his principle of population as the basis of representation in the session on Saturday, July 14. He "expressed his apprehensions that if the proper foundation of government was destroyed, by substituting an equality in place of a proportional representation, no proper superstructure would be raised." His last-ditch effort at a compromise that would satisfy him was the proposition that "In all cases where the general government is to act on the people, let the people be represented and the votes be proportional. In all cases where the government is to act on the states as such, in like manner as Congress now act on them, let the states be represented and the votes be equal. This was the true ground of compromise if there was any ground at all." But Madison then retreated to his principle and "denied that there was any ground" for compromise.

Madison's words became increasingly sharp and bitter. He challenged his opponents to show "a single instance in which the general government was not to operate on the people individually." He leveled a veiled insult at Delaware, whose five delegates outnumbered both Massachusetts and New York. "No one would say that either in Congress or out of Congress Delaware had equal weight with Pennsylvania," Madison said. He repeated his earlier disquisition on the

Dutch confederacy, and then outlined five objections to equality of states in the Senate, arguing that small states "could extort measures" from the larger states and frustrate "the will of the majority of the people." He finally lashed out at the southern states as the fomenters of discord and division. "It seemed now to be pretty well understood," Madison said, "that the real difference of interest lay, not between the large and small but between the northern and southern states. The institution of slavery and its consequences formed the line of discrimination." Giving the slave states extra weight in Congress by counting, even at three fifths, persons who were barred from voting struck Madison as unjust, on both moral and practical grounds.

Madison used strong words in the Saturday session. By Monday morning, the battle was over. The Great Compromise, allowing the southern states to count slaves as three fifths of a person for House seats and providing for equal votes for each state in the Senate, was adopted without further debate. Four of the small states—Connecticut, New Jersey, Delaware, and Maryland—found an ally in North Carolina, a large state in population but also a slave state. These five states outvoted Pennsylvania, Virginia, South Carolina, and Georgia. Four of the thirteen states in the Confederation were divided or did not vote. The four delegates from Massachusetts were split, two on each side; Rhode Island did not send delegates to Philadelphia; and New York and New Hampshire each lacked a quorum. Based on the white population, states with less than one third of the total population prevailed over those with two thirds. The outcome was hardly a ringing endorsement of democracy; in fact, it represented a victory for slavery, aristocracy, and elitism. But the rules of the convention had been followed, and five was a larger number than four.

Edmund Randolph was the first to speak after this momentous decision. He voiced the concerns of those from the larger states who felt the closeness of the vote robbed the convention of legitimacy. "The vote of this morning had embarrassed the business extremely," he began. Randolph then spoke of the Constitution the delegates had assembled in Philadelphia to draft. "It will probably be in vain to come to any final decision with a bare majority on either side." He proposed that the convention adjourn, "that the large states might consider the steps proper to be taken in the present solemn crisis of the business, and that the small states might also deliberate on the means of conciliation."

William Paterson of New Jersey, who had opposed counting slaves in any representation plan but whose delegation had voted for the Great Compromise, took Randolph's remarks a step further. He thought "it was high time for the convention to adjourn, that the rule of secrecy ought to be rescinded, and that our constituents should be consulted." Paterson challenged Randolph to move for adjournment "sine die"—that is, without specifying a day to reconvene—which would have ended the convention for good. Randolph replied that he had not proposed an indefinite adjournment and "was sorry that his meaning had been so readily and strangely misinterpreted." John Rutledge of South Carolina did not wish to "abandon everything to hazard" and wanted to proceed. He was adamant on this issue. "The little states were fixed," he said. "All that the large states then had to do, was to decide whether they would yield or not."

And yield they did. The delegates voted to adjourn until the next day. That morning, before the convention resumed, Madison attended a meeting of delegates from several states—large and small—to discuss the seeming impasse. "The time was wasted in vague conversation," he noted, "without any specific proposition or agreement." Some delegates from large states held firm against the Great Compromise, but others "seemed inclined to yield to the smaller states" and move on. When the delegates met on July 17 in the State House, the battle was over. Counting slaves as "three fifths" of a person for House seats and providing equal votes for each state in the Senate were now parts of the Constitution.

Flushed with victory, the slave states pressed for even greater protection of their "property" in fellow humans. Before the convention ended, they succeeded in securing two additional provisions. Pierce Butler and Charles Cotesworth Pinckney of South Carolina moved on August 28 "to require fugitive slaves and servants to be delivered up like criminals." Roger Sherman of Connecticut objected that he "saw no more propriety in the public seizing and surrendering a slave or servant, than a horse." The South Carolinians withdrew their motion and came back the next day with a longer, more detailed motion providing that—even in free states—fugitive slaves "shall be delivered up to the person justly claiming their service or labor." The delegates agreed to this provision by voice vote, with no recorded debate. The final version in the Constitution, polished by the Committee on Style, differed only slightly in wording and was adopted once more without debate.

The third provision about slavery did provoke debate, much of it heated. Luther Martin of Maryland, himself the owner of "domestic" slaves as household help, moved on August 21 that Congress be allowed to prohibit the further importation of slaves. He argued that slavery "weakened one part of the Union which the other parts were bound to protect: the privilege of importing them was therefore unreasonable." He also objected that slavery "was inconsistent with the principles of the Revolution and dishonorable to the American character to have such a feature in the Constitution." John Rutledge of South Carolina immediately responded for the slave states. "Religion and humanity had nothing to do with this question," he said dismissively. "Interest alone is the governing principle with nations." He felt that "If the northern states consult their interest, they will not oppose the increase of slaves which will increase the commodities of which they will become the carriers." Rutledge issued an implied threat, reminding Martin that the convention had not yet adopted a Constitution and that the "true question" was whether the slave states "shall or shall not be parties to the Union."

The debate over slavery consumed most of the next day. Roger Sherman of Connecticut "disapproved of the slave trade" but found it "expedient to have as few objections as possible" to the Constitution. He proposed allowing the southern states to continue importing slaves and "urged on the convention the necessity of dispatching its business." Sherman wanted to move on to such pressing issues as the number of days each house of Congress could adjourn without consent from the other. George Mason, the Virginia radical, jumped to his feet and answered Sherman with indignation. Despite being a slave owner himself, he denounced the "infernal traffic" in slaves and rebuked those northern states that allowed a "lust of gain" from commerce to cloud their moral vision. Mason added that "the judgement of heaven" fell on countries that allowed the "nefarious traffic" in slaves. "As nations cannot be rewarded or punished in the next world they must be in this," he continued. "By an inevitable chain of causes and effects providence punishes national sins, by national calamities." Mason spoke like an Old Testament prophet, but his fellow delegates did not "incline their ear" to his words, as Jeremiah had lamented of those who ignored his prophecy that "the land will become a ruin" if they did not repent "the evil of their ways."

Oliver Ellsworth of Connecticut was deaf to moral appeals. "Let us not intermeddle," he replied to Mason, and "be unjust" toward the states whose commerce depended on slavery. Delegates from the slave states warned those who would prohibit further importation that intransigence on this question would imperil the Constitution. "If the convention thinks," said John Rutledge, that the slave states "will ever agree to the plan, unless their right to import slaves be untouched, the expectation is vain. The people of those states will never be such fools as to give up so important an interest."

Despite the southern threats, enough delegates voiced support for allowing Congress to ban the slave trade that both sides agreed with the proposal of Gouverneur Morris of Pennsylvania that the issue be sent to a committee that "may form a bargain among the northern and southern states." The committee returned on August 24 with a bargain in hand: Congress would be allowed to prohibit the importation of slaves, but could not exercise this power before 1800, thirteen years later. When the delegates reached this provision the next day, Charles Cotesworth Pinckney of South Carolina moved to extend the time to 1808. James Madison was the only voice in opposition. "Twenty years will produce all the mischief that can be apprehended from the liberty to import slaves," he warned. "So long a term will be more dishonorable to the national character than to say nothing about it in the Constitution." The delegates ignored Madison's counsel and adopted the provision with Pinckney's amendment.

Slavery was not the only issue that divided the delegates in Philadelphia. But there was, in retrospect, no issue that more affected the Union over the next two centuries—and into the next millennium—than slavery and its legacy in racial segregation and discrimination. Every branch of the government the delegates fashioned in Philadelphia—Congress, the executive, and the judiciary—has struggled to resolve the conflicts that stemmed from the Great Compromise in 1787. Those who praise the Framers as farsighted statesmen and champions of democracy tend to ignore or brush aside the slavery provisions of the Constitution. Not one delegate refused to sign the document because of moral objections to these provisions. And, as George Mason had warned, national sins were punished by national calamities.

* * *

The adoption of the Great Compromise by delegates to the Philadelphia convention in 1787, with its legitimation of slavery in the Constitution, did not end debate over other contentious issues. Divisions over the structure of Congress, how members of the House and Senate would be elected, and what powers they could exercise largely reflected conflicts between larger and smaller states, compounded by the demands of states—both small and large—whose "wealth" depended on slavery. Even while debate continued over the provisions of what finally became Article I of the Constitution, vesting "all legislative powers" in Congress, the delegates argued over the structure and powers of the executive and judicial branches of the national government.

The Virginia Plan, drafted by James Madison, provided for a "national executive" with "general authority to execute the national laws" and for a "national judiciary" with jurisdiction over "questions which may involve the national peace and harmony." More questions were raised than answered by Madison's proposals for these two branches of government. Madison himself, who prepared for the convention with months of reading on different forms of government, had no inflexible positions on how to choose executive and judicial officers, what powers they should wield in their respective spheres, and their relations with Congress. In his first speech to the convention on "executive authority," delivered on June 1, Madison professed doubt in deciding whether that department should be "administered by one or more persons." He then proposed that executive officers, in addition to their authority to "carry into effect the national laws," also exercise "such other powers" which were "not legislative nor judiciary in their nature." Madison's remarks added nothing of substance to the vague contours of his plan.

The convention first took up the question of executive power on June 1, in an atmosphere of gravity and anticipation. The session opened with a motion by James Wilson of Pennsylvania that "the executive consist of a single person." Madison recorded in his *Notes* that a "considerable pause" followed the motion, as delegates hesitated to commit themselves on this issue. Benjamin Franklin, who had been assisted to his special chair to attend a session he considered vital, finally broke the silence. Franklin "observed that it was a point of great importance and wished that the gentlemen would deliver their sentiments on it" before they voted. John Rutledge of South Carolina obliged the elder statesman. He spoke of the "shyness of gentlemen" on this question, suggesting that delegates who, "having frankly disclosed their opinions" on choosing the executive, might feel precluded from "afterwards changing them." Rutledge supported "vesting the executive power in a single person, though he was not for giving him the power of war and peace."

During the debate that followed Rutledge's speech, Edmund Randolph of Virginia—himself the chief executive of a large and powerful state—chafed in his seat and finally jumped to his feet. Randolph "strenuously opposed a unity in the executive magistracy," Madison reported. "He regarded it as the fetus of monarchy." Randolph "could not see why the great requisites for the executive department, vigor, despatch, and responsibility, could not be found in three men, as well as in one man." James Wilson answered that "unity in the executive instead of being the fetus of monarchy would be the best safeguard against tyranny."

With the delegates unable to agree on how many men should occupy the "executive magistracy," debate shifted to the method of election. Again, divisions on this issue reflected attitudes toward "the people" as participants in the political process. During the session on June 9, Elbridge Gerry of Massachusetts moved that the state governors select the national executive, with each state having the same number of votes as it had senators. He reasoned that governors "would be most likely to select the fittest men" for the post, whether one or more. Not a single delegate rose to support Gerry's motion, and not a single state—including his own—voted for his motion.

During the Philadelphia convention, a few delegates did urge that "the people" be allowed to elect the president directly. On July 17, after the states voted without dissent that the "national executive consist of a single person," the delegates took up the proposal in the Virginia Plan that the executive "be chosen by the national legislature." Gouverneur Morris of Pennsylvania spoke "pointedly" against this motion, Madison noted in recording his speech. "He ought to be elected by the people at large," Morris said of the president. "If the people should elect, they will never fail to prefer some man of distinguished character, or services; some man, if he might so speak, of continental reputation." Madison did not record in his notes whether heads turned in the chamber toward General Washington, seated before them in the presiding chair. Virtually all the delegates assumed that Washington would be elected by acclamation as the first "national executive" by whatever method they chose; it was the question of who would follow Washington that led most delegates to question the proposal for direct election.

Morris outlined his objections to the Virginia Plan. "If the legislature elect," he argued, "it will be the work of intrigue, of cabal, and of faction; it will be like the election of a pope by a conclave of cardinals; real merit will rarely be the title to the appointment." Roger Sherman of Connecticut voiced the concern of the smaller states on this question. He countered Morris that "the people at large . . . will never be sufficiently informed of characters" of the candidates. "They will generally vote for some man in their own state, and the largest state will have the best chance for the appointment." George Mason of Virginia, who fervently supported the rights of "the people" on most issues, and who represented both the largest state in delegates and the home of George Washington, surprisingly sided with Sherman. "He conceived it would be as unnatural," Madison recorded, "to refer the choice of a proper character for Chief Magistrate to the people, as it would to refer a trial of colors to a blind man. The extent of the country renders it impossible that the people can have the requisite capacity to judge of the respective pretensions of the candidates." When the delegates voted, only Morris's home state of Pennsylvania supported his motion for "an election by the people" of the president.

Debate over varying proposals for the election of the president—although that title for the chief executive was not widely used until the convention neared its end—dragged on throughout the summer, with no agreement in sight. On July 19, Gouverneur Morris restated his position that "the executive magistrate should be the guardian of the people, even of the lower classes, against legislative tyranny, against the great and the wealthy who in the course of things will necessarily compose the legislative body." His long and eloquent speech fell on deaf ears. Even Madison, who supported direct election of the president in principle, yielded to sentiment against it and observed that electors chosen by

state legislatures "seemed on the whole to be liable to fewest objections."

Frustration on this issue mounted to such levels that George Mason, speaking on July 26, listed seven different proposals that had been moved and rejected, from direct election by the people to choosing a president by lottery. Mason opposed direct election because a choice which should be made "by those who know most of eminent characters" should not be made "by those who know least." About the lottery proposal, which was totally facetious, Mason wryly remarked that "the tickets do not appear to be in much demand."

Not until September did the delegates take any real steps toward settling this vexing issue. Opinions seemed to be moving toward proposals for a single presidential term of seven years, with the president elected by Congress, and with a provision for impeachment. But the convention refused to make a decision, and the weary delegates finally dumped the issue on a newly created Committee on Postponed Matters. When that group reported on September 4, it laid before the convention a proposal that became—with minor changes—the text of Article II of the Constitution. The country would not only have a president, elected for a term of four years, but a vice president as well, chosen by electors who were themselves chosen by the state legislatures. The election plan was complex, giving both houses of Congress a role in choosing the president in case a majority of state electors could not agree; the vice president would be the man with the second-largest number of electoral votes.

By September 12, after dozens of motions to amend the committee's report had been debated and voted up or down, the convention finally adopted a detailed plan for election of the "national executive" that Madison had proposed in vague outline on May 29. The president was now designated as "commander in chief" of the armed forces, was empowered to "make treaties" with the concurrence of two thirds of the Senate, and was authorized to appoint "judges of the Supreme Court, and all other officers of the United States," subject to approval by a Senate majority. The provisions of Article II did not satisfy Gouverneur Morris's plea that "the people" directly elect the president, but the sharing of powers with Congress muted Edmund Randolph's fears of an executive "monarchy" that might impose a "tyranny" on the country. In the end, the Framers of 1787 adopted yet another compromise that diluted the principles of democracy. But this compromise on presidential election and powers—like the Great Compromise on congressional structure and powers in Article I—allowed the Framers to submit to the states for ratification a constitution that established a strong national government.

* * *

Looking back from the perspective of more than two centuries, it seems astounding that delegates to the Philadelphia convention of 1787 spent so little time—and so few words—debating the structure and powers of the "national judiciary" that Madison first proposed in the Virginia Plan. Since its establishment by Article III of the Constitution, the Supreme Court has exercised "the judicial power of the United States" in thousands of cases that have decided whether state and federal laws conform to the Constitution, which is sanctified by Article VI as the "supreme law of the land." This awesome power—limited only by the equally awesome power of Congress and the states to amend the Constitution—appears at first glance to have been granted as an afterthought by the Philadelphia delegates.

On closer inspection, however, it seems clear that the delegates who drafted the final version of the Constitution's judicial provisions were united in supporting a "national judiciary" with expansive powers over state and federal legislation. They arrived at this destination by varied routes, but the notion of "judicial review" of legislation was not foreign to them. Once the concept of an independent judiciary gained majority support, the delegates did not shrink from vesting the Supreme Court with the powers needed for its role as the dominant branch of the national government.

On August 6, the Committee on Detail, which had worked diligently for weeks to prepare a draft of the Constitution, based on the tentative votes of the Committee of the Whole, reported its efforts to the convention. During the weeks that followed the submission of the draft Constitution by the Committee on Detail, the delegates laboriously slogged their way through every clause of every article, taking literally hundreds of votes on motions to strike or add words and phrases. The convention devoted little of its time to the Supreme Court, which was dealt with in Article III, about halfway through the lengthy document. The delegates finally reached this article on August 27, and almost hurried their way through it, with little discussion or debate. They agreed to vesting "the judicial power of the United States" in a Supreme Court "and in such inferior courts" as Congress might create. They also agreed to give the Supreme Court jurisdiction over "all cases under laws passed by the legislature of the United States" and to "controversies" between states, "between a state and citizens of another state," and "between citizens of different states." Through this jurisdictional scheme, the delegates intended to place all cases that did not arise solely within a single state into a federal judicial forum. Although only a few delegates voiced their underlying concerns on this issue, these jurisdictional provisions obviously reflected fears that state judges might be biased against out-of-state litigants or against the federal government itself.

During the debate on August 27, William Johnson of Connecticut, a noted scholar with degrees from Yale and Harvard, who would shortly become president of Columbia College, offered an amendment to change the provision to give the Court jurisdiction over "all cases arising under this Constitution and laws" enacted by Congress. Some delegates may have considered this a trivial change, or simply one that was assumed, but Madison rose to object. He recorded himself as doubting "whether it was not going too far to extend the jurisdiction of the Court generally to cases arising under the Constitution and whether it ought not to be limited to cases of a judiciary nature. The right of expounding the Constitution in cases not of this nature ought not to be given to that department." Madison did not define what he meant by "cases of a judiciary nature," but he presumably intended to prevent the Supreme Court from issuing advisory opinions on constitutional questions, a power that some delegates had suggested giving the Court in earlier sessions. At any rate, the delegates promptly passed Johnson's motion without dissent, "it being generally

supposed that the jurisdiction given was constructively limited to cases of a judiciary nature," Madison recorded approvingly.

With hardly any debate, the delegates approved the creation of a branch of the national government with sweeping jurisdiction and awesome—if still untested—powers to strike down laws of both the states and Congress. Many delegates, in fact, seemed unaware that they had granted these powers to the national judiciary. During the extended debate over proposals to join the president and Supreme Court into a "Council of Revision" with power to veto laws passed by Congress, Madison proposed on August 15 a complicated scheme to allow Congress to override such vetoes. His motion, by far the most complicated of any on this issue, would have entangled members of all three branches in the business of the others.

During the debate that followed, as Madison reported, John Mercer of Maryland "disapproved of the doctrine that judges as expositors of the Constitution should have the authority to declare a law void. He thought laws ought to be well and cautiously made, and then to be uncontrollable." John Dickinson of Delaware was "strongly impressed" with Mercer's comment. "He thought no such power ought to exist. He was at the same time at a loss what expedient to substitute." No other delegate rose to suggest a substitute for Madison's proposal, but his notion of involving the Supreme Court in deciding the constitutionality of legislation before it took effect—giving it, in other words, the power of issuing advisory opinions—never came close to passage. On this particular motion, Madison lost by a vote of eight states to three. Later on, the convention voted to give Congress the power to override presidential vetoes by a two-thirds vote of both the House and Senate. The delegates left the Supreme Court out of these battles among the other two branches of the national government.

A majority of the delegates in Philadelphia shared Madison's "Federalist" belief in a strong national government, with varying degrees of intensity. At the same time, every delegate represented his state and was loath to hand over to the new government they were framing the essential powers of the states. Yet in designing the judicial branch of government, the delegates added to its sweeping jurisdiction in Article III the additional power to make the Constitution and federal laws "the supreme law of the land," binding every state judge to their enforcement.

This provision, which became the Supremacy Clause of Article VI, first took shape in Madison's proposal in the Virginia Plan to give the national legislature a "negative" over state laws that contravened the "articles of Union." Debate over this proposal continued for almost three months, from its introduction on May 29 until August 23, when the delegates finally buried it. During that final debate, Roger Sherman of Connecticut also proposed that "all acts" of Congress "shall be the supreme law of the respective states" and that "the judiciary of the several states shall be bound thereby in their decisions, anything in the respective laws of the individual states to the contrary notwithstanding."

Paterson clearly had no intention of placing the federal judiciary in a position of "supremacy" over the states. He envisioned a Congress in which the states—particularly the smaller states like New Jersey—dominated the federal government, and in which the national executive had very limited powers. Paterson's proposal that "all acts" of Congress would be the "supreme law" of the states hardly threatened state power, especially since his plan limited the jurisdiction of federal judges to cases that involved impeachments, piracies, treaties, and "collection of the federal revenue." But in his choice of words, Paterson—unwittingly for sure—gave the advocates of a strong national government the design of a judicial battering ram that would knock down hundreds of state laws over the next two centuries.

When the Committee on Detail submitted its draft Constitution to the delegates on August 6, it adopted Paterson's "supreme law" wording with little change. But the committee's draft, of course, also proposed a Congress with sweeping powers over the states. With hardly another word on the convention floor, the delegates approved the Supremacy Clause in their final vote on September 12, 1787. The ultimate irony of the Constitution is that the provision giving the Supreme Court a veto power over state laws, the most important power it exercises, was first proposed by a vehement advocate of state sovereignty. To compound this irony, George Washington nominated William Paterson to the Supreme Court in 1793, a position he held until his death in 1806. Paterson remained a firm advocate of constitutional supremacy during his judicial service, ruling in one case that "every act of the legislature repugnant to the constitution is absolutely void."

* * *

Surprisingly, it was not until August 20, after three months of deliberation, that any delegate raised the question of including a bill of rights in the Constitution. Many had thought about this issue and talked about it over dinners in the surrounding taverns and in meetings of state delegations. All but two of the state constitutions that were adopted after the states declared their independence from England in 1776 contained "bills of rights" that protected citizens against arbitrary governmental power. Many of these constitutions included specific guarantees for rights of speech, press, and religion. The Virginia constitution, which James Madison had helped to draft, offered protection against unreasonable search or seizure, provided that defendants in criminal trials could not be forced to testify against themselves, and barred the state from infringing the freedom of the press. Pennsylvania, where the first colonial newspaper was published and which was settled by Quakers, who preached and practiced religious toleration, protected the freedoms of press and religion in its constitution.

Although a large majority of delegates came to Philadelphia with the resolve to create a strong federal union—one with "positive" powers to make and execute national laws—most also believed that the state governments should be primarily responsible for protecting citizens in the "negative" sense of barring legislators and executive officials from infringing their basic rights. Many of these "inalienable" rights—summed up as "life, liberty, and the pursuit of happiness" in the Declaration of Independence—had first been "enumerated" in the Magna Carta. The notion of listing such rights in a written constitution gained many supporters before and after the American Revolution. Few of those who advocated bills of rights in state constitutions, however, felt

that the federal constitution they were creating should add to—or subtract from—the rights provided by the states.

Ironically, it was a delegate from the slave-owning state of South Carolina who first proposed a federal bill of rights. When the session opened on August 20, Charles Cotesworth Pinckney submitted thirteen "propositions" to the convention, asking that they be referred to the Committee on Detail. Pinckney, who rose the very next day to denounce proposals to give Congress the power "of meddling with the importation of negroes," proposed that "the liberty of the press shall be inviolably preserved" and that "no soldier shall be quartered in any house in time of peace without consent of the owner." With changes only of wording, Pinckney's proposals were incorporated—four years later—into the Bill of Rights as parts of the First and Third Amendments. But the delegates in 1787 referred them "without debate or consideration" to the Committee on Detail, from which they never emerged.

On September 12, three weeks after Pinckney offered his proposal, the Committee on Style submitted its draft of the Constitution, laying out in detail the "positive" powers of the three branches of the national government. Along with its draft, the committee appended a letter to the delegates. Noting that "the full and entire approbation of every state is not perhaps to be expected," the committee expressed its hope that the draft Constitution "may promote the lasting welfare of that country so dear to us all, and secure her freedom and happiness." George Mason of Virginia was not happy with the result. "He wished the plan had been prefaced with a Bill of Rights," Madison recorded his Virginia colleague as saying. Mason added that such a provision "would give great quiet to the people; and with the aid of the state declarations, a bill might be prepared in a few hours." Elbridge Gerry of Massachusetts "concurred in the idea and moved for a committee to prepare a Bill of Rights."

Only two delegates addressed Gerry's motion. Roger Sherman of Connecticut spoke for the "localists" in the convention. "The state Declarations of Rights are not repealed by this Constitution," he argued, "and being in force are sufficient." Mason rose from his seat again. "The laws of the United States are to be paramount to state Bills of Rights," he replied. These brief remarks, on both sides of this momentous question, barely scratched the surface of a question that later divided those who supported or opposed the ratification of the Constitution. Eager to conclude their deliberations, the state delegations—with the abstention of Gerry's colleagues from Massachusetts—unanimously rejected his motion.

Three days after deciding not to include a bill of rights in the Constitution, the delegates took their final vote on the provisions of the document they had labored to produce. On September 15, George Mason offered a motion that no "navigation act" regarding the shipping trade be enacted without the concurrence of two thirds of each house of Congress, rather than a simple majority as provided by the draft Constitution. Mason lost on this issue by a vote of seven states to three. Within seconds of the tally, Edmund Randolph sought and received George Washington's permission to address the convention. Almost four months earlier, Randolph had yielded to Madison's entreaties to introduce the Virginia Plan to the convention, prefaced by his own proposal that the Articles of Confederation "be so corrected and enlarged as to accomplish" their objectives of ensuring the "common defense, security of liberty and general welfare" of the confederated states. Randolph was bitterly disappointed with the results of the succeeding four months of debate and deliberation. Scribbling furiously to record his friend's remarks, Madison wrote that Randolph denounced the "dangerous power given by the Constitution to Congress" and expressed "the pain he felt at differing from the body of the convention, on the close of the great and awful subject of their labors."

Randolph knew that his fellow delegates were eager to submit the Constitution to the states for final ratification. Keenly aware that he spoke for a small minority, he nonetheless moved that "amendments to the plan might be offered by the state conventions, which should be submitted to and finally decided on by another general convention." Should his motion be rejected, Randolph said with obvious sadness, it would "be impossible for him to put his name to the instrument." Randolph spoke to the convention not only as a single delegate but as the governor of Virginia, the state whose legislature had called for the Philadelphia convention. His introduction of the Virginia Plan had carried special weight because of his position.

George Mason, who followed Randolph in addressing the delegates, enjoyed his own eminence as the author of Virginia's Declaration of Rights and from his indefatigable labors in framing the Constitution he now rose to reject. Mason spoke in even stronger words than Randolph. The "dangerous power" given to Congress in the Constitution, he predicted, "would end either in monarchy, or a tyrannical aristocracy; which, he was in doubt, but one or other, he was sure." Mason complained that the Constitution "had been formed without the knowledge or idea of the people." He followed Randolph in proposing another convention, one that could add a bill of rights to the version before the delegates. "It was improper to say to the people, take this or nothing," Mason argued.

The arguments of Randolph and Mason, made by delegates who were widely respected by their fellows, did not fall on deaf ears in the State House chamber. But they did not sway any votes that were not already committed. Charles Pinckney of South Carolina responded to his fellow southerners. "These declarations from members so respectable," he said, "give a particular solemnity to the present moment." But Pinckney saw no reason for a second convention. "Nothing but confusion and contrariety could spring from the experiment," he predicted. "He was not without objections as well as others to the plan," Pinckney said of the draft Constitution. "But apprehending the danger of a general confusion, and an ultimate decision by the sword, he should give the plan his support."

The last delegate to speak before the convention took its final votes on the Constitution had, like Randolph and Mason, labored hard over the past four months. Elbridge Gerry had risen to speak more than a hundred times, most often to denounce the "Federalist" provisions that Madison had drafted, which Gerry considered incursions on the rights of the states. In his speech of September 15, Gerry listed in detail his accumulated objections to the Constitution. Some points were minor, such as "the power of Congress over the places of election." Others were substantial,

such as the Great Compromise on counting slaves as three fifths of a "person" in allocating House seats. But on each of Gerry's objections, other delegates had voted with him in the minority and then swallowed their doubts when the time came for a final vote on the Constitution.

Gerry assured his fellow delegates that he, too, could "get over all these" objections. But he could not sign a document in which "the rights of the citizens" had been "rendered insecure by the general power of the legislature to make what laws they please to call necessary and proper." Gerry was not a diehard on the states' rights issue; he had earlier spoken in favor of a federal union as "an umpire to decide controversies" between the states. Neither did he support "the people" as best qualified to make political decisions, as shown by his remarks about the "excesses" of democracy. But Gerry equally distrusted legislative supremacy, and his advocacy of a national bill of rights fit into his political philosophy, which sought a broad dispersal of power between the states and federal government and between their separate branches. Having opened his speech by stating that he felt compelled "to withhold his name from the Constitution," Gerry ended with a plea for "a second general convention," as Randolph had moved.

As soon as Gerry sat down, the convention voted on Randolph's motion for "another general convention" to consider amendments "offered by the state conventions" when they met to consider ratification of the Constitution. Madison recorded the verdict on Randolph's motion: "All the states answered—no." Madison then scribbled in his notes: "On the question to agree to the Constitution, as amended. All the states aye. The Constitution was then ordered to be engrossed. And the House adjourned."

Madison later shared with Thomas Jefferson—who observed the Philadelphia convention from his diplomatic post in Paris—his concern that the Constitution, "should it be adopted, will neither effectually answer its national object nor prevent the local mischiefs which everywhere excite disgust against the state governments." In this gloomy assessment of his labors, Madison took little account of the combination of principle and practicality that he brought to the monumental task of framing the Constitution. There is, in retrospect, significance in the fact that Madison's last words to the convention—spoken on September 15—responded to a motion that every state have an equal vote in the Senate, a proposal he had consistently opposed. "Begin with these special provisos," he said, "and every state will insist on them." When the convention ended, Madison had agreed to this provision in the Constitution. More than any delegate in Philadelphia, Madison knew that ratification of the Constitution depended on the many compromises that he had initially opposed and then grudgingly accepted.

One of these compromises dealt with the number of states necessary to ratify the Constitution. The delegates resolved this question near the end of their deliberations. This was, they all recognized, an important and delicate issue, since the Articles of Confederation they were supposedly "revising" provided that amendments must be approved by unanimous vote of the states. It was almost certain that at least one state, and probably two or three, would vote in the Confederation Congress to reject the Constitution. Rhode Island, after all, had refused to send any delegates to Philadelphia, and its political leaders had denounced the whole notion of a new constitution. New York's governor, George Clinton, also opposed the idea, and two of the state's three delegates to the Philadelphia convention had walked out in July, leaving Alexander Hamilton with a voice but no vote.

To lessen the risk of rejection, the delegates voted on August 31 that ratification by nine of the thirteen states "shall be sufficient" to establish the Constitution as binding among the ratifying states. During the debate on what became Article VII, motions were made to set the number at seven, eight, nine, ten, and thirteen of the states. Ironically, two delegates who refused to sign the Constitution helped to assure its final ratification. Edmund Randolph proposed nine as "a respectable majority" of the states, and George Mason agreed this was the "preferable" number. Compounding the irony, Madison and the other Virginia delegates voted against the motion, placing their state in the minority on this motion, which passed by a vote of eight states to three.

The delegates also decided to bypass the Confederation Congress and submit the Constitution to conventions in each state. This was also a risky move, since they could not dictate to the states how to choose the members of these conventions. Madison urged this move, rather than allowing the state legislatures to vote on ratification, for the quite pragmatic reason that, as he put it, "the powers given to the general government being taken from the state governments, the legislatures would be more disinclined" to ratify the Constitution. Madison ended on a loftier note: "The people were in fact," he proclaimed, "the fountain of all power, and by resorting to them, all difficulties were got over."

The difficulties of securing ratification by conventions of at least nine states would not easily be "got over," as Madison well knew. The day after they adjourned, the Philadelphia delegates sent the Constitution to New York, on a stagecoach with Major Jackson, for submission to the Confederation Congress. Considering that the delegates had voted to bypass that body, this step was largely, as Madison confessed to George Washington, "a matter of form and respect." Along with eight other signers, Madison was a member of Congress, and he hoped that it would send the Constitution to the states without delay. He also hoped to secure a resolution from Congress that endorsed the ratification of the Constitution by the state conventions.

Madison accomplished his first goal, but only after his fellow Virginian Richard Henry Lee—who listened to George Mason's objections after the convention's veil of secrecy had been lifted—urged that the Congress amend the Constitution to add a bill of rights. Ironically, Madison, the man we now honor as "the Father of the Bill of Rights," argued strenuously against Lee's motion and prevailed. On September 28, 1787, the Confederation Congress—with eleven states voting—unanimously agreed that the Constitution "be transmitted to the several legislatures, in order to be submitted to a convention of delegates chosen in each state by the people thereof." His fellow congressmen, however, frustrated Madison's second goal, withholding any endorsement of the Constitution. After all, the document they sent to the states would replace their body with another, more powerful Congress, one that would wield enormous powers over the states they had been chosen to represent.

Two days after this vote, Madison wrote from New York to George Washington, who had returned to his Mount Vernon estate. The refusal of Congress to endorse the Constitution pained Madison. "A more direct approbation would have been of advantage" in securing ratification, he lamented. The man who accepted many compromises in Philadelphia was now afraid that too many compromises might doom his ultimate goal of a strong national government. "The country must finally decide," he wrote to Washington, "the sense of which is as yet wholly unknown" (Irons, 1999).

SECTION 2

~~~

THE STRUGGLE FOR RATIFICATION

James Madison and other Framers of the Constitution feared that the document they had labored so hard to create might be ripped to shreds in the state conventions to which it was sent—without endorsement—by the Confederation Congress. Their deliberations in Philadelphia had been conducted behind closed doors and sealed windows, raising suspicions that the delegates had conspired to impose an executive "monarchy" or a legislative "tyranny" on the people. Many delegates were regarded—quite rightly—as representatives of the old colonial aristocracy or the newer economic elite. The "Federalists" who dominated the Constitutional Convention were largely from the cities of the Eastern Seaboard, spread from Boston in Massachusetts to Charleston in South Carolina. More than half of the Framers were lawyers or had legal training, which raised more suspicions among those who distrusted "pettifoggers" in the courts. Only a handful worked the land as farmers, although many of the southern delegates owned or lived on plantations, where the land was plowed, planted, and harvested by slaves. In short, the Framers had little in common with the backcountry farmers, small-town tradesmen, and urban "mechanics" who made up a majority of the American population in 1787. To be more correct, the white, male population that owned enough property or paid enough taxes to vote in most states.

Factors that might seem to hobble the Framers and their supporters in the ratification debate also became sources of political strength. First—and very important in their campaign for the Constitution—the Framers took the initiative and adopted the "Federalist" name for themselves. This left their opponents with the weak and negative label "Antifederalist," despite the efforts of some to call themselves "Federal Republicans" or some more appealing name. Second, the Federalists enjoyed the support of most of the country's newspapers, which were largely published in cities like Boston, New York, and Philadelphia. Access to the media has always been a crucial factor in political success. Third, the Federalists had the advantage of having a concrete proposal—a detailed Constitution—while their opponents had nothing to offer except criticism. The text of the Constitution was widely published and avidly read by those who voted for delegates to the state ratifying conventions. The

Antifederalists, among them men of great oratorical and rhetorical skill, made speeches and wrote pamphlets that presented their case with logic and polish. But their only alternatives to the Constitution were amendment and delay.

The Federalists moved quickly to capitalize on their advantages. Most important, they only needed the support of nine states, the number proposed for ratification by Edmund Randolph. In the first three months after the Confederation Congress sent the document to the states, conventions in three of the smaller states voted unanimously for ratification. Delaware took first place in the race (its license plates now boast "The First State") on December 7, 1787. John Dickinson and George Read, two of the most active and articulate delegates in Philadelphia, persuaded the Delaware convention to ratify by a vote of thirty to zero. Led by James Paterson, who swallowed his states'-rights objections and signed the Constitution, the New Jersey convention ratified by a vote of thirty-eight to zero on December 18. Georgia, the most southern state and probably the most in need of national protection to fend off Indian attacks and predatory land speculators, ratified on the last day of 1787 by a vote of twenty-six to zero. George Washington said of Georgia that "if a weak state with the Indians on its back and the Spaniards on its flank does not see the necessity of a general government, there must I think be wickedness or insanity in the way."

The victories in these small states produced a welcome momentum for ratification. But the larger states posed greater problems for the Federalists. The first major obstacle was Pennsylvania, which seemed on the surface an easy state to persuade. After all, the state's most eminent citizen, Benjamin Franklin, had signed the Constitution and urged its adoption before the state legislature. Another of the Framers, James Wilson, helped to draft the Pennsylvania constitution and was widely respected around the state. But the Constitution's supporters faced two serious problems in Pennsylvania. First, although Federalists controlled the one-house state legislature, the Antifederalist bloc—mostly from the western and rural areas—held more than a third of the sixty-nine seats. If the Federalists could not muster a quorum of forty-six members, their opponents could block a vote to send the Constitution to a state convention. Second, the ratification debate, waged primarily in the state's newspapers, had become ferocious and fevered.

The Federalists solved the first problem with strongarm tactics. When the roll call in the legislative session, called to propose a ratification convention, turned up only forty-four members, the Pennsylvania Assembly sent its sergeant at arms to round up at least two of the Antifederalist members, who had boycotted the meeting to prevent a vote they knew they would lose. Surrounded by a self-appointed posse, the sergeant canvassed the taverns and lodging houses near the State House and finally located two of the boycotters, James M'Calmont and Jacob Miley. A later report by the dissenting members described their treatment by the Federalist posse: "Their lodgings were violently broken open, their clothes torn, and after much abuse and insult, they were forcibly dragged through the streets of Philadelphia to the State House, and there detained by force." Federalist members held M'Calmont and Miley in their seats while the Assembly—with its press-gang quorum—voted forty-six to twenty-three

to hold elections for a ratification convention. This was hardly a victory for democracy, but neither side in the ratification debate played by the rules of genteel debate. For them, the stakes were too high.

The rhetoric of the debaters reached equally violent levels. Many of those who penned essays in the newspapers employed pseudonyms to conceal their identity, perhaps fearing the wrath of another partisan mob. Writing under the name "Centinel," one Pennsylvania Antifederalist argued in the *Independent Gazetteer* of Philadelphia that the "most perfect system of local government in the world" would be replaced under the Constitution by "the supremacy of the lordly and profligate few." Centinel could see "no alternative between adoption and absolute ruin." He even insinuated that "the weakness and indecision attendant on old age" had influenced Benjamin Franklin to sign the Constitution.

These charges against his dear friend, and the publication in the *Pennsylvania Packet* of George Mason's objections to the Constitution, prompted James Wilson to fight back. He was particularly stung by criticism that the Constitution did not include a bill of rights, which the Pennsylvania charter provided in detail. Wilson argued in the state ratification debate that "such an idea never entered the mind" of the Framers. "To every suggestion concerning a Bill of Rights, the citizens of the United States may always say, 'We reserve the right to do what we please.'" Wilson prevailed in the Pennsylvania convention, which ratified the Constitution by a vote of forty-six to twenty-three on December 12, 1787.

By the end of that fateful year, four of the nine states required for final ratification had given their assent to the Constitution. But ratification by three of the larger states—Massachusetts, Virginia, and New York—lay ahead. Without the approval of all three, the Constitution had little chance of success. It would be possible, of course, to secure final ratification with the votes of smaller states. But the ultimate goal of the Federalists—the creation of a powerful national government—would be frustrated if even one of these crucial states rejected the Constitution. Political reality, far more than principle, dictated the Federalist strategy of securing unanimous support in the state conventions.

The Massachusetts convention posed more problems for the Federalists. The town meetings that elected delegates sent a large number of farmers to Boston, and the western part of the state still harbored resentment at the politicians—many of them Federalists—whose tax laws had fueled Shays' Rebellion. And, in contrast to Pennsylvania, the Massachusetts Antifederalists were well organized, boasting the leadership of Elbridge Gerry, the renowned patriot and pamphleteer Sam Adams, and men like James Winthrop, James Warren, and Benjamin Austin, whose family roots went deep in the state's rocky soil. The Antifederalists also offered their own proposal: if the convention did ratify the Constitution, it should attach amendments to secure a federal bill of rights.

Passions ran high as the Massachusetts convention began on January 9, 1788. The delegates first elected Governor John Hancock as president, but Hancock—who looked at the political weathervane and saw it swinging wildly—pled an attack of gout and stayed home until the convention's final days. The debate in Massachusetts, which the public followed avidly in the state's newspapers, revolved around

Antifederalist calls for a bill of rights. Writing under the name "Agrippa," one opponent published sixteen essays against the Constitution in the *Massachusetts Gazette.* "There is no bill of rights, and consequently a continental law may control any of those sacred principles" the state's constitution provided its citizens, Agrippa complained. The Federalist answer to this argument, made at the convention by Joseph Varnum, did little to mollify the opponents. The powers granted to Congress in the Constitution, Varnum claimed, were the sole extent of federal power; therefore, a bill of rights as a check on these powers would be superfluous. The problem with this response, as Antifederalists quickly noted, lay in the provision which gave to Congress the additional power "to make all laws which shall be necessary and proper" to implement the specified powers, which included a broad authority to provide for the "general welfare of the United States."

Exchanges like these may not have swayed votes, but they revealed the views that each side in the ratification debates had of the other. Those in the middle recognized that compromise was necessary to avoid a bitter conflict. William Heath, a moderate Federalist, suggested that the convention "ratify the Constitution, and instruct our first Members of Congress, to exert their utmost endeavors to have such checks, and guards provided as appears to be necessary" to the delegates. Talk of compromise brought Governor Hancock from his sickbed to the convention, where he asked to "hazard a proposition" that would bridge the differences. Hancock quickly drafted nine proposed amendments—he probably had them ready—and put them before the convention. The first, and most important, provided "that all powers not expressly delegated by the aforesaid Constitution are reserved to the several states, to be by them exercised."

The response to Hancock's move exceeded his expectations. Sam Adams, perhaps the most respected Antifederalist, rose to announce that he now supported ratification. The delegates then voted by the narrow margin of 187 to 168 to ratify the Constitution, directing the state's future congressmen to "exert all their influence" in pressing for the amendments Hancock had drafted. As a reward, the Federalists promised to support Hancock's reelection as governor. Watching from Mount Vernon, George Washington expressed his qualified relief. "The decision of Massachusetts would have been more influential had the majority been greater," he wrote, "and the ratification unaccompanied by the recommendatory Act. As it stands, however, the blow is severely felt by antifederalists in the equivocal states."

Another three of the smaller states were not equivocal. By a vote of 128 to 40, Connecticut had ratified the Constitution a month before Massachusetts. Maryland held its convention in April 1788. The delegates listened for hours to the vituperative Antifederalist railings of Luther Martin, who had walked out of the Philadelphia convention in disgust. George Washington's secretary wrote that Martin "is a man whose character is so infamous that anything advanced by him against the Constitution, would where he is known, bias the people in favor of it." This proved an accurate prediction. After Martin sat down, the delegates voted for ratification by a tally of sixty-three to eleven. South Carolina followed in May by a vote of 149 to 73, although it joined Massachusetts

in proposing amendments that would reserve to the states the powers not granted to Congress.

*   *   *

Five days after South Carolina became the eighth state to ratify the Constitution, George Washington wrote to his French friend the Marquis de Lafayette: "The plot thickens fast. A few short weeks will determine the political fate of America for the present generation, and probably no small influence on the happiness of society through a succession of ages to come." Although his prose was portentous, Washington did not exaggerate. Ratification by any of the remaining five states was far from certain. From New Hampshire to North Carolina, Antifederalists were determined to fight to the finish.

Washington hoped, of course, that Virginia would provide the crucial ninth vote for the Constitution. He remained aloof from the fray and did not stand for election to the state convention, which opened in Richmond on June 2, 1788.

The delegates in Richmond included some of the most illustrious men in American political and judicial history. Among the Federalists were James Madison; George Wythe, the state's chancellor and its most noted lawyer; and John Marshall, a brilliant young lawyer who everyone knew was destined for national prominence. Their opponents were equally distinguished. George Mason had published his objections to the Constitution in a widely read pamphlet, Edmund Randolph was the state's governor, and Richard Henry Lee was a respected member of the Confederation Congress. These eminent men, however, had little of the luster of Patrick Henry, the golden-tongued orator who stirred the country to revolution in 1775 with his cry, "Give me liberty, or give me death!"

Henry waved a rhetorical copy of the Declaration of Independence before the delegates. The document "which separated us from Great Britain," he declaimed, had asserted the rights of the people against arbitrary governmental power. But the Constitution protected none of these rights. "The rights of conscience, trial by jury, liberty of the press," he thundered, "all pretensions to human rights and privileges, are rendered insecure, if not lost, by this change." Echoing his stirring call to rebellion against the British, Henry urged the delegates to rebel against the Federalists. "Liberty, greatest of all earthly blessings—give us that precious jewel, and you may take everything else!"

Despite his rhetorical excesses, Patrick Henry made a point that appealed to many delegates. Virginia had enshrined in its constitution in 1776 a Declaration of Rights, drafted by George Mason, that protected rights of religion, speech, and press. James Madison, who sat quietly during Henry's lengthy speeches, listened carefully and decided to take the wind out of his opponent's billowing sails. Madison, who had publicly opposed any amendments to the Constitution as a condition of ratification, conferred with Edmund Randolph and proposed a compromise. If Madison agreed to amendments, would Randolph support ratification? The two former adversaries in Philadelphia reached agreement in Richmond. Speaking in quiet tones, Randolph told the convention that he would support the Constitution if the delegates asked Congress to adopt a bill of rights.

Just before the Virginia convention voted to ratify the Constitution, by the close vote of eighty-nine to seventy-nine,

Patrick Henry conceded defeat in a gracious speech. "If I shall be in the minority," he said, "I shall have those painful sensations which arise from a conviction of being overpowered in a good cause. Yet I will be a peaceable citizen." Henry spoke wistfully of his revolutionary efforts. He expressed the hope "that the spirit which predominated in the revolution is not yet gone, nor the cause of those who are attached to the revolution yet lost. I shall therefore patiently wait in expectation of seeing that government changed, so as to be compatible with the safety, liberty, and happiness, of the people."

Patrick Henry lost the battle in Virginia, but he won the war he waged against the Federalists. James Madison agreed, as a condition for ratification, to press the new Congress to adopt a bill of rights. With that concession, the debate over the Constitution shifted from the "positive" powers of Congress to the "negative" limitations that would protect "the people" from their federal lawmakers.

As it turned out, Virginia was not the ninth state to ratify. That honor went to New Hampshire, whose convention first met in February 1788. When the state's Federalists realized they had been outvoted in the town meetings that elected delegates, they pulled all their parliamentary strings and succeeded in postponing the convention until June 17, two weeks after Virginia began its sessions. By that time, the New Hampshire Federalists had flexed their political muscles—promising federal offices to their opponents—and they prevailed on June 21 by the narrow margin of fifty-seven to forty-seven. New Hampshire bested Virginia by four days in the race for ratification, but neither side in this political battle could claim victory until New York decided to adopt or reject the Constitution.

Without New York, there could be no United States. Not only in population but in commerce and finance, this was the largest state, the linchpin of the union. Alexander Hamilton, New York's sole delegate in Philadelphia after Robert Yates and John Lansing departed, turned his immense talents and energy to the ratification campaign. He had founded the Federalist Party in New York before the Constitutional Convention, and its members represented the state's landowning, mercantile, banking, and legal interests. Governor George Clinton headed the Antifederalist forces, which drew support—as in most states—from farmers and "upstate" voters.

Hamilton turned the momentum for ratification to his advantage, maneuvering to delay the state convention until adoption of the Constitution seemed assured. This put the burden on his opponents to either accept or destroy the union. He also waged a masterful propaganda campaign, through the eighty-five essays that were published in the New York press under the name "Publius." Hamilton recruited John Jay, who became the first Chief Justice of the United States, and James Madison to help write the essays, which the authors churned out every two or three days between October 1787 and May 1788. The Publius essays gained later fame, and wide circulation, as *The Federalist Papers,* but they had little circulation or influence outside New York at the time.

The men who wrote the Publius essays were actually responding to "Brutus," a pseudonymous Antifederalist who was never identified but may have been Robert Yates. Brutus wrote sixteen essays during the same months as the Publius letters. His attack on the Constitution stressed the country's size—"it now contains near three millions of souls"—and its diverse and discordant interests, from north to south. "Now, in a large, extended country," Brutus wrote, "it is impossible to have a representation, possessing the sentiments, and of integrity, to declare the minds of the people, without having it so numerous and unwieldy, as to be subject in great measure to the inconveniency of a democratic government." A national legislature, Brutus concluded, "would be composed of such heterogenous and discordant principles, as would constantly be contending with each other."

In a brilliant essay, later known as "Federalist No. 10," Madison—disguised as Publius—answered Brutus by accepting his premise and turning his logic around. "A landed interest, a manufacturing interest, a mercantile interest, a moneyed interest, with many lesser interests, grow up of necessity in civilized nations," Madison wrote, listing the groups that dominated Hamilton's Federalist Party, "and divide them into different classes, actuated by different sentiments and views." However, the existence of these "factions" was not a vice but a virtue in a national government. In a large and diverse country, Madison argued, no single faction was likely to control a legislative majority. "If a faction controls less than a majority," he wrote, "relief is supplied by the republican principle, which enables the majority to defeat its sinister views by regular vote." The more "factions" the better, he claimed. The "increased number of parties comprised within the Union" would better protect the people from "local prejudices," Madison concluded, and "make it less probable that a majority of the whole will have a common motive to invade the rights of other citizens."

The essays of Publius and Brutus, which powerfully and persuasively stated the arguments for and against a strong national government, probably changed few votes in the New York convention. What did change votes was the defection of a prominent Antifederalist to Hamilton's side. Sam Adams in Massachusetts and Edmund Randolph in Virginia had switched sides and swayed votes in their conventions. Melancton Smith—an upstate merchant—played this role in New York, although he had secretly changed sides before the convention began, convinced that his state's interests could not be protected outside the Union. Without revealing his true feelings, Smith debated the Constitution with Hamilton. He pointed out that a majority of a quorum in Congress would be twenty-four. "Can the liberties of three millions of people be securely trusted in the hands of twenty-four men?" Smith asked. He charged Hamilton with proposing an "aristocratic" government. Hamilton, in fact, hardly concealed his admiration for an aristocracy of the wellborn and wealthy.

Sensing defeat on an up-or-down ratification vote, the New York Antifederalists—unaware of Smith's secret defection—adopted the strategy of their Massachusetts and Virginia compatriots and pressed for amendments to the Constitution. John Lansing proposed adding a bill of rights, including an amendment providing that "no person" could be deprived of "life, liberty, or property but by due process of law." With only minor changes in wording, Lansing's proposal later formed the basis of the Fifth Amendment to the Constitution, which has protected Americans from arbitrary governmental power since the Supreme Court "rescued" the

Liberty Clause from corporations—which had used it as a weapon against workers—in the 1930s.

Lansing also proposed an amendment providing that all powers not expressly granted to Congress "shall be reserved to the respective states, to be by them exercised." This proposal, which echoed the words of Governor Hancock in Massachusetts, later formed the basis of the Tenth Amendment to the Constitution. That last—but certainly not least—article in the Bill of Rights provided that all powers not delegated to Congress "are reserved to the states respectively, or to the people." The nature and extent of these "unenumerated" powers have caused much debate in the Supreme Court's chambers over the past two centuries.

Lansing's move, endorsed by the Federalists, paved the way for Melancton Smith's motion that the Constitution be ratified with "confidence" that the proposed amendments would be adopted by Congress. Smith brought several wavering delegates with him to the Federalist side. On July 26, 1788, the convention voted thirty to twenty-seven to ratify the Constitution.

The New York vote sealed the victory of the Federalists, even though North Carolina and Rhode Island stubbornly refused to join the ratification parade. North Carolina, in fact, initially voted in August 1788 to reject the Constitution by a decisive vote of 184 to 84. The delegates to this first convention heatedly denounced the failure of the Framers to include a bill of rights. In November 1789, a month after the first Congress sent twelve proposed amendments to the states for ratification, North Carolina held a second convention and ratified the Constitution by the more decisive vote of 194 to 77. And the stubborn Rhode Islanders—who boycotted the Philadelphia convention—finally and grudgingly joined the Union in May 1790 by the closest vote of any state, thirty-four to thirty-two. Ironically, the only state with no constitution of its own was now subject to one it played no role in framing (Irons, 1999).

SECTION 3

THE BILL OF RIGHTS

James Madison and his fellow Federalists rejoiced at the final ratification of the Constitution they had labored to produce in Philadelphia and later guided through the state conventions. Their efforts had come perilously close to disaster; the switch of two votes in New York, six in Virginia and New Hampshire, or ten in Massachusetts could have doomed the Constitution. And the jubilation of the victorious Federalists was tempered by political reality. They had promised, as a campaign strategy during the ratification debates, to propose a bill of rights to the First Congress. Madison and other leading Federalists, who had opposed adding a bill of rights in Philadelphia, now found themselves under pressure to fulfill their campaign promise.

Despite the slowness of the mails in the age of sailing ships—it took weeks, sometimes months, for a letter to cross the Atlantic—one keen observer kept up a voluminous correspondence from his diplomatic post in Paris. Before and after ratification, Thomas Jefferson sent dozens of letters to America, all with the same message: the Constitution must contain a bill of rights. "I do not like," he wrote to Madison in December 1787, "the omission of a bill of rights providing clearly and without the aid of sophisms for freedom of religion, freedom of the press," and other guarantees against governmental oppression. Jefferson pounded his drum for more than a year. Writing in March 1789, just before the First Congress began its first session, Jefferson replied to Madison's letter of the previous October: "How it happened to be four months on the way," he wrote, "I cannot tell, as I never knew by what hand it came."

Madison had raised in this letter—reporting, he said, the sentiments of others—several objections to a bill of rights. Jefferson answered them point by point. "1. That the rights in question are reserved [to the states] by the manner in which the federal powers are granted. Answer. A constitutive act . . . which leaves some precious articles unnoticed, and raises implications against others, a declaration of rights becomes necessary by way of supplement. This is the case of our new federal constitution." Jefferson moved on. "2. A positive declaration of some essential rights could not be obtained in the requisite latitude. Answer. Half a loaf is better than no bread. If we cannot secure all our rights, let us secure what we can." Jefferson reminded Madison of the "tyranny of the legislatures" and of executives. "In the arguments in favor of a declaration of rights," he noted, "you omit one which has great weight with me, the legal check which it puts into the hands of the judiciary." The third objection Madison raised—whether for himself or others—was that the "limited powers of the federal government" could not compel the states to protect their citizens' rights. Although Jefferson did not mention the Supremacy Clause of Article VI, his answer reflected its premise. "The declaration of rights will be the text whereby they will try all the acts of the federal government," he wrote. "In this view it is necessary to the federal government also: as by the same text they may try the opposition of the subordinate governments." In other words, state and federal governments alike would be bound to enforce the Constitution as "the supreme law of the land."

Keenly aware of Madison's ambivalence on the need for a bill of rights, Jefferson made a final appeal in his letter of March 1789. "There is a remarkable difference between the characters of the inconveniences which attend a declaration of rights, and those which attend the want of it," he wrote. "The inconveniences of the declaration are that it may cramp government in its useful exertions. But the evil of this is shortlived, moderate, and reparable. The inconveniences of the want of a declaration are permanent, afflicting, and irreparable: they are in constant progression from bad to worse."

Just at the time he received this letter from his mentor and friend, Madison was taking his seat in the First Congress—which met in the nation's first capital, New York City—as a representative from Virginia. Presidential electors had already been chosen under the Constitution's indirect plan, and they voted unanimously on February 4, 1789, for George Washington, with John Adams of Massachusetts as vice president. On the same day, Madison faced the voters in Virginia. It had been a tough campaign, in which he faced

James Monroe, a young protégé of Patrick Henry's and like Madison a future president. The state legislature, controlled by Antifederalists, sent two of its members, Richard Henry Lee and William Grayson, to the Senate.

Madison faced attack for his failure to support a bill of rights. He had "never thought the omission a material defect" in the Constitution, Madison explained, and was "not anxious to supply it even by subsequent amendments." But his election over Monroe by a scant 366 votes, and the fact that both Virginia and New York had called on Congress for a second—and wide-open—constitutional convention persuaded Madison to honor his promise, made in Virginia's ratifying convention, to press Congress for a bill of rights. Jefferson's letter provided the final push that Madison needed to begin the amendment process he had long resisted.

The First Congress met in New York City on March 4, 1789, but it lacked a quorum, with only eight senators and thirteen representatives on hand; another month passed before the House held its first official session and elected its speaker, Frederick Muhlenberg of Pennsylvania. The Senate lagged behind, conducting business with temporary officers until both chambers met on April 30 for the inauguration of President Washington, who spoke to members of Congress and a cheering throng of citizens from the balcony of Federal Hall, at the corner of Wall and Broad Streets in lower Manhattan.

Near the end of his inaugural address, Washington spoke directly to the members of Congress. They would need to "decide how far an exercise of the occasional power" conferred on them to propose amending the Constitution "is rendered expedient at the present juncture by the nature of objections which have been urged against the system, or by the degree of inquietude which has given birth to them." With this florid language, Washington seemingly hinted that Congress should respond to popular pressure for a bill of rights. Disclaiming "any particular recommendations on this subject," he nonetheless expressed hope that "a reverence for the characteristic rights of freemen and a regard for public harmony will sufficiently influence your deliberations on the question" of amendments.

The new president did not propose any particular amendment. He left that job to Madison, who had already begun the laborious task of sifting through some two hundred proposed amendments that eight of the state ratifying conventions had submitted. After eliminating duplicates, the list still approached a hundred. Even when Madison eliminated amendments he considered outside the Constitution's scope, there still remained dozens from various states. Madison imposed his own rule of thumb on the stack that remained; he would only consider amendments that had been proposed—with allowance for different wording—by at least four states. This made his task much easier, and reduced the pile to twenty-two potential amendments.

Madison informed the House on May 4 that he planned to introduce the final list of proposed amendments within the month. He hurried to complete this task, worried that Antifederalist calls for a second Constitutional Convention would spread from Virginia and New York to other states. The prospect of a second convention horrified Madison, who confessed his fear that such a convention would "mutilate" the Constitution that had emerged from Philadelphia. Another concern was that Congress had already bogged down

in debate over "tonnage duties" and other revenue measures. Several representatives responded to Madison's announcement on May 4 with arguments that the House had more pressing business than debating a bill of rights. He made a conciliatory reply, expressing hope that the people would "wait with patience" until the House was "at leisure" to consider the issue.

Madison did not meet his self-imposed deadline, but he finally rose in the House chamber on June 8, 1789. Facing his fellow representatives, who numbered sixty-five, he placed a substantial pile of paper on his desk. Over the past several days, Madison had laboriously written in longhand a speech that would take him at least three hours to deliver. He knew that this might well be the most important address of his political life, certainly one that might rescue the Constitution from its enemies. The men who sat before Madison included Elbridge Gerry, his adversary in Philadelphia, and a bloc of Antifederalists who had switched positions and no longer supported a bill of rights. Their goal now was to press for a second convention and return to the Articles of Confederation, dressed up in new clothes.

His lengthy speech contained not a hint that Madison himself considered a bill of rights essential or even necessary. His goal was simply "to satisfy the public mind that their liberties will be perpetual" and to accomplish this "without endangering any part of the Constitution, which is considered as essential by those who promoted its adoption." Madison painted those who had pressed for state bills of rights as desiring to "raise barriers against power in all forms and departments of the Government," a vast exaggeration of their aims. Lumping together the state bills and the amendments he was introducing, Madison damned both with faint praise, saying that "although some of them are rather unimportant, yet, upon the whole, they will have a salutary tendency." Many declarations of rights "do no more than state the perfect equality of mankind," he sniffed. "This, to be sure, is an absolute truth, yet it is not absolutely necessary to be inserted at the head of a Constitution."

Madison clearly resented those who stirred up fears of an omnipotent and oppressive national government. In his mind, "the great danger lies rather in the abuse of the community than in the Legislative body" referring to Congress. The real danger, he argued, "is not found in either the Executive or Legislative departments of government, but in the body of the people, operating by the majority against the minority." The majorities he meant by this phrase were not those which elected members of Congress, but those which elected local and state lawmakers. Madison implied that the people had little to fear from the body he addressed, stating that the powers granted to Congress by the Constitution were "circumscribed" and "directed to particular objects" that were limited to those listed in Article I. He conceded that these powers "may admit of abuse to a certain extent" and even pointed to the "necessary and proper" clause as tempting Congress to exceed its powers. His concessions over, Madison concluded with a triumphant flourish, pointing to the federal courts as "independent tribunals of justice" that "will be an impenetrable bulwark against every assumption of power in the Legislative and Executive" branches.

Madison made no secret of his disdain for state governments, which he said "are as liable to attack" their citizens' rights "as the General Government is, and therefore ought to be as cautiously guarded against." Why, then, did he make the effort to draft a bill of rights, if he saw the states as more dangerous than Congress? His answer to this unstated question was smoothly phrased, but revealed his true feelings. It would be "highly politic," he said, "for the tranquility of the public mind, and the stability of the government, that we should offer something, in the form I have proposed, to be incorporated in the system of Government, as a declaration of the rights of the people." Soothing the public with a bill of rights he considered "unnecessary" was good politics, and Madison was certainly a good politician. The "something" he offered, after all, was better than nothing. And giving Congress nothing to consider might stir more calls to scrap the Constitution.

* * *

What *did* Madison offer to Congress as a bill of rights? He listed "the amendments which have occurred to me" in order from "firstly" to "ninthly." His first proposed amendment took inspiration from the Declaration of Independence, suggesting that "there be prefixed to the Constitution a declaration, that all power is originally vested in, and consequently derived from, the people." Madison continued with words borrowed from Thomas Jefferson. Governments existed to protect "the enjoyment of life and liberty, with the right of acquiring and using property and generally of pursuing and obtaining happiness and safety." He went on to state—in words that only a lawyer could love—that "the people have an indubitable, unalienable, and indefeasible right to change their Government" when they find it "adverse" to their interests. This was precisely the kind of language that Madison considered "unnecessary" in a Constitution. Perhaps he hoped with this verbiage to placate Jefferson, who considered a bill of rights essential, which Madison clearly did not.

Madison's second proposed amendment responded to complaints by the smaller states, like Delaware and Rhode Island, that the Constitution penalized them by granting one representative for every thirty thousand inhabitants. These two states, in fact, each had just one House member in the First Congress. Madison considered this a petty issue, but he nonetheless proposed that each state have "at least two Representatives" in Congress. His third amendment proposed that changes in congressional salaries could not take effect "before the next ensuing election of Representatives."

Not until his fourth proposed amendment did Madison address the real concerns of those who pressed for a bill of rights. He suggested inserting several new clauses in the Constitution, after the provisions in Article I that barred Congress from enacting any "bill of attainder" or "ex post facto" law. It had been Elbridge Gerry of Massachusetts—who had vainly pressed for a bill of rights in 1787—who convinced the delegates in Philadelphia to include in the Constitution these protections against governmental power to punish individuals without trial and for acts that were lawful when they were committed. Madison had not spoken a word in support of Gerry's motion in Philadelphia. Now he spoke in New York to press for additional rights in the Constitution.

Madison's fourth proposed amendment had ten separate paragraphs and included all but a few of the provisions adopted in the Bill of Rights that was later ratified by the states. The first paragraph dealt with religion: "The civil rights of none shall be abridged on account of religious belief or worship, nor shall any national religion be established, nor shall the full and equal rights of conscience be in any manner, or on any pretext, infringed." The next two paragraphs provided that the "right to speak" and "freedom of the press" should remain "inviolable," and that "the people shall not be restrained from peaceably assembling" and petitioning the government "for redress of their grievances." These paragraphs formed the basis of what later became the First Amendment.

The next paragraph in the proposed amendment had three clauses. The first provided that "The right of the people to keep and bear arms shall not be infringed" by the federal government. The second clause—separated by a semicolon from the first—stated that this right stemmed from the need for "a well armed and well regulated militia" to protect the "security of a free country," presumably from insurrection or invasion. The third clause provided that "no person religiously scupulous of bearing arms shall be compelled to render military service in person." This last clause did not survive the congressional gauntlet, but the first two were blended into the Second Amendment, with their order reversed and the semicolon replaced by a comma.

Madison followed this proposed amendment with one that reflected old resentments at the British army's practice of forcing the American colonists to house and feed its redcoated soldiers. The First Congress debated no more than ten minutes before adopting Madison's proposal that "No soldier shall in time of peace be quartered in any house without the consent of the owner; nor at any time, but in a manner warranted by law." With only minor wording changes, this became the Third Amendment to the Constitution.

The next four paragraphs that Madison read to Congress dealt with the rights of criminal defendants. Politicians today—responding to the "majority" against which Madison warned—are quick to denounce as "soft on crime" anyone who questions the need for quicker trials, longer sentences, and bigger prisons. More than two centuries ago, Madison spoke for most Americans in urging protections for ordinary citizens against the arbitrary practices of British officials that provoked their colonial subjects to revolt. He proposed that no person be subjected to more than "one trial for the same offence," which became the Double Jeopardy Clause of the Fifth Amendment. Madison also proposed that no person be "compelled to be a witness against himself," be "deprived of life, liberty, or property without due process of law," or be "obliged to relinquish his property, where it may be necessary for public use, without a just compensation." With minor wording changes, these proposals became part of the Fifth Amendment.

Madison also proposed the protection of criminal defendants against "excessive bail" before trial and "excessive fines" after conviction. These provisions, which became part of the Eighth Amendment, raised no opposition. But his proposal that Congress ban the infliction of "cruel and unusual punishments" prompted Samuel Livermore of New Hampshire to reply. He argued that "it is sometimes necessary to hang a man, villains often deserve whipping, and perhaps even having their ears cut off; but are we in future to be prevented from inflicting these punishments because they are cruel?"

Madison included a provision that citizens be "secured in their persons, their houses, their papers, and their other property, from all unreasonable searches and seizures." He went on to propose jury trials in civil cases, the right to an "impartial jury" in criminal cases, and—near the bottom of the list—a guarantee that "no state" shall abridge "the freedom of the press." From this hodgepodge emerged parts of the First, Fourth, Sixth, and Seventh Amendments.

Another proposed amendment was phrased in convoluted words, but in the middle was a provision that the Bill of Rights—if adopted—"shall not be so construed as to diminish the just importance of other rights retained by the people." Madison stated his final proposal in clear words: "The powers not delegated by this Constitution, nor prohibited by it to the States, are reserved to the States respectively." These two provisions emerged from Congress, after polishing by committees and debate on the floor, as the Ninth and Tenth Amendments to the Constitution.

Madison outlined in his lengthy speech almost every provision that later became part of the Bill of Rights. He worked long hours, for more than a month, to perfect his list of proposed amendments and polish the words he spoke to Congress. But his heart was not really behind his careful preparation. Ending his speech, Madison confessed to his fellow representatives that his work "may be deemed unnecessary," but he saw "no harm in making such a declaration" of rights. "I am sure I understand it so," he concluded, "and do therefore propose it." With that ambivalent endorsement of his labors, Madison sat down.

* * *

Madison's halfhearted speech to Congress seems at odds with the accolades showered on him since his death—and even during his lifetime—as the "Father of the Bill of Rights." The facts are that he did *not* consider a federal bill of rights essential, and that he proposed amendments partly to placate his political mentor, Thomas Jefferson, and partly to blunt the Antifederalist campaign for a second constitutional convention. He even referred to "the nauseous project of amendments" in a letter to a Federalist friend. Nonetheless, Madison loyally and diligently performed the task he had assumed, and pressed ahead for adoption of the Bill of Rights by Congress and ratification by the states.

The immediate response to Madison's speech and list of proposed amendments was compounded by apathy and annoyance. Representative James Jackson of Georgia stated his opinion that "we ought not be in a hurry with respect to altering the Constitution." He urged that his colleagues "not neglect the more important business which is now unfinished before them." Madison shot back that Jackson was "unfriendly to the object I have in contemplation" but assured the House that "I only wish to introduce the great work" of the Bill of Rights and that "I do not expect it will be decided immediately."

Roger Sherman of Connecticut, who had often sparred with Madison at the Philadelphia convention, noted that his state ratified the Constitution "by a very great majority, because they wished for the Government; but they desired no amendments." He suggested to the House that "it will therefore be imprudent to neglect much more important concerns for this." Sherman had signed the Constitution in Philadelphia, and he saw no need for amendments. "I have strong objections to being interrupted in completing the more important business" of Congress, he complained, "because I am well satisfied it will alarm the fears of twenty of our constituents where it will please one." Madison seemed discouraged by these remarks. He replied to Sherman, in plaintive words, that he was "compelled to beg a patient hearing to what I have to lay before you."

Madison's patience was sorely tested over the month that followed his speech. Hardly any member of the House offered full support for the Bill of Rights, and Madison struggled to put his proposals into better shape. On July 21, he "begged the House to indulge him in the further consideration of Amendments to the Constitution." Once again, House members claimed they had more pressing business, although Madison succeeded in having the project sent to a select committee with a member from each state.

The Committee of Eleven reported back on July 28. It made few substantive changes to the list Madison had proposed on June 8. Busy with revenue bills, the House promptly tabled the report. Madison faced a constant struggle during the summer of 1789 to force his reluctant colleagues to consider the amendments. Debate did not begin in earnest until August 14. Antifederalists heaped scorn on the whole project. Representative Aedanus Burke of South Carolina dismissed the proposals as "not those solid and substantial amendments which the people expect" but "frothy and full of wind." He thought "we have done nothing but lose our time, and that it will be better to drop the subject now, and proceed to the organization of the Government." Even the representative who chaired the Committee of Eleven, John Vining of Delaware, apologized for diverting the House from considering "the bill for establishing a Land Office for the disposal of the vacant lands in the Western Territory."

The House debates on the Bill of Rights did not rise to the rhetorical heights, or rival the political passions, of those in the Philadelphia convention in 1787. In truth, they were dull and dispiriting. At one point, John Vining ridiculed a motion by Roger Sherman as reminding him of "an act to amend a supplement to an act entitled an act for altering part of an act entitled an act for certain purposes therein mentioned." The substantive provisions of the amendments submitted by the Committee of Eleven underwent numerous wording changes and finally emerged on August 24 as a resolution to the Senate. The House recommended seventeen amendments; the first and longest revised the apportionment of House seats by a complicated formula, designed to keep the total number in check as the nation's population grew. The second, to which little objection was voiced, prevented laws that raised congressional salaries from taking effect before the next House elections.

The ten amendments we now call the Bill of Rights began in the House resolution with the third, which stated that "Congress shall make no law establishing religion or prohibiting the free exercise thereof, nor shall the rights of conscience be infringed." The fourth on the list contained the rest of what became the First Amendment, protecting freedom of speech and of the press, and rights of assembly and petition. Those dealing with the rights of criminal defendants were presented in forms that emerged in the final Bill of Rights with minor wording changes. The House list also included what are now the Ninth and Tenth Amendments, guaranteeing to "the people" those "rights" not enumerated in the Constitution, and reserving to the states those powers not granted to Congress by the Constitution.

The Senate began consideration of the House resolution on September 2. But that body met in closed session until 1794, and no record exists of its debates on the Bill of Rights, although the *Senate Journal* includes a record of motions and votes. We do know that the Senate tinkered with the apportionment proposal and removed protection against military service by conscientious objectors to war. In their most significant action, the senators dropped the article in the House resolution that Madison considered "the most valuable" of the lot. This proposed amendment, fourteenth on the House list, read: "No state shall infringe the right of trial by jury in criminal cases, nor the rights of conscience, nor the freedom of speech, or of the press." Had it remained, and been adopted, the rights of the people against oppression by the states would have been secured well before the Supreme Court finally began applying the Bill of Rights to the states. That did not happen until 1925, when it ruled that the First Amendment was binding on the states as part of the "liberty" protected against state infringement by the Fourteenth Amendment, ratified in 1868.

The Senate concluded its debates on the Bill of Rights on September 10, sending back to the House a revised and pared-down list of twelve amendments. Since it was clear the House would not accept the Senate version without further revision, the two bodies each named three members to a conference committee, which Madison chaired. The most significant change to emerge from this committee was that Madison succeeded in restoring the House version of what became the first clause of the First Amendment, providing that "Congress shall make no law respecting an establishment or religion." Madison had labored for years in Virginia against state support for established religions, and he now imposed the same ban on the national government.

The House adopted the final version of the twelve proposed amendments by a vote of thirty-seven to twenty-four on September 24, and the Senate followed suit the next day, without a recorded vote. On October 2, President Washington sent copies to each state governor, with a brief letter of transmittal.

*   *   *

There remains virtually no record of debates over the Bill of Rights in the state legislatures. Few lawmakers spoke from written texts, and speeches were not transcribed by reporters. We must rely on letters by partisans and on newspaper accounts, which often reflected personal or political bias. We do know that ratification of the Bill of Rights, which required the assent of eleven states, dragged on for more than two years.

New Jersey was the first to ratify, on November 20, 1789, although it rejected the second proposed amendment, dealing with congressional salaries. Before the process was completed, the first two of the twelve amendments adopted by Congress were defeated in the states. In recent years, many people—including Supreme Court justices—have noted that the protections of religion, speech, press, and assembly were placed in the First Amendment. They argue from this fact that the Framers intended to elevate these rights to a "preferred position" in the Bill of Rights, to underscore their primacy in protecting the people's rights. Of course, had the states not rejected the first two proposed amendments, the First Amendment would now be the Third. Claims that "my rights are protected by the Third Amendment" do not have quite the force of invoking the First.

Maryland, the two Carolinas, New Hampshire, and Delaware approved the Bill of Rights with little dissent. North Carolina actually first joined the Union when it finally ratified the Constitution on November 21, 1789. One month later, its legislature adopted all twelve proposed amendments. New York, with Antifederalist George Clinton still its governor, ratified all but the second proposed amendment in February 1790. Clinton had rallied his troops against the Constitution with appeals for a bill of rights, and he was stuck with that record. Privately, he regretted his earlier enthusiasm. After his state's ratification, he wrote to a relative that his legislature "has transacted no business of very great consequence, unless the adoption of the trivial and equivocal amendments may be so styled."

After the New York vote, Pennsylvania and Rhode Island joined the parade. That made nine of the required eleven states; the Constitution required ratification by three fourths of the states, which now numbered fourteen. Vermont gave up its status as an independent republic and joined the Union in 1791. Its legislature ratified all thirteen proposed amendments in November 1791, two years after President Washington submitted them to the states. One state was still needed before the Bill of Rights became part of the Constitution. Connecticut and Georgia, which were both Federalist strongholds, refused to ratify the amendments, largely because their political leaders felt that the Constitution left such matters to the states. Massachusetts also withheld its vote, the result more of legislative bumbling than clear intent. The two houses of the "Great and General Court" of Massachusetts bickered over the amendments and never joined in a final vote. As a result, the failure of Connecticut, Georgia, and Massachusetts to ratify the Bill of Rights made Virginia the crucial eleventh state.

Virginia actually took up the proposed amendments shortly after President Washington submitted them in October 1789. But the state senate, in which Patrick Henry served, was firmly in Antifederalist hands. The state's two federal senators, Richard Henry Lee and William Grayson, sent a letter to Governor Beverly Randolph—the brother of Edmund—stating that "it is with grief that we now send forward propositions inadequate to the purpose of real and substantial Amendments, and so far short of the wishes of our Country." Amazingly, the Virginia senate even rejected the proposed Third Amendment—now the First—which drew its inspiration from that state's Declaration of Religious Freedom. The Virginia Antifederalists were so consumed with hostility to the national government that they would deny federal protection of rights they jealously claimed for themselves.

The legislative logjam was finally broken when Senator Lee and George Mason—who had refused to sign the Constitution in Philadelphia—changed their minds and grudgingly agreed to support ratification of the Bill of Rights. Both men feared that the Antifederalists, who looked ahead to the next congressional elections, would be tarred as opponents of the people's rights. Mason, who had first blasted Madison's proposals as "milk and water propositions," now found "much satisfaction" in the Bill of Rights. Even the oratory of Patrick Henry could not overcome these defections, and the Virginia legislature finally ratified all twelve proposed amendments on December 15, 1791, a day now celebrated by federal proclamation as "Bill of Rights Day."

James Madison had stated in the Virginia convention that ratified the Constitution his belief that amendments to that document would be both "unnecessary and dangerous—unnecessary, because it was evident that the general government had no power but what was given it" by the Constitution, and "dangerous, because an enumeration which is not complete is not safe." He also dismissed the need for "parchment barriers" against the powers of Congress. Two years later, after the states ratified ten of the twelve proposed amendments, Madison wrote that adoption of the Bill of Rights "will kill the opposition everywhere, and by putting an end to dissatisfaction with the Government itself, enable the Administration to venture on measures not otherwise safe." The primary advocate in Congress of a bill of rights

displayed an attitude toward the "nauseous project" that moved, grudgingly and solely for political reasons, from hostile opposition to lukewarm support.

Considering the ambivalence of its sponsor, why should Americans now celebrate—even venerate—the Bill of Rights? The reasons have much to do with the survival of the Constitution over more than two centuries, despite a bloody Civil War and continuing discord between the "factions" that Madison felt were inevitable in a democratic society. Adoption of the Bill of Rights was the price we paid for the Constitution, and its protections of fundamental freedoms—for religious and political dissenters, even for those charged with serious crimes—have been applied by the Supreme Court to reach every government official in the land. As Justice Robert Jackson wrote in 1943, "The very purpose of a Bill of Rights was to withdraw certain subjects from the vicissitudes of political controversy, to place them beyond the reach of majorities and officials and to establish them as legal principles to be applied by the courts." With the ratification of the Constitution in 1789 and the Bill of Rights in 1791, it became the task of the Supreme Court to breathe life into their "parchment" provisions (Irons, 1999).

*   *   *   *   *   *

⁓ FEDERALIST PAPER ⁓

Number 78

[ALEXANDER HAMILTON]

WE PROCEED now to an examination of the judiciary department of the proposed government.

In unfolding the defects of the existing Confederation, the utility and necessity of a federal judicature have been clearly pointed out. It is the less necessary to recapitulate the considerations there urged, as the propriety of the institution in the abstract is not disputed; the only questions which have been raised being relative to the manner of constituting it, and to its extent. To these points, therefore, our observations shall be confined. . . .

Whoever attentively considers the different departments of power must perceive that, in a government in which they are separated from each other, the judiciary, from the nature of its functions, will always be the least dangerous to the political rights of the Constitution; because it will be least in a capacity to annoy or injure them. The Executive not only dispenses the honours, but holds the sword of the community. The legislature not only commands the purse, but prescribes the rules by which the duties and rights of every citizen are to be regulated. The judiciary, on the contrary, has no influence over either the sword or the purse; no direction either of the strength or of the wealth of the society; and can take no active resolution, whatever. It may truly be said to have neither FORCE nor WILL, but merely judgment; and must ultimately depend upon the aid of the executive arm even for the efficacy of its judgments.

This simple view of the matter suggests several important consequences. It proves incontestably that the judiciary is beyond comparison the weakest of the three departments of power; that it can never attack with success either of the other two; and that all possible care is requisite to enable it to defend

itself against their attacks. It equally proves that though individual oppression may now and then proceed from the courts of justice, the general liberty of the people can never be endangered from that quarter; I mean so long as the judiciary remains truly distinct from both the legislature and the Executive. For I agree that "there is no liberty, if the power of judging be not separated from the legislative and executive powers." And it proves, in the last place, that as liberty can have nothing to fear from the judiciary alone, but would have everything to fear from its union with either of the other departments; that as all the effects of such a union must ensue from a dependence of the former on the latter, notwithstanding a nominal and apparent separation; that as from the natural feebleness of the judiciary; it is in continual jeopardy of being overpowered, awed, or influenced by its co-ordinate branches; and that as nothing can contribute so much to its firmness and independence as permanency in office, this quality may therefore be justly regarded as an indispensable ingredient in its constitution, and, in a great measure, as the citadel of the public justice and the public security.

The complete independence of the courts of justice is peculiarly essential in a limited Constitution. By a limited Constitution I understand one which contains certain specified exceptions to the legislative authority; such, for instance, as that it shall pass no bills of attainder, no *ex post facto* laws, and the like: Limitations of this kind can be preserved in practice no other way than through the medium of courts of justice, whose duty it must be to declare all acts contrary to the manifest tenor of the Constitution void. Without this, all the reservations of particular rights or privileges would amount to nothing.

Some perplexity respecting the rights of the courts to pronounce legislative acts void, because contrary to the Constitution, has arisen from an imagination that the doctrine would imply a superiority of the judiciary to the legislative power. It is urged that the authority which can declare the acts of another void must necessarily be superior to the one whose acts may be declared void. As this doctrine is of great importance in all the American constitutions, a brief discussion of the ground on which it rests cannot be unacceptable.

There is no position which depends on clearer principles than that every act of a delegated authority, contrary to the tenor of the commission under which it is exercised, is void. No legislative act, therefore, contrary to the Constitution can be valid. To deny this would be to affirm that the deputy is greater than his principal; that the servant is above his master; that the representatives of the people are superior to the people themselves; that men acting by virtue of powers may do not only what their powers do not authorise, but what they forbid.

If it be said that the legislative body are themselves the constitutional judges of their own powers, and that the construction they put upon them is conclusive upon the other departments, it may be answered that this cannot be the natural presumption where it is not to be collected from any particular provisions in the Constitution. It is not otherwise to be supposed that the Constitution could intend to enable the representatives of the people to substitute their *will* to that of their constituents. It is far more rational to suppose that the courts were designed to be an intermediate body between the people and the legislature, in order, among other things, to keep the latter within the limits assigned to their authority. The interpretation of the laws is the proper and peculiar province of the courts. A constitution is, in fact, and must be regarded by the judges, as a fundamental law. It therefore belongs to them to ascertain its meaning, as well as the meaning of any particular act proceeding from the legislative body. If there should happen to be an irreconcilable variance between the two, that which has the superior obligation and validity ought, of course, to be preferred; or, in other words, the Constitution ought to be preferred to the statute, the intention of the people to the intention of their agents.

Nor does this conclusion by any means suppose a superiority of the judicial to the legislative power. It only supposes that the power of the people is superior to both; and that where the will of the legislature, declared in its statutes, stands in opposition to that of the people, declared in the Constitution, the judges ought to be governed by the latter rather than the former. They ought to regulate their decisions by the fundamental laws, rather than by those which are not fundamental.

This exercise of judicial discretion, in determining between two contradictory laws, is exemplified in a familiar instance. It not uncommonly happens that there are two statutes existing at one time, clashing in whole or in part with each other, and neither of them containing any repealing clause or expression. In such a case it is the province of the courts to liquidate and fix their meaning and operation. So far as they can, by any fair construction, be reconciled to each other, reason and law conspire to dictate that this should be done; where this is impracticable, it becomes a matter of necessity to give effect to one in exclusion of the other. The rule which has obtained in the courts for determining their relative validity is, that the last in order of time shall be preferred to the first. But this is a mere rule of construction, not derived from any positive law, but from the nature and reason of the thing. It is a rule not enjoined upon the courts by legislative provision, but adopted by themselves, as consonant to truth and propriety, for the direction of their conduct as interpreters of the law. They thought it reasonable that between the interfering acts of an *equal* authority, that which was the last indication of its will should have the preference.

But in regard to the interfering acts of a superior and subordinate authority, of an original and derivative power, the nature and reason of the thing indicate the converse of that rule as proper to be followed. They teach us that the prior act of a superior ought to be preferred to the subsequent act of an inferior and subordinate authority; and that accordingly, whenever a particular statute contravenes the Constitution, it will be the duty of the judicial tribunals to adhere to the latter and disregard the former.

It can be of no weight to say that the courts, on the pretence of a repugnancy, may substitute their own pleasure to the constitutional intentions of the legislature. This might as well happen in the case of two contradictory statutes; or it might as well happen in every adjudication upon any single statute. The courts must declare the sense of the law; and if they should be disposed to exercise WILL instead of JUDGMENT, the consequence would equally be the substitution of their pleasure to that of the legislative body. The observation, if it prove anything, would prove that there ought to be no judges distinct from that body.

If, then, the courts of justice are to be considered as the bulwarks of a limited Constitution against legislative encroachments, this consideration will afford a strong argument for the permanent tenure of judicial offices, since nothing will contribute so much as this to that independent spirit in the judges which must be essential to the faithful performance of so arduous a duty.

This independence of the judges is equally requisite to guard the Constitution and the rights of individuals from the effects of those ill humours, which the arts of designing men, or the influence of particular conjunctures, sometimes disseminate among the people themselves, and which, though they speedily give place to better information, and more deliberate reflection, have a tendency, in the meantime, to occasion dangerous innovations in the government, and serious oppressions of the minor party in the community. Though I trust the friends of the proposed Constitution will never concur with its enemies, in questioning that fundamental principle of republican government which admits the right of the people to alter or abolish the established Constitution, whenever they find it inconsistent with their happiness, yet it is not to be inferred from this principle that the representatives of the people, whenever a momentary inclination happens to lay hold of a majority of their constituents, incompatible with the provisions in the existing constitution, would, on that account, be justifiable in a violation of those provisions; or that the courts would be under a greater obligation to connive at infractions in this shape than when they had proceeded wholly from the cabals of the representative body. Until the people have, by some solemn and authoritative act, annulled or changed the established form, it is binding upon themselves collectively, as well as individually; and no presumption, or even knowledge, of their sentiments, can warrant their representatives in a departure from it, prior to such an act. But it is easy to see that it would require an uncommon portion of fortitude in the judges to do their duty as faithful guardians of the Constitution where legislative invasions of it had been instigated by the major voice of the community.

But it is not with a view to infractions of the Constitution only that the independence of the judges may be an essential safeguard against the effects of occasional ill humours in the society. These sometimes extend no farther than to the injury of the private rights of particular classes of citizens by unjust and partial laws. Here also the firmness of the judicial magistracy is of vast importance in mitigating the severity and confining the operation of such laws. It not only serves to moderate the immediate mischiefs of those which may have been passed, but it operates as a check upon the legislative body in passing them; who, perceiving that obstacles to the success of iniquitous intention are to be expected from the scruples of the courts, are in a manner compelled, by the very motives of the injustice they meditate to qualify their attempts. This is a circumstance calculated to have more influence upon the character of our governments than but few may be aware of. The benefits of the integrity and moderation of the judiciary have already been felt in more States than one; and though they may have displeased those whose sinister expectations they may have disappointed, they must have commanded the esteem and applause of all the virtuous and disinterested. Considerate men, of every description, ought to prize whatever will tend to be get or fortify that temper in the courts; as no man can be sure that he may not be to-morrow the victim of a spirit of injustice, by which he may be a gainer to-day. And every man must now feel that the inevitable tendency of such a spirit is to sap the foundations of public and private confidence, and to introduce in its stead universal distrust and distress.

That inflexible and uniform adherence to the rights of the Constitution, and of individuals, which we perceive to be indispensable in the courts of justice, can certainly not be expected from judges who hold their offices by a temporary commission. Periodical appointments, however regulated, or by whomsoever made, would, in some way or other, be fatal to their necessary independence. If the power of making them was committed either to the Executive or legislature, there would be danger of an improper complaisance to the branch which possessed it; if to both, there would be an unwillingness to hazard the displeasure of either; if to the people, or to persons chosen by them for the special purpose, there would be too great a disposition to consult popularity, to justify a reliance that nothing would be consulted but the Constitution and the laws.

There is yet a further and a weightier reason for the permanency of the judicial offices which is deducible from the nature of the qualifications they require. It has been frequently remarked, with great propriety, that a voluminous code of laws is one of the inconveniences necessarily connected with the advantages of a free government. To avoid an arbitrary discretion in the courts, it is indispensable that they should be bound down by strict rules and precedents, which serve to define and point out their duty in every particular case that comes before them; and it will readily be conceived from the variety of controversies which grow out of the folly and wickedness of mankind that the records of those precedents must unavoidably swell to a very considerable bulk, and must demand long and laborious study to acquire a competent knowledge of them. Hence it is, that there can be but few men in the society who will have sufficient skill in the laws to qualify them for the stations of judges. And making the proper deductions for the ordinary depravity of human nature, the number must be still smaller of those who unite the requisite integrity with the requisite knowledge. These considerations apprise us that the government can have no great option between fit character; and that a temporary duration in office, which would naturally discourage such characters from quitting a lucrative line of practice to accept a seat on the bench, would have a tendency to throw the administration of justice into hands less able, and less well qualified, to conduct it with utility and dignity.

CHAPTER 2

"To Say What the Law Is"

SECTION 1

"A LAW REPUGNANT TO THE CONSTITUTION"

INTRODUCTION

The Framers provided in Article VI of the Constitution that its provisions "shall be the supreme law of the land" and gave the Supreme Court in Article III jurisdiction over all cases "arising under this Constitution" as well as cases involving "the laws of the United States." Read together, these clauses make clear the intent of the Framers to invest the Court with power to nullify laws that conflicted with its reading of the Constitution. However, the constitutional text left several important questions unanswered. One stemmed from the wording of Article III, giving the Supreme Court "original jurisdiction" over "cases affecting ambassadors, other public ministers and consuls, and those in which a state shall be a party." This clause meant that such cases could begin in the Court, without first being decided by lower federal courts. In all other cases, "the Supreme Court shall have appellate jurisdiction, both as to law and fact, with such exceptions, and under such regulations as the Congress shall make." The wording of this provision left no doubt that Congress could not expand the original jurisdiction of the Supreme Court; only a constitutional amendment could accomplish that.

A dispute over these clauses of the Constitution gave rise to the Court's first test of its power to nullify acts of Congress. The case of *Marbury v. Madison* also gave Chief Justice John Marshall, a staunch Federalist and judicial nationalist, his first opportunity to assert the Court's power, after more than a decade in which it had labored in virtual obscurity. The

Court's only significant decision in the years before Marshall became Chief Justice in 1801, ruling in *Chisholm v. Georgia* in 1793 that citizens of one state could sue another state, had provoked such a political uproar that Congress had enacted and the states ratified the Eleventh Amendment, barring such suits as invasions of state sovereignty. Marshall, who had been placed at the Court's helm by President John Adams, was determined to restore its tarnished reputation. The case of *Marbury v. Madison* confronted the Court with a dispute in which Marshall himself had played a leading role, as secretary of state under President Adams, who lost his post to Thomas Jefferson in the 1800 election. Jefferson had led the Republican party to victory, but the defeated Federalists were reluctant to relinquish the power they had wielded during the Adams administration. Four months elapsed between the national election in November and the change of administration the following March, a delay provided by the first Congress out of concern for bad roads and winter storms, which might keep electors from meeting and sending their votes to Congress. Hardly anyone foresaw the potential mischief that lame-duck lawmakers and presidents could create for their successors, particularly when control of Congress and the White House changed parties. The defeated Federalists in Congress met for their last session in December 1800 and passed a Judiciary Act that President Adams signed in February 1801. The law's most notable provision would reduce the Supreme Court from six to five members after the next vacancy. Many people expected the elderly and frail Justice Cushing to retire soon, and the Federalists wanted to prevent Jefferson from choosing a Republican to replace him. Cushing, although noticeably senile, depended on his judicial salary and hobbled to the Court until 1810.

The Judiciary Act also created twenty-six new posts in the federal district and circuit courts, to relieve the Supreme

Court of the detested burden of circuit-riding. With the nation's capital moved to the District of Columbia, Congress established forty-five positions as "justice of the peace," a minor judicial office that provided a small salary and fees for notarizing papers and handling small claims. Washington was still a small city in 1801 and hardly needed forty-five new judges. But as one Republican paper accurately noted, Congress had passed "a bill providing sinecure places and pensions for thoroughgoing Federal partisans." President Adams and Congress spent considerable time picking and confirming the new district and circuit judges in the weeks before Jefferson took office. Faced with a deadline of midnight on March 3, Congress met into the night and rushed through confirmations of the new justices of the peace. Clerks quickly delivered their commissions to Secretary of State Marshall, who signed the parchment documents and stacked them on his desk.

In the last-minute rush, however, Marshall neglected to have the commissions delivered to the "midnight judges," as Republicans derisively called them. One account—probably apocryphal—had the incoming attorney general, Levi Lincoln, dramatically striding into Marshall's office with Jefferson's watch in his hand. Pointing to the timepiece, Lincoln informed Marshall that midnight had arrived and directed him to leave the office. Humiliated by this order, Marshall laid down his pen and departed. Whether or not this actually happened, Marshall did keep signing judicial commissions until at least nine o'clock that night. Shortly after Jefferson took his oath as president on March 4, 1801, James Madison took Marshall's office as secretary of state and sat behind the desk on which the undelivered commissions rested.

This was the odd beginning of the famous case of *Marbury v. Madison,* which started with Marshall's oversight in 1801 as secretary of state and culminated in 1803 with his forceful assertion of judicial review as Chief Justice. The two years in between were marked by Republican efforts to hobble the federal courts that remained as Federalist redoubts. "The Federalists have retired into the judiciary as a stronghold," Jefferson complained after taking office, "and from that battery all the works of republicanism are to be beaten down and erased." He directed Madison to deliver only twenty-five of the forty-two commissions Marshall left on his desk, perhaps to cut expenses for judicial salaries, even the small amount for these minor posts.

Of the seventeen slighted judges, only four—including William Marbury—took their claims to court, filing suit in the Supreme Court and asking for a "writ of mandamus" against Secretary Madison. This common-law writ, with roots in English practice, empowers judges to order recalcitrant officials to carry out their duties; the Latin term comes from the word for "hand." In effect, the judge issuing the writ is forcing the official to move his hand. Marshall had not lifted his hand to deliver Marbury's commission and Madison now refused to complete the task.

Marbury's suit against Madison languished in the Supreme Court clerk's office for two years before it was argued. The Court, in fact, did not conduct any business for more than a year, as the Republican majority in Congress exacted revenge on the Federalists for passing the Sedition Act in 1798 and for packing the federal courts in 1801. Over Federalist protests, Congress repealed the Judiciary Act of 1801 and

then passed a law moving the Court's next term, scheduled for June 1802, to February 1803. This move did not remove any sitting judges from their posts, but the Republicans wanted to prevent the Court from striking down the repeal bill as unconstitutional while they prepared impeachment charges against federal judges (and perhaps even Supreme Court justices) for partisan bias in Sedition Act prosecutions.

Although some extreme Federalists implored Marshall to convene the Court in June 1802 as originally scheduled, he prudently decided to avoid a confrontation with Congress that might have provoked even further efforts to cripple the Court. But when the justices did meet in February 1803, for the first time in fourteen months, Marshall was ready to respond. Both sides in *Marbury v. Madison* expected the justices to issue the requested writ of mandamus, which would likely have precipitated the constitutional crisis that political moderates feared and that extremists in both parties welcomed as an overdue showdown between the Republican "Jacobins" and the Federalist "Tories."

Anticipating defeat, James Madison did not even send a lawyer to defend him, passing up the chance to blame Marshall for the entire mess. William Marbury's lawyer, former attorney general Charles Lee, brimmed with confidence as he addressed the justices. The Court had three simple questions before it, Lee argued, and the answer to each was obvious. First, was Marbury entitled to his commission? Article I of the Constitution empowers Congress to create federal offices. Marbury was duly nominated for the post that Congress established, he was duly confirmed by the Senate, and his commission was duly signed by the secretary of state, as the law provided. The answer to Lee's first question was obviously yes. Second, did the law provide Marbury a remedy for Madison's refusal to deliver his commission? The answer came from the old maxim "Every wrong provides a remedy." Otherwise, courts would have no power or even purpose.

The only remaining question was whether mandamus provided the remedy in Marbury's suit. Lee did not even consider this a question but a settled fact. The First Congress had authorized the Supreme Court in Section 13 of the Judiciary Act of 1789 to issue writs of mandamus against "persons holding office under the authority of the United States." Secretary Madison was such a person, and the writ of mandamus was necessary to force his compliance with a clear legal duty to Marbury. Lee stated his case as if he were reciting a simple syllogism.

Chief Justice Marshall issued the Court's opinion in *Marbury v. Madison* on February 24, 1803, just two weeks after Lee's argument. Given the rhetorical polish of this momentous opinion, Marshall had most likely decided the case and begun writing before Lee opened his mouth. He wrote for himself and three other justices; because of illness, William Cushing and Alfred Moore did not hear argument or vote in the case. Marshall posed the three questions Charles Lee had asked and answered each in turn. The first and second gave Marshall no trouble. It was "the opinion of the Court," he wrote, that "by signing the commission of Mr. Marbury, the president of the United States appointed him a justice of the peace" and that "the seal of the United States, affixed thereto by the secretary of state," conferred on Marbury "a legal right to the office" he sought. Madison's refusal to deliver that commission "is a plain violation of that right, for which the laws of his country afford him a remedy."

Marbury won the right to his commission, but could the Court order Madison to deliver it? Marshall's answer to this question surprised everyone and cleverly defused the constitutional crisis he hoped to avoid. Congress had authorized the Supreme Court to issue writs of mandamus, but Article III of the Constitution limited the Court's "original jurisdiction" to cases involving ambassadors, foreign consuls, and states. In all other cases, the Court had only "appellate jurisdiction" over decisions of lower courts, both state and federal. William Marbury made the fatal mistake of filing his suit in the Supreme Court, wrongly assuming that it had jurisdiction under Section 13 of the Judiciary Act to decide his claim. Marshall concluded that "the jurisdiction must be appellate, not original," for the Court to authorize writs of mandamus.

With that conclusion, Marbury's suit against Madison was over. He could, of course, ask a lower court to issue the writ; Marshall had not offered this advice in his opinion, but a good lawyer like Charles Lee would know how to remedy the error. Normally, if a judge decides that his (or her) court lacks jurisdiction over a case, the judge refrains from expressing an opinion on the merits of that case. But Marshall did not stop with his holding that Marbury had filed suit in the wrong court. He continued with a stern lecture to Congress, asserting the Court's power to declare the offending Section 13 unconstitutional. His words rang with certitude and confidence. He began with a rhetorical question. "If an act of the legislature, repugnant to the Constitution, is void, does it, notwithstanding its invalidity, bind the courts, and oblige them to give it effect?" Answering yes to this question, Marshall wrote, would be "an absurdity too gross to be insisted on."

Marshall's next question was implied by the first. Who decides if a law is unconstitutional? His answer was clear and simple. "It is emphatically the province and duty of the judicial department to say what the law is," he wrote. Because "the Constitution is superior to any ordinary act of the legislature," the provisions of the Constitution "must govern the case to which they both apply." Arguments that "courts must close their eyes on the Constitution, and see only the law," Marshall wrote, "would subvert the very foundation of all written constitutions."

In going beyond the questions raised in *Marbury* and proclaiming the Supreme Court's power to strike down congressional acts, Marshall deliberately threw down a gauntlet before Congress. He took a calculated risk, knowing that President Jefferson had recently asked Congress to impeach a Federalist judge, John Pickering of New Hampshire, for partisan bias in Sedition Act prosecutions. Marshall must have known that if Pickering—who was both alcoholic and insane—was removed from office, the Republicans might turn their guns on the Supreme Court. The political stakes were high, but Marshall did not flinch.

Several generations of historians have elevated Marshall to the pantheon of judicial greatness and have annointed his *Marbury* opinion as the most important in American constitutional history. Marshall certainly led the Supreme Court from obscurity to a position of power. But his *Marbury* opinion did not break new legal ground. The doctrine of judicial review had been stated by several Framers of the Constitution in 1787, was refined in *The Federalist Papers* during the ratification debates, and was forcefully restated by Justice Paterson in 1795, when he wrote in a circuit court decision that "every act of the legislature repugnant to the Constitution is absolutely void." What transformed *Marbury* from a simple "jurisdiction" case, sending the plaintiff back to a lower court, into a constitutional landmark was John Marshall's determination to force a showdown with Thomas Jefferson—his political foe and personal enemy—over the most basic question in politics: Who rules?

The *Marbury* case presented this question in its clearest form. If Congress ruled in authorizing the Supreme Court to issue writs of mandamus, then Congress could expand or contract the Court's jurisdiction at will. And if the president ruled in directing James Madison to withhold judicial commissions that Congress had confirmed and Marshall had signed, the executive branch could evade judicial orders. But if the Supreme Court could strike down legislative acts, and invalidate executive actions based on such laws, the justices would hold the power "to say what the law is" and bind the Congress and president to their decisions.

Marshall's opinion in *Marbury* is best understood not as a legal opinion but as a political act. As a committed Federalist, he knew that his nationalist views could only survive Jefferson's "Jacobin" regime if the Supreme Court employed the power of judicial review to keep the president and Congress in check. Marshall won his first duel with Jefferson in the *Marbury* case. There were, in fact, no more shots fired in public before Marshall died in 1835 (Irons, 1999).

MARBURY V. MADISON
5 U.S. 137 (1803)

CHIEF JUSTICE MARSHALL delivered the opinion of the Court.

At the last term on the affidavits then read and filed with the clerk, a rule was granted in this case, requiring the Secretary of State to show cause why a mandamus should not issue, directing him to deliver to William Marbury his commission as a justice of the peace for the county of Washington, in the district of Columbia.

No cause has been shown, and the present motion is for a mandamus. The peculiar delicacy of this case, the novelty of some of its circumstances, and the real difficulty attending the points which occur in it, require a complete exposition of the principles on which the opinion to be given by the court is founded. . . .

In the order in which the court has viewed this subject, the following questions have been considered and decided:

1st. Has the applicant a right to the commission he demands?
2d. If he has a right, and that right has been violated, do the laws of his country afford him a remedy?
3d. If they do afford him a remedy, is it a mandamus issuing from this court?

The first object of inquiry is: Has the applicant a right to the commission he demands? . . . It [is] decidedly the opinion of the court, that when a commission has been signed by the president, the appointment is made; and that the commission is complete, when the seal of the United States has been affixed to it by the secretary of state. . . . To withhold his commission, therefore, is an act deemed by the court not warranted by law, but violative of a vested legal right.

This brings us to the second inquiry; which is: If he has a right, and that right has been violated, do the laws of his country afford him a remedy? The very essence of civil liberty certainly consists in the right of every individual to claim the protection of the laws, whenever he receives an injury. One of the first duties of government is to afford that protection. [The] government of the United States has been emphatically termed a government of laws, and not of men. It will certainly cease to deserve this high appellation, if the laws furnish no remedy for the violation of a vested legal right. . . .

By the constitution of the United States, the President is invested with certain important political powers, in the exercise of which he is to use his own discretion, and is accountable only to his country in his political character, and to his own conscience. To aid him in the performance of these duties, he is authorized to appoint certain officers, who act by his authority and in conformity with his orders. In such cases, their acts are his acts; and whatever opinion may be entertained of the manner in which executive discretion may be used, still there exists, and can exist, no power to control that discretion. The subjects are political. They respect the nation, not individual rights, and being entrusted to the executive, the decision of the executive is conclusive. . . . But when the legislature proceeds to impose on that officer other duties; when he is directed peremptorily to perform certain acts; when the rights of individuals are dependent on the performance of those acts; he is so far the officer of the law; is amenable to the laws for his conduct; and cannot at his discretion sport away the vested rights of others. The conclusion from this reasoning is, that where the heads of departments are the political or confidential agents of the executive, merely to execute the will of the President, or rather to act in cases in which the executive possesses a constitutional or legal discretion, nothing can be more perfectly clear than that their acts are only politically examinable. But where a specific duty is assigned by law, and individual rights depend upon the performance of that duty, it seems equally clear, that the individual who considers himself injured, has a right to resort to the laws of his country for a remedy. . . . It is, then, the opinion of the court [that Marbury has a] right to the commission; a refusal to deliver which is a plain violation of that right, for which the laws of his country afford him a remedy.

It remains to be enquired whether, thirdly, [h]e is entitled to the remedy for which he applies. This depends on [t]he nature of the writ applied for, and [t]he power of this court. First, [t]he nature of the writ. . . . This, then, is a plain case for a mandamus, either to deliver the commission, or a copy of it from the record; and it only remains to be enquired, [w]hether it can issue from this court. The act to establish the judicial courts of the United States authorizes the Supreme Court "to issue writs of mandamus in cases warranted by the principles and usages of law, to any courts appointed, or persons holding office, under the authority of the United States." The Secretary of State, being a person holding an office under the authority of the United States, is precisely within the letter of the description; and if this court is not authorized to issue a writ of mandamus to such an officer, it must be because the law is unconstitutional, and therefore incapable of conferring the authority, and assigning the duties which its words purport to confer and assign.

The constitution vests the whole judicial power of the United States in one Supreme Court, and such inferior courts as congress shall, from time to time, ordain and establish. This power is expressly extended to all cases arising under the laws of the United States; and, consequently, in some form, may be exercised over the present case; because the right claimed is given by a law of the United States. In the distribution of this power it is declared that "the Supreme Court shall have original jurisdiction in all cases affecting ambassadors, other public ministers and consuls, and those in which a state shall be a party. In all other cases, the Supreme Court shall have appellate jurisdiction." It has been insisted, at the bar, that as the original grant of jurisdiction, to the supreme and inferior courts, is general, and the clause, assigning original jurisdiction to the Supreme Court, contains no negative or restrictive words, the power remains to the legislature, to assign original jurisdiction to that court in other cases than those specified in the article which has been recited; provided those cases belong to the judicial power of the United States. If it had been intended to leave it in the discretion of the legislature to apportion the judicial power between the supreme and inferior courts according to the will of that body, it would certainly have been useless to have proceeded further than to have defined the judicial power, and the tribunals in which it should be vested. The subsequent part of the section is mere surplusage, is entirely without meaning, if such is to be the construction. If congress remains at liberty to give this court appellate jurisdiction, where the constitution has declared their jurisdiction shall be original; and original jurisdiction where the constitution has declared it shall be appellate; the distribution of jurisdiction, made in the constitution, is form without substance. Affirmative words are often, in their operation, negative of other objects than those affirmed; and in this case, a negative or exclusive sense must be given to them or they have no operation at all. It cannot be presumed that any clause in the constitution is intended to be without effect; and, therefore, such a construction is inadmissible, unless the words require it. . . .

To enable this court, then, to issue a mandamus, it must be shown to be an exercise of appellate jurisdiction, or to be necessary to enable them to exercise appellate jurisdiction. It has been stated at the bar that the appellate jurisdiction may be exercised in a variety of forms, and that if it be the will of the legislature that a mandamus should be used for that purpose, that will must be obeyed. This is true, yet the jurisdiction must be appellate, not original. It is the essential criterion of appellate jurisdiction, that it revises and corrects the proceedings in a cause already instituted, and does not create that cause. Although, therefore, a mandamus may be directed to courts, yet to issue such a writ to an officer for the delivery of a paper, is in effect the same as to sustain an original action for that paper, and, therefore, seems not to belong to appellate, but to original jurisdiction. Neither is it necessary in such a case as this, to enable the court to exercise its appellate jurisdiction. The authority, therefore, given to the Supreme Court, by the act establishing the judicial courts of the United States, to issue writs of mandamus to public officers, appears not to be warranted by the constitution; and it becomes necessary to enquire whether a jurisdiction, so conferred, can be exercised.

The question, whether an act, repugnant to the constitution, can become the law of the land, is a question deeply interesting to the United States; but happily, not of an intricacy proportioned to its interest. It seems only necessary to recognize certain principles, supposed to have been long and well established, to decide it. That the people have an original right to establish, for their future government, such principles as, in their opinion, shall most conduce to their own happiness, is the basis on which the whole American fabric has been erected. The exercise of this original right is a very great exertion; nor can it, nor ought it, to be frequently repeated. The principles, therefore, so established, are deemed fundamental. And as the authority from which they proceed is supreme, and can seldom act, they are designed to be permanent.

This original and supreme will organizes the government, and assigns to different departments their respective powers. It may either stop here, or establish certain limits not to be transcended by those departments. The government of the United States is of the latter description. The powers of the legislature are defined and limited; and that those limits may not be mistaken, or forgotten, the constitution is written. To what purpose are powers limited, and to what purpose is that limitation committed to writing, if these limits may, at any time, be passed by those intended to be restrained? The distinction between a government with limited and unlimited powers is abolished, if those limits do not confine the persons on whom they are imposed, and if acts prohibited and acts allowed, are of equal obligation. It is a proposition too plain to be contested, that the constitution controls any legislative act repugnant to it; or, that the legislature may alter the constitution by an ordinary act. Between these alternatives there is no middle ground. The constitution is either a superior, paramount law, unchangeable by ordinary means, or it is on a level with ordinary legislative acts, and, like other acts, is alterable when the legislature shall please to alter it. If the former part of the alternative be true, then a legislative act contrary to the constitution is not law: if the latter part be true, then written constitutions are absurd attempts, on the part of the people, to limit a power in its own nature illimitable.

Certainly all those who have framed written constitutions contemplate them as forming the fundamental and paramount law of the nation, and consequently, the theory of every such government must be, that an act of the legislature, repugnant to the constitution, is void. This theory is essentially attached to a written constitution, and is, consequently, to be considered, by this court, as one of the fundamental principles of our society. It is not therefore to be lost sight of in the further consideration of this subject.

If an act of the legislature, repugnant to the constitution, is void, does it, notwithstanding its invalidity, bind the courts, and oblige them to give it effect? Or, in other words, though it be not law, does it constitute a rule as operative as if it was a law? This would be to overthrow in fact what was established in theory; and would seem, at first view, an absurdity too gross to be insisted on. It shall, however, receive a more attentive consideration.

It is emphatically the province and duty of the judicial department to say what the law is. Those who apply the rule to particular cases, must of necessity expound and interpret that rule. If two laws conflict with each other, the courts must decide on the operation of each. So if a law be in opposition to the constitution; if both the law and the constitution apply to a particular case, so that the court must either decide that case conformably to the law, disregarding the constitution; or conformably to the constitution, disregarding the law; the court must determine which of these conflicting rules governs the case. This is of the very essence of judicial duty. If, then, the courts are to regard the constitution, and the constitution is superior to any ordinary act of the legislature, the constitution, and not such ordinary act, must govern the case to which they both apply. Those then who controvert the principle that the constitution is to be considered, in court, as a paramount law, are reduced to the necessity of maintaining that the courts must close their eyes on the constitution, and see only the law. This doctrine would subvert the very foundation of all written constitutions. It would declare that an act which, according to the principles and theory of our government, is entirely void, is yet, in practice, completely obligatory. It would declare that if the legislature shall do what is expressly forbidden, such act, notwithstanding the express prohibition, is in reality effectual. It would be giving to the legislature a practical and real omnipotence, with the same breath which professes to restrict their powers within narrow limits. It is prescribing limits, and declaring that those limits may be passed at pleasure.

That it thus reduces to nothing what we have deemed the greatest improvement on political institutions—a written constitution—would of itself be sufficient, in America, where written constitutions have been viewed with so much reverence, for rejecting the construction. But the peculiar expressions of the constitution of the United States furnish additional arguments in favor of its rejection. The judicial power of the United States is extended to all cases arising under the constitution. Could it be the intention of those who gave this power, to say that in using it the constitution should not be looked into? That a case arising under the constitution should be decided without examining the instrument under which it arises? This is too extravagant to be maintained. In some cases, then, the constitution must be looked into by the judges. And if they can open it at all, what part of it are they forbidden to read or to obey? . . . There are many other parts of the constitution which serve to illustrate this subject.

It is declared that "no tax or duty shall be laid on articles exported from any state." Suppose a duty on the export of cotton, of tobacco, or of flour; and a suit instituted to recover it. Ought judgment to be rendered in such a case? Ought the judges to close their eyes on the constitution, and only see the law? The constitution declares that "no bill of attainder or ex post facto law shall be passed." If, however, such a bill should be passed, and a person should be prosecuted under it; must the court condemn to death those victims whom the constitution endeavors to preserve? "No person," says the constitution, "shall be convicted of treason unless on the testimony of two witnesses to the same overt act, or on confession in open court." Here the language of the constitution is addressed especially to the courts. It prescribes, directly for them, a rule of evidence not to be departed from. If the legislature should change that rule, and declare one witness, or a confession out of court, sufficient for conviction, must the constitutional principle yield to the legislative act? From these, and many other selections which might be made, it is apparent, that the framers of the constitution contemplated that instrument as a rule for the government of courts, as well as of the legislature. . . .

It is also not entirely unworthy of observation that in declaring what shall be the supreme law of the land, the constitution itself is first mentioned; and not the laws of the United States generally, but those only which shall be made in pursuance of the constitution, have that rank. Thus, the particular phraseology of the constitution of the United States confirms and strengthens the principle, supposed to be essential to all written constitutions, that a law repugnant to the constitution is void; and that courts, as well as other departments, are bound by that instrument. The rule must be discharged.

SECTION 2

"A SCHEME OF ORDERED LIBERTY"

INTRODUCTION

Chief Justice Marshall's opinion in the *Marbury* case was handed down two years after he assumed the Court's leadership in 1801. He wrote another landmark opinion just two years before his death in 1835, in a case that Marshall also considered equally simple to decide. In *Barron v. Baltimore,* decided in 1833, the justices faced the question of whether the Constitution prohibits the states as well as Congress from depriving "any person" of their "life, liberty, or property, without due process of law," as provided by the Fifth Amendment. The *Barron* case required the Court to decide, for the first time, whether the Bill of Rights applied to the states or just to the federal government. As has often happened in American constitutional history, a question of great significance was presented in a run-of-the-mill case.

The suit between John Barron and the city of Baltimore began with a road-building project in 1815. Barron's family operated a shipping wharf in Baltimore's harbor, and the largest vessels could dock at the wharf. But the soil dumped into the harbor as roads were graded and washed into it by rains gradually blocked access to the wharf for the large ships that had previously loaded and unloaded goods into nearby warehouses. Barron sued the city in state court in 1822, claiming that its actions violated the Fifth Amendment provision barring the taking of "private property . . . for public use without just compensation." A jury awarded Barron $4,500 in damages, but the state's highest court reversed this judgment, holding that the city was not subject to the provisions of the Bill of Rights.

Chief Justice Marshall disposed of this case in one of his shortest opinions. He stated Barron's claim to the protection of the Fifth Amendment in these words: "He insists that this amendment, being in favor of the liberty of the citizen, ought to be so construed as to restrain the legislative power of a state, as well as that of the United States." Marshall brushed aside Barron's argument: "The question thus presented is, we think, of great importance, but not of much difficulty." The Constitution was "established by the people of the United States for themselves, for their own government, and not for the government of the individual states," he wrote. But the question was not as simple, nor the answer as clear, as Marshall presumed. For one thing, the Framers had placed in the Constitution, in Section 10 of Article I, several express limitations on state powers. One of them—as we have seen—barred states from passing laws "impairing the obligation of contracts," a provision Marshall had used to strike down many state laws. But he attempted to turn the provisions of Section 10 to his advantage. "It is worthy of remark," he wrote, "that these inhibitions generally restrain state legislation on subjects entrusted to the general government, or in which the people of all the states feel an interest." Legislation regarding contracts, however, was not solely entrusted to Congress, and the people of all the states had an interest in protecting their property from "taking" without just compensation. Why could they not turn to federal courts for protection of rights granted in the Constitution?

Marshall answered this question by asserting that the express limitations on state power in Section 10 were the only ones intended by the Framers. He required some "strong reason" for departing from this "safe and judicious" reading of their intent. "We search in vain for that reason," Marshall wrote. He noted that the Constitution was ratified over the "immense opposition" of those who demanded a bill of rights to restrain the powers of Congress. Marshall had voted in the Virginia ratification convention against Antifederalist demands for a bill of rights. But with the Fifth Amendment before him for interpretation, he took the "safe and judicious" course of deciding that it "is not applicable to the legislation of the states." Marshall ruled in John Barron's lawsuit that the Supreme Court "has no jurisdiction of the cause; and it is dismissed."

The Court's unanimous decision in *Barron v. Baltimore* came near the end of Marshall's long tenure as Chief Justice. His opinion attracted little notice in 1833, and little discussion since then; one recent history of the Supreme Court relegated the *Barron* case to a footnote. Most constitutional scholars have simply assumed that Marshall reached the right conclusion in this case, and that those who framed the Bill of Rights had not intended to protect the people against oppression by the states, as they did from Congress. But Marshall was a fervent nationalist and almost always gave an expansive reading to the Constitution. It would have been more in character for him to force the states into compliance with federal standards. However, he had little respect for the rights of "the people" against the government—state or federal. Forced to choose between these countering principles, he did not find "much difficulty" in rejecting the argument based on individual rights (Irons, 1999).

BARRON V. BALTIMORE
32 U.S. 243 (1833)

MR. CHIEF JUSTICE MARSHALL delivered the opinion of the Court.

The constitution was ordained and established by the people of the United States for themselves, for their own government, and not for the government of the individual states. Each state established a constitution for itself, and, in that constitution, provided such limitations and restrictions on the powers of its particular government as its judgment dictated. The people of the United States framed such a government for the United States as they supposed best adapted to their situation, and best calculated to promote their interests. The powers they conferred on this government were to be exercised by itself; and the limitations on power, if expressed in general terms, are naturally, and, we think, necessarily applicable to the government created by the instrument. They are limitations of power granted in the instrument itself; not of distinct governments, framed by different persons and for different purposes.

If these propositions be correct, the fifth amendment must be understood as restraining the power of the general government, not as applicable to the states. In their several constitutions they have imposed such restrictions on their respective governments as their own wisdom suggested; such as they deemed most proper for themselves. It is a subject on which they judge exclusively, and with which others interfere no farther than they are supposed to have a common interest. . . .

Had the people of the several states, or any of them, required changes in their constitutions; had they required additional safeguards to liberty from the apprehended encroachments of their particular governments: the remedy was in their own hands, and would have been applied by themselves. A convention would have been assembled by the discontented state, and the required improvements would have been made by itself. The unwieldy and cumbrous machinery of procuring a recommendation from two-thirds of congress, and the assent of three-fourths of their sister states, could never have occurred to any human being as a mode of doing that which might be effected by the state itself. Had the framers of these amendments intended them to be limitations on the powers of the state governments, they would have imitated the framers of the original constitution, and have expressed that intention. Had congress engaged in the extra-ordinary occupation of improving the constitutions of the several states by affording the people additional protection from the exercise of power by their own governments in matters which concerned themselves alone, they would have declared this purpose in plain and intelligible language.

But it is universally understood, it is a part of the history of the day, that the great revolution which established the constitution of the United States, was not effected without immense opposition. Serious fears were extensively entertained that those powers which the patriot statesmen, who then watched over the interests of our country, deemed essential to union, and to the attainment of those invaluable objects for which union was sought, might be exercised in a manner dangerous to liberty. In almost every convention by which the constitution was adopted, amendments to guard against the abuse of power were recommended. These amendments demanded security against the apprehended encroachments of the general government not against those of the local governments.

In compliance with a sentiment thus generally expressed, to quiet fears thus extensively entertained, amendments were proposed by the required majority in congress, and adopted by the states. These amendments contain no expression indicating an intention to apply them to the state governments. This court cannot so apply them.

We are of opinion that the provision in the fifth amendment to the constitution, declaring that private property shall not be taken for public use without just compensation, is intended solely as a limitation on the exercise of power by the government of the United States, and is not applicable to the legislation of the states. We are therefore of opinion that there is no repugnancy between the several acts of the general assembly of Maryland, given in evidence by the defendants at the trial of this cause, in the court of that state, and the constitution of the United States. This court, therefore, has no jurisdiction of the cause; and it is dismissed.

Chief Justice Marshall's emphatic opinion in the *Barron* case slammed the courthouse door on claims that state laws violated the provisions of the Bill of Rights. Forty years after this decision, however, American society and the Constitution had been profoundly changed by the struggle over slavery and the Civil War, for which the Court bore a major responsibility with its 1857 decision in the *Dred Scott* case (see Chapter 8). Under the control of Radical Republicans, the

Congress adopted and the states ratified the Fourteenth Amendment in 1868. Designed to reverse the Court's holding in *Dred Scott* that no person of African ancestry, not only slaves but free blacks as well, could be a citizen of the United States or of the states in which they lived, the Fourteenth Amendment provided that no state could "deprive any person of life, liberty, or property, without due process of law; nor deny to any person within its jurisdiction the equal protection of the laws."

Over the past century, the due process and equal protection clauses of the Fourteenth Amendment have been transformed by the Supreme Court into bulwarks of protection against arbitrary and discriminatory action by the states. However, another clause of the amendment gave rise in the nineteenth century to claims against the states, which cannot "make or enforce any law which shall abridge the privileges or immunities of citizens of the United States." The meaning and scope of the "privileges and immunities" clause produced considerable debate over the extent to which it "incorporated" into the Fourteenth Amendment the provisions of the Bill of Rights. Those who advocated the position that the amendment's Framers intended to "incorporate" some or all of the Bill of Rights into the Fourteenth Amendment and apply them to the states were met with arguments that incorporation would violate the rights of states to legislate on any subject that might involve civil rights and liberties.

Significantly, the Supreme Court first addressed the incorporation issue in a case decided in 1873, the year after the "stolen election" of 1872 placed in the White House a Republican president, Rutherford B. Hayes, who proceeded to honor his campaign pledge to end the Reconstruction policies that had placed the former Confederate states under federal rule. The demise of Reconstruction signaled the victory of the adherents of state sovereignty. In this changed political landscape, the Supreme Court decided a case that had nothing to do with the rights of the former slaves but which nonetheless turned the Fourteenth Amendment into a toothless pledge of protection against state oppression.

The issue before the Court in the *Slaughterhouse Cases* stemmed from a law passed by the Louisiana legislature—most of whose members had sold their votes—that established a monopoly in New Orleans over livestock slaughtering. The butchers who had been excluded from the monopoly charged in federal court that the law and the monopoly it created had violated their "privileges and immunities" under the Fourteenth Amendment. One of these "privileges," dating back to the common-law tradition of England and the colonies, was the right to pursue an occupation on equal terms with other merchants or tradesmen. In deciding the *Slaughterhouse Cases*, the Supreme Court slammed the door on claims against the states by their citizens that were based on the provisions of the Bill of Rights.

SLAUGHTER HOUSE CASES
83 U.S. 36 (1873)

Opinion for the Court by Justice Miller

Was it the purpose of the fourteenth amendment, by the simple declaration that no State should make or enforce any law which shall abridge the privileges and immunities of *citizens of the United States*, to transfer the security and protection of all the civil rights which we have mentioned, from the States to the Federal government? And where it is declared that Congress shall have the power to enforce that article, was it intended to bring within the power of Congress the entire domain of civil rights heretofore belonging exclusively to the States?

All this and more must follow, if the proposition of the plaintiffs . . . be sound. For not only are these rights subject to the control of Congress whenever in its discretion any of them are supposed to be abridged by State legislation, but that body may also pass laws in advance, limiting and restricting the exercise of legislative power by the States, in their most ordinary and usual functions, as in its judgment it may think proper on all such subjects. And still further, such a construction followed by the reversal of the judgments of the Supreme Court of Louisiana in these cases, would constitute this court a perpetual censor upon all legislation of the States, on the civil rights of their own citizens, with authority to nullify such as it did not approve as consistent with those rights, as they existed at the time of the adoption of this amendment. The argument we admit is not always the most conclusive which is drawn from the consequences urged against the adoption of a particular construction of an instrument. But when, as in the case before us, these consequences are so serious, so far-reaching and pervading, so great a departure from the structure and spirit of our institutions; when the effect is to fetter and degrade the State governments by subjecting them to the control of Congress, in the exercise of powers heretofore universally conceded to them of the most ordinary and fundamental character; when in fact it radically changes the whole theory of the relations of the State and Federal governments to each other and of both these governments to the people; the argument has a force that is irresistible, in the absence of language which expresses such a purpose too clearly to admit of doubt.

We are convinced that no such results were intended by the Congress which proposed these amendments, nor by the legislatures of the States which ratified them.

The debate over the "incorporation" of the Bill of Rights into the Fourteenth Amendment, seemingly decided by the

Supreme Court in the *Slaughterhouse Cases,* was revived in the years that followed World War I, which produced a spate of state laws that restricted rights of free speech and press. Many state legislatures, alarmed by the growth and appeal of radical political groups, including the Communist parties that advocated violent revolution to overthrow the capitalist system, passed "criminal anarchy" and "criminal syndicalism" laws that subjected members of these groups to prosecution and prison terms. Those who challenged such laws again raised the incorporation argument, and found a receptive audience at the Supreme Court, as the process of "selective incorporation" began in 1925 with the Court's ruling in *Gitlow v. New York* (see Chapter 5). This case involved a Communist leader, Benjamin Gitlow, who had been convicted and sentenced to prison for violating New York's criminal anarchy law by publishing and distributing a revolutionary manifesto. Ironically, the Court upheld Gitlow's conviction, but in the majority opinion, Justice Edward Sanford stated:

> For present purposes we may and do assume that freedom of speech and of the press—which are protected by the First Amendment from abridgement by Congress—are among the fundamental personal rights and "liberties" protected by the due process clause of the Fourteenth Amendment from impairment by the states.

Justices Oliver Wendell Holmes and Louis Brandeis issued a dissenting opinion in the *Gitlow* case, arguing that Gitlow's manifesto presented "no present danger of an attempt to overthrow the government" of New York. But the dissenters agreed with the majority that the protection of speech against state abridgement "must be taken to be included in the Fourteenth Amendment." On this "incorporation" issue, all the justices sided with those who argued that the duplication of the wording of the due process clause in both the Fifth and Fourteenth Amendments clearly established the intent of those who framed the latter amendment to protect such "fundamental personal rights" as free speech and press from unreasonable state infringement.

The Court left unanswered in its *Gitlow* decision the larger question of just which "fundamental" rights and liberties in the Bill of Rights were incorporated into the Fourteenth Amendment, aside from the protection of free speech and press in the First Amendment. The advocates of "total incorporation" made their argument forcefully, but unsuccessfully, in a case decided in 1937. The issue in *Palko v. Connecticut* was whether the Fifth Amendment's protection against "double jeopardy" banned the state from a second trial for a criminal defendant who had been convicted of murder but whose conviction had been reversed by a state court, on grounds that the trial judge had improperly excluded Frank Palko's confession at his trial. Palko had been convicted and sentenced to life imprisonment for killing two police officers during a robbery. The state prosecutors had successfully urged the appellate court to allow the introduction of his confession and to retry the case before a new jury, which again convicted Palko and sentenced him to die in the electric chair.

Ironically, as had occurred in the *Gitlow* case, the Supreme Court upheld the defendant's conviction, while at the same time advancing the cause of incorporating provisions of the Bill of Rights into the Fourteenth Amendment. The Court, however, rejected the "total incorporation" argument of Palko's lawyers and held that the Fifth Amendment's command that no person shall "be subject for the same offense to be twice put in jeopardy of life and limb" was not among rights protected against state abridgement, because it was "not of the very essence of a scheme of ordered liberty." In contrast, the Court said in the opinion of Justice Benjamin Cardozo (himself a former state judge), the "specific pledges" of the First Amendment were so important that "neither liberty nor justice would exist if they were sacrificed." The *Palko* decision extended the *Gitlow* ruling to include the rights of free exercise of religion and of peaceable assembly within the incorporation doctrine, while leaving open for later cases the question of which other "fundamental rights" might be "implicit in the concept of ordered liberty, and thus, through the Fourteenth Amendment, become valid as against the states."

PALKO V. CONNECTICUT
302 U.S. 319 (1937)

MR. JUSTICE CARDOZO delivered the opinion of the Court.

The argument for appellant is that whatever is forbidden by the Fifth Amendment is forbidden by the Fourteenth also. The Fifth Amendment, which is not directed to the states, but solely to the federal government, creates immunity from double jeopardy. No person shall be "subject for the same offense to be twice put in jeopardy of life or limb." The Fourteenth Amendment ordains, "nor shall any State deprive any person of life, liberty, or property, without due process of law." To retry a defendant, though under one indictment

and only one, subjects him, it is said, to double jeopardy in violation of the Fifth Amendment, if the prosecution is one on behalf of the United States. From this the consequence is said to follow that there is a denial of life or liberty without due process of law, if the prosecution is one on behalf of the People of a State. . . .

We have said that in appellant's view the Fourteenth Amendment is to be taken as embodying the prohibitions of the Fifth. His thesis is even broader. Whatever would be a violation of the original bill of rights (Amendments I to VIII) if done by the federal government is now equally unlawful by force of the Fourteenth Amendment if done by a state. There is no such general rule.

The Fifth Amendment provides, among other things, that no person shall be held to answer for a capital or otherwise infamous crime unless on presentment or indictment of a grand jury. This court has held that, in prosecutions by a state, presentment or indictment by a grand jury may give way to information at the instance of a public officer. The Fifth Amendment provides also that no person shall be compelled in any criminal case to be a witness against himself. This court has said that, in prosecutions by a state, the exemption will fail if the state elects to end it. The Sixth Amendment calls for a jury trial in criminal cases and the Seventh for a jury trial in civil cases at common law where the value in controversy shall exceed twenty dollars. This court has ruled that consistently with those amendments trial by jury may be modified by a state or abolished altogether. . . .

On the other hand, the due process clause of the Fourteenth Amendment may make it unlawful for a state to abridge by its statutes the freedom of speech which the First Amendment safeguards against encroachment by the Congress, or the like freedom of the press, or the free exercise of religion, or the right of peaceable assembly, without which speech would be unduly trammeled, or the right of one accused of crime to the benefit of counsel. In these and other situations immunities that are valid as against the federal government by force of the specific pledges of particular amendments have been found to be implicit in the concept of ordered liberty, and thus, through the Fourteenth Amendment, become valid as against the states.

The line of division may seem to be wavering and broken if there is a hasty catalogue of the cases on the one side and the other. Reflection and analysis will induce a different view. There emerges the perception of a rationalizing principle which gives to discrete instances a proper order and coherence. The right to trial by jury and the immunity from prosecution except as the result of an indictment may have value and importance. Even so, they are not of the very essence of a scheme of ordered liberty. To abolish them is not to violate a "principle of justice so rooted in the traditions and conscience of our people as to be ranked as fundamental." Few would be so narrow or provincial as to maintain that a fair and enlightened system of justice would be impossible without them. What is true of jury trials and indictments is true also, as the cases show, of the immunity from compulsory self-incrimination. This too might be lost, and justice still be done. Indeed, today as in the past there are students of our penal system who look upon the immunity as a mischief rather than a benefit, and who would limit its scope, or destroy it altogether. No doubt there would remain the need to give protection against torture, physical or mental. Justice, however, would not perish if the accused were subject to a duty to respond to orderly inquiry. The exclusion of these immunities and privileges from the privileges and immunities protected against the action of the states has not been arbitrary or casual. It has been dictated by a study and appreciation of the meaning, the essential implications, of liberty itself.

We reach a different plane of social and moral values when we pass to the privileges and immunities that have been taken over from the earlier articles of the federal bill of rights and brought within the Fourteenth Amendment by a process of absorption. These in their origin were effective against the federal government alone. If the Fourteenth Amendment has absorbed them, the process of absorption has had its source in the belief that neither liberty nor justice would exist if they were sacrificed. This is true, for illustration, of freedom of thought and speech. Of that freedom one may say that it is the matrix, the indispensable condition, of nearly every other form of freedom. With rare aberrations a pervasive recognition of that truth can be traced in our history, political and legal. So it has come about that the domain of liberty, withdrawn by the Fourteenth Amendment from encroachment by the states, has been enlarged by latter-day judgments to include liberty of the mind as well as liberty of action. The extension became, indeed, a logical imperative when once it was recognized, as long ago it was, that liberty is something more than exemption from physical restraint, and that even in the field of substantive rights and duties the legislative judgment, if oppressive and arbitrary, may be overridden by the courts.

Our survey of the cases serves, we think, to justify the statement that the dividing line between them, if not unfaltering throughout its course, has been true for the most part to a unifying principle. On which side of the line the case made out by the appellant has appropriate location must be the next inquiry and the final one. Is that kind of double jeopardy to which the statute has subjected him a hardship so acute and shocking that our polity will not endure it? Does it violate those "fundamental principles of liberty and justice which lie at the base of all our civil and political institutions"? The answer surely must be "no." What the answer would have to be if the state were permitted after a trial free from error to try the accused over again or to bring another case against him, we have no occasion to consider. We deal with the statute before us and no other. The state is not attempting to wear the accused out by a multitude of cases with accumulated trials. It asks no more than this, that the case against him shall go on until there shall be a trial free from the corrosion of substantial legal error. This is not cruelty at all nor even vexation in any immoderate degree. If the trial had been infected with error adverse to the accused, there might have been review at his instance and as often as necessary to purge the vicious taint. A reciprocal privilege, subject at all times to the discretion of the presiding judge, has now been granted to the state. There is here no seismic innovation. The edifice of justice stands, its symmetry, to many, greater than before. . . .

The debate over incorporation of the Bill of Rights into the Fourteenth Amendment continued after the *Palko* decision, with the advocates of "total incorporation" winning many of the battles but not the final victory. One notable loss in 1947 came in the case of *Adamson v. California*, in which the Supreme Court's majority declined to extend the Fifth Amendment's protection against self-incrimination to the states. The dissenters in this case, Justices William Douglas and Hugo Black, expressed their belief in what they considered "the original purpose of the Fourteenth Amendment— to extend to all the people of the nation the complete protection of the Bill of Rights." Most of the cases that raised the incorporation issue involved criminal defendants, whose lawyers pointed to the protections given defendants in federal trials and argued that allowing the states to limit the rights provided by the Fourth, Fifth, Sixth, and Eighth Amendments was both illogical and unfair.

The Supreme Court took another step toward full incorporation in 1968, during the most liberal period of the Warren Court. Over the objections of two dissenters, the majority ruled in *Duncan v. Louisiana* that the Sixth Amendment guarantee of a jury trial in federal cases applied to the states as well. In this case, a black defendant, Gary Duncan, was charged with battery, having been accused of hitting a white youth during a racially charged confrontation. The offense was punishable under state law by a maximum prison term of two years, but the trial judge refused Duncan's request for a jury trial on the charge, citing the provision of the Louisiana Constitution that allowed judges to try criminal cases without a jury except in cases in which the maximum penalty was "hard labor" or death. After Duncan appealed this ruling to the Supreme Court, having been rebuffed by the Louisiana courts, the state's lawyers pointed the justices to a ruling in a case decided in 1900, *Maxwell v. Dow,* in which the Supreme Court held that jury trial in state courts had "never been affirmed as a necessary requisite of due process of law." The *Maxwell* ruling, of course, came before any of the decisions in which the Court had incorporated provisions of the Bill of Rights into the Fourteenth Amendment, and the Court in *Duncan* reversed this decision. Both the majority and dissenting opinions in the *Duncan* case express the views of the differing sides in this judicial battle.

DUNCAN V. LOUISIANA
391 U.S. 145 (1968)

MR. JUSTICE WHITE delivered the opinion of the Court.

The test for determining whether a right extended by the Fifth and Sixth Amendments with respect to federal criminal proceedings is also protected against state action by the Fourteenth Amendment has been phrased in a variety of ways in the opinions of this Court. The question has been asked whether a right is among those "fundamental principles of liberty and justice which lie at the base of all our civil and political institutions," . . . whether it is "basic in our system of jurisprudence," . . . and whether it is "a fundamental right, essential to a fair trial." . . . The claim before us is that the right to trial by jury guaranteed by the Sixth Amendment meets these tests. The position of Louisiana, on the other hand, is that the Constitution imposes upon the States no duty to give a jury trial in any criminal case, regardless of the seriousness of the crime or the size of the punishment which may be imposed. Because we believe that trial by jury in criminal cases is fundamental to the American scheme of justice, we hold that the Fourteenth Amendment guarantees a right of jury trial in all criminal cases which—were they to be tried in a federal court—would come within the Sixth Amendment's guarantee. Since we consider the appeal before us to be such a case, we hold that the Constitution was violated when appellant's demand for jury trial was refused. . . .

We are aware of prior cases in this Court in which the prevailing opinion contains statements contrary to our holding today that the right to jury trial in serious criminal cases is a fundamental right and hence must be recognized by the States as part of their obligation to extend due process of law to all persons within their jurisdiction. Louisiana relies especially on *Maxwell v. Dow* (1900); *Palko v. Connecticut* (1937); and *Snyder v. Massachusetts* (1934). None of these cases, however, dealt with a State which had purported to dispense entirely with a jury trial in serious criminal cases. *Maxwell* held that no provision of the Bill of Rights applied to the States—a position long since repudiated—and that the Due Process Clause of the Fourteenth Amendment did not prevent a State from trying a defendant for a noncapital offense with fewer than 12 men on the jury. It did not deal with a case in which no jury at all had been provided. In neither *Palko* nor *Snyder* was jury trial actually at issue, although both cases contain important dicta asserting that the right to jury trial is not essential to ordered liberty and may be dispensed with by the States regardless of the Sixth and Fourteenth Amendments. These observations, though weighty and respectable, are nevertheless dicta, unsupported by holdings in this Court that a State may refuse a defendant's demand for a jury trial when he is charged with a serious crime. . . . Respectfully, we reject the prior dicta regarding jury trial in criminal cases.

The guarantees of jury trial in the Federal and State Constitutions reflect a profound judgment about the way in which law should be enforced and justice administered. A right to jury trial is granted to criminal defendants in order to prevent oppression by the Government. Those who wrote our constitutions knew from history and experience that it was necessary to protect against unfounded criminal charges brought to eliminate enemies and against judges too responsive to the voice of higher authority. The framers of the constitutions strove to create an independent judiciary but insisted upon further protection against arbitrary action. Providing an accused with the right to be tried by a jury of his peers gave him an inestimable safeguard against the corrupt or overzealous prosecutor and against the compliant, biased, or eccentric judge. If the defendant preferred the common-sense judgment of a jury to the more tutored but perhaps less sympathetic reaction of the single judge, he was to have it. Beyond this, the jury trial provisions in the Federal and State Constitutions reflect a fundamental decision about the exercise of official power—a reluctance to entrust plenary powers over the life and liberty of the citizen to one judge or to a group of judges. Fear of unchecked power, so typical of our State and Federal Governments in other respects, found expression in the criminal law in this insistence upon community participation in the determination of guilt or innocence. The deep commitment of the Nation to the right of jury trial in serious criminal cases as a defense against arbitrary law enforcement qualifies for protection under the Due Process Clause of the Fourteenth Amendment, and must therefore be respected by the States. . . .

MR. JUSTICE HARLAN, whom MR. JUSTICE STEWART joins, dissenting.

The States have always borne primary responsibility for operating the machinery of criminal justice within their borders, and adapting it to their particular circumstances. In exercising this responsibility, each State is compelled to conform its procedures to the requirements of the Federal Constitution. The Due Process Clause of the Fourteenth Amendment requires that those procedures be fundamentally fair in all respects. It does not, in my view, impose or encourage nationwide uniformity for its own sake; it does not command adherence to forms that happen to be old; and it does not impose on the States the rules that may be in force in the federal courts except where such rules are also found to be essential to basic fairness.

The Court's approach to this case is an uneasy and illogical compromise among the views of various Justices on how the Due Process Clause should be interpreted. The Court does not say that those who framed the Fourteenth Amendment intended to make the Sixth Amendment applicable to the States. And the Court concedes that it finds nothing unfair about the procedure by which the present appellant was tried. Nevertheless, the Court reverses his conviction: it holds, for some reason not apparent to me, that the Due Process Clause incorporates the particular clause of the Sixth Amendment that requires trial by jury in federal criminal cases—including, as I read its opinion, the sometimes trivial accompanying baggage of judicial interpretation in federal contexts. I have raised my voice many times before against the Court's continuing undiscriminating insistence upon fastening on the States federal notions of criminal justice, and I must do so again in this instance. With all respect, the Court's approach and its reading of history are altogether topsy-turvy. . . .

In my view, often expressed elsewhere, the first section of the Fourteenth Amendment was meant neither to incorporate, nor to be limited to, the specific guarantees of the first eight Amendments. The overwhelming historical evidence . . . demonstrates, to me conclusively, that the Congressmen and state legislators who wrote, debated, and ratified the Fourteenth Amendment did not think they were "incorporating" the Bill of Rights and the very breadth and generality of the Amendment's provisions suggest that its authors did not suppose that the Nation would always be limited to mid-19th century conceptions of "liberty" and "due process of law" but that the increasing experience and evolving conscience of the American people would add new "intermediate premises." In short, neither history, nor sense, supports using the Fourteenth Amendment to put the States in a constitutional straitjacket with respect to their own development in the administration of criminal or civil law.

Today's Court still remains unwilling to accept the total incorporationists' view of the history of the Fourteenth Amendment. This, if accepted, would afford a cogent reason for applying the Sixth Amendment to the States. The Court is also, apparently, unwilling to face the task of determining whether denial of trial by jury in the situation before us, or in other situations, is fundamentally unfair. Consequently, the Court has compromised on the ease of the incorporationist position, without its internal logic. It has simply assumed that the question before us is whether the Jury Trial Clause of the Sixth Amendment should be incorporated into the Fourteenth, jot-for-jot and case-for-case, or ignored. Then the Court merely declares that the clause in question is "in" rather than "out." . . .

This Court, other courts, and the political process are available to correct any experiments in criminal procedure that prove fundamentally unfair to defendants. That is not what is being done today: instead, and quite without reason, the Court has chosen to impose upon every State one means of trying criminal cases; it is a good means, but it is not the only fair means, and it is not demonstrably better than the alternatives States might devise.

SECTION 3

~~~

"MORE EXACTING JUDICIAL SCRUTINY"

INTRODUCTION

The outcome of debates in the Supreme Court over the incorporation of the Bill of Rights into the Fourteenth Amendment centered on the marriage of Justice Edward Sanford's statement in his *Gitlow* opinion that "fundamental personal rights" are deserving of protection against both federal and state abridgement and Justice Benjamin Cardozo's claim in his *Palko* opinion that such rights are "implicit in the concept of ordered liberty." The backdrop to these debates lies in Chief Justice John Marshall's assertion of the doctrine of judicial review in his *Marbury* opinion, in which he forcefully claimed for the Supreme Court the power "to say what the law is," regardless of the legislative or executive will.

What these statements did not answer, however, was the question of what standards judges should apply in cases that raised issues of civil rights and liberties. One approach, rooted in the common-law tradition, is that in deciding cases arising under the Constitution, judges should presume that laws enacted by legislative bodies, which are elected by and represent the people, are constitutional. Under this approach, the burden falls on a law's challengers to convince the judges that the legislature failed to follow the commands of the Constitution. Lawmakers at all levels of government, from the president to city council members, are bound by oath to "protect and defend the Constitution of the United States." The democratic foundation of American government rests on the fidelity of public officials to this oath. Unelected judges should not, under this view, assume that elected lawmakers will deliberately enact laws that violate the Constitution.

Flowing from this approach is the corollary judicial doctrine that judges should uphold laws against constitutional challenge if lawmakers had a "rational basis" for passing the law. It did not matter if the reasons advanced for the law's necessity struck judges as imprudent or unwise, so long as they were not "arbitrary or capricious" and totally lacking in reason. The reasons most often advanced by those who defended laws against a constitutional challenge were that lawmakers were exercising the "police powers" of the state. Another judicial doctrine rooted in the common-law era, the "police powers" included the state's basic purpose to protect the "health, safety, welfare, and morals" of the citizens. The "rational basis" test was applied by the Supreme Court, most often without being stated, in virtually every case—regardless of subject matter—decided before 1938. Consequently, the Court rebuffed most challenges to laws that were assailed as violating the provisions of the First Amendment, including the free speech cases that reached the Court after World War I.

Ironically, the "rational basis" test, and its presumption of constitutionality, were displaced in civil rights and liberties cases by a series of decisions by the Supreme Court in the "Constitutional Revolution" of 1937, in which the Court abruptly changed course and invoked the "police powers" doctrine to uphold state and federal laws that were designed to protect the American people against the economic and social ravages of the Great Depression. Between 1935 and 1937, the conservative majority on the Court had struck down the most important and far-reaching efforts of the New Deal administration of President Franklin Roosevelt to revive the shattered economy and restore the nation to economic health. In other cases that challenged state laws setting maximum work hours and minimum wages, the Court invoked the doctrine of "liberty of contract" to invalidate the "Little New Deal" laws.

The political uproar that followed the Court's rulings in these cases prompted President Roosevelt to launch an attack on the "Nine Old Men" whose "horse-and-buggy" approach to the Constitution had virtually crippled the government. Roosevelt's audacious proposal in February 1937 to "pack" the Court by increasing its membership to a maximum of fifteen justices created another political uproar. The American public solidly opposed the Court's rulings against New Deal laws, but most people also felt the Court should be immune from the retaliation that motivated the court-packing plan. The growing constitutional crisis was averted when the Court repudiated the "liberty of contact" doctrine in ruling, by a narrow five-to-four vote, that states could exercise their "police powers" to set minimum wages for workers. Chief Justice Charles Evans Hughes put the new doctrine of "economic due process" into these words in his March 1937 opinion in *West Coast Hotel v. Parrish*, upholding a Washington state law that set minimum wages for women. Speaking of the Fourteenth Amendment's "liberty" clause, Justice Harlan Fiske Stone wrote:

> Liberty in each of its phases has its history and connotation. But the liberty safeguarded is liberty in a social organization which requires the protection of law against the evils which

menace the health, safety, morals and welfare of the people. Liberty under the Constitution is thus necessarily subject to the restraints of due process, and regulation which is reasonable in relation to its subject and is adopted in the interests of the community is due process.

The Court's ruling in the *West Coast Hotel* case, and its decision the following month to uphold the National Labor Relations Act in *NLRB v. Jones & Laughlin Steel Corporation,* effectively removed the Court from its self-assumed role as arbiter of economic regulation, returning that function to elected lawmakers. These decisions also scuttled Roosevelt's court-packing plan, although—contrary to the assumptions and assertions of many historians—the Court had decided the momentous *West Coast Hotel* case in December 1936, two months before the president unveiled his plan. What really decided the case was the Court's recognition that the American people, who had given Roosevelt a second term in the November 1936 elections by an overwhelming margin and had reduced the Republican party in Congress to an ineffective and tiny minority.

The "Constitutional Revolution" of 1937 also gave Roosevelt the chance to reshape the Supreme Court and to achieve the goal of his court-packing plan by replacing conservative justices who died or retired over the next several years. He added such liberal justices to the Court as Hugo Black, William Douglas, Felix Frankfurter, and Frank Murphy. The New Deal justices that Franklin Roosevelt added to the Supreme Court continued the "Constitutional Revolution" their predecessors had begun in 1937 by shifting their agenda from property rights to human rights. They were led in this judicial crusade by Harlan Fiske Stone, who had served on the Court since 1925 and was a nominal Republican. But his Yankee conscience was affronted by intolerance and bigotry, and Stone read the newspapers in 1937 and 1938 with growing concern. Stone expressed his concerns in an unusual way, by adding an important footnote to an opinion in an otherwise unimportant case. Almost unnoticed when it appeared in 1938, Footnote Four in *United States v. Carolene Products* soon became the deadliest weapon in the judicial war against those who deny minorities their rights.

The story of Footnote Four deserves far more space than it occupies in Stone's opinion. It really began in 1933 with the rise to power of two men, Franklin Roosevelt and Adolf Hitler. One courted the votes of blacks and Jews; the other vowed to maintain "Aryan" racial purity and to purge his country of Jewish influence. Despite their political differences, both men headed parties with powerful factions that employed violence against the minorities they despised. Roosevelt could not control the white-hooded Klansmen, many of them loyal Democrats, who waved the Confederate flag, while Hitler totally controlled the brown-shirted thugs who marched under the Nazi swastika in Germany. But the Great Depression, which swept both men into office, also fueled racial and religious violence in both countries. During the 1930s, American blacks and German Jews became victims of lawless mobs. More than a hundred blacks, most accused of raping white women, were lynched in the South, while Nazi mobs beat hundreds of Jews and murdered dozens suspected of Communist sympathies.

Justice Stone viewed these atrocities with disgust and growing alarm. Early in 1938, he decided to offer the

Supreme Court as a refuge for persecuted minorities. The *West Coast Hotel* and *Jones & Laughlin* decisions had effectively cleared the Court's docket of economic regulation cases, but several remained for argument and decision. Searching the list, Stone picked an unlikely podium for his announcement of a new judicial agenda. The case of *United States v. Carolene Products Company* involved the Filled Milk Act of 1923, in which Congress prohibited the shipment in interstate commerce of "skimmed milk compounded with any fat or oil other than milk fat." The Carolene Products company made something called Milnut, a compound of condensed milk and coconut oil. During the Depression, many families could not afford whole milk for their children and turned to products like Milnut, cheaper than whole milk but lacking its nutritional value. After the company's indictment for selling "an adulterated article of food, injurious to the public health," its lawyers challenged the law as violating both the Commerce and Due Process Clauses. They won the first round in federal court and the government appealed to the Supreme Court.

The *Carolene Products* case was argued on April 6, 1938. Justice Stone read in that morning's *New York Times* that, under Nazi rule in Austria, "2,000 Jewish lawyers in Vienna will be excluded from the bar" and that "Jewish physicians and surgeons have been removed from all hospitals." That week's *Time* magazine reported a speech by Hitler's propaganda minister, Joseph Goebbels: "Our racial theory is the sole basis for the correct solution of the Jewish problem." Stone had earlier read in the *New York Times* that Roosevelt Townes, accused of murder in Duck Hill, Mississippi, was tied to a tree, his "eyes were gouged out with an ice pick," and he was "tortured slowly to death with flames from a blow-torch." The week before the *Carolene Products* argument, Stone read about the death of the federal antilynching law at the hands of southern Democrats. Mississippi senator Theodore Bilbo, whose racist diatribes rivaled those of Goebbels, railed against "the Ethiopian who has inspired this proposed legislation" and "the lust and lasciviousness of the rape fiend in his diabolical effort to despoil the womanhood of the Caucasian race."

Justice Stone expressed his reaction to these reports in a letter to Irving Lehman, a New York judge: "I have been deeply concerned about the increasing racial and religious intolerance which seems to bedevil the world, and which I greatly fear may be augmented in this country." With the aid of his Jewish law clerk, Louis Lusky, Stone drafted a footnote for his *Carolene Products* opinion, which reversed the district judge and upheld the Filled Milk Act as "an appropriate means of preventing injury to the public." Stone emphasized that the Court would presume the constitutionality of regulatory laws "affecting ordinary commercial transactions" if they rested upon "some rational basis within the knowledge and experience of the legislators." He did not invent the "rational basis" test but applied it to *Carolene Products* like a schoolmaster.

Stone could have ended the lesson on that note, but he continued his lecture in Footnote Four. "There may be narrower scope for operation of the presumption of constitutionality," he wrote, "when legislation appears on its face to be within a specific prohibition of the Constitution, such as those of the first ten amendments, which are deemed equally specific when held to be embraced within the Fourteenth." Boiled down, this lengthy sentence expressed the doctrine that the Fourteenth Amendment "incorporated" at least some provisions of the Bill of Rights and applied them to the states. Stone warned that "legislation which restricts those political processes which can ordinarily be expected to bring about repeal of undesirable legislation" would in the future "be subjected to more exacting judicial scrutiny" than regulatory laws such as the Filled Milk Act. Stone devised in this sentence what soon became known as the "strict scrutiny" test for laws that were challenged as violations of the Bill of Rights. Under the "rational basis" test, regulatory laws enjoyed a presumption of constitutionality; Stone's new test reversed that presumption for laws that restricted political rights.

Stone continued with another warning to lawmakers who might be swayed by "popular passions" against religious, national, or racial minorities. Laws directed at members of these groups would also lose their presumption of constitutionality and trigger "more searching judicial inquiry" of the motives behind their passage. Stone provided examples by citing prior cases that dealt with Catholics, people of German or Japanese origin, and blacks. He added that laws reflecting "prejudice against discrete and insular minorities" of other kinds would also be subjected to the "strict scrutiny" test. Stone left this category open, but his wording suggested that members of groups "set apart" from the majority by some characteristic other than religion, nationality, or race would be equally protected from official prejudice (Irons, 1999).

UNITED STATES V. CAROLENE PRODUCTS CO.
304 U.S. 144 (1938)

MR. JUSTICE STONE delivered the opinion of the Court.

The question for decision is whether the "Filled Milk Act" of Congress of March 4, 1923 which prohibits the shipment in interstate commerce of skimmed milk compounded with any fat or oil other than milk fat, so as to resemble milk or cream, transcends the power of Congress to regulate interstate commerce or infringes the Fifth Amendment.

Appellee was indicted in the district court for southern Illinois for violation of the Act by the shipment in interstate commerce of certain packages of "Milnut," a compound of condensed skimmed milk and coconut oil made in imitation or semblance of condensed milk or cream. The indictment states, in the words of the statute, that Milnut "is an adulterated article of food, injurious to the public health," and that it is not a prepared food product of the type excepted from the prohibition of the Act. . . .

Appellee assails the statute as beyond the power of Congress over interstate commerce, and hence an invasion of a field of action said to be reserved to the states by the Tenth Amendment. Appellee also complains that the statute denies to it equal protection of the laws and, in violation of the Fifth Amendment, deprives it of its property without due process of law, particularly in that the statute purports to make binding and conclusive upon appellee the legislative declaration that appellee's product "is an adulterated article of food injurious to the public health and its sale constitutes a fraud on the public."

Congress is free to exclude from interstate commerce articles whose use in the states for which they are destined it may reasonably conceive to be injurious to the public health, morals or welfare. . . . Such regulation is not a forbidden invasion of state power either because its motive or its consequence is to restrict the use of articles of commerce within the states of destination, and is not prohibited unless by the due process clause of the Fifth Amendment. And it is no objection to the exertion of the power to regulate interstate commerce that its exercise is attended by the same incidents which attend the exercise of the police power of the states. . . .

In twenty years evidence has steadily accumulated of the danger to the public health from the general consumption of foods which have been stripped of elements essential to the maintenance of health. The Filled Milk Act was adopted by Congress after committee hearings, in the course of which eminent scientists and health experts testified. An extensive investigation was made of the commerce in milk compounds in which vegetable oils have been substituted for natural milk fat, and of the effect upon the public health of the use of such compounds as a food substitute for milk. . . .

We may assume for present purposes that no pronouncement of a legislature can forestall attack upon the constitutionality of the prohibition which it enacts by applying opprobrious epithets to the prohibited act, and that a statute would deny due process which precluded the disproof in judicial proceedings of all facts which would show or tend to show that a statute depriving the suitor of life, liberty or property had a rational basis.

But such we think is not the purpose or construction of the statutory characterization of filled milk as injurious to health and as a fraud upon the public. There is no need to consider it here as more than a declaration of the legislative findings deemed to support and justify the action taken as a constitutional exertion of the legislative power, aiding informed judicial review, as do the reports of legislative committees, by revealing the rationale of the legislation. Even in the absence of such aids the existence of facts supporting the legislative judgment is to be presumed, for regulatory legislation affecting ordinary commercial transactions is not to be pronounced unconstitutional unless in the light of the facts made known or generally assumed it is of such a character as to preclude the assumption that it rests upon some rational basis within the knowledge and experience of the legislators.[4]

Justice Stone's opinion in the *Carolene Products* case, and his statement in Footnote Four of what came to be known as the "strict scrutiny" test, displaced the "presumption of constitutionality" in cases that dealt with civil rights and liberties and imposed the burden of defending a challenged law in these areas on the government, whether local, state, or federal. Government lawyers could prevail under this test only if they showed that the law served a "compelling state interest" and was "narrowly tailored" to achieve its purpose. As one eminent constitutional scholar, Gerald Gunther, later wrote, Stone's new test was "strict in theory, and fatal in fact." Few laws that were challenged as abridging the protections of the First Amendment, or as depriving individuals of "fundamental personal rights," could survive this constitutional gauntlet.

However, the defenders of the "police powers" doctrine and the "rational basis" test did not give up. Judges who continued to adhere to the "presumption of constitutionality" in civil rights and liberties cases fought a tenacious battle on behalf of "judicial restraint" in these areas. Justice Felix Frankfurter, who had been named to the Court by President Franklin Roosevelt in 1939 over the objection of conservatives who feared he would become a judicial radical, quickly shed his liberal label and emerged as the intellectual leader of those who decried the "strict scrutiny" test. A pair of Supreme Court decisions in 1940 and 1943, in cases that both involved challenges by members of the Jehovah's Witnesses denomination to compulsory flag salutes in public schools,

---

[4]There may be narrower scope for operation of the presumption of constitutionality when legislation appears on its face to be within a specific prohibition of the Constitution, such as those of the first ten amendments, which are deemed equally specific when held to be embraced within the Fourteenth. See *Stromberg* v. *California*, 283 U.S. 359, 369–370; *Lovell* v. *Griffin*, 303 U.S. 444, 452.

It is unnecessary to consider now whether legislation which restricts those political processes which can ordinarily be expected to bring about repeal of undesirable legislation, is to be subjected to more exacting judicial scrutiny under the general prohibitions of the Fourteenth Amendment than are most other types of legislation. On restrictions upon the right to vote, see *Nixon* v. *Herndon*, 273 U.S. 536; *Nixon* v. *Condon*, 286 U.S. 73; on restraints upon the dissemination of information, see *Near* v. *Minnesota ex rel. Olson*, 283 U.S. 697, 713–714, 718–720, 722; *Grosjean* v. *American Press Co.*, 297 U.S. 233; *Lovell* v. *Griffin, supra*; on interferences with political organizations, see *Stromberg* v. *California, supra*, 369; *Fiske* v. *Kansas*, 274 U.S. 380; *Whitney* v. *California*, 274 U.S. 357, 373–378; *Herndon* v. *Lowry*, 301 U.S. 242; and see Holmes, J., in *Gitlow* v. *New York*, 268 U.S. 652, 673; as to prohibition of peaceable assembly, see *De Jonge* v. *Oregon*, 299 U.S. 353, 365.

Nor need we enquire whether similar considerations enter into the review of statutes directed at particular religious, *Pierce* v. *Society of Sisters*, 268 U.S. 510, or national, *Meyer* v. *Nebraska*, 262 U.S. 390; *Bartels* v. *Iowa*, 262 U.S. 404; *Farrington* v. *Tokushige*, 273 U.S. 484, or racial minorities, *Nixon* v. *Herndon, supra*; *Nixon* v. *Condon, supra*: whether prejudice against discrete and insular minorities may be a special condition, which tends seriously to curtail the operation of those political processes ordinarily to be relied upon to protect minorities, and which may call for a correspondingly more searching judicial inquiry. Compare *McCulloch* v. *Maryland*, 4 Wheat. 316, 428; *South Carolina* v. *Barnwell Bros.*, 303 U.S. 177, 184, n. 2, and cases cited.

place in sharp contrast the positions of the two sides in this judicial battle. Frankfurter's majority opinion in *Minersville School District v. Gobitis,* decided in 1940, provoked a solitary dissent by Justice Harlan Fiske Stone, the author of Footnote Four. And the majority opinion of Justice Robert Jackson in *West Virginia Board of Education v. Barnette,* in which the Court reversed the *Gobitis* decision in 1943, in turn provoked a heated and bitter dissent by Frankfurter. Excerpts of these opinions (see Chapter 4) set forth the contrasting views in a judicial debate that is still going on, as Frankfurter's disciples on the Supreme Court continue to denounce the "strict scrutiny" test and promote a view of "judicial restraint" that would reverse the abortion-rights decision in *Roe v. Wade* and other landmark cases. One final case excerpt in this chapter has been included for two reasons: first, to illustrate the "rational basis" test in operation and, second, because the 1955 opinion in this case, *Williamson v. Lee Optical,* has been cited many times over the past three decades by one of the most fervent opponents of the "strict scrutiny" test, Chief Justice William Rehnquist. He relied on *Williamson* in his first opinion on the Court, dissenting in a case decided in 1972 that struck down a federal law designed to prevent "hippies" from receiving food stamps, and that also re-

moved many poor and disabled people from the program. Rehnquist also cited *Williamson* in dissenting from the Court's ruling in 1973 that states could not make abortions a criminal offense, striking down a Texas law in *Roe v. Wade.*

The author of the *Williamson* opinion, Justice William Douglas, was one of the staunchest liberals on the Court, an advocate of the "strict scrutiny" test in civil rights and liberties cases. Douglas believed, as he wrote in *Williamson,* that the "rational basis" test should be limited to laws that affected "business and industrial conditions." The fact that Rehnquist and other judicial conservatives have cited *Williamson* in cases that raised issues of "fundamental personal rights" such as abortion, far removed from economic regulation, shows that judges do not always look to factual similarities in their search for doctrinal support. Justice Harry Blackmun, author of the majority opinion in the *Roe* case, found support for a "right to privacy" in cases that involved wiretapping, possession of pornography, and "stop-and-frisk" searches by police officers. Justice Oliver Wendell Holmes once wrote that "consistency is the hobgoblin of the law." The fact that an opinion by Justice Douglas has become a favored citation by Chief Justice Rehnquist underscores this trenchant observation.

WILLIAMSON V. LEE OPTICAL CO.
348 U.S. 483 (1955)

MR. JUSTICE DOUGLAS delivered the opinion of the Court.

This suit was instituted in the District Court to have an Oklahoma law declared unconstitutional and to enjoin state officials from enforcing it for the reason that it allegedly violated various provisions of the Federal Constitution. The matter was heard by a District Court of three judges. . . .

The District Court held unconstitutional three sections of the Act. First, it held invalid under the Due Process Clause of the Fourteenth Amendment the portions of § 2 which make it unlawful for any person not a licensed optometrist or ophthalmologist to fit lenses to a face or to duplicate or replace into frames lenses or other optical appliances, except upon written prescriptive authority of an Oklahoma licensed ophthalmologist or optometrist.

An ophthalmologist is a duly licensed physician who specializes in the care of the eyes. An optometrist examines eyes for refractive error, recognizes (but does not treat) diseases of the eye, and fills prescriptions for eyeglasses. The optician is an artisan qualified to grind lenses, fill prescriptions, and fit frames.

The effect of § 2 is to forbid the optician from fitting or duplicating lenses without a prescription from an ophthalmologist or optometrist. In practical effect, it means that no optician can fit old glasses into new frames or supply a lens, whether it be a new lens or one to duplicate a lost or broken

lens, without a prescription. The District Court conceded that it was in the competence of the police power of a State to regulate the examination of the eyes. But it rebelled at the notion that a State could require a prescription from an optometrist or ophthalmologist "to take old lenses and place them in new frames and then fit the completed spectacles to the *face* of the eyeglass wearer."

It held that such a requirement was not "reasonably and rationally related to the health and welfare of the people." The court found that through mechanical devices and ordinary skills the optician could take a broken lens or a fragment thereof, measure its power, and reduce it to prescriptive terms. The court held that "Although on this precise issue of duplication, the legislature in the instant regulation was dealing with a matter of public interest, the particular means chosen are neither reasonably necessary nor reasonably related to the end sought to be achieved."

It was, accordingly, the opinion of the court that this provision of the law violated the Due Process Clause by arbitrarily interfering with the optician's right to do business. . . .

The Oklahoma law may exact a needless, wasteful requirement in many cases. But it is for the legislature, not the courts, to balance the advantages and disadvantages of the new requirement. It appears that in many cases the optician can easily supply the new frames or new lenses without reference to the old written prescription. It also appears that many written prescriptions contain no directive data in regard to fitting spectacles to the face. But in some cases the directions contained in the prescription are essential, if the glasses are to be fitted so as to correct the particular defects of vision or alleviate the eye condition. The legislature might have concluded that the frequency of occasions when a prescription is necessary was sufficient to justify this regulation of the fitting of eyeglasses. Likewise, when it is necessary to duplicate a lens, a written prescription may or may not be necessary. But the legislature might have concluded that one was needed often enough to require one in every case. Or the legislature may have concluded that eye examinations were so critical, not only for correction of vision but also for detection of latent ailments or diseases, that every change in frames and every duplication of a lens should be accompanied by a prescription from a medical expert. To be sure, the present law does not require a new examination of the eyes every time the frames are changed or the lenses duplicated. For if the old prescription is on file with the optician, he can go ahead and make the new fitting or duplicate the lenses. But the law need not be in every respect logically consistent with its aims to be constitutional. It is enough that there is an evil at hand for correction, and that it might be thought that the particular legislative measure was a rational way to correct it.

The day is gone when this Court uses the Due Process Clause of the Fourteenth Amendment to strike down state laws, regulatory of business and industrial conditions, because they may be unwise, improvident, or out of harmony with a particular school of thought.

We emphasize again what Chief Justice Waite said in *Munn v. Illinois*, 94 U. S. 113, 134, "For protection against abuses by legislatures the people must resort to the polls, not to the courts." . . .

The problem of legislative classification is a perennial one, admitting of no doctrinaire definition. Evils in the same field may be of different dimensions and proportions, requiring different remedies. Or so the legislature may think. Or the reform may take one step at a time, addressing itself to the phase of the problem which seems most acute to the legislative mind.

The legislature may select one phase of one field and apply a remedy there, neglecting the others.

The prohibition of the Equal Protection Clause goes no further than the invidious discrimination. We cannot say that that point has been reached here. For all this record shows, the ready-to-wear branch of this business may not loom large in Oklahoma or may present problems of regulation distinct from the other branch. . . .

It seems to us that this regulation is on the same constitutional footing as the denial to corporations of the right to practice dentistry.

It is an attempt to free the profession, to as great an extent as possible, from all taints of commercialism. It certainly might be easy for an optometrist with space in a retail store to be merely a front for the retail establishment. In any case, the opportunity for that nexus may be too great for safety, if the eye doctor is allowed inside the retail store. Moreover, it may be deemed important to effective regulation that the eye doctor be restricted to geographical locations that reduce the temptations of commercialism. Geographical location may be an important consideration in a legislative program which aims to raise the treatment of the human eye to a strictly professional level. We cannot say that the regulation has no rational relation to that objective and therefore is beyond constitutional bounds.

PART II

The First Amendment: Religion, Speech, Press, and Assembly

CHAPTER 3

"An Establishment of Religion"

INTRODUCTION

The two most divisive issues in American society, over the entire course of the nation's history, have been religion and race. These two issues are connected in many ways. Conflicts over race, during the periods of slavery and legal segregation, brought forth arguments based on religious belief on both sides. Many defenders of slavery claimed that God had tainted black people, and made them fit only for servitude, as the descendents of Ham. On the other side, many abolitionists denounced slavery as morally wrong and an affront to the biblical command to "love your brother as yourself." Religious belief has also motivated those who take opposite sides on such issues as abortion and military service.

Religion has been such a powerful force in American history because it forms the core of most people's values and provides a sense of identity. At the same time, religion has divided our society because of the diversity of denominations and sects, many of which consider the adherents of other religions to be misled or even sinful. Advocates of religious tolerance have always confronted the persistence of intolerance, which has led to acts of violence, with victims among groups as varied as Quakers, Roman Catholics, Jews, Mormons, and followers of "New Age" cults and sects. As a preface to this chapter on cases that stem from the command of the First Amendment that "Congress shall make no law respecting an establishment of religion," two related episodes of religious intolerance in colonial Massachusetts bear telling.

There is a powerful irony in the disparity between the myth of colonial America as a haven for religious dissenters from the orthodoxy of the Church of England and the reality of intolerance toward those who challenged the new orthodoxy of the colonists. It was an awareness of this irony, and a revulsion at religious intolerance, that prompted the men who framed the Bill of Rights to provide in the First Amendment that Congress "shall make no law respecting an establishment of religion, or prohibiting the free exercise thereof." During the century and a half that separated the Body of Liberties of the Massachusetts Bay Colony from the adoption of the Bill of Rights in 1791, religious conflict affected virtually every village and town in every colony.

Two episodes in Massachusetts illustrate the divisive effects of religious intolerance. The first was the expulsion of Roger Williams from the colony in 1636, which led to the establishment of the new colony of Rhode Island. Williams had come to Boston in 1631 as a Puritan pastor; he soon became minister of the church in Salem. During his formative years in England, Williams studied under the great jurist Edward Coke, who defended both political and religious freedom within the narrow confines of laws against "seditious libel." Williams became a controversial figure in Salem, from whose pulpit he denounced the notion that civil authorities could enforce religious edicts. These views so offended his parishioners and the political leaders of the colony that Williams left Salem after a few months for the relative tolerance of the church in Plymouth, where he continued his attacks on the Puritan theocracy. "Let any man show me a commission given by the Son of God to civil powers in these spiritual affairs of His Christian kingdom and worship," Williams demanded in a pamphlet that enraged Puritan leaders. For this heresy, the General Court of Massachusetts expelled Williams from their midst.

The second religious dissident was poles apart from Roger Williams in theology, but equally a threat to Puritan orthodoxy. Williams was, in some ways, more of a Puritan than those who condemned and expelled him. He argued against admitting to worship those "unregenerant" Puritans who attended Church of England services on visits to

England. Anne Hutchinson, on the other hand, resisted Puritan worship altogether. She held services in her home and preached to those who attended her "study" sessions—mostly women—the heretical doctrines that salvation comes through grace and not through work, and that the Holy Spirit can dwell within every person through individual revelation. Despite her social prominence—her husband was a close friend and ally of Governor John Winthrop—Anne Hutchinson so directly challenged Puritan orthodoxy that she found herself facing trial before the General Court in 1637, with Governor Winthrop as the chief prosecutor and interrogator.

The transcript of this historic trial offers an insight into the conflict between individual conscience and state power that continues to divide Americans. Far more knowledgeable than Winthrop on biblical scripture, Hutchinson continually bested him in debates over fine points of theology. She turned the tables on Winthrop, questioning him so relentlessly that he finally admitted that Hutchinson had biblical support for the main charge against her, that of preaching a doctrine of personal revelation of God's word. "How did Abraham know that it was God that bid him offer his son" for sacrifice? she demanded to know from Winthrop. "By an immediate voice," he responded. Hutchinson pounced on the governor. "So to me by an immediate revelation," she said of her views on salvation by grace. "By the voice of his own spirit to my soul." Winthrop was so enraged at falling into Hutchinson's trap that he quickly called a vote on the heresy charges and secured a conviction with only three dissents. The penalty was banishment from the colony. Anne Hutchinson and John Winthrop had one last exchange. "I desire to know wherefore I am banished," she asked. The governor's answer spoke volumes about colonial limits on the rule of law. "Say no more," Winthrop replied; "the court knows wherefore and is satisfied." Anne Hutchinson left the colony in 1637 and settled in Rhode Island, the tiny outpost of religious tolerance in New England.

The expulsions of Roger Williams and Anne Hutchinson took place early in the colonial era, and they exemplify the extremes of religious intolerance in the most intolerant colony. By the time of the Revolution, advocates of toleration spoke with louder voices and demanded the "disestablishment" of the churches that controlled most of the colonies. James Madison of Virginia, the primary author of the Bill of Rights, deserves the greatest credit for moving the country toward religious toleration of dissenters. In 1774, Madison wrote to a friend that the "diabolical, hell-conceived principle of persecution rages among some" in Virginia. "There are at this time in the adjacent county not less than five or six well-meaning men in close jail, for publishing their religious sentiments, which in the main are very orthodox. . . . I have squabbled and scolded, abused and ridiculed so long about it, that I am without common patience."

Madison continued his crusade for religious toleration through the Revolution and into the period of independence. His patience was still taxed by efforts of the Church of England in Virginia, renamed the Episcopal Church, to retain its status as the established denomination. Working closely with his friend and mentor Thomas Jefferson, Madison drafted and the Virginia legislature enacted in 1785 "An Act Establishing Religious Freedom." The law provided

that "no man shall be compelled to frequent or support any religious worship, place, or ministry whatever, . . . nor shall otherwise suffer on account of his religious opinions or belief; but that all men shall be free to profess, and by argument to maintain, their opinions in matters of religion, and that the same shall in no wise diminish, enlarge, or affect their civil capacities." Jefferson later wrote that Madison's law was "meant to comprehend within the mantle of its protection the Jew and the Gentile, the Christian and Mahometan, the Hindu and Infidel of every denomination" (Irons, 1999).

Long after the expulsions of Roger Williams and Anne Hutchinson from colonial Massachusetts, efforts to impose religious orthodoxy and uniformity were tried in many areas and have failed. American society today is a religious mosaic, with churches, synagogues, mosques, temples, and other houses of worship in almost every city and town. However, many communities in America, especially small towns in the South and Midwest, are religiously homogenous, with virtually all residents of the same faith. The religious diversity and tolerance of most big cities, often more apparent than real, is strained in smaller towns where Jews, Muslims, or Catholics are scarce or even absent. And the residents of many communities or states, who make up a majority of the population, often attempt to obtain financial or material support for their denomination's activities from public funds. Such efforts, particularly when they are directed at public schools, have given rise to many cases brought under the Establishment Clause of the First Amendment over the past six decades, when the Supreme Court first dealt with these issues. Most Establishment Clause cases, in fact, begin in schools and spill into the courts, often with the support of such groups as Americans United for Separation of Church and State and the American Civil Liberties Union.

In deciding Establishment Clause cases, the Supreme Court has itself become a battleground between judicial adherents of "differing constitutional faiths," to adapt a phrase from legal scholar Sanford Levinson. On one side are the "strict separationists," among whom Justices Hugo Black and William Douglas have been the most vehement and vocal. Any state aid to religious groups that furthers their programs offends judges in this group, as does prayer and any form of religious proselytizing in schools or other public forums. On the other side are the "accommodationists," such as Chief Justice William Rehnquist and Justice Antonin Scalia in recent years. They would allow state aid to religious groups that is dispensed on a "neutral" basis and find no constitutional bar to prayer in public places that is not overtly denominational. In the middle, often as the swing votes in religion cases, are those justices (Sandra O'Connor and Anthony Kennedy are recent examples) who argue that state aid to religion is permissible so long as it is not "coercive."

The cases in this chapter deal with state aid to religious groups in several forms: religious teaching in public schools; direct payments or subsidies to parents who send their children to religious schools; school prayer from the classroom to the football field; the erection of Christmas nativity scenes in public places; and the teaching of "creationism" in public schools. Notably, all these cases except the nativity scene cases begin in schools, a reflection of the fact that all

Table 3.1 Religious Bodies—Selected Data

Religious Body	Year Reported	Churches Reported	Membership* (1,000)	Pastors Serving Parishes[1]
African Methodist Episcopal Church	1999	6,200	2,500	NA
African Methodist Episcopal Zion Church	1999	3,125	1,277	2,731
American Baptist Association, The	1998	1,760	275	1,740
American Baptist Churches in the U.S.A	1999	5,775	1,454	4,895
Antiochian Orthodox Christian Archdiocese of North America, The	1999	227	65	290
Armenian Apostolic Church of America	1999	36	360	35
Armenian Apostolic Church, Diocese of America	1991	72	414	49
Assemblies of God	1999	12,055	2,575	18,159
Baptist Bible Fellowship International	1997	4,500	1,200	NA
Baptist General Conference	1999	880	143	NA
Baptist Missionary Association of America	1999	1,334	235	1,525
Buddhist[2]	1990	NA	401	NA
Christian and Missionary Alliance, The	1999	1,973	348	1,493
Christian Brethren (a.k.a. Plymouth Brethren)	1997	1,150	100	NA
Christian Church (Disciples of Christ)	1999	3,765	831	3,307
Christian Churches and Churches of Christ	1998	5,579	1,072	5,525
Christian Congregation, Inc., The	1999	1,438	118	1,436
Christian Methodist Episcopal Church	1999	3,069	784	2,058
Christian Reformed Church in North America	1999	732	198	675
Church of God in Christ, The	1991	15,300	5,500	28,988
Church of God of Prophecy	1999	1,862	75	2,000
Church of God (Anderson, Indiana)	1998	2,353	234	3,034
Church of God (Cleveland, Tennessee)	1999	6,328	870	3,352
Church of Jesus Christ of Latter-day Saints, The	1999	11,315	5,113	33,945
Church of the Brethren	1997	1,095	141	827
Church of the Nazarene	1998	5,101	627	4,598
Churches of Christ	1999	15,000	1,500	14,500
Conservative Baptist Association of America	1998	1,200	200	NA
Coptic Orthodox Church	1992	85	180	65
Cumberland Presbyterian Church	1999	775	86	535
Episcopal Church	1998	7,390	2,318	NA
Evangelical Covenant Church, The	1999	636	99	607
Evangelical Free Church of America, The	1995	1,224	243	1,936
Evangelical Lutheran Church in America	1999	10,851	5,150	9,542
Free Methodist Church of North America	1999	971	71	NA
Full Gospel Fellowship of Churches and Ministers International	2000	896	325	2,070
General Association of General Baptists	1998	719	67	780
General Association of Regular Baptist Churches	1999	1,398	92	NA
General Conference of Mennonite Brethren Churches	1996	368	82	590
Greek Orthodox Archdiocese of America	1998	523	1,955	596
Hindu[2]	1990	NA	227	NA
International Church of the Foursquare Gospel	1999	1,836	253	4,802
International Council of Community Churches	1999	180	200	198
International Pentecostal Holiness Church	1999	1,771	185	1,609
Jehovah's Witnesses	1999	11,257	990	NA
Jewish[3]	1999	NA	6,061	NA
Lutheran Church—Missouri Synod (LCMS), The	1999	6,220	2,582	5,210
Mennonite Church	1999	935	92	NA
Muslim/Islamic[2]	1990	NA	527	NA
National Association of Congregational Christian Churches	1999	426	66	506
National Association of Free Will Baptists	1999	2,476	217	2,800
National Baptist Convention of America, Inc.	1987	2,500	3,500	8,000
National Missionary Baptist Convention of America	1992	NA	2,500	NA
Old Order Amish Church	1993	898	81	3,592
Orthodox Church in America, The	1999	710	1,000	735
Pentecostal Assemblies of the World, Inc.	1998	1,750	1,500	4,500
Pentecostal Church of God	1999	1,237	105	NA
Presbyterian Church in America	1999	1,206	299	NA
Presbyterian Church (U.S.A.)	1999	11,216	3,561	9,292
Progressive National Baptist Convention, Inc	1995	2,000	2,500	NA
Reformed Church in America	1999	901	293	880
Religious Society of Friends (Conservative)	1994	1,200	104	NA

Table 3.1 *(Continued)*

Religious Body	Year Reported	Churches Reported	Membership* (1,000)	Pastors Serving Parishes[1]
Reorganized Church of Jesus Christ of Latter Day Saints	1999	1,236	137	NA
Roman Catholic Church, The	1999	19,627	62,391	NA
Salvation Army, The	1999	1,410	473	3,072
Serbian Orthodox Church in the U.S.A. and Canada	1986	68	67	60
Seventh-day Adventist Church	1999	4,421	862	2,501
Southern Baptist Convention	1998	40,870	15,729	NA
Unitarian Universalist Association of Congregations	1999	NA	217	NA
United Church of Christ	1999	5,961	1,402	4,264
United Methodist Church, The	1999	35,609	8,378	24,998
Wesleyan Church, The	1999	1,594	121	1,946
Wisconsin Evangelical Lutheran Synod	1999	1,239	723	1,230

*Membership data: **2,500 represents 2,500,000.** Includes the self-reported membership of religious bodies with 65,000 or more as reported to the *Yearbook of American and Canadian Churches*. Groups may be excluded if they do not supply information. The data are not standardized so comparisons between groups are difficult. The definition of *church member* is determined by the religious body.

NA Not available.

[1]Does not include retired clergy or clergy not working with congregations.   [2]Figures obtained from the National Survey of Religious Identification, a survey conducted by the City University of New York in 1990 and published in *One Nation Under God: Religion in Contemporary American Society*, by Barry, Kosmin and Seymour Lachman (1993).   [3]Source: *American Jewish Year Book*, American Jewish Committee, New York, NY, See table 67.

Table 3.2   Religious Preference, Church Membership, and Attendance: 1980 to 2000

Year	Religious Preference							Church/Synagogue Members	Persons Attending Church/Synagogue[1]
	Protestant	Catholic	Jewish	Orthodox	Mormon	Other Specific	None		
1980	61	28	2	NA	NA	2	7	69	40
1985	57	28	2	NA	NA	4	9	71	42
1990	56	25	2	NA	NA	6	11	65	40
1995	56	27	2	1	1	5	8[2]	69	43
1996	58	25	3	1	1	3	9[2]	65	38
1997	58	26	2	1	1	4	8[2]	67	40
1998	59	27	2	2	1	4	8[2]	70	40
1999	55	28	2	1	2	2	10[2]	70	43
2000	56	27	2	1	1	5	8[2]	68	44

Data shown in percentages. Covers civilian noninstitutional population, 18 years old and over. Data represent averages of the combined results of several surveys during year or period indicated. Data are subject to sampling variability.

NA Not available.

[1]Persons who attended a church or synagogue in the last 7 days.   [2]Includes those respondents who did not designate.

children are compelled by law to attend school, whether in public, private, parochial, or home-school settings. The state directs the curriculum, certifies the teachers, and provides the facilities for schooling. And in many communities, schools have become battlegrounds for religious wars.

As a setting for this chapter, Tables 3.1, 3.2, and 3.3, taken from the 2001 volume of the *Statistical Abstract of the United States*, illustrate the religious diversity of contemporary American society. A total of 74 denominations report a membership of more than 65,000, with 24 having more than one million members. Some 86 percent of the American public who report church membership belong to Christian denominations, with Jews, Muslims, Buddhists, Hindus, and those who profess no religion making up a small and often stigmatized minority.

Not surprisingly, most cases that have challenged state aid to religious groups under the Establishment Clause have involved members of the Christian majority who have more influence with lawmakers who share their beliefs and are responsive to the voters among the religious majority, especially those who belong to such large and established denominations as Roman Catholics and Baptists. In contrast, most of the Free Exercise Clause cases decided by the Supreme Court (see Chapter 4) have been brought by members of smaller and less influential religious groups such as the Old Order Amish, Orthodox Jews, Seventh-day Adventists, and the Native American Church. But the Supreme Court has upheld most challenges to state preference for religion under the Establishment Clause, particularly in school prayer cases, while ruling for members of religious minorities in Free Exercise Clause cases. These differences in judicial outcome reflect the Court's acknowledgement, as Justice Robert Jackson wrote in *West Virginia Board of Education v. Barnette* in 1943, that constitutional rights "depend on the outcome of no election."

Table 3.3   Christian Church Adherents, 1990, and Jewish Population, 1999—States

| State | Christian Adherents, 1990 | | Jewish Population, 1999 | | State | Christian Adherents, 1990 | | Jewish Population, 1999 | |
	Number (1,000)	Percent of Population[1]	Number (1,000)	Percent of Population[1]		Number (1,000)	Percent of Population[1]	Number (1,000)	Percent of Population[1]
U.S.	131,084	52.7	6,061	2.2	MO	2,892	56.6	62	1.1
AL	2,858	70.7	9	0.2	MT	341	42.7	1	0.1
AK	175	31.8	4	0.6	NE	1,000	63.4	7	0.4
AZ	1,505	41.1	82	1.7	NV	366	29.6	58	3.2
AR	1,423	60.5	2	0.1	NH	431	38.9	10	0.8
CA	11,665	39.2	967	2.9	NJ	4,305	55.7	465	5.7
CO	1,244	37.8	68	1.7	NM	883	58.3	10	0.6
CT	1,933	58.9	101	3.1	NY	9,970	55.5	1,651	9.1
DE	297	44.6	14	1.8	NC	3,949	59.6	25	0.3
DC	349	57.5	25	4.9	ND	485	75.9	1	0.1
FL	5,106	39.5	637	4.2	OH	5,313	48.9	144	1.3
GA	3,659	56.5	88	1.1	OK	2,097	66.5	5	0.1
HI	391	35.3	7	0.6	OR	904	31.8	30	0.9
ID	507	50.4	1	0.1	PA	6,960	58.6	282	2.4
IL	6,579	57.5	270	2.2	RI	754	75.1	16	1.6
IN	2,615	47.1	18	0.3	SC	2,149	61.7	10	0.3
IA	1,674	60.3	6	0.2	SD	474	68.1	(Z)	0.1
KS	1,346	54.3	14	0.5	TN	2,968	60.8	18	0.3
KY	2,213	60.1	11	0.3	TX	10,788	63.5	124	0.6
LA	2,959	70.1	16	0.4	UT	1,371	79.6	4	0.2
ME	439	36.1	8	0.6	VT	233	40.4	6	1.0
MD	2,101	43.9	216	4.1	VA	2,898	46.8	76	1.1
MA	3,666	60.9	274	4.4	WA	1,579	32.4	35	0.6
MI	4,580	49.2	107	1.1	WV	740	41.3	2	0.1
MN	2,807	64.2	42	0.9	WI	3,125	63.9	28	0.5
MS	1,804	70.1	1	0.1	WY	216	47.6	(Z)	0.1

Christian church adherents were defined as "all members, including full members, their children and the estimated number of other regular participants who are not considered as communicant, confirmed or full members." Data on Christian church adherents are based on reports of 133 church groupings and exclude 34 church bodies that reported more than 100,000 members to the *Yearbook of American and Canadian Churches*. The Jewish population includes Jews who define themselves as Jewish by religion as well as those who define themselves as Jewish in cultural terms. Data on Jewish population are based primarily on a compilation of individual estimates made by local Jewish federations. Additionally, most large communities have completed Jewish demographic surveys from which the Jewish population can be determined.

Z Fewer than 500.

[1]Based on U.S. Census Bureau data for resident population enumerated as of April 1, 1990, and estimated as of July 1, 1999.

EVERSON V. BOARD OF EDUCATION OF EWING TOWNSHIP, NEW JERSEY
330 U.S. 1 (1947)

"[The] First Amendment requires the state to be a neutral in its relations with groups of religious believers and non-believers; it does not require the state to be their adversary. State power is no more to be used so as to handicap religions, than it is to favor them."

The Question: Can a state use public tax funds to subsidize the bus transportation of students who attend Catholic parochial schools?

The Arguments: PRO

Parents have a right, established by the Supreme Court, to send their children to private schools, both secular or religious. Many states and local school districts provide bus transportation to students in public schools. Although public tax funds cannot be used to support religious teaching in private schools, there is nothing about riding a bus to school that supports or endorses the religious message of the denomination that operates the school. Finally, states and local governments provide fire and police protection to all schools, whether they are public or private, and bus transportation also serves a safety function for students who might otherwise be forced to walk to school along busy streets and across dangerous intersections.

CON

The Constitution forbids any direct aid to religious institutions, whether they are churches or schools that are operated by churches. Any public tax funds that indirectly aid religious groups, even through subsidies to church members or those who use church facilities or programs, reduce the financial burden on the church and its programs, and thus constitute a taxpayer-funded contribution to religion. Bus transportation is not like police or fire protection, and parents who send their children to religious schools should not receive tax funds for any purpose connected to those schools. Further, if taxpayers subsidize bus transportation, there will be pressure to fund other school programs, and keeping the secular and religious parts of school activities separate would entangle public officials in religious matters.

MR. JUSTICE BLACK delivered the opinion of the Court.

A New Jersey statute authorizes its local school districts to make rules and contracts for the transportation of children to and from schools. The appellee, a township board of education, acting pursuant to this statute authorized reimbursement to parents of money expended by them for the bus transportation of their children on regular busses operated by the public transportation system. Part of this money was for the payment of transportation of some children in the community to Catholic parochial schools. These church schools give their students, in addition to secular education, regular religious instruction conforming to the religious tenets and modes of worship of the Catholic Faith. The superintendent of these schools is a Catholic priest.

The appellant, in his capacity as a district taxpayer, filed suit in a State court challenging the right of the Board to reimburse parents of parochial school students. He contended [t]hat the statute and the resolution passed pursuant to it violated both the State and the Federal Constitutions. That court held that the legislature was without power to authorize such payment under the State constitution. The New Jersey Court of Errors and Appeals reversed, holding that neither the statute nor the resolution passed pursuant to it was in conflict with the State constitution or the provisions of the Federal Constitution in issue. . . .

The New Jersey statute is challenged as a "law respecting an establishment of religion." The First Amendment . . . commands that a state "shall make no law respecting an establishment of religion, or prohibiting the free exercise thereof." These words of the First Amendment reflected in the minds of early Americans a vivid mental picture of conditions and practices which they fervently wished to stamp out in order to preserve liberty for themselves and for their posterity. Doubtless their goal has not been entirely reached; but so far has the Nation moved toward it that the expression "law respecting an establishment of religion," probably does not so vividly remind present-day Americans of the evils, fears, and political problems that caused that expression to be written into our Bill of Rights. Whether this New Jersey law is one respecting the "establishment of religion" requires an understanding of the

meaning of that language, particularly with respect to the imposition of taxes. Once again, therefore, it is not inappropriate briefly to review the background and environment of the period in which that constitutional language was fashioned and adopted.

A large proportion of the early settlers of this country came here from Europe to escape the bondage of laws which compelled them to support and attend government favored churches. The centuries immediately before and contemporaneous with the colonization of America had been filled with turmoil, civil strife, and persecutions, generated in large part by established sects determined to maintain their absolute political and religious supremacy. With the power of government supporting them, at various times and places, Catholics had persecuted Protestants, Protestants had persecuted Catholics, Protestant sects had persecuted other Protestant sects, Catholics of one shade of belief had persecuted Catholics of another shade of belief, and all of these had from time to time persecuted Jews. In efforts to force loyalty to whatever religious group happened to be on top and in league with the government of a particular time and place, men and women had been fined, cast in jail, cruelly tortured, and killed. Among the offenses for which these punishments had been inflicted were such things as speaking disrespectfully of the views of ministers of government-established churches, nonattendance at those churches, expressions of non-belief in their doctrines, and failure to pay taxes and tithes to support them.

These practices of the old world were transplanted to and began to thrive in the soil of the new America. The very charters granted by the English Crown to the individuals and companies designated to make the laws which would control the destinies of the colonials authorized these individuals and companies to erect religious establishments which all, whether believers or non-believers, would be required to support and attend. An exercise of this authority was accompanied by a repetition of many of the old world practices and persecutions. Catholics found themselves hounded and proscribed because of their faith; Quakers who followed their conscience went to jail; Baptists were peculiarly obnoxious to certain dominant Protestant sects; men and women of varied faiths who happened to be in a minority in a particular locality were persecuted because they steadfastly persisted in worshipping God only as their own consciences dictated. And all of these dissenters were compelled to pay tithes and taxes to support government-sponsored churches whose ministers preached inflammatory sermons designed to strengthen and consolidate the established faith by generating a burning hatred against dissenters.

These practices became so commonplace as to shock the freedom-loving colonials into a feeling of abhorrence. The imposition of taxes to pay ministers' salaries and to build and maintain churches and church property aroused their indignation. It was these feelings which found expression in the First Amendment. No one locality and no one group throughout the Colonies can rightly be given entire credit for having aroused the sentiment that culminated in adoption of the Bill of Rights' provisions embracing religious liberty. But Virginia, where the established church had achieved a dominant influence in political affairs and where many excesses attracted wide public attention, provided a great stimulus and able leadership for the movement. The people there, as elsewhere, reached the conviction that individual religious liberty could be achieved best under a government which was stripped of all power to tax, to support, or otherwise to assist any or all religions, or to interfere with the beliefs of any religious individual or group.

The movement toward this end reached its dramatic climax in Virginia in 1785–86 when the Virginia legislative body was about to renew Virginia's tax levy for the support of the established church. Thomas Jefferson and James Madison led the fight against this tax. Madison wrote his great Memorial and Remonstrance against the law. In it, he eloquently argued that a true religion did not need the support of law; that no person, either believer or nonbeliever, should be taxed to support a religious institution of any kind; that the best interest of a society required that the minds of men always be wholly free; and that cruel persecutions were the inevitable result of government-established religions. Madison's Remonstrance received strong support throughout Virginia, and the Assembly postponed consideration of the proposed tax measure until its next session. When the proposal came up for consideration at that session, it not only died in committee, but the Assembly enacted the famous "Virginia Bill for Religious Liberty" originally written by Thomas Jefferson. The preamble to that Bill stated among other things that "Almighty God hath created the mind free; that all attempts to influence it by temporal punishments, or burthens, or by civil incapacitations, tend only to beget habits of hypocrisy and meanness, and are a departure from the plan of the Holy author of our religion who being Lord both of body and mind, yet chose not to propagate it by coercions on either . . . ; that to compel a man to furnish contributions of money for the propagation of opinions which he disbelieves, is sinful and tyrannical; that even forcing him to support this or that teacher of his own religious persuasion, is depriving him of the comfortable liberty of giving his contributions to the particular pastor, whose morals he would make his pattern. . . ."

In recent years, so far as the provision against the establishment of a religion is concerned, the question has most frequently arisen in connection with proposed state aid to church schools and efforts to carry on religious teachings in the public schools in accordance with the tenets of a particular sect. Some churches have either sought or accepted state financial support for their schools. Here again the efforts to obtain state aid or acceptance of it have not been limited to any one particular faith. The state courts, in the main, have remained faithful to the language of their own constitutional provisions designed to protect religious freedom and to separate religions and governments. Their decisions, however, show the difficulty in drawing the line between tax legislation which provides funds for the welfare of the general public and that which is designed to support institutions which teach religion. . . .

The "establishment of religion" clause of the First Amendment means at least this: Neither a state nor the Federal Government can set up a church. Neither can pass laws which aid one religion, aid all religions, or prefer one religion over another. Neither can force nor influence a person to go to or to remain away from church against his will or force him to profess a belief or disbelief in any religion. No person can be punished for entertaining or professing religious beliefs or disbeliefs, for church attendance or nonattendance. No tax in any amount, large or small, can be levied to support any religious activities or institutions, whatever they may be called, or whatever form they may adopt to teach or practice religion. Neither a state nor the Federal Government can, openly or secretly, participate in the affairs of any religious organizations or groups and vice versa. In the words of Jefferson, the clause against establishment of religion by law was intended to erect "a wall of separation between Church and State."

We must consider the New Jersey statute in accordance with the foregoing limitations imposed by the First Amendment. But we must not strike that state statute down if it is within the state's constitutional power even though it approaches the verge of that power. New Jersey cannot consistently with the "establishment of religion" clause of the First Amendment contribute tax-raised funds to the support of an institution which teaches the tenets and faith of any church. On the other hand, other language of the amendment commands that New Jersey cannot hamper its citizens in the free exercise of their own religion. Consequently, it cannot exclude individual Catholics, Lutherans, Mohammedans, Baptists, Jews, Methodists, Non-believers, Presbyterians, or the members of any other faith, because of their faith, or lack of it, from receiving the benefits of public welfare legislation. While we do not mean to intimate that a state could not provide transportation only to children attending public schools, we must be careful, in protecting the citizens of New Jersey against state-established churches, to be sure that we do not inadvertently prohibit New Jersey from extending its general State law benefits to all its citizens without regard to their religious belief.

Measured by these standards, we cannot say that the First Amendment prohibits New Jersey from spending tax-raised funds to pay the bus fares of parochial school pupils as a part of a general program under which it pays the fares of pupils attending public and other schools. It is undoubtedly true that children are helped to get to church schools. There is even a possibility that some of the children might not be sent to the church schools if the parents were compelled to pay their children's bus fares out of their own pockets when transportation to a public school would have been paid for by the State. The same possibility exists where the state requires a local transit company to provide reduced fares to school children including those attending parochial schools, or where a municipally owned transportation system undertakes to carry all school children free of charge. Moreover, state-paid policemen, detailed to protect children going to and from church schools from the very real hazards of traffic, would serve much the same purpose and accomplish much the same result as state provisions intended to guarantee free transportation of a kind which the state deems to be best for the school children's welfare. And parents might refuse to risk their children to the serious danger of traffic accidents going to and from parochial schools, the approaches to which were not protected by policemen. Similarly, parents might be reluctant to permit their children to attend schools which the state had cut off from such general government services as ordinary police and fire protection, connections for sewage disposal, public highways and sidewalks. Of course, cutting off church schools from these services, so separate and so indisputably marked off from the religious function, would make it far more difficult for the schools to operate. But such is obviously not the purpose of the First Amendment. That Amendment requires the state to be a neutral in its relations with groups of religious believers and non-believers; it does not require the state to be their adversary. State power is no more to be used so as to handicap religions, than it is to favor them.

This Court has said that parents may, in the discharge of their duty under state compulsory education laws, send their children to a religious rather than a public school if the school meets the secular educational requirements which the state has power to impose. It appears that these parochial schools meet New Jersey's requirements. The State contributes no money to the schools. It does not support them. Its legislation, as applied, does no more than provide a general program to help parents get their children, regardless of their religion, safely and expeditiously to and from accredited schools. The First Amendment has erected a wall between church and state. That wall must be kept high and impregnable. We could not approve the slightest breach. New Jersey has not breached it here.

Affirmed.

MR. JUSTICE JACKSON, dissenting.

I find myself, contrary to first impressions, unable to join in this decision. I have a sympathy, though it is not ideological, with Catholic citizens who are compelled by law to pay taxes for public schools, and also feel constrained by conscience and discipline to support other schools for their own children. Such relief to them as this case involves is not in itself a serious burden to taxpayers and I had assumed it to be as little serious in principle. Study of this case convinces me otherwise. The Court's opinion marshals every argument in favor of state aid and puts the case in its most favorable light, but much of its reasoning confirms my conclusions that there are no good grounds upon which to support the present legislation. In fact, the undertones of the opinion, advocating complete and uncompromising separation of Church from

State, seem utterly discordant with its conclusion yielding support to their commingling in educational matters. The case which irresistibly comes to mind as the most fitting precedent is that of Julia who, according to Byron's reports, "whispering 'I will ne'er consent,'—consented."

The Court sustains this legislation by assuming two deviations from the facts of this particular case; first, it assumes a state of facts the record does not support, and secondly, it refuses to consider facts which are inescapable on the record. The Court concludes that this "legislation, as applied, does no more than provide a general program to help parents get their children, regardless of their religion, safely and expeditiously to and from accredited schools," and it draws a comparison between "state provisions intended to guarantee free transportation" for school children with services such as police and fire protection, and implies that we are here dealing with "laws authorizing new types of public services. . . ." This hypothesis permeates the opinion. The facts will not bear that construction.

The Township of Ewing is not furnishing transportation to the children in any form; it is not operating school buses itself or contracting for their operation; and it is not performing any public service of any kind with this taxpayer's money. All school children are left to ride as ordinary paying passengers on the regular buses operated by the public transportation system. What the Township does, and what the taxpayer complains of, is at stated intervals to reimburse parents for the fares paid, provided the children attend either public schools or Catholic Church schools. This expenditure of tax funds has no possible effect on the child's safety or expedition in transit. As passengers on the public busses they travel as fast and no faster, and are as safe and no safer, since their parents are reimbursed as before.

In addition to thus assuming a type of service that does not exist, the Court also insists that we must close our eyes to a discrimination which does exist. The resolution which authorizes disbursement of this taxpayer's money limits reimbursement to those who attend public schools and Catholic schools. That is the way the Act is applied to this taxpayer. The New Jersey Act in question makes the character of the school, not the needs of the children determine the eligibility of parents to reimbursement. The Act permits payment for transportation to parochial schools or public schools but prohibits it to private schools operated in whole or in part for profit. Children often are sent to private schools because their parents feel that they require more individual instruction than public schools can provide, or because they are backward or defective and need special attention. If all children of the state were objects of impartial solicitude, no reason is obvious for denying transportation reimbursement to students of this class, for these often are as needy and as worthy as those who go to public or parochial schools. Refusal to reimburse those who attend such schools is understandable only in the light of a purpose to aid the schools, because the state might well abstain from aiding a profit-making private enterprise. Thus, under the Act and resolution brought to us by this case children are classified according to the schools they attend and are to be aided if they attend the public schools or private Catholic schools, and they are not allowed to be aided if they attend private secular schools or private religious schools of other faiths. . . .

If we are to decide this case on the facts before us, our question is simply this: Is it constitutional to tax this complainant to pay the cost of carrying pupils to Church schools of one specified denomination? Whether the taxpayer constitutionally can be made to contribute aid to parents of students because of their attendance at parochial schools depends upon the nature of those schools and their relation to the Church. The Constitution says nothing of education. It lays no obligation on the states to provide schools and does not undertake to regulate state systems of education if they see fit to maintain them. But they cannot, through school policy any more than through other means, invade rights secured to citizens by the Constitution of the United States. One of our basic rights is to be free of taxation to support a transgression of the constitutional command that the authorities "shall make no law respecting an establishment of religion, or prohibiting the free exercise thereof." U.S. Const., Amend. I.

The function of the Church school is a subject on which this record is meager. It shows only that the schools are under superintendence of a priest and that "religion is taught as part of the curriculum." But we know that such schools are parochial only in name—they, in fact, represent a worldwide and age-old policy of the Roman Catholic Church. Under the rubric "Catholic Schools," the Canon Law of the Church by which all Catholics are bound, provides: "Catholic children are to be educated in schools where not only nothing contrary to Catholic faith and morals is taught, but rather in schools where religious and moral training occupy the first place. . . . In every elementary school the children must, according to their age, be instructed in Christian doctrine. The young people who attend the higher schools are to receive a deeper religious knowledge, and the bishops shall appoint priests qualified for such work by their learning and piety.". . .

I should be surprised if any Catholic would deny that the parochial school is a vital, if not the most vital, part of the Roman Catholic Church. If put to the choice, that venerable institution, I should expect, would forego its whole service for mature persons before it would give up education of the young, and it would be a wise choice. Its growth and cohesion, discipline and loyalty, spring from its schools. Catholic education is the rock on which the whole structure rests, and to render tax aid to its Church school is indistinguishable to me from rendering the same aid to the Church itself.

It is of no importance in this situation whether the beneficiary of this expenditure of tax-raised funds is primarily the parochial school and incidentally the pupil, or whether the aid is directly bestowed on the pupil with indirect benefits to the school. The state cannot maintain a Church and it can no more tax its citizens to furnish free carriage to those who attend a Church. The prohibition against establishment of religion cannot be circumvented by a subsidy, bonus or reimbursement of expense to individuals for receiving religious instruction and indoctrination. . . .

It seems to me that the basic fallacy in the Court's reasoning, which accounts for its failure to apply the principles it avows, is in ignoring the essentially religious test by which beneficiaries of this expenditure are selected. A policeman protects a Catholic, of course—but not because he is a Catholic; it is because he is a man and a member of our society. The fireman protects the Church school—but not because it is a Church school; it is because it is property, part of the assets of our society. Neither the fireman nor the policeman has to ask before he renders aid "Is this man or building identified with the Catholic Church?" But before these school authorities draw a check to reimburse for a student's fare they must ask just that question, and if the school is a Catholic one they may render aid because it is such, while if it is of any other faith or is run for profit, the help must be withheld. To consider the converse of the Court's reasoning will best disclose its fallacy. That there is no parallel between police and fire protection and this plan of reimbursement is apparent from the incongruity of the limitation of this Act if applied to police and fire service. Could we sustain an Act that said police shall protect pupils on the way to or from public schools and Catholic schools but not while going to and coming from other schools, and firemen shall extinguish a blaze in public or Catholic school buildings but shall not put out a blaze in Protestant Church schools or private schools operated for profit? That is the true analogy to the case we have before us and I should think it pretty plain that such a scheme would not be valid.

The Court's holding is that this taxpayer has no grievance because the state has decided to make the reimbursement a public purpose and therefore we are bound to regard it as such. I agree that this Court has left, and always should leave to each state, great latitude in deciding for itself, in the light of its own conditions, what shall be public purposes in its scheme of things. It may socialize utilities and economic enterprises and make taxpayers' business out of what conventionally had been private business. It may make public business of individual welfare, health, education, entertainment or security. But it cannot make public business of religious worship or instruction, or of attendance at religious institutions of any character. There is no answer to the proposition . . . that the effect of the religious freedom Amendment to our Constitution was to take every form of propagation of religion out of the realm of things which could directly or indirectly be made public business and thereby be supported in whole or in part at taxpayers' expense. That is a difference which the Constitution sets up between religion and almost every other subject matter of legislation, a difference which goes to the very root of religious freedom and which the Court is overlooking today. This freedom was first in the Bill of Rights because it was first in the forefathers' minds; it was set forth in absolute terms, and its strength is its rigidity. It was intended not only to keep the states' hands out of religion, but to keep religion's hands off the state, and above all, to keep bitter religious controversy out of public life by denying to every denomination any advantage from getting control of public policy or the public purse. Those great ends I cannot but think are immeasurably compromised by today's decision.

This policy of our Federal Constitution has never been wholly pleasing to most religious groups. They all are quick to invoke its protections; they all are irked when they feel its restraints. This Court has gone a long way, if not an unreasonable way, to hold that public business of such paramount importance as maintenance of public order, protection of the privacy of the home, and taxation may not be pursued by a state in a way that even indirectly will interfere with religious proselyt[iz]ing. But we cannot have it both ways. Religious teaching cannot be a private affair when the state seeks to impose regulations which infringe on it indirectly, and a public affair when it comes to taxing citizens of one faith to aid another, or those of no faith to aid all. If these principles seem harsh in prohibiting aid to Catholic education, it must not be forgotten that it is the same Constitution that alone assures Catholics the right to maintain these schools at all when predominant local sentiment would forbid them. Nor should I think that those who have done so well without this aid would want to see this separation between Church and State broken down. If

the state may aid these religious schools, it may therefore regulate them. Many groups have sought aid from tax funds only to find that it carried political controls with it. . . . But in any event, the great purposes of the Constitution do not depend on the approval or convenience of those they restrain. I cannot read the history of the struggle to separate political from ecclesiastical affairs . . . without a conviction that the Court today is unconsciously giving the clock's hands a backward turn.

MR. JUSTICE FRANKFURTER joins in this opinion.

McCollum v. Board of Education of Champaign-Urbana, Illinois
333 U.S. 203 (1948)

"The First Amendment rests upon the premise that both religion and government can best work to achieve their lofty aims if each is left free from the other within its respective sphere. . . . The First Amendment had erected a wall between Church and State which must be kept high and impregnable."

The Question: Can a local school board establish a "released time" program of religious instruction in public schools, in classes taught by ministers, priests, and rabbis and conducted during school hours?

The Arguments: PRO

Allowing students, with their parents' permission, to attend classes taught by religious leaders adds an important topic to the school curriculum. No students are coerced to attend these classes, and attendance is voluntary. The classes are not taught by public school teachers, and the school takes no position on the truth or falsity of the religious doctrines being presented. Many parents find this a better way for their children to learn about their religion than through Sunday school or other kinds of religious instruction. The schools are not preferring any one religion over another or even endorsing religion in general, by giving students the choice of adding religious classes to their studies.

CON

Religious instruction in public schools, conducted on school premises and during class time, has the inescapable effect of aiding religious groups in proselytizing their doctrines. The proper place for religious training is in the home and in churches and synagogues. Students who choose not to participate in religious classes, either from their own choice or that of their parents, might be subject to peer pressure, ostracism, or teasing from those who take religious classes. Public school teachers and officials should not be in the position of monitoring what is taught in religious classes to make sure it is not harmful to students or undermines the school's curriculum.

MR. JUSTICE BLACK delivered the opinion of the Court.

This case relates to the power of a state to utilize its tax-supported public school system in aid of religious instruction insofar as that power may be restricted by the First and Fourteenth Amendments to the Federal Constitution.

The appellant, Vashti McCollum, began this action for mandamus against the Champaign Board of Education in the Circuit Court of Champaign County, Illinois. Her

asserted interest was that of a resident and taxpayer of Champaign and of a parent whose child was then enrolled in the Champaign public schools. . . . Appellant's petition for mandamus alleged that religious teachers, employed by private religious groups, were permitted to come weekly into the school buildings during the regular hours set apart for secular teaching, and then and there for a period of thirty minutes substitute their religious teaching for the secular education provided under the compulsory education law.

The petitioner charged that this joint public-school religious-group program violated the First and Fourteenth Amendments to the United States Constitution. The prayer of her petition was that the Board of Education be ordered to "adopt and enforce rules and regulations prohibiting all instruction in and teaching of all religious education in all public schools in Champaign District Number 71, and in all public school houses and buildings in said district when occupied by public schools.". . .

Although there are disputes between the parties as to various inferences that may or may not properly be drawn from the evidence concerning the religious program, the following facts are shown by the record without dispute. In 1940 interested members of the Jewish, Roman Catholic, and a few of the Protestant faiths formed a voluntary association called the Champaign Council on Religious Education. They obtained permission from the Board of Education to offer classes in religious instruction to public school pupils in grades four to nine inclusive. Classes were made up of pupils whose parents signed printed cards requesting that their children be permitted to attend; they were held weekly, thirty minutes for the lower grades, forty-five minutes for the higher. The council employed the religious teachers at no expense to the school authorities, but the instructors were subject to the approval and supervision of the superintendent of schools. The classes were taught in three separate religious groups by Protestant teachers, Catholic priests, and a Jewish rabbi, although for the past several years there have apparently been no classes instructed in the Jewish religion. Classes were conducted in the regular classrooms of the school building. Students who did not choose to take the religious instruction were not released from public school duties; they were required to leave their classrooms and go to some other place in the school building for pursuit of their secular studies. On the other hand, students who were released from secular study for the religious instructions were required to be present at the religious classes. Reports of their presence or absence were to be made to their secular teachers.

The foregoing facts, without reference to others that appear in the record, show the use of tax-supported property for religious instruction and the close cooperation between the school authorities and the religious council in promoting religious education. The operation of the state's compulsory education system thus assists and is integrated with the program of religious instruction carried on by separate religious sects. Pupils compelled by law to go to school for secular education are released in part from their legal duty upon the condition that they attend the religious classes. This is beyond all question a utilization of the tax-established and tax-supported public school system to aid religious groups to spread their faith. And it falls squarely under the ban of the First Amendment (made applicable to the States by the Fourteenth) as we interpreted it in Everson v. Board of Education. . . .

Recognizing that the Illinois program is barred by the First and Fourteenth Amendments if we adhere to the views expressed both by the majority and the minority in the Everson case, counsel for the respondents challenge those views as dicta and urge that we reconsider and repudiate them. They argue that historically the First Amendment was intended to forbid only government preference of one religion over another, not an impartial governmental assistance of all reli-

gions. In addition they ask that we distinguish or overrule our holding in the Everson case that the Fourteenth Amendment made the "establishment of religion" clause of the First Amendment applicable as a prohibition against the States. After giving full consideration to the arguments presented we are unable to accept either of these contentions.

To hold that a state cannot consistently with the First and Fourteenth Amendments utilize its public school system to aid any or all religious faiths or sects in the dissemination of their doctrines and ideals does not, as counsel urges, manifest a governmental hostility to religion or religious teachings. A manifestation of such hostility would be at war with our national tradition as embodied in the First Amendment's guarantee of the free exercise of religion. For the First Amendment rests upon the premise that both religion and government can best work to achieve their lofty aims if each is left free from the other within its respective sphere. Or, as we said in the Everson case, the First Amendment had erected a wall between Church and State which must be kept high and impregnable.

Here not only are the state's tax-supported public school buildings used for the dissemination of religious doctrines. The State also affords sectarian groups an invaluable aid in that it helps to provide pupils for their religious classes through use of the state's compulsory public school machinery. This is not separation of Church and State.

The cause is reversed and remanded to the State Supreme Court for proceedings not inconsistent with this opinion.

Reversed and remanded.

MR. JUSTICE FRANKFURTER delivered the following opinion, in which MR. JUSTICE JACKSON, MR. JUSTICE RUTLEDGE and MR. JUSTICE BURTON join.

We dissented in Everson v. Board of Education, because in our view the Constitutional principle requiring separation of Church and State compelled invalidation of the ordinance sustained by the majority. Illinois has here authorized the commingling of sectarian with secular instruction in the public schools. The Constitution of the United States forbids this.

The case, in the light of the Everson decision, demonstrates anew that the mere formulation of a relevant Constitutional principle is the beginning of the solution of a problem, not its answer. This is so because the meaning of a spacious conception like that of the separation of Church from State is unfolded as appeal is made to the principle from case to case. We are all agreed that the First and the Fourteenth Amendments have a secular reach far more penetrating in the conduct of Government than merely to forbid an "established church." But agreement, in the abstract, that the First Amendment was designed to erect a "wall of separation between Church and State," does not preclude a clash of views as to what the wall separates. Involved is not only the Constitutional principle but the implications of judicial review in its enforcement. Accommodation of legislative freedom and Constitutional limitations upon that freedom cannot be achieved by a mere phrase. We cannot illuminatingly apply the "wall-of-separation" metaphor until we have considered the relevant history of religious education in America, the place of the "released time" movement in that history, and its precise manifestation in the case before us.

To understand the particular program now before us as a conscientious attempt to accommodate the allowable functions of Government and the special concerns of the Church within the framework of our Constitution and with due regard to the kind of society for which it was designed, we must put this Champaign program of 1940 in its historic setting. Traditionally, organized education in the Western world was Church education. It could hardly be otherwise when the education of children was primarily study of the Word and the ways of God. Even in the Protestant countries, where there was a less close identification of Church and State, the basis of education was largely the Bible, and its chief purpose inculcation of piety. To the extent that the State intervened, it used its authority to further aims of the Church.

The emigrants who came to these shores brought this view of education with them. Colonial schools certainly started with a religious orientation. When the common problems of the early settlers of the Massachusetts Bay Colony revealed the need for common schools, the object was the defeat of "one chief project of that old deluder, Satan, to keep men from the knowledge of the Scriptures."

The evolution of colonial education, largely in the service of religion, into the public school system of today is the story of changing conceptions regarding the American democratic society, of the functions of State-maintained education in such a society, and of the role therein of the free exercise of religion by the people. The modern public school derived from a philosophy of freedom reflected in the First Amendment. It is appropriate to recall that the Remonstrance of James Madison, an event basic in the history of religious liberty, was called forth by a proposal which involved support to religious education. As the momentum for popular education increased and in turn evoked strong claims for State support of religious education, contests not unlike that which in Virginia had produced Madison's Remonstrance appeared in various form in other States. New York and Massachusetts provide famous chapters in the history that established disassociation of religious teaching from State-maintained schools. In New York, the rise of the common schools led, despite fierce sectarian opposition, to the barring of tax founds to church schools, and later to any school in which sectarian doctrine was taught. In Massachusetts, largely through the efforts of Horace Mann, all sectarian teachings were barred from the common school to save it from being rent by denominational conflict. The upshot of these controversies, often long and fierce, is fairly summarized by saying that long before the Fourteenth Amendment subjected the States to new limitations, the prohibition of furtherance by the State of religious instruction became the guiding principle, in law and feeling, of the American people. . . .

Separation in the field of education, then, was not imposed upon unwilling States by force of superior law. In this respect the Fourteenth Amendment merely reflected a principle then dominant in our national life. To the extent that the Constitution thus made it binding upon the States, the basis of the restriction is the whole experience of our people. Zealous watchfulness against fusion of secular and religious activities by Government itself, through any of its instruments but especially through its educational agencies, was the democratic response of the American community to the particular needs of a young and growing nation, unique in the composition of its people. . . . The secular public school did not imply indifference to the basic role of religion in the life of the people, nor rejection of religious education as a means of fostering it. The claims of religion were not minimized by refusing to make the public schools agencies for their assertion. The non-sectarian or secular public school was the means of reconciling freedom in general with religious freedom. The sharp confinement of the public schools to secular education was a recognition of the need of a democratic society to educate its children, insofar as the State undertook to do so, in an atmosphere free from pressures in a realm in which pressures are most resisted and where conflicts are most easily and most bitterly engendered. Designed to serve as perhaps the most powerful agency for promoting cohesion among a heterogeneous democratic people, the public school must keep scrupulously free from entanglement in the strife of sects. The preservation of the community from divisive conflicts, of Government from irreconcilable pressures by religious groups, of religion from censorship and coercion however subtly exercised, requires strict confinement of the State to instruction other than religious, leaving to the individual's church and home, indoctrination in the faith of his choice. . . .

Separation means separation, not something less. Jefferson's metaphor in describing the relation between Church and State speaks of a "wall of separation," not of a fine line easily overstepped. The public school is at once the symbol of our democracy and the most pervasive means for promoting our common destiny. In no activity of the State is it more vital to keep out divisive forces than in its schools, to avoid confusing, not to say fusing, what the Constitution sought to keep strictly apart.". . . It is the Court's duty to enforce this principle in its full integrity. If nowhere else, in the relation between Church and State, "good fences make good neighbors."

Mr. Justice Reed, dissenting.

The decisions reversing the judgment of the Supreme Court of Illinois interpret the prohibition of the First Amendment against the establishment of religion, made effective as to the states by the Fourteenth Amendment, to forbid pupils of the public schools electing, with the approval of their parents, courses in religious education. . . . As I am convinced that this interpretation of the First Amendment is erroneous, I feel impelled to express the reasons for my disagreement. By directing attention to the many instances of close association of church and state in American society and by recalling that many of these relations are so much a part of our tradition and culture that they are accepted without more, this dissent may help in an appraisal of the meaning of the clause of the First Amendment concerning the establishment of religion and of the reasons which lead to the approval or disapproval of the judgment below. . . .

I find it difficult to extract from the opinions any conclusion as to what it is in the Champaign plan that is unconstitutional. Is it the use of school buildings for religious instruction; the release of pupils by the schools for religious instruction during school hours; the so-called assistance by teachers in handing out the request cards to pupils, in keeping lists of them for release and records of their attendance; or the action of the principals in arranging an opportunity for the classes and the appearance of the Council's instructors?

None of the reversing opinions say whether the purpose of the Champaign plan for religious instruction during school hours is unconstitutional or whether it is some ingredient used in or omitted from the formula that makes the plan unconstitutional.

From the tenor of the opinions I conclude that their teachings are that any use of a pupil's school time whether that use is on or off the school grounds, with the necessary school regulations to facilitate attendance, falls under the ban.... The opinions do not say in words that the condemned practice of religious education is a law respecting an establishment of religion contrary to the First Amendment.... It seems obvious that the action of the School Board in permitting religious education in certain grades of the schools by all faiths did not prohibit the free exercise of religion. Even assuming that certain children who did not elect to take instruction are embarrassed to remain outside of the classes, one can hardly speak of that embarrassment as a prohibition against the free exercise of religion. As no issue of prohibition upon the free exercise of religion is before us, we need only examine the School Board's action to see if it constitutes an establishment of religion....

The phrase "an establishment of religion" may have been intended by Congress to be aimed only at a state church. When the First Amendment was pending in Congress in substantially its present form, "Mr. Madison said, he apprehended the meaning of the words to be, that Congress should not establish a religion, and enforce the legal observation of it by law, nor compel men to worship God in any manner contrary to their conscience." Passing years, however, have brought about acceptance of a broader meaning, although never until today, I believe, has this Court widened its interpretation to any such degree as holding that recognition of the interest of our nation in religion, through the granting, to qualified representatives of the principal faiths, of opportunity to present religion as an optional, extracurricular subject during released school time in public school buildings, was equivalent to an establishment of religion....

This Court summarized the amendment's accepted reach into the religious field, as I understand its scope, in Everson v. Board of Education. The Court's opinion quotes the gist of the Court's reasoning in Everson. I agree as there stated that none of our governmental entities can "set up a church." I agree that they cannot "aid" all or any religions or prefer one "over another." But "aid" must be understood as a purposeful assistance directly to the church itself or to some religious group or organization doing religious work of such a character that it may fairly be said to be performing ecclesiastical functions. "Prefer" must give an advantage to one "over another." I agree that pupils cannot "be released in part from their legal duty" of school attendance upon condition that they attend religious classes. But as Illinois has held that it is within the discretion of the School Board to permit absence from school for religious instruction no legal duty of school attendance is violated....

With the general statements in the opinions concerning the constitutional requirement that the nation and the states, by virtue of the First and Fourteenth Amendments, may "make no law respecting an establishment of religion," I am in agreement. But, in the light of the meaning given to those words by the precedents, customs, and practices which I have detailed above, I cannot agree with the Court's conclusion that when pupils compelled by law to go to school for secular education are released from school so as to attend the religious classes, churches are unconstitutionally aided. Whatever may be the wisdom of the arrangement as to the use of the school buildings made with the Champaign Council of Religious Education, it is clear to me that past practice shows such cooperation between the schools and a non-ecclesiastical body is not forbidden by the First Amendment. When actual church services have always been permitted on government property, the mere use of the school buildings by a non-sectarian group for religious education ought not to be condemned as an establishment of religion. For a non-sectarian organization to give the type of instruction here offered cannot be said to violate our rule as to the establishment of religion by the state....

This Court cannot be too cautious in upsetting practices embedded in our society by many years of experience. A state is entitled to have great leeway in its legislation when dealing with the important social problems of its population. A definite violation of legislative limits must be established. The Constitution should not be stretched to forbid national customs in the way courts act to reach arrangements to avoid federal taxation. Devotion to the great principle of religious liberty should not lead us into a rigid interpretation of the constitutional guarantee that conflicts with accepted habits of our people. This is an instance where, for me, the history of past practices is determinative of the meaning of a constitutional clause not a decorous introduction to the study of its text. The judgment should be affirmed.

Engel v. Vitale
370 U.S. 421 (1962)

"The constitutional prohibition against laws respecting an establishment of religion must at least mean that . . .
it is no part of the business of government to compose official prayers for any group of the American people to
recite as part of a religious program carried on by government."

The Question: Can state educational officials require that a particular prayer, directed to "Almighty God," be recited each day by students in public schools?

The Arguments: PRO

Our nation was founded by people who prayed at public events and who firmly believed in asking for divine guidance. Chaplains lead prayer in Congress and state legislative bodies, and the word *God* appears on our currency and in the national anthem. As long as the prayer is nonsectarian and does not promote a particular denomination, students in public school classes are free to participate or not. In addition, beginning a school day with prayer sets a tone of reverence, thankfulness, and concern for others that will promote good behavior and a serious attitude toward learning. There is nothing harmful about prayer, and its benefits are obvious.

CON

Any prayer that begins with a reference to "Almighty God" confers the school's endorsement of a theistic religion and excludes those who are not religious or who are offended by public prayer. Students who remain silent, who do not bow their heads, or who leave the room during prayer are likely to be singled out by other students as deviant, or even devil worshipers, as has happened in several communities. Schools have no business taking sides on religious questions, and promoting a belief in God is something that should be left to parents and churches. Religion should not become a divisive issue in our schools.

MR. JUSTICE BLACK delivered the opinion of the Court.

The respondent Board of Education of Union Free School District No. 9, New Hyde Park, New York, acting in its official capacity under state law, directed the School District's principal to cause the following prayer to be said aloud by each class in the presence of a teacher at the beginning of each school day: "Almighty God, we acknowledge our dependence upon Thee, and we beg Thy blessings upon us, our parents, our teachers and our Country."

This daily procedure was adopted on the recommendation of the State Board of Regents, a governmental agency created by the State Constitution to which the New York Legislature has granted broad supervisory, executive, and legislative powers over the State's public school system. These state officials composed the prayer which they recommended and published as a part of their "Statement on Moral and Spiritual Training in the Schools," saying: "We believe that this Statement will be subscribed to by all men and women of good will, and we call upon all of them to aid in giving life to our program."

Shortly after the practice of reciting the Regents' prayer was adopted by the School District, the parents of ten pupils brought this action in a New York State Court insisting that use of this official prayer in the public schools was contrary to the beliefs, religions, or religious practices of both themselves and their children. Among other things, these parents challenged the constitutionality of both the state law authorizing the School District to direct the use of prayer in public schools and the School District's regulation ordering the recitation of this particular prayer on the ground that these actions of official governmental agencies violate that part of the First Amendment of the Federal Constitution which commands that "Congress shall make no law respecting an establishment of religion"—a command which was "made applicable to the State of New York by the Fourteenth Amendment of the said Constitution." The New York Court of Appeals . . . sustained an order of the lower state courts which had upheld the power of New York to use the Regents' prayer as a part of the daily procedures of its public schools

so long as the schools did not compel any pupil to join in the prayer over his or her parents' objection. We granted certiorari to review this important decision involving rights protected by the First and Fourteenth Amendments.

We think that by using its public school system to encourage recitation of the Regents' prayer, the State of New York has adopted a practice wholly inconsistent with the Establishment Clause. There can, of course, be no doubt that New York's program of daily classroom invocation of God's blessings as prescribed in the Regents' prayer is a religious activity. It is a solemn avowal of divine faith and supplication for the blessings of the Almighty. . . .

The petitioners contend among other things that the state laws requiring or permitting use of the Regents' prayer must be struck down as a violation of the Establishment Clause because that prayer was composed by governmental officials as a part of a governmental program to further religious beliefs. For this reason, petitioners argue, the State's use of the Regents' prayer in its public school system breaches the constitutional wall of separation between Church and State. We agree with that contention since we think that the constitutional prohibition against laws respecting an establishment of religion must at least mean that in this country it is no part of the business of government to compose official prayers for any group of the American people to recite as a part of a religious program carried on by government.

It is a matter of history that this very practice of establishing governmentally composed prayers for religious services was one of the reasons which caused many of our early colonists to leave England and seek religious freedom in America. The Book of Common Prayer, which was created under governmental direction and which was approved by Acts of Parliament in 1548 and 1549, set out in minute detail the accepted form and content of prayer and other religious ceremonies to be used in the established, tax-supported Church of England. The controversies over the Book and what should be its content repeatedly threatened to disrupt the peace of that country as the accepted forms of prayer in the established church changed with the views of the particular ruler that happened to be in control at the time.

Powerful groups representing some of the varying religious views of the people struggled among themselves to impress their particular views upon the Government and obtain amendments of the Book more suitable to their respective notions of how religious services should be conducted in order that the official religious establishment would advance their particular religious beliefs. Other groups, lacking the necessary political power to influence the Government on the matter, decided to leave England and its established church and seek freedom in America from England's governmentally ordained and supported religion.

It is an unfortunate fact of history that when some of the very groups which had most strenuously opposed the established Church of England found themselves sufficiently in control of colonial governments in this country to write their own prayers into law, they passed laws making their own religion the official religion of their respective colonies. Indeed, as late as the time of the Revolutionary War, there were established churches in at least eight of the thirteen former colonies and established religions in at least four of the other five. But the successful Revolution against English political domination was shortly followed by intense opposition to the practice of establishing religion by law. This opposition crystallized rapidly into an effective political force in Virginia where the minority religious groups such as Presbyterians, Lutherans, Quakers and Baptists had gained such strength that the adherents to the established Episcopal Church were actually a minority themselves. In 1785–1786, those opposed to the established Church, led by James Madison and Thomas Jefferson, who, though themselves not members of any of these dissenting religious groups, opposed all religious establishments by law on grounds of principle, obtained the enactment of the famous "Virginia Bill for Religious Liberty" by which all religious groups were placed on an equal footing so far as the State was concerned. Similar though less far-reaching legislation was being considered and passed in other States.

By the time of the adoption of the Constitution, our history shows that there was a widespread awareness among many Americans of the dangers of a union of Church and State. These people knew, some of them from bitter personal experience, that one of the greatest dangers to the freedom of the individual to worship in his own way lay in the Government's placing its official stamp of approval upon one particular kind of prayer or one particular form of religious services. They knew the anguish, hardship and bitter strife that could come when zealous religious groups struggled with one another to obtain the Government's stamp of approval from each King, Queen, or Protector that came to temporary power. The Constitution was intended to avert a part of this danger by leaving the government of this country in the hands of the people rather than in the hands of any monarch. But this safeguard was not enough. Our Founders were no more willing to let the content of their prayers and their privilege of praying whenever they pleased be influenced by the ballot box than they were to let these vital matters of personal conscience depend upon the succession of monarchs. The First Amendment was added to the Constitution to stand as a guarantee that neither the power nor the prestige of the Federal Government would be used to control, support or influence the kinds of prayer the American people can say—that

the people's religious must not be subjected to the pressures of government for change each time a new political administration is elected to office. Under that Amendment's prohibition against governmental establishment of religion, as reinforced by the provisions of the Fourteenth Amendment, government in this country, be it state or federal, is without power to prescribe by law any particular form of prayer which is to be used as an official prayer in carrying on any program of governmentally sponsored religious activity.

There can be no doubt that New York's state prayer program officially establishes the religious beliefs embodied in the Regents' prayer. The respondents' argument to the contrary, which is largely based upon the contention that the Regents' prayer is "non-denominational" and the fact that the program, as modified and approved by state courts, does not require all pupils to recite the prayer but permits those who wish to do so to remain silent or be excused from the room, ignores the essential nature of the program's constitutional defects. Neither the fact that the prayer may be denominationally neutral nor the fact that its observance on the part of the students is voluntary can serve to free it from the limitations of the Establishment Clause, as it might from the Free Exercise Clause, of the First Amendment, both of which are operative against the States by virtue of the Fourteenth Amendment. Although these two clauses may in certain instances overlap, they forbid two quite different kinds of governmental encroachment upon religious freedom. The Establishment Clause, unlike the Free Exercise Clause, does not depend upon any showing of direct governmental compulsion and is violated by the enactment of laws which establish an official religion whether those laws operate directly to coerce nonobserving individuals or not. This is not to say, of course, that laws officially prescribing a particular form of religious worship do not involve coercion of such individuals. When the power, prestige and financial support of government is placed behind a particular religious belief, the indirect coercive pressure upon religious minorities to conform to the prevailing officially approved religion is plain. But the purposes underlying the Establishment Clause go much further than that. Its first and most immediate purpose rested on the belief that a union of government and religion tends to destroy government and to degrade religion.

The history of governmentally established religion, both in England and in this country, showed that whenever government had allied itself with one particular form of religion, the inevitable result had been that it had incurred the hatred, disrespect and even contempt of those who held contrary beliefs. That same history showed that many people had lost their respect for any religion that had relied upon the support of government to spread its faith. The Establishment Clause thus stands as an expression of principle on the part of the Founders of our Constitution that religion is too personal, too sacred, too holy, to permit its "unhallowed perversion" by a civil magistrate. . . . The New York laws officially prescribing the Regents' prayer are inconsistent both with the purposes of the Establishment Clause and with the Establishment Clause itself.

It has been argued that to apply the Constitution in such a way as to prohibit state laws respecting an establishment of religious services in public schools is to indicate a hostility toward religion or toward prayer. Nothing, of course, could be more wrong. The history of man is inseparable from the history of religion. And perhaps it is not too much to say that since the beginning of that history many people have devoutly believed that "More things are wrought by prayer than this world dreams of." It was doubtless largely due to men who believed that there grew up a sentiment that caused men to leave the cross-currents of officially established state religions and religious persecution in Europe and come to this country filled with the hope that they could find a place in which they could pray when they pleased to the God of their faith in the language they chose. And there were men of this same faith in the power of prayer who led the fight for adoption of our Constitution and also for our Bill of Rights with the very guarantees of religious freedom that forbid the sort of governmental activity which New York has attempted here. These men knew that the First Amendment, which tried to put an end to governmental control of religion and of prayer, was not written to destroy either. They knew rather that it was written to quiet well-justified fears which nearly all of them felt arising out of an awareness that governments of the past had shackled men's tongues to make them speak only the religious thoughts that government wanted them to speak and to pray only to the God that government wanted them to pray to. It is neither sacrilegious nor antireligious to say that each separate government in this country should stay out of the business of writing or sanctioning official prayers and leave that purely religious function to the people themselves and to those the people choose to look to for religious guidance. . . .

The judgment of the Court of Appeals of New York is reversed and the cause remanded for further proceedings not inconsistent with this opinion.

MR. JUSTICE FRANKFURTER took no part in the decision of this case.

MR. JUSTICE WHITE took no part in the consideration or decision of this case.

MR. JUSTICE STEWART, dissenting.

A local school board in New York has provided that those pupils who wish to do so may join in a brief prayer at the beginning of each school day, acknowledging their dependence upon God and asking His blessing upon them and upon their parents, their teachers, and their country. The Court today decides that in permitting this brief nondenominational prayer the school board has violated the Constitution of the United States. I think this decision is wrong. . . .

The Court does not hold, nor could it, that New York has interfered with the free exercise of anybody's religion. For the state courts have made clear that those who object to reciting the prayer must be entirely free of any compulsion to do so, including any "embarrassments and pressures." But the Court says that in permitting school children to say this simple prayer, the New York authorities have established "an official religion."

With all respect, I think the Court has misapplied a great constitutional principle. I cannot see how an "official religion" is established by letting those who want to say a prayer say it. On the contrary, I think that to deny the wish of these school children to join in reciting this prayer is to deny them the opportunity of sharing in the spiritual heritage of our Nation.

The Court's historical review of the quarrels over the Book of Common Prayer in England throws no light for me on the issue before us in this case. England had then and has now an established church. Equally unenlightening, I think, is the history of the early establishment and later rejection of an official church in our own States. For we deal here not with the establishment of a state church, which would, of course, be constitutionally impermissible, but with whether school children who want to begin their day by joining in prayer must be prohibited from doing so. Moreover, I think that the Court's task, in this as in all areas of constitutional adjudication, is not responsibly aided by the uncritical invocation of metaphors like the "wall of separation," a phrase nowhere to be found in the Constitution. What is relevant to the issue here is not the history of an established church in sixteenth century England or in eighteenth century America, but the history of the religious traditions of our people, reflected in countless practices of the institutions and officials of our government.

At the opening of each day's Session of this Court we stand, while one of our officials invokes the protection of God. Since the days of John Marshall our Crier has said, "God save the United States and this Honorable Court." Both the Senate and the House of Representatives open their daily Sessions with prayer. Each of our Presidents, from George Washington to John F. Kennedy, has upon assuming his Office asked the protection and help of God.

The Court today says that the state and federal governments are without constitutional power to prescribe any particular form of words to be recited by any group of the American people on any subject touching religion. One of the stanzas of "The Star-Spangled Banner," made our National Anthem by Act of Congress in 1931, contains these verses:

> Blest with victory and peace, may the heav'n rescued land
> Praise the Pow'r that hath made and preserved us a nation!
> Then conquer we must, when our cause it is just,
> And this be our motto "In God is our Trust."

In 1954 Congress added a phrase to the Pledge of Allegiance to the Flag so that it now contains the words "one Nation under God, indivisible, with liberty and justice for all." In 1952 Congress enacted legislation calling upon the President each year to proclaim a National Day of Prayer. Since 1865 the words "IN GOD WE TRUST" have been impressed on our coins. Countless similar examples could be listed, but there is no need to belabor the obvious. It was all summed up by this Court just ten years ago in a single sentence: "We are a religious people whose institutions presuppose a Supreme Being." Zorach v. Clauson.

I do not believe that this Court, or the Congress, or the President has by the actions and practices I have mentioned established an "official religion" in violation of the Constitution. And I do not believe the State of New York has done so in this case. What each has done has been to recognize and to follow the deeply entrenched and highly cherished spiritual traditions of our Nation—traditions which come down to us from those who almost two hundred years ago avowed their "firm Reliance on the Protection of divine Providence" when they proclaimed the freedom and independence of this brave new world.

I dissent.

SCHOOL DISTRICT OF ABINGTON TOWNSHIP, PENNSYLVANIA V. SCHEMPP
374 U.S. 203 (1963)

"In the relationship between man and religion, the State is firmly committed to a position of neutrality. Though the application of that rule requires interpretation of a delicate sort, the rule itself is clearly and concisely stated in the words of the First Amendment."

The Question: Can a state require that public schools begin each day's session with readings from the Bible and recitation of the Lord's Prayer?

The Arguments: PRO

There has long been a tradition in American schools of beginning the day with prayer. The Bible includes many stories that have moral lessons and that help students to understand what is good behavior. Also, the majority of students in Pennsylvania schools are from Christian or Jewish families, and the Old and New Testaments are a common source of morality for the Judeo-Christian tradition. No students are required to participate in the Bible readings and prayer, and they can be excused if their parents object. The majority of the American people support school prayer, and the minority should not be able to block this traditional religious practice.

CON

The Bible is a religious book that promotes a particular set of beliefs, based on an omnipotent God. The New Testament teaches that Jesus Christ is God and places the blame for Christ's death on Jews. The Lord's Prayer comes straight from the New Testament. Students from other religious traditions, such as Islam or Buddhism, or who profess no religion can be subject to ostracism for not taking part in the Lord's Prayer. The fact that most students are Christian does not justify public schools' presenting a Christian message at the beginning of every school day.

MR. JUSTICE CLARK delivered the opinion of the Court.

The Commonwealth of Pennsylvania by law . . . requires that "At least ten verses from the Holy Bible shall be read, without comment, at the opening of each public school on each school day. Any child shall be excused from such Bible reading, or attending such Bible reading, upon the written request of his parent or guardian." The Schempp family, husband and wife and two of their three children, brought suit to enjoin enforcement of the statute, contending that their rights under the Fourteenth Amendment to the Constitution of the United States are, have been, and will continue to be violated unless this statute be declared unconstitutional as violative of these provisions of the First Amendment. They sought to enjoin the appellant school district, wherein the Schempp children attend school, and its officers and the Superintendent of Public Instruction of the Commonwealth from continuing to conduct such readings and recitation of the Lord's Prayer in the public schools of the district pursuant to the statute. A three-judge statutory District Court for the Eastern District of Pennsylvania held that the statute is violative of the Establishment Clause of the First Amendment as applied to the States by the Due Process Clause of the Fourteenth Amendment and directed that appropriate injunctive relief issue. On appeal by the District, its officials and the Superintendent . . . we noted probable jurisdiction.

The appellees Edward Lewis Schempp, his wife Sidney, and their children, Roger and Donna, are of the Unitarian faith and are members of the Unitarian church in Germantown, Philadelphia, Pennsylvania, where they, as well as another son, Ellory, regularly attend religious services. The latter was originally a party but having graduated from the school system pendente lite was voluntarily dismissed from the action. The other children attend the Abington Senior High School, which is a public school operated by appellant district.

On each school day at the Abington Senior High School between 8:15 and 8:30 a.m., while the pupils are attending their home rooms or advisory sections, opening exercises are conducted pursuant to the statute. The exercises are broadcast into each room in the school building through an intercommunications system and are conducted under the supervision of a teacher by students attending the school's radio and television workshop. Selected students from this course gather each morning in the school's workshop studio for the exercises, which include readings by one of the students of 10 verses of the Holy Bible, broadcast to each room in the building. This is followed by the recitation of the Lord's Prayer, likewise over the intercommunications system, but also by the students in the various classrooms, who are asked to stand and join in repeating the prayer in unison. The exercises are closed with the flag salute and such pertinent announcements as are of interest to the students. Participation in the opening exercises, as directed by the statute, is voluntary. The student reading the verses from the Bible may select the passages and read from any version he chooses, although the only copies furnished by the school are the King James version, copies of which were circulated to each teacher by the school district. During the period in which the exercises have been conducted the King James, the Douay and the Revised Standard versions of the Bible have been used, as well as the Jewish Holy Scriptures. There are no prefatory statements, no questions asked or solicited, no comments or explanations made and no interpretations given at or during the exercises. The students and parents are advised that the student may absent himself from the classroom or, should he elect to remain, not participate in the exercises. . . .

Edward Schempp and the children testified [before the district court] as to specific religious doctrines purveyed by a literal reading of the Bible "which were contrary to the religious beliefs which they held and to their familial teaching." The children testified that all of the doctrines to which they referred were read to them at various times as part of the exercises. Edward Schempp testified . . . that he had considered having Roger and Donna excused from attendance at the exercises but decided against it for several reasons, including his belief that the children's relationships with their teachers and classmates would be adversely affected. Expert testimony was introduced by both appellants and appellees, which testimony was summarized by the trial court as follows:

> Dr. Solomon Grayzel testified that there were marked differences between the Jewish Holy Scriptures and the Christian Holy Bible, the most obvious of which was the absence of the New Testament in the Jewish Holy Scriptures. Dr. Grayzel testified that portions of the New Testament were offensive to Jewish tradition and that, from the standpoint of Jewish faith, the concept of Jesus Christ as the Son of God was "practically blasphemous." He cited instances in the New Testament which, assertedly, were not only sectarian in nature but tended to bring the Jews into ridicule or scorn. Dr. Grayzel gave as his expert opinion that such material from the New Testament could be explained to Jewish children in such a way as to do no harm to them. But if portions of the New Testament were read without explanation, they could be, and in his specific experience with children Dr. Grayzel observed, had been, psychologically harmful to the child and had caused a divisive force within the social media of the school. . . .
>
> Dr. Luther A. Weigle, an expert witness for the defense, testified in some detail as to the reasons for and the methods employed in developing the King James and the Revise Standard Versions of the Bible. On direct examination, Dr. Weigle stated that the Bible was non-sectarian. He later stated that the phrase "non-sectarian" meant to him non-sectarian within the Christian faiths. Dr. Weigle stated that his definition of the Holy Bible would include the Jewish Holy Scriptures, but also stated that the "Holy Bible" would not be complete without the New Testament. He stated that the New Testament "conveyed the message of Christians." In his opinion, reading of the Holy Scriptures to the exclusion of the New Testament would be a sectarian practice. Dr. Weigle stated that the Bible was of great moral, historical and literary value. This is conceded by all the parties and is also the view of the court. . . .

It is true that religion has been closely identified with our history and government. . . . The fact that the Founding Fathers believed devotedly that there was a God and that the unalienable rights of man were rooted in Him is clearly evidenced in their writings, from the Mayflower Compact to the Constitution itself. This background is evidenced today in our public life through the continuance in our oaths of office from the Presidency to the Alderman of the final supplication, "So help me God." Likewise each House of the Congress provides through its Chaplain an opening prayer, and the sessions of this Court are declared open by the crier in a short ceremony, the final phrase of which invokes the grace of God. Again, there are such manifestations in our military forces, where those of our citizens who are under the restrictions of military service wish to engage in voluntary worship. Indeed, only last year an official survey of the country indicated that 64% of our people have church membership, while less than 3% profess no religion whatever. It can be truly said, therefore, that today, as in the beginning, our national life reflects a religious people who, in the words of Madison, are "earnestly praying, as . . . in duty bound, that the Supreme Lawgiver of the Universe . . . guide them into every measure which may be worthy of his [blessing]. . . ."

This is not to say, however, that religion has been so identified with our history and government that religious freedom is not likewise as strongly imbedded in our public and private life. Nothing but the most telling of personal experiences in religious persecution suffered by our forebears, could have planted our belief in liberty of religious opinion any more deeply in our heritage. It is true that this liberty frequently was not realized by the colonists, but this is readily accountable by their close ties to the Mother Country. However, the views of Madison and Jefferson, preceded by Roger Williams, came to be incorporated not only in the Federal Constitution but likewise in those of most of our States. This freedom to worship was indispensable in a country whose people came from the four quarters of the earth and brought with them a diversity of religious opinion. Today authorities list 83 separate religious bodies, each with membership exceeding 50,000, existing among our people, as well as innumerable smaller groups. . . .

The wholesome "neutrality" of which this Court's cases speak . . . stems from a recognition of the teachings of history that powerful sects or groups might bring about a fusion of governmental and religious functions or a concert or dependency of one upon the other to the end that official support of the State or Federal Government would be placed behind the tenets of one or of all orthodoxies. This the Establishment Clause prohibits. . . . Applying the Establishment Clause principles to the cases at bar we find that the States are requiring the selection and reading at the opening of the school day of verses from the Holy Bible and the recitation of the Lord's Prayer by the students in unison. These exercises are prescribed as part of the curricular activities of students who are required by law to attend school. They are held in the school buildings under the supervision and with the participation of teachers employed in those schools. . . . We agree with the trial court's finding as to the religious character of the exercises. Given that finding, the exercises and the law requiring them are in violation of the Establishment Clause. . . .

The conclusion follows that in both cases the laws require religious exercises and such exercises are being conducted in direct violation of the rights of the appellees and petitioners.

Nor are these required exercises mitigated by the fact that individual students may absent themselves upon parental request, for that fact furnishes no defense to a claim of unconstitutionality under the Establishment Clause. Further, it is no defense to urge that the religious practices here may be relatively minor encroachments on the First Amendment. The breach of neutrality that is today a trickling stream may all too soon become a raging torrent and, in the words of Madison, "it is proper to take alarm at the first experiment on our liberties."

It is insisted that unless these religious exercises are permitted a "religion of secularism" is established in the schools. We agree of course that the State may not establish a "religion of secularism" in the sense of affirmatively opposing or showing hostility to religion, thus "preferring those who believe in no religion over those who do believe." We do not agree, however, that this decision in any sense has that effect. In addition, it might well be said that one's education is not complete without a study of comparative religion or the history of religion and its relationship to the advancement of civilization. It certainly may be said that the Bible is worthy of study for its literary and historic qualities. Nothing we have said here indicates that such study of the Bible or of religion, when presented objectively as part of a secular program of education, may not be effected consistently with the First Amendment. But the exercises here do not fall into those categories. They are religious exercises, required by the States in violation of the command of the First Amendment that the Government maintain strict neutrality, neither aiding nor opposing religion. . . .

The place of religion in our society is an exalted one, achieved through a long tradition of reliance on the home, the church and the inviolable citadel of the individual heart and mind. We have come to recognize through bitter experience that it is not within the power of government to invade that citadel, whether its purpose or effect be to aid or oppose, to advance or retard. In the relationship between man and religion, the State is firmly committed to a position of neutrality. Though the application of that rule requires interpretation of a delicate sort, the rule itself is clearly and concisely stated in the words of the First Amendment. Applying that rule to the facts of these cases, we affirm the judgment [of the trial court].

MR. JUSTICE STEWART, dissenting.

The First Amendment declares that "Congress shall make no law respecting an establishment of religion, or prohibiting the free exercise thereof. . . ." It is, I think, a fallacious oversimplification to regard these two provisions as establishing a single constitutional standard of "separation of church and state," which can be mechanically applied in every case to delineate the required boundaries between government and religion. We err in the first place if we do not recognize, as a matter of history and as a matter of the imperatives of our free society, that religion and government must necessarily interact in countless ways. Secondly, the fact is that while in many contexts the Establishment Clause and the Free Exercise Clause fully complement each other, there are areas in which a doctrinaire reading of the Establishment Clause leads to irreconcilable conflict with the Free Exercise Clause.

A single obvious example should suffice to make the point. Spending federal funds to employ chaplains for the armed forces might be said to violate the Establishment Clause. Yet a lonely soldier stationed at some faraway outpost could surely complain that a government which did not provide him the opportunity for pastoral guidance was affirmatively prohibiting the free exercise of his religion. And such examples could readily be multiplied. The short of the matter is simply that the two relevant clauses of the First Amendment cannot accurately be reflected in a sterile metaphor which by its very nature may distort rather than illumine the problems involved in a particular case. . . .

That the central value embodied in the First Amendment—and, more particularly, in the guarantee of "liberty" contained in the Fourteenth—is the safeguarding of an individual's right to free exercise of his religion has been consistently recognized. . . . It is this concept of constitutional protection embodied in our decisions which makes the cases before us such difficult ones for me. For there is involved in these cases a substantial free exercise claim on the part of those who affirmatively desire to have their children's school day open with the reading of passages from the Bible. . . .

It might . . . be argued that parents who want their children exposed to religious influences can adequately fulfill that wish off school property and outside school time. With all its surface persuasiveness, however, this argument seriously misconceives the basic constitutional justification for permitting the exercises at issue in these cases. For a compulsory state educational system so structures a child's life that if religious exercises are held to be an impermissible activity in schools, religion is placed at an artificial and state-created disadvantage. Viewed in this light, permission of such exercises for those who want them is necessary if the schools are truly to be neutral in the matter of religion. And a refusal to permit religious exercises thus is seen, not as the realization of state neutrality, but rather as the establishment of a religion of secularism, or at the least, as government support of the beliefs of those who think that religious exercises should be conducted only in private.

What seems to me to be of paramount importance, then, is recognition of the fact that the claim advanced here in favor of Bible reading is sufficiently substantial to make simple reference to the constitutional phrase "establishment of religion" as inadequate an analysis of the cases before us as the ritualistic invocation of the nonconstitutional phrase "separation of church and state." What these cases compel, rather, is an analysis of just what the "neutrality" is which is required by the interplay of the Establishment and Free Exercise Clauses of the First Amendment. . . .

The dangers both to government and to religion inherent in official support of instruction in the tenets of various religious sects are absent in the present cases, which involve only a reading from the Bible unaccompanied by comments which might otherwise constitute instruction. Indeed, since, from all that appears in either record, any teacher who does not wish to do so is free not to participate, it cannot even be contended that some infinitesimal part of the salaries paid by the State are made contingent upon the performance of a religious function. . . .

In the absence of coercion upon those who do not wish to participate—because they hold less strong beliefs, other beliefs, or no beliefs at all—such provisions cannot, in my view, be held to represent the type of support of religion barred by the Establishment Clause. For the only support which such rules provide for religion is the withholding of state hostility—a simple acknowledgment on the part of secular authorities that the Constitution does not require extirpation of all expression of religious belief.

I have said that these provisions authorizing religious exercises are properly to be regarded as measures making possible the free exercise of religion. But it is important to stress that, strictly speaking, what is at issue here is a privilege rather than a right. In other words, the question presented is not whether exercises such as those at issue here are constitutionally compelled, but rather whether they are constitutionally invalid. And that issue, in my view, turns on the question of coercion.

It is clear that the dangers of coercion involved in the holding of religious exercises in a schoolroom differ qualitatively from those presented by the use of similar exercises or affirmations in ceremonies attended by adults. Even as to children, however, the duty laid upon government in connection with religious exercises in the public schools is that of refraining from so structuring the school environment as to put any kind of pressure on a child to participate in those exercises; it is not that of providing an atmosphere in which children are kept scrupulously insulated from any awareness that some of their fellows may want to open the school day with prayer, or of the fact that there exist in our pluralistic society differences of religious belief. . . .

The governmental neutrality which the First and Fourteenth Amendments require in the cases before us, in other words, is the extension of evenhanded treatment to all who believe, doubt, or disbelieve a refusal on the part of the State to weight the scales of private choice. In these cases, therefore, what is involved is not state action based on impermissible categories, but rather an attempt by the State to accommodate those differences which the existence in our society of a variety of religious beliefs makes inevitable. The Constitution requires that such efforts be struck down only if they are proven to entail the use of the secular authority of government to coerce a preference among such beliefs.

It may well be, as has been argued to us, that even the supposed benefits to be derived from noncoercive religious exercises in public schools are incommensurate with the administrative problems which they would create. The choice involved, however, is one for each local community and its school board, and not for this Court. For, as I have said, religious exercises are not constitutionally invalid if they simply reflect differences which exist in the society from which the school draws its pupils. They become constitutionally invalid only if their administration places the sanction of secular authority behind one or more particular religious or irreligious beliefs. . . .

What our Constitution indispensably protects is the freedom of each of us, be he Jew or Agnostic, Christian or Atheist, Buddhist or Freethinker, to believe or disbelieve, to worship or not worship, to pray or keep silent, according to his own conscience, uncoerced and unrestrained by government. It is conceivable that these school boards, or even all school boards, might eventually find it impossible to administer a system of religious exercises during school hours in

such a way as to meet this constitutional standard—in such a way as completely to free from any kind of official coercion those who do not affirmatively want to participate. But I think we must not assume that school boards so lack the qualities of inventiveness and good will as to make impossible the achievement of that goal.

MEET ELLERY SCHEMPP

Ellery is the eldest child of Sidney and Ed Schempp. He says that he was "raised in a family that believed in free inquiry"; his parents encouraged the challenging of ideas. They belonged to the local Unitarian Church. Because he was an excellent student at Abington Senior High School, as a junior in the 1957–1958 school year, he was enrolled in advanced classes in science, math, and history. Students in these classes were "encouraged to think and to write in an expository fashion." Even today he remembers the most influential teacher in his life at the school, Allan Gladhorn. Gladhorn invited his students to his home each Thursday evening for a discussion of ideas and current events. During that fall Ellery explored history and government, examining the Bill of Rights. As he compared the First Amendment with the prayer and Bible reading required each morning, he concluded "there was a genuine issue here." Some of his fellow students agreed and Ellery and two or three others decided to protest. "They all chickened out when they thought of the principal calling their parents. I determined that if I believed the prayer to be unconstitutional I had to do something." It was Thanksgiving and

> I was riding with my family in the car when I told them what I planned to do. . . . My parents had no strong reaction but they offered no opposition.
> The next week I decided I would not participate in the prayer. My friend George lent me a copy of the Koran and the next morning as the Bible was read and the Lord's Prayer was recited by all the students standing I sat, opened the Koran and read to myself. When they said the flag pledge I stood up and joined in.

The reaction was very quick. "My home room teacher asked what was going on. He said he noticed I had not participated in morning devotions and that in the future I was to stand up and pay attention. I said to him that in good conscience I don't believe I can do that any longer." Ellery was then sent to the vice-principal who was "flabbergasted by my behavior." He told Ellery he had a lot of friends in the Unitarian Church and none of them would ever do this. He said it was a matter of respect. "Eleven hundred others show respect," the vice-principal said. "I cited the First Amendment and was soon on my way to the guidance counselor." Ellery was to become well acquainted with Evelyn Brehm over the next few months. She asked a lot of questions in her role as school psychologist. After about an hour she apparently was satisfied that he was sane and "hinted that she was sympathetic with my actions."

Ellery went home and told his family about it. They supported him and told him he was right but they "left it up to me." His father was an ACLU member, so Ellery found the address and wrote for help. When he returned to school the next day, Ms. Brehm had arranged for Ellery to come in each morning and sign in as being in attendance and then go to her office during the devotions. "We had many conversations over that year and she soon ceased trying to talk me out of my stand."

> Sometime in January or February of 1958 the ACLU came to our home and interviewed me and my parents. Dad and mother said we wanted to pursue the case. From the beginning it was understood that the case would be filed in the name of Edward Schempp and his children. The ACLU attorney, Spencer Coxe, made it clear that we would be entering at least a five-year period of litigation. The fact that my sister Donna was five years younger than I meant we could maintain standing in court long enough to see the matter through.

When the news came out that the suit was filed Ellery saw little change in his daily routine at school. "One teacher attacked my position in the classroom, but those of us in advanced placement were somewhat isolated from the rest of the school. We had the best teachers and most were sympathetic."

In the fall of 1958 the school refused to allow Ellery to miss morning "devotions" any longer. The Pennsylvania law made no provision for such excuse. The family and the ACLU determined that rather than make a stand on "civil disobedience" Ellery should remain in the class with everyone and participate in the prayer and listen to the Bible reading. This would show the coercive nature of the law. So he went through the exercises.

Ellery graduated in the spring of 1959 and was no longer a plaintiff, although he did testify in the Pennsylvania State District Court on August 5, 1959.

Ellery was, by then, enrolled at Tufts University in Boston. CBS News decided to do a story on television and invited Ellery to be on the program. In preparation for that appearance Ellery spoke with the admissions officer at Tufts to discover whether his participation in the suit in any way affected the decision to admit him. The admissions officer smiled and commented, "You don't know, do you?" He related the following story: Principal Eugene Stuhl had taken the authority away from the school registrar to send any information concerning Ellery Schempp to any college. Stuhl assumed that responsibility and ordered all matters pertaining to Ellery be sent to his desk. Stuhl called the admissions office at Tufts, told them they had made a terrible mistake in accepting Ellery, who was perhaps a communist or worse, and that Tufts should rescind the admission. Obviously that did not occur and the admissions officer told Ellery, "We put it in context" and that he was certain the admissions office was right in their decision.

Ellery has a vivid memory of attending the oral arguments at the Supreme Court in February 1963. He sat in the front row and marvelled at the informality of the justices as they posed questions. He was also deeply impressed by the family's attorney, Henry W. Sawyer. When the Court handed down its opinion on June 17, 1963, Ellery had graduated from Tufts and was on his honeymoon. After a long and highly successful career as a scientist and scholar he is comfortable with everything that transpired and feels pleased to have been a part of a critically important moment in First Amendment jurisprudence. Today Ellery has his own consulting firm, Harvard Consulting Group, in Massachusetts.

After leaving high school he attended Tufts University where he graduated with Phi Beta Kappa honors and a degree in physics and geology. He earned his Ph.D. at Brown University (Alley, 1996).

THE "LEMON TEST"

Until 1971, the Supreme Court applied the test of governmental "neutrality" toward religion in cases brought under the Establishment Clause. As Justice Hugo Black wrote in the *Everson* case in 1947:

> The "establishment of religion" clause of the First Amendment means at least this: Neither a state nor the federal government can set up a church. Neither can pass laws which aid one religion, aid all religions, or prefer one religion over another. Neither can force nor influence a person to go to or to remain away from church against his will or force him to profess a belief or disbelief in any religion. No person can be punished for entertaining or professing religious beliefs or disbeliefs, for church attendance or nonattendance. No tax in any amount, large or small, can be levied to support any religious activities or institutions, whatever they may be called, or whatever they may adopt to teach or practice religion. Neither a state nor the Federal Government can, openly or secretly, participate in the affairs of any religious organizations or groups and vice versa. In the words of Jefferson, the clause against establishment of religion by law was intended to erect "a wall of separation between Church and State."

Justice Black's lengthy catalog of prohibited governmental activities seemingly made the "wall of separation" an absolute barrier. The Court remained committed to this principle in the years that followed the *Everson* decision, and later rulings reaffirmed that principle. Justice Tom Clark returned to this theme in the *Schempp* case, writing in 1963 that "the State is firmly committed to a position of 'neutrality' between state and religion." However, the Court faced dozens of Establishment Clause cases in succeeding years, and the justices felt the need to draw more precise lines of demarcation in this area. Writing in 1971, Chief Justice Warren Burger fashioned in the case of *Lemon v. Kurtzman* what came to be known as the "Lemon test," in a decision that struck down a Rhode Island law that provided salary supplements for teachers in Catholic parochial schools, in a state whose residents were largely Catholic. Burger put the refined test in these words:

> Every analysis in this area must begin with consideration of the cumulative criteria developed by the Court over many years. Three such tests may be gleaned from our cases. First, the statute must have a secular legislative purpose; second, its principal or primary effect must be one that neither advances nor inhibits religion; finally, the statute must not foster an excessive government entanglement with religion.

In practice, application of the "Lemon test" mandated that if a challenged law violated any one of the three "prongs" of the test, the law violated the Establishment Clause. In the years that followed the *Lemon* decision, the Court applied the "Lemon test" in more than thirty cases, striking down the challenged statute or practice in all but a few. Most often, the Court based its ruling on the second prong of the test, finding that challenged laws had the "primary effect" of advancing religious doctrine or practice. In effect, the "Lemon test" gave judges a tool with which to measure the extent to which the "wall of separation" had been breached in any particular case.

As the Court became more conservative during the years, it was led by Chief Justice Burger. Under his successor, Chief Justice William Rehnquist, the "Lemon test" came under judicial fire and prompted calls for lowering the wall of separation between state and religion. Burger himself lamented in 1985, in the school prayer case of *Wallace v. Jaffree*, that the Court's repeated application of the "Lemon test" to strike down challenged laws "suggests a naive preoccupation with an easy, bright-line approach for addressing constitutional issues." The harshest criticism came from Justice Rehnquist, whose dissent in this case argued for scrapping the test altogether and replacing it with an "accommodationist" position

that better reflected, in Rehnquist's view, the position of the men who had framed the First Amendment. Rehnquist asserted that the Establishment Clause simply "forbade the establishment of a national religion and forbade preference among religious sects or denominations. . . . [I]t did not prohibit the . . . government from providing nondiscriminatory aid to religion." Under this view of "original intent," governments would be free to provide aid to religion, in the form of tax payments for schools and other programs, or through religious activities such as school prayer, so long as that aid did not prefer one denomination over others. During his tenure as Chief Justice, Rehnquist continued to press for judicial repudiation of the "Lemon test," but his position has not yet persuaded a majority of the justices to join him.

LEE V. WEISMAN
505 U.S. 577 (1992)

"In the hands of government, what might begin as a tolerant expression of religious views may end in a policy to indoctrinate and coerce. A state-created orthodoxy puts at grave risk that freedom of belief and conscience which is the sole assurance that religious faith is real, not imposed."

The Question: Can a public school invite a Christian minister or Jewish rabbi to deliver an invocation and benediction at a school graduation ceremony?

The Arguments: PRO

A graduation ceremony is a solemn occasion for students and their families, and an invocation and benediction lends a proper tone to the event. Public school graduations are not the same as classrooms, where students have no choice about whether to attend. Anyone who objects to the prayers at a graduation ceremony can remain silent and does not have to stand or otherwise signify their agreement with the religious message. Graduation prayers have been traditional in most communities for generations, and turning the graduation ceremonies into purely secular events would remove much of the solemnity of the occasion.

CON

The Supreme Court has ruled that classroom prayers violate the Constitution, and that public schools cannot promote religion in any of their activities. Graduation ceremonies are important to students and their families, and forcing a student to listen to a prayer can take away the enjoyment of this important event. School officials choose the religious leader, whether minister or rabbi, who deliver the prayers, and they exercise control over the content of the message by setting guidelines for the prayers. Graduation ceremonies are official school events, and there is no real difference between prayers in classrooms or graduations.

JUSTICE KENNEDY delivered the opinion of the Court.

School principals in the public school system of the city of Providence, Rhode Island, are permitted to invite members of the clergy to offer invocation and benediction prayers as part of the formal graduation ceremonies for middle schools and for high schools. The question before us is whether including clerical members who offer prayers as part of the

official school graduation ceremony is consistent with the Religion Clauses of the First Amendment, provisions the Fourteenth Amendment makes applicable with full force to the States and their school districts.

Deborah Weisman graduated from Nathan Bishop Middle School, a public school in Providence, at a formal ceremony in June, 1989. She was about 14 years old. For many years, it has been the policy of the Providence School

Committee and the Superintendent of Schools to permit principals to invite members of the clergy to give invocations and benedictions at middle school and high school graduations. Many, but not all, of the principals elected to include prayers as part of the graduation ceremonies. Acting for himself and his daughter, Deborah's father, Daniel Weisman, objected to any prayers at Deborah's middle school graduation, but to no avail. The school principal, petitioner Robert E. Lee, invited a rabbi to deliver prayers at the graduation exercises for Deborah's class. Rabbi Leslie Gutterman, of the Temple Beth El in Providence, accepted.

It has been the custom of Providence school officials to provide invited clergy with a pamphlet entitled "Guidelines for Civic Occasions," prepared by the National Conference of Christians and Jews. The Guidelines recommend that public prayers at nonsectarian civic ceremonies be composed with "inclusiveness and sensitivity," though they acknowledge that "[p]rayer of any kind may be inappropriate on some civic occasions." The principal gave Rabbi Gutterman the pamphlet before the graduation, and advised him the invocation and benediction should be nonsectarian. Rabbi Gutterman's prayers were as follows:

Invocation

God of the Free, Hope of the Brave: For the legacy of America where diversity is celebrated and the rights of minorities are protected, we thank You. May these young men and women grow up to enrich it. For the liberty of America, we thank You. May these new graduates grow up to guard it. For the political process of America in which all its citizens may participate, for its court system where all may seek justice, we thank You. May those we honor this morning always turn to it in trust. For the destiny of America, we thank You. May the graduates of Nathan Bishop Middle School so live that they might help to share it. May our aspirations for our country and for these young people, who are our hope for the future, be richly fulfilled. Amen.

Benediction

O God, we are grateful to You for having endowed us with the capacity for learning which we have celebrated on this joyous commencement. Happy families give thanks for seeing their children achieve an important milestone. Send Your blessings upon the teachers and administrators who helped prepare them.

The graduates now need strength and guidance for the future; help them to understand that we are not complete with academic knowledge alone. We must each strive to fulfill what You require of us all: to do justly, to love mercy, to walk humbly. We give thanks to You, Lord, for keeping us alive, sustaining us, and allowing us to reach this special, happy occasion. Amen.

The school board (and the United States, which supports it as amicus curi[a]e) argued that these short prayers and others like them at graduation exercises are of profound meaning to many students and parents throughout this country who consider that due respect and acknowledgment for divine guidance and for the deepest spiritual aspirations of our people ought to be expressed at an event as important in life as a graduation. We assume this to be so in addressing the difficult case now before us, for the significance of the prayers lies also at the heart of Daniel and Deborah Weisman's case. . . .

These dominant facts mark and control the confines of our decision: State officials direct the performance of a formal religious exercise at promotional and graduation ceremonies for secondary schools. Even for those students who object to the religious exercise, their attendance and participation in the state-sponsored religious activity are, in a fair and real sense, obligatory, though the school district does not require attendance as a condition for receipt of the diploma. . . .

The principle that government may accommodate the free exercise of religion does not supersede the fundamental limitations imposed by the Establishment Clause. It is beyond dispute that, at a minimum, the Constitution guarantees that government may not coerce anyone to support or participate in religion or its exercise, or otherwise act in a way which "establishes a [state] religion or religious faith, or tends to do so." The State's involvement in the school prayers challenged today violates these central principles.

That involvement is as troubling as it is undenied. A school official, the principal, decided that an invocation and a benediction should be given; this is a choice attributable to the State, and, from a constitutional perspective, it is as if a state statute decreed that the prayers must occur. The principal chose the religious participant, here a rabbi, and that choice is also attributable to the State. The reason for the choice of a rabbi is not disclosed by the record, but the potential for divisiveness over the choice of a particular member of the clergy to conduct the ceremony is apparent.

Divisiveness, of course, can attend any state decision respecting religions, and neither its existence nor its potential necessarily invalidates the State's attempts to accommodate religion in all cases. The potential for divisiveness is of particular relevance here, though, because it centers around an overt religious exercise in a secondary school environment where subtle coercive pressures exist, and where the student had no real alternative which would have allowed her to avoid the fact or appearance of participation.

The State's role did not end with the decision to include a prayer and with the choice of clergyman. Principal Lee provided Rabbi Gutterman with a copy of the "Guidelines for Civic Occasions" and advised him that his prayers should be nonsectarian. Through these means, the principal directed and controlled the content of the prayers. Even if the only sanction for ignoring the instructions were that the rabbi would not be invited back, we think no religious representative who valued his or her continued reputation and effectiveness in the community would incur the State's displeasure in this regard. It is a cornerstone principle of our Establishment Clause jurisprudence that "it is no part of the business of government to compose official prayers for any group of the American people to recite as a part of a religious program carried on by government," and that is what the school officials attempted to do.

Petitioners argue, and we find nothing in the case to refute it, that the directions for the content of the prayers were a good-faith attempt by the school to ensure that the sectarianism which is so often the flashpoint for religious animosity be removed from the graduation ceremony. The concern is understandable, as a prayer which uses ideas or images identified with a particular religion may foster a different sort of sectarian rivalry than an invocation or benediction in terms more neutral. The school's explanation, however, does not resolve the dilemma caused by its participation. The question is not the good faith of the school in attempting to make the prayer acceptable to most persons, but the legitimacy of its undertaking that enterprise at all when the object is to produce a prayer to be used in a formal religious exercise which students, for all practical purposes are obliged to attend. . . .

The degree of school involvement here made it clear that the graduation prayers bore the imprint of the State, and thus put school-age children who objected in an untenable position. We turn our attention now to consider the position of the students, both those who desired the prayer and she who did not.

To endure the speech of false ideas or offensive content and then to counter it is part of learning how to live in a pluralistic society, a society which insists upon open discourse towards the end of a tolerant citizenry. And tolerance presupposes some mutuality of obligation. It is argued that our constitutional vision of a free society requires confidence in our own ability to accept or reject ideas of which we do not approve, and that prayer at a high school graduation does nothing more than offer a choice. By the time they are seniors, high school students no doubt have been required to attend classes and assemblies and to complete assignments exposing them to ideas they find distasteful or immoral or absurd, or all of these. Against this background, students may consider it an odd measure of justice to be subjected during the course of their educations to ideas deemed offensive and irreligious, but to be denied a brief, formal prayer ceremony that the school offers in return. This argument cannot prevail, however. It overlooks a fundamental dynamic of the Constitution.

The First Amendment protects speech and religion by quite different mechanisms. Speech is protected by ensuring its full expression even when the government participates, for the very object of some of our most important speech is to persuade the government to adopt an idea as its own. The method for protecting freedom of worship and freedom of conscience in religious matters is quite the reverse. In religious debate or expression, the government is not a prime participant, for the Framers deemed religious establishment antithetical to the freedom of all. The Free Exercise Clause embraces a freedom of conscience and worship that has close parallels in the speech provisions of the First Amendment, but the Establishment Clause is a specific prohibition on forms of state intervention in religious affairs, with no precise counterpart in the speech provisions. The explanation lies in the lesson of history that was and is the inspiration for the Establishment Clause, the lesson that, in the hands of government, what might begin as a tolerant expression of religious views may end in a policy to indoctrinate and coerce. A state-created orthodoxy puts at grave risk that freedom of belief and conscience which are the sole assurance that religious faith is real, not imposed. . . .

As we have observed before, there are heightened concerns with protecting freedom of conscience from subtle coercive pressure in the elementary and secondary public schools. Our decisions in Engel v. Vitale and School Dist. of Abington recognize, among other things, that prayer exercises in public schools carry a particular risk of indirect coercion. The concern may not be limited to the context of schools, but it is most pronounced there. What to most believers may seem nothing more than a reasonable request that the nonbeliever respect their religious practices, in a school context may appear to the nonbeliever or dissenter to be an attempt to employ the machinery of the State to enforce a religious orthodoxy.

We need not look beyond the circumstances of this case to see the phenomenon at work. The undeniable fact is that the school district's supervision and control of a high school graduation ceremony places public pressure, as well as peer pressure, on attending students to stand as a group or, at least, maintain respectful silence during the invocation and benediction. This pressure, though subtle and indirect, can be as real as any overt compulsion. Of course, in our culture, standing or remaining silent can signify adherence to a view or simple respect for the views of others. And no doubt some persons who have no desire to join a prayer have little objection to standing as a sign of respect for those who do. But for the dissenter of high school age, who has a reasonable perception that she is being forced by the State to pray in a manner her conscience will not allow, the injury is no less real. There can be no doubt that for many, if not most, of the students at the graduation, the act of standing or remaining silent was an expression of participation in the rabbi's prayer. That was the very point of the religious exercise. It is of little comfort to a dissenter, then, to be told that, for her, the act of standing or remaining in silence signifies mere respect, rather than participation. What matters is that, given our social conventions, a reasonable dissenter in this milieu could believe that the group exercise signified her own participation or approval of it.

Finding no violation under these circumstances would place objectors in the dilemma of participating, with all that implies, or protesting. We do not address whether that choice is acceptable if the affected citizens are mature adults, but we think the State may not, consistent with the Establishment Clause, place primary and secondary school children in this position. Research in psychology supports the common assumption that adolescents are often susceptible to pressure from their peers towards conformity, and that the influence is strongest in matters of social convention. To recognize that the choice imposed by the State constitutes an unacceptable constraint only acknowledges that the government may no more use social pressure to enforce orthodoxy than it may use more direct means.

The injury caused by the government's action, and the reason why Daniel and Deborah Weisman object to it, is that the State, in a school setting, in effect required participation in a religious exercise. It is, we concede, a brief exercise during which the individual can concentrate on joining its message, meditate on her own religion, or let her mind wander. But the embarrassment and the intrusion of the religious exercise cannot be refuted by arguing that these prayers, and similar ones to be said in the future, are of a de minimis character. To do so would be an affront to the rabbi who offered them and to all those for whom the prayers were an essential and profound recognition of divine authority. And for the same reason, we think that the intrusion is greater than the two minutes or so of time consumed for prayers like these. Assuming, as we must, that the prayers were offensive to the student and the parent who now object, the intrusion was both real and, in the context of a secondary school, a violation of the objector rights. That the intrusion was in the course of promulgating religion that sought to be civic or nonsectarian, rather than pertaining to one sect, does not lessen the offense or isolation to the objectors. At best it narrows their number, at worst, increases their sense of isolation and affront.

There was a stipulation in the District Court that attendance at graduation and promotional ceremonies is voluntary. . . . The argument lacks all persuasion. Law reaches past formalism. And to say a teenage student has a real choice not to attend her high school graduation is formalistic in the extreme. True, Deborah could elect not to attend commencement without renouncing her diploma; but we shall not allow the case to turn on this point. Everyone knows that, in our society and in our culture, high school graduation is one of life's most significant occasions. A school rule which excuses attendance is beside the point. Attendance may not be required by official decree, yet it is apparent that a student is not free to absent herself from the graduation exercise in any real sense of the term "voluntary," for absence would require forfeiture of those intangible benefits which have motivated the student through youth and all her high school years. Graduation is a time for family and those closest to the student to celebrate success and express mutual wishes of gratitude and respect, all to the end of impressing upon the young person the role that it is his or her right and duty to assume in the community and all of its diverse parts.

The importance of the event is the point the school district and the United States rely upon to argue that a formal prayer ought to be permitted, but it becomes one of the principal reasons why their argument must fail. Their contention, one of considerable force were it not for the constitutional constraints applied to state action, is that the prayers are an essential part of these ceremonies because, for many persons, an occasion of this significance lacks meaning if there is no recognition, however brief, that human achievements cannot be understood apart from their spiritual essence. We think the Government's position that this interest suffices to force students to choose between compliance or forfeiture demonstrates fundamental inconsistency in its argumentation. It fails to acknowledge that what for many of Deborah's classmates and their parents was a spiritual imperative was, for Daniel and Deborah Weisman, religious conformance compelled by the State. While in some societies the wishes of the majority might prevail, the Establishment Clause of the First Amendment is addressed to this contingency, and rejects the balance urged upon us. The Constitution forbids the State to exact religious conformity from a student as the price of attending her own high school graduation. This is the calculus the Constitution commands.

The Government's argument gives insufficient recognition to the real conflict of conscience faced by the young student. The essence of the Government's position is that, with regard to a civic, social occasion of this importance, it is the objector, not the majority, who must take unilateral and private action to avoid compromising religious scruples, hereby electing to miss the graduation exercise. This turns conventional First Amendment analysis on its head. It is a tenet of the First Amendment that the State cannot require one of its citizens to forfeit his or her rights and benefits as the price of resisting conformance to state-sponsored religious practice. To say that a student must remain apart from the ceremony at the opening invocation and closing benediction is to risk compelling conformity in an environment analogous to the classroom setting, where we have said the risk of compulsion is especially high. . . .

Our society would be less than true to its heritage if it lacked abiding concern for the values of its young people, and we acknowledge the profound belief of adherents to many faiths that there must be a place in the student's life for precepts of a morality higher even than the law we today enforce. We express no hostility to those aspirations, nor would our oath permit us to do so. A relentless and all-pervasive attempt to exclude religion from every aspect of public life could itself become inconsistent with the Constitution. We recognize that, at graduation time and throughout the course of the educational process, there will be instances when religious values, religious practices, and religious persons will have some interaction with the public schools and their students. But these matters, often questions of accommodation of religion, are not before us. The sole question presented is whether a religious exercise may be conducted at a graduation ceremony in circumstances where, as we have found, young graduates who object are induced to conform. No holding by this Court suggests that a school can persuade or compel a student to participate in a religious exercise. That is being done here, and it is forbidden by the Establishment Clause of the First Amendment.

For the reasons we have stated, the judgment of the Court of Appeals is Affirmed.

JUSTICE SCALIA, with whom the Chief Justice, JUSTICE WHITE, and JUSTICE THOMAS join, dissenting.

Three Terms ago, I joined an opinion recognizing that the Establishment Clause must be construed in light of the "[g]overnment policies of accommodation, acknowledgment, and support for religion [that] are an accepted part of our political and cultural heritage." That opinion affirmed that "the meaning of the Clause is to be determined by reference to historical practices and understandings." It said that "[a] test for implementing the protections of the Establishment Clause that, if applied with consistency, would invalidate longstanding traditions cannot be a proper reading of the Clause." County of Allegheny v. American Civil Liberties Union, Greater Pittsburgh Chapter.

These views, of course, prevent me from joining today's opinion, which is conspicuously bereft of any reference to history. In holding that the Establishment Clause prohibits invocations and benedictions at public school graduation ceremonies, the Court—with nary a mention that it is doing so—lays waste a tradition that is as old as public school graduation ceremonies themselves, and that is a component of an even more longstanding American tradition of nonsectarian prayer to God at public celebrations generally. As its instrument of destruction, the bulldozer of its social engineering, the Court invents a boundless, and boundlessly manipulable, test of psychological coercion. . . . Today's opinion shows more forcefully than volumes of argumentation why our Nation's protection, that fortress which is our Constitution, cannot possibly rest upon the changeable philosophical predilections of the Justices of this Court, but must have deep foundations in the historic practices of our people. . . .

The history and tradition of our Nation are replete with public ceremonies featuring prayers of thanksgiving and petition. . . . From our Nation's origin, prayer has been a prominent part of governmental ceremonies and proclamations. The Declaration of Independence, the document marking our birth as a separate people, "appeal[ed] to the Supreme Judge of the world for the rectitude of our intentions" and avowed "a firm reliance on the protection of divine Providence." In his first inaugural address, after swearing his oath of office on a Bible, George Washington deliberately made a prayer a part of his first official act as President. . . .

In addition to this general tradition of prayer at public ceremonies, there exists a more specific tradition of invocations and benedictions at public school graduation exercises. . . . As the Court obliquely acknowledges in describing the "customary features" of high school graduations, the invocation and benediction have long been recognized to be "as traditional as any other parts of the [school] graduation program and are widely established."

The Court presumably would separate graduation invocations and benedictions from other instances of public "preservation and transmission of religious beliefs" on the ground that they involve "psychological coercion.". . . A few citations of "[r]esearch in psychology" that have no particular bearing upon the precise issue here cannot disguise the fact that the Court has gone beyond the realm where judges know what they are doing. The Court's argument that state officials have "coerced" students to take part in the invocation and benediction at graduation ceremonies is, not to put too fine a point on it, incoherent. . . .

The opinion manifests that the Court itself has not given careful consideration to its test of psychological coercion. For if it had, how could it observe, with no hint of concern or disapproval, that students stood for the Pledge of Allegiance, which immediately preceded Rabbi Gutterman's invocation? . . . If students were psychologically coerced to remain standing during the invocation, they must also have been psychologically coerced, moments before, to stand for (and thereby, in the Court's view, take part in or appear to take part in) the Pledge. Must the Pledge therefore be barred from the public schools (both from graduation ceremonies and from the classroom)? . . . Logically, that ought to be the next project for the Court's bulldozer.

The reader has been told much in this case about the personal interest of Mr. Weisman and his daughter, and very little about the personal interests on the other side. They are not inconsequential. Church and state would not be such a difficult subject if religion were, as the Court apparently thinks it to be, some purely personal avocation that can be indulged entirely in secret, like pornography, in the privacy of one's room. For most believers, it is not that, and has never been. Religious men and women of almost all denominations have felt it necessary to acknowledge and beseech the blessing of God as a people, and not just as individuals, because they believe in the "protection of divine Providence," as the Declaration of Independence put it, not just for individuals but for societies; because they believe God to be, as Washington's first Thanksgiving Proclamation put it,

the "Great Lord and Ruler of Nations." One can believe in the effectiveness of such public worship, or one can deprecate and deride it. But the longstanding American tradition of prayer at official ceremonies displays with unmistakable clarity that the Establishment Clause does not forbid the government to accommodate it.

The narrow context of the present case involves a community's celebration of one of the milestones in its young citizens' lives, and it is a bold step for this Court to seek to banish from that occasion, and from thousands of similar celebrations throughout this land, the expression of gratitude to God that a majority of the community wishes to make. The issue before us today is not the abstract philosophical question whether the alternative of frustrating this desire of a religious majority is to be preferred over the alternative of imposing "psychological coercion," or a feeling of exclusion, upon nonbelievers. Rather, the question is whether a mandatory choice in favor of the former has been imposed by the United States Constitution. As the age-old practices of our people show, the answer to that question is not at all in doubt.

I must add one final observation: the Founders of our Republic knew the fearsome potential of sectarian religious belief to generate civil dissension and civil strife. And they also knew that nothing, absolutely nothing, is so inclined to foster among religious believers of various faiths a toleration—no, an affection—for one another than voluntarily joining in prayer together, to the God whom they all worship and seek. Needless to say, no one should be compelled to do that, but it is a shame to deprive our public culture of the opportunity, and indeed the encouragement, for people to do it voluntarily. The Baptist or Catholic who heard and joined in the simple and inspiring prayers of Rabbi Gutterman on this official and patriotic occasion was inoculated from religious bigotry and prejudice in a manner that cannot be replicated. To deprive our society of that important unifying mechanism in order to spare the nonbeliever what seems to me the minimal inconvenience of standing, or even sitting in respectful nonparticipation, is as senseless in policy as it is unsupported in law.

For the foregoing reasons, I dissent.

MEET DEBORAH WEISMAN

Hi, I'm Deborah Weisman. My involvement with the issue of church/state separation began in 1986 when my older sister, Merith, was graduating from junior high in Providence, Rhode Island. I'll never forget how uncomfortable I felt when a Baptist minister led us in a prayer at the ceremony. I had always felt that religion is important and has its place, but I didn't think a public school was that place. My parents sent the school a letter that was never answered.

Three years later, just before my own eighth grade graduation, my parents called the school to bring up the prayer issue again. A teacher told them, "We got you a rabbi." They thought we objected to the minister just because we're Jewish! But a rabbi wouldn't have made it any better: Prayer in public school was what we objected to. The school board told us that graduation prayer was a tradition. If we had a problem with the practice, they said, we could sue. And that's just what we did. The ACLU of Rhode Island assigned us a lawyer, who asked the federal court to order the school board to stop having graduation prayers. The court ruled in our favor, the school board appealed, we won again, and the school board appealed again—this time to the U.S. Supreme Court. The Supreme Court hears less than 5 percent of the cases brought before it, so we were surprised when the Justices agreed to hear our case.

Almost three years after my eighth grade graduation and nine days after my high school commencement (where there was no prayer), we won: When a public school sponsors a prayer of any faith, the Supreme Court said, it violates the First Amendment.

Throughout the years of waiting for a ruling, we were harassed by hate mail and even death threats, and the media attention often bothered me. But I was encouraged by the support we received from friends, and at no time did I regret having taken our case to court. What amazes me is that it only took me and my family to make a difference (ACLU Online Archives).

SANTA FE INDEPENDENT SCHOOL DISTRICT V. DOE
530 U.S. 290 (2000)

"School sponsorship of a religious message is impermissible because it sends the ancillary message to members of the audience who are non-adherents 'that they are outsiders, not full members of the political community, and an accompanying message to adherents that they are insiders, favored members of the political community.'"

The Question: Can a school district allow students to elect a fellow student to deliver an "invocation" at high school football games that may include a prayer or other religious message?

The Arguments: PRO

High school football games are competitive events, but they should also foster good sportsmanship and community spirit. One way to set the proper tone before a game is to offer prayers for the athletes on both sides and their friends and families in the audience. Offering students a chance to elect a fellow student to deliver an invocation before games does not promote religion, and the message does not have to be religious in nature. In addition, attendance at football games is purely voluntary, and those who object to a prayer can leave the stands until the invocation is over or arrive at the game after the message. School officials should not be able to tell the student who delivers the invocation what to say in the message.

CON

In many American communities, high school football is almost a religion, and attendance at games is expected of students as well as the athletes' families. There is nothing about a football game that requires a religious message. By setting up the election process for the student who delivers the invocation at football games, and by instructing the student to avoid certain topics in the message, the school retains control over the event. There is very little doubt that students who deliver invocations will present a prayer, and it is virtually certain that the prayer will be sectarian in nature. Although attendance at games is voluntary for most spectators, the athletes, members of high school bands, and team staff members are required to attend in order to receive academic credit.

JUSTICE STEVENS delivered the opinion of the Court.

The Santa Fe Independent School District (District) is a political subdivision of the State of Texas, responsible for the education of more than 4,000 students in a small community in the southern part of the State. The District includes the Santa Fe High School, two primary schools, an intermediate school and the junior high school. Respondents are two sets of current or former students and their respective mothers. One family is Mormon and the other is Catholic. The District

Court permitted respondents (Does) to litigate anonymously to protect them from intimidation or harassment.

Respondents commenced this action in April 1995 and moved for a temporary restraining order to prevent the District from violating the Establishment Clause [by allowing students] to deliver overtly Christian prayers over the public address system at home football games. . . . On May 10, 1995, the District Court entered an interim order. . . . In response to that order, the District adopted a series of policies over several months dealing with prayer at school functions. . . . The policy which was titled "Prayer at Football Games". . . authorized two student elections, the first to determine whether "invocations" should be delivered, and the second to select the spokesperson to deliver them. . . . On August 31, 1995, "the district's high school students voted to determine whether a student would deliver prayer at varsity football games. . . . The students chose to allow a student to say a prayer at football games. "A week later, in a separate election, they selected a student" to deliver the prayer at varsity football games.". . . The District Court [ruled] that delivering a prayer "over the school's public address system prior to each football and baseball game coerces student participation in religious events.". . . [The Fifth Circuit Court of Appeals upheld the District Court ruling]. We granted the District's petition for certiorari, limited to the following question: "Whether petitioner's policy permitting student-led, student-initiated prayer at football games violates the Establishment Clause." We conclude, as did the Court of Appeals, that it does.

The first Clause in the First Amendment to the Federal Constitution provides that "Congress shall make no law respecting an establishment of religion, or prohibiting the free exercise thereof." In Lee v. Weisman (1992), we held that a prayer delivered by a rabbi at a middle school graduation ceremony violated that Clause. Although this case involves student prayer at a different type of school function, our analysis is properly guided by the principles that we endorsed in Lee. As we held in that case: "The principle that government may accommodate the free exercise of religion does not supersede the fundamental limitations imposed by the Establishment Clause. It is beyond dispute that, at a minimum, the Constitution guarantees that government may not coerce anyone to support or participate in religion or its exercise, or otherwise act in a way which 'establishes a [state] religion or religious faith, or tends to do so.'"

In this case the District first argues that this principle is inapplicable to its policy because the messages are private student speech, not public speech. It reminds us that "there is a crucial difference between government speech endorsing religion, which the Establishment Clause forbids, and private speech endorsing religion, which the Free Speech and Free Exercise Clauses protect." We certainly agree with that distinction, but we are not persuaded that the pre-game invocations should be regarded as "private speech." These invocations are authorized by a government policy and take place on government property at government-sponsored school-related events. . . . The statement or invocation, moreover, is subject to particular regulations that confine the content and topic of the student's message. . . . Santa Fe's student election system ensures that only those messages deemed "appropriate" under the District's policy may be delivered. That is, the majoritarian process implemented by the District guarantees, by definition, that minority candidates will never prevail and that their views will be effectively silenced. . . . [T]his student election does nothing to protect minority views but rather places the students who hold such views at the mercy of the majority. Because "fundamental rights may not be submitted to vote; they depend on the outcome of no elections," West Virginia Bd. of Ed. v. Barnette (1943), the District's elections are insufficient safeguards of diverse student speech. . . . Moreover, the District has failed to divorce itself from the religious content in the invocations.

It has not succeeded in doing so, either by claiming that its policy is one of neutrality rather than endorsement or by characterizing the individual student as the "circuit-breaker" in the process. Contrary to the District's repeated assertions that it has adopted a "hands-off" approach to the pre-game invocation, the realities of the situation plainly reveal that its policy involves both perceived and actual endorsement of religion. In this case, as we found in Lee, the "degree of school involvement" makes it clear that the pre-game prayers bear "the imprint of the State and thus put school-age children who objected in an untenable position."

The District has attempted to disentangle itself from the religious messages by developing the two-step student election process. The text of the policy, however, exposes the extent of the school's entanglement. The elections take place at all only because the school "board has chosen to permit students to deliver a brief invocation and/or message." The elections thus "shall" be conducted "by the high school student council" and "[u]pon advice and direction of the high school principal." The decision whether to deliver a message is first made by majority vote of the entire student body, followed by a choice of the speaker in a separate, similar majority election. Even though the particular words used by the speaker are not determined by those votes, the policy . . . invites and encourages religious messages. . . . In fact, as used in the past at Santa Fe High School, an "invocation" has always entailed a focused religious message. Thus, the expressed purposes of the policy encourage the selection of a religious message, and that is precisely how the students understand the policy. The results of the elections make it clear that the students understood that the central question before them was whether prayer should be a part of the pre-game ceremony. We recognize the important role that public worship plays in many communities, as well as the sincere desire to include public prayer as a part of various occasions so as to mark those occasions' significance. But such religious activity in public schools, as elsewhere, must comport with the First Amendment.

The actual or perceived endorsement of the message, moreover, is established by factors beyond just the text of the policy. Once the student speaker is selected and the message composed, the invocation is then delivered to a large audience assembled as part of a regularly scheduled, school-sponsored function conducted on school property. The message is broadcast over the school's public address system, which remains subject to the control of school officials. It is fair to assume that the pre-game ceremony is clothed in the traditional indicia of school sporting events, which generally include not just the team, but also cheerleaders and band members dressed in uniforms sporting the school name and mascot. The school's name is likely written in large print across the field and on banners and flags. The crowd will certainly include many who display the school colors and insignia on their school T-shirts, jackets, or hats and who may also be waving signs displaying the school name. It is in a setting such as this that "[t]he board has chosen to permit" the elected student to rise and give the "statement or invocation."

In this context the members of the listening audience must perceive the pre-game message as a public expression of the views of the majority of the student body delivered with the approval of the school administration. In cases involving state participation in a religious activity, one of the relevant questions is "whether an objective observer, acquainted with the text, legislative history, and implementation of the statute, would perceive it as a state endorsement of prayer in public schools." Regardless of the listener's support for, or objection to, the message, an objective Santa Fe High School student will unquestionably perceive the inevitable pre-game prayer as stamped with her school's seal of approval. . . .

School sponsorship of a religious message is impermissible because it sends the ancillary message to members of the audience who are non-adher[e]nts "that they are outsiders, not full members of the political community, and an accompanying message to adher[e]nts that they are insiders, favored members of the political community." Lynch v. Donnelly (1984). The delivery of such a message—over the school's public address system, by a speaker representing the student body, under the supervision of school faculty, and pursuant to a school policy that explicitly and implicitly encourages public prayer—is not properly characterized as "private" speech.

The reasons just discussed explaining why the alleged "circuit-breaker" mechanism of the dual elections and student speaker do not turn public speech into private speech also demonstrate why these mechanisms do not insulate the school from the coercive element of the final message. In fact, this aspect of the District's argument exposes anew the concerns that are created by the majoritarian election system. The . . . controversy in this case demonstrates that the views of the students are not unanimous on that issue. One of the purposes served by the Establishment Clause is to remove debate over this kind of issue from governmental supervision or control. We explained in Lee that the "preservation and transmission of religious beliefs and worship is a responsibility and a choice committed to the private sphere." The two student elections authorized by the policy, coupled with the debates that presumably must precede each, impermissibly invade that private sphere. The election mechanism, when considered in light of the history in which the policy in question evolved, reflects a device the District put in place that determines whether religious messages will be delivered at home football games. The mechanism encourages divisiveness along religious lines in a public school setting, a result at odds with the Establishment Clause. . . .

The District further argues that attendance at the commencement ceremonies at issue in Lee "differs dramatically" from attendance at high school football games, which it contends "are of no more than passing interest to many student[s]" and are "decidedly extracurricular," thus dissipating any coercion. Attendance at a high school football game, unlike showing up for class, is certainly not required in order to receive a diploma. Moreover, we may assume that the District is correct in arguing that the informal pressure to attend an athletic event is not as strong as a senior's desire to attend her own graduation ceremony. There are some students, however, such as cheerleaders, members of the band, and, of course, the team members themselves, for whom seasonal commitments mandate their attendance, sometimes for class credit.

The District also minimizes the importance to many students of attending and participating in extracurricular activities as part of a complete educational experience. To assert that high school students do not feel immense social pressure, or have a truly genuine desire, to be involved in the extracurricular event that is American high school football is "formalistic in the extreme." We stressed in Lee the obvious observation that "adolescents are often susceptible to pressure from their peers towards conformity, and that the influence is strongest in matters of social convention." High school home football games are traditional gatherings of a school community; they bring together students and faculty as well as friends and family from years present and past to root for a common cause. Undoubtedly, the games are not important to some students, and they voluntarily choose not to attend. For many others, however, the choice between whether to attend these games or to risk facing a personally offensive religious ritual is in no practical sense an easy one. The Constitution, moreover, demands that the school may not force this difficult choice upon these students for "[i]t is a tenet of the First Amendment that the State cannot require one of its citizens to forfeit his or her rights and benefits as the price of resisting conformance to state-sponsored religious practice."

Even if we regard every high school student's decision to attend a home football game as purely voluntary, we are nevertheless persuaded that the delivery of a pre-game prayer has the improper effect of coercing those present to participate in an act of religious worship. . . . The District, nevertheless, asks us to pretend that we do not recognize what every Santa Fe High School student understands clearly—that this policy is about prayer. The District further asks us to accept what is obviously untrue: that these messages are necessary to "solemnize" a football game and that this single-student, year-long position is essential to the protection of student speech. We refuse to turn a blind eye to the context in which this policy arose, and that context quells any doubt that this policy was implemented with the purpose of endorsing school prayer. . . . The judgment of the Court of Appeals is, accordingly, affirmed.

CHIEF JUSTICE REHNQUIST, with whom JUSTICE SCALIa and JUSTICE THOMAS join, dissenting.

The Court distorts existing precedent to conclude that the school district's student-message program is invalid on its face under the Establishment Clause. But even more disturbing than its holding is the tone of the Court's opinion; it bristles with hostility to all things religious in public life. Neither the holding nor the tone of the opinion is faithful to the meaning of the Establishment Clause, when it is recalled that George Washington himself, at the request of the very Congress which passed the Bill of Rights, proclaimed a day of "public thanksgiving and prayer, to be observed by acknowledging with grateful hearts the many and signal favors of Almighty God.". . .

First, the Court misconstrues the nature of the "majoritarian election" permitted by the policy as being an election on "prayer" and "religion." To the contrary, the election permitted by the policy is a two-fold process whereby students vote first on whether to have a student speaker before football games at all, and second, if the students vote to have such a speaker, on who that speaker will be. It is conceivable that the election could become one in which student candidates campaign on platforms that focus on whether or not they will pray if elected. It is also conceivable that the election could lead to a Christian prayer before 90 percent of the football games. . . . But it is possible that the students might vote not to have a pre-game speaker, in which case there would be no threat of a constitutional violation. It is also possible that the election would not focus on prayer, but on public speaking ability or social popularity. And if student campaigning did begin to focus on prayer, the school might decide to implement reasonable campaign restrictions.

But the Court ignores these possibilities by holding that merely granting the student body the power to elect a speaker that may choose to pray, "regardless of the students' ultimate use of it, is not acceptable." The Court so holds despite that any speech that may occur as a result of the election process here would be private, not government, speech. The elected student, not the government, would choose what to say. Support for the Court's holding cannot be found in any of our cases. And it essentially invalidates all student elections. A newly elected student body president, or even a newly elected prom king or queen, could use opportunities for public speaking to say prayers. Under the Court's view, the mere grant of power to the students to vote for such offices, in light of the fear that those elected might publicly pray, violates the Establishment Clause.

Second, with respect to the policy's purpose, the Court holds that "the simple enactment of this policy, with the purpose and perception of school endorsement of student prayer, was a constitutional violation." But the policy itself has plausible secular purposes: "[T]o solemnize the event, to promote good sportsmanship and student safety, and to establish the appropriate environment for the competition." Where a governmental body "expresses a plausible secular purpose" for an enactment, "courts should generally defer to that stated intent." The Court grants no deference to—and appears openly hostile toward—the policy's stated purposes, and wastes no time in concluding that they are a sham.

For example, the Court dismisses the secular purpose of solemnization by claiming that it "invites and encourages religious messages." The Court so concludes based on its rather strange view that a "religious message is the most obvious means of solemnizing an event." But it is easy to think of solemn messages that are not religious in nature, for example urging that a game be fought fairly. And sporting events often begin with a solemn rendition of our national anthem, with its concluding verse "And this be our motto: 'In God is our trust.'" Under the Court's logic, a public school that sponsors the singing of the national anthem before football games violates the Establishment Clause. Although the Court apparently believes that solemnizing football games is an illegitimate purpose, the voters in the school district seem to disagree. Nothing in the Establishment Clause prevents them from making this choice. . . . I would reverse the judgment of the Court of Appeals.

COMMENTARY: "HOW COULD A MORMON FAMILY SUE OVER SCHOOL PRAYER?"

Santa Fe, Texas—This week's news that the Supreme Court had ruled against allowing the Santa Fe, Texas Independent School District to have "student-led voluntary prayers" before high school football games was disappointing to many conservative Mormons. It was also shocking for many that a lawsuit had been filed by a Mormon family. But an analysis of the case history shows why a Mormon family might file such a lawsuit.

The case was originally filed in 1995, in response to the way that the Mormon family, and a Catholic family that joined them in the suit, were treated by teachers and other students in the school district. Both families felt that their children had been discriminated against and harassed for belonging to a minority religion in the majority Southern Baptist town, according to Mormon News' analysis of news reports and contacts with those involved in the case.

Both families experienced a pattern of teachers and students promoting their religion at school. One junior high school teacher passed out fliers for a Baptist revival in class. Invitations to religious camps and other religious materials were handed out in the classroom. Teachers included denominational religious teachings in their lessons. Bibles were distributed in the schools by the Gideons. At lunch time, students were told to bow their heads and pray before eating.

The families soon discovered that religion was included in the school system's policies. At the time the original lawsuit was filed, the district had a written policy of designating a minister at the beginning of each school year who was to give invocations at school events, including not only football games and graduation, but school assemblies. The district court found that the school district had encouraged and preferred religion clubs over other clubs.

But the problem faced by the Mormon and Catholic families wasn't limited to simple promotion of a church. It included outright harassment of their children, simply because they weren't part of the dominant church. When one of the children in the Mormon family questioned a teacher's promotion of a revival, the teacher asked the student what religion she belonged to. When told that the child was Mormon, the teacher launched into an attack on Mormonism, calling it a "non-Christian cult," saying it was of the devil, and telling the child that she was going to hell. The court also heard "uncontradicted" evidence that students who declined to accept Bibles or objected to prayers and religious observances in school were verbally harassed.

Because of the climate, the families decided that they needed protection, and filed their lawsuit anonymously. But the district actively sought to find out their identities, according to one report going as far as to interrogate some students in an effort to discover the identities of the families. These efforts led the district court to threaten "the harshest possible contempt sanctions" if school employees continued trying "to ferret out the identities of" the families. It specifically enjoined the district from using "bogus petitions, questionnaires, individual interrogation, or downright 'snooping'" to discover who the families are.

The court also closed the courtroom when the children in the families testified because of "the possibility of social ostracization and violence due to militant religious attitudes. One of the witnesses who testified in the case (not a member of either family), chose to home-school her youngest daughter to avoid persistent verbal harassment, with pushing and shoving, over issues of religion in the public school.

Faced with the lawsuit, the school district quickly changed its policies, instead of trying to defend them. But in practice, the attorney for the plaintiffs claims that the school district never fixed the problems. "A number of school board members were a very strong and vocal religious right, and they took a position in concert with some local churches that they were going to infuse religion into the school," says Anthony Griffin, who represents the families. "And it's still going on. It's a policy that comes from higher up."

Because the families remain anonymous, it isn't possible to know how the Mormon family felt about the issue of prayer in the school before they experienced this harassment. But, the family is pleased with the results. A friend of the families, Debbie Mason, told the Associated Press that the families were elated by the Supreme Court's decision on Monday. "Thank God, thank God," Mason said. "This time it was football games, next it could have been the classroom. It is a slippery slope. This school district knew what it was doing and kept pushing and pushing" (Larsen, 2000).

EPPERSON V. ARKANSAS
393 U.S. 97 (1968)

"The State's undoubted right to prescribe the curriculum for its public schools does not carry with it the right to prohibit, on pain of criminal penalty, the teaching of a scientific theory or doctrine where that prohibition is based upon reasons that violate the First Amendment."

The Question: Can a state prohibit the teaching in public schools of "the theory or doctrine that mankind ascended or descended from a lower order of animals" and thus make it unlawful to teach the theory of evolution?

The Arguments: PRO

Elected state lawmakers have both a right and duty to establish the public school curriculum. The state can prohibit the teaching of theories that are considered unproven by reputable scientists. In addition, the theory that mankind is descended from lower orders of animals, such as apes and monkeys, is highly offensive to the majority of voters who hold a sincere belief that man was created by God in His image. Public school teachers do not have the "academic freedom" to teach subjects or doctrines that are not approved for the school curriculum. The subject of biology can be taught without reference to the theory of evolution.

CON

The sole motivation for passing the "anti-evolution" law was to prevent the teaching of a scientific theory that conflicted with the Christian fundamentalist doctrine of man's creation by God, set forth in the Book of Genesis. The Supreme Court has ruled that legislatures cannot prevent schools from teaching particular foreign languages, because of public hostility toward people who speak that language. Similarly, teachers cannot be prohibited from teaching a particular scientific theory because a majority of the public is hostile toward it. Allowing the voters or legislators to censor the public school curriculum would set a dangerous precedent and place teachers at risk if they taught any subject that offended a majority of the public, or even a vocal minority that is determined to ban certain topics from the school curriculum.

BACKGROUND

"Teacher at Central High Challenges Constitutionality of Evolution Law." This front-page headline jolted readers of *The Arkansas Gazette* on December 7, 1965. During the previous decade, Little Rock's prestigious Central High School had dominated headlines in Arkansas and the nation during the pitched battles, in both courts and streets, over school integration. After two years of turmoil, quiet returned to Central High in 1959 as the school admitted a token number of black students.

On the surface, this new headline about Central High had nothing to do with racial integration. But the evolution controversy tapped the deep roots of Southern racism: those who called black people "monkeys" recoiled at the notion that humans had evolved from apes. And for those Fundamentalists who mixed racism with religion, the Genesis account of creation allowed a separate origin for blacks and whites. Not all opponents of evolution also fought school integration, but the groups had considerable overlap in the South. For many in the Bible Belt, banning evolution from the schools was part of the crusade to protect the "Southern Way of Life" from "atheists" and "race mixers," equally evil in Dixie demonology.

The *Gazette* headline framed a picture of Susan Epperson, the Central High teacher whose lawsuit challenged an Arkansas law enacted in 1928 which imposed criminal penalties for teaching that "mankind ascended or descended from a lower order of animals." The 24-year-old biology teacher hardly fit the image of the Yankee carpetbagger, intent on imposing a new Reconstruction on the old South. The *Gazette* reported that Susan Epperson was a graduate of The College of the Ozarks in Clarksville, Arkansas, where her father, Dr. T.L. Smith, had taught biology since 1919. The story quoted Susan as saying that her parents "both are dedicated Christians who see no conflict between their belief in God and the scientific search for truth. I share this belief." Susan held a master's degree from the University of Illinois, the article noted, and was "married to First Lt. Jon O. Epperson, who is a member of a missile crew stationed at the Little Rock Air Force Base."

The newspaper picture of the smiling young teacher may have disarmed some Arkansas residents who in the Sputnik era considered the law against teaching evolution an embarrassing anachronism. Science became king of the curriculum in American high schools as the nation scrambled to catch the Soviets in space. Biology as well as physics and math prospered in the new pedagogy, and high-school textbooks discarded the caution of past decades and returned Charles Darwin and his theory of natural selection to its central place in human evolution. Susan Epperson, who began her second year of teaching at Central High in 1965, had selected a brand-new edition of an old textbook, *Modern Biology* by James Otto and Albert Towle, for her tenth-grade students. Evolution had vanished from this text in 1926, but the new edition stated that evidence of "changes in plants and animals" over time indicated that humans and apes "may have had a common, generalized ancestor in the remote past." Cautious and qualified, this statement still clashed with the Arkansas law and confronted Susan Epperson with the risks of firing and fines.

The crusade against teaching evolution in public schools began some fifty years after the publication in 1859 of Darwin's seminal book *The Origin of Species*. Before the twentieth century, only a handful of American youngsters, most from affluent families, attended public high schools, and evolution was the reigning orthodoxy in biology. The new century brought with it a rapid expansion of public school education; the number of high schools doubled in the first decade. This period also saw rapid growth in cities, factories, and immigration from Southern and Eastern Europe. The new Americans were mostly Jews and Catholics. Leaders of the mainstream churches adapted to change and welcomed Darwin's theory to the Social Gospel movement, which preached an "onward and upward" brand of theology.

Protestant, conservative, rural America viewed these social changes with suspicion and denounced the Social Gospel as heresy. Evangelical leaders responded between 1909 and 1912 with "The Fundamentals," a pamphlet series which proclaimed biblical literalism as the antidote to "modernism." Few of the Fundamentalists, as they soon called themselves, were Bible-thumping bookburners; many joined Progressive campaigns against child labor and sweatshops, seen as the evil spawn of secular greed. The two religious camps agreed on many social reforms but parted ways over evolution, which Fundamentalists could not square with the Genesis account of creation. The issue quickly moved from pamphlets to pulpits and then to political rallies.

The Progressive era died in World War I, and the Social Gospel was badly wounded in the postwar Red Scare. Fundamentalists took the offensive in midwestern and southern states and made evolution a leading target of legislative restriction. Between 1920 and 1926, eight southern states barred the teaching of evolution in public schools, and local school boards in many other states told their teachers not to present Darwin's theory to students. The growing movement gained a leader in William Jennings Bryan, three-time Democratic presidential candidate and a spell-binding orator. "All the ills from which America suffers can be traced back to the teaching of evolution," Bryan thundered in 1924. "It would be better to destroy every other book ever written, and just save the first three verses of Genesis."

Tennessee became the battleground for the first courtroom war over evolution. Bryan's support had prompted the passage in March 1925 of the first state law against teaching evolution. Several weeks later, the American Civil Liberties Union placed an ad in a Chattanooga newspaper: "We are looking for a Tennessee teacher who is willing to accept our services in testing this law in the courts." John T. Scopes, a 24-year-old biology teacher in rural Dayton, volunteered as a test-case plaintiff and wired the ACLU for help. Meeting the same day in Memphis, the World's Christian Fundamentals Association denounced "the teaching of the unscientific, anti-Christian, atheistic, anarchistic, pagan rationalistic evolutionary theory," and delegates voted to ask Bryan to prosecute Scopes for the Dayton school board. Vowing to wage "a battle royal between the Christian people of Tennessee and the so-called scientists," Bryan agreed and the board hired him without salary.

The "Monkey Trial" in Dayton pitted Bryan against Clarence Darrow, the legendary lawyer for underdogs. Conducted in a carnival atmosphere for two humid weeks, the trial ended with the anticlimax of Scopes' conviction. The main act was Bryan's duel on the witness stand—as an expert on the Bible—with Darrow, who jumped his opponent through the hoops of biblical literalism until he collapsed. Those who followed the trial, broadcast by radio and covered by the press like summer sweat, either grinned or winced at Bryan's humiliation by the master of cross-examination. Two weeks later, Bryan collapsed and died of a heart attack. The loss of its leader slowed the crusade against evolution to a crawl. And the Tennessee Supreme Court reversed Scopes' conviction on a technicality, preventing the U.S. Supreme Court from reviewing the case.

Following the Dayton debacle, only two southern states—Arkansas and Mississippi—enacted laws against evolution. The Arkansas legislature declined in 1927 to pass a bill which Fundamentalists pushed; mainstream church leaders opposed the bill at the cost of vilification and heresy trials. The bill's main sponsor then gathered enough signatures to place the measure on the statewide ballot in 1928. Civic and academic leaders, including a former governor, leading ministers, and the presidents of the University of Arkansas and other colleges pleaded with voters to protect "our schools from foolish and futile legislation and the good name of our state from ridicule." Supporters of Act No. 1 countered with an effective newspaper ad, titled "The Bible or Atheism, Which?" The choice was simple: "If you agree with atheism, vote against Act No. 1. If you agree with the Bible, vote for Act No. 1." Atheists were scarce in Arkansas, and voters approved the law by a 63 percent margin.

After this final electoral victory, the crusade against evolution lost its zeal and became dormant for three decades. The economic collapse of 1929 and the Great Depression took people's minds off the issue, and southern support of Franklin Roosevelt's liberal New Deal blunted the Fundamentalist movement. But in fact the evolutionists had retreated in the face of public hostility; timid textbook editors snipped out any mention of Darwin, and fearful high-school biology teachers avoided conflict with parents and school boards. Only after the Cold War eased and the Science War began did another biology teacher dare to risk the legal defeat that John Scopes had suffered.

Thirty years separated the Scopes trial and the hearing on Susan Epperson's case, but light-years separated their atmosphere. The first dragged on for two weeks; the second was briskly halted after two hours on April 1, 1966. Witnesses paraded to the stand in Dayton to declaim on religion and biology; Judge Murray O. Reed in Little Rock barred testimony on either topic, limiting the case to constitutional issues. . . . Susan's testimony was directed to just one point: "I brought this law suit because I have a text book which includes the theory about the origin or the descent or the ascent of man from a lower form of animals. This seemed to be a widely accepted theory and I feel it is my responsibility to acquaint my students with it."

The most striking contrast between Dayton and Little Rock was that Arkansas Attorney General Bruce Bennett, who defended the state law, was no William Jennings Bryan. Although he swaggered into court with Bryan's bombast and braggadocio, Bennett was cut down by Warren's objections when he tried to put evolution on trial. Judge Reed sustained every one of Warren's objections. Bennett was so poorly prepared, so obviously ignorant of science, that the audience frequently tittered. "This is a serious matter," Judge Reed admonished. "The only question here is a constitutional question of law and it is a serious one." Bennett left the courtroom in a pique, his play to the galleries frustrated.

Judge Reed did not reject "Creation" in his written opinion, issued two months later, but he rejected the law against teaching evolution: "This Court is of the opinion that a chapter in a biology book, adopted by the school administrative authorities, stating that a specific theory has been advanced by an individual that man ascended or descended from a lower form of animal life, does not constitute such a hazard to the safety, health and morals of the community that the constitutional freedoms may justifiably be suppressed by the state." Two decades of Supreme Court opinions which raised the "wall of separation" between church and school convinced Reed that "the unconstitutionality of the statute under consideration is not subject to doubt."

Attorney General Bennett's appeal of this ruling went to the Arkansas Supreme Court without oral argument; the justices and both lawyers saw the court as a quick whistle stop on the road to Washington, D.C. The court's opinion, issued on June 5, 1967, set a two-sentence record for brevity. The first sentence ruled that the state law "is a valid exercise of the state's power to specify the curriculum in its public schools." No precedent was cited, no issues discussed. The second sentence left lawyers and judges scratching their heads in puzzlement. "The court expresses no opinion on the question whether the Act prohibits any explanation of the theory of evolution or merely prohibits teaching that the theory is true," the judges wrote. Whether Susan Epperson could assign chapter 39 of *Modern Biology* to her students was a question the justices left unanswered (Irons, 1988).

* * *

MR. JUSTICE FORTAS delivered the opinion of the Court.

This appeal challenges the constitutionality of the "anti-evolution" statute which the State of Arkansas adopted in 1928 to prohibit the teaching in its public schools and universities of the theory that man evolved from other species of life. The statute was a product of the upsurge of "fundamentalist" religious fervor of the twenties. The Arkansas statute was an adaptation of the famous Tennessee "monkey law" which that State adopted in 1925. The constitutionality of the Tennessee law was upheld by the Tennessee Supreme Court in the celebrated Scopes case in 1927.

The Arkansas law makes it unlawful for a teacher in any state-supported school or university "to teach the theory or doctrine that mankind ascended or descended from a lower order of animals," or "to adopt or use in any such institution a textbook that teaches" this theory. Violation is a misdemeanor and subjects the violator to dismissal from his position.

The present case concerns the teaching of biology in a high school in Little Rock. According to the testimony, until the events here in litigation, the official textbook furnished for the high school biology course did not have a section on the Darwinian Theory. Then, for the academic year 1965–1966, the school administration, on recommendation of the teachers of biology in the school system, adopted and prescribed a textbook which contained a chapter setting forth "the theory about the origin . . . of man from a lower form of animal."

Susan Epperson, a young woman who graduated from Arkansas' school system and then obtained her master's degree in zoology at the University of Illinois, was employed by the Little Rock school system in the fall of 1964 to teach 10th grade biology at Central High School. At the start of the next academic year, 1965, she was confronted by the new textbook (which one surmises from the record was not unwelcome to her). She faced at least a literal dilemma because she was supposed to use the new textbook for classroom instruction and presumably to teach the statutorily condemned chapter; but to do so would be a criminal offense and subject her to dismissal.

She instituted the present action in the Chancery Court of the State, seeking a declaration that the Arkansas statute is void and enjoining the State and the defendant officials of the Little Rock school system from dismissing her for violation of the statute's provisions. . . . The Chancery Courts . . . held that the statute violated the Fourteenth Amendment to the United States Constitution. The court noted that this Amendment encompasses the prohibitions upon state interference with freedom of speech and thought which are contained in the First Amendment. Accordingly, it held that the challenged statute is unconstitutional because, in violation of the First Amendment, it "tends to hinder the quest for knowledge, restrict the freedom to learn, and restrain the freedom to teach." In this perspective, the Act, it held, was an unconstitutional and void restraint upon the freedom of speech guaranteed by the Constitution. On appeal, the Supreme Court of Arkansas reversed. Its two-sentence opinion . . . sustained the statute as an exercise of the State's power to specify the curriculum in public schools. It did not address itself to the competing constitutional considerations. . . .

At the outset, it is urged upon us that the challenged statute is vague and uncertain and therefore within the condemnation of the Due Process Clause of the Fourteenth Amendment. The contention that the Act is vague and uncertain is supported by language in the brief opinion of Arkansas' Supreme Court. That court, perhaps reflecting the discomfort which the statute's quixotic prohibition necessarily engenders in the modern mind, stated that it "expresses no opinion" as to whether the Act prohibits "explanation" of the theory of evolution or merely forbids "teaching that the theory is true." Regardless of this uncertainty, the court held that the statute is constitutional. On the other hand, counsel for the State, in oral argument in this Court, candidly stated that, despite the State Supreme Court's equivocation, Arkansas would interpret the statute "to mean that to make a student aware of the theory . . . just to teach that there was such a theory" would be grounds for dismissal and for prosecution under the statute; and he said "that the Supreme Court of Arkansas' opinion should be interpreted in that manner." He said: "If Mrs. Epperson would tell her students that 'Here is Darwin's theory, that man ascended or descended from a lower form of being,' then I think she would be under this statute liable for prosecution."

In any event, we do not rest our decision upon the asserted vagueness of the statute. On either interpretation of its language, Arkansas' statute cannot stand. It is of no moment whether the law is deemed to prohibit mention of Darwin's theory, or to forbid any or all of the infinite varieties of communication embraced within the term "teaching." Under either interpretation, the law must be stricken because of its conflict with the constitutional prohibition of state laws respecting an establishment of religion or prohibiting the free exercise thereof. The overriding fact is that Arkansas' law selects from the body of knowledge a particular segment which it proscribes for the sole reason that it is deemed to conflict with a particular religious doctrine; that is, with a particular interpretation of the Book of Genesis by a particular religious group.

The antecedents of today's decision are many and unmistakable. They are rooted in the foundation soil of our Nation. They are fundamental to freedom. Government in our democracy, state and national, must be neutral in matters of religious theory, doctrine, and practice. It may not be hostile to any religion or to the advocacy of no-religion; and it may not aid, foster, or promote one religion or religious theory against another or even against the militant opposite. The First Amendment mandates governmental neutrality between religion and religion, and between religion and nonreligion. . . .

Judicial interposition in the operation of the public school system of the Nation raises problems requiring care and restraint. Our courts, however, have not failed to apply the First Amendment's mandate in our educational system where essential to safeguard the fundamental values of freedom of speech and inquiry and of belief. By and large, public education in our Nation is committed to the control of state and local authorities. Courts do not and cannot intervene in the resolution of conflicts which arise in the daily operation of school systems and which do not directly and sharply implicate basic constitutional values. On the other hand, "[t]he vigilant protection of constitutional freedoms is nowhere more vital than in the community of American schools," Shelton v. Tucker. As this Court said in Keyishian v. Board of Regents, the First Amendment "does not tolerate laws that cast a pall of orthodoxy over the classroom.". . .

There is and can be no doubt that the First Amendment does not permit the State to require that teaching and learning must be tailored to the principles or prohibitions of any religious sect or dogma. . . . While study of religions and of the Bible from a literary and historic viewpoint, presented objectively as part of a secular program of education, need not collide with the First Amendment's prohibition, the State may not adopt programs or practices in its public schools or colleges which "aid or oppose" any religion. This prohibition is absolute. It forbids alike the preference of a religious doctrine or the prohibition of theory which is deemed antagonistic to a particular dogma. . . . The State's undoubted right to prescribe the curriculum for its public schools does not carry with it the right to prohibit, on pain of criminal penalty, the teaching of a scientific theory or doctrine where that prohibition is based upon reasons that violate the First Amendment. It is much too late to argue that the State may impose upon the teachers in its schools any conditions that it chooses, however restrictive they may be of constitutional guarantees.

In the present case, there can be no doubt that Arkansas has sought to prevent its teachers from discussing the theory of evolution because it is contrary to the belief of some that the Book of Genesis must be the exclusive source of doctrine as to the origin of man. No suggestion has been made that Arkansas' law may be justified by considerations of state policy other than the religious views of some of its citizens. It is clear that fundamentalist sectarian conviction was and is the law's reason for existence. Its antecedent, Tennessee's "monkey law," candidly stated its purpose: to make it unlawful "to teach any theory that denies the story of the Divine Creation of man as taught in the Bible, and to teach instead that man has descended from a lower order of animals." Perhaps the sensational publicity attendant upon the Scopes trial induced Arkansas to adopt less explicit language. It eliminated Tennessee's reference to "the story of the Divine Creation of man" as taught in the Bible, but there is no doubt that the motivation for the law was the same: to suppress the teaching of a theory which, it was thought, "denied" the divine creation of man.[1]

Arkansas' law cannot be defended as an act of religious neutrality. Arkansas did not seek to excise from the curricula of its schools and universities all discussion of the origin of man. The law's effort was confined to an attempt to blot out a particular theory because of its supposed conflict with the Biblical account, literally read. Plainly, the law is contrary to the mandate of the First, and in violation of the Fourteenth, Amendment to the Constitution.

The judgment of the Supreme Court of Arkansas is Reversed.

MEET SUSAN EPPERSON

I was born in 1941 in Little Rock, Arkansas. My parents lived in Clarksville, Arkansas, near the Ozark mountains, about a hundred miles west of Little Rock. My dad was a biology professor at a small Presbyterian college, The College of the Ozarks. I spent my entire childhood in Clarksville, which, compared to my married life traveling a lot, is a completely different thing.

My father was born in Alabama in 1890, so he was in his fifties when I was born. He was in the First World War; and after the war he went back to Wooster College in Ohio, where he had received his bachelor's degree, to see about job possibilities. They said, There's a small Presbyterian college in Arkansas that needs a biology teacher, and so he went down. The school was very small, not many facilities, but he ended up being there fifty years, with times off to go back for further degrees.

I grew up right across the street from the college chapel. My mother still lives in the same house. I have wonderful memories of going over in the late afternoons to the science building where my dad taught. Classes would be over, it would be about time for him to come home, so I would go over and meet him. And usually the janitor would be buffing the floors to a high shine, and the late-afternoon sun would be hitting that newly waxed, shiny floor, and I would smell the wax. It's amazing how those things stick with you. I'd walk into the lab and there was the big swordfish snout and skeletons and specimens on the shelves, and beautiful rocks in the rock collection. I really have lots of nice memories of the science lab.

I went to The College of the Ozarks, right there at home. Because my math test scores were very good, it seemed that

mathematics was what I should major in, so I began with that. The mathematics didn't work out, and then I considered English. I still enjoy English, I still entertain thoughts of going back and getting a master's degree in English for the pure fun of it, because I like to read and I like literature. But the more I took courses in biology, which I enjoyed, and talked with my folks about what to major in, I decided to major in biology. . . .

Evolution was certainly dealt with in our courses. Because of where he was teaching, in the Bible Belt, Daddy often referred to "progressive change" rather than using the word evolution, since the word can get people excited. Yet he certainly talked about evolution, about change, and the evidence in the rocks. . . .

I was raised with the idea that you could certainly be a Christian, which both of my parents were, and still accept the evidence for evolution that we see in the rocks. It's not just the rocks—there's a lot of biochemical evidence and serological evidence—and it's just not a problem. It never has been for me.

I received my bachelor's degree in 1962 and went away that next fall to graduate school at the University of Illinois in Champaign-Urbana. I lived there for two years and got my masters in zoology. I worked half-time during those two years, in a mosquito genetics lab where they were studying DDT resistance in various strains of mosquitos—which is another evidence for the kinds of changes that can bring about evolutionary change.

Teaching was always an option for me, something I wanted to consider. . . . I applied a few places in Arkansas, including Little Rock Central; went down and interviewed, and got the job. I was teaching tenth-grade biology, with a straight schedule of biology classes.

When I started teaching at Central, I knew there was some kind of evolution law in Arkansas. I hadn't really heard it talked about a whole lot, but I knew there was some kind of restriction on teaching evolution. There had been some articles in *The Arkansas Gazette*, in Little Rock, about "Let's get rid of this old law, there's a problem here." And there were letters back and forth—people who were very much opposed to trying to get rid of it, and others who thought that it was old and antiquated and being ignored, and should be taken off the books. So there was already some controversy. I also knew the law was disregarded by-and-large. Certainly the courses at the University of Arkansas would teach evolution concepts, in contradiction to the law. So it was sort of in the back of my mind.

In the fall of my second year at Central, in 1965, Mrs. Virginia Minor came to see me one afternoon. She was a fellow teacher and a friend; she taught home economics and ran the kindergarten program at Central. Mrs. Minor told me that the Arkansas Education Association was considering a lawsuit to try to have the evolution law declared unconstitutional. She asked me, Do you think you'd be interested?

I was terrified at the prospect. But I thought, Well, it sounds interesting.

I agreed to talk with the lawyer for the AEA, Mr. Eugene Warren, who was a super fellow, a marvelous lawyer. One afternoon that fall we met after school in Mrs. Minor's kindergarten room, and we sat in little, tiny chairs at little, tiny tables. It was sort of funny. Mr. Warren had prepared a

---

[1]The following advertisement is typical of the public appeal which was used in the campaign to secure adoption of the statute:

The Bible or Atheism, Which?

All atheists favor evolution. If you agree with atheism vote against Act No. 1. If you agree with the Bible vote for Act No. 1. . . . Shall conscientious church members be forced to pay taxes to support teachers to teach evolution which will undermine the faith of their children? The Gazette said Russian Bolshevists laughed at Tennessee. True, and that sort will laugh at Arkansas. Who cares? Vote FOR ACT NO. 1.

Letters from the public expressed the fear that teaching of evolution would be "subversive of Christianity," and that it would cause school children "to disrespect the Bible." One letter read: "The cosmogony taught by [evolution] runs contrary to that of Moses and Jesus, and as such is nothing, if anything at all, but atheism. . . . Now let the mothers and fathers of our state that are trying to raise their children in the Christian faith arise in their might and vote for this anti-evolution bill that will take it out of our tax supported schools. When they have saved the children, they have saved the state."

five-page complaint to file in court. All of it, the idea of courts and lawsuits, was really foreign to me. I wasn't familiar with the process at all. But he was very good, and explained the case to me and told me how it compared with the Scopes case.

As I read the complaint, even though I hadn't carefully thought about the law, it expressed very clearly the kind of things that I really did think, when it was actually put into words. One, that the law was being disregarded. So in that sense, a message was being sent to students that if you don't like a law, then just go ahead and break it. Which, of course, is civil disobedience, a wonderful thing that we can do in America; but I also thought that maybe that wasn't the best way to try to handle it. I felt very strongly, and still do, that a teacher is someone who should set an example and *be* an example to students. So this presented a dilemma.

The other dilemma was, I'm a science teacher and if you've studied some science, and the more you study, you understand that evolution is a very unifying principle in the understanding of all kinds of biology. To leave it out, to not be able to say anything about it, is really shortchanging your students, not giving them the full picture. And also not giving them something that helps to tie the whole discipline together. So there was this dilemma—do I not teach this, which I feel is important to teach?

Mr. Warren told me the day he'd go down to the courthouse to file the complaint and said it would probably be in the morning paper. All these interesting things you learn along the way! Reporters go every day to the courthouse to see what kind of suits have been filed, so you knew that would get into the paper. Somewhere they got ahold of a picture of me, and that was on the front page of the *Gazette* the next day, with an article, "Teacher Challenges Evolution Law."

The next day it was in the paper, and several of my students came and waved the clipping. Oh, Mrs. Epperson, look! Your picture's in the paper! Are you for it or against it? I thought, That's typical—they see the picture but they don't read the article to find out what's happening. I spent a little time in each class that day, briefly telling them what we were doing and how I was involved.

We went to court the first of April, and a lot of people joked about April Fools Day. The case was tried in the chancery court in Little Rock, before Judge Murray O. Reed. I thought he was a good judge. Of course, when someone decides in your favor, you'll think they were a good judge.

Mr. Warren put me on the witness stand, and he asked about my educational background; how I happened to be teaching at Central; would I teach evolution as a fact or a theory. It seems to be reassuring to people if you say, I'm only going to teach it as a theory. There are different uses of the word "theory," and to someone like Stephen Jay Gould, those educated in science, a scientific theory is something with a great deal of support. Mr. Warren established that I was under some kind of threat from this law and that I thought it should be declared unconstitutional.

One interesting aspect of the case was that I got to meet John Scopes through Jerry Tompkins, a Presbyterian minister who had written a book about the Scopes trial. Jerry had interviewed John Scopes, who was a very quiet, retiring kind of person. Jerry said he'd really like for us to meet John

Scopes, that it would be historic. Scopes was living in Shreveport, Louisiana, and at Christmas one year we were going to southern Arkansas to see my grandmother. Jon and I drove down with Jerry one day to Shreveport and we all met at a Holiday Inn and had lunch in a private room with Mr. Scopes and his wife. We had a nice, quiet visit and a friendly chat. As we were leaving, he made a point of letting me know that he was really supportive of me. He had wanted to come to our trial and show his support, but he knew it would just create a furor, which it probably would have. But he assured me that his absence didn't mean that he didn't support what we had done.

Since my case was decided, the so-called creationism movement has come to the forefront. I'm really opposed to how they're trying to put religion into biology classes. I heard from the Creation Research Society when my case came about, a letter saying I was wrong and shouldn't be doing this, and there's just as much scientific evidence for creation as there is for evolution. I remember thinking, What kind of fly-by-night group is this? They were saying the earth is much younger than the paleontological evidence shows and that carbon dating is bunk, and that God just put all the fossil evidence there to make the earth *look* old! Why, I don't know. This doesn't sound like the omnipotent God that I worship, it just sounds cockeyed to me.

They say they're scientific, but I do not see evidence of the scientific method and the kind of investigative approach that has given us the evidence we have for evolution. As far as I understand it, creationism is not science. Therefore, it does not belong in a science classroom. If they want to teach these ideas in a history course of philosophy course, I'm not opposed to their talking about their ideas. This is not just an effort to get rid of evolution in the schools, it's an effort to debunk a lot of science—techniques like carbon dating. The scientific method as such is under fire. It's kind of like, Let's go back to medieval days and let's not account for what we see.

I don't think creationism is good science, and I don't think it's good religion. They say they're not coming from the Bible, but of course they are. They're trying to equate the creations of the world with an established scientific theory. I believe God made the world, although I can't explain how He did it. And there are gaps in the evolutionary record, there are things we just don't know, and I'm willing to live with that. But there is a preponderance of evidence for evolutionary change.

The creationists say, you can't *show* evolution. Well, you can show it in insects, in things that have a faster generation time than humans. To me, there's an awful lot of evidence to support it. One of the basic differences between creationism and science is that a scientist looks at things, just like Darwin did when he went sailing on the Beagle. He hadn't even thought of coming up with the theory of evolution, but he saw all these life forms and these islands and he thought, Hmmm, how does this fit together? A scientist sees mold growing on something and puts it on a plate and it kills bacteria, and he says, Hmmm, what's happening here? You *see* things and observe, and you draw conclusions and try to make some kind of unity out of that, and then you come up with a theory about bactericides or whatever. The creationists, on the other hand, already have a conclusion, and they eliminate whatever evidence they don't want. It's just not science to start with a foregone conclusion and they try to find evidence to support it.

I was very happy to read that the Supreme court declared that the Louisiana "equal time" creationism law was unconstitutional. It was obviously a correct decision. Of course I'm opposed to such laws because of the confusion they would cause for science teachers and students. I really believe young people need to study the Bible and learn about God—but these are not for public schools to teach, and certainly not for science teachers (Irons, 1988).

EDWARDS V. AGUILLARD
482 U.S. 578 (1987)

"Requiring schools to teach creation science with evolution does not advance academic freedom. . . . The preeminent purpose of the Louisiana Legislature was clearly to advance the religious viewpoint that a supernatural being created humankind."

The Question: Can a state require that the theories of evolution and creationism receive "balanced treatment" in the public school biology curriculum and prohibit teaching the theory of evolution unless it is accompanied by instruction in "creation science"?

The Arguments: PRO

Although the Supreme Court has ruled that states cannot prohibit the teaching of the theory of evolution in public schools, state lawmakers have the constitutional authority to require that schools in which the theory of evolution is taught balance that teaching with the opposing theory of "creation science." Many reputable scientists believe that evolution is a flawed theory, and that substantial evidence exists for "creation science" as an alternative—and plausible—theory of the origins of life on earth. This is a question of academic freedom, in making sure that more than one point of view is presented on this important question. Creation science can be taught without any reference to God or the Genesis account of creation.

CON

The "balanced treatment" law is really just a thinly disguised effort to get around the Supreme Court ruling that evolution cannot be banned from the public school curriculum. Even the sponsors of the law at issue admitted that their primary motivation was to expose students in biology classes to the biblical doctrine of human creation. The weight of scientific evidence is strongly in support of evolution as the best theory of the development of species. "Creation science" is not really science, since its premises cannot be subject to tests of reliability, replication, and falsification. Therefore, efforts to inject religious doctrine into the science curriculum must be rejected, whatever the supposedly "scientific" label their sponsors put on them.

JUSTICE BRENNAN delivered the opinion of the Court.

The question for decision is whether Louisiana's "Balanced Treatment for Creation-Science and Evolution-Science in Public School Instruction" Act (Creationism Act), is facially invalid as violative of the Establishment Clause of the First Amendment. The Creationism Act forbids the teaching of the theory of evolution in public schools unless accompanied by instruction in "creation science." No school is required to teach evolution or creation science. If either is taught, however, the other must also be taught. The theories of evolution and creation science are statutorily defined as "the scientific evidences for [creation or evolution] and inferences from those scientific evidences."

Appellees, who include parents of children attending Louisiana public schools, Louisiana teachers, and religious leaders, challenged the constitutionality of the Act in District Court, seeking an injunction and declaratory relief. Appellants, Louisiana officials charged with implementing the Act, defended on the ground that the purpose of the Act is to protect a legitimate secular interest, namely, academic freedom. Appellees attacked the Act as facially invalid because it violated the Establishment Clause and made a motion for summary judgment. The District Court granted the motion. The court held that there can be no valid secular reason for prohibiting the teaching of evolution, a theory historically opposed by some religious denominations. The court further concluded that "the teaching of 'creation-science' and 'creationism,' as contemplated by the statute, involves teaching 'tailored to the principles' of a particular religious sect or group of sects." The District Court therefore held that the Creationism Act violated the Establishment Clause either because it prohibited the teaching of evolution or because it required the teaching of creation science with the purpose of advancing a particular religious doctrine.

The Court of Appeals affirmed. The court observed that the statute's avowed purpose of protecting academic freedom was inconsistent with requiring, upon risk of sanction, the teaching of creation science whenever evolution is taught. The court found that the Louisiana Legislature's actual intent was "to discredit evolution by counterbalancing its teaching at every turn with the teaching of creationism, a religious belief." Because the Creationism Act was thus a law furthering a particular religious belief, the Court of Appeals held that the Act violated the Establishment Clause. . . . We noted probable jurisdiction, and now affirm.

The Establishment Clause forbids the enactment of any law "respecting an establishment of religion." The Court has applied a three-pronged test to determine whether legislation comports with the Establishment Clause. First, the legislature must have adopted the law with a secular purpose. Second, the statute's principal or primary effect must be one that neither advances nor inhibits religion. Third, the statute must not result in an excessive entanglement of government with religion. Lemon v. Kurtzman. State action violates the Establishment Clause if it fails to satisfy any of these prongs. . . .

Lemon's first prong focuses on the purpose that animated adoption of the Act. "The purpose prong of the Lemon test asks whether government's actual purpose is to endorse or disapprove of religion." A governmental intention to promote religion is clear when the State enacts a law to serve a religious purpose. If the law was enacted for the purpose of endorsing religion, "no consideration of the second or third criteria [of Lemon] is necessary." In this case, appellants have identified no clear secular purpose for the Louisiana Act. True, the Act's stated purpose is to protect academic freedom. This phrase might, in common parlance, be understood as referring to enhancing the freedom of teachers to teach what they will. The Court of Appeals, however, correctly concluded that the Act was not designed to further that goal. . . . Even if "academic freedom" is read to mean "teaching all of the evidence" with respect to the origin of human beings, the Act does not further this purpose. The goal of providing a more comprehensive science curriculum is not furthered either by outlawing the teaching of evolution or by requiring the teaching of creation science.

While the Court is normally deferential to a State's articulation of a secular purpose, it is required that the statement of such purpose be sincere and not a sham. It is clear from the legislative history that the purpose of the legislative sponsor, Senator Bill Keith, was to narrow the science curriculum. During the legislative hearings, Senator Keith stated: "My preference would be that neither [creationism nor evolution] be taught." Such a ban on teaching does not promote—indeed, it undermines—the provision of a comprehensive scientific education.

It is equally clear that requiring schools to teach creation science with evolution does not advance academic freedom. The Act does not grant teachers a flexibility that they did not already possess to supplant the present science curriculum with the presentation of theories, besides evolution, about the origin of life. Indeed, the Court of Appeals found that no law prohibited Louisiana public school teachers from teaching any scientific theory. As the president of the Louisiana Science Teachers Association testified, "[a]ny scientific concept that's based on established fact can be included in our curriculum already, and no legislation allowing this is necessary." The Act provides Louisiana schoolteachers with no new authority. Thus the stated purpose is not furthered by it. . . .

If the Louisiana Legislature's purpose was solely to maximize the comprehensiveness and effectiveness of science instruction, it would have encouraged the teaching of all scientific theories about the origins of humankind. But under the Act's requirements, teachers who were once free to teach any and all facets of this subject are now unable to do so. Moreover, the Act fails even to ensure that creation science will be taught, but instead requires the teaching of this theory only when the theory of evolution is taught. Thus we agree with the Court of Appeals' conclusion that the Act does not serve to protect academic freedom, but has the distinctly different purpose of discrediting "evolution by counterbalancing its teaching at every turn with the teaching of creationism. . . ."

There is a historic and contemporaneous link between the teachings of certain religious denominations and the teaching of evolution. It was this link that concerned the Court in Epperson v. Arkansas, which also involved a facial challenge to a statute regulating the teaching of evolution. In that case, the Court reviewed an Arkansas statute that made it unlawful for an instructor to teach evolution or to use a textbook that referred to this scientific theory. Although the Arkansas antievolution law did not explicitly state its predominate religious purpose, the Court could not ignore that "[t]he statute was a product of the upsurge of 'fundamentalist' religious fervor" that has long viewed this particular scientific theory as contradicting the literal interpretation of the Bible. . . .

These same historic and contemporaneous antagonisms between the teachings of certain religious denominations and the teaching of evolution are present in this case. The preeminent purpose of the Louisiana Legislature was clearly to advance the religious viewpoint that a supernatural being created humankind. The term "creation science" was defined as embracing this particular religious doctrine by those responsible for the passage of the Creationism Act. Senator Keith's leading expert on creation science, Edward Boudreaux, testified at the legislative hearings that the theory of creation science included belief in the existence of a supernatural creator. The legislative history therefore reveals that the term "creation science," as contemplated by the legislature that adopted this Act, embodies the religious belief that a supernatural creator was responsible for the creation of humankind.

Furthermore, it is not happenstance that the legislature required the teaching of a theory that coincided with this religious view. The legislative history documents that the Act's primary purpose was to change the science curriculum of public schools in order to provide persuasive advantage to a particular religious doctrine that rejects the factual basis of evolution in its entirety. The sponsor of the Creationism Act,

Senator Keith, explained during the legislative hearings that his disdain for the theory of evolution resulted from the support that evolution supplied to views contrary to his own religious beliefs. According to Senator Keith, the theory of evolution was consonant with the "cardinal principle[s] of religious humanism, secular humanism, theological liberalism, aetheistism [sic]." The state senator repeatedly stated that scientific evidence supporting his religious views should be included in the public school curriculum to redress the fact that the theory of evolution incidentally coincided with what he characterized as religious beliefs antithetical to his own. The legislation therefore sought to alter the science curriculum to reflect endorsement of a religious view that is antagonistic to the theory of evolution.

In this case, the purpose of the Creationism Act was to restructure the science curriculum to conform with a particular religious viewpoint. Out of many possible science subjects taught in the public schools, the legislature chose to affect the teaching of the one scientific theory that historically has been opposed by certain religious sects. As in Epperson, the legislature passed the Act to give preference to those religious groups which have as one of their tenets the creation of humankind by a divine creator. The "overriding fact" that confronted the Court in Epperson was "that Arkansas' law selects from the body of knowledge a particular segment which it proscribes for the sole reason that it is deemed to conflict with . . . a particular interpretation of the Book of Genesis by a particular religious group." Similarly, the Creationism Act is designed either to promote the theory of creation science which embodies a particular religious tenet by requiring that creation science be taught whenever evolution is taught or to prohibit the teaching of a scientific theory disfavored by certain religious sects by forbidding the teaching of evolution when creation science is not also taught. The Establishment Clause, however, "forbids alike the preference of a religious doctrine or the prohibition of theory which is deemed antagonistic to a particular dogma." Because the primary purpose of the Creationism Act is to advance a particular religious belief, the Act endorses religion in violation of the First Amendment. . . .

The Louisiana Creationism Act advances a religious doctrine by requiring either the banishment of the theory of evolution from public school classrooms or the presentation of a religious viewpoint that rejects evolution in its entirety. The Act violates the Establishment Clause of the First Amendment because it seeks to employ the symbolic and financial support of government to achieve a religious purpose. The judgment of the Court of Appeals therefore is Affirmed.

JUSTICE SCALIA, with whom the Chief Justice joins, dissenting.

Even if I agreed with the questionable premise that legislation can be invalidated under the Establishment Clause on the basis of its motivation alone, without regard to its effects, I would still find no justification for today's decision. The Louisiana legislators who passed the "Balanced Treatment for Creation-Science and Evolution-Science Act" (Balanced Treatment Act), each of whom had sworn to support the Constitution, were well aware of the potential Establishment Clause problems and considered that aspect of the legislation with great care. After seven hearings and several months of study, resulting in substantial revision of the original proposal, they approved the Act overwhelmingly and specifically articulated the secular purpose they meant it to serve. Although the record contains abundant evidence of the sincerity of that purpose (the only issue pertinent to this case), the Court today holds, essentially on the basis of "its visceral knowledge regarding what must have motivated the legislators," that the members of the Louisiana Legislature knowingly violated their oaths and then lied about it. I dissent. . . .

Our cases in no way imply that the Establishment Clause forbids legislators merely to act upon their religious convictions. We surely would not strike down a law providing money to feed the hungry or shelter the homeless if it could be demonstrated that, but for the religious beliefs of the legislators, the funds would not have been approved. Also, political activism by the religiously motivated is part of our heritage. Notwithstanding the majority's implication to the contrary, we do not presume that the sole purpose of a law is to advance religion merely because it was supported strongly by organized religions or by adherents of particular faiths. To do so would deprive religious men and women of their right to participate in the political process. Today's religious activism may give us the Balanced Treatment Act, but yesterday's resulted in the abolition of slavery, and tomorrow's may bring relief for famine victims. . . .

Similarly, we will not presume that a law's purpose is to advance religion merely because it "happens to coincide or harmonize with the tenets of some or all religions," or because it benefits religion, even substantially. . . . Thus, the fact that creation science coincides with the beliefs of certain religions, a fact upon which the majority relies heavily, does not itself justify invalidation of the Act.

With the foregoing in mind, I now turn to the purposes underlying adoption of the Balanced Treatment Act. . . . We cannot accurately assess whether this purpose is a "sham," until we first examine the evidence presented to the legislature far more carefully than the Court has done. Before summarizing the testimony of Senator Keith and his supporters, I wish to make clear that I by no means intend to endorse its accuracy. But my views (and the views of this Court) about creation science and evolution are (or should be) beside the point. Our task is not to judge the debate about teaching the origins of life, but to ascertain what the members of the Louisiana Legislature believed. The vast majority of them voted to approve a bill which explicitly stated a secular purpose; what is crucial is not their wisdom in believing that purpose would be achieved by the bill, but their sincerity in believing it would be.

Most of the testimony in support of Senator Keith's bill came from the Senator himself and from scientists and educators he presented, many of whom enjoyed academic credentials that may have been regarded as quite impressive by members of the Louisiana Legislature. To a substantial extent, their testimony was devoted to lengthy, and, to the layman, seemingly expert scientific expositions on the origin of life. These scientific lectures touched upon, inter alia, biology, paleontology, genetics, astronomy, astrophysics, probability analysis, and biochemistry. The witnesses repeatedly assured committee members that "hundreds and hundreds" of highly respected, internationally renowned scientists believed in creation science and would support their testimony. Senator Keith and his witnesses testified essentially as set forth in the following numbered paragraphs:

(1) There are two and only two scientific explanations for the beginning of life—evolution and creation science. Both are bona fide "sciences." Both posit a theory of the origin of life and subject that theory to empirical testing. Evolution posits that life arose out of inanimate chemical compounds and has gradually evolved over millions of years. Creation science posits that all life forms now on earth appeared suddenly and relatively recently and have changed little. Since there are only two possible explanations of the origin of life, any evidence that tends to disprove the theory of evolution necessarily tends to prove the theory of creation science, and vice versa. For example, the abrupt appearance in the fossil record of complex life, and the extreme rarity of transitional life forms in that record, are evidence for creation science.

(2) The body of scientific evidence supporting creation science is as strong as that supporting evolution. In fact, it may be stronger. The evidence for evolution is far less compelling than we have been led to believe. Evolution is not a scientific "fact," since it cannot actually be observed in a laboratory. Rather, evolution is merely a scientific theory or "guess." It is a very bad guess at that. The scientific problems with evolution are so serious that it could accurately be termed a "myth."

(3) Creation science is educationally valuable. Students exposed to it better understand the current state of scientific evidence about the origin of life. Those students even have a better understanding of evolution. Creation science can and should be presented to children without any religious content.

(4) Although creation science is educationally valuable and strictly scientific, it is now being censored from or misrepresented in the public schools. Evolution, in turn, is misrepresented as an absolute truth. Teachers have been brainwashed by an entrenched scientific establishment composed almost exclusively of scientists to whom evolution is like a "religion." These scientists discriminate against creation scientists so as to prevent evolution's weaknesses from being exposed.

(5) The censorship of creation science has at least two harmful effects. First, it deprives students of knowledge of one of the two scientific explanations for the origin of life and leads them to believe that evolution is proven fact; thus, their education suffers and they are wrongly taught that science has proved their religious beliefs false. Second, it violates the Establishment Clause. The United States Supreme Court has held that secular humanism is a religion. Belief in evolution is a central tenet of that religion. Thus, by censoring creation science and instructing students that evolution is fact, public school teachers are now advancing religion in violation of the Establishment Clause.

Senator Keith repeatedly and vehemently denied that his purpose was to advance a particular religious doctrine. At the outset of the first hearing on the legislation, he testified: "We are not going to say today that you should have some kind of religious instructions in our schools. . . . We are not talking about religion today. . . . I am not proposing that we take the Bible in each science class and read the first chapter of Genesis.". . . We have no way of knowing, of course, how many legislators believed the testimony of Senator Keith and his witnesses. But in the absence of evidence to the contrary,

we have to assume that many of them did. Given that assumption, the Court today plainly errs in holding that the Louisiana Legislature passed the Balanced Treatment Act for exclusively religious purposes. . . .

The Act's reference to "creation" is not convincing evidence of religious purpose. The Act defines creation science as "scientific evidenc[e]," and Senator Keith and his witnesses repeatedly stressed that the subject can and should be presented without religious content. We have no basis on the record to conclude that creation science need be anything other than a collection of scientific data supporting the theory that life abruptly appeared on earth. Creation science, its proponents insist, no more must explain whence life came than evolution must explain whence came the inanimate materials from which it says life evolved. But even if that were not so, to posit a past creator is not to posit the eternal and personal God who is the object of religious veneration. Indeed, it is not even to posit the "unmoved mover" hypothesized by Aristotle and other notably nonfundamentalist philosophers. Senator Keith suggested this when he referred to "a creator however you define a creator.". . .

Legislators other than Senator Keith made only a few statements providing insight into their motives, but those statements cast no doubt upon the sincerity of the Act's articulated purpose. The legislators were concerned primarily about the manner in which the subject of origins was presented in Louisiana schools—specifically, about whether scientifically valuable information was being censored and students misled about evolution. . . . It is undoubtedly true that what prompted the legislature to direct its attention to the misrepresentation of evolution in the schools (rather than the inaccurate presentation of other topics) was its awareness of the tension between evolution and the religious beliefs of many children. But even appellees concede that a valid secular purpose is not rendered impermissible simply because its pursuit is prompted by concern for religious sensitivities. . . .

In sum, even if one concedes, for the sake of argument, that a majority of the Louisiana Legislature voted for the Balanced Treatment Act partly in order to foster (rather than merely eliminate discrimination against) Christian fundamentalist beliefs, our cases establish that that alone would not suffice to invalidate the Act, so long as there was a genuine secular purpose as well. We have, moreover, no adequate basis for disbelieving the secular purpose set forth in the Act itself, or for concluding that it is a sham enacted to conceal the legislators' violation of their oaths of office. I am astonished by the Court's unprecedented readiness to reach such a conclusion, which I can only attribute to an intellectual predisposition created by the facts and the legend of Scopes v. State, an instinctive reaction that any governmentally imposed requirements bearing upon the teaching of evolution must be a manifestation of Christian fundamentalist repression. In this case, however, it seems to me the Court's position is the repressive one. The people of Louisiana, including those who are Christian fundamentalists, are quite entitled, as a secular matter, to have whatever scientific evidence there may be against evolution presented in their schools, just as Mr. Scopes was entitled to present whatever scientific evidence there was for it. Perhaps what the Louisiana Legislature has done is unconstitutional because there is no such evidence, and the scheme they have established will amount to no more than a presentation of the Book of Genesis. But we cannot say that on the evidence before us in this summary judgment context, which includes ample uncontradicted testimony that "creation science" is a body of scientific knowledge rather than revealed belief. Infinitely less can we say (or should we say) that the scientific evidence for evolution is so conclusive that no one could be gullible enough to believe that there is any real scientific evidence to the contrary, so that the legislation's stated purpose must be a lie. Yet that illiberal judgment, that Scopes-in-reverse, is ultimately the basis on which the Court's facile rejection of the Louisiana Legislature's purpose must rest.

Because I believe that the Balanced Treatment Act had a secular purpose, which is all the first component of the Lemon test requires, I would reverse the judgment of the Court of Appeals and remand for further consideration.

MEET DON AGUILLARD

Donald Aguillard was one of six children in his family. While growing up, his family lived on a big farm in Louisiana. Aguillard became interested in science education ever since high school. As he explains in an interview with Randy Moore, in the "American Biology Teacher," "I attended a small high school in which one teacher taught all the sciences—biology, chemistry, physics, and geology. Everyone was expected to take all of those courses. From the outset, I was fascinated by the logic and beauty of science, especially the way it built on prior knowledge and was based on big, underlying concepts." Aguillard claims that he always knew that he wanted to be a science teacher. He majored in science education, taking many biology courses in particular. His twin brother also ended up majoring in science education however; he minored in math as well.

Upon graduating from college, Aguillard became a student teacher at Acadiana High School, which is one of five high schools in Lafayette Parish in Scott, Louisiana. [Aguillard's] certification in biology allowed him to teach an honors-biology course. After one of the biology teachers at the high school moved away, Aguillard was granted the position, teaching full-time; five sections of general biology. After the assistant principal observed Aguillard's teaching and noticed that no one understood what he taught, he was assigned instead to teach two sections of honors biology and three sections of general biology the following year.

As a biology teacher at Acadiana high school, evolution proved to be a central part of Aguillard's courses. He used Holt's *Modern Biology,* which presented evolution as an important theme of biology. Evolution was presented as a fundamental tenet of biology, as a logical development of structure and function. Creationism was not taught, nor mentioned at Acadiana High School.

Aguillard became involved in the case because as he alleges, "I knew that creationism didn't belong in science classrooms. I couldn't stand by and do nothing." The ACLU asked Aguillard if he would be willing to be the lead plaintiff in the case. Not knowing exactly what this involved,

Aguillard agreed, with the intent of helping fight against the creationist cause. He never had any second thoughts about getting involved for he knew that it was important. As he explains, "I was very concerned about how this law would affect science teachers, science teaching, and science students. I was not ready to pretend that 'creation science' was legitimate or that evolution didn't matter. I felt an obligation to get involved. It was not acceptable to get on the sidelines and watch this happen."

Aguillard immediately informed his principal and superintendent about his decision to get involved in the case. He found both supportive. They both assured him that he should not worry about losing his job or about being chastised by scientists or science educators. As Aguillard describes, "They both wanted me to do what I believed in. Their support was very reassuring."

While he had the support of many, there were also many who disagreed with Aguillard's involvement in the case. Each time there was a decision made in the case, Aguillard would receive 75 negative letters accusing him of being an atheist and going to hell. All of them were unsigned. He threw out all of the letters. He further received literature and telephone calls from all over the country accusing him of doing the wrong thing. Many also questioned Aguillard's religious beliefs.

Aguillard never thought that the case would make it to the Supreme Court, nor did he know how the judges would rule in the end. As he explains, "My intent was to correct the law in Louisiana. However, the State Attorney General of Louisiana continually challenged the decisions; every time we won a case, he appealed." Aguillard did not attend the momentous day that the Supreme Court decision for *Edwards v. Aguillard* was made. The ACLU immediately contacted him after the decision was announced. Aguillard was quite pleased with the decision.

Several years after the decision. . . , Aguillard began pursuing a doctoral degree in science education at Louisiana State University (LSU). Although he originally intended to do his dissertation on pre-service training, he ended up doing it on evolution and creationism after discovering that the issue "is alive and well among biology teachers." Aguillard moved on to be an assistant principal at Acadiana High School. He then became principal at Carencro High School, in Lafayette, Louisiana, in which he currently serves.

Reflecting back on the case thirteen years later, in his interview in "The American Biology Teacher," Aguillard admits what he believes about the case now. He professes, "The case showed me what a particular special-interest group can do to impact public education. It's not just science educators that must be wary; all educators must be wary. What topics will be pushed because some groups have the ear of a sympathetic legislator?" Aguillard cautions biology teachers, "we must continually be at meetings of textbook adoption committees. We must continually be wary of parents who are members of curriculum-writing teams. We can't turn the curriculum over to the community; if we do, we shouldn't be surprised if they insert their agenda into the curriculum and quality goes down." After all, Aguillard concludes, "If biologists lose this battle, there would be no other battles to fight."

LYNCH V. DONNELLY
465 U.S. 668 (1984)

"In our modern, complex society, whose traditions and constitutional underpinnings rest on and encourage diversity and pluralism in all areas, an absolutist approach in applying the Establishment Clause is simplistic and has been uniformly rejected by the Court."

The Question: Can a city erect a Christmas display in the central business district that includes a nativity scene with figures of Mary, Joseph, and Jesus, along with a Christmas tree, a large candy-striped pole, and a banner that reads, "Seasons Greetings"?

The Arguments: PRO

The Christmas season is a time of good feeling and cheer, along with the religious celebration of the birth of Jesus. A display that reflects the holiday spirit does not violate the Constitution. The secular aspects of the display, including Santa Claus, candy canes, and holiday lights, make it clear that every member of the community is invited to join the festivities of the holiday season. Including a nativity scene is simply an acknowledgment of the fact that this is a special time for Christians. But no one is excluded from enjoying the display, and the religious message is not the central focus of the display. Further, to have a Christmas holiday scene without any part of the display showing the "reason for the season" would be offensive to many people.

CON

No matter how much "Christmas clutter" is placed around the display, the religious message of celebrating the birth of Jesus is unmistakable. By erecting the display in a central location, the city has placed its support behind the sectarian message of the nativity scene. There is no way for the city to dissociate itself from the Christian scene at the center of the display, and no way for members of the public to avoid that message. The fact that Christmas displays are traditional in many cities and towns does not make them constitutional. And by including only a Christian nativity scene, other religions are slighted.

CHIEF JUSTICE BURGER delivered the opinion of the Court.

We granted certiorari to decide whether the Establishment Clause of the First Amendment prohibits a municipality from including a creche, or Nativity scene, in its annual Christmas display.

Each year, in cooperation with the downtown retail merchants' association, the city of Pawtucket, R. I., erects a Christmas display as part of its observance of the Christmas holiday season. The display is situated in a park owned by a nonprofit organization and located in the heart of the shopping district. The display is essentially like those to be found in hundreds of towns or cities across the Nation—often on public grounds—during the Christmas season. The Pawtucket display comprises many of the figures and decorations traditionally associated with Christmas, including, among other things, a Santa Claus house, reindeer pulling Santa's sleigh, candy-striped poles, a Christmas tree, carolers, cutout figures representing such characters as a clown, an elephant, and a teddy bear, hundreds of colored lights, a large banner that reads "SEASONS GREETINGS," and the creche at issue here. All components of this display are owned by the city.

The creche, which has been included in the display for 40 or more years, consists of the traditional figures, including the Infant Jesus, Mary and Joseph, angels, shepherds, kings, and animals, all ranging in height from 5" to 5'. In 1973, when the present creche was acquired, it cost the city $1,365; it now is valued at $200. The erection and dismantling of the creche costs the city about $20 per year; nominal expenses are incurred in lighting the creche. No money has been expended on its maintenance for the past 10 years.

Respondents, Pawtucket residents and individual members of the Rhode Island affiliate of the American Civil Liberties Union, and the affiliate itself, brought this action in the United States District Court for Rhode Island, challenging the city's inclusion of the creche in the annual display. The District Court held that the city's inclusion of the creche in the display violates the Establishment Clause, which is binding on the states through the Fourteenth Amendment. The District Court found that, by including the creche in the Christmas display, the city has "tried to endorse and promulgate religious beliefs," and that "erection of the creche has the real and substantial effect of affiliating the City with the Christian beliefs that the creche represents." A divided panel of the Court of Appeals for the First Circuit affirmed. We granted certiorari, and we reverse. . . .

In every Establishment Clause case, we must reconcile the inescapable tension between the objective of preventing unnecessary intrusion of either the church or the state upon the other, and the reality that, as the Court has so often noted, total separation of the two is not possible. The Court has sometimes described the Religion Clauses as erecting a "wall" between church and state. The concept of a "wall" of separation is a useful figure of speech probably deriving from views of Thomas Jefferson. The metaphor has served as a reminder that the Establishment Clause forbids an established church or anything approaching it. But the metaphor itself is not a wholly accurate description of the practical aspects of the relationship that in fact exists between church and state. . . .

There is an unbroken history of official acknowledgment by all three branches of government of the role of religion in American life from at least 1789. . . . Our history is replete with official references to the value and invocation of Divine guidance in deliberations and pronouncements of the Founding Fathers and contemporary leaders. Beginning in the early colonial period long before Independence, a day of Thanksgiving was celebrated as a religious holiday to give thanks for the bounties of Nature as gifts from God. President Washington and his successors proclaimed Thanksgiving, with all its religious overtones, a day of national celebration and Congress made it a National Holiday more than a century ago. That holiday has not lost its theme of expressing thanks for Divine aid any more than has Christmas lost its religious significance. . . .

This history may help explain why the Court consistently has declined to take a rigid, absolutist view of the Establishment Clause. We have refused "to construe the Religion Clauses with a literalness that would undermine the ultimate constitutional objective as illuminated by history." In our modern, complex society, whose traditions and constitutional underpinnings rest on and encourage diversity and pluralism in all areas, an absolutist approach in applying the Establishment Clause is simplistic and has been uniformly rejected by the Court.

Rather than mechanically invalidating all governmental conduct or statutes that confer benefits or give special recognition to religion in general or to one faith—as an absolutist approach would dictate—the Court has scrutinized challenged legislation or official conduct to determine whether, in reality, it establishes a religion or religious faith, or tends to do so. . . . In each case, the inquiry calls for line-drawing; no fixed, per se rule can be framed. The Establishment Clause like the Due Process Clauses is not a precise, detailed provision in a legal code capable of ready application. The purpose of the Establishment Clause "was to state an objective, not to write a statute." The line between permissible relationships and those barred by the Clause can no more be straight and unwavering than due process can be defined in a single stroke or phrase or test. The Clause erects a "blurred, indistinct, and variable barrier depending on all the circumstances of a particular relationship.". . .

The Court has invalidated legislation or governmental action on the ground that a secular purpose was lacking, but only when it has concluded there was no question that the statute or activity was motivated wholly by religious considerations. . . . The District Court inferred from the religious nature of the creche that the city has no secular purpose for the display. In so doing, it rejected the city's claim that its reasons for including the creche are essentially the same as its reasons for sponsoring the display as a whole. The District Court plainly erred by focusing almost exclusively on the creche. When viewed in the proper context of the Christmas Holiday season, it is apparent that, on this record, there is insufficient evidence to establish that the inclusion of the creche is a purposeful or surreptitious effort to express some kind of subtle governmental advocacy of a particular religious message. In a pluralistic society a variety of motives and purposes are implicated. The city, like the Congresses and Presidents, however, has principally taken note of a significant historical religious event long celebrated in the Western World. The creche in the display depicts the historical origins of this traditional event long recognized as a National Holiday.

The narrow question is whether there is a secular purpose for Pawtucket's display of the creche. The display is sponsored by the city to celebrate the Holiday and to depict the origins of that Holiday. These are legitimate secular purposes. The District Court's inference, drawn from the religious nature of the creche, that the city has no secular purpose was, on this record, clearly erroneous. The District Court found that the primary effect of including the creche is to confer a substantial and impermissible benefit on religion in general and on the Christian faith in particular. Comparisons of the relative benefits to religion of different forms of governmental support are elusive and difficult to make. But to conclude that the primary effect of including the creche is to advance religion in violation of the Establishment Clause would require that we view it as more beneficial to and more an endorsement of religion, for example, than expenditure of large sums of public money for textbooks supplied throughout the country to students attending church-sponsored schools. . . .

The dissent asserts some observers may perceive that the city has aligned itself with the Christian faith by including a Christian symbol in its display and that this serves to advance religion. We can assume, arguendo, that the display advances religion in a sense; but our precedents plainly contemplate that on occasion some advancement of religion will result from governmental action. . . . Here, whatever benefit there is to one faith or religion or to all religions, is indirect, remote, and incidental; display of the creche is no more an advancement or endorsement of religion than the Congressional and Executive recognition of the origins of the Holiday itself as "Christ's Mass," or the exhibition of literally hundreds of religious paintings in governmentally supported museums. . . .

We are satisfied that the city has a secular purpose for including the creche, that the city has not impermissibly advanced religion, and that including the creche does not create excessive entanglement between religion and government. . . . The display engenders a friendly community spirit of goodwill in keeping with the season. The creche may well have special meaning to those whose faith includes the celebration of religious Masses, but none who sense the origins of the Christmas celebration would fail to be aware of its religious implications. That the display brings people into the central city, and serves commercial interests and benefits merchants and their employees, does not, as the dissent points out, determine the character of the display. . . . To forbid the use of this one passive symbol—the creche—at the very time people are taking note of the season with Christmas hymns and carols in public schools and other public places, and while the Congress and legislatures open sessions with prayers by paid chaplains, would be a stilted overreaction contrary to our history and to our holdings. If the presence of the creche in this display violates the Establishment Clause, a host of other forms of taking official note of Christmas, and of our religious heritage, are equally offensive to the Constitution. . . . We hold that, notwithstanding the religious significance of the creche, the city of Pawtucket has not violated the Establishment Clause of the First Amendment. Accordingly, the judgment of the Court of Appeals is reversed.

JUSTICE BRENNAN, with whom JUSTICE MARSHALL, JUSTICE BLACKMUN, and JUSTICE STEVENS join, dissenting.

The Court advances two principal arguments to support its conclusion that the Pawtucket creche satisfies the Lemon test. Neither is persuasive.

First. The Court, by focusing on the holiday "context" in which the nativity scene appeared, seeks to explain away the clear religious import of the creche and the findings of the District Court that most observers understood the creche as both a symbol of Christian beliefs and a symbol of the city's support for those beliefs. . . . The effect of the creche, of course, must be gauged not only by its inherent religious significance but also by the overall setting in which it appears. But it blinks reality to claim, as the Court does, that by including such a distinctively religious object as the creche in its Christmas display, Pawtucket has done no more than make use of a "traditional" symbol of the holiday, and has thereby purged the creche of its religious content and conferred only an "incidental and indirect" benefit on religion.

The Court's struggle to ignore the clear religious effect of the creche seems to me misguided for several reasons. In the first place, the city has positioned the creche in a central and highly visible location within the Hodgson Park display. . . . Moreover, the city has done nothing to disclaim government approval of the religious significance of the creche, to suggest that the creche represents only one religious symbol among many others that might be included in a seasonal display truly aimed at providing a wide catalog of ethnic and religious celebrations, or to disassociate itself from the religious content of the creche. . . . Finally, and most importantly, even in the context of Pawtucket's seasonal celebration, the creche retains a specifically Christian religious meaning. I refuse to accept the notion implicit in today's decision that non-Christians would find that the religious content of the creche is eliminated by the fact that it appears as part of the city's otherwise secular celebration of the Christmas holiday. The nativity scene is clearly distinct in its purpose and effect from the rest of the Hodgson Park display for the simple reason that it is the only one rooted in a biblical account of Christ's birth. It is the chief symbol of the characteristically Christian belief that a divine Savior was brought into the world and that the purpose of this miraculous birth was to illuminate a path toward salvation and redemption. For Christians, that path is exclusive, precious, and holy. But for those who do not share these beliefs, the symbolic reenactment of the birth of a divine being who has been miraculously incarnated as a man stands as a dramatic reminder of their differences with Christian faith. . . . To be so excluded on religious grounds by one's elected government is an insult and an injury that, until today, could not be countenanced by the Establishment Clause.

Second. The Court also attempts to justify the creche by entertaining a beguilingly simple, yet faulty syllogism. The Court begins by noting that government may recognize Christmas Day as a public holiday; the Court then asserts that the creche is nothing more than a traditional element of Christmas celebrations; and it concludes that the inclusion of a creche as part of a government's annual Christmas celebration is constitutionally permissible. The Court apparently believes that once it finds that the designation of Christmas as a public holiday is constitutionally acceptable, it is then free to conclude that virtually every form of governmental association with the celebration of the holiday is also constitutional. The vice of this dangerously superficial argument is that it overlooks the fact that the Christmas holiday in our national culture contains both secular and sectarian elements. To say that government may recognize the holiday's traditional, secular elements of gift-giving, public festivities, and community spirit, does not mean that government may indiscriminately embrace the distinctively sectarian aspects of the holiday. . . .

When government decides to recognize Christmas Day as a public holiday, it does no more than accommodate the calendar of public activities to the plain fact that many Americans will expect on that day to spend time visiting with their families, attending religious services, and perhaps enjoying some respite from preholiday activities. The Free Exercise Clause, of course, does not necessarily compel the government to provide this accommodation, but neither is the Establishment Clause offended by such a step. . . . If public officials go further and participate in the secular celebration of Christmas—by, for example, decorating public places with such secular images as wreaths, garlands, or Santa Claus figures—they move closer to the limits of their constitutional power but nevertheless remain within the boundaries set by the Establishment Clause. But when those officials participate in or appear to endorse the distinctively religious elements of this otherwise secular event, they encroach upon First Amendment freedoms. For it is at that point that the government brings to the forefront the theological content of the holiday, and places the prestige, power, and financial support of a civil authority in the service of a particular faith.

The inclusion of a creche in Pawtucket's otherwise secular celebration of Christmas clearly violates these principles. Unlike such secular figures as Santa Claus, reindeer, and carolers, a nativity scene represents far more than a mere "traditional" symbol of Christmas. The essence of the creche's symbolic purpose and effect is to prompt the observer to experience a sense of simple awe and wonder appropriate to the contemplation of one of the central elements of Christian dogma—that God sent His Son into the world to be a Messiah. Contrary to the Court's suggestion, the creche is far from a mere representation of a "particular historic religious event." It is, instead, best understood as a mystical recreation of an event that lies at the heart of Christian faith. To suggest, as the Court does, that such a symbol is merely "traditional" and therefore no different from Santa's house or reindeer is not only offensive to those for whom the creche has profound significance, but insulting to those who insist for religious or personal reasons that the story of Christ is in no sense a part of "history" nor an unavoidable element of our national "heritage.". . .

The American historical experience concerning the public celebration of Christmas, if carefully examined, provides no support for the Court's decision. The opening sections of the Court's opinion, while seeking to rely on historical evidence, do no more than recognize the obvious: because of the strong religious currents that run through our history, an inflexible or absolutistic enforcement of the Establishment Clause would be both imprudent and impossible. . . . Indeed, the Court's approach suggests a fundamental misapprehension of the proper uses of history in constitutional interpretation. Certainly, our decisions reflect the fact that an awareness of historical practice often can provide a useful guide in interpreting the abstract language of the Establishment Clause. . . . Although invoking these decisions in support of its result, the Court wholly fails to discuss the history of the public celebration of Christmas or the use of publicly displayed nativity scenes. The Court, instead, simply asserts, without any historical analysis or support whatsoever, that the now familiar celebration of Christmas springs from an unbroken history of acknowledgment "by the people, by the Executive Branch, by the Congress, and the courts for 2 centuries. . . ." The Court's complete failure to offer any explanation of its assertion is perhaps understandable, however, because the historical record points in precisely the opposite direction. Two features of this history are worth noting. First, at the time of the adoption of the Constitution and the Bill of Rights, there was no settled pattern of celebrating Christmas, either as a purely religious holiday or as a public event. Second, the historical evidence, such as it is, offers no uniform pattern of widespread acceptance of the holiday and indeed suggests that the development of Christmas as a public holiday is a comparatively recent phenomenon.

The intent of the Framers with respect to the public display of nativity scenes is virtually impossible to discern primarily because the widespread celebration of Christmas did not emerge in its present form until well into the 19th century. Carrying a well-defined Puritan hostility to the celebration of Christ's birth with them to the New World, the founders of the Massachusetts Bay Colony pursued a vigilant policy of opposition to any public celebration of the holiday. To the Puritans, the celebration of Christmas represented a "Popish" practice lacking any foundation in Scripture. This opposition took legal form in 1659 when the Massachusetts Bay Colony made the observance of Christmas Day, "by abstinence from labor, feasting, or any other way," an offense punishable by fine. Although the Colony eventually repealed this ban in 1681, the Puritan objection remained firm.

During the 18th century, sectarian division over the celebration of the holiday continued. As increasing numbers of members of the Anglican and the Dutch and German Reformed Churches arrived, the practice of celebrating Christmas as a purely religious holiday grew. But denominational differences continued to dictate differences in attitude toward the holiday. American Anglicans, who carried with them the Church of England's acceptance of the holiday, Roman Catholics, and various German groups all made the celebration of Christmas a vital part of their religious life. By contrast, many nonconforming Protestant groups, including the Presbyterians, Congregationalists, Baptists, and Methodists, continued to regard the holiday with suspicion and antagonism well into the 19th century. This pattern of sectarian division concerning the holiday suggests that for the Framers of the Establishment Clause, who were acutely sensitive to such sectarian controversies, no single view of how government should approach the celebration of Christmas would be possible. . . .

In sum, there is no evidence whatsoever that the Framers would have expressly approved a federal celebration of the Christmas holiday including public displays of a nativity scene. Nor is there any suggestion that publicly financed and supported displays of Christmas creches are supported by a record of widespread, undeviating acceptance that extends throughout our history. Therefore, our prior decisions which relied upon concrete, specific historical evidence to support a particular practice simply have no bearing on the question presented in this case. Contrary to today's careless decision, those prior cases have all recognized that the "illumination" provided by history must always be focused on the particular practice at issue in a given case. Without that guiding principle and the intellectual discipline it imposes, the Court is at sea, free to select random elements of America's varied history solely to suit the views of five Members of this Court. . . . I dissent.

***

ALLEGHENY COUNTY, PENNSYLVANIA V. GREATER PITTSBURGH AMERICAN CIVIL LIBERTIES UNION
492 U.S. 573 (1989)

"The government may acknowledge Christmas as a cultural phenomenon, but under the First Amendment it may not observe it as a Christian holy day by suggesting that people praise God for the birth of Jesus."

The question: Can a county government, during the Christmas holiday season, allow the display in the county courthouse of a Christian nativity scene, and the display outside the county administration building of a large Jewish menorah, next to a Christmas tree?

The Arguments: PRO

The Supreme Court has upheld the display of Christmas holiday displays that include nativity scenes, as long as the display includes nonsectarian items that are traditional parts of the holiday. Although the nativity display in this case does not include such items as Santa Claus and snowmen, there is a large sign that informs courthouse visitors that the display is owned and was erected by a private group, and that the county does not endorse its religious message. The menorah display also shows that the county is not endorsing one religion over another. Further, public buildings should not be off-limits for displays by private groups, and to prevent religious groups from using public spaces is a form of discrimination.

CON

The Christmas display in this case does not fit within the Supreme Court ruling that allowed such displays, along with nonsectarian items. The Nativity scene in the county courthouse is purely sectarian, and the banner with the words "Gloria in Excelsis Deo" makes the Christian message perfectly clear. Putting up a sign that says the display is owned by a private group cannot overcome the perception by visitors that the county endorses the religious message. Allowing a Jewish group to erect a menorah outside another county building places the county's endorsement behind another religious message. Trying to "balance" the religious scales in this manner only compounds the constitutional violation.

JUSTICE BLACKMUN announced the judgment of the Court.

This litigation concerns the constitutionality of two recurring holiday displays located on public property in downtown Pittsburgh. The first is a creche placed on the Grand Staircase of the Allegheny County Courthouse. The second is a Chanukah menorah placed just outside the City-County Building, next to a Christmas tree and a sign saluting liberty. The Court of Appeals for the Third Circuit ruled that each display violates the Establishment Clause of the First Amendment because each has the impermissible effect of endorsing religion. We agree that the creche display has that unconstitutional effect but reverse the Court of Appeals' judgment regarding the menorah display. . . .

Since 1981, the county has permitted the Holy Name Society, a Roman Catholic group, to display a creche in the county courthouse during the Christmas holiday season. . . . The creche includes figures of the infant Jesus, Mary, Joseph, farm animals, shepherds, and wise men, all placed in or before a wooden representation of a manger, which has at its crest an angel bearing a banner that proclaims "Gloria in Excelsis Deo!". . .

The City-County Building is separate and a block removed from the county courthouse and, as the name implies, is jointly owned by the city of Pittsburgh and Allegheny County. The city's portion of the building houses the city's principal offices, including the mayor's. The city is responsible for the building's Grant Street entrance which has three rounded arches supported by columns. At least since 1982, the city has expanded its Grant Street holiday display to include a symbolic representation of Chanukah, an 8-day Jewish holiday that begins on the 25th day of the Jewish lunar month of Kislev. The 25th of Kislev usually occurs in December, and thus Chanukah is the annual Jewish holiday that falls closest to Christmas Day each year. . . .

This litigation began on December 10, 1986, when respondents, the Greater Pittsburgh Chapter of the American Civil Liberties Union and seven local residents, filed suit against the county and the city, seeking permanently to enjoin the county from displaying the creche in the county courthouse and the city from displaying the menorah in front of the City-County Building. Respondents claim that the displays of the creche and the menorah each violate the Establishment Clause of the First Amendment, made applicable to state governments by the Fourteenth Amendment. . . .

We have had occasion in the past to apply Establishment Clause principles to the government's display of objects with religious significance. In Stone v. Graham, we held that the display of a copy of the Ten Commandments on the walls of public classrooms violates the Establishment Clause. Closer to the facts of this litigation is Lynch v. Donnelly, in which we considered whether the city of Pawtucket, R. I., had violated the Establishment Clause by including a creche in its annual Christmas display, located in a private park within the downtown shopping district. By a 5-to-4 decision in that difficult case, the Court upheld inclusion of the creche in the Pawtucket display, holding, inter alia, that the inclusion of the creche did not have the impermissible effect of advancing or promoting religion.

The rationale of the majority opinion in Lynch is none too clear: the opinion contains two strands, neither of which provides guidance for decision in subsequent cases. First, the opinion states that the inclusion of the creche in the display was "no more an advancement or endorsement of religion" than other "endorsements" this Court has approved in the past, but the opinion offers no discernible measure for distinguishing between permissible and impermissible endorsements. Second, the opinion observes that any benefit the government's display of the creche gave to religion was no more than "indirect, remote, and incidental," without saying how or why. . . .

Since Lynch, the Court has made clear that, when evaluating the effect of government conduct under the Establishment Clause, we must ascertain whether "the challenged governmental action is sufficiently likely to be perceived by adherents of the controlling denominations as an endorsement, and by the nonadherents as a disapproval, of their individual religious choices." Accordingly, our present task is to determine whether the display of the creche and the menorah, in their respective "particular physical settings," has the effect of endorsing or disapproving religious beliefs.

We turn first to the county's creche display. There is no doubt, of course, that the creche itself is capable of communicating a religious message. Indeed, the creche in this lawsuit uses words, as well as the picture of the Nativity scene, to make its religious meaning unmistakably clear. "Glory to God in the Highest!" says the angel in the creche—Glory to God because of the birth of Jesus. This praise to God in Christian terms is indisputably religious—indeed sectarian—just as it is when said in the Gospel or in a church service.

Under the Court's holding in Lynch, the effect of a creche display turns on its setting. Here, unlike in Lynch, nothing in the context of the display detracts from the creche's religious message. The Lynch display comprised a series of figures and objects, each group of which had its own focal point. Santa's house and his reindeer were objects of attention separate from the creche, and had their specific visual story to tell. Similarly, whatever a "talking" wishing well may be, it obviously was a center of attention separate from the creche. Here, in contrast, the creche stands alone: it is the single element of the display on the Grand Staircase. . . .

The fact that the creche bears a sign disclosing its ownership by a Roman Catholic organization does not alter this conclusion. On the contrary, the sign simply demonstrates that the government is endorsing the religious message of that organization, rather than communicating a message of its own. But the Establishment Clause does not limit only the religious content of the government's own communications. It also prohibits the government's support and promotion of religious communications by religious organizations. Indeed, the very concept of "endorsement" conveys the sense of promoting someone else's message. Thus, by prohibiting government endorsement of religion, the Establishment Clause prohibits precisely what occurred here: the government's lending its support to the communication of a religious organization's religious message.

Finally, the county argues that it is sufficient to validate the display of the creche on the Grand Staircase that the display celebrates Christmas, and Christmas is a national holiday. This argument obviously proves too much. It would allow the celebration of the Eucharist inside a courthouse on Christmas Eve. While the county may have doubts about the constitutional status of celebrating the Eucharist inside the courthouse under the government's auspices, this Court does not. The government may acknowledge Christmas as a cultural phenomenon, but under the First Amendment it may not observe it as a Christian holy day by suggesting that people praise God for the birth of Jesus.

In sum, Lynch teaches that government may celebrate Christmas in some manner and form, but not in a way that endorses Christian doctrine. Here, Allegheny County has transgressed this line. It has chosen to celebrate Christmas in a way that has the effect of endorsing a patently Christian message: Glory to God for the birth of Jesus Christ. Under Lynch, and the rest of our cases, nothing more is required to demonstrate a violation of the Establishment Clause. The

display of the creche in this context, therefore, must be permanently enjoined. . . .

The display of the Chanukah menorah in front of the City-County Building may well present a closer constitutional question. The menorah, one must recognize, is a religious symbol: it serves to commemorate the miracle of the oil as described in the Talmud. But the menorah's message is not exclusively religious. The menorah is the primary visual symbol for a holiday that, like Christmas, has both religious and secular dimensions. Moreover, the menorah here stands next to a Christmas tree and a sign saluting liberty. While no challenge has been made here to the display of the tree and the sign, their presence is obviously relevant in determining the effect of the menorah's display. The necessary result of placing a menorah next to a Christmas tree is to create an "overall holiday setting" that represents both Christmas and Chanukah—two holidays, not one.

The mere fact that Pittsburgh displays symbols of both Christmas and Chanukah does not end the constitutional inquiry. If the city celebrates both Christmas and Chanukah as religious holidays, then it violates the Establishment Clause. The simultaneous endorsement of Judaism and Christianity is no less constitutionally infirm than the endorsement of Christianity alone. Conversely, if the city celebrates both Christmas and Chanukah as secular holidays, then its conduct is beyond the reach of the Establishment Clause. Because government may celebrate Christmas as a secular holiday, it follows that government may also acknowledge Chanukah as a secular holiday. Simply put, it would be a form of discrimination against Jews to allow Pittsburgh to celebrate Christmas as a cultural tradition while simultaneously disallowing the city's acknowledgment of Chanukah as a contemporaneous cultural tradition.

Accordingly, the relevant question for Establishment Clause purposes is whether the combined display of the tree, the sign, and the menorah has the effect of endorsing both Christian and Jewish faiths, or rather simply recognizes that both Christmas and Chanukah are part of the same winter-holiday season, which has attained a secular status in our society. Of the two interpretations of this particular display, the latter seems far more plausible and is also in line with Lynch. The Christmas tree, unlike the menorah, is not itself a religious symbol. Although Christmas trees once carried religious connotations, today they typify the secular celebration of Christmas. Numerous Americans place Christmas trees in their homes without subscribing to Christian religious beliefs, and when the city's tree stands alone in front of the City-County Building, it is not considered an endorsement of Christian faith. Indeed, a 40-foot Christmas tree was one of the objects that validated the creche in Lynch. The widely accepted view of the Christmas tree as the preeminent secular symbol of the Christmas holiday season serves to emphasize the secular component of the message communicated by other elements of an accompanying holiday display, including the Chanukah menorah.

The tree, moreover, is clearly the predominant element in the city's display. The 45-foot tree occupies the central position beneath the middle archway in front of the Grant Street entrance to the City-County Building; the 18-foot menorah is positioned to one side. Given this configuration, it is much more sensible to interpret the meaning of the menorah in light of the tree, rather than vice versa. In the shadow of the tree, the menorah is readily understood as simply a recognition that Christmas is not the only traditional way of observing the winter-holiday season. In these circumstances, then, the combination of the tree and the menorah communicates, not a simultaneous endorsement of both the Christian and Jewish faiths, but instead, a secular celebration of Christmas coupled with an acknowledgment of Chanukah as a contemporaneous alternative tradition. . . .

Lynch v. Donnelly confirms, and in no way repudiates, the longstanding constitutional principle that government may not engage in a practice that has the effect of promoting or endorsing religious beliefs. The display of the creche in the county courthouse has this unconstitutional effect. The display of the menorah in front of the City-County Building, however, does not have this effect, given its "particular physical setting."

The judgment of the Court of Appeals is affirmed in part and reversed in part, and the cases are remanded for further proceedings.

JUSTICE BRENNAN, with whom JUSTICE MARSHALL and JUSTICE STEVENS join, concurring in part and dissenting in part.

I have previously explained at some length my views on the relationship between the Establishment Clause and government-sponsored celebrations of the Christmas holiday. See Lynch v. Donnelly. I continue to believe that the display of an object that "retains a specifically Christian [or other] religious meaning," is incompatible with the separation of church and state demanded by our Constitution. I therefore agree with the Court that Allegheny County's display of a creche at the county courthouse signals an endorsement of the Christian faith in violation of the Establishment Clause. . . . I cannot agree, however, that the city's display of a 45-foot Christmas tree and an 18-foot Chanukah menorah at the entrance to the building housing the mayor's office shows no favoritism towards Christianity, Judaism, or both. Indeed, I should have thought that the answer as to the first display supplied the answer to the second.

According to the Court, the creche display sends a message endorsing Christianity because the creche itself bears a religious meaning, because an angel in the display carries a banner declaring "Glory to God in the highest!," and because the floral decorations surrounding the creche highlight it rather than secularize it. The display of a Christmas tree and Chanukah menorah, in contrast, is said to show no endorsement of a particular faith or faiths, or of religion in general, because the Christmas tree is a secular symbol which brings out the secular elements of the menorah. And, Justice Blackmun concludes, even though the menorah has religious aspects, its display reveals no endorsement of religion because no other symbol could have been used to represent the secular aspects of the holiday of Chanukah without mocking its celebration. Rather than endorsing religion, therefore, the display merely demonstrates that "Christmas is not the only traditional way of observing the winter-holiday season," and confirms our "cultural diversity."

Thus, the decision as to the menorah rests on three premises: the Christmas tree is a secular symbol; Chanukah is a holiday with secular dimensions, symbolized by the menorah; and the government may promote pluralism by sponsoring or condoning displays having strong religious associations on its property. None of these is sound. . . . Positioned as it was, the Christmas tree's religious significance was bound to come to the fore. Situated next to the menorah—which, Justice Blackmun acknowledges, is "a symbol with religious meaning," and indeed, is "the central religious symbol and ritual object of" Chanukah—the Christmas tree's religious dimension could not be overlooked by observers of the display. Even though the tree alone may be deemed predominantly secular, it can hardly be so characterized when placed next to such a forthrightly religious symbol. Consider a poster featuring a star of David, a statute of Buddha, a Christmas tree, a mosque, and a drawing of Krishna. There can be no doubt that, when found in such company, the tree serves as an unabashedly religious symbol.

The second premise on which today's decision rests is the notion that Chanukah is a partly secular holiday, for which the menorah can serve as a secular symbol. It is no surprise and no anomaly that Chanukah has historical and societal roots that range beyond the purely religious. I would venture that most, if not all, major religious holidays have beginnings and enjoy histories studded with figures, events, and practices that are not strictly religious. It does not seem to me that the mere fact that Chanukah shares this kind of background makes it a secular holiday in any meaningful sense. The menorah is indisputably a religious symbol, used ritually in a celebration that has deep religious significance. That, in my view, is all that need be said. Whatever secular practices the holiday of Chanukah has taken on in its contemporary observance are beside the point. . . . Justice Blackmun, in his acceptance of the city's message of "diversity," appear[s] to believe that, where seasonal displays are concerned, more is better. Whereas a display might be constitutionally problematic if it showcased the holiday of just one religion, those problems vaporize as soon as more than one religion is included. I know of no principle under the Establishment Clause, however, that permits us to conclude that governmental promotion of religion is acceptable so long as one religion is not favored. We have, on the contrary, interpreted that Clause to require neutrality, not just among religions, but between religion and nonreligion. . . . To lump the ritual objects and holidays of religions together without regard to their attitudes toward such inclusiveness, or to decide which religions should be excluded because of the possibility of offense, is not a benign or beneficent celebration of pluralism: it is instead an interference in religious matters precluded by the Establishment Clause.

The government-sponsored display of the menorah alongside a Christmas tree also works a distortion of the Jewish religious calendar. As Justice Blackmun acknowledges, "the proximity of Christmas [may] accoun[t] for the social prominence of Chanukah in this country." It is the proximity of Christmas that undoubtedly accounts for the city's decision to participate in the celebration of Chanukah, rather than the far more significant Jewish holidays of Rosh Hashanah and Yom Kippur. . . . Thus, the city's erection alongside the Christmas tree of the symbol of a relatively minor Jewish religious holiday, far from conveying "the city's secular recognition of different traditions for celebrating the winter-holiday season," has the effect of promoting a Christianized version of Judaism. The holiday calendar they appear willing to accept revolves exclusively around a Christian holiday. . . . And those religions that have no holiday at all during the period between Thanksgiving and New Year's Day will not benefit, even in a second-class manner, from the city's once-a-year tribute to "liberty" and "freedom of belief." This is not "pluralism" as I understand it.

JUSTICE KENNEDY, with whom the Chief Justice, JUSTICE WHITE, and JUSTICE SCALIA join, concurring in the judgment in part and dissenting in part.

The majority holds that the County of Allegheny violated the Establishment Clause by displaying a creche in the county courthouse, because the "principal or primary effect" of the display is to advance religion within the meaning of Lemon v. Kurtzman. This view of the Establishment Clause reflects an unjustified hostility toward religion, a hostility inconsistent with our history and our precedents, and I dissent from this holding. The creche display is constitutional, and, for the same reasons, the display of a menorah by the city of Pittsburgh is permissible as well. On this latter point, I concur in the result, but not the reasoning, of Justice Blackmun's opinion. . . .

Rather than requiring government to avoid any action that acknowledges or aids religion, the Establishment Clause permits government some latitude in recognizing and accommodating the central role religion plays in our society. Any approach less sensitive to our heritage would border on latent hostility toward religion, as it would require government in all its multifaceted roles to acknowledge only the secular, to the exclusion and so to the detriment of the religious. A categorical approach would install federal courts as jealous guardians of an absolute "wall of separation," sending a clear message of disapproval. In this century, as the modern administrative state expands to touch the lives of its citizens in such diverse ways and redirects their financial choices through programs of its own, it is difficult to maintain the fiction that requiring government to avoid all assistance to religion can in fairness be viewed as serving the goal of neutrality. . . .

The ability of the organized community to recognize and accommodate religion in a society with a pervasive public sector requires diligent observance of the border between accommodation and establishment. Our cases disclose two limiting principles: government may not coerce anyone to support or participate in any religion or its exercise; and it may not, in the guise of avoiding hostility or callous indifference, give direct benefits to religion in such a degree that it in fact "establishes a [state] religion or religious faith, or tends to do so. "Lynch v. Donnelly. These two principles, while distinct, are not unrelated, for it would be difficult indeed to establish a religion without some measure of more or less subtle coercion, be it in the form of taxation to supply the substantial benefits that would sustain a state-established faith, direct compulsion to observance, or governmental exhortation to religiosity that amounts in fact to proselytizing.

It is no surprise that without exception we have invalidated actions that further the interests of religion through the coercive power of government. . . . The freedom to worship as one pleases without government interference or oppression is the great object of both the Establishment and the Free Exercise Clauses. Barring all attempts to aid religion through government coercion goes far toward attainment of this object. . . . Absent coercion, the risk of infringement of religious liberty by passive or symbolic accommodation is minimal. Our cases reflect this reality by requiring a showing that the symbolic recognition or accommodation advances religion to such a degree that it actually "establishes a religion or religious faith, or tends to do so.". . .

These principles are not difficult to apply to the facts of the cases before us. In permitting the displays on government property of the menorah and the creche, the city and county sought to do no more than "celebrate the season," and to acknowledge, along with many of their citizens, the historical background and the religious, as well as secular, nature of the Chanukah and Christmas holidays. This interest falls well within the tradition of government accommodation and acknowledgment of religion that has marked our history from the beginning. It cannot be disputed that government, if it chooses, may participate in sharing with its citizens the joy of the holiday season, by declaring public holidays, installing or permitting festive displays, sponsoring celebrations and parades, and providing holiday vacations for its employees. All levels of our government do precisely that. As we said in Lynch, "Government has long recognized—indeed it has subsidized—holidays with religious significance."

If government is to participate in its citizens' celebration of a holiday that contains both a secular and a religious component, enforced recognition of only the secular aspect would signify the callous indifference toward religious faith that our cases and traditions do not require; for by commemorating the holiday only as it is celebrated by nonadherents, the government would be refusing to acknowledge the plain fact, and the historical reality, that many of its citizens celebrate its religious aspects as well. Judicial invalidation of government's attempts to recognize the religious underpinnings of the holiday would signal not neutrality but a pervasive intent to insulate government from all things religious. The Religion Clauses do not require government to acknowledge these holidays or their religious component; but our strong tradition of government accommodation and acknowledgment permits government to do so.

There is no suggestion here that the government's power to coerce has been used to further the interests of Christianity or Judaism in any way. No one was compelled to observe or participate in any religious ceremony or activity. Neither the city nor the county contributed significant amounts of tax money to serve the cause of one religious faith. The creche and the menorah are purely passive symbols of religious holidays. Passersby who disagree with the message conveyed by these displays are free to ignore them, or even to turn their backs, just as they are free to do when they disagree with any other form of government speech. . . .

If Lynch is still good law—and until today it was—the judgment below cannot stand. I accept and indeed approve both the holding and the reasoning of Chief Justice Burger's opinion in Lynch, and so I must dissent from the judgment that the creche display is unconstitutional. On the same reasoning, I agree that the menorah display is constitutional.

CHAPTER 4

"The Free Exercise of Religion"

INTRODUCTION

The Supreme Court's recurring effort to deal with cases that involve religion has confronted the justices with the difficult task of balancing the commands of two separate clauses of the First Amendment, the first barring the government from supporting an "establishment of religion" and the second prohibiting it from interfering with the "free exercise" of religion. The line between these two clauses is not always easy to discern and apply. For example, if local school districts bar the use of their facilities for religious activities that include prayer, in order to comply with the Establishment Clause, do they violate the Free Exercise Clause if they prohibit students from gathering around a flagpole on school grounds to pray? The answers to this and other questions most often turn on a fact-specific inquiry into the circumstances of the situation. If the students gather around the flagpole during a scheduled school activity, whether it be lunchtime or a period devoted to library use, the prayer might be seen as violating the Establishment Clause if a teacher or administrator is supervising that activity. On the other hand, if students are free to use that time without official supervision, the prayer might be viewed as protected by the Free Exercise Clause. Examples of this potential conflict between the two clauses, both real and hypothetical, are easy to find or imagine.

Chief Justice William Rehnquist, writing in 1993 for a unanimous Supreme Court in one of the cases in this chapter, *Church of Lukumi Babalu Aye v. City of Hialeah, Florida,* noted that most Establishment Clause cases "have addressed governmental efforts to benefit religion or particular religions," while most Free Exercise Clause cases raise challenges by members of religious minorities to legislative attempts "to disfavor their religion because of the religious ceremonies it commands." This distinction between the two classes of religion cases generally holds true, although exceptions to this general rule have come before the Court in several important cases.

The eight cases in this chapter have been selected from more than two hundred cases decided by the Supreme Court under the Free Exercise Clause, chosen because they raise important constitutional issues and have resulted in major doctrinal statements by the Court. These eight cases also present a wide variety of factual situations that illustrate the remarkable diversity of religious beliefs and practices in American society, stemming in almost every case from the interpretation by members of a religious group of a sacred book or scripture that includes commands to believers in its teaching that they perform (or refrain from performing) some act. Virtually every religion requires of its members that they conform their behavior, in some aspect of their devotional exercises or daily life, to the injunctions of the scriptures or teachings of their leaders in which they believe.

Some of the actions, or behavior, of religious believers are part of religious services. Many of these actions, such as drinking wine as part of a communion service, are engaged in by millions of worshipers in Roman Catholic and other Christian denominations. Others, such as the ritual slaughter of animals such as chickens and goats during religious services, are performed by members of much smaller groups such as the adherents of the Santaria religion. And a few, including the handling of poisonous snakes, are part of the services of scattered groups of Pentecostal religions. Generally, the smaller and more esoteric the religious group, the more likely practices such as these are to fall under some legislative ban. Claims that religious practices such as ritual animal slaughter and snake handling are protected under the Free Exercise Clause are often met with arguments based on the "police powers" of government to protect the public health and safety.

Other religious actions or behaviors stem from beliefs about the commands of scripture or the teachings of religious leaders about how to live one's life in a "holy" way. Many religions prescribe or proscribe certain foods, such as the bans on eating pork for Muslims and Jews. Others relate to dress and bodily appearance, such as the wearing of yarmulkes by Jews, turbans by Sikhs, or keeping hair in "dreadlocks" by Rastafarians. Mormons wear "temple garments" under their outer clothing, the Old Order Amish use hooks rather than buttons or zippers on their clothing, and some Hindus have "caste marks" on their foreheads. Whether visible or not, such divergent practices in apparel and appearance often subject those who follow their religion's commands to ridicule and rudeness. And legislative bans on some of these practices have reached the courts through challenges based on the Free Exercise Clause. Would a public school, for example, violate the First Amendment rights of teachers who wore yarmulkes or kept their hair in dreadlocks? If schools did allow these practices, might they be challenged as violating the Establishment Clause by "endorsing" the religious precepts of their teachers? Questions such as these illustrate the difficult constitutional issues raised by the adherents of the many, and highly diverse, religions in American society.

The Supreme Court first confronted the meaning and reach of the Free Exercise Clause in 1878, in a case that challenged a federal law that made polygamy, or plural marriage, a criminal offense. This case, *Reynolds v. United States,* came from the state of Utah, first settled as a territory by members of the Church of Jesus Christ of Latter-day Saints, more commonly known as Mormons. Members of this church, which began in New York under the leadership of Joseph Smith, had been literally driven across the country by hostility and violence from those who feared or detested its teachings, which included a command that male members of the church, if able, should have more than one wife. After the Mormons were attacked by mobs in Illinois and Missouri, and their founder murdered, they found refuge in Utah, where they prospered and formed the great majority of the territorial population. However, hostility to polygamy by opponents of Mormonism led Congress to place federal criminal penalties on the practice of plural marriage and impose this ban as a condition of statehood for Utah. A Mormon named George Reynolds, who had two wives, offered himself as a "test case" for a challenge to the federal law and was convicted in the territorial court, although the U.S. attorney had great trouble finding a jury that did not include polygamists.

The Supreme Court upheld the conviction of George Reynolds, basing its opinion on claims that polygamy was "odious among the northern and western nations of Europe" and had been, until the Mormon church was founded, "almost exclusively a feature of the life of Asiatic and African people." This claim, in fact, constituted the sole basis of the Court's opinion in the case, despite the fact that neither of Reynolds' wives had raised any objection to their shared marriage with him. The more important aspect of the Court's decision, one that has remained at the core of the Court's decisions in later Free Exercise cases, is the so-called "belief/action" distinction. "Laws are made for the government of actions," the Court ruled, "and while they cannot interfere with mere religious belief and opinions, they may with practices." As examples, the Court listed a "parade of horribles" that included human sacrifice as a religious practice. However, did this argument of extremes, highly unlikely to exist in American society or to seek protection under the Free Exercise Clause, provide a reasonable basis for upholding the law against polygamy, absent any evidence of harm to those who willingly engaged in this practice commanded by their religion?

This chapter begins with the *Reynolds* case, not only because of its lasting doctrinal significance but also because it raises the central question under the Free Exercise Clause. To what extent should religious practices, or refusals to participate in behavior commanded by law (such as compulsory flag salutes in public schools), be tolerated by those who do not share the beliefs of those who engage in such practices or refuse to conform their behavior to the laws enacted by the majority? Secondly, how are judges to decide what forms of behavior motivated by religious belief constitute such a demonstrable harm to individuals or society that they can be regulated or punished without damaging the command of the Free Exercise Clause?

The cases that follow the *Reynolds* decision in this chapter illustrate the widely divergent answers the Supreme Court has given to these questions, demonstrating that religious belief and practice in American society remain sources of political, cultural, and legal conflict. All of the succeeding cases were decided after the Court "incorporated" the First Amendment, and the Free Exercise Clause, into the Fourteenth Amendment's protection of "liberty" against deprivation by the states. All but one, the case of *Goldman v. Weinberger,* involve challenges to local or state laws or regulations that "disfavored" the members of religious minorities; the *Goldman* case stemmed from a regulation of the U.S. Air Force that banned the wearing of any head covering indoors, provoking a challenge by an Air Force officer who was an Orthodox Jew and felt compelled to wear his yarmulke at all times. Two of these cases, *Minersville School District of Pennsylvania v. Gobitis* and *West Virginia Board of Education v. Barnette,* involved children in public schools who belonged to the Jehovah's Witness denomination and who refused on religious grounds to salute the American flag at the beginning of the school day. The conflicting opinions of Justices Felix Frankfurter and Harlan Fiske Stone in the *Gobitis* case, and the even more divergent opinions of Frankfurter and Justice Robert Jackson, who wrote the majority opinion in 1943 that overturned the *Gobitis* ruling, issued just three years earlier, offer perhaps the sharpest contrast between the position of "judicial restraint" and deference to legislative judgment on one hand and that of finding a "preferred place" in the Constitution for First Amendment protections of religious and other minorities on the other. The sharp judicial debates in these pairs of opinions illustrate the difficulty of what Frankfurter aptly called the Court's obligation in such cases to "reconcile the conflicting claims of liberty and authority." The Court faced that obligation, in fact, in each of the cases included in this chapter, all of which involve the members of religious minorities.

The difficulties confronting the Court in meeting its judicial obligation to reconcile claims of liberty and authority have led to some rulings that are themselves difficult to reconcile. For example, in the case of *Wisconsin v. Yoder,* the Court upheld a challenge by members of the Old Order Amish to a state law requiring children to attend school until the age of sixteen. This law had "general application" to all children, and imposed criminal penalties on parents who did not comply. In contrast, the Court rejected in *Employment Division of Oregon v. Smith* a challenge by members of the Native American Church who were dismissed from their jobs and denied unemployment benefits for using peyote in religious services, another law of "general application" that imposed criminal penalties for using that hallucinogenic drug for any purpose. In the *Yoder* case, members of the Old Order Amish received an exemption from the state law, while members of the Native American Church were denied such an exemption in the *Smith* case. Arguments that laws designed to punish the use of a drug such as peyote serve a more "legitimate" governmental purpose than laws designed to ensure that children receive an adequate education

seem to many scholars (and members of the public as well) to fall short of plausibility. But the Supreme Court majority in the *Smith* case, in an opinion written by Justice Antonin Scalia, simply brushed aside the *Yoder* ruling as irrelevant. In fact, many legal scholars feel that Justice Scalia completely mischaracterized the *Yoder* decision in his *Smith* opinion, saying that it "involved not the Free Exercise Clause alone, but the Free Exercise Clause in conjunction with other constitutional protections, such as freedom of speech and of the press," a claim that finds no basis in the *Yoder* case.

The point of this discussion of the *Yoder* and *Smith* decisions is not to cast aspersions on Justice Scalia, however unsound his reading of precedent, but to underscore the difficult task the Court faces in reconciling the conflicting claims of liberty and authority in Free Exercise cases. Along with cases that raise issues of racial discrimination and the right to abortions, no other issues that have come before the Court in the past two centuries have put the Constitution to such a test.

REYNOLDS V. UNITED STATES
98 U.S. 145 (1878)

"Laws are made for the government of actions, and while they cannot interfere with mere religious belief and opinions, they may with practices. . . . Can a man excuse his practices to the contrary [of the law] because of his religious belief? To permit this would be to make the professed doctrines of religious belief superior to the law of the land and in effect to permit every citizen to become a law unto himself."

The Question: Can Congress pass a law making polygamy a federal crime and enforce such a law against members of the Mormon church who hold a sincere religious belief that polygamy is required of male church members who are able to support more than one wife?

The Arguments: PRO

Being married to more than one person has been a crime under common-law rules that go back hundreds of years. Laws against polygamy are based on the doctrines of the Christian religion and are also supported by many non-Christian religions. The fact that polygamy is required by the doctrines of any religious denomination does not give its members a special exemption from a law that is designed to protect the monogamous family and that members of all other religious groups must obey. Allowing an exemption for this practice would also open the door for claims that practices such as adultery, drug use, and homosexuality are required by sincere religious belief.

CON

Laws against polygamy are based on the beliefs of orthodox Christianity and were passed solely to punish the members of one unorthodox religious denomination, the Mormons. There is no evidence in this case that either of the two women who married the Mormon husband were coerced into plural marriage or suffered in any way from it. Consenting adults should be free to choose their own marriage partners, subject only to laws that protect children from early marriage and that prevent coercion. Marriage itself is not a criminal act, and the number of spouses any person has should not be subject to criminal penalties.

COMMENTARY: POLYGAMY AND THE MORMON CHURCH

The following excerpt, from *Isn't One Wife Enough?* by the Mormon historian Kimball Young, chronicles the church's painful and reluctant decision to repudiate its doctrine and practice of polygamy in the face of forceful pressure from Congress and opponents of the church. The Manifesto announcing the changes the church adopted in 1890 was a product more of fear of renewed prosecutions than of a true change of heart and mind by church members and leaders.

It should be noted that polygamy did not disappear after the Manifesto took effect; many Mormons simply ignored it, and many suffered excommunication as a result. Experts have estimated that at least 50,000 members of breakaway Mormon groups, who call themselves "fundamentalist" Mormons, live today in polygamous families, many in southern Utah and northern Arizona. Most of those who have chosen to live in "plural marriages" do so quietly, some openly and others secretly, and are not bothered by local officials, many of them polygamists themselves. Others live in and around cities such as Salt Lake City, known to neighbors but keeping a low profile. There have been recent prosecutions of polygamists in Utah; one man with five wives and more than a dozen children was convicted and sentenced in 2001 to a five-year prison term, the result of a crackdown by Utah officials who have targeted vocal advocates of polygamy for prosecution.

Legal challenges to laws against polygamy have little chance of success, but some constitutional scholars have argued that polygamous relationships deserve protection under the Free Exercise and Equal Protection clauses of the Constitution. The current legal and political debate over same-sex marriages, which are now recognized as "civil unions" with all the benefits of marriage by the state of Vermont, may presage a change over time in public acceptance of polygamy as a legitimate form of marriage. However, those who defend traditional marriage, limited to couples of opposite genders, form a majority of the public and most likely would oppose proposals to give legal status to polygamy with the same fervor they have displayed in lobbying against proposals in other states to legitimize same-sex marriages.

"Isn't One Wife Enough?"

The years from 1870 to the Manifesto in 1890 were marked by an intensification of the conflict between the Mormons and the Gentiles. What had started out as a local and somewhat tangential issue had become a central problem for the entire American public. Millions of words were poured out in public discussion. Strong emotions were evoked by the federal judges as well as by the reformers who wished to get rid of the cancer of polygamy. This whole period provides an excellent illustration of the interplay of public sentiment and judicial action. Moreover, among the Mormons there is evidence of a gradual decline of enthusiasm for the Principle and a good deal of readiness to compromise so that they might obtain certain other benefits, especially that of statehood.

The first definite legislation against polygamy, the Morrill Act of 1862, had not been effective. While the bill was directed against the practice of polygamy, it had been so framed as not to interfere with the dictates of conscience. Nevertheless, the bill was viewed by the Mormons as put by the *Deseret News,* April 26, 1866, as a means of getting them to deny their "faith" and in particular as a method of "bastardizing our children" and "making shipwreck of our salvation for disobeying an unconstitutional stretch of the law-making department."

The first serious attempt to put teeth into the anti-polygamy laws came during the administration of President U. S. Grant. Various proposals were advanced to disfranchise the Mormons, disincorporate the Church, and take away its property.

In his message to Congress in December, 1871, President Grant stated among other things:

> In Utah there still remains a remnant of barbarism, repugnant to civilization, decency, and to the law of the United States. . . . Neither polygamy nor any other violation of existing statutes will be permitted in the territory of the United States. It is not with the religion of self-styled saints that we are now dealing, but their practices. They will be protected in the worship of God according to the dictates of their consciences, but they will not be permitted to violate laws under the cloak of religion. . . .

One of the basic difficulties with the administration of justice in Utah, particularly in reference to polygamy, arose from the fact that there was really a dual set of courts: (a) probate courts which also had civil and criminal jurisdictions at the local levels; these courts were with few exceptions manned by Mormons. (b) In addition there were the federal district courts—three in number—and the territorial supreme court. The three federal judges, appointed from Washington, were without exception Gentiles. These men served as the supreme court, consisting of a chief justice and two associate justices.

The re-election of Grant in 1872 was viewed by the Gentile forces as indicative of more severe measures to come. In his annual message to Congress, December 1, 1873, he requested legislation for Utah which would modify the system of obtaining jurors and sharply limit the power of the probate courts. Most of Grant's recommendations were embodied in a bill by Representative Luke P. Poland of Vermont introduced on January 5, 1874, and finally passed in the early summer of that year.

The "Poland law," as it was called, took from the probate courts in Utah all civil, chancery, and criminal jurisdictions. These were now allotted to the district and supreme courts of the territory. It provided further that when a woman filed a bill to declare void a marriage because of a previous marriage, the court could grant alimony. Furthermore, in any prosecution for adultery, bigamy, or polygamy, a juror could be challenged for belief in, or practice of, plural marriage. In short, this law removed the power of the Mormon Church to control the territorial courts. The probate courts had only to do with matters of inheritance and guardianship.

The *Salt Lake Tribune* for June 24, 1874, was happy over the passage of the Poland Bill and its headline screamed out in such phrases as: "Polygamy and murder no longer justified"; "Human slavery abolished forever and priesthood rule killed"; and "The last rites of barbarism extirpated from the earth."

The official church view, as expressed in the *Deseret News* was that the law "takes from the people and their legislative representatives powers and rights enjoyed by them for a quarter of a century . . . a thing entirely foreign to constitutional and republican principles."

Then, as later, the Mormons argued that polygamy was not the basic issue in the attack but a camouflage under which the Gentiles would destroy their Church. In truth, this view was freely admitted by some non-Mormons who continually harped on the stranglehold, both economically and politically, of the Mormon Church.

Although the Saints made every effort to preserve their civil rights, the campaign was on. On October 2, 1871, Brigham Young, along with George Q. Cannon and others, was arrested for lascivious cohabitation under the law of 1852. This act had been drawn against adultery by the Mormons themselves and was never intended to apply to plural marriages. Young was released on $5,000.00 bail and allowed to stay in his own home under guard.

On October 9, 1871, the case was called before Judge McKean. The defense first raised the question as to the legal competence of the Grand Jury to indict but this motion was denied by the judge. McKean then went on to indicate clearly his emotional involvement in this whole matter. He rendered an opinion from the bench in which he said, among other things, ". . . while the case at bar is called 'The people versus Brigham Young,' its other and real title is, 'Federal authority versus polygamic theocracy.' . . . A system is on trial in the person of Brigham Young."

Young went to court and pled not guilty. In the courtroom he was so dignified that he impressed everybody. Even Judge McKean, who on other occasions had been quick to snap and cackle at the Mormons, refrained from his usual tirades.

The Eastern press continued to be supplied with inflammatory messages charging the Mormons with outright treason. However, some of the Gentile press by no means approved the conduct of the federal courts in these cases. For example, the *Montana Herald* in October, 1871, commented editorially, "The conduct of Judge McKean does not look to us like that of a democratic judge in a free country, but more like that of Judge Jeffreys in the most gloomy and despotic era of English history."

That Judge McKean viewed himself as a crusader against Mormonism is neatly illustrated in his charge to the grand and petit juries on one occasion. He said: "I apologize to nobody for being here. . . . I know . . . that the day is not far in the future, when the disloyal high priesthood of the so-called 'Church of Jesus Christ of Latter-day Saints,' shall bow to and obey the laws that are elsewhere respected, or else those laws will grind them into powder."

Finally, there was an unofficial and informal agreement between the federal officials and the leaders of the Church to produce a test case. The man chosen for this trial was George Reynolds, then secretary to Brigham Young. Reynolds had but recently taken a second wife. He was found guilty and given a fine of $500.00 and sentenced to two years in the penitentiary.

The territorial supreme court upheld the action of the lower court and two and a half years later on January 6, 1876, the United States Supreme Court concurred in the action of the lower court and declared the law of 1862 to be constitutional.

The significance of the Reynolds case cannot be overlooked. While Reynolds served out his full time, the whole episode represented a definite shift in judicial action. It was a precedent for the convictions that followed. Moreover, it foreshadowed the increasing hostility of the government toward the Mormons. It was a sanction of the Gentile crusade and certainly facilitated the passage of more proscriptive legislation regarding polygamy.

All during this time the Mormon forces were defending their course in terms of freedom of conscience and the divinity of polygamy as witnessed by Joseph Smith's revelation and by the Old Testament practices of the same. But there was a growing view of both judges and federal legislators that plural marriage could not be defended or excused in terms of any "constitutional guarantee of religious freedom," as Justice Waite put it in the opinion of the Supreme Court which upheld the Morrill Act. And, in his message to Congress in December, 1880, President Hayes remarked: "It is the duty and purpose of the people of the United States, to suppress polygamy where it now exists in one territory and prevent its extension. . . ." In the year following President Arthur asked for strong legislation to abolish "this odious crime.". . .

At the same time among the rank and file of the Mormons, the notion was growing up that the practice of polygamy was more a matter of permissiveness than of outright obligation. The severe prosecutions had begun to pay dividends in weakening the Saints' faith in the Principle.

While the official Church had persisted in saying that it would not capitulate to non-Mormon pressure against polygamy, it is clear that both the general authorities and the bulk of Mormons realized more and more that the system could not continue without some compromise. . . .

All during the 1880's whenever the matter of statehood was proposed, the Gentile forces were quick to argue that although various proposed constitutions contained articles to suppress polygamy such proposals were mere subterfuges.

In midsummer of 1887, the *Salt Lake Tribune* approvingly quoted the *New York Times*: "Utah should not be admitted to the Union until the Mormon Church formally renounces the doctrine of polygamy and the people have abandoned the practice for a period sufficient to guarantee that both the doctrine and practice had been absolutely given up.". . .

Bound up in this whole desire for statehood was the fundamental loyalty of the Mormons to their country. While they viewed the prosecutions for polygamy as downright persecution nevertheless they suffered a considerable sense of guilt and shame at breaking the law.

There is some evidence that the Mormon lobby made promises to leading members of both parties in Washington that the Church would do something specific and official about polygamy if they could get ahead with their program for statehood. At home their leaders were giving ever more serious thought to develop some formula which would save face as far as polygamy was concerned and at the same time facilitate the steps toward statehood.

On September 24, 1890, Wilford Woodruff, President of the Mormon Church, issued what has been termed the "Manifesto."

In as much as laws have been enacted by Congress forbidding plural marriages, which laws have been pronounced constitutional by the court of last resource, I hereby declare my intention to submit to those laws and to use my influence with the members of the Church over which I preside to have them do likewise. . . .

There is nothing in my teachings to the Church or in those of my associates, during the time specified, which can be reasonably construed to inculcate or encourage polygamy; and when any Elder of the Church has used language which appeared to convey any such teaching, he has been promptly reproved. And I now publicly declare that my advice to the Latter-day Saints is to refrain from contracting any marriage forbidden by the law of the land.

This Manifesto was the product not of Woodruff alone but of the First Presidency and the Apostles as well. At the general conference of the Church on October 6, 1890, Lorenzo Snow, one of the Twelve Apostles, presented a motion to sustain and approve the Manifesto and this was done unanimously by those assembled (Young, 1954).

MR. CHIEF JUSTICE WAITE delivered the opinion of the court.

This is an indictment found in the District Court for the third judicial district of the Territory of Utah, charging George Reynolds with bigamy, in violation of Section 5352 of the Revised Statutes, which, omitting its exceptions, is as follows:

Every person having a husband or wife living, who marries another, whether married or single, in a Territory, or other place over which the United States have exclusive jurisdiction, is guilty of bigamy, and shall be punished by a fine of not more than $500, and by imprisonment for a term of not more than five years.

On the trial, the plaintiff in error, the accused, proved that at the time of his alleged second marriage he was, and for many years before had been, a member of the Church of Jesus Christ of Latter-Day Saints, commonly called the Mormon Church, and a believer in its doctrines; that it was an accepted doctrine of that church "that it was the duty of male members of said church, circumstances permitting, to practice polygamy; . . . that this duty was enjoined by different books which the members of said church believed to be of divine origin, and among others the Holy Bible, and also that the members of the church believed that the practice of polygamy was directly enjoined upon the male members thereof by the Almighty God, in a revelation to Joseph Smith, the founder and prophet of said church; that the failing or refusing to practice polygamy by such male members of said church, when circumstances would admit, would be punished, and that the penalty for such failure and refusal would be damnation in the life to come." He also proved "that he had received permission from the recognized authorities in said church to enter into polygamous marriage; . . . that Daniel H. Wells, one having authority in said church to perform the marriage ceremony, married the said defendant on or about the time the crime is alleged to have been committed, to some woman by the name of Schofield, and that such marriage ceremony was performed under and pursuant to the doctrines of said church."

Upon this proof he asked the court to instruct the jury that if they found from the evidence that he "was married as charged—if he was married—in pursuance of and in conformity with what he believed at the time to be a religious duty, that the verdict must be 'not guilty.'" This request was refused, and the court did charge "that there must have been a criminal intent, but that if the defendant, under the influence of a religious belief that it was right—under an inspiration, if you please, that it was right—deliberately married a second time, having a first wife living, the want of consciousness of evil intent—the want of understanding on his part that he was committing a crime—did not excuse him; but the law inexorably in such case implies the criminal intent."

Upon this charge and refusal to charge the question is raised, whether religious belief can be accepted as a justification of an overt act made criminal by the law of the land. The inquiry is not as to the power of Congress to prescribe criminal laws for the Territories, but as to the guilt of one who knowingly violates a law which has been properly enacted, if he entertains a religious belief that the law is wrong.

Congress cannot pass a law for the government of the Territories which shall prohibit the free exercise of religion. The first amendment to the Constitution expressly forbids such legislation. Religious freedom is guaranteed everywhere throughout the United States, so far as congressional interference is concerned. The question to be determined is, whether the law now under consideration comes within this prohibition.

The word "religion" is not defined in the Constitution. We must go elsewhere, therefore, to ascertain its meaning, and nowhere more appropriately, we think, than to the history of the times in the midst of which the provision was adopted. The precise point of the inquiry is, what is the religious freedom which has been guaranteed.

Before the adoption of the Constitution, attempts were made in some of the colonies and States to legislate not only in respect to the establishment of religion, but in respect to its doctrines and precepts as well. The people were taxed, against their will, for the support of religion, and sometimes for the support of particular sects to whose tenets they could not and did not subscribe. Punishments were prescribed for a failure to attend upon public worship, and sometimes for entertaining heretical opinions. The controversy upon this general subject was animated in many of the States, but seemed at last to culminate in Virginia. In 1784, the House of Delegates of that State having under consideration "a bill establishing provision for teachers of the Christian religion," postponed it until the next session, and directed that the bill should be published and distributed, and that the people be requested "to signify their opinion respecting the adoption of such a bill at the next session of assembly."

This brought out a determined opposition. Amongst others, Mr. Madison prepared a "Memorial and Remonstrance," which was widely circulated and signed, and in which he demonstrated "that religion, or the duty we owe the Creator," was not within the cognizance of civil government. At the next session the proposed bill was not only defeated, but another, "for establishing religious freedom," drafted by Mr. Jefferson, was passed. In the preamble of this act religious freedom is defined; and after a recital "that to suffer the civil magistrate to intrude his powers into the field of opinion, and to restrain the profession or propagation of principles on supposition of their ill tendency, is a dangerous fallacy which at once destroys all religious liberty," it is declared "that it is time enough for the rightful purposes of civil government for its officers to interfere when principles break out into overt acts against peace and good order." In these two sentences is found the true distinction between what properly belongs to the church and what to the State.

In a little more than a year after the passage of this statute the convention met which prepared the Constitution of the United States. Of this convention Mr. Jefferson was not a member, he being then absent as minister to France. As soon as he saw the draft of the Constitution proposed for adoption, he, in a letter to a friend, expressed his disappointment at the absence of an express declaration insuring the freedom of religion, but was willing to accept it as it was, trusting that the good sense and honest intentions of the people would bring about the necessary alterations. Five of the States, while adopting the Constitution, proposed amendments. Three—New Hampshire, New York, and Virginia—included in one form or another a declaration of religious freedom in the changes they desired to have made, as did also North Carolina, where the convention at first declined to ratify the Constitution until the proposed amendments were acted upon. Accordingly, at the first session of the first Congress the amendment now under consideration was proposed with others by Mr. Madison. It met the views of the advocates of religious freedom, and was adopted. Mr. Jefferson afterwards, in reply to an address to him by a committee of the Danbury Baptist Association, took occasion to say: "Believing with you that religion is a matter which lies solely between man and his God; that he owes account to none other for his faith or his worship; that the legislative powers of the government reach actions only, and not opinions—I contemplate with sovereign reverence that act of the whole American people which declared that their legislature should "make no law respecting an establishment of religion or prohibiting the free exercise thereof,' thus building a wall of separation between church and State. Adhering to this expression of the supreme will of the nation in behalf of the rights of conscience, I shall see with sincere satisfaction the progress of those sentiments which tend to restore man to all his natural rights, convinced he has no natural right in opposition to his social duties." Coming as this does from an acknowledged leader of the advocates of the measure, it may be accepted almost as an authoritative declaration of the scope and effect of the amendment thus secured. Congress was deprived of all legislative power over mere opinion, but was left free to reach actions which were in violation of social duties or subversive of good order.

Polygamy has always been odious among the northern and western nations of Europe, and, until the establishment of the Mormon Church, was almost exclusively a feature of the life of Asiatic and of African people. At common law, the second marriage was always void, and from the earliest history of England polygamy has been treated as an offence against society. After the establishment of the ecclesiastical courts, and until the time of James I., it was punished through the instrumentality of those tribunals, not merely because ecclesiastical rights had been violated, but because upon the separation of the ecclesiastical courts from the civil the ecclesiastical were supposed to be the most appropriate for the trial of matrimonial causes and offences against the rights of marriage, just as they were for testamentary causes and the settlement of the estates of deceased persons.

By the statute of James I, the offence, if committed in England or Wales, was made punishable in the civil courts, and the penalty was death. As this statute was limited in its operation to England and Wales, it was at a very early period re-enacted, generally with some modifications, in all the colonies. In connection with the case we are now considering, it is a significant fact that on the 8th of December, 1788, after the passage of the act establishing religious freedom, and after the convention of Virginia had recommended as an amendment to the Constitution of the United States the declaration in a bill of rights that "all men have an equal, natural, and unalienable right to the free exercise of religion, according to the dictates of conscience," the legislature of that State substantially enacted the statute of James I, death penalty included, because, as recited in the preamble, "it hath been doubted whether bigamy or polgamy be punishable by the laws of this Commonwealth." From that day to this we think it may safely be said there never has been a time in any State of the Union when polygamy has not been an offence against society, cognizable by the civil courts and punishable with more or less severity. In the face of all this evidence, it is impossible to believe that the constitutional guaranty of religious freedom was intended to prohibit legislation in respect to this most important feature of social life. Marriage, while from its very nature a sacred obligation, is nevertheless, in most civilized nations, a civil contract, and usually regulated by law. Upon it society may be said to be built, and out of its fruits spring social relations and social obligations and duties, with which government is necessarily required to deal. In fact, according as monogamous or polygamous marriages are allowed, do we find the principles on which the government of the people, to a greater or less extent, rests. Professor Lieber says, polygamy leads to the patriarchal principle, and which, when applied to large communities, fetters the people in stationary despotism, while that principle cannot long exist in connection with monogamy. Chancellor Kent observes that this remark is equally striking and profound. An exceptional colony of polygamists under an exceptional leadership may sometimes exist for a time without appearing to disturb the social condition of the people who surround it; but there cannot be a doubt that, unless restricted by some form of constitution, it is within the legitimate scope of the power of every civil government to determine whether polygamy or monogamy shall be the law of social life under its dominion.

In our opinion, the statute immediately under consideration is within the legislative power of Congress. It is constitutional and valid as prescribing a rule of action for all those residing in the Territories, and in places over which the United States have exclusive control. This being so, the only question which remains is, whether those who make polygamy a part of their religion are excepted from the operation of the statute. If they are, then those who do not make polygamy a part of their religious belief may be found guilty and punished, while those who do, must be acquitted and go free. This would be introducing a new element into criminal law. Laws are made for the government of actions, and while they cannot interfere with mere religious belief and opinions, they may with practices. Suppose one believed that human sacrifices were a necessary part of religious worship, would it be seriously contended that the civil government under which he lived could not interfere to prevent a sacrifice? Or if a wife religiously believed it was her duty to burn herself upon the funeral pile of her dead husband, would it be beyond the power of the civil government to prevent her carrying her belief into practice?

So here, as a law of the organization of society under the exclusive dominion of the United States, it is provided that plural marriages shall not be allowed. Can a man excuse his practices to the contrary because of his religious belief? To permit this would be to make the professed doctrines of religious belief superior to the law of the land, and in effect to permit every citizen to become a law unto himself. Government could exist only in name under such circumstances.

MINERSVILLE SCHOOL DISTRICT V. GOBITIS
310 U.S. 586 (1940)

"Judicial review, itself a limitation on popular government, is a fundamental part of our constitutional scheme. But to the legislature no less than to courts is committed the guardianship of deeply-cherished liberties. . . . To fight out the wise use of legislative authority in the forum of public opinion and before legislative assemblies rather than to transfer such a contest to the judicial arena serves to vindicate the self-confidence of a free people."

The Question: Can local school boards or state boards of education have the power to require all public school students to join in the ceremony of saluting the American flag and to expel students who object to the flag salute because of their sincere religious beliefs, including members of the Jehovah's Witness denomination?

The Arguments: PRO

School officials should have the authority to require participation of all students in the flag-salute ceremony, as a means of inculcating patriotism and respect for the flag as America's national symbol. Allowing any student to refuse to participate would create a special exemption and perhaps encourage other, more impressionable students to join that refusal. Therefore, it is essential for discipline that all students take part in the ceremony. Further, members of the Jehovah's Witness denomination also refuse to serve in the military and claim they owe no allegiance to the American government, which undermines the country's solidarity.

CON

Forcing anyone to participate in a ceremony that violates their deeply held religious beliefs is a totalitarian act and smacks of the Nazi and fascist regimes that Americans fought against in World War II. There is no evidence that the refusal of the Jehovah's Witness students harmed any other student, undermined school discipline, or threatened the nation's security. To punish a student for an act of religious conscience sets a poor example of this country's democratic beliefs and subjects members of religious minorities to the tyranny of the majority. Expulsion from school is a drastic punishment and far exceeds any need to impose discipline or to enforce uniformity of behavior.

BACKGROUND: THE PLEDGE OF ALLEGIANCE

Only one item appeared on the agenda of the Minersville, Pennsylvania school board at its meeting on November 6, 1935. Superintendent Charles E. Roudabush reported that three students had refused to join the daily ceremony of saluting the American flag that had been customary in Minersville schools since Roudabush arrived in 1914. The superintendent, who prided himself on firm discipline, was particularly annoyed at Walter Gobitis, whose children Lillian and William had first objected to the flag salute. Roudabush and Gobitis had argued about the issue over the past month, but heated debates had failed to resolve their dispute.

Walter Gobitis and his family belonged to Jehovah's Witnesses, a religious group whose energetic door-to-door preaching and hostility to Roman Catholicism combined to make Witnesses unpopular in towns such as Minersville, where close to 90 percent of the residents were Catholic. Gobitis was a Minersville native who was raised in the Catholic faith, and who took part in the flag-salute ceremony as a schoolboy. He and his family became Witnesses in 1931, when Lillian was eight and William was six, and the children saluted the flag every day until early October, 1935. (Although the family name was properly spelled "Gobitas," a court clerk's mistake perpetuated the spelling that the Supreme Court adopted and that persists to this day.)

The clash in Minersville, a town of ten thousand in the hilly anthracite coal region north of Philadelphia, was rooted in conflicting visions of patriotism and contrasting ideas of religious freedom.

Flag-salute ceremonies in public schools began during wartime: The New York legislature passed the first mandatory salute law in 1898, the day after the United States declared war on Spain. Only five states enacted flag-salute laws before World War I, but a national campaign began in 1919 as a project of the American Legion, founded that year by veterans to foster "one hundred per cent Americanism." During the next decade, the Legion campaign was joined by the Veterans of Foreign Wars, the Daughters of the American Revolution, and the Ku Klux Klan, the lattermost of which sought respectability in the 1920s through involvement in "patriotic" activities. By 1935, eighteen states had enacted flag-salute statutes, and hundreds of local school boards in other states had voted to compel all students to participate in the ceremony.

The Gobitis children were not the first objectors to the flag-salute ceremonies that began the school day in thousands of American communities. As early as 1918, when patriotic fervor and anti-German hostility swept the country during World War I, a handful of Mennonite children, members of a pacifist and largely German church, faced expulsion for refusal to salute the flag. Over the next fifteen years, the American Civil Liberties Union recorded a scattering of flag-salute cases around the country, but none had raised any constitutional challenge to compulsory participation in the ceremonies.

Beginning in 1935, Jehovah's Witnesses became the first religious group to promote a campaign of refusal to join classroom ceremonies and to press their challenges in court on a constitutional basis. Ironically, in view of later claims that "unpatriotic" Witnesses were aiding Nazi propagandists, the sect's objections to compulsory flag-salute ceremonies began in Nazi Germany, which banned the Witnesses in 1933 on Hitler's orders. German Witnesses defied Nazi edicts to join the "raised-palm" Fascist salute in schools and at all public events, and ultimately more than ten thousand were imprisoned in concentration camps. In response to this persecution, the leader of American Witnesses, Joseph F. Rutherford, denounced compulsory flag-salute laws at the sect's national convention in 1935. Witnesses "do not 'Heil Hitler' nor any other creature," Rutherford told his followers.

Shortly after Rutherford's speech, his admonition was heeded by Carleton Nicholls, a third-grade student in Lynn, Massachusetts. Earlier that year, the Bay State had enacted a mandatory flag-salute law which required students to face the flag with a "raised-palm" salute, identical to the Nazi version. After Carleton's refusal to continue saluting, his father was arrested when he accompanied Carleton to school and they both refused to stand during the ceremony. This arrest prompted Rutherford, a lawyer whose followers called him "Judge," to praise Carleton in a national radio address for making a "wise choice" and to proclaim that other Witnesses "who act wisely will do the same thing."

Walter Gobitis and his family—along with every Witness who could—listened to Rutherford's speech on their radios, and within a few days Lillian and William, then in the seventh and fifth grades respectively, decided to emulate Carleton Nicholls. Their defiance upset Superintendent Roudabush, who knew he could not lawfully punish them. Neither the state legislature nor the local school board had made the salute mandatory or provided any penalties for refusal to participate. After his appeals to Walter Gobitis failed, Roudabush secured an opinion from the State Department of Public Instruction that the school board could enact a regulation to compel participation in the salute and to expel students who refused.

When the board met in November 1935, its members sat impatiently as Walter Gobitis and the mother of Edmund Wasliewski, a sixth-grader who had joined the objectors, explained the Witness position on the flag salute. "We are not desecrating the American flag," Gobitis said. "We show no disrespect for the flag, but we cannot salute it. The Bible tells us this, and we must obey." Gobitis pointed the board members to chapter 20 of Exodus, which warned believers not to "bow down" to any "graven image" which portrayed false gods. The flags of nations were images of Satan, who ruled the secular governments of the world, Gobitis told his unsympathetic listeners.

On the motion of Dr. Thomas J. McGurl, an Irish Catholic physician and influential Minersville resident, the board unanimously adopted a resolution requiring all students "to salute the flag of our Country as a part of the daily exercises" and providing that refusal to participate "shall be regarded as an act of insubordination and shall be dealt with accordingly." Roudabush immediately declared that "I hereby expel from the Minersville schools Lillian Gobitis, William Gobitis and Edmund Wasliewski for this act of insubordination, to wit, failure to salute the flag in our school exercises." Walter Gobitis left the meeting with a parting shot to Roudabush and the board: "I'm going to take you to court for this!" (Irons, 1988).

MR. JUSTICE FRANKFURTER delivered the opinion of the Court.

A grave responsibility confronts this Court whenever in course of litigation it must reconcile the conflicting claims of liberty and authority. But when the liberty invoked is liberty of conscience, and the authority is authority to safeguard the nation's fellowship, judicial conscience is put to its severest test. Of such a nature is the present controversy.

Lillian Gobitis, aged twelve, and her brother William, aged ten, were expelled from the public schools of Minersville, Pennsylvania, for refusing to salute the national flag as part of a daily school exercise. The local Board of Education required both teachers and pupils to participate in this ceremony. The ceremony is a familiar one. The right hand is placed on the breast and the following pledge recited in unison: "I pledge allegiance to my flag, and to the Republic for which it stands; one nation indivisible, with liberty and justice for all." While the words are spoken, teachers and pupils extend their right hands in salute to the flag. The Gobitis family are affiliated with "Jehovah's Witnesses," for whom the Bible as the Word of God is the supreme authority. The children had been brought up conscientiously to believe that such a gesture of respect for the flag was forbidden by command of scripture.[1]

The Gobitis children were of an age for which Pennsylvania makes school attendance compulsory. Thus they were denied a free education and their parents had to put them into private schools. To be relieved of the financial burden thereby entailed, their father, on behalf of the children and in his own behalf, brought this suit. He sought to enjoin the authorities from continuing to exact participation in the flag-salute ceremony as a condition of his children's attendance at the Minersville school. After trial of the issues, Judge Maris gave at a preliminary stage of the litigation relief in the District Court, on the basis of a thoughtful opinion; his decree was affirmed by the Circuit Court of Appeals. Since this decision ran counter to several per curiam dispositions of this Court, we granted certiorari to give the matter full reconsideration. . . .

We must decide whether the requirement of participation in such a ceremony, exacted from a child who refuses upon sincere religious grounds, infringes without due process of law the liberty guaranteed by the Fourteenth Amendment.

Centuries of strife over the erection of particular dogmas as exclusive or all-comprehending faiths led to the inclusion of a guarantee for religious freedom in the Bill of Rights. The First Amendment, and the Fourteenth through its absorption of the First, sought to guard against repetition of those bitter religious struggles by prohibiting the establishment of a state religion and by securing to every sect the free exercise of its faith. So pervasive is the acceptance of this precious right that its scope is brought into question, as here, only when the conscience of individuals collides with the felt necessities of society.

Certainly the affirmative pursuit of one's convictions about the ultimate mystery of the universe and man's relation to it is placed beyond the reach of law. Government may not interfere with organized or individual expression of belief or disbelief. Propagation of belief—or even of disbelief in the supernatural—is protected, whether in church or chapel, mosque or synagogue, tabernacle or meetinghouse. Likewise the Constitution assures generous immunity to the individual from imposition of penalties for offending, in the course of his own religious activities, the religious views of others, be they a minority or those who are dominant in government.

But the manifold character of man's relations may bring his conception of religious duty into conflict with the secular interests of his fellow-men. When does the constitutional guarantee compel exemption from doing what society thinks necessary for the promotion of some great common end, or from a penalty for conduct which appears dangerous to the general good? To state the problem is to recall the truth that no single principle can answer all of life's complexities. The right to freedom of religious belief, however dissident and however obnoxious to the cherished beliefs of others—even of a majority—is itself the denial of an absolute. But to affirm that the freedom to follow conscience has itself no limits in the life of a society would deny that very plurality of principles which, as a matter of history, underlies protection of religious toleration. Our present task then, as so often the case with courts, is to reconcile two rights in order to prevent either from destroying the other. But, because in safeguarding conscience we are dealing with interests so subtle and so dear, every possible leeway should be given to the claims of religious faith.

In the judicial enforcement of religious freedom we are concerned with a historic concept. The religious liberty which the Constitution protects has never excluded legislation of general scope not directed against doctrinal loyalties of particular sects. Judicial nullification of legislation cannot be justified by attributing to the framers of the Bill of Rights views for which there is no historic warrant. Conscientious scruples have not, in the course of the long struggle for religious toleration, relieved the individual from obedience to a general law not aimed at the promotion or restriction of religious beliefs. The mere possession of religious convictions which contradict the relevant concerns of a political society does not relieve the citizen from the discharge of political responsibilities. . . . Even if it were assumed that freedom of speech goes beyond the historic concept of full opportunity to utter and to disseminate views, however heretical or offensive to dominant opinion, and includes freedom from conveying what may be deemed an implied but rejected affirmation, the question remains whether school children, like the Gobitis children, must be excused from conduct required of all the other children in the promotion of national cohesion. We are dealing with an interest inferior to none in the hierarchy of legal values. National unity is the basis of national security. To deny the legislature the right to select appropriate means for its attainment presents a totally different order of problem from that of the propriety of subordinating the possible ugliness of littered streets to the free expression of opinion through distribution of handbills.

Situations like the present are phases of the profoundest problem confronting a democracy—the problem which Lincoln cast in memorable dilemma: "Must a government of necessity be too strong for the liberties of its people, or too weak to maintain its own existence?". . . The ultimate foundation of a free society is the binding tie of cohesive sentiment. Such a sentiment is fostered by all those agencies of the mind and spirit which may serve to gather up the traditions of a people, transmit them from generation to generation, and thereby create that continuity of a treasured common life which constitutes a civilization. "We live by symbols." The flag is the symbol of our national unity, transcending all internal differences, however large, within the framework of the Constitution. . . .

---

[1]Reliance is especially placed on the following verses from Chapter 20 of Exodus:

3. Thou shalt have no other gods before me.

4. Thou shalt not make unto thee any graven image, or any likeness of any thing that is in heaven above, or that is in the earth beneath, or that is in the water under the earth.

5. Thou shalt not bow down thyself to them, nor serve them . . .

The case before us must be viewed as though the legislature of Pennsylvania had itself formally directed the flag-salute for the children of Minersville; had made no exemption for children whose parents were possessed of conscientious scruples like those of the Gobitis family; and had indicated its belief in the desirable ends to be secured by having its public school children share a common experience at those periods of development when their minds are supposedly receptive to its assimilation, by an exercise appropriate in time and place and setting, and one designed to evoke in them appreciation of the nation's hopes and dreams, its sufferings and sacrifices. The precise issue, then, for us to decide is whether the legislatures of the various states and the authorities in a thousand counties and school districts of this country are barred from determining the appropriateness of various means to evoke that unifying sentiment without which there can ultimately be no liberties, civil or religious.

To stigmatize legislative judgment in providing for this universal gesture of respect for the symbol of our national life in the setting of the common school as a lawless inroad on that freedom of conscience which the Constitution protects, would amount to no less than the pronouncement of pedagogical and psychological dogma in a field where courts possess no marked and certainly no controlling competence. The influences which help toward a common feeling for the common country are manifold. Some may seem harsh and others no doubt are foolish. Surely, however, the end is legitimate. And the effective means for its attainment are still so uncertain and so unauthenticated by science as to preclude us from putting the widely prevalent belief in flag-saluting beyond the pale of legislative power. It mocks reason and denies our whole history to find in the allowance of a requirement to salute our flag on fitting occasions the seeds of sanction for obeisance to a leader.

The wisdom of training children in patriotic impulses by those compulsions which necessarily pervade so much of the educational process is not for our independent judgment. Even were we convinced of the folly of such a measure, such belief would be no proof of its unconstitutionality. For ourselves, we might be tempted to say that the deepest patriotism is best engendered by giving unfettered scope to the most crochety beliefs. Perhaps it is best, even from the standpoint of those interests which ordinances like the one under review seek to promote, to give to the least popular sect leave from conformities like those here in issue. But the court-room is not the arena for debating issues of educational policy. It is not our province to choose among competing considerations in the subtle process of securing effective loyalty to the traditional ideals of democracy, while respecting at the same time individual idiosyncracies among a people so diversified in racial origins and religious allegiances. So to hold would in effect make us the school board for the country. That authority has not been given to this Court, nor should we assume it.

We are dealing here with the formative period in the development of citizenship. Great diversity of psychological and ethical opinion exists among us concerning the best way to train children for their place in society. Because of these differences and because of reluctance to permit a single, iron-cast system of education to be imposed upon a nation compounded of so many strains, we have held that, even though public education is one of our most cherished democratic institutions, the Bill of Rights bars a state from compelling all children to attend the public schools. But it is a very different thing for this Court to exercise censorship over the conviction of legislatures that a particular program or exercise will best promote in the minds of children who attend the common schools an attachment to the institutions of their country.

What the school authorities are really asserting is the right to awaken in the child's mind considerations as to the significance of the flag contrary to those implanted by the parent. In such an attempt the state is normally at a disadvantage in competing with the parent's authority, so long—and this is the vital aspect of religious toleration—as parents are unmolested in their right to counteract by their own persuasiveness the wisdom and rightness of those loyalties which the state's educational system is seeking to promote. Except where the transgression of constitutional liberty is too plain for argument, personal freedom is best maintained—so long as the remedial channels of the democratic process remain open and unobstructed—when it is ingrained in a people's habits and not enforced against popular policy by the coercion of adjudicated law. That the flag-salute is an allowable portion of a school program for those who do not invoke conscientious scruples is surely not debatable. But for us to insist that, though the ceremony may be required, exceptional immunity must be given to dissidents, is to maintain that there is no basis for a legislative judgment that such an exemption might introduce elements of difficulty into the school discipline, might cast doubts in the minds of the other children which would themselves weaken the effect of the exercise.

The preciousness of the family relation, the authority and independence which give dignity to parenthood, indeed the enjoyment of all freedom, presuppose the kind of ordered society which is summarized by our flag. A society which is dedicated to the preservation of these ultimate values of civilization may in self-protection utilize the educational process for inculcating those almost unconscious feelings which bind men together in a comprehending loyalty, whatever may be their lesser differences and difficulties. That is to say, the process may be utilized so long as men's right to believe as they please, to win others to their way of belief, and their right to assemble in their chosen places of worship for the devotional ceremonies of their faith, are all fully respected.

Judicial review, itself a limitation on popular government, is a fundamental part of our constitutional scheme. But to the legislature no less than to courts is committed the guardianship of deeply-cherished liberties. Where all the effective means of inducing political changes are left free from interference, education in the abandonment of foolish legislation is itself a training in liberty. To fight out the wise use of legislative authority in the forum of public opinion and before legislative assemblies rather than to transfer such a contest to the judicial arena, serves to vindicate the self-confidence of a free people.

Reversed.

Mr. Justice McReynolds concurs in the result.

Mr. Justice Stone, dissenting.

I think the judgment below should be affirmed.

Two youths, now fifteen and sixteen years of age, are by the judgment of this Court held liable to expulsion from the public schools and to denial of all publicly supported educational privileges because of their refusal to yield to the compulsion of a law which commands their participation in a school ceremony contrary to their religious convictions. They and their father are citizens and have not exhibited by any action or statement of opinion, any disloyalty to the Government of the United States. They are ready and willing to obey all its laws which do not conflict with what they sincerely believe to be the higher commandments of God. It is not doubted that these convictions are religious, that they are genuine, or that the refusal to yield to the compulsion of the law is in good faith and with all sincerity. It would be a denial of their faith as well as the teachings of most religions to say that children of their age could not have religious convictions.

The law which is thus sustained is unique in the history of Anglo-American legislation. It does more than suppress freedom of speech and more than prohibit the free exercise of religion, which concededly are forbidden by the First Amendment and are violations of the liberty guaranteed by the Fourteenth. For by this law the state seeks to coerce these children to express a sentiment which, as they interpret it, they do not entertain, and which violates their deepest religious convictions. It is not denied that such compulsion is a prohibited infringement of personal liberty, freedom of speech and religion, guaranteed by the Bill of Rights, except in so far as it may be justified and supported as a proper exercise of the state's power over public education. Since the state, in competition with parents, may through teaching in the public schools indoctrinate the minds of the young, it is said that in aid of its undertaking to inspire loyalty and devotion to constituted authority and the flag which symbolizes it, it may coerce the pupil to make affirmation contrary to his belief and in violation of his religious faith. And, finally, it is said that since the Minersville School Board and others are of the opinion that the country will be better served by conformity than by the observance of religious liberty which the Constitution prescribes, the courts are not free to pass judgment on the Board's choice.

Concededly the constitutional guaranties of personal liberty are not always absolutes. Government has a right to survive and powers conferred upon it are not necessarily set at naught by the express prohibitions of the Bill of Rights. It may make war and raise armies. To that end it may compel citizens to give military service, and subject them to military training despite their religious objections. It may suppress religious practices dangerous to morals, and presumably those also which are inimical to public safety, health and good order. But it is a long step, and one which I am unable to take, to the position that government may, as a supposed educational measure and as a means of disciplining the young, compel public affirmations which violate their religious conscience. . . .

The guaranties of civil liberty are but guaranties of freedom of the human mind and spirit and of reasonable freedom and opportunity to express them. They presuppose the right of the individual to hold such opinions as he will and to give them reasonably free expression, and his freedom, and that of the state as well, to teach and persuade others by the communication of ideas. The very essence of the liberty which they guaranty is the freedom of the individual from compulsion as to what he shall think and what he shall say, at least where the compulsion is to bear false witness to his religion. If these guaranties are to have any meaning they must, I think, be deemed to withhold from the state any authority to compel belief or the expression of it where that expression violates religious convictions, whatever may be the legislative view of the desirability of such compulsion.

History teaches us that there have been but few infringements of personal liberty by the state which have not been justified, as they are here, in the name of righteousness and the public good, and few which have not been directed, as they are now, at politically helpless minorities. The framers were not unaware that under the system which they created most governmental curtailments of personal liberty would have the support of a legislative judgment that the public interest would be better served by its curtailment than by its constitutional protection. I cannot conceive that in prescribing, as limitations upon the powers of government, the freedom of the mind and spirit secured by the explicit guaranties of freedom of speech and religion, they intended or rightly could have left any latitude for a legislative judgment that the compulsory expression of belief which violates religious convictions would better serve the public interest than their protection. The Constitution may well elicit expressions of loyalty to it and to the government which it created, but it does not command such expressions or otherwise give any indication that compulsory expressions of loyalty play any such part in our scheme of government as to override the constitutional protection of freedom of speech and religion. And while such expressions of loyalty, when voluntarily given, may promote national unity, it is quite another matter to say that their compulsory expression by children in violation of their own and their parents' religious convictions can be regarded as playing so important a part in our national unity as to leave school boards free to exact it despite the constitutional guarantee of freedom of religion. The very terms of the Bill of Rights preclude, it seems to me, any reconciliation of such compulsions with the constitutional guaranties by a legislative declaration that they are more important to the public welfare than the Bill of Rights.

But even if this view be rejected and it is considered that there is some scope for the determination by legislatures whether the citizen shall be compelled to give public expression of such sentiments contrary to his religion, I am not persuaded that we should refrain from passing upon the legislative judgment "as long as the remedial channels of the democratic process remain open and unobstructed." This seems to me no more than the surrender of the constitutional protection of the liberty of small minorities to the popular will. We have previously pointed to the importance of a searching judicial inquiry into the legislative judgment in situations where prejudice against discrete and insular minorities may tend to curtail the operation of those political processes ordinarily to be relied on to protect minorities. See United States v. Carolene Products Co., 304 U.S. 144, 152, note 4. And until now we have not hesitated similarly to scrutinize legislation restricting the civil liberty of racial and religious minorities although no political process was affected. Here we have such a small minority entertaining in good faith a religious belief, which is such a departure from the usual course of human conduct, that most persons are disposed to regard it with little toleration or concern. In such circumstances careful scrutiny of legislative efforts to secure conformity of belief and opinion by a compulsory affirmation of the desired belief, is especially needful if civil rights are to receive any protection. Tested by this standard, I am not prepared to say that the right of this small and helpless minority, including children having a strong religious conviction, whether they understand its nature or not, to refrain from an expression obnoxious to their religion, is to be overborne by the interest of the state in maintaining discipline in the schools.

The Constitution expresses more than the conviction of the people that democratic processes must be preserved at all costs. It is also an expression of faith and a command that freedom of mind and spirit must be preserved, which government must obey, if it is to adhere to that justice and moderation without which no free government can exist. For this reason it would seem that legislation which operates to repress the religious freedom of small minorities, which is admittedly within the scope of the protection of the Bill of Rights, must at least be subject to the same judicial scrutiny as legislation which we have recently held to infringe the constitutional liberty of religious and racial minorities.

With such scrutiny I cannot say that the inconveniences which may attend some sensible adjustment of school discipline in order that the religious convictions of these children may be spared, presents a problem so momentous or pressing as to outweigh the freedom from compulsory violation of religious faith which has been thought worthy of constitutional protection.

COMMENTARY: "RECENT RESTRICTIONS UPON RELIGIOUS LIBERTY"

Within the last five years [1937–1942], the Supreme Court of the United States has added decisions of greater importance to the case law of religious freedom than had been accumulated in all the years since the adoption of the Bill of Rights. It will be well to examine them in the light of the history of the federally secured right of religious freedom and in the light of the immediate public reactions to them.

A considerable proportion of the early emigration to the thirteen original colonies was undoubtedly due to a desire to escape religious persecution in England and on the Continent. Those colonists, however, were as insistent that their own particular form of religion be adhered to as their oppressors had been. The story of Roger Williams, who was expelled from the colony of Massachusetts because of his nonconformist views and who established the colony of Rhode Island as a sanctuary of religious tolerance, and that of Ann Hutchinson, who also was exiled from the Bay Colony for a like reason, are monuments to the intolerance of the Puritans.

But by the time of the adoption of the Constitution, the principle of religious freedom which Roger Williams so stoutly advocated and put into practice in Rhode Island had gained such headway that its omission from the law of the land was at once protested; and, significantly, the first tenet of the so-called Bill of Rights was a cure of that want: "Congress shall make no law respecting an establishment of religion, or prohibiting the free exercise thereof. . . ."

It will be observed that this declaration is an inhibition only on the federal government. It does not prevent the states from doing the things thus prohibited to the Congress. The amendment embodies the principle of the separation of church and state. In the words of the Supreme Court, it was designed to allow everyone under the jurisdiction of the United States to entertain such notions respecting his relation to his Maker and the duties they impose as may be approved by his judgment and conscience, and to exhibit his sentiments in such form of worship as he may think proper, not injurious to the rights of others, and to prohibit legislation for the support of any religious tenets or the modes of worship of any sect.

The right to think as one wishes regarding religion can scarcely be doubted; the question which today seems to prompt the action of the secular authorities is the right to practice religious dictates. The rule in this regard is old and sound. It is, briefly, that there is a right to practice any religious principle and teach any religious doctrine which does not, as above indicated, injure the personal rights of others, nor offend the laws established by society for peace and morality.

The Fourteenth Amendment has now become recognized as a bulwark against state infringement of the same religious liberties which the First Amendment secured from federal interference. Religious freedom is so elementary to the concept of ordered "liberty" that it must be said to be within the meaning of that term in the Fourteenth Amendment, which reads, in pertinent parts, as follows: ". . . nor shall any state deprive any person of . . . liberty, . . . without due process of law. . . ." The liberty of religion protected from state interference by this amendment includes the absolute right of any person to entertain whatever views regarding religion his conscience may dictate, and the right to exercise those beliefs in such ceremonies and practices as do not conflict with the laws of society for peace and good morals. Any invasion by a state of the right to believe as one sees fit would undoubtedly be considered arbitrary, and hence violative of due process; and so would a state infringement of the right to exercise those religious beliefs unless such exercise conflicted with the secular laws regarding peace and good morals.

This brief review brings us to a consideration of the cases decided by the Supreme Court in the last five years. A small religious sect or society known as Jehovah's Witnesses has served as the guinea pig for all the important cases in this period.

The Jehovah's Witnesses are the followers of the religious doctrines formulated by the late pastor, Charles T. Russell. Russell was born in Pittsburgh in 1852 and was brought up in the Presbyterian faith. At the age of sixteen, he decided that the then existing schools of religious thought were wrong, and he built up a religion of his own, centered around calculations as to the second coming of Christ and the battle of Armageddon. His followers, formerly known as "Russellites" but adopting the name "Jehovah's Witnesses" in 1931, believe that their highest function is to disseminate their interpretations of the Bible and their religious beliefs. To accomplish this purpose, a non-profit, non-stock corporation was founded in 1884 under the laws of Pennsylvania, and now known as the Watch Tower Bible and Tract Society. The corporation owns printing plants located in Brooklyn, New York, Berne (Switzerland), and other places, and these plants are devoted to the printing of books, magazines, and pamphlets embodying the Witnesses' beliefs. The corporation also supplies Witnesses with phonographs, public address cars, and recorded explanations of the contents of the large volume of printed matter. Armed with the Society's publications and with the portable phonographs, individual Witnesses carry out their conviction that they must spread the gospel as they see it by street corner and door-to-door distribution of the books and bulletins.

Publications of the Society contain highly contentious teachings. They attack all institutionalized churches and sects as things of Satan. The members decry any form of religious ceremony and, in this connection, they refuse to salute the flag because they believe that that practice runs counter to the commandment that they should not bow down to any "graven image." The Society teaches "that we are not of this world" and discourages Witnesses from participation in politics or the support of war. Each Witness claims to be a minister of the gospel.

These beliefs have occasioned intense animosity in every state of the Union, and the virulent attacks on institutionalized religion, particularly the Catholic church, are highly offensive to many people. Small town officials are flooded with protests on those days when the "witnessing" activities are being carried on. As a result, peddling and solicitation ordinances have been applied as a restraining mechanism. The religious convictions against the flag salute and against military service have aroused the ire of patriotic groups such as veterans' organizations, and this has occasioned further protests and often mob violence. In those communities where local or state law requires that children in public schools salute the flag, numerous school children adhering to the Jehovah's Witnesses' belief have been expelled for refusing to do so.

The school board of the Minersville school district made a ruling that all children attending the public schools of the district should give the flag salute at the opening of the school day. The children of Walter Gobitis attended those schools being, however, Jehovah's Witnesses and as such holding the religious conviction that to salute the flag was to disobey the commandment of the Bible against obeisance to a graven image. They were expelled; and Gobitis applied to the federal district court for an injunction against enforcement of the expulsion order.

On December 1, 1937, Federal District Judge Maris denied the defendant school district's motion to dismiss the injunction suit. He said public officials should not question the religious basis of a sincere refusal to act when public safety, health, or morals, or personal or property rights were not prejudiced by such refusal; the refusal to salute the flag because of religious convictions did not involve such dangers. It was pointed out that the effect of the ruling of the school board was to make the flag, which is a symbol of religious liberty, a means of imposing a religious test as a condition of receiving the benefits of public education. Later, Judge Maris granted the requested injunction against the enforcement of the "salute or be expelled" order of the school board. It may be noted parenthetically here that in the years 1937 and 1938 the Department of Justice received exactly three letters concerning the Jehovah's Witnesses; the following year, 1939, apparently as a result of American reactions to the spreading conflict in Europe, numerous complaints were made to the Department regarding attacks upon the Witnesses.

On March 4, 1940, the United States Circuit Court of Appeals for the Third Circuit sustained the Gobitis injunction in a cogent opinion. The Court noted that the conflict boiled down to a question of whether the flag-salute requirement was such a rule of society for safety and good morals as must take precedence over liberty of conscience. It observed that the Minersville school board rule imposed not a prohibition upon action, but rather a command to do an act, and concluded that it was not of sufficient moment as a device for instilling respect for country to outweigh freedom of religious conscience. If invoked, it was held, the rule denied the religious freedom on which is based a great measure of the respect due this nation and its flag.

But both lower courts were reversed in the federal Supreme Court on June 3, 1940. Mr. Justice Frankfurter, speaking for the eight-to-one majority of the Court, acknowledged the question as being one of balancing a rule of political society against considerations of religious freedom. His conclusion, however, ran contrary to that of the circuit court. The necessity for cohesive patriotic sentiments was felt to be more important than the non-conformist religious views of the Witnesses. . . .

The Court then declined to question the choice by the school board of the flag exercise as an appropriate means to instill patriotic sentiment.

Admittedly, there are difficult questions involved here. Before attempting to suggest a solution, it will be well to review the effect of the decision.

Between June 12 and June 20, 1940, hundreds of attacks upon the Witnesses were reported to the Department of Justice. Several were of such violence that it was deemed advisable to have the Federal Bureau of Investigation look into them. At Kennebunk, Maine, the Kingdom Hall was burned. At Rockville, Maryland, the police assisted a mob in dispersing a Bible meeting. At Litchfield, Illinois, practically the entire town mobbed a company of some sixty Witnesses who were canvassing it, and it was necessary to call on the state troopers to protect the members of the sect. Several Witnesses were charged with riotous conspiracy at Connersville, Indiana, their attorney was mobbed, and he and several other Witnesses who had attended the arraignment were beaten and driven out of town. At Jackson, Mississippi, members of a veterans' organization, led by an individual claiming the rank of major, forcibly removed a number of Witnesses and their trailer homes from the town.

Three instances of such vigilantism led by state or municipal officers caused the Department of Justice to seek indictments against the officers for violation of the Civil Rights Act. Jehovah's Witnesses conventions in July, 1940, were held in twenty cities in some fifteen states. At the urgent request of the Department of Justice, through the United States attorneys, local law enforcement officers were induced to give these conventions adequate protection, so that no violence attended. In this connection, it should be noted also that persecution of the Witnesses is peculiarly a small town and rural community phenomenon, whereas the conventions were held in larger cities.

In the two years following the decision, the files of the Department of Justice reflect an uninterrupted record of violence and persecution of the Witnesses. Almost without exception, the flag and the flag salute can be found as the percussion cap that sets off these acts.

This ugly picture of the two years following the Gobitis decision is an eloquent argument in support of the minority contention of Mr. Justice Stone. The placing of symbolic exercises on a higher plane than freedom of conscience has made this symbol an instrument of oppression of a religious minority. The flag has been violated by its misuse to deny the very freedoms it is intended to represent—the freedoms which themselves best engender a healthy "cohesive" respect for national institutions. In short, public health, safety, and morals have not been fortified by the compulsory flag salute laws. Indeed, the result has been quite the contrary.

It seems probable that a reversal of that ruling would profoundly enhance respect for the flag. The vigor of constitutional guarantees such as religious freedom, on which respect for flag and country must depend, stems from their ever renewed public recognition and observance. How much more effective an instrument of patriotic education it would be if the flag salute itself were made a practical daily exercise of a fundamental liberty, a liberty which is one of the four great freedoms for which this nation is now fighting! (Rotnem & Folson, 1942).

MEET LILLIAN GOBITAS

I was born in Minersville, Pennsylvania, in 1923. Both of my parents were also born in Minersville. Mother was Pennsylvania Dutch, and her family had been there more than two hundred years. Dad's family came straight to Minersville from a month-long trip from Lithuania. There are a lot of Lithuanians and Middle Europeans in Minersville. I think they must have known someone, and came straight to work in the coal mines, like my grandfather did. My grandmother was a self-made woman, who didn't even know how to read. She just bought property. Europeans believe in getting property. She opened up a bar, and she took in boarders. Later she opened a grocery store, which became my father's. As all of her children got married, she gave them a business, and she sent one of my uncles to college. For a little peasant woman, that was something.

We lived in a big house, over the store which was called the Economy Grocery. There were six of us finally, and I was the first. We had to work in the grocery store and we were very glad about that. The majority of the fathers worked in the coal mines, so having a grocery store was much nicer. Some children would lose their fathers with black damp, or a rock fall in the mine.

It was hard in Minersville during the Depression years. I remember Dad had a little account book for the bills that people ran up, all yellow and old. Some people never paid, but he never went after them. When the WPA [Works Progress Administration] and relief finally came along, it

was quite a help. Those measures were very good. My uncle died on the WPA, from a heart attack, and my aunt was on relief. At least we had food. Everything else was do-it-yourself. We learned to sew, and make do with a lot of hand-me-downs. It was not awful. We were really a jolly family. While we worked we would listen to those old radio shows.

Dad was raised Catholic and Mother was Methodist, although her parents had been Jehovah's Witnesses since 1904. Mother and all the children were very active in the Methodist church. It was my father that first delved into being a Witness, when my grandparents came to live with us for a while. He started just out of curiosity. What takes so much of their time? When they were gone, he would look into their literature, because they didn't want to make him a captive audience. So we would come home from Sunday school and he would ask what we had learned, and he would say, Oh, look at this, look at that! Dad would enthusiastically call attention to Scriptures that indicated hell was man's common grave instead of torment, and also delightful verses from Isaiah that we felt would mean also a literal earthly paradise. Pretty soon we were having a Bible study in our home and not going to church.

In the summer of 1935, Judge Rutherford, the president of the Watchtower Society of Jehovah's Witnesses, gave this talk on the radio about what the Scriptures say on emblems. He said that he himself wouldn't give a salute to the flag, not because he didn't respect the flag as a symbol of the country but because of what the Scripture says about worshipping an image of the State.

We were all at different schools, but we liked them very much. I loved school, and I was with a nice group. I was actually kind of popular. I was class president in the seventh grade, and I had good grades. And I felt that, Oh, if I stop saluting the flag, I will blow all this! And I did. It sure worked out that way. I really was so fearful that, when the teacher would look my way, I would quick put out my hand and move my lips. We knew that Carleton Nicholls up in Lynn, Massachusetts, took a stand against the salute in school. He was expelled from school, and the story was in the newspapers.

My brother William was in the fifth grade at that time, the fall of 1935. The next day Bill came home and said, I stopped saluting the flag. So I knew this was the moment! This wasn't something my parents forced on us. They were very firm about that, that what you do is your decision, and you should understand what you're doing. I did a lot of reading and checking in the Bible and I really took my own stand.

I went first to my teacher, Miss Anna Shofstal, so I couldn't chicken out of it. She listened to my explanation and surprisingly, she just hugged me and said she thought it was very nice, to have courage like that. But the students were awful. I really should have explained to the whole class but I was fearful. I didn't know whether it was right to stand up or sit down. These days, we realize that the salute itself is the motions and the words. So I sat down and the whole room was aghast. After that, when I'd come to school, they would throw a hail of pebbles and yell things like, Here comes Jehovah! They were just jeering at me. Some of my girl friends would come and ask what it was about. That was nice. One-on-one is a lot easier.

They watched us for two weeks, my brother and I and Edmund Wasliewski, who was another Witness who wouldn't salute. With my brother, the teacher tried to force his arm up and he just held onto his pocket. After two weeks, they had the school-board meeting and Dad and Mom both went. They had grown up with these men on the school board and gone to school with them. The superintendent, Dr. Roudabush, was a very firm type of person, and Dr. McGurl, the board president, was also very firm. The others kind of followed suit.

Dad told the school board why we couldn't take part in the flag salute. Dad told us he was very nervous at the meeting. The board made its decision right then, without much discussion. The idea was that we were insubordinate, and there would be immediate expulsion. They said at the meeting, Don't even come to school tomorrow!

After we had been expelled, one of the Catholic churches in Minersville announced a boycott of our store, and it meant a great deal to us. More children had been born, and it was our living, so it was very important. Business fell off quite a lot. Sometimes my Dad sent my brother to my aunt's house next door for a loan, because it was kind of critical. After a while, though, time went by and the people felt that

this was kind of ridiculous, that the priest would tell them where to buy their groceries. Dad was really well known and he made a go of it by making farmer sausage and kielbasi. People came from everywhere for these things and this is how we survived the boycott. So they came back.

We wouldn't have done anything about our expulsion, but since the school board was so firm in our case, the Watchtower Society said they would like to use ours as a test case. Some schools were very kind and took the children back, but there were thousands that had hard, hard treatment, who were knocked against the wall and beaten and went home crying and almost hysterical.

It has been more than fifty years since I took a stand on the flag salute, but I would do it again in a second. Without reservations! Jehovah's Witnesses do feel that we're trying to follow the Scriptures, and Jesus said, They persecuted me, and they will persecute you also. We do expect that before the end there will be a tremendous, all-out wave of persecution. Jehovah's Witnesses are now banned in over forty countries. So we really try to build up our faith, to meet the apathy about religion that we meet from door to door (Irons, 1988).

WEST VIRGINIA BOARD OF EDUCATION V. BARNETTE
319 U.S. 624 (1943)

"The very purpose of a Bill of Rights was to withdraw certain subjects from the vicissitudes of political controversy, to place them beyond the reach of majorities and officials, and to establish them as legal principles to be applied by the courts. One's right to life, liberty, and property, to free speech, a free press, freedom of worship and assembly, and other fundamental rights may not be submitted to vote; they depend on the outcome of no elections."

MR. JUSTICE JACKSON delivered the opinion of the Court.

Following the decision by this Court on June 3, 1940, in Minersville School District v. Gobitis, the West Virginia legislature amended its statutes to require all schools therein to conduct courses of instruction in history, civics, and in the Constitutions of the United States and of the State "for the purpose of teaching, fostering and perpetuating the ideals, principles and spirit of Americanism, and increasing the knowledge of the organization and machinery of the government.". . . The Board of Education on January 9, 1942, adopted a resolution containing recitals taken largely from the Court's Gobitis opinion and ordering that the salute to the flag become "a regular part of the program of activities in the public schools," that all teachers and pupils "shall be required to participate in the salute honoring the Nation represented by the Flag; provided, however, that refusal to salute the Flag be regarded as an Act of insubordination, and shall be dealt with accordingly.". . .

Appellees, citizens of the United States and of West Virginia, brought suit in the United States District Court for

themselves and others similarly situated asking its injunction to restrain enforcement of these laws and regulations against Jehovah's Witnesses. . . . Children of this faith have been expelled from school and are threatened with exclusion for no other cause. Officials threaten to send them to reformatories maintained for criminally inclined juveniles. Parents of such children have been prosecuted and are threatened with prosecutions for causing delinquency.

The Board of Education moved to dismiss the complaint setting forth these facts and alleging that the law and regulations are an unconstitutional denial of religious freedom, and of freedom of speech, and are invalid under the "due process" and "equal protection" clauses of the Fourteenth Amendment to the Federal Constitution. The cause was submitted on the pleadings to a District Court of three judges. It restrained enforcement as to the plaintiffs and those of that class. The Board of Education brought the case here by direct appeal.

This case calls upon us to reconsider a precedent decision, as the Court throughout its history often has been required to do. Before turning to the Gobitis case, however, it is desirable to notice certain characteristics by which this controversy is distinguished. The freedom asserted by these appellees does not bring them into collision with rights asserted by any other individual. It is such conflicts which most frequently require intervention of the State to determine where the rights of one end and those of another begin. But the refusal of these persons to participate in the ceremony does not interfere with or deny rights of others to do so. Nor is there any question in this case that their behavior is peaceable and orderly. The sole conflict is between authority and rights of the individual. The State asserts power to condition access to public education on making a prescribed sign and profession and at the same time to coerce attendance by punishing both parent and child. The latter stand on a right of self-determination in matters that touch individual opinion and personal attitude. . . .

There is no doubt that, in connection with the pledges, the flag salute is a form of utterance. Symbolism is a primitive but effective way of communicating ideas. The use of an emblem or flag to symbolize some system, idea, institution, or personality, is a short cut from mind to mind. Causes and nations, political parties, lodges and ecclesiastical groups seek to knit the loyalty of their followings to a flag or banner, a color or design. The State announces rank, function, and authority through crowns and maces, uniforms and black robes; the church speaks through the Cross, the Crucifix, the altar and shrine, and clerical raiment. Symbols of State often convey political ideas just as religious symbols come to convey theological ones. Associated with many of these symbols are appropriate gestures of acceptance or respect: a salute, a bowed or bared head, a bended knee. A person gets from a symbol the meaning he puts into it, and what is one man's comfort and inspiration is another's jest and scorn. . . .

It is also to be noted that the compulsory flag salute and pledge requires affirmation of a belief and an attitude of mind. It is not clear whether the regulation contemplates that pupils forego any contrary convictions of their own and become unwilling converts to the prescribed ceremony or whether it will be acceptable if they simulate assent by words without belief and by a gesture barren of meaning. It is now a commonplace that censorship or suppression of expression of opinion is tolerated by our Constitution only when the expression presents a clear and present danger of action of a kind the State is empowered to prevent and punish. It would seem that involuntary affirmation could be commanded only on even more immediate and urgent grounds than silence. But here the power of compulsion is invoked without any allegation that remaining passive during a flag salute ritual creates a clear and present danger that would justify an effort even to muffle expression. To sustain the compulsory flag salute we are required to say that a Bill of Rights which guards the individual's right to speak his own mind, left it open to public authorities to compel him to utter what is not in his mind.

Whether the First Amendment to the Constitution will permit officials to order observance of ritual of this nature does not depend upon whether as a voluntary exercise we would think it to be good, bad or merely innocuous. Any credo of nationalism is likely to include what some disapprove or to omit what others think essential, and to give off different overtones as it takes on different accents or interpretations. If official power exists to coerce acceptance of any patriotic creed, what it shall contain cannot be decided by courts, but must be largely discretionary with the ordaining authority, whose power to prescribe would no doubt include power to amend. Hence validity of the asserted power to force an American citizen publicly to profess any statement of belief or to engage in any ceremony of assent to one presents questions of power that must be considered independently of any idea we may have as to the utility of the ceremony in question.

Nor does the issue as we see it turn on one's possession of particular religious views or the sincerity with which they are held. While religion supplies appellees' motive for enduring the discomforts of making the issue in this case, many citizens who do not share these religious views hold such a compulsory rite to infringe constitutional liberty of the individual. It is not necessary to inquire whether nonconformist beliefs will exempt from the duty to salute unless we first find power to make the salute a legal duty.

The Gobitis decision, however, assumed, as did the argument in that case and in this, that power exists in the State to impose the flag salute discipline upon school children in general. The Court only examined and rejected a claim based on religious beliefs of immunity from an unquestioned general rule. The question which underlies the flag salute controversy is whether such a ceremony so touching matters of opinion and political attitude may be imposed upon the individual by official authority under powers committed to any political organization under our Constitution. We examine rather than assume existence of this power and, against this broader definition of issues in this case, reexamine specific grounds assigned for the Gobitis decision. . . .

The Fourteenth Amendment, as now applied to the States, protects the citizen against the State itself and all of its creatures—Boards of Education not excepted. These have, of course, important, delicate, and highly discretionary functions, but none that they may not perform within the limits of the Bill of Rights. That they are educating the young for citizenship is reason for scrupulous protection of Constitutional freedoms of the individual, if we are not to strangle the free mind at its source and teach youth to discount important principles of our government as mere platitudes.

Such Boards are numerous and their territorial jurisdiction often small. But small and local authority may feel less sense of responsibility to the Constitution, and agencies of publicity may be less vigilant in calling it to account. The action of Congress in making flag observance voluntary and respecting the conscience of the objector in a matter so vital as raising the Army contrasts sharply with these local regulations in matters relatively trivial to the welfare of the nation. There are village tyrants as well as village Hampdens, but none who acts under color of law is beyond reach of the Constitution.

The Gobitis opinion reasoned that this is a field "where courts possess no marked and certainly no controlling competence," that it is committed to the legislatures as well as the courts to guard cherished liberties and that it is constitutionally appropriate to "fight out the wise use of legislative authority in the forum of public opinion and before legislative assemblies rather than to transfer such a contest to the judicial arena," since all the "effective means of inducing political changes are left free." The very purpose of a Bill of Rights was to withdraw certain subjects from the vicissitudes of political controversy, to place them beyond the reach of majorities and officials and to establish them as legal principles to be applied by the courts. One's right to life, liberty, and property, to free speech, a free press, freedom of worship and assembly, and other fundamental rights may not be submitted to vote; they depend on the outcome of no elections. . . .

Lastly, and this is the very heart of the Gobitis opinion, it reasons that "National unity is the basis of national security," that the authorities have "the right to select appropriate means for its attainment," and hence reaches the conclusion that such compulsory measures toward "national unity" are constitutional. Upon the verity of this assumption depends our answer in this case. National unity as an end which officials may foster by persuasion and example is not in question. The problem is whether under our Constitution compulsion as here employed is a permissible means for its achievement.

Struggles to coerce uniformity of sentiment in support of some end thought essential to their time and country have been waged by many good as well as by evil men. Nationalism is a relatively recent phenomenon but at other times and places the ends have been racial or territorial security, support of a dynasty or regime, and particular plans for saving souls. As first and moderate methods to attain unity have failed, those bent on its accomplishment must resort to an ever-increasing severity. As governmental pressure toward unity becomes greater, so strife becomes more bitter as to whose unity it shall be. Probably no deeper division of our people could proceed from any provocation than from finding it necessary to choose what doctrine and whose program public educational officials shall compel youth to unite in embracing. Ultimate futility of such attempts to compel coherence is the lesson of every such effort from the Roman drive to stamp out Christianity as a disturber of its pagan unity, the Inquisition, as a means to religious and dynastic unity, the Siberian exiles as a means to Russian unity, down to the fast failing efforts of our present totalitarian enemies. Those who begin coercive elimination of dissent soon find themselves exterminating dissenters. Compulsory unification of opinion achieves only the unanimity of the graveyard.

It seems trite but necessary to say that the First Amendment to our Constitution was designed to avoid these ends by avoiding these beginnings. There is no mysticism in the American concept of the State or of the nature or origin of its authority. We set up government by consent of the governed, and the Bill of Rights denies those in power any legal opportunity to coerce that consent. Authority here is to be controlled by public opinion, not public opinion by authority.

The case is made difficult not because the principles of its decision are obscure but because the flag involved is our own. Nevertheless, we apply the limitations of the Constitution with no fear that freedom to be intellectually and spiritually diverse or even contrary will disintegrate the social organization. To believe that patriotism will not flourish if patriotic ceremonies are voluntary and spontaneous instead of a compulsory routine is to make an unflattering estimate of the appeal of our institutions to free minds. We can have intellectual individualism and the rich cultural diversities that we owe to exceptional minds only at the price of

occasional eccentricity and abnormal attitudes. When they are so harmless to others or to the State as those we deal with here, the price is not too great. But freedom to differ is not limited to things that do not matter much. That would be a mere shadow of freedom. The test of its substance is the right to differ as to things that touch the heart of the existing order.

If there is any fixed star in our constitutional constellation, it is that no official, high or petty, can prescribe what shall be orthodox in politics, nationalism, religion, or other matters of opinion or force citizens to confess by word or act their faith therein. If there are any circumstances which permit an exception, they do not now occur to us.

We think the action of the local authorities in compelling the flag salute and pledge transcends constitutional limitations on their power and invades the sphere of intellect and spirit which it is the purpose of the First Amendment to our Constitution to reserve from all official control.

The decision of this Court in Minersville School District v. Gobitis and the holdings of those few per curiam decisions which preceded and foreshadowed it are overruled, and the judgment enjoining enforcement of the West Virginia Regulation is affirmed.

Mr. Justice Roberts and Mr. Justice Reed adhere to the views expressed by the Court in Minersville School District v. Gobitis, and are of the opinion that the judgment below should be reversed.

Mr. Justice Frankfurter, dissenting.

One who belongs to the most vilified and persecuted minority in history is not likely to be insensible to the freedoms guaranteed by our Constitution. Were my purely personal attitude relevant I should wholeheartedly associate myself with the general libertarian views in the Court's opinion, representing as they do the thought and action of a lifetime. But as judges we are neither Jew nor Gentile, neither Catholic nor agnostic. We owe equal attachment to the Constitution and are equally bound by our judicial obligations whether we derive our citizenship from the earliest or the latest immigrants to these shores. As a member of this Court I am not justified in writing my private notions of policy into the Constitution, no matter how deeply I may cherish them or how mischievous I may deem their disregard. The duty of a judge who must decide which of two claims before the Court shall prevail, that of a State to enact and enforce laws within its general competence or that of an individual to refuse obedience because of the demands of his conscience, is not that of the ordinary person. It can never be emphasized too much that one's own opinion about the wisdom or evil of a law should be excluded altogether when one is doing one's duty on the bench. The only opinion of our own even looking in that direction that is material is our opinion whether legislators could in reason have enacted such a law. In the light of all the circumstances, including the history of this question in this Court, it would require more daring than I possess to deny that reasonable legislators could have taken the action which is before us for review. Most unwillingly, therefore, I must differ from my brethren with regard to legislation like this. I cannot bring my mind to believe that the "liberty" secured by the Due Process Clause gives this Court authority to deny to the State of West Virginia the attainment of that which we all recognize as a legitimate legislative end, namely, the promotion of good citizenship, by employment of the means here chosen. . . .

The reason why from the beginning even the narrow judicial authority to nullify legislation has been viewed with a jealous eye is that it serves to prevent the full play of the democratic process. The fact that it may be an undemocratic aspect of our scheme of government does not call for its rejection or its disuse. But it is the best of reasons, as this Court has frequently recognized, for the greatest caution in its use. . . .

Under our constitutional system the legislature is charged solely with civil concerns of society. If the avowed or intrinsic legislative purpose is either to promote or to discourage some religious community or creed, it is clearly within the constitutional restrictions imposed on legislatures and cannot stand. But it by no means follows that legislative power is wanting whenever a general non-discriminatory civil regulation in fact touches conscientious scruples or religious beliefs of an individual or a group. Regard for such scruples or beliefs undoubtedly presents one of the most reasonable claims for the exertion of legislative accommodation. It is, of course, beyond our power to rewrite the state's requirement, by providing exemptions for those who do not wish to participate in the flag salute or by making some other accommodations to meet their scruples. That wisdom might suggest the making of such accommodations and that school administration would not find it too difficult to make them and yet maintain the ceremony for those not refusing to conform, is outside our province to suggest. Tact, respect, and generosity toward variant views will always commend themselves to those charged with the duties of legislation so as to achieve a maximum of good will and to require a minimum of unwilling submission to a general law. But the real question is, who is to make such accommodations, the courts or the legislature?

This is no dry, technical matter. It cuts deep into one's conception of the democratic process—it concerns no less the practical differences between the means for making these accommodations that are open to courts and to legislatures. A court can only strike down. It can only say "This or that law is void." It cannot modify or qualify, it cannot make exceptions to a general requirement. And it strikes down not merely for a day. At least the finding of unconstitutionality ought not to have ephemeral significance unless the Constitution is to be reduced to the fugitive importance of mere legislation. . . .

Conscientious scruples, all would admit, cannot stand against every legislative compulsion to do positive acts in conflict with such scruples. We have been told that such compulsions override religious scruples only as to major concerns of the state. But the determination of what is major and what is minor itself raises questions of policy. For the way in which men equally guided by reason appraise importance goes to the very heart of policy. Judges should be very diffident in setting their judgment against that of a state in determining what is and what is not a major concern, what means are appropriate to proper ends, and what is the total social cost in striking the balance of imponderables. . . .

The constitutional protection of religious freedom terminated disabilities, it did not create new privileges. It gave religious equality, not civil immunity. Its essence is freedom from conformity to religious dogma, not freedom from conformity to law because of religious dogma. Religious loyalties may be exercised without hindrance from the state, not the state may not exercise that which except by leave of religious loyalties is within the domain of temporal power. Otherwise each individual could set up his own censor against obedience to laws conscientiously deemed for the public good by those whose business it is to make laws. . . . That which to the majority may seem essential for the welfare of the state may offend the consciences of a minority. But, so long as no inroads are made upon the actual exercise of religion by the minority, to deny the political power of the majority to enact laws concerned with civil matters, simply because they may offend the consciences of a minority, really means that the consciences of a minority are more sacred and more enshrined in the Constitution than the consciences of a majority. . . .

I am fortified in my view of this case by the history of the flag salute controversy in this Court. Five times has the precise question now before us been adjudicated. Four times the Court unanimously found that the requirement of such a school exercise was not beyond the powers of the states. . . . The fifth case, Minersville District v. Gobitis, was brought here because the decision of the Circuit Court of Appeals for the Third Circuit ran counter to our rulings. They were reaffirmed after full consideration, with one Justice dissenting. What may be even more significant than this uniform recognition of state authority is the fact that every Justice—thirteen in all—who has hitherto participated in judging this matter has at one or more times found no constitutional infirmity in what is now condemned. Only the two Justices sitting for the first time on this matter have not heretofore found this legislation inoffensive to the "liberty" guaranteed by the Constitution. . . .

One's conception of the Constitution cannot be severed from one's conception of a judge's function in applying it. The Court has no reason for existence if it merely reflects the pressures of the day. Our system is built on the faith that men set apart for this special function, freed from the influences of immediacy and from the deflections of worldly ambition, will become able to take a view of longer range than the period of responsibility entrusted to Congress and legislatures. We are dealing with matters as to which legislators and voters have conflicting views. Are we as judges to impose our strong convictions on where wisdom lies? That which three years ago had seemed to five successive Courts to lie within permissible areas of legislation is now outlawed by the deciding shift of opinion of two Justices. What reason is there to believe that they or their successors may not have another view a few years hence? Is that which was deemed to be of so fundamental a nature as to be written into the Constitution to endure for all times to be the sport of shifting winds of doctrine? Of course, judicial opinions, even as to questions of constitutionality, are not immutable. As has been true in the past, the Court will from time to time reverse its position. But I believe that never before these Jehovah's Witnesses cases (except for minor deviations subsequently retraced) has this Court overruled decisions so as to restrict the powers of democratic government. Always heretofore, it has withdrawn narrow views of legislative authority so as to authorize what formerly it had denied.

In view of this history it must be plain that what thirteen Justices found to be within the constitutional authority of a state, legislators can not be deemed unreasonable in enacting. Therefore, in denying to the states what heretofore has received such impressive judicial sanction, some other tests of unconstitutionality must surely be guiding the Court than the absence of a rational justification for the legislation. But I know of no other test which this Court is authorized to apply in nullifying legislation.

In the past this Court has from time to time set its views of policy against that embodied in legislation by finding laws in conflict with what was called the "spirit of the Constitution." Such undefined destructive power was not conferred on this Court by the Constitution. Before a duly enacted law can be judicially nullified, it must be forbidden by some explicit restriction upon political authority in the Constitution. Equally inadmissible is the claim to strike down legislation because to us as individuals it seems opposed to the "plan and purpose" of the Constitution. That is too tempting a basis for finding in one's personal views the purposes of the Founders.

The uncontrollable power wielded by this Court brings it very close to the most sensitive areas of public affairs. As appeal from legislation to adjudication becomes more frequent, and its consequences more far-reaching, judicial self-restraint becomes more and not less important, lest we unwarrantably enter social and political domains wholly outside our concern. I think I appreciate fully the objections to the law before us. But to deny that it presents a question upon which men might reasonably differ appears to me to be intolerance. And since men may so reasonably differ, I deem it beyond my constitutional power to assert my view of the wisdom of this law against the view of the State of West Virginia. . . .

Of course patriotism cannot be enforced by the flag salute. But neither can the liberal spirit be enforced by judicial invalidation of illiberal legislation. Our constant preoccupation with the constitutionality of legislation rather than with its wisdom tends to preoccupation of the American mind with a false value. The tendency of focusing attention on constitutionality is to make constitutionality synonymous with wisdom, to regard a law as all right if it is constitutional. Such an attitude is a great enemy of liberalism. Particularly in legislation affecting freedom of thought and freedom of speech much which should offend a free-spirited society is constitutional. Reliance for the most precious interests of civilization, therefore, must be found outside of their vindication in courts of law. Only a persistent positive translation of the faith of a free society into the convictions and habits and actions of a community is the ultimate reliance against unabated temptations to fetter the human spirit.

SHERBERT V. VERNER
374 U.S. 398 (1963)

"The ruling [of the lower court that Adell Sherbert, a Seventh-day Adventist, could be denied unemployment benefits for refusing to work on Saturdays] forces her to choose between following the precepts of her religion and forfeiting benefits . . . and abandoning one of the precepts of her religion in order to accept work. . . . Governmental imposition of such a choice puts the same kind of burden upon the free exercise of religion as would a fine imposed against [Sherbert] for her Saturday worship."

The Question: Can a state refuse to pay unemployment benefits to a person who lost her job because she refused to work on Saturdays, the Sabbath day of her religious denomination, the Seventh-day Adventists?

The Arguments: PRO

Payment of unemployment benefits is limited to workers who lose their jobs for reasons beyond their control, such as layoffs, closing a factory or business, and natural disasters such as floods and hurricanes. The law does not allow benefits to persons who refuse "without good cause" to accept available work assignments from an employer. To allow any worker to refuse to work on Saturdays, or other days that might not suit them, would open the gates for workers to make unreasonable demands on their employers for work schedules that might disrupt production. Even sincere religious beliefs do not exempt a worker from rules that apply to everyone and that were not designed to punish workers for their religious beliefs.

CON

The state cannot single out those with religious scruples against working on their Sabbath day and deny them unemployment benefits, without violating their rights to freely practice their religion. There are ample means to determine if workers are abusing the unemployment benefit system with claims that are not based on sincere religious belief. The law does not punish those who belong to denominations whose Sabbath day is Sunday for refusing to work on that day; it is only those whose Sabbath falls on Saturday, such as Seventh-day Adventists or Orthodox Jews, who are barred from receiving benefits if they lose their jobs for this reason.

MR. JUSTICE BRENNAN delivered the opinion of the Court.

Appellant, a member of the Seventh-day Adventist Church, was discharged by her South Carolina employer because she would not work on Saturday, the Sabbath Day of her faith. When she was unable to obtain other employment because from conscientious scruples she would not take Saturday work, she filed a claim for unemployment compensation benefits under the South Carolina Unemployment Compensation Act. That law provides that, to be eligible for benefits, a claimant must be "able to work and . . . available for work"; and, further, that a claimant is ineligible for benefits "[i]f . . . he has failed, without good cause . . . to accept available suitable work when offered him by the employment office or the employer. . . ." The Employment Security Commission, in administrative proceedings under the statute, found that appellant's restriction upon her availability for Saturday work brought her within the provision disqualifying for benefits insured workers who fail, without good cause, to accept "suitable work when offered . . . by the employment office or the employer. . . ." The Commission's finding was sustained by the Court of Common Pleas for Spartanburg County. That court's judgment was in turn affirmed by the South Carolina Supreme Court, which rejected appellant's contention that, as applied to her, the disqualifying provisions of the South Carolina statute abridged her right to the free exercise of her religion secured under the Free Exercise Clause of the First Amendment. . . . We reverse the judgment of the South Carolina Supreme Court and remand for further proceedings not inconsistent with this opinion.

The door of the Free Exercise Clause stands tightly closed against any governmental regulation of religious beliefs as such. Government may neither compel affirmation of a repugnant belief, nor penalize or discriminate against individuals or groups because they hold religious views abhorrent to the authorities. . . . On the other hand, the Court has rejected challenges under the Free Exercise Clause to governmental regulation of certain overt acts prompted by religious beliefs or principles, for "even when the action is in accord with one's religious convictions, [it] is not totally free from legislative restrictions." The conduct or actions so regulated have invariably posed some substantial threat to public safety, peace or order.

Plainly enough, appellant's conscientious objection to Saturday work constitutes no conduct prompted by religious principles of a kind within the reach of state legislation. If, therefore, the decision of the South Carolina Supreme Court is to withstand appellant's constitutional challenge, it must be either because her disqualification as a beneficiary represents no infringement by the State of her constitutional rights of free exercise, or because any incidental burden on the free exercise of appellant's religion may be justified by a "compelling state interest in the regulation of a subject within the State's constitutional power to regulate. . . ."

We turn first to the question whether the disqualification for benefits imposes any burden on the free exercise of appellant's religion. We think it is clear that it does. In a sense the consequences of such a disqualification to religious principles and practices may be only an indirect result of welfare legislation within the State's general competence to enact; it is true that no criminal sanctions directly compel appellant to work a six-day week. But this is only the beginning, not the end, of our inquiry. Here not only is it apparent that appellant's declared ineligibility for benefits derives solely from the practice of her religion, but the pressure upon her to forego that practice is unmistakable. The ruling forces her to choose between following the precepts of her religion and forfeiting benefits, on the one hand, and abandoning one of the precepts of her religion in order to accept work, on the other hand. Governmental imposition of such a choice puts the same kind of burden upon the free exercise of religion as would a fine imposed against appellant for her Saturday worship.

Nor may the South Carolina court's construction of the statute be saved from constitutional infirmity on the ground that unemployment compensation benefits are not appellant's "right" but merely a "privilege." It is too late in the day to doubt that the liberties of religion and expression may be infringed by the denial of or placing of conditions upon a benefit or privilege. [T]o condition the availability of benefits upon this appellant's willingness to violate a cardinal principle of her religious faith effectively penalizes the free exercise of her constitutional liberties.

Significantly South Carolina expressly saves the Sunday worshipper from having to make the kind of choice which we here hold infringes the Sabbatarian's religious liberty. When in times of "national emergency" the textile plants are authorized by the State Commissioner of Labor to operate on Sunday, "no employee shall be required to work on Sunday . . . who is conscientiously opposed to Sunday work; and if any employee should refuse to work on Sunday on account of conscientious . . . objections he or she shall not jeopardize his or her seniority by such refusal or be discriminated against in any other manner." No question of the disqualification of a Sunday worshipper for benefits is likely to arise, since we cannot suppose that an employer will discharge him in violation of this statute. The unconstitutionality of the disqualification of the Sabbatarian is thus compounded by the religious discrimination which South Carolina's general statutory scheme necessarily effects.

We must next consider whether some compelling state interest enforced in the eligibility provisions of the South Carolina statute justifies the substantial infringement of appellant's First Amendment right. It is basic that no showing merely of a rational relationship to some colorable state interest would suffice; in this highly sensitive constitutional area . . . The appellees suggest no more than a possibility that the filing of fraudulent claims by unscrupulous claimants feigning religious objections to Saturday work might not only dilute the unemployment compensation fund but also hinder the scheduling by employers of necessary Saturday work. But that possibility is not apposite here because . . . even if the possibility of spurious claims did threaten to dilute the fund and disrupt the scheduling of work, it would plainly be incumbent upon the appellees to demonstrate that no alternative forms of regulation would combat such abuses without infringing First Amendment rights. . . .

In holding as we do, plainly we are not fostering the "establishment" of the Seventh-day Adventist religion in South Carolina, for the extension of unemployment benefits to Sabbatarians in common with Sunday worshippers reflects nothing more than the governmental obligation of neutrality in the face of religious differences, and does not represent that involvement of religious with secular institutions which it is the object of the Establishment Clause to forestall. Nor does the recognition of the appellant's right to unemployment benefits under the state statute serve to abridge any other person's religious liberties. Nor do we, by our decision today, declare the existence of a constitutional right to unemployment benefits on the part of all persons whose religious convictions are the cause of their unemployment. This is not a case in which an employee's religious convictions serve to make him a nonproductive member of society. Finally, nothing we say today constrains the States to adopt any particular form or scheme of unemployment compensation. Our holding today is only that South Carolina may not constitutionally apply the eligibility provisions so as to constrain a worker to abandon his religious convictions respecting the day of rest.

The judgment of the South Carolina Supreme Court is reversed and the case is remanded for further proceedings not inconsistent with this opinion.

Mr. Justice Harlan, whom Mr. Justice White joins, dissenting.

Today's decision is disturbing both in its rejection of existing precedent and in its implications for the future. The significance of the decision can best be understood after an examination of the state law applied in this case.

South Carolina's Unemployment Compensation Law was enacted in 1936 in response to the grave social and economic problems that arose during the depression of that period. Thus the purpose of the legislature was to tide people over, and to avoid social and economic chaos, during periods when work was unavailable. But at the same time there was clearly no intent to provide relief for those who for purely personal reasons were or became unavailable for work. In accordance with this design, the legislature provided that "[a]n unemployed insured worker shall be eligible to receive benefits with respect to any week only if the Commission finds that . . . [h]e is able to work and is available for work. . . ."

The South Carolina Supreme Court has uniformly applied this law in conformity with its clearly expressed purpose. It has consistently held that one is not "available for work" if his unemployment has resulted not from the inability of industry to provide a job but rather from personal circumstances, no matter how compelling. The reference to "involuntary unemployment" in the legislative statement of policy, whatever a sociologist, philosopher, or theologian might say, has been interpreted not to embrace such personal circumstances. In the present case all that the state court has done is to apply these accepted principles. Since virtually all of the mills in the Spartanburg area were operating on a six-day week, the appellant was "unavailable for work," and thus ineligible for benefits, when personal considerations prevented her from accepting employment on a fulltime basis in the industry and locality in which she had worked. The fact that these personal considerations sprang from her religious convictions was wholly without relevance to the state court's application of the law. Thus in no proper sense can it be said that the State discriminated against the appellant on the basis of her religious beliefs or that she was denied benefits because she was a Seventh-day Adventist. She was denied benefits just as any other claimant would be denied benefits who was not "available for work" for personal reasons.

With this background, this Court's decision comes into clearer focus. What the Court is holding is that if the State chooses to condition unemployment compensation on the applicant's availability for work, it is constitutionally compelled to carve out an exception—and to provide benefits—for those whose unavailability is due to their religious convictions. Such a holding has particular significance in two respects.

First, despite the Court's protestations to the contrary, the decision necessarily overrules Braunfeld v. Brown, which held that it did not offend the "Free Exercise" Clause of the Constitution for a State to forbid a Sabbatarian to do business on Sunday. The secular purpose of the statute before us today is even clearer than that involved in Braunfeld. And just as in Braunfeld—where exceptions to the Sunday closing laws for Sabbatarians would have been inconsistent with the purpose to achieve a uniform day of rest and would have required case-by-case inquiry into religious beliefs—so here, an exception to the rules of eligibility based on religious convictions would necessitate judicial examination of those convictions and would be at odds with the limited purpose of the statute to smooth out the economy during periods of industrial instability. Finally, the indirect financial burden of the present law is far less than that involved in Braunfeld. Forcing a store owner to close his business on Sunday may well have the effect of depriving him of a satisfactory livelihood if his religious convictions require him to close on Saturday as well. Here we are dealing only with temporary benefits, amounting to a fraction of regular weekly wages and running for not more than 22 weeks. Clearly, any difference between this case and Braunfeld cut against the present appellant.

Second, the implications of the present decision are far more troublesome than its apparently narrow dimensions would indicate at first glance. The meaning of today's holding, as already noted, is that the State must furnish unemployment benefits to one who is unavailable for work if the unavailability stems from the exercise of religious convictions. The State, in other words, must single out for financial assistance those whose behavior is religiously motivated, even though it denies such assistance to others whose identical behavior (in this case, inability to work on Saturdays) is not religiously motivated. . . .

It has been suggested that such singling out of religious conduct for special treatment may violate the constitutional limitations on state action. My own view, however, is that at least under the circumstances of this case it would be a permissible accommodation of religion for the State, if it chose to do so, to create an exception to its eligibility requirements for persons like the appellant. The constitutional obligation of "neutrality" is not so narrow a channel that the slightest deviation from an absolutely straight course leads to condemnation. There are too many instances in which no such course can be charted, too many areas in which the pervasive

activities of the State justify some special provision for religion to prevent it from being submerged by an all-embracing secularism. . . . But there is, I believe, enough flexibility in the Constitution to permit a legislative judgment accommodating an unemployment compensation law to the exercise of religious beliefs such as appellant's.

For very much the same reasons, however, I cannot subscribe to the conclusion that the State is constitutionally compelled to carve out an exception to its general rule of eligibility in the present case. Those situations in which the Constitution may require special treatment on account of religion are, in my view, few and far between, . . . Such compulsion in the present case is particularly inappropriate in light of the indirect, remote, and insubstantial effect of the decision below on the exercise of appellant's religion and in light of the direct financial assistance to religion that today's decision requires. For these reasons I respectfully dissent from the opinion and judgment of the Court.

WISCONSIN V. YODER
406 U.S. 205 (1972)

"The programs and values of the modern secondary school are in sharp conflict with the fundamental mode of life mandated by the Amish religion; modern laws requiring compulsory secondary education [interfere with] the religious development of the Amish child and his integration into the way of life of the Amish faith community at the crucial adolescent stage of development [and contravene] the basic religious tenets and practice of the Amish community."

The Question: Can a state impose criminal penalties on parents who belong to religious groups that believe children should not attend public schools past the eighth grade, such as the Old Order Amish or Conservative Mennonites, for violations of state law that requires attendance in school until age sixteen?

The Arguments: PRO

States have the power to set the minimum age for leaving school; in this case, the state of Wisconsin has set that age at sixteen. The reasons for this policy are that students need the skills that are taught in grades nine through eleven in order to obtain good jobs and to participate in society and government as an informed citizen. Allowing students to leave school before age sixteen, simply because they belong to a religious denomination that does not believe in education past that level, would open the door for other parents to take their children out of school for other reasons. The interests of the child in being able to pursue topics such as science, math, and foreign languages should not be subject to a parent's decision.

CON

This case involves a very limited and narrow exemption from school-attendance laws for members of particular religious groups whose beliefs and practices are rooted in hundreds of years of tradition. There is evidence that Amish and Mennonite children might be unable to function in their traditional, farm-based culture if they were subjected to the mores, music, and manners of teenagers from very different backgrounds. In addition, it is clear that Amish and Mennonite children are well trained after they leave school in the skills they need, farming for boys and household management for girls. The state has shown no compelling reason to violate the sincere religious beliefs of Amish and Mennonite parents.

MR. CHIEF JUSTICE BURGER delivered the opinion of the Court.

On petition of the State of Wisconsin, we granted the writ of certiorari in this case to review a decision of the Wisconsin Supreme Court holding that respondents' convictions of violating the State's compulsory school-attendance law were invalid under the Free Exercise Clause of the First Amendment to the United States Constitution made applicable to the States by the Fourteenth Amendment. For the reasons hereafter stated we affirm the judgment of the Supreme Court of Wisconsin.

Respondents Jonas Yoder and Wallace Miller are members of the Old Order Amish religion, and respondent Adin Yutzy is a member of the Conservative Amish Mennonite Church. They and their families are residents of Green County, Wisconsin. Wisconsin's compulsory school-attendance law required them to cause their children to attend public or private school until reaching age 16 but the respondents declined to send their children, ages 14 and 15, to public school after they completed the eighth grade. The children were not enrolled in any private school, or within any recognized exception to the compulsory-attendance law, and they are conceded to be subject to the Wisconsin statute.

On complaint of the school district administrator for the public schools, respondents were charged, tried, and convicted of violating the compulsory-attendance law in Green Country Court and were fined the sum of $5 each. Respondents defended on the ground that the application of the compulsory-attendance law violated their rights under the First and Fourteenth Amendments. The trial testimony showed that respondents believed, in accordance with the tenets of Old Order Amish communities generally, that their children's attendance at high school, public or private, was contrary to the Amish religion and way of life. They believed that by sending their children to high school, they would not only expose themselves to the danger of the censure of the church community, but, as found by the county court, also endanger their own salvation and that of their children. The State stipulated that respondents' religious beliefs were sincere. . . .

In support of their position, respondents presented as expert witnesses scholars on religion and education whose testimony is uncontradicted. They expressed their opinions on the relationship of the Amish belief concerning school attendance to the more general tenets of their religion, and described the impact that compulsory high school attendance could have on the continued survival of Amish communities as they exist in the United States today. The history of the Amish sect was given in some detail, beginning with the Swiss Anabaptists of the 16th century who rejected institutionalized churches and sought to return to the early, simple, Christian life de-emphasizing material success, rejecting the competitive spirit, and seeking to insulate themselves from the modern world. As a result of their common heritage, Old Order Amish communities today are characterized by a fundamental belief that salvation requires life in a church community separate and apart from the world and worldly influence. This concept of life aloof from the world and its values is central to their faith.

A related feature of Old Order Amish communities is their devotion to a life in harmony with nature and the soil, as exemplified by the simple life of the early Christian era that continued in America during much of our early national life. Amish beliefs require members of the community to make their living by farming or closely related activities. Broadly speaking, the Old Order Amish religion pervades and determines the entire mode of life of its adherents. Their conduct is regulated in great detail by the Ordnung, or rules, of the church community. Adult baptism, which occurs in late adolescence, is the time at which Amish young people voluntarily undertake heavy obligations, not unlike the Bar Mitzvah of the Jews, to abide by the rules of the church community.

Amish objection to formal education beyond the eighth grade is firmly grounded in these central religious concepts. They object to the high school, and higher education generally, because the values they teach are in marked variance with Amish values and the Amish way of life; they view secondary school education as an impermissible exposure of their children to a "worldly" influence in conflict with their beliefs. The high school tends to emphasize intellectual and scientific accomplishments, self-distinction, competitiveness, worldly success, and social life with other students. Amish society emphasizes informal learning-through-doing; a life of "goodness," rather than a life of intellect; wisdom, rather than technical knowledge; community welfare, rather than competition; and separation from, rather than integration with, contemporary worldly society.

Formal high school education beyond the eighth grade is contrary to Amish beliefs, not only because it places Amish children in an environment hostile to Amish beliefs with increasing emphasis on competition in class work and sports and with pressure to conform to the styles, manners, and ways of the peer group, but also because it takes them away from their community, physically and emotionally, during the crucial and formative adolescent period of life. During this period, the children must acquire Amish attitudes favoring manual work and self-reliance and the specific skills needed to perform the adult role of an Amish farmer or housewife. They must learn to enjoy physical labor. Once a child has learned basic reading, writing, and elementary mathematics, these traits, skills, and attitudes admittedly fall within the category of those best learned through example and "doing" rather than in a classroom. And, at this time in life, the Amish child must also grow in his faith and his relationship to the Amish community if he is to be prepared to accept the heavy obligations imposed by adult baptism. . . . The Amish do not object to elementary education through the first eight grades as a general proposition because they agree that their children must have basic skills in the "three R's" in order to read the Bible, to be good farmers and citizens, and to be able to deal with non-Amish people when necessary in the course of daily affairs. They view such a basic education as acceptable because it does not significantly expose their children to worldly values or interfere with their development in the Amish community during the crucial adolescent period. While Amish accept compulsory elementary education generally, wherever possible they have established their own elementary schools in many respects like the small local schools of the past. In the Amish belief higher learning tends to develop values they reject as influences that alienate man from God. . . .

There is no doubt as to the power of a State, having a high responsibility for education of its citizens, to impose reasonable regulations for the control and duration of basic education. See, e.g., Pierce v. Society of Sisters. Providing public schools ranks at the very apex of the function of a State. Yet even this paramount responsibility was, in Pierce, made to yield to the right of parents to provide an equivalent education in a privately operated system. There the Court held that Oregon's statute compelling attendance in a public school from age eight to age 16 unreasonably interfered with the interest of parents in directing the rearing of their offspring, including their education in church-operated schools. . . .

The record shows that the respondents' religious beliefs and attitude toward life, family, and home have remained constant—perhaps some would say static—in a period of unparalleled progress in human knowledge generally and great changes in education. The respondents freely concede, and indeed assert as an article of faith, that their religious beliefs and what we would today call "life style" have not altered in fundamentals for centuries. Their way of life in a church-oriented community, separated from the outside world and "worldly" influences, their attachment to nature and the soil, is a way inherently simple and uncomplicated, albeit difficult to preserve against the pressure to conform. Their rejection of telephones, automobiles, radios, and television, their mode of dress, of speech, their habits of manual work do indeed set them apart from much of contemporary society; these customs are both symbolic and practical.

As the society around the Amish has become more populous, urban, industrialized, and complex, particularly in this century, government regulation of human affairs has correspondingly become more detailed and pervasive. The Amish mode of life has thus come into conflict increasingly with requirements of contemporary society exerting a hydraulic insistence on conformity to majoritarian standards. So long as compulsory education laws were confined to eight grades of elementary basic education imparted in a nearby rural schoolhouse, with a large proportion of students of the Amish faith, the Old Order Amish had little basis to fear that school attendance would expose their children to the worldly influence they reject. But modern compulsory secondary education in rural areas is now largely carried on in a consolidated school, often remote from the student's home and alien to his daily home life. As the record so strongly shows, the values and programs of the modern secondary school are in sharp conflict with the fundamental mode of life mandated by the Amish religion; modern laws requiring compulsory secondary education have accordingly engendered great concern and conflict. The conclusion is inescapable that secondary schooling, by exposing Amish children to worldly influences in terms of attitudes, goals, and values contrary to beliefs, and by substantially interfering with the religious development of the Amish child and his integration into the way of life of the Amish faith community at the crucial adolescent stage of development, contravenes the basic religious tenets and practice of the Amish faith, both as to the parent and the child. . . .

In sum, the unchallenged testimony of acknowledged experts in education and religious history, almost 300 years of consistent practice, and strong evidence of a sustained faith pervading and regulating respondents' entire mode of life support the claim that enforcement of the State's requirement of compulsory formal education after the eighth grade would gravely endanger if not destroy the free exercise of respondents' religious beliefs.

Neither the findings of the trial court nor the Amish claims as to the nature of their faith are challenged in this Court by the State of Wisconsin. Its position is that the State's interest in universal compulsory formal secondary education to age 16 is so great that it is paramount to the undisputed claims of respondents that their mode of preparing their youth for Amish life, after the traditional elementary education, is an essential part of their religious belief and practice. Nor does the State undertake to meet the claim that the Amish mode of life and education is inseparable from and a part of the basic tenets of their religion—indeed, as much a part of their religious belief and practices as baptism, the confessional, or a sabbath may be for others.

Wisconsin concedes that under the Religion Clauses religious beliefs are absolutely free from the State's control, but it argues that "actions," even though religiously grounded, are outside the protection of the First Amendment. But our decisions have rejected the idea that religiously grounded conduct is always outside the protection of the Free Exercise Clause. It is true that activities of individuals, even when religiously based, are often subject to regulation by the States in the exercise of their undoubted power to promote the health, safety, and general welfare, or the Federal Government in the exercise of its delegated powers. But to agree that religiously grounded conduct must often be subject to the broad police power of the State is not to deny that there are areas of conduct protected by the Free Exercise Clause of the First Amendment and thus beyond the power of the State to control, even under regulations of general applicability. . . .

We turn, then, to the State's broader contention that its interest in its system of compulsory education is so compelling that even the established religious practices of the Amish must give way. Where fundamental claims of religious freedom are at stake, however, we cannot accept such a sweeping claim; despite its admitted validity in the generality of cases, we must searchingly examine the interests that the State seeks to promote by its requirement for compulsory education to age 16, and the impediment to those objectives that would flow from recognizing the claimed Amish exemption. The State advances two primary arguments in support of its system of compulsory education. It notes, as Thomas Jefferson pointed out early in our history, that some degree of education is necessary to prepare citizens to participate effectively and intelligently in our open political system if we are to preserve freedom and independence. Further, education prepares individuals to be self-reliant and self-sufficient participants in society. We accept these propositions.

However, the evidence adduced by the Amish in this case is persuasively to the effect that an additional one or two years of formal high school for Amish children in place of their long-established program of informal vocational education would do little to serve those interests. Respondents' experts testified at trial, without challenge, that the value of all education must be assessed in terms of its capacity to prepare the child for life. It is one thing to say that compulsory education for a year or two beyond the eighth grade may be necessary when its goal is the preparation of the child for life in modern society as the majority live, but it is quite another if the goal of education be viewed as the preparation of the child for life in the separated agrarian community that is the keystone of the Amish faith.

The State attacks respondents' position as one fostering "ignorance" from which the child must be protected by the State. No one can question the State's duty to protect children from ignorance but this argument does not square with the facts disclosed in the record. Whatever their idiosyncrasies as seen by the majority, this record strongly shows that the Amish community has been a highly successful social unit within our society, even if apart from the conventional "mainstream." Its members are productive and very law-abiding members of society; they reject public welfare in any of its usual modern forms. The Congress itself recognized their self-sufficiency by authorizing exemption of such groups as the Amish from the obligation to pay social security taxes. . . .

For the reasons stated we hold, with the Supreme Court of Wisconsin, that the First and Fourteenth Amendments prevent the State from compelling respondents to cause their children to attend formal high school to age 16. Our disposition of this case, however, in no way alters our recognition of the obvious fact that courts are not school boards or legislatures, and are ill-equipped to determine the "necessity" of discrete aspects of a State's program of compulsory education. This should suggest that courts must move with great circumspection in performing the sensitive and delicate task of weighing a State's legitimate social concern when faced with religious claims for exemption from generally applicable educational requirements. It cannot be overemphasized that we are not dealing with a way of life and mode of education by a group claiming to have recently discovered some "progressive" or more enlightened process for rearing children for modern life. . . .

Nothing we hold is intended to undermine the general applicability of the State's compulsory school-attendance statutes or to limit the power of the State to promulgate reasonable standards that, while not impairing the free exercise of religion, provide for continuing agricultural vocational education under parental and church guidance by the Old Order Amish or others similarly situated. The States have had a long history of amicable and effective relationships with church-sponsored schools, and there is no basis for assuming that, in this related context, reasonable standards cannot be established concerning the content of the continuing vocational education of Amish children under parental guidance, provided always that state regulations are not inconsistent with what we have said in this opinion.

Affirmed.

Mr. Justice Douglas, dissenting in part.

I agree with the Court that the religious scruples of the Amish are opposed to the education of their children beyond the grade schools, yet I disagree with the Court's conclusion that the matter is within the dispensation of parents alone. The Court's analysis assumes that the only interests at stake in the case are those of the Amish parents on the one hand, and those of the State on the other. The difficulty with this approach is that, despite the Court's claim, the parents are seeking to vindicate not only their own free exercise claims, but also those of their high-school-age children.

It is argued that the right of the Amish children to religious freedom is not presented by the facts of the case, as the issue before the Court involves only the Amish parents' religious freedom to defy a state criminal statute imposing upon them an affirmative duty to cause their children to attend high school. . . .

Religion is an individual experience. It is not necessary, nor even appropriate, for every Amish child to express his views on the subject in a prosecution of a single adult. Crucial, however, are the views of the child whose parent is the subject of the suit. Frieda Yoder has in fact testified that her own religious views are opposed to high-school education. I therefore join the judgment of the Court as to respondent Jonas Yoder. But Frieda Yoder's views may not be those of Vernon Yutzy or Barbara Miller. I must dissent, therefore, as to respondents Adin Yutzy and Wallace Miller as their motion to dismiss also raised the question of their children's religious liberty.

This issue has never been squarely presented before today. Our opinions are full of talk about the power of the parents over the child's education. See Pierce v. Society of Sisters, Meyer v. Nebraska. And we have in the past analyzed similar conflicts between parent and State with little regard for the views of the child. See Prince v. Massachusetts, supra. Recent cases, however, have clearly held that the children themselves have constitutionally protectible interests. . . .

On this important and vital matter of education, I think the children should be entitled to be heard. While the parents, absent dissent, normally speak for the entire family, the education of the child is a matter on which the child will often have decided views. He may want to be a pianist or an astronaut or an oceanographer. To do so he will have to break from the Amish tradition.

It is the future of the student, not the future of the parents, that is imperiled by today's decision. If a parent keeps his child out of school beyond the grade school, then the child will be forever barred from entry into the new and amazing world of diversity that we have today. The child may decide that that is the preferred course, or he may rebel. It is the student's judgment, not his parents', that is essential if we are to give full meaning to what we have said about the Bill of Rights and of the right of students to be masters of their own destiny. If he is harnessed to the Amish way of life by those in authority over him and if his education is truncated, his entire life may be stunted and deformed. The child, therefore, should be given an opportunity to be heard before the State gives the exemption which we honor today.

The views of the two children in question were not canvassed by the Wisconsin courts. The matter should be explicitly reserved so that new hearings can be held on remand of the case.

GOLDMAN V. WEINBERGER
475 U.S. 503 (1986)

"The military need not encourage debate or tolerate protest to the extent that such tolerance is required of the civilian state by the First Amendment; to accomplish its mission the military must foster instinctive obedience, unity, commitment, and esprit de corps."

The Question: Can the Air Force discipline an officer who is an Orthodox Jew for wearing a yarmulke, a small, round cap that is required by religious belief and practice to be worn indoors, in violation of military regulations that ban the wearing of any headgear while indoors, except for security personnel?

The Arguments: PRO

The very word *uniform* implies that all military personnel will be uniform in appearance while on duty, both indoors and out. The reasons for this policy are based on the military's need for strict obedience to orders, the feeling among personnel that all are treated equally and that none are given special exemptions from military rules and regulations. An officer who insists on adhering to the practices of Orthodox Judaism is free to leave the service if his or her religious beliefs are paramount. Creating special exemptions might encourage personnel with other religious practices relating to dress or grooming, such as the beards and turbans of Sikhs or the dreadlocks of Rastafarians, to further undermine uniform appearance and discipline, and might also create safety hazards.

CON

There is simply no evidence that the wearing of a small, unobtrusive yarmulke by an Orthodox Jewish officer creates any danger to discipline or morale. The officer is not impeded in his military duties, nor does his yarmulke create a safety hazard. The military should be willing to accommodate the sincere religious practices of personnel whose dress does not interfere with their duties. Furthermore, regulations can be drafted that would distinguish between yarmulkes, beards, turbans, or dreadlocks that might cause safety hazards or interfere with duties such as wearing helmets. There is no evidence, in fact, that any significant number of military personnel would ask for religious exemptions under such carefully drafted regulations.

JUSTICE REHNQUIST delivered the opinion of the Court.

Petitioner S. Simcha Goldman contends that the Free Exercise Clause of the First Amendment to the United States Constitution permits him to wear a yarmulke while in uniform, notwithstanding an Air Force regulation mandating uniform dress for Air Force personnel. The District Court for the District of Columbia permanently enjoined the Air Force from enforcing its regulation against petitioner and from penalizing him for wearing his yarmulke. The Court of Appeals for the District of Columbia Circuit reversed on the ground that the Air Force's strong interest in discipline justified the strict enforcement of its uniform dress requirements. We granted certiorari because of the importance of the question, and now affirm.

Petitioner Goldman is an Orthodox Jew and ordained rabbi. In 1973, he was accepted into the Armed Forces Health Professions Scholarship Program and placed on inactive reserve status in the Air Force while he studied clinical psychology at Loyola University of Chicago. During his three years in the scholarship program, he received a monthly stipend and an allowance for tuition, books, and fees. After completing his Ph.D. in psychology, petitioner entered active service in the United States Air Force as a commissioned officer, in accordance with a requirement that participants in the scholarship program serve one year of active duty for each year of subsidized education. Petitioner was stationed at March Air Force Base in Riverside, California, and served as a clinical psychologist at the mental health clinic on the base.

Until 1981, petitioner was not prevented from wearing his yarmulke on the base. He avoided controversy by remaining close to his duty station in the health clinic and by wearing his service cap over the yarmulke when out of doors. But in April 1981, after he testified as a defense witness at a court-martial wearing his yarmulke but not his service cap, opposing counsel lodged a complaint with Colonel Joseph Gregory, the Hospital Commander, arguing that petitioner's practice of wearing his yarmulke was a violation of Air Force Regulation (AFR) 35-10. This regulation states in pertinent part that "[h]eadgear will not be worn ... [w]hile indoors except by armed security police in the performance of their duties."

Colonel Gregory informed petitioner that wearing a yarmulke while on duty does indeed violate AFR 35-10, and ordered him not to violate this regulation outside the hospital. Although virtually all of petitioner's time on the base was spent in the hospital, he refused. Later, after petitioner's attorney protested to the Air Force General Counsel, Colonel Gregory revised his order to prohibit petitioner from wearing the yarmulke even in the hospital. Petitioner's request to report for duty in civilian clothing pending legal resolution of the issue was denied. The next day he received a formal letter of reprimand, and was warned that failure to obey AFR 35-10 could subject him to a court-martial. Colonel Gregory also withdrew a recommendation that petitioner's application to extend the term of his active service be approved, and substituted a negative recommendation.

Petitioner then sued respondent Secretary of Defense and others, claiming that the application of AFR 35-10 to prevent him from wearing his yarmulke infringed upon his First Amendment freedom to exercise his religious beliefs. The United States District Court for the District of Columbia ... permanently enjoined the Air Force from prohibiting petitioner from wearing a yarmulke while in uniform. Respondents appealed to the Court of Appeals for the District of Columbia Circuit, which reversed. As an initial matter, the Court of Appeals determined that the appropriate level of scrutiny of a military regulation that clashes with a constitutional right is neither strict scrutiny nor rational basis. Instead, it held that a military regulation must be examined to determine whether "legitimate military ends are sought to be achieved," and whether it is "designed to accommodate the individual right to an appropriate degree." Applying this test, the court concluded that "the Air Force's interest in uniformity renders the strict enforcement of its regulation permissible." ...

Our review of military regulations challenged on First Amendment grounds is far more deferential than constitutional review of similar laws or regulations designed for civilian society. The military need not encourage debate or tolerate protest to the extent that such tolerance is required of the civilian state by the First Amendment; to accomplish its mission the military must foster instinctive obedience, unity, commitment, and esprit de corps. The essence of military service "is the subordination of the desires and interests of the individual to the needs of the service." These aspects of military life do not, of course, render entirely nugatory in the military context the guarantees of the First Amendment. But "within the military community there is simply not the same [individual] autonomy as there is in the larger civilian community." In the context of the present case, when evaluating whether military needs justify a particular restriction on religiously motivated conduct, courts must give great deference to the professional judgment of military authorities concerning the relative importance of a particular military interest. Not only are courts "ill-equipped to determine the impact upon discipline that any particular intrusion upon military authority might have," but the military authorities have been charged by the Executive and Legislative Branches with carrying out our Nation's military policy.

The considered professional judgment of the Air Force is that the traditional outfitting of personnel in standardized uniforms encourages the subordination of personal preferences and identities in favor of the overall group mission. Uniforms encourage a sense of hierarchical unity by tending to eliminate outward individual distinctions except for those of rank. The Air Force considers them as vital during peacetime as during war because its personnel must be ready to provide an effective defense on a moment's notice; the necessary habits of discipline and unity must be developed in advance of trouble. We have acknowledged that "[t]he inescapable demands of military discipline and obedience to orders cannot be taught on battlefields; the habit of immediate compliance with military procedures and orders must be virtually reflex with no time for debate or reflection." ...

Petitioner Goldman contends that the Free Exercise Clause of the First Amendment requires the Air Force to make an exception to its uniform dress requirements for religious apparel unless the accouterments create a "clear danger" of undermining discipline and esprit de corps. He asserts that in general, visible but "unobtrusive" apparel will not create such a danger and must therefore be accommodated. He argues that the Air Force failed to prove that a specific exception for his practice of wearing an unobtrusive yarmulke would threaten discipline. He contends that the Air Force's assertion to the contrary is mere ipse dixit, with no support from actual experience or a scientific study in the record, and is contradicted by expert testimony that religious exceptions to AFR 35-10 are in fact desirable and will increase morale by making the Air Force a more humane place.

But whether or not expert witnesses may feel that religious exceptions to AFR 35-10 are desirable is quite beside the point. The desirability of dress regulations in the military is decided by the appropriate military officials, and they are under no constitutional mandate to abandon their considered professional judgment. Quite obviously, to the extent the regulations do not permit the wearing of religious apparel such as a yarmulke, a practice described by petitioner as silent devotion akin to prayer, military life may be more objectionable for petitioner and probably others. But the First Amendment does not require the military to accommodate such practices in the face of its view that they would detract from the uniformity sought by the dress regulations. The Air Force has drawn the line essentially between religious apparel that is visible and that which is not, and we hold that those portions of the regulations challenged here reasonably and evenhandedly regulate dress in the interest of the military's perceived need for uniformity. The First Amendment therefore does not prohibit them from being applied to petitioner even though their effect is to restrict the wearing of the headgear required by his religious beliefs.

The judgment of the Court of Appeals is Affirmed.

JUSTICE BRENNAN, with whom JUSTICE MARSHALL joins, dissenting.

Simcha Goldman invokes this Court's protection of his First Amendment right to fulfill one of the traditional religious obligations of a male Orthodox Jew—to cover his head before an omnipresent God. The Court's response to Goldman's request is to abdicate its role as principal expositor of the

Constitution and protector of individual liberties in favor of credulous deference to unsupported assertions of military necessity. I dissent.

In ruling that the paramount interests of the Air Force override Dr. Goldman's free exercise claim, the Court overlooks the sincere and serious nature of his constitutional claim. It suggests that the desirability of certain dress regulations, rather than a First Amendment right, is at issue. The Court declares that in selecting dress regulations, "military officials . . . are under no constitutional mandate to abandon their considered professional judgment." If Dr. Goldman wanted to wear a hat to keep his head warm or to cover a bald spot I would join the majority. Mere personal preferences in dress are not constitutionally protected. The First Amendment, however, restrains the Government's ability to prevent an Orthodox Jewish serviceman from, or punish him for, wearing a yarmulke.

The Court also attempts, unsuccessfully, to minimize the burden that was placed on Dr. Goldman's rights. The fact that "the regulations do not permit the wearing of . . . a yarmulke," does not simply render military life for observant Orthodox Jews "objectionable." It sets up an almost absolute bar to the fulfillment of a religious duty. Dr. Goldman spent most of his time in uniform indoors, where the dress code forbade him even to cover his head with his service cap. Consequently, he was asked to violate the tenets of his faith virtually every minute of every workday.

Dr. Goldman has asserted a substantial First Amendment claim, which is entitled to meaningful review by this Court. The Court, however, evades its responsibility by eliminating, in all but name only, judicial review of military regulations that interfere with the fundamental constitutional rights of service personnel.

Our cases have acknowledged that in order to protect our treasured liberties, the military must be able to command service members to sacrifice a great many of the individual freedoms they enjoyed in the civilian community and to endure certain limitations on the freedoms they retain. Notwithstanding this acknowledgment, we have steadfastly maintained that "our citizens in uniform may not be stripped of basic rights simply because they have doffed their civilian clothes." And, while we have hesitated, due to our lack of expertise concerning military affairs and our respect for the delegated authority of a coordinate branch, to strike down restrictions on individual liberties which could reasonably be justified as necessary to the military's vital function, we have never abdicated our obligation of judicial review.

Today the Court eschews its constitutionally mandated role. It adopts for review of military decisions affecting First Amendment rights a subrational-basis standard—absolute, uncritical "deference to the professional judgment of military authorities." If a branch of the military declares one of its rules sufficiently important to outweigh a service person's constitutional rights, it seems that the Court will accept that conclusion, no matter how absurd or unsupported it may be. A deferential standard of review, however, need not, and should not, mean that the Court must credit arguments that defy common sense. When a military service burdens the free exercise rights of its members in the name of necessity, it must provide, as an initial matter and at a minimum, a credible explanation of how the contested practice is likely to interfere with the proffered military interest. Unabashed ipse dixit cannot outweigh a constitutional right.

In the present case, the Air Force asserts that its interests in discipline and uniformity would be undermined by an exception to the dress code permitting observant male Orthodox Jews to wear yarmulkes. The Court simply restates these assertions without offering any explanation how the exception Dr. Goldman requests reasonably could interfere with the Air Force's interests. Had the Court given actual consideration to Goldman's claim, it would have been compelled to decide in his favor.

The Government maintains in its brief that discipline is jeopardized whenever exceptions to military regulations are granted. Service personnel must be trained to obey even the most arbitrary command reflexively. Non-Jewish personnel will perceive the wearing of a yarmulke by an Orthodox Jew as an unauthorized departure from the rules and will begin to question the principle of unswerving obedience. Thus shall our fighting forces slip down the treacherous slope toward unkempt appearance, anarchy, and, ultimately, defeat at the hands of our enemies.

The contention that the discipline of the Armed Forces will be subverted if Orthodox Jews are allowed to wear yarmulkes with their uniforms surpasses belief. It lacks support in the record of this case, and the Air Force offers no basis for it as a general proposition. While the perilous slope permits the services arbitrarily to refuse exceptions requested to satisfy mere personal preferences, before the Air Force may burden free exercise rights it must advance, at the very least, a rational reason for doing so. . . .

The Government also argues that the services have an important interest in uniform dress, because such dress establishes the preeminence of group identity, thus fostering esprit de corps and loyalty to the service that transcends individual bonds. In its brief, the Government characterizes the yarmulke as an assertion of individuality and as a badge of religious and ethnic identity, strongly suggesting that, as such, it could drive a wedge of divisiveness between members of the services. . . .

It cannot be seriously contended that a serviceman in a yarmulke presents so extreme, so unusual, or so faddish an image that public confidence in his ability to perform his duties will be destroyed. Under the Air Force's own standards, then, Dr. Goldman should have and could have been granted an exception to wear his yarmulke.

I find totally implausible the suggestion that the overarching group identity of the Air Force would be threatened if Orthodox Jews were allowed to wear yarmulkes with their uniforms. To the contrary, a yarmulke worn with a United States military uniform is an eloquent reminder that the shared and proud identity of United States serviceman embraces and unites religious and ethnic pluralism. . . .

Through our Bill of Rights, we pledged ourselves to attain a level of human freedom and dignity that had no parallel in history. Our constitutional commitment to religious freedom and to acceptance of religious pluralism is one of our greatest achievements in that noble endeavor. Almost 200 years after the First Amendment was drafted, tolerance and respect for all religions still set us apart from most other countries and draws to our shores refugees from religious persecution from around the world.

Guardianship of this precious liberty is not the exclusive domain of federal courts. It is the responsibility as well of the States and of the other branches of the Federal Government. Our military services have a distinguished record of providing for many of the religious needs of their personnel. But that they have satisfied much of their constitutional obligation does not remove their actions from judicial scrutiny. Our Nation has preserved freedom of religion, not through trusting to the good faith of individual agencies of government alone, but through the constitutionally mandated vigilant oversight and checking authority of the judiciary.

It is not the province of the federal courts to second-guess the professional judgments of the military services, but we are bound by the Constitution to assure ourselves that there exists a rational foundation for assertions of military necessity when they interfere with the free exercise of religion. . . . The military, with its strong ethic of conformity and unques-

tioning obedience, may be particularly impervious to minority needs and values. A critical function of the Religion Clauses of the First Amendment is to protect the rights of members of minority religions against quiet erosion by majoritarian social institutions that dismiss minority beliefs and practices as unimportant, because unfamiliar. It is the constitutional role of this Court to ensure that this purpose of the First Amendment be realized.

The Court and the military services have presented patriotic Orthodox Jews with a painful dilemma—the choice between fulfilling a religious obligation and serving their country. Should the draft be reinstated, compulsion will replace choice. Although the pain the services inflict on Orthodox Jewish servicemen is clearly the result of insensitivity rather than design, it is unworthy of our military because it is unnecessary. The Court and the military have refused these servicemen their constitutional rights; we must hope that Congress will correct this wrong.

EMPLOYMENT DIVISION OF OREGON V. SMITH
494 U.S. 872 (1990)

"The government's ability to enforce generally applicable prohibitions of . . . harmful conduct, like its ability to carry out other aspects of public policy, "cannot depend on measuring the effects of a governmental action on a religious objector's spiritual development." To make an individual's obligation to obey such a law contingent upon the law's coincidence with his religious beliefs, . . . contradicts both constitutional tradition and common sense."

The Question: Can a state deny unemployment benefits to workers who are fired from their jobs because they ingested the psychoactive plant peyote in religious rituals of the Native American Church, of which they were members, in violation of a state law that classified peyote as a "controlled substance" and made its use unlawful?

The Arguments: PRO

States have the power to impose criminal penalties on the possession, sale, or use of drugs that are considered harmful. Laws that make drug use unlawful apply to every person, and states are not required to make exemptions from drug laws for those who claim that use of particular drugs is a required religious practice or ritual. Creating such an exemption for peyote use by Native American Church members could open the door to claims from persons who wish to use drugs like marijuana, cocaine, or heroin for alleged "religious" rituals. The state is not allowed by the Supreme Court to decide which religious beliefs or practices are sincere and which are shams.

CON

There is ample and undisputed evidence that members of the Native American Church have long used peyote in their religious ceremonies, without physical or mental harm. The use of peyote is a central element of rituals that produce visions of the "Great Spirit" in those who ingest the plant. The peyote plant is very bitter in taste and would be unlikely to appeal to casual drug users who could more easily and cheaply obtain drugs such as marijuana. Finally, the state could not ban the use of other mind-altering drugs, such as alcohol, in the religious ceremonies of churches that use wine in their sacraments, although states have the power to prohibit the consumption of alcohol.

JUSTICE SCALIA delivered the opinion of the Court.

This case requires us to decide whether the Free Exercise Clause of the First Amendment permits the State of Oregon to include religiously inspired peyote use within the reach of its general criminal prohibition on use of that drug, and thus permits the State to deny unemployment benefits to persons dismissed from their jobs because of such religiously inspired use.

Oregon law prohibits the knowing or intentional possession of a "controlled substance" unless the substance has been prescribed by a medical practitioner. The law defines "controlled substance" as a drug classified in Schedules I through V of the Federal Controlled Substances Act. Persons who violate this provision by possessing a controlled substance listed on Schedule I are "guilty of a Class B felony." Schedule I contains the drug peyote, a hallucinogen derived from the plant Lophophora williamsii Lemaire.

Respondents Alfred Smith and Galen Black (hereinafter respondents) were fired from their jobs with a private drug rehabilitation organization because they ingested peyote for sacramental purposes at a ceremony of the Native American Church, of which both are members. When respondents applied to petitioner Employment Division (hereinafter petitioner) for unemployment compensation, they were determined to be ineligible for benefits because they had been discharged for work-related "misconduct." The Oregon Court of Appeals reversed that determination, holding that the denial of benefits violated respondents' free exercise rights under the First Amendment.

On appeal to the Oregon Supreme Court, petitioner argued that the denial of benefits was permissible because respondents' consumption of peyote was a crime under Oregon law. The Oregon Supreme Court reasoned, however, that the criminality of respondents' peyote use was irrelevant to resolution of their constitutional claim—since the purpose of the "misconduct" provision under which respondents had been disqualified was not to enforce the State's criminal laws but to preserve the financial integrity of the compensation fund, and since that purpose was inadequate to justify the burden that disqualification imposed on respondents' religious practice. [T]he court concluded that respondents were entitled to payment of unemployment benefits. We granted certiorari . . .

The free exercise of religion means, first and foremost, the right to believe and profess whatever religious doctrine one desires. Thus, the First Amendment obviously excludes all "governmental regulation of religious beliefs as such." . . . But the "exercise of religion" often involves not only belief and profession but the performance of (or abstention from) physical acts: assembling with others for a worship service, participating in sacramental use of bread and wine, proselytizing, abstaining from certain foods or certain modes of transportation. It would be true, we think (though no case of ours has involved the point), that a State would be "prohibiting the free exercise [of religion]" if it sought to ban such acts or abstentions only when they are engaged in for religious reasons, or only because of the religious belief that they display. It would doubtless be unconstitutional, for example, to ban the casting of "statues that are to be used for worship purposes," or to prohibit bowing down before a golden calf.

Respondents in the present case, however, seek to carry the meaning of "prohibiting the free exercise [of religion]" one large step further. They contend that their religious motivation for using peyote places them beyond the reach of a criminal law that is not specifically directed at their religious practice, and that is concededly constitutional as applied to those who use the drug for other reasons. They assert, in other words, that "prohibiting the free exercise [of religion]" includes requiring any individual to observe a generally applicable law that requires (or forbids) the performance of an act that his religious belief forbids (or requires). As a textual matter, we do not think the words must be given that meaning. It is no more necessary to regard the collection of a general tax, for example, as "prohibiting the free exercise [of religion]" by those citizens who believe support of organized government to be sinful, than it is to regard the same tax as "abridging the freedom . . . of the press" of those publishing companies that must pay the tax as a condition of staying in business. It is a permissible reading of the text, in the one case as in the other, to say that if prohibiting the exercise of religion (or burdening the activity of printing) is not the object of the tax but merely the incidental effect of a generally applicable and otherwise valid provision, the First Amendment has not been offended. . . .

The only decisions in which we have held that the First Amendment bars application of a neutral, generally applicable law to religiously motivated action have involved not the Free Exercise Clause alone, but the Free Exercise Clause in conjunction with other constitutional protections, such as freedom of speech and of the press, see . . . Wisconsin v. Yoder; West Virginia Bd. of Education v. Barnette. The present case does not present such a hybrid situation, but a free exercise claim unconnected with any communicative activity or parental right. Respondents urge us to hold, quite simply, that when otherwise prohibitable conduct is accompanied by religious convictions, not only the convictions but the conduct itself must be free from governmental regulation. We have never held that, and decline to do so now. There being no contention that Oregon's drug law represents an attempt to regulate religious beliefs, the communication of religious beliefs, or the raising of one's children in those beliefs, the rule to which we have adhered ever since Reynolds plainly controls.

Respondents argue that even though exemption from generally applicable criminal laws need not automatically be extended to religiously motivated actors, at least the claim for a religious exemption must be evaluated under the balancing test set forth in Sherbert v. Verner. . . . Even if we were inclined to breathe into Sherbert some life beyond the unemployment compensation field, we would not apply it to require exemptions from a generally applicable criminal law. The Sherbert test, it must be recalled, was developed in a context that lent itself to individualized governmental assessment of the reasons for the relevant conduct. . . . Whether or not the decisions are that limited, they at least have nothing to do with an across-the-board criminal prohibition on a particular form of conduct. . . . We conclude today that the sounder approach, and the approach in accord with the vast majority of our precedents, is to hold the test inapplicable to such challenges. The government's ability to enforce generally applicable prohibitions of socially harmful conduct, like its ability to carry out other aspects of public policy, "cannot depend on measuring the effects of a governmental action on a religious objector's spiritual development." To make an individual's obligation to obey such a law contingent upon the law's coincidence with his religious beliefs, except where the State's interest is "compelling"—permitting him, by virtue of his beliefs, "to become a law unto himself," Reynolds v. United States, contradicts both constitutional tradition and common sense. . . .

If the "compelling interest" test is to be applied at all, then, it must be applied across the board, to all actions thought to be religiously commanded. Moreover, if "compelling interest" really means what it says (and watering it down here would subvert its rigor in the other fields where it is applied), many laws will not meet the test. Any society adopting such a system would be courting anarchy, but that danger increases in direct proportion to the society's diversity of religious beliefs, and its determination to coerce or suppress none of them. Precisely because "we are a cosmopolitan nation made up of people of almost every conceivable religious preference," and precisely because we value and protect that religious divergence, we cannot afford the luxury of deeming presumptively invalid, as applied to the religious objector, every regulation of conduct that does not protect an interest of the highest order. The rule respondents favor would open the prospect of constitutionally required religious exemptions from civic obligations of almost every conceivable kind. . . .

Values that are protected against government interference through enshrinement in the Bill of Rights are not thereby banished from the political process. Just as a society that believes in the negative protection accorded to the press by the First Amendment is likely to enact laws that affirmatively foster the dissemination of the printed word, so also a society that believes in the negative protection accorded to religious belief can be expected to be solicitous of that value in its legislation as well. It is therefore not surprising that a number of States have made an exception to their drug laws for sacramental peyote use. But to say that a nondiscriminatory religious-practice exemption is permitted, or even that it is desirable, is not to say that it is constitutionally required, and that the appropriate occasions for its creation can be discerned by the courts. It may fairly be said that leaving accommodation to the political process will place at a relative disadvantage those religious practices that are not widely engaged in; but that unavoidable consequence of democratic government must be preferred to a system in which each conscience is a law unto itself or in which judges weigh the social importance of all laws against the centrality of all religious beliefs.

Because respondents' ingestion of peyote was prohibited under Oregon law, and because that prohibition is constitutional, Oregon may, consistent with the Free Exercise Clause, deny respondents unemployment compensation when their dismissal results from use of the drug. The decision of the Oregon Supreme Court is accordingly reversed.

JUSTICE BLACKMUN, with whom JUSTICE BRENNAN and JUSTICE MARSHALL join, dissenting.

This Court over the years painstakingly has developed a consistent and exacting standard to test the constitutionality of a state statute that burdens the free exercise of religion. Such a statute may stand only if the law in general, and the State's refusal to allow a religious exemption in particular, are justified by a compelling interest that cannot be served by less restrictive means.

Until today, I thought this was a settled and inviolate principle of this Court's First Amendment jurisprudence. The majority, however, perfunctorily dismisses it as a "constitutional anomaly." The Court discards leading free exercise cases such as Cantwell v. Connecticut, and Wisconsin v. Yoder, as "hybrid." The Court views traditional free exercise analysis as somehow inapplicable to criminal prohibitions (as opposed to conditions on the receipt of benefits), and to state laws of general applicability (as opposed, presumably, to laws that expressly single out religious practices). The Court cites cases in which, due to various exceptional circumstances, we found strict scrutiny inapposite, to hint that the Court has repudiated that standard altogether. In short, it effectuates a wholesale overturning of settled law concerning the Religion Clauses of our Constitution. One hopes that the Court is aware of the consequences, and that its result is not a product of overreaction to the serious problems the country's drug crisis has generated.

This distorted view of our precedents leads the majority to conclude that strict scrutiny of a state law burdening the free exercise of religion is a "luxury" that a well-ordered society cannot afford, and that the repression of minority religions is an "unavoidable consequence of democratic government." I do not believe the Founders thought their dearly bought freedom from religious persecution a "luxury," but an essential element of liberty—and they could not have thought religious intolerance "unavoidable," for they drafted the Religion Clauses precisely in order to avoid that intolerance. . . .

In weighing the clear interest of respondents Smith and Black (hereinafter respondents) in the free exercise of their religion against Oregon's asserted interest in enforcing its drug laws, it is important to articulate in precise terms the state interest involved. It is not the State's broad interest in fighting the critical "war on drugs" that must be weighed against respondents' claim, but the State's narrow interest in refusing to make an exception for the religious, ceremonial use of peyote.

The State's interest in enforcing its prohibition, in order to be sufficiently compelling to outweigh a free exercise claim, cannot be merely abstract or symbolic. The State cannot plausibly assert that unbending application of a criminal prohibition is essential to fulfill any compelling interest, if it does not, in fact, attempt to enforce that prohibition. In this case, the State actually has not evinced any concrete interest in enforcing its drug laws against religious users of peyote. Oregon has never sought to prosecute respondents, and does not claim that it has made significant enforcement efforts against other religious users of peyote. The State's asserted interest thus amounts only to the symbolic preservation of an unenforced prohibition. But a government interest in "symbolism, even symbolism for so worthy a cause as the abolition of unlawful drugs," cannot suffice to abrogate the constitutional rights of individuals.

Similarly, this Court's prior decisions have not allowed a government to rely on mere speculation about potential harms, but have demanded evidentiary support for a refusal to allow a religious exception. In this case, the State's justification for refusing to recognize an exception to its criminal laws for religious peyote use is entirely speculative. The State proclaims an interest in protecting the health and safety of its citizens from the dangers of unlawful drugs. It offers, however, no evidence that the religious use of peyote has ever harmed anyone. The factual findings of other courts cast doubt on the State's assumption that religious use of peyote is harmful. The fact that peyote is classified as a Schedule I controlled substance does not, by itself, show that any and all uses of peyote, in any circumstance, are inherently harmful and dangerous. The Federal Government, which created the classifications of unlawful drugs from which Oregon's drug laws are derived, apparently does not find peyote so dangerous as to preclude an exemption for religious use. . . .

Moreover, just as in Yoder, the values and interests of those seeking a religious exemption in this case are congruent, to a great degree, with those the State seeks to promote through its drug laws. Not only does the church's doctrine forbid nonreligious use of peyote; it also generally advocates self-reliance, familial responsibility, and abstinence from alcohol. There is considerable evidence that the spiritual and social support provided by the church has been effective in combating the tragic effects of alcoholism on the Native American population. . . . Far from promoting the lawless and irresponsible use of drugs, Native American Church members' spiritual code exemplifies values that Oregon's drug laws are presumably intended to foster. . . .

The State also seeks to support its refusal to make an exception for religious use of peyote by invoking its interest in abolishing drug trafficking. There is, however, practically no illegal traffic in peyote. Also, the availability of peyote for religious use, even if Oregon were to allow an exemption from its criminal laws, would still be strictly controlled by federal regulations. Peyote simply is not a popular drug; its distribution for use in religious rituals has nothing to do with the vast and violent traffic in illegal narcotics that plagues this country.

Finally, the State argues that granting an exception for religious peyote use would erode its interest in the uniform, fair, and certain enforcement of its drug laws. The State fears that, if it grants an exemption for religious peyote use, a flood of other claims to religious exemptions will follow. It would then be placed in a dilemma, it says, between allowing a patchwork of exemptions that would hinder its law enforcement efforts, and risking a violation of the Establishment Clause by arbitrarily limiting its religious exemptions. This argument, however, could be made in almost any free exercise case. This Court, however, consistently has rejected similar arguments in past free exercise cases, and it should

do so here as well. The State's apprehension of a flood of other religious claims is purely speculative. Almost half the States, and the Federal Government, have maintained an exemption for religious peyote use for many years, and apparently have not found themselves overwhelmed by claims to other religious exemptions. Allowing an exemption for religious peyote use would not necessarily oblige the State to grant a similar exemption to other religious groups. The unusual circumstances that make the religious use of peyote compatible with the State's interests in health and safety and in preventing drug trafficking would not apply to other religious claims. Some religions, for example, might not restrict drug use to a limited ceremonial context, as does the Native American Church. Some religious claims involve drugs such as marijuana and heroin, in which there is significant illegal traffic, with its attendant greed and violence, so that it would be difficult to grant a religious exemption without seriously compromising law enforcement efforts. That the State might grant an exemption for religious peyote use, but deny other religious claims arising in different circumstances, would not violate the Establishment Clause. Though the State must treat all religions equally, and not favor one over another, this obligation is fulfilled by the uniform application of the "compelling interest" test to all free exercise claims, not by reaching uniform results as to all claims. . . .

Respondents believe, and their sincerity has never been at issue, that the peyote plant embodies their deity, and eating it is an act of worship and communion. Without peyote, they could not enact the essential ritual of their religion. If Oregon can constitutionally prosecute them for this act of worship, they, like the Amish, may be "forced to migrate to some other and more tolerant region." This potentially devastating impact must be viewed in light of the federal policy—reached in reaction to many years of religious persecution and intolerance—of protecting the religious freedom of Native Americans. . . .

For these reasons, I conclude that Oregon's interest in enforcing its drug laws against religious use of peyote is not sufficiently compelling to outweigh respondents' right to the free exercise of their religion. Since the State could not constitutionally enforce its criminal prohibition against respondents, the interests underlying the State's drug laws cannot justify its denial of unemployment benefits. . . . The State of Oregon cannot, consistently with the Free Exercise Clause, deny respondents unemployment benefits.

I dissent.

CHURCH OF LUKUMI BABALU AYE V. CITY OF HIALEAH, FLORIDA
508 U.S. 520 (1993)

"The Free Exercise Clause commits government itself to religious tolerance and, upon even slight suspicion that proposals for state intervention stem from animosity to religion or distrust of its practices, all officials must pause to remember their own high duty to the Constitution and to the rights it secures. Legislators may not devise mechanisms, overt or disguised, designed to persecute or oppress a religion or its practices."

The Question:	Can a city prohibit the sacrifice of animals in a public or private ritual or ceremony if the purpose of such a prohibition is to prevent the members of a particular religious denomination, the Santeria Church, from engaging in the ritual slaughter of animals such as chickens, goats, and sheep as a central element in religious ceremonies?
The Arguments:	PRO

Animal sacrifice is cruel, inhumane, and barbaric and violates the norms of American culture. It can also be dangerous to participants in the sacrificial rituals, with the use of sharp knives, and poses the possibility of transmitting diseases from animals to humans. Courts have upheld prohibitions against the handling of poisonous snakes in religious ceremonies, even of denominations that have a sincere belief that snake handling is required by biblical injunction. Animal sacrifice is potentially as dangerous as snake handling and is equally subject to legislative prohibition.

CON

Legislative bodies should not have the power to decide which religious practices, however offensive to the sentiments of many people, should be allowed and which should be prohibited. The state is not the arbiter of religious practices, unless they can be shown by clear evidence to pose a substantial danger to the participants or others. Animal sacrifice is not analogous to snake handling, and the dangers from sharp knives or animal blood can be dealt with through regulations that do not prohibit the practice of sacrifice itself. Animal sacrifice has roots in the Bible and the traditions of many religions, and it is central to the Santeria faith.

JUSTICE KENNEDY delivered the opinion of the Court, except as to Part II-A-2.

The principle that government may not enact laws that suppress religious belief or practice is so well understood that few violations are recorded in our opinions. Our review confirms that the laws in question were enacted by officials who did not understand, failed to perceive, or chose to ignore the fact that their official actions violated the Nation's essential commitment to religious freedom. The challenged laws had an impermissible object; and in all events, the principle of general applicability was violated because the secular ends asserted in defense of the laws were pursued only with respect to conduct motivated by religious beliefs. We invalidate the challenged enactments, and reverse the judgment of the Court of Appeals.

This case involves practices of the Santeria religion, which originated in the 19th century. When hundreds of thousands of members of the Yoruba people were brought as slaves from western Africa to Cuba, their traditional African religion absorbed significant elements of Roman Catholicism. The resulting syncretion, or fusion, is Santeria, "the way of the saints." The Cuban Yoruba express their devotion to spirits, called orishas, through the iconography of Catholic saints, Catholic symbols are often present at Santeria rites, and Santeria devotees attend the Catholic sacraments.

The Santeria faith teaches that every individual has a destiny from God, a destiny fulfilled with the aid and energy of the orishas. The basis of the Santeria religion is the nurture of a personal relation with the orishas, and one of the principal forms of devotion is an animal sacrifice. The sacrifice of animals as part of religious rituals has ancient roots. Animal sacrifice is mentioned throughout the Old Testament, and it played an important role in the practice of Judaism before destruction of the second Temple in Jerusalem. In

modern Islam, there is an annual sacrifice commemorating Abraham's sacrifice of a ram in the stead of his son. According to Santeria teaching, the orishas are powerful, but not immortal. They depend for survival on the sacrifice. Sacrifices are performed at birth, marriage, and death rites, for the cure of the sick, for the initiation of new members and priests, and during an annual celebration. Animals sacrificed in Santeria rituals include chickens, pigeons, doves, ducks, guinea pigs, goats, sheep, and turtles. The animals are killed by the cutting of the carotid arteries in the neck. The sacrificed animal is cooked and eaten, except after healing and death rituals. . . .

Santeria adherents faced widespread persecution in Cuba, so the religion and its rituals were practiced in secret. The open practice of Santeria and its rites remains infrequent. The religion was brought to this Nation most often by exiles from the Cuban revolution. The District Court estimated that there are at least 50,000 practitioners in South Florida today.

Petitioner Church of the Lukumi Babalu Aye, Inc. (Church), is a not-for-profit corporation organized under Florida law in 1973. The Church and its congregants practice the Santeria religion. The president of the Church is petitioner Ernesto Pichardo, who is also the Church's priest and holds the religious title of Italero, the second highest in the Santeria faith. In April, 1987, the Church leased land in the city of Hialeah, Florida, and announced plans to establish a house of worship as well as a school, cultural center, and museum. Pichardo indicated that the Church's goal was to bring the practice of the Santeria faith, including its ritual of animal sacrifice, into the open. The Church began the process of obtaining utility service and receiving the necessary licensing, inspection, and zoning approvals. Although the Church's efforts at obtaining the necessary licenses and permits were far from smooth, it appears that it received all needed approvals by early August, 1987.

The prospect of a Santeria church in their midst was distressing to many members of the Hialeah community, and the announcement of the plans to open a Santeria church in Hialeah prompted the city council to hold an emergency public session on June 9, 1987. First, the city council adopted Resolution 87-66, which noted the "concern" expressed by residents of the city "that certain religions may propose to engage in practices which are inconsistent with public morals, peace or safety," and declared that "[t]he City reiterates its commitment to a prohibition against any and all acts of any and all religious groups which are inconsistent with public morals, peace or safety." . . .

In September, 1987, the city council adopted three substantive ordinances addressing the issue of religious animal sacrifice. Ordinance 87-52 defined "sacrifice" as "to unnecessarily kill, torment, torture or mutilate an animal in a public or private ritual or ceremony not for the primary purpose of food consumption," and prohibited owning or possessing an animal "intending to use such animal for food purposes." It restricted application of this prohibition, however, to any individual or group that "kills, slaughters or sacrifices animals for any type of ritual, regardless of whether or not the flesh or blood of the animal is to be consumed." The ordinance contained an exemption for slaughtering by "licensed establishment[s]"of animals "specifically raised for food purposes." Declaring, moreover, that the city council has determined that the sacrificing of animals within the city limits is contrary to the public health, safety, welfare and morals of the community," the city council adopted Ordinance 87-71. That ordinance defined sacrifice as had Ordinance 87-52, and then provided that "[i]t shall be unlawful for any person, persons, corporations or associations to sacrifice any animal within the corporate limits of the City of Hialeah, Florida.". . .

The city does not argue that Santeria is not a "religion" within the meaning of the First Amendment. Nor could it. Although the practice of animal sacrifice may seem abhorrent to some, "religious beliefs need not be acceptable, logical, consistent, or comprehensible to others in order to merit First Amendment protection." Given the historical association between animal sacrifice and religious worship, petitioners' assertion that animal sacrifice is an integral part of their religion "cannot be deemed bizarre or incredible." Neither the city nor the courts below, moreover, have questioned the sincerity of petitioners' professed desire to conduct animal sacrifices for religious reasons. We must consider petitioners' First Amendment claim. . . .

In our Establishment Clause cases, we have often stated the principle that the First Amendment forbids an official purpose to disapprove of a particular religion or of religion in general. See, e.g., Wallace v. Jaffree, Epperson v. Arkansas, School Dist. of Abington v. Schempp, Everson v. Board of Ed. of Ewing. These cases, however, for the most part, have addressed governmental efforts to benefit religion or particular religions, and so have dealt with a question different, at least in its formulation and emphasis, from the issue here. Petitioners allege an attempt to disfavor their religion because of the religious ceremonies it commands, and the Free Exercise Clause is dispositive in our analysis. . . .

The record in this case compels the conclusion that suppression of the central element of the Santeria worship service was the object of the ordinances. First, though use of the words "sacrifice" and "ritual" does not compel a finding of improper targeting of the Santeria religion, the choice of these words is support for our conclusion. There are further respects in which the text of the city council's enactments discloses the improper attempt to target Santeria. Resolution 87-66, adopted June 9, 1987, recited that "residents and citizens of the City of Hialeah have expressed their concern that certain religions may propose to engage in practices which are inconsistent with public morals, peace or safety," and "reiterate[d]" the city's commitment to prohibit "any and all [such] acts of any and all religious groups." No one suggests, and, on this record, it cannot be maintained, that city officials had in mind a religion other than Santeria.

It becomes evident that these ordinances target Santeria sacrifice when the ordinances' operation is considered. Apart from the text, the effect of a law in its real operation is strong evidence of its object. To be sure, adverse impact will not always lead to a finding of impermissible targeting. For example, a social harm may have been a legitimate concern of government for reasons quite apart from discrimination. The subject at hand does implicate, of course, multiple concerns unrelated to religious animosity, for example, the suffering or mistreatment visited upon the sacrificed animals and health hazards from improper disposal. But the ordinances, when considered together, disclose an object remote from these legitimate concerns. The design of these laws accomplishes, instead, a "religious gerrymander," an impermissible attempt to target petitioners and their religious practices.

It is a necessary conclusion that almost the only conduct subject to [these ordinances] is the religious exercise of Santeria church members. The texts show that they were drafted in tandem to achieve this result. We begin with Ordinance 87-71. It prohibits the sacrifice of animals, but defines sacrifice as "to unnecessarily kill . . . an animal in a public or private ritual or ceremony not for the primary purpose of food consumption." The definition excludes almost all killings of animals except for religious sacrifice, and the primary purpose requirement narrows the proscribed category even further, in particular by exempting kosher slaughter. We need not discuss whether this differential treatment of two religions is, itself, an independent constitutional violation. It suffices to recite this feature of the law as support for our conclusion that Santeria alone was the exclusive legislative concern. The net result of the gerrymander is that few, if any, killings of animals are prohibited other than Santeria sacrifice, which is proscribed because it occurs during a ritual or ceremony and its primary purpose is to make an offering to the orishas, not food consumption. Indeed, careful drafting ensured that, although Santeria sacrifice is prohibited, killings that are no more necessary or humane in almost all other circumstances are unpunished. . . .

Although respondent claimed at oral argument that it had experienced significant problems resulting from the sacrifice of animals within the city before the announced opening of the Church, the city council made no attempt to address the supposed problem before its meeting in June, 1987, just weeks after the Church announced plans to open. The minutes and taped excerpts of the June 9 session, both of which are in the record, evidence significant hostility exhibited by residents, members of the city council, and other city officials toward the Santeria religion and its practice of animal sacrifice. The public crowd that attended the June 9 meetings interrupted statements by council members critical of Santeria with cheers and the brief comments of Pichardo with taunts. When Councilman Martinez, a supporter of the ordinances, stated that, in prerevolution Cuba, "people were put in jail for practicing this religion," the audience applauded. Other statements by members of the city council were in a similar vein. For example, Councilman Martinez, after noting his belief that Santeria was outlawed in Cuba, questioned: "If we could not practice this [religion] in our homeland [Cuba], why bring it to this country?" Councilman Cardoso said that Santeria devotees at the Church "are in violation of everything this country stands for." Councilman Mejides indicated that he was "totally against the sacrificing of animals," and distinguished kosher slaughter because it had a "real purpose." The "Bible says we are allowed to sacrifice an animal for consumption," he continued, "but for any other purposes, I don't believe that the Bible allows that." The president of the city council, Councilman Echevarria, asked: "What can we do to prevent the Church from opening?"

Various Hialeah city officials made comparable comments. The chaplain of the Hialeah Police Department told the city council that Santeria was a sin, "foolishness," "an abomination to the Lord," and the worship of "demons." He advised the city council: "We need to be helping people and sharing with them the truth that is found in Jesus Christ." He concluded: "I would exhort you . . . not to permit this Church to exist." The city attorney commented that Resolution 87-66 indicated: "This community will not tolerate religious practices which are abhorrent to its citizens. . . ." Similar comments were made by the deputy city attorney. This history discloses the object of the ordinances to target animal sacrifice by Santeria worshippers because of its religious motivation.

In sum, the neutrality inquiry leads to one conclusion: the ordinances had as their object the suppression of religion. The pattern we have recited discloses animosity to Santeria adherents and their religious practices; the ordinances, by their own terms, target this religious exercise; the texts of the ordinances were gerrymandered with care to proscribe religious killings of animals but to exclude almost all secular killings; and the ordinances suppress much more religious conduct than is necessary in order to achieve the legitimate ends asserted in their defense. These ordinances are not neutral, and the court below committed clear error in failing to reach this conclusion. . . .

We conclude, in sum, that each of Hialeah's ordinances pursues the city's governmental interests only against conduct motivated by religious belief. . . . This precise evil is what the requirement of general applicability is designed to prevent.

The Free Exercise Clause commits government itself to religious tolerance, and upon even slight suspicion that proposals for state intervention stem from animosity to religion or distrust of its practices, all officials must pause to remember their own high duty to the Constitution and to the rights it secures. Those in office must be resolute in resisting importunate demands and must ensure that the sole reasons for imposing the burdens of law and regulation are secular. Legislators may not devise mechanisms, overt or disguised, designed to persecute or oppress a religion or its practices. The laws here in question were enacted contrary to these constitutional principles, and they are void.

Reversed.

CHAPTER 5

Freedom of Speech

INTRODUCTION

There is probably no metaphor more powerful, nor a single sentence more remembered, from any Supreme Court opinion than these words of Justice Oliver Wendell Holmes: "The most stringent protection of free speech would not protect a man in falsely shouting fire in a theater and causing a panic." Holmes was writing for a unanimous Court in a case that arose during World War I, upholding the conviction of a Socialist party leader who had circulated leaflets urging young men facing the wartime draft to "assert your opposition to the draft." Like many evocative metaphors, the image Holmes conveyed of fire in a crowded theater was vivid and conveyed a feeling of fear and horror. In the same opinion in *Schenck v. United States*, the first case in this chapter, Holmes minted the doctrine that speech presenting a "clear and present danger" to the government, and to the public, could be proscribed and punished.

Justice Holmes was perhaps the best writer who ever served on the Supreme Court, and his mastery of words and phrases was matched by the clarity of his thought on constitutional issues. But those who employ metaphor, however vivid, often raise more questions than they answer. In the case of Charles Schenck, sentenced to prison for urging draft-age young men to sign a petition to Congress against the draft, was the "impassioned language" of his leaflet—hardly a match for Holmes—in any way comparable to "falsely shouting fire in a crowded theater"? However strongly the leaflet denounced the draft and the country's participation in the war, Schenck did not urge anyone to violate the draft law. Holmes did not consider this fact relevant to his conclusion that the "tendency and the intent" of the leaflet were directed to "obstruction of the recruiting service" during wartime. Consequently, Holmes saw "no ground for saying that success alone warrants making the act a crime."

Significantly, Holmes changed his mind just eight months after the *Schenck* decision in 1919. He dissented from the *Abrams v. United States* decision that upheld the convictions of four Russian immigrants who circulated leaflets denouncing American military intervention against the Bolshevik government in their native country. In their leaflets, circulated in the Lower East Side of Manhattan, the Russians had in fact urged workers in munitions factories to engage in a general strike against the production of "bullets, bayonets, cannon" that would be used against Russians. However unlikely, such a general strike would have been illegal. The Court's majority relied on the *Schenck* decision to uphold the convictions for "sedition," but Holmes shrank from applying his "clear and present danger" test to this case. He decried the Court's ruling that sent the Russians to prison for twenty years for circulating leaflets they "had as much right to publish as the Government has to publish the Constitution of the United States now vainly invoked by them."

The contrasting opinions of Justice Holmes in the *Schenck* and *Abrams* cases provide a vivid illustration of the difficulties faced by the Supreme Court in cases that raise challenges to governmental efforts to suppress or punish speech. Holmes wrote in *Schenck* that "the character of every act depends upon the circumstances in which it is done." This statement is clearly true: swinging a bat on a baseball field to hit a ball is different from swinging a bat to hit someone's head. And falsely shouting "fire" in a crowded theater is different from truthfully shouting "fire" to alert those in the theater to danger. In each example, the circumstances are relevant to a judicial decision as to which act can be punished and which cannot. But those circumstances flow from the factual situation and the intent of the actor in each case. Applying a test such as the "clear and present danger" test to varied situations and circumstances in which speech results in prosecution eludes any "bright-line" rule to distinguish between allowable and punishable speech.

The cases that follow *Schenck* and *Abrams* in this chapter were all decided on the basis of some variant or descendent of the "clear and present" danger test that Holmes devised close to a century ago. They vary considerably in the facts and "circumstances" in which they arose, but they all involve a prosecution by some governmental body—from local school boards to the federal government—against a person who communicated an idea or opinion through words or writings, or by such forms of "symbolic speech" as wearing a black armband or burning the American flag. The penalties imposed in these cases ranged from suspension from junior high school for Mary Beth Tinker to twenty-year prison terms for the Russian defendants in the *Abrams* case. Some involved just one person whose speech offended a government official, such as the case in which Walter Chaplinsky, a Jehovah's Witness, called a police office a "fascist" and "racketeer" during World War II. Others involved the leaders of groups with thousands of members, such as Eugene Dennis and other top officials of the Communist party, convicted of "sedition" during the height of the Cold War with the Soviet Union. What these cases all have in common is that each provides a test of the limits of free expression, and of the Supreme Court's judgment about those limits.

One factor of great significance in free speech cases is that, most often, the speaker—through spoken words, writings, or some form of "symbolic speech"—has upset or offended his or her listeners, whether they be fellow citizens on a street corner who are simply passing by or government officials. Speech is rarely prosecuted when it voices sentiments or opinions with which the listeners agree. But, as the Supreme Court wrote in *Terminiello v. Chicago* in 1949, striking down the conviction of an anti-Semitic rabble-rouser in 1949 for provoking a near riot with tirades against Jews, a principal "function of free speech under our system of government is to invite dispute. It may indeed best serve its high purpose when it induces a condition of unrest, creates dissatisfaction with conditions as they are, or even stirs people to anger."

Most of the cases in this chapter *did* involve speech that created unrest or stirred listeners to anger, from the face-to-face confrontation of Walter Chaplinsky and the police officer he called a "fascist" to the angry response of government officials who feared the Communist party as a "fifth column" of Soviet sympathizers during the Cold War period. These cases raise the issue of the "hecklers' veto," in which speech is suppressed or punished because of the angry, often violent, reaction of onlookers or audience members. Subjecting a speaker to prosecution because of such hostile reactions, the Supreme Court has said in several opinions, would place speech at the mercy of those who find it offensive. However, speech can also have the effect of inciting listeners to violence, and if this was the speaker's intent, or a likely consequence of his or her speech, laws that punish "incitement to riot" can be legitimately invoked by the authorities. Speech may also fall within prohibitions against harassment if punishment is imposed, not for the ideas it expresses, no matter how offensive, but for the speaker's intent to place others in fear of bodily harm or personal security.

Another category of cases in which the Supreme Court has upheld "reasonable" restrictions on speech that would otherwise be protected involves the "time, place, and manner" of expression. For example, in 1949, the Court upheld in *Kovacs v. Cooper* a municipal ordinance that banned the use of sound-amplifying equipment to broadcast messages (in this case to advise the public about a labor dispute) at high volume and in a "raucous" manner. The Court noted in its *Kovacs* opinion that "even the fundamental rights of the Bill of Rights are not absolute. . . . Opportunity to gain the public's ears by objectionably amplified sound on the streets is no more assured by the right of free speech than is the unlimited opportunity to address gatherings on the streets. The preferred place of freedom of speech in a society that cherishes liberty for all does not require legislators to be insensible to claims by citizens to comfort and convenience."

Even the "time, place, and manner" doctrine raises difficult questions, especially that of determining what is a "reasonable" regulation of speech. For example, a sound truck promoting a political candidate may "gain the public's ears" on a busy city street during the daytime, without creating such a "raucous" noise that it can be banned from the streets. But the same sound truck, broadcasting the same message at the same volume, could "reasonably" be prohibited from blaring its message in a residential neighborhood at midnight, when residents expect peace and quiet. Each such case, obviously, requires consideration of the "circumstances" to which Justice Holmes referred in his *Schenck* opinion.

Another issue related to "time, place, and manner" restrictions on speech arises in cases that challenge laws requiring "solicitors" and other persons who distribute messages to the public to obtain licenses from public officials as a condition of going door-to-door in residential areas or handing out material in public places. The Supreme Court has almost invariably struck down such "licensing" ordinances, most of them adopted to keep Jehovah's Witnesses from engaging in their religious proselytizing. The Court struck down one such ordinance in 1939, in *Schneider v. State*, holding that "to require a censorship through license which makes impossible the free and unhampered distribution of pamphlets strikes at the very heart of the constitutional guarantees" of free speech and press. The next year, in *Cantwell v. Connecticut*, the Court struck down an ordinance requiring solicitors to obtain a license from a city official, who was authorized to withhold a license if the solicitor's "cause" was not related to a legitimate religious and charitable purpose. "He is not to issue a certificate as a matter of course," the Court noted in its *Cantwell* decision. "His decision to issue or refuse it involves appraisal of facts, the exercise of judgment, and the formation of an opinion" about the legitimacy of the cause.

As recently as June 2002, the Court relied on the *Schneider* and *Cantwell* decisions in striking down a licensing ordinance from the small town of Stratton, Ohio, in another case brought by Jehovah's Witnesses. Ruling in *Watchtower Bible and Tract Society v. Village of Stratton,* the Court held that even an ordinance requiring city officials to issue licenses to every solicitor who applied was unconstitutional because it might deter those, like the Jehovah's Witnesses, who refuse as a matter of principle to apply for licenses to distribute messages to the public. "It is offensive—not only to the values protected by the First Amendment, but to the very notion of a free society—that in the context of everyday public discourse a citizen must first inform the government of her desire to speak to her neighbors and then obtain a permit to do so," Justice John Paul Stevens wrote in the *Stratton* case. "Even if the issuance of permits by the mayor's office is a ministerial task that is performed promptly and at no cost to the applicant, a law requiring a permit to engage in such speech constitutes a dramatic departure from our national heritage and constitutional tradition."

This chapter includes one final category of speech which has been singled out, through most of American history, for moral condemnation and legal suppression. In his opinion in *Chaplinsky v. New Hampshire,* Justice Frank Murphy included "lewd and obscene" speech as being among those forms of expression "the prevention and punishment of which have never been thought to raise any Constitutional problem." Murphy explained that "such utterances are no essential part of any exposition of ideas, and are of such slight social value as a step to truth that any benefit that may be derived from them is clearly outweighed by the social interest in order and morality."

Despite the dogged and often impassioned efforts of such crusaders against "vice" as Anthony Comstock, who led the nineteenth-century campaign to suppress everything he and his followers considered salacious, even the most innocuous display of nudity, the fact remains that books and films that portrayed sexuality found a large audience among the American public. Even such indisputably literary works as *Lady Chatterley's Lover,* by the renowned author D.H. Lawrence, and the path-breaking work by James Joyce, *Ulysses,* became the objects of legal suppression. Both of these books survived lawsuits brought by zealous prosecutors, but many books and films that had no pretensions of literary merit were banned as obscene.

Until the 1950s, judges who ruled in obscenity cases looked for precedent to an English decision of 1868, *Regina v. Hicklin.* In that case, the English court applied this test in deciding whether a work was obscene: "Whether the tendency of the matter charged as obscenity is to deprave or corrupt those whose minds are open to such immoral influences and into whose hands a publication of this sort might fall." Needless to say, such a test was highly subjective and gave judges almost total discretion to uphold bans on any work a prosecutor might consider "immoral."

The *Hicklin* test stood as precedent in American courts until 1957, when the Supreme Court first attempted its own definition of obscenity in *Roth v. United States,* a case in which Samuel Roth was convicted under a federal law which banned "obscene, indecent, and filthy matter" from distribution through the mail. Roth had sent out advertising circulars for such picture magazines as *Photo and Body* and *American Aphrodite,* which included photographs of nude women, although none of the women depicted were engaged in any sexual act. In an opinion by Justice William Brennan, the Court defined *obscenity* as "material which deals with sex in a manner appealing to prurient interest." Very few people drop the word *prurient* into their everyday conversation, and its dictionary definition traces its origin to the Latin *prurire,* which means "to itch." The medical term *pruritis* comes from the same Latin root and defines a condition of "intense itching of the skin." A "prurient interest" in sex, by definition, then, is one that produces a mental itch that can be scratched by exposure to sexual material. Quite obviously, applying such a definition to magazines, books, or films that are allegedly obscene involves as much subjectivity as the outmoded *Hicklin* test had allowed judges to exercise.

Many people confuse *obscenity* with *pornography* and use the two words interchangeably. There is, in fact, a substantial legal difference between them, along with a linguistic difference. The word *pornography* comes from the Greek words for "writing about prostitutes" and is defined as writings and pictures "intended primarily to arouse sexual desire." But sexual desire can be aroused by words and pictures that simply portray or depict nudity, partial or complete, without any sexual act involved. And what arouses sexual desire in one person may leave another cold. The law has never held pornography, as a class of expression, unlawful. It is the subcategory of pornography that arouses "prurient interest" that met the legal definition of obscenity, which could be prosecuted under the *Roth* test. Justice Brennan added to his test a set of guidelines to judges in deciding whether material met that test: "whether to the average person, applying contemporary community standards, the dominant theme of the material taken as a whole appeals to prurient interest."

Justice Brennan's effort to guide judges in obscenity cases raised several difficult questions: What is the "average person"? How are "contemporary community standards" to be discerned, and in terms of what community, the community in which the allegedly obscene material was produced, the community in which a prosecutor brought suit against it, or a "national community" composed of millions of people, with differing tastes and tolerances for sexual material? How can judges decide what the "dominant theme" of a work is, particularly in a book or film in which descriptions or depictions of sex is part of a broader work? And, once more, how can judges determine whether such material "appeals to prurient interest"?

The Court's opinion in the *Roth* case, however diligent an effort to provide guidance to prosecutors and judges, did little to stem the growing flood of pornography, which became widely available in the 1960s through videocassettes. People with a "prurient interest" in sex no longer had to visit seedy movie theaters to watch depictions of intercourse, oral sex, masturbation, and other forms of sexual activity, much of it filmed in motel rooms. They could purchase these cassettes in adult bookstores and view them in the privacy of their own homes. However, many prosecutors continued to bring criminal charges against theater operators who showed films such as *Carnal Knowledge*, which starred Jack Nicholson and Ann Margret, and was nominated for an Academy Award. The Supreme Court overturned the conviction of a theater owner in rural Georgia who had exhibited this film, as well as the conviction of a Cleveland operator for showing the French film *Les Amants* (The Lovers).

In a Cleveland case, *Jacobellis v. Ohio*, Justice Brennan again wrote for the Court and took pains to warn local prosecutors that juries would be instructed to apply "national community standards" in obscenity cases. What was legally obscene in rural Iowa would be judged by a standard that included the tastes in sexual material of residents of Las Vegas. Justice Brennan's refinement of the *Roth* test in the *Jacobellis* case created even more problems. How can a "national" standard be discerned, through public opinion polls? The difficulties in applying, let alone finding, such a standard led Justice Potter Stewart to literally throw up his hands in frustration. In a concurring opinion in the *Jacobellis* case, Stewart wrote: "I shall not today attempt further to define [obscenity]. But I know it when I see it."

The Supreme Court made another effort to clear the muddy legal waters in 1973, in the case of *Miller v. California*, which involved prosecution for mailing advertising brochures that depicted simulated acts of intercourse and oral sex. By this time, Justice Brennan had repudiated his *Roth* opinion and joined the four *Miller* dissenters. However, Chief Justice Warren Burger, who can fairly be labeled a prude in sexual matters, wrote for the majority, offering state and local officials a guide for writing new obscenity laws. Lawmakers could now enact laws that prohibited: "(a) Patently offensive representation or descriptions of ultimate sexual acts, normal or perverted, actual or simulated. (b) Patently offensive representation or descriptions of masturbation, excretory functions, and lewd exhibition of the genitals." Burger proudly announced that, "for the first time since *Roth* was decided in 1957, a majority of this Court has agreed on concrete guidelines to isolate 'hard core' pornography from expression protected by the First Amendment."

Chief Justice Burger's "concrete guidelines" turned to sand in the 1980s with the advent of the Internet and the World Wide Web that linked anyone with a computer to sites around the globe and offered the most explicit sex, including bestiality and child pornography. Local and state prosecutors virtually gave up their efforts to convict theater and adult-bookstore operators for purveying obscenity, and legislators turned their attention to child pornography, undoubtedly the most "patently offensive" form of sexual exploitation to most people. The Supreme Court had upheld in 1982 the conviction of a man who sold videotapes that depicted young boys who were masturbating. Writing for the Court in *New York v. Ferber*, Justice Byron White noted that virtually all the states had made a legislative judgment that "the use of children as subjects of pornographic materials is harmful to the physiological, emotional, and mental health of the child. That judgment, we think, easily passes muster under the First Amendment."

Justice Brennan concurred in this decision, writing in a separate opinion that a state could express its "special interest in protecting the well-being of its youth" by regulating child pornography, "even though the State does not have such leeway when it seeks only to protect consenting adults from such material."

However, the legislative shift of focus from obscene films and videos in which adults engaged in sexual activities (the Court had already ruled that words alone could not be prosecuted as obscene) to the banning of child pornography, which did not have to meet the *Miller* test, came up against the relentless advance of computer technology. In the 1990s it became possible to create "virtual child pornography," in which videos could be produced that showed children engaged in sex, even though the children were not real but simply the products of computer programming. Confronted with this brand-new form of child pornography, Congress enacted in 1996 the Child Pornography Prevention Act, which banned sexually explicit images that appeared to depict children but were produced without using any actual children.

In the final case in this chapter, *Ashcroft v. Free Speech Coalition*, the Supreme Court in April 2002 struck down the Child Pornography Prevention Act, on the ground that it "proscribes a significant universe of speech that is neither obscene under *Miller* nor child pornography under *Ferber*." The federal law failed the *Miller* test because it banned the depiction of any form of sexual activity by persons who "appear" to be under 18 years of age, and it failed the *Ferber* test because computer-generated images "do not involve, let alone harm, any children in the production process." The Court's ruling provoked outrage from many people, who argued that the purveyors of child pornography were now free to produce the most graphic and offensive material if they used computers to simulate children who looked real. Defenders of the *Ashcroft* decision, a decided minority of those who commented on the case, replied that lawmakers could still protect real children from sexual exploitation, which had been the rationale of the *Ferber* decision.

Viewed together, the free speech cases in this chapter illustrate the long-standing and continuing debate—both among the public and within the Supreme Court—over the limits of free expression in the diverse and not always tolerant American society. There are few First Amendment "absolutists" in this nation, and few who would ban any form of expression that offends or "invites dispute" about matters of religion, politics, or morality. Most people remain in the middle, generally supportive of the principle of free speech but willing to support laws that punish such forms of speech as flag burning and pornography. Meanwhile, the Supreme Court steers a course in free speech cases that remains committed to the admonition of Justice Robert Jackson in his *Barnette* opinion, that "fundamental rights may not be submitted to vote; they depend on the outcome of no elections."

POLITICAL SPEECH: SOCIALISTS, ANARCHISTS, COMMUNISTS, AND RACISTS

SCHENCK V. UNITED STATES
249 U.S. 47 (1919)

"The character of every act depends upon the circumstances in which it is done. The most stringent protection of free speech would not protect a man in falsely shouting fire in a theater and causing a panic. . . . The question in every case is whether the words used are used in such circumstances and are of such a nature . . . that they will bring about the substantive evils that Congress has a right to prevent."

The Question: Can the Congress pass a law that makes it a federal crime during wartime to "utter" in words or print anything that is intended to "obstruct" recruitment into the armed forces or to hinder the production of munitions of other military supplies?

The Arguments: PRO

The government has the power and the obligation during wartime to raise armed forces through recruitment or by a military draft, and to make sure the production of munitions and other military supplies is not obstructed. Physical obstructions, such as blockades of recruiting stations or of munitions factories, can be punished. The same principle applies to speech, in verbal or written form, which can persuade those who hear or read it to take actions that could hinder the war effort. Persuading young men not to register for the draft or to refuse induction, or encouraging strikes in munitions factories could seriously hinder the war effort and put the lives of military troops and civilians at risk. Free speech is not a license to endanger the nation during wartime.

CON

The protection of free speech is one of the main things that distinguishes American society from the repressive governments against which we fight during wartime. Citizens have a right to criticize our government, its leaders, and their policies, without fear of prosecution. There are laws that allow the punishment of overt acts to hinder military recruitment and the production of war supplies. But without clear evidence that speech has directly provoked these acts, such as blockades or strikes, there is no constitutional basis for punishing the speaker or publisher of critical words, even those that insult our political leaders or heap scorn on their policies.

MR. JUSTICE HOLMES delivered the opinion of the Court.

The [indictment in this case] charges a conspiracy to violate the Espionage Act of June 15, 1917, by causing and attempting to cause insubordination, &c., in the military and naval forces of the United States, and to obstruct the recruiting and enlistment service of the United States, when the United States was at war with the German Empire, to-wit, that the defendant wilfully conspired to have printed and circulated to men who had been called and accepted for military service . . . a document set forth and alleged to be calculated to cause such insubordination and obstruction. . . .

According to the testimony Schenck said he was general secretary of the Socialist party and had charge of the Socialist headquarters from which the documents were sent. He identified a book found there as the minutes of the Executive Committee of the party. The book showed a resolution of August 13, 1917, that 15,000 leaflets should be printed on the other side of one of them in use, to be mailed to men who had passed exemption boards, and for distribution. Schenck personally attended to the printing.

The document in question upon its first printed side recited the first section of the Thirteenth Amendment, and said that the idea embodied in it was violated by the conscription act and that a conscript is little better than a convict. In impassioned language it intimated that conscription was despotism in its worst form and a monstrous wrong against humanity in the interest of Wall Street's chosen few. It said, "Do not submit to intimidation," but in form at least confined itself to peaceful measures such as a petition for the repeal of the act. The other and later printed side of the sheet was headed "Assert Your Rights." It stated reasons for alleging that any one violated the Constitution when he refused to recognize "your right to assert your opposition to the draft," and went on, "If you do not assert and support your rights, you are helping to deny or disparage rights which it is the solemn duty of all citizens and residents of the United States to retain." It described the arguments on the other side as coming from cunning politicians and a mercenary capitalist press, and even silent consent to the conscription law as helping to support an infamous conspiracy. It denied the power to send our citizens away to foreign shores to shoot up the people of other lands, and added that words could not express the condemnation such cold-blooded ruthlessness deserves, &c., &c., winding up, "You must do your share to maintain, support and uphold the rights of the people of this country." Of course the document would not have been sent unless it had been intended to have some effect, and we do not see what effect it could be expected to have upon persons subject to the draft except to influence them to obstruct the carrying of it out. . . .

But it is said, suppose that that was the tendency of this circular, it is protected by the First Amendment to the Constitution. . . . We admit that in many places and in ordinary times the defendants in saying all that was said in the circular would have been within their constitutional rights. But the character of every act depends upon the circumstances in which it is done. The most stringent protection of free speech would not protect a man in falsely shouting fire in a theatre and causing a panic. It does not even protect a man from an injunction against uttering words that may have all the effect of force. The question in every case is whether the words used are used in such circumstances and are of such a nature as to create a clear and present danger that they will bring about the substantive evils that Congress has a right to prevent. It is a question of proximity and degree. When a nation is at war many things that might be said in time of peace are such a hindrance to its effort that their utterance will not be endured so long as men fight and that no Court could regard them as protected by any constitutional right. It seems to be admitted that if an actual obstruction of the recruiting service were proved, liability for words that produced that effect might be enforced. If the act (speaking, or circulating a paper), its tendency and the intent with which it is done are the same, we perceive no ground for saying that success alone warrants making the act a crime.

Abrams v. United States
250 U.S. 616 (1919)

"While the immediate occasion for this particular outbreak of lawlessness, on the part of the defendant alien anarchists, may have been resentment caused by our government sending troops into Russia . . . the plain purpose of their propaganda was to excite, at the supreme crisis of the war, disaffection, sedition, riots, and . . . revolution, in this country."

BACKGROUND

One week after the Court issued its *Schenck* decision, the justices unanimously upheld a ten-year sentence imposed on Eugene Debs for violating the Espionage Act. The charismatic Socialist leader had been prosecuted for making a two-hour speech at Nimasilla Park in Canton, Ohio, on June 16, 1918. Speaking on a Sunday afternoon at an outdoor picnic and rally, Debs larded his speech with indignation, humor, bombast, and passion. Among the crowd of several thousand was E. R. Sterling, who scribbled out Debs's words in shorthand for the Justice Department, whose agents had shadowed Debs on a national tour to protest the imprisonment of other Socialists.

Pointing to the county jail across the street from the park, Debs told the crowd, "I have just returned from a visit over yonder, where three of our most loyal comrades are paying the penalty for their devotion to the cause of the working class." He had visited three young men serving sentences for obstructing military recruitment. "They have come to realize," Debs said of his imprisoned followers, "that it is extremely dangerous to exercise the constitutional right of free speech in a country fighting to make Democracy safe in the world." (Sterling noted "applause" at these words; the crowd applauded, cheered, and laughed more than three hundred times during the speech.)

Debs was well aware that government agents were recording his words. "I realize that, in speaking to you this afternoon," he said, "there are certain limitations placed upon the right of free speech. I must be exceedingly careful, prudent, as to what I say, and even more careful and more prudent as to how I say it." The crowd laughed. "I may not be able to say all that I think (laughter and applause); but I am not going to say anything that I do not think (applause). But, I would rather a thousand times be a free soul in jail than to be a sycophant and coward on the streets (applause and shouts)."

During his Canton speech, Debs cast blame for the war on both sides, denouncing both the Allies and Germany for seeking "profits" at home and "plunder" abroad. "The master class has always declared the war," he declaimed; "the subject class has always fought the battles; the master class has all to gain, nothing to lose, and the subject class has had nothing to gain and all to lose including their lives (applause). They have always taught you that it is your patriotic duty to go to war and to have yourselves slaughtered at a command." This was as close as Debs came to mentioning the draft, perhaps from the "prudence" of knowing his words were being recorded.

The fact that Debs had not urged draft resistance failed to sway Justice Holmes. The Socialist Party had adopted a resolution calling for "continuous, active, and public opposition to the war, through demonstrations, mass petitions, and all other means within our power." Holmes read this statement, and Debs's speech, as "evidence that if in that speech he used words tending to obstruct the recruiting service he meant that they should have that effect."

Holmes made only a passing reference to the First Amendment in his *Debs v. United States* opinion. All he said, in fact, was that objections to the conviction "based upon the First Amendment to the Constitution" had been "disposed of in *Schenck v. United States.*" Holmes did not repeat, or rely on, the "clear and present danger" test in *Debs*, perhaps because he thought its application was implied in his opinion. More likely, he realized it would be more difficult to find a "clear and present danger" to the draft in Debs's words than in Schenck's leaflet. It was enough for Holmes that the "natural tendency" of the Canton speech was to "obstruct the recruiting service." What legal scholars later called the "bad tendency" test, which cast a much wider net over speech, owes its genesis to the *Debs* opinion, much less remembered than *Schenck* but more dangerous to dissenters.

The opinion Holmes wrote sent Debs to prison, and President Woodrow Wilson refused all appeals to release his political opponent. Debs campaigned for the presidency in 1920 from his cell in Atlanta Penitentiary against Republican Warren Harding and Democrat James Cox, and again garnered almost a million votes. Harding won by the largest margin in American history and set Debs free in 1921 after three years in prison. By this time, the Socialist firebrand was tired and ill at sixty-six, and the party he had built into a real force in American politics never regained its electoral strength.

Justice Holmes issued his *Schenck* and *Debs* opinions in March 1919. Something happened to him during the next eight months. The man who found that Charles Schenck's leaflet posed a "clear and present danger" to the draft and that the "natural tendency" of Eugene Debs's speech would obstruct military recruiting changed his mind about the First Amendment by November 1919. The story of his move from certitude to skepticism is not entirely clear, but Holmes obviously listened to his critics and heeded their words. One of the first to suggest that he had erred was Judge Learned Hand, who exchanged letters with Holmes after the two men shared a train ride and began a dialogue on free speech issues. Shortly after Holmes issued his *Debs* opinion, Hand wrote to argue that speech only violated the Espionage Act "when the words were directly an incitement" to break the law. Hand questioned whether the evidence met this test. Holmes replied that "I don't quite get your point," adding that he saw little difference between a "direct incitement" test and his own standard of "clear and present danger."

Holmes received more pointed, and more public, criticism from Ernst Freund of the University of Chicago Law School. Writing in *The New Republic* on "The Debs Case and Freedom of Speech," Freund attacked the notion of "implied provocation" to violate laws and argued that only "direct provocation" could satisfy the First Amendment. Freund also dismissed the example Holmes offered in *Schenck* to support the "clear and present danger" test. "Justice Holmes would make us believe that the relation of the speech to obstruction is like that of the shout of Fire! in a crowded theatre to the resulting panic! Surely implied provocation in connection with political offenses is an unsafe doctrine if it has to be made plausible by a parallel so manifestly inappropriate." Holmes composed a reply to Freund that stood by his opinions but admitted some doubts. "I hated to have to write the Debs case," he confessed. "I could not see the wisdom of pressing the cases, especially when the fighting was over and I think it quite possible that if I had been on the jury I should have been for acquittal," he added. Holmes had second thoughts about debating his opinions in public and did not send his letter to *The New Republic.*

A more persuasive—and more tactfully phrased— response to the *Schenck* and *Debs* opinions came from Zechariah Chafee of Harvard Law School. In his *Harvard Law Review* article "Freedom of Speech in War Time," Chafee admitted the difficulty of deciding "where the line runs" between lawful and unlawful speech. He suggested that Holmes had missed a "magnificent opportunity'" to draw such a line by comparing Schenck's leaflet with a false shout of "Fire!" Chafee offered a better example: "How about the man who gets up in a theater between the acts and informs the audience honestly but perhaps mistakenly that the fire exits are too few or locked. He is a much closer parallel to Schenck or Debs." He supported the "direct incitement" test that Learned Hand had proposed to Holmes, adding that "absolutely unlimited discussion" of public issues—even during wartime— was necessary for "the discovery and spread of truth on subjects of general concern." Holmes read Chafee's article and met with him over tea during the summer of 1919. Perhaps he read the leaves in his cup with an eye toward First Amendment cases on the Court's docket for argument that fall.

* * *

The case that led Holmes to revise his First Amendment views began on a Thursday evening, August 22, 1918, on Second Avenue near Eighth Street in New York City. The Lower East Side in Manhattan was home to thousands of Russian Jews, most of them refugees over the past decade from the anti-Semitic "pogroms" of the czarist government, which had fallen to the Communist Bolsheviks in the October Revolution of 1917. Passersby noticed dozens of leaflets falling onto the sidewalks from a rooftop. Those who picked up copies discovered that some were printed in English, others in Yiddish. A storekeeper picked up one in English and was incensed by its contents, printed under the heading "The Hypocrisy of the United States and Her Allies." He rushed up the stairs to the rooftop but could not find the culprit. He then brought copies of both the English and Yiddish leaflets to the police, who conducted a house-to-house search without locating the perpetrator. Newspaper headlines the next day alerted New Yorkers: "Seditious Circulars Scattered in Streets" and "Wilson Attacked in Circulars from Roofs of East Side."

On the morning of August 23, four men brought more copies to the police and said they saw the leaflets floating from a window at 610 Broadway. Two detectives from the army's Military Intelligence Division visited the building, checked the time cards of workers at the American Hat Company on the third floor, and found that Hyman Rosansky had punched in earlier than usual. They approached Rosansky and asked to see his draft card; he pulled it out of his coat pocket with other papers, including copies of both the English and Yiddish leaflets. Rosansky claimed he had found them on the fire escape, but no one had seen him near it that morning. The detectives took him to his apartment in East Harlem, where they found more leaflets and a loaded .32 caliber revolver.

Grilled at police headquarters, Rosansky said he was born in Russia and had entered the United States in 1910. He admitted being an anarchist but claimed he had nothing to do with producing the leaflets. He had been approached the night before by some men he knew from anarchist circles. "I know the fellows but don't know exactly the names," he said. "Lachowsky I know by name." The men gave Rosansky leaflets to distribute. "I says, 'What kind of leaflets?' 'It is all right, you don't have to know what kind of leaflets.' 'What I got to do with this?' He says, 'You have got to throw them from the window.'" Thoroughly frightened, Rosansky told the detectives he had arranged to meet Lachowsky and other members of his shadowy "Group" that evening on East 104th Street to receive more leaflets. Military agents staked out the block while Rosansky nervously waited for his contacts to appear. By ones and twos, several people approached Rosansky; one handed him a bundle of leaflets. Detectives followed them into apartments and restaurants and arrested four young men and one woman: Jacob Abrams, Hyman Lachowsky, Samuel Lipman, Jacob Schwartz, and Mollie Steimer. They were all held in the city jail, charged with violating the Sedition Act of 1918, arraigned the next morning, and held on $10,000 bail. The *New York World* reported that all five belonged to "the Blast Group and all are long-haired anarchists who came here from Russia."

What had so alarmed the shopkeeper who picked up a leaflet on Second Avenue that he took it to the police? The English-language circular denounced American military intervention in Russia and efforts "to crush the russian revolution." The previous month, President Wilson had approved sending 7,500 American troops to eastern Russia, purportedly to divert German forces from the European front. The Wilson administration had yielded to pressure from its wartime allies for military action against the Bolsheviks, who had signed a separate peace treaty with the Germans in March 1918. Many Americans paid little attention to this faraway military adventure, but most Russian immigrants opposed the Allied intervention. The leaflets that Abrams and his fellow Blast Group members had tossed from rooftops and windows denounced Wilson for failing to inform the American public about his real purpose in sending troops to Siberia, to support the "White" soldiers who battled the "Red" forces of the Bolshevik regime. "His shameful, cowardly silence about the intervention in Russia reveals the hypocrisy of the plutocratic gang in Washington," read the English version. The Blast Group took

pains to distance themselves from German sympathizers. "It is absurd to call us pro-German," they wrote. "We hate and despise German militarism more than do your hypocritical tyrants."

The English leaflet did no more than exhort "workers of America, workers of Germany" to be "AWAKE!" to their governments' efforts to destroy the Russian Revolution. However, the Yiddish version—headed "Workers, Wake Up!"—appealed to workers in munitions factories who "are producing bullets, bayonets, cannon, to murder not only the Germans, but also your dearest, best, who are in Russia and are fighting for freedom." The Blast Group urged direct action: "Workers, our reply to the barbaric intervention has to be a general strike!" Taking its heated rhetoric at face value, this leaflet was hardly likely to foment a "general strike" or any disruption of war production. The "sweatshops" of the Lower East Side produced clothing and buttons, not cannons and bullets. Even if workers in munitions factories read the Yiddish leaflet, few if any would risk their jobs by striking for any reason. But these facts did not dissuade government prosecutors from charging the Blast Group members with violating the Sedition Act by publishing "disloyal, scurrilous and abusive language about the form of Government of the United States" and with inciting "curtailment of production of things and products, to wit, ordnance and ammunition, necessary and essential to the prosecution of the war."

The trial of the Russian anarchists took place in October 1918 while German and Allied diplomats were negotiating the Armistice that ended the bloody carnage of World War I the next month. But the assault on the First Amendment continued in the courtroom of Judge Henry D. Clayton Jr., who came from Alabama to help shoulder the burden of wartime prosecutions in New York City. The son of a Confederate officer, Clayton faced the Russian defendants not only across his judicial bench but across a cultural and political chasm. He belittled their broken English and openly disparaged their beliefs. When the jury returned with its inevitable "guilty" verdicts, Clayton sentenced Jacob Abrams, Samuel Lipman, and Hyman Lachowsky—Jacob Schwartz, who suffered numerous police beatings, died in jail the night before the trial began—to maximum terms of twenty years. In a gesture of southern chivalry, Clayton cut five years from the maximum for Mollie Steimer.

The Supreme Court heard the appeals of the convicted anarchists in October 1919, a year after their trial and sentences. Their lawyer, Harry Weinberger, submitted a brief that took an uncompromising view of First Amendment rights. Not only did he reject the "clear and present danger" test of Justice Holmes, he went beyond the "direct incitement" standard of Judge Learned Hand to argue that only "overt acts" could be punished; speech itself must be "perfectly unrestrained" by government. Weinberger asserted that "absolute freedom of speech is the only basis upon which the Government can stand and remain free." The government's brief took an equally extreme position, claiming that the First Amendment's framers did not intend to protect "the unlimited right to publish a seditious libel." This effort to revive the doctrine that any criticism of government could be punished had little historical support, but it reflected the hard-line position of

Justice Department officials. The brief also claimed that the Yiddish leaflet calling for a general strike was intended "to stop the production of munitions, and to overthrow by force the form of government of the United States by law established."

Jacob Abrams's name went first in alphabetical order on the appeal, and the Supreme Court decided *Abrams v. United States* on November 10, 1919. Seven justices lined up with the government; only Oliver Wendell Holmes and Louis Brandeis stood behind the First Amendment. Justice John H. Clarke, a "progressive" on most issues, wrote for the majority. His opinion dismissed in one sentence Harry Weinberger's argument that the Sedition Act violated the First Amendment. "This contention is sufficiently discussed and is definitely negatived in *Schenck v. United States*" is all Clarke wrote on this issue.

The Court's majority sent the four Russian anarchists from the New York jails where they had been held since their arrests to state and federal prisons in November 1919. Mollie Steimer, just twenty years old, was sent to the Missouri state penitentiary; the three young men—Jacob Abrams, Hyman Lachowsky, and Samuel Lipman—went to the Atlanta federal penitentiary, where they joined Eugene Debs, who was serving his ten-year sentence. All the anarchists endured "hard time" behind bars, forced to work at exhausting prison jobs and punished with solitary confinement for any violation of prison rules. Harry Weinberger, who defended them in court, mounted a campaign for an "amnesty" that would allow their deportation to Soviet Russia. Friends and supporters of President Wilson urged that he commute the sentences of all those imprisoned for Espionage Act violations, but he adamantly refused. "I do not think the men you refer to are in any proper sense political prisoners," he replied to Norman Hapgood, a prominent journalist. Rather, all those in prison had "violated criminal statutes." Not until Wilson relinquished the White House to Warren Harding did amnesty appeals finally succeed.

On November 23, 1921, the four young anarchists boarded a ship in New York that took them to Latvia, from where they traveled by train to Moscow. Having endured prison in the United States for supporting the Soviet revolution, they encountered persecution by the Bolshevik government. Vladimir Lenin ordered a crackdown on anarchists after a mutiny at the Kronstadt naval base in March 1921 in which they played leading roles. Bolshevik troops killed six hundred insurgents and marched several thousand to prisons, while thousands more fled to neighboring Finland. "The time has come," Lenin warned, "to put an end to opposition, to put a lid on it; we have had enough opposition." The Bolsheviks put an end to Russian anarchism, and the four young people who chose deportation over prison all met sad ends. Samuel Lipman—who was more of a Marxist than an anarchist—joined the Communist Party but could not escape his past and was murdered in the Stalinist purges of the 1930s. Hyman Lachowsky moved from Moscow to Minsk in 1922 and most likely died when German troops overran the city in 1941 and systematically murdered all Jews who remained. Quickly disillusioned, Jacob Abrams and Mollie Steimer left Russia and found exile in Mexico by different paths. Abrams died in 1953 and Steimer in 1980. Mollie Steimer, the most uncompromising of the group,

wrote in 1960 what could serve as an epitaph for them all: "We fought injustice in our humble way as best we could; and if the result was prison, hard labour, deportations and lots of suffering, well, this was something that every human being who fights for a better humanity has to expect" (Irons, 1999).

MR. JUSTICE CLARKE delivered the opinion of the Court.

On a single indictment, containing four counts, the five plaintiffs in error, hereinafter designated the defendants, were convicted of conspiring to violate provisions of the Espionage Act of Congress, as amended by the Act of May 16, 1918.

Each of the first three counts charged the defendants with conspiring, when the United States was at war with the Imperial Government of Germany, to unlawfully utter, print, write and publish: In the first count, "disloyal, scurrilous and abusive language about the form of government of the United States. . . ." The charge in the fourth count was that the defendants conspired "when the United States was at war with the Imperial German Government, . . . unlawfully and willfully, by utterance, writing, printing and publication to urge, incite and advocate curtailment of production of things and products, to wit, ordnance and ammunition, necessary and essential to the prosecution of the war." It was charged in each count of the indictment that it was a part of the conspiracy that the defendants would attempt to accomplish their unlawful purpose by printing, writing and distributing in the city of New York many copies of a leaflet or circular, printed in the English language, and of another printed in the Yiddish language, copies of which, properly identified, were attached to the indictment.

All of the five defendants were born in Russia. They were intelligent, had considerable schooling, and at the time they were arrested they had lived in the United States terms varying from five to ten years, but none of them had applied for naturalization. Four of them testified as witnesses in their own behalf, and of these three frankly avowed that they were "rebels," "revolutionists," "anarchists," that they did not believe in government in any form, and they declared that they had no interest whatever in the government of the United States. The fourth defendant testified that he was a "Socialist" and believed in "a proper kind of government, not capitalistic," but in his classification the government of the United States was "capitalistic."

It was admitted on the trial that the defendants had united to print and distribute the described circulars and that 5,000 of them had been printed and distributed about the 22d day of August, 1918. . . . The circulars were distributed, some by throwing them from a window of a building where one of the defendants was employed and others secretly, in New York City. . . .

On the record thus described it is argued, somewhat faintly, that the acts charged against the defendants were not unlawful because within the protection of that freedom of speech and of the press which is guaranteed by the First Amendment to the Constitution of the United States, and that the entire Espionage Act is unconstitutional because in conflict with that amendment. . . .

The first of the two articles attached to the indictment is conspicuously headed, "The Hypocrisy of the United States and her Allies." After denouncing President Wilson as a hypocrite and a coward because troops were sent into Russia, it proceeds to assail our government in general, saying: "His [the President's] shameful, cowardly silence about the intervention in Russia reveals the hypocrisy of the plutocratic gang in Washington and vicinity."

It continues: "He [the President] is too much of a coward to come out openly and say: 'We capitalistic nations cannot afford to have a proletarian republic in Russia.'" Among the capitalistic nations Abrams testified the United States was included.

Growing more inflammatory as it proceeds, the circular culminates in:

The Russian Revolution cries: Workers of the World! Awake! Rise! Put down your enemy and mine!

Yes friends, there is only one enemy of the workers of the world and that is CAPITALISM.

This is clearly an appeal to the "worker" of this country to arise and put down by force the government of the United States which they characterize as their "hypocritical," "cowardly" and "capitalistic" enemy.

It concludes:

"Awake! Awake, you Workers of the World! REVOLUTIONISTS."

The second of the articles was printed in the Yiddish language and in the translation is headed, "Workers—Wake Up." After referring to "his Majesty, Mr. Wilson, and the rest of the gang, dogs of all colors!" it continues:

Workers, Russian emigrants, you who had the least belief in the honesty of our government,

—which defendants admitted referred to the United States government—

must now throw away all confidence, must spit in the face the false, hypocritic, military propaganda which has fooled you so relentlessly, calling forth your sympathy, your help, to the prosecution of the war.

The purpose of this obviously was to persuade the persons to whom it was addressed to turn a deaf ear to patriotic appeals in behalf of the government of the United States, and to cease to render it assistance in the prosecution of the war.

It goes on:

With the money which you have loaned, or are going to loan, them they will make bullets not only for the Germans, but also for the Workers Soviets of Russia. Workers in the ammunition factories, you are producing bullets, bayonets, cannon, to murder not only the Germans, but also your dearest, best, who are in Russia and are fighting for freedom.

It will not do to say, as is now argued, that the only intent of these defendants was to prevent injury to the Russian cause. Men must be held to have intended, and to be accountable for, the effects which their acts were likely to produce. Even if their primary purpose and intent was to aid the cause of the Russian Revolution, the plan of action which they adopted necessarily involved, before it could be realized, defeat of the war program of the United States, for the obvious effect of this appeal, if it should become effective, as they hoped it might, would be to persuade persons of character such as those whom they regarded themselves as addressing, not to aid government loans and not to work in ammunition factories, where their work would produce "bullets, bayonets, cannon" and other munitions of war, the use of which would cause the "murder" of Germans and Russians. . . .

These excerpts sufficiently show, that while the immediate occasion for this particular outbreak of lawlessness, on the part of the defendant alien anarchists, may have been resentment caused by our government sending troops into Russia as a strategic operation against the Germans on the eastern battle front, yet the plain purpose of their propaganda was to excite, at the supreme crisis of the war, disaffection, sedition, riots, and, as they hoped, revolution, in this country for the purpose of embarrassing and if possible defeating the military plans of the government in Europe. A technical distinction may perhaps be taken between disloyal and abusive language applied to the form of our government or language intended to bring the form of our government into contempt and disrepute, and language of like character and intended to produce like results directed against the President and Congress, the agencies through which that form of government must function in time of war. But it is not necessary to a decision of this case to consider whether such distinction is vital or merely formal, for the language of these circulars was obviously intended to provoke and to encourage resistance to the United States in the war, as the third count runs, and, the defendants, in terms, plainly urged and advocated a resort to a general strike of workers in ammunition factories for the purpose of curtailing the production of ordnance and munitions necessary and essential to the prosecution of the war as is charged in the fourth count. Thus it is clear not only that some evidence but that much persuasive evidence was before the jury tending to prove that the defendants were guilty as charged in both the third and fourth counts of the indictment and under the long established rule of law hereinbefore stated the judgment of the District Court must be

Affirmed.

MR. JUSTICE HOLMES, dissenting.

I never have seen any reason to doubt that the questions of law that alone were before this Court in the cases of Schenck, Frohwerk, and Debs, were rightly decided. I do not doubt for a moment that by the same reasoning that would justify punishing persuasion to murder, the United States constitutionally may punish speech that produces or is intended to produce a clear and imminent danger that it will bring about forthwith certain substantive evils that the United States constitutionally may seek to prevent. The power undoubtedly is greater in time of war than in time of peace because war opens dangers that do not exist at other times.

But as against dangers peculiar to war, as against others, the principle of the right to free speech is always the same. It is only the present danger of immediate evil or an intent to bring it about that warrants Congress in setting a limit to the expression of opinion where private rights are not concerned. Congress certainly cannot forbid all effort to change the mind of the country. Now nobody can suppose that the surreptitious publishing of a silly leaflet by an unknown man, without more, would present any immediate danger that its opinions would hinder the success of the government arms or have any appreciable tendency to do so. Publishing those opinions for the very purpose of obstructing, however, might indicate a greater danger and at any rate would have the quality of an attempt. So I assume that the second leaflet if published for the purposes alleged in the fourth count might be punishable. But it seems pretty clear to me that nothing less than that would bring these papers within the scope of this law. . . .

In this case sentences of twenty years imprisonment have been imposed for the publishing of two leaflets that I believe the defendants had as much right to publish as the Government has to publish the Constitution of the United States now vainly invoked by them. Even if I am technically wrong and enough can be squeezed from these poor and puny anonymities to turn the color of legal litmus paper; I will add, even if what I think the necessary intent were shown; the most nominal punishment seems to me all that possible could be inflicted, unless the defendants are to be made to suffer not for what the indictment alleges but for the creed that they avow—a creed that I believe to be the creed of ignorance and immaturity when honestly held, as I see no reason to doubt that it was held here but which, although made the subject of examination at the trial, no one has a right even to consider in dealing with the charges before the Court.

Persecution for the expression of opinions seems to me perfectly logical. If you have no doubt of your premises or your power and want a certain result with all your heart you naturally express your wishes in law and sweep away all opposition. To allow opposition by speech seems to indicate that you think the speech impotent, as when a man says that he has squared the circle, or that you do not care wholeheartedly for the result, or that you doubt either your power or your premises. But when men have realized that time has upset many fighting faiths, they may come to believe even

more than they believe the very foundations of their own conduct that the ultimate good desired is better reached by free trade in ideas—that the best test of truth is the power of the thought to get itself accepted in the competition of the market, and that truth is the only ground upon which their wishes safely can be carried out. That at any rate is the theory of our Constitution. It is an experiment, as all life is an experiment. Every year if not every day we have to wager our salvation upon some prophecy based upon imperfect knowledge. While that experiment is part of our system I think that we should be eternally vigilant against attempts to check the expression of opinions that we loathe and believe to be fraught with death, unless they so imminently threaten immediate interference with the lawful and pressing purposes of the law that an immediate check is required to save the country. I wholly disagree with the argument of the Government that the First Amendment left the common law as to seditious libel in force. History seems to me against the notion. I had conceived that the United States through many years had shown its repentance for the Sedition Act of 1798, by repaying fines that it imposed. Only the emergency that makes it immediately dangerous to leave the correction of evil counsels to time warrants making any exception to the sweeping command, "Congress shall make no law abridging the freedom of speech." Of course I am speaking only of expressions of opinion and exhortations, which were all that were uttered here, but I regret that I cannot put into more impressive words my belief that in their conviction upon this indictment the defendants were deprived of their rights under the Constitution of the United States.

MR. JUSTICE BRANDEIS concurs with the foregoing opinion.

GITLOW v. NEW YORK
268 U.S. 652 (1925)

"[Utterances inciting to the overthrow of government by unlawful means], by their very nature, involve danger to the public peace and to the security of the State. . . . A single revolutionary spark may kindle a fire that, smouldering for a time, may burst into a sweeping and destructive conflagration. . . . [The State may] suppress the threatened danger in its incipiency."

The Question: Can a state or the Congress pass laws that make it a crime to "advocate" the doctrine that "government should be overthrown by force or violence" or by other unlawful means, whether the advocacy is by word or printed matter? And, can membership in a political party that advocates such acts be made a criminal offense?

The Arguments: PRO

The most basic principle of government is defending its institutions, and the people they serve, from attacks that might lead to its overthrow or destruction. These attacks can come from outside the country's borders or from within. The most dangerous threats to government come from those within its borders who sympathize with and conspire with foreign enemies against their own country. Those who advocate the violent overthrow of the government have relinquished the protection of the First Amendment for speech and writings that are intended to bring about violence or revolution. Whenever such advocacy moves beyond theoretical discussion to organizing a political party whose members are willing to join revolutionary acts, the government has a right and duty to punish the advocates of such violent acts.

CON

Free speech in a democratic society includes the right to advocate revolutionary change. Indeed, the men who advocated and joined a revolution against British rule in the American colonies are lauded today as patriots. The First Amendment draws a clear line between the advocacy of change, even revolutionary change, and the commission of overt acts that are designed to set a revolutionary effort into violent action. Drilling troops, stockpiling weapons, and plotting a violent overthrow of government can be punished, but there must first be clear evidence of a "clear and present danger."

MR. JUSTICE SANFORD delivered the opinion of the Court.

Benjamin Gitlow was indicted in the Supreme Court of New York, with three others, for the statutory crime of criminal anarchy. He was separately tried, convicted, and sentenced to imprisonment. The judgment was affirmed by the Appellate Division and by the Court of Appeals.... The contention here is that the statute, by its terms and as applied in this case, is repugnant to the due process clause of the Fourteenth Amendment. Its material provisions are:

Sec. 160. Criminal anarchy is the doctrine that organized government should be overthrown by force or violence, or by assassination of the executive head or of any of the executive officials of government, or by any unlawful means. The advocacy of such doctrine either by word of mouth or writing is a felony.

Sec. 161. Any person who ... by word of mouth or writing advocates, advises or teaches the duty, necessity or propriety of overthrowing or overturning organized government by force or violence, or by assassination of the executive head or of any of the executive officials of government, or by any unlawful means ... is guilty of a felony and punishable by imprisonment or fine, or both.

The indictment was in two counts. The first charged that the defendant had advocated, advised and taught the duty, necessity and propriety of overthrowing and overturning organized government by force, violence and unlawful means, by certain writings therein set forth entitled "The Left Wing Manifesto"; the second that he had printed, published and knowingly circulated and distributed a certain paper called "The Revolutionary Age," containing the writings set forth in the first count advocating, advising and teaching the doctrine that organized government should be overthrown by force, violence and unlawful means.

The following facts were established on the trial by undisputed evidence and admissions: The defendant is a member of the Left Wing Section of the Socialist Party, a dissenting branch or faction of that party formed in opposition to its dominant policy of "moderate Socialism." Membership in both is open to aliens as well as citizens. The Left Wing Section was organized nationally at a conference in New York City in June, 1919, attended by ninety delegates from twenty different States. The conference elected a National Council, of which the defendant was a member, and left to it the adoption of a "Manifesto." This was published in The Revolutionary Age, the official organ of the Left Wing. The defendant was on the board of managers of the paper and was its business manager.... There was no evidence of any effect resulting from the publication and circulation of the Manifesto....

Coupled with a review of the rise of Socialism, [the Manifesto] condemned the dominant "moderate Socialism" for its recognition of the necessity of the democratic parliamentary state; repudiated its policy of introducing Socialism by legislative measures; and advocated, in plain and unequivocal language, the necessity of accomplishing the "Communist Revolution" by a militant and "revolutionary Socialism," based on "the class struggle" and mobilizing the "power of the proletariat in action," through mass industrial revolts developing into mass political strikes and "revolutionary mass action," for the purpose of conquering and destroying the parliamentary state and establishing in its place, through a "revolutionary dictatorship of the proletariat," the system of Communist Socialism. The then recent strikes in Seattle and Winnepeg were cited as instances of a development already verging on revolutionary action and suggestive of proletarian dictatorship, in which the strike-workers were "trying to usurp the functions of municipal government"; and revolutionary Socialism, it was urged, must use these mass industrial revolts to broaden the strike, make it general and militant, and develop it into mass political strikes and revolutionary mass action for the annihilation of the parliamentary state....

The sole contention here is, essentially, that as there was no evidence of any concrete result flowing from the publication of the Manifesto or of circumstances showing the likelihood of such result, the statute as construed and applied by the trial court penalizes the mere utterance, as such, of "doctrine" having no quality of incitement, without regard either to the circumstances of its utterance or to the likelihood of unlawful sequences; and that, as the exercise of the right of free expression with relation to government is only punishable "in circumstances involving likelihood of substantive evil," the statute contravenes the due process clause of the Fourteenth Amendment....

The statute does not penalize the utterance or publication of abstract "doctrine" or academic discussion having no quality of incitement to any concrete action. It is not changes in the form of government by constitutional and lawful means. What it prohibits is language advocating, advising or teaching the overthrow of organized government by unlawful means. These words imply urging to action....

The Manifesto, plainly, is neither the statement of abstract doctrine nor, as suggested by counsel, mere prediction that industrial disturbances and revolutionary mass strikes will result spontaneously in an inevitable process of evolution in the economic system. It advocates and urges in fervent language mass action which shall progressively foment industrial disturbances and through political mass strikes and revolutionary mass action overthrow and destroy organized parliamentary government. It concludes with a call to action in these words:

> The proletariat revolution and the Communist reconstruction of society—the struggle for these—is now indispensable. . . . The Communist International calls the proletariat of the world to the final struggle!

This is not the expression of philosophical abstraction, the mere prediction of future events; it is the language of direct incitement. . . .

For present purposes we may and do assume that freedom of speech and of the press—which are protected by the First Amendment from abridgment by Congress—are among the fundamental personal rights and "liberties" protected by the due process clause of the Fourteenth Amendment from impairment by the States. . . . It is a fundamental principle, long established, that the freedom of speech and of the press which is secured by the Constitution, does not confer an absolute right to speak or publish, without responsibility, whatever one may choose, or an unrestricted and unbridled license that gives immunity for every possible use of language and prevents the punishment of those who abuse this freedom. . . .

That a State in the exercise of its police power may punish those who abuse this freedom by utterances inimical to the public welfare, tending to corrupt public morals, incite to crime, or disturb the public peace, is not open to question. . . . And, for yet more imperative reasons, a State may punish utterances endangering the foundations of organized government and threatening its overthrow by unlawful means. These imperil its own existence as a constitutional State. Freedom of speech and press, said Story, supra, does not protect disturbances to the public peace or the attempt to subvert the government. It does not protect publications or teachings which tend to subvert or imperil the government or to impede or hinder it in the performance of its governmental duties. It does not protect publications prompting the overthrow of government by force; the punishment of those who publish articles which tend to destroy organized society being essential to the security of freedom and the stability of the state. . . .

By enacting the present statute the State has determined, through its legislative body, that utterances advocating the overthrow of organized government by force, violence and unlawful means, are so inimical to the general welfare and involve such danger of substantive evil that they may be penalized in the exercise of its police power. . . . That utterances inciting to the overthrow of organized government by unlawful means, present a sufficient danger of substantive evil to bring their punishment within the range of legislative discretion, is clear. Such utterances, by their very nature, involve danger to the public peace and to the security of the State. They threaten breaches of the peace and ultimate revolution. And the immediate danger is none the less real and substantial, because the effect of a given utterance cannot be accurately foreseen. The State cannot reasonably be required to measure the danger from every such utterance in the nice balance of a jeweler's scale. A single revolutionary spark may kindle a fire that, smouldering for a time, may burst into a sweeping and destructive conflagration. It cannot be said that the State is acting arbitrarily or unreasonably when in the exercise of its judgment as to the measures necessary to protect the public peace and safety, it seeks to extinguish the spark without waiting until it has enkindled the flame or blazed into the conflagration. It cannot reasonably be required to defer the adoption of measures for its own peace and safety until the revolutionary utterances lead to actual disturbances of the public peace or imminent and immediate danger of its own destruction; but it may, in the exercise of its judgment, suppress the threatened danger in its incipiency.

We cannot hold that the present statute is an arbitrary or unreasonable exercise of the police power of the State unwarrantably infringing the freedom of speech or press; and we must and do sustain its constitutionality.

This being so it may be applied to every utterance—not too trivial to be beneath the notice of the law—which is of such a character and used with such intent and purpose as to bring it within the prohibition of the statute. . . . In other words, when the legislative body has determined generally, in the constitutional exercise of its discretion, that utterances of a certain kind involve such danger of substantive evil that they may be punished, the question whether any specific utterance coming within the prohibited class is likely, in and of itself, to bring about the substantive evil, is not open to consideration. It is sufficient that the statute itself be constitutional and that the use of the language comes within its prohibition. . . .

And finding, for the reasons stated, that the statute is not in itself unconstitutional, and that it has not been applied in the present case in derogation of any constitutional right, the judgment of the Court of Appeals is

Affirmed.

Mr. Justice Holmes, dissenting.

Mr. Justice Brandeis and I are of opinion that this judgment should be reversed. The general principle of free speech, it seems to me, must be taken to be included in the Fourteenth Amendment, in view of the scope that has been given to the word "liberty" as there used, although perhaps it may be accepted with a somewhat larger latitude of interpretation than is allowed to Congress by the sweeping language that governs or ought to govern the laws of the United States. . . .

If what I think the correct test is applied it is manifest that there was no present danger of an attempt to overthrow the government by force on the part of the admittedly small minority who shared the defendant's views. It is said that this manifesto was more than a theory, that it was an incitement. Every idea is an incitement. It offers itself for belief and if believed it is acted on unless some other belief outweighs it or some failure of energy stifles the movement at its birth. The only difference between the expression of an opinion and an incitement in the narrower sense is the speaker's enthusiasm for the result. Eloquence may set fire to reason. But whatever may be thought of the redundant discourse before us it had no chance of starting a present conflagration. If in the long run the beliefs expressed in proletarian dictatorship are destined to be accepted by the dominant forces of the community, the only meaning of free speech is that they should be given their chance and have their way.

If the publication of this document had been laid as an attempt to induce an uprising against government at once and not at some indefinite time in the future it would have presented a different question. The object would have been one with which the law might deal, subject to the doubt whether there was any danger that the publication could produce any result, or in other words, whether it was not futile and too remote from possible consequences. But the indictment alleges the publication and nothing more.

WHITNEY V. CALIFORNIA
274 U.S. 357 (1927)

"The State has declared . . . that to knowingly . . . become a member of or assist in organizing an association to advocate . . . the commission of crimes or unlawful acts of force, violence, or terrorism . . . involves such danger to the public peace and the security of the State that these acts should be penalized in the exercise of its police power."

MR. JUSTICE SANFORD delivered the opinion of the Court.

By a criminal information filed in the Superior Court of Alameda County, California, the plaintiff in error was charged, in five counts, with violations of the Criminal Syndicalism Act of that State. She was tried, convicted on the first count, and sentenced to imprisonment. . . .

The pertinent provisions of the Criminal Syndicalism Act are:

Section 1. The term "criminal syndicalism" as used in this act is hereby defined as any doctrine or precept advocating, teaching or aiding and abetting the commission of crime, sabotage (which word is hereby defined as meaning willful and malicious physical damage or injury to physical property), or unlawful acts of force and violence or unlawful methods of terrorism as a means of accomplishing a change in industrial ownership or control or effecting any political change.

Sec. 2. Any person who: . . . organizes or assists in organizing, or is or knowingly becomes a member of, any organization, society, group or assemblage of persons organized or assembled to advocate, teach or aid and abet criminal syndicalism; . . . is guilty of a felony and punishable by imprisonment. . . .

The following facts, among many others, were established on the trial by undisputed evidence: The defendant, a resident of Oakland, in Alameda County, California, had been a member of the Local Oakland branch of the Socialist Party. This Local sent delegates to the national convention of the Socialist Party held in Chicago in 1919, which resulted in a split between the "radical" group and the old-wing Socialists. The "radicals"—to whom the Oakland delegates adhered—being ejected, went to another hall, and formed the Communist Labor Party of America. Its Constitution provided for the membership of persons subscribing to the principles of the Party and pledging themselves to be guided by its Platform, and for the formation of state organizations conforming to its Platform as the supreme declaration of the Party. In its "Platform and Program" the Party declared that it was in full harmony with "the revolutionary working class parties of all countries" and adhered to the principles of Communism laid down in the Manifesto of the Third International at Moscow, and that its purpose was "to create a unified revolutionary working class movement in America," organizing the workers as a class, in a revolutionary class struggle to conquer the capitalist state, for the overthrow of capitalist rule, the conquest of political power and the establishment of a working class government, the Dictatorship of the Proletariat, in place of the state machinery of the capitalists. . . .

Shortly thereafter the Local Oakland withdrew from the Socialist Party, and sent accredited delegates, including the defendant, to a convention held in Oakland in November, 1919, for the purpose of organizing a California branch of the Communist Labor Party. The defendant, after taking out a temporary membership in the Communist Labor Party, attended this convention as a delegate and took an active part in its proceedings. She was elected a member of the Credentials Committee, and, as its chairman, made a report to the convention upon which the delegates were seated. She was also appointed a member of the Resolutions Committee, and as such signed the following resolution in reference to political action, among others proposed by the Committee:

The C. L. P. of California fully recognizes the value of political action as a means of spreading communist propaganda; it insists that in proportion to the development of the economic strength of the working class, it, the working class, must also develop its political power. The C. L. P. of California proclaims and insists that the capture of political power, locally or nationally by the revolutionary working class can be of tremendous assistance to the workers in their struggle of emancipation. Therefore, we again urge the workers who are possessed of the right of franchise to cast their votes for the party which represents their immediate and final interest— the C. L. P.—at all elections, being fully convinced of the utter futility of obtaining any real measure of justice or freedom under officials elected by parties owned and controlled by the capitalist class.

The minutes show that this resolution, with the others proposed by the committee, was read by its chairman to the convention before the Committee on the Constitution had submitted its report. According to the recollection of the defendant, however, she herself read this resolution. Thereafter, before the report of the Committee on the Constitution had been acted upon, the defendant was elected an alternate member of the State Executive Committee. The Constitution, as finally read, was then adopted. This provided that the organization should be named the Communist Labor Party of California; that it should be "affiliated with" the Communist Labor Party of America, and subscribe to its Program, Platform and Constitution, and "through this affiliation" be "joined with the Communist International of Moscow"; and that the qualifications for membership should be those prescribed in the National Constitution. The proposed resolutions were later taken up and all adopted, except that on political action, which caused a lengthy debate, resulting in its defeat and the acceptance of the National Program in its place. After this action, the defendant, without, so far as appears, making any protest, remained in the convention until it adjourned. She later attended as an alternate member one or two meetings of the State Executive Committee in San Jose and San Francisco, and stated, on the trial, that she was then a member of the Communist Labor Party. She also testified that it was not her intention that the Communist Labor Party of California should be an instrument of terrorism or violence, and that it was not her purpose or that of the Convention to violate any known law.

That the freedom of speech which is secured by the Constitution does not confer an absolute right to speak, without responsibility, whatever one may choose, or an unrestricted and unbridled license giving immunity for every possible use of language and preventing the punishment of those who abuse this freedom; and that a State in the exercise of its police power may punish those who abuse this freedom by utterances inimical to the public welfare, tending to incite to crime, disturb the public peace, or endanger the foundations of organized government and threaten its overthrow by unlawful means, is not open to question. Gitlow v. New York.

By enacting the provisions of the Syndicalism Act the State has declared, through its legislative body, that to knowingly be or become a member of or assist in organizing an association to advocate, teach or aid and abet the commission of crimes or unlawful acts of force, violence or terrorism as a means of accomplishing industrial or political changes, involves such danger to the public peace and the security of the State, that these acts should be penalized in the exercise of its police power. . . . The essence of the offense denounced by the Act is the combining with others in an association for the accomplishment of the desired ends through the advocacy and use of criminal and unlawful methods. It partakes of the nature of a criminal conspiracy. That such united and joint action involves even greater danger to the public peace and security than the isolated utterances and acts of individuals is clear. We cannot hold that, as here applied, the Act is an unreasonable or arbitrary exercise of the police power of the State, unwarrantably infringing any right of free speech,

assembly or association, or that those persons are protected from punishment by the due process clause who abuse such rights by joining and furthering an organization thus menacing the peace and welfare of the State.

We find no repugnancy in the Syndicalism Act as applied in this case to either the due process or equal protection clauses of the Fourteenth Amendment on any of the grounds upon which its validity has been here challenged.

The order dismissing the writ of error will be vacated and set aside, and the judgment of the Court of Appeal

Affirmed.

MR. JUSTICE BRANDEIS, concurring.

Miss Whitney was convicted of the felony of assisting in organizing, in the year 1919, the Communist Labor Party of California, of being a member of it, and of assembling with it. These acts are held to constitute a crime, because the party was formed to teach criminal syndicalism. The statute which made these acts a crime restricted the right of free speech and of assembly theretofore existing. The claim is that the statute, as applied, denied to Miss Whitney the liberty guaranteed by the Fourteenth Amendment.

The felony which the statute created is a crime very unlike the old felony of conspiracy or the old misdemeanor of unlawful assembly. The mere act of assisting in forming a society for teaching syndicalism, of becoming a member of it, or assembling with others for that purpose is given the dynamic quality of crime. There is guilt although the society may not contemplate immediate promulgation of the doctrine. Thus the accused is to be punished, not for attempt, incitement or conspiracy, but for a step in preparation, which, if it threatens the public order at all, does so only remotely. The novelty in the prohibition introduced is that the statute aims, not at the practice of criminal syndicalism, nor even directly at the preaching of it, but at association with those who propose to preach it. . . .

The right of free speech, the right to teach and the right of assembly are, of course, fundamental rights. These may not be denied or abridged. But, although the rights of free speech and assembly are fundamental, they are not in their nature absolute. Their exercise is subject to restriction, if the particular restriction proposed is required in order to protect the state from destruction or from serious injury, political, economic or moral. That the necessity which is essential to a valid restriction does not exist unless speech would produce, or is intended to produce, a clear and imminent danger of some substantive evil which the state constitutionally may seek to prevent has been settled. See Schenck v. United States. It is said to be the function of the Legislature to determine whether at a particular time and under the particular circumstances the formation of, or assembly with, a society organized to advocate criminal syndicalism constitutes a clear and present danger of substantive evil; and that by enacting the law here in question the Legislature of California determined that question in the affirmative. . . .

This court has not yet fixed the standard by which to determine when a danger shall be deemed clear; how remote the danger may be and yet be deemed present; and what degree of evil shall be deemed sufficiently substantial to justify resort to abridgment of free speech and assembly as the means of protection. To reach sound conclusions on these matters, we must bear in mind why a state is, ordinarily, denied the power to prohibit dissemination of social, economic and political doctrine which a vast majority of its citizens believes to be false and fraught with evil consequence. Those who won our independence believed that the final end of the state was to make men free to develop their faculties, and that in its government the deliberative forces should prevail over the arbitrary. They valued liberty both as an end and as a means. They believed liberty to be the secret of happiness and courage to be the secret of liberty. They believed that freedom to think as you will and to speak as you think are means indispensable to the discovery and spread of political truth; that without free speech and assembly discussion would be futile; that with them, discussion affords ordinarily adequate protection against the dissemination of noxious doctrine; that the greatest menace to freedom is an inert people; that public discussion is a political duty; and that this should be a fundamental principle of the American government. They recognized the risks to which all human institutions are subject. But they knew that order cannot be secured merely through fear of punishment for its infraction; that it is hazardous to discourage thought, hope and imagination; that fear breeds repression; that repression breeds hate; that hate menaces stable government; that the path of safety lies in the opportunity to discuss freely supposed grievances and proposed remedies; and that the fitting remedy for evil counsels is good ones. Believing in the power of reason as applied through public discussion, they eschewed silence coerced by law—the argument of force in its worst form. Recognizing the occasional tyrannies of governing majorities, they amended the Constitution so that free speech and assembly should be guaranteed.

Fear of serious injury cannot alone justify suppression of free speech and assembly. Men feared witches and burnt women. It is the function of speech to free men from the bondage of irrational fears. To justify suppression of free speech there must be reasonable ground to fear that serious evil will result if free speech is practiced. There must be reasonable ground to believe that the danger apprehended is imminent. There must be reasonable ground to believe that the evil to be prevented is a serious one. Every denunciation of existing law tends in some measure to increase the probability that there will be violation of it. Condonation of a breach enhances the probability. Expressions of approval add to the probability. Propagation of the criminal state of mind by teaching syndicalism increases it. Advocacy of lawbreaking heightens it still further. But even advocacy of violation, however reprehensible morally, is not a justification for denying free speech where the advocacy falls short of incitement and there is nothing to indicate that the advocacy would be immediately acted on. The wide difference between advocacy and incitement, between preparation and attempt, between assembling and conspiracy, must be borne in mind. In order to support a finding of clear and present danger it must be shown either that immediate serious violence was to be expected or was advocated, or that the past conduct furnished reason to believe that such advocacy was then contemplated. Those who won our independence by revolution were not cowards. They did not fear political change. They did not exalt order at the cost of liberty. To courageous, self reliant men, with confidence in the power of free and fearless reasoning applied through the processes of popular government, no danger flowing from speech can be deemed clear and present, unless the incidence of the evil apprehended is so imminent that it may befall before there is opportunity for full discussion. If there be time to expose through discussion the falsehood and fallacies, to avert the evil by the processes of education, the remedy to be applied is more speech, not enforced silence. Only an emergency can justify repression. Such must be the rule if authority is to be reconciled with freedom. Such, in my opinion, is the command of the Constitution. It is therefore always open to Americans to challenge a law abridging free speech and assembly by showing that there was no emergency justifying it.

Moreover, even imminent danger cannot justify resort to prohibition of these functions essential to effective democracy, unless the evil apprehended is relatively serious. Prohibition of free speech and assembly is a measure so stringent that it would be inappropriate as the means for averting a relatively trivial harm to society. A police measure may be unconstitutional merely because the remedy, although effective as means of protection, is unduly harsh or oppressive. Thus, a state might, in the exercise of its police power, make any trespass upon the land of another a crime, regardless of the results or of the intent or purpose of the trespasser. It might, also, punish an attempt, a conspiracy, or an incitement to commit the trespass. But it is hardly conceivable that this court would hold constitutional a statute which punished as a felony the mere voluntary assembly with a society formed to teach that pedestrians had the moral right to cross uninclosed, unposted, waste lands and to advocate their doing so, even if there was imminent danger that advocacy would lead to a trespass. The fact that speech is likely to result in some violence or in destruction of property is not enough to justify its suppression. There must be the probability of serious injury to the State. Among free men, the deterrents ordinarily to be applied to prevent crime are education and punishment for violations of the law, not abridgment of the rights of free speech and assembly.

Whenever the fundamental rights of free speech and assembly are alleged to have been invaded, it must remain open to a defendant to present the issue whether there actually did exist at the time a clear danger, whether the danger, if any, was imminent, and whether the evil apprehended was one so substantial as to justify the stringent restriction interposed by the Legislature. The legislative declaration, like the fact that the statute was passed and was sustained by the highest court of the State, creates merely a rebuttable presumption that these conditions have been satisfied.

Whether in 1919, when Miss Whitney did the things complained of, there was in California such clear and present danger of serious evil, might have been made the important issue in the case. She might have required that the issue be determined either by the court or the jury. She claimed [in the court] that the statute as applied to her violated the federal Constitution; but she did not claim that it was void because there was no clear and present danger of serious evil, nor did she request that the existence of these conditions of a valid measure thus restricting the rights of free speech and assembly be passed upon by the court of a jury. On the other hand, there was evidence on which the court or jury might have found that such danger existed. I am unable to assent to the suggestion in the opinion of the court that assembling with a political party, formed to advocate the desirability of a proletarian revolution by mass action at some date necessarily far in the future, is not a right within the protection of the Fourteenth Amendment. In the present case, however, there was other testimony which tended to establish the existence of a conspiracy, on the part of members of the [Industrial] Workers of the World, to commit present serious crimes, and likewise to show that such a conspiracy would be furthered by the activity of the society of which Miss Whitney was a member. Under these circumstances the judgment of the State court cannot be disturbed. . . . Because we may not inquire into the errors now alleged I concur in affirming the judgment of the state court.

MR. JUSTICE HOLMES joins in this opinion.

DENNIS V. UNITED STATES
341 U.S. 494 (1951)

"If Government is aware that a group aiming at its overthrow is attempting to indoctrinate its members and to commit them to a course whereby they will strike when the leaders feel the circumstances permit, action by the Government is required."

The Question: Can the Congress pass a law that makes it a federal crime for any person to "advocate the overthrow of the government by force and violence" or to publish or distribute any literature which includes such advocacy?

The Arguments: PRO

The government has a right to protect itself and the American people from those groups or individuals that organize and conspire to overthrow it by force and violence. The Communist party is especially dangerous, because it is allied with the Soviet Union, which came to power through a violent revolution and has exported that ideology to other countries, including the United States. The advocacy of violent revolution is a "clear and present danger" to this country and does not deserve the protection of the First Amendment.

CON

The government has all the means necessary to protect itself from those who actually take concrete steps to use violence to overthrow the government, with a definite and immediate plan to take such action. But the mere advocacy of revolution, through speech or publications, is protected by the First Amendment. Under such a law, the men who advocated a revolution against British rule of the American colonies could have been jailed for their speeches and writings. Punishing those who advocate ideas of any kind would set a dangerous precedent.

BACKGROUND

On June 5, 1950, North Korean soldiers crossed the 38th parallel to invade South Korea. The Cold War suddenly turned hot. American troops joined the United Nations "police action" in Korea and pushed the North Koreans back into their own territory, almost to the Yalu River border with Communist China. General Douglas MacArthur, who commanded the American military forces, promised they would be home for Christmas. But he could not keep that promise, as Chinese "volunteers" poured across the Yalu River and forced MacArthur's troops down the bloody peninsula in disordered retreat.

The rout of American forces in Korea took place as the Supreme Court heard arguments in a case that threatened a retreat from First Amendment values. This case, *Dennis v. United States*, began in July 1948 with the federal indictment of twelve Communist Party leaders for conspiring to "teach and advocate the overthrow and destruction of the government of the United States by force and violence." Eugene Dennis, the party's general secretary, headed the list of defendants, which included most of the party's national committee. They were charged with violating the Alien Registration Act of 1940, better known as the Smith Act after its House sponsor, Howard Smith of Virginia. Congress decided to punish American Communists for backing the Hitler-Stalin pact of 1939, which created the "unholy alliance" of German Nazis and Soviet Communists while France and England fought for their lives against Hitler's forces. The Smith Act made it unlawful to advocate "the propriety of overthrowing or destroying any government in the United States by force and violence." The law also punished those who organized any group that advocated revolution or circulated literature with such advocacy.

The case against Eugene Dennis and his fellow Communists resembled the earlier prosecution of left-wing propagandist Benjamin Gitlow, whose conviction for violating New York's "criminal anarchy" law was based solely on his distribution of literature calling for "proletarian revolution" against the "capitalist state." No evidence connected Gitlow to any concrete plans to instigate an insurrection at any time, but the Supreme Court ruled in 1925 that his "utterances" endangered "the security of the State" and threatened "ultimate revolution." Very few of the "utterances" for which the government prosecuted Eugene Dennis and his comrades came from their mouths or pens; Justice Department lawyers based their case largely on the words of foreign revolutionaries who had never set foot in the United States. The bulk of the government's evidence, in fact, came from the writings of Karl Marx, Vladimir Lenin, and Joseph Stalin, published between 1848 and 1929.

The trial of the American Communists began in March 1949 at the federal courthouse in New York City. Outside the Foley Square judicial fortress, pickets chanted, "Hey judge, we won't budge, until the twelve are free." Inside the courtroom, Judge Harold Medina presided over his first criminal trial; his short temper and obvious sympathy for the prosecution sparked outbursts from defense lawyers and prompted reporters to call the trial "the Battle of Foley Square." Prosecutors asked the jurors, carefully screened by FBI agents for loyalty, to connect the Communist Party leaders with the Soviet government. Given the American party's membership in the Communist International, which was headquartered in Moscow, this proved an easy task.

Prosecutors had a harder time showing that the defendants themselves advocated "force and violence" against the American government. Judge Medina helped out by ruling that, because Lenin and Stalin had advocated "the violent shattering of the capitalist states," circulating their writings showed that American Communists were "basically committed to the overthrow of the Government of the United States" by violent means. But the writings of Lenin and Stalin conflicted with the American party's 1945 constitution, subjecting any member who conspired or acted to overthrow "the institutions of American democracy" to immediate expulsion. Medina allowed Louis Budenz, a former *Daily Worker* editor and now the government's prize witness, to tell jurors that such "Aesopian" language was merely "window dressing asserted for protective purposes" against Smith Act prosecutions. Medina's ruling placed the defendants in a Catch-22 dilemma: their disavowal of revolutionary acts proved their intention to commit them. The judge virtually instructed jurors to disregard the protestations of defense witnesses that the party's constitution meant exactly what it said.

When the Foley Square trial concluded in October 1949, Medina instructed jurors that all they needed to convict the defendants was "language" in Communist literature showing the party's intention to overthrow the government "as speedily as circumstances would permit." They could infer that intention from the words of Marx, Lenin, and Stalin, even though the defendants had denied endorsing their calls for violent revolution. The jurors worked speedily as well; after hearing eight months of testimony, they deliberated just eight hours before returning guilty verdicts against eleven Communist leaders (William Z. Foster, the party's elderly chairman, had his case severed for health reasons). Judge Medina imposed five-year sentences on all but one defendant, who had won the Distinguished Service Cross for heroism in the South Pacific and received a three-year term in reward. For good measure, Medina sentenced five party lawyers to jail terms for contempt of court, getting the last word in his courtroom arguments.

Eugene Dennis and his fellow Communists, now branded as felons by Judge Medina, asked a federal appellate panel to reverse their convictions on First Amendment grounds. Three judges of the Second Circuit Court of Appeals, all elderly Republicans appointed by President Calvin Coolidge, heard the case in June 1950. Even before argument began, Judges Harrie Chase and Thomas Swan made clear their hostility toward the defendants, refusing them permission to travel outside New York to make speeches and raise funds for their appeal. Chase denounced the "shocking" idea of letting the Communists "try their cause in public." Swan commented sourly that he was prepared to "have all the oral argument we can stomach." In a highly unusual move, armed guards were stationed outside the courthouse and inside the courtroom.

With two votes almost certainly against them, lawyers for the Communists—themselves under sentence for contempt—viewed the hearing as a trial run for the Supreme Court. But they hoped for a dissent by Judge Learned Hand, who had ruled in 1917 that governments could only punish direct incitement to criminal acts. Hand had argued with Justice Holmes over this issue in 1919 and lost when Holmes devised the "clear and present danger" test in his *Schenck* opinion. Hand did not agree with Holmes that leaflets against the World War I draft posed much danger to military recruitment, but the prospect of nuclear war in 1950 was a real danger in his mind. Hand expressed his fears in writing for the Second Circuit panel in the *Dennis* case. "We must not close our eyes to our position in the world," he cautioned. Citing the Berlin airlift of 1949, Hand warned that any border flare-up or diplomatic incident might spark warfare. "We do not understand how one could ask for a more probable danger," he concluded.

Still uneasy about the "clear and present danger" test, Hand devised his own First Amendment formula. Judges must ask, he wrote, "whether the gravity of the 'evil,' discounted by its improbability, justifies such invasion of free speech as is necessary to avoid the danger." Like an algebraic equation, the answer in each case depended upon the value assigned to each factor. The danger in *Schenck* was disruption of military recruitment in Philadelphia, while the danger in *Dennis* was violent overthrow of the national government. Totting up his mental calculations, Hand concluded that the "gravity" of revolution far outweighed the "improbability" that American Communists might overthrow the government.

The *Dennis* appeal reached the Supreme Court at a bad time for the defendants. Arguments began on December 4, 1950; that morning's headlines read, "Enemy Is Closing on Pyongyang" and "Scorched Earth Aids Chinese Korean Drive." Against this backdrop of grim news, First

Amendment appeals seemed unlikely to sway justices who read the newspapers. Conceding their clients' sympathy for the Soviet Union, lawyers for the American Communists defended their right to voice their political views. Upholding the Second Circuit decision "would merely be a confession of our unwillingness to take the risk of permitting political dissent to be heard," they wrote. "This is a suppression of the democratic process itself."

Government lawyers replied that Soviet-sponsored "aggression and disruption" around the world created a clear and present danger from domestic Communists. "Recent events in Korea" provided evidence of this danger, as did Communist participation in "such overt activities as sabotage and espionage" carried out "to assist the Soviet Union and its policies." But the government's brief offered no evidence of such acts; requiring proof that Communists were plotting insurrection, its authors stated, "would mean that the First Amendment protects their preparations until they are ready to attempt a seizure of power, or to act as a fifth column in time of crisis."

The oral arguments on both sides offered the justices more rhetoric than reflection. Speaking for the defendants, Abraham Isserman warned that upholding the Smith Act might prompt the government to prosecute "the 500,000 Americans who, according to J. Edgar Hoover, do the bidding of the Communist party." He pointed to Senator Joseph McCarthy, the Red-hunting Wisconsin Republican whose charges that Communists "were shaping the policy of the State Department" sent tremors around the country. "Already men in high places have suffered from McCarthyism," Isserman told the Court. He might have looked at Justice Frankfurter, whose former law clerk, Dean Acheson, was now secretary of state and McCarthy's prime target. Solicitor General Philip Perlman spoke for the government in *Dennis*. "When Justices Holmes and Brandeis talked about 'clear and present danger,'" he said, "they were thinking about isolated agitators, not about these tightly organized, rigidly disciplined people, operating under orders from a foreign country" (Irons, 1999).

MR. CHIEF JUSTICE VINSON announced the judgment of the Court and an opinion in which MR. JUSTICE REED, MR. JUSTICE BURTON, and MR. JUSTICE MINTON join.

Petitioners were indicted in July, 1948, for violation of the conspiracy provisions of the Smith Act, during the period of April, 1945, to July, 1948. The pretrial motion to quash the indictment on the grounds, inter alia, that the statute was unconstitutional was denied, and the case was set for trial on January 17, 1949. A verdict of guilty as to all the petitioners was returned by the jury on October 14, 1949. The Court of Appeals affirmed the convictions. . . .

Sections 2 and 3 of the Smith Act provide as follows:

Sec. 2. (a) It shall be unlawful for any person—

(1) to knowingly or willfully advocate, abet, advise, or teach the duty, necessity, desirability, or propriety of overthrowing or destroying any government in the United States by force or violence, or by the assassination of any officer of any such government;

(2) with intent to cause the overthrow or destruction of any government in the United States, to print, publish, edit, issue, circulate, sell, distribute, or publicly display any written or printed matter advocating, advising, or teaching the duty, ne-

cessity, desirability, or propriety of overthrowing or destroying any government in the United States by force or violence;

(3) to organize or help to organize any society, group, or assembly of persons who teach, advocate, or encourage the overthrow or destruction of any government in the United States by force or violence; or to be or become a member of, or affiliate with, any such society, group, or assembly of persons, knowing the purposes thereof.

Sec. 3. It shall be unlawful for any person to attempt to commit, or to conspire to commit, any of the acts prohibited by the provisions of this title.

The indictment charged the petitioners with willfully and knowingly conspiring (1) to organize as the Communist Party of the United States of America a society, group and assembly of persons who teach and advocate the overthrow and destruction of the Government of the United States by force and violence, and (2) knowingly and willfully to advocate and teach the duty and necessity of overthrowing and destroying the Government of the United States by force and violence. . . .

The obvious purpose of the statute is to protect existing Government, not from change by peaceable, lawful and constitutional means, but from change by violence, revolution and terrorism. That it is within the power of the Congress to protect the Government of the United States from armed rebellion is a proposition which requires little discussion. Whatever theoretical merit there may be to the argument that there is a "right" to rebellion against dictatorial governments is without force where the existing structure of the government provides for peaceful and orderly change. We reject any principle of governmental helplessness in the face of preparation for revolution, which principle, carried to its logical conclusion, must lead to anarchy. No one could conceive that it is not within the power of Congress to prohibit acts intended to overthrow the Government by force and violence. The question with which we are concerned here is not whether Congress has such power, but whether the means which it has employed conflict with the First and Fifth Amendments to the Constitution.

One of the bases for the contention that the means which Congress has employed are invalid takes the form of an attack on the face of the statute on the grounds that by its terms it prohibits academic discussion of the merits of Marxism-Leninism, that it stifles ideas and is contrary to all concepts of a free speech and a free press. . . . The very language of the Smith Act negates the interpretation which petitioners would have us impose on that Act. It is directed at advocacy, not discussion. Thus, the trial judge properly charged the jury that they could not convict if they found that petitioners did "no more than pursue peaceful studies and discussions or teaching and advocacy in the realm of ideas." He further charged that it was not unlawful "to conduct in an American college or university a course explaining the philosophical theories set forth in the books which have been placed in evidence." Such a charge is in strict accord with the statutory language, and illustrates the meaning to be placed on those words. Congress did not intend to eradicate the free discussion of political theories, to destroy the traditional rights of Americans to discuss and evaluate ideas without fear of governmental sanction. Rather Congress was concerned with the very kind of activity in which the evidence showed these petitioners engaged.

But although the statute is not directed at the hypothetical cases which petitioners have conjured, its application in this case has resulted in convictions for the teaching and advocacy of the overthrow of the Government by force and violence, which, even though coupled with the intent to accomplish that overthrow, contains an element of speech. For this reason, we must pay special heed to the demands of the First Amendment marking out the boundaries of speech. . . .

No important case involving free speech was decided by this Court prior to Schenck v. United States. Writing for a unanimous Court, Justice Holmes stated that the "question in every case is whether the words used are used in such circumstances and are of such a nature as to create a clear and present danger that they will bring about the substantive evils that Congress has a right to prevent." . . .

In this case we are squarely presented with the application of the "clear and present danger" test, and must decide what that phrase imports. We first note that many of the cases in which this Court has reversed convictions by use of this or similar tests have been based on the fact that the interest which the State was attempting to protect was itself too insubstantial to warrant restriction of speech. . . . Overthrow of the Government by force and violence is certainly a substantial enough interest for the Government to limit speech. Indeed, this is the ultimate value of any society, for if a society cannot protect its very structure from armed internal attack, it must follow that no subordinate value can be protected. If, then, this interest may be protected, the literal problem which is presented is what has been meant by the use of the phrase "clear and present danger" of the utterances bringing about the evil within the power of Congress to punish.

Obviously, the words cannot mean that before the Government may act, it must wait until the putsch is about to be executed, the plans have been laid and the signal is awaited. If Government is aware that a group aiming at its overthrow is attempting to indoctrinate its members and to commit them to a course whereby they will strike when the leaders feel the circumstances permit, action by the Government is required. The argument that there is no need for Government to concern itself, for Government is strong, it possesses ample powers to put down a rebellion, it may defeat the revolution with ease needs no answer. For that is not the question. Certainly an attempt to overthrow the Government by force, even though doomed from the outset because of inadequate numbers or power of the revolutionists, is a sufficient evil for Congress to prevent. The damage which such attempts create both physically and politically to a nation makes it impossible to measure the validity in terms of the probability of success, or the immediacy of a successful attempt. In the instant case the trial judge charged the jury that they could not convict unless they found that petitioners intended to overthrow the Government "as speedily as circumstances would permit." This does not mean, and could not properly mean, that they would not strike until there was certainty of success. What was meant was that the revolutionists would strike when they thought the time was ripe. We must therefore reject the contention that success or probability of success is the criterion. . . .

Chief Judge Learned Hand, writing for the majority [in the court] below, interpreted the phrase ["clear and present danger"] as follows: "In each case [courts] must ask whether the gravity of the 'evil,' discounted by its improbability, justifies such invasion of free speech as is necessary to avoid the danger." We adopt this statement of the rule. As articulated by Chief Judge Hand, it is as succinct and inclusive as any other we might devise at this time. It takes into consideration those factors which we deem relevant, and relates their significances. More we cannot expect from words.

Likewise, we are in accord with the court below, which affirmed the trial court's finding that the requisite danger existed. The mere fact that from the period 1945 to 1948 petitioners' activities did not result in an attempt to overthrow the Government by force and violence is of course no answer to the fact that there was a group that was ready to make the attempt. The formation by petitioners of such a highly organized conspiracy, with rigidly disciplined members subject to call when the leaders, these petitioners, felt that the time had come for action, coupled with the inflammable nature of world conditions, similar uprisings in other countries, and the touch-and-go nature of our relations with countries with whom petitioners were in the very least ideologically attuned, convince us that their convictions were justified on this score. And this analysis disposes of the contention that a conspiracy to advocate, as distinguished from the advocacy itself, cannot be constitutionally restrained, because it comprises only the preparation. It is the existence of the conspiracy which creates the danger. If the ingredients of the reaction are present, we cannot bind the Government to wait until the catalyst is added. . . .

We hold that [sections] 2 (a) (1), 2 (a) (3) and 3 of the Smith Act do not inherently, or as construed or applied in the instant case, violate the First Amendment and other provisions of the Bill of Rights, or the First and Fifth Amendments because of indefiniteness. Petitioners intended to overthrow the Government of the United States as speedily as the circumstances would permit. Their conspiracy to organize the Communist Party and to teach and advocate the overthrow of the Government of the United States by force and violence created a "clear and present danger" of an attempt to overthrow the Government by force and violence. They were properly and constitutionally convicted for violation of the Smith Act. The judgments of conviction are Affirmed.

Mr. Justice Black, dissenting.

At the outset I want to emphasize what the crime involved in this case is, and what it is not. These petitioners were not charged with an attempt to overthrow the Government. They were not charged with overt acts of any kind designed to overthrow the Government. They were not even charged with saying anything or writing anything designed to overthrow the Government. The charge was that they agreed to assemble and to talk and publish certain ideas at a later date: The indictment is that they conspired to organize the Communist Party and to use speech or newspapers and other publications in the future to teach and advocate the forcible overthrow of the Government. No matter how it is worded, this is a virulent form of prior censorship of speech and press, which I believe the First Amendment forbids. I would hold [section] 3 of the Smith Act authorizing this prior restraint unconstitutional on its face and as applied.

But let us assume, contrary to all constitutional ideas of fair criminal procedure, that petitioners although not indicted for the crime of actual advocacy, may be punished for it. Even on this radical assumption, the other opinions in this case show that the only way to affirm these convictions is to repudiate directly or indirectly the established "clear and present danger" rule. This the Court does in a way which greatly restricts the protections afforded by the First Amendment. The opinions for affirmance indicate that the chief reason for jettisoning the rule is the expressed fear that advocacy of Communist doctrine endangers the safety of the Republic. Undoubtedly, a governmental policy of unfettered communication of ideas does entail dangers. To the Founders of this Nation, however, the benefits derived from free expression were worth the risk. They embodied this philosophy in the First Amendment's command that "Congress shall make no law . . . abridging the freedom of speech, or of the press. . . ." I have always believed that the First Amendment is the keystone of our Government, that the freedoms it guarantees provide the best insurance against destruction of all freedom. At least as to speech in the realm of public matters, I believe that the "clear and present danger" test does not "mark the furthermost constitutional boundaries of protected expression" but does "no more than recognize a minimum compulsion of the Bill of Rights." Bridges v. California.

So long as this Court exercises the power of judicial review of legislation, I cannot agree that the First Amendment permits us to sustain laws suppressing freedom of speech and press on the basis of Congress' or our own notions of mere "reasonableness." Such a doctrine waters down the First Amendment so that it amounts to little more than an admonition to Congress. The Amendment as so construed is not likely to protect any but those "safe" or orthodox views which rarely need its protection. . . . Public opinion being what it now is, few will protest the conviction of these Communist petitioners. There is hope, however, that in calmer times, when present pressures, passions and fears subside, this or some later Court will restore the First Amendment liberties to the high preferred place where they belong in a free society.

MR. JUSTICE DOUGLAS, dissenting.

If this were a case where those who claimed protection under the First Amendment were teaching the techniques of sabotage, the assassination of the President, the filching of documents from public files, the planting of bombs, the art of street warfare, and the like, I would have no doubts. The freedom to speak is not absolute; the teaching of methods of terror and other seditious conduct should be beyond the pale along with obscenity and immorality. This case was argued as if those were the facts. The argument imported much seditious conduct into the record. That is easy and it has popular appeal, for the activities of Communists in plotting and scheming against the free world are common knowledge. But the fact is that no such evidence was introduced at the trial. There is a statute which makes a seditious conspiracy unlawful. Petitioners, however, were not charged with a "conspiracy to overthrow" the Government. They were charged with a conspiracy to form a party and groups and assemblies of people who teach and advocate the overthrow of our Government by force or violence and with a conspiracy to advocate and teach its overthrow by force and violence. It may well be that indoctrination in the techniques of terror to destroy the Government would be indictable under either statute. But the teaching which is condemned here is of a different character.

So far as the present record is concerned, what petitioners did was to organize people to teach and themselves teach the Marxist-Leninist doctrine contained chiefly in four books: Stalin, Foundations of Leninism (1924); Marx and Engels, Manifesto of the Communist Party (1848); Lenin, The State and Revolution (1917); History of the Communist Party of the Soviet Union (B.) (1939).

Those books are to Soviet Communism what Mein Kampf was to Nazism. If they are understood, the ugliness of Communism is revealed, its deceit and cunning are exposed, the nature of its activities becomes apparent, and the chances of its success less likely. That is not, of course, the reason why petitioners chose these books for their classrooms. They are fervent Communists to whom these volumes are gospel. They preached the creed with the hope that some day it would be acted upon.

The opinion of the Court does not outlaw these texts nor condemn them to the fire, as the Communists do literature offensive to their creed. But if the books themselves are not outlawed, if they can lawfully remain on library shelves, by what reasoning does their use in a classroom become a crime? It would not be a crime under the Act to introduce these books to a class, though that would be teaching what the creed of violent overthrow of the Government is. The Act, as construed, requires the element of intent—that those who teach the creed believe in it. The crime then depends not on what is taught but on who the teacher is. That is to make freedom of speech turn not on what is said, but on the intent with which it is said. Once we start down that road we enter territory dangerous to the liberties of every citizen. . . .

Free speech has occupied an exalted position because of the high service it has given our society. Its protection is essential to the very existence of a democracy. The airing of ideas releases pressures which otherwise might become destructive. When ideas compete in the market for acceptance, full and free discussion exposes the false and they gain few adherents. Full and free discussion even of ideas we hate encourages the testing of our own prejudices and preconceptions. Full and free discussion keeps a society from becoming stagnant and unprepared for the stresses and strains that work to tear all civilizations apart.

The nature of Communism as a force on the world scene would, of course, be relevant to the issue of clear and present danger of petitioners' advocacy within the United States. But the primary consideration is the strength and tactical position of petitioners and their converts in this country. On that there is no evidence in the record. If we are to take judicial notice of the threat of Communists within the nation, it should not be difficult to conclude that as a political party they are of little consequence. Communists in this country have never made a respectable or serious showing in any election. I would doubt that there is a village, let alone a city or county or state, which the Communists could carry. Communism in the world scene is no bogeyman; but Communism as a political faction or party in this country plainly is. Communism has been so thoroughly exposed in this country that it has been crippled as a political force. Free speech has destroyed it as an effective political party. It is inconceivable that those who went up and down this country preaching the doctrine of revolution which petitioners espouse would have any success. In days of trouble and confusion, when bread lines were long, when the unemployed walked the streets, when people were starving, the advocates of a short-cut by revolution might have a chance to gain adherents. But today there are no such conditions. The country is not in despair; the people know Soviet Communism; the doctrine of Soviet revolution is exposed in all of its ugliness and the American people want none of it.

How it can be said that there is a clear and present danger that this advocacy will succeed is, therefore, a mystery. Some nations less resilient than the United States, where illiteracy is high and where democratic traditions are only budding, might have to take drastic steps and jail these men for merely speaking their creed. But in America they are miserable merchants of unwanted ideas; their wares remain unsold. The fact that their ideas are abhorrent does not make them powerful.

The political impotence of the Communists in this country does not, of course, dispose of the problem. Their numbers; their positions in industry and government; the extent to which they have in fact infiltrated the police, the armed services, transportation, stevedoring, power plants, munitions works, and other critical places—these facts all bear on the likelihood that their advocacy of the Soviet theory of revolution will endanger the Republic. But the record is silent on these facts. If we are to proceed on the basis of judicial notice, it is impossible for me to say that the Communists in this country are so potent or so strategically deployed that they must be suppressed for their speech. I could not so hold unless I were willing to conclude that the activities in recent years of committees of Congress, of the Attorney General, of labor unions, of state legislatures, and of Loyalty Boards were so futile as to leave the country on the edge of grave peril. To believe that petitioners and their following are placed in such critical positions as to endanger the Nation is to believe the incredible. It is safe to say that the followers of the creed of Soviet Communism are known to the F. B. I.; that in case of war with Russia they will be picked up overnight as were all prospective saboteurs at the commencement of World War II; that the invisible army of petitioners is the best known, the most beset, and the least thriving of any fifth column in history. Only those held by fear and panic could think otherwise.

CHAPLINSKY V. NEW HAMPSHIRE
315 U.S. 568 (1942)

"There are certain well-defined and narrowly limited classes of speech, the prevention and punishment of which has never been thought to raise any Constitutional problem. These include the lewd and obscene, the profane, the libelous, and the insulting or "fighting" words—those which by their very utterance inflict injury or tend to incite an immediate breach of the peace."

The Question: Can a state punish a person for addressing "offensive, derisive, or annoying" words to another person in a public place, if the words used are "insulting" or "fighting" words that might incite an immediate breach of the peace?

The Arguments: PRO

The right of free speech does not protect anyone from leveling such verbal abuse at another person, through words that are meant to insult or provoke them, that a breach of the peace is likely to result from such insulting or "fighting words." Calling a police officer a "damn fascist," as was done in this case, does not further the exchange of ideas; rather, it is likely to provoke a violent response. The category of insulting or "fighting" words is limited to those which have no use in communicating an idea, even a derogatory idea. Such words are the equivalent of a slap in the face or an invitation to fight and serve no useful function in society.

CON

There are some very limited categories of speech that are not protected by the First Amendment, including overt threats to another person. "Shut up, or I'll hit you" is not the same as calling another person an offensive or derogatory name. We have to tolerate some kinds of speech that offend or upset people in order to protect the expression of ideas and feelings. Calling a police officer a "damn fascist" does express an idea and is not the same as a threat to injure him or to pick a fight. In this case, the officer's order to stop speaking about religion in a public place, simply because some listeners object loudly to the message, is not lawful. Thus, a rude or insulting remark in return should not be punished as a criminal offense.

MR. JUSTICE MURPHY delivered the opinion of the Court.

Appellant, a member of the sect known as Jehovah's Witnesses, was convicted in the municipal court of Rochester, New Hampshire, for violation of Chapter 378, Section 2, of the Public Laws of New Hampshire: "No person shall address any offensive, derisive or annoying word to any other person who is lawfully in any street or other public place, nor call him by any offensive or derisive name, nor make any noise or exclamation in his presence and hearing with intent to deride, offend or annoy him, or to prevent him from pursuing his lawful business or occupation."

The complaint charged that appellant "with force and arms, in a certain public place in said city of Rochester, to wit, on the public sidewalk on the easterly side of Wakefield Street, near unto the entrance of the City Hall, did unlawfully repeat, the words following, addressed to the complainant, that is to say, "You are a God damned racketeer" and "a damned Fascist and the whole government of Rochester are Fascists or agents of Fascists' the same being offensive, derisive and annoying words and names."

Upon appeal there was a trial de novo of appellant before a jury in the Superior Court. He was found guilty and the judgment of conviction was affirmed by the Supreme Court of the State.

By motions and exceptions, appellant raised the questions that the statute was invalid under the Fourteenth Amendment of the Constitution of the United States in that it placed an unreasonable restraint on freedom of speech, freedom of the press, and freedom of worship, and because it was vague and indefinite. These contentions were overruled and the case comes here on appeal.

There is no substantial dispute over the facts. Chaplinsky was distributing the literature of his sect on the streets of Rochester on a busy Saturday afternoon. Members of the local citizenry complained to the City Marshal, Bowering, that Chaplinsky was denouncing all religion as a "racket." Bowering told them that Chaplinsky was lawfully engaged, and then warned Chaplinsky that the crowd was getting restless. Some time later a disturbance occurred and the traffic officer on duty at the busy intersection started with Chaplinsky for the police station, but did not inform him that he was under arrest or that he was going to be arrested. On the way they encountered Marshal Bowering who had been advised that a riot was under way and was therefore hurrying to the scene. Bowering repeated his earlier warning to Chaplinsky who then addressed to Bowering the words set forth in the complaint.

Chaplinsky's version of the affair was slightly different. He testified that when he met Bowering, he asked him to arrest the ones responsible for the disturbance. In reply Bowering cursed him and told him to come along. Appellant admitted that he said the words charged in the complaint with the exception of the name of the Deity. . . .

Appellant assails the statute as a violation of all three freedoms, speech, press and worship, but only an attack on the basis of free speech is warranted. The spoken, not the written, word is involved. And we cannot conceive that cursing a public officer is the exercise of religion in any sense of the term. But even if the activities of the appellant which preceded the incident could be viewed as religious in character, and therefore entitled to the protection of the Fourteenth Amendment, they would not cloak him with immunity from the legal consequences for concomitant acts committed in violation of a valid criminal statute. We turn, therefore, to an examination of the statute itself.

Allowing the broadest scope to the language and purpose of the Fourteenth Amendment, it is well understood that the right of free speech is not absolute at all times and under all circumstances. There are certain well-defined and narrowly limited classes of speech, the prevention and punishment of which has never been thought to raise any Constitutional problem. These include the lewd and obscene, the profane, the libelous, and the insulting or "fighting" words—those which by their very utterance inflict injury or tend to incite an immediate breach of the peace. It has been well observed that such utterances are no essential part of any exposition of ideas, and are of such slight social value as a step to truth that any benefit that may be derived from them is clearly outweighed by the social interest in order and morality. "Resort to epithets or personal abuse is not in any proper sense communication of information or opinion safeguarded by the Constitution, and its punishment as a criminal act would raise no question under that instrument." Cantwell v. Connecticut.

The state statute here challenged comes to us authoritatively construed by the highest court of New Hampshire. . . . On the authority of its earlier decisions, the state court declared that the statute's purpose was to preserve the public peace, no words being "forbidden except such as have a direct tendency to cause acts of violence by the person to whom, individually, the remark is addressed." . . . "The statute, as construed, does no more than prohibit the face-to-face words plainly likely to cause a breach of the peace by the addressee, words whose speaking constitute a breach of the peace by the speaker—including 'classical fighting words,' words in current use less 'classical' but equally likely to cause violence, and other disorderly words, including profanity, obscenity and threats."

We are unable to say that the limited scope of the statute as thus construed contravenes the constitutional right of free expression. It is a statute narrowly drawn and limited to define and punish specific conduct lying within the domain of state power, the use in a public place of words likely to cause a breach of the peace. This conclusion necessarily disposes of appellant's contention that the statute is so vague and indefinite as to render a conviction thereunder a violation of due process. A statute punishing verbal acts, carefully drawn so as not unduly to impair liberty of expression, is not too vague for a criminal law.

Nor can we say that the application of the statute to the facts disclosed by the record substantially or unreasonably impinges upon the privilege of free speech. Argument is unnecessary to demonstrate that the appellations "damn racketeer" and "damn Fascist" are epithets likely to provoke the average person to retaliation, and thereby cause a breach of the peace. . . .

Affirmed.

BEAUHARNAIS V. ILLINOIS
343 U.S. 250 (1952)

"If an utterance directed at an individual may be the object of criminal sanctions, we cannot deny to a State power to punish the same utterance directed at a defined group. . . . We would deny experience to say that the . . . legislature was without reason in seeking ways to curb false or malicious defamation of racial and religious groups."

The Question: Can a state punish a person for circulating written material that "portrays depravity, criminality, unchastity, or lack of virtue" of a racial or religious group, in this case a flyer that accused African Americans of committing crimes such as rape, robbery, and drug use?

The Arguments: PRO

The laws of libel and slander—both known as defamation—are designed to punish those persons who falsely accuse another person of criminal or immoral behavior. Attributing the same crimes and immorality to all the members of a racial or ethnic group can be just as harmful as making such accusations against a single individual. The growth and spread of racial and religious hostility and intolerance is a serious problem and needs to be stopped. The concept of "group libel" is a logical extension of libeling a person. Writings that portray an entire racial or religious group as criminal or immoral are directed at every member of those groups. Such "group libel" laws are a reasonable means of dealing with the purveyors of racial and religious intolerance.

CON

There is a real difference between the libel or slander of an individual and "group libel" that is based on race or religion. Defamation laws can be applied only in cases where the charges of criminal or immoral behavior can be shown to be false and thus injure the reputation of the person falsely accused. There is no way to prove the falsity of charges against an entire racial or religious group or to prove that any member of such groups has been injured in his or her reputation. As much as society condemns such intolerance, it is dangerous to First Amendment rights to punish those who circulate intolerant words. Terms such as "lack of virtue" are so vague and undefined that anyone who criticizes a racial or religious group runs the risk of criminal punishment.

MR. JUSTICE FRANKFURTER delivered the opinion of the Court.

The petitioner was convicted upon information in the Municipal Court of Chicago of violating [section] 224a of the Illinois Criminal Code. He was fined $200. The section provides:

> It shall be unlawful for any person, firm or corporation to manufacture, sell, or offer for sale, advertise or publish, present or exhibit in any public place in this state any lithograph, moving picture, play, drama or sketch, which publication or exhibition portrays depravity, criminality, unchastity, or lack of virtue of a class of citizens, of any race, color, creed or religion which said publication or exhibition exposes the citizens of any race, color, creed or religion to contempt, derision, or obloquy or which is productive of breach of the peace or riots. . . .

Beauharnais challenged the statute as violating the liberty of speech and of the press guaranteed as against the States by the Due Process Clause of the Fourteenth Amendment, and as too vague, under the restrictions implicit in the same Clause, to support conviction for crime. The Illinois courts rejected these contentions and sustained defendant's conviction. We granted certiorari in view of the serious questions raised concerning the limitations imposed by the Fourteenth Amendment on the power of a State to punish utterances promoting friction among racial and religious groups.

The information, cast generally in the terms of the statute, charged that Beauharnais "did unlawfully . . . exhibit in public places lithographs, which publications portray depravity, criminality, unchastity or lack of virtue of citizens of Negro race and color and which exposes [sic] citizens of Illinois of the Negro race and color to contempt, derision, or obloquy. . . ." The lithograph complained of was a leaflet setting forth a petition calling on the Mayor and City Council of Chicago "to halt the further encroachment, harassment and invasion of white people, their property, neighborhoods and persons, by the Negro. . . ." Below was a call for "One million self respecting white people in Chicago to unite . . ." with the statement added that "If persuasion and the need to prevent the white race from becoming mongrelized by the negro will not unite us, then the aggressions . . . rapes, robberies, knives, guns and marijuana of the negro, surely will." This, with more language, similar if not so violent, concluded with an attached application for membership in the White Circle League of America, Inc.

The testimony at the trial was substantially undisputed. From it the jury could find that Beauharnais was president of the White Circle League; that, at a meeting on January 6, 1950, he passed out bundles of the lithographs in question, together with other literature, to volunteers for distribution on downtown Chicago street corners the following day; that he carefully organized that distribution, giving detailed instructions for it; and that the leaflets were in fact distributed on January 7 in accordance with his plan and instructions. . . .

The Illinois Supreme Court tells us that 224a "is a form of criminal libel law.". . . Libel of an individual was a common-law crime, and thus criminal in the colonies. Indeed, at common law, truth or good motives was no defense. In the first decades after the adoption of the Constitution, this was changed by judicial decision, statute or constitution in most States, but nowhere was there any suggestion that the crime of libel be abolished. . . . No one will gainsay that it is libelous falsely to charge another with being a rapist, robber, carrier of knives and guns, and user of marijuana. The precise question before us, then, is whether the protection of "liberty" in the Due Process Clause of the Fourteenth Amendment prevents a State from punishing such libels—as criminal libel has been defined, limited and constitutionally recognized time out of mind—directed at designated collectivities and flagrantly disseminated. . . . But if an utterance directed at an individual may be the object of criminal sanctions, we cannot deny to a State power to punish the same utterance directed at a defined group, unless we can say that this is a willful and purposeless restriction unrelated to the peace and well-being of the State.

Illinois did not have to look beyond her own borders or await the tragic experience of the last three decades to conclude that willful purveyors of falsehood concerning racial and religious groups promote strife and tend powerfully to obstruct the manifold adjustments required for free, ordered life in a metropolitan, polyglot community. From the murder of the abolitionist Lovejoy in 1837 to the Cicero riots of 1951, Illinois has been the scene of exacerbated tension between races, often flaring into violence and destruction. . . . In the face of this history and its frequent obligato of extreme racial and religious propaganda, we would deny experience to say that the Illinois legislature was without reason in seeking ways to curb false or malicious defamation of racial and religious groups, made in public places and by means calculated to have a powerful emotional impact on those to whom it was presented. . . .

It may be argued, and weightily, that this legislation will not help matters; that tension and on occasion violence between racial and religious groups must be traced to causes more deeply embedded in our society than the rantings of modern Know-Nothings. Only those lacking responsible humility will have a confident solution for problems as intractable as the frictions attributable to differences of race, color or religion. This being so, it would be out of bounds for the judiciary to deny the legislature a choice of policy, pro-

vided it is not unrelated to the problem and not forbidden by some explicit limitation on the State's power. That the legislative remedy might not in practice mitigate the evil, or might itself raise new problems, would only manifest once more the paradox of reform. It is the price to be paid for the trial-and-error inherent in legislative efforts to deal with obstinate social issues. . . . This being so, we are precluded from saying that speech concededly punishable when immediately directed at individuals cannot be outlawed if directed at groups with whose position and esteem in society the affiliated individual may be inextricably involved. . . .

We find no warrant in the Constitution for denying to Illinois the power to pass the law here under attack. But it bears repeating—although it should not—that our finding that the law is not constitutionally objectionable carries no implication of approval of the wisdom of the legislation or of its efficacy. These questions may raise doubts in our minds as well as in others. It is not for us, however, to make the legislative judgment. We are not at liberty to erect those doubts into fundamental law.

Affirmed.

MR. JUSTICE BLACK, with whom MR. JUSTICE DOUGLAS concurs, dissenting.

This case is here because Illinois inflicted criminal punishment on Beauharnais for causing the distribution of leaflets in the city of Chicago. The conviction rests on the leaflet's contents, not on the time, manner or place of distribution. Beauharnais is head of an organization that opposes amalgamation and favors segregation of white and colored people. After discussion, an assembly of his group decided to petition the mayor and council of Chicago to pass laws for segregation. Volunteer members of the group agreed to stand on street corners, solicit signers to petitions addressed to the city authorities, and distribute leaflets giving information about the group, its beliefs and its plans. In carrying out this program a solicitor handed out a leaflet which was the basis of this prosecution. . . .

That Beauharnais and his group were making a genuine effort to petition their elected representatives is not disputed. Even as far back as 1689, the Bill of Rights exacted of William & Mary said: "It is the Right of the Subjects to petition the King, and all Commitments and Prosecutions for such petitioning are illegal." And 178 years ago the Declaration of Rights of the Continental Congress proclaimed to the monarch of that day that his American subjects had "a right peaceably to assemble, consider of their grievances, and petition the King; and that all prosecutions, prohibitory proclamations, and commitments for the same, are illegal." After independence was won, Americans stated as the first unequivocal command of their Bill of Rights: "Congress shall make no law . . . abridging the freedom of speech, or of the press; or the right of the people peaceably to assemble, and to petition the Government for a redress of grievances." Without distortion, this First Amendment could not possibly be read so as to hold that Congress has power to punish Beauharnais and others for petitioning Congress as they have here sought to petition the Chicago authorities. . . .

The Court's holding here and the constitutional doctrine behind it leave the rights of assembly, petition, speech and press almost completely at the mercy of state legislative, executive, and judicial agencies. I say "almost" because state curtailment of these freedoms may still be invalidated if a majority of this Court conclude that a particular infringement is "without reason," or is "a willful and purposeless restriction unrelated to the peace and well being of the State." But lest this encouragement should give too much hope as to how and when this Court might protect these basic freedoms from state invasion, we are cautioned that state legislatures must be left free to "experiment" and to make "legislative" judgments. We are told that mistakes may be made during the legislative process of curbing public opinion. In such event the Court fortunately does not leave those mistakenly curbed, or any of us for that matter, unadvised. Consolation can be sought and must be found in the philosophical reflection that state legislative error in stifling speech and press "is the price to be paid for the trial-and-error inherent in legislative efforts to deal with obstinate social issues." My own belief is that no legislature is charged with the duty or vested with the power to decide what public issues Americans can discuss. In a free country that is the individual's choice, not the state's. State experimentation in curbing freedom of expression is startling and frightening doctrine in a country dedicated to self-government by its people. I reject the holding that either state or nation can punish people for having their say in matters of public concern. . . .

The Court condones this expansive state censorship by painstakingly analogizing it to the law of criminal libel. As a result of this refined analysis, the Illinois statute emerges labeled a "group libel law." This label may make the Court's holding more palatable for those who sustain it, but the sugar-coating does not make the censorship less deadly. . . . Every expansion of the law of criminal libel so as to punish discussions of matters of public concern means a corresponding invasion of the area dedicated to free expression by the First Amendment. . . .

This Act sets up a system of state censorship which is at war with the kind of free government envisioned by those who forced adoption of our Bill of Rights. The motives behind the state law may have been to do good. But the same can be said about most laws making opinions punishable as crimes. History indicates that urges to do good have led to the burning of books and even to the burning of "witches."

No rationalization on a purely legal level can conceal the fact that state laws like this one present a constant overhanging threat to freedom of speech, press and religion. Today Beauharnais is punished for publicly expressing strong views in favor of segregation. Ironically enough, Beauharnais, convicted of crime in Chicago, would probably be given a hero's reception in many other localities, if not in some parts of Chicago itself. Moreover, the same kind of state law that makes Beauharnais a criminal for advocating segregation in Illinois can be utilized to send people to jail in other states for advocating equality and nonsegregation. What Beauharnais said in his leaflet is mild compared with usual arguments on both sides of racial controversies. . . .

If there be minority groups who hail this holding as their victory, they might consider the possible relevancy of this ancient remark: "Another such victory and I am undone."

BRANDENBURG V. OHIO
395 U.S. 444 (1969)

"The constitutional guarantees of free speech and free press do not permit a State to forbid or proscribe advocacy of the use of force or of law violation except where such advocacy is directed to inciting or producing imminent lawless action and is likely to incite or produce such action."

The Question: Can a state impose criminal penalties on any person who advocates the doctrines of "criminal syndicalism," which is the use of "sabotage, violence, or unlawful methods of terrorism as a means of accomplishing industrial or political reform"?

The Arguments: PRO

Much like the laws designed to punish the advocacy of "sedition" or the overthrow of the government, "criminal syndicalism" laws have the same purpose of protecting society from those who advocate the use of terrorist acts against any person or group. The speech in this case by a Ku Klux Klan leader whose followers carried guns and burned a cross was designed to inflame racial and religious hatred, and could lead to terrorist acts. The Klan and other groups based on doctrines of racial and religious hatred have committed many acts of violence, including the bombing of churches and the murder of African Americans and Jews. Protecting members of these minority groups, and society as a whole, from the possibility of violence that is instigated by incendiary speeches does not violate the First Amendment.

CON

There are ample laws on the books to punish the commission of terrorist acts such as the bombing of the federal building in Oklahoma City by Timothy McVeigh. But it stretches the First Amendment too far when persons are punished, or threatened with prosecution, for expressing hateful ideas about racial and religious minorities. However much we may deplore these ideas and the words that express them, society cannot punish speech that does not lead to "imminent lawless acts," such as speech that directly incites listeners to riot or assault. The speech in this case did not provoke or incite any violent acts, and it was protected by the First Amendment. Protecting the speech that we hate is essential if we are to protect the speech that we support.

PER CURIAM.

The appellant, a leader of a Ku Klux Klan group, was convicted under the Ohio Criminal Syndicalism statute for "advocat[ing] . . . the duty, necessity, or propriety of crime, sabotage, violence, or unlawful methods of terrorism as a means of accomplishing industrial or political reform" and for "voluntarily assembl[ing] with any society, group, or assemblage of persons formed to teach or advocate the doctrines of criminal syndicalism." He was fined $1,000 and sentenced to one to 10 years' imprisonment. The appellant challenged the constitutionality of the criminal syndicalism statute under the First and Fourteenth Amendments to the United States Constitution, but the intermediate appellate court of Ohio affirmed his conviction without opinion. The Supreme Court of Ohio dismissed his appeal, sua sponte, "for the reason that no substantial constitutional question exists herein." It did not file an opinion or explain its conclusions. Appeal was taken to this Court, and we noted probable jurisdiction. We reverse.

The record shows that a man, identified at trial as the appellant, telephoned an announcer-reporter on the staff of a Cincinnati television station and invited him to come to a Ku Klux Klan "rally" to be held at a farm in Hamilton County. With the cooperation of the organizers, the reporter and a cameraman attended the meeting and filmed the events. Portions of the films were later broadcast on the local station and on a national network.

The prosecution's case rested on the films and on testimony identifying the appellant as the person who communicated with the reporter and who spoke at the rally. The State also introduced into evidence several articles appearing in the film, including a pistol, a rifle, a shotgun, ammunition, a Bible, and a red hood worn by the speaker in the films.

One film showed 12 hooded figures, some of whom carried firearms. They were gathered around a large wooden cross, which they burned. No one was present other than the participants and the newsmen who made the film. Most of the words uttered during the scene were incomprehensible when the film was projected, but scattered phrases could be understood that were derogatory of Negroes and, in one instance, of Jews.[1]

Another scene on the same film showed the appellant, in Klan regalia, making a speech. The speech, in full, was as follows:

This is an organizers' meeting. We have had quite a few members here today which are—we have hundreds, hundreds of members throughout the State of Ohio. I can quote from a newspaper clipping from the Columbus, Ohio Dispatch, five weeks ago Sunday morning. The Klan has more members in the State of Ohio than does any other organization. We're not a revengent organization, but if our President, our Congress, our Supreme Court, continues to suppress the white, Caucasian race, it's possible that there might have to be some revengeance taken.

We are marching on Congress July the Fourth, four hundred thousand strong. From there we are dividing into two groups, one group to march on St. Augustine, Florida, the other group to march into Mississippi. Thank you.

The second film showed six hooded figures one of whom, later identified as the appellant, repeated a speech very similar to that recorded on the first film. The reference to the possibility of "revengeance" was omitted, and one sentence was added:

"Personally, I believe the nigger should be returned to Africa, the Jew returned to Israel." Though some of the figures in the films carried weapons, the speaker did not.

The Ohio Criminal Syndicalism Statute was enacted in 1919. From 1917 to 1920, identical or quite similar laws were adopted by 20 States and two territories. In 1927, this Court sustained the constitutionality of California's Criminal Syndicalism Act, the text of which is quite similar to that of the laws of Ohio. Whitney v. California. The Court upheld the statute on the ground that, without more, "advocating" violent means to effect political and economic change involves such danger to the security of the State that the State may outlaw it. But Whitney has been thoroughly discredited by later decisions. See Dennis v. United States. These later decisions have fashioned the principle that the constitutional guarantees of free speech and free press do not permit a State to forbid or proscribe advocacy of the use of force or of law violation except where such advocacy is directed to inciting or producing imminent lawless action and is likely to incite or produce such action. . . . As we said in

---

[1]The significant portions that could be understood were:

"How far is the nigger going to—yeah."
"This is what we are going to do to the niggers."
"A dirty nigger."
"Send the Jews back to Israel."
"Let's give them back to the dark garden."
"Save America."

"Let's go back to constitutional betterment."
"Bury the niggers."
"We intend to do our part."
"Give us our state rights."
"Freedom for the whites."
"Nigger will have to fight for every inch he gets from now on."

Noto v. United States, "the mere abstract teaching . . . of the moral propriety or even moral necessity for a resort to force and violence, is not the same as preparing a group for violent action and steeling it to such action." A statute which fails to draw this distinction impermissibly intrudes upon the freedoms guaranteed by the First and Fourteenth Amendments. It sweeps within its condemnation speech which our Constitution has immunized from governmental control.

Measured by this test, Ohio's Criminal Syndicalism Act cannot be sustained. The Act punishes persons who "advocate or teach the duty, necessity, or propriety" of violence "as a means of accomplishing industrial or political reform"; or who publish or circulate or display any book or paper containing such advocacy; or who "justify" the commission of violent acts "with intent to exemplify, spread or advocate the propriety of the doctrines of criminal syndicalism"; or who "voluntarily assemble" with a group formed "to teach or advocate the doctrines of criminal syndicalism." Neither the indictment nor the trial judge's instructions to the jury in any way refined the statute's bald definition of the crime in terms of mere advocacy not distinguished from incitement to imminent lawless action.

Accordingly, we are here confronted with a statute which, by its own words and as applied, purports to punish mere advocacy and to forbid, on pain of criminal punishment, assembly with others merely to advocate the described type of action. Such a statute falls within the condemnation of the First and Fourteenth Amendments. The contrary teaching of Whitney v. California cannot be supported, and that decision is therefore overruled.

Reversed.

SECTION 2

Symbolic Speech: Draft Cards, Armbands, Crosses, and Flags

United States v. O'Brien
391 U.S. 367 (1968)

"David O'Brien and three companions burned their Selective Service registration certificates on the steps of the South Boston Courthouse. . . . O'Brien . . . argues that . . . his act . . . was protected "symbolic speech" within the First Amendment. . . . When "speech" and "nonspeech" elements are combined in the same course of conduct, a sufficiently important governmental interest in regulating the nonspeech element can justify incidental limitations on First Amendment freedoms."

The Question: Can Congress make it a criminal offense for any person to knowingly destroy or mutilate a Selective Service certificate, better known as a draft card, if the purpose of the law is to punish those who burn their cards as a protest against the Vietnam War?

The Arguments: PRO

The government has a legitimate interest in the physical integrity of the Selective Service certificates that young men who are subject to the military draft are required to carry on their persons. The draft cards are a form of identification, and government officials may have a need to inspect them to carry out the "smooth functioning" of the draft system. Congress also had the authority to add the phrase "knowingly destroys, knowingly mutilates" to the law in order to cope with a rash of draft-card burnings. The fact that the amended law may subject to criminal punishment a form of "symbolic protest" against the war does not override the government's interest in keeping the draft cards intact, and those who protest the war, or the draft system, have many other forms of expression available.

CON

The record of congressional debates when the Selective Service Act was amended to add "knowingly destroys, knowingly mutilates" makes it clear that the amendment's sponsors really wanted to punish the "beatniks" who were burning their draft cards as a protest against the Vietnam War. The Selective Service System does not have a need for draft-age men to carry their cards at all times, and numerous means of locating and identifying draft registrants are available. The symbolic effect of burning a draft card is to make a political statement of opposition to the war and the draft, and to censor this means of expression in the guise of protecting a small piece of cardboard is clearly an effort to punish this dramatic but harmless form of protest.

MR. CHIEF JUSTICE WARREN delivered the opinion of the Court.

On the morning of March 31, 1966, David Paul O'Brien and three companions burned their Selective Service registration certificates on the steps of the South Boston Courthouse. A sizable crowd, including several agents of the Federal Bureau of Investigation, witnessed the event. Immediately after the burning, members of the crowd began attacking O'Brien and his companions. An FBI agent ushered O'Brien to safety inside the courthouse. After he was advised of his right to counsel and to silence, O'Brien stated to FBI agents that he had burned his registration certificate because of his beliefs, knowing that he was violating federal law. He produced the charred remains of the certificate, which, with his consent, were photographed.

For this act, O'Brien was indicted, tried, convicted, and sentenced in the United States District Court for the District of Massachusetts. He did not contest the fact that he had burned the certificate. He stated in argument to the jury that he burned the certificate publicly to influence others to adopt his antiwar beliefs, as he put it, "so that other people would reevaluate their positions with Selective Service, with the armed forces, and reevaluate their place in the culture of today, to hopefully consider my position."

The indictment upon which he was tried charged that he "willfully and knowingly did mutilate, destroy, and change by burning . . . [his] Registration Certificate (Selective Service System Form No. 2); in violation of Title 50, App., United States Code, Section 462 (b)." Section 462 (b) (3) . . . was amended by Congress in 1965, adding the words italicized below, so that at the time O'Brien burned his certificate an offense was committed by any person "who forges, alters, *knowingly destroys, knowingly mutilates,* or in any manner changes any such certificate. . . ."

In the District Court, O'Brien argued that the 1965 Amendment prohibiting the knowing destruction or mutilation of certificates was unconstitutional because it was enacted to abridge free speech, and because it served no legitimate legislative purpose. The District Court rejected these arguments, holding that the statute on its face did not abridge First Amendment rights, that the court was not competent to inquire into the motives of Congress in enacting the 1965 Amendment, and that the Amendment was a reasonable exercise of the power of Congress to raise armies.

On appeal, the Court of Appeals for the First Circuit held the 1965 Amendment unconstitutional as a law abridging freedom of speech. At the time the Amendment was enacted, a regulation of the Selective Service System required registrants to keep their registration certificates in their "personal possession at all times." . . . The Court of Appeals, therefore, was of the opinion that conduct punishable under the 1965 Amendment was already punishable under the nonpossession regulation, and consequently that the Amendment served no valid purpose; further, that in light of the prior reg-

ulation, the Amendment must have been "directed at public as distinguished from private destruction." On this basis, the court concluded that the 1965 Amendment ran afoul of the First Amendment by singling out persons engaged in protests for special treatment. . . . We hold that the 1965 Amendment is constitutional both as enacted and as applied. . . .

When a male reaches the age of 18, he is required by the Universal Military Training and Service Act to register with a local draft board. He is assigned a Selective Service number, and within five days he is issued a registration certificate. . . . [T]he registration . . . certificates are small white cards, approximately 2 by 3 inches. The registration certificate specifies the name of the registrant, the date of registration, and the number and address of the local board with which he is registered. Also inscribed upon it are the date and place of the registrant's birth, his residence at registration, his physical description, his signature, and his Selective Service number. . . .

By the 1965 Amendment, Congress added to 12 (b) (3) of the 1948 Act the provision here at issue, subjecting to criminal liability not only one who "forges, alters, or in any manner changes" but also one who "knowingly destroys, [or] knowingly mutilates" a certificate. We note at the outset that the 1965 Amendment plainly does not abridge free speech on its face, and we do not understand O'Brien to argue otherwise. Amended 12 (b) (3) on its face deals with conduct having no connection with speech. It prohibits the knowing destruction of certificates issued by the Selective Service System, and there is nothing necessarily expressive about such conduct. . . . A law prohibiting destruction of Selective Service certificates no more abridges free speech on its face than a motor vehicle law prohibiting the destruction of drivers' licenses, or a tax law prohibiting the destruction of books and records.

O'Brien nonetheless argues that the 1965 Amendment is unconstitutional in its application to him, and is unconstitutional as enacted because what he calls the "purpose" of Congress was "to suppress freedom of speech." We consider these arguments separately.

O'Brien first argues that the 1965 Amendment is unconstitutional as applied to him because his act of burning his registration certificate was protected "symbolic speech" within the First Amendment. His argument is that the freedom of expression which the First Amendment guarantees includes all modes of "communication of ideas by conduct," and that his conduct is within this definition because he did it in "demonstration against the war and against the draft."

We cannot accept the view that an apparently limitless variety of conduct can be labeled "speech" whenever the person engaging in the conduct intends thereby to express an idea. However, even on the assumption that the alleged communicative element in O'Brien's conduct is sufficient to bring into play the First Amendment, it does not necessarily follow that the destruction of a registration certificate is constitutionally protected activity. This Court has held that when "speech" and "nonspeech" elements are combined in the same course of conduct, a sufficiently important governmental interest in regulating the nonspeech element can justify incidental limitations on First Amendment freedoms.... [W]e think it clear that a government regulation is sufficiently justified if it is within the constitutional power of the Government; if it furthers an important or substantial governmental interest; if the governmental interest is unrelated to the suppression of free expression; and if the incidental restriction on alleged First Amendment freedoms is no greater than is essential to the furtherance of that interest. We find that the 1965 Amendment to 12 (b) (3) of the Universal Military Training and Service Act meets all of these requirements, and consequently that O'Brien can be constitutionally convicted for violating it. . . .

O'Brien's argument to the contrary is necessarily premised upon his unrealistic characterization of Selective Service certificates. He essentially adopts the position that such certificates are so many pieces of paper designed to notify registrants of their registration or classification, to be retained or tossed in the wastebasket according to the convenience or taste of the registrant. Once the registrant has received notification, according to this view, there is no reason for him to retain the certificates. O'Brien notes that most of the information on a registration certificate serves no notification purpose at all; the registrant hardly needs to be told his address and physical characteristics. We agree that the registration certificate contains much information of which the registrant needs no notification. This circumstance, however, does not lead to the conclusion that the certificate serves no purpose, but that, like the classification certificate, it serves purposes in addition to initial notification. Many of these purposes would be defeated by the certificates' destruction or mutilation. . . .

We think it apparent that the continuing availability to each registrant of his Selective Service certificates substantially furthers the smooth and proper functioning of the system that Congress has established to raise armies. We think it also apparent that the Nation has a vital interest in having a system for raising armies that functions with maximum efficiency and is capable of easily and quickly responding to continually changing circumstances. For these reasons, the Government has a substantial interest in assuring the continuing availability of issued Selective Service certificates.

It is equally clear that the 1965 Amendment specifically protects this substantial governmental interest. We perceive no alternative means that would more precisely and narrowly assure the continuing availability of issued Selective Service certificates than a law which prohibits their willful mutilation or destruction. The 1965 Amendment prohibits such conduct and does nothing more. In other words, both the governmental interest and the operation of the 1965 Amendment are limited to the noncommunicative aspect of O'Brien's conduct. The governmental interest and the scope of the 1965 Amendment are limited to preventing harm to the smooth and efficient functioning of the Selective Service System. When O'Brien deliberately rendered unavailable his registration certificate, he willfully frustrated this governmental interest. For this noncommunicative impact of his conduct, and for nothing else, he was convicted. . . .

In conclusion, we find that because of the Government's substantial interest in assuring the continuing availability

of issued Selective Service certificates, because amended 462 (b) is an appropriately narrow means of protecting this interest and condemns only the independent noncommunicative impact of conduct within its reach, and because the noncommunicative impact of O'Brien's act of burning his registration certificate frustrated the Government's interest, a sufficient governmental interest has been shown to justify O'Brien's conviction.

O'Brien finally argues that the 1965 Amendment is unconstitutional as enacted because what he calls the "purpose" of Congress was "to suppress freedom of speech." We reject this argument because under settled principles the purpose of Congress, as O'Brien uses that term, is not a basis for declaring this legislation unconstitutional. It is a familiar principle of constitutional law that this Court will not strike down an otherwise constitutional statute on the basis of an alleged illicit legislative motive.... Inquiries into congressional motives or purposes are a hazardous matter. When the issue is simply the interpretation of legislation, the Court will look to statements by legislators for guidance as to the purpose of the legislature, because the benefit to sound decision-making in this circumstance is thought sufficient to risk the possibility of misreading Congress' purpose. It is entirely a different matter when we are asked to void a statute that is, under well-settled criteria, constitutional on its face, on the basis of what fewer than a handful of Congressmen said about it. What motivates one legislator to make a speech about a statute is not necessarily what motivates scores of others to enact it, and the stakes are sufficiently high for us to eschew guesswork. We decline to void essentially on the ground that it is unwise legislation which Congress had the undoubted power to enact and which could be reenacted in its exact form if the same or another legislator made a "wiser" speech about it. . . .

We think it not amiss, in passing, to comment upon O'Brien's legislative-purpose argument. There was little floor debate on this legislation in either House. Only Senator Thurmond commented on its substantive features in the Senate. . . . In the House debate only two Congressmen addressed themselves to the Amendment—Congressmen Rivers and Bray. The bill was passed after their statements without any further debate by a vote of 393 to 1. It is principally on the basis of the statements by these three Congressmen that O'Brien makes his congressional-"purpose" argument. We note that if we were to examine legislative purpose in the instant case, we would be obliged to consider not only these statements but also the more authoritative reports of the Senate and House Armed Services Committees.... While both reports make clear a concern with the "defiant" destruction of so-called "draft cards" and with "open" encouragement to others to destroy their cards, both reports also indicate that this concern stemmed from an apprehension that unrestrained destruction of cards would disrupt the smooth functioning of the Selective Service System.

Since the 1965 Amendment to 12 (b) (3) of the Universal Military Training and Service Act is constitutional as enacted and as applied, the Court of Appeals should have affirmed the judgment of conviction entered by the District Court. Accordingly, we vacate the judgment of the Court of Appeals, and reinstate the judgment and sentence of the District Court.

TINKER V. SCHOOL DISTRICT OF DES MOINES, IOWA
393 U.S. 503 (1969)

"In our system, . . . schools may not be enclaves of totalitarianism. It can hardly be argued that either students or teachers shed their constitutional rights to freedom of speech or expression at the schoolhouse gate. The prohibition . . . of one particular opinion, . . . without evidence that it is necessary to avoid material and substantial interference with schoolwork or discipline, is not constitutionally permissible."

The Question: Can a local school board pass a regulation that bans the wearing of armbands by students in the public schools, in this case as a form of protest against the Vietnam War, and subject any student who wears an armband to suspension from school?

The Arguments: PRO

Public schools are not appropriate places in which to conduct political demonstrations, even those that employ symbols to express a position. There is a potential for disruption of school activities, in classrooms, cafeterias, hallways, and athletic fields, as well as the possibility of violence if the protest activity arouses strong feelings on both sides of the issue. In this case, the potential for disruption was great because a graduate of a local high school had recently been killed in Vietnam and his friends may have resented those who expressed their opposition to the nation's war effort. School officials have the authority to impose reasonable regulations on student behavior, and those who oppose the war are free to express their views outside the school grounds.

CON

The regulation in this case was adopted solely to prevent a particular view from being expressed by students in the public schools, in a silent and nondisruptive manner. The wearing of a narrow armband, without any words or other symbols attached, could not reasonably be expected to disrupt school activities. School officials cannot act as censors of viewpoints they disagree with, so long as expression of those views is not disruptive. Arguments that community feeling about the war is too "tense" to allow any protest against it is a form of "heckler's veto," which the First Amendment does not allow. And a regulation that singles out armbands but does not prohibit wearing Iron Crosses or other expressive symbols is a form of "viewpoint discrimination" that allows school officials to pick and choose the views they will permit students to express.

BACKGROUND

On the morning of December 16, 1965, Mary Beth Tinker wore a black armband to her eighth-grade classes at Warren Harding Junior High School in Des Moines, Iowa. Her morning classes passed without incident, and she had lunch in the school cafeteria with friends who discussed the armband and topics more typical of conversation among thirteen-year-olds. Mary went from lunch to her algebra class. Before the bell rang, she was summoned to the office of Chester Pratt, the Harding principal. He demanded that Mary remove the armband, and she complied. Pratt did not allow Mary to return to algebra class but suspended her from school and sent her home for violating a school-board edict which banned armbands from all Des Moines schools.

Mary wore her black armband to school in the American heartland as a symbol of mourning for those who were dying 10,000 miles from Des Moines, in Vietnam. The armband also expressed support for a Christmas truce and

cease-fire in Vietnam. Mary's act of symbolic protest put her on the front page of *The Des Moines Register* the next morning. "Wear Black Arm Bands, Two Students Sent Home," the paper reported. Chris Eckhardt, a sophomore at Roosevelt High School, had also been suspended for defying the armband edict. Don Blackman, the Roosevelt vice-principal who suspended Chris, told the *Register* that "no commotion or disturbance" had taken place in the school. The school-board president, Ora Niffenegger, defended the ban on armbands as a "disciplinary measure" against any "disturbing influence" in Des Moines schools. Niffenegger pounded a patriotic drum: "Our country's leaders have decided on a course of action and we should support them." Mary and Chris followed a different drummer and found themselves out of school; they could return when they removed their armbands and rejoined the parade.

That same Thursday night, about twenty-five students and parents met to discuss the armband issue and decide on a response to the suspensions. The meeting was called by Mary's father, Rev. Leonard Tinker, a Methodist minister who worked as peace education director of the American Friends Service Committee regional office in Des Moines. The group issued a statement expressing "deep concern" that students were being "deprived of an important opportunity to participate in this form of expression" about the war. Earlier that day, students had asked the school board for an "emergency meeting" on the ban. Ora Niffenegger refused, saying the issue "wasn't important enough" to warrant review before the next scheduled meeting. Friday morning, three more students were suspended, including Mary's brother John, a tenth-grade student at North High School.

Following the five suspensions, the battle over the armband issue began with moderate words on both sides. Craig Sawyer, a Drake University law professor, spoke for the Iowa Civil Liberties Union in asking the school board to rescind its edict. The Union's statement recognized the need to protect "the educational atmosphere of the school" from disruption, but also recognized "the students' right to freely express themselves" on controversial issues. School superintendent Dwight Davis disavowed any intent to ban the expression of student views on Vietnam: "There should be an opportunity to discuss controversial issues in school," he said. "You have to draw the line somewhere," Davis added. The board drew the line at armbands because they threatened "a disruptive influence at the school." The board's policy had been adopted two days before Mary Tinker was suspended, and the front-page *Register* story about the ban appeared under an editorial cartoon of an American soldier stabbed in the back with a knife that read "Viet Cong Propaganda."

Calls for a truce had no more impact in Des Moines than in Vietnam, although one battle was largely rhetorical and the other was fought with bombs and bullets. Despite the cease-fire campaign, fighting in Vietnam continued as Christmas approached. More than 250 American troops died in combat that week, the war's highest toll yet. One of those casualties was Pvt. James Flagg of Des Moines, a nineteen-year-old black paratrooper and graduate of John Tinker's school, North High. Flagg's picture and the report of his death appeared on the *Register's* front page, next to a story about fighting in the Des Moines schools over the armband issue. Ross Peterson, a Roosevelt High Senior who wore black clothes to school but not an armband, was "slugged in the mouth" at the lunch break on Friday. Bruce Clark, a suspended Roosevelt senior, claimed that football coach Donald Prior called those who wore armbands "Communists" and encouraged students in gym class to shout "Beat the Viet Cong" during jumping-jack exercises. Prior supported the shouters: "They are proving their Americanism. They are on the side of President Johnson."

On December 21, 1965, a State Department spokesman said the United States was considering the Viet Cong's proposal for a Christmas truce. American agreement was announced the next day. The Des Moines school board also met on December 21, but no truce was reached on the armband issue. More than 200 people jammed the meeting room for a two-hour debate. Craig Sawyer, speaking for the Iowa Civil Liberties Union and parents of the five suspended students, asked for their immediate reinstatement and repeal of the armband edict. Board member George Caudill asked Sawyer if he also supported a student's right to wear an armband with a Nazi swastika. "Yes," Sawyer replied, "and the Jewish Star of David and the Cross of the Catholic Church and an armband saying 'Down with the School Board.'"

In the best tradition of American town meetings, the Des Moines school-board debate exposed the roots of the conflict between free expression and public order. One board member, Rev. Robert Keck of St. John's Methodist Church, supported the suspended students. "Controversy is at the heart of education," he said, "and the disturbance of set thinking is the catalyst." Referring to physical attacks on students who wore armbands or black clothing, Rev. Keck said the board had let "the ruffian element dictate educational policy." George Caudill, a pediatric physician, responded that classrooms "should not and cannot be used for demonstrations" on any issue. "Regardless of the type of demonstration," he said, "it will be disruptive to some degree." Speaking from the audience, an elderly citizen asked the board to "maintain law and order in the schools" and recalled his school days: "If we did something wrong, we got the stick" from teachers and parents alike.

Bruce Clark, one of the suspended students, reminded the board that black armbands had been allowed in 1963 to mourn the four black girls killed in a church bombing in Birmingham, Alabama. Lorena Tinker, Mary and John's mother, assured the board that she and her husband had "not encouraged our children to be defiant." Mary and John, and the four other Tinker children, were raised "to be responsible citizens in a democracy," their mother said. "Our children have been raised in a home where we've held certain values. They are, in their way, witnessing to the values we believe in." After one board member moved to postpone any action on the issue, Craig Sawyer burst out, "I am demanding that you decide it. Take a stand! That's what you're here for." The board finally took a stand, voting 4–3 to continue the ban on armbands. Speaking for the Iowa Civil Liberties Union, Sawyer suggested that the board would soon meet Mary Beth Tinker in court.

Following the suspensions in December 1965, the armband issue moved from the classroom to the courtroom. Mary and the other students returned to school after Christmas without their armbands, while the Iowa Civil Liberties Union filed suit in federal court against the Des Moines school board, seeking an injunction against the armband policy. Dan L. Johnston, a twenty-eight-year-old graduate of Drake Law School in Des Moines, represented the students. The board's lawyer was Allan A. Herrick, seventy-year-old partner in one of the city's largest firms, whose practice was centered on defending insurance companies against claimants. The case was assigned to Chief District Judge Roy L. Stephenson, who had been awarded the Bronze and Silver stars during World War II combat duty and who remained in the Iowa National Guard as a Lt. Colonel. An active Republican, Stephenson was named to the federal bench in 1960 by President Eisenhower.

The hearing before Judge Stephenson was brief, and Johnston and Herrick directed their legal arguments solely at the First Amendment and its limits. Mary and John Tinker and Chris Eckhardt each testified, Stephenson wrote in his opinion, "that their purpose in wearing the armbands was to mourn those who had died in the Vietnam war and to support Senator Robert F. Kennedy's proposal that the truce proposed for Christmas Day, 1965, be extended indefinitely." None of the school officials who testified cited any actual disruption of school activities by the armband protest.

Stephenson's opinion, issued on September 1, 1966, made clear his belief that students left their First Amendment rights at the school door. He admitted—citing the Supreme Court's decision in the *Barnette* case of 1943, striking down the school expulsion of Jehovah's Witnesses who refused to join flag-salute ceremonies—that wearing an armband "is a symbolic act and falls within the protection of the first amendment's free speech clause." But he countered that precedent with the Supreme Court's 1951 decision that Communist party leaders presented a "clear and present danger" to American society and that free speech protections "are not absolute."

Judge Stephenson's opinion reached beyond Mary, John, and Chris to put all Vietnam War protesters on trial. He noted that the school-board's armband edict was adopted when "debate over the Vietnam war had become vehement in many localities. A protest march against the war had been recently held in Washington, D.C. A wave of draft card burning incidents protesting the war had swept the country." Stephenson also noted that supporters and opponents of the war "were quite vocal in expressing their views" at the board meeting to debate the armband policy. "It is against this background that the Court must review the reasonableness of the regulation."

Stephenson bowed to the First Amendment in writing that an issue "should never be excluded from the classroom merely because it is controversial." But the board's concern for "the disciplined atmosphere of the classroom" took first prize in this balancing test. Stephenson allowed the "heckler's veto" to prevail over the lack of evidence of any actual classroom disruption. "While the armbands themselves may not be disruptive," he wrote, "the reactions and comments from other students as a result of the armbands would be likely to disturb the disciplined atmosphere required for any classroom." What the judge considered "likely" had not in fact happened, as school officials conceded. But Stephenson considered the armband policy "reasonable" and denied the injunction request (Irons, 1988).

MR. JUSTICE FORTAS delivered the opinion of the Court.

Petitioner John F. Tinker, 15 years old, and petitioner Christopher Eckhardt, 16 years old, attended high schools in Des Moines, Iowa. Petitioner Mary Beth Tinker, John's sister, was a 13-year-old student in junior high school.

In December 1965, a group of adults and students in Des Moines held a meeting at the Eckhardt home. The group determined to publicize their objections to the hostilities in Vietnam and their support for a truce by wearing black armbands during the holiday season and by fasting on December 16 and New Year's Eve. Petitioners and their parents had previously engaged in similar activities, and they decided to participate in the program.

The principals of the Des Moines schools became aware of the plan to wear armbands. On December 14, 1965, they met and adopted a policy that any student wearing an armband to school would be asked to remove it, and if he refused he would be suspended until he returned without the armband. Petitioners were aware of the regulation that the school authorities adopted.

On December 16, Mary Beth and Christopher wore black armbands to their schools. John Tinker wore his armband the next day. They were all sent home and suspended from school until they would come back without their armbands. They did not return to school until after the planned period for wearing armbands had expired—that is, until after New Year's Day.

This complaint was filed in the United States District Court by petitioners, through their fathers, under Section 1983 of Title 42 of the United States Code. It prayed for an injunction restraining the respondent school officials and the respondent members of the board of directors of the school district from disciplining the petitioners, and it sought nominal damages. After an evidentiary hearing the District Court dismissed the complaint. It upheld the constitutionality of the school authorities' action on the ground that it was reasonable in order to prevent disturbance of school discipline. . . . On appeal, the Court of Appeals for the Eighth Circuit considered the case en banc. The court was equally divided, and the District Court's decision was accordingly affirmed, without opinion. . . .

First Amendment rights, applied in light of the special characteristics of the school environment, are available to teachers and students. It can hardly be argued that either students or teachers shed their constitutional rights to freedom of speech or expression at the schoolhouse gate. This has been the unmistakable holding of this Court for almost 50 years. . . . In West Virginia v. Barnette, this Court held that under the First Amendment, the student in public school may not be compelled to salute the flag. . . . On the other hand, the Court has repeatedly emphasized the need for affirming the comprehensive authority of the States and of school officials, consistent with fundamental constitutional safeguards, to prescribe and control conduct in the schools. Our problem lies in the area where students in the exercise of First Amendment rights collide with the rules of the school authorities. . . .

The problem posed by the present case does not relate to regulation of the length of skirts or the type of clothing, to hair style, or deportment. It does not concern aggressive, disruptive action or even group demonstrations. Our problem involves direct, primary First Amendment rights akin to "pure speech." The school officials banned and sought to punish petitioners for a silent, passive expression of opinion, unaccompanied by any disorder or disturbance on the part of petitioners. There is here no evidence whatever of petitioners' interference, actual or nascent, with the schools' work or of collision with the rights of other students to be secure and to be let alone. Accordingly, this case does not concern speech or action that intrudes upon the work of the schools or the rights of other students.

Only a few of the 18,000 students in the school system wore the black armbands. Only five students were suspended for wearing them. There is no indication that the work of the schools or any class was disrupted. Outside the classrooms, a few students made hostile remarks to the children wearing armbands, but there were no threats or acts of violence on school premises.

The District Court concluded that the action of the school authorities was reasonable because it was based upon their fear of a disturbance from the wearing of the armbands. But, in our system, undifferentiated fear or apprehension of disturbance is not enough to overcome the right to freedom of expression. Any departure from absolute regimentation may cause trouble. Any variation from the majority's opinion may inspire fear. Any word spoken, in class, in the lunchroom, or on the campus, that deviates from the views of another person may start an argument or cause a disturbance. But our Constitution says we must take this risk, and our history says that it is this sort of hazardous freedom—this kind of openness—that is the basis of our national strength and of the independence and vigor of Americans who grow up and live in this relatively permissive, often disputatious, society.

In order for the State in the person of school officials to justify prohibition of a particular expression of opinion, it must be able to show that its action was caused by something more than a mere desire to avoid the discomfort and unpleasantness that always accompany an unpopular viewpoint. Certainly where there is no finding and no showing that engaging in the forbidden conduct would "materially and substantially interfere with the requirements of appropriate discipline in the operation of the school," the prohibition cannot be sustained.

In the present case, the District Court made no such finding, and our independent examination of the record fails to yield evidence that the school authorities had reason to anticipate that the wearing of the armbands would substantially interfere with the work of the school or impinge upon the rights of other students. Even an official memorandum prepared after the suspension that listed the reasons for the ban on wearing the armbands made no reference to the anticipation of such disruption. . . .

It is also relevant that the school authorities did not purport to prohibit the wearing of all symbols of political or controversial significance. The record shows that students in some of the schools wore buttons relating to national political campaigns, and some even wore the Iron Cross, traditionally a symbol of Nazism. The order prohibiting the wearing of armbands did not extend to these. Instead, a particular symbol—black armbands worn to exhibit opposition to this Nation's involvement in Vietnam—was singled out for prohibition. Clearly, the prohibition of expression of one particular opinion, at least without evidence that it is necessary to avoid material and substantial interference with schoolwork or discipline, is not constitutionally permissible.

In our system, state-operated schools may not be enclaves of totalitarianism. School officials do not possess absolute authority over their students. Students in school as well as out of school are "persons" under our Constitution. They are possessed of fundamental rights which the State must respect, just as they themselves must respect their obligations to the State. In our system, students may not be regarded as closed-circuit recipients of only that which the State chooses to communicate. They may not be confined to the expression of those sentiments that are officially approved. In the absence of a specific showing of constitutionally valid reasons to regulate their speech, students are entitled to freedom of expression of their views. . . .

The principal use to which the schools are dedicated is to accommodate students during prescribed hours for the purpose of certain types of activities. Among those activities is personal intercommunication among the students. This is not only an inevitable part of the process of attending school; it is also an important part of the educational process. A student's rights, therefore, do not embrace merely the classroom hours. When he is in the cafeteria, or on the playing field, or on the campus during the authorized hours, he may express his opinions, even on controversial subjects like the conflict in Vietnam, if he does so without "materially and substantially interfer[ing] with the requirements of appropriate discipline in the operation of the school" and without colliding with the rights of others. But conduct by the student, in class or out of it, which for any reason—whether it stems from time, place, or type of behavior—materially disrupts classwork or involves substantial disorder or invasion of the rights of others is, of course, not immunized by the constitutional guarantee of freedom of speech.

Under our Constitution, free speech is not a right that is given only to be so circumscribed that it exists in principle but not in fact. Freedom of expression would not truly exist if the right could be exercised only in an area that a benevolent government has provided as a safe haven for crackpots. The Constitution says that Congress (and the States) may not abridge the right to free speech. This provision means what it says. We properly read it to permit reasonable regulation of speech-connected activities in carefully restricted circumstances. But we do not confine the permissible exercise of First Amendment rights to a telephone booth or the four corners of a pamphlet, or to supervised and ordained discussion in a school classroom.

If a regulation were adopted by school officials forbidding discussion of the Vietnam conflict, or the expression by any student of opposition to it anywhere on school property except as part of a prescribed classroom exercise, it would be obvious that the regulation would violate the constitutional rights of students, at least if it could not be justified by a showing that the students' activities would materially and substantially disrupt the work and discipline of the school. In the circumstances of the present case, the prohibition of the silent, passive "witness of the armbands," as one of the children called it, is no less offensive to the Constitution's guarantees.

Reversed and remanded.

Mr. Justice Black, dissenting.

The Court's holding in this case ushers in what I deem to be an entirely new era in which the power to control pupils by the elected "officials of state supported public schools . . ." in the United States is in ultimate effect transferred to the Supreme Court. The Court brought this particular case here on a petition for certiorari urging that the First and Fourteenth Amendments protect the right of school pupils to express their political views all the way "from kindergarten through high school." Here the constitutional right to "political expression" asserted was a right to wear black armbands during school hours and at classes in order to demonstrate to the other students that the petitioners were mourning because of the death of United States soldiers in Vietnam and to protest that war which they were against. Ordered to refrain from wearing the armbands in school by the elected school officials and the teachers vested with state authority to do so, apparently only seven out of the school system's 18,000 pupils deliberately refused to obey the order. One defying pupil was Paul Tinker, 8 years old, who was in the second grade; another, Hope Tinker, was 11 years old and in the fifth grade; a third member of the Tinker family was 13, in the eighth grade; and a fourth member of the same family was John Tinker, 15 years old, an 11th grade high school pupil. Their father, a Methodist minister without a church, is paid a salary by the American Friends Service Committee. Another student who defied the school order and insisted on wearing an armband in school was Christopher Eckhardt, an 11th grade pupil and a petitioner in this case. His mother is an official in the Women's International League for Peace and Freedom.

As I read the Court's opinion it relies upon the following grounds for holding unconstitutional the judgment of the Des Moines school officials and the two courts below. First, the Court concludes that the wearing of armbands is "symbolic speech" which is "akin to 'pure speech'" and therefore protected by the First and Fourteenth Amendments. Secondly, the Court decides that the public schools are an appropriate place to exercise "symbolic speech" as long as normal school functions are not "unreasonably" disrupted. Finally, the Court arrogates to itself, rather than to the State's elected officials charged with running the schools, the decision as to which school disciplinary regulations are "reasonable."

Assuming that the Court is correct in holding that the conduct of wearing armbands for the purpose of conveying political ideas is protected by the First Amendment, the crucial remaining questions are whether students and teachers may use the schools at their whim as a platform for the exercise of free speech—"symbolic" or "pure"—and whether the courts will allocate to themselves the function of deciding how the pupils' school day will be spent. While I have always believed that under the First and Fourteenth Amendments neither the State nor the Federal Government has any authority to regulate or censor the content of speech, I have never believed that any person has a right to give speeches or engage in demonstrations where he pleases and when he pleases. . . .

While the record does not show that any of these armband students shouted, used profane language, or were violent in any manner, detailed testimony by some of them shows their armbands caused comments, warnings by other students, the poking of fun at them, and a warning by an older football player that other, nonprotesting students had better let them alone. There is also evidence that a teacher of mathematics had his lesson period practically "wrecked" chiefly by disputes with Mary Beth Tinker, who wore her armband for her "demonstration." Even a casual reading of the record shows that this armband did divert students' minds from their regular lessons, and that talk, comments, etc., made John Tinker "self-conscious" in attending school with his armband. While the absence of obscene remarks or boisterous and loud disorder perhaps justifies the Court's statement that the few armband students did not actually "disrupt" the classwork, I think the record overwhelmingly shows that the armbands did exactly what the elected school officials and principals foresaw they would, that is, took the students' minds off their classwork and diverted them to thoughts about the highly emotional subject of the Vietnam war. And I repeat that if the time has come when pupils of state-supported schools, kindergartens, grammar schools, or high schools, can defy and flout orders of school officials to keep their minds on their own schoolwork, it is the beginning of a new revolutionary era of permissiveness in this country fostered by the judiciary. The next logical step, it appears to me, would be to hold unconstitutional laws that bar pupils under 21 or 18 from voting, or from being elected members of the boards of education. . . .

I deny . . . that it has been the "unmistakable holding of this Court for almost 50 years" that "students" and "teachers" take with them into the "schoolhouse gate" constitutional rights to "freedom of speech or expression." . . . The truth is that a teacher of kindergarten, grammar school, or high school pupils no more carries into a school with him a complete right to freedom of speech and expression than an anti-Catholic or anti-Semite carries with him a complete freedom of speech and religion into a Catholic church or Jewish synagogue. Nor does a person carry with him into the United States Senate or House, or into the Supreme Court, or any other court, a complete constitutional right to go into those places contrary to their rules and speak his mind on any subject he pleases. It is a myth to say that any person has a constitutional right to say what he pleases, where he pleases, and when he pleases. . . . Nor are public school students sent to the schools at public expense to broadcast political or any other views to educate and inform the public. The original idea of schools, which I do not believe is yet abandoned as worthless or out of date, was that children had not yet reached the point of experience and wisdom which enabled them to teach all of their elders. It may be that the Nation has outworn the old-fashioned slogan that "children are to be seen not heard," but one may, I hope, be permitted to harbor the thought that taxpayers send children to school on the premise that at their age they need to learn, not teach. . . .

Here the Court should accord Iowa educational institutions the same right to determine for themselves to what extent free expression should be allowed in its schools as it accorded Mississippi with reference to freedom of assembly. But even if the record were silent as to protests against the Vietnam war distracting students from their assigned class work, members of this Court, like all other citizens, know, without being told, that the disputes over the wisdom of the Vietnam war have disrupted and divided this country as few other issues ever have. Of course students, like other people, cannot concentrate on lesser issues when black armbands are being ostentatiously displayed in their presence to call attention to the wounded and dead of the war, some of the wounded and the dead being their friends and neighbors. It was, of course, to distract the attention of other students that some students insisted up to the very point of their own suspension from school that they were determined to sit in school with their symbolic armbands.

Change has been said to be truly the law of life but sometimes the old and the tried and true are worth holding. The schools of this Nation have undoubtedly contributed to giving us tranquility and to making us a more law-abiding people. Uncontrolled and uncontrollable liberty is an enemy to domestic peace. We cannot close our eyes to the fact that some of the country's greatest problems are crimes committed by the youth, too many of school age. School discipline, like parental discipline, is an integral and important part of training our children to be good citizens—to be better citizens. Here a very small number of students have crisply and summarily refused to obey a school order designed to give pupils who want to learn the opportunity to do so. One does not need to be a prophet or the son of a prophet to know that after the Court's holding today some students in Iowa schools and indeed in all schools will be ready, able, and willing to defy their teachers on practically all orders. This is the more unfortunate for the schools since groups of students all over the land are already running loose, conducting break-ins, sit-ins, lie-ins, and smash-ins. Many of these student groups, as is all too familiar to all who read the newspapers and watch the television news programs, have already engaged in rioting, property seizures, and destruction. They have picketed schools to force students not to cross their picket lines and have too often violently attacked earnest but frightened students who wanted an education that the pickets did not want them to get. Students engaged in such activities are apparently confident that they know far more about how to operate public school systems than do their parents, teachers, and elected school officials. It is no answer to say that the particular students here have not yet reached such high points in their demands to attend classes in order to exercise their political pressures. Turned loose with lawsuits for damages and injunctions against their teachers as they are here, it is nothing but wishful thinking to imagine that young, immature students will not soon believe it is their right to control the schools rather than the right of the States that collect the taxes to hire the teachers for the benefit of the pupils. This case, therefore, wholly without constitutional reasons in my judgment, subjects all the public schools in the country to the whims and caprices of their loudest-mouthed, but maybe not their brightest, students. I, for one, am not fully persuaded that school pupils are wise enough, even with this Court's expert help from Washington, to run the 23,390 public school systems in our 50 States. I wish, therefore, wholly to disclaim any purpose on my part to hold that the Federal Constitution compels the teachers, parents, and elected school officials to surrender control of the American public school system to public school students.

I dissent.

MEET MARY BETH TINKER

I was born in Burlington, Iowa, in 1952. My father was a Methodist minister at the time I was born. He was raised in Hudson, New York, but he was making the circuit of small Iowa towns as a Methodist minister. We lived in Burlington, and we lived in Atlantic, Iowa, and eventually when I was about five or six we moved to Des Moines, Iowa. My father was assigned to a fairly big church there, Epworth Methodist Church. My mother was pretty much a housewife at that time. There were six kids in the family, three girls and three boys, and I was the fourth. I had an older sister and two older brothers, and a younger sister and brother.

My parents met in seminary school, at Scarritt College, which was in Nashville, Tennessee. My mother was interested in the ministry also, although only my father got ordained as a minister. They both had very strong views about racial equality, and that's what caused most of the problems my family had when I was young. I think going to seminary in Tennessee in the 1940s, when the South was still segregated, had a lot to do with their feelings about the evils of racism.

My mother is very unusual. She's very outspoken and has a lot of courage, and she has kind of paid a price for that, in terms of employment. She was strong, and believed in standing up for what you think is right. My father was much more quiet, strong in a sort of quiet way. He was very religious and taught us this love of life, and a higher meaning in life, and a love of nature.

Their controversial life started in Atlantic, before we moved to Des Moines, when they had some trouble with integrating a swimming pool there. That must have been in the late fifties, and that's when swimming pools were really hot, because you didn't want to get contaminated with black people's skin or germs or whatever. I was five when we moved from Atlantic to Des Moines, and I didn't understand a lot of what was going on when I was so young. But I do remember about the swimming pool, and I certainly couldn't understand why people couldn't all go to the same swimming pool.

After we moved to Des Moines, my mother started getting more involved in civil-rights things and my father did, too. I remember there were a lot of civil-rights demonstrations that we all took part in, my parents and all the kids who could hold picket signs. We would go to the courthouse in Des Moines and picket around housing issues and voting rights. This was around the time when the Southern civil-rights movement was becoming active and the freedom rides were going on. I remember there was a call by the Southern Christian Leadership Conference for ministers in the north to come down to the South to witness what was going on there and help protect the freedom riders, because they'd be under less attack if the news was focusing on these northern ministers coming down. So my parents went to Mississippi for a few weeks.

A very important incident happened when I was about ten. It was in about '62, I guess, when my father was removed from the Methodist church. He was not allowed to preach any more, because they were trying to integrate the Epworth Church where he was the minister. We lived in a racially mixed, kind of working-class neighborhood, where Epworth was, on the east side of town. The board of directors of the church was mad at him and gave him all kinds of hell, so he was basically put out of the Methodist church. They kept him as a Methodist minister, technically, but he didn't have anywhere to preach and he couldn't find another church. That was hard on him, because he really enjoyed preaching.

After that, we looked around at different churches. I remember my parents were shopping for churches, going to different ones, and thinking where would they fit in. About a year later, in about '64, he went to work for the Quakers. They took him on as a peace education coordinator for the American Friends Service Committee, which had a regional office in Des Moines. His job was to do a lot of education around a five-state area in the midwest. He'd stop at places, mostly churches, and talk to them about the Vietnam War, which was his job with the Friends. He'd take all kinds of literature and leaflets and movies, to promote the idea of resolving the Vietnam War and having peace in Vietnam.

After the Vietnam War started to escalate and became controversial, we were going to these various demonstrations and pickets against the war. There was a teen group also that had its own activities. I was kind of a hanger-on because I was a little young. I remember sitting at Bill and Maggie Eckhardt's house one night—their son, Chris, was also involved in our group, along with my older brother, John—and we decided to wear these black armbands to school. I think the idea came nationally from something that Bobby Kennedy started. It was part of a call for a Christmas truce in '65, when there was this tremendous bombing of North Vietnam.

By then the movement against the Vietnam War was beginning to grow. It wasn't nearly what it became later, but there were quite a few people involved nationally. I remember it all being very exciting; everyone was joining together with this great idea, and our meetings had a lot of creativity and enthusiasm. I was a young kid, but I could still be part of it and still be important. It wasn't just for the adults, and the kids were respected: When we had something to say, people would listen.

So then we just planned this little thing of wearing these armbands to school. It was moving forward and we didn't think it was going to be that big of a deal. We had no idea it was going to be such a big thing because we were already doing these other little demonstrations and nothing much came of them. All the kids at this meeting went to different schools. The one I went to was Warren Harding Junior High School; I was in eighth grade.

Kids at my school must have already had some opinion about me, because I remember one boy, when I told him that we were planning to wear armbands, he said, Oh, there you go again! I think I was already speaking out. I remember one incident where I raised something in a history class about the war, and the teacher said, Mary, there's a pep rally this Friday—don't you *ever* think of having fun?

That kind of hurt my feelings, to think I was no fun. I had a big social life and a lot of friends. I ran around and got in trouble and went to the movie shows at night and snuck around with boys, like all the other kids. My best friend's dad owned a tavern; we used to spend all our weekends together and think up little plots and plans and run around like that. I remember another kid in our friendship group whose father owned a fruit stand. One time, I had this little date with this black boy who I'd known since I was a child, and that weekend I went by her father's fruit stand and she said, Oh, you're a nigger lover! I guess there was some fall-out from that.

After we had our meeting at the Eckhardt's and decided to wear the black armbands, we were all going to do it on the same day. I told this kid at school about it, and the day before we were going to wear the armbands it came up somehow in my algebra class. The teacher got really mad and he said, If anybody in this class wears an armband to school they'll get kicked out of my class. I went back and told the group and the next thing we knew, the school board made this policy against wearing armbands. They had a special meeting and decided that any student who wore an armband would be suspended from school.

The next day I went to school and I wore the armband all morning. The kids were kind of talking, but it was all friendly, nothing hostile. Then I got to my algebra class, right after lunch, and sat down. The teacher came in, and everyone was kind of whispering; they didn't know what was going to happen. Then this guy came to the door of the class and he said, Mary Tinker, you're wanted out here in the hall. Then they called me down to the principal's office.

The girls' counselor was there in the office. She was real nice. She said, Mary, you know we're going to have to suspend you from school unless you take off that armband. Oddly enough, I took it off. I took off the armband because I was intimidated. I was in this office with these people, the principal was there, and they were giving me these threats and I didn't know what was going to happen, so I took it off. The principal was pretty hostile. Then they suspended me anyway. That's the ironic thing about it. There was a moment there where I thought, This is the *end* of it.

The principal sent me home and called my parents. I went home, and everyone was getting a little bit hysterical. It was getting to be a big deal. Everyone was sort of milling around the house. My brother John, who was in the eleventh grade at another school, didn't wear an armband until the next day, and he got suspended right after he got to school. The two little kids in the family, Hope and Paul, were in elementary school. Hope was in the fifth grade and Paul was in the second grade. They wore black armbands too, but nothing happened to them. I don't think the schools thought people would support suspending *little* kids for something like that.

We got suspended about a week before the Christmas holiday started. We were out of school that week, and every day there was a lot of activity. We were going to meetings, discussing this, figuring out what was going on. The school board had a meeting after we were suspended that hundreds of people went to, and there was a lot of argument and coverage in the newspapers and television. We all went there, wearing these armbands, and they decided to maintain their policy.

After the Christmas holiday, we went back to school but we didn't wear armbands. What we did was to wear black clothes every day for a long time, I think until school ended for the year. We wore all black because there was nothing they could do about that, but it was still this statement. It was our way of fighting back. By then, I think some of the kids were thinking, That's just the nutty Tinker kids. But they got used to it real quick.

After all the publicity about what we did, we got a lot of repercussions. People threw red paint at our house, and we got lots of calls. We got all kinds of threats to our family, even death threats. They even threatened my little brothers and sisters, which was *really* sick. People called our house on Christmas Eve and said the house would be blown up by morning. There was a radio talk-show host in Des Moines who was a right-wing war hawk, and he would always start in on our family, the Tinker family. My mother used to listen to this all the time. I couldn't stand to listen to it, but she loved to tune in and see what they were saying. One night he said that if anyone wanted to use a shotgun on my father he would pay for the court costs if anything happened.

I was leaving for school one morning, on my way out the door, and the phone rang and I picked it up. This woman said, Is this Mary Tinker? And I said yes. And she said, I'm going to *kill* you! At that time, I started a policy I still have today; it's a habit. When anyone calls, I always find out who it is before I talk to them, because of that happening that one morning. It's made me a lot more hardened in certain ways, when you learn in a personal way what the repercussions are for doing unpopular things.

By the time the Supreme Court decided our case in 1969, we had moved from Des Moines to St. Louis. My father transferred to St. Louis with the AFSC, in the fall of '68. By that time, he was doing a lot of draft counseling. We had just moved to St. Louis. I was a junior in high school by then, sixteen years old. I was new in town, and I didn't know anyone. When you're that age, your friends are so important. I was like a fish out of water; I was kind of scared and shy.

When the Supreme Court decided the case, in our favor, suddenly it was mass hysteria. All these national papers and magazines wrote articles when the case broke. *Time* magazine came and did this whole photo session at the school. They came to my chemistry class; it was really crazy. I was trying to make sense of it all. Where does this all fit in with my personal life? I was trying to make new friends and here I am, this maniac who's all over the news. All the kids were talking about it. I think in a way I just wanted to put it out of my mind. I didn't want to be a big star, because I was a teen-ager. Teen-agers never want to stand out in a crowd. They just want to blend in. It was kind of a rough time when it broke.

Even though I went through a period of being cynical about the armband case, I'm not at all sorry I did it. I'm glad that it all happened. I feel it was a privilege to be part of that whole time period and I'm really proud that we had a part in ending the crazy Vietnam War (Irons, 1988).

R.A.V. v. City of St. Paul, Minnesota
505 U.S. 377 (1992)

"[St. Paul] has proscribed fighting words of whatever manner that communicate messages of racial, gender, or religious intolerance. Selectivity of this sort creates the possibility that the city is seeking to handicap the expression of particular ideas. . . . Burning a cross in someone's front yard is reprehensible. But St. Paul has sufficient means at its disposal to prevent such behavior without adding the First Amendment to the fire."

The Question: Can a city pass a law to punish a person who places on private or public property a "symbol," such as a burning cross or Nazi swastika, if that person knows or should know that the symbol will arouse "anger, alarm or resentment in others on the basis of race, color, creed, religion or gender" in those who observe the symbol?

The Arguments: PRO

The placing of a burning cross on the front lawn of a black family, as in this case, is a form of terrorism and a direct threat to the physical and psychological well-being of that family. The fact that the threat is expressed in a "symbol" instead of menacing words or club brandishing does not change the impact of the symbol and the threat it conveys. The fact that members of racial and religious minorities, and women, are more likely to become targets of such threatening behavior means they are deserving of protection because of their membership in these vulnerable groups. Furthermore, the city does not have to list every possible group that might be the target of "alarming" symbols in order to protect members of those groups listed in the ordinance.

CON

There are ample laws on the books to protect members of minority groups and women—in fact, any member of society—from acts of trespass, vandalism, arson, or overt threats. The persons who placed the burning cross on the black family's lawn in this case could have been prosecuted under more than one of those laws. But they were prosecuted instead for the hateful thought behind their symbolic act, and the First Amendment does not allow punishment for thoughts alone. In addition, singling out certain groups for protection against these acts is a form of "content discrimination" that allows officials to decide which kinds of symbolic expression should be punished and which should be allowed.

BACKGROUND: "THE BURNING CROSS"

The story begins on the evening of June 20, 1990, in a neighborhood on the east side of St. Paul, Minnesota, called Mounds Park. Mounds Park was not one of those old and tired urban neighborhoods with poorly maintained houses crowded together, voicing despair and frustration. It was a nice, working-class neighborhood whose homes were large and well kept and whose lawns were well trimmed, where neighbors knew one another, cared for the appearance of their street, and raised their children in the American way. It was, in short, the kind of neighborhood that one expects to find in the upper Midwest. Mounds Park was also predominantly white, but not exclusively so. Black families lived in nearby apartments and had purchased homes in the neighborhood as well.

East Ivy Avenue is one of the streets running through Mounds Park. On one side of the street was the home in which Arthur M. Miller III lived. Miller was eighteen years old at the time and living with his father. He had a number of young friends in the neighborhood who would often gather at his house. Friendship and good, wholesome fun, however, were not the only things that brought the boys together. The bond that tied them was recreational in a different way as well, for when they gathered on that Wednesday evening in June 1990, marijuana, LSD, and alcohol were also on their minds.

Miller's father wasn't home that evening, so Miller was there alone with his girlfriend. During the course of the evening he and his girlfriend got into an argument and in the midst of the ensuing fight he broke a window in the house. So when five or six of Miller's friends came to the door of the house, Miller was cleaning up the broken glass. The friends came by to sit and talk and bum around, as one does in one's youth on summer evenings; they came also, according to one of them, in the hope that Arthur would have some "weed." The friends drank, used drugs, and apparently just lounged around. As the evening turned to early morning, the need for a new outlet apparently emerged from the increasingly hazy mists beclouding their minds.

"I drank all night. If I was sober I wouldn't even have thought about going along." This is what Miller said in his statement to the police, made some days later, after his arrest. According to Miller, whose objectivity can well be doubted, one of the youths "came up with the idea about a cross-burning. Everybody agreed." He continued, "I heard them talking about one of them getting chased by a bunch of black people by their house because they had a skin head." No longer languid, the group's conversation now became active and focused, and the boys' thoughts, dimmed by the effects of alcohol and drugs, turned to action.

The group proceeded downstairs to Miller's basement. There they searched for material with which to make a cross. They found two wooden dowels that would form the cross, tape to bind the wood pieces together, rags to wrap around the dowels, and paint solvent to soak the rags for the coming conflagration. Then, armed with the cross, they turned their attention to an object for their ill-begotten enterprise. They found it immediately at hand: the home of Russ and Laura Jones, located just across the street.

Russ and Laura Jones had recently moved into the Mounds Hill neighborhood with their children, attracted by the well-kept homes and the prospects of raising a family in a safe and clean and wholesome area with good schools and lots of other children. Being African American, the Joneses no doubt moved to the largely white working-class neighborhood with some apprehension but also with hope and optimism. Since their move they had experienced a few small acts of vandalism, but in a neighborhood with many children playing outside—children to whom property lines were irrelevant and a front-yard fence just another obstacle to be overcome—the source of the vandalism was ambiguous. Russ Jones was inclined to presume the best, not the worst.

There was cause for concern, however, for St. Paul had experienced its share of racial incidents. Indeed, concern about race relations and incidents springing from racial bias had motivated the City Council in 1982 to enact a law entitled "St. Paul Bias-Motivated Crime Ordinance." While other laws already in effect would provide ample grounds for prosecuting cases of vandalism, disturbing the peace, and assault growing out of racial tension, the politics of the late twentieth century required, in St. Paul as elsewhere around the nation, a more explicit and direct legislative response—an opportunity, perhaps, for those in elected political office to claim a hand in arresting racial hatred, or at least an excuse that they had done all that they could do about it. So under the ponderous heading of the ordinance, the City Council enacted the following law:

> Whoever places on public or private property a symbol, object, appellation, characterization, or graffiti, including but not limited to, a burning cross or Nazi Swastika, which one knows or has reasonable grounds to know arouses anger, alarm or resentment in others on the basis of race, color, creed, religion or gender commits disorderly conduct and shall be guilty of a misdemeanor.

In its reference to "a burning cross" the ordinance seems to have exhibited prescience, at least as one now looks upon the events of that June evening in 1990. But of course the St. Paul ordinance was just a law. It could not anticipate what was to happen. Indeed, it could not prevent it. It could only punish the act after the fact.

Sometime after midnight of June 20, 1990, in the wee hours of the morning, Miller and his young friends, most of whom were under eighteen and therefore juveniles in the eyes of the law, turned their attention—and their paint-solvent–soaked, handmade cross—toward the Jones house across the street. Accompanying Miller were five or six others, including Jason Olson, age eighteen, who had come to Miller's house with two of his friends, hoping to get some marijuana, and Robert Viktora, seventeen, who was charged with Miller as a leader in the incident and whose prosecution under the St. Paul ordinance would find its way to the Supreme Court of the United States. Because Viktora was a juvenile, his case, *R.A.V. v. City of St. Paul, Minnesota*, would not bear his name, only his initials.

The youths were in a state of inebriated recklessness; they had now been drinking, smoking marijuana, and using LSD since the previous evening. With inept stealth the motley and disorderly group crossed the street and entered the Jones yard. The house was dark, for the Jones family had gone to bed. As they placed the cross in the front yard, the boys were anything but silent, their ineffectual attempts at whispers piercing the dark night air. No one, of course, admitted placing the cross and setting it afire; as with most such incidents, the act itself simply emerged from thin air as if produced by the force of will alone. But the boys were all in it together, and it really doesn't matter whose hand struck the match, for that hand moved as if directed by the passion of each.

"Everybody went in the yard," Miller would later tell the police. "I don't remember who lit it." But a match was struck and placed on the soaked fabric of the erected cross, and the cross was engulfed in flames, its shape leaping forth from the darkness, the reckless and hungry fire bringing the cross to life. The boys watched the evil symbol emerge from the darkness, transfixed in their drunken excitement, and then fled the scene, returning to the darkness.

Russ and Laura Jones were asleep in their bedroom. Sometime after midnight they were awakened by the sound of voices outside. As they listened, it became apparent that the voices were coming from their yard. They got out of bed and went to the window. There, in horror, they witnessed a black family's worst nightmare: a cross burning in front of their house. Shocked and frightened, for themselves and, especially, for their children, they called 911. Police were quickly dispatched to their home.

Miller and his friends watched the scene from his house. Still high on drugs and alcohol, they felt no remorse or guilt—they couldn't have, or they wouldn't have done what they did next. Their watching was instead accompanied by a frenzied excitement—the kind, perhaps, that accompanies a childhood prank. Only this was no childhood prank, and these were not children. The squad cars were in the street and police officers were examining the scene. Miller and his friends awaited the departure of the police.

"Let's go burn some more and be crazy," one of the boys said as the police departed. And they did.

With their emotions now raised to an even higher fever pitch by a mixture of drugs, alcohol, and adrenaline, Miller and his friends returned to the basement to begin the next stage of their loathsome enterprise. They built two more crosses, this time out of broken-furniture legs. Again they taped the crosses together, wrapped them in cloth, and soaked them in paint solvent. With the police gone and the neighborhood returned to darkness, they left Miller's house and proceeded first to the corner. There they lit a second cross across the street from the Jones house. They then proceeded two blocks up the street to an apartment house where other African-American families lived, where they lit the third cross. Twice more they witnessed their crosses emerge from the night's darkness, engulfed by hungry flames.

Russ Jones was quickly jolted out of his benign complacency by the events of the early morning of June 21, 1990. Whatever the source of the earlier incidents of vandalism, there could be no doubt about the motivation behind the cross-burning in his front yard and the second across the street. A powerful combination of emotions—fear, helplessness, danger, anger, shock, isolation—buffeted Russ and Laura Jones with an intensity that few white Americans could understand. The burning cross was the evil symbol of the Ku Klux Klan. It conveyed a message not of oppression but of stark, unmitigated fear.

Morning finally dawned, following what must have been a sleepless night of fear and apprehension, confusion and despair. One can imagine the Joneses looking out at the spot where the symbol of hatred and anarchy and bigotry had burned, perhaps guarding the truth from their children, who wouldn't understand and shouldn't have to know, finding little solace in the light of day. Their world—their optimism and hope—had been cruelly and crudely wrested from them.

But it turns out that they were not alone, nor were they unwelcome. With the morning came also an outpouring of sympathy and support from their neighbors and from city officials. The police investigation of the three incidents—as well as other incidents that were never linked to Miller and his friends—was swift, and within a few days Miller and his friends were tracked down. Miller and Viktora, alleged to have been the leaders in the incidents, were quickly charged with violating the St. Paul Bias-Motivated Crime Ordinance. It was the first time the ordinance had been used, even though it had been on the books since 1982. Miller was charged as an adult, pleaded guilty, and was sentenced to thirty days in jail. He, at least, admitted his guilt and accepted his punishment.

The same cannot be said of Viktora, who would come to be known in the annals of the law as R. A. V. He did not plead guilty but, instead, challenged the law's constitutionality under the First Amendment's guarantee of free speech. The juvenile court judge who first heard his case agreed with him and dismissed the charges. But the judge's decision was appealed by the City of St. Paul to the Minnesota Supreme Court, where the juvenile court decision was reversed and the case sent back for trial. The trial never took place, however, because Viktora appealed the Minnesota Supreme Court decision to the United States Supreme Court, which agreed to review the case (Bezanson, 1998).

JUSTICE SCALIA delivered the opinion of the Court.

In the predawn hours of June 21, 1990, petitioner and several other teenagers allegedly assembled a crudely made cross by taping together broken chair legs. They then allegedly burned the cross inside the fenced yard of a black family that lived across the street from the house where petitioner was staying. Although this conduct could have been punished under any of a number of laws, one of the two provisions under which respondent city of St. Paul chose to charge petitioner (then a juvenile) was the St. Paul Bias-Motivated Crime Ordinance, which provides:

> Whoever places on public or private property a symbol, object, appellation, characterization or graffiti, including, but not limited to, a burning cross or Nazi swastika, which one knows or has reasonable grounds to know arouses anger, alarm or resentment in others on the basis of race, color, creed, religion or gender commits disorderly conduct and shall be guilty of a misdemeanor.

Petitioner moved to dismiss this count on the ground that the St. Paul ordinance was substantially overbroad and impermissibly content based, and therefore facially invalid under the First Amendment. The trial court granted this motion, but the Minnesota Supreme Court reversed. That court rejected petitioner's overbreadth claim [and] also concluded that the ordinance was not impermissibly content based because, in its view, "the ordinance is a narrowly tailored means toward accomplishing the compelling governmental interest in protecting the community against bias-motivated threats to public safety and order." We granted certiorari.

In construing the St. Paul ordinance . . . we accept the Minnesota Supreme Court's authoritative statement that the ordinance reaches only those expressions that constitute "fighting words" within the meaning of Chaplinsky. Petitioner and his amici urge us to modify the scope of the Chaplinsky formulation, thereby invalidating the ordinance as "substantially overbroad." We find it unnecessary to consider this issue. Assuming, arguendo, that all of the expression reached by the ordinance is proscribable under the "fighting words" doctrine, we nonetheless conclude that the ordinance is facially unconstitutional in that it prohibits otherwise permitted speech solely on the basis of the subjects the speech addresses.

The First Amendment generally prevents government from proscribing speech, see, e.g., Cantwell v. Connecticut, or even expressive conduct, see, e.g., Texas v. Johnson, because of disapproval of the ideas expressed. Content-based regulations are presumptively invalid. From 1791 to the present, however, our society, like other free but civilized societies, has permitted restrictions upon the content of speech in a few limited areas, which are "of such slight social value as a step to truth that any benefit that may be derived from them is clearly outweighed by the social interest in order and morality." Chaplinsky. We have recognized that "the freedom of speech" referred to by the First Amendment does not include a freedom to disregard these traditional limitations. Our decisions since the 1960's have narrowed the scope of the traditional categorical exceptions for defamation, see New York Times Co. v. Sullivan, and for obscenity, see Miller v. California, but a limited categorical approach has remained an important part of our First Amendment jurisprudence.

We have sometimes said that these categories of expression are "not within the area of constitutionally protected speech"; or that the "protection of the First Amendment does not extend" to them. Such statements must be taken in context, however, and are no more literally true than is the occasionally repeated shorthand characterizing obscenity "as not being speech at all." What they mean is that these areas of speech can, consistently with the First Amendment, be regulated because of their constitutionally proscribable content (obscenity, defamation, etc.)—not that they are categories of speech entirely invisible to the Constitution, so that they may be made the vehicles for content discrimination unrelated to their distinctively proscribable content. Thus, the government may proscribe libel; but it may not make the further content discrimination of proscribing only libel critical of the government. . . .

The proposition that a particular instance of speech can be proscribable on the basis of one feature (e.g., obscenity) but not on the basis of another (e.g., opposition to the city government) is commonplace and has found application in many contexts. We have long held, for example, that nonverbal expressive activity can be banned because of the action it entails, but not because of the ideas it expresses—so that

burning a flag in violation of an ordinance against outdoor fires could be punishable, whereas burning a flag in violation of an ordinance against dishonoring the flag is not. See [Texas v.] Johnson. Similarly, we have upheld reasonable "time, place, or manner" restrictions, but only if they are "justified without reference to the content of the regulated speech." And just as the power to proscribe particular speech on the basis of a non-content element (e.g., noise) does not entail the power to proscribe the same speech on the basis of a content element, so also the power to proscribe it on the basis of one content element (e.g., obscenity) does not entail the power to proscribe it on the basis of other content elements.

In other words, the exclusion of "fighting words" from the scope of the First Amendment simply means that, for purposes of that Amendment, the unprotected features of the words are, despite their verbal character, essentially a "nonspeech" element of communication. Fighting words are thus analogous to a noisy sound truck. . . . As with the sound truck, however, so also with fighting words: the government may not regulate use based on hostility—or favoritism—towards the underlying message expressed. . . . Even the prohibition against content discrimination that we assert the First Amendment requires is not absolute. It applies differently in the context of proscribable speech than in the area of fully protected speech. The rationale of the general prohibition, after all, is that content discrimination "raises the specter that the Government may effectively drive certain ideas or viewpoints from the marketplace." But content discrimination among various instances of a class of proscribable speech often does not pose this threat.

When the basis for the content discrimination consists entirely of the very reason the entire class of speech at issue is proscribable, no significant danger of idea or viewpoint discrimination exists. Such a reason, having been adjudged neutral enough to support exclusion of the entire class of speech from First Amendment protection, is also neutral enough to form the basis of distinction within the class. To illustrate: a State might choose to prohibit only that obscenity which is the most patently offensive in its prurience—i.e., that which involves the most lascivious displays of sexual activity. But it may not prohibit, for example, only that obscenity which includes offensive political messages. . . .

Applying these principles to the St. Paul ordinance, we conclude that, even as narrowly construed by the Minnesota Supreme Court, the ordinance is facially unconstitutional. Although the phrase in the ordinance, "arouses anger, alarm or resentment in others," has been limited by the Minnesota Supreme Court's construction to reach only those symbols or displays that amount to "fighting words," the remaining, unmodified terms make clear that the ordinance applies only to "fighting words" that insult, or provoke violence, "on the basis of race, color, creed, religion or gender." Displays containing abusive invective, no matter how vicious or severe, are permissible unless they are addressed to one of the specified disfavored topics. Those who wish to use "fighting words" in connection with other ideas—to express hostility, for example, on the basis of political affiliation, union membership, or homosexuality—are not covered. The First Amendment does not permit St. Paul to impose special prohibitions on those speakers who express views on disfavored subjects.

In its practical operation, moreover, the ordinance goes even beyond mere content discrimination to actual viewpoint discrimination. Displays containing some words—odious racial epithets, for example—would be prohibited to proponents of all views. But "fighting words" that do not themselves invoke race, color, creed, religion, or gender—aspersions upon a person's mother, for example—would seemingly be usable ad libitum in the placards of those arguing in favor of racial, color, etc., tolerance and equality, but could not be used by those speakers' opponents. One could hold up a sign saying, for example, that all "anti-Catholic bigots" are misbegotten; but not that all "papists" are, for that would insult and provoke violence "on the basis of religion." St. Paul has no such authority to license one side of a debate to fight freestyle, while requiring the other to follow Marquis of Queensberry rules. . . .

The content-based discrimination reflected in the St. Paul ordinance comes within neither any of the specific exceptions to the First Amendment prohibition we discussed earlier nor a more general exception for content discrimination that does not threaten censorship of ideas. It assuredly does not fall within the exception for content discrimination based on the very reasons why the particular class of speech at issue (here, fighting words) is proscribable. As explained earlier, the reason why fighting words are categorically excluded from the protection of the First Amendment is not that their content communicates any particular idea, but that their content embodies a particularly intolerable (and socially unnecessary) mode of expressing whatever idea the speaker wishes to convey. St. Paul has not singled out an especially offensive mode of expression—it has not, for example, selected for prohibition only those fighting words that communicate ideas in a threatening (as opposed to a merely obnoxious) manner. Rather, it has proscribed fighting words of whatever manner that communicate messages of racial, gender, or religious intolerance. Selectivity of this sort creates the possibility that the city is seeking to handicap the expression of particular ideas. That possibility would alone be enough to render the ordinance presumptively invalid, but St. Paul's comments and concessions in this case elevate the possibility to a certainty. . . .

Finally, St. Paul and its amici defend the conclusion of the Minnesota Supreme Court that, even if the ordinance regulates expression based on hostility towards its protected ideological content, this discrimination is nonetheless justified because it is narrowly tailored to serve compelling state interests. Specifically, they assert that the ordinance helps to ensure the basic human rights of members of groups that have historically been subjected to discrimination, including the right of such group members to live in peace where they wish. We do not doubt that these interests are compelling, and that the ordinance can be said to promote them. . . . The dispositive question in this case, therefore, is whether content discrimination is reasonably necessary to achieve St. Paul's compelling interests; it plainly is not. An ordinance not limited to the favored topics, for example, would have precisely the same beneficial effect. In fact, the only interest distinctively served by the content limitation is that of displaying the city council's special hostility towards the particular biases thus singled out. That is precisely what the First Amendment forbids. The politicians of St. Paul are entitled to express that hostility—but not through the means of imposing unique limitations upon speakers who (however benightedly) disagree.

Let there be no mistake about our belief that burning a cross in someone's front yard is reprehensible. But St. Paul has sufficient means at its disposal to prevent such behavior without adding the First Amendment to the fire.

The judgment of the Minnesota Supreme Court is reversed, and the case is remanded for proceedings not inconsistent with this opinion.

JUSTICE WHITE, with whom JUSTICE BLACKMUN and JUSTICE O'CONNOR join, and with whom JUSTICE STEVENS joins except as to Part I-A, concurring in the judgment.

I agree with the majority that the judgment of the Minnesota Supreme Court should be reversed. However, our agreement ends there.

This case could easily be decided within the contours of established First Amendment law by holding, as petitioner argues, that the St. Paul ordinance is fatally overbroad because it criminalizes not only unprotected expression but expression protected by the First Amendment. . . . But in the present case, the majority casts aside long-established First Amendment doctrine without the benefit of briefing and adopts an untried theory. This is hardly a judicious way of proceeding, and the Court's reasoning in reaching its result is transparently wrong.

This Court's decisions have plainly stated that expression falling within certain limited categories so lacks the values the First Amendment was designed to protect that the Constitution affords no protection to that expression. Chaplinsky v. New Hampshire, made the point in the clearest possible terms:

> There are certain well-defined and narrowly limited classes of speech, the prevention and punishment of which have never been thought to raise any Constitutional problem. . . . It has been well observed that such utterances are no essential part of any exposition of ideas, and are of such slight social value as a step to truth that any benefit that may be derived from them is clearly outweighed by the social interest in order and morality.

Thus, as the majority concedes, this Court has long held certain discrete categories of expression to be proscribable on the basis of their content. For instance, the Court has held that the individual who falsely shouts "fire" in a crowded theater may not claim the protection of the First Amendment. Schenck v. United States. All of these categories are content-based. But the Court has held that the First Amendment does not apply to them, because their expressive content is worthless or of de minimis value to society. . . . This categorical approach has provided a principled and narrowly focused means for distinguishing between expression that the government may regulate freely and that which it may regulate on the basis of content only upon a showing of compelling need.

Today, however, the Court announces that earlier Courts did not mean their repeated statements that certain categories of expression are "not within the area of constitutionally protected speech." The present Court submits that such clear statements "must be taken in context," and are not "literally true." To the contrary, those statements meant precisely what they said: the categorical approach is a firmly entrenched part of our First Amendment jurisprudence. . . . Nevertheless, the majority holds that the First Amendment protects those narrow categories of expression long held to be undeserving of First Amendment protection—at least to the extent that lawmakers may not regulate some fighting words more strictly than others because of their content. The Court announces that such content-based distinctions violate the First Amendment because "[t]he government may not regulate use based on hostility—or favoritism—towards the underlying message expressed." Should the government want to criminalize certain fighting words, the Court now requires it to criminalize all fighting words.

To borrow a phrase: "Such a simplistic, all-or-nothing-at-all approach to First Amendment protection is at odds with common sense, and with our jurisprudence as well." It is inconsistent to hold that the government may proscribe an entire category of speech because the content of that speech is evil, but that the government may not treat a subset of that category differently without violating the First Amendment; the content of the subset is, by definition, worthless and undeserving of constitutional protection.

The majority's observation that fighting words are "quite expressive indeed," is no answer. Fighting words are not a means of exchanging views, rallying supporters, or registering a protest; they are directed against individuals to provoke violence or to inflict injury. Therefore, a ban on all fighting words or on a subset of the fighting words category would restrict only the social evil of hate speech, without creating the danger of driving viewpoints from the marketplace. Therefore, the Court's insistence on inventing its brand of First Amendment underinclusiveness puzzles me. The overbreadth doctrine has the redeeming virtue of attempting to avoid the chilling of protected expression, but the Court's new "underbreadth" creation serves no desirable function. Instead, it permits, indeed invites, the continuation of expressive conduct that, in this case, is evil and worthless in First Amendment terms, until the city of St. Paul cures the underbreadth by adding to its ordinance a catchall phrase such as "and all other fighting words that may constitutionally be subject to this ordinance."

Any contribution of this holding to First Amendment jurisprudence is surely a negative one, since it necessarily signals that expressions of violence, such as the message of intimidation and racial hatred conveyed by burning a cross on someone's lawn, are of sufficient value to outweigh the social interest in order and morality that has traditionally placed such fighting words outside the First Amendment. Indeed, by characterizing fighting words as a form of "debate," the majority legitimates hate speech as a form of public discussion.

Furthermore, the Court obscures the line between speech that could be regulated freely on the basis of content (i.e., the narrow categories of expression falling outside the First Amendment) and that which could be regulated on the basis of content only upon a showing of a compelling state interest (i.e., all remaining expression). By placing fighting words, which the Court has long held to be valueless, on at least equal constitutional footing with political discourse and other forms of speech that we have deemed to have the greatest social value, the majority devalues the latter category.

In a second break with precedent, the Court refuses to sustain the ordinance even though it would survive under the strict scrutiny applicable to other protected expression. Assuming, arguendo, that the St. Paul ordinance is a content-based regulation of protected expression, it nevertheless would pass First Amendment review under settled law upon a showing that the regulation "is necessary to serve a compelling state interest and is narrowly drawn to achieve that end." St. Paul has urged that its ordinance, in the words of the majority, "helps to ensure the basic human rights of members of groups that have historically been subjected to discrimination. . . ." The Court expressly concedes that this interest is compelling, and is promoted by the ordinance. Nevertheless, the Court treats strict scrutiny analysis as irrelevant to the constitutionality of the legislation. Under the majority's view, a narrowly drawn, content-based ordinance could never pass constitutional muster if the object of that legislation could be accomplished by banning a wider category of speech. This appears to be a general renunciation of strict scrutiny review, a fundamental tool of First Amendment analysis. . . .

As with its rejection of the Court's categorical analysis, the majority offers no reasoned basis for discarding our firmly established strict scrutiny analysis at this time. The majority appears to believe that its doctrinal revisionism is necessary to prevent our elected lawmakers from prohibiting libel against members of one political party, but not another, and from enacting similarly preposterous laws. The majority is misguided. . . .

Turning to the St. Paul ordinance and assuming, arguendo, as the majority does, that the ordinance is not constitutionally overbroad, there is no question that it would pass equal protection review. The ordinance proscribes a subset of "fighting words," those that injure "on the basis of race, color, creed, religion or gender." This selective regulation reflects the city's judgment that harms based on race, color, creed, religion, or gender are more pressing public concerns than the harms caused by other fighting words. In light of our Nation's long and painful experience with discrimination, this determination is plainly reasonable. Indeed, as the majority concedes, the interest is compelling. . . .

Although I disagree with the Court's analysis, I do agree with its conclusion: the St. Paul ordinance is unconstitutional. However, I would decide the case on overbreadth grounds. We have emphasized time and again that overbreadth doctrine is an exception to the established principle that "a person to whom a statute may constitutionally be applied will not be heard to challenge that statute on the ground that it may conceivably be applied unconstitutionally to others, in other situations not before the Court." A defendant being prosecuted for speech or expressive conduct may challenge the law on its face if it reaches protected expression, even when that person's activities are not protected by the First Amendment. This is because "the possible harm to society in permitting some unprotected speech to go unpunished is outweighed by the possibility that protected speech of others may be muted.". . .

I agree with petitioner that the ordinance is invalid on its face. Although the ordinance, as construed, reaches categories of speech that are constitutionally unprotected, it also criminalizes a substantial amount of expression that—however repugnant—is shielded by the First Amendment. . . . In construing the St. Paul ordinance, the Minnesota Supreme Court drew upon the definition of fighting words that appears in Chaplinsky—words "which, by their very utterance, inflict injury or tend to incite an immediate breach of the peace.". . . I therefore understand the court to have ruled that St. Paul may constitutionally prohibit expression that, "by its very utterance," causes "anger, alarm or resentment." Our fighting words cases have made clear, however, that such generalized reactions are not sufficient to strip expression of its constitutional protection. The mere fact that expressive activity causes hurt feelings, offense, or resentment does not render the expression unprotected. In the First Amendment context, criminal statutes must be scrutinized with particular care;

those that make unlawful a su[...] tionally protected conduct ma[...] if they also have legitimate ap[...] ordinance is such a law. Althou[...] duct that is unprotected, it als[...] conduct that causes only hurt fe[...] and is protected by the First A[...] therefore fatally overbroad an[...]

Today, the Court has disre[...] ciples of First Amendment la[...] ent replacement theory. Its de[...] interpretation, driven by the f[...] of judges to tinker with the [...] sion is mischievous at best, [...] lower courts. I join the judgm[...] opinion.

VIRGINIA V. BLACK
___U.S.___(2003)

"Burning a cross in the United States is inextricably intertwined with the history of the K[...] this day, regardless of whether the message is a political one or whether the message is [...] intimidate, the burning of a cross is a "symbol of hate." . . . And when a cross bur[...] to intimidate, few if any messages are more powerful."

The Question: Can a state make it a crime to burn a cross on public or private [...] pose or effect of the cross burning is to "intimidate" any pers[...] sons. Also, can such a law include a presumption that burning[...] of an intent to intimidate others?

The Arguments: PRO

There is no doubt that cross burning is meant to intimidate m[...] groups, especially African Americans. Cross burning is his[...] with the Ku Klux Klan, which has a long record of violen[...] against blacks and other groups such as Jews, Catholics, and u[...] First Amendment does not protect "conduct" like cross burn[...] "symbolic speech" along with the conduct. It seems obvious th[...] itself, is evidence of an intent to intimidate those who witness[...]

CON

Virtually every person considers cross burning to be repug[...] But it clearly is a form of "symbolic speech" that is protected[...] ment. The Supreme Court has ruled that burning the America[...] repugnant to almost everyone, is a protected form of symbol[...] ing an exception to this rule would allow further incursions[...] ment. There are laws that allow states to punish direct acts of i[...] mere act of burning a cross may not be a direct threat to anyo[...]

JUSTICE O'CONNOR announced the judgment of the Court and delivered the opinion of the Court with respect to Parts I, II, and III, and an opinion with respect to Parts IV and V, in which The Chief Justice, JUSTICE STEVENS, and JUSTICE BREYER join.

In this case we consider w[...] Virginia's statute banning c[...] intimidate a person or grou[...] Amendment. Va. Code Ann[...]

that while a State, consistent with the First Amendment, may ban cross burning carried out with the intent to intimidate, the provision in the Virginia statute treating any cross burning as prima facie evidence of intent to intimidate renders the statute unconstitutional in its current form.

I

Respondents Barry Black, Richard Elliott, and Jonathan O'Mara were convicted separately of violating Virginia's cross-burning statute. That statute provides:

> It shall be unlawful for any person or persons, with the intent of intimidating any person or group of persons, to burn, or cause to be burned, a cross on the property of another, a highway or other public place. Any person who shall violate any provision of this section shall be guilty of a Class 6 felony.
>
> Any such burning of a cross shall be prima facie evidence of an intent to intimidate a person or group of persons.

On August 22, 1998, Barry Black led a Ku Klux Klan rally in Carroll County, Virginia. Twenty-five to thirty people attended this gathering, which occurred on private property with the permission of the owner, who was in attendance. The property was located on an open field just off Brushy Fork Road (State Highway 690) in Cana, Virginia.

When the sheriff of Carroll County learned that a Klan rally was occurring in his county, he went to observe it from the side of the road.... Eight to ten houses were located in the vicinity of the rally. Rebecca Sechrist, who was related to the owner of the property where the rally took place, "sat and watched to see wha[t] [was] going on" from the lawn of her in-laws' house.... During the rally, Sechrist heard Klan members speak about "what they were" and "what they believed in." The speakers "talked real bad about the blacks and the Mexicans." One speaker told the assembled gathering that "he would love to take a .30/.30 and just random[ly] shoot the blacks."... Sechrist testified that this language made her "very ... scared." At the conclusion of the rally, the crowd circled around a 25- to 30-foot cross. The cross was between 300 and 350 yards away from the road. According to the sheriff, the cross "then all of a sudden ... went up in a flame."... The sheriff then went down the driveway, entered the rally, and asked "who was responsible for burning the cross." Black responded, "I guess I am because I'm the head of the rally." The sheriff then told Black, "[T]here's a law in the State of Virginia that you cannot burn a cross and I'll have to place you under arrest for this."

Black was charged with burning a cross with the intent of intimidating a person or group of persons, in violation of §18.2—423. At his trial, the jury was instructed that "intent to intimidate means the motivation to intentionally put a person or a group of persons in fear of bodily harm. Such fear must arise from the willful conduct of the accused rather than from some mere temperamental timidity of the victim." The trial court also instructed the jury that "the burning of a cross by itself is sufficient evidence from which you may infer the required intent."... The jury found Black guilty, and fined him $2,500. The Court of Appeals of Virginia affirmed Black's conviction.

On May 2, 1998, respondents Richard Elliott and Jonathan O'Mara, as well as a third individual, attempted to burn a cross on the yard of James Jubilee. Jubilee, an African American, was Elliott's next-door neighbor in Virginia Beach, Virginia.... Before the cross burning, Jubilee spoke to Elliott's mother to inquire about shots being fired from behind the Elliott home. Elliott's mother explained to Jubilee that her son shot firearms as a hobby, and that he used the backyard as a firing range.

On the night of May 2, respondents drove a truck onto Jubilee's property, planted a cross, and set it on fire. Their apparent motive was to "get back" at Jubilee for complaining about the shooting in the backyard. Respondents were not affiliated with the Klan. The next morning, as Jubilee was pulling his car out of the driveway, he noticed the partially burned cross approximately 20 feet from his house. After seeing the cross, Jubilee was "very nervous" because he "didn't know what would be the next phase," and because "a cross burned in your yard ... tells you that it's just the first round."

Elliott and O'Mara were charged with attempted cross burning and conspiracy to commit cross burning. O'Mara pleaded guilty to both counts, reserving the right to challenge the constitutionality of the cross-burning statute. The judge sentenced O'Mara to 90 days in jail and fined him $2,500.... At Elliott's trial ... the court instructed the jury that the Commonwealth must prove that "the defendant intended to commit cross burning" ... and that "the defendant had the intent of intimidating any person or group of persons."... The jury found Elliott guilty of attempted cross burning and acquitted him of conspiracy to commit cross burning. It sentenced Elliott to 90 days in jail and a $2,500 fine. The Court of Appeals of Virginia affirmed the convictions of both Elliott and O'Mara.

Each respondent appealed to the Supreme Court of Virginia, arguing that §18.2—423 is facially unconstitutional. The Supreme Court of Virginia consolidated all three cases, and held that the statute is unconstitutional on its face. It held that the Virginia cross-burning statute "is analytically indistinguishable from the ordinance found unconstitutional in R. A. V. [v. St. Paul (1992)]." The Virginia statute, the court held, discriminates on the basis of content since it "selectively chooses only cross burning because of its distinctive message." The court also held that the prima facie evidence provision renders the statute overbroad because "[t]he enhanced probability of prosecution under the statute chills the expression of protected speech."... We granted certiorari.

II

Cross burning originated in the 14th century as a means for Scottish tribes to signal each other.... Cross burning in this country, however, long ago became unmoored from its Scottish ancestry. Burning a cross in the United States is inextricably intertwined with the history of the Ku Klux Klan.

The first Ku Klux Klan began in Pulaski, Tennessee, in the spring of 1866. Although the Ku Klux Klan started as a social club, it soon changed into something far different. The Klan fought Reconstruction and the corresponding drive to allow freed blacks to participate in the political process. Soon the Klan imposed "a veritable reign of terror" throughout the South. The Klan employed tactics such as whipping, threatening to burn people at the stake, and murder. The Klan's victims included blacks, Southern whites who disagreed with the Klan, and "carpetbagger" northern whites.

The activities of the Ku Klux Klan prompted legislative action at the national level. In 1871, . . . Congress passed what is now known as the Ku Klux Klan Act. President Grant used these new powers to suppress the Klan in South Carolina, the effect of which severely curtailed the Klan in other States as well. By the end of Reconstruction in 1877, the first Klan no longer existed.

The genesis of the second Klan began in 1905, with the publication of Thomas Dixon's The Clansmen: An Historical Romance of the Ku Klux Klan. Dixon's book was a sympathetic portrait of the first Klan, depicting the Klan as a group of heroes "saving" the South from blacks and the "horrors" of Reconstruction. Although the first Klan never actually practiced cross burning, Dixon's book depicted the Klan burning crosses to celebrate the execution of former slaves. Cross burning thereby became associated with the first Ku Klux Klan. When D. W. Griffith turned Dixon's book into the movie The Birth of a Nation in 1915, the association between cross burning and the Klan became indelible. . . .

From the inception of the second Klan, cross burnings have been used to communicate both threats of violence and messages of shared ideology. . . . Often, the Klan used cross burnings as a tool of intimidation and a threat of impending violence. . . . Throughout the history of the Klan, cross burnings have . . . remained potent symbols of shared group identity and ideology. The burning cross became a symbol of the Klan itself and a central feature of Klan gatherings. . . . At Klan gatherings across the country, cross burning became the climax of the rally or the initiation. . . .

To this day, regardless of whether the message is a political one or whether the message is also meant to intimidate, the burning of a cross is a "symbol of hate." And while cross burning sometimes carries no intimidating message, at other times the intimidating message is the *only* message conveyed. . . . Indeed, as the cases of respondents Elliott and O'Mara indicate, individuals without Klan affiliation who wish to threaten or menace another person sometimes use cross burning because of this association between a burning cross and violence.

In sum, while a burning cross does not inevitably convey a message of intimidation, often the cross burner intends that the recipients of the message fear for their lives. And when a cross burning is used to intimidate, few if any messages are more powerful.

III

A

The First Amendment, applicable to the States through the Fourteenth Amendment, provides that "Congress shall make no law . . . abridging the freedom of speech." The hallmark of the protection of free speech is to allow "free trade in ideas"—even ideas that the overwhelming majority of people might find distasteful or discomforting. . . . The First Amendment affords protection to symbolic or expressive conduct as well as to actual speech. The protections afforded by the First Amendment, however, are not absolute, and we have long recognized that the government may regulate certain categories of expression consistent with the Constitution. . . . Thus, for example, a State may punish those words "which by their very utterance inflict injury or tend to incite an immediate breach of the peace." Chaplinsky v. New Hampshire . . . and the First Amendment also permits a State to ban a "true threat." "True threats" encompass those statements where the speaker means to communicate a serious expression of an intent to commit an act of unlawful violence to a particular individual or group of individuals. The speaker need not actually intend to carry out the threat. Rather, a prohibition on true threats "protect[s] individuals from the fear of violence" and "from the disruption that fear engenders," in addition to protecting people "from the possibility that the threatened violence will occur." Intimidation in the constitutionally proscribable sense of the word is a type of true threat, where a speaker directs a threat to a person or group of persons with the intent of placing the victim in fear of bodily harm or death. Respondents do not contest that some cross burnings fit within this meaning of intimidating speech, and rightly so. . . .

B

The Supreme Court of Virginia ruled that in light of R. A. V. v. City of St. Paul, even if it is constitutional to ban cross burning in a content-neutral manner, the Virginia cross-burning statute is unconstitutional because it discriminates on the basis of content and viewpoint. . . . We disagree.

In R. A. V., we held that a local ordinance that banned certain symbolic conduct, including cross burning, when done with the knowledge that such conduct would "arouse anger, alarm or resentment in others on the basis of race, color, creed, religion or gender" was unconstitutional. . . . We held that the ordinance did not pass constitutional muster because it discriminated on the basis of content by targeting only those individuals who "provoke violence" on a basis specified in the law. . . . This content-based discrimination was unconstitutional because it allowed the city "to impose special prohibitions on those speakers who express views on disfavored subjects."

We did not hold in R. A. V. that the First Amendment prohibits *all* forms of content-based discrimination within a proscribable area of speech. . . . Indeed, we noted that it would be constitutional to ban only a particular type of threat: "[T]he Federal Government can criminalize only those threats of violence that are directed against the President . . . since the reasons why threats of violence are outside the First Amendment . . . have special force when applied to the person of the President." . . . Similarly, Virginia's statute does not run afoul of the First Amendment insofar as it bans cross burning with intent to intimidate. Unlike the statute at issue in R. A. V., the Virginia statute does not single out for opprobrium only that speech directed toward "one of the specified disfavored topics." It does not matter whether an individual burns a cross with intent to intimidate because of the victim's race, gender, or religion. . . . The First Amendment permits Virginia to outlaw cross burnings done with the intent to intimidate because burning a cross is a particularly virulent form of intimidation. Instead of prohibiting all intimidating messages, Virginia may choose to regulate this subset of intimidating messages in light of cross burning's long and pernicious history as a signal of impending violence. . . . A ban on cross burning carried out with the intent to intimidate is fully consistent with our holding in R. A. V. and is proscribable under the First Amendment.

IV

The Supreme Court of Virginia ruled in the alternative that Virginia's cross-burning statute was unconstitutionally overbroad due to its provision stating that "[a]ny such burning of a cross shall be prima facie evidence of an intent to intimidate a person or group of persons." . . . The prima facie evidence provision, as interpreted by the jury instruction, renders the statute unconstitutional. . . . As construed by the jury instruction, the prima facie provision strips away the very reason why a State may ban cross burning with the intent to intimidate. The prima facie evidence provision permits a jury to convict in every cross-burning case in which defendants exercise their constitutional right not to put on a defense. And even where a defendant like Black presents a defense, the prima facie evidence provision makes it more likely that the jury will find an intent to intimidate regardless of the particular facts of the case. The provision permits the Commonwealth to arrest, prosecute, and convict a person based solely on the fact of cross burning itself.

It is apparent that the provision as so interpreted "would create an unacceptable risk of the suppression of ideas." The act of burning a cross may mean that a person is engaging in constitutionally proscribable intimidation. But that same act may mean only that the person is engaged in core political speech. The prima facie evidence provision in this statute blurs the line between these two meanings of a burning cross. As interpreted by the jury instruction, the provision chills constitutionally protected political speech because of the possibility that a State will prosecute—and potentially convict—somebody engaging only in lawful political speech at the core of what the First Amendment is designed to protect.

As the history of cross burning indicates, a burning cross is not always intended to intimidate. Rather, sometimes the cross burning is a statement of ideology, a symbol of group solidarity. . . . Indeed, occasionally a person who burns a cross does not intend to express either a statement of ideology or intimidation. Cross burnings have appeared in movies such as Mississippi Burning, and in plays such as the stage adaptation of Sir Walter Scott's The Lady of the Lake. The prima facie provision makes no effort to distinguish among these different types of cross burnings. . . . It does not distinguish between a cross burning at a public rally or a cross burning on a neighbor's lawn. It does not treat the cross burning directed at an individual differently from the cross burning directed at a group of like-minded believers. It allows a jury to treat a cross burning on the property of another with the owner's acquiescence in the same manner as a cross burning on the property of another without the owner's permission. . . .

For these reasons, the prima facie evidence provision, as interpreted through the jury instruction and as applied in Barry Black's case, is unconstitutional on its face. . . . With respect to Barry Black, we agree with the Supreme Court of Virginia that his conviction cannot stand, and we affirm the judgment of the Supreme Court of Virginia. With respect to Elliott and O'Mara, we vacate the judgment of the Supreme Court of Virginia, and remand the case for further proceedings. It is so ordered.

JUSTICE SOUTER, with whom JUSTICE KENNEDY and JUSTICE GINSBURG join, concurring in the judgment in part and dissenting in part.

I agree with the majority that the Virginia statute makes a content-based distinction within the category of punishable intimidating or threatening expression, the very type of distinction we considered in R. A. V. v. St. Paul. I disagree that any exception should save Virginia's law from unconstitutionality under the holding in R. A. V. or any acceptable variation of it. . . .

The issue is whether the statutory prohibition restricted to this symbol falls within one of the exceptions to R. A. V.'s general condemnation of limited content-based proscription within a broader category of expression proscribable generally. Because of the burning cross's extraordinary force as a method of intimidation, the R. A. V. exception most likely to cover the statute is the . . . exception for content discrimination on a basis that "consists entirely of the very reason the entire class of speech at issue is proscribable." This is the exception the majority speaks of here as covering statutes prohibiting "particularly virulent" proscribable expression.

I do not think that the Virginia statute qualifies for this virulence exception as R. A. V. explained it. The statute fits poorly with the illustrative examples given in R. A. V., none of which involves communication generally associated with a particular message, and in fact, the majority's discussion of a special virulence exception here moves that exception toward a more flexible conception than the version in R. A. V. I will reserve judgment on that doctrinal development, for even on a pragmatic conception of R. A. V. and its exceptions the Virginia statute could not pass muster, the most obvious hurdle being the statute's prima facie evidence provision. That provision is essential to understanding why the statute's tendency to suppress a message disqualifies it from any rescue by exception from R. A. V.'s general rule. . . .

My concern here, in any event, is not with the merit of a pragmatic doctrinal move. For whether or not the Court should conceive of exceptions to R.A.V.'s general rule in a more practical way, no content-based statute should survive even under a pragmatic recasting of R.A.V. without a high probability that no "official suppression of ideas is afoot." I believe the prima facie evidence provision stands in the way of any finding of such a high probability here. . . .

As I see the likely significance of the evidence provision, its primary effect is to skew jury deliberations toward conviction in cases where the evidence of intent to intimidate is relatively weak and arguably consistent with a solely ideological reason for burning. To understand how the provision may work, recall that the symbolic act of burning a cross, without more, is consistent with both intent to intimidate and intent to make an ideological statement free of any aim to threaten. One can tell the intimidating instance from the wholly ideological one only by reference to some further circumstance. In the real world, of course, and in real-world prosecutions, there will always be further circumstances, and the factfinder will always learn something more than the isolated fact of cross burning. Sometimes those circumstances will show an intent to intimidate, but sometimes they will be at least equivocal, as in cases where a white supremacist group burns a cross at an initiation ceremony or political rally visible to the public. In such a case, if the factfinder is aware of the prima facie evidence provision, as the jury was in respondent Black's case, the provision will have the practical effect of tilting the jury's thinking in favor of the prosecution.... To the extent the prima facie evidence provision skews prosecutions, then, it skews the statute toward suppressing ideas. Thus, the appropriate way to consider the statute's prima facie evidence term, in my view, is not as if it were an overbroad statutory definition amenable to severance or a narrowing construction. The question here is not the permissible scope of an arguably overbroad statute, but the claim of a clearly content-based statute to an exception from the general prohibition of content-based proscriptions, an exception that is not warranted if the statute's terms show that suppression of ideas may be afoot....

I conclude that the statute under which all three of the respondents were prosecuted violates the First Amendment, since the statute's content-based distinction was invalid at the time of the charged activities, regardless of whether the prima facie evidence provision was given any effect in any respondent's individual case. In my view, severance of the prima facie evidence provision now could not eliminate the unconstitutionality of the whole statute at the time of the respondents' conduct. I would therefore affirm the judgment of the Supreme Court of Virginia vacating the respondents' convictions and dismissing the indictments. Accordingly, I concur in the Court's judgment as to respondent Black and dissent as to respondents Elliott and O'Mara.

JUSTICE THOMAS, dissenting.

Although I agree with the majority's conclusion that it is constitutionally permissible to "ban ... cross burning carried out with intent to intimidate," I believe that the majority errs in imputing an expressive component to the activity in question.... In my view, whatever expressive value cross burning has, the legislature simply wrote it out by banning only intimidating conduct undertaken by a particular means. A conclusion that the statute prohibiting cross burning with intent to intimidate sweeps beyond a prohibition on certain conduct into the zone of expression overlooks not only the words of the statute but also reality....

To me, the majority's brief history of the Ku Klux Klan only reinforces this common understanding of the Klan as a terrorist organization, which, in its endeavor to intimidate, or even eliminate those it dislikes, uses the most brutal of methods.... For those not easily frightened, cross burning has been followed by more extreme measures, such as beatings and murder.... In our culture, cross burning has almost invariably meant lawlessness and understandably instills in its victims well-grounded fear of physical violence.... It is simply beyond belief that, in passing the statute now under review, the Virginia legislature was concerned with anything but penalizing conduct it must have viewed as particularly vicious.

Accordingly, this statute prohibits only conduct, not expression. And, just as one cannot burn down someone's house to make a political point and then seek refuge in the First Amendment, those who hate cannot terrorize and intimidate to make their point. In light of my conclusion that the statute here addresses only conduct, there is no need to analyze it under any of our First Amendment tests. Even assuming that the statute implicates the First Amendment, in my view, the fact that the statute permits a jury to draw an inference of intent to intimidate from the cross burning itself presents no constitutional problems. Therein lies my primary disagreement with the plurality.... Considering the horrific effect cross burning has on its victims, it is also reasonable to presume intent to intimidate from the act itself....

The plurality, however, is troubled by the presumption because this is a First Amendment case. The plurality laments the fate of an innocent cross-burner who burns a cross, but does so without an intent to intimidate. The plurality fears the chill on expression because, according to the plurality, the inference permits "the Commonwealth to arrest, prosecute and convict a person based solely on the fact of cross burning itself." ... Yet, here, the plurality strikes down the statute because one day an individual might wish to burn a cross, but might do so without an intent to intimidate anyone. That cross burning subjects its targets, and, sometimes, an unintended audience, to extreme emotional distress, and is virtually never viewed merely as "unwanted communication," but rather, as a physical threat, is of no concern to the plurality. Henceforth, under the plurality's view, physical safety will be valued less than the right to be free from unwanted communications. Because I would uphold the validity of this statute, I respectfully dissent.

TEXAS V. JOHNSON
491 U.S. 397 (1989)

"If there is a bedrock principle underlying the First Amendment, it is that the government may not prohibit the expression of an idea simply because society finds the idea itself offensive or disagreeable.... We can imagine no more appropriate response to burning a flag than waving one's own.... We do not consecrate the flag by punishing its desecration, for in doing so we dilute the freedom that this cherished emblem represents."

The Question:	Can a state make it a criminal offense to "desecrate" a flag, in this case by burning an American flag in a public place as a form of political protest, if the act of burning the flag "offends" any person who witnesses the act?
The Arguments:	PRO

Just as the Supreme Court has upheld a federal law that punishes those who burn draft cards as a form of political protest, states have an equal right to punish those who burn the American flag as a form of "symbolic protest." Even more than a draft card, the flag is a unique symbol of our nation and its commitment to "liberty and justice for all." Anyone is free to burn a copy of the Constitution, or to speak disrespectfully of the flag, but the act of burning the flag is inherently likely to offend those who witness the act, and to provoke a breach of the peace by those who are offended. The principle of free speech is not absolute, and conferring special protection on the American flag is a reasonable way of ensuring that it is treated with respect.

CON

Even if the burning of draft cards can be punished in order to ensure the "smooth functioning" of the military draft system, no such reason would support a law that punishes flag burning. There is no doubt that many people are highly offended when they witness the burning of our nation's flag, but political expression cannot be censored because it offends someone. The outrage provoked by this case shows that flag burning does attract attention as an act of political expression, in a much more effective and dramatic fashion than making a speech or handing out leaflets. The American flag as our national symbol will endure this act of disrespect, and to punish anyone for burning the flag undermines the values of the First Amendment.

JUSTICE BRENNAN delivered the opinion of the Court.

After publicly burning an American flag as a means of political protest, Gregory Lee Johnson was convicted of desecrating a flag in violation of Texas law. This case presents the question whether his conviction is consistent with the First Amendment. We hold that it is not.

While the Republican National Convention was taking place in Dallas in 1984, respondent Johnson participated in a political demonstration dubbed the "Republican War Chest Tour." As explained in literature distributed by the demonstrators and in speeches made by them, the purpose of this event was to protest the policies of the Reagan administration and of certain Dallas-based corporations. The demonstrators marched through the Dallas streets, chanting political slogans and stopping at several corporate locations to stage "die-ins" intended to dramatize the consequences of nuclear war. On several occasions they spray-painted the walls of buildings and overturned potted plants, but Johnson himself took no part in such activities. He did, however, accept an American flag handed to him by a fellow protester who had taken it from a flagpole outside one of the targeted buildings.

The demonstration ended in front of Dallas City Hall, where Johnson unfurled the American flag, doused it with kerosene, and set it on fire. While the flag burned, the protestors chanted: "America, the red, white, and blue, we spit on you." After the demonstrators dispersed, a witness to the flag burning collected the flag's remains and buried them in his backyard. No one was physically injured or threatened with injury, though several witnesses testified that they had been seriously offended by the flag burning.

Of the approximately 100 demonstrators, Johnson alone was charged with a crime. The only criminal offense with which he was charged was the desecration of a venerated object in violation of Tex. Penal Code. After a trial, he was convicted, sentenced to one year in prison, and fined $2,000. The Court of Appeals for the Fifth District of Texas at Dallas affirmed Johnson's conviction, but the Texas Court of Criminal Appeals reversed, holding that the State could not, consistent with the First Amendment, punish Johnson for burning the flag in these circumstances. . . . We granted certiorari, and now affirm. . . .

The First Amendment literally forbids the abridgment only of "speech," but we have long recognized that its protection does not end at the spoken or written word. While we have rejected "the view that an apparently limitless variety of conduct can be labeled 'speech' whenever the person engaging in the conduct intends thereby to express an idea," we have acknowledged that conduct may be "sufficiently imbued with elements of communication to fall within the scope of the First and Fourteenth Amendments." . . .

The State of Texas conceded for purposes of its oral argument in this case that Johnson's conduct was expressive conduct. . . . Johnson burned an American flag as part—indeed, as the culmination—of a political demonstration that coincided with the convening of the Republican Party and its renomination of Ronald Reagan for President. The expressive, overtly political nature of this conduct was both intentional and overwhelmingly apparent. At his trial, Johnson explained his reasons for burning the flag as follows: "The American Flag was burned as Ronald Reagan was being renominated as President. And a more powerful statement of symbolic speech, whether you agree with it or not, couldn't have been made at that time. It's quite a just position [juxtaposition]. We had new patriotism and no patriotism." In these circumstances, Johnson's burning of the flag was conduct "sufficiently imbued with elements of communication."

The government generally has a freer hand in restricting expressive conduct than it has in restricting the written or spoken word. It may not, however, proscribe particular conduct because it has expressive elements. It is, in short, not simply the verbal or nonverbal nature of the expression, but the governmental interest at stake, that helps to determine whether a restriction on that expression is valid. . . .

Texas claims that its interest in preventing breaches of the peace justifies Johnson's conviction for flag desecration. However, no disturbance of the peace actually occurred or threatened to occur because of Johnson's burning of the flag. Although the State stresses the disruptive behavior of the protesters during their march toward City Hall, it admits that "no actual breach of the peace occurred at the time of the flagburning or in response to the flagburning." The State's emphasis on the protestors' disorderly actions prior to arriving at City Hall is not only somewhat surprising given that no charges were brought on the basis of this conduct, but it also fails to show that a disturbance of the peace was a likely reaction to Johnson's conduct. The only evidence offered by the State at trial to show the reaction to Johnson's actions was the testimony of several persons who had been seriously offended by the flag burning.

The State's position, therefore, amounts to a claim that an audience that takes serious offense at particular expression is necessarily likely to disturb the peace and that the expression may be prohibited on this basis. Our precedents do not countenance such a presumption. On the contrary, they recognize that a principal "function of free speech under our system of government is to invite dispute. It may indeed best serve its high purpose when it induces a condition of unrest, creates dissatisfaction with conditions as they are, or even stirs people to anger." It would be odd indeed to conclude . . . that the government may ban the expression of certain disagreeable ideas on the unsupported presumption that their very disagreeableness will provoke violence.

Thus, we have not permitted the government to assume that every expression of a provocative idea will incite a riot, but have instead required careful consideration of the actual circumstances surrounding such expression, asking whether the expression "is directed to inciting or producing imminent lawless action and is likely to incite or produce such action." Brandenburg v. Ohio. To accept Texas' arguments that it need only demonstrate "the potential for a breach of the peace," and that every flag burning necessarily possesses that potential, would be to eviscerate our holding in Brandenburg. This we decline to do. . . .

We thus conclude that the State's interest in maintaining order is not implicated on these facts. The State need not worry that our holding will disable it from preserving the peace. We do not suggest that the First Amendment forbids a State to prevent "imminent lawless action." Brandenburg. And, in fact, Texas already has a statute specifically prohibiting breaches of the peace, which tends to confirm that Texas need not punish this flag desecration in order to keep the peace. . . .

It remains to consider whether the State's interest in preserving the flag as a symbol of nationhood and national unity justifies Johnson's conviction. . . . The State's argument is not that it has an interest simply in maintaining the flag as a symbol of something, no matter what it symbolizes; indeed, if that were the State's position, it would be difficult to see how that interest is endangered by highly symbolic conduct such as Johnson's. Rather, the State's claim is that it has an interest in preserving the flag as a symbol of nationhood and national unity, a symbol with a determinate range of meanings. According to Texas, if one physically treats the flag in a way that would tend to cast doubt on either the idea that nationhood and national unity are the flag's referents or that national unity actually exists, the message conveyed thereby is a harmful one and therefore may be prohibited.

If there is a bedrock principle underlying the First Amendment, it is that the government may not prohibit the expression of an idea simply because society finds the idea itself offensive or disagreeable. We have not recognized an exception to this principle even where our flag has been involved. . . . To bring its argument outside our precedents, Texas attempts to convince us that even if its interest in preserving the flag's symbolic role does not allow it to prohibit words or some expressive conduct critical of the flag, it does permit it to forbid the outright destruction of the flag. The State's argument cannot depend here on the distinction between written or spoken words and nonverbal conduct. That distinction, we have shown, is of no moment where the nonverbal conduct is expressive, as it is here, and where the regulation of that conduct is related to expression, as it is here. . . . Texas' focus on the precise nature of Johnson's expression, moreover, misses the point of our prior decisions: their enduring lesson, that the government may not prohibit expression simply because it disagrees with its message, is not dependent on the particular mode in which one chooses to express an idea. If we were to hold that a State may forbid flag burning wherever it is likely to endanger the flag's symbolic role, but allow it wherever burning a flag promotes that role—as where, for example, a person ceremoniously burns a dirty flag—we would be saying that when it comes to impairing the flag's physical integrity, the flag itself may be used as a symbol—as a substitute for the written or spoken word or a "short cut from mind to mind"—only in one direction. We would be permitting a State to "prescribe what shall be orthodox" by saying that one may burn the flag to convey one's attitude toward it and its referents only if one does not endanger the flag's representation of nationhood and national unity. . . .

To conclude that the government may permit designated symbols to be used to communicate only a limited set of messages would be to enter territory having no discernible or defensible boundaries. Could the government, on this theory, prohibit the burning of state flags? Of copies of the Presidential seal? Of the Constitution? In evaluating these choices under the First Amendment, how would we decide which symbols were sufficiently special to warrant this unique status? To do so, we would be forced to consult our own political preferences, and impose them on the citizenry, in the very way that the First Amendment forbids us to do. There is, moreover, no indication—either in the text of the Constitution or in our cases interpreting it—that a separate juridical category exists for the American flag alone. Indeed, we would not be surprised to learn that the persons who framed our Constitution and wrote the Amendment that we now construe were not known for their reverence for the Union Jack. The First Amendment does not guarantee that other concepts virtually sacred to our Nation as a whole—such as the principle that discrimination on the basis of race is odious and destructive—will go unquestioned in the marketplace of ideas. We decline, therefore, to create for the flag an exception to the joust of principles protected by the First Amendment. . . .

We are tempted to say, in fact, that the flag's deservedly cherished place in our community will be strengthened, not weakened, by our holding today. Our decision is a reaffirmation of the principles of freedom and inclusiveness that the flag best reflects, and of the conviction that our toleration of criticism such as Johnson's is a sign and source of our strength. Indeed, one of the proudest images of our flag, the one immortalized in our own national anthem, is of the bombardment it survived at Fort McHenry. It is the Nation's resilience, not its rigidity, that Texas sees reflected in the flag—and it is that resilience that we reassert today.

The way to preserve the flag's special role is not to punish those who feel differently about these matters. It is to persuade them that they are wrong. . . . We can imagine no more appropriate response to burning a flag than waving one's own, no better way to counter a flag burner's message than by saluting the flag that burns, no surer means of preserving the dignity even of the flag that burned than by—as one witness here did—according its remains a respectful burial. We do not consecrate the flag by punishing its desecration, for in doing so we dilute the freedom that this cherished emblem represents.

Johnson was convicted for engaging in expressive conduct. The State's interest in preventing breaches of the peace does not support his conviction because Johnson's conduct did not threaten to disturb the peace. Nor does the State's interest in preserving the flag as a symbol of nationhood and national unity justify his criminal conviction for engaging in political expression. The judgment of the Texas Court of Criminal Appeals is therefore

Affirmed.

JUSTICE KENNEDY, concurring.

I write not to qualify the words Justice Brennan chooses so well, for he says with power all that is necessary to explain our ruling. I join his opinion without reservation, but with a keen sense that this case, like others before us from time to time, exacts its personal toll. This prompts me to add to our pages these few remarks.

The case before us illustrates better than most that the judicial power is often difficult in its exercise. We cannot here ask another Branch to share responsibility, as when the argument is made that a statute is flawed or incomplete. For we are presented with a clear and simple statute to be judged against a pure command of the Constitution. The outcome can be laid at no door but ours.

The hard fact is that sometimes we must make decisions we do not like. We make them because they are right, right in the sense that the law and the Constitution, as we see them, compel the result. And so great is our commitment to the process that, except in the rare case, we do not pause to express distaste for the result, perhaps for fear of undermining a valued principle that dictates the decision. This is one of those rare cases.

Our colleagues in dissent advance powerful arguments why respondent may be convicted for his expression, reminding us that among those who will be dismayed by our holding will be some who have had the singular honor of carrying the flag in battle. And I agree that the flag holds a lonely place of honor in an age when absolutes are distrusted and simple truths are burdened by unneeded apologetics.

With all respect to those views, I do not believe the Constitution gives us the right to rule as the dissenting Members of the Court urge, however painful this judgment is to announce. Though symbols often are what we ourselves make of them, the flag is constant in expressing beliefs Americans share, beliefs in law and peace and that freedom which sustains the human spirit. The case here today forces recognition of the costs to which those beliefs commit us. It is poignant but fundamental that the flag protects those who hold it in contempt.

For all the record shows, this respondent was not a philosopher and perhaps did not even possess the ability to comprehend how repellent his statements must be to the Republic itself. But whether or not he could appreciate the enormity of the offense he gave, the fact remains that his acts were speech, in both the technical and the fundamental meaning of the Constitution. So I agree with the Court that he must go free.

CHIEF JUSTICE REHNQUIST, with whom JUSTICE WHITE and JUSTICE O'CONNOR join, dissenting.

In holding this Texas statute unconstitutional, the Court ignores Justice Holmes' familiar aphorism that "a page of history is worth a volume of logic." For more than 200 years, the American flag has occupied a unique position as the symbol of our Nation, a uniqueness that justifies a governmental prohibition against flag burning in the way respondent Johnson did here.

At the time of the American Revolution, the flag served to unify the Thirteen Colonies at home, while obtaining recognition of national sovereignty abroad. Ralph Waldo Emerson's "Concord Hymn" describes the first skirmishes of the Revolutionary War in these lines:

> By the rude bridge that arched the flood
> Their flag to April's breeze unfurled,
> Here once the embattled farmers stood
> And fired the shot heard round the world.

During the War of 1812, British naval forces sailed up Chesapeake Bay and marched overland to sack and burn the city of Washington. They then sailed up the Patapsco River to invest the city of Baltimore, but to do so it was first necessary to reduce Fort McHenry in Baltimore Harbor. Francis Scott Key, a Washington lawyer, had been granted permission by the British to board one of their warships to negotiate the release of an American who had been taken prisoner. That night, waiting anxiously on the British ship, Key watched the British fleet firing on Fort McHenry. Finally, at daybreak, he saw the fort's American flag still flying; the British attack had failed. Intensely moved, he began to scribble on the back of an envelope the poem that became our national anthem:

> O say can you see by the dawn's early light
> What so proudly we hail'd at the twilight's last gleaming,
> Whose broad stripes & bright stars through the perilous fight

O'er the ramparts we watch'd, were so gallantly streaming?
And the rocket's red glare, the bomb bursting in air,
Gave proof through the night that our flag was still there,
O say does that star-spangled banner yet wave
O'er the land of the free & the home of the brave?

In the First and Second World Wars, thousands of our countrymen died on foreign soil fighting for the American cause. At Iwo Jima in the Second World War, United States Marines fought hand to hand against thousands of Japanese. By the time the Marines reached the top of Mount Suribachi, they raised a piece of pipe upright and from one end fluttered a flag. That ascent had cost nearly 6,000 American lives. The Iwo Jima Memorial in Arlington National Cemetery memorializes that event. . . .

The flag symbolizes the Nation in peace as well as in war. It signifies our national presence on battleships, airplanes, military installations, and public buildings from the United States Capitol to the thousands of county courthouses and city halls throughout the country. Two flags are prominently placed in our courtroom. Countless flags are placed by the graves of loved ones each year on what was first called Decoration Day, and is now called Memorial Day. . . . No other American symbol has been as universally honored as the flag. . . .

The American flag, then, throughout more than 200 years of our history, has come to be the visible symbol embodying our Nation. It does not represent the views of any particular political party, and it does not represent any particular political philosophy. The flag is not simply another "idea" or "point of view" competing for recognition in the marketplace of ideas. Millions and millions of Americans regard it with an almost mystical reverence regardless of what sort of social, political, or philosophical beliefs they may have. I cannot agree that the First Amendment invalidates the Act of Congress, and the laws of 48 of the 50 States, which make criminal the public burning of the flag. . . .

Here it may equally well be said that the public burning of the American flag by Johnson was no essential part of any exposition of ideas, and at the same time it had a tendency to incite a breach of the peace. Johnson was free to make any verbal denunciation of the flag that he wished; indeed, he was free to burn the flag in private. He could publicly burn other symbols of the Government or effigies of political leaders. He did lead a march through the streets of Dallas, and conducted a rally in front of the Dallas City Hall. He engaged in a "die-in" to protest nuclear weapons. He shouted out various slogans during the march, including: "Reagan, Mondale which will it be? Either one means World War III"; "Ronald Reagan, killer of the hour, Perfect example of U.S. power"; and "red, white and blue, we spit on you, you stand for plunder, you will go under." For none of these acts was he arrested or prosecuted; it was only when he proceeded to burn publicly an American flag stolen from its rightful owner that he violated the Texas statute. . . .

The result of the Texas statute is obviously to deny one in Johnson's frame of mind one of many means of "symbolic speech." Far from being a case of "one picture being worth a thousand words," flag burning is the equivalent of an inarticulate grunt or roar that, it seems fair to say, is most likely to be indulged in not to express any particular idea, but to antagonize others. . . . The Texas statute deprived

Johnson of only one rather inarticulate symbolic form of protest—a form of protest that was profoundly offensive to many—and left him with a full panoply of other symbols and every conceivable form of verbal expression to express his deep disapproval of national policy. Thus, in no way can it be said that Texas is punishing him because his hearers—or any other group of people—were profoundly opposed to the message that he sought to convey. Such opposition is no proper basis for restricting speech or expression under the First Amendment. It was Johnson's use of this particular symbol, and not the idea that he sought to convey by it or by his many other expressions, for which he was punished. . . .

The Court concludes its opinion with a regrettably patronizing civics lecture, presumably addressed to the Members of both Houses of Congress, the members of the 48 state legislatures that enacted prohibitions against flag burning, and the troops fighting under that flag in Vietnam who objected to its being burned: "The way to preserve the flag's special role is not to punish those who feel differently about these matters. It is to persuade them that they are wrong." The Court's role as the final expositor of the Constitution is well established, but its role as a Platonic guardian admonishing those responsible to public opinion as if they were truant schoolchildren has no similar place in our system of government. The cry of "no taxation without representation" animated those who revolted against the English Crown to found our Nation—the idea that those who submitted to government should have some say as to what kind of laws would be passed. Surely one of the high purposes of a democratic society is to legislate against conduct that is regarded as evil and profoundly offensive to the majority of people—whether it be murder, embezzlement, pollution, or flag burning.

Our Constitution wisely places limits on powers of legislative majorities to act, but the declaration of such limits by this Court "is, at all times, a question of much delicacy, which ought seldom, if ever, to be decided in the affirmative, in a doubtful case." Uncritical extension of constitutional protection to the burning of the flag risks the frustration of the very purpose for which organized governments are instituted. The Court decides that the American flag is just another symbol, about which not only must opinions pro and con be tolerated, but for which the most minimal public respect may not be enjoined. The government may conscript men into the Armed Forces where they must fight and perhaps die for the flag, but the government may not prohibit the public burning of the banner under which they fight. I would uphold the Texas statute as applied in this case.

COMMENTARY: STATEMENT OF PRESIDENT GEORGE BUSH: REMARKS ANNOUNCING THE PROPOSED CONSTITUTIONAL AMENDMENT ON DESECRATION OF THE FLAG

June 30, 1989

We stand today at the Tomb of the Unknown Soldier before a symbol of hope and of triumph. All across America—above farmhouses and statehouses, schools and courts and capitols—our flag is borne on the breeze of freedom. And it reminds Americans how much they've been given and how much they have to give. Our flag represents freedom and the unity of our nation. And our flag flies in peace, thanks to the sacrifices of so many Americans.

A woman in Florida recently shared with me a letter written by her cousin, a young soldier named Wayne Thomas. On December 16, 1966, he wrote: "Every time we go out on patrol, it gets a little scarier. The only thing that gives us a sense of security is when we walk back into camp and our flag is still flying high." She told me that Wayne stepped on a landmine 11 days later and was killed. He was 18 years old. He understood this banner of freedom and ultimately gave his life for the flag to give others the freedom that it represents.

You know, she also pointed out to me, parenthetically, that she was a registered Democrat. And to me that simply states that patriotism is not a partisan issue; it's not a political issue. Our purpose today transcends politics and partisanship.

And we feel in our hearts, and we know from our experience, that the surest way to preserve liberty is to protect the spirit that sustains it. And this flag sustains that spirit, and it's one of our most powerful ideas. And like all powerful ideas, if it is not defended, it is defamed. To the touch, this flag is merely fabric. But to the heart, the flag represents and reflects the fabric of our nation—our dreams, our destiny, our very fiber as a people.

And when we consider the importance of the colors to this nation, we do not question the right of men to speak freely. For it is this very symbol, with its stripes and stars, that has guaranteed and nurtured those precious rights—for those who've championed the cause of civil rights here at home, to those who fought for democracy abroad.

Free speech is a right that is dear and close to all. It is in defense of that right, and the others enshrined in our Constitution, that so many have sacrificed. But before we accept dishonor to our flag, we must ask ourselves how many have died following the order to "Save the Colors!" We must ask how many have fought for the ideals it represents. And we must honor those who have been handed the folded flag from the casket at Arlington.

If the debate here is about liberty, then we cannot turn our backs on those who fought to win it for us. We can't forget the importance of the flag to the ideals of liberty and honor and freedom. To burn the flag, to dishonor it, is simply wrong.

And today we remember one of the most vivid images of our flag—the one you see behind me—Joe Rosenthal's stunning photograph immortalized in bronze. As you view this memorial, think of its flag and of these men and of how they honor the living and the dead. Remember their heroism and their sacrifice, giving of themselves and others of their lives, fighting bravely, daring greatly, so that freedom could survive.

The Battle of Iwo Jima wrote one of the greatest chapters in the story of America. And even now, it humbles us, inspires us, reminds us of how Henry Ward Beecher said, "A thoughtful mind, when it sees a nation's flag, sees not the flag only but the nation itself."

The Nation itself was ennobled by the Battle of Iwo Jima. It was fought in early 1945, fought on 8 square miles of sand, caves, and volcanic rubble. And it cost our Armed Forces almost 7,000 killed and more than 19,000 wounded—almost a third of the landing force. But like Tarawa and Guadalcanal and the Philippines before, it had to be won. For victory at

Iwo would be yet another step towards bringing that ghastly war to a close.

These marines wrote a profile in courage, enduring a torrent of shells, pushing their way up that extinct volcano. And they stormed Mount Suribachi. And when they reached the top, the five men behind me raised a piece of pipe upright, and from one end flew a flag. And in the most famous image of World War II, a photograph was taken of these men and that flag. And what that flag embodies is too sacred to be abused.

As Justice Stevens stated so eloquently in his dissenting opinion in the recent Supreme Court case: "The ideas of liberty and equality have been an irresistible force in motivating leaders like Patrick Henry, Susan B. Anthony, Abraham Lincoln; schoolteachers like Nathan Hale and Booker T. Washington; the Philippine Scouts who fought at Bataan; and the soldiers who scaled the bluff at Omaha Beach. If those ideas are worth fighting for—and our history demonstrates that they are—it cannot be true," he says, "that the flag that uniquely symbolizes their power is not itself worthy of protection from unnecessary desecration." The Justice is right.

And today I am grateful to the leaders here and the leaders of the Congress with us in this audience who have proposed a constitutional amendment to protect the flag. Its language is stark, and it's simple and to the point: "The Congress and the States shall have power to prohibit the physical desecration of the flag of the United States." Simple and to the point, this amendment preserves the widest conceivable range of options for free expression. It applies only to the flag, the unique symbol of our nation.

Senator Dole, Senator Dixon, Congressmen Michel and Montgomery, I know that you have already taken the lead, but please take the lead, working with others here today, in moving this bill forward. With the help of you Members of the Senate and House here today, and with the help of the many more of your colleagues who couldn't be with us today, I am confident that we will succeed. I've seen predictions that this will take a long time; it need not. It is simple, to the point, direct; and it addresses itself to only one thing: Our flag will not be desecrated.

Let me close with a letter from a man named Augusto Moreno. Born in Argentina, now a naturalized citizen, he likes to say that he's more proud to be an American than most of those born in this country. I'm not sure he's right about that, but that's what he likes to say, anyway. He's very serious when he states: "I am proud to say that my blood is represented on our flag. I was wounded while fighting for democracy with the United State Marine Corps in Vietnam. I am now a disabled veteran. I am sure that there is not one day that goes by without you seeing the faces of those who were not so fortunate to return as you and I:" And he says: "We must continue our struggle to protect the flag now, as when we were in uniform—if not for us, then for those fallen veterans. We've been entrusted by those who have fought for freedom before us to protect our flag. I cannot allow anyone to desecrate the only symbol of freedom in the world." And he ends saying, "Sir, I realize that you're a Navy veteran, but Semper Fi anyway." [*Laughter*] Those darn marines, I'll tell you.

Well, Mr. Moreno, you have our word on it: For the sake of the fallen, for the men behind the guns, for every American, we will defend the flag of the United States of America.

Thank you. God bless this flag, and God bless the United States of America.

COMMENTARY: CONGRESSIONAL DEBATE ON FLAG-BURNING AMENDMENT

Mr. MITCHELL. Mr. President. I am pleased to cosponsor the legislation proposed by the chairman of the Judiciary Committee, the purpose of which is to make Federal law on the destruction of the American flag conform to the requirements of the first amendment.

This bill will ensure that the flag will be protected against physical destruction or abuse, for whatever purpose, with the appropriate penalties under law.

This legislation is what is needed to make certain that the Federal flag statute can withstand challenge by making the act of destruction itself the offense, rather than the purpose for which the act is carried out. The flag law would thereby punish vandalism against the flag, just as other, similar laws, punish vandalism against other national monuments.

The freedom of speech clause of the first amendment to the Constitution explicitly protects the right of all Americans to speak freely. It says nothing about actions. The speech provision of the Constitution protects the right of Americans to say things, but does not create a right to do things.

The Supreme Court has both limited and expanded the first amendment's protection.

As a limitation, it has imposed restrictions on some forms of speech. In the 1919 case of Schenk versus United States, Justice Oliver Wendell Homes wrote that:

> The character of every act depends on the circumstances in which it is done. The most stringent protection of free speech would not protect a man in falsely shouting fire in a theater and causing a panic.

Those words represented a commonsense principle of behavior that is essential to preserve a civil society with free speech. Clearly, no first amendment right would today protect a statement by an airplane passenger that he was about to explode a bomb, even if his purpose was to call attention to his political views.

The Court has expanded first amendment protection to certain actions, even though the amendment itself specifically protects only speech. The Court has reasoned that certain actions are closely related to speech and should be regarded as a form of speech, particularly where political ideas are involved.

In those cases involving action—the Court calls it "symbolic speech" or "expressive conduct"—the Court balances the governmental interest in prohibiting the conduct against the burden placed on the individual by not permitting the conduct to occur.

In reaching that balance, reasonable people can, do, and have disagreed.

In the flag burning case itself, the Court divided 5 to 4.

In another case, a divided court ruled that homeless persons wishing to demonstrate their destitution could not sleep in the square before the White House. The Supreme Court said that sleeping was not a form of speech protected by the Constitution.

In another case, local statutes barring demonstration within a certain distance of foreign embassies have been upheld, because they do not unduly burden speech, and they serve valuable government purposes.

In my judgment, the principle applied in those earlier cases applies to the actions in the flag case.

The protesters were not denied the right to speak. They chose to burn the flag as an addition to that right, not as a substitute when speech was impossible or endangering.

The facts in the case are not in dispute. Gregory L. Johnson, apparently leading a group of demonstrators outside the 1984 Republican Convention, poured kerosene on an American flag and set a match to it, while his group chanted: "America, the red, white, and blue, we spit on you."

Those words, offensive as they are to me and the vast majority of Americans, are protected by the first amendment. To my knowledge, no one disputed their right to say those words. Nobody interfered with their right to speak freely. They were not prevented from speaking.

But they did not merely speak. They also acted. It was this action which was punished, not the speech.

Indeed, they may well have burned the flag in order to obtain the attention that their speech itself would not have garnered.

The first amendment may guarantee the freedom to speak. It guarantees nobody an audience for his words.

And if these protestors' purpose was to compel attention that their words alone could not attract, there is no constitutional obligation to provide that attention.

I agree with the dissent of Justice Stevens in this case, when he said, "The case has nothing to do with 'disagreeable ideas'. . . it involves disagreeable conduct. . . ." Justice Stevens is right. The five-man majority of the Court is wrong.

JUSTICE STEVENS made the point succinctly:

> Had [Johnson] chosen to spray paint . . . his message of dissatisfaction on the facade of the Lincoln Memorial, there would be no question about the power of the government to prohibit his means of expression. The prohibition would be supported by the legitimate interest in preserving the quality of an important national asset.

The flag is also a national asset, although admittedly an intangible one.

We need not permit acts that undermine its value for all Americans in order to avoid burdening in slight fashion the speech rights of those who seek to be heard in the face of indifference, not persecution.

* * *

Mr. KERREY. Mr. President, I rise today to express my thoughts concerning the June 21, 1989, Supreme Court decision known as Texas versus Johnson, in which the Supreme Court protected the right to express an opinion by burning an American flag.

At first I, like most Americans, was outraged by the decision. It seemed ridiculous to me that flag burning could be a protected act. My anger grew when I watched a replay of the 1984 incident, which also included the expression of derogatory chants and epithets against the United States of America.

I joined with 96 other Senators expressing our disagreement with the decision. As I prepared to head home for the

Fourth of July recess. I declared my disbelief at our apparent impotence in protecting this symbol of American freedom.

Then, during the recess, I read the decision. Mr. President, I was surprised to discover that I agreed with the majority. I was surprised to discover that I found the majority argument to be reasonable, understandable, and consistent with those values which I believe make America so wonderful.

Further, I was surprised to discover that after reading this decision my anger was not directed at Justices Brennan, Scalia, Kennedy, Marshall, and Blackmun who joined in the majority. Rather, it was the language of the dissent which angered me, particularly that of Chief Justice Rehnquist whose argument appears to stand not on 200 years of case law which has supported greater and greater freedom of speech for Americans, but on a sentimental nationalism which seems to impose a functional litmus test of loyalty before expression is permitted.

Today, I declare that I do not support any of the constitutional amendments which are being offered by my colleagues and friends as a necessary remedy to this decision. I will not yield in my belief that these amendments create problems rather than solving them.

Today, I am even skeptical about the need to pass antiflag burning laws at the State or the Federal level. Even this response seems more patronizing than necessary.

Today, I am disappointed that the strength of leadership shown by President Bush in his travels to Poland and Hungary was not shown here at home. President Bush did not stand before the angry and distressed mob to stop us in our tracks before we had done something we would regret. He did not offer words that calmed us and gave us assurance that the Nation was not endangered. Instead of leading us, President Bush joined us.

The polls showed support for a constitutional amendment and so the President yielded to his political advisers. Even though most Americans had not read the decision prior to being polled, even though they did not understand what is potentially at stake if our Bill of Rights was altered, the President chose the path of least resistance and greatest political gain.

I believe we should slow down and examine what it is we are about to do. I believe we should look at the decision carefully. And I believe if we do, we are less likely to conclude that action is even needed.

I believe that we should look first at the two States of the 50 States in this Nation that do [not] have antiflag burning laws. Ask yourself how it is that Alaska and Wyoming have survived without such laws. Is it because they are less patriotic than the citizens of 48 other States? Is it because they simply were not aware of the great danger that exists to each of them if such laws were not passed?

Or is it because they simply recognize that no danger exists? Is it because they recognize there is already a sufficient amount of unwritten negative sanctions against flag burning without the need for the law makers to act further? I suspect it is the latter. I suspect that a law making it illegal to burn the American flag in Wyoming or Alaska is simply seen as unnecessary.

Mr. President, there is simply no line of Americans outside this building or in this Nation queuing up to burn our flag. On the face of the evidence at hand it seems to me that there is no need for us to do anything. The only reason to speak at all is to give credence to the cynical observation of H.L. Mencken who said: "Whenever you hear a man speak of his love for his country, it is a sign that he expects to be paid for it."

Mr. President, America is the beacon of hope for the people of this world who yearn for freedom from the despotism of repressive government. This hope is diluted when we advise others that we are frightened by flag burning.

John Stuart Mill, in his 1859 essay "On Liberty" offered three reasons that the expression of opinion should rarely be limited. First, the suppressed opinion might be right; its suppression might deprive mankind of the opportunity of "exchanging error for truth." Second, even though the opinion might be false, it may contain "a portion of truth," and "it is only by the collision of adverse opinions," each of which contains partial truth, "that the remainder of the truth has any chance of being supplied." Third, even if the opinion to be silenced is completely wrong, in silencing it mankind loses "what is almost as great a benefit as that (of truth), the clearer perception and livelier impression of truth, produced by its collision with error."

Mr. President, flag burning is clearly in the third category. It does not persuade us that the burner holds an opinion that is true. It persuades us that his opinion is untrue. And it gives us the opportunity to see what true freedom and true patriotism is.

Patriotism means loving one's country. And like any kind of love, it is fundamentally a personal, even private act.

It is the patriotism of mothers and fathers who provide a loving environment for their children to grow to their full potential. It is the patriotism of the men and women who farm our farms, toiling tirelessly to make ends meet while producing food for the rest of us. It is the patriotism of teachers who put in the extra hours to help their students do better in school. It is the patriotism of our local police who go in harm's way to keep us feeling safe and secure.

It is the patriotism of nurses and doctors who help us heal. And it is the patriotism of all of us who pay our taxes, register to vote, contribute to church and charity, and love our country.

Finally, Mr. President, Chief Justice Rehnquist, in his disappointing dissent, asserts that men and women fought for our flag in Vietnam. In my case I do not remember feeling this way.

I remember that my first impulse to fight was the result of a feeling that it was my duty. My Nation called and I went. In the short time that I was there, I do not remember giving the safety of our flag anywhere near the thought that I gave the safety of my men.

I do remember thinking about going home and I remember why that home felt so good to me. I remember realizing how wonderful my mother and father were. I remember longing to be back in the old neighborhood. I remember most vividly on the night that I was wounded, with the smell of my own burning flesh in my head, that I knew I was going home, and how happy I was with that certainty.

America—the home of the free and the brave—is my home, and I give thanks to God that it is. America—the home of the free and the brave—does not need our Government to protect us from those who burn a flag.

SECTION 3

〜〜〜

DEFAMATION: LIBEL AND SLANDER

NEW YORK TIMES V. SULLIVAN
376 U.S. 254 (1964)

*"We consider this case against the background of a profound national commitment to the principle that debate
on public issues should be uninhibited, robust, and wide-open, and that it may well include vehement,
caustic, and sometimes unpleasantly sharp attacks on government and public officials. . . .
The Constitution delimits a State's power to award damages for libel in actions brought
by public officials against critics of their official conduct."*

The Question: Can a public official, in this case the police commissioner of Montgomery, Alabama, recover damages from a newspaper for publishing an advertisement that did not mention his name but contained statements a jury found had damaged his reputation?

The Arguments: PRO

The New York Times published an advertisement, designed to raise funds to pay for bail and legal expenses of "sit-in" demonstrators, stating that "truckloads of police armed with shotguns and tear-gas ringed the . . . campus" of a black college in Montgomery, Alabama. The *Times* does not deny this statement was false. Readers of the *Times* could infer that Police Commissioner L.B. Sullivan had ordered the police to "ring" the campus and that he was among the "Southern violators" who used "intimidation and violence" against peaceful civil rights demonstrators, as the ad claimed. The jury's finding that these false statements injured his reputation should not be reversed simply because Southern officials are not popular in other areas of the country.

CON

The *Times* did not write the advertisement in question and should not be held responsible for the minor errors in it. To hold the press to a standard of complete accuracy in every article and advertisement would make publishers and editors wary of printing anything that might suggest wrongdoing by public officials. The ad in question did not name Commissioner Sullivan, and a reasonable reader would not infer that he was personally responsible for acts of "intimidation and violence" against peaceful demonstrators. Even if the police had "ringed" the college campus, the ad did not accuse them or Sullivan of any unlawful act. The minor errors in the ad do not justify a damage judgment of $500,000 against the *Times*.

MR. JUSTICE BRENNAN delivered the opinion of the Court.

We are required in this case to determine for the first time the extent to which the constitutional protections for speech and press limit a State's power to award damages in a libel action brought by a public official against critics of his official conduct.

Respondent L. B. Sullivan is one of the three elected Commissioners of the City of Montgomery, Alabama. He testified that he was "Commissioner of Public Affairs and the duties are supervision of the Police Department, Fire Department, Department of Cemetery and Department of Scales." He brought this civil libel action against the four individual petitioners, who are Negroes and Alabama clergymen, and against petitioner the New York Times Company, a New York corporation which publishes the New York Times, a daily newspaper. A jury in the Circuit Court of Montgomery County awarded him damages of $500,000, the full amount claimed, against all the petitioners, and the Supreme Court of Alabama affirmed.

Respondent's complaint alleged that he had been libeled by statements in a full-page advertisement that was carried in the New York Times on March 29, 1960. Entitled "Heed Their Rising Voices," the advertisement began by stating that "As the whole world knows by now, thousands of Southern Negro students are engaged in widespread non-violent demonstrations in positive affirmation of the right to live in human dignity as guaranteed by the U.S. Constitution and the Bill of Rights." It went on to charge that "in their efforts to uphold these guarantees, they are being met by an unprecedented wave of terror by those who would deny and negate that document which the whole world looks upon as setting the pattern for modern freedom. . . ." Succeeding paragraphs purported to illustrate the "wave of terror" by describing certain alleged events. The text concluded with an appeal for funds for three purposes: support of the student movement, "the struggle for the right-to-vote," and the legal defense of Dr. Martin Luther King, Jr., leader of the movement, against a perjury indictment then pending in Montgomery.

The text appeared over the names of 64 persons, many widely known for their activities in public affairs, religion, trade unions, and the performing arts. Below these names, and under a line reading "We in the south who are struggling daily for dignity and freedom warmly endorse this appeal," appeared the names of the four individual petitioners and of 16 other persons, all but two of whom were identified as clergymen in various Southern cities. The advertisement was signed at the bottom of the page by the "Committee to Defend Martin Luther King and the Struggle for Freedom in the South," and the officers of the Committee were listed.

Of the 10 paragraphs of text in the advertisement, the third and a portion of the sixth were the basis of respondent's claim of libel. They read as follows: "In Montgomery, Alabama, after students sang 'My Country, 'Tis of Thee' on the State Capitol steps, their leaders were expelled from school, and truckloads of police armed with shotguns and tear-gas ringed the Alabama State College Campus. When the entire student body protested to state authorities by re-fusing to re-register, their dining hall was padlocked in an attempt to starve them into submission. Again and again the Southern violators have answered Dr. King's peaceful protests with intimidation and violence. They have bombed his home almost killing his wife and child. They have assaulted his person. They have arrested him seven times—for 'speeding,' 'loitering' and similar 'offenses.' And now they have charged him with 'perjury'—a felony under which they could imprison him for ten years. . . ."

Although neither of these statements mentions respondent by name, he contended that the word "police" in the third paragraph referred to him as the Montgomery Commissioner who supervised the Police Department, so that he was being accused of "ringing" the campus with police. He further claimed that the paragraph would be read as imputing to the police, and hence to him, the padlocking of the dining hall in order to starve the students into submission. As to the sixth paragraph, he contended that since arrests are ordinarily made by the police, the statement "They have arrested [Dr. King] seven times" would be read as referring to him; he further contended that the "They" who did the arresting would be equated with the "They" who committed the other described acts and with the "Southern

violators." Thus, he argued, the paragraph would be read as accusing the Montgomery police, and hence him, of answering Dr. King's protests with "intimidation and violence," bombing his home, assaulting his person, and charging him with perjury. Respondent and six other Montgomery residents testified that they read some or all of the statements as referring to him in his capacity as Commissioner.

It is uncontroverted that some of the statements contained in the paragraphs were not accurate descriptions of events which occurred in Montgomery. Although Negro students staged a demonstration on the State Capitol steps, they sang the National Anthem and not "My Country, 'Tis of Thee." Although nine students were expelled by the State Board of Education, this was not for leading the demonstration at the Capitol, but for demanding service at a lunch counter in the Montgomery County Courthouse on another day. Not the entire student body, but most of it, had protested the expulsion, not by refusing to register, but by boycotting classes on a single day; virtually all the students did register for the ensuing semester. The campus dining hall was not padlocked on any occasion, and the only students who may have been barred from eating there were the few who had neither signed a preregistration application nor requested temporary meal tickets. Although the police were deployed near the campus in large numbers on three occasions, they did not at any time "ring" the campus, and they were not called to the campus in connection with the demonstration on the State Capitol steps, as the third paragraph implied. Dr. King had not been arrested seven times, but only four; and although he claimed to have been assaulted some years earlier in connection with his arrest for loitering outside a courtroom, one of the officers who made the arrest denied that there was such an assault. . . .

Respondent made no effort to prove that he suffered actual pecuniary loss as a result of the alleged libel. One of his witnesses, a former employer, testified that if he had believed the statements, he doubted whether he "would want to be associated with anybody who would be a party to such things that are stated in that ad," and that he would not reemploy respondent if he believed "that he allowed the Police Department to do the things that the paper says he did." But neither this witness nor any of the others testified that he had actually believed the statements in their supposed reference to respondent. . . .

The trial judge submitted the case to the jury under instructions that the statements in the advertisement were "libelous per se" and were not privileged, so that petitioners might be held liable if the jury found that they had published the advertisement and that the statements were made "of and concerning" respondent. The jury was instructed that, because the statements were libelous per se, "the law . . . implies legal injury from the bare fact of publication itself," "falsity and malice are presumed," "general damages need not be alleged or proved but are presumed," and "punitive damages may be awarded by the jury even though the amount of actual damages is neither found nor shown." . . . The judge rejected petitioners' contention that his rulings abridged the freedoms of speech and of the press that are guaranteed by the First and Fourteenth Amendments. . . .

In affirming the judgment, the Supreme Court of Alabama sustained the trial judge's rulings and instructions in all respects. It held that "where the words published tend to injure a person libeled by them in his reputation, profession, trade or business, or charge him with an indictable offense, or tend to bring the individual into public contempt," they are "libelous per se"; that "the matter complained of is, under the above doctrine, libelous per se, if it was published of and concerning the plaintiff"; and that it was actionable without "proof of pecuniary injury . . ., such injury being implied." . . .

Because of the importance of the constitutional issues involved, we granted the separate petitions for certiorari of the individual petitioners and of the Times. We reverse the judgment. We hold that the rule of law applied by the Alabama courts is constitutionally deficient for failure to provide the safeguards for freedom of speech and of the press that are required by the First and Fourteenth Amendments in a libel action brought by a public official against critics of his official conduct. We further hold that under the proper safeguards the evidence presented in this case is constitutionally insufficient to support the judgment for respondent. . . .

Under Alabama law as applied in this case, a publication is "libelous per se" if the words "tend to injure a person . . . in his reputation" or to "bring [him] into public contempt"; the trial court stated that the standard was met if the words are such as to "injure him in his public office, or impute misconduct to him in his office, or want of official integrity, or want of fidelity to a public trust. . . ." The jury must find that the words were published "of and concerning" the plaintiff, but where the plaintiff is a public official his place in the governmental hierarchy is sufficient evidence to support a finding that his reputation has been affected by statements that reflect upon the agency of which he is in charge. Once "libel per se" has been established, the defendant has no defense as to stated facts unless he can persuade the jury that they were true in all their particulars. . . . Unless he can discharge the burden of proving truth, general damages are presumed, and may be awarded without proof of pecuniary injury. A showing of actual malice is apparently a prerequisite to recovery of punitive damages, and the defendant may in any event forestall a punitive award by a retraction meeting the statutory requirements. Good motives and belief in truth do not negate an inference of malice, but are relevant only in mitigation of punitive damages if the jury chooses to accord them weight.

The question before us is whether this rule of liability, as applied to an action brought by a public official against critics of his official conduct, abridges the freedom of speech and of the press that is guaranteed by the First and Fourteenth Amendments. . . .

The general proposition that freedom of expression upon public questions is secured by the First Amendment has long been settled by our decisions. The constitutional safeguard, we have said, "was fashioned to assure unfettered interchange of ideas for the bringing about of political and social changes desired by the people." . . . Thus we consider this case against the background of a profound national commitment to the principle that debate on public issues should be unin-

hibited, robust, and wide-open, and that it may well include vehement, caustic, and sometimes unpleasantly sharp attacks on government and public officials. The present advertisement, as an expression of grievance and protest on one of the major public issues of our time, would seem clearly to qualify for the constitutional protection. The question is whether it forfeits that protection by the falsity of some of its factual statements and by its alleged defamation of respondent.

Authoritative interpretations of the First Amendment guarantees have consistently refused to recognize an exception for any test of truth—whether administered by judges, juries, or administrative officials—and especially one that puts the burden of proving truth on the speaker. The constitutional protection does not turn upon "the truth, popularity, or social utility of the ideas and beliefs which are offered." As Madison said, "Some degree of abuse is inseparable from the proper use of every thing; and in no instance is this more true than in that of the press." . . .

Injury to official reputation affords no more warrant for repressing speech that would otherwise be free than does factual error. Where judicial officers are involved, this Court has held that concern for the dignity and reputation of the courts does not justify the punishment as criminal contempt of criticism of the judge or his decision. . . . If judges are to be treated as "men of fortitude, able to thrive in a hardy climate," surely the same must be true of other government officials, such as elected city commissioners. Criticism of their official conduct does not lose its constitutional protection merely because it is effective criticism and hence diminishes their official reputations. If neither factual error nor defamatory content suffices to remove the constitutional shield from criticism of official conduct, the combination of the two elements is no less inadequate. . . .

A rule compelling the critic of official conduct to guarantee the truth of all his factual assertions—and to do so on pain of libel judgments virtually unlimited in amount—leads to a comparable "self-censorship." Allowance of the defense of truth, with the burden of proving it on the defendant, does not mean that only false speech will be deterred. Even courts accepting this defense as an adequate safeguard have recognized the difficulties of adducing legal proofs that the alleged libel was true in all its factual particulars. Under such a rule, would-be critics of official conduct may be deterred from voicing their criticism, even though it is believed to be true and even though it is in fact true, because of doubt whether it can be proved in court or fear of the expense of having to do so. They tend to make only statements which "steer far wider of the unlawful zone." The rule thus dampens the vigor and limits the variety of public debate. It is inconsistent with the First and Fourteenth Amendments. The constitutional guarantees require, we think, a federal rule that prohibits a public official from recovering damages for a defamatory falsehood relating to his official conduct unless he proves that the statement was made with "actual malice"—that is, with knowledge that it was false or with reckless disregard of whether it was false or not. . . .

We hold today that the Constitution delimits a State's power to award damages for libel in actions brought by public officials against critics of their official conduct. Since this is such an action, the rule requiring proof of actual malice is applicable. . . . Since respondent may seek a new trial, we deem that considerations of effective judicial administration require us to review the evidence in the present record to determine whether it could constitutionally support a judgment for respondent. This Court's duty is not limited to the elaboration of constitutional principles; we must also in proper cases review the evidence to make certain that those principles have been constitutionally applied. . . . Applying these standards, we consider that the proof presented to show actual malice lacks the convincing clarity which the constitutional standard demands, and hence that it would not constitutionally sustain the judgment for respondent under the proper rule of law. . . .

The judgment of the Supreme Court of Alabama is reversed and the case is remanded to that court for further proceedings not inconsistent with this opinion.

MR. JUSTICE BLACK, with whom MR. JUSTICE DOUGLAS joins, concurring.

I concur in reversing this half-million-dollar judgment against the New York Times Company and the four individual defendants. In reversing, the Court holds that "the Constitution delimits a State's power to award damages for libel in actions brought by public officials against critics of their official conduct." I base my vote to reverse on the belief that the First and Fourteenth Amendments not merely "delimit" a State's power to award damages to "public officials against critics of their official conduct" but completely prohibit a State from exercising such a power. The Court goes on to hold that a State can subject such critics to damages if "actual malice" can be proved against them. "Malice," even as defined by the Court, is an elusive, abstract concept, hard to prove and hard to disprove. The requirement that malice be proved provides at best an evanescent protection for the right critically to discuss public affairs and certainly does not measure up to the sturdy safeguard embodied in the First Amendment. Unlike the Court, therefore, I vote to reverse exclusively on the ground that the Times and the individual defendants had an absolute, unconditional constitutional right to publish in the Times advertisement their criticisms of the Montgomery agencies and officials. I do not base my vote to reverse on any failure to prove that these individual defendants signed the advertisement or that their criticism of the Police Department was aimed at the plaintiff Sullivan, who was then the Montgomery City Commissioner having supervision of the city's police; for present purposes I assume these things were proved. Nor is my reason for reversal the size of the half-million-dollar judgment, large as it is. If Alabama has constitutional power to use its civil libel law to impose damages on the press for criticizing the way public officials perform or fail to perform their duties, I know of no provision in the Federal Constitution which either expressly or impliedly bars the State from fixing the amount of damages.

The half-million-dollar verdict does give dramatic proof, however, that state libel laws threaten the very existence of an American press virile enough to publish unpopular views on public affairs and bold enough to criticize the conduct of public officials. The factual background of this case emphasizes the imminence and enormity of that threat. One of the acute and highly emotional issues in this country arises out of efforts of many people, even including some public officials, to continue state-commanded segregation of races in the public schools and other public places, despite our several holdings that such a state practice is forbidden by the Fourteenth Amendment. Montgomery is one of the localities in which widespread hostility to desegregation has been manifested. This hostility has sometimes extended itself to persons who favor desegregation, particularly to so-called "outside agitators," a term which can be made to fit papers like the Times, which is published in New York. The scarcity of testimony to show that Commissioner Sullivan suffered any actual damages at all suggests that these feelings of hostility had at least as much to do with rendition of this half-million-dollar verdict as did an appraisal of damages. Viewed realistically, this record lends support to an inference that instead of being damaged Commissioner Sullivan's political, social, and financial prestige has likely been enhanced by the Times' publication. . . .

In my opinion the Federal Constitution has dealt with this deadly danger to the press in the only way possible without leaving the free press open to destruction—by granting the press an absolute immunity for criticism of the way public officials do their public duty. Stopgap measures like those the Court adopts are in my judgment not enough. This record certainly does not indicate that any different verdict would have been rendered here whatever the Court had charged the jury about "malice," "truth," "good motives," "justifiable ends," or any other legal formulas which in theory would protect the press. Nor does the record indicate that any of these legalistic words would have caused the courts below to set aside or to reduce the half-million-dollar verdict in any amount. . . .

We would, I think, more faithfully interpret the First Amendment by holding that at the very least it leaves the people and the press free to criticize officials and discuss public affairs with impunity. This Nation of ours elects many of its important officials; so do the States, the municipalities, the counties, and even many precincts. These officials are responsible to the people for the way they perform their duties. . . . This Nation, I suspect, can live in peace without libel suits based on public discussions of public affairs and public officials. But I doubt that a country can live in freedom where its people can be made to suffer physically or financially for criticizing their government, its actions, or its officials. An unconditional right to say what one pleases about public affairs is what I consider to be the minimum guarantee of the First Amendment. I regret that the Court has stopped short of this holding indispensable to preserve our free press from destruction.

GERTZ V. ROBERT WELCH, INC.
418 U.S. 323 (1974)

"The communications media are entitled to act on the assumption that public officials and public figures have voluntarily exposed themselves to increased risk of injury from defamatory falsehood concerning them. No such assumption is justified with respect to a private individual. . . . He has a more compelling call on the courts for redress of injury inflicted by defamatory falsehood."

The Question: Can a person who is not a public official or a public figure recover damages for defamation against the publisher of a magazine that ran a story falsely accusing the person of being a "Leninist" and "Communist-fronter"?

The Arguments: PRO

The Supreme Court has ruled that public officials should expect criticism in the press, and publishers should not be held liable for minor errors in articles and advertisements. This does not mean that private citizens, who have not thrust themselves into public controversy, should not be protected against false statements that seriously damage their reputations. In this case, the magazine of the right-wing John Birch Society published an article, which the editors had sufficient time to check for accuracy, that falsely accused a respected attorney of being a "Leninist" and "Communist-fronter." There are few accusations more likely to damage an attorney's professional standing and even his or her livelihood, and the publisher should be liable for the gross negligence of its authors and editors.

CON

The Supreme Court ruling that public officials cannot recover damages for defamation without a finding of "reckless disregard" for the truth on the part of the publisher should be followed in this case. The article in question examined an issue of great public concern, the supposed "war on the police" by Communists and "front-groups" that follow the party line. The plaintiff, a lawyer who represented the family of a man who was shot and killed by a police officer, had belonged to a legal group that had been labeled a "Communist front" by the U.S. Attorney General. Whatever mistakes were made in researching the article in question, they do not rise to the level of "reckless disregard" of the truth.

BACKGROUND

On March 22, 1969, someone thrust a pamphlet into the hands of Mary Giampietro while she strolled through a shopping mall in Chicago, Illinois. Only after she returned home did she browse idly through the unsolicited literature. The pamphlet bore the title, "Frame-Up, Richard Nuccio and the War on Police." Mary learned from small print that the pamphlet was a reprinted article from a magazine known as *American Opinion.* The article's author, Alan Stang, was identified as "a former business editor for Prentice Hall" who had "just returned from an investigative trip to Chicago, where he conducted extensive research into the Richard Nuccio Case." Flipping through the pamphlet, Mary was shocked to find a picture of her husband Wayne's employer, Elmer Gertz. The caption under the picture read, "Elmer Gertz of Red Guild harasses Nuccio."

Within hours of Mary's shopping trip, Elmer read the pamphlet she brought him. What prompted Stang's article, Elmer discovered, was the murder conviction in August 1968 of a Chicago policeman, Richard Nuccio, for the shoot-

ing death of a young man named Ronald Nelson. What prompted Stang's charge against Elmer Gertz was the Chicago lawyer's role in representing Nelson's family in a civil damage suit against Nuccio. Stang drew a conspiratorial connection between the two separate cases. His article accused Elmer of active participation in "the Communist War on Police," a national conspiracy aimed at destroying local police "so that Communists can impose their totalitarian dictatorship." Portraying Elmer as the mastermind of the "carefully orchestrated" campaign to frame Officer Nuccio for Nelson's murder, Stang labeled the Chicago lawyer as a "Leninist" and "Communist-fronter." Stang's evidence for these charges, and "the only thing Chicagoans need to know about Gertz," was Elmer's association—no dates were listed—with "the Communist National Lawyers Guild."

The pamphlet did not identify the organization that published *American Opinion* and that paid Alan Stang for his article. Elmer Gertz quickly discovered that Stang's journalistic assault had been sponsored by the John Birch Society. During the 1960s, the Birch Society was the largest and most active of the Radical Right groups that were spawned by

McCarthyism and fed on Cold War paranoia. Notorious for their "Impeach Earl Warren" campaign and their crusade against American membership in the United Nations, Birchers consciously adopted the tactics of their enemies and set up "fronts" which promoted their goals under cover of innocuous titles. Birch fronts often promoted fringe causes, like the "Committee to Warn of the Arrival of Communist Merchandise on the Local Business Scene," which opposed Polish hams and Czech glassware. Others tried to exploit more popular causes. The "Support Your Local Police" campaign, which peddled bumper stickers and 86,000 copies of Stang's article on the Nuccio case, allied the Birchers with an issue of widespread public concern.

Among the Radical Right groups, Birchers specialized in tossing around "treason" charges. Robert Welch, who had worked for a family confectionary business in Boston, abandoned candy to attack Communists in 1958, when he founded the Birch Society. Welch had no partisan bias in labeling American leaders as traitors. In the two-day speech that he delivered at the founding Birch meeting, and repeated every two weeks to Birch recruits, Welch accused President Franklin Roosevelt of "pure unadulterated treason" for his wartime agreements with the Soviets. Welch later branded President Dwight Eisenhower a "conscious agent of the Communist conspiracy." Although Welch soon disavowed this charge, it sent shivers through conservatives like Barry Goldwater, who slithered away from Welch's endorsement of his 1964 presidential effort. With friends like Welch, conservatives did not need enemies.

Although the Birch Society kept its membership figures under wraps, observers estimated that some 50,000 Americans became Birchers in the early 1960s. Three California congressmen admitted Birch affiliation, although each fell victim to the voters after his membership became an election issue. Birchers had an insatiable appetite for exposures of "treason" in high places. *American Opinion,* a glossy monthly, fed this appetite with articles by a stable of freelance authors. Alan Stang, who wrote more than a hundred pieces for the Birch journal between 1963 and its demise in 1985, excelled at the kind of cut-and-paste, hit-and-run journalism that drew on newspaper snippets, quotations from Communists, and the indexes of congressional Red-hunting panels. Stang had no time for subtlety or nuance in his Radical Right writings. He favored three-word sentences and "treason" charges. Stang could not resist linking Elmer Gertz with the "traitors" who marched in Chicago against the Vietnam War.

The Birchers had not anticipated libel suits from their victims. Supreme Court precedent made it difficult for well-known figures to recover damages in defamation suits. But the Birchers had also not anticipated Elmer Gertz's reaction to Alan Stang's charge that he was a "Leninist" and "Communist-fronter." Only a few weeks after Mary Giampietro brought him the Birch pamphlet, Elmer sued the Birch Society's corporate body, Robert Welch, Inc. Wayne Giampietro, a young lawyer who had recently joined Elmer in law practice, filed the suit in Chicago's federal court. Elmer's complaint stated that he had practiced law in Chicago since 1930, that he belonged to many "professional, literary, historical, religious, educational, philanthropic and civic" organizations and had "received awards and citations for public services from several groups." The complaint added, without

undue modesty, that Elmer "has deservedly enjoyed a good reputation as a lawyer and citizen" and that he "has always been a loyal and respected citizen of the United States."

The editorial tag-line to Stang's article claimed he had conducted "extensive research" into the Nuccio case. Stang's research, however, stopped short of talking with Elmer Gertz about his involvement in the case, or his background. This proved to be a fatal mistake for the Birch Society. The most cursory research would have disclosed that Elmer had never been a Communist, had never supported the Communists, and had in fact actively opposed the Communists on many issues. Stang had picked the wrong person to libel. Elmer *had* once belonged to the National Lawyers Guild, but he left the liberal group more than fifteen years before Stang's article appeared. Three members of the U.S. Supreme Court had also been Guild members, along with many lawyers—some of them Communists—who rejected the conservative positions of the American Bar Association. Elmer had certainly never been a "Leninist" of any sort, and Stang's "guilt by association" tactics had no factual basis.

Because the Birch Society was based in Massachusetts, Elmer was entitled to file his libel suit in federal court under the "diversity" rule that governs disputes between citizens of different states. But these diversity cases are decided on the basis of state law, and Illinois judges had given Elmer an advantage—which he and Wayne Giampietro well knew. Prior decisions by Illinois courts made clear that falsely accusing someone of "Communist" membership or sympathy was libelous, regardless of motive or mistake. The reason for what judges called the *per se* rule of libel was that Communist activity was criminal in Illinois, and false accusations of criminal behavior would certainly damage a person's reputation.

Elmer's suit against the Birch Society put two rights into conflict. On the one hand, the law gave citizens legal protection against false statements which might damage their reputations and professions. Calling a respected lawyer a "Communist" might well scare away present or potential clients. On the other hand, threatening the press with huge damage claims for errors made in the heat of polemical battle might lead to editorial timidity and journalistic tiptoeing around issues. The judge who first handled Elmer's case faced an unenviable task in balancing these contending rights.

Elmer's suit came before District Judge Bernard M. Decker. The quirks of Chicago politics led a Democratic president, John F. Kennedy, to appoint Decker, a Republican, to the federal bench. But in Chicago, politics has many quirks, and lawyers considered Judge Decker competent and fair. Decker first ruled in Elmer's favor, denying the Birch Society's motion to dismiss the case. James A. Boyle, a respected Chicago lawyer with no Birch ties, argued without success that calling someone a Communist, even falsely, could not damage them enough to bring a case under federal jurisdiction. Judge Decker cited Illinois cases which upheld claims based on damage to professional reputation. "An allegation of Communist affiliations," Decker held, "must necessarily cast grave doubts" on a lawyer's adherence to American law, and fitness to practice. He set the case for trial before a jury and put the Birch Society in the dock.

Alan Stang, who stuck the "Leninist" label on Elmer Gertz, did not appear at the trial. The Birchers rested their defense on Scott Stanley, managing editor of *American*

Opinion. Stanley had asked Stang, he told the jurors, to visit Chicago and determine whether "the Nuccio murder trial and the publicity around it were part of a continuing Communist effort to blacken the reputation of America's police officers." Not surprisingly, Stang reached the conclusion that Stanley had suggested. The article's purpose, Stanley testified, was to support the Birch Society's "national Support Your Local Police campaign."

Wayne Giampietro, who represented Elmer at the trial, hammered at Stanley's quick-and-dirty editorial work. Under Illinois law, editorial negligence would suffice for libel damages. Stanley admitted that because of deadline pressures he sent Stang's article to the printer "within twenty-four hours" of its submission. Wayne asked if Stanley had any personal knowledge of the facts in the article. "No first-hand knowledge," the editor confessed. "I relied upon Mr. Stang." Had Stanley ever heard of Elmer Gertz before he read Stang's article? The answer was no. Did he personally check any of the charges about Elmer before the article went to press? Again, the answer was no.

Wayne pressed Stanley on whether Elmer's former membership in the National Lawyers Guild justified calling him a "Communist-fronter." Stanley tried to distance himself from the term. He preferred to call the Guild "a Red organization." Weren't the terms synonymous, Wayne asked. Red was known "as early as the French Revolution as the color of International Socialism," Stanley explained. Calling someone a French Revolutionist would not be libelous. But any claim that Elmer had Communist sympathies, Stanley knew, exposed the Birch Society to libel damages. Stang's article, of course, made just that claim.

The next witness caught Boyle and Stanley by surprise. Michael Kachigian identified himself as a Chicago lawyer who knew Elmer Gertz personally. Wayne asked if he knew Elmer's reputation among other lawyers for honesty and integrity. "Very good," Kachigian answered. What about Elmer's reputation as a loyal American? "Excellent." Kachigian had never heard Elmer espouse any Communist ideas. Wayne then asked the witness if he knew Officer Nuccio. "Yes, I do, as his attorney." Wayne then asked if Elmer had been "involved in any way in any prosecution or harassment of Mr. Nuccio." Kachigian had no knowledge of any involvement. Wayne then asked, "Did you ever hear of a man named Alan Stang?" Kachigian's answer struck Boyle and Stanley like a brick. "I don't believe so." Wayne pressed on. "Did Mr. Stang ever contact you about the Nuccio case?" "No." Boyle was so shaken by this testimony that he only asked Kachigian one question: "I'm sorry, I didn't hear your name?"

The trial testimony left Boyle without much defense on the facts. His closing argument reflected this reality. "I think you are entitled," Boyle told the jurors, to presume "that Stang wasn't right in all respects in this case. I don't think there are any two ways about it. As I stand here today, I can speak on behalf of my client and say that we don't think that Elmer Gertz is a Communist." With that concession, and Stang's article on the record, Judge Decker instructed the jurors that Elmer had been libeled and directed them to assess damages. The jury returned quickly with an award of $50,000 against the Birch Society.

Judge Decker promptly took the check out of Elmer's hands. Ruling before the trial that Elmer was not a "public figure" under Supreme Court standards, Decker did not require him to prove "malice" on Stanley's part. After the trial, Decker changed his mind. The murder prosecution of Officer Nuccio, Decker wrote, "commanded wide public attention and interest." Stang's article reflected that interest. "By representing the victim's family in litigation brought against the policeman, Gertz thrust himself into the vortex of this important public controversy." Although Stanley's failure to check the accuracy of Stang's article was negligent, Decker held that "Stanley clearly did not act with actual malice or with reckless disregard for the truth."

Elmer asked the federal appellate court in Chicago to return his award. The judges sat on his appeal for eighteen months and then ruled against him in August 1972. Judge John Paul Stevens, later appointed by President Gerald Ford to the Supreme Court, agreed with Judge Decker that a false statement on a matter of public interest "is protected unless made with knowledge of its falsity or with reckless disregard of its truth or falsity." Stevens noted Stanley's "failure to verify Stang's facts" and his "apparent disposition" to believe that any lawyer who filed suit against a policeman might be a "Communist-fronter." But the trial record showed "no evidence that Stanley actually knew that Stang's article was false," Stevens wrote. Without proof of malice, Elmer could not recover damages for the admitted libel. "We cannot," Stevens concluded, "apply a fundamental protection in one fashion to the New York Times and Time Magazine and in another way to the John Birch Society." Judge Roger Kiley concurred in the decision "with considerable reluctance" because he felt that Stevens had "pushed through" the "outer limits of the First Amendment" and had stripped ordinary citizens of "their personal privacy" (Irons, 1988).

MEET ELMER GERTZ

I was born September 14, 1906 in Chicago, and I've lived in Chicago most of my life. I was born on Blue Island Avenue, on the East Side of Chicago, an area where many immigrant Jews lived in those days. My father, Morris, was a presser with Hart, Schaffner & Marx, and later he opened his own clothing shop. I was the fourth child of six, the third son in a close-knit family. We later moved to the "Back of the Yards" area of the stockyards and slaughterhouses that Upton Sinclair wrote about in *The Jungle.*

My mother died when I was ten, and my younger brother Bob and I were sent for a while to the Jewish Orphans Asylum in Cleveland. Although I later found it difficult to tell people I had lived in an orphanage, it had an excellent school, where I developed my lifelong love of books, and we went to see Tris Speaker and Babe Ruth play baseball at the Indians' park.

Like every good little Jewish boy, I was interested in law. Two experiences in particular helped to push me in that direction. At the time I was about to graduate from high school, I got a bond as a gift. Somewhere in the chain of title, the bond had been stolen. Of course, I knew nothing about it and the person who gave it to me didn't know it. One day in 1924 while I was taking care of my father's clothing store, two plainclothes men who looked like they were going to hold me up came in and arrested me. "Come with us, kid!" was all they said. They took me to another part of the city— didn't permit me to call my father and tell him that I had to leave the store. They must have violated about every right of mine. This was at the time that Loeb and Leopold had been picked up for the kidnapping and murder of Bobby Franks. The captain in the police station noticed I was about the same age as Loeb and Leopold and began talking to me about the case, and was apparently interested in what I had to say. After midnight, he permitted me to call my father. The next day the theft charge against me was thrown out. That had a great effect on me.

A little later, the Sacco—Vanzetti case had a profound impact on me. I was deeply moved by the case of the two immigrant anarchists charged with murder, and I studied all the literature on the case. I felt then and I feel now that they were innocent, and when they were finally killed in 1927, I was terribly shaken.

I graduated from law school just a few months after the stockmarket crash of 1929, and it took me four months to get located in a law firm. I got all of fifteen bucks a week as a lawyer, but it was a politically well-connected firm, the Epstein and Arvey firm. I handled *every* kind of case. They paid me in compliments rather than money! They used to say that I could handle anything in the field of law. I used to get down there at seven in the morning and they'd scold me: "Who expects you to *work* so hard?" I was working to become a lawyer. I handled everything under the sun, and had some very interesting experiences. We had a very big estate that was highly contested, and one day we went to court when the case was being tried. I was carrying the briefcase of the senior partner, McInerney, and when the case was called, McInerney answered, Ready!—and then to my shock he turned to me and said, It's *your* case, Elmer. I was fortunate enough to win the case.

Even before I went to college, I knew Clarence Darrow. I attended lectures of his and corresponded with him. I saw him on behalf of Frank Harris, who asked me to arrange for him to be defended by Darrow if he came to this country and were arrested because of *My Life and Loves*. Darrow agreed to do so. I took very seriously what Darrow had said many times, that you had to be not only a lawyer for your clients, but a friend. And I became that. Some of my dearest friends were clients. I always was very careful in preparation. In the *Tropic of Cancer* case, the head of Grove Press, Barney Rossett, said the extent of my preparation was almost terrifying. In every case, I would never think in terms of what I could afford. I have always worked very hard. Throughout my entire practice, I was always embarrassed by having to charge fees. I never knew what to charge. I was always glad when there was a conventional fee, an hourly fee, or a percentage. My son, who's a very good lawyer in a different field, makes several times more than I ever made in my practice.

My libel case started this way, in 1969. I knew a young woman, Ralla Klepak, who was a lawyer with a criminal practice and who was interested in literature and the theater. She was retained by the family of Ronald Nelson, who was killed by a police officer, Richard Nuccio. She had represented Ronald when he was being persecuted by the police when he was still alive. She asked if I would associate myself with her in the case. I knew nothing about the circumstances of the case, but when she told me what it was all about, I readily agreed, and then I took the lead in the case.

The circumstances of the case were simply outrageous! Ronald Nelson, who was a white kid, may not have been a nice kid in some respects. He and a group of friends that you might call young hoodlums used to frequent this hot-dog place across from the Cubs' park, Wrigley Field, and the owner called in the police. A judge in the juvenile court ordered Nelson and his friends not to go there for six months, and he violated the order, which the judge had no right to enter. When they appeared again, the owner called the police and this Nuccio, who had harassed young Nelson on other occasions, responded. Nelson took off down the alley, and he was ninety feet away when Nuccio shot him in the back and killed him. There was no reason for this cop to think his life was in danger. And the cops planted a knife nearby to cover up the murder!

Shortly after I became attorney with Ralla Klepak the wife of my associate, Mary Giampietro, called me up, all excited. She had been shopping and a pamphlet, a reprint of an article from *American Opinion*, the Birch Society magazine, was thrust upon her. She looked at it and there was a picture of me, and an article dealing with me. So I asked her to come down, and I was very much upset and angered and shocked by this thing. The article accused me of being part of a Communist conspiracy to undermine respect for the police across the country, and being part of a conspiracy to frame Officer Nuccio for Ronald Nelson's murder. The article based these totally false charges on my former membership in the National Lawyers Guild, and referred to me as a "Leninist." A large part of my practice was not civil rights—they were property cases, estates, business matters. I thought that many of my clients could have been prejudiced by these claims about me, so I decided to sue the Birch Society.

My only role in the case was to help Nelson's family get a civil judgment against Officer Nuccio, which we did, but they never recovered because Nuccio had nothing. It was an *absurdity* for the Birch Society to say that I had anything to do with Officer Nuccio's criminal indictment or prosecution or conviction. I didn't have the *slightest* thing to do with it! One of the paradoxical things was that I had been the director of public relations for the Illinois Police Association. I had represented the police on many occasions, including some McCarthyite police, because I thought their civil rights were violated. So it was an absurdity for anyone to say that I was the architect of a communist conspiracy to frame a police officer for murder.

My role in the National Lawyers Guild had a direct effect on my libel case, because the Birch Society article claimed that I actively supported the Communist cause as a Guild officer. I was outraged because they didn't have sense enough to check. Actually, I had not been a Guild member for fifteen years, although I had once been president of the Guild in Chicago, and national vice-president. I became involved almost at the beginning of the Guild in the late 1930s, when Arthur Goldberg was president of the Chicago chapter and the Guild was a very respectable organization. We had presidents of the United States and senators and justices of the Supreme Court speaking at our meetings. I was consulted as the Guild president by the Navy and the State Department about applicants for jobs.

I left the Guild later. When it was attacked by the Un-American Activities Committee, I felt I ought to remain in there. When the Lawyers Guild was admitting blacks and was concerned with New Deal legislation, it was a very useful organization. The American Bar Association and other lawyers' groups wouldn't admit blacks. But when foreign affairs became the Guild's preoccupation, I felt it was losing its effectiveness and I became increasingly impatient. Now, if I had remained a member, I would understand its concern with Vietnam, Central America, and other things, where I feel those foreign-affairs issues are really domestic issues as well.

After I learned of the Birch Society article, my associate, Wayne Giampietro, and I did some research and concluded that we would have a good cause of action for libel. We weren't thinking of the fourteen-and-a-half-year history that would follow. Wayne was a brilliant young attorney whom I had hired originally in connection with the appeal of Jack Ruby from his death sentence for the murder of Lee Harvey Oswald. Wayne was a law student then, and I was so impressed by him that I asked him to join me when he finished law school. This suit illustrated for me what time and place mean. First of all, if they had defamed me at the time of the Leopold case, which was before the Supreme Court decision in New York *Times* versus Sullivan, I was clearly a public figure. I couldn't go anywhere in Chicago without being instantly recognized. People would stop me on the streets and say, How's your client getting along? And then I receded into being an ordinary lawyer. I was well-known in my profession, but nobody on the jury panel had ever heard of me. And if the article had appeared a few weeks later, I would have been a public official, because I was elected as a delegate to the Illinois Constitutional Convention. I learned later that nobody expected me to win, but I did!

One interesting thing about the case is that actually my earnings did not decrease. They went up! And I was elected to public office. But nonetheless, by the Supreme Court test of humiliation, embarrassment, injury to reputation, I did suffer greatly. Nobody knows how many clients I may have lost because of this article. I learned later that some of the board members of the Chicago Bar Association said maybe I was a Communist. Undoubtedly, it had an adverse effect in many quarters.

I've often analyzed, Why did I file this suit? It was a very complicated process. I knew the John Birch Society had called General Marshall and Eisenhower, and others I respected, Communists or Communist influenced. And I felt that *somebody* ought to call a halt to that kind of thing. In a sense, I nominated myself to do the job. If I had been defamed by some obscure group, I might not have done it. But it was the John Birch Society. I knew the effect of Red-baiting and McCarthyism. I never had the feeling that I was a brave character, going forth to fight the John Birch Society. Never in my life did I have a martyr complex. But once I got involved in the case, I was determined to carry it through (Irons, 1988).

MR. JUSTICE POWELL delivered the opinion of the Court.

This Court has struggled for nearly a decade to define the proper accommodation between the law of defamation and the freedoms of speech and press protected by the First Amendment. With this decision we return to that effort. We granted certiorari to reconsider the extent of a publisher's constitutional privilege against liability for defamation of a private citizen.

In 1968 a Chicago policeman named Nuccio shot and killed a youth named Nelson. The state authorities prosecuted Nuccio for the homicide and ultimately obtained a conviction for murder in the second degree. The Nelson family retained petitioner Elmer Gertz, a reputable attorney, to represent them in civil litigation against Nuccio.

Respondent publishes American Opinion, a monthly outlet for the views of the John Birch Society. Early in the 1960's the magazine began to warn of a nationwide conspiracy to discredit local law enforcement agencies and create in their stead a national police force capable of supporting a Communist dictatorship. As part of the continuing effort to alert the public to this assumed danger, the managing editor of American Opinion commissioned an article on the murder trial of Officer Nuccio. For this purpose he engaged a regular contributor to the magazine. In March 1969 respondent published the resulting article under the title "FRAME-UP: Richard Nuccio And The War On Police." The article purports to demonstrate that the testimony against Nuccio at his criminal trial was false and that his prosecution was part of the Communist campaign against the police.

In his capacity as counsel for the Nelson family in the civil litigation, petitioner attended the coroner's inquest into the boy's death and initiated actions for damages, but he neither discussed Officer Nuccio with the press nor played any part in the criminal proceeding. Notwithstanding petitioner's remote connection with the prosecution of Nuccio, respondent's magazine portrayed him as an architect of the "frame-up." According to the article, the police file on petitioner took "a big, Irish cop to lift." The article stated that petitioner had been an official of the "Marxist League for Industrial Democracy, originally known as the Intercollegiate Socialist Society, which has advocated the violent seizure of our government." It labeled Gertz a "Leninist" and a "Communist-fronter." It also stated that Gertz had been an officer of the National Lawyers Guild, described as a Communist organization that "probably did more than any other outfit to plan the Communist attack on the Chicago police during the 1968 Democratic Convention."

These statements contained serious inaccuracies. The implication that petitioner had a criminal record was false. Petitioner had been a member and officer of the National Lawyers Guild some 15 years earlier, but there was no evidence that he or that organization had taken any part in planning the 1968 demonstrations in Chicago. There was also no basis for the charge that petitioner was a "Leninist" or a "Communist-fronter." And he had never been a member of the "Marxist League for Industrial Democracy" or the "Intercollegiate Socialist Society."

The managing editor of American Opinion made no effort to verify or substantiate the charges against petitioner. Instead, he appended an editorial introduction stating that the author had "conducted extensive research into the Richard Nuccio Case." And he included in the article a photograph of petitioner and wrote the caption that appeared under it: "Elmer Gertz of Red Guild harrasses Nuccio." Respondent placed the issue of American Opinion containing the article on sale at newsstands throughout the country and distributed reprints of the article on the streets of Chicago.

Petitioner filed a diversity action for libel in the United States District Court for the Northern District of Illinois. He claimed that the falsehoods published by respondent injured his reputation as a lawyer and a citizen. . . . After answering the complaint, respondent filed a pretrial motion for summary judgment, claiming a constitutional privilege against liability for defamation. It asserted that petitioner was a public official or a public figure and that the article concerned an issue of public interest and concern. For these reasons, respondent argued, it was entitled to invoke the privilege enunciated in New York Times Co. v. Sullivan. Under this rule respondent would escape liability unless petitioner could prove publication of defamatory falsehood "with 'actual malice'—that is, with knowledge that it was false or with reckless disregard of whether it was false or not." Respondent claimed that petitioner could not make such a showing and submitted a supporting affidavit by the magazine's managing editor. The editor denied any knowledge of the falsity of the statements concerning petitioner and stated that he had relied on the author's reputation and on his prior experience with the accuracy and authenticity of the author's contributions to American Opinion. . . .

After all the evidence had been presented but before submission of the case to the jury, the court ruled in effect that petitioner was neither a public official nor a public figure. It added that, if he were, the resulting application of the New York Times standard would require a directed verdict for respondent. Because some statements in the article constituted libel per se under Illinois law, the court submitted the case to the jury under instructions that withdrew from its consideration all issues save the measure of damages. The jury awarded $50,000 to petitioner. . . .

The principal issue in this case is whether a newspaper or broadcaster that publishes defamatory falsehoods about an individual who is neither a public official nor a public figure may claim a constitutional privilege against liability for the injury inflicted by those statements. . . . Under the First Amendment there is no such thing as a false idea. However pernicious an opinion may seem, we depend for its correction not on the conscience of judges and juries but on the competition of other ideas. But there is no constitutional value in false statements of fact. Neither the intentional lie nor the careless error materially advances society's interest in "uninhibited, robust, and wide-open" debate on public issues. New York Times Co. v. Sullivan. They belong to that category of utterances which "are no essential part of any exposition of ideas, and are of such slight social value as a step to truth that any benefit that may be derived from them is clearly outweighed by the social interest in order and morality." Chaplinsky v. New Hampshire. Although the erroneous statement of fact is not worthy of constitutional protection, it is nevertheless inevitable in free debate. And punishment of error runs the risk of inducing a cautious and restrictive exercise of the constitutionally guaranteed freedoms of speech and press. Our decisions recognize that a rule of strict liability that compels a publisher or broadcaster to guarantee the accuracy of his factual assertions may lead to intolerable self-censorship. Allowing the media to avoid liability only by proving the truth of all injurious statements does not accord adequate protection to First Amendment liberties. The First Amendment requires that we protect some falsehood in order to protect speech that matters.

The need to avoid self-censorship by the news media is, however, not the only societal value at issue. If it were, this Court would have embraced long ago the view that publishers and broadcasters enjoy an unconditional and indefeasible immunity from liability for defamation. Such a rule would, indeed, obviate the fear that the prospect of civil liability for injurious falsehood might dissuade a timorous press from the effective exercise of First Amendment freedoms. Yet absolute protection for the communications media requires a total sacrifice of the competing value served by the law of defamation.

The legitimate state interest underlying the law of libel is the compensation of individuals for the harm inflicted on them by defamatory falsehood. . . . Some tension necessarily exists between the need for a vigorous and uninhibited press and the legitimate interest in redressing wrongful injury. . . . The New York Times standard defines the level of constitutional protection appropriate to the context of defamation of a public person. Those who, by reason of the notoriety of their achievements or the vigor and success with which they seek the public's attention, are properly classed as public figures and those who hold governmental office may recover for injury to reputation only on clear and convincing proof that the defamatory falsehood was made with knowledge of its falsity or with reckless disregard for the truth. This standard administers an extremely powerful antidote to the inducement to media self-censorship of the common-law rule of strict liability for libel and slander. And it exacts a correspondingly high price from the victims of defamatory falsehood. Plainly many deserving plaintiffs, including some intentionally subjected to injury, will be unable to surmount the barrier of the New York Times test. . . . For the reasons stated below, we conclude that the state interest in compensating injury to the reputation of private individuals requires that a different rule should obtain with respect to them. . . .

The first remedy of any victim of defamation is self-help—using available opportunities to contradict the lie or correct the error and thereby to minimize its adverse impact on reputation. Public officials and public figures usually enjoy significantly greater access to the channels of effective communication and hence have a more realistic opportunity to counteract false statements than private individuals normally enjoy. Private individuals are therefore more vulnerable to injury, and the state interest in protecting them is correspondingly greater. More important than the likelihood that private individuals will lack effective opportunities for rebuttal, there is a compelling normative consideration underlying the distinction between public and private defamation plaintiffs. An individual who decides to seek governmental office must accept certain necessary consequences of that involvement in public affairs. He runs the risk of closer public scrutiny than might otherwise be the case. And society's interest in the officers of government is not strictly limited to the formal discharge of official duties.

Those classed as public figures stand in a similar position. Hypothetically, it may be possible for someone to become a public figure through no purposeful action of his own, but the instances of truly involuntary public figures must be exceedingly rare. For the most part those who attain this status have assumed roles of especial prominence in the affairs of society. Some occupy positions of such persuasive power and influence that they are deemed public figures for all purposes. More commonly, those classed as public figures have thrust themselves to the forefront of particular public controversies in order to influence the resolution of the issues involved. In either event, they invite attention and comment. . . .

Even if the foregoing generalities do not obtain in every instance, the communications media are entitled to act on the assumption that public officials and public figures have voluntarily exposed themselves to increased risk of injury from defamatory falsehood concerning them. No such assumption is justified with respect to a private individual. He has not accepted public office or assumed an "influential role in ordering society." He has relinquished no part of his interest in the protection of his own good name, and consequently he has a more compelling call on the courts for redress of injury inflicted by defamatory falsehood. Thus, private individuals are not only more vulnerable to injury than public officials and public figures; they are also more deserving of recovery. . . .

We hold that, so long as they do not impose liability without fault, the States may define for themselves the appropriate standard of liability for a publisher or broadcaster of defamatory falsehood injurious to a private individual. This approach provides a more equitable boundary between the competing concerns involved here. It recognizes the strength of the legitimate state interest in compensating private individuals for wrongful injury to reputation, yet shields the press and broadcast media from the rigors of strict liability for defamation. . . .

We therefore conclude that the New York Times standard is inapplicable to this case and that the trial court erred in entering judgment for respondent. Because the jury was allowed to impose liability without fault and was permitted to presume damages without proof of injury, a new trial is necessary. We reverse and remand for further proceedings in accord with this opinion.

Mr. Justice Brennan, dissenting.

The Court does not hold that First Amendment guarantees do not extend to speech concerning private persons' involvement in events of public or general interest. It recognizes that self-governance in this country perseveres because of our "profound national commitment to the principle that debate on public issues should be uninhibited, robust, and wide-open." New York Times v. Sullivan. Thus, guarantees of free speech and press necessarily reach "far more than knowledge and debate about the strictly official activities of various levels of government," for "[f]reedom of discussion, if it would fulfill its historic function in this nation, must embrace all issues about which information is needed or appropriate to enable the members of society to cope with the exigencies of their period." . . .

Although acknowledging that First Amendment values are of no less significance when media reports concern private persons' involvement in matters of public concern, the Court refuses to provide, in such cases, the same level of constitutional protection that has been afforded the media in the context of defamation of public persons. The accommodation that this Court has established between free speech and libel laws in cases involving public officials and public figures—that defamatory falsehood be shown by clear and convincing evidence to have been published with knowledge of falsity or with reckless disregard of truth—is not apt, the Court holds, because the private individual does not have the same degree of access to the media to rebut defamatory comments as does the public person and he has not voluntarily exposed himself to public scrutiny. While these arguments are forcefully and eloquently presented, I cannot accept them. . . .

[T]he argument that private persons should not be required to prove New York Times knowing-or-reckless falsity because they do not assume the risk of defamation by freely entering the public arena "bears little relationship either to the values protected by the First Amendment or to the nature of our society." Social interaction exposes all of us to some degree of public view. This Court has observed that "[t]he risk of this exposure is an essential incident of life in a society which places a primary value on freedom of speech and of press."

We recognized in New York Times Co. v. Sullivan that a rule requiring a critic of official conduct to guarantee the truth of all of his factual contentions would inevitably lead to self-censorship when publishers, fearful of being unable to prove truth or unable to bear the expense of attempting to do so, simply eschewed printing controversial articles. Adoption, by many States, of a reasonable-care standard in cases where private individuals are involved in matters of public interest—the probable result of today's decision—will likewise lead to self-censorship since publishers will be required carefully to weigh a myriad of uncertain factors before publication. The reasonable-care standard . . . saddles the press with "the intolerable burden of guessing how a jury might assess the reasonableness of steps taken by it to verify the accuracy of every reference to a name, picture or portrait." Under a reasonable-care regime, publishers and broadcasters will have to make pre-publication judgments about juror assessment of such diverse considerations as the size, operating procedures, and financial condition of the newsgathering system, as well as the relative costs and benefits of instituting less frequent and more costly reporting at a higher level of accuracy. . . .

The Court does not discount altogether the danger that jurors will punish for the expression of unpopular opinions. This probability accounts for the Court's limitation that "the States may not permit recovery of presumed or punitive damages, at least when liability is not based on a showing of knowledge of falsity or reckless disregard for the truth." But plainly a jury's latitude to impose liability for want of due care poses a far greater threat of suppressing unpopular views than does a possible recovery of presumed or punitive damages. Moreover, the Court's broad-ranging examples of "actual injury," including impairment of reputation and standing in the community, as well as personal humiliation, and mental anguish and suffering, inevitably allow a jury bent on punishing expression of unpopular views a formidable weapon for doing so. Finally, even a limitation of recovery to "actual injury"—however much it reduces the size or frequency of recoveries—will not provide the necessary elbowroom for First Amendment expression. . . .

Since petitioner failed, after having been given a full and fair opportunity, to prove that respondent published the disputed article with knowledge of its falsity or with reckless disregard of the truth, I would affirm the judgment of the Court of Appeals (Irons, 1988).

HUSTLER MAGAZINE V. FALWELL
485 U.S. 46 (1988)

"We conclude that public figures and public officials may not recover for the tort of intentional infliction of emotional distress . . . without showing that the publication contains a false statement of fact which was made with . . . knowledge that the statement was false or with reckless disregard as to whether or not it was true."

The Question: Can a prominent public figure, who is a Baptist minister, recover damages for the "intentional infliction of emotional distress" against the publisher of a magazine that ran a so-called parody ad alleging that the minister's first sexual experience was with his mother in an outhouse while he was drunk?

The Arguments: PRO

The advertisement in question looked almost exactly like those for a popular liqueur, Campari, and duplicated the format and style of real Campari ads. The phrase "parody ad" was printed in very small type at the bottom of the page in *Hustler Magazine* and could easily be overlooked by readers. The Rev. Jerry Falwell has achieved prominence as a minister and as the founder of the organization called Moral Majority. His reputation as a moral person was seriously damaged by charges that he engaged in sex with his mother, and the publisher should have known that this ad, even meant as a parody, would inflict great emotional distress on Falwell. The First Amendment does not protect those who engage in such acts of gratuitous cruelty.

CON

There is a long tradition in the press, going back to colonial times, of cartoons and other forms of ridicule and parody. Political leaders such as Abraham Lincoln and Franklin Roosevelt were lampooned, often in bad taste and with cruel intent. Thus, prominent public figures such as Rev. Falwell should expect to endure such treatment in the press. In this case, Falwell is a natural target for parody for leading a group called the Moral Majority. Those who disagree with his political views, including the publisher of *Hustler*, are likely to poke fun at him by suggesting that he has engaged in immoral behavior. In addition, the ad was clearly labeled as a parody, and it is unlikely that *Hustler* readers actually believed what was in the ad.

BACKGROUND:
"THE FIRST AMENDMENT ON TRIAL"

"Reverend Falwell, have you seen this?"

The question was put to Jerry Falwell by a reporter as Falwell was leaving a Washington, D.C., news conference in November of 1983. The reporter was brandishing the latest edition of *Hustler Magazine*.

Falwell was in a hurry; he quickly glanced at the cover of *Hustler* in the reporter's hand and shrugged off the question. "That is probably nothing new," he said, walking away.

When Falwell returned that day to his hometown in Lynchburg, Virginia, however, he decided that perhaps he ought to take a closer look. He asked a staff member to buy a current issue of *Hustler* (one cannot imagine Jerry Falwell *himself* in line at the local 7-Eleven with a copy in his hand), and when he got the magazine, he opened it to the front inside cover. Falwell then saw what appeared to be, at its first embarrassing blush, an advertisement for Campari Liqueur, with himself as the featured celebrity endorsing the product! Falwell was stunned. But the initial shock was nothing compared to the wave of disgust he felt as he read the Campari ad more closely. Entitled "Jerry Falwell talks about his first time," it includes a picture of Falwell, an illustration of a Campari bottle next to a glass of Campari on the rocks, and an "interview" in which Falwell describes his "first time":

FALWELL: My first time was in an outhouse outside Lynchburg, Virginia.

INTERVIEWER: Wasn't it a little cramped?

FALWELL: Not after I kicked the goat out.

INTERVIEWER: I see. You must tell me all about it.

FALWELL: I never *really* expected to make it with Mom, but then after she showed all the other guys in town such a good time, I figured, "What the hell!"

INTERVIEWER: But your mom? Isn't that a bit odd?

FALWELL: I don't think so. Looks don't mean that much to me in a woman.

INTERVIEWER: Go on.

FALWELL: Well, we were drunk off our God-fearing asses on Campari, ginger ale and soda—that's called a Fire and Brimstone—at the time. And Mom looked better than a Baptist whore with a $100 donation.

INTERVIEWER: Campari in the crapper with Mom . . . how interesting. Well, how was it?

FALWELL: The Campari was great, but Mom passed out before I could come.

INTERVIEWER: Did you ever try it again?

FALWELL: Sure . . . lots of times. But not in the outhouse. Between Mom and the shit, the flies were too much to bear.

INTERVIEWER: We meant the Campari.

FALWELL: Oh, yeah. I always get sloshed before I go out to the pulpit. You don't think I could lay down all that bullshit *sober*, do you?

Located below the "interview" is an additional paragraph purporting to tout the merits of Campari:

Campari, like all liquor, was made to mix you up. It's a light, 48-proof, refreshing spirit, just mild enough to make you drink too much before you know you're schnockered. For your first time, mix it with orange juice. Or maybe some white wine. Then you won't remember anything the next morning. *Campari. The mixable that smarts.*

The ad ends with the catchline "Campari. You'll never forget your first time."

This page in *Hustler*'s November issue is listed in its table of contents (yes, *Hustler* has a table of contents) as "Fiction. Ad & Personality Parody." At the very top of the ad, following the title "Jerry Falwell talks about his first time," a small asterisk appears. At the bottom of the page, the asterisk is repeated with a disclaiming footnote that says, in, relatively fine print: "Ad Parody—Not to Be Taken Seriously."

Jerry Falwell, however, took it quite seriously— "As seriously," he said, "as anything I have ever read in my life." Falwell was outraged. "I think I have never been as angry as I was at that moment," he said. "I somehow felt that in all of my life I had never believed that human beings could do something like this. I really felt like weeping." Instead of weeping, however, Falwell commenced a $45 million lawsuit against *Hustler* and its publisher, Larry Flynt.

The lawsuit *Jerry Falwell v. Larry Flynt and Hustler Magazine* is destined to be an American classic. It is one of those few cases selected each year for resolution by the United States Supreme Court, but the majesty of a final decision by the Supreme Court is only a small part of what makes the case *Falwell v. Flynt* one of the most extraordinary legal battles in recent memory. The case was at once high moral drama and farcical passion play, a tragicomic mélange of bombastic lawyers, contemptuous witnesses, and scathing cross-examinations. The case became much more than a battle of lawyers over the legal consequences of a dirty joke. It was also a cultural battle: Presenting to the Supreme Court deep conflicts reaching into the very soul of the American First Amendment tradition, the case involved a battle over the very nature of free expression in a pluralistic society, a battle over competing visions of American life.

The jurors saw Falwell spin out before them his entire vision of a morally rejuvenated America and heard conservative North Carolina Senator Jesse Helms take the stand as a character witness to praise Falwell as one of the greatest living Americans. The jurors also came to know Larry Flynt "up close and personal." They saw Flynt, in deposition testimony, stubbornly refusing to use Falwell's correct name, insisting instead on calling him "Farwell." And they heard wild exchanges between Flynt and Falwell's lawyer, Norman Roy Grutman.

"To save a lot of time," they heard Flynt say, "why don't you just ask them questions direct, so we can get to the meat of things."

"Well," Grutman responded, "I'm trying. I have to do—"

"I'm talking about Farwell fucking his mother," Flynt interrupted.

"Let's talk about Jerry and his mother. Just get right to the meat of it."

"Talk about whom?"

"Jerry Farwell."

"And his what?"

"And his mother, about him fucking his mother in the outhouse, you know, let's just get—"

"Well, I'm going to come to that in a moment. You know that I'm here for that purpose."

Many other witnesses appeared in the trial, but Falwell and Flynt jointly held center stage, and their performances dominated the case. The trial was the sort of political and cultural drama that periodically plays itself out in American courtrooms, reminiscent of Tennessee's Scopes "Monkey Trial" of 1925 or the battle between Abbie Hoffman and his cohorts against Judge Julius J. Hoffman and Mayor Richard J. Daley in the "Chicago Seven" trial, which arose from the violence at the 1968 Chicago Democratic National Convention. The drama was heightened by the personalities of the two principal trial lawyers—Norman Roy Grutman for Falwell and Alan Isaacman for Flynt. Grutman bombarded the jury at every turn with righteous indignation at the horrible, sleazy sinfulness of Larry Flynt. Isaacman fought back valiantly, against all odds, desperately trying to achieve the litigation upset of the century, a victory for Larry Flynt and *Hustler Magazine* against Reverend Jerry Falwell in Roanoke, Virginia, only a short distance from Falwell's Lynchburg, Virginia, home.

The wild circus of a trial in Roanoke was followed by an appeal to a federal appellate court, the United States Court of Appeals for the Fourth Circuit, and finally by a decision in the nation's highest tribunal, the United States Supreme Court. These appellate decisions took the raw, violent confrontations of the trial and distilled from them several of the most profound freedom-of-speech questions ever decided by American courts, questions that reach to the very heart of the type of nation we want to be (Smolla, 1988).

CHIEF JUSTICE REHNQUIST delivered the opinion of the Court.

Petitioner Hustler Magazine, Inc., is a magazine of nation-wide circulation. Respondent Jerry Falwell, a nationally known minister who has been active as a commentator on politics and public affairs, sued petitioner and its publisher, petitioner Larry Flynt, to recover damages for invasion of privacy, libel, and intentional infliction of emotional distress. The District Court directed a verdict against respondent on the privacy claim, and submitted the other two claims to a jury. The jury found for petitioners on the defamation claim, but found for respondent on the claim for intentional infliction of emotional distress and awarded damages. We now consider whether this award is consistent with the First and Fourteenth Amendments of the United States Constitution.

The inside front cover of the November 1983 issue of Hustler Magazine featured a "parody"of an advertisement for Campari Liqueur that contained the name and picture of respondent and was entitled "Jerry Falwell talks about his first time." This parody was modeled after actual Campari ads that included interviews with various celebrities about their "first times." Although it was apparent by the end of each interview that this meant the first time they sampled Campari, the ads clearly played on the sexual double entendre of the general subject of "first times." Copying the form and layout of these Campari ads, Hustler's editors chose respondent as the featured celebrity and drafted an alleged "interview" with him in which he states that his "first time" was during a drunken incestuous rendezvous with his mother in an outhouse. The Hustler parody portrays respondent and his mother as drunk and immoral, and suggests that respondent is a hypocrite who preaches only when he is drunk. In small print at the bottom of the page, the ad contains the disclaimer, "ad parody—not to be taken seriously." The magazine's table of contents also lists the ad as "Fiction; Ad and Personality Parody."

Soon after the November issue of Hustler became available to the public, respondent brought this diversity action in the United States District Court for the Western District of Virginia against Hustler Magazine, Inc., Larry C. Flynt, and Flynt Distributing Co., Inc. Respondent stated in his complaint that publication of the ad parody in Hustler entitled him to recover damages for libel, invasion of privacy, and intentional infliction of emotional distress. The case proceeded to trial. At the close of the evidence, the District Court granted a directed verdict for petitioners on the invasion of privacy claim. The jury then found against respondent on the libel claim, specifically finding that the ad parody could not "reasonably be understood as describing actual facts about [respondent] or actual events in which [he] partici-

pated." The jury ruled for respondent on the intentional infliction of emotional distress claim, however, and stated that he should be awarded $100,000 in compensatory damages, as well as $50,000 each in punitive damages from petitioners. Petitioners' motion for judgment notwithstanding the verdict was denied.

On appeal, the United States Court of Appeals for the Fourth Circuit affirmed the judgment against petitioners. . . . Given the importance of the constitutional issues involved, we granted certiorari.

This case presents us with a novel question involving First Amendment limitations upon a State's authority to protect its citizens from the intentional infliction of emotional distress. We must decide whether a public figure may recover damages for emotional harm caused by the publication of an ad parody offensive to him, and doubtless gross and repugnant in the eyes of most. Respondent would have us find that a State's interest in protecting public figures from emotional distress is sufficient to deny First Amendment protection to speech that is patently offensive and is intended to inflict emotional injury, even when that speech could not reasonably have been interpreted as stating actual facts about the public figure involved. This we decline to do.

At the heart of the First Amendment is the recognition of the fundamental importance of the free flow of ideas and opinions on matters of public interest and concern. "[T]he freedom to speak one's mind is not only an aspect of individual liberty—and thus a good unto itself—but also is essential to the common quest for truth and the vitality of society as a whole." We have therefore been particularly vigilant to ensure that individual expressions of ideas remain free from governmentally imposed sanctions. The First Amendment recognizes no such thing as a "false" idea. As Justice Holmes wrote, "when men have realized that time has upset many fighting faiths, they may come to believe even more than they believe the very foundations of their own conduct that the ultimate good desired is better reached by free trade in ideas—that the best test of truth is the power of the thought to get itself accepted in the competition of the market. . . ." Abrams v. United States.

The sort of robust political debate encouraged by the First Amendment is bound to produce speech that is critical of those who hold public office or those public figures who are "intimately involved in the resolution of important public questions or, by reason of their fame, shape events in areas of concern to society at large." Such criticism, inevitably, will not always be reasoned or moderate; public figures as well as public officials will be subject to "vehement, caustic, and sometimes unpleasantly sharp attacks." New York Times.

Of course, this does not mean that any speech about a public figure is immune from sanction in the form of damages. Since New York Times Co. v. Sullivan, we have consistently ruled that a public figure may hold a speaker liable for the damage to reputation caused by publication of a defamatory falsehood, but only if the statement was made "with knowledge that it was false or with reckless disregard of whether it was false or not." False statements of fact are particularly valueless; they interfere with the truth-seeking function of the marketplace of ideas, and they cause damage to an individual's reputation that cannot easily be repaired by counterspeech, however persuasive or effective. See Gertz. But even though falsehoods have little value in and of themselves, they are "nevertheless inevitable in free debate," and a rule that would impose strict liability on a publisher for false factual assertions would have an undoubted "chilling" effect on speech relating to public figures that does have constitutional value. "Freedoms of expression require" breathing space. "This breathing space is provided by a constitutional rule that allows public figures to recover for libel or defamation only when they can prove both that the statement was false and that the statement was made with the requisite level of culpability.

Respondent argues, however, that a different standard should apply in this case because here the State seeks to prevent not reputational damage, but the severe emotional distress suffered by the person who is the subject of an offensive publication. In respondent's view, and in the view of the Court of Appeals, so long as the utterance was intended to inflict emotional distress, was outrageous, and did in fact inflict serious emotional distress, it is of no constitutional import whether the statement was a fact or an opinion, or whether it was true or false. It is the intent to cause injury that is the gravamen of the tort, and the State's interest in preventing emotional harm simply outweighs whatever interest a speaker may have in speech of this type.

Generally speaking the law does not regard the intent to inflict emotional distress as one which should receive much solicitude, and it is quite understandable that most if not all jurisdictions have chosen to make it civilly culpable where the conduct in question is sufficiently "outrageous." But in the world of debate about public affairs, many things done with motives that are less than admirable are protected by the First Amendment. . . . Thus while such a bad motive may be deemed controlling for purposes of tort liability in other areas of the law, we think the First Amendment prohibits such a result in the area of public debate about public figures.

Were we to hold otherwise, there can be little doubt that political cartoonists and satirists would be subjected to damage awards without any showing that their work falsely defamed its subject. . . . The appeal of the political cartoon or caricature is often based on exploitation of unfortunate physical traits or politically embarrassing events—an exploitation often calculated to injure the feelings of the subject of the portrayal. The art of the cartoonist is often not reasoned or evenhanded, but slashing and one-sided. . . .

Several famous examples of this type of intentionally injurious speech were drawn by Thomas Nast, probably the greatest American cartoonist to date, who was associated for many years during the post–Civil War era with Harper's Weekly. In the pages of that publication Nast conducted a graphic vendetta against William M. "Boss" Tweed and his corrupt associates in New York City's "Tweed Ring." It has been described by one historian of the subject as "a sustained attack which in its passion and effectiveness stands alone in the history of American graphic art." . . .

Despite their sometimes caustic nature, from the early cartoon portraying George Washington as an ass down to the present day, graphic depictions and satirical cartoons have played a prominent role in public and political debate. Nast's castigation of the Tweed Ring . . . and numerous other efforts have undoubtedly had an effect on the course and outcome of contemporaneous debate. Lincoln's tall, gangling posture, Teddy Roosevelt's glasses and teeth, and Franklin D. Roosevelt's jutting jaw and cigarette holder have been memorialized by political cartoons with an effect that could not have been obtained by the photographer or the portrait artist. From the viewpoint of history it is clear that our political discourse would have been considerably poorer without them.

Respondent contends, however, that the caricature in question here was so "outrageous" as to distinguish it from more traditional political cartoons. There is no doubt that the caricature of respondent and his mother published in Hustler is at best a distant cousin of the political cartoons described above, and a rather poor relation at that. If it were possible by laying down a principled standard to separate the one from the other, public discourse would probably suffer little or no harm. But we doubt that there is any such standard, and we are quite sure that the pejorative description "outrageous" does not supply one. "Outrageousness" in the area of political and social discourse has an inherent subjectiveness about it which would allow a jury to impose liability on the basis of the jurors' tastes or views, or perhaps on the basis of their dislike of a particular expression. An "outrageousness" standard thus runs afoul of our longstanding refusal to allow damages to be awarded because the speech in question may have an adverse emotional impact on the audience.

We conclude that public figures and public officials may not recover for the tort of intentional infliction of emotional distress by reason of publications such as the one here at issue without showing in addition that the publication contains a false statement of fact which was made with "actual malice," i.e., with knowledge that the statement was false or with reckless disregard as to whether or not it was true. This is not merely a "blind application" of the New York Times standard, it reflects our considered judgment that such a standard is necessary to give adequate "breathing space" to the freedoms protected by the First Amendment.

Here it is clear that respondent Falwell is a "public figure" for purposes of First Amendment law. The jury found against respondent on his libel claim when it decided that the Hustler ad parody could not "reasonably be understood as describing actual facts about [respondent] or actual events in which [he] participated." . . . Respondent is thus relegated to his claim for damages awarded by the jury for the intentional infliction of emotional distress by "outrageous" conduct. But for reasons heretofore stated this claim cannot, consistently with the First Amendment, form a basis for the award of damages when the conduct in question is the publication of a caricature such as the ad parody involved here. The judgment of the Court of Appeals is accordingly reversed.

SECTION 4

〜〜

OBSCENITY: BOOKS, MAGAZINES, FILMS, DANCING, AND COMPUTERS

ROTH V. UNITED STATES
354 U.S. 476 (1957)*

"All ideas having even the slightest redeeming social importance—unorthodox ideas, controversial ideas, even ideas hateful to the prevailing climate of opinion—have the full protection of the [First Amendment] guaranties, unless excludable because they encroach upon the limited area of more important interests. But implicit in the history of the First Amendment is the rejection of obscenity as utterly without redeeming social importance."

The Question: Can the states and Congress pass laws that make it a criminal offense to publish, sell, or distribute material that is found by a jury to be obscene?

The Arguments: PRO

The sole purpose of obscenity is to arouse lustful thoughts and to detract from the normal enjoyment and practice of sex. Furthermore, there is considerable evidence that exposure to obscenity is associated with immoral behavior and the sexual abuse of women and children. The Supreme Court has ruled that obscenity is a category of speech that is not protected by the First Amendment because it is "no essential part of any exposition of ideas" and undermines society's interest in morality. Although it may be difficult to define obscenity with precision, the law should allow jurors to rely on their common sense in deciding if a book, magazine, or film is obscene.

CON

Laws that prohibit the distribution of obscenity are reflections of Victorian notions of morality, in which sex is considered "dirty" and having "lustful thoughts" is abnormal and perverted. In fact, the research of reputable scientists such as Alfred Kinsey shows that most adults engage in sexual behavior that would be considered "obscene" under the laws in question. Portraying this behavior in words or pictures has been done since the early days of Greece and Rome, and efforts to stamp out depictions of sexuality as "obscene" have always failed. In addition, definitions of obscenity are impossible to draft with enough precision to avoid punishing the publishers of works that have undoubted artistic or literary merit.

MR. JUSTICE BRENNAN delivered the opinion of the Court.

The constitutionality of a criminal obscenity statute is the question in each of these cases. In Roth, the primary constitutional question is whether the federal obscenity statute violates the provision of the First Amendment that "Congress shall make no law . . . abridging the freedom of speech, or of the press. . . ." In Alberts, the primary constitutional question is whether the obscenity provisions of the California Penal Code invade the freedoms of speech and press as they may be incorporated in the liberty protected

---
*Together with **Alberts v. California,** appeal from the Superior Court of California, Los Angeles County, Appellate Department.

from state action by the Due Process Clause of the Fourteenth Amendment. . . .

Roth conducted a business in New York in the publication and sale of books, photographs and magazines. He used circulars and advertising matter to solicit sales. He was convicted by a jury in the District Court for the Southern District of New York upon 4 counts of a 26-count indictment charging him with mailing obscene circulars and advertising, and an obscene book, in violation of the federal obscenity statute. His conviction was affirmed by the Court of Appeals for the Second Circuit. Alberts conducted a mail-order business from Los Angeles. He was convicted by the Judge of the Municipal Court of the Beverly Hills Judicial District (having waived a jury trial) under a misdemeanor complaint which charged him with lewdly keeping for sale obscene and indecent books, and with writing, composing and publishing an obscene advertisement of them, in violation of the California Penal Code. The conviction was affirmed by the Appellate Department of the Superior Court of the State of California in and for the County of Los Angeles.

The dispositive question is whether obscenity is utterance within the area of protected speech and press. Although this is the first time the question has been squarely presented to this Court, either under the First Amendment or under the Fourteenth Amendment, expressions found in numerous opinions indicate that this Court has always assumed that obscenity is not protected by the freedoms of speech and press. Chaplinsky v. New Hampshire. . . .

[I]t is apparent that the unconditional phrasing of the First Amendment was not intended to protect every utterance. This phrasing did not prevent this Court from concluding that libelous utterances are not within the area of constitutionally protected speech. At the time of the adoption of the First Amendment, obscenity law was not as fully developed as libel law, but there is sufficiently contemporaneous evidence to show that obscenity, too, was outside the protection intended for speech and press. . . .

All ideas having even the slightest redeeming social importance—unorthodox ideas, controversial ideas, even ideas hateful to the prevailing climate of opinion—have the full protection of the guaranties, unless excludable because they encroach upon the limited area of more important interests. But implicit in the history of the First Amendment is the rejection of obscenity as utterly without redeeming social importance. This rejection for that reason is mirrored in the universal judgment that obscenity should be restrained, reflected in the international agreement of over 50 nations, in the obscenity laws of all of the 48 States, and in the 20 obscenity laws enacted by the Congress from 1842 to 1956. This is the same judgment expressed by this Court in Chaplinsky v. New Hampshire:

> There are certain well-defined and narrowly limited classes of speech, the prevention and punishment of which have never been thought to raise any Constitutional problem. These include the lewd and obscene. . . . It has been well observed that such utterances are no essential part of any exposition of ideas, and are of such slight social value as a step to truth that any benefit that may be derived from them is clearly outweighed by the social interest in order and morality. . . .

We hold that obscenity is not within the area of constitutionally protected speech or press. It is strenuously urged that these obscenity statutes offend the constitutional guaranties because they punish incitation to impure sexual thoughts, not shown to be related to any overt antisocial conduct which is or may be incited in the persons stimulated to such thoughts. . . . It is insisted that the constitutional guaranties are violated because convictions may be had without proof either that obscene material will perceptibly create a clear and present danger of antisocial conduct, or will probably induce its recipients to such conduct. . . .

However, sex and obscenity are not synonymous. Obscene material is material which deals with sex in a manner appealing to prurient interest. The portrayal of sex, e.g., in art, literature and scientific works, is not itself sufficient reason to deny material the constitutional protection of freedom of speech and press. Sex, a great and mysterious motive force in human life, has indisputably been a subject of absorbing interest to mankind through the ages; it is one of the vital problems of human interest and public concern. . . .

The fundamental freedoms of speech and press have contributed greatly to the development and well-being of our free society and are indispensable to its continued growth. Ceaseless vigilance is the watchword to prevent their erosion by Congress or by the States. The door barring federal and state intrusion into this area cannot be left ajar; it must be kept tightly closed and opened only the slightest crack necessary to prevent encroachment upon more important interests. It is therefore vital that the standards for judging obscenity safeguard the protection of freedom of speech and press for material which does not treat sex in a manner appealing to prurient interest. . . .

The early leading standard of obscenity allowed material to be judged merely by the effect of an isolated excerpt upon particularly susceptible persons. Regina v. Hicklin, 1868. Some American courts adopted this standard but later decisions have rejected it and substituted this test: whether to the average person, applying contemporary community standards, the dominant theme of the material taken as a whole appeals to prurient interest. The Hicklin test, judging obscenity by the effect of isolated passages upon the most susceptible persons, might well encompass material legitimately treating with sex, and so it must be rejected as unconstitutionally restrictive of the freedoms of speech and press. On the other hand, the substituted standard provides safeguards adequate to withstand the charge of constitutional infirmity. . . .

In summary, then, we hold that these statutes, applied according to the proper standard for judging obscenity, do not offend constitutional safeguards against convictions based upon protected material, or fail to give men in acting adequate notice of what is prohibited. . . . The judgments are affirmed.

MR. JUSTICE DOUGLAS, with whom MR. JUSTICE BLACK concurs, dissenting.

When we sustain these convictions, we make the legality of a publication turn on the purity of thought which a book or tract instills in the mind of the reader. I do not think we can approve that standard and be faithful to the command of the First Amendment, which by its terms is a restraint on Congress and which by the Fourteenth is a restraint on the States.

In the Roth case the trial judge charged the jury that the statutory words "obscene, lewd and lascivious" describe "that form of immorality which has relation to sexual impurity and has a tendency to excite lustful thoughts." He stated that the term "filthy" in the statute pertains "to that sort of treatment of sexual matters in such a vulgar and indecent way, so that it tends to arouse a feeling of disgust and revulsion." He went on to say that the material "must be calculated to corrupt and debauch the minds and morals" of "the average person in the community," not those of any particular class. "You judge the circulars, pictures and publications which have been put in evidence by present-day standards of the community. You may ask yourselves does it offend the common conscience of the community by present-day standards."

The trial judge who, sitting without a jury, heard the Alberts case and the appellate court that sustained the judgment of conviction, took California's definition of "obscenity" from People v. Wepplo. That case held that a book is obscene "if it has a substantial tendency to deprave or corrupt its readers by inciting lascivious thoughts or arousing lustful desire."

By these standards punishment is inflicted for thoughts provoked, not for overt acts nor antisocial conduct. This test cannot be squared with our decisions under the First Amendment. Even the ill-starred Dennis case conceded that speech to be punishable must have some relation to action which could be penalized by government. This issue cannot be avoided by saying that obscenity is not protected by the First Amendment. The question remains, what is the constitutional test of obscenity? . . .

The test of obscenity the Court endorses today gives the censor free range over a vast domain. To allow the State to step in and punish mere speech or publication that the judge or the jury thinks has an undesirable impact on thoughts but that is not shown to be a part of unlawful action is drastically to curtail the First Amendment. . . . If we were certain that impurity of sexual thoughts impelled to action, we would be on less dangerous ground in punishing the distributors of this sex literature. But it is by no means clear that obscene literature, as so defined, is a significant factor in influencing substantial deviations from the community standards.

The absence of dependable information on the effect of obscene literature on human conduct should make us wary. It should put us on the side of protecting society's interest in literature, except and unless it can be said that the particular publication has an impact on action that the government can control.

As noted, the trial judge in the Roth case charged the jury in the alternative that the federal obscenity statute outlaws literature dealing with sex which offends "the common conscience of the community." That standard is, in my view, more inimical still to freedom of expression. . . . The standard of what offends "the common conscience of the community" conflicts, in my judgment, with the command of the First Amendment that "Congress shall make no law . . . abridging the freedom of speech, or of the press." Certainly that standard would not be an acceptable one if religion, economics, politics or philosophy were involved. How does it become a constitutional standard when literature treating with sex is concerned?

Any test that turns on what is offensive to the community's standards is too loose, too capricious, too destructive of freedom of expression to be squared with the First Amendment. Under that test, juries can censor, suppress, and punish what they don't like, provided the matter relates to "sexual impurity" or has a tendency "to excite lustful thoughts." This is community censorship in one of its worst forms. It creates a regime where in the battle between the literati and the Philistines, the Philistines are certain to win. If experience in this field teaches anything, it is that "censorship of obscenity has almost always been both irrational and indiscriminate." The test adopted here accentuates that trend. . . .

The legality of a publication in this country should never be allowed to turn either on the purity of thought which it instills in the mind of the reader or on the degree to which it offends the community conscience. By either test the role of the censor is exalted, and society's values in literary freedom are sacrificed.

The Court today suggests a third standard. It defines obscene material as that "which deals with sex in a manner appealing to prurient interest." Like the standards applied by the trial judges below, that standard does not require any nexus between the literature which is prohibited and action which the legislature can regulate or prohibit. Under the First Amendment, that standard is no more valid than those which the courts below adopted.

I do not think that the problem can be resolved by the Court's statement that "obscenity is not expression protected by the First Amendment." With the exception of Beauharnais v. Illinois, none of our cases has resolved problems of free speech and free press by placing any form of expression beyond the pale of the absolute prohibition of the First Amendment. Unlike the law of libel, wrongfully relied on in Beauharnais, there is no special historical evidence that literature dealing with sex was intended to be treated in a special manner by those who drafted the First Amendment. In fact, the first reported court decision in this country involving obscene literature was in 1821. I reject too the implication that problems of freedom of speech and of the press are to be resolved by weighing against the values of free expression, the judgment of the Court that a particular form of that expression has "no redeeming social importance." The First Amendment, its prohibition in terms absolute, was designed to preclude courts as well as legislatures from weighing the values of speech against silence. The First Amendment puts free speech in the preferred position.

Freedom of expression can be suppressed if, and to the extent that, it is so closely brigaded with illegal action as to be an inseparable part of it. As a people, we cannot afford to relax that standard. For the test that suppresses a cheap tract today can suppress a literary gem tomorrow. All it need do is to incite a lascivious thought or arouse a lustful desire. The list of books that judges or juries can place in that category is endless. I would give the broad sweep of the First Amendment full support. I have the same confidence in the ability of our people to reject noxious literature as I have in their capacity to sort out the true from the false in theology, economics, politics, or any other field.

MILLER V. CALIFORNIA
413 U.S. 15 (1973)

"Sex and nudity may not be exploited without limit by films or pictures exhibited or sold in places of public accommodation any more than live sex and nudity can be exhibited or sold without limit in such public places. At a minimum, prurient, patently offensive depiction or description of sexual conduct must have serious literary, artistic, political, or scientific value to merit First Amendment protection."

MR. CHIEF JUSTICE BURGER delivered the opinion of the Court.

This is one of a group of "obscenity-pornography" cases being reviewed by the Court in a re-examination of standards enunciated in earlier cases involving what Mr. Justice Harlan called "the intractable obscenity problem." Appellant conducted a mass mailing campaign to advertise the sale of illustrated books, euphemistically called "adult" material. After a jury trial, he was convicted of violating California Penal Code by knowingly distributing obscene matter, and the Appellate Department, Superior Court of California, County of Orange, summarily affirmed the judgment without opinion. Appellant's conviction was specifically based on his conduct in causing five unsolicited advertising brochures to be sent through the mail in an envelope addressed to a restaurant in Newport Beach, California. The envelope was opened by the manager of the restaurant and his mother. They had not requested the brochures; they complained to the police.

The brochures advertise four books entitled "Intercourse," "Man-Woman," "Sex Orgies Illustrated," and "An Illustrated History of Pornography," and a film entitled "Marital Intercourse." While the brochures contain some descriptive printed material, primarily they consist of pictures and drawings very explicitly depicting men and women in groups of two or more engaging in a variety of sexual activities, with genitals often prominently displayed.

This case involves the application of a State's criminal obscenity statute to a situation in which sexually explicit materials have been thrust by aggressive sales action upon unwilling recipients who had in no way indicated any desire to receive such materials. This Court has recognized that the States have a legitimate interest in prohibiting dissemination or exhibition of obscene material when the mode of dissemination carries with it a significant danger of offending the sensibilities of unwilling recipients or of exposure to juveniles. It is in this context that we are called on to define the standards which must be used to identify obscene material that a State may regulate without infringing on the First Amendment as applicable to the States through the Fourteenth Amendment. . . .

[S]ince the Court now undertakes to formulate standards more concrete than those in the past, it is useful for us to focus on two of the landmark cases in the somewhat tortured history of the Court's obscenity decisions. In Roth v. United States the Court sustained a conviction under a federal statute punishing the mailing of "obscene, lewd, lascivious or filthy . . ." materials. The key to that holding was the Court's rejection of the claim that obscene materials were protected by the First Amendment. Five Justices joined in the opinion stating: "All ideas having even the slightest redeeming social importance—unorthodox ideas, controversial ideas, even ideas hateful to the prevailing climate of opinion—have the full protection of the [First Amendment] guaranties, unless excludable because they encroach upon the limited area of more important interests. But implicit in the history of the First Amendment is the rejection of obscenity as utterly without redeeming social importance. . . . We hold that obscenity is not within the area of constitutionally protected speech or press."

Nine years later, in Memoirs v. Massachusetts, the Court veered sharply away from the Roth concept and, with only three Justices in the plurality opinion, articulated a new test of obscenity. The plurality held that under the Roth definition "as elaborated in subsequent cases, three elements must coalesce: it must be established that (a) the dominant theme of the material taken as a whole appeals to a prurient interest in sex; (b) the material is patently offensive because it affronts contemporary community standards relating to the description or representation of sexual matters; and (c) the material is utterly without redeeming social value.". . .

While Roth presumed "obscenity" to be "utterly without redeeming social importance," Memoirs required that to prove obscenity it must be affirmatively established that the material is "utterly without redeeming social value." Thus, even as they repeated the words of Roth, the Memoirs plurality produced a drastically altered test that called on the prosecution to prove a negative, i.e., that the material was "utterly without redeeming social value"—a burden virtually impossible to discharge under our criminal standards of proof. Such considerations caused Mr. Justice Harlan to wonder if the "utterly without redeeming social value" test had any meaning at all.

Apart from the initial formulation in the Roth case, no majority of the Court has at any given time been able to agree on a standard to determine what constitutes obscene, pornographic material subject to regulation under the States' police power. We have seen "a variety of views among the members of the Court unmatched in any other course of constitutional adjudication." This is not remarkable, for in the area of freedom of speech and press the courts must always remain sensitive to any infringement on genuinely serious literary, artistic, political, or scientific expression. This is an area in which there are few eternal verities. . . .

We acknowledge . . . the inherent dangers of undertaking to regulate any form of expression. State statutes designed to regulate obscene materials must be carefully limited. As a result, we now confine the permissible scope of such regulation to works which depict or describe sexual conduct. That conduct must be specifically defined by the applicable state law, as written or authoritatively construed. A state offense must also be limited to works which, taken as a whole, appeal to the prurient interest in sex, which portray sexual conduct in a patently offensive way, and which, taken as a whole, do not have serious literary, artistic, political, or scientific value.

The basic guidelines for the trier of fact must be: (a) whether "the average person, applying contemporary community standards" would find that the work, taken as a whole, appeals to the prurient interest; (b) whether the work depicts or describes, in a patently offensive way, sexual conduct specifically defined by the applicable state law; and (c) whether the work, taken as a whole, lacks serious literary, artistic, political, or scientific value. . . . If a state law that regulates obscene material is thus limited, as written or construed, the First Amendment values applicable to the States through the Fourteenth Amendment are adequately protected by the ultimate power of appellate courts to conduct an independent review of constitutional claims when necessary.

We emphasize that it is not our function to propose regulatory schemes for the States. That must await their concrete legislative efforts. It is possible, however, to give a few plain examples of what a state statute could define for regulation under part (b) of the standard announced in this opinion:

> (a) Patently offensive representations or descriptions of ultimate sexual acts, normal or perverted, actual or simulated.
> (b) Patently offensive representations or descriptions of masturbation, excretory functions, and lewd exhibition of the genitals.

Sex and nudity may not be exploited without limit by films or pictures exhibited or sold in places of public accommodation any more than live sex and nudity can be exhibited or sold without limit in such public places. At a minimum, prurient, patently offensive depiction or description of sexual conduct must have serious literary, artistic, political, or scientific value to merit First Amendment protection. . . . In resolving the inevitably sensitive questions of fact and law, we must continue to rely on the jury system, accompanied by the safeguards that judges, rules of evidence, presumption of innocence, and other protective features provide, as we do with rape, murder, and a host of other offenses against society and its individual members. . . .

Under the holdings announced today, no one will be subject to prosecution for the sale or exposure of obscene materials unless these materials depict or describe patently offensive "hard core" sexual conduct specifically defined by the regulating state law, as written or construed. We are satisfied that these specific prerequisites will provide fair notice to a dealer in such materials that his public and commercial activities may bring prosecution. If the inability to define regulated materials with ultimate, god-like precision altogether removes the power of the States or the Congress to regulate,

then "hard core" pornography may be exposed without limit to the juvenile, the passerby, and the consenting adult alike, as, indeed, Mr. Justice Douglas contends. In this belief, however, Mr. Justice Douglas now stands alone. . . .

Under a National Constitution, fundamental First Amendment limitations on the powers of the States do not vary from community to community, but this does not mean that there are, or should or can be, fixed, uniform national standards of precisely what appeals to the "prurient interest" or is "patently offensive." These are essentially questions of fact, and our Nation is simply too big and too diverse for this Court to reasonably expect that such standards could be articulated for all 50 States in a single formulation, even assuming the prerequisite consensus exists. When triers of fact are asked to decide whether "the average person, applying contemporary community standards" would consider certain materials "prurient," it would be unrealistic to require that the answer be based on some abstract formulation. The adversary system, with lay jurors as the usual ultimate factfinders in criminal prosecutions, has historically permitted triers of fact to draw on the standards of their community, guided always by limiting instructions on the law. To require a State to structure obscenity proceedings around evidence of a national "community standards" would be an exercise in futility. . . .

It is neither realistic nor constitutionally sound to read the First Amendment as requiring that the people of Maine or Mississippi accept public depiction of conduct found tolerable in Las Vegas, or New York City. People in different States vary in their tastes and attitudes, and this diversity is not to be strangled by the absolutism of imposed uniformity. . . . [T]he primary concern with requiring a jury to apply the standard of "the average person, applying contemporary community standards" is to be certain that, so far as material is not aimed at a deviant group, it will be judged by its impact on an average person, rather than a particularly susceptible or sensitive person—or indeed a totally insensitive one. We hold that the requirement that the jury evaluate the materials with reference to "contemporary standards of the State of California" serves this protective purpose and is constitutionally adequate. . . .

The dissenting Justices sound the alarm of repression. But, in our view, to equate the free and robust exchange of ideas and political debate with commercial exploitation of obscene material demeans the grand conception of the First Amendment and its high purposes in the historic struggle for freedom. The First Amendment protects works which, taken as a whole, have serious literary, artistic, political, or scientific value, regardless of whether the government or a majority of the people approve of the ideas these works represent. But the public portrayal of hard-core sexual conduct for its own sake, and for the ensuing commercial gain, is a different matter. . . . One can concede that the "sexual revolution" of recent years may have had useful byproducts in striking layers of prudery from a subject long irrationally kept from needed ventilation. But it does not follow that no regulation of patently offensive "hard-core" materials is needed or permissible; civilized people do not allow unregulated access to heroin because it is a derivative of medicinal morphine.

In sum, we (a) reaffirm the Roth holding that obscene material is not protected by the First Amendment; (b) hold that such material can be regulated by the States, subject to the specific safeguards enunciated above, without a showing that the material is "utterly without redeeming social value"; and (c) hold that obscenity is to be determined by applying "contemporary community standards," not "national standards." The judgment of the Appellate Department of the Superior Court, Orange County, California, is vacated and the case remanded to that court for further proceedings not inconsistent with the First Amendment standards established by this opinion.

MR. JUSTICE DOUGLAS, dissenting.

Today we leave open the way for California to send a man to prison for distributing brochures that advertise books and a movie under freshly written standards defining obscenity which until today's decision were never the part of any law.

The Court has worked hard to define obscenity and concededly has failed. In Roth v. United States, it ruled that "[o]bscene material is material which deals with sex in a manner appealing to prurient interest." Obscenity, it was said, was rejected by the First Amendment because it is "utterly without redeeming social importance." The presence of a "prurient interest" was to be determined by "contemporary community standards." That test, it has been said, could not be determined by one standard here and another standard there, but "on the basis of a national standard." . . .

In Memoirs v. Massachusetts the Roth test was elaborated to read as follows: "[T]hree elements must coalesce: it must be established that (a) the dominant theme of the material taken as a whole appeals to a prurient interest in sex; (b) the material is patently offensive because it affronts contemporary community standards relating to the description or representation of sexual matters; and (c) the material is utterly without redeeming social value." . . .

But even those members of this Court who had created the new and changing standards of "obscenity" could not agree on their application. And so we adopted a per curiam treatment of so-called obscene publications that seemed to pass constitutional muster under the several constitutional tests which had been formulated. Some condemn it if its "dominant tendency might be to 'deprave or corrupt' a reader." Others look not to the content of the book but to whether it is advertised "to appeal to the erotic interests of customers." Some condemn only "hardcore pornography"; but even then a true definition is lacking. It has indeed been said of that definition [by Justice Stewart], "I could never succeed in [defining it] intelligibly," but "I know it when I see it." . . .

Today the Court retreats from the earlier formulations of the constitutional test and undertakes to make new definitions. This effort, like the earlier ones, is earnest and well intentioned. The difficulty is that we do not deal with constitutional terms, since "obscenity" is not mentioned in the Constitution or Bill of Rights. And the First Amendment makes no such exception from "the press" which it undertakes to protect nor, as I have said on other occasions, is an exception necessarily implied, for there was no recognized exception to the free press at the time the Bill of Rights was adopted which treated "obscene" publications differently from other types of papers, magazines, and books. So there are no constitutional guidelines for deciding what is and what is not "obscene." The Court is at large because we deal with tastes and standards of literature. What shocks me may be sustenance for my neighbor. What causes one person to boil up in rage over one pamphlet or movie may reflect only his neurosis, not shared by others. We deal here with a regime of censorship which, if adopted, should be done by constitutional amendment after full debate by the people.

Obscenity cases usually generate tremendous emotional outbursts. They have no business being in the courts. If a constitutional amendment authorized censorship, the censor would probably be an administrative agency. Then criminal prosecutions could follow as, if, and when publishers defied the censor and sold their literature. Under that regime a publisher would know when he was on dangerous ground. Under the present regime—whether the old standards or the new ones are used—the criminal law becomes a trap. A brand new test would put a publisher behind bars under a new law improvised by the courts after the publication. . . . My contention is that until a civil proceeding has placed a tract beyond the pale, no criminal prosecution should be sustained. For no more vivid illustration of vague and uncertain laws could be designed than those we have fashioned. . . . Obscenity—which even we cannot define with precision—is a hodge-podge. To send men to jail for violating standards they cannot understand, construe, and apply is a monstrous thing to do in a Nation dedicated to fair trials and due process. . . .

If there are to be restraints on what is obscene, then a constitutional amendment should be the way of achieving the end. There are societies where religion and mathematics are the only free segments. It would be a dark day for America if that were our destiny. But the people can make it such if they choose to write obscenity into the Constitution and define it.

We deal with highly emotional, not rational, questions. To many the Song of Solomon is obscene. I do not think we, the judges, were ever given the constitutional power to make definitions of obscenity. If it is to be defined, let the people debate and decide by a constitutional amendment what they want to ban as obscene and what standards they want the legislatures and the courts to apply. Perhaps the people will decide that the path towards a mature, integrated society requires that all ideas competing for acceptance must have no censor. Perhaps they will decide otherwise. Whatever the choice, the courts will have some guidelines. Now we have none except our own predilections.

STANLEY V. GEORGIA
394 U.S. 557 (1969)

"Given the present state of knowledge, the State may no more prohibit mere possession of obscene matter on the ground that it may lead to antisocial conduct than it may prohibit possession of chemistry books on the ground that they may lead to the manufacture of homemade spirits."

The Question: Can the state make the private possession of obscene material a crime, without evidence that the material has been sold or distributed to others?

The Arguments: PRO

The Supreme Court has ruled that obscene material is not protected by the First Amendment. That ruling was based on a finding that obscenity is harmful to society and consequently to persons who are exposed to it. This finding justifies the state's decision to protect its citizens against a harmful substance, in much the same way that possession of drugs can be prohibited. The fact that the defendant in this case did not sell or distribute the obscene material found in his home does not change the case, just as keeping drugs in one's home can be punished even if they are not sold or distributed. The state can assume that persons who possess obscene material not only injure themselves but also pose a greater risk of harming others through sexual assault or deviant sexual practices.

CON

The first rule of law is, "a man's home is his castle." The state cannot tell a person what he cannot read, listen to, or look at in the privacy of his home. In this case, police officers who searched the defendant's home with a warrant that authorized them to search for evidence of illegal bookmaking found some films they considered obscene. The defendant was not suspected of, or ever charged with committing, any crimes related to viewing the allegedly obscene films. Upholding the conviction in this case would encourage the police to obtain search warrants on any pretext, and then to search for material the police consider obscene. This is "Big Brother" government at its most intrusive.

MR. JUSTICE MARSHALL delivered the opinion of the Court.

An investigation of appellant's alleged bookmaking activities led to the issuance of a search warrant for appellant's home. Under authority of this warrant, federal and state agents secured entrance. They found very little evidence of bookmaking activity, but while looking through a desk drawer in an upstairs bedroom, one of the federal agents, accompanied by a state officer, found three reels of eight-millimeter film. Using a projector and screen found in an upstairs living room, they viewed the films. The state officer concluded that they were obscene and seized them. Since a further examination of the bedroom indicated that appellant occupied it, he was charged with possession of obscene matter and placed under arrest. He was later indicted for "knowingly hav[ing] possession of . . . obscene matter" in violation of Georgia law. Appellant was tried before a jury and convicted. The Supreme Court of Georgia affirmed.

Appellant raises several challenges to the validity of his conviction. We find it necessary to consider only one. Appellant argues here, and argued below, that the Georgia obscenity statute, insofar as it punishes mere private possession of

obscene matter, violates the First Amendment, as made applicable to the States by the Fourteenth Amendment. For reasons set forth below, we agree that the mere private possession of obscene matter cannot constitutionally be made a crime. . . .

Georgia . . . contends that since "obscenity is not within the area of constitutionally protected speech or press," Roth v. United States, the States are free, subject to the limits of other provisions of the Constitution, to deal with it any way deemed necessary, just as they may deal with possession of other things thought to be detrimental to the welfare of their citizens. If the State can protect the body of a citizen, may it not, argues Georgia, protect his mind?

It is true that Roth does declare, seemingly without qualification, that obscenity is not protected by the First Amendment. That statement has been repeated in various forms in subsequent cases. However, neither Roth nor any subsequent decision of this Court dealt with the precise problem involved in the present case. Roth was convicted of mailing obscene circulars and advertising, and an obscene book, in violation of a federal obscenity statute. . . . None of the statements cited by the Court in Roth for the proposition that "this Court has always assumed that obscenity is not protected by the freedoms of speech and press" were made in the context of a statute punishing mere private possession of obscene material; the cases cited deal for the most part with use of the mails to distribute objectionable material or with some form of public distribution or dissemination. Moreover, none of this Court's decisions subsequent to Roth involved prosecution for private possession of obscene materials. Those cases dealt with the power of the State and Federal Governments to prohibit or regulate certain public actions taken or intended to be taken with respect to obscene matter. In this context, we do not believe that this case can be decided simply by citing Roth.... That holding cannot foreclose an examination of the constitutional implications of a statute forbidding mere private possession of such material.

It is now well established that the Constitution protects the right to receive information and ideas. This right . . . is fundamental to our free society. Moreover, in the context of this case—a prosecution for mere possession of printed or filmed matter in the privacy of a person's own home—that right takes on an added dimension. For also fundamental is the right to be free, except in very limited circumstances, from unwanted governmental intrusions into one's privacy.

These are the rights that appellant is asserting in the case before us. He is asserting the right to read or observe what he pleases—the right to satisfy his intellectual and emotional needs in the privacy of his own home. He is asserting the right to be free from state inquiry into the contents of his library. Georgia contends that appellant does not have these rights, that there are certain types of materials that the individual may not read or even possess. Georgia justifies this assertion by arguing that the films in the present case are obscene. But we think that mere categorization of these films as "obscene" is insufficient justification for such a drastic invasion of personal liberties guaranteed by the First and Fourteenth Amendments. Whatever may be the justifications for other statutes regulating obscenity, we do not think they reach into the privacy of one's own home. If the First Amendment means anything, it means that a State has no business telling a man, sitting alone in his own house, what books he may read or what films he may watch. Our whole constitutional heritage rebels at the thought of giving government the power to control men's minds.

And yet, in the face of these traditional notions of individual liberty, Georgia asserts the right to protect the individual's mind from the effects of obscenity. We are not certain that this argument amounts to anything more than the assertion that the State has the right to control the moral content of a person's thoughts. To some, this may be a noble purpose, but it is wholly inconsistent with the philosophy of the First Amendment. Nor is it relevant that obscene materials in general, or the particular films before

the Court, are arguably devoid of any ideological content. The line between the transmission of ideas and mere entertainment is much too elusive for this Court to draw, if indeed such a line can be drawn at all. Whatever the power of the state to control public dissemination of ideas inimical to the public morality, it cannot constitutionally premise legislation on the desirability of controlling a person's private thoughts.

Perhaps recognizing this, Georgia asserts that exposure to obscene materials may lead to deviant sexual behavior or crimes of sexual violence. There appears to be little empirical basis for that assertion. But more important, if the State is only concerned about printed or filmed materials inducing antisocial conduct, we believe that in the context of private consumption of ideas and information we should adhere to the view that "[a]mong free men, the deterrents ordinarily to be applied to prevent crime are education and punishment for violations of the law . . ." Whitney v. California. Given the present state of knowledge, the State may no more prohibit mere possession of obscene matter on the ground that it may lead to antisocial conduct than it may prohibit possession of chemistry books on the ground that they may lead to the manufacture of homemade spirits.

It is true that in Roth this Court rejected the necessity of proving that exposure to obscene material would create a clear and present danger of antisocial conduct or would probably induce its recipients to such conduct. But that case dealt with public distribution of obscene materials and such distribution is subject to different objections. For example, there is always the danger that obscene material might fall into the hands of children, or that it might intrude upon the sensibilities or privacy of the general public. No such dangers are present in this case.

Finally, we are faced with the argument that prohibition of possession of obscene materials is a necessary incident to statutory schemes prohibiting distribution. That argument is based on alleged difficulties of proving an intent to distribute or in producing evidence of actual distribution. We are not convinced that such difficulties exist, but even if they did we do not think that they would justify infringement of the individual's right to read or observe what he pleases. Because that right is so fundamental to our scheme of individual liberty, its restriction may not be justified by the need to ease the administration of otherwise valid criminal laws.

We hold that the First and Fourteenth Amendments prohibit making mere private possession of obscene material a crime. Roth and the cases following that decision are not impaired by today's holding. As we have said, the States retain broad power to regulate obscenity; that power simply does not extend to mere possession by the individual in the privacy of his own home. Accordingly, the judgment of the court below is reversed and the case is remanded for proceedings not inconsistent with this opinion.

BARNES V. GLEN THEATRE, INC.
501 U.S. 560 (1991)

"Public indecency statutes such as the one before us reflect moral disapproval of people appearing in the nude among strangers in public places. . . . Thus, the public indecency statute furthers a substantial government interest in protecting order and morality."

The Question: Can a state enforce its "public indecency" statute to prohibit nude dancing in clubs whose patrons choose to view such performances?

The Arguments: PRO

The legal definition of "public indecency" is not limited to nudity in public places such as beaches and parks, at which members of the public could be offended. A club in which nude dancing is not visible to passersby on the sidewalk is still a public place, and the state's prohibition of nudity applies to such clubs. Society can express its "moral disapproval" of public nudity even if the performances of nude dancers are not legally obscene. Nude dancing in clubs that serve alcohol is not the kind of artistic expression that is protected by the First Amendment, since its primary purpose is to provide erotic stimulation for the club's patrons, and not to express any ideas. Dancers in these clubs are free to perform as long as they wear "pasties" and "G-strings" to conceal their nipples and genitals.

CON

In this case, the state clearly could not—and would not—prohibit a performance by a renowned dance company in which the dancers appeared nude. The prohibition against "public indecency" is only applied to nude dancers in clubs that are largely patronized by men who enjoy watching nude women. This would not be illegal if the nude dancers were viewed on film or video. There is no reason other than prudery for prohibiting a live performance of nude dancing. The state concedes that these dances are not obscene, just that they offend "public morality." In addition, dancing—both nude and clothed—can be "expressive" of ideas, even erotic ideas.

CHIEF JUSTICE REHNQUIST announced the judgment of the Court and delivered an opinion, in which JUSTICE O'CONNOR and JUSTICE KENNEDY join.

Respondents are two establishments in South Bend, Indiana, that wish to provide totally nude dancing as entertainment, and individual dancers who are employed at these establishments. They claim that the First Amendment's guarantee of freedom of expression prevents the State of Indiana from enforcing its public indecency law to prevent this form of dancing. We reject their claim.

The facts appear from the pleadings and findings of the District Court, and are uncontested here. The Kitty Kat Lounge, Inc. (Kitty Kat) is located in the city of South Bend. It sells alcoholic beverages and presents "go-go dancing." Its proprietor desires to present "totally nude dancing," but an applicable Indiana statute regulating public nudity requires that the dancers wear "pasties" and a "G-string" when they dance. The dancers are not paid an hourly wage, but work on commission. They receive a 100 percent commission on the first $60 in drink sales during their performances. Darlene Miller, one of the respondents in the action, had worked at the Kitty Kat for about two years at the time this action was brought. Miller wishes to dance nude because she believes she would make more money doing so.

Respondent Glen Theatre, Inc., is an Indiana corporation with a place of business in South Bend. Its primary business is supplying so-called adult entertainment through written and printed materials, movie showings, and live entertainment at an enclosed "bookstore." The live entertainment at the "bookstore" consists of nude and seminude performances and showings of the female body through glass panels. Customers sit in a booth and insert coins into a timing mechanism that permits them to observe the live nude and seminude dancers for a period of time. One of Glen Theatre's dancers, Gayle Ann Marie Sutro, has danced, modeled, and acted professionally for more than 15 years, and in addition to her performances at the Glen Theatre, can be seen in a pornographic movie at a nearby theater.

Respondents sued in the United States District Court for the Northern District of Indiana to enjoin the enforcement of the Indiana public indecency statute, asserting that its prohibition against complete nudity in public places violated the First Amendment. The District Court . . . concluded that "the type of dancing these plaintiffs wish to perform is not expressive activity protected by the Constitution of the United States," and rendered judgment in favor of the defendants. The Court of Appeals . . . concluded that non-obscene nude dancing performed for entertainment is expression protected by the First Amendment, and that the public indecency statute was an improper infringement of that expressive activity because its purpose was to prevent the message of eroticism and sexuality conveyed by the dancers. We granted certiorari, and now hold that the Indiana statutory requirement that the dancers in the establishments involved in this case must wear pasties and a G-string does not violate the First Amendment. . . .

Indiana, of course, has not banned nude dancing as such, but has proscribed public nudity across the board. The Supreme Court of Indiana has construed the Indiana statute to preclude nudity in what are essentially places of public accommodation such as the Glen Theatre and the Kitty Kat Lounge. In such places, respondents point out, minors are excluded and there are no nonconsenting viewers. Respondents contend that, while the state may license establishments such as the ones involved here and limit the geographical area in which they do business, it may not in any way limit the performance of the dances within them without violating the First Amendment. The petitioner contends, on the other hand, that Indiana's restriction on nude dancing is a valid "time, place or manner" restriction. . . .

[W]e turn . . . to the rule enunciated in United States v. O'Brien. O'Brien burned his draft card on the steps of the South Boston courthouse in the presence of a sizable crowd, and was convicted of violating a statute that prohibited the knowing destruction or mutilation of such a card. He claimed that his conviction was contrary to the First Amendment because his act was "symbolic speech"—expressive conduct. The court rejected his contention that symbolic speech is entitled to full First Amendment protection, saying: "This Court has held that, when 'speech' and 'nonspeech' elements are combined in the same course of conduct, a sufficiently important governmental interest in regulating the nonspeech element can justify incidental limitations on First Amendment freedoms. . . . [W]e think it clear that a government regulation is sufficiently justified if it is within the constitutional power of the Government; if it furthers an important or substantial governmental interest; if the governmental interest is unrelated to the suppression of free expression; and if the incidental restriction on alleged First Amendment freedoms is no greater than is essential to the furtherance of that interest."

Applying the four-part O'Brien test enunciated above, we find that Indiana's public indecency statute is justified despite its incidental limitations on some expressive activity. The public indecency statute is clearly within the constitutional power of the State, and furthers substantial governmental interests. . . . Public indecency statutes such as the one before us reflect moral disapproval of people appearing in the nude among strangers in public places. . . . Thus, the public indecency statute furthers a substantial government interest in protecting order and morality.

This interest is unrelated to the suppression of free expression. Some may view restricting nudity on moral grounds as necessarily related to expression. We disagree.

It can be argued, of course, that almost limitless types of conduct—including appearing in the nude in public—are "expressive," and in one sense of the word this is true. People who go about in the nude in public may be expressing something about themselves by so doing. But the court rejected this expansive notion of "expressive conduct" in O'Brien, saying: "We cannot accept the view that an apparently limitless variety of conduct can be labelled 'speech' whenever the person engaging in the conduct intends thereby to express an idea." . . .

Respondents contend that, even though prohibiting nudity in public generally may not be related to suppressing expression, prohibiting the performance of nude dancing is related to expression because the state seeks to prevent its erotic message. Therefore, they reason that the application of the Indiana statute to the nude dancing in this case violates the First Amendment, because it fails the third part of the O'Brien test, viz: the governmental interest must be unrelated to the suppression of free expression.

But we do not think that, when Indiana applies its statute to the nude dancing in these nightclubs it is proscribing nudity because of the erotic message conveyed by the dancers. Presumably numerous other erotic performances are presented at these establishments and similar clubs without any interference from the state, so long as the performers wear a scant amount of clothing. Likewise, the requirement that the dancers don pasties and a G-string does not deprive the dance of whatever erotic message it conveys; it simply makes the message slightly less graphic. The perceived evil that Indiana seeks to address is not erotic dancing, but public nudity. The appearance of people of all shapes, sizes and ages in the nude at a beach, for example, would convey little if any erotic message, yet the state still seeks to prevent it. Public nudity is the evil the state seeks to prevent, whether or not it is combined with expressive activity. . . .

The fourth part of the O'Brien test requires that the incidental restriction on First Amendment freedom be no greater than is essential to the furtherance of the governmental interest. As indicated in the discussion above, the governmental interest served by the text of the prohibition is societal disapproval of nudity in public places and among strangers. The statutory prohibition is not a means to some greater end, but an end in itself. It is without cavil that the public indecency statute is "narrowly tailored"; Indiana's requirement that the dancers wear at least pasties and a G-string is modest, and the bare minimum necessary to achieve the state's purpose.

The judgment of the Court of Appeals accordingly is reversed.

JUSTICE WHITE, with whom JUSTICE MARSHALL, JUSTICE BLACKMUN, and JUSTICE STEVENS join, dissenting.

The first question presented to us in this case is whether nonobscene nude dancing performed as entertainment is expressive conduct protected by the First Amendment. The Court of Appeals held that it is, observing that our prior decisions permit no other conclusion. Not surprisingly, then, the Court now concedes that "nude dancing of the kind sought to be performed here is expressive conduct within the outer perimeters of the First Amendment. . . ." This is no more than recognizing, as the Seventh Circuit observed, that dancing is an ancient art form and "inherently embodies the expression and communication of ideas and emotions."

Having arrived at the conclusion that nude dancing performed as entertainment enjoys First Amendment protection, the Court states that it must "determine the level of protection to be afforded to the expressive conduct at issue, and must determine whether the Indiana statute is an impermissible infringement of that protected activity." For guidance, the plurality turns to United States v. O'Brien, which held that expressive conduct could be narrowly regulated or forbidden in pursuit of an important or substantial governmental interest that is unrelated to the content of the expression. The plurality finds that the Indiana statute satisfies the O'Brien test in all respects.

The plurality acknowledges that it is impossible to discern the exact state interests which the Indiana legislature had in mind when it enacted the Indiana statute, but the Court nonetheless concludes that it is clear from the statute's text and history that the law's purpose is to protect "societal order and morality." The plurality goes on to conclude that Indiana's statute "was enacted as a general prohibition" on people appearing in the nude among strangers in public places. The plurality then points to cases in which we upheld legislation based on the State's police power, and ultimately concludes that the Indiana statute "furthers a substantial government interest in protecting order and morality." The plurality also holds that the basis for banning nude dancing is unrelated to free expression, and that it is narrowly drawn to serve the State's interest.

The plurality's analysis is erroneous in several respects. [T]he Court . . . overlook[s] a fundamental and critical aspect of our cases upholding the States' exercise of their police powers. None of the cases they rely upon, including O'Brien and Bowers v. Hardwick, involved anything less than truly general proscriptions on individual conduct. In O'Brien, for example, individuals were prohibited from destroying their draft cards at any time and in any place, even in completely private places such as the home. Likewise, in Bowers, the State prohibited sodomy, regardless of where the conduct might occur, including the home, as was true in that case. . . . By contrast, in this case, Indiana does not suggest that its statute applies to, or could be applied to, nudity wherever it occurs, including the home. We do not understand the Court . . . to be suggesting that Indiana could constitutionally enact such an intrusive prohibition, nor do we think such a suggestion would be tenable in light of our decision in Stanley v. Georgia, in which we held that States could not punish the mere possession of obscenity in the privacy of one's own home. . . .

[T]he Indiana Supreme Court held that the statute at issue here cannot and does not prohibit nudity as a part of some larger form of expression meriting protection when the communication of ideas is involved. Petitioners also state that the evils sought to be avoided by applying the statute in this case would not obtain in the case of theatrical productions, such as Salome or Hair. Neither is there any evidence that the State has attempted to apply the statute to nudity in performances such as plays, ballets or operas. "No arrests have ever been made for nudity as part of a play or ballet."

Thus, the Indiana statute is not a general prohibition of the type we have upheld in prior cases. As a result, the Court's . . . simple references to the State's general interest in promoting societal order and morality are not sufficient justification for a statute which concededly reaches a significant amount of protected expressive activity. Instead, in applying the O'Brien test, we are obligated to carefully examine the reasons the State has chosen to regulate this expressive conduct in a less than general statute. In other words, when the State enacts a law which draws a line between expressive conduct which is regulated and nonexpressive conduct of the same type which is not regulated, O'Brien places the burden on the State to justify the distinctions it has made. Closer inquiry as to the purpose of the statute is surely appropriate.

Legislators do not just randomly select certain conduct for proscription; they have reasons for doing so, and those reasons illuminate the purpose of the law that is passed. Indeed, a law may have multiple purposes. The purpose of forbidding people to appear nude in parks, beaches, hot dog stands, and like public places is to protect others from offense. But that could not possibly be the purpose of preventing nude dancing in theaters and barrooms, since the viewers are exclusively consenting adults who pay money to see these dances. The purpose of the proscription in these contexts is to protect the viewers from what the State believes is the harmful message that nude dancing communicates. . . . [T]he perceived damage to the public interest caused by appearing nude on the streets or in the parks, as I have said, is not what the State seeks to avoid in preventing nude dancing in theaters and taverns. There the perceived harm is the communicative aspect of the erotic dance. As the State now tells us, the State's goal in applying what it describes as its "content-neutral" statute to the nude dancing in this case is "deterrence of prostitution, sexual assaults, criminal activity, degradation of women, and other activities which break down family structure." The attainment of these goals, however, depends on preventing an expressive activity.

The plurality nevertheless holds that the third requirement of the O'Brien test, that the governmental interest be unrelated to the suppression of free expression, is satisfied, because, in applying the statute to nude dancing, the State is not "proscribing nudity because of the erotic message conveyed by the dancers." The plurality suggests that this is so because the State does not ban dancing that sends an erotic message; it is only nude erotic dancing that is forbidden. The perceived evil is not erotic dancing, but public nudity, which may be prohibited despite any incidental impact on expressive activity. This analysis is transparently erroneous.

In arriving at its conclusion, the Court concedes that nude dancing conveys an erotic message, and concedes that the message would be muted if the dancers wore pasties and G-strings. Indeed, the emotional or erotic impact of the dance is intensified by the nudity of the performers. As Judge Posner argued in his thoughtful concurring opinion in the Court of Appeals, the nudity of the dancer is an integral part of the emotions and thoughts that a nude dancing performance evokes. The sight of a fully clothed, or even a partially clothed, dancer generally will have a far different impact on a spectator than that of a nude dancer, even if the same dance is performed. The nudity is itself an expressive component of the dance, not merely incidental "conduct." We have previously pointed out that "'[n]udity alone' does not place otherwise protected material outside the mantle of the First Amendment."

This being the case, it cannot be that the statutory prohibition is unrelated to expressive conduct. Since the State permits the dancers to perform if they wear pasties and G-strings, but forbids nude dancing, it is precisely because of the distinctive, expressive content of the nude dancing performances at issue in this case that the State seeks to apply the statutory prohibition. It is only because nude dancing performances may generate emotions and feelings of eroticism and sensuality among the spectators that the State seeks to regulate such expressive activity, apparently on the assumption that creating or emphasizing such thoughts and ideas in the minds of the spectators may lead to increased prostitution and the degradation of women. But generating thoughts, ideas, and emotions is the essence of communication. The nudity element of nude dancing performances cannot be neatly pigeonholed as mere "conduct" independent of any expressive component of the dance. . . .

That the performances in the Kitty Kat Lounge may not be high art, to say the least, and may not appeal to the Court, is hardly an excuse for distorting and ignoring settled doctrine. The plurality's assessment of the artistic merits of nude dancing performances should not be the determining factor in deciding this case. In the words of Justice Harlan, "[I]t is largely because governmental officials cannot make principled decisions in this area that the Constitution leaves matters of taste and style so largely to the individual" Cohen v. California. . . .

Accordingly, I would affirm the judgment of the Court of Appeals, and dissent from this Court's judgment.

ASHCROFT V. FREE SPEECH COALITION
535 U.S. 234 (2002)

"First Amendment freedoms are most in danger when the government seeks to control thought or to justify its laws for that impermissible end. The right to think is the beginning of freedom, and speech must be protected from the government because speech is the beginning of thought."

The Question: Can the federal government ban the production, sale, or possession of "virtual child pornography," which is produced by computer-generated images and does not involve the filming of any real children?

The Arguments: PRO

Society has an essential interest in preventing the sexual exploitation of children and minors below the age of 18. Statistics show that child sexual abuse is a major problem, and the use of children to engage in sexual acts or to pose in sexually provocative ways is harmful to the emotional, physiological, and mental health of children who are exploited in this manner. Child pornography is also likely to encourage pedophiles to seek out children whom they can abuse or expose to this material. The fact that "virtual child pornography" can be produced by computer imaging, without the use of real children, does not distinguish it from actual child pornography; since those who seek out such material are not concerned with whether the images are "real" or not but simply whether it satisfies their urge to see children engaged in sexual conduct.

CON

No one disputes that child pornography, including the use of children in producing this material, is harmful to the children involved and to society. However, the laws that prohibit the use of real children in pornography are based on the legitimate interest in protecting them from sexual abuse and exploitation. The material that is banned by the federal Child Pornography Prevention Act includes images that do no meet the legal definition of obscenity, and the law could be used to punish film makers and other artists whose work deals with childhood sexuality. Several recent films of acknowledged artistic merit, such as *Traffic* and *American Beauty*, could fall under the law's ban.

JUSTICE KENNEDY delivered the opinion of the Court.

We consider in this case whether the Child Pornography Prevention Act of 1996 (CPPA) . . . abridges the freedom of speech. The CPPA extends the federal prohibition against child pornography to sexually explicit images that appear to depict minors but were produced without using any real children. The statute prohibits, in specific circumstances, possessing or distributing these images, which may be created by using adults who look like minors or by using computer imaging. The new technology, according to Congress, makes it possible to create realistic images of children who do not exist.

By prohibiting child pornography that does not depict an actual child, the statute goes beyond New York v. Ferber (1982), which distinguished child pornography from other sexually explicit speech because of the State's interest in protecting the children exploited by the production process. As a general rule, pornography can be banned only if obscene, but under *Ferber*, pornography showing minors can be proscribed whether or not the images are obscene under the definition set forth in Miller v. California (1973).

While we have not had occasion to consider the question, we may assume that the apparent age of persons engaged in sexual conduct is relevant to whether a depiction offends community standards. Pictures of young children engaged in certain acts might be obscene where similar depictions of adults, or perhaps even older adolescents, would not. The CPPA, however, is not directed at speech that is obscene; Congress has proscribed those materials through a separate statute.

Like the law in Ferber, the CPPA seeks to reach beyond obscenity, and it makes no attempt to conform to the Miller standard. For instance, the statute would reach visual depictions, such as movies, even if they have redeeming social value.

The principal question to be resolved, then, is whether the CPPA is constitutional where it proscribes a significant universe of speech that is neither obscene under *Miller* nor child pornography under Ferber.

I

Before 1996, Congress defined child pornography as the type of depictions at issue in Ferber, images made using actual minors. The CPPA retains that prohibition at 18 U. S. C. §2256(8)(A) and adds three other prohibited categories of speech, of which the first, §2256(8)(B), and the third, §2256(8)(D), are at issue in this case. Section 2256(8)(B) prohibits "any visual depiction, including any photograph, film, video, picture, or computer or computer-generated image or picture" that "is, or appears to be, of a minor engaging in sexually explicit conduct." The prohibition on "any visual depiction" does not depend at all on how the image is produced. The section captures a range of depictions, sometimes called "virtual child pornography," which include computer-generated images, as well as images produced by more traditional means. For instance, the literal terms of the statute embrace a Renaissance painting depicting a scene from classical mythology, a "picture" that "appears to be, of a minor engaging in sexually explicit conduct." The statute also prohibits Hollywood movies, filmed without any child actors, if a jury believes an actor "appears to be" a minor engaging in "actual or simulated . . . sexual intercourse." §2256(2).

These images do not involve, let alone harm, any children in the production process; but Congress decided the materials threaten children in other, less direct, ways. Pedophiles might use the materials to encourage children to participate in sexual activity. "[A] child who is reluctant to engage in sexual activity with an adult, or to pose for sexually explicit photographs, can sometimes be convinced by viewing depictions of other children 'having fun' participating in such activity."

Furthermore, pedophiles might "whet their own sexual appetites" with the pornographic images, "thereby increasing the creation and distribution of child pornography and the sexual abuse and exploitation of actual children." Under these rationales, harm flows from the content of the images, not from the means of their production. In addition, Congress identified another problem created by computer-generated images: Their existence can make it harder to prosecute pornographers who do use real minors.

As imaging technology improves, Congress found, it becomes more difficult to prove that a particular picture was produced using actual children. To ensure that defendants possessing child pornography using real minors cannot evade prosecution, Congress extended the ban to virtual child pornography.

Fearing that the CPPA threatened the activities of its members, respondent Free Speech Coalition and others challenged the statute in the United States District Court for the Northern District of California. The Coalition, a California trade association for the adult-entertainment industry, alleged that its members did not use minors in their sexually explicit works, but they believed some of these materials might fall within the CPPA's expanded definition of child pornography. The other respondents are Bold Type, Inc., the publisher of a book advocating the nudist lifestyle; Jim Gingerich, a painter of nudes; and Ron Raffaelli, a photographer specializing in erotic images. Respondents alleged that the "appears to be" and "conveys the impression" provisions are overbroad and vague, chilling them from producing works protected by the First Amendment. The District Court disagreed and granted summary judgment to the Government. The court dismissed the overbreadth claim because it was "highly unlikely" that any "adaptations of sexual works like 'Romeo and Juliet,' will be treated as 'criminal contraband.'"

The Court of Appeals for the Ninth Circuit reversed. The court reasoned that the Government could not prohibit speech because of its tendency to persuade viewers to commit illegal acts. The court held the CPPA to be substantially overbroad because it bans materials that are neither obscene nor produced by the exploitation of real children as in New York v. Ferber (1982). Judge Ferguson dissented on the ground that virtual images, like obscenity and real child pornography, should be treated as a category of speech unprotected by the First Amendment.

II

The First Amendment commands, "Congress shall make no law . . . abridging the freedom of speech." The government may violate this mandate in many ways, e.g., Rosenberger v. Rector and Visitors of Univ. of Va. (1995), Keller v. State Bar of Cal. (1990), but a law imposing criminal penalties on protected speech is a stark example of speech suppression. The CPPA's penalties are indeed severe. A first offender may be imprisoned for 15 years. A repeat offender faces a prison sentence of not less than 5 years and not more than 30 years in prison. While even minor punishments can chill protected speech, see Wooley v. Maynard (1977), this case provides a textbook example of why we permit facial challenges to statutes that burden expression. With these severe penalties in force, few legitimate movie producers or book publishers, or few other speakers in any capacity, would risk distributing images in or near the uncertain reach of this law. The Constitution gives significant protection from overbroad laws that chill speech within the First Amendment's vast and privileged sphere. Under this principle, the CPPA is unconstitutional on its face if it prohibits a substantial amount of protected expression. See Broadrick v. Oklahoma (1973).

The sexual abuse of a child is a most serious crime and an act repugnant to the moral instincts of a decent people. In its legislative findings, Congress recognized that there are subcultures of persons who harbor illicit desires for children and commit criminal acts to gratify the impulses.

As a general principle, the First Amendment bars the government from dictating what we see or read or speak or hear. The freedom of speech has its limits; it does not embrace certain categories of speech, including defamation, incitement, obscenity, and pornography produced with real children.

As we have noted, the CPPA is much more than a supplement to the existing federal prohibition on obscenity. Under Miller v. California (1973), the Government must prove that the work, taken as a whole, appeals to the prurient interest, is patently offensive in light of community standards, and lacks serious literary, artistic, political, or scientific value. The CPPA, however, extends to images that appear to depict a minor engaging in sexually explicit activity without regard to the Miller requirements. The materials need not appeal to the prurient interest. Any depiction of sexually explicit activity, no matter how it is presented, is proscribed. The CPPA applies to a picture in a psychology manual, as well as a movie depicting the horrors of sexual abuse. It is not necessary, moreover, that the image be patently offensive. Pictures of what appear to be 17-year-olds engaging in sexually explicit activity do not in every case contravene community standards.

The CPPA prohibits speech despite its serious literary, artistic, political, or scientific value. The statute proscribes the visual depiction of an idea—that of teenagers engaging in sexual activity—that is a fact of modern society and has been a theme in art and literature throughout the ages.

Both themes—teenage sexual activity and the sexual abuse of children—have inspired countless literary works. William Shakespeare created the most famous pair of teenage lovers, one of whom is just 13 years of age. See Romeo and Juliet, act I, sc. 2, 1. 9 ("She hath not seen the change of fourteen years"). In the drama, Shakespeare portrays the relationship as something splendid and innocent, but not juvenile. The work has inspired no less than 40 motion pictures, some of which suggest that the teenagers consummated their relationship. E.g., Romeo and Juliet

(B. Luhrmann director, 1996). Shakespeare may not have written sexually explicit scenes for the Elizabethan audience, but were modern directors to adopt a less conventional approach, that fact alone would not compel the conclusion that the work was obscene.

Contemporary movies pursue similar themes. Last year's Academy Awards featured the movie, Traffic, which was nominated for Best Picture. The film portrays a teenager, identified as a 16-year-old, who becomes addicted to drugs. The viewer sees the degradation of her addiction, which in the end leads her to a filthy room to trade sex for drugs. The year before, American Beauty won the Academy Award for Best Picture. In the course of the movie, a teenage girl engages in sexual relations with her teenage boyfriend, and another yields herself to the gratification of a middle-aged man. The film also contains a scene where, although the movie audience understands the act is not taking place, one character believes he is watching a teenage boy performing a sexual act on an older man.

Our society, like other cultures, has empathy and enduring fascination with the lives and destinies of the young. Art and literature express the vital interest we all have in the formative years we ourselves once knew, when wounds can be so grievous, disappointment so profound, and mistaken choices so tragic, but when moral acts and self-fulfillment are still in reach. Whether or not the films we mention violate the CPPA, they explore themes within the wide sweep of the statute's prohibitions. If these films, or hundreds of others of lesser note that explore those subjects, contain a single graphic depiction of sexual activity within the statutory definition, the possessor of the film would be subject to severe punishment without inquiry into the work's redeeming value. This is inconsistent with an essential First Amendment rule: The artistic merit of a work does not depend on the presence of a single explicit scene.

Ferber upheld a prohibition on the distribution and sale of child pornography, as well as its production, because these acts were "intrinsically related" to the sexual abuse of children in two ways. First, as a permanent record of a child's abuse, the continued circulation itself would harm the child who had participated. Like a defamatory statement, each new publication of the speech would cause new injury to the child's reputation and emotional well-being. Second, because the traffic in child pornography was an economic motive for its production, the State had an interest in closing the distribution network.

Ferber did not hold that child pornography is by definition without value. On the contrary, the Court recognized some works in this category might have significant value, see id., at 761, but relied on virtual images—the very images prohibited by the CPPA—as an alternative and permissible means of expression: "[I]f it were necessary for literary or artistic value, a person over the statutory age who perhaps looked younger could be utilized. Simulation outside of the prohibition of the statute could provide another alternative." Ferber, then, not only referred to the distinction between actual and virtual child pornography, it relied on it as a reason supporting its holding. Ferber provides no support for a statute that eliminates the distinction and makes the alternative mode criminal as well.

III

The CPPA, for reasons we have explored, is inconsistent with Miller and finds no support in Ferber. The Government seeks to justify its prohibitions in other ways. It argues that the CPPA is necessary because pedophiles may use virtual child pornography to seduce children. There are many things innocent in themselves, however, such as cartoons, video games, and candy, that might be used for immoral purposes, yet we would not expect those to be prohibited because they can be misused. The Government, of course, may punish adults who provide unsuitable materials to children, see Ginsberg v. New York (1968), and it may enforce criminal penalties for unlawful solicitation. The precedents establish, however, that speech within the rights of adults to hear may not be silenced completely in an attempt to shield children from it.

Here, the Government wants to keep speech from children not to protect them from its content but to protect them from those who would commit other crimes. The principle, however, remains the same: The Government cannot ban speech fit for adults simply because it may fall into the hands of children. The evil in question depends upon the actor's unlawful conduct, conduct defined as criminal quite apart from any link to the speech in question. This establishes that the speech ban is not narrowly drawn. The objective is to prohibit illegal conduct, but this restriction goes well beyond that interest by restricting the speech available to law-abiding adults.

The Government submits further that virtual child pornography whets the appetites of pedophiles and encourages them to engage in illegal conduct. This rationale cannot sustain the provision in question. The mere tendency of speech to encourage unlawful acts is not a sufficient reason for banning it. The government "cannot constitutionally premise legislation on the desirability of controlling a person's private thoughts." Stanley v. Georgia, (1969). First Amendment freedoms are most in danger when the government seeks to control thought or to justify its laws for that impermissible end. The right to think is the beginning of freedom, and speech must be protected from the government because speech is the beginning of thought.

In sum, §2256(8)(B) covers materials beyond the categories recognized in Ferber and Miller, and the reasons the Government offers in support of limiting the freedom of speech have no justification in our precedents or in the law of the First Amendment. The provision abridges the freedom to engage in a substantial amount of lawful speech. For this reason, it is overbroad and unconstitutional.

JUSTICE O'CONNOR, with whom THE CHIEF JUSTICE and JUSTICE SCALIA join as to Part II, concurring in the judgment in part and dissenting in part.

II

I disagree with the Court that the CPPA's prohibition of virtual-child pornography is overbroad. The basis for this holding is unclear. Although a content-based regulation may serve a compelling state interest, and be as narrowly tailored as possible while substantially serving that interest, the regulation may unintentionally ensnare speech that has serious literary, artistic, political, or scientific value or that does not threaten the harms sought to be combated by the Government. If so, litigants may challenge the regulation on its face as overbroad, but in doing so they bear the heavy burden of demonstrating that the regulation forbids a substantial amount of valuable or harmless speech. Respondents have not made such a demonstration. Respondents provide no examples of films or other materials that are wholly computer-generated and contain images that "appea[r] to be . . . of minors" engaging in indecent conduct, but that have serious value or do not facilitate child abuse. Their overbreadth challenge therefore fails.

III

Although in my view the CPPA's ban on youthful-adult pornography appears to violate the First Amendment, the ban on virtual-child pornography does not. It is true that both bans are authorized by the same text: The statute's definition of child pornography to include depictions that "appea[r] to be" of children in sexually explicit poses.

Invalidating a statute due to overbreadth, however, is an extreme remedy, one that should be employed "sparingly and only as a last resort."

Heeding this caution, I would strike the "appears to be" provision only insofar as it is applied to the subset of cases involving youthful-adult pornography.

Although 18 U. S. C. §2256(8)(B) does not distinguish between youthful-adult and virtual-child pornography, the CPPA elsewhere draws a line between these two classes of speech. The statute provides an affirmative defense for those who produce, distribute, or receive pornographic images of individuals who are actually adults, but not for those with pornographic images that are wholly computer generated. This is not surprising given that the legislative findings enacted by Congress contain no mention of youthful-adult pornography. Those findings focus explicitly only on actual-child pornography and virtual-child pornography. See, e.g., finding (9) following §2251 ("[T]he danger to children who are seduced and molested with the aid of child sex pictures is just as great when the child pornographer or child molester uses visual depictions of child sexual activity produced wholly or in part by electronic, mechanical, or other means, including by computer, as when the material consists of unretouched photographic images of actual children engaging in sexually explicit conduct"). Drawing a line around, and striking just, the CPPA's ban on youthful-child pornography not only is consistent with Congress' understanding of the categories of speech encompassed by §2256(8)(B), but also preserves the CPPA's prohibition of the material that Congress found most dangerous to children.

In sum, I would strike down the CPPA's ban on material that "conveys the impression" that it contains actual-child pornography, but uphold the ban on pornographic depictions that "appea[r] to be" of minors so long as it is not applied to youthful-adult pornography.

CHAPTER 6

Freedom of the Press

INTRODUCTION

"Freedom of the press," the noted critic and satirist H. L. Mencken once wrote, "belongs to those who own one." In years past, from colonial days through much of the twentieth century, Mencken's statement was largely true. The publication of newspapers, magazines, and books required the labor of typesetters, the operation of large and complicated printing presses, and a distribution network to deliver the publications to the public through newsstands, home delivery, or bookstores. However, there have long been those with news or views to sell who printed "broadsheets" in small numbers on smaller presses, and who often ran afoul of the authorities by printing material that thin-skinned officials considered dangerous or unduly critical of their acts and opinions. With the advent in recent years of low-cost printing equipment, radio and television, and now the Internet, publications—whether on paper or through computer images—have proliferated and can be produced and distributed by virtually anyone. And with the growing number of media that qualify for designation as "the press" in various forms, the number of legal challenges—by government and private individuals—to the press has grown as well.

The men and women who settled in the American colonies brought with them a dislike and distrust of official censorship of the press, which the English government had used for centuries to deter and punish—with death in some cases—those brave and often foolhardy critics of the Crown and its officers with the temerity to put their opinions in print. The system of British censorship, which required the approval of an official censor before publication and the risk of punishment for surreptitious or "seditious" publications, met with disapproval and outright flouting by critics of colonial rule.

The most important "free press" case in the colonial era took place in 1735, when jurors in New York found John Peter Zenger not guilty of seditious libel. An outspoken newspaper publisher, Zenger had printed articles that accused colonial governor William Cosby of trampling on the legal rights of New York's residents. Zenger's lawyer, Alexander Hamilton, appealed to the jurors to disregard the direct instructions of Judge James Delaney (a political ally of Governor Cosby) that the "truth" of the published accusations was no defense under English law. The jurors heeded Hamilton's passionate argument and promptly acquitted Zenger, a verdict that not only set a precedent for later American law but also showed the disdain of the jurors for claims that any criticism of public officials, true or not, could be punished.

The men who framed and ratified the Bill of Rights had Zenger and other colonial publishers like him in mind when they provided in the First Amendment that "Congress shall make no law" abridging the freedom of the press. They also drew inspiration and support from Sir William Blackstone, whose influential four-volume *Commentaries on the Laws of England* declared, "The liberty of the press is indeed essential to the nature of a free state; but this consists in laying no *previous* restraints upon publications, and not in freedom from censure for criminal matter when published." Blackstone expanded on this statement in these words: "Every freeman has an undoubted right to lay what sentiments he pleases before the public; to forbid this is to destroy the freedom of the press; but if he publishes what is improper, mischievous or illegal, he must take the consequence of his own temerity." Blackstone's condemnation of "prior restraints" on publication by official censorship or suppression did not provide an absolute protection for publishers, who faced criminal or civil prosecution for the content of what they printed.

The distinction between prior restraint before publication and subsequent prosecution after publication has become critical in the development of free press law. The Supreme Court has long held that the government faces a "heavy burden" in justifying any form of prior restraint, but the laws of "sedition" and defamation imposed a lesser burden on government prosecutors and private litigants until recent years. Congress passed the first "sedition act" in 1798, making it a federal crime to "write, print, utter or publish . . . any false, scandalous and malicious writing" against the government, Congress, or the president. Members of the Federalist party of President John Adams had enacted this law to punish their critics in the Republican party of Thomas Jefferson, whom they accused of supporting the revolutionary Jacobin regime in France. Under the Sedition Act, more than twenty of Jefferson's supporters were fined or jailed, including a Republican member of Congress, Matthew Lyon of Vermont. But the first sedition law expired in 1801, after Jefferson defeated Adams for the presidency, and the act never came before the courts for a test of its constitutionality.

Although the rise of the mass press in the late nineteenth century, both daily newspapers and the "penny dreadfuls" that enticed readers with lurid tales of scandal and romance stories, gave rise to calls by latter-day Puritans for curbs on the press, the Supreme Court did not address the Free Press Clause in a significant case until 1931. The case of *Near v. Minnesota* confronted the Court with a clear issue of prior restraint, during the waning days of the Prohibition era. Jay Near published the weekly Minneapolis paper *Saturday Press*, which accused numerous city officials, including the police chief, of colluding with and taking bribes from bootleggers who smuggled alcohol across the border from Canada. Near lambasted his targets in virulently anti-Semitic language. "I simply state a fact when I say that ninety percent of the crimes committed against society in this city are committed by Jew gangsters. It is Jew, Jew, Jew as long as one cares to comb over the records." Near also attacked Minnesota governor Floyd Olsen as a "Jew lover." For publishing these diatribes, Olsen and other officials moved to block further publication of the *Saturday Press* under a state law that permitted "the abatement, as a public nuisance, of a malicious, scandalous, and defamatory newspaper, magazine, or other periodical."

Near's challenge to the restraining order of a state judge reached the Supreme Court, which found the state law to be "the essence of censorship." Chief Justice Charles Evans Hughes wrote for the majority in a five-to-four decision, putting the case in these words: "The fact that the liberty of the press may be abused by miscreant purveyors of scandal does not make any the less necessary the immunity of the press from previous restraint in dealing with official misconduct. Subsequent punishment for such abuses as may exist is the appropriate remedy, consistent with constitutional privilege."

The Court lifted the restraining order against Near's paper, but Hughes made clear in his opinion that "the protection even as to previously restraint is not absolutely unlimited." He went on to list the possible exceptions to the ban on prior restraint: "No one would question but that a government might prevent actual obstruction to its recruiting service or the publication of the sailing dates of transports and location of troops [during wartime]. On similar grounds, the primary requirements of decency may be enforced against obscene publications. The security of the community life may be protected against incitements to acts of violence and the overthrow by force of orderly government." The "troop ship" exception is perhaps the most defensible of the exceptions Hughes listed, and a case raising that issue has not yet reached the Court. The Court has, of course, decided cases involving "obstruction to its recruiting service" in *Schenck* and other cases, and many cases that dealt with obscenity, incitement to violence, and advocacy of the overthrow of the government. However, these cases raised issues, not of prior restraint, but of "subsequent punishment" for the publication of supposedly unlawful material.

The closest the Supreme Court has come to the "troop ship" exemption was in the 1971 case of *New York Times v. United States,* the "Pentagon Papers" case in which the *Times* was restrained by a federal judge in June 1971 from publishing further excerpts of a 7,000-page Defense Department report entitled "History of U.S. Decision-Making Process on Viet Nam Policy." Shortly after the *Times* was enjoined from further publication, the *Washington Post* printed excerpts from the same study, which had been given to both papers by Daniel Ellsberg, a former defense official who had helped to prepare the historical study. Ellsberg had become disaffected with the war and felt that the American public needed to know how the country had been dragged into what he called the "quagmire" in Vietnam.

Although federal judges in Washington, D.C. had refused to restrain the *Post* from further publication, that paper's editors voluntarily agreed not to print further excerpts from the Pentagon Papers until the Supreme Court ruled on the government's appeal in that case. Confronted with conflicting lower-court orders, and fully aware that this historic case involved two of the nation's most influential newspapers, the Supreme Court hastily convened a rare summer session and issued a brief per curiam decision lifting the judicial orders. The Court issues such unsigned per curiam opinions (from the Latin for "by the court") when the Court needs to announce its result quickly, or when the justices agree that a case does not require a full opinion. In the "Pentagon Papers" case, the Court issued its ruling less than two weeks after the *Times* published its first article. Chief Justice Burger, one of three dissenters, chided his colleagues for their "unseemly haste" in deciding a case of such importance. The Court's majority, however, had concluded that *any* delay in allowing the *Times* and *Post* to resume publication of excerpts from and articles about the Pentagon Papers was damaging to the First Amendment.

Because none of the opinions issued on both sides in *New York Times v. United States* spoke for a majority on the Court, this historic case produced no sweeping doctrine or lasting precedent, except the agreement of six justices in the per curiam decision that the government had not met the "heavy burden" imposed in prior restraint cases. How the Court would rule in a true "troop ship" case remains to be seen. For example, if reporters discovered that terrorists had firm plans to detonate a massive bomb in the U.S. Capitol and that American troops had been gathered to launch a preemptive attack on the terrorists, could a court restrain a newspaper or television network from publishing or broadcasting what its reporters had learned? Even Justice Brennan, who denounced the prior restraint in the "Pentagon Papers" case, suggested that "the suppression of information that would set in motion a nuclear holocaust" might be legitimately restrained. Obviously, the prospect of such a horrifying event would give pause to even the most "absolutist" defenders of the Free Press Clause.

None of the cases that follow *New York Times v. United States* in this chapter involve anything close to nuclear holocaust. But they all raise serious issues of press freedom. The questions posed in these cases affect students who write for high school newspapers, reporters who want to protect their confidential sources and inform the public about criminal proceedings, and public officials and private citizens who claim the press has damaged their reputations. In three of these six cases, the Supreme Court ruled for the press, and in three the press lost. Viewed together, these cases illustrate the Court's basic commitment to freedom of the press, while at the same time balancing that "fundamental right" against the competing rights of school officials to monitor and possibly to censor what their students publish, of law enforcement officials to provide relevant information to grand jurors, and of private citizens to protect their reputations against the publication of falsehoods about them.

NEAR V. MINNESOTA
283 U.S. 697 (1931)

"Public officers, whose character and conduct remain open to debate and free discussion in the press, find their remedies for false accusations in actions under libel laws providing for redress and punishment and not in proceedings to restrain the publication of newspapers and periodicals."

The Question: Can a state pass a law that allows a newspaper or magazine to be banned prior to its publication because it has in the past contained articles that state or local officials consider "malicious, scandalous and defamatory," as a form of "prior restraint" of the press?

The Arguments: PRO

Freedom of the press is not absolute and abuse of that freedom can seriously damage the reputations of public officials and members of the public. In this case, the publishers of a weekly newspaper had repeatedly accused public officials of corruption and collusion with "Jew gangsters," an expression of anti-Semitism that was calculated to stir up religious hostility. Just as the Supreme Court has upheld "group libel" laws designed to protect members of racial and religious minorities, the repeated attribution of criminal conduct to a religious group can reasonably be expected to continue if the newspaper or magazine is not enjoined from future publication.

CON

The imposition of prior restraint on publications, which the British government employed during the colonial period to ban newspapers that criticized royal officials and their policies, was the primary target of the First Amendment. The notion that periodicals could be censored before their publication is totally at odds with freedom of the press. The laws of libel and slander are available to public officials and anyone else who can show that the publication of false statements has damaged their reputation. This case illustrates that any publisher who offends an official can be silenced by an injunction, and other publishers will think twice before printing anything critical if this form of prior restraint is upheld.

BACKGROUND

Chiseled in marble on the facade of the *Chicago Tribune* building is a statement by Chief Justice Charles Evans Hughes. Taken from the 1931 Supreme Court case *Near v. Minnesota*, it reads:

The administration of government has become more complex, the opportunities for malfeasance and corruption have multiplied, crime has grown to most serious proportions, and the danger of its protection by unfaithful officials and of the impairment of the fundamental security of life and property by criminal alliances and official neglect, emphasize the need of a vigilant and courageous press, especially in great cities. The fact that liberty of the press may be abused by miscreant purveyors of scandal does not make any less necessary the immunity of the press from prior restraint in dealing with official misconduct.

The case that produced this landmark ruling also generated a massive body of argumentation on both sides as to the true meaning of freedom of the press, its history as a concept and instrument, and its role in relation to the Constitution and constitutional government. The ruling has become vital in the censorship area, as its frequent use as a precedent attests.

The ruling involved a small newspaper, widely recognized as a scandal sheet; a future mayor of Minneapolis; a future governor of Minnesota; two publishers, one a millionaire and the other a pauper; a national civil liberties organization; and the First Amendment to the Constitution. The time was the famous Jazz Age—the socially irrepressible but politically conservative Twenties. The fact that the case drew extended national attention was a measure of the sensitive, vital, and often contradictory national feelings it tapped.

The 1920s also saw the emergence of a number of cheap, ephemeral scandal sheets, which were used for extortion, blackmailing petty crooks, or pressuring concessions from venal public officials. Many, however, while their tone was deplorable, actually filled an information gap. In a number of cities, the politicians *were* in collusion with the business world, which was closely tied to big newspapers and more interested in circulation based upon scandal and gossip than in performing honest public information functions.

The Minnesota situation was not atypical. Because of Prohibition, the state had become a crossroads in the illegal Canadian liquor trade, and with such law defiance had come vice and crime, both in Duluth and in Minneapolis and St. Paul. Ordinary law-abiding citizens looked the other way, concerning themselves with their private affairs, leaving law enforcement and civic administration to corrupt politicians and gangsters. Numerous gang killings accompanied gambling and trade in illegal booze. Respectable newspapers refused to investigate the association between the law breakers and law enforcement officials, and scandal sheets moved in to fill the void. In Duluth, John Morrison's *Duluth Rip-Saw* trumpeted sin, vice, and corruption so raucously and attacked vulnerable politicians so aggressively that the Minnesota legislature, responding to public demands for censorship, enacted a statute in 1925 to protect the community against the evils of these forms of business. The law was pushed by State Senator Mike Boylan and State Representative George Lommen, both of whom had been targets of the *Rip-Saw*. Subsequently dubbed the Minnesota Gag Law, it permitted a judge, acting without a jury, to stop the publication of a newspaper if the judge found it "obscene, lewd, and lascivious" or "malicious, scandalous, and defamatory." More specifically, it provided that the county attorney or, in his absence, the attorney general or any citizen acting in behalf of the county attorney might petition the district court for a temporary restraining order against any periodical that allegedly had violated the provisions of the act.

After a trial on the merits of the case, the district court judge could grant a permanent injunction, by which, in the language of the law, "such a nuisance may be wholly abated." Thus, the law allowed the enjoining of any publication which, in the opinion of a single judge, was contrary to public morals. It was, as a popular commentator wrote later, "a shining example . . . of that kind of police power which makes for governmental tyranny." If the law was effective, political corruption and business fraud could flourish without fear of exposure. Failure to comply with the order of the court would be contempt, punishable by a fine of a thousand dollars or a year in the county jail.

Jay M. Near and Howard Guilford had established the *Saturday Press* in 1927. Both had come to the Twin Cities a decade or so earlier, Near from Fort Atkinson, Iowa, and Guilford from Northampton, Massachusetts. They had previously practiced a brand of journalism that teetered on the edge of legality, and frequently toppled over. Guilford had had a particularly checkered career. Though never convicted of any crime, he had been indicted nineteen times. Rumor had it that he was a skillful con man who was not above blackmail and extortion. He had founded a weekly paper, *The Reporter,* in St. Paul in 1913. It was a sensationalist sheet that exposed gambling, prostitution, and the sexual adventures of the Twin Cities elite. In 1916, Guilford hired Near as a reporter. Near, who was something of a dandy, had a different flair. He was anti-Catholic, anti-Semitic, antiblack, and antilabor, frequently blasting the "Communist unions." These values crept into even his exposé stories about the Twin Cities establishment. Political corruption, and the truce between bootleggers, gamblers, and prostitution merchants and the police and city fathers, provided endless material for the two. But although their articles were sensational and often overstated, much that they published was true, or at least more true than false.

The *Saturday Press,* the object of the *Near* case, was to be a paper primarily to reveal corruption, including corrupt ties between the police and the Twin Cities underworld. Minneapolis Chief of Police Frank Brunskill learned of its purpose, as did figures with whom he was working. He sought to ban it before a single issue was published, threatening to send out his men to get it off the newsstands. He failed, but shortly after the first issue did hit the streets, a touring car overtook Howard Guilford on his way home, and before he could pull his own gun, two assailants pumped four bullets into his car. The last struck him in the abdomen as the car careened to a stop. Guilford was rushed to the hospital in critical condition. "I headed into the city on September 26, ran across three Jews in a Chevrolet, stopped a lot of lead and won a bed for myself in St. Barnabas Hospital for six weeks," he later reported. "Wherefore, I have withdrawn all allegiance to anything with a hook nose that eats herring." The respectable Minneapolis *Morning Tribune,* in reporting the episode, included an editorial indicating that "gangland [which clearly included people like Guilford] cannot settle its differences with impunity in our streets."

But in the next issue of the *Saturday Press,* Near made clear that there were links between gambling syndicates and the police. He warned the mob and the police that: "If the ochre-hearted rodents who fired those shots into the defenseless body of my buddy thought for a moment that they were ending the light against gang rule in this city, they were mistaken." The paper went on from there to get particularly tough with city and county government officials, attacking among others the county prosecutor, Floyd B. Olson, who later became a three-term Minnesota governor. It called him a "Jew Lover" and accused him of dragging his feet in the investigation of gangland pursuits.

Olson was enraged. Politically ambitious and savvy about whom to play ball with, Olson had occasionally blinked at some of the minor infractions of small-time gamblers. Having certain Robin Hood proclivities, he hoped to build a base from which to move into state politics, and he certainly wanted no insinuations as to his motives. He promised to "put out of business forever the *Saturday Press* and other sensational weeklies."

On November 21, 1927, Olson filed a complaint with Hennepin County District Judge Mathias Baldwin, alleging that the *Saturday Press* had defamed Mayor George Leach, Police Chief Brunskill, and Charles G. Davis, head of the Law Enforcement League, as well as the Minneapolis *Tribune,* the Minneapolis *Journal,* the Hennepin County Grand Jury, Olson himself, and the entire Jewish community. He described the paper as a "malicious, scandalous, and defamatory publication" and asked that "said nuisance be abated." He wanted the court to issue a temporary restraining order barring Near and Guilford or anyone else from "conducting or maintaining said nuisance under the name of the *Saturday Press,* or any other name." Judge Baldwin complied, and went on to forbid Near and Guilford "to produce, edit, publish, circulate, have in their possession, sell, or give away any publication known by any other name whatsoever containing matter of the kind alleged in the plaintiff's complaint."

However, the Minnesota constitution contained a clear statement that "the liberty of the press shall forever remain inviolate, and all persons may freely speak, write, and publish their sentiments on all subjects." Baldwin, conscious of this guarantee, certified an appeal of the case to the Minnesota supreme court, leaving to it the question of the law's constitutionality.

Three months after the request for an expedited hearing, the Minnesota supreme court convened to hear oral arguments on the constitutionality of the 1925 Public Nuisance Bill. If the court sustained it, the case would then be sent back to Baldwin's court to decide whether the *Saturday Press* had violated the law and whether the temporary restraining order should be made permanent. By this time Guilford's interest was waning. Nursing his gunshot wound, he left it to Near to fight the law and keep the case in the courts. However, Thomas Latimer (who in 1935 became mayor of Minneapolis) made an eloquent argument that the law was indeed a violation of the state constitution and was "null, void and invalid, being in contravention of the Fourteenth Amendment to the Constitution of the United States."

The court was unimpressed. It ruled unanimously to uphold the state law. Comparing the *Saturday Press* to houses of prostitution and noxious weeds, Chief Justice Samuel B. Wilson asserted that the legislature had the power to do away with such nuisances. In Minnesota, Wilson argued, no one could stifle the truthful voice of the press, but the Constitution's drafters never intended it to protect malice, scandal, and defamation.

Minneapolis newspapers refused to see the broader implications which sustaining the Gag Law carried. To them, the issue was the damage blackmailers and scandalmongers would do the community. They scoffed at the fears of the ACLU.

But the editor of the Chicago *Tribune* was not nearly so myopic. Colonel Robert Rutherford ("Bertie") McCormick admired Near for many of the same reasons that the ACLU was apprehensive about him. Rich and powerful, isolationist in his politics, and constantly at battle with Chicago officials over crime and corruption in that city, McCormick disliked black, Jews, and other minorities, to say nothing of labor unions. He had fought many legal battles over expose-type articles published in his newspapers. He certainly did not want the Illinois legislature to copy the Minnesota Gag Law. The interests of the rich publisher in Chicago and those of the poor scandalmonger in Minnesota coincided. McCormick therefore committed the *Tribune*'s resources to the case, indicating that he would strongly consider providing representation for Near in future legal proceedings.

So the stage was finally set for Near, with McCormick's help, to bring his case to the United States Supreme Court, and on April 26, 1930, the clerk of the Court notified the Minnesota supreme court that *Near* v. *Minnesota* had been docketed. Thus the highest court in the land for the first time took a freedom-of-the-press case involving the vital and ancient principle of prior restraint (Murphy, 1987).

Mr. CHIEF JUSTICE HUGHES delivered the opinion of the Court.

Chapter 285 of the Session Laws of Minnesota provides for the abatement, as a public nuisance, of a "malicious, scandalous and defamatory newspaper, magazine or other periodical." . . . Under this statute, the county attorney of Hennepin county brought this action to enjoin the publication of what was described as a "malicious, scandalous and defamatory newspaper, magazine or other periodical," known as The Saturday Press, published by the defendants in the city of Minneapolis. . . .

Without attempting to summarize the contents of the voluminous exhibits attached to the complaint, we deem it sufficient to say that the articles charged, in substance, that a Jewish gangster was in control of gambling, bootlegging, and racketeering in Minneapolis, and that law enforcing officers and agencies were not energetically performing their duties. Most of the charges were directed against the chief of police; he was charged with gross neglect of duty, illicit relations with gangsters, and with participation in graft. The county attorney was charged with knowing the existing conditions and with failure to take adequate measures to remedy them. The mayor was accused of inefficiency and dereliction. One member of the grand jury was stated to be in sympathy with the gangsters. . . . There is no question but that the articles made serious accusations against the public officers named and others in connection with the prevalence of crimes and the failure to expose and punish them. . . .

Thereupon the defendant Near, the present appellant, answered the complaint. He averred that he was the sole owner and proprietor of the publication in question. He admitted the publication of the articles in the issues described in the complaint, but denied that they were malicious, scandalous, or defamatory as alleged. He expressly invoked the protection of the due process clause of the Fourteenth Amendment. The case then came on for trial. . . . The district court . . . perpetually enjoined the defendants "from producing, editing, publishing, circulating, having in their possession, selling or giving away any publication whatsoever which is a malicious, scandalous or defamatory newspaper, as defined by law," and also "from further conducting said nuisance under the name and title of said The Saturday Press or any other name or title."

The defendant Near appealed from this judgment to the Supreme Court of the State, again asserting his right under the Federal Constitution, and the judgment was affirmed . . . From the judgment as thus affirmed, the defendant Near appeals to this Court.

This statute, for the suppression as a public nuisance of a newspaper or periodical, is unusual, if not unique, and raises questions of grave importance transcending the local interests involved in the particular action. It is no longer open to doubt that the liberty of the press and of speech is within the liberty safeguarded by the due process clause of the Fourteenth Amendment from invasion by state action. . . . Liberty of speech and of the press is also not an absolute right, and the state may punish its abuse. Liberty, in each of its phases, has its history and connotation, and, in the present instance, the inquiry is as to the historic conception of the liberty of the press and whether the statute under review violates the essential attributes of that liberty. . . .

If we cut through mere details of procedure, the operation and effect of the statute in substance is that public authorities may bring the owner or publisher of a newspaper or periodical before a judge upon a charge of conducting a business of publishing scandalous and defamatory matter—in particular that the matter consists of charges against public officers of official dereliction—and, unless the owner or publisher is able and disposed to bring competent evidence to satisfy the judge that the charges are true and are published with good motives and for justifiable ends, his newspaper or periodical is suppressed and further publication is made punishable as a contempt. This is the essence of censorship.

The question is whether a statute authorizing such proceedings in restraint of publication is consistent with the conception of the liberty of the press as historically conceived and guaranteed. In determining the extent of the constitutional protection, it has been generally, if not universally, considered that it is the chief purpose of the guaranty to prevent previous restraints upon publication. The struggle in England, directed against the legislative power of the licenser, resulted in renunciation of the censorship of the press. The liberty deemed to be established was thus described by Blackstone: "The liberty of the press is indeed essential to the nature of a free state; but this consists in laying no previous restraints upon publications, and not in freedom from censure for criminal matter when published. Every freeman has an undoubted right to lay what sentiments he pleases before the public; to forbid this, is to destroy the freedom of the press; but if he publishes what is improper, mischievous or illegal, he must take the consequence of his own temerity." . . . In the present case, we have no occasion to inquire as to the permissible scope of subsequent punishment.

For whatever wrong the appellant has committed or may commit, by his publications, the state appropriately affords both public and private redress by its libel laws. As has been noted, the statute in question does not deal with punishments; it provides for no punishment, except in case of contempt for violation of the court's order, but for suppression and injunction—that is, for restraint upon publication.

The objection has also been made that the principle as to immunity from previous restraint is stated too broadly, if every such restraint is deemed to be prohibited. That is undoubtedly true; the protection even as to previous restraint is not absolutely unlimited. But the limitation has been recognized only in exceptional cases. "When a nation is at war many things that might be said in time of peace are such a hindrance to its effort that their utterance will not be endured so long as men fight and that no Court could regard them as protected by any constitutional right." Schenck v. United States. No one would question but that a government might prevent actual obstruction to its recruiting service or the publication of the sailing dates of transports or the number and location of troops. On similar grounds, the primary requirements of decency may be enforced against obscene publications. The security of the community life may be protected against incitements to acts of violence and the overthrow by force of orderly government. The constitutional guaranty of free speech does not "protect a man from an injunction against uttering words that may have all the effect of force. . . . These limitations are not applicable here. Nor are we now concerned with questions as to the extent of authority to prevent publications in order to protect private rights according to the principles governing the exercise of the jurisdiction of courts of equity. . . .

The fact that for approximately one hundred and fifty years there has been almost an entire absence of attempts to impose previous restraints upon publications relating to the malfeasance of public officers is significant of the deep-seated conviction that such restraints would violate constitutional right. Public officers, whose character and conduct remain open to debate and free discussion in the press, find their remedies for false accusations in actions under libel laws providing for redress and punishment, and not in proceedings to restrain the publication of newspapers and periodicals. The general principle that the constitutional guaranty of the liberty of the press gives immunity from previous restraints has been approved in many decisions under the provisions of state constitutions.

The importance of this immunity has not lessened. While reckless assaults upon public men, and efforts to bring obloquy upon those who are endeavoring faithfully to discharge official duties, exert a baleful influence and deserve the severest condemnation in public opinion, it cannot be said that this abuse is greater, and it is believed to be less, than that which characterized the period in which our institutions took shape. Meanwhile, the administration of government has become more complex, the opportunities for malfeasance and corruption have multiplied, crime has grown to most serious proportions, and the danger of its protection by unfaithful officials and of the impairment of the fundamental security of life and property by criminal alliances and official neglect, emphasizes the primary need of a vigilant and courageous press, especially in great cities. The fact that the liberty of the press may be abused by miscreant purveyors of scandal does not make any the less necessary the immunity of the press from previous restraint in dealing with offical misconduct. Subsequent punishment for such abuses as may exist is the appropriate remedy, consistent with constitutional privilege. . . .

For these reasons we hold the statute, so far as it authorized the proceedings in this action, to be an infringement of the liberty of the press guaranteed by the Fourteenth Amendment. We should add that this decision rests upon the operation and effect of the statute, without regard to the question of the truth of the charges contained in the particular periodical. The fact that the public officers named in this case, and those associated with the charges of official dereliction, may be deemed to be impeccable, cannot affect the conclusion that the statute imposes an unconstitutional restraint upon publication.

Judgment reversed.

MR. JUSTICE BUTLER, dissenting.

The decision of the Court in this case declares Minnesota and every other state powerless to restrain by injunction the business of publishing and circulating among the people malicious, scandalous, and defamatory periodicals that in due course of judicial procedure has been adjudged to be a public nuisance. It gives to freedom of the press a meaning and a scope not heretofore recognized, and construes "liberty" in the due process clause of the Fourteenth Amendment to put upon the states a federal restriction that is without precedent. . . .

The record shows, and it is conceded, that defendants' regular business was the publication of malicious, scandalous, and defamatory articles concerning the principal public officers, leading newspapers of the city, many private persons, and the Jewish race. It also shows that it was their purpose at all hazards to continue to carry on the business. In every edition slanderous and defamatory matter predominates to the practical exclusion of all else. Many of the statements are so highly improbable as to compel a finding that they are false. The articles themselves show malice. The defendant here has no standing to assert that the statute is invalid because it might be construed so as to violate the Constitution. His right is limited solely to the inquiry whether, having regard to the points properly raised in his case, the effect of applying the statute is to deprive him of his liberty without due process of law. This court should not reverse the judgment below upon the ground that in some other case the statute may be applied in a way that is repugnant to the freedom of the press protected by the Fourteenth Amendment. This record requires the Court to consider the statute as applied to the business of publishing articles that are in fact malicious, scandalous, and defamatory. . . .

The Minnesota statute does not operate as a previous restraint on publication within the proper meaning of that phrase. It does not authorize administrative control in advance such as was formerly exercised by the licensers and censors, but prescribes a remedy to be enforced by a suit in equity. In this case there was previous publication made in the course of the business of regularly producing malicious, scandalous, and defamatory periodicals. The business and publications unquestionably constitute an abuse of the right of free press. . . . It is fanciful to suggest similarity between the granting or enforcement of the decree authorized by this statute to prevent further publication of malicious, scandalous, and defamatory articles and the previous restraint upon the press by licensers as referred to by Blackstone and described in the history of the times to which he alludes. . . . The doctrine that measures such as the one before us are invalid because they operate as previous restraints to infringe freedom of press exposes the peace and good order of every community and the business and private affairs of every individual to the constant and protracted false and malicious assaults of any insolvent publisher who may have purpose and sufficient capacity to contrive and put into effect a scheme or program for oppression, blackmail or extortion.

The judgment should be affirmed.

MR. JUSTICE VAN DEVANTER, MR. JUSTICE MCREYNOLDS, and MR. JUSTICE SUTHERLAND concur in this opinion.

NEW YORK TIMES V. UNITED STATES
403 U.S. 713 (1971)

"In the First Amendment the Founding Fathers gave the free press the protection it must have to fulfill its essential role in our democracy. . . . Only a free and unrestrained press can effectively expose deception in government. . . . In revealing the workings of government that led to the Vietnam war, the newspapers did precisely that which the Founders hoped and trusted they would do."

The Question: Can a federal judge issue an injunction and impose a "prior restraint" on the further publication by the *New York Times* and *Washington Post* of portions of a "top secret" history of American involvement in the Vietnam War? The Pentagon Papers, prepared by Department of Defense personnel, were leaked to the newspapers by a former Pentagon employee.

The Arguments: PRO

The federal government has an inherent right to protect military secrets from unauthorized disclosure. In this case, the top secret history of the Vietnam War contained documents that responsible officials considered potentially damaging to the national security and that might, if published, jeopardize negotiations to end the war and endanger the lives of American troops and prisoners of war. This case falls within the "troop ship" exception to the rule against prior restraint, because the nation's enemies might learn from published excerpts details of American military operations that would compromise the safety of future operations, or details about past negotiations that might make it difficult or impossible to conduct future negotiations.

CON

This case does not involve a "troop ship" exception to the rule against prior restraint; that exception is limited to publication of the details of troop movements and other military plans that will occur in the future. In this case, the Pentagon Papers are entirely about events that took place in the past. Placing a "top secret" stamp on a government study does not forbid the press from publishing documents it has obtained from any source. There is no evidence in the record of this case that any material in the Pentagon Papers would so gravely endanger the conduct of the Vietnam War or negotiations to end the war that future publication should be enjoined. The statements of government officials that publication of excerpts of the study would endanger national security are suspect for bias and should not be relied upon by the courts.

MEET DANIEL ELLSBERG

For over seven years, like many other Americans I have been preoccupied with our involvement in Vietnam. In that time I have seen it first as a problem; then as a stalemate; then as a crime.

Each of these perspectives called for a different mode of personal commitment: a problem, to help solve it; a stalemate, to help extricate ourselves with grace; a crime, to expose and resist it, to try to stop it immediately, to seek moral and political change.

None of these aims—mine or, I would suppose, anyone else's—has met with success. It may be that five individuals, our Presidents from Truman to Nixon, should be excepted from this generalization, if I am right in concluding that each of them aimed mainly to avoid a definitive failure, "losing Indochina to Communism" during his tenure, so that renewed stalemate has been for them a kind of success. For the rest of us, efforts to *end* the conflict—whether it is seen as failed test, quagmire, or moral disaster—have been no more rewarded than efforts to win it. We fail or tire, it persists.

There are some who have been resisting for years, by a variety of means, what they saw clearly as an unjust war, a brutal fraud, a lawless imperial adventure. I deeply respect their courage, their insight, and commitment; I have, belatedly, joined them in spirit and action; indeed, although most Americans do not admire "antiwar activists," polls now indicate that a majority agree with them that the war is morally wrong. But the war persists. Why?

Is it simply because the forces maintaining the war are too strong? Too strong, say, to be defeated "quickly": i.e., by seven years of teach-ins and demonstrations, five years of large-scale draft resistance and emigration, four years of universal disillusionment (the Tet offensive took place four years ago this spring!); by an electoral drive in the primaries that unseated an incumbent President (again, four years ago),

the creation of a mood among voters that defeated his designated successor and produced a Presidential mandate to "end the war"; by another year, 1969–70, that saw the largest demonstrations yet, two years of unprecedented legislative challenges in the Senate (though not yet to defense appropriations), the largest action of nonviolent civil disobedience in U.S. history (producing 13,000 arrests in May, 1971, mostly illegal); by the draft board raids of the Catholic Left, small mutinies in Vietnam, the My Lai prosecutions; by twenty-five years of continuous resistance by the Vietnamese, making even the largest, most violent phase—from 1965 to the present—our longest war? Is more of just this opposition what is called for; is it simply too soon to expect an end?

Perhaps. In any case, without each of these forms of protest and resistance (except of the Vietnamese), the war might well be even larger and more murderous than it has been. Yet perhaps the failure to end the war reflects not only the undoubtedly great strength of the forces sustaining it, but reflects, as well, the limits and defects of the best current understanding of those forces and of the overall system in which they operate: an inadequate grasp of all the motives and institutions that matter, and of their vulnerabilities to change. That is not so necessarily; but I believe that it is the case. As the war goes on, the meaning of its nature and of its continuance becomes more and more challenging.

In my opinion this war, even at this late stage, needs not only to be resisted; it remains to be understood. . . . My research and governmental experience over the decade prior to the Pentagon Papers includes studies of "decision-making under uncertainty"; of Presidential "command and control," and of Presidential decision-making in specific crises. It also includes my actual experience in the Pentagon as Special Assistant to the Assistant Secretary of Defense (International Security Affairs), in the election-and-escalation period 1964–65; and in my two years in Vietnam, 1965–67, as a State

Department volunteer on General Edward Lansdale's senior liaison team, and then as Special Assistant to the Deputy Ambassador, William Porter.

All of this experience made it natural for me on my return from Vietnam to be urged, and to agree, to participate from the outset in the McNamara task force studying "the history of United States involvement in Vietnam from World War II to the present." At a later period I was, in fact, the only researcher in the country with authorized access to the completed McNamara Study. Indeed, it was these earlier interests in studying the decision-making process that had brought me to join the Defense Department full-time in 1964 and were among my motives in going to Vietnam in 1965. . . .

What I had learned, by June, 1966, or before it, was that the war was stalemated. By the next year I knew it would remain so. Two years of field work had discredited, in my eyes, any hopes of success, in almost any terms, in Vietnam, given the courses we were following and the increasingly obvious unlikelihood of our changing them. The prospect I saw was one of continued conflict, at increasing levels of violence, followed some day—probably later rather than sooner, and after more and more deaths, costs, destruction, and dissension at home—by U.S. withdrawal and NLF dominance.

It was not to find this—or to find out the shortcomings of American officials, practices and policies that seemed heavily at fault—that I had come to Vietnam two years earlier. The process of reaching these conclusions was, quite simply, the most frustrating, disappointing, disillusioning period of my life. I had come to Vietnam to learn, but also to help us succeed; and the learning was as bitter as the failure.

Yet my observations in Vietnam did not, in themselves, discredit the intentions of the policy-makers or the legitimacy of our original involvement, despite our evident "mistakes." The explanation that inadequate, misguided policies in Washington had been based on "bad information" from Vietnam seemed almost inescapable, watching the cable traffic from the transmitting end of the channel. It is easy for most Americans to guess that the President receives misleadingly optimistic reports from the field; in Vietnam, it is easy to *know* this is so. . . .

Whatever it was each President thought privately he might achieve from what he had decided to do, it must have differed from the written estimates and much of the advice he was receiving in those years; it could not simply be the product of bureaucratic euphoria or deception. Indeed, in each of those crisis years—in contrast to the years in-between—there had been enough realistic intelligence analyses and even operational reporting available to the President that it was hard to imagine that *more* truth-telling or even pessimism would have made any difference to his choices.

Could it be, then, that none of the lying to the Presidents had mattered? Or that it had mainly mirrored and supported their own deception of Congress and the public? If each President had been told at the point of escalation—as it appeared from the record—that what he was ordering would probably not solve the problem, what then was he up to? Why did he not do more—or less? And why did each President mislead the public and Congress about what he was doing and what he had been told?. . .

Here are some things I understood when I had finished reading the Pentagon Papers.

There have been no First and Second Indochina Wars, no Third War: just one war, continuously for a quarter of a century. In practical terms, it has been an American war almost from its beginning: a war of Vietnamese—not all of them but enough to persist—against American policy and American financing, proxies, technicians, firepower, and finally, troops and pilots. Since at least the late 1940's there has probably never been a year when political violence in Vietnam would have reached or stayed at the scale of a "war," had not the U.S. President, Congress, and citizens fueled it with money, weapons, and ultimately, manpower: first through the French, then wholly owned client regimes, and at last directly.

The popular critique that we have "interfered" in what is "really a civil war"—a notion long held privately by many of my former colleagues as a pledge to themselves of their secret realism—is as much a myth as the earlier official one of "aggression from the North." To call a conflict in which one army is financed and equipped entirely by foreigners a "civil war" simply screens a more painful reality: that the war is, after all, a foreign aggression. Our aggression. . . .

For myself, to read, through our own official documents, about the origins of the conflict and of our participation in it, is to see our involvement—and the killing we do—naked of any shred of legitimacy. That applies just as strongly to our deliberately prolonging it by a single additional day, or bomb, or death. Can it ever be precipitate to end a policy of murder? . . .

To ask myself, a man who had spent the last decade serving four . . . Presidents, to act on such perceptions was asking me to jump out of my skin. Something harder than risking it: that I had done already, along with some three million, mostly younger Americans who had gone to Vietnam. Most of us had seen our going as the response of loyal Americans to our President; until recently, few had supposed that might conflict with serving the legitimate interests of our country. What was needed now, to go beyond that reflex response, was the inspiration to find in oneself loyalties long unconsulted, deeper and broader than loyalty to the President: loyalties to America's founding concepts, to our Constitutional system, to countrymen, to one's own humanity—and to our "allies," the people we were bombing.

At this point it was other young Americans who helped me by their example. That same month of August, 1969, that I began to read the origins of the war and to learn the President's plans, I met for the first time, face-to-face, Americans who were on their way to prison or refusing to collaborate in an unjust war. I found them to be sober, intelligent, principled; they showed, in fact, the dedication I had respected in many officials I had known in Vietnam, but they were acting on different premises, which I now shared. These personal acts of "witness" gave me what reading alone could not.

In October, I joined my five colleagues at Rand in the first critical statement on Vietnam policy addressed to the public that any of us had ever signed: a letter to the *New York Times* calling for U.S. unilateral withdrawal within one year. At the same time, without the knowledge of anyone at Rand, I acted privately to reveal the information in the Pentagon Papers, beginning with the Senate Foreign Relations Committee.

As it worked out, nearly twenty months went by before the information finally reached the public and the rest of

Congress (or, for that matter, the Executive, which till then had neglected totally to unlock and study its own copies of the McNamara Study). Meanwhile, as warned, two more invasions had taken place; another million tons of bombs had fallen; nearly ten thousand more Americans had died, as well as hundreds of thousands of Indochinese. It had become painfully clear that much of Congress, too, was part of the problem; so I acted, as well, to inform the sovereign public through the "fourth branch of government," the press. . . .

Will the Pentagon Papers in the hands of the public eventually do more? Or is it possible that the American people, too, are part of the problem; that our passivity, fears, obedience weld us, unresisting, into the stalemate machine: that *we* are the problem for much of the rest of the world?

It is too soon to conclude that. There is too much information to be absorbed from the Pentagon Papers and the disclosures and analyses that are beginning to follow; too many myths and lies to be unlearned; habits too strong to be changed so quickly in a public that has let its sovereignty in foreign affairs atrophy for thirty years. . . .

In releasing the Pentagon Papers I acted in hope I still hold: that truths that changed me could help Americans free themselves and other victims from our longest war (Ellsberg, 1972).

PER CURIAM.

We granted certiorari in these cases in which the United States seeks to enjoin the New York Times and the Washington Post from publishing the contents of a classified study entitled "History of U.S. Decision-Making Process on Viet Nam Policy."

> "Any system of prior restraints of expression comes to this Court bearing a heavy presumption against its constitutional validity." Bantam Books, Inc. v. Sullivan (1963); see also Near v. Minnesota (1931). The Government "thus carries a heavy burden of showing justification for the imposition of such a restraint." Organization for a Better Austin v. Keefe (1971). The District Court for the Southern District of New York in the New York Times case and the District Court for the District of Columbia and the Court of Appeals for the District of Columbia Circuit in the Washington Post case held that the Government had not met that burden. We agree.

The judgment of the Court of Appeals for the District of Columbia Circuit is therefore affirmed. The order of the Court of Appeals for the Second Circuit is reversed and the case is remanded with directions to enter a judgment affirming the judgment of the District Court for the Southern District of New York. The stays entered June 25, 1971, by the Court are vacated. The judgments shall issue forthwith.

So ordered.

MR. JUSTICE BLACK, with whom MR. JUSTICE DOUGLAS joins, concurring.

I adhere to the view that the Government's case against the Washington Post should have been dismissed and that the injunction against the New York Times should have been vacated without oral argument when the cases were first presented to this Court. I believe that every moment's continuance of the injunctions against these newspapers amounts to a flagrant, indefensible, and continuing violation of the First Amendment. Furthermore, after oral argument, I agree completely that we must affirm the judgment of the Court of Appeals for the District of Columbia Circuit and reverse the judgment of the Court of Appeals for the Second Circuit for the reasons stated by my Brothers Douglas and Brennan. In my view it is unfortunate that some of my Brethren are apparently willing to hold that the publication of news may sometimes be enjoined. Such a holding would make a shambles of the First Amendment.

Our Government was launched in 1789 with the adoption of the Constitution. The Bill of Rights, including the First Amendment, followed in 1791. Now, for the first time in the 182 years since the founding of the Republic, the federal courts are asked to hold that the First Amendment does not mean what it says, but rather means that the Government can halt the publication of current news of vital importance to the people of this country.

In seeking injunctions against these newspapers and in its presentation to the Court, the Executive Branch seems to have forgotten the essential purpose and history of the First Amendment. When the Constitution was adopted, many people strongly opposed it because the document contained no Bill of Rights to safeguard certain basic freedoms. They especially feared that the new powers granted to a central government might be interpreted to permit the government to curtail freedom of religion, press, assembly, and speech. In response to an overwhelming public clamor, James Madison offered a series of amendments to satisfy citizens that these great liberties would remain safe and beyond the power of government to abridge. Madison proposed what later became the First Amendment in three parts, two of which are set out below, and one of which proclaimed: "The people shall not be deprived or abridged of their right to speak, to write, or to publish their sentiments; and the freedom of the press, as one of the great bulwarks of liberty, shall be inviolable." The amendments were offered to curtail and restrict the general powers granted to the Executive, Legislative, and Judicial Branches two years before in the original Constitution. The Bill of Rights changed the original Constitution into a new charter under which no branch of government could abridge the people's freedoms of press, speech, religion, and assembly. Yet the Solicitor General argues and some members of the Court appear to agree that the general powers of the Government adopted in the original Constitution should be interpreted to limit and restrict the specific and emphatic guarantees of the Bill of Rights adopted later. I can imagine no greater perversion of history. Madison and the other Framers of the First Amendment, able men that they were, wrote in language they earnestly believed could never be misunderstood: "Congress shall make no law . . . abridging the freedom . . . of the press. . . ." Both the history and language of the First Amendment support the view that the press must be left free to publish news, whatever the source, without censorship, injunctions, or prior restraints.

In the First Amendment the Founding Fathers gave the free press the protection it must have to fulfill its essential role in our democracy. The press was to serve the governed, not the governors. The Government's power to censor the press was abolished so that the press would remain forever free to censure the Government. The press was protected so that it could bare the secrets of government and inform the people. Only a free and unrestrained press can effectively expose deception in government. And paramount among the responsibilities of a free press is the duty to prevent any part of the government from deceiving the people and sending them off to distant lands to die of foreign fevers and foreign shot and shell. In my view, far from deserving condemnation for their courageous reporting, the New York Times, the Washington Post, and other newspapers should be commended for serving the purpose that the Founding Fathers saw so clearly. In revealing the workings of government that led to the Vietnam war, the newspapers nobly did precisely that which the Founders hoped and trusted they would do.

The Government's case here is based on premises entirely different from those that guided the Framers of the First Amendment. The Solicitor General has carefully and emphatically stated:

> Now, Mr. Justice [BLACK], your construction of . . . [the First Amendment] is well known, and I certainly respect it. You say that no law means no law, and that should be obvious. I can only say, Mr. Justice, that to me it is equally obvious that "no law" does not mean "no law", and I would seek to persuade the Court that is true. . . . [T]here are other parts of the Constitution that grant powers and responsibilities to the Executive, and . . . the First Amendment was not intended to make it impossible for the Executive to function or to protect the security of the United States.

And the Government argues in its brief that in spite of the First Amendment, "[t]he authority of the Executive Department to protect the nation against publication of information whose disclosure would endanger the national security stems from two interrelated sources: the constitutional power of the President over the conduct of foreign affairs and his authority as Commander-in-Chief."

In other words, we are asked to hold that despite the First Amendment's emphatic command, the Executive Branch, the Congress, and the Judiciary can make laws enjoining publication of current news and abridging freedom of the press in the name of "national security." The Government does not even attempt to rely on any act of Congress. Instead it makes the bold and dangerously far-reaching contention that the courts should take it upon themselves to "make" a law abridging freedom of the press in the name of equity, presidential power and national security, even when the representatives of the people in Congress have adhered to the command of the First Amendment and refused to make such a law. To find that the President has "inherent power" to halt the publication of news by resort to the courts would wipe out the First Amendment and destroy the fundamental liberty and security of the very people the Government hopes to make "secure." No one can read the history of the adoption of the First Amendment without being convinced beyond any doubt that it was injunctions like those sought here that Madison and his collaborators intended to outlaw in this Nation for all time.

The word "security" is a broad, vague generality whose contours should not be invoked to abrogate the fundamental law embodied in the First Amendment. The guarding of military and diplomatic secrets at the expense of informed representative government provides no real security for our Republic. The Framers of the First Amendment, fully aware of both the need to defend a new nation and the abuses of the English and Colonial governments, sought to give this new society strength and security by providing that freedom of speech, press, religion, and assembly should not be abridged. . . .

MR. JUSTICE BRENNAN, concurring.

I write separately in these cases only to emphasize what should be apparent: that our judgments in the present cases may not be taken to indicate the propriety, in the future, of issuing temporary stays and restraining orders to block the publication of material sought to be suppressed by the Government. So far as I can determine, never before has the United States sought to enjoin a newspaper from publishing information in its possession. The relative novelty of the questions presented, the necessary haste with which decisions were reached, the magnitude of the interests asserted, and the fact that all the parties have concentrated their arguments upon the question whether permanent restraints were proper may have justified at least some of the restraints heretofore imposed in these cases.

Certainly it is difficult to fault the several courts below for seeking to assure that the issues here involved were preserved for ultimate review by this Court. But even if it be assumed that some of the interim restraints were proper in the two cases before us, that assumption has no bearing upon the propriety of similar judicial action in the future. To begin with, there has now been ample time for reflection and judgment; whatever values there may be in the preservation of novel questions for appellate review may not support any restraints in the future. More important, the First Amendment stands as an absolute bar to the imposition of judicial restraints in circumstances of the kind presented by these cases.

The error that has pervaded these cases from the outset was the granting of any injunctive relief whatsoever, interim or otherwise. The entire thrust of the Government's claim throughout these cases has been that publication of the material sought to be enjoined "could," or "might," or "may" prejudice the national interest in various ways. But the First Amendment tolerates absolutely no prior judicial restraints of the press predicated upon surmise or conjecture that untoward consequences may result. Our cases, it is true, have indicated that there is a single, extremely narrow class of cases in which the First Amendment's ban on prior judicial restraint may be overridden. Our cases have thus far indicated that such cases may arise only when the Nation "is at war," Schenck v. United States (1919), during which times "[n]o one would question but that a government might prevent actual obstruction to its recruiting service or the publication of the sailing dates of transports or the number and location of troops." Near v. Minnesota (1931). Even if the present world situation were assumed to be tantamount to a time of war, or if the power of presently available armaments would justify even in peacetime the suppression of information that would set in motion a nuclear holocaust, in neither of these actions has the Government presented or even alleged that publication of items from or based upon the material at issue would cause the happening of an event of that nature. "[T]he chief purpose of [the First Amendment's] guaranty [is] to prevent previous restraints upon publication." Near v. Minnesota. Thus, only governmental allegation and proof that publication must inevitably, directly, and immediately cause the occurrence of an event kindred to imperiling the safety of a transport already at sea can support even the issuance of an interim restraining order. In no event may mere conclusions be sufficient: for if the Executive Branch seeks judicial aid in preventing publication, it must inevitably submit the basis upon which that aid is sought to scrutiny by the judiciary. And therefore, every restraint issued in this case, whatever its form, has violated the First Amendment—and not less so because that restraint was justified as necessary to afford the courts an opportunity to examine the claim more thoroughly. Unless and until the Government has clearly made out its case, the First Amendment commands that no injunction may issue. . . . Here there is no question but that the material sought to be suppressed is within the protection of the First Amendment; the only question is whether, notwithstanding that fact, its publication may be enjoined for a time because of the presence of an overwhelming national interest. Similarly, copyright cases have no pertinence here: the Government is not asserting an interest in the particular form of words chosen in the documents, but is seeking to suppress the ideas expressed therein. And the copyright laws, of course, protect only the form of expression and not the ideas expressed.

MR. CHIEF JUSTICE BURGER, dissenting.

So clear are the constitutional limitations on prior restraint against expression, that from the time of Near v. Minnesota (1931), until recently in Organization for a Better Austin v. Keefe (1971), we have had little occasion to be concerned with cases involving prior restraints against news reporting on matters of public interest. There is, therefore, little variation among the members of the Court in terms of resistance to prior restraints against publication. Adherence to this basic constitutional principle, however, does not make these cases simple. In these cases, the imperative of a free and unfettered press comes into collision with another imperative, the effective functioning of a complex modern government and specifically the effective exercise of certain constitutional powers of the Executive. Only those who view the First Amendment as an absolute in all circumstances—a view I respect, but reject—can find such cases as these to be simple or easy.

These cases are not simple for another and more immediate reason. We do not know the facts of the cases. No District Judge knew all the facts. No Court of Appeals judge knew all the facts. No member of this Court knows all the facts.

Why are we in this posture, in which only those judges to whom the First Amendment is absolute and permits of no restraint in any circumstances or for any reason, are really in a position to act? I suggest we are in this posture because these cases have been conducted in unseemly haste. . . . The prompt setting of these cases reflects our universal abhorrence of prior restraint. But prompt judicial action does not mean unjudicial haste.

Here, moreover, the frenetic haste is due in large part to the manner in which the Times proceeded from the date it obtained the purloined documents. It seems reasonably clear now that the haste precluded reasonable and deliberate judicial treatment of these cases and was not warranted. The precipitate action of this Court aborting trials not yet completed is not the kind of judicial conduct that ought to attend the disposition of a great issue.

The newspapers make a derivative claim under the First Amendment; they denominate this right as the public "right to know"; by implication, the Times asserts a sole trusteeship of that right by virtue of its journalistic "scoop." The right is asserted as an absolute. Of course, the First Amendment right itself is not an absolute, as Justice Holmes so long ago pointed out in his aphorism concerning the right to shout "fire" in a crowded theater if there was no fire. There are other exceptions, some of which Chief Justice Hughes mentioned by way of example in Near v. Minnesota. There are no doubt other exceptions no one has had occasion to describe or discuss. Conceivably such exceptions may be lurking in these cases and would have been flushed had they been properly considered in the trial courts, free from unwarranted deadlines and frenetic pressures. An issue of this importance should be tried and heard in a judicial atmosphere conducive to thoughtful, reflective deliberation, especially when haste, in terms of hours, is unwarranted in light of the long period the Times, by its own choice, deferred publication.

It is not disputed that the Times has had unauthorized possession of the documents for three to four months, during which it has had its expert analysts studying them, presumably digesting them and preparing the material for publication. During all of this time, the Times, presumably in its capacity as trustee of the public's "right to know," has held up publication for purposes it considered proper and thus public knowledge was delayed. No doubt this was for a good reason; the analysis of 7,000 pages of complex material drawn from a vastly greater volume of material would inevitably take time and the writing of good news stories takes time. But why should the United States Government, from whom this information was illegally acquired by someone, along with all the counsel, trial judges, and appellate judges be placed under needless pressure? After these months of deferral, the alleged "right to know" has somehow and suddenly become a right that must be vindicated instanter.

Would it have been unreasonable, since the newspaper could anticipate the Government's objections to release of secret material, to give the Government an opportunity to review the entire collection and determine whether agreement could be reached on publication? Stolen or not, if security was not in fact jeopardized, much of the material could no doubt have been declassified, since it spans a period ending in 1968. With such an approach—one that great newspapers have in the past practiced and stated editorially to be the duty of an honorable press—the newspapers and Government might well have narrowed the area of disagreement as to what was and was not publishable, leaving the remainder to be resolved in orderly litigation, if necessary. To me it is hardly believable that a newspaper long regarded as a great institution in American life would fail to perform one of the basic and simple duties of every citizen with respect to the discovery or possession of stolen property or secret government documents. That duty, I had thought—perhaps naively—was to report forthwith, to responsible public officers. This duty rests on taxi drivers, Justices, and the New York Times. The course followed by the Times, whether so calculated or not, removed any possibility of orderly litigation of the issues. If the action of the judges up to now has been correct, that result is sheer happenstance. Our grant of the writ of certiorari before final judgment in the Times case aborted the trial in the District Court before it had made a complete record pursuant to the mandate of the Court of Appeals for the Second Circuit.

The consequence of all this melancholy series of events is that we literally do not know what we are acting on. As I see it, we have been forced to deal with litigation concerning rights of great magnitude without an adequate record, and surely without time for adequate treatment either in the prior proceedings or in this Court. It is interesting to note that counsel on both sides, in oral argument before this Court, were frequently unable to respond to questions on factual points. Not surprisingly they pointed out that they had been working literally "around the clock" and simply were unable to review the documents that give rise to these cases and were not familiar with them. This Court is in no better posture. . . .

I would affirm the Court of Appeals for the Second Circuit and allow the District Court to complete the trial aborted by our grant of certiorari, meanwhile preserving the status quo in the Post case. I would direct that the District Court on remand give priority to the Times case to the exclusion of all other business of that court but I would not set arbitrary deadlines. . . . We all crave speedier judicial processes but when judges are pressured as in these cases the result is a parody of the judicial function.

MR. JUSTICE HARLAN, with whom THE CHIEF JUSTICE and MR. JUSTICE BLACKMUN join, dissenting.

With all respect, I consider that the Court has been almost irresponsibly feverish in dealing with these cases. Both the Court of Appeals for the Second Circuit and the Court of Appeals for the District of Columbia Circuit rendered judgment on June 23. The New York Times' petition for certiorari, its motion for accelerated consideration thereof, and its application for interim relief were filed in this Court on June 24 at about 11 a.m. The application of the United States for interim relief in the Post case was also filed here on June 24 at about 7:15 p.m. This Court's order setting a hearing before us on June 26 at 11 a.m., a course which I joined only to avoid the possibility of even more peremptory action by the Court, was issued less than 24 hours before. The record in the Post case was filed with the Clerk shortly before 1 p.m. on June 25; the record in the Times case did not arrive until 7 or 8 o'clock that same night. The briefs of the parties were received less than two hours before argument on June 26.

This frenzied train of events took place in the name of the presumption against prior restraints created by the First Amendment. Due regard for the extraordinarily important and difficult questions involved in these litigations should have led the Court to shun such a precipitate timetable. . . . The time which has been available to us, to the lower courts, and to the parties has been wholly inadequate for giving these cases the kind of consideration they deserve. It is a re-flection on the stability of the judicial process that these great issues—as important as any that have arisen during my time on the Court—should have been decided under the pressures engendered by the torrent of publicity that has attended these litigations from their inception.

Forced as I am to reach the merits of these cases, I dissent from the opinion and judgments of the Court. Within the severe limitations imposed by the time constraints under which I have been required to operate, I can only state my reasons in telescoped form, even though in different circumstances I would have felt constrained to deal with the cases in the fuller sweep indicated above. . . .

It is plain to me that the scope of the judicial function in passing upon the activities of the Executive Branch of the Government in the field of foreign affairs is very narrowly restricted. This view is, I think, dictated by the concept of separation of powers upon which our constitutional system rests. . . . I agree that, in performance of its duty to protect the values of the First Amendment against political pressures, the judiciary must review the initial Executive determination to the point of satisfying itself that the subject matter of the dispute does lie within the proper compass of the President's foreign relations power. Constitutional considerations forbid "a complete abandonment of judicial control." Moreover, the judiciary may properly insist that the determination that disclosure of the subject matter would irreparably impair the national security be made by the head of the Executive Department concerned—here the Secretary of State or the Secretary of Defense—after actual personal consideration by that officer. This safeguard is required in the analogous area of executive claims of privilege for secrets of state. But in my judgment the judiciary may not properly go beyond these two inquiries and redetermine for itself the probable impact of disclosure on the national security.

Even if there is some room for the judiciary to override the executive determination, it is plain that the scope of review must be exceedingly narrow. I can see no indication in the opinions of either the District Court or the Court of Appeals in the Post litigation that the conclusions of the Executive were given even the deference owing to an administrative agency, much less that owing to a co-equal branch of the Government operating within the field of its constitutional prerogative.

Accordingly, I would vacate the judgment of the Court of Appeals for the District of Columbia Circuit on this ground and remand the case for further proceedings in the District Court. Before the commencement of such further proceedings, due opportunity should be afforded the Government for procuring from the Secretary of State or the Secretary of Defense or both an expression of their views on the issue of national security. The ensuing review by the District Court should be in accordance with the views expressed in this opinion. And for the reasons stated above I would affirm the judgment of the Court of Appeals for the Second Circuit.

Pending further hearings in each case conducted under the appropriate ground rules, I would continue the restraints on publication. I cannot believe that the doctrine prohibiting prior restraints reaches to the point of preventing courts from maintaining the status quo long enough to act responsibly in matters of such national importance as those involved here.

HAZELWOOD SCHOOL DISTRICT V. KUHLMEIER
484 U.S. 260 (1988)

*"Educators are entitled to exercise greater control over [school-sponsored publications] to assure that . . .
readers or listeners are not exposed to material that may be inappropriate for their level of maturity
and that the views of the individual speaker are not erroneously attributed to the school."*

The Question: Can a school principal order that particular articles in a newspaper prepared by high school students be removed before publication on the ground that they deal with issues—teen pregnancy and the impact of divorce on students in this case— that are inappropriate in content and that might invade the privacy of students or parents who are quoted or referred to in the articles, even if their names are withheld?

The Arguments: PRO

Student newspapers, which are funded by the schools and supervised by teachers, are not the same as other newspapers. In this case, the students who researched and wrote the two articles in question were subject to final approval by teachers and the principal, who are responsible for making sure that articles are appropriate in content and style for a student audience, and that articles do not contain quotations or details that might identify persons whose privacy should be protected. High school students are not professional or independent journalists, and school officials have a legitimate concern for the accuracy and fairness of what is published in school newspapers.

CON

The censorship of high school newspapers sends a message to student journalists that they can print only what pleases their teachers and principals. The articles at issue in this case dealt with topics that concern every student, and the record does not show that anything in the censored articles was false or violated standards of journalistic ethics. In this case, school officials had approved a statement that gave student journalists the protection of the First Amendment in what they printed. The fact that the school funds the newspaper does not give teachers or administrators the authority to censor articles they consider inappropriate.

JUSTICE WHITE delivered the opinion of the Court.

This case concerns the extent to which educators may exercise editorial control over the contents of a high school newspaper produced as part of the school's journalism curriculum. Petitioners are the Hazelwood School District in St. Louis County, Missouri; various school officials; Robert Eugene Reynolds, the principal of Hazelwood East High School; and Howard Emerson, a teacher in the school district. Respondents are three former Hazelwood East students who were staff members of Spectrum, the school newspaper. They contend that school officials violated their First Amendment rights by deleting two pages of articles from the May 13, 1983, issue of Spectrum.

Spectrum was written and edited by the Journalism II class at Hazelwood East. The newspaper was published every three weeks or so during the 1982–1983 school year. More than 4,500 copies of the newspaper were distributed during that year to students, school personnel, and members of the community. . . . The practice at Hazelwood East during the spring 1983 semester was for the journalism teacher to submit page proofs of each Spectrum issue to Principal Reynolds for his review prior to publication. On May 10, Emerson delivered the proofs of the May 13 edition to Reynolds, who objected to two of the articles scheduled to appear in that edition. One of the stories described three Hazelwood East students' experiences with pregnancy; the other discussed the impact of divorce on students at the school.

Reynolds was concerned that, although the pregnancy story used false names "to keep the identity of these girls a secret," the pregnant students still might be identifiable from the text. He also believed that the article's references to sexual activity and birth control were inappropriate for some of the younger students at the school. In addition, Reynolds was concerned that a student identified by name in the divorce story had complained that her father "wasn't spending enough time with my mom, my sister and I" prior to the divorce, "was always out of town on business or out late playing cards with the guys," and "always argued about everything" with her mother. Reynolds believed that the student's parents should have been given an opportunity to respond to these remarks or to consent to their publication. He was unaware that Emerson had deleted the student's name from the final version of the article.

Reynolds believed that there was no time to make the necessary changes in the stories before the scheduled press run and that the newspaper would not appear before the end of the school year if printing were delayed to any significant extent. He concluded that his only options under the circumstances were to publish a four-page newspaper instead of the planned six-page newspaper, eliminating the two pages on which the offending stories appeared, or to publish no newspaper at all. Accordingly, he directed Emerson to withhold from publication the two pages containing the stories on pregnancy and divorce. He informed his superiors of the decision, and they concurred.

Respondents subsequently commenced this action in the United States District Court for the Eastern District of Missouri seeking a declaration that their First Amendment rights had been violated, injunctive relief, and monetary damages. After a bench trial, the District Court denied an injunction, holding that no First Amendment violation had occurred. . . . The Court of Appeals for the Eighth Circuit reversed. The court held that Spectrum was not only "a part of the school adopted curriculum," but also a public forum, because the newspaper was "intended to be and operated as a conduit for student viewpoint." The court then concluded that Spectrum's status as a public forum precluded school officials from censoring its contents except when "necessary to avoid material and substantial interference with school work or discipline . . . or the rights of others." Accordingly, the court held that school officials had violated respondents' First Amendment rights by deleting the two pages of the newspaper. . . . We granted certiorari, and we now reverse.

Students in the public schools do not "shed their constitutional rights to freedom of speech or expression at the schoolhouse gate." Tinker. They cannot be punished merely for expressing their personal views on the school premises— whether "in the cafeteria, or on the playing field, or on the campus during the authorized hours," unless school authorities have reason to believe that such expression will "substantially interfere with the work of the school or impinge upon the rights of other students." We have nonetheless recognized that the First Amendment rights of students in the public schools "are not automatically coextensive with the rights of adults in other settings," and must be "applied in light of the special characteristics of the school environment." A school need not tolerate student speech that is inconsistent with its "basic educational mission," even though the government could not censor similar speech outside the school. . . . We thus recognized that "[t]he determination of what manner of speech in the classroom or in school assembly is inappropriate properly rests with the school board," rather than with the federal courts. It is in this context that respondents' First Amendment claims must be considered. . . .

The Hazelwood East Curriculum Guide described the Journalism II course as a "laboratory situation in which the students publish the school newspaper applying skills they have learned in Journalism I." The lessons that were to be learned from the Journalism II course, according to the Curriculum Guide, included development of journalistic skills

under deadline pressure, "The legal, moral, and ethical restrictions imposed upon journalists within the school community," and "responsibility and acceptance of criticism for articles of opinion." . . . Journalism II was taught by a faculty member during regular class hours. Students received grades and academic credit for their performance in the course.

School officials did not deviate in practice from their policy that production of Spectrum was to be part of the educational curriculum and a "regular classroom activit[y]." Robert Stergos, the journalism teacher during most of the 1982–1983 school year, selected the editors of the newspaper, scheduled publication dates, decided the number of pages for each issue, assigned story ideas to class members, advised students on the development of their stories, reviewed the use of quotations, edited stories, selected and edited the letters to the editor, and dealt with the printing company. Many of these decisions were made without consultation with the Journalism II students. . . . Accordingly, school officials were entitled to regulate the contents of Spectrum in any reasonable manner. It is this standard, rather than our decision in Tinker, that governs this case.

The question whether the First Amendment requires a school to tolerate particular student speech—the question that we addressed in Tinker—is different from the question whether the First Amendment requires a school affirmatively to promote particular student speech. The former question addresses educators' ability to silence a student's personal expression that happens to occur on the school premises. The latter question concerns educators' authority over school-sponsored publications, theatrical productions, and other expressive activities that students, parents, and members of the public might reasonably perceive to bear the imprimatur of the school. These activities may fairly be characterized as part of the school curriculum, whether or not they occur in a traditional classroom setting, so long as they are supervised by faculty members and designed to impart particular knowledge or skills to student participants and audiences.

Educators are entitled to exercise greater control over this second form of student expression to assure that participants learn whatever lessons the activity is designed to teach, that readers or listeners are not exposed to material that may be inappropriate for their level of maturity, and that the views of the individual speaker are not erroneously attributed to the school. Hence, a school may in its capacity as publisher of a school newspaper or producer of a school play "disassociate itself" from speech that is, for example, ungrammatical, poorly written, inadequately researched, biased or prejudiced, vulgar or profane, or unsuitable for immature audiences. A school must be able to set high standards for the student speech that is disseminated under its auspices— standards that may be higher than those demanded by some newspaper publishers or theatrical producers in the "real" world—and may refuse to disseminate student speech that does not meet those standards. In addition, a school must be able to take into account the emotional maturity of the intended audience in determining whether to disseminate student speech on potentially sensitive topics, which might range from the existence of Santa Claus in an elementary school setting to the particulars of teenage sexual activity in a high school setting. A school must also retain the authority to refuse to sponsor student speech that might reasonably be perceived to advocate drug or alcohol use, irresponsible sex, or conduct otherwise inconsistent with "the shared values of a civilized social order," or to associate the school with any position other than neutrality on matters of political controversy. Otherwise, the schools would be unduly constrained from fulfilling their role as "a principal instrument in awakening the child to cultural values, in preparing him for later professional training, and in helping him to adjust normally to his environment."

Accordingly, we conclude that the standard articulated in Tinker for determining when a school may punish student expression need not also be the standard for determining when a school may refuse to lend its name and resources to the dissemination of student expression. Instead, we hold that educators do not offend the First Amendment by exercising editorial control over the style and content of student speech in school-sponsored expressive activities so long as their actions are reasonably related to legitimate pedagogical concerns. . . .

We also conclude that Principal Reynolds acted reasonably in requiring the deletion from the May 13 issue of Spectrum of the pregnancy article, the divorce article, and the remaining articles that were to appear on the same pages of the newspaper. The initial paragraph of the pregnancy article declared that "[a]ll names have been changed to keep the identity of these girls a secret." The principal concluded that the students' anonymity was not adequately protected, however, given the other identifying information in the article and the small number of pregnant students at the school. Indeed, a teacher at the school credibly testified that she could positively identify at least one of the girls and possibly all three. It is likely that many students at Hazelwood East would have been at least as successful in identifying the girls. . . . The student who was quoted by name in the version of the divorce article seen by Principal Reynolds made comments sharply critical of her father. The principal could reasonably have concluded that an individual publicly identified as an inattentive parent—indeed, as one who chose "playing cards with the guys" over home and family—was entitled to an opportunity to defend himself as a matter of journalistic fairness. . . .

In sum, we cannot reject as unreasonable Principal Reynolds' conclusion that neither the pregnancy article nor the divorce article was suitable for publication in Spectrum. Reynolds could reasonably have concluded that the students who had written and edited these articles had not sufficiently mastered those portions of the Journalism II curriculum that pertained to the treatment of controversial issues and personal attacks, the need to protect the privacy of individuals whose most intimate concerns are to be revealed in the newspaper, and "the legal, moral, and ethical restrictions imposed upon journalists within [a] school community" that includes adolescent subjects and readers. Finally, we conclude that the principal's decision to delete two pages of Spectrum, rather than to delete only the offending articles or to require that they be modified, was reasonable under the circumstances as he understood them. Accordingly, no violation of First Amendment rights occurred.

The judgment of the Court of Appeals for the Eighth Circuit is therefore reversed.

JUSTICE BRENNAN, with whom JUSTICE MARSHALL and JUSTICE BLACKMUN join, dissenting.

When the young men and women of Hazelwood East High School registered for Journalism II, they expected a civics lesson. Spectrum, the newspaper they were to publish, "was not just a class exercise in which students learned to prepare papers and hone writing skills, it was a . . . forum established to give students an opportunity to express their views while gaining an appreciation of their rights and responsibilities under the First Amendment to the United States Constitution. . . . [A]t the beginning of each school year," the student journalists published a Statement of Policy—tacitly approved each year by school authorities—announcing their expectation that "Spectrum, as a student-press publication, accepts all rights implied by the First Amendment. . . . Only speech that 'materially and substantially interferes with the requirements of appropriate discipline' can be found unacceptable and therefore prohibited." The school board itself affirmatively guaranteed the students of Journalism II an atmosphere conducive to fostering such an appreciation and exercising the full panoply of rights associated with a free student press. "School sponsored student publications," it vowed, "will not restrict free expression or diverse viewpoints within the rules of responsible journalism."

This case arose when the Hazelwood East administration breached its own promise, dashing its students' expectations. The school principal, without prior consultation or explanation, excised six articles—comprising two full pages—of the May 13, 1983, issue of Spectrum. He did so not because any of the articles would "materially and substantially interfere with the requirements of appropriate discipline," but simply because he considered two of the six "inappropriate, personal, sensitive, and unsuitable" for student consumption. In my view the principal broke more than just a promise. He violated the First Amendment's prohibitions against censorship of any student expression that neither disrupts classwork nor invades the rights of others, and against any censorship that is not narrowly tailored to serve its purpose.

Public education serves vital national interests in preparing the Nation's youth for life in our increasingly complex society and for the duties of citizenship in our democratic Republic. The public school conveys to our young the information and tools required not merely to survive in, but to contribute to, civilized society. . . . The public educator's task is weighty and delicate indeed. It demands particularized and supremely subjective choices among diverse curricula, moral values, and political stances to teach or inculcate in students, and among various methodologies for doing so. Accordingly, we have traditionally reserved "daily operation of school systems" to the States and their local school boards. We have not, however, hesitated to intervene where their decisions run afoul of the Constitution. . . . See e.g., Edwards v. Aguillard, Epperson v. Arkansas, West Virginia Board of Education v. Barnette.

Free student expression undoubtedly sometimes interferes with the effectiveness of the school's pedagogical functions. Some brands of student expression do so by directly preventing the school from pursuing its pedagogical mission: The young polemic who stands on a soapbox during calculus class to deliver an eloquent political diatribe interferes with the legitimate teaching of calculus. And the student who delivers a lewd endorsement of a student-government candidate might so extremely distract an impressionable high school audience as to interfere with the orderly operation of the school. Other student speech, however, frustrates the school's legitimate pedagogical purposes merely by expressing a message that conflicts with the school's, without directly interfering with the school's expression of its message: A student who responds to a political science teacher's question with the retort, "socialism is good," subverts the school's inculcation of the message that capitalism is better. Even the maverick who sits in class passively sporting a symbol of protest against a government policy, Tinker v. Des Moines, or the gossip who sits in the student commons swapping stories of sexual escapade could readily muddle a clear official message condoning the government policy or condemning teenage sex. Likewise, the student newspaper that, like Spectrum, conveys a moral position at odds with the school's official stance might subvert the administration's legitimate inculcation of its own perception of community values.

If mere incompatibility with the school's pedagogical message were a constitutionally sufficient justification for the suppression of student speech, school officials could censor each of the students or student organizations in the foregoing hypotheticals, converting our public schools into "enclaves of totalitarianism" that "strangle the free mind at its source." The First Amendment permits no such blanket censorship authority. While the "constitutional rights of students in public school are not automatically coextensive with the rights of adults in other settings," students in the public schools do not "shed their constitutional rights to freedom of speech or expression at the schoolhouse gate," Tinker. . . . [P]ublic educators must accommodate some student expression even if it offends them or offers views or values that contradict those the school wishes to inculcate. . . . I fully agree with the Court that the First Amendment should afford an educator the prerogative not to sponsor the publication of a newspaper article that is "ungrammatical, poorly written, inadequately researched, biased or prejudiced," or that falls short of the "high standards for . . . student speech that is disseminated under [the school's] auspices. . . ." But we need not abandon Tinker to reach that conclusion; we need only apply it. The enumerated criteria reflect the skills that the curricular newspaper "is designed to teach." The educator may, under Tinker, constitu-

tionally "censor" poor grammar, writing, or research because to reward such expression would "materially disrup[t]" the newspaper's curricular purpose.

The same cannot be said of official censorship designed to shield the audience or dissociate the sponsor from the expression. Censorship so motivated might well serve some other school purpose. But it in no way furthers the curricular purposes of a student newspaper, unless one believes that the purpose of the school newspaper is to teach students that the press ought never report bad news, express unpopular views, or print a thought that might upset its sponsors. Unsurprisingly, Hazelwood East claims no such pedagogical purpose. . . .

Tinker teaches us that the state educator's undeniable, and undeniably vital, mandate to inculcate moral and political values is not a general warrant to act as "thought police" stifling discussion of all but state-approved topics and advocacy of all but the official position. Otherwise educators could transform students into "closed-circuit recipients of only that which the State chooses to communicate," and cast a perverse and impermissible "pall of orthodoxy over the classroom." . . . The mere fact of school sponsorship does not, as the Court suggests, license such thought control in the high school, whether through school suppression of disfavored viewpoints or through official assessment of topic sensitivity. . . . The State's prerogative to dissolve the student newspaper entirely (or to limit its subject matter) no more entitles it to dictate which viewpoints students may express on its pages, than the State's prerogative to close down the schoolhouse entitles it to prohibit the nondisruptive expression of antiwar sentiment within its gates. . . .

The Court opens its analysis in this case by purporting to reaffirm Tinker's time-tested proposition that public school students "do not shed their constitutional rights to freedom of speech or expression at the schoolhouse gate." That is an ironic introduction to an opinion that denudes high school students of much of the First Amendment protection that Tinker itself prescribed. . . . The young men and women of Hazelwood East expected a civics lesson, but not the one the Court teaches them today.

I dissent.

BRANZBURG V. HAYES
408 U.S. 665 (1972)

"We perceive no basis for holding that the public interest in law enforcement and in ensuring effective grand jury proceedings is insufficient to override the consequential, but uncertain, burden on news gathering that is said to result from insisting that reporters, like other citizens, respond to relevant questions put to them in the course of a valid grand jury investigation."

The Question: Can a state judge order a journalist to reveal to a grand jury the names of persons who were sources for articles about criminal activities being investigated by the grand jurors, if those sources had been given assurances their names would not be disclosed?

The Arguments: PRO

The law does not recognize a "reporter's privilege" that is analogous to the privileges given to spouses, the clergy, doctors, and therapists. Reporters have a legitimate interest in protecting the confidentiality of their sources, but that interest must yield to the interests of law enforcement, if the reporter has published accounts of criminal activity and if the prosecutors have no other source for the information contained in the articles. These exceptions to the rule of confidentiality are narrow and limited, and the press should not fear that prosecutors will engage in "fishing expeditions" and rummage through their files for evidence of criminal activity.

CON

The press would not be able to operate if prosecutors could force reporters to disclose their confidential sources for any reason. Sources of news, particularly reporting on criminal activity, will dry up if reporters cannot assure their sources that their identities will be protected. Reporters should have a privilege against disclosing confidential sources similar to the privileges given to spouses, doctors, and the clergy, and for the same reason: the relationship between a reporter and a confidential source would be damaged or destroyed if information given on a promise of confidentiality were open to scrutiny by law enforcement officials.

Opinion of the Court by Mr. Justice White.

The issue in these cases is whether requiring newsmen to appear and testify before state or federal grand juries abridges the freedom of speech and press guaranteed by the First Amendment. We hold that it does not.

The writ of certiorari in Branzburg v. Hayes brings before us two judgments of the Kentucky Court of Appeals, both involving petitioner Branzburg, a staff reporter for the Courier-Journal, a daily newspaper published in Louisville, Kentucky. On November 15, 1969, the Courier-Journal carried a story under petitioner's by-line describing in detail his observations of two young residents of Jefferson County synthesizing hashish from marihuana, an activity which, they asserted, earned them about $5,000 in three weeks. The article included a photograph of a pair of hands working above a laboratory table on which was a substance identified by the caption as hashish. The article stated that petitioner had promised not to reveal the identity of the two hashish makers. Petitioner was shortly subpoenaed by the Jefferson County grand jury; he appeared, but refused to identify the individuals he had seen possessing marihuana or the persons he had seen making hashish from marihuana. A state trial court judge ordered petitioner to answer these questions and rejected his contention that the Kentucky reporters' privilege statute, the First Amendment of the United States Constitution, or the Kentucky Constitution authorized his refusal to answer. . . .

In re Pappas originated when petitioner Pappas, a television newsman-photographer working out of the Providence, Rhode Island, office of a New Bedford, Massachusetts, television station, was called to New Bedford on July 30, 1970, to report on civil disorders there which involved fires and other turmoil. He intended to cover a Black Panther news conference at that group's headquarters in a boarded-up store. Petitioner found the streets around the store barricaded, but he ultimately gained entrance to the area and recorded and photographed a prepared statement read by one of the Black Panther leaders at about 3 p.m. He then

asked for and received permission to re-enter the area. Returning at about 9 o'clock, he was allowed to enter and remain inside Panther headquarters. As a condition of entry, Pappas agreed not to disclose anything he saw or heard inside the store except an anticipated police raid, which Pappas, "on his own," was free to photograph and report as he wished. Pappas stayed inside the headquarters for about three hours, but there was no police raid, and petitioner wrote no story and did not otherwise reveal what had occurred in the store while he was there. Two months later, petitioner was summoned before the Bristol County Grand Jury and appeared, answered questions as to his name, address, employment, and what he had seen and heard outside Panther headquarters, but refused to answer any questions about what had taken place inside headquarters while he was there, claiming that the First Amendment afforded him a privilege to protect confidential informants and their information. A second summons was then served upon him, again directing him to appear before the grand jury and "to give such evidence as he knows relating to any matters which may be inquired of on behalf of the Commonwealth before . . . the Grand Jury." His motion to quash on First Amendment and other grounds was denied by the trial judge who, noting the absence of a statutory newsman's privilege in Massachusetts, ruled that petitioner had no constitutional privilege to refuse to divulge to the grand jury what he had seen and heard, including the identity of persons he had observed. . . .

United States v. Caldwell arose from subpoenas issued by a federal grand jury in the Northern District of California to respondent Earl Caldwell, a reporter for the New York Times assigned to cover the Black Panther Party and other black militant groups. A subpoena duces tecum was served on respondent on February 2, 1970, ordering him to appear before the grand jury to testify and to bring with him notes and tape recordings of interviews given him for publication by officers and spokesmen of the Black Panther Party concerning the aims, purposes, and activities of that organization. . . . Respondent and his employer, the New York Times, moved to quash on the ground that the unlimited breadth of the subpoenas and the fact that Caldwell would have to appear in secret before the grand jury would destroy his working relationship with the Black Panther Party and "suppress vital First Amendment freedoms . . . by driving a wedge of distrust and silence between the news media and the militants." Respondent argued that "so drastic an incursion upon First Amendment freedoms" should not be permitted "in the absence of a compelling governmental interest—not shown here—in requiring Mr. Caldwell's appearance before the grand jury." . . .

Petitioners Branzburg and Pappas and respondent Caldwell press First Amendment claims that may be simply put: that to gather news it is often necessary to agree either not to identify the source of information published or to publish only part of the facts revealed, or both; that if the reporter is nevertheless forced to reveal these confidences to a grand jury, the source so identified and other confidential sources of other reporters will be measurably deterred from furnishing publishable information, all to the detriment of the free flow of information protected by the First Amendment. Although the newsmen in these cases do not claim an absolute privilege against official interrogation in all circumstances, they assert that the reporter should not be forced either to appear or to testify before a grand jury or at trial until and unless sufficient grounds are shown for believing that the reporter possesses information relevant to a crime the grand jury is investigating, that the information the reporter has is unavailable from other sources, and that the need for the information is sufficiently compelling to override the claimed invasion of First Amendment interests occasioned by the disclosure. . . . The heart of the claim is that the burden on news gathering resulting from compelling reporters to disclose confidential information outweighs any public interest in obtaining the information.

We do not question the significance of free speech, press, or assembly to the country's welfare. Nor is it suggested that news gathering does not qualify for First Amendment protection; without some protection for seeking out the news, freedom of the press could be eviscerated. But these cases involve no intrusions upon speech or assembly, no prior restraint or restriction on what the press may publish, and no express or implied command that the press publish what it prefers to withhold. No exaction or tax for the privilege of publishing, and no penalty, civil or criminal, related to the content of published material is at issue here. The use of confidential sources by the press is not forbidden or restricted; reporters remain free to seek news from any source by means within the law. No attempt is made to require the press to publish its sources of information or indiscriminately to disclose them on request.

The sole issue before us is the obligation of reporters to respond to grand jury subpoenas as other citizens do and to answer questions relevant to an investigation into the commission of crime. Citizens generally are not constitutionally immune from grand jury subpoenas; and neither the First Amendment nor any other constitutional provision protects the average citizen from disclosing to a grand jury information that he has received in confidence. The claim is, however, that reporters are exempt from these obligations because if forced to respond to subpoenas and identify their sources or disclose other confidences, their informants will refuse or be reluctant to furnish newsworthy information in the future. This asserted burden on news gathering is said to make compelled testimony from newsmen constitutionally suspect and to require a privileged position for them. . . .

It has generally been held that the First Amendment does not guarantee the press a constitutional right of special access to information not available to the public generally. . . . Despite the fact that news gathering may be hampered, the press is regularly excluded from grand jury proceedings, our own conferences, the meetings of other official bodies gathered in executive session, and the meetings of private organizations. Newsmen have no constitutional right of access to the scenes of crime or disaster when the general public is excluded, and they may be prohibited from attending or publishing information about trials if such restrictions are necessary to assure a defendant a fair trial before an impartial tribunal. . . . It is thus not surprising that the great weight of authority is that newsmen are not exempt from the normal duty of appearing before a grand jury and answering questions relevant to a criminal investigation. At common law, courts consistently refused to recognize the existence of any privilege authorizing a newsman to refuse to reveal confidential information to a grand jury. . . . A number of States have provided newsmen a statutory privilege of varying breadth, but the majority have not done so, and none has been provided by federal statute. Until now the only testimonial privilege for unofficial witnesses that is rooted in the Federal Constitution is the Fifth Amendment privilege against compelled self-incrimination. We are asked to create another by interpreting the First Amendment to grant newsmen a testimonial privilege that other citizens do not enjoy. This we decline to do. Fair and effective law enforcement aimed at providing security for the person and property of the individual is a fundamental function of government, and the grand jury plays an important, constitutionally mandated role in this process. On the records now before us, we perceive no basis for holding that the public interest in law enforcement and in ensuring effective grand jury proceedings is insufficient to override the consequential, but uncertain, burden on news gathering that is said to result from insisting that reporters, like other citizens, respond to relevant questions put to them in the course of a valid grand jury investigation or criminal trial.

This conclusion itself involves no restraint on what newspapers may publish or on the type or quality of information reporters may seek to acquire, nor does it threaten the vast bulk of confidential relationships between reporters and their sources. Grand juries address themselves to the issues of whether crimes have been committed and who committed them. Only where news sources themselves are implicated in crime or possess information relevant to the grand jury's task need they or the reporter be concerned about grand jury subpoenas. Nothing before us indicates that a large number or percentage of all confidential news sources falls into either category and would in any way be deterred by our holding that the Constitution does not, as it never has, exempt the newsman from performing the citizen's normal duty of appearing and furnishing information relevant to the grand jury's task.

The preference for anonymity of those confidential informants involved in actual criminal conduct is presumably a product of their desire to escape criminal prosecution, and this preference, while understandable, is hardly deserving of constitutional protection. It would be frivolous to assert—and no one does in these cases—that the First Amendment, in the interest of securing news or otherwise, confers a license on either the reporter or his news sources to violate valid criminal laws. Although stealing documents or private wiretapping could provide newsworthy information, neither reporter nor source is immune from conviction for such conduct, whatever the impact on the flow of news. Neither is immune, on First Amendment grounds, from testifying against the other, before the grand jury or at a criminal trial. The Amendment does not reach so far as to override the interest of the public in ensuring that neither reporter nor source is invading the rights of other citizens through reprehensible conduct forbidden to all other persons. Thus, we cannot seriously entertain the notion that the First Amendment protects a newsman's agreement to conceal the criminal conduct of his source, or evidence thereof, on the theory that it is better to write about crime than to do something about it. Insofar as any reporter in these cases undertook not to reveal or testify about the crime he witnessed, his claim of privilege under the First Amendment presents no substantial question. The crimes of news sources are no less reprehensible and threatening to the public interest when witnessed by a reporter than when they are not.

There remain those situations where a source is not engaged in criminal conduct but has information suggesting illegal conduct by others. Newsmen frequently receive information from such sources pursuant to a tacit or express agreement to withhold the source's name and suppress any information that the source wishes not published. Such informants presumably desire anonymity in order to avoid being entangled as a witness in a criminal trial or grand jury investigation. They may fear that disclosure will threaten their job security or personal safety or that it will simply result in dishonor or embarrassment.

The argument that the flow of news will be diminished by compelling reporters to aid the grand jury in a criminal investigation is not irrational, nor are the records before us silent on the matter. But we remain unclear how often and to what extent informers are actually deterred from furnishing information when newsmen are forced to testify before a grand jury. The available data indicate that some newsmen rely a great deal on confidential sources and that some informants are particularly sensitive to the threat of exposure and may be silenced if it is held by this Court that, ordinarily, newsmen must testify pursuant to subpoenas, but the evidence fails to demonstrate that there would be a significant constriction of the flow of news to the public if this Court reaffirms the prior common-law and constitutional rule regarding the testimonial obligations of newsmen. . . . Accepting the fact, however, that an undetermined number of informants not themselves implicated in crime will nevertheless, for whatever reason, refuse to talk to newsmen

if they fear identification by a reporter in an official investigation, we cannot accept the argument that the public interest in possible future news about crime from undisclosed, unverified sources must take precedence over the public interest in pursuing and prosecuting those crimes reported to the press by informants and in thus deterring the commission of such crimes in the future. . . .

It is said that currently press subpoenas have multiplied, that mutual distrust and tension between press and officialdom have increased, that reporting styles have changed, and that there is now more need for confidential sources, particularly where the press seeks news about minority cultural and political groups or dissident organizations suspicious of the law and public officials. These developments, even if true, are treacherous grounds for a far-reaching interpretation of the First Amendment fastening a nationwide rule on courts, grand juries, and prosecuting officials everywhere. The obligation to testify in response to grand jury subpoenas will not threaten these sources not involved with criminal conduct and without information relevant to grand jury investigations, and we cannot hold that the Constitution places the sources in these two categories either above the law or beyond its reach. . . .

MR. JUSTICE STEWART, with whom MR. JUSTICE BRENNAN and MR. JUSTICE MARSHALL join, dissenting.

The Court's crabbed view of the First Amendment reflects a disturbing insensitivity to the critical role of an independent press in our society. The question whether a reporter has a constitutional right to a confidential relationship with his source is of first impression here, but the principles that should guide our decision are as basic as any to be found in the Constitution. . . . [T]he Court in these cases holds that a newsman has no First Amendment right to protect his sources when called before a grand jury. The Court thus invites state and federal authorities to undermine the historic independence of the press by attempting to annex the journalistic profession as an investigative arm of government. Not only will this decision impair performance of the press' constitutionally protected functions, but it will, I am convinced, in the long run harm rather than help the administration of justice. I respectfully dissent.

The reporter's constitutional right to a confidential relationship with his source stems from the broad societal interest in a full and free flow of information to the public. It is this basic concern that underlies the Constitution's protection of a free press, because the guarantee is "not for the benefit of the press so much as for the benefit of all of us."

Enlightened choice by an informed citizenry is the basic ideal upon which an open society is premised, and a free press is thus indispensable to a free society. Not only does the press enhance personal self-fulfillment by providing the people with the widest possible range of fact and opinion, but it also is an incontestable precondition of self-government. . . . As private and public aggregations of power burgeon in size and the pressures for conformity necessarily mount, there is obviously a continuing need for an independent press to disseminate a robust variety of information and opinion through reportage, investigation, and criticism, if we are to preserve our constitutional tradition of maximizing freedom of choice by encouraging diversity of expression.

In keeping with this tradition, we have held that the right to publish is central to the First Amendment and basic to the existence of constitutional democracy. A corollary of the right to publish must be the right to gather news. The full flow of information to the public protected by the free-press guarantee would be severely curtailed if no protection whatever were afforded to the process by which news is assembled and disseminated.... No less important to the news dissemination process is the gathering of information. News must not be unnecessarily cut off at its source, for without freedom to acquire information the right to publish would be impermissibly compromised. Accordingly, a right to gather news, of some dimensions, must exist.

The right to gather news implies, in turn, a right to a confidential relationship between a reporter and his source. This proposition follows as a matter of simple logic once three factual predicates are recognized: (1) newsmen require informants to gather news; (2) confidentiality—the promise or understanding that names or certain aspects of communications will be kept off the record—is essential to the creation and maintenance of a news-gathering relationship with informants; and (3) an unbridled subpoena power—the absence of a constitutional right protecting, in any way, a confidential relationship from compulsory process—will either deter sources from divulging information or deter reporters from gathering and publishing information.

It is obvious that informants are necessary to the news-gathering process as we know it today. If it is to perform its constitutional mission, the press must do far more than merely print public statements or publish prepared handouts. Familiarity with the people and circumstances involved in the myriad background activities that result in the final product called "news" is vital to complete and responsible journalism, unless the press is to be a captive mouthpiece of "newsmakers."

It is equally obvious that the promise of confidentiality may be a necessary prerequisite to a productive relationship between a newsman and his informants. An officeholder may fear his superior; a member of the bureaucracy, his associates; a dissident, the scorn of majority opinion. All may have information valuable to the public discourse, yet each may be willing to relate that information only in confidence to a reporter whom he trusts, either because of excessive caution or because of a reasonable fear of reprisals or censure for unorthodox views. The First Amendment concern must not be with the motives of any particular news source, but rather with the conditions in which informants of all shades of the spectrum may make information available through the press to the public....

After today's decision, the potential informant can never be sure that his identity or off-the-record communications will not subsequently be revealed through the compelled testimony of a newsman. A public-spirited person inside government, who is not implicated in any crime, will now be fearful of revealing corruption or other governmental wrongdoing, because he will now know he can subsequently be identified by use of compulsory process. The potential source must, therefore, choose between risking exposure by giving information or avoiding the risk by remaining silent.

The reporter must speculate about whether contact with a controversial source or publication of controversial material will lead to a subpoena. In the event of a subpoena, under today's decision, the newsman will know that he must choose between being punished for contempt if he refuses to testify, or violating his profession's ethics and impairing his resourcefulness as a reporter if he discloses confidential information. Again, the commonsense understanding that such deterrence will occur is buttressed by concrete evidence.... Surveys have verified that an unbridled subpoena power will substantially impair the flow of news to the public, especially in sensitive areas involving governmental officials, financial affairs, political figures, dissidents, or minority groups that require in-depth, investigative reporting.... The impairment of the flow of news cannot, of course, be proved with scientific precision, as the Court seems to demand. Obviously, not every news-gathering relationship requires confidentiality. And it is difficult to pinpoint precisely how many relationships do require a promise or understanding of nondisclosure. But we have never before demanded that First Amendment rights rest on elaborate empirical studies demonstrating beyond any conceivable doubt that deterrent effects exist; we have never before required proof of the exact number of people potentially affected by governmental action, who would actually be dissuaded from engaging in First Amendment activity....

Thus, we cannot escape the conclusion that when neither the reporter nor his source can rely on the shield of confidentiality against unrestrained use of the grand jury's subpoena power, valuable information will not be published and the public dialogue will inevitably be impoverished....

The error in the Court's absolute rejection of First Amendment interests in these cases seems to me to be most profound. For in the name of advancing the administration of justice, the Court's decision, I think, will only impair the achievement of that goal. People entrusted with law enforcement responsibility, no less than private citizens, need general information relating to controversial social problems. Obviously, press reports have great value to government, even when the newsman cannot be compelled to testify before a grand jury. The sad paradox of the Court's position is that when a grand jury may exercise an unbridled subpoena power, and sources involved in sensitive matters become fearful of disclosing information, the newsman will not only cease to be a useful grand jury witness; he will cease to investigate and publish information about issues of public import. I cannot subscribe to such an anomalous result, for, in my view, the interests protected by the First Amendment are not antagonistic to the administration of justice. Rather, they can, in the long run, only be complementary, and for that reason must be given great "breathing space."

NEBRASKA PRESS ASSOCIATION V. STUART
427 U.S. 539 (1976)

"If it can be said that a threat of criminal or civil sanctions . . . "chills" speech, prior restraint "freezes" it at least for the time. The damage can be particularly great when the prior restraint falls upon the communication of news and commentary on current events. . . . The protection against prior restraint should have particular force as applied to reporting of criminal proceedings."

The Question: Can a state judge issue an order barring the news media from publishing or broadcasting accounts of confessions made by a person accused of murder, or reporting facts that implicate the accused person in the crime?

The Arguments: PRO

The First Amendment rights of the press are not absolute and, in cases such as this, where six persons were murdered in a gruesome manner, the Sixth Amendment rights of the accused defendant to a fair trial and an impartial jury are paramount. The press will be able to report on the confessions and the details of the crime once the jury has been seated, and there is no need to publish these facts before the trial begins. In this case, where the crime took place in a rural area, publication of the confessions and details of the crime might make it difficult or impossible to find jurors who have not been exposed to these reports. The defendant's right to an impartial jury requires that the media wait a short time before reporting details that might prejudice the jurors.

CON

This case involves a prior restraint on the press, and the Supreme Court has made clear that such bans on the publication of truthful matters can be justified only by the most pressing and urgent needs of the state. The press in this case is not seeking to publish anything that is not disclosed in a public proceeding. Granted, the defendant in this murder case has a constitutional right to an impartial jury, but there are alternative means to assure such a jury without abridging the freedom of the press to report on matters of public concern. For example, the court could grant a change of venue or delay the trial until the publicity had abated. Making the press responsible for producing an impartial jury is not a function it should be required to assume.

MR. CHIEF JUSTICE BURGER delivered the opinion of the Court.

The respondent State District Judge entered an order restraining the petitioners from publishing or broadcasting accounts of confessions or admissions made by the accused or facts "strongly implicative" of the accused in a widely reported murder of six persons. We granted certiorari to decide whether the entry of such an order on the showing made before the state court violated the constitutional guarantee of freedom of the press.

On the evening of October 18, 1975, local police found the six members of the Henry Kellie family murdered in their home in Sutherland, Neb., a town of about 850 people. Police released the description of a suspect, Erwin Charles Simants, to the reporters who had hastened to the scene of the crime. Simants was arrested and arraigned in Lincoln County Court the following morning, ending a tense night for this small rural community.

The crime immediately attracted widespread news coverage, by local, regional, and national newspapers, radio and television stations. Three days after the crime, the County Attorney and Simants' attorney joined in asking the County Court to enter a restrictive order relating to "matters that may or may not be publicly reported or disclosed to the public," because of the "mass coverage by news media" and the "reasonable likelihood of prejudicial news which would make difficult, if not impossible, the impaneling of an impartial jury and tend to prevent a fair trial." The County Court heard oral argument but took no evidence; no attorney for members of the press appeared at this stage. The County Court granted the prosecutor's motion for a restrictive order and entered it the next day, October 22. The order prohibited everyone in attendance from "releas[ing] or authoriz[ing] the release for public dissemination in any form or manner whatsoever any testimony given or evidence adduced." Simants' preliminary hearing was held the same day, open to the public but subject to the order. The County Court bound over the defendant for trial to the State District Court. The charges, as amended to reflect the autopsy findings, were that Simants had committed the murders in the course of a sexual assault.

Petitioners—several press and broadcast associations, publishers, and individual reporters—moved for leave to intervene in the District Court, asking that the restrictive order imposed by the County Court be vacated. The District Court conducted a hearing, at which the County Judge testified and newspaper articles about the Simants case were admitted in evidence. The District Judge granted petitioners' motion to intervene and entered his own restrictive order. The judge found "because of the nature of the crimes charged in the complaint that there is a clear and present danger that pre-trial publicity could impinge upon the defendant's right to a fair trial." The order applied only until the jury was impaneled, and specifically prohibited petitioners from reporting five subjects: (1) the existence or contents of a confession Simants had made to law enforcement officers, which had been introduced in open court at arraignment; (2) the fact or nature of statements Simants had made to other persons; (3) the contents of a note he had written the night of the crime; (4) certain aspects of the medical testimony at the preliminary hearing; and (5) the identity of the victims of the alleged sexual assault and the nature of the assault. It also prohibited reporting the exact nature of the restrictive order itself. . . .

In practice, of course, even the most ideal guidelines are subjected to powerful strains when a case such as Simants' arises, with reporters from many parts of the country on the scene. Reporters from distant places are unlikely to consider themselves bound by local standards. They report to editors outside the area covered by the guidelines, and their editors are likely to be guided only by their own standards. To contemplate how a state court can control acts of a newspaper or broadcaster outside its jurisdiction, even though the newspapers and broadcasts reach the very community from which jurors are to be selected, suggests something of the practical difficulties of managing such guidelines.

The problems presented in this case have a substantial history outside the reported decisions of courts, in the efforts of many responsible people to accommodate the competing interests. We cannot resolve all of them, for it is not the function of this Court to write a code. We look instead to this particular case and the legal context in which it arises.

The Sixth Amendment in terms guarantees "trial, by an impartial jury. . . ." In the overwhelming majority of criminal trials, pretrial publicity presents few unmanageable threats to this important right. But when the case is a "sensational" one tensions develop between the right of the accused to trial by an impartial jury and the rights guaranteed others by the First Amendment. . . . The relevant decisions of this Court, even if not dispositive, are instructive by way of background. . . .

Taken together, these cases demonstrate that pretrial publicity—even pervasive, adverse publicity—does not inevitably lead to an unfair trial. The capacity of the jury eventually impaneled to decide the case fairly is influenced by the tone and extent of the publicity, which is in part, and often in large part, shaped by what attorneys, police, and other officials do to precipitate news coverage. The trial judge has a major responsibility. What the judge says about a case, in or out of the courtroom, is likely to appear in newspapers and broadcasts. More important, the measures a judge takes or fails to take to mitigate the effects of pretrial publicity—the measures described in Sheppard—may well determine whether the defendant receives a trial consistent with the requirements of due process. . . .

The state trial judge in the case before us acted responsibility, out of a legitimate concern, in an effort to protect the defendant's right to a fair trial. What we must decide is not simply whether the Nebraska courts erred in seeing the possibility of real danger to the defendant's rights, but whether in the circumstances of this case the means employed were foreclosed by another provision of the Constitution.

The First Amendment provides that "Congress shall make no law . . . abridging the freedom . . . of the press," and it is "no longer open to doubt that the liberty of the press, and of speech, is within the liberty safeguarded by the due process clause of the Fourteenth Amendment from invasion by state action." Near v. Minnesota. The Court has interpreted these guarantees to afford special protection against orders that prohibit the publication or broadcast of particular information or commentary—orders that impose a "previous" or "prior" restraint on speech. None of our decided cases on prior restraint involved restrictive orders entered to protect a defendant's right to a fair and impartial jury, but the opinions on prior restraint have a common thread relevant to this case. . . .

The thread running through all these cases is that prior restraints on speech and publication are the most serious and the least tolerable infringement on First Amendment rights. A criminal penalty or a judgment in a defamation case is subject to the whole panoply of protections afforded by deferring the impact of the judgment until all avenues of appellate review have been exhausted. Only after judgment has become final, correct or otherwise, does the law's sanction become fully operative.

A prior restraint, by contrast and by definition, has an immediate and irreversible sanction. If it can be said that a threat of criminal or civil sanctions after publication "chills" speech, prior restraint "freezes" it at least for the time. The damage can be particularly great when the prior restraint falls upon the communication of news and commentary on current events. Truthful reports of public judicial proceedings have been afforded special protection against subsequent punishment. For the same reasons the protection against prior restraint should have particular force as applied to reporting of criminal proceedings, whether the crime in question is a single isolated act or a pattern of criminal conduct. . . .

Of course, the order at issue . . . does not prohibit but only postpones publication. Some news can be delayed and most commentary can even more readily be delayed without serious injury, and there often is a self-imposed delay when responsible editors call for verification of information. But such delays are normally slight and they are self-imposed. Delays imposed by governmental authority are a different matter. As a practical matter, moreover, the element of time is not unimportant if press coverage is to fulfill its traditional function of bringing news to the public promptly. . . .

We turn now to the record in this case. . . . In assessing the probable extent of publicity, the trial judge had before him newspapers demonstrating that the crime had already drawn intensive news coverage, and the testimony of the County Judge, who had entered the initial restraining order based on the local and national attention the case had attracted. The District Judge was required to assess the probable publicity that would be given these shocking crimes prior to the time a jury was selected and sequestered. He then had to examine the probable nature of the publicity and determine how it would affect prospective jurors.

Our review of the pretrial record persuades us that the trial judge was justified in concluding that there would be intense and pervasive pretrial publicity concerning this case. He could also reasonably conclude, based on common human experience, that publicity might impair the defendant's right to a fair trial. He did not purport to say more, for he found only "a clear and present danger that pre-trial publicity could impinge upon the defendant's right to a fair trial." His conclusion as to the impact of such publicity on prospective jurors was of necessity speculative, dealing as he was with factors unknown and unknowable. . . .

We have noted earlier that pretrial publicity, even if pervasive and concentrated, cannot be regarded as leading automatically and in every kind of criminal case to an unfair trial. The decided cases "cannot be made to stand for the proposition that juror exposure to information about a state defendant's prior convictions or to news accounts of the crime with which he is charged alone presumptively deprives the defendant of due process." Appellate evaluations as to the impact of publicity take into account what other measures were used to mitigate the adverse effects of publicity. The more difficult prospective or predictive assessment that a trial judge must make also calls for a judgment as to whether other precautionary steps will suffice.

We have therefore examined this record to determine the probable efficacy of the measures short of prior restraint on the press and speech. There is no finding that alternative measures would not have protected Simants' rights, and the Nebraska Supreme Court did no more than imply that such measures might not be adequate. Moreover, the record is lacking in evidence to support such a finding. . . . The Nebraska Supreme Court narrowed the scope of the restrictive order, and its opinion reflects awareness of the tensions between the need to protect the accused as fully as possible and the need to restrict publication as little as possible. The dilemma posed underscores how difficult it is for trial judges to predict what information will in fact undermine the impartiality of jurors, and the difficulty of drafting an order that will effectively keep prejudicial information from prospective jurors. When a restrictive order is sought, a court can anticipate only part of what will develop that may injure the accused. But information not so obviously prejudicial may emerge, and what may properly be published in these "gray zone" circumstances may not violate the restrictive order and yet be prejudicial.

Finally, we note that the events disclosed by the record took place in a community of 850 people. It is reasonable to assume that, without any news accounts being printed or broadcast, rumors would travel swiftly by word of mouth. One can only speculate on the accuracy of such reports, given the generative propensities of rumors; they could well be more damaging than reasonably accurate news accounts. But plainly a whole community cannot be restrained from discussing a subject intimately affecting life within it. Given these practical problems, it is far from clear that prior restraint on publication would have protected Simants' rights. . . .

The record demonstrates, as the Nebraska courts held, that there was indeed a risk that pretrial news accounts, true or false, would have some adverse impact on the attitudes of those who might be called as jurors. But on the record now before us it is not clear that further publicity, unchecked, would so distort the views of potential jurors that 12 could not be found who would, under proper instructions, fulfill their sworn duty to render a just verdict exclusively on the evidence presented in open court. We cannot say on this record that alternatives to a prior restraint on petitioners would not have sufficiently mitigated the adverse effects of pretrial publicity so as to make prior restraint unnecessary. Nor can we conclude that the restraining order actually entered would serve its intended purpose. Reasonable minds can have few doubts about the gravity of the evil pretrial publicity can work, but the probability that it would do so here was not demonstrated with the degree of certainty our cases on prior restraint require. . . .

Our analysis ends as it began, with a confrontation between prior restraint imposed to protect one vital constitutional guarantee and the explicit command of another that the freedom to speak and publish shall not be abridged. We reaffirm that the guarantees of freedom of expression are not an absolute prohibition under all circumstances, but the barriers to prior restraint remain high and the presumption against its use continues intact. We hold that, with respect to the order entered in this case prohibiting reporting or commentary on judicial proceedings held in public, the barriers have not been overcome; to the extent that this order restrained publication of such material, it is clearly invalid. To the extent that it prohibited publication based on information gained from other sources, we conclude that the heavy burden imposed as a condition to securing a prior restraint was not met and the judgment of the Nebraska Supreme Court is therefore reversed.

CHAPTER 7

Freedom of Assembly and Association

INTRODUCTION

One of the oldest and most honored principles of the common law of England was that "the streets have been held in public trust from time immemorial." The freemen of England enjoyed the right to gather in the streets and other public places, such as parks, to express their own views and to communicate these views to others. The images of a person standing on a soapbox in London's Hyde Square, haranguing a crowd of passersby, or of striking workers parading down a street with picket signs, bring to mind the historic roots of the First Amendment's protection of "the right of the people peaceably to assemble, and to petition the government for a redress of grievances." The rights of assembly and petition are both linked and separate; it is not required that persons who assemble in public places must gather to discuss or prepare a petition to the government. But if *petition* is read broadly, in its dictionary meaning of "asking for something," most public assemblies do ask for something, even the willingness of those who hear or see the message of those assembled to stop and listen.

The Supreme Court has decided many freedom of assembly cases over the past century, since the provisions of the First Amendment were "incorporated" into the Fourteenth and applied to the states in the 1930s. Most of the assembly cases raised challenges to state and local laws that barred entirely, or placed restrictions on, the use of public places to gather in organized groups and to communicate a message. Some of these cases involved laws that required a permit to march in the streets or gather in parks, and challenged the power of local officials to refuse permits to groups whose goals and aims they considered dangerous or subversive. Others involved challenges to the use of criminal laws that punish trespassing, breaches of the peace, and other "public order" regulations. Still others dealt with the actions of public officials, usually police officers, to break up and disperse gatherings because of ostensible concerns about noise, congestion, traffic disruption, and similar public safety and convenience reasons.

A related group of cases involve what the Supreme Court has called "freedom of association," a right not mentioned by name in the First Amendment but one the Court has recognized as a logical outgrowth of the "enumerated" rights of speech, assembly, and petition. Can the government ban an organization from meeting because officials consider its purposes dangerous or illegal? Can officials require organized groups to disclose their membership lists for public scrutiny? Many groups, particularly those whose activities include fund-raising and are incorporated for tax purposes, are required by law to register with state or local officials and to report their income and identify their officers and employees. Can the government refuse to give a business permit or charter to groups whose activities they consider fraudulent or disruptive of public order? These are broad questions, but local and state laws of these kinds have been applied to such varied groups as the Ku Klux Klan and Black Panthers, the Hare Krishnas and Jews for Jesus, civil rights and antiwar protesters, labor unions, and others spanning the religious, political, and religious spectrum.

The four cases in this chapter are just a small fraction of the freedom of assembly and association cases the Supreme Court has decided over the past six decades. Between them, however, these four cases raise the basic questions in this area of constitutional law, and provide in the Court's opinions the guidance that officials and lower courts require to apply its rulings. Needless to say, not all officials or judges read or heed the Court's opinions, and new cases arise with new facts or new laws. In most of these cases, the Court either upholds or reverses the decisions of lower courts with summary orders, or by refusing to hear an appeal, based on its prior rulings in assembly and association cases. Infrequently, the Court will hear argument and decide a case in this area, either to refine its earlier decisions or to send a pointed message to lower-court judges who did not apply precedent correctly. The basic judicial doctrine in this area is fairly clear and simple. Government officials can impose reasonable "time, place, and manner" restrictions on public assembly, to avoid congestion, traffic disruption, or excessive noise. But they cannot use such regulations to block an assembly because they disapprove of its message. Permits to assemble and to use the streets for marches and demonstrations may be required, but must be "content neutral" in regard to the views expressed by marchers or demonstrators. Organizations that engage in fund-raising may be required to register their officers and employees and disclose their finances, but registration may not be withheld or restricted for reasons of political or religious bias, and such groups can keep their membership lists from government scrutiny or disclosure.

HAGUE V. COMMITTEE FOR INDUSTRIAL ORGANIZATION
307 U.S. 496 (1939)

"Wherever the title of streets and parks may rest, they have immemorially been held in trust for the use of the public and, time out of mind, have been used for purposes of assembly, communicating thoughts between citizens, and discussing public questions."

The Question: Can the mayor and other officials of a city deny labor union members and their supporters the right to gather and speak in public places, and to evict union members from the city on grounds that they are spreading communist doctrines?

The Argument: PRO

In this case, union members and their supporters were flooding into Jersey City, New Jersey, holding meetings that created public disturbances and blocked access to streets and sidewalks for city residents. In addition, the union members were advocating doctrines that promoted communism, and created a danger to the public peace. City officials have a duty to ensure that advocacy of "the destruction or overthrow of the government of the United States" is not spread in the city. City officials also have a right to exclude from the city those persons who are reasonably thought to pose a "clear and present danger" of creating public disturbances or spreading subversive doctrines.

CON

The basic principle in this case is the common-law doctrine that "the streets have been held in public trust from time immemorial" and cannot be closed to peaceful gatherings. Refusing to grant permits to hold meetings and forcibly evicting union members from Jersey City are clearly violations of First Amendment rights to free speech and assembly. Any public disturbances in Jersey City have been caused by police officers who have arrested union members for exercising their constitutional rights. The statement of Frank Hague, mayor of Jersey City, that "I am the law," demonstrates the city's contemptuous attitude toward the Constitution.

MR. JUSTICE ROBERTS delivered an opinion in which MR. JUSTICE BLACK concurred.

We granted certiorari as the case presents important questions in respect of the asserted privilege and immunity of citizens of the United States to advocate action pursuant to a federal statute, by distribution of printed matter and oral discussion in peaceable assembly; and the jurisdiction of federal courts of suits to restrain the abridgment of such privilege and immunity.

The respondents [Committee for Industrial Organization, members of the CIO, and the American Civil Liberties Union] brought suit in the United States District Court against the petitioners, the Mayor, the Director of Public

Safety, and the Chief of Police of Jersey City, New Jersey, and the Board of Commissioners, the governing body of the city.

The bill alleges that acting under a city ordinance forbidding the leasing of any hall, without a permit from the Chief of Police, for a public meeting at which a speaker shall advocate obstruction of the Government of the United States or a state, or a change of government by other than lawful means, the petitioners, and their subordinates, have denied respondents the right to hold lawful meetings in Jersey City on the ground that they are Communists or Communist organizations; that pursuant to an unlawful plan, the petitioners have caused the eviction from the municipality of persons they considered undesirable because of their labor organization activities, and have announced that they will continue so to do. It further alleges that . . . the petitioners have discriminated against the respondents by prohibiting and interfering with distribution of leaflets and pamphlets by the respondents while permitting others to distribute similar printed matter; that . . . the petitioners have caused respondents, and those acting with them, to be arrested for distributing printed matter in the streets, and have caused them, and their associates, to be carried beyond the limits of the city or to remote places therein, and have compelled them to board ferry boats destined for New York; have, with violence and force, interfered with the distribution of pamphlets discussing the rights of citizens under the National Labor Relations Act; have unlawfully searched persons coming into the city and seized printed matter in their possession; have arrested and prosecuted respondents, and those acting with them, for attempting to distribute such printed matter; and have threatened that if respondents attempt to hold public meetings in the city to discuss rights afforded by the National Labor Relations Act, they would be arrested; and unless restrained, the petitioners will continue in their unlawful conduct. The bill further alleges that . . . the petitioners have consistently refused to issue any permits for meetings to be held by, or sponsored by, respondents, and have thus prevented the holding of such meetings; that the respondents did not, and do not, purpose to advocate the destruction or overthrow of the government of the United States, or that of New Jersey, but that their sole purpose is to explain to workingmen the purposes of the National Labor Relations Act, the benefits to be derived from it, and the aid which the Committee for Industrial Organization would furnish workingmen to that end; and all the activities in which they seek to engage in Jersey City were, and are, to be performed peacefully, without intimidation, fraud, violence, or other unlawful methods.

The bill . . . alleges that the petitioners' conduct has been "in pursuance of an unlawful conspiracy . . . to injure, oppress, threaten, and intimidate citizens of the United States, including the individual plaintiffs herein, . . . in the free exercise and enjoyment of the rights and privileges secured to them by the Constitution and laws of the United States." The bill charges that the ordinances are unconstitutional and void, or are being enforced against respondents in an unconstitutional and discriminatory way; and that the petitioners, as officials of the city, purporting to act under the ordinances, have deprived respondents of the privileges of free speech and peaceable assembly secured to them, as citizens of the United States, by the Fourteenth Amendment. It prays an injunction against continuance of petitioners' conduct. . . . The answer denies generally, or qualifies, the allegations of the bill [and] alleges that the supposed grounds of federal jurisdiction are frivolous, no facts being alleged sufficient to show that any substantial federal question is involved.

After trial upon the merits the District Court entered findings of fact and conclusions of law and a decree in favor of respondents. In brief, the court found that the purposes of respondents, other than the American Civil Liberties Union, were the organization of unorganized workers into labor unions, causing such unions to exercise the normal and legal functions of labor organizations, such as collective bargaining with respect to the betterment of wages, hours of work and other terms and conditions of employment, and that these purposes were lawful; that the petitioners, acting in their official capacities, have adopted and enforced the deliberate policy of excluding and removing from Jersey City the agents of the respondents; have interfered with their right of passage upon the streets and access to the parks of the city; that these ends have been accomplished by force and violence despite the fact that the persons affected were acting in an orderly and peaceful manner; that exclusion, removal, personal restraint and interference, by force and violence, is accomplished without authority of law and without promptly bringing the persons taken into custody before a judicial officer for hearing. . . . The court concluded that . . . the respondents had established a cause of action under the Constitution of the United States. . . . The Circuit Court of Appeals concurred in the findings of fact; held the District Court had jurisdiction, modified the decree in respect of one of its provisions, and, as modified, affirmed it. . . .

Section 24(14) [of the federal Judicial Code] grants jurisdiction of suits at law or in equity authorized by law to be brought by any person to redress the deprivation, under color of any law, statute, ordinance, regulation, custom, or usage, of any State, of any right, privilege, or immunity, secured by the Constitution of the United States, or of any right secured by any law of the United States providing for equal rights of citizens of the United States, or of all persons within the jurisdiction of the United States.

The petitioners insist that the rights of which the respondents say they have been deprived are not within those described in subsection (14). The courts below have held that citizens of the United States possess such rights by virtue of their citizenship; that the Fourteenth Amendment secures these rights against invasion by a state, and authorizes legislation by Congress to enforce the Amendment. . . . Prior to the Civil War there was confusion and debate as to the relation between United States citizenship and state citizenship. Beyond dispute, citizenship of the United States, as such, existed. The Constitution, in various clauses, recognized it but nowhere defined it. Many thought state citizenship, and that only, created United States citizenship. . . .

The first sentence of the [Fourteenth] Amendment settled the old controversy as to citizenship by providing that "All persons born or naturalized in the United States, and subject to the jurisdiction thereof, are citizens of the United States and of the State wherein they reside." Thenceforward citizenship of the United States became primary and citizenship of a state secondary. The first section of the Amendment further provides: "No State shall make or enforce any law which shall abridge the privileges or immunities of citizens of the United States." . . .

[The] Civil Rights Act, adopted [by Congress in 1871], provided "That any person who, under color of any law, statute, ordinance, regulation, custom, or usage of any State, shall subject, or cause to be subjected, any person within the jurisdiction of the United States to the deprivation of any rights, privileges, or immunities secured by the Constitution of the United States, shall . . . be liable to the party injured in any action at law, suit in equity, or other proper proceeding for redress." . . .

The question now presented is whether freedom to disseminate information concerning the provisions of the National Labor Relations Act, to assemble peaceably for discussion of the Act, and of the opportunities and advantages offered by it, is a privilege or immunity of a citizen of the United States secured against State abridgment by Section 1 of the Fourteenth Amendment; and whether . . . Section 24(14) of the Judicial Code afford[s] redress in a federal court for such abridgment. This is the narrow question presented by the record, and we confine our decision to it, without consideration of broader issues which the parties urge. . . . Although it has been held that the Fourteenth Amendment created no rights in citizens of the United States, but merely secured existing rights against state abridgment, it is clear that the right peaceably to assemble and to discuss these topics, and to communicate respecting them, whether orally or in writing, is a privilege inherent in citizenship of the United States which the Amendment protects. . . . No expression of a contrary view has ever been voiced by this court. . . .

Citizenship of the United States would be little better than a name if it did not carry with it the right to discuss national legislation and the benefits, advantages, and opportunities to accrue to citizens therefrom. All of the respondents' proscribed activities had this single end and aim. . . . What has been said demonstrates that, in the light of the facts found, privileges and immunities of the individual respondents as citizens of the United States, were infringed by the petitioners, by virtue of their official positions, under color of ordinances of Jersey City, unless, as petitioners contend, the city's ownership of streets and parks is as absolute as one's ownership of his home, with consequent power altogether to exclude citizens from the use thereof. . . .

Wherever the title of streets and parks may rest, they have immemorially been held in trust for the use of the public and, time out of mind, have been used for purposes of assembly, communicating thoughts between citizens, and discussing public questions. Such use of the streets and public places has, from ancient times, been a part of the privileges, immunities, rights, and liberties of citizens. The privilege of a citizen of the United States to use the streets and parks for communication of views on national questions may be regulated in the interest of all; it is not absolute, but relative, and must be exercised in subordination to the general comfort and convenience, and in consonance with peace and good order; but it must not, in the guise of regulation, be abridged or denied.

We think the court below was right in holding the ordinance [requiring a permit to use the parks] void upon its face. It does not make comfort or convenience in the use of streets or parks the standard of official action. It enables the Director of Safety to refuse a permit on his mere opinion that such refusal will prevent "riots, disturbances or disorderly assemblage." It can thus, as the record discloses, be made the instrument of arbitrary suppression of free expression of views on national affairs for the prohibition of all speaking will undoubtedly "prevent" such eventualities. But uncontrolled official suppression of the privilege cannot be made a substitute for the duty to maintain order in connection with the exercise of the right. . . .

[The trial court's decree] prohibits the petitioners from excluding or removing the respondents or persons acting with them from Jersey City, exercising personal restraint over them without warrant or confining them without lawful arrest . . . or interfering with their free access to the streets, parks, or public places of the city. The argument is that this section of the decree is so vague in its terms as to be impractical of enforcement or obedience. We agree with the court below that the objection is not well founded.

[The decree also] enjoins the petitioners from interfering with the right of the respondents, their agents and those acting with them, to communicate their views as individuals to others on the streets in an orderly and peaceable manner. It reserves to the petitioners full liberty to enforce law and order by lawful search and seizure or by arrest and production before a judicial officer. We think this paragraph unassailable. . . .

Although the court below held the ordinance [requiring a permit to hold public meetings] void, the decree enjoins the petitioners as to the manner in which they shall administer it. There is an initial command that the petitioners shall not place "any previous restraint" upon the respondents in respect of holding meetings provided they apply for a permit as required by the ordinance. This is followed by an enumeration of the conditions under which a permit may be granted or denied. We think this is wrong. As the ordinance is void, the respondents are entitled to a decree so declaring and an injunction against its enforcement by the petitioners. They are free to hold meetings without a permit and without regard to the terms of the void ordinance. The courts cannot rewrite the ordinance, as the decree, in effect, does.

[The provisions of the decree discussed above] should be modified as indicated. In other respects the decree should be affirmed.

MR. JUSTICE STONE, concurring.

I do not doubt that the decree below, modified as has been proposed, is rightly affirmed, but I am unable to follow the path by which some of my brethren have attained that end, and I think the matter is of sufficient importance to merit discussion in some detail. It has been explicitly and repeatedly affirmed by this Court, without a dissenting voice, that freedom of speech and of assembly for any lawful purpose are rights of personal liberty secured to all persons, without regard to citizenship, by the due process clause of the Fourteenth Amendment. It has never been held that either is a privilege or immunity peculiar to citizenship of the United States, to which alone the privileges and immunities clause refers, and neither can be brought within the protection of that clause without enlarging the category of privileges and immunities of United States citizenship as it has hitherto been defined.

. . . [T]he right to maintain a suit in equity to restrain state officers, acting under a state law, from infringing the rights of freedom of speech and of assembly guaranteed by the due process clause, is given by Act of Congress to every person within the jurisdiction of the United States whether a citizen or not. . . . Hence there is no occasion, for jurisdictional purposes or any other, to consider whether freedom of speech and of assembly are immunities secured by the privileges and immunities clause of the Fourteenth Amendment to citizens of the United States. . . .

The respondents in their bill of complaint . . . made no specific allegation that any of those whose freedom had been interfered with by petitioners was a citizen of the United States. . . . There is no finding by either court below that any of respondents or any of those whose freedom of speech and assembly has been infringed are citizens of the United States, and we are referred to no part of the evidence in which their citizenship is mentioned or from which it can be inferred. . . . The court below rightly omitted any such limitation from the decree, evidently because, as it declared, petitioners' acts infringed the due process clause, which guarantees to all persons freedom of speech and of assembly for any lawful purpose.

No more grave and important issue can be brought to this Court than that of freedom of speech and assembly, which the due process clause guarantees to all persons regardless of their citizenship, but which the privileges and immunities clause secures only to citizens, and then only to the limited extent that their relationship to the national government is affected. I am unable to rest decision here on the assertion, which I think the record fails to support, that respondents must depend upon their limited privileges as citizens of the United States in order to sustain their cause, or upon so palpable an avoidance of the real issue in the case, which . . . is whether the present proceeding can be maintained . . . as a

suit for the protection of rights and privileges guaranteed by the due process clause. I think respondents' right to maintain it does not depend on their citizenship and cannot rightly be made to turn on the existence or non-existence of a purpose to disseminate information about the National Labor Relations Act. It is enough that petitioners have prevented respondents from holding meetings and disseminating information whether for the organization of labor unions or for any other lawful purpose.

If it be the part of wisdom to avoid unnecessary decision of constitutional questions, it would seem to be equally so to avoid the unnecessary creation of novel constitutional doctrine, inadequately supported by the record, in order to attain an end easily and certainly reached by following the beaten paths of constitutional decision. The right to maintain the present suit is conferred upon the individual respondents by the due process clause and Acts of Congress, regardless of their citizenship. . . .

MR. JUSTICE McREYNOLDS, dissenting.

I am of opinion that the decree of the Circuit Court of Appeals should be reversed and the cause remanded to the District Court with instructions to dismiss the bill. In the circumstances disclosed, I conclude that the District Court should have refused to interfere by injunction with the essential rights of the municipality to control its own parks and streets. Wise management of such intimate local affairs, generally, at least, is beyond the competency of federal courts, and essays in that direction should be avoided. There was ample opportunity for respondents to assert their claims through an orderly proceeding in courts of the state empowered authoritatively to interpret her laws with final review here in respect of federal questions.

NAACP v. ALABAMA
357 U.S. 449 (1958)

"Effective advocacy of both public and private points of view, particularly controversial ones, is undeniably enhanced by group association, as this Court has more than once recognized by remarking upon the close nexus between the freedoms of speech and assembly."

The Question: Can a state compel an organization with its headquarters in another state, as a condition of doing business, to reveal to public officials the names and addresses of all its members in the state?

The Arguments: PRO

Most states require corporations with headquarters in other states to file their corporate charters and other records with public officials. These rules are necessary to provide for service of legal process on corporation officers. The requirement in this case that the NAACP also file with the Alabama secretary of state a list of the group's members and their addresses is necessary to assist in the state's investigation of activities by the NAACP and its members that may violate state law, such as organizing and conducting illegal boycotts of businesses and trespassing on private property. State officials will not themselves disclose the names or addresses of NAACP members, and any private actions against them are not actions of the state.

CON

There is only one reason for Alabama's demand that the NAACP turn over to state officials a list of its members and their addresses: the state intends to make the membership list public, so that segregationists can intimidate and retaliate against civil rights activists. The state has made no similar demand of any other group that is licensed to do business in Alabama. The NAACP is willing to turn over records of its corporate charter, offices and officers in Alabama, and other records that serve legitimate state interests. But the membership list is not a record for which the state has demonstrated any legitimate need, and the demand for its production abridges the freedom of association that is protected by the First Amendment.

MR. JUSTICE HARLAN delivered the opinion of the Court.

We review from the standpoint of its validity under the Federal Constitution a judgment of civil contempt entered against petitioner, the National Association for the Advancement of Colored People, in the courts of Alabama. The question presented is whether Alabama, consistently with the Due Process Clause of the Fourteenth Amendment, can compel petitioner to reveal to the State's Attorney General the names and addresses of all its Alabama members and agents, without regard to their positions or functions in the Association. The judgment of contempt was based upon petitioner's refusal to comply fully with a court order requiring in part the production of membership lists. Petitioner's claim is that the order, in the circumstances shown by this record, violated rights assured to petitioner and its members under the Constitution.

Alabama has a statute similar to those of many other States which requires a foreign [out-of-state] corporation, except as exempted, to qualify before doing business by filing its corporate charter with the Secretary of State and designating a place of business and an agent to receive service of process. The statute imposes a fine on a corporation transacting intrastate business before qualifying and provides for criminal prosecution of officers of such a corporation. The National Association for the Advancement of Colored People is a nonprofit membership corporation organized under the laws of New York. Its purposes, fostered on a nationwide basis, are those indicated by its name, and it operates through chartered affiliates which are independent unincorporated associations, with membership therein equivalent to membership in petitioner. The first Alabama affiliates were chartered in 1918. Since that time the aims of the Association have been advanced through activities of its affiliates, and in 1951 the Association itself opened a regional office in Alabama, at which it employed two supervisory persons and one clerical worker. The Association has never complied with the qualification statute, from which it considered itself exempt.

In 1956 the Attorney General of Alabama brought an equity suit in the State Circuit Court, Montgomery County, to enjoin the Association from conducting further activities within, and to oust it from, the State. Among other things the bill in equity alleged that the Association had opened a regional office and had organized various affiliates in Alabama; had recruited members and solicited contributions within the State; had given financial support and furnished legal assistance to Negro students seeking admission to the state university; and had supported a Negro boycott of the bus lines in Montgomery to compel the seating of passengers without regard to race. The bill recited that the Association, by continuing to do business in Alabama without complying with the qualification statute, was "causing irreparable injury to the property and civil rights of the residents and citizens of the State of Alabama for which criminal prosecution and civil actions at law afford no adequate relief." On the day the complaint was filed, the Circuit Court issued ex parte an order restraining the Association, pendente lite, from engaging in further activities within the State and forbidding it to take any steps to qualify itself to do business therein.

Petitioner demurred to the allegations of the bill and moved to dissolve the restraining order. It contended that its activities did not subject it to the qualification requirements of the statute and that in any event what the State sought to accomplish by its suit would violate rights to freedom of speech and assembly guaranteed under the Fourteenth Amendment to the Constitution of the United States. Before the date set for a hearing on this motion, the State moved for the production of a large number of the Association's records and papers, including bank statements, leases, deeds, and records containing the names and addresses of all Alabama "members" and "agents" of the Association. It alleged that all such documents were necessary for adequate preparation for the hearing, in view of petitioner's denial of the conduct of intrastate business within the meaning of the qualification statute. Over petitioner's objections, the court ordered the production of a substantial part of the requested records, including the membership lists, and postponed the hearing on the restraining order to a date later than the time ordered for production.

Thereafter petitioner filed its answer to the bill in equity. It admitted its Alabama activities substantially as alleged in the complaint and that it had not qualified to do business in the State. . . . However petitioner did not comply with the production order, and for this failure was adjudged in civil contempt and fined $10,000. The contempt judgment provided that the fine would be subject to reduction or remission if compliance were forthcoming within five days but otherwise would be increased to $100,000.

At the end of the five-day period petitioner produced substantially all the data called for by the production order except its membership lists, as to which it contended that Alabama could not constitutionally compel disclosure. . . . [T]he Circuit Court made a further order adjudging petitioner in continuing contempt and increasing the fine already imposed to $100,000. . . . The State Supreme Court thereafter twice dismissed petitions for certiorari to review this final contempt judgment. . . . We granted certiorari because of the importance of the constitutional questions presented. . . .

We . . . reach petitioner's claim that the production order in the state litigation trespasses upon fundamental freedoms protected by the Due Process Clause of the Fourteenth Amendment. Petitioner argues that in view of the facts and circumstances shown in the record, the effect of compelled disclosure of the membership lists will be to abridge the rights of its rank-and-file members to engage in lawful association in support of their common beliefs. It contends that governmental action which, although not directly suppressing association, nevertheless carries this consequence, can be justified only upon some overriding valid interest of the State.

Effective advocacy of both public and private points of view, particularly controversial ones, is undeniably enhanced by group association, as this Court has more than once recognized by remarking upon the close nexus between the freedoms of speech and assembly. It is beyond debate that freedom to engage in association for the advancement of beliefs and ideas is an inseparable aspect of the "liberty" assured by the Due Process Clause of the Fourteenth Amendment, which embraces freedom of speech. Of course, it is immaterial whether the beliefs sought to be advanced by association pertain to political, economic, religious or cultural matters, and state action which may have the effect of curtailing the freedom to associate is subject to the closest scrutiny.

The fact that Alabama . . . has taken no direct action to restrict the right of petitioner's members to associate freely, does not end inquiry into the effect of the production order. In the domain of these indispensable liberties, whether of speech, press, or association, the decisions of this Court recognize that abridgment of such rights, even though unintended, may inevitably follow from varied forms of governmental action. . . . The governmental action challenged may appear to be totally unrelated to protected liberties. Statutes imposing taxes upon rather than prohibiting particular activity have been struck down when perceived to have the consequence of unduly curtailing the liberty of freedom of press assured under the Fourteenth Amendment.

It is hardly a novel perception that compelled disclosure of affiliation with groups engaged in advocacy may constitute as effective a restraint on freedom of association as the forms of governmental action in the cases above were thought likely to produce upon the particular constitutional rights there involved. This Court has recognized the vital relationship between freedom to associate and privacy in one's associations. When referring to the varied forms of governmental action which might interfere with freedom of assembly, it said: "A requirement that adherents of particular religious faiths or political parties wear identifying armbands, for example, is obviously of this nature." Compelled disclosure of membership in an organization engaged in advocacy of particular beliefs is of the same order. Inviolability of privacy in group association may in many circumstances be indispensable to preservation of freedom of association, particularly where a group espouses dissident beliefs.

We think that the production order, in the respects here drawn in question, must be regarded as entailing the likelihood of a substantial restraint upon the exercise by petitioner's members of their right to freedom of association. Petitioner has made an uncontroverted showing that on past occasions revelation of the identity of its rank-and-file members has exposed these members to economic reprisal, loss of employment, threat of physical coercion, and other manifestations of public hostility. Under these circumstances, we think it apparent that compelled disclosure of petitioner's Alabama membership is likely to affect adversely the ability of petitioner and its members to pursue their collective effort to foster beliefs which they admittedly have the right to advocate, in that it may induce members to withdraw from the Association and dissuade others from joining it because of fear of exposure of their beliefs shown through their associations and of the consequences of this exposure.

It is not sufficient to answer, as the State does here, that whatever repressive effect compulsory disclosure of names of petitioner's members may have upon participation by Alabama citizens in petitioner's activities follows not from state action but from private community pressures. The crucial factor is the interplay of governmental and private action, for it is only after the initial exertion of state power represented by the production order that private action takes hold.

We turn to the final question whether Alabama has demonstrated an interest in obtaining the disclosures it seeks from petitioner which is sufficient to justify the deterrent effect which we have concluded these disclosures may well have on the free exercise by petitioner's members of their constitutionally protected right of association. Such a "subordinating interest of the State must be compelling." It is not of moment that the State has here acted solely through its judicial branch, for whether legislative or judicial, it is still the application of state power which we are asked to scrutinize.

It is important to bear in mind that petitioner asserts no right to absolute immunity from state investigation, and no right to disregard Alabama's laws. As shown by its substantial compliance with the production order, petitioner does not deny Alabama's right to obtain from it such information as the State desires concerning the purposes of the Association and its activities within the State. Petitioner has not objected to divulging the identity of its members who are employed by or hold official positions with it. It has urged the rights solely of its ordinary rank-and-file members. This is therefore not analogous to a case involving the interest of a State in protecting its citizens in their dealings with paid solicitors or agents of foreign corporations by requiring identification.

Whether there was "justification" in this instance turns solely on the substantiality of Alabama's interest in obtaining the membership lists. During the course of a hearing before the Alabama Circuit Court on a motion of petitioner to set aside the production order, the State Attorney General presented at length, under examination by petitioner, the State's reason for requesting the membership lists. . . . The issues in the litigation . . . were whether the character of petitioner and its activities in Alabama had been such as to make petitioner subject to the registration statute, and whether the extent of petitioner's activities without qualifying suggested its permanent ouster from the State. Without intimating the slightest view upon the merits of these issues, we are unable to perceive that the disclosure of the names of petitioner's rank-and-file members has a substantial bearing on either of them. . . . As matters stand in the state court, petitioner . . . has apparently complied satisfactorily with the production order, except for the membership lists, by furnishing the Attorney General with varied business records, its charter and statement of purposes, the names of all of its directors and officers, and with the total number of its Alabama members and the amount of their dues. These last items would not on this record appear subject to constitutional challenge and have been furnished, but whatever interest the State may have in obtaining names of ordinary members has

not been shown to be sufficient to overcome petitioner's constitutional objections to the production order. . . .

We hold that the immunity from state scrutiny of membership lists which the Association claims on behalf of its members is here so related to the right of the members to pursue their lawful private interests privately and to associate freely with others in so doing as to come within the protection of the Fourteenth Amendment. And we conclude that Alabama has fallen short of showing a controlling justification for the deterrent effect on the free enjoyment of the right to associate which disclosure of membership lists is likely to have. Accordingly, the judgment of civil contempt and the $100,000 fine which resulted from petitioner's refusal to comply with the production order in this respect must fall. . . .

For the reasons stated, the judgment of the Supreme Court of Alabama must be reversed and the case remanded for proceedings not inconsistent with this opinion.

Cox v. Louisiana
379 U.S. 536 (1965)

"Unfettered discretion in local officials in the regulation of the use of the streets for peaceful parades and meetings is an unwarranted abridgment of . . . freedom of speech and assembly secured . . . by the First Amendment."

The Question: Can state and local officials lawfully prosecute civil rights demonstrators for disturbing the peace, obstructing public passages, and trespass when the demonstrations are peaceful and take place on public property?

The Arguments: PRO

The records in both of these cases show that large groups of civil rights demonstrators marched through public streets to a courthouse in one case and a county jail in the other. Outside these public buildings, the demonstrators created congestion, made loud noises, disrupted traffic, and interfered with access to these buildings. The laws in question have been applied simply to preserve the public peace and protect the right of citizens and public officials to conduct their business. In both of these cases, demonstrators ignored and disobeyed lawful orders from police officers to disperse and to cease their disturbances of the peace.

CON

Both of these cases involve peaceful civil rights demonstrations which designed to show support for fellow demonstrators who had been arrested and jailed. Further, both demonstrations were conducted in ways that allowed vehicular and foot traffic free access to the streets, sidewalks, and public buildings. The demonstrators sang, chanted slogans, and made speeches, but there was no disturbance of the peace. Therefore, the trespass statutes should not be used to prevent peaceful assemblies on public grounds. The right of the people "peaceably to assemble and to petition for a redress of grievances" is protected by the First Amendment.

MR. JUSTICE GOLDBERG delivered the opinion of the Court.

Appellant, the Reverend Mr. B. Elton Cox, the leader of a civil rights demonstration, was arrested and charged with four

offenses under Louisiana law—criminal conspiracy, disturbing the peace, obstructing public passages, and picketing before a courthouse. In a consolidated trial before a judge without a jury, and on the same set of facts, he was acquitted of criminal conspiracy but convicted of the other three offenses. He was sentenced to serve four months in jail and pay a $200 fine for disturbing the peace, to serve five months in jail and pay a $500 fine for obstructing public passages, and to serve one year in jail and pay a $5,000 fine for picketing before a courthouse. The sentences were cumulative.... [T]he Louisiana Supreme Court ... affirmed all three convictions.

On December 14, 1961, 23 students from Southern University, a Negro college, were arrested in downtown Baton Rouge, Louisiana, for picketing stores that maintained segregated lunch counters. This picketing, urging a boycott of those stores, was part of a general protest movement against racial segregation, directed by the local chapter of the Congress of Racial Equality, a civil rights organization. The appellant, an ordained Congregational minister, the Reverend Mr. B. Elton Cox, a Field Secretary of CORE, was an advisor to this movement. On the evening of December 14, appellant and Ronnie Moore, student president of the local CORE chapter, spoke at a mass meeting at the college. The students resolved to demonstrate the next day in front of the courthouse in protest of segregation and the arrest and imprisonment of the picketers who were being held in the parish jail located on the upper floor of the courthouse building.

The next morning about 2,000 students left the campus, which was located approximately five miles from downtown Baton Rouge. Most of them had to walk into the city since the drivers of their busses were arrested.... When Cox arrived, 1,500 of the 2,000 students were assembling at the site of the old State Capitol building, two and one-half blocks from the courthouse. Cox walked up and down cautioning the students to keep to one side of the sidewalk while getting ready for their march to the courthouse. The students circled the block in a file two or three abreast occupying about half of the sidewalk. The police had learned of the proposed demonstration the night before from news media and other sources. Captain Font of the City Police Department and Chief Kling of the Sheriff's office, two high-ranking subordinate officials, approached the group and spoke to Cox at the northeast corner of the capitol grounds. Cox identified himself as the group's leader, and, according to Font and Kling, he explained that the students were demonstrating to protest "the illegal arrest of some of their people who were being held in jail." The version of Cox and his witnesses throughout was that they came not "to protest just the arrest but ... [also] to protest the evil of discrimination." Kling asked Cox to disband the group and "take them back from whence they came." Cox did not acquiesce in this request but told the officers that they would march by the courthouse, say prayers, sing hymns, and conduct a peaceful program of protest. The officer repeated his request to disband, and Cox again refused. Kling and Font then returned to their car in order to report by radio to the Sheriff and Chief of Police who were in the immediate vicinity; while this was going on, the students, led by Cox, began their walk toward the courthouse....

As Cox, still at the head of the group, approached the vicinity of the courthouse, he was stopped by Captain Font and Inspector Trigg and brought to Police Chief Wingate White, who was standing in the middle of St. Louis Street. The Chief then inquired as to the purpose of the demonstra-

tion. Cox, reading from a prepared paper, outlined his program to White, stating that it would include a singing of the Star Spangled Banner and a "freedom song," recitation of the Lord's Prayer and the Pledge of Allegiance, and a short speech. White testified that he told Cox that "he must confine" the demonstration "to the west side of the street." White added, "This, of course, was not—I didn't mean it in the import that I was giving him any permission to do it, but I was presented with a situation that was accomplished, and I had to make a decision." Cox testified that the officials agreed to permit the meeting....

The students were then directed by Cox to the west sidewalk, across the street from the courthouse, 101 feet from its steps. They were lined up on this sidewalk about five deep and spread almost the entire length of the block. The group did not obstruct the street. It was close to noon and, being lunch time, a small crowd of 100 to 300 curious white people, mostly courthouse personnel, gathered on the east sidewalk and courthouse steps, about 100 feet from the demonstrators. Seventy-five to eighty policemen, including city and state patrolmen and members of the Sheriff's staff, as well as members of the fire department and a fire truck were stationed in the street between the two groups. Rain fell throughout the demonstration.

Several of the students took from beneath their coats picket signs similar to those which had been used the day before. These signs bore legends such as "Don't buy discrimination for Christmas," "Sacrifice for Christ, don't buy," and named stores which were proclaimed "unfair." They then sang "God Bless America," pledged allegiance to the flag, prayed briefly, and sang one or two hymns, including "We Shall Overcome." The 23 students, who were locked in jail cells in the courthouse building out of the sight of the demonstrators, responded by themselves singing; this in turn was greeted with cheers and applause by the demonstrators. Appellant gave a speech, described by a State's witness as follows: "He said that in effect that it was a protest against the illegal arrest of some of their members and that other people were allowed to picket ... and he said that they were not going to commit any violence, that if anyone spit on them, they would not spit back on the person that did it."

Cox then said: "All right. It's lunch time. Let's go eat. There are twelve stores we are protesting. A number of these stores have twenty counters; they accept your money from nineteen. They won't accept it from the twentieth counter. This is an act of racial discrimination. These stores are open to the public. You are members of the public. We pay taxes to the Federal Government and you who live here pay taxes to the State." In apparent reaction to these last remarks, there was what state witnesses described as "muttering" and "grumbling" by the white onlookers.

The Sheriff, deeming, as he testified, Cox's appeal to the students to sit in at the lunch counters to be "inflammatory," then took a power microphone and said, "Now, you have been allowed to demonstrate. Up until now your demonstration has been more or less peaceful, but what you are doing now is a direct violation of the law, a disturbance of the peace, and it has got to be broken up immediately." The testimony as to what then happened is disputed. Some of the State's witnesses testified that Cox said, "don't move"; others stated that he made a "gesture of defiance." It is clear from the record, however, that Cox and the demonstrators did not then and there break up the demonstration. Two of the Sheriff's deputies immediately started across the street and told the group, "You have heard what the Sheriff said, now, do what he said." A state witness testified that they put their hands on the shoulders of some of the students "as though to shove them away."

Almost immediately thereafter—within a time estimated variously at two to five minutes—one of the policemen exploded a tear gas shell at the crowd. This was followed by several other shells. The demonstrators quickly dispersed, running back towards the State Capitol and the downtown area; Cox tried to calm them as they ran and was himself one of the last to leave. No Negroes participating in the demonstration were arrested on that day. The only person then arrested was a young white man, not a part of the demonstration, who was arrested "because he was causing a disturbance." The next day appellant was arrested and charged with the four offenses above described.

THE BREACH OF THE PEACE CONVICTION

Appellant was convicted of violating a Louisiana "disturbing the peace" statute, which provides: "Whoever with intent to provoke a breach of the peace, or under circumstances such that a breach of the peace may be occasioned thereby . . . crowds or congregates with others . . . in or upon . . . a public street or public highway, or upon a public sidewalk, or any other public place or building . . . and who fails or refuses to disperse and move on . . . when ordered so to do by any law enforcement officer . . . shall be guilty of disturbing the peace." . . .

We hold that Louisiana may not constitutionally punish appellant under this statute for engaging in the type of conduct which this record reveals, and also that the statute as authoritatively interpreted by the Louisiana Supreme Court is unconstitutionally broad in scope. The Louisiana courts have held that appellant's conduct constituted a breach of the peace under state law . . . but our independent examination of the record, which we are required to make, shows no conduct which the State had a right to prohibit as a breach of the peace.

Appellant led a group of young college students who wished "to protest segregation" and discrimination against Negroes and the arrest of 23 fellow students. They assembled peaceably at the State Capitol building and marched to the courthouse where they sang, prayed and listened to a speech. A reading of the record reveals agreement on the part of the State's witnesses that Cox had the demonstration "very well controlled," and until the end of Cox's speech, the group was perfectly "orderly." Sheriff Clemmons testified that the crowd's activities were not "objectionable" before that time. They became objectionable, according to the Sheriff himself, when Cox, concluding his speech, urged the students to go uptown and sit in at lunch counters. The Sheriff testified that the sole aspect of the program to which he objected was "[t]he inflammatory manner in which he [Cox] addressed that crowd and told them to go on up town, go to four places on the protest list, sit down and if they don't feed you, sit there for one hour." Yet this part of Cox's speech obviously did not deprive the demonstration of its protected character under the Constitution as free speech and assembly.

The State argues, however, that while the demonstrators started out to be orderly, the loud cheering and clapping by the students in response to the singing from the jail converted the peaceful assembly into a riotous one. The record, however, does not support this assertion. It is true that the students, in response to the singing of their fellows who were in custody, cheered and applauded. However, the meeting was an outdoor meeting and a key state witness testified that while the singing was loud, it was not disorderly. There is, moreover, no indication that the mood of the students was ever hostile, aggressive, or unfriendly. . . .

There is an additional reason why this conviction cannot be sustained. The statute at issue in this case, as authoritatively interpreted by the Louisiana Supreme Court, is unconstitutionally vague in its overly broad scope. The statutory crime consists of two elements: (1) congregating with others "with intent to provoke a breach of the peace, or under circumstances such that a breach of the peace may be occasioned," and (2) a refusal to move on after having been ordered to do so by a law enforcement officer. While the second part of this offense is narrow and specific, the first element is not. The Louisiana Supreme Court in this case defined the term "breach of the peace" as "to agitate, to arouse from a state of repose, to molest, to interrupt, to hinder, to disquiet."

The Louisiana statute, as interpreted by the Louisiana court, is at least as likely to allow conviction for innocent speech. . . . Therefore, the conviction under this statute must be reversed as the statute is unconstitutional in that it sweeps within its broad scope activities that are constitutionally protected free speech and assembly. Maintenance of the opportunity for free political discussion is a basic tenet of our constitutional democracy.

For all these reasons we hold that appellant's freedoms of speech and assembly, secured to him by the First Amendment, as applied to the States by the Fourteenth Amendment, were denied by his conviction for disturbing the peace. The conviction on this charge cannot stand.

THE OBSTRUCTING PUBLIC PASSAGES CONVICTION

We now turn to the issue of the validity of appellant's conviction for violating the Louisiana statute which provides: "No person shall wilfully obstruct the free, convenient and normal use of any public sidewalk, street, highway . . . or other passageway, or the entrance, corridor or passage of any public building . . . by impeding, hindering, stifling, retarding or restraining traffic or passage thereon or therein."

Appellant was convicted under this statute, not for leading the march to the vicinity of the courthouse, which the Louisiana Supreme Court stated to have been "orderly," but for leading the meeting on the sidewalk across the street from the courthouse. In upholding appellant's conviction under this statute, the Louisiana Supreme Court thus construed the statute so as to apply to public assemblies which do not have as their specific purpose the obstruction of traffic. There is no doubt from the record in this case that this far sidewalk was obstructed, and thus, as so construed, appellant violated the statute.

Appellant, however, contends that as so construed and applied in this case, the statute is an unconstitutional infringement on freedom of speech and assembly. This contention on the facts here presented raises an issue with which this Court has dealt in many decisions, that is, the right of a State or municipality to regulate the use of city streets and other facilities to assure the safety and convenience of the people in their use and the concomitant right of the people of free speech and assembly. . . . From these decisions certain clear principles emerge. The rights of free speech and assembly, while fundamental in our democratic society, still do not mean that everyone with opinions or beliefs to express may address a group at any public place and at any time. The constitutional guarantee of liberty implies the existence of an organized society maintaining public order, without which liberty itself would be lost in the excesses of anarchy. The control of travel on the streets is a clear example of governmental responsibility to insure this necessary order. . . . One would not be justified in ignoring the familiar red light because this was thought to be a means of social protest. Nor could one, contrary to traffic regulations, insist upon a street meeting in the middle of Times Square at the rush hour as a form of freedom of speech or assembly. Governmental authorities have the duty and responsibility to keep their streets open and available for movement. A group of demonstrators could not insist upon the right to cordon off a street, or entrance to a public or private building, and allow no one to pass who did not agree to listen to their exhortations. . . . We emphatically reject the notion urged by appellant that the First and Fourteenth Amendments afford the same kind of freedom to those who would communicate ideas by conduct such as patrolling, marching, and picketing on streets and highways, as these amendments afford to those who communicate ideas by pure speech. . . .

City officials who testified for the State clearly indicated that certain meetings and parades are permitted in Baton Rouge, even though they have the effect of obstructing traffic, provided prior approval is obtained. . . . The statute itself provides no standards for the determination of local officials as to which assemblies to permit or which to prohibit. Nor are there any administrative regulations on this subject which have been called to our attention. From all the evidence before us it appears that the authorities in Baton Rouge permit or prohibit parades or street meetings in their completely uncontrolled discretion. . . .

The situation is thus the same as if the statute itself expressly provided that there could only be peaceful parades or demonstrations in the unbridled discretion of the local officials. . . . This Court has recognized that the lodging of such broad discretion in a public official allows him to determine which expressions of view will be permitted and which will not. This thus sanctions a device for the suppression of the communication of ideas and permits the official to act as a censor. Also inherent in such a system allowing parades or meetings only with the prior permission of an official is the obvious danger to the right of a person or group not to be denied equal protection of the laws. It is clearly unconstitutional to enable a public official to determine which expressions of view will be permitted and which will not or to engage in invidious discrimination among persons or groups either by use of a statute providing a system of broad discretionary licensing power or, as in this case, the equivalent of such a system by selective enforcement of an extremely broad prohibitory statute.

It is, of course, undisputed that appropriate, limited discretion, under properly drawn statutes or ordinances, concerning the time, place, duration, or manner of use of the streets for public assemblies may be vested in administrative officials. . . . But here it is clear that the practice in Baton Rouge allowing unfettered discretion in local officials in the regulation of the use of the streets for peaceful parades and meetings is an unwarranted abridgment of appellant's freedom of speech and assembly secured to him by the First Amendment, as applied to the States by the Fourteenth Amendment. It follows, therefore, that appellant's conviction for violating the statute as so applied and enforced must be reversed.

For the reasons discussed above the judgment of the Supreme Court of Louisiana is reversed.

ADDERLEY V. FLORIDA
385 U.S. 39 (1966)

"The State, no less than a private owner of property, has power to preserve the property under its control for the use to which it is lawfully dedicated."

MR. JUSTICE BLACK delivered the opinion of the Court.

Petitioners, Harriett Louise Adderley and 31 other persons, were convicted by a jury in a joint trial in the County Judge's Court of Leon County, Florida, on a charge of "trespass with a malicious and mischievous intent" upon the premises of the county jail contrary to [the Florida trespass statute: "Every trespass upon the property of another, committed with a malicious and mischievous intent, the punishment of which is not specially provided for, shall be punished by imprisonment not exceeding three months, or by fine not exceeding one hundred dollars"].

Petitioners, apparently all students of the Florida A. & M. University in Tallahassee, had gone from the school to the jail about a mile away, along with many other students, to "demonstrate" at the jail their protests of arrests of other protesting students the day before, and perhaps to protest more generally against state and local policies and practices of racial segregation, including segregation of the jail. The county sheriff, legal custodian of the jail and jail grounds, tried to persuade the students to leave the jail grounds. When this did not work, he notified them that they must leave, that if they did not leave he would arrest them for trespassing, and that if they resisted he would charge them with that as well. Some of the students left but others, including petitioners, remained and they were arrested. On appeal the convictions were affirmed by the Florida Circuit Court and then by the Florida District Court of Appeal. . . .

Petitioners have insisted from the beginning of this case that it is controlled by and must be reversed because of our prior cases of Edwards v. South Carolina, and Cox v. Louisiana. We cannot agree.

The Edwards case, like this one, did come up when a number of persons demonstrated on public property against their State's segregation policies. They also sang hymns and danced, as did the demonstrators in this case. But here the analogies to this case end. In Edwards, the demonstrators went to the South Carolina State Capitol grounds to protest. In this case they went to the jail. Traditionally, state capitol grounds are open to the public. Jails, built for security purposes, are not. The demonstrators at the South Carolina Capitol went in through a public driveway and as they entered they were told by state officials there that they had a right as citizens to go through the State House grounds as long as they were peaceful. Here the demonstrators entered the jail grounds through a driveway used only for jail purposes and without warning to or permission from the sheriff. More importantly, South Carolina sought to prosecute its State Capitol demonstrators by charging them with the common-law crime of breach of the peace. This Court in Edwards took pains to point out at length the indefinite, loose, and broad nature of this charge . . . The South Carolina breach-of-the-peace statute was thus struck down as being so broad and all-embracing as to jeopardize speech, press, assembly and petition. . . . And it was on this same ground of vagueness that in Cox v. Louisiana the Louisiana breach-of-the-peace law used to prosecute Cox was invalidated.

The Florida trespass statute under which these petitioners were charged cannot be challenged on this ground. It is aimed at conduct of one limited kind, that is, for one person or persons to trespass upon the property of another with a malicious and mischievous intent. There is no lack of notice in this law, nothing to entrap or fool the unwary.

Petitioners seem to argue that the Florida trespass law is void for vagueness because it requires a trespass to be "with a malicious and mischievous intent." But these words do not broaden the scope of trespass so as to make it cover a multitude of types of conduct as does the common-law breach-of-the-peace charge. On the contrary, these words narrow the scope of the offense. . . . The use of these terms in the statute, instead of contributing to uncertainty and misunderstanding, actually makes its meaning more understandable and clear. . . .

Petitioners here contend that "Petitioners' convictions are based on a total lack of relevant evidence." If true, this would be a denial of due process. . . . [But] petitioners' summary of facts, as well as that of the Circuit Court, shows an abundance of facts to support the jury's verdict of guilty in this case. In summary both these statements show testimony ample to prove this: Disturbed and upset by the arrest of their schoolmates the day before, a large number of Florida A. & M. students assembled on the school grounds and decided to march down to the county jail. Some apparently wanted to be put in jail too, along with the students already there. A group of around 200 marched from the school and arrived at the jail singing and clapping. They went directly to the jail-door entrance where they were met by a deputy sheriff, evidently surprised by their arrival. He asked them to move back, claiming they were blocking the entrance to the jail and fearing that they might attempt to enter the jail. They moved back part of the way, where they stood or sat, singing, clapping and dancing, on the jail driveway and on an adjacent grassy area upon the jail premises. This particular jail entrance and driveway were not normally used by the public, but by the sheriff's department for transporting prisoners to and from the courts several blocks away and by commercial concerns for servicing the jail. Even after their partial retreat, the demonstrators continued to block vehicular passage over this driveway up to the entrance of the jail.

Someone called the sheriff who was at the moment apparently conferring with one of the state court judges about incidents connected with prior arrests for demonstrations. When the sheriff returned to the jail, he immediately inquired if all was safe inside the jail and was told it was. He then engaged in a conversation with two of the leaders. He told them that they were trespassing upon jail property and that he would give them 10 minutes to leave or he would arrest them. Neither of the leaders did anything to disperse the crowd, and one of them told the sheriff that they wanted to get arrested. A local minister talked with some of the demonstrators and told them not to enter the jail, because they could not arrest themselves, but just to remain where they were. After about 10 minutes, the sheriff, in a voice loud enough to be heard by all, told the demonstrators that he was the legal custodian of the jail and its premises, that they were trespassing on county property in violation of the law, that they should all leave forthwith or he would arrest them, and that if they attempted to resist arrest, he would charge them with that as a separate offense. Some of the group then left. Others, including all petitioners, did not leave. Some of them sat down. In a few minutes, realizing that the remaining demonstrators had no intention of leaving, the sheriff ordered his deputies to surround those remaining on jail premises and placed them, 107 demonstrators, under arrest. . . .

[We now consider] the question of whether conviction of the state offense, thus defined, unconstitutionally deprives petitioners of their rights to freedom of speech, press, assembly or petition. We hold it does not. The sheriff, as jail custodian, had power, as the state courts have here held, to direct that this large crowd of people get off the grounds. There is not a shred of evidence in this record that this power was exercised . . . because the sheriff objected to what was being sung or said by the demonstrators or because he disagreed with the objectives of their protest. The record reveals that he objected only to their presence on that part of the jail grounds reserved for jail uses. There is no evidence at all that on any other occasion had similarly large groups of the public been permitted to gather on this portion of the jail grounds for any purpose. Nothing in the Constitution of the United States prevents Florida from even-handed enforcement of its general trespass statute against those refusing to obey the sheriff's order to remove themselves from what amounted to the curtilage of the jailhouse. The State, no less than a private owner of property, has power to preserve the property under its control for the use to which it is lawfully dedicated. For this reason there is no merit to the petitioners' argument that they had a constitutional right to stay on the property, over the jail custodian's objections, because this "area chosen for the peaceful civil rights demonstration was not only 'reasonable' but also particularly appropriate. . . . "Such an argument has as its major unarticulated premise the assumption that people who want to propagandize protests or views have a constitutional right to do so whenever and however and wherever they please. That concept of constitutional law was vigorously and forthrightly rejected in Cox v. Louisiana. We reject it again. The United States Constitution does not forbid a State to control the use of its own property for its own lawful nondiscriminatory purpose.

These judgments are affirmed.

MR. JUSTICE DOUGLAS, with whom THE CHIEF JUSTICE, MR. JUSTICE BRENNAN, and MR. JUSTICE FORTAS concur, dissenting.

The First Amendment . . . provides that "Congress shall make no law . . . abridging . . . the right of the people peaceably to assemble, and to petition the Government for a redress of grievances." These rights, along with religion, speech, and press, are preferred rights of the Constitution, made so by reason of that explicit guarantee. . . . With all respect, therefore, the Court errs in treating the case as if it were an ordinary trespass case or an ordinary picketing case.

The jailhouse, like an executive mansion, a legislative chamber, a courthouse, or the statehouse itself is one of the seats of government, whether it be the Tower of London, the Bastille, or a small county jail. And when it houses political prisoners or those who many think are unjustly held, it is an obvious center for protest. The right to petition for the redress of grievances has an ancient history and is not limited to writing a letter or sending a telegram to a congressman; it is not confined to appearing before the local city council, or writing letters to the President or Governor or Mayor. Conventional methods of petitioning may be, and often have been, shut off to large groups of our citizens. Legislators may turn deaf ears; formal complaints may be routed endlessly through a bureaucratic maze; courts may let the wheels of justice grind very slowly. Those who do not control television and radio, those who cannot afford to advertise in newspapers or circulate elaborate pamphlets may have only a more limited type of access to public officials. Their meth-

ods should not be condemned as tactics of obstruction and harassment as long as the assembly and petition are peaceable, as these were.

There is no question that petitioners had as their purpose a protest against the arrest of Florida A. & M. students for trying to integrate public theatres. The sheriff's testimony indicates that he well understood the purpose of the rally. The petitioners who testified unequivocally stated that the group was protesting the arrests, and state and local policies of segregation, including segregation of the jail. This testimony was not contradicted or even questioned. The fact that no one gave a formal speech, that no elaborate handbills were distributed, and that the group was not laden with signs would seem to be immaterial. Such methods are not the sine qua non of petitioning for the redress of grievances. The group did sing "freedom" songs. And history shows that a song can be a powerful tool of protest. There was no violence; no threat of violence; no attempted jail break; no storming of a prison; no plan or plot to do anything but protest.

The evidence is uncontradicted that the petitioners' conduct did not upset the jailhouse routine; things went on as they normally would. None of the group entered the jail. Indeed, they moved back from the entrance as they were instructed. There was no shoving, no pushing, no disorder or threat of riot. It is said that some of the group blocked part of the driveway leading to the jail entrance. The chief jailer, to be sure, testified that vehicles would not have been able to use the driveway. Never did the students locate themselves so as to cause interference with persons or vehicles going to or coming from the jail. Indeed, it is undisputed that the sheriff and deputy sheriff, in separate cars, were able to drive up the driveway to the parking places near the entrance and that no one obstructed their path. Further, it is undisputed that the entrance to the jail was not blocked. And whenever the students were requested to move they did so. If there was congestion, the solution was a further request to move to lawns or parking areas, not complete ejection and arrest. . . . Finally, the fact that some of the protestants may have felt their cause so just that they were willing to be arrested for making their protest outside the jail seems wholly irrelevant. A petition is nonetheless a petition, though its futility may make martyrdom attractive.

We do violence to the First Amendment when we permit this "petition for redress of grievances" to be turned into a trespass action. It does not help to analogize this problem to the problem of picketing. Picketing is a form of protest usually directed against private interests. I do not see how rules governing picketing in general are relevant to this express constitutional right to assemble and to petition for redress of grievances. In the first place the jailhouse grounds were not marked with "NO TRESPASSING!" signs, nor does respondent claim that the public was generally excluded from the grounds. Only the sheriff's fiat transformed lawful conduct into an unlawful trespass. To say that a private owner could have done the same if the rally had taken place on private property is to speak of a different case, as an assembly and a petition for redress of grievances run to government, not to private proprietors.

The Court forgets that prior to this day our decisions have drastically limited the application of state statutes inhibiting the right to go peacefully on public property to exercise First Amendment rights. As Mr. Justice Roberts wrote in Hague v. C. I. O.: "Wherever the title of streets and parks may rest, they have immemorially been held in trust for the use of the public and, time out of mind, have been used for purposes of assembly, communicating thoughts between citizens, and discussing public questions. Such use of the streets and public places has, from ancient times, been a part of the privileges, immunities, rights, and liberties of citizens." . . .

There may be some public places which are so clearly committed to other purposes that their use for the airing of grievances is anomalous. There may be some instances in which assemblies and petitions for redress of grievances are not consistent with other necessary purposes of public property. A noisy meeting may be out of keeping with the serenity of the statehouse or the quiet of the courthouse. No one, for example, would suggest that the Senate gallery is the proper place for a vociferous protest rally. And in other cases it may be necessary to adjust the right to petition for redress of grievances to the other interests inhering in the uses to which the public property is normally put. But this is quite different from saying that all public places are off limits to people with grievances. And it is farther yet from saying that the "custodian" of the public property in his discretion can decide when public places shall be used for the communication of ideas, especially the constitutional right to assemble and petition for redress of grievances. For to place such discretion in any public official, be he the "custodian" of the public property or the local police commissioner is to place those who assert their First Amendment rights at his mercy. It gives him the awesome power to decide whose ideas may be expressed and who shall be denied a place to air their claims and petition their government. Such power is out of step with all our decisions prior to today where we have insisted that before a First Amendment right may be curtailed under the guise of a criminal law, any evil that may be collateral to the exercise of the right must be isolated and defined in a "narrowly drawn" statute lest the power to control excesses of conduct be used to suppress the constitutional right itself. That tragic consequence happens today when a trespass law is used to bludgeon those who peacefully exercise a First Amendment right to protest to government against one of the most grievous of all modern oppressions which some of our States are inflicting on our citizens. . . .

Today a trespass law is used to penalize people for exercising a constitutional right. Tomorrow a disorderly conduct statute, a breach-of-the-peace statute, a vagrancy statute will be put to the same end. It is said that the sheriff did not make the arrests because of the views which petitioners espoused. That excuse is usually given, as we know from the many cases involving arrests of minority groups for breaches of the peace, unlawful assemblies, and parading without a permit. . . . Yet by allowing these orderly and civilized protests against injustice to be suppressed, we only increase the forces of frustration which the conditions of second-class citizenship are generating amongst us.

PART III

Race, Gender, and the Equal Protection Clause

CHAPTER 8

Race: Slavery and Segregation

INTRODUCTION

There has been no more divisive and disruptive issue in American history than race. From the time the first Africans were transported to Virginia in 1619, first as indentured servants but soon after as slaves, most of the white settlers considered them "beings of an inferior order," as the Supreme Court bluntly but accurately stated in the infamous *Dred Scott* decision in 1857. Between those two years, more than 4 million Africans were brought to this country in chains, sold at auction, and forced into back-breaking labor on plantations and farms, and in the homes of their white owners. From a human perspective, the condition of slaves was nothing short of degradation, however "humane" their treatment. Every attempt to sanitize the history of slavery, to portray the "happy" slave, to excuse or minimize the brutality of plantation overseers, paints a false picture. The record of slave uprisings, led by men like Nat Turner and Denmark Vesey, shows the courage in the face of almost certain death of people whose abortive insurrections provide an ironic twist to the state motto of New Hampshire, "Live free or die."

Close to five centuries after slavery was first established in the colonies, and continued after the successful revolution against England, the social, political, and legal consequences of slavery can be seen in almost every American city and many towns, in residential segregation, income disparities, and the return of "separate and unequal" education in the resegregation of American schools. The Supreme Court's decision in *Brown v. Board of Education* in 1954 that school segregation violated the Constitution (see Chapter 9), and congressional enactment of civil rights laws in the 1960s, finally ended four centuries of legalized racism. But judicial decisions and civil rights laws have not come close to bringing African Americans and members of other racial and ethnic minorities to parity with the white majority that instituted slavery, imposed the Jim Crow system after slavery was abolished, and continues to decry affirmative action to redress the racial discrimination that remains as the legacy of slavery and segregation.

There is, in reality, no way to study and examine the Supreme Court's decisions on slavery and segregation without a frank acknowledgment of the historical record just summarized. The Court has survived what Chief Justice Charles Evans Hughes called the "self-inflicted wound" of the *Dred Scott* decision, and has made some courageous rulings in the past half-century, most notably in the *Brown* case. But many of the benefits that blacks and other minorities gained from those decisions have been subsequently limited by the Court, by ending judicial oversight of school integration plans and by prohibiting government agencies and universities from adopting "race conscious" programs to give racial minorities their fair share of public contracts, jobs, and higher education.

Reading the Supreme Court's opinions in this area without an awareness of and exposure to the historical context in which the cases arose is akin to visiting a Civil War cemetery to study the calligraphy on the tombstones. This book is based on the premise that Supreme Court opinions should be viewed, not individually and separately, but as joined parts of the historical record of race in American society, a record in which judicial decisions are reflections of social, political, and economic currents that shift over time, sometimes moving toward greater racial equality and at other times falling back into episodes of intolerance and discrimination. There is no inevitable progression toward the ideal of equality; the Fourteenth Amendment's promise of the "equal protection of the laws" has as often been broken as it has been honored by the Supreme Court.

This book also invites students and readers to look more closely at the racial attitudes of the Supreme Court justices who decided the cases in this section. They include Chief Justice Roger Taney, a fervent defender of slavery who wrote the majority opinion in the *Dred Scott* case, declaring that "persons of African descent," whether slave or free, had "no rights which the white man was bound to respect." They also include such "genteel" racists as Justice Henry Brown, who asserted in his majority opinion in *Plessy v. Ferguson* that if legal segregation "stamps the colored race with a badge of inferiority" that was "solely because the colored race chooses to put that construction upon it." And they include Chief Justice William Rehnquist, who wrote as a law clerk to Justice Robert Jackson in 1953, while the Supreme Court was considering the *Brown* case, that "I think *Plessy v. Ferguson* was right and should be reaffirmed."

Of course, the Court has also had justices who spoke out forcefully against slavery and segregation. Justice John McLean, one of the two dissenters in the *Dred Scott* case, denounced the "infamous traffic in slaves" and "the degradation of negro slavery in our country." Justice John Marshall Harlan (whose grandson, with the same illustrious name, later sat on the Court) wrote the sole dissent in the *Plessy* case. "Our Constitution is color-blind," Harlan stated, "and neither knows nor tolerates classes among citizens." And Justice Thurgood Marshall, whose grandfather had been a slave, shared the Court's bench with Justice Rehnquist for twenty years. Dissenting from Rehnquist's majority opinion in a case that terminated judicial oversight of a "resegregated" school system, Marshall wrote that its holding "perpetuates the message of racial inferiority associated with segregation."

Another premise of this book is that the constitutional doctrine that flows from the Court's opinions puts into judicial language the underlying personal attitudes and values of the justices who join them. Particularly in the area of race, these attitudes and values are often masked by solicitude for members of racial minorities. Justice Henry Brown asserted in his *Plessy* opinion, for example, that the Fourteenth Amendment was designed "to enforce the absolute equality of the two races before the law." During his Senate confirmation hearings in 1971, Justice Rehnquist promised to obey the *Brown* decision as "the established constitutional law of the land" and referring to civil rights laws told one senator, "I have come to realize the strong concern that minorities have for the recognition of these rights." But the votes of the justices in cases that raise issues of racial segregation and discrimination count for more than professions of concern for those who challenge these practices.

This chapter includes only a handful of the hundreds of Supreme Court cases that have dealt with racial issues since the era of slavery. All but the *Dred Scott* case were decided after the ratification of the Fourteenth Amendment in 1868, which guarantees "the equal protection of the laws" to "all persons" in this country. The Equal Protection Clause is where civil rights law begins, but hardly where it ends. Judicial interpretation and application of the clause raise myriad questions. The basic constitutional principle is that "similarly situated" persons should be treated equally by the law, and not be subject to "invidious" discrimination (that is, designed to harm or disadvantage a person, or deny them a benefit given to others) on the basis of some "immutable characteristic" over which they have no control and cannot change. In some areas of law, such as the rights of homosexuals, this principle has provoked much debate, since many people believe that sexual orientation is a lifestyle "choice" and not a characteristic with genetic or neurological roots. In the area of racial segregation, however, this principle leads to a clear and simple answer: race is an immutable characteristic, and subjecting any person to invidious discrimination because of their race violates the Equal Protection Clause. The Supreme Court repudiated school segregation in its *Brown* decision on the basis of this principle, unstated but implicit in the Court's unanimous opinion. This and other school cases are dealt with in the following chapter, since they form a distinct area of civil rights law, but they share with the cases in this chapter the same grounding in the Equal Protection Clause.

DRED SCOTT V. SANDFORD
60 U.S. 393 (1857)

"At the time the Constitution was adopted, negroes had for more than a century before been regarded as beings of an inferior order and altogether unfit to associate with the white race, either in social or political relations; and so far inferior, that they had no rights which the white man was bound to respect; and that the negro might justly and lawfully be reduced to slavery for his benefit."

The Question: Can a person held in slavery bring suit in federal court against a citizen of another state, under the Constitution's "diversity of citizenship" clause, seeking his freedom on grounds that his residence in a state and a territory in which slavery was unlawful had emancipated him?

The Arguments: PRO

The Constitution allows citizens to file suit in federal court against citizens of another state. In this case, a person held in slavery was taken by his owner and resided in the state of Illinois and in Wisconsin Territory; in both places slavery is unlawful. These periods of residence effectively emancipated the slave under the doctrine "once free, always free." The Constitution does not define the term *citizen* and there is no provision in the Constitution that bars persons of African descent, whether free or slave, from this status. The federal courts have jurisdiction over this case, the person seeking his freedom has standing to bring the suit, and the courts should reach the merits of the suit.

CON

The historical record makes it clear that the Framers of the Constitution did not intend to include persons of African descent in the category of "citizens of the United States"; nor are persons of African descent who are lawfully held in slavery citizens of the states in which they reside. Accordingly, the person who brought this suit in federal court does not have standing to bring suit, and it must be dismissed. In addition, Congress did not have the authority in passing the Missouri Compromise in 1820 to prohibit the further admission of states to the Union under constitutions or laws that allow slavery, north of the line specified by Congress in that law.

BACKGROUND

No individual litigant in American constitutional history has equaled the fame of Dred Scott, whose suit for freedom brought the slavery issue to a boil in the political cauldron of the 1850s. Every student of constitutional history knows Dred Scott by name, but hardly anyone knows anything about him beyond his name. Just who *was* the man whose Supreme Court case pushed the nation over the brink of sectional conflict and into the Civil War? This is not a trivial question. Every Supreme Court case that involves a claim of individual rights is brought by a real person, who has sought legal redress for some kind of oppression. American constitutional history is the history of real people with real grievances. Judges—who are also real people—do not always uphold these claims, but their decisions affect many lives: first, of the individuals who brought the case, and second, of those whose rights are determined by the Court's ruling. We often learn more from the personal stories of these real people than from the impersonal pages of Supreme Court decisions.

One thing we learn about Dred Scott is that, like most slaves, his identity and history are riddled with historical gaps. This fact tells us a great deal about an institution that robbed its victims not only of rights but often of their names. This was true of Dred Scott, who may have been known simply as "Sam" for most of his life, and acquired the name "Dred Scott" after his sale in 1833 to Dr. John Emerson in St. Louis, Missouri. His previous owner, Peter Blow, arrived in St. Louis from Alabama in 1830 with six slaves, five male and one female. He set up a boardinghouse but died in 1832, a year after his wife's death. After Blow's death, his executor sold two male slaves to settle claims against the estate, one named Sam and the other with no recorded name. No one knows which of these two slaves was purchased by Dr. Emerson, whether Sam became Dred Scott, or whether the unnamed slave was in fact named Dred Scott. No one even knows for sure when or where Dred Scott was born. He was literally a man without a past, or at least one known to white people.

We do know that the Blow family remained close to their former slave and supported Dred Scott during his long struggle for freedom. Three months after the Supreme Court ruled in March 1857 that Scott was still a slave, Peter Blow's son Taylor regained title to him and promptly freed him. But Dred lived only fifteen months as a free man, working as a hotel porter in St. Louis; he died of "consumption" in September 1858. He never sought the limelight, although he did talk with several newspaper reporters about his case. One report, published in 1857, described Dred Scott as "illiterate but not ignorant" and as a person with a "strong common sense." An article in 1858 called him "a small, pleasant-looking negro" with an "imperial" beard, wearing a "seedy" black suit and looking "somewhat the worse for wear and tear."

Life imposed a great deal of "wear and tear" on Dred Scott, particularly after Dr. Emerson purchased him from the Blows. By all accounts, Emerson was a poor doctor and a chronic malcontent. He finagled a position in 1832 as an army medical officer and was posted in 1834 to Fort Armstrong in the "free" state of Illinois. Dred Scott—then in his early thirties—accompanied his new owner, who disliked life on the frontier and asked to return to St. Louis for treatment of a "syphiloid disease." After several rebuffs by the army brass, Dr. Emerson finally secured a new post in 1836 when Fort Armstrong was closed. He and Dred moved to Fort Snelling, located in Wisconsin Territory (later renamed Iowa Territory and now part of Minnesota).

These chapters in Dred Scott's life have great significance. Fort Armstrong and Fort Snelling both lay in "free" territory, north of the line drawn by the Missouri Compromise in 1820. Slavery was illegal in both Illinois and Wisconsin Territory, and Dred could not lawfully be held as a slave by Dr. Emerson in either place. While he lived at Fort Snelling, Dred met Harriet Robinson, a teenage girl, also held as a slave by the resident Indian agent, Major Taliaferro. He either sold Harriet to Emerson or gave her to Dred as a wife, and they were married by the major as a local justice of the peace. The Scotts had four children; two sons died in infancy, but two girls—Eliza and Lizzie—grew up and joined their parents' suit for freedom.

Dr. Emerson complained about the cold weather in the North (the weather never suited him) and secured a transfer back to St. Louis in 1837, only to find orders when he arrived that he report to Fort Jesup in Louisiana. The weather was too damp in the South for his taste, and he wangled a return to Fort Snelling in 1838. But during his stay in Louisiana, Emerson got married and Dred and Harriet Scott—who had remained at Fort Snelling—traveled down the Mississippi by steamboat to join them. The Emersons and the Scotts journeyed back to Fort Snelling by boat; Eliza Scott was born on this trip, north of the Missouri Compromise line in "free" territory.

Emerson got into violent quarrels with the personnel at Fort Snelling, and he was ordered in 1840 to Florida, where the army was engaged in the Seminole War against the Indians. Emerson's wife returned from Fort Snelling to St. Louis with the Scotts. Dr. Emerson's complaints became too much for the army, and he was dismissed from service in 1842. He returned to St. Louis but could not build a private practice there. He moved to Davenport, Iowa, in 1843, and died there—most likely of syphilis—at the end of that year. The Scotts remained in Missouri, although where they lived at the time of Emerson's death is unclear.

The sad story of Dr. Emerson bears recounting largely because it shows that Dred Scott and his family lived at least twice in "free" territory where slavery was illegal. Did their residence on free soil in Illinois and Wisconsin Territory remove the chains of slavery? Surprisingly, this question had a fairly clear answer in 1846, when Dred and Harriet Scott filed identical suits for their freedom in Missouri state court in St. Louis.

Their suits did, however, raise two puzzling questions. First, who actually owned the Scotts, or claimed ownership? Second, who encouraged them to file suit and put up the money to hire lawyers? In his exhaustive account of the *Dred Scott* case, Don Fehrenbacher concluded that the answer to both "remains a mystery." John Sanford, the brother of Emerson's wife, Eliza, claimed ownership during the lawsuits, but there are no records to support his claim. It is possible that Dred Scott himself decided to sue for his freedom, with help from his former owners, the Blow family. Fehrenbacher notes that Dred Scott possessed "some measure of self-reliance, as well as a fund of practical knowledge, and suits for freedom occurred often enough to be common talk among St. Louis slaves."

* * *

Missouri law was on the Scotts' side, at least when they filed their suits. The state's highest court had repeatedly held that masters who took slaves into "free" territory thereby emancipated them, and that slavery did not reattach when they returned to Missouri. The legal doctrine of that time was "once free, always free." But Dred and Harriet Scott had the misfortune to find their suits caught in the shifting currents of Missouri (and national) politics. That misfortune stemmed from the snail's pace at which their cases proceeded through the state courts. More than a year passed between the time the Scotts filed their suits in 1846 and

their first trial in June 1847. Dred's complaint alleged that Dr. Emerson's widow, Irene, had "beat, bruised, and ill-treated him" and then "imprisoned" him for twelve hours on April 4, 1846, two days before he filed suit against her for assault and false imprisonment, asking for damages of $10. Dred also claimed to be a "free person" in his complaint. His claims that Irene Emerson beat and imprisoned him may or may not have been true; she was apparently not a cruel or violent person, and may not even have seen Dred on April 4. But charges like these were necessary in suits for freedom. If the defendant had beaten or imprisoned a slave, those acts constituted lawful "chastisement" and slaves could receive no damages. But a "free person" could not be lawfully beaten or imprisoned, and juries could award them damages. So the jurors in Dred's case had to determine, before they reached the damage issue, whether he was a free man or a slave.

Whoever put up the funds for the Scotts' lawsuit picked a prominent lawyer in Samuel Bay, Missouri's former attorney general. But prominent lawyers make mistakes just like obscure ones, and Bay made a serious error. Before he could argue that the Scotts' residence in Illinois and Wisconsin Territory had freed them from slavery, he needed to show that Irene Emerson claimed their ownership and controlled them. Unfortunately, Bay's witnesses failed to produce satisfactory evidence on this issue. A man named Samuel Russell testified that he "hired out" the Scotts from Mrs. Emerson and paid her father, Alexander Sanford, for their labor. But Russell had no personal knowledge that Mrs. Emerson owned the Scotts; he testified that his wife made all the arrangements. Without evidence on the important—and disputed—issue of whether Irene Emerson "owned" Dred Scott, the jury returned a verdict in her favor.

Hoping to correct his legal error, Samuel Bay filed a motion for a new trial, which the state judge granted after some delay. But Irene Emerson had a prominent lawyer as well, George Goode, a Virginian who held strong proslavery views. He opposed the judge's order for a new trial, and the dispute came before the Missouri supreme court in April 1848. Although that court dismissed Mrs. Emerson's claim two months later and sent the case back for a second trial, proceedings did not begin until January 1850. By this time, the Scotts' cases were almost four years old, and the sectional battles over slavery in Congress—which produced the Compromise of 1850—had affected Missouri politics as well.

The second time around, Dred Scott's case went to the jury with testimony from Mrs. Russell that Irene Emerson had hired out the Scotts to the Russells, claiming "ownership" of her slaves. This testimony, along with evidence that the Scotts had lived in "free" territory, convinced the jurors that Dred Scott was a free man under Missouri law. But the law allows for appeals from jury verdicts, and appeals take time. And Mrs. Emerson and her lawyers—hired by her brother, John Sanford—were determined to carry the issue to higher courts. They filed an appeal with the Missouri supreme court in March 1850, but that court did not decide the case until 1852. By that time, Missouri voters had placed two new judges on the state's supreme court. One of them, William Scott, was a fervent proslavery Democrat, and he persuaded the court to reverse the trial jury's decision that Dred Scott was a free man.

The Missouri judges ruled that they were bound by an 1851 decision of the United States Supreme Court in a case called *Strader v. Graham*. This case began when two black musicians—both of them slaves—traveled from Kentucky to Ohio to perform in minstrel shows. They had been to Ohio many times and had always returned to Kentucky. But on this last trip they kept on traveling to Canada, where they reached freedom. Kentucky was a slave state and Ohio a free state, and the musicians' owner in Kentucky brought a suit for damages against several Ohio residents who allegedly helped them escape from slavery. The defendants relied on the Northwest Ordinance of 1787, in which Congress banned slavery in the territories of the United States. Kentucky's highest court rejected this argument, on the ground that Ohio was now a state, and no longer part of the Northwest Territory. Consequently, the Northwest Ordinance no longer governed the case and the dispute became purely a matter of state law. Not surprisingly, the Kentucky judges ruled that their state's laws prevailed over those of Ohio. Because the escaped minstrels, had they been apprehended and returned to Kentucky, would have been slaves—and thus the "property" of their master—in that state, the master was entitled to damages against the Ohioans who helped them escape. The Kentucky judges, of course, dismissed the "once free, always free" doctrine in their ruling.

When the *Strader* case reached the Supreme Court, the "states' rights" decision of the Kentucky judges found a receptive audience. Chief Justice Roger Taney wrote for a unanimous Court, dismissing the case for lack of federal jurisdiction. However, he took sides in the dispute, writing that if the slave musicians had returned to Kentucky—willingly or not—their status would have "depended altogether upon the laws of that State and could not be influenced by the laws of Ohio." Since they never returned to Kentucky, Taney's opinion on this issue was the rankest form of dictum, the Latin term for judicial statements that go beyond—in this case, far beyond—the questions presented in the case. But the Chief Justice seemed determined in *Strader* to instruct state judges that the doctrine of "once free, always free" no longer applied in suits for freedom.

The Missouri judges followed Taney's instructions in Dred Scott's case, which they finally decided in March 1852. Judge Scott—certainly no relation to Dred—echoed Taney in writing that Missouri was not "bound to carry into effect enactments conceived in a spirit hostile to that which pervades her own laws." And what enactment of hostile spirit did Judge Scott have in mind? The Missouri Compromise of 1820, which banned slavery in the northern territories. Just as Chief Justice Taney ruled that the Northwest Ordinance no longer had effect, Judge Scott ruled that the Missouri Compromise had no effect in his state. And just as Taney wrote his racial views into the *Strader* opinion, Judge Scott added his to the *Dred Scott* decision. He rejected his court's earlier rulings on the grounds that "circumstances" had changed. "Times are not now as they were when the former decisions on this subject were made," Scott wrote. "Since then not only individuals but States have been possessed with a dark and fell spirit in relation to slavery, whose gratification is sought in the pursuit of measures, whose inevitable consequences must be in the overthrow and destruction of our government." After these ominous words,

Scott offered praise to God for instituting slavery to raise men like Dred Scott above the level of "miserable" Africans. He was convinced "that the introduction of slavery amongst us was, in the providence of God, who makes the evil passions of men subservient to His own glory, a means of placing that unhappy race within the pale of civilized nations."

Five years passed between this ruling in 1852 and the final decision of the United States Supreme Court in 1857. During these years, Dred Scott's case moved from state to federal court, new lawyers appeared on both sides, the legal issues changed, and national politics once again affected judicial opinions. Irene Emerson's brother, John Sanford, still claimed ownership of the Scott family, although he had supposedly moved to New York. After their defeat in state court, Dred's lawyers filed suit against Sanford in federal court in St. Louis, claiming jurisdiction under the "Diversity of Citizenship" Clause of the Constitution, which gave federal courts jurisdiction over suits between citizens of different states. There is much doubt that Sanford actually resided in New York, and much speculation that the suit was contrived by lawyers on both sides to reach the Supreme Court. Nonetheless, the federal judge who presided at the trial in May 1854, Robert Wells, ruled that he was bound by the Supreme Court's decision in *Strader v. Graham* and instructed the jury to return a verdict in Sanford's favor.

In his opinion, Judge Wells overlooked a crucial question. The Diversity Clause of the Constitution allows only "citizens" of one state to bring suit against those of another state in federal court. Wells did not decide this critical issue. He merely ruled that Dred Scott was a "resident" of Missouri, and allowed his suit to go before the jurors. But in ruling that Dred had always been a slave, Wells left open the question of whether Dred was a "citizen" of Missouri, a requirement for bringing suit in federal court. The judge's failure—deliberate or not—to decide this issue made Dred's "citizenship" the central question when the case reached the Supreme Court.

After their defeat in federal district court, Dred's lawyers filed an appeal with the Supreme Court in December 1854. They had little money, and little chance of success. What they needed, most of all, was a lawyer of national renown to argue the case. John Sanford had already recruited a former United States attorney general, Reverdy Johnson of Maryland. Johnson was an old friend of Chief Justice Taney and a formidable lawyer. Dred's supporters appealed for help in a twelve-page pamphlet he supposedly wrote, despite his illiteracy. Whether it was written by Dred or not, the pamphlet spoke volumes about his plight. "I have no money to pay anybody at Washington to speak for me," he said. "My fellowmen, can any of you help me in my day of trial? Will nobody speak for me at Washington, even without hope of other reward than the blessings of a poor black man and his family?" On Christmas Eve of 1854, Dred Scott's appeal for help reached Montgomery Blair, a prominent lawyer and former West Point cadet. After years of practice in St. Louis, Blair had moved to Washington (where he lived in Blair House, now the official guest house of the president) and established a legal practice before the Supreme Court. Blair gave Dred Scott the Christmas present of his services without fee.

The most dramatic consequence of Taney's ruling in *Dred Scott*, and the one most Americans recall from history lessons, came in the face-to-face debates between Abraham Lincoln and Stephen Douglas in 1858, when the two men campaigned across Illinois for the Senate seat Douglas then held. Douglas tried to distance himself from Taney's effort to "nationalize" slavery by advocating "popular sovereignty" on slavery in the territories—letting the voters in each territory decide the question. Ironically, six months before the *Dred Scott* ruling, Abraham Lincoln had spoken for Republicans in telling Democrats that the Supreme Court was the body charged with deciding the issue of slavery in the territories and that "we will submit to its decisions; and if you do also, there will be an end to the matter." Shortly after the ruling, Lincoln changed his tune and claimed that "the *Dred Scott* decision is erroneous. We know the court that made it has often overruled its own decisions, and we shall do what we can to have it overrule this. We offer no resistance to it."

During the twenty months between the *Dred Scott* decision and the 1858 elections, Lincoln and Douglas spoke to hundreds of audiences in Illinois and around the country, and they discussed the case in almost every speech. The seven formal—and now famous—debates between the two senatorial candidates focused largely on the Court's ruling and its consequences for national unity, as talk of secession grew louder in the South. The Constitution had become the topic of stump speeches, barroom debate, and dinner-table conversation across the nation. During the Lincoln-Douglas debates, each man charged his opponent with hostility to the Constitution. Douglas accused Lincoln of conducting "warfare on the Supreme Court," while Lincoln shot back that Douglas was complicit in a "conspiracy to perpetuate and nationalize slavery."

As the Senate election neared, the campaign rhetoric became more heated. Douglas insinuated that Lincoln favored the "amalgamation" of the races, which drew an indignant denial. He had no desire to "set the niggers and white people to marry together," Lincoln assured his listeners in Ottawa, Illinois. During their debate in Charleston, Lincoln declared that "I am not, nor ever have been, in favor of bringing about the social and political equality of the white and black races." In their last debate in Alton, Lincoln spoke for more than two hours on *Dred Scott*, tearing apart the ruling on the Missouri Compromise. But he pointedly denied any difference with Taney on the issue of black citizenship. "I am not in favor of Negro citizenship," Lincoln stated firmly.

Douglas narrowly bested Lincoln in this crucial electoral test of public sentiment on the slavery issue. Shortly after his defeat, Lincoln wrote to a friend that "Douglas had the ingenuity to be supported in the late contest both as the best means to break down and to uphold the slave interest. No ingenuity can keep these antagonistic elements in harmony long. Another explosion will soon come." Lincoln was prophetic in more than one way. Douglas continued to support "popular sovereignty" in voting on slavery, which prompted the southern Democrats in the Senate to depose him as chairman of the Committee on Territories after eleven years in that post. As the presidential campaign of 1860 neared, the Democrats fought bitterly over southern demands for federal legislation to protect slavery in the territories. Douglas opposed the bill sponsored by Senator Jefferson Davis of Mississippi, and the Republicans exulted at the internecine warfare among their opponents. "The *Dred*

Scott decision," one Republican stated, "is the only Democratic platform that now exists."

The Democratic convention in 1860, which met in the proslavery stronghold of Charleston, South Carolina, turned conflict into chaos. Party rules required a two-thirds majority to nominate a candidate, but only a simple majority to adopt a platform. Delegates who favored Douglas outnumbered those who supported other candidates, but southerners had enough votes to block Douglas. The platform committee, with one delegate from each state, adopted by a one-vote margin a proslavery document that rejected Douglas's "popular sovereignty" position and called for support of the Jefferson Davis bill to protect slavery. The Douglas forces on the convention floor rejected the proposed platform, which prompted the delegates from eight Southern states to walk out.

The convention promptly adjourned in confusion, and the delegates assembled two months later in Baltimore. After a bitter wrangle over seating rival delegations, the southerners again walked out, leaving Douglas with the nomination but without half of his party. Those who bolted in Baltimore later nominated Vice President John Breckinridge as the second Democratic candidate, running on a platform that endorsed the *Dred Scott* decision. Meanwhile, the Republicans surprised many, including Abraham Lincoln, by nominating him for president over Senator William Seward, a party stalwart with more national prominence than Lincoln. A fourth candidate, John Bell of Tennessee, represented diehard Whigs who now called themselves the Constitutional Union Party. The presidential campaign of 1860 had none of the drama or suspense of the Senate contest between Douglas and Lincoln. With the Democrats fatally split, Lincoln won easily; although he received less than 40 percent of the popular vote, he garnered 60 percent of the electoral votes.

Lincoln had predicted the "explosion" in the Democratic Party, which blew apart over the *Dred Scott* decision. But a much greater explosion shook the nation soon after Lincoln's inauguration on March 4, 1861. The new president, the first Republican in the White House, spoke to a throng at the Capitol for an hour about the Constitution and the Supreme Court in measured, sober words. Lincoln appealed to the Constitution more than twenty times, as the foundation of the Union and protector of minorities, alluding to Southern defenders of slavery and not to the slaves. "All the vital rights of minorities," he said, "are so plainly assured . . . in the Constitution, that controversies never arise concerning them." But the Constitution cannot "express provisions for all possible questions."

Lincoln turned to the burning questions of the time. "May Congress prohibit slavery in the Territories? The Constitution does not expressly say. Must Congress protect slavery in the Territories? The Constitution does not expressly say. From questions of this class spring all our constitutional controversies, and we divide upon them into majorities and minorities. If the minority will not acquiesce, the majority must, or the government must cease." Lincoln had discussed *Dred Scott* in hundreds of speeches over the past four years, deploring the Court's decision, but he spoke in general terms in his inaugural address. He agreed that "constitutional questions are to be decided by the Supreme Court" and that its decisions were binding "upon the parties to a suit, as to the object of that suit," but Lincoln did not show much deference to the Court. Its decisions were "entitled to very high respect and consideration" by the other branches of government, a far cry from the position of judicial supremacy that Marshall had fashioned and that Taney had shaped to his own uses.

With the Chief Justice sitting uncomfortably behind him, Lincoln spoke critically of the Court, asserting that "if the policy of the government, upon vital questions affecting the whole people, is to be irrevocably fixed by decisions of the Supreme Court, the instant they are made, in ordinary litigation between parties in personal actions, the people will have ceased to be their own rulers, having to that extent practically resigned their government into the hands of that eminent tribunal." In this lengthy sentence, and without mention of the *Dred Scott* decision, Lincoln delivered a forceful rebuke to Taney and those who had voted with him, although he disclaimed "any assault upon the court or the judges." The justices were not to blame "if others seek to turn their decisions to political purposes." But the president *did* blame Taney for writing a political tract in his opinion, and for handing ammunition to his fellow proslavery extremists.

Many presidents have criticized the Supreme Court, before and since Lincoln, from Jefferson's campaign to impeach Justice Samuel Chase to Franklin Roosevelt's attack on the "nine old men" who blocked his New Deal program. But never has a president spoken at such length of the Constitution and its role in national life. Lincoln, of course, came to office during the greatest constitutional crisis the nation ever faced, and he brought to his speech—delivered as the country slid ever more quickly into civil war—a profound respect for the Constitution, tempered with an appreciation of the Court's role as a political body.

Just five weeks after Lincoln's inaugural address, on April 12, Confederate forces fired on Fort Sumter in South Carolina, and its beleaguered defenders waved the white flag of surrender on April 14. That same day, Lincoln called the Congress into special session, citing "the power in me vested by the Constitution" to call out the state militias and "to cause the laws to be duly executed." The Civil War had begun. Before it ended in 1865, some 600,000 Americans—most of them young men in blue or gray uniforms—lost their lives in battles whose first shots were fired by the Supreme Court in 1857 (Irons, 1999).

STATEMENT OF FACTS

In the year 1834, the plaintiff was a negro slave belonging to Dr. Emerson, who was a surgeon in the army of the United States. In that year, 1834, Dr. Emerson took the plaintiff from the State of Missouri to the military post at Rock Island, in the State of Illinois, and held him there as a slave until the month of April or May, 1836. At the time last mentioned, said Dr. Emerson removed the plaintiff from said military post at Rock Island to the military post at Fort Snelling, on the west bank of the Mississippi river, in the Territory known as Upper Louisiana, and situate north of the latitude of thirty-six degrees thirty minutes north, and north of the State of Missouri. Dr. Emerson held the plaintiff in slavery at said Fort Snelling until the year 1838.

In the year 1835, Harriet, who is named in the second count of the plaintiff's declaration, was the negro slave of Major Taliaferro, who belonged to the army of the United States. In 1835, said Major Taliaferro took said Harriet to said Fort Snelling, and kept her there as a slave until the year 1836, and then sold her as a slave to Dr. Emerson, [who] held Harriet in slavery at Fort Snelling until the year 1838.

In the year 1836, the plaintiff and Harriet at Fort Snelling, with the consent of Dr. Emerson, who then claimed to be their master and owner, intermarried, and took each other for husband and wife. Eliza and Lizzie, named in the third count of the plaintiff's declaration, are the fruit of that marriage. Eliza is about fourteen years old, and was born on board the steamboat Gipsey, north of the north line of the State of Missouri, and upon the river Mississippi. Lizzie is about seven years old, and was born in the State of Missouri, at the military post called Jefferson Barracks. In the year 1838, Dr. Emerson removed the plaintiff and Harriet and their daughter Eliza, from Fort Snelling to the State of Missouri, where they have ever since resided.

Before the commencement of this suit, Dr. Emerson sold and conveyed the plaintiff, Harriet, Eliza, and Lizzie, to the defendant [John Sanford], as slaves, and the defendant has ever since claimed to hold each of them as slaves.

At the times mentioned in the plaintiff's declaration, the defendant, claiming to be owner as aforesaid, laid his hands upon plaintiff, Harriet, Eliza, and Lizzie, and imprisoned them, doing in this respect, however, no more than what he might lawfully do if they were of right his slaves at such times. Further proof may be given on the trial for either party.

It is agreed that Dred Scott brought suit for his freedom in the Circuit Court of St. Louis county; that there was a verdict and judgment in his favor; that on a writ of error to the Supreme Court, the judgment below was reversed, and the same remanded to the Circuit Court, where it has been continued to await the decision of this case.

* * *

MR. CHIEF JUSTICE TANEY delivered the opinion of the court.

There are two leading questions presented by the record: 1. Had the Circuit Court of the United States jurisdiction to hear and determine the case between these parties? And 2. If it had jurisdiction, is the judgment it has given erroneous or not? The plaintiff in error . . . was, with his wife and children, held as slaves by the defendant, in the State of Missouri; and he brought this action in the Circuit Court of the United States for that district, to assert the title of himself and his family to freedom. The declaration . . . contains the averment necessary to give the court jurisdiction; that he and the defendant are citizens of different States; that is, that he is a citizen of Missouri, and the defendant a citizen of New York. The defendant pleaded . . . that the plaintiff was not a citizen of the State of Missouri, as alleged in his declaration, being a negro of African descent, whose ancestors were of pure African blood, and who were brought into this country and sold as slaves. To this plea the plaintiff demurred, and the defendant joined in demurrer. The court overruled the plea, and . . . at the trial the verdict and judgment were in [defendant's] favor. Whereupon the plaintiff brought this writ of error . . .

[Defendant] denies the right of the plaintiff to sue in a court of the United States, for the reasons therein stated. If . . . the court should be of [the] opinion that the facts stated in it disqualify the plaintiff from becoming a citizen, in the sense in which that word is used in the Constitution of the United States, then the judgment of the Circuit Court is erroneous, and must be reversed. . . .

[W]hen a plaintiff sues in a court of the United States, it is necessary that he should show, in his pleading, that the suit he brings is within the jurisdiction of the court, and that he is entitled to sue there. And if he omits to do this, and should, by any oversight of the Circuit Court, obtain a judgment in his favor, the judgment would be reversed in the appellate court for want of jurisdiction in the court below. . . . And if the plaintiff claims a right to sue in a Circuit Court of the United States, under that provision of the Constitution which gives jurisdiction in controversies between citizens of different States, he must distinctly aver in his pleading that they are citizens of different States; and he cannot maintain his suit without showing that fact in the pleadings. . . .

In this case, the citizenship is averred, but it is denied by the defendant in the manner required by the rules of pleading. . . . [I]t becomes, therefore, our duty to decide whether the facts stated in the plea are or are not sufficient to show that the plaintiff is not entitled to sue as a citizen in a court of the United States. This is certainly a very serious question, and one that now for the first time has been brought for decision before this court. But it is brought here by those who have a right to bring it, and it is our duty to meet it and decide it.

The question is simply this: Can a negro, whose ancestors were imported into this country, and sold as slaves, become a member of the political community formed and brought into existence by the Constitution of the United States, and as such become entitled to all the rights, and privileges, and immunities, guarantied by that instrument to the citizen? One of which rights is the privilege of suing in a court of the United States in the cases specified in the Constitution.

It will be observed, that the plea applies to that class of persons only whose ancestors were negroes of the African race, and imported into this country, and sold and held as slaves. The only matter in issue before the court, therefore, is, whether the descendants of such slaves, when they shall be emancipated, or who are born of parents who had become free before their birth, are citizens of a State, in the sense in which the word citizen is used in the Constitution of the United States. And this being the only matter in dispute on the pleadings, the court must be understood as speaking in this opinion of that class only, that is, of those persons who are the descendants of Africans who were imported into this country, and sold as slaves. . . .

The words "people of the United States" and "citizens" are synonymous terms, and mean the same thing. They both describe the political body who, according to our republican institutions, form the sovereignty, and who hold the power and conduct the Government through their representatives. They are what we familiarly call the "sovereign people," and every citizen is one of this people, and a constituent member of this sovereignty. The question before us is, whether the

class of persons described in the plea in abatement compose a portion of this people, and are constituent members of this sovereignty? We think they are not, and that they are not included, and were not intended to be included, under the word "citizens" in the Constitution, and can therefore claim none of the rights and privileges which that instrument provides for and secures to citizens of the United States. On the contrary, they were at that time considered as a subordinate and inferior class of beings, who had been subjugated by the dominant race, and, whether emancipated or not, yet remained subject to their authority, and had no rights or privileges but such as those who held the power and the Government might choose to grant them. . . .

It is not the province of the court to decide upon the justice or injustice, the policy or impolicy, of these laws. The decision of that question belonged to the political or law-making power; to those who formed the sovereignty and framed the Constitution. The duty of the court is, to interpret the instrument they have framed, with the best lights we can obtain on the subject, and to administer it as we find it, according to its true intent and meaning when it was adopted. . . .

It becomes necessary, therefore, to determine who were citizens of the several States when the Constitution was adopted. And in order to do this, we must recur to the Governments and institutions of the thirteen colonies, when they separated from Great Britain and formed new sovereignties, and took their places in the family of independent nations. We must inquire who, at that time, were recognised as the people or citizens of a State, whose rights and liberties had been outraged by the English Government; and who declared their independence, and assumed the powers of Government to defend their rights by force of arms.

In the opinion of the court, the legislation and histories of the times, and the language used in the Declaration of Independence, show, that neither the class of persons who had been imported as slaves, nor their descendants, whether they had become free or not, were then acknowledged as a part of the people, nor intended to be included in the general words used in that memorable instrument.

It is difficult at this day to realize the state of public opinion in relation to that unfortunate race, which prevailed in the civilized and enlightened portions of the world at the time of the Declaration of Independence, and when the Constitution of the United States was framed and adopted. But the public history of every European nation displays it in a manner too plain to be mistaken.

They had for more than a century before been regarded as beings of an inferior order, and altogether unfit to associate with the white race, either in social or political relations; and so far inferior, that they had no rights which the white man was bound to respect; and that the negro might justly and lawfully be reduced to slavery for his benefit. He was bought and sold, and treated as an ordinary article of merchandise and traffic, whenever a profit could be made by it. This opinion was at that time fixed and universal in the civilized portion of the white race. It was regarded as an axiom in morals as well as in politics, which no one thought of disputing, or supposed to be open to dispute; and men in every grade and position in society daily and habitually acted upon it in their private pursuits, as well as in matters of public concern, without doubting for a moment the correctness of this opinion.

And in no nation was this opinion more firmly fixed or more uniformly acted upon than by the English Government and English people. They not only seized them on the coast of Africa, and sold them or held them in slavery for their own use; but they took them as ordinary articles of merchandise to every country where they could make a profit on them, and were far more extensively engaged in this commerce than any other nation in the world.

The opinion thus entertained and acted upon in England was naturally impressed upon the colonies they founded on this side of the Atlantic. And, accordingly, a negro of the African race was regarded by them as an article of property, and held, and bought and sold as such, in every one of the thirteen colonies which united in the Declaration of Independence, and afterwards formed the Constitution of the United States. The slaves were more or less numerous in the different colonies, as slave labor was found more or less profitable. But no one seems to have doubted the correctness of the prevailing opinion of the time. . . .

The legislation of the different colonies furnishes positive and indisputable proof of this fact. . . . The province of Maryland, in 1717, passed a law declaring "that if any free negro or mulatto intermarry with any white woman, or if any white man shall intermarry with any negro or mulatto woman, such negro or mulatto shall become a slave during life, excepting mulattoes born of white women, who, for such intermarriage, shall only become servants for seven years. . . . The other colonial law to which we refer was passed by Massachusetts in 1705. It is entitled "An act for the better preventing of a spurious and mixed issue"; and it provides . . . "that none of her Majesty's English or Scottish subjects, nor of any other Christian nation, within this province, shall contract matrimony with any negro or mulatto. . . ." We give both of these laws in the words used by the respective legislative bodies, because the language in which they are framed, as well as the provisions contained in them, show, too plainly to be misunderstood, the degraded condition of this unhappy race. They were still in force when the Revolution began, and are a faithful index to the state of feeling towards the class of persons of whom they speak, and of the position they occupied throughout the thirteen colonies, in the eyes and thoughts of the men who framed the Declaration of Independence and established the State Constitutions and Governments. They show that a perpetual and impassable barrier was intended to be erected between the white race and the one which they had reduced to slavery, and governed as subjects with absolute and despotic power, and which they then looked upon as so far below them in the scale of created beings, that intermarriages between white persons and negroes or mulattoes were regarded as unnatural and immoral, and punished as crimes, not only in the parties, but in the person who joined them in marriage. And no distinction in this respect was made between the free negro or mulatto and the slave, but this stigma, of the deepest degradation, was fixed upon the whole race.

We refer to these historical facts for the purpose of showing the fixed opinions concerning that race, upon which the statesmen of that day spoke and acted. It is necessary to do this, in order to determine whether the general terms used in the Constitution of the United States, as to the rights of man and the rights of the people, was intended to include them, or to give to them or their posterity the benefit of any of its provisions.

The language of the Declaration of Independence is equally conclusive: . . . "We hold these truths to be self-evident: that all men are created equal; that they are endowed by their Creator with certain unalienable rights; that among them is life, liberty, and the pursuit of happiness; that to secure these rights, Governments are instituted, deriving their just powers from the consent of the governed."

The general words above quoted would seem to embrace the whole human family, and if they were used in a similar instrument at this day would be so understood. But it is too clear for dispute, that the enslaved African race were not intended to be included, and formed no part of the people who framed and adopted this declaration; for if the language, as understood in that day, would embrace them, the conduct of the distinguished men who framed the Declaration of Independence would have been utterly and flagrantly inconsistent with the principles they asserted; and instead of the sympathy of mankind, to which they so confidently appealed, they would have deserved and received universal rebuke and reprobation.

Yet the men who framed this declaration were great men—high in literary acquirements—high in their sense of honor, and incapable of asserting principles inconsistent with those on which they were acting. They perfectly understood the meaning of the language they used, and how it would be understood by others; and they knew that it would not in any part of the civilized world be supposed to embrace the negro race, which, by common consent, had been excluded from civilized Governments and the family of nations, and doomed to slavery. They spoke and acted according to the then established doctrines and principles, and in the ordinary language of the day, and no one misunderstood them. The unhappy black race were separated from the white by indelible marks, and laws long before established, and were never thought of or spoken of except as property, and when the claims of the owner or the profit of the trader were supposed to need protection.

This state of public opinion had undergone no change when the Constitution was adopted, as is equally evident from its provisions and language. The brief preamble sets forth by whom it was formed, for what purposes, and for whose benefit and protection. It declares that it is formed by the people of the United States; that is to say, by those who were members of the different political communities in the several States; and its great object is declared to be to secure the blessings of liberty to themselves and their posterity. It speaks in general terms of the people of the United States, and of citizens of the several States, when it is providing for the exercise of the powers granted or the privileges secured to the citizen. It does not define what description of persons are intended to be included under these terms, or who shall be regarded as a citizen and one of the people. It uses them as terms so well understood, that no further description or definition was necessary.

But there are two clauses in the Constitution which point directly and specifically to the negro race as a separate class of persons, and show clearly that they were not regarded as a portion of the people or citizens of the Government then formed.

One of these clauses reserves to each of the thirteen States the right to import slaves until the year 1808, if it thinks proper. And the importation which it thus sanctions was unquestionably of persons of the race of which we are speaking, as the traffic in slaves in the United States had always been confined to them. And by the other provision the States pledge themselves to each other to maintain the right of property of the master, by delivering up to him any slave who may have escaped from his service, and be found within their respective territories. By the first above-mentioned clause, therefore, the right to purchase and hold this property is directly sanctioned and authorized for twenty years by the people who framed the Constitution. And by the second, they pledge themselves to maintain and uphold the right of the master in the manner specified, as long as the Government they then formed should endure. And these two provisions show, conclusively, that neither the description of persons therein referred to, nor their descendants, were embraced in any of the other provisions of the Constitution; for certainly these two clauses were not intended to confer on them or their posterity the blessings of liberty, or any of the personal rights so carefully provided for the citizen.

No one of that race had ever migrated to the United States voluntarily; all of them had been brought here as articles of merchandise. The number that had been emancipated at that time were but few in comparison with those held in slavery; and they were identified in the public mind with the race to which they belonged, and regarded as a part of the slave population rather than the free. It is obvious that they were not even in the minds of the framers of the Constitution when they were conferring special rights and privileges upon the citizens of a State in every other part of the Union. . . .

No one, we presume, supposes that any change in public opinion or feeling, in relation to this unfortunate race, in the civilized nations of Europe or in this country, should induce the court to give to the words of the Constitution a more liberal construction in their favor than they were intended to bear when the instrument was framed and adopted. Such an argument would be altogether inadmissible in any tribunal called on to interpret it. If any of its provisions are deemed unjust, there is a mode prescribed in the instrument itself by which it may be amended; but while it remains unaltered, it must be construed now as it was understood at the time of its adoption. . . . What the construction was at that time, we think can hardly admit of doubt. We have the language of the Declaration of Independence and of the Articles of Confederation, in addition to the plain words of the Constitution itself; we have the legislation of the different States, before, about the time, and since, the Constitution was adopted; we have the legislation of Congress, from the time of its adoption to a recent period; and we have the constant and uniform action of the Executive Department, all concurring together, and leading to the same result. And if anything in relation to the construction of the Constitution can be regarded as settled, it is that which we now give to the word "citizen" and the word "people."

And upon a full and careful consideration of the subject, the court is of [the] opinion, that, upon the facts stated in the plea in abatement, Dred Scott was not a citizen of Missouri within the meaning of the Constitution of the United States, and not entitled as such to sue in its courts; and, consequently, that the Circuit Court had no jurisdiction of the case. . . .

Mr. Justice McLean dissenting.

An action of trespass was brought, which charges the defendant with an assault and imprisonment of the plaintiff, and also of Harriet Scott, his wife, Eliza and Lizzie, his two children, on the ground that they were his slaves, which was without right on his part, and against law.

The defendant filed a plea in abatement . . . that "plaintiff, Dred Scott, is not a citizen of the State of Missouri, as alleged in his declaration, because he is a negro of African descent, his ancestors were of pure African blood, and were brought into this country and sold as negro slaves." . . .

[T]he plea which raises the question of jurisdiction, in my judgment, is radically defective. . . . There is no averment in this plea which shows . . . an inability in the plaintiff to sue in the Circuit Court. It does not allege that the plaintiff had his domicil in any other State, nor that he is not a free man in Missouri. He is averred to have had a negro ancestry, but this does not show that he is not a citizen of Missouri, within the meaning of the act of Congress authorizing him to sue in the Circuit Court. It has never been held necessary, to constitute a citizen within the act, that he should have the qualifications of an elector. Females and minors may sue in the Federal courts, and so may any individual who has a permanent domicil in the State under whose laws his rights are protected, and to which he owes allegiance.

Being born under our Constitution and laws, no naturalization is required, as one of foreign birth, to make him a citizen. The most general and appropriate definition of the term citizen is "a freeman." Being a freeman, and having his domicil in a State different from that of the defendant, he is a citizen within the act of Congress, and the courts of the Union are open to him. . . .

The pleader has not the boldness to allege that the plaintiff is a slave, as that would assume against him the matter in controversy, and embrace the entire merits of the case in a plea to the jurisdiction. But beyond the facts set out in the plea, the court, to sustain it, must assume the plaintiff to be a slave, which is decisive on the merits. This is a short and an effectual mode of deciding the cause; but I am yet to learn that it is sanctioned by any known rule of pleading.

The defendant's counsel complain, that if the court take jurisdiction on the ground that the plaintiff is free, the assumption is against the right of the master. This argument is easily answered. In the first place, the plea does not show him to be a slave; it does not follow that a man is not free whose ancestors were slaves. . . . No injustice can result to the master, from an exercise of jurisdiction in this cause. Such a decision does not in any degree affect the merits of the case; it only enables the plaintiff to assert his claims to freedom before this tribunal. If the jurisdiction be ruled against him, on the ground that he is a slave, it is decisive of his fate. . . .

In the argument, it was said that a colored citizen would not be an agreeable member of society. This is more a matter of taste than of law. Several of the States have admitted persons of color to the right of suffrage, and in this view have recognised them as citizens; and this has been done in the slave as well as the free States. On the question of citizenship, it must be admitted that we have not been very fastidious. Under the late treaty with Mexico, we have made citizens of all grades, combinations, and colors. The same was done in the admission of Louisiana and Florida. No one ever doubted, and no court ever held, that the people of these Territories did not become citizens under the treaty. They have exercised all the rights of citizens, without being naturalized under the acts of Congress. . . .

We need not refer to the mercenary spirit which introduced the infamous traffic in slaves, to show the degradation of negro slavery in our country. This system was imposed upon our colonial settlements by the mother country, and it is due to truth to say that the commercial colonies and States were chiefly engaged in the traffic. But we know as a historical fact, that James Madison, that great and good man, a leading member in the Federal Convention, was solicitous to guard the language of that instrument so as not to convey the idea that there could be property in man.

I prefer the lights of Madison, Hamilton, and Jay, as a means of construing the Constitution in all its bearings, rather than to look behind that period, into a traffic which is now declared to be piracy, and punished with death by Christian nations. I do not like to draw the sources of our domestic relations from so dark a ground. Our independence was a great epoch in the history of freedom; and while I admit the Government was not made especially for the colored race, yet many of them were citizens of the New England States, and exercised, the rights of suffrage when the Constitution was adopted, and it was not doubted by any intelligent person that its tendencies would greatly ameliorate their condition. . . .

MR. JUSTICE CURTIS dissenting.

I dissent from the opinion pronounced by the Chief Justice, and from the judgment which the majority of the court think it proper to render in this case. The plaintiff alleged, in his declaration, that he was a citizen of the State of Missouri, and that the defendant was a citizen of the State of New York. It is not doubted that it was necessary to make each of these allegations, to sustain the jurisdiction of the Circuit Court. The defendant denied, by a plea to the jurisdiction . . . that the plaintiff was a citizen of the State of Missouri. . . . Now, the plea to the jurisdiction in this case does not controvert the fact that the plaintiff resided in Missouri at the date of the writ. If he did then reside there, and was also a citizen of the United States, no provisions contained in the Constitution or laws of Missouri can deprive the plaintiff of his right to sue citizens of States other than Missouri, in the courts of the United States.

So that, under the allegations contained in this plea, and admitted by the demurrer, the question is, whether any person of African descent, whose ancestors were sold as slaves in the United States, can be a citizen of the United States. If any such person can be a citizen, this plaintiff has the right to the judgment of the court that he is so; for no cause is shown by the plea why he is not so, except his descent and the slavery of his ancestors.

The first section of the second article of the Constitution uses the language, "a citizen of the United States at the time of the adoption of the Constitution." One mode of approaching this question is, to inquire who were citizens of the United States at the time of the adoption of the Constitution.

Citizens of the United States at the time of the adoption of the Constitution can have been no other than citizens of the United States under the Confederation. By the Articles of Confederation, a Government was organized, the style whereof was, "The United States of America." This Government was in existence when the Constitution was framed and proposed for adoption, and was to be superseded by the new Government of the United States of America, organized under the Constitution. When, therefore, the Constitution speaks of citizenship of the United States, existing at the time of the adoption of the Constitution, it must necessarily refer to citizenship under the Government which existed prior to and at the time of such adoption.

Without going into any question concerning the powers of the Confederation to govern the territory of the United States out of the limits of the States, and consequently to sustain the relation of Government and citizen in respect to the inhabitants of such territory, it may safely be said that the citizens of the several States were citizens of the United States under the Confederation.

That Government was simply a confederacy of the several States, possessing a few defined powers over subjects of general concern, each State retaining every power, jurisdiction, and right, not expressly delegated to the United States in Congress assembled. And no power was thus delegated to the Government of the Confederation, to act on any question of citizenship, or to make any rules in respect thereto. The whole matter was left to stand upon the action of the several States, and to the natural consequence of such action, that the citizens of each State should be citizens of that Confederacy into which that State had entered, the style whereof was, "The United States of America."

To determine whether any free persons, descended from Africans held in slavery, were citizens of the United States under the Confederation, and consequently at the time of the adoption of the Constitution of the United States, it is only necessary to know whether any such persons were citizens of either of the States under the Confederation, at the time of the adoption of the Constitution.

Of this there can be no doubt. At the time of the ratification of the Articles of Confederation, all free native-born inhabitants of the States of New Hampshire, Massachusetts, New York, New Jersey, and North Carolina, though descended from African slaves, were not only citizens of those States, but such of them as had the other necessary qualifications possessed the franchise of electors, on equal terms with other citizens. . . .

On review of the status of persons of color in the states making up the Confederation, and of debates at the Constitutional Convention, it is clear, that under the Confederation, and at the time of the adoption of the Constitution, free colored persons of African descent might be, and, by reason of their citizenship in certain States, were entitled to the privileges and immunities of general citizenship of the United States.

Did the Constitution of the United States deprive them or their descendants of citizenship? That Constitution was ordained and established by the people of the United States, through the action, in each State, or those persons who were qualified by its laws to act thereon, in behalf of themselves and all other citizens of that State. In some of the States, as we have seen, colored persons were among those qualified by law to act on this subject. These colored persons were not only included in the body of "the people of the United States," by whom the Constitution was ordained and established, but in at least five of the States they had the power to act, and doubtless did act, by their suffrages, upon the question of its adoption. It would be strange, if we were to find in that instrument anything which deprived of their citizenship any part of the people of the United States who were among those by whom it was established.

I can find nothing in the Constitution which . . . deprives of their citizenship any class of persons who were citizens of the United States at the time of its adoption, or who should be native-born citizens of any State after its adoption; nor any power enabling Congress to disfranchise persons born on the soil of any State, and entitled to citizenship of such State by its Constitution and laws. And my opinion is, that, under the Constitution of the United States, every free person born on the soil of a State, who is a citizen of that State by force of its Constitution or laws, is also a citizen of the United States. . . .

It has been often asserted that the Constitution was made exclusively by and for the white race. It has already been shown that in five of the thirteen original States, colored persons then possessed the elective franchise, and were among those by whom the Constitution was ordained and established. If so, it is not true, in point of fact, that the Constitution was made exclusively by the white race. And that it was made exclusively for the white race is, in my opinion, not only an assumption not warranted by anything in the Constitution, but contradicted by its opening declaration, that it was ordained and established by the people of the United States, for themselves and their posterity. And as free colored persons were then citizens of at least five States, and so in every sense part of the people of the United States, they were among those for whom and whose posterity the Constitution was ordained and established. . . .

The conclusions at which I have arrived on this part of the case are:

First. That the free native-born citizens of each State are citizens of the United States.

Second. That as free colored persons born within some of the States are citizens of those States, such persons are also citizens of the United States.

Third. That every such citizen, residing in any State, has the right to sue and is liable to be sued in the Federal courts, as a citizen of that State in which he resides.

Fourth. That as the plea to the jurisdiction in this case shows no facts, except that the plaintiff was of African descent, and his ancestors were sold as slaves, and as these facts are not inconsistent with his citizenship of the United States, and his residence in the State of Missouri, the plea to the jurisdiction was bad, and the judgment of the Circuit Court overruling it was correct.

I dissent, therefore, from that part of the opinion of the majority of the court, in which it is held that a person of African descent cannot be a citizen of the United States.

STRAUDER V. WEST VIRGINIA
100 U.S. 303 (1879)

"It is not easy to comprehend how it can be said that while every white man is entitled to a trial by a jury selected . . . without discrimination against his color, and a negro is not, the latter is equally protected by the law with the former."

The Question: Can a state pass a law that limits service as grand or petit jurors to white men and thus bars any black man from serving on juries in state courts?

The Arguments: PRO

The people of a state have the power to determine which persons are qualified to serve as grand or petit jurors, and are free to limit service to those persons they consider best qualified to serve. The federal constitution does not limit the state's power on this issue, as no person has a positive right to serve on a jury. The provision in the Fourteenth Amendment that guarantees "the equal protection of the laws" applies only to rights provided to all persons by law, and jury service is not such a right.

CON

The law in question is a clear violation of the "equal protection of the laws" clause of the Fourteenth Amendment, which was designed and intended by its Framers to make unlawful any discrimination on the basis of race against those persons formerly held in slavery. Although no person has an unqualified right to serve as a juror, limiting that office to white men is a discrimination against black men. There is no evidence in the record of this case that black men are less capable of serving as jurors, the only qualification or service being the ability to be "impartial" between the parties in the case.

MR. JUSTICE STRONG delivered the opinion of the court.

The plaintiff in error, a colored man, was indicated for murder in the Circuit Court of Ohio County, in West Virginia, on the 20th of October, 1874, and upon trial was convicted and sentenced. The record was then removed to the Supreme Court of the State, and there the judgment of the Circuit Court was affirmed. The present case is a writ of error to that court, and it is now, in substance, averred that at the trial in the State court the defendant (now plaintiff in error) was denied rights to which he was entitled under the Constitution and laws of the United States.

In the Circuit Court of the State, before the trial of the indictment was commenced, the defendant [petitioned] for a removal of the cause into the Circuit Court of the United States, assigning, as ground for the removal, that "by virtue of the laws of the State of West Virginia no colored man was eligible to be a member of the grand jury or to serve on a petit jury in the State; that white men are so eligible, and that by reason of his being a colored man and having been a slave, he had reason to believe, and did believe, he could not have the full and equal benefit of all laws and proceedings in the State of West Virginia for the security of his person as is enjoyed by white citizens. . . ." This petition was denied by the State court, and the cause was forced to trial. . . .

The law of the State . . . is as follows: "All white male persons who are twenty-one years of age and who are citizens of this State shall be liable to serve as jurors, except as herein provided." The persons excepted are State officials.

. . . [T]he controlling question [in this case is] whether, by the Constitution and laws of the United States, every citizen of the United States has a right to a trial of an indictment against him by a jury selected and impaneled without discrimination against his race or color, because of race or color. . . . It is to be observed that the question is not whether a colored man, when an indictment has been preferred against him, has a right to a grand or a petit jury composed in whole or in part of persons of his own race or color, but it is whether, in the composition or selection of jurors by whom he is to be indicted or tried, all persons of his race or color may be excluded by law, solely because of their race or color, so that by no possibility can any colored man sit upon the jury. . . .

. . . [When the Fourteenth Amendment was adopted], it required little knowledge of human nature to anticipate that those who had long been regarded as an inferior and subject race would, when suddenly raised to the rank of citizenship, be looked upon with jealousy and positive dislike, and that State laws might be enacted or enforced to perpetuate the distinctions that had before existed. Discriminations against them had been habitual. It was well known that in some States laws making such discriminations then existed, and others might well be expected. The colored race, as a race, was abject and ignorant, and in that condition was unfitted to command the respect of those who had superior intelligence. Their training had left them mere children, and as such they needed the protection which a wise government extends to those who are unable to protect themselves. They especially needed protection against unfriendly action in the States where they were resident. It was in view of these considerations the Fourteenth Amendment was framed and adopted. It was designed to assure to the colored race the enjoyment of all the civil rights that under the law are enjoyed by white persons, and to give to that race the protection of the general government, in that enjoyment, whenever it should be denied by the States. It not only gave citizenship and the privileges of citizenship to persons of color, but it denied to any State the power to withhold from them the equal protection of the laws, and authorized Congress to enforce its provisions by appropriate legislation. . . .

If this is the spirit and meaning of the amendment, whether it means more or not, it is to be construed liberally, to carry out the purposes of its framers. It ordains that no State shall make or enforce any laws which shall abridge the privileges or immunities of citizens of the United States. . . . It ordains that no State shall deprive any person of life, liberty, or property, without due process of law, or deny to any person within its jurisdiction the equal protection of the laws. What is this but declaring that the law in the States shall be the same for the black as for the white; that all persons, whether colored or white, shall stand equal before the laws of the States, and, in regard to the colored race, for whose protection the amendment was primarily designed, that no discrimination shall be made against them by law because of their color? The words of the amendment, it is true, are prohibitory, but they contain a necessary implication of a positive immunity, or right, most valuable to the colored race, the right to exemption from unfriendly legislation against them distinctively as colored, exemption from legal discriminations, implying inferiority in civil society, lessening the security of their enjoyment of the rights which others enjoy, and discriminations which are steps towards reducing them to the condition of a subject race.

That the West Virginia statute respecting juries—the statute that controlled the selection of the grand and petit jury in the case of the plaintiff in error—is such a discrimination ought not to be doubted. Nor would it be if the persons excluded by it were white men. If in those States where the colored people constitute a majority of the entire population a law should be enacted excluding all white men from jury service, thus denying to them the privilege of participating equally with the blacks in the administration of justice, we apprehend no one would be heard to claim that it would not be a denial to white men of the equal protection of the laws. Nor if a law should be passed excluding all naturalized Celtic Irishmen, would there be any doubt of its inconsistency with the spirit of the amendment. The very fact that colored people are singled out and expressly denied by a statute all right to participate in the administration of the law, as jurors, because of their color, though they are citizens, and may be in other respects fully qualified, is practically a brand upon them, affixed by the law, an assertion of their inferiority, and a stimulant to that race prejudice which is an impediment to securing to individuals of the race that equal justice which the law aims to secure to all others.

The right to a trial by jury is guaranteed to every citizen of West Virginia by the Constitution of that State, and the constitution of juries is a very essential part of the protection such a mode of trial is intended to secure. The very idea of a jury is a body of men composed of the peers or equals of the person whose rights it is selected or summoned to determine; that is, of his neighbors, fellows, associates, persons having the same legal status in society as that which he holds. . . . In view of these considerations, it is hard to see why the statute of West Virginia should not be regarded as discriminating against a colored man when he is put upon trial for an alleged criminal offence against the State. It is not easy to comprehend how it can be said that while every white man is entitled to a trial by a jury selected from persons of his own race or color, or, rather, selected without discrimination against his color, and a negro is not, the latter is equally protected by the law with the former. Is not protection of life and liberty against race or color prejudice, a right, a legal right, under the constitutional amendment? And how can it be maintained that compelling a colored man to submit to a trial for his life by a jury drawn from a panel from which the State has expressly excluded every man of his race, because of color alone, however well qualified in other respects, is not a denial to him of equal legal protection? . . .

The Fourteenth Amendment makes no attempt to enumerate the rights it designed to protect. It speaks in general terms, and those are as comprehensive as possible. Its language is prohibitory; but every prohibition implies the existence of rights and immunities, prominent among which is an immunity from inequality of legal protection, either for life, liberty, or property. Any State action that denies this immunity to a colored man is in conflict with the Constitution. . . .

The judgment of the Supreme Court of West Virginia will be reversed, and the case remitted with instructions to reverse the judgment of the Circuit Court of Ohio county; and it is so ordered.

MR. JUSTICE FIELD.

I dissent from the judgment of the court in this case, and Mr. Justice Clifford concurs with me.

CIVIL RIGHTS CASES*
109 U.S. 3 (1883)

"When a man has emerged from slavery, and by the aid of beneficent legislation has shaken off the inseparable concomitants of that state, there must be some stage in the progress of his elevation when he takes the ranks of a mere citizen and ceases to be the special favorite of the laws."

The Question: Can the Congress pass a law, based on the Enforcement Clause of the Fourteenth Amendment, that prohibits discrimination on the ground of race in access to and use of places of public accommodation, including theaters, restaurants, hotels, and transportation?

The Arguments: PRO

The overriding purpose of the Fourteenth Amendment was to prohibit discrimination based on race, including any place to which the public was invited. Places of public accommodation, including those from which the black persons who brought these suits were excluded, are licensed by and regulated by the states, and the common law provides that all well-behaved persons have a right to use such

---

*United States v. Stanley (Circuit Court of the United States for the District of Kansas)

United States v. Ryan (Circuit Court of the United States for the District of California)

United States v. Nichols (Circuit Court of the United States for the Western District of Missouri)

United States v. Singleton (Circuit Court of the United States for the Southern District of New York)

Robinson and wife v. Memphis & Charleston R. Co. (Circuit Court of the United States for the Western District of Tennessee)

accommodations. The right of access to these places is among the "privileges" that are protected from infringement by the Fourteenth Amendment. The fact that the businesses against which suits were brought in these cases are privately owned does not remove them from regulation under the Fourteenth Amendment.

CON

The Fourteenth Amendment, by its terms, applies only to the actions of states or their officials. The businesses in these cases are all privately owned, and their proprietors have the right to exclude any person from their premises, for any reason. For Congress to bring all places of public accommodation under its regulation would set a precedent that would allow federal officials to determine who should be admitted to private clubs, or even homes, on the ground that state licenses must be obtained to serve food or drink, or to construct a building. The end result would be the destruction of the principle of private property.

BACKGROUND

The Union's military forces won the Civil War in 1865, but its political leaders surrendered that hard-won victory to the former Confederates over the next twelve years. The two men who succeeded Abraham Lincoln as president—Andrew Johnson and Ulysses Grant—followed appeasement policies that encouraged violent resistance to Reconstruction and weakened Republican resolve to protect the civil rights of the former slaves. Despite the presence of federal troops in southern states, the Ku Klux Klan and other groups that vowed to "redeem" the South were able to terrorize and murder blacks with virtual impunity. Intimidation and violence escalated as the 1874 elections neared. Blacks appealed vainly for protection from bands of armed whites, many of them former Confederate soldiers. "They are going around the streets at night dressed in soldiers clothes and making colored people run for their lives," black residents of Vicksburg, Mississippi, wrote to the Reconstruction governor. "We are intimidated by the whites. We will not vote at all, unless there are troops to protect us." A group of Mississippi whites attacked a gathering of black voters in Coahoma County and killed six. The black sheriff, who had been addressing the crowd, fled the area and never returned.

The tactics of terror succeeded. Blacks—and the dwindling number of southern white Republicans—stayed away from the polls in 1874 and Democrats won two thirds of the region's congressional seats, giving them control of the House, although Republicans still controlled the Senate. Before the new members took office, however, Republicans pushed the Civil Rights Act of 1875 through Congress, a law declaring "that all persons within the jurisdiction of the United States shall be entitled to the full and equal enjoyment of the accommodations" in restaurants, theaters, hotels, and railroads. Based on the enforcement clauses of the Thirteenth and Fourteenth Amendments, early drafts of this law would have required integration of public schools and provided federal enforcement of its provisions.

Before its final passage, the Civil Rights Act was weakened by compromises. Congress eliminated the school integration and federal enforcement provisions, turning the enforcement burden over to individual litigants. Since few blacks had the money to file suits under the law or the fortitude to pursue them in the courts, the new law proved virtually toothless. Even the bill's supporters expressed weariness and resignation. "Is it possible that you can find

power in the Constitution to declare war . . . and pass laws upon all conceivable subjects," one House Republican challenged his reluctant colleagues, "but can find no power to protect American citizens . . . in the enjoyment and exercise of their constitutional rights?"

The Civil Rights Act of 1875 proved to be the last gasp of the exhausted and embittered remnant of Radical Republicans in Congress. By then, many had deserted their positions and waved the white flag of surrender. Just before House Republicans turned their chamber over to the Democrats, who thirsted for more power and vowed to end Reconstruction, Joseph Hawley of Connecticut spoke in words of resignation. "I have been a radical abolitionist from my earliest days," he said, but he now felt that "social, and educational, and moral reconstruction" in the South could "never come from any legislative halls."

As Reconstruction faltered and finally died, one Southern editor boasted that the Fourteenth and Fifteenth Amendments "may stand forever; but we intend . . . to make them dead letters on the statute-book." The Supreme Court did the job for the unrepentant South.

The Court imposed a judicial death sentence on the Civil Rights Act of 1875 eight years after its passage. Under the caption *Civil Rights Cases*, the justices decided five cases from New York, Kansas, California, Tennessee, and Missouri. The dry legal wording of the federal indictments in these disparate cases illustrates the humiliation that black citizens endured every day, north and south and across the continent; these musty records put human faces on cases decided without names.

In Topeka, Kansas (the home of Linda Brown of the celebrated *Brown* case in 1954), "on the tenth day of October, in the year of our Lord one thousand eight hundred and seventy-five, one Murray Stanley, having management and control of a certain inn, did unlawfully deny to one Bird Gee the full enjoyment of the accommodations of said inn by denying to said Bird Gee the privilege of partaking of a meal, to wit, of a supper, at the table of said inn, for the reason that he, the said Bird Gee, was a person of color and of the African race, and for no other reason whatever, contrary to the act of Congress, and against the peace and dignity of the United States of America."

The California indictment charged that "on the 4th day of January, A.D. 1876, Michael Ryan did unlawfully deny to George M. Tyler, the full enjoyment of accommodations of Maguire's Theatre in the city of San Francisco, as follows, that the said George M. Tyler did purchase a ticket of admission, for the sum of one dollar, to the orchestra seats, and said orchestra seats did possess superior advantages to any other portion of said theatre, and that the said Michael Ryan, who was the ticket-taker of said theatre, did then and there, by force and arms, deny to said George M. Tyler, admission to said theatre, solely for the reason that said George M. Tyler was and is of the African or negro race, being what is commonly called a colored man, and not a white man."

The third indictment charged the Memphis & Charleston Railroad Company with discriminating against Sallie J. Robinson, stating that "on the 22nd of May, 1879, Mrs. Robinson, wishing to be carried from Grand Junction, Tennessee, to Lynchburg, Virginia, purchased tickets entitling her to be carried as a first-class passenger over the defendant's railway, and that being so entitled Mrs. Robinson got upon defendant's train of cars at Grand Junction, Tennessee, and attempted to go into the ladies' car, being the car provided for ladies and first-class passengers, when the conductor of the train refused to admit her into the car, and that in so refusing her admission the conductor took Mrs. Robinson by the arm and jerked her roughly around, wherefore she was damaged $500, and therefore the plaintiff sues."

The final indictment, printed without dates, alleged that in St. Louis, Missouri, "one Samuel Nichols was the proprietor of a certain common inn called the Nichols House, for the accommodation of travelers and the general public, that one W. H. R. Agee, was an applicant to the said Samuel Nichols for the accommodations of said inn as a guest therein, but the said Samuel Nichols did deny to the said W. H. R. Agee admission as a guest in said inn, for the sole reason that the said W. H. R. Agee, was a person of color and one of the Negro race" (Irons, 1999).

STATEMENT OF FACTS

These cases are all founded on the first and second sections of the act of Congress known as the "Civil Rights Act," passed March 1, 1875, entitled "An act to protect all citizens in their civil and legal rights." Two of the cases, those against Stanley and Nichols, are indictments for denying to persons of color the accommodations and privileges of an inn or hotel; two of them, those against Ryan and Singleton, are, one an information, the other an indictment, for denying to individuals the privileges and accommodations of a theater, the information against Ryan being for refusing a colored person a seat in the dress circle of Maguire's theater in San Francisco; and the indictment against Singleton being for denying to another person, whose color is not stated, the full enjoyment of the accommodations of the theater known as the Grand Opera House in New York. . . . The case of Robinson and wife against the Memphis & Charleston Railroad Company was an action brought in the circuit court of the United States for the western district of Tennessee, to recover the penalty of $500 given by the second section of the act; and the gravamen was the refusal by the conductor of the railroad company to allow the wife to ride in the ladies' car, for the reason, as stated in one of the counts, that she was a person of African descent. . . .

* * *

BRADLEY, J. [wrote the opinion of the court]

It is obvious that the primary and important question in all the cases is the constitutionality of the law; for if the law is unconstitutional none of the prosecutions can stand.

The sections of the law referred to provide as follows:

Section 1. That all persons within the jurisdiction of the United States shall be entitled to the full and equal enjoyment of the accommodations, advantages, facilities, and privileges of inns, public conveyances on land or water, theaters, and other places of public amusement; subject only to the conditions and limitations established by law, and applicable alike to citizens of every race and color, regardless of any previous condition of servitude.

Sec. 2. That any person who shall violate the foregoing section by denying to any citizen, except for reasons by law applicable to citizens of every race and color, and regardless of any previous condition of servitude, the full enjoyment of any of the accommodations, advantages, facilities, or privileges in said section enumerated, or by aiding or inciting such denial, shall, for every such offense, forfeit and pay the sum of $500 to the person aggrieved thereby, to be recovered in an action of debt, with full costs; and shall, also, for every such offense, be deemed guilty of a misdemeanor, and upon conviction thereof shall be fined not less than $500 nor more than $1,000, or shall be imprisoned not less than 30 days nor more than one year. . . .

Are these sections constitutional? . . . The essence of the law is, not to declare broadly that all persons shall be entitled to the full and equal enjoyment of the accommodations, advantages, facilities, and privileges of inns, public conveyances, and theaters; but that such enjoyment shall not be subject to any conditions applicable only to citizens of a particular race or color, or who had been in a previous condition of servitude. . . .

The first section of the fourteenth amendment . . . declares that "no state shall make or enforce any law which shall abridge the privileges or immunities of citizens of the United States; nor shall any state deprive any person of life, liberty, or property without due process of law; nor deny to any person within its jurisdiction the equal protection of the laws." It is state action of a particular character that is prohibited. Individual invasion of individual rights is not the subject matter of the amendment. It has a deeper and broader scope. It nullifies and makes void all state legislation, and state action of every kind, which impairs the privileges and immunities of citizens of the United States, or which injures them in life, liberty, or property without due process of law, or which denies to any of them the equal protection of the laws. It not only does this, but . . . the last section of the amendment invests congress with power to enforce it by appropriate legislation. To enforce what? To enforce the prohibition. To adopt appropriate legislation for correcting the effects of such prohibited state law and state acts, and thus to render them effectually null, void, and innocuous. This is the legislative power conferred upon congress, and this is the whole of it. It does not invest congress with power to legislate upon subjects which are within the domain of state legislation; but to provide modes of relief against state legislation, or state action, of the kind referred to. It does not authorize congress to create a code of municipal law for the regulation of private rights; but to provide modes of redress against the operation of state laws, and the action of state officers, executive or judicial, when these are subversive of the fundamental rights specified in the amendment. Positive rights and privileges are undoubtedly secured by the fourteenth amendment; but they are secured by way of prohibition against state laws and state proceedings affecting those rights and privileges, and by power given to congress to legislate for the purpose of carrying such prohibition into effect; and such legislation must necessarily be predicated upon such supposed state laws or state proceedings, and be directed to the correction of their operation and effect. . . .

And so in the present case, until some state law has been passed, or some state action through its officers or agents has been taken, adverse to the rights of citizens sought to be protected by the fourteenth amendment, no legislation of the United States under said amendment, nor any proceeding under such legislation, can be called into activity, for the prohibitions of the amendment are against state laws and acts done under state authority. . . . Such legislation cannot properly cover the whole domain of rights appertaining to life, liberty, and property, defining them and providing for their vindication. That would be to establish a code of municipal law regulative of all private rights between man and man in society. It would be to make congress take the place of the state legislatures and to supersede them. . . .

If the principles of interpretation which we have laid down are correct, as we deem them to be, . . . it is clear that the law in question cannot be sustained by any grant of legislative power made to congress by the fourteenth amendment. That amendment prohibits the states from denying to any person the equal protection of the laws, and declares that congress shall have power to enforce, by appropriate legislation, the provisions of the amendment. The law in question, without any reference to adverse state legislation on the subject, declares that all persons shall be entitled to equal accommodation and privileges of inns, public conveyances, and places of public amusement, and imposes a penalty upon any individual who shall deny to any citizen such equal accommodations and privileges. This is not corrective legislation; it is primary and direct; it takes immediate and absolute possession of the subject of the right of admission to inns, public conveyances, and places of amusement. It supersedes and displaces state legislation on the same subject, or only allows it permissive force. It ignores such legislation, and assumes that the matter is one that belongs to the domain of national regulation. Whether it would not have been a more effective protection of the rights of citizens to have clothed congress with plenary power over the whole subject, is not now the question. What we have to decide is, whether such plenary power has been conferred upon congress by the fourteenth amendment, and, in our judgment, it has not. . . .

When a man has emerged from slavery, and by the aid of beneficent legislation has shaken off the inseparable concomitants of that state, there must be some stage in the progress of his elevation when he takes the rank of a mere citizen, and ceases to be the special favorite of the laws, and when his rights as a citizen, or a man, are to be protected in the ordinary modes by which other men's rights are protected. There were thousands of free colored people in this country before the abolition of slavery, enjoying all the essential rights of life, liberty, and property the same as white citizens; yet no one, at that time, thought that it was any invasion of their personal status as freemen because they were not admitted to all the privileges enjoyed by white citizens, or because they were subjected to discriminations in the enjoyment of accommodations in inns, public conveyances, and places of amusement. Mere discriminations on account of race or color were not regarded as badges of slavery. If, since that time, the enjoyment of equal rights in all these respects has become established by constitutional enactment, it is not by force of the thirteenth amendment (which merely abolishes slavery), but by force of the fourteenth and fifteenth amendments.

On the whole, we are of [the] opinion that no countenance of authority for the passage of the law in question can be found in either the thirteenth or fourteenth amendment of the constitution; and no other ground of authority for its passage being suggested, it must necessarily be declared void, at least so far as its operation in the several states is concerned.

Harlan, J., dissenting.

The opinion in these cases proceeds, as it seems to me, upon grounds entirely too narrow and artificial. The substance and spirit of the recent amendments of the constitution have been sacrificed by a subtle and ingenious verbal criticism. "It is not the words of the law but the internal sense of it that makes the law. The letter of the law is the body; the sense and reason of the law is the soul." Constitutional provisions, adopted in the interest of liberty, and for the purpose of securing, through national legislation, if need be, rights inhering in a state of freedom, and belonging to American citizenship, have been so construed as to defeat the ends the people desired to accomplish, which they attempted to accomplish, and which they supposed they had accomplished by changes in their fundamental law. By this I do not mean that the determination of these cases should have been materially controlled by considerations of mere expediency or policy. I mean only, in this form, to express an earnest conviction that the court has departed from the familiar rule requiring, in the interpretation of constitutional provisions, that full effect be given to the intent with which they were adopted.

The purpose of the first section of the act of congress of March 1, 1875, was to prevent race discrimination. It does not assume to define the general conditions and limitations under which inns, public conveyances, and places of public amusement may be conducted, but only declares that such conditions and limitations, whatever they may be, shall not be applied, by way of discrimination, on account of race, color, or previous condition of servitude. The second section provides a penalty against any one denying, or aiding or inciting the denial, to any citizen that equality of right given by the first section, except for reasons by law applicable to citizens of every race or color, and regardless of any previous condition of servitude.

There seems to be no substantial difference between my brethren and myself as to what was the purpose of congress;

for they say that the essence of the law is, not to declare broadly that all persons shall be entitled to the full and equal enjoyment of the accommodations, advantages, facilities, and privileges of inns, public conveyances, and theaters, but that such enjoyment shall not be subject to any conditions applicable only to citizens of a particular race or color, or who had been in a previous condition of servitude. The effect of the statute, the court says, is that colored citizens, whether formerly slaves or not, and citizens of other races, shall have the same accommodations and privileges in all inns, public conveyances, and places of amusement as are enjoyed by white persons, and vice versa. . . .

Before the adoption of the recent amendments it had become . . . the established doctrine of this court that negroes, whose ancestors had been imported and sold as slaves, could not become citizens of a state, or even of the United States, with the rights and privileges guarantied to citizens by the national constitution; further, that one might have all the rights and privileges of a citizen of a state without being a citizen in the sense in which that word was used in the national constitution, and without being entitled to the privileges and immunities of citizens of the several states. Still further, between the adoption of the thirteenth amendment and the proposal by congress of the fourteenth amendment, on June 16, 1866, the statute-books of several of the states, as we have seen, had become loaded down with enactments which, under the guise of apprentice, vagrant, and contract regulations, sought to keep the colored race in a condition, practically, of servitude. It was openly announced that whatever rights persons of that race might have as freemen, under the guaranties of the national constitution, they could not become citizens of a state, with the rights belonging to citizens, except by the consent of such state; consequently, that their civil rights, as citizens of the state, depended entirely upon state legislation. To meet this new peril to the black race, that the purposes of the nation might not be doubted or defeated, and by way of further enlargement of the power of congress, the fourteenth amendment was proposed for adoption. . . .

If . . . exemption from discrimination in respect of civil rights is a new constitutional right, secured by the grant of state citizenship to colored citizens of the United States, why may not the nation, by means of its own legislation of a primary direct character, guard, protect, and enforce that right? It is a right and privilege which the nation conferred. It did not come from the states in which those colored citizens reside. It has been the established doctrine of this court during all its history, accepted as vital to the national supremacy, that congress, in the absence of a positive delegation of power to the state legislatures, may by legislation enforce and protect any right derived from or created by the national constitution. . . . Will any one claim, in view of the declarations of this court in former cases, or even without them, that exemption of colored citizens within their states from race discrimination, in respect of the civil rights of citizens, is not an immunity created or derived from the national constitution? . . .

The opinion of the court, as I have said, proceeds upon the ground that the power of congress to legislate for the protection of the rights and privileges secured by the fourteenth amendment cannot be brought into activity except with the view, and as it may become necessary, to correct and annul state laws and state proceedings in hostility to such rights and privileges. In the absence of state laws or state action, adverse to such rights and privileges, the nation may not actively interfere for their protection and security. Such I understand to be the position of my brethren. If the grant to colored citizens of the United States of citizenship in their respective states imports exemption from race discrimination, in their states, in respect of the civil rights belonging to citizenship, then, to hold that the amendment remits that right to the states for their protection, primarily, and stays the hands of the nation, until it is assailed by state laws or state proceedings, is to adjudge that the amendment, so far from enlarging the powers of congress—as we have heretofore said it did—not only curtails them, but reverses the policy which the general government has pursued from its very organization. Such an interpretation of the amendment is a denial to congress of the power, by appropriate legislation, to enforce one of its provisions. In view of the circumstances under which the recent amendments were incorporated into the constitution, and especially in view of the peculiar character of the new rights they created and secured, it ought not to be presumed that the general government has abdicated its authority, by national legislation, direct and primary in its character, to guard and protect privileges and immunities secured by that instrument. . . .

It was perfectly well known that the great danger to the equal enjoyment by citizens of their rights, as citizens, was to be apprehended, not altogether from unfriendly state legislation, but from the hostile action of corporations and individuals in the states. And it is to be presumed that it was intended, by that section, to clothe congress with power and authority to meet that danger. If the rights intended to be secured by the act of 1875 are such as belong to the citizen, in common or equally with other citizens in the same state, then it is not to be denied that such legislation is appropriate to the end which congress is authorized to accomplish, viz., to protect the citizen, in respect of such rights, against discrimination on account of his race. As to the prohibition in the fourteenth amendment upon the making or enforcing of state laws abridging the privileges of citizens of the United States, it was impossible for any state to have enforced laws of that character. . . . Consequently, the prohibition upon state laws hostile to the rights belonging to citizens of the United States, was intended only as an express limitation on the powers of the states, and was not intended to diminish, in the slightest degree, the authority which the nation has always exercised, of protecting, by means of its own direct legislation, rights created or secured by the constitution. The purpose not to diminish the national authority is distinctly negatived by the express grant of power, by legislation, to enforce every provision of the amendment, including that which, by the grant of citizenship in the state, secures exemption from race discrimination in respect of the civil rights of citizens. . . .

My brethren say that when a man has emerged from slavery, and by the aid of beneficent legislation has shaken off the inseparable concomitants of that state, there must be some stage in the progress of his elevation when he takes the rank of a mere citizen, and ceases to be the special favorite of the laws, and when his rights as a citizen, or a man, are to be protected in the ordinary modes by which other men's rights are protected. It is, I submit, scarcely just to say that the colored race has been the special favorite of the laws. What the nation, through congress, has sought to accomplish in reference to that race is, what had already been done in every state in the Union for the white race, to secure and protect rights belonging to them as freemen and citizens; nothing more. The one underlying purpose of congressional legislation has been to enable the black race to take the rank of mere citizens. The difficulty has been to compel a recognition of their legal right to take that rank, and to secure the enjoyment of privileges belonging, under the law, to them as a component part of the people for whose welfare and happiness government is ordained. At every step in this direction the nation has been confronted with class tyranny, which a contemporary English historian says is, of all tyrannies, the most intolerable, "for it is ubiquitous in its operation, and weighs, perhaps, most heavily on those whose obscurity or distance would withdraw them from the notice of a single despot." To-day it is the colored race which is denied, by corporations and individuals wielding public authority, rights fundamental in their freedom and citizenship. At some future time it may be some other race that will fall under the ban. If the constitutional amendments be enforced, according to the intent with which, as I conceive, they were adopted, there cannot be, in this republic, any class of human beings in practical subjection to another class, with power in the latter to dole out to the former just such privileges as they may choose to grant. The supreme law of the land has decreed that no authority shall be exercised in this country upon the basis of discrimination, in respect of civil rights, against freemen and citizens because of their race, color, or previous condition of servitude. To that decree—for the due enforcement of which, by appropriate legislation, congress has been invested with express power—every one must bow, whatever may have been, or whatever now are, his individual views as to the wisdom or policy, either of the recent changes in the fundamental law, or of the legislation which has been enacted to give them effect.

For the reasons stated I feel constrained to withhold my assent to the opinion of the court.

YICK WO V. HOPKINS
118 U.S. 356 (1886)

"Though the law itself be fair on its face, and impartial in appearance, yet, if it is applied and administered by public authority with an evil eye and an unequal hand, so as practically to make unjust and illegal discriminations between persons in similar circumstances, material to their rights, the denial of equal justice is still within the prohibition of the constitution."

The Question: Can a local government pass a regulation that requires all persons who operate laundries to obtain a permit from city officials if the laundry is located in a building constructed of wood, as a public safety measure, if such a regulation is applied to deny permits to all laundry operators of Chinese descent?

The Arguments: PRO

The regulation at issue in this case is a reasonable means of protecting the public safety. Laundries use heating devices that may set fire to the buildings in which they are located, and an inspection by the fire marshal prior to issuing a business permit is reasonable. The city officials who grant such permits have the power to exercise their discretion in deciding which persons are qualified to operate laundries, and that discretion should not be subject to judicial oversight.

CON

This case involves a clear pattern of racial discrimination, for which no legitimate reason can be advanced. The record of this case shows that all of the laundry operators of Chinese descent were denied permits in the city of San Francisco, and that all but one of the Caucasian operators were granted permits. The Fourteenth Amendment guarantees all persons the "equal protection of the laws," but the application of the law at issue is clearly unequal, based solely on the race and ancestry of the persons who are discriminated against.

BACKGROUND

Dissenting in the *Civil Rights Cases,* Justice John Marshall Harlan had reminded his colleagues—and the nation—that "class tyranny" could be imposed by any group that controlled power. "Today, it is the colored race which is denied, by corporations and individuals wielding public authority, rights fundamental in their freedom and citizenship," Harlan wrote. "At some future time, it may be that some other race will fall under the ban of race discrimination."

Justice Harlan was right; another race did "fall under the ban of race discrimination" and appealed to the Court for protection. This time, the race was Oriental, and the discrimination fell on Chinese laundrymen in San Francisco. And this time, in 1886, the Court struck down a law because it violated the Equal Protection Clause of the Fourteenth Amendment. Perhaps his colleagues had read Harlan's dissent in the *Civil Rights Cases* and found it convincing. A more likely explanation for the Court's ruling in *Yick Wo v. Hopkins* is that there was clearly "state action" behind the discrimination and no good reason for treating Chinese laundrymen differently from their Caucasian competitors.

Who *was* Yick Wo, and how did his case wind up in the Supreme Court? The record is sparse, because most documents in the case were burned in the fires that followed the San Francisco earthquake of 1906. We do know that Yick Wo was born in China, came to California in 1861, and operated a laundry in downtown San Francisco until the city's fire marshal (a man named Hopkins) denied his application to renew his license in 1885. Five years earlier, the city's board of supervisors had passed an ordinance making it unlawful to operate a laundry "without having first obtained the consent of the board of supervisors," unless the laundry "be located in a building constructed either of brick or stone." Of some 320 laundries in San Francisco, only ten were housed in brick or stone structures. The rest were in wooden buildings, subject to the licensing power of Fire Marshal Hopkins.

More than two hundred Chinese laundrymen, including Yick Wo, applied to Hopkins for licenses, which required a prior safety inspection. Hopkins turned down every Chinese applicant, but he granted licenses to all but one of eighty Caucasians; the sole exception was Mary Meagles. (Because almost every non-Chinese laundry operator was either French or Belgian, we can speculate that Mrs. Meagles was handicapped by either her gender or her Irish name). At any rate, Yick Wo and another Chinese laundryman, Wo Lee, refused to obey the order to close down their laundries and wound up in jail, unwilling to pay their fines after being convicted of violating the city ordinance (Irons, 1999).

The plaintiff in error, Yick Wo, on August 24, 1885, petitioned the supreme court of California for the writ of habeas corpus, alleging that he was illegally deprived of his personal liberty by the defendant as sheriff of the city and county of San Francisco. The sheriff made return to the writ that he held the petitioner in custody by virtue of a sentence of the police judge's court No. 2 of the city and county of San Francisco, whereby he was found guilty of a violation of certain ordinances of the board of supervisors of that county, and adjudged to pay a fine of $10 and, in default of payment, be imprisoned in the county jail at the rate of one day for each dollar of fine until said fine should be satisfied; and a commitment in consequence of nonpayment of said fine. The ordinances for the violation of which he had been found guilty are set out as follows:

> Order No. 1,569, passed May 26, 1880, prescribing the kind of buildings in which laundries may be located: "The people of the city and county of San Francisco do ordain as follows: It shall be unlawful, from and after the passage of this order, for any person or persons to establish, maintain, or carry on a laundry, within the corporate limits of the city and county of San Francisco, without having first obtained the consent of the board of supervisors, except the same be located in a building constructed either of brick or stone. Any person who shall violate any of the provisions of this order shall be deemed guilty of a misdemeanor, and upon conviction thereof shall be punished by a fine of not more than one thousand dollars, or by imprisonment in the county jail not more than six months, or by both such fine and imprisonment."

The following facts are also admitted on the record: That petitioner is a native of China, and came to California in 1861, and is still a subject of the emperor of China; that he has been engaged in the laundry business in the same premises and building for 22 years last past; that he had a license from the board of fire-wardens, dated March 3, 1884, from which it appeared "that the above-described premises have been inspected by the board of fire-wardens, and upon such inspection said board found all proper arrangements for carrying on the business; that the stoves, washing and drying apparatus, and the appliances for heating smoothing-irons, are in good condition, and that their use is not dangerous to the surrounding property from fire; . . . that the petitioner applied to the board of supervisors, June 1, 1885, for consent of said board to maintain and carry on his laundry, but that said board, on July 1, 1885, refused said consent." It is also admitted to be true . . . that on February 24, 1880, "there were about 320 laundries in the city and county of San Francisco, of which about 240 were owned and conducted by subjects of China, and of the whole number, about 310 were constructed of wood, the same material that constitutes nine-tenths of the houses in the city of San Francisco." . . . It is also admitted "that petitioner and 200 of his countrymen similarly situated petitioned the board of supervisors for permission to continue their business in the various houses which they had been occupying and using for laundries for more than twenty years, and such petitions were denied, and all the petitions of those who were not Chinese, with one exception of Mrs. Mary Meagles, were granted."

By section 11 of article 11 of the constitution of California it is provided that "any county, city, town, or township may make and enforce within its limits all such local, police, sanitary, and other regulations as are not in conflict with general laws." By section 74 of the act of April 19, 1856, usually known as the "Consolidation Act," the board of supervisors is empowered, among other things, "to provide by regulation for the prevention and summary removal of nuisances to public health, the prevention of contagious diseases; . . . to prohibit the erection of wooden buildings within any fixed limits where the streets shall have been established and graded; . . . to regulate the sale, storage, and use of gunpowder, or other explosive or combustible materials and substances, and make all needful regulations for protection against fire; to make such regulations concerning the erection and use of buildings as may be necessary for the safety of the inhabitants."

The supreme court of California, in the opinion pronouncing the judgment in this case, said: "The board of supervisors, under the several statutes conferring authority upon them, has the power to prohibit or regulate all occupations which are against good morals, contrary to public order and decency, or dangerous to the public safety. Clothes-washing is certainly not opposed to good morals, or subversive of public order or decency, but when conducted in given localities it may be highly dangerous to the public safety. Of this fact the supervisors are made the judges, and, having taken action in the premises, we do not find that they have prohibited the establishment of laundries, but they have, as they well might do, regulated the places at which they should be established, the character of the buildings in which they are to be maintained, etc. The process of washing is not prohibited by thus regulating the places at which and the surroundings by which it must be exercised. The [ordinances] are not in contravention of common right, or unjust, unequal, partial, or oppressive, in such sense as authorizes us in this proceeding to pronounce them invalid." . . .

MATTHEWS, J. [delivered the opinion of the court].

In the case of the petitioner, brought here by writ of error to the supreme court of California, our jurisdiction is limited to the question whether the plaintiff in error has been denied a right in violation of the constitution, laws, or treaties of the United States. The question whether his imprisonment is illegal, under the constitution and laws of the state, is not open to us. . . . That, however, does not preclude this court from putting upon the ordinances of the supervisors of the county and city of San Francisco an independent construction; for the determination of the question whether the proceedings under these ordinances, and in enforcement of them, are in conflict with the constitution and laws of the United States, necessarily involves the meaning of the ordinances, which, for that purpose, we are required to ascertain and adjudge.

We are consequently constrained, at the outset, to differ from the supreme court of California upon the real meaning of the ordinances in question. That court considered these ordinances as vesting in the board of supervisors a not unusual discretion in granting or withholding their assent to the use of wooden buildings as laundries, to be exercised in reference to the circumstances of each case, with a view to the protection of the public against the dangers of fire. We are not able to concur in that interpretation of the power conferred upon the supervisors. There is nothing in the ordinances which points to such a regulation of the business of keeping and conducting laundries. They seem intended to confer, and actually do confer, not a discretion to be exercised upon a consideration of the circumstances of each case, but a naked and arbitrary power to give or withhold consent, not only as to places, but as to persons; so that, if an applicant for such consent, being in every way a competent and qualified person, and having complied with every reasonable condition demanded by any public interest, should, failing to obtain the requisite consent of the supervisors to

the prosecution of his business, apply for redress by the judicial process of mandamus to require the supervisors to consider and act upon his case, it would be a sufficient answer for them to say that the law had conferred upon them authority to withhold their assent, without reason and without responsibility. The power given to them is not confided to their discretion in the legal sense of that term, but is granted to their mere will. It is purely arbitrary, and acknowledges neither guidance nor restraint. . . .

The ordinance drawn in question in the present case . . . does not prescribe a rule and conditions, for the regulation of the use of property for laundry purposes, to which all similarly situated may conform. It allows, without restriction, the use for such purposes of buildings of brick or stone; but, as to wooden buildings, constituting nearly all those in previous use, it divides the owners or occupiers into two classes, not having respect to their personal character and qualifications for the business, nor the situation and nature and adaptation of the buildings themselves, but merely by an arbitrary line, on one side of which are those who are permitted to pursue their industry by the mere will and consent of the supervisors, and on the other those from whom that consent is withheld, at their mere will and pleasure. And both classes are alike only in this: that they are tenants at will, under the supervisors, of their means of living. . . .

When we consider the nature and the theory of our institutions of government, the principles upon which they are supposed to rest, and review the history of their development, we are constrained to conclude that they do not mean to leave room for the play and action of purely personal and arbitrary power. Sovereignty itself is, of course, not subject to law, for it is the author and source of law; but in our system, while sovereign powers are delegated to the agencies of government, sovereignty itself remains with the people, by whom and for whom all government exists and acts. And the law is the definition and limitation of power. It is, indeed, quite true that there must always be lodged somewhere, and in some person or body, the authority of final decision; and in many cases of mere administration, the responsibility is purely political, no appeal lying except to the ultimate tribunal of the public judgment, exercised either in the pressure of opinion, or by means of the suffrage. But the fundamental rights to life, liberty, and the pursuit of happiness, considered as individual possessions, are secured by those maxims of constitutional law which are the monuments showing the victorious progress of the race in securing to men the blessings of civilization under the reign of just and equal laws, so that, in the famous language of the Massachusetts bill of rights, the government of the commonwealth "may be a government of laws and not of men." For the very idea that one man may be compelled to hold his life, or the means of living, or any material right essential to the enjoyment of life, at the mere will of another, seems to be intolerable in any country where freedom prevails, as being the essence of slavery itself. . . .

In the present cases, we are not obliged to reason from the probable to the actual, and pass upon the validity of the ordinances complained of, as tried merely by the opportunities which their terms afford, of unequal and unjust discrimination in their administration; for the cases present the ordinances in actual operation, and the facts shown establish an administration directed so exclusively against a particular class of persons as to warrant and require the conclusion that, whatever may have been the intent of the ordinances as adopted, they are applied by the public authorities charged with their administration, and thus representing the state itself, with a mind so unequal and oppressive as to amount to a practical denial by the state of that equal protection of the laws which is secured to the petitioners, as to all other persons, by the broad and benign provisions of the fourteenth amendment to the constitution of the United States. Though the law itself be fair on its face, and impartial in appearance, yet, if it is applied and administered by public authority with an evil eye and an unequal hand, so as practically to make unjust and illegal discriminations between persons in similar circumstances, material to their rights, the denial of equal justice is still within the prohibition of the constitution.

The present cases, as shown by the facts disclosed in the record, are within this class. It appears that both petitioners have complied with every requisite deemed by the law, or by the public officers charged with its administration, necessary for the protection of neighboring property from fire, or as a precaution against injury to the public health. No reason whatever, except the will of the supervisors, is assigned why they should not be permitted to carry on, in the accustomed manner, their harmless and useful occupation, on which they depend for a livelihood; and while this consent of the supervisors is withheld from them, and from 200 others who have also petitioned, all of whom happen to be Chinese subjects, 80 others, not Chinese subjects, are permitted to carry on the same business under similar conditions. The fact of this discrimination is admitted. No reason for it is shown, and the conclusion cannot be resisted that no reason for it exists except hostility to the race and nationality to which the petitioners belong, and which, in the eye of the law, is not justified. The discrimination is therefore illegal, and the public administration which enforces it is a denial of the equal protection of the laws, and a violation of the fourteenth amendment of the constitution. The imprisonment of the petitioners is therefore illegal, and they must be discharged.

PLESSY V. FERGUSON
163 U.S. 537 (1896)

"Legislation is powerless to eradicate racial instincts, or to abolish distinctions based upon physical differences, and the attempt to do so can only result in accentuating the difficulties of the present situation. . . . If one race be inferior to the other socially, the constitution of the United States cannot put them upon the same plane."

The Question: Can a state pass a law that requires "equal but separate" railroad cars for white and black passengers on all trains that operate within the state?

The Arguments: PRO

The law in question, passed by the Louisiana legislature in 1890, is a reasonable exercise of the state's police powers to protect the public welfare. All persons, whether black or white, are treated equally by the law, as white persons are barred from siting in coaches for black persons and the law requires that the separate coaches be equal in quality. Furthermore, the state is allowed to provide for the "comfort" of railroad passengers who do not wish to share a coach with persons of another race. Its law is based upon the established traditions and customs of the people of Louisiana, and the federal courts have no jurisdiction in this area.

CON

This law was passed, not to prevent white persons from sitting in railroad coaches with black persons, but simply to keep blacks out of coaches reserved exclusively for whites. This is racial discrimination, imposed by the state, in clear violation of the Fourteenth Amendment's command that all persons enjoy "the equal protection of the laws." In addition, the law does not define *race* in any manner and allows a railroad employee to make such determinations based on his subjective views and subject to his prejudices. This is not a "welfare" issue; rather, it is an unlawful discrimination based on race.

BACKGROUND

Confronted with mounting legal challenges to the "Jim Crow" laws that Southern lawmakers had passed in the 1890s to enforce racial segregation, the Supreme Court decided the most important of these cases in *Plessy v. Ferguson*, which arrived in Washington after a four-year journey from Louisiana. The case began on June 7, 1892, when Homer Adolph Plessy entered the New Orleans station of the East Louisiana Railway and bought a first-class ticket to Covington, Louisiana, a trip of about fifty miles around Lake Pontchartrain. Most passengers wanted to arrive at their destination for pleasure or business. Plessy, however, took no pleasure in his trip and had no particular business in Covington. What he wanted—and expected—was to be arrested for violating the 1890 state law requiring that "no person or persons shall be permitted to occupy seats in coaches, other than the ones assigned to them on account of the race they belong to." The law required that railroads provide "equal but separate" facilities for those of different races; however, it did not define "race" and left to conductors the job of assigning passengers to the proper cars.

Plessy had almost certainly arranged his arrest before he bought his ticket, although perhaps not the way it was carried out. According to the Supreme Court's later statement of facts, Plessy "entered a passenger train, and took possession of a vacant seat in a coach where passengers of the white race were accommodated." The conductor then ordered him "to vacate said coach" and move to one "for persons not of the white race." When Plessy refused to move, "he was, with the aid of a police officer, forcibly ejected from said coach and hurried off to and imprisoned in the parish jail of New Orleans." His stay in jail was brief, and Plessy was released after arraignment in the local recorder's court.

Plessy was a friend of Rodolphe Desdunes, a leader of the American Citizens' Equal Rights Association in New Orleans and a prominent figure in the city's Creole community. Desdunes also helped to organize a "Citizens' Committee to Test the Constitutionality of the Separate Car Law," and most likely he recruited Plessy to challenge the law.

Plessy had to arrange his arrest because he looked white and "passed" the color line in the racial gumbo of New Orleans. He was an "octoroon," the word then used to describe people with seven white great-grandparents and one (most often a female slave) who was black. His name suggests that Plessy was a Creole of French ancestry; most of the men who founded the citizens' committee in New Orleans—like Rodolphe Desdunes—had "roots" going back to French control of Louisiana. The legal papers filed in Plessy's case noted that "the mixture of colored blood was not discernible in him." If he could "pass" for white, why did Plessy court arrest to challenge the Jim Crow law? The answer is not certain, but it might reflect the "marginal" status of Creoles in New Orleans. They were "almost" white, but under state law they had no more rights than the darkest black. Even in the same family, some could pass and others could not. Those with darker skin certainly resented their segregation from whites, but people like Plessy must have felt more anxious when they boarded a "white" railroad car and came under the conductor's gaze.

Louis Martinet, a prominent Creole physician and lawyer, joined Rodolphe Desdunes as the guiding force behind the *Plessy* case. Shortly after the Louisiana legislature passed the "separate cars" law in 1890, Martinet launched a campaign in his column in the *New Orleans Crusader*. "We'll make a case," he wrote, "a test case, and bring it before the Federal Court on the ground of the invasion of the right of a person to travel through the States unmolested." It took Martinet almost two years to find a good test case; one problem was that most Louisiana railroads did not support the Jim Crow law, which cost them money for separate cars. Officials of two railroads told Martinet that "the law was a bad and mean one; they would like us to get rid of it."

Even before Desdunes recruited Homer Plessy for the test case and arranged with the East Louisiana Railway to have him arrested, Martinet had recruited the nation's leading civil rights lawyer to handle the court battle. Albion W. Tourgee of New York was a former Union army officer who moved to North Carolina during Reconstruction; he helped to write its radical constitution and served as a state judge for six years. After the white "Redeemers" took control in 1877, Tourgee returned to New York and became—in his biographer's words—"the most vocal, militant, persistent, and widely heard advocate of racial equality, in the United States, black or white." He agreed to represent Plessy without fee (what we now call "pro bono" work). Because Tourgee did not belong to the Louisiana bar, Martinet hired a local white attorney, James C. Walker, to assist him for a fee of $1,000. The case of *State v. Plessy* began slowly on its journey through the lower courts. Louis Martinet had first planned to ask a federal judge to rule that the "separate cars" law interfered with interstate travel and violated the Commerce Clause of the Constitution. But a federal court had recently held that Louisiana railroads could not segregate passengers who held tickets for travel across state lines. That decision, although favorable to blacks, forced the *Plessy* case into state court. In July 1892, Assistant District Attorney Lionel Adams formally charged Plessy with violating the Jim Crow law, and in October he appeared before Judge John H. Ferguson in the criminal district court of New Orleans.

Normally, judges ask criminal defendants at arraignments to enter pleas of "guilty" or "not guilty" and set trial dates for those in the latter group. Homer Plessy, however, did not make a plea. His lawyers filed a lengthy document with Judge Ferguson, asking him to dismiss the charges on the grounds that the state law violated the Thirteenth and Fourteenth Amendments. Ferguson heard several hours of oral argument on October 28, 1892. Albion Tourgee and James Walker claimed that the law imposed a "badge of servitude" on Plessy and deprived him of the "privileges and immunities" of citizenship. Lionel Adams defended the law as a "reasonable" exercise of the state's "police powers" to protect the public health, safety, welfare, and morals. Just which of these four powers he relied on is unclear, but Adams did claim that "the foul odors of blacks in close quarters" made the law reasonable. The record does not show that he presented any evidence for this claim, or mentioned that most blacks lived in homes without bathtubs (or even running water) and labored for long hours in hot, humid weather.

Judge Ferguson issued his ruling on November 18, 1892. Not surprisingly, he denied Plessy's constitutional challenge, citing the Supreme Court decisions in the *Slaughterhouse Cases* of 1873 and the *Civil Rights Cases* of 1883. Tourgee and Walker had originally planned to appeal Ferguson's decision—which they fully expected—to the federal court in New Orleans, but they abruptly shifted course and took the case to the Louisiana supreme court. Most likely, they decided that waiting for decisions in two lower federal courts would delay their case longer than one stop in state court. Chief Justice Francis T. Nicholls, despite the fact that he had signed the Jim Crow law as governor in 1890, promptly issued a "writ of prohibition" that ordered Judge Ferguson to "show cause" why his ruling should not be reversed. But after hearing oral argument, the Louisiana supreme court upheld Ferguson's ruling on January 2, 1893. Three days later, Plessy's lawyers asked Justice Nicholls to issue a "writ of error" to the United States Supreme Court. He granted this request the same day, and the legal documents in *Plessy v. Ferguson* arrived in Washington by mail train before the end of February.

The *Plessy* case completed its journey through the Louisiana courts in less than eight months, but it then sat on a siding in the Supreme Court clerk's office for another three years. One reason for this lengthy delay stemmed from the Court's swollen docket; appeals from state and federal courts flooded the justices with hundreds of cases each year (the Court decided 392 in the 1895 term).

Another factor slowed down the *Plessy* case: Albion Tourgee looked at the justices and did not like what he saw. The Court's rules allowed for expedited hearings in criminal cases, but Tourgee decided to wait his turn on the regular docket. "Of the whole number of Justices there is but one who is known to favor the view we must stand upon," he wrote to James Walker in October 1893, obviously counting Justice John Marshall Harlan on his side. Tourgee saw four certain votes against Plessy; these justices—he did not name them—would "probably stay where they are until Gabriel blows his horn," he lamented. The remaining four would probably uphold the Jim Crow law, but shifts in public sentiment might affect their votes. "The Court has always been the foe of liberty," Tourgee wrote, "until forced to move on by public opinion."

Public opinion *did* shift before the Court ruled in 1896, but it became even more hostile toward blacks. Southern states passed more Jim Crow laws and began to purge blacks from voting rolls; in 1894 Congress repealed almost every Reconstruction law that remained on the books. Faced with this gloomy outlook, Tourgee's brief to the Supreme Court reflected his refusal to temporize; he threw caution to the wind and challenged the justices to look racism in the face. "Suppose a member of this court, nay, suppose every member of it," he wrote, "should wake tomorrow with black skin and curly hair—the two obvious and controlling indications of race—and in traveling through that portion of the country where the 'Jim Crow Car' abounds, should be ordered into it by the conductor. It is easy to imagine what would be the result, the indignation, the protests, the assertion of pure Caucasian ancestry. But the conductor, the autocrat of Caste, armed with the power of the State conferred by this statute, will listen neither to denial or protest."

Tourgee continued his philippic: "What humiliation, what rage would then fill the judicial mind! How would the resources of language not be taxed in objurgation! Why would this sentiment prevail in your minds? Simply because you would then feel and know that such assortment of citizens on the line of race was a discrimination intended to humiliate and degrade the former subject and dependent class—an attempt to perpetuate the caste distinctions on which slavery rested."

Although his brief included more lawyerly argument on the Thirteenth and Fourteenth Amendments, Tourgee also asked the justices to imagine the possible consequences of upholding Jim Crow laws. "Why not require all colored people to walk on one side of the street and whites on the other? Why not require every white man's house to be painted white and every colored man's black?" (The Court's majority opinion considered these hypotheticals—as lawyers call them—and dismissed them as not being "reasonable" exercises of the state's police powers.) Tourgee added a sentence that wound up, slightly changed, in the solitary dissent: "Justice is pictured blind and her daughter, the Law, ought at least to be color-blind," he wrote (Irons, 1999).

STATEMENT OF FACTS

This was a petition for writs of prohibition and certiorari originally filed in the supreme court of the state by [Homer Adolphe] Plessy, the plaintiff in error, against the Hon. John H. Ferguson, judge of the criminal district court for the parish of Orleans, and setting forth, in substance, the following facts:

That petitioner was a citizen of the United States and a resident of the state of Louisiana, of mixed descent, in the proportion of seven-eighths Caucasian and one-eighth African blood; that the mixture of colored blood was not discernible in him, and that he was entitled to every recognition, right, privilege, and immunity secured to the citizens of the United States of the white race by its constitution and laws; that on June 7, 1892, he engaged and paid for a first-class passage on the East Louisiana Railway, from New Orleans to Covington, in the same state, and thereupon entered a passenger train, and took possession of a vacant seat in a coach where passengers of the white race were accommodated; that such railroad company was incorporated by the laws of Louisiana as a common carrier, and was not authorized to distinguish between citizens according to their race, but, notwithstanding this, petitioner was required by the conductor, under penalty of ejection from said train and imprisonment, to vacate said coach, and occupy another seat, in a coach assigned by said company for persons not of the white race, and for no other reason than that petitioner was of the colored race; that, upon petitioner's refusal to comply with such order, he was, with the aid of a police officer, forcibly ejected from said coach, and hurried off to, and imprisoned in, the parish jail of New Orleans, and there held to answer a charge made by such officer to the effect that he was guilty of having criminally violated an act of the general assembly of the state, approved July 10, 1890, in such case made and provided.

The petitioner was subsequently brought before the recorder of the city for preliminary examination, and committed for trial to the criminal district court for the parish of Orleans . . . where an information was filed against him . . . for a violation of the above act, which act the petitioner affirmed to be null and void, because in conflict with the constitution of the United States; that petitioner interposed a plea to such information, based upon the unconstitutionality of the act. . . .

The case coming on for hearing before the supreme court, that court was of opinion that the law under which the prosecution was had was constitutional and denied the relief prayed for by the petitioner; whereupon petitioner prayed for a writ of error from this court, which was allowed by the chief justice of the supreme court of Louisiana.

*   *   *

MR. JUSTICE BROWN, after stating the facts in the foregoing language, delivered the opinion of the court.

This case turns upon the constitutionality of an act of the general assembly of the state of Louisiana, passed in 1890, providing for separate railway carriages for the white and colored races. Acts [of] 1890.

The first section of the statute enacts "that all railway companies carrying passengers in their coaches in this state, shall provide equal but separate accommodations for the white, and colored races, by providing two or more passenger coaches for each passenger train, or by dividing the passenger coaches by a partition so as to secure separate accommodations provided: that this section shall not be construed to apply to street railroads. No person or persons shall be permitted to occupy seats in coaches, other than the ones assigned to them, on account of the race they belong to." . . .

By the second section it was enacted "that the officers of such passenger trains shall have power and are hereby required to assign each passenger to the coach or compartment used for the race to which such passenger belongs; any passenger insisting on going into a coach or compartment to which by race he does not belong, shall be liable to a fine of twenty-five dollars, or in lieu thereof to imprisonment for a period of not more than twenty days in the parish prison. . . ."

The constitutionality of this act is attacked upon the ground that it conflicts both with the thirteenth amendment of the constitution, abolishing slavery, and the fourteenth amendment, which prohibits certain restrictive legislation on the part of the states.

1. That it does not conflict with the thirteenth amendment, which abolished slavery and involuntary servitude, except a punishment for crime, is too clear for argument. Slavery implies involuntary servitude—a state of bondage; the ownership of mankind as a chattel, or, at least, the control of the labor and services of one man for the benefit of another, and the absence of a legal right to the disposal of his own person, property, and services. This amendment was . . . intended primarily to abolish slavery, as it had been previously known in this country, and that it equally forbade Mexican peonage or the Chinese coolie trade, when they amounted to slavery or involuntary servitude, and that the use of the word "servitude" was intended to prohibit the use of all forms of involuntary slavery, of whatever class or name. . . .

A statute which implies merely a legal distinction between the white and colored races—a distinction which is founded in the color of the two races, and which must always exist so long as white men are distinguished from the other race by color—has no tendency to destroy the legal equality of the two races, or re-establish a state of involuntary servitude. Indeed, we do not understand that the thirteenth amendment is strenuously relied upon by the plaintiff in error in this connection.

2. By the fourteenth amendment, all persons born or naturalized in the United States, and subject to the jurisdiction thereof, are made citizens of the United States and of the state wherein they reside; and the states are forbidden from making or enforcing any law which shall abridge the privileges or immunities of citizens of the United States, or shall deprive any person of life, liberty, or property without due process of law, or deny to any person within their jurisdiction the equal protection of the laws. . . .

[I]ts main purpose was to establish the citizenship of the negro, to give definitions of citizenship of the United States and of the states, and to protect from the hostile legislation of the states the privileges and immunities of citizens of the United States, as distinguished from those of citizens of the states. The object of the amendment was undoubtedly to enforce the absolute equality of the two races before the law, but, in the nature of things, it could not have been intended to abolish distinctions based upon color, or to enforce social, as distinguished from political, equality, or a commingling of the two races upon terms unsatisfactory to either. Laws permitting, and even requiring, their separation, in places where they are liable to be brought into contact, do not necessarily imply the inferiority of either race to the other, and have been generally, if not universally, recognized as within the competency of the state legislatures in the exercise of their police power. The most common instance of this is connected with the establishment of separate schools for white and colored children, which have been held to be a valid exercise of the legislative power even by courts of states where the political rights of the colored race have been longest and most earnestly enforced. . . .

[I]t is . . . suggested by the learned counsel for the plaintiff in error that the same argument that will justify the state legislature in requiring railways to provide separate accommodations for the two races will also authorize them to require separate cars to be provided for people whose hair is of a certain color, or who are aliens, or who belong to certain nationalities, or to enact laws requiring colored people to walk upon one side of the street, and white people upon the other, or requiring white men's houses to be painted white, and colored men's black, or their vehicles or business signs to be of different colors, upon the theory that one side of the street is as good as the other, or that a house or vehicle of one color is as good as one of another color. The reply to all this is that every exercise of the police power must be reasonable, and extend only to such laws as are enacted in good faith for the promotion of the public good, and not for the annoyance or oppression of a particular class. . . .

So far, then, as a conflict with the fourteenth amendment is concerned, the case reduces itself to the question whether the statute of Louisiana is a reasonable regulation, and with respect to this there must necessarily be a large discretion on the part of the legislature. In determining the question of reasonableness, it is at liberty to act with reference to the established usages, customs, and traditions of the people, and with a view to the promotion of their comfort, and the preservation of the public peace and good order. Gauged by this standard, we cannot say that a law which authorizes or even requires the separation of the two races in public conveyances is unreasonable, or more obnoxious to the fourteenth amendment than the acts of congress requiring separate schools for colored children in the District of Columbia, the constitutionality of which does not seem to have been questioned, or the corresponding acts of state legislatures.

We consider the underlying fallacy of the plaintiff's argument to consist in the assumption that the enforced separation of the two races stamps the colored race with a badge of inferiority. If this be so, it is not by reason of anything found in the act, but solely because the colored race chooses to put that construction upon it. The argument necessarily assumes that if, as has been more than once the case, and is not unlikely to be so again, the colored race should become the dominant power in the state legislature, and should enact a law in precisely similar terms, it would thereby relegate the white race to an inferior position. We imagine that the white race, at least, would not acquiesce in this assumption. The argument also assumes that social prejudices may be overcome by legislation, and that equal rights cannot be secured to the negro except by an enforced commingling of the two races. We cannot accept this proposition. If the two races are to meet upon terms of social equality, it must be the result of natural affinities, a mutual appreciation of each other's merits, and a voluntary consent of individuals. . . . Legislation is powerless to eradicate racial instincts, or to abolish distinctions based upon physical differences, and the attempt to do so can only result in accentuating the difficulties of the present situation. If the civil and political rights of both races be equal, one cannot be inferior to the other civilly or politically. If one race be inferior to the other socially, the constitution of the United States cannot put them upon the same plane. . . .

The judgment of the court below is therefore affirmed.

MR. JUSTICE HARLAN dissenting.

In respect of civil rights, common to all citizens, the constitution of the United States does not, I think, permit any public authority to know the race of those entitled to be protected in the enjoyment of such rights. Every true man has pride of race, and under appropriate circumstances, when the rights of others, his equals before the law, are not to be affected, it is his privilege to express such pride and to take such action based upon it as to him seems proper. But I deny that any legislative body or judicial tribunal may have regard to the race of citizens when the civil rights of those citizens are involved. Indeed, such legislation as that here in question is inconsistent not only with that equality of rights which pertains to citizenship, national and state, but with the personal liberty enjoyed by every one within the United States.

The thirteenth amendment does not permit the withholding or the deprivation of any right necessarily inhering in freedom. It not only struck down the institution of slavery as previously existing in the United States, but it prevents the imposition of any burdens or disabilities that constitute badges of slavery or servitude. It decreed universal civil freedom in this country. This court has so adjudged. But, that amendment having been found inadequate to the protection of the rights of those who had been in slavery, it was followed by the fourteenth amendment, which added greatly to the dignity and glory of American citizenship, and to the security of personal liberty. . . . These two amendments, if enforced according to their true intent and meaning, will protect all the civil rights that pertain to freedom and citizenship. . . .

It was said in argument that the statute of Louisiana does not discriminate against either race, but prescribes a rule applicable alike to white and colored citizens. But this argument does not meet the difficulty. Every one knows that the statute in question had its origin in the purpose, not so much to exclude white persons from railroad cars occupied by blacks, as to exclude colored people from coaches occupied by or assigned to white persons. Railroad corporations of Louisiana did not make discrimination among whites in the matter of accommodation for travelers. The thing to accomplish was, under the guise of giving equal accommodation for whites and blacks, to compel the latter to keep to themselves while traveling in railroad passenger coaches. No one would be so wanting in candor as to assert the contrary. The fundamental objection, therefore, to the statute, is that it interferes with the personal freedom of citizens. If a white man and a black man choose to occupy the same public conveyance on a public highway, it is their right to do so; and no government, proceeding alone on grounds of race, can prevent it without infringing the personal liberty of each.

It is one thing for railroad carriers to furnish, or to be required by law to furnish, equal accommodations for all whom they are under a legal duty to carry. It is quite another thing for government to forbid citizens of the white and black races from traveling in the same public conveyance, and to punish officers of railroad companies for permitting persons of the two races to occupy the same passenger coach. If a state can prescribe, as a rule of civil conduct, that whites and blacks shall not travel as passengers in the same railroad coach, why may it not so regulate the use of the streets of its cities and towns as to compel white citizens to keep on one side of a street, and black citizens to keep on the other? Why may it not, upon like grounds, punish whites and blacks who ride together in street cars or in open vehicles on a public road or street? Why may it not require sheriffs to assign whites to one side of a courtroom, and blacks to the other? And why may it not also prohibit the commingling of the two races in the galleries of legislative halls or in public assemblages convened for the consideration of the political questions of the day? Further, if this statute of Louisiana is consistent with the personal liberty of citizens, why may not the state require the separation in railroad coaches of native and naturalized citizens of the United States, or of Protestants and Roman Catholics? . . .

The white race deems itself to be the dominant race in this country. And so it is, in prestige, in achievements, in education, in wealth, and in power. So, I doubt not, it will continue to be for all time, if it remains true to its great heritage, and holds fast to the principles of constitutional liberty. But in view of the constitution, in the eye of the law, there is in this country no superior, dominant, ruling class of citizens. There is no caste here. Our constitution is color-blind, and neither knows nor tolerates classes among citizens. In respect of civil rights, all citizens are equal before the law. The humblest is the peer of the most powerful. The law regards man as man, and takes no account of his surroundings or of his color when his civil rights as guaranteed by the supreme law of the land are involved. It is therefore to be regretted that this high tribunal, the final expositor of the fundamental law of the land, has reached the conclusion that it is competent for a state to regulate the enjoyment by citizens of their civil rights solely upon the basis of race.

In my opinion, the judgment this day rendered will, in time, prove to be quite as pernicious as the decision made by this tribunal in the Dred Scott Case. It was adjudged in that case that the descendants of Africans who were imported into this country, and sold as slaves, were not included nor intended to be included under the word "citizens" in the constitution, and could not claim any of the rights and privileges which that instrument provided for and secured to citizens of the United States; that, at time of the adoption of the constitution, they were "considered as a subordinate and inferior class of beings, who had been subjugated by the dominant race, and, whether emancipated or not, yet remained subject to their authority, and had no rights or privileges but such as those who held the power and the government might choose to grant them." The recent amendments of the constitution, it was supposed, had eradicated these principles from our institutions. But it seems that we have yet, in some of the states, a dominant race—a superior class of citizens—which assumes to regulate the enjoyment of civil rights, common to all citizens, upon the basis of race. The present decision, it may well be apprehended, will not only stimulate aggressions, more or less brutal and irritating, upon the admitted rights of colored citizens, but will encourage the belief that it is possible, by means of state enactments, to defeat the beneficent purposes which the people of the United States had in view when they adopted the recent amendments of the constitution, by one of which the blacks of this country were made citizens of the United States and of the states in which they respectively reside, and whose privileges and immunities, as citizens, the states are forbidden to abridge. Sixty millions of whites are in no danger from the presence here of eight millions of blacks. The destinies of the two races, in this country, are indissolubly linked together, and the interests of both require that the common government of all shall not permit the seeds of race hate to be planted under the sanction of law. What can more certainly arouse race hate, what more certainly create and perpetuate a feeling of distrust between these races, than state enactments which, in fact, proceed on the ground that colored citizens are so inferior and degraded that they cannot be allowed to sit in public coaches occupied by white citizens? That, as all will admit, is the real meaning of such legislation as was enacted in Louisiana.

The sure guaranty of the peace and security of each race is the clear, distinct, unconditional recognition by our governments, national and state, of every right that inheres in civil freedom, and of the equality before the law of all citizens of the United States, without regard to race. State enactments regulating the enjoyment of civil rights upon the basis of race, and cunningly devised to defeat legitimate results of the war, under the pretense of recognizing equality of rights, can have no other result than to render permanent peace impossible, and to keep alive a conflict of races, the continuance of which must do harm to all concerned. This question is not met by the suggestion that social equality cannot exist between the white and black races in this country. That argument, if it can be properly regarded as one, is scarcely worthy of consideration; for social equality no more exists between two races when traveling in a passenger coach or a public highway than when members of the same races sit by each other in a street car or in the jury box, or stand or sit with each other in a political assembly, or when they use in common the streets of a city or town, or when they are in the same room for the purpose of having their names placed on the registry of voters, or when they approach the ballot box in order to exercise the high privilege of voting. . . .

It is scarcely just to say that a colored citizen should not object to occupying a public coach assigned to his own race. He does not object, nor, perhaps, would he object to separate coaches for his race if his rights under the law were recognized. But he does object, and he ought never to cease objecting, that citizens of the white and black races can be adjudged criminals because they sit, or claim the right to sit, in the same public coach on a public highway. The arbitrary separation of citizens, on the basis of race, while they are on a public highway, is a badge of servitude wholly inconsistent with the civil freedom and the equality before the law established by the constitution. It cannot be justified upon any legal grounds.

If evils will result from the commingling of the two races upon public highways established for the benefit of all, they will be infinitely less than those that will surely come from state legislation regulating the enjoyment of civil rights upon the basis of race. We boast of the freedom enjoyed by our people above all other peoples. But it is difficult to reconcile that boast with a state of the law which, practically, puts the brand of servitude and degradation upon a large class of our fellow citizens,—our equals before the law. The thin disguise of "equal" accommodations for passengers in railroad coaches will not mislead any one, nor atone for the wrong this day done. . . .

For the reason stated, I am constrained to withhold my assent from the opinion and judgment of the majority.

SHELLEY V. KRAEMER*
334 U.S. 1 (1948)

"The rights created by the Fourteenth Amendment are, by its terms, guaranteed to the individual. The rights established are personal rights. . . . The Constitution confers upon no individual the right to demand action by the State which results in the denial of equal protection of the laws to other individuals."

The Question: Can the courts be enlisted to enforce a real-estate contract of sale that includes a "racial covenant," in this case barring any person of "the Negro or Mongolian race" from purchasing, leasing, or occupying the property covered by the covenant?

The Arguments: PRO

Real-estate contracts of sale are private agreements between the parties, and the inclusion in them of racial covenants is not unlawful. All persons who purchase, lease, or occupy property covered by such covenants are bound by their terms. In this case, the sale of a house to a black person was done in violation of a racial covenant, and the owners of other property covered by the same covenant are entitled to enforce its terms by seeking a court order to rescind the sale. Without judicial enforcement of their terms, all contracts—for real estate or otherwise—would be useless. The courts are not being asked to judge the morality of such covenants, just to enforce their lawful terms.

CON

Racial covenants in real-estate contracts are contrary to public policy. Congress has barred racial discrimination in many areas, and it violates basic American values. The fact that racial covenants are included in many real-estate contracts should not make this form of prejudice enforceable in state or federal courts. These contracts could not be enforced if they were drafted by state officials, and the state should not enforce private contracts that the state itself could not enter into. The owners of adjacent or nearby properties should not be able to prohibit any willing seller to convey real estate to any willing buyer, simply because of the buyer's race.

BACKGROUND

J.D. and Ethel Lee Shelley moved into their new home at 4600 Labadie Avenue, a tree-shaded street in the Grande Prairie neighborhood of St. Louis, Missouri, on September 11, 1945. With six active children to house, J.D. and Ethel were eager to leave their crowded apartment on North 9th Street, backed against the Mississippi River in a crime-ridden black ghetto. The Shelleys had arrived in St. Louis from rural Mississippi just before World War II, part of the growing black migration from the Deep South to northern cities, driven from fields to factories by Depression poverty. They asked their pastor, Robert Bishop, to help them, using savings from their wartime jobs, to find a more spacious residence. Elder Bishop, who combined ministry with real-estate sales, found a yellow-brick, two-apartment house on Labadie Avenue, and arranged its purchase from Geraldine Fitzgerald for $5,700. The Shelleys, who never met Mrs. Fitzgerald, were delighted to escape the ghetto with their children.

Just a few days later, an unexpected visitor knocked on the door and handed Ethel a summons to appear in court. Louis and Fern Kraemer, who lived ten blocks east on Labadie, had filed suit in the Circuit Court of St. Louis to evict J.D. and Ethel from their new home. According to the summons, the Shelleys had unlawfully purchased a building which was "covered" by a restrictive racial covenant. Recorded in 1911, the covenant was limited to the block on which the Shelleys lived, bounded by Cora Avenue on the west and Taylor Avenue on the east. "This contract of restrictions," the covenant read, was designed to prevent ownership or occupancy of the covered houses "by people of the Negro or Mongolian Race." Fern Kraemer's parents had been among the thirty property owners, of thirty-nine on the block, who signed the joint covenant, which purported to bind all future purchasers for a period of fifty years.

Behind the Kraemers stood the Marcus Avenue Improvement Association, founded in 1910 by white residents of the Grande Prairie neighborhood. Urging its members to adopt restrictive covenants, the group's officers promised that "in the event an attempt was made to sell to colored, the Association would back up the property owners to the fullest extent of the law." The use of such covenants to enforce

---

*Decided with McGhee v. Sipes

residential segregation became widespread after 1917, when the U.S. Supreme Court struck down municipal laws which attempted to prevent blacks from purchasing or occupying property in "white" areas. Although cities were barred from adopting such laws, property owners could accomplish the same end through private agreements, under the "freedom of contract" doctrine the Court had constructed to block Progressive Era regulation of business and commerce.

During the first four decades of this century, the black population of northern cities tripled, while racial covenants helped to force this unwanted minority into crowded slums. Between 1910 and 1940, more than sixty thousand blacks arrived in St. Louis, with thousands more spilling across the Mississippi into East St. Louis, Illinois. During the mass migration of World War I, blacks pushed against their ghetto walls and met with resistance from the poor whites who competed for jobs and housing. Racial violence erupted in East St. Louis in June 1917. Carlos Hurd, reporting for the St. Louis *Post-Dispatch,* wrote that "a black skin was a death warrant" for those who faced white mobs. "I saw man after man, with his hands raised pleading for his life," Hurd wrote, executed by "the historic sentence of intolerance, death by stoning." More than one hundred blacks died in four days of rioting.

The growing use of racial covenants to maintain residential apartheid led the National Association for the Advancement of Colored People to begin, in 1922, a legal campaign against their enforcement. The first case to reach the U.S. Supreme Court began with a lawsuit between two white neighbors in the District of Columbia, who had both signed a racial covenant. One signer, Irene Corrigan, sold her property to a black woman named Helen Curtis and was sued by another signer, John Buckley, who sought to restrain the sale. Coming to the aid of Corrigan and Curtis, NAACP lawyers argued that judicial enforcement of such covenants placed the state behind a form of racial segregation which violated the "equal protection" clause of the Fourteenth Amendment. Ruling in 1926, the Supreme Court evaded a decision on this issue by dismissing the NAACP appeal in *Corrigan* v. *Buckley* as "insubstantial" and "frivolous." But the court issued an opinion holding that Fourteenth Amendment prohibitions "have reference to state action exclusively" and could not bar "private individuals from entering into contracts respecting the control and disposition of their own property." Judicial enforcement of the covenants did not constitute "state action" in such private suits.

Despite this setback, NAACP lawyers included legal attacks on racial covenants in their long-term campaign against all forms of state-enforced segregation. Members of other minorities joined the crusade against covenants. "The issue is much broader than that of simply preventing discrimination against Negroes," the NAACP noted in 1930, "for already such restrictive covenants have been used against Jews and Catholics." By the end of World War II, prospects for success in the Supreme Court seemed bright. The wartime migration of blacks to northern cities, pressure for access to decent housing, awareness of the horrors that Nazi racial ideology had created, and the dominance of "liberals" on the Supreme Court—all these factors encouraged NAACP lawyers and their allies.

Strategy for a renewed assault on racial covenants emerged from a two-day conference in Chicago in July 1945.

Thurgood Marshall, NAACP special counsel, guided the attending lawyers toward a coordinated legal campaign in courts around the country, designed to force the Supreme Court to accept one or more cases for decision. One lawyer at the conference, George L. Vaughn of St. Louis, suggested that lawyers not ignore the "political angle" in selecting test cases: "Because the Negro vote played such an important part in the election of judges" in St. Louis, Vaughn predicted success in his city. The son of a slave, Vaughn held influential positions in both the NAACP and the Democratic party . . . in St. Louis. He was also acquainted with Robert Bishop, who later sold the house on Labadie Avenue to J.D. and Ethel Shelley. Two months after the Chicago conference, the Shelleys presented George Vaughn with an ideal test case.

The suit brought by the Kraemers against the Shelleys proceeded rapidly to trial in October 1945. Fern Kraemer, nervous on the witness stand, testified briefly that she had inherited property covered by the racial covenant on Labadie Avenue from her parents, who had signed that document. Robert Bishop explained that Geraldine Fitzgerald, for whom he purchased the house from other signatories to the covenant, had been a "straw party" in the sale to the Shelleys. Judge William K. Koerner, who heard the case, recognized that Bishop had enlisted Mrs. Fitzgerald to shield the Shelleys from knowledge of the racial covenant.

Ethel Shelley told Judge Koerner from the witness stand that she knew nothing of the covenant until the Kraemers filed their suit. Judge Koerner asked if she knew "why you have been sued and why you are here?" Mrs. Shelley certainly did know. "Well, I understand the white people didn't want me back." George Vaughn came to trial with an arsenal of arguments against the covenant. He first claimed that the covenant had never been enforceable, because nine of the thirty-nine owners on the block in 1911 had failed to sign the document. Vaughn also pointed out that five houses on the block had been occupied by blacks, going back to 1882. The purpose of the covenant, to keep any blacks from living on the block, had never been met.

Vaughn also attacked the covenant on constitutional and social grounds, adopting material supplied by Thurgood Marshall and the NAACP staff. Judicial enforcement of the covenant, he claimed, would violate the federal Civil Rights Act of 1866, which extended to newly emancipated blacks the same right to buy and sell real property "as is enjoyed by white citizens." Vaughn blamed racial covenants for creating a ghetto that "narrowed, surrounded and circumscribed almost completely" the housing available to blacks in St. Louis. He also quoted from a report submitted to President Hoover in 1932, which found that residential segregation had confined blacks in slums that were "fatally unwholesome places, a menace to health, morals, and general decency of cities and plague spots for race exploitation, friction and riots."

Judge Koerner's ruling in the case justified Vaughn's prediction of judicial sympathy in St. Louis. Although he declined to address constitutional objections to the covenant, Koerner inferred from the document's wording that it was intended to bind property owners on Labadie Avenue only if "all the landowners should sign." Because nine of the initial owners had not signed, and black families had lived on the block for many years, Judge Koerner refused to enforce the covenant against the Shelleys.

Jubilation at this victory turned to gloom after the Missouri Supreme Court reversed Judge Koerner in December 1946. Gerald Seegers, counsel to the Marcus Avenue Improvement Association and nephew of its founder, convinced the appellate judges that the covenant had bound only the initial signatories and those who later purchased the covered property. Stressing the repeated use of "the undersigned" in the document, Judge James N. Douglas held that "the agreement by its terms intended to cover only the property of those owners who signed it." The signatories knew that blacks owned property on the block and "it must have been their intention to prevent greatly increased occupancy by negroes." Judge Douglas also cited the *Corrigan* ruling of the U.S. Supreme Court as precedent for holding that judicial enforcement of racial covenants did not constitute "state action" under the Fourteenth Amendment.

Defeat in the Shelley case, along with similar setbacks in Michigan and the District of Columbia, prompted Thurgood Marshall to call a second conference on racial covenants, held in January 1947 at Howard University in Washington, D.C. Urging the submission of appeals to the Supreme Court, Marshall noted two recent developments. First, although the Supreme Court had declined in 1945 to review the *Corrigan* ruling, two justices had voted to hear the challenge; only two more votes were needed to grant review in a new case. Second, President Harry Truman had appointed fifteen eminent citizens in December 1946 to the President's Committee on Civil Rights, and high on the panel's agenda was possible federal action against racial covenants.

The Howard conferees reviewed the available test cases and agreed that none presented an adequate trial record of evidence on "the effect of overcrowded slum conditions and black ghettos upon both the victims of discrimination and their fellow citizens." One NAACP lawyer reported the preparation of a Chicago case that would include testimony by economists and sociologists on the impact of restrictive covenants on racial tensions. Expert testimony on these issues, Marshall argued, might persuade the Supreme Court to accept a test case for argument. George Vaughn, who did not attend this conference, upset this cautious strategy when he filed an appeal for the Shelleys with the Supreme Court in April 1947. Marshall quickly arranged to rush the Michigan and the District of Columbia cases along, and the Supreme Court agreed to hear all the appeals in January 1948.

Thurgood Marshall also organized the preparation of *amicus curiae* briefs by fifteen organizations which joined the attack on racial covenants. These groups spanned the religious, ethnic, and political spectrums, and included the American Jewish Committee, Protestant Council of New York, Japanese American Citizens League, American Indian Council, American Civil Liberties Union, and Congress of Industrial Organizations. The *amicus* effort was designed to impress the Supreme Court with the broad coalition that opposed racial covenants.

Another influential voice, that of the federal government, joined the chorus in October 1947. The day after the President's Committee on Civil Rights issued its lengthy report, which recommended "intervention by the Department of Justice" in the campaign against racial covenants, Solicitor General Philip Perlman announced the government's intention to file a supporting *amicus* brief. The efforts of federal agencies to "clear

and replace slum areas," the brief argued, were hindered by racial covenants, which deprived "minority racial groups" of access to decent housing. Several *amicus* briefs, including the government's, cited the Supreme Court holding in the *Hirabayashi* case that racial discrimination was "odious to a free people," an ironic reversal of the government's support for the wartime internment in that case (Irons, 1999).

MR. CHIEF JUSTICE VINSON delivered the opinion of the Court.

These cases present for our consideration questions relating to the validity of court enforcement of private agreements, generally described as restrictive covenants, which have as their purpose the exclusion of persons of designated race or color from the basic constitutional issues of obvious importance [which] have been raised.

The first of these cases comes to this Court on certiorari to the Supreme Court of Missouri. On February 16, 1911, thirty out of a total of thirty-nine owners of property fronting both sides of Labadie Avenue between Taylor Avenue and Cora Avenue in the city of St. Louis, signed an agreement, which was subsequently recorded, providing in part: "the said property is hereby restricted to the use and occupancy for the term of Fifty (50) years from this date, so that it shall be a condition . . . precedent to the sale of the same, that hereafter no part of said property or any portion thereof shall be . . . occupied by any person not of the Caucasian race, it being intended hereby to restrict the use of said property . . . against the occupancy as owners or tenants of any portion of said property for resident or other purpose by people of the Negro or Mongolian Race." . . .

On August 11, 1945, pursuant to a contract of sale, petitioners Shelley, who are Negroes, for valuable consideration received from one Fitzgerald a warranty deed to the parcel in question. The trial court found that petitioners had no actual knowledge of the restrictive agreement at the time of the purchase. On October 9, 1945, respondents, as owners of other property subject to the terms of the restrictive covenant, brought suit in Circuit Court of the city of St. Louis praying that petitioners Shelley be restrained from taking possession of the property and that judgment be entered divesting title out of petitioners Shelley and revesting title in the immediate grantor or in such other person as the court should direct. The trial court denied the requested relief on the ground that the restrictive agreement, upon which respondents based their action, had never become final and complete because it was the intention of the parties to that agreement that it was not to become effective until signed by all property owners in the district, and signatures of all the owners had never been obtained.

The Supreme Court of Missouri reversed and directed the trial court to grant the relief for which respondents had prayed. That court held the agreement effective and concluded that enforcement of its provisions violated no rights guaranteed to petitioners by the Federal Constitution. At the time the court rendered its decision, petitioners were occupying the property in question.

The second of the cases under consideration comes to this Court from the Supreme Court of Michigan. The circumstances presented do not differ materially from the Missouri case. In June, 1934, one Ferguson and his wife, who then owned the property located in the city of Detroit which is involved in this case, executed a contract providing in part: "This property shall not be used or occupied by any person or persons except those of the Caucasian race. . . ." By deed dated November 30, 1944, petitioners, who were found by the trial court to be Negroes, acquired title to the property and thereupon entered into its occupancy. On January 30, 1945, respondents, as owners of property subject to the terms of the restrictive agreement, brought suit against petitioners in the Circuit Court of Wayne County. After a hearing, the court entered a decree directing petitioners to move from the property within ninety days. Petitioners were further enjoined and restrained from using or occupying the premises in the future. On appeal, the Supreme Court of Michigan affirmed, deciding adversely to petitioners' contentions that they had been denied rights protected by the Fourteenth Amendment.

Petitioners have placed primary reliance on their contentions, first raised in the state courts, that judicial enforcement of the restrictive agreements in these cases has violated rights guaranteed to petitioners by the Fourteenth Amendment of the Federal Constitution and Acts of Congress passed pursuant to that Amendment. Specifically, petitioners urge that they have been denied the equal protection of the laws, deprived of property without due process of law, and have been denied privileges and immunities of citizens of the United States. We pass to a consideration of those issues.

Whether the equal protection clause of the Fourteenth Amendment inhibits judicial enforcement by state courts of restrictive covenants based on race or color is a question which this Court has not heretofore been called upon to consider. Only two cases have been decided by this Court which in any way have involved the enforcement of such agreements. The first of these was the case of Corrigan v. Buckley, 1926. There, suit was brought in the courts of the District of Columbia to enjoin a threatened violation of certain restrictive covenants relating to lands situated in the city of Washington. Relief was granted, and the case was brought here on appeal. It is apparent that that case, which had originated in the federal courts and involved the enforcement of covenants on land located in the District of Columbia, could present no issues under the Fourteenth Amendment; for that Amendment by its terms applies only to the States. . . . The only constitutional issue which the appellants had raised in the lower courts, and hence the only constitutional issue before this Court on appeal, was the validity of the covenant agreements as such. This Court concluded that since the inhibitions of the constitutional provisions invoked, apply only to governmental action, as contrasted to action of private individuals, there was no showing that the covenants, which were simply agreements between private property owners, were invalid. Accordingly, the appeal was dismissed for want of a substantial question. Nothing in the opinion of this Court, therefore, may properly be regarded as an adjudication on the merits of the constitutional issues presented by these cases, which raise the question of the validity, not of the private agreements as such, but of the judicial enforcement of those agreements.

The second of the cases involving racial restrictive covenants was Hansberry v. Lee, 1940. In that case, petitioners, white property owners, were enjoined by the state courts from violating the terms of a restrictive agreement. The state Supreme Court had held petitioners bound by an earlier judicial determination, in litigation in which petitioners were not parties, upholding the validity of the restrictive agreement. . . . This Court reversed the judgment of the state Supreme Court upon the ground that petitioners had been denied due process of law in being held estopped to challenge the validity of the agreement. . . . In arriving at its result, this Court did not reach the issues presented by the cases now under consideration. . . .

It should be observed that these covenants do not seek to proscribe any particular use of the affected properties. Use of the properties for residential occupancy, as such, is not forbidden. The restrictions of these agreements, rather, are directed toward a designated class of persons and seek to determine who may and who may not own or make use of the properties for residential purposes. The excluded class is defined wholly in terms of race or color.; simply that and nothing more.

It cannot be doubted that among the civil rights intended to be protected from discriminatory state action by the Fourteenth Amendment are the rights to acquire, enjoy, own and dispose of property. Equality in the enjoyment of property rights was regarded by the framers of that Amendment as an essential pre-condition to the realization of other basic civil rights and liberties which the Amendment was intended to guarantee. Thus, the Civil Rights Act of 1866 which was enacted by Congress while the Fourteenth Amendment was also under consideration, provides: "All citizens of the United States shall have the same right, in every State and Territory, as is enjoyed by white citizens thereof to inherit, purchase, lease, sell, hold, and convey real and personal property."

It is likewise clear that restrictions on the right of occupancy of the sort sought to be created by the private agreements in these cases could not be squared with the requirements of the Fourteenth Amendment if imposed by state statute or local ordinance. We do not understand respondents to urge the contrary. In the case of Buchanan v. Warley, a unanimous Court declared unconstitutional the provisions of a city ordinance which denied to colored persons the right to occupy houses in blocks in which the greater number of houses were occupied by white persons, and imposed similar restrictions on white persons with respect to blocks in which the greater number of houses were occupied by colored persons. During the course of the opinion in that case, this Court stated: "The Fourteenth Amendment and these statutes enacted in furtherance of its purpose operate to qualify and entitle a colored man to acquire property without state legislation discriminating against him solely because of color.". . .

Since the decision of this Court in the Civil Rights Cases, 1883, the principle has become firmly embedded in our constitutional law that the action inhibited by the first section of the Fourteenth Amendment is only such action as may fairly be said to be that of the States. That Amendment erects no shield against merely private conduct, however discriminatory or wrongful. We conclude, therefore, that the restrictive agreements standing alone cannot be regarded as a violation of any rights guaranteed to petitioners by the Fourteenth Amendment. So long as the purposes of those agreements are effectuated by voluntary adherence to their terms, it would appear clear that there has been no action by the State and the provisions of the Amendment have not been violated.

But here there was more. These are cases in which the purposes of the agreements were secured only by judicial enforcement by state courts of the restrictive terms of the agreements. The respondents urge that judicial enforcement of private agreements does not amount to state action; or, in any event, the participation of the State is so attenuated in character as not to amount to state action within the meaning of the Fourteenth Amendment. Finally, it is suggested, even if the States in these cases may be deemed to have acted in the constitutional sense, their action did not deprive petitioners of rights guaranteed by the Fourteenth Amendment. We move to a consideration of these matters.

That the action of state courts and of judicial officers in their official capacities is to be regarded as action of the State within the meaning of the Fourteenth Amendment, is a proposition which has long been established by decisions of this Court. . . . One of the earliest applications of the prohibitions contained in the Fourteenth Amendment to action of state judicial officials occurred in cases in which Negroes had been excluded from jury service in criminal prosecutions by reason of their race or color. These cases demonstrate, also, the early recognition by this Court that state action in violation of the Amendment's provisions is equally repugnant to the constitutional commands whether directed by state statute or taken by a judicial official in the absence of statute. Thus, in Strauder v. West Virginia, 1880, this Court declared invalid a state statute restricting jury service to white persons as amounting to a denial of the equal protection of the laws to the colored defendant in that case. . . .

The short of the matter is that from the time of the adoption of the Fourteenth Amendment until the present, it has been the consistent ruling of this Court that the action of the States to which the Amendment has reference, includes action of state courts and state judicial officials. Although, in construing the terms of the Fourteenth Amendment, differences have from time to time been expressed as to whether particular types of state action may be said to offend the Amendment's prohibitory provisions, it has never been suggested that state court action is immunized from the operation of those provisions simply because the act is that of the judicial branch of the state government.

Against this background of judicial construction, extending over a period of some three-quarters of a century, we are called upon to consider whether enforcement by state courts of the restrictive agreements in these cases may be deemed to be the acts of those States; and, if so, whether that action has denied these petitioners the equal protection of the laws which the Amendment was intended to insure. We have no doubt that there has been state action in these cases in the full and complete sense of the phrase. The undisputed facts disclose that petitioners were willing purchasers of properties upon which they desired to establish homes. The owners of the properties were willing sellers; and contracts of sale were accordingly consummated. It is clear that but for the active intervention of the state courts, supported by the full panoply of state power, petitioners would have been free to occupy the properties in question without restraint.

These are not cases, as has been suggested, in which the States have merely abstained from action, leaving private individuals free to impose such discriminations as they see fit. Rather, these are cases in which the States have made available to such individuals the full coercive power of government to deny to petitioners, on the grounds of race or color, the enjoyment of property rights in premises which petitioners are willing and financially able to acquire and which the grantors are willing to sell. The difference between judicial enforcement and nonenforcement of the restrictive covenants is the difference to petitioners between being denied rights of property available to other members of the community and being accorded full enjoyment of those rights on an equal footing. . . .

We hold that in granting judicial enforcement of the restrictive agreements in these cases, the States have denied petitioners the equal protection of the laws and that, therefore, the action of the state courts cannot stand. . . . Respondents urge, however, that since the state courts stand ready to enforce restrictive covenants excluding white persons from the ownership or occupancy of property covered by such agreements, enforcement of covenants excluding colored persons may not be deemed a denial of equal protection of the laws to the colored persons who are thereby affected. This contention does not bear scrutiny. The parties have directed our attention to no case in which a court, state or federal, has been called upon to enforce a covenant excluding members of the white majority from ownership or occupancy of real property on grounds of race or color. But there are more fundamental considerations. The rights created by the first section of the Fourteenth Amendment are, by its terms, guaranteed to the individual. The rights established are personal rights. It is, therefore, no answer to these petitioners to say that the courts may also be induced to deny white persons rights of ownership and occupancy on grounds of race or color. Equal protection of the laws is not achieved through indiscriminate imposition of inequalities.

Nor do we find merit in the suggestion that property owners who are parties to these agreements are denied equal protection of the laws if denied access to the courts to enforce the terms of restrictive covenants and to assert property rights which the state courts have held to be created by such agreements. The Constitution confers upon no individual the right to demand action by the State which results in the denial of equal protection of the laws to other individuals. And it would appear beyond question that the power of the State to create and enforce property interests must be exercised within the boundaries defined by the Fourteenth Amendment. . . .

For the reasons stated, the judgment of the Supreme Court of Missouri and the judgment of the Supreme Court of Michigan must be reversed.

MR. JUSTICE REED, MR. JUSTICE JACKSON, and MR. JUSTICE RUTLEDGE took no part in the consideration or decision of these cases.

MEET J.D. SHELLEY

I was born in Starkville, Mississippi, on Christmas Day in 1907. My folks worked on farms around there; they worked for white people. They named me J.D., but the initials don't stand for nothing. People call me J.D. or some people call me Shelley. Me and my wife, Ethel, got married on December 14, 1923. I wasn't quite sixteen and she was younger than me.

I been working all my life. When I was down South, I did sawmill work, railroad, construction, all like that. In Mississippi I did mostly construction work; just before I left they was building a highway in Starkville and I worked on that. After they completed that then I started doing construction work at the A & M college; they was building houses out there. That's where I was working when I left and came here to St. Louis. That was in the fall of '39. . . .

When I first come to St. Louis, my wife and kids they stayed in Mississippi and I stayed here for a year. When I first came here I was only making $17 a week. I was working at a medical place where they made pills, and I was paying $12 a month rent at that time. It was cheap; I didn't have to pay much for nothing. White people here was prejudiced against colored at that time. When I came to St. Louis, they had places like the Fox Theater, no colored could go there; and the baseball diamond up on Sportsman's Park, they don't allow no colored in there at one time. When they did open up Sportsman's Park for colored, onliest place they could sit was in the bleachers. That changed after the war. Down in South St. Louis, there's places now you can't go if you're colored.

After I was here for a year, I went back down to Mississippi and came back with my wife and kids. The first place I rented was on Francis Avenue and I moved from there to North 9th St. My wife was working at a baby-care company and during the war I was working out at the small-arms bullet plant, out on Goodfellow. They had women operating the machines that make bullets. The mechanics, they were all men, and they had to fix the machines when they broke down. The colored men, they had to fix the colored girls' machines; the white men, they fixed the white.

Some of the colored mechanics, they complained about this, they figure they should fix whatever machine is broke. So they had a meeting at the Kiel Auditorium downtown, which was called by the union. A union man come from up north somewhere, and the man say we got a war and colored is over there fighting for this country. And he say, There's got to be a change made; we going to fix it where the colored man going to be the mechanic on the machine for the white girl and the white men for the colored. And one white man get up and says he would rather work with a dog than work with a nigger. And they told him, You just have to work with a dog; if you want to stay out there you going to be a mechanic on the colored girls' machine. So they changed that.

With me having so many kids, they put me in 4F during the war. I had six kids, and it was hard fitting us all in the places we was living during the war. At that time it was hard for you to find a place when you had children, so every place we'd go they didn't want us. We had been wanting to buy us a house, but we thought we better save up some money while we was both working. I told my wife, I tell you what we'll do. My check is more than yours, and we'll just save my check and we'll use your check to take care of the family and the household.

So we had some money saved up, and I wanted to buy a new car. My wife says, J.D., no! We got these kids and it's hard for us to find a place. What we'll do, we'll take what money we got and buy us a home. And when we get it straight and I'm still working, then we'll buy us a car. I told her we couldn't pay for no home and she said we pay rent, so we can make the payments on a house.

I talked to my supervisor the next day when I got to work and he say, Shelley, you know what? Your wife is right. So I came home and told her, Well, we'll just go ahead and find a place. This was just about when the war was over in Japan. Ethel went to the Church of God in Christ and her pastor, Elder Robert Bishop, he was also in real estate. So we went and talked to him and he said, Yeah, I know a place on Labadie that's for sale. It's got two apartments, so you can rent one out. So we went and looked at it and decided we would buy it. The price of the house was five thousand, seven hundred.

The day we supposed to move, I got a fellow with a truck to move me. That evening when I got off work, I was riding the bus, and I got off at Cora. That's about two blocks from where my house was on Labadie. At that time, the police were walking the beat. This one police, he come up and he ask me what was my name and I told him, J.D. Shelley. He ask me what was I doing out here, and I told him I'm going home. He say, Home? Where you live? I say, 4600 Labadie. He say, Labadie? I say, I just moved; my family just moved today. I had a fellow to move me. I didn't take off from work, I just hired this fellow to move me. So the police, he followed me all the way to the house. He stopped on the sidewalk, and I went on up the steps and got my key out of my pocket and went on in the house. So he left.

Later on, it was just a few days later, I come home one evening and my wife, she says, J.D., we got to go to court. I said, Court for what? She say, This supposed to be a restricted area, no colored on this side of Taylor Avenue. We're not supposed to be living out here. A man just came here and gave me a summons when I got back from work. He'll be back to give you one. He got one for you too.

Around about seven o'clock the doorbell rang and I went to the door, and this man say, Are you Shelley? I say, yes. He say, I got some papers here for you. I say, Papers? For what? He say, It's just some papers. You going to take them? I say, I ain't going to take no papers unless you tell me what it's for. And he say, Mr. Shelley, I'm trying to help you. I say, I still ain't going to take no papers unless you tell me what's the papers for. Just like that. So he throwed the papers down on the floor and walked on out.

So I didn't have to go to court, because if you don't receive a summons in your hand, you don't got to go to court. But my wife had to go to court. Elder Bishop, he got lawyer Vaughn. George Vaughn was his name; he was a colored lawyer. I didn't know him, but I guess he was Elder Bishop's lawyer. A couple of weeks after this man come around with the papers, Ethel went to court. When we bought the house, there was a family living downstairs; he was a street-car motorman. When he saw the sign says the property was sold, he moved. So that's why I got to move in downstairs. The family that was living upstairs, they was renting from the real-estate agent and they stayed for a while. This man and his wife upstairs, they had to go to court too, and the judge wanted to know, how did we treat them. This white lady that lived upstairs, she say, They seem just like when the white were living downstairs. When I go down to the basement to wash, Miz Shelley, she come down and we laugh and talk. And she say, They treat us nice. We don't have no trouble.

What they say in court was that this was supposed to be a restricted area, no colored live on this side of Taylor Avenue. That's one or two blocks from where my house was on

Labadie. This Jack Kraemer that sued us, he didn't even *own* no property on this block. I never even seen him around here. Nobody who lived on this block never say they want us to move.

I liked that house on Labadie. There was white on this side of me, and white on that side, and all the way down. I knowed all of them, and they treated us nice. None of the white never did say nothing about us living here. My supervisor say, Shelley, you might have to move, man. I says, Man, I ain't moving nowhere. Long as they don't mess with my kids. I ain't worried about them messing with me, but they better not mess with my kids. My kids was teenagers then.

There was some white boys that messed with my little daughter. She went to the store down on the corner and they messed with my daughter and throwed something at her, and my boy went out there and beat them. After that, the kids was all right. The white kids played with my kids, and their parents would have to come to the house sometimes to get them to come home.

After I moved out here, other colored started to buy and they started throwing stink bombs in their house. Every time they'd buy a house, they'd have trouble. They throw bricks in their window. But they never did bother me. My wife, she was going to church and praying. I'd go, but I wasn't like she was.

After the first time we went to court, the lawyers took the case up to the Supreme Court. . . .

When they took it to the Supreme Court they passed a decision, they say it don't make no difference, white or colored, long as they was able to buy property, anywhere in the United States. When I got home that evening, my wife was sitting on the front porch reading the paper that says we won the case. That night, the photographer come, and we was sitting on the couch, with the kids sitting betwixt us, and some on the floor, and they had it in the newspaper.

When we won the case, we didn't sleep that night. People was calling me from overseas, congratulating me. Say they heard it on the news, they saw it in the paper. People called from everywhere. Every time we'd hang up, the phone rings.

The way I see it, it was a good thing that we done this case. When all this happened, when I bought the property, I didn't think there was going to be anything about it. But I knowed it was important. We was the first ones to live where they said colored can't live (Irons, 1988).

HEART OF ATLANTA MOTEL V. UNITED STATES
379 U.S. 241 (1964)

"Negroes in particular have been the subject of discrimination in transient accommodations, having to travel great distances to secure the same. . . . This uncertainty stemming from racial discrimination had the effect of discouraging travel on the part of a substantial portion of the Negro community."

The Question: Can Congress pass a law, based on the Commerce Clause of the Constitution, that makes it a federal offense for the owner of any place of public accommodation to refuse service to black persons solely on account of their race?

The Arguments: PRO

The Congress has passed many laws that prohibit racial discrimination in areas such as voting, housing, and transportation. The law at issue in this case is based on lengthy congressional hearings and voluminous testimony that established beyond dispute that black persons who travel between the states are often unable to obtain lodging or meals because of racial segregation in hotels, motels, and restaurants. This pattern of discrimination constitutes an obstruction of interstate commerce, and Congress has the power to remove such obstructions to the free flow of commerce. Travel by persons is just as much a part of commerce as the transportation of goods.

CON

The Supreme Court's 1883 ruling in the *Civil Rights Cases* that Congress did not have the power under the Fourteenth Amendment to bar the owners of private businesses from choosing their customers. Having been rebuffed in this first attempt to regulate private choices, Congress cannot pick another provision of the Constitution to reverse the Court's earlier decision. Stretching the definition of commerce power to include a prohibition of racial discrimination would go far beyond the intent of the Constitution's Framers, who clearly had no such purpose in mind when they drafted the Commerce Clause.

MR. JUSTICE CLARK delivered the opinion of the Court.

This is a declaratory judgment action, attacking the constitutionality of Title II of the Civil Rights Act of 1964. . . . A three-judge court . . . sustained the validity of the Act and issued a permanent injunction . . . restraining appellant from continuing to violate the Act. We affirm the judgment.

The case comes here on admissions and stipulated facts. Appellant owns and operates the Heart of Atlanta Motel which has 216 rooms available to transient guests. The motel is located on Courtland Street, two blocks from downtown Peachtree Street. It is readily accessible to interstate highways 75 and 85 and state highways 23 and 41. Appellant solicits patronage from outside the State of Georgia through various national advertising media, including magazines of national circulation; it maintains over 50 billboards and highway signs within the State, soliciting patronage for the motel; it accepts convention trade from outside Georgia and approximately 75% of its registered guests are from out of State. Prior to passage of the Act the motel had followed a practice of refusing to rent rooms to Negroes, and it alleged that it intended to continue to do so. In an effort to perpetuate that policy this suit was filed.

The appellant contends that Congress in passing this Act exceeded its power to regulate commerce under Art. I, Sec. 8, cl. 3, of the Constitution of the United States; that the Act violates the Fifth Amendment because appellant is deprived of the right to choose its customers and operate its business as it wishes, resulting in a taking of its liberty and property without due process of law and a taking of its property without just compensation; and, finally, that by requiring appellant to rent available rooms to Negroes against its will, Congress is subjecting it to involuntary servitude in contravention of the Thirteenth Amendment.

The appellees counter that the unavailability to Negroes of adequate accommodations interferes significantly with interstate travel, and that Congress, under the Commerce Clause, has power to remove such obstructions and restraints; that the Fifth Amendment does not forbid reasonable regulation and that consequential damage does not constitute a "taking" within the meaning of that amendment; that the Thirteenth Amendment claim fails because it is entirely frivolous to say that an amendment directed to the abolition of human bondage and the removal of widespread disabilities associated with slavery places discrimination in public accommodations beyond the reach of both federal and state law. . . .

Congress first evidenced its interest in civil rights legislation in the Civil Rights or Enforcement Act of April 9, 1866. There followed four Acts, with a fifth, the Civil Rights Act of March 1, 1875, culminating the series. In 1883 this Court struck down the public accommodations sections of the 1875 Act in the Civil Rights Cases. No major legislation in this field had been enacted by Congress for 82 years when the Civil Rights Act of 1957 became law. It was followed by the Civil Rights Act of 1960. Three years later, on June 19, 1963, the late President Kennedy called for civil rights legislation in a message to Congress to which he attached a proposed bill. Its stated purpose was

> to promote the general welfare by eliminating discrimination based on race, color, religion, or national origin in . . . public accommodations through the exercise by Congress of the

powers conferred upon it . . . to enforce the provisions of the fourteenth and fifteenth amendments, to regulate commerce among the several States, and to make laws necessary and proper to execute the powers conferred upon it by the Constitution.

Bills were introduced in each House of the Congress, embodying the President's suggestion. However, it was not until July 2, 1964, upon the recommendation of President Johnson, that the Civil Rights Act of 1964, here under attack, was finally passed. . . .

The Act as finally adopted was most comprehensive, undertaking to prevent through peaceful and voluntary settlement discrimination in voting, as well as in places of accommodation and public facilities, federally secured programs and in employment. Since Title II is the only portion under attack here, we confine our consideration to those public accommodation provisions. This Title is divided into seven sections beginning with 201 (a) which provides that:

> All persons shall be entitled to the full and equal enjoyment of the goods, services, facilities, privileges, advantages, and accommodations of any place of public accommodation, as defined in this section, without discrimination or segregation on the ground of race, color, religion, or national origin.

There are listed in 201 (b) four classes of business establishments, each of which "serves the public" and "is a place of public accommodation" within the meaning of 201 (a) "if its operations affect commerce, or if discrimination or segregation by it is supported by State action." The covered establishments [include]:

> (1) any inn, hotel, motel, or other establishment which provides lodging to transient guests, other than an establishment located within a building which contains not more than five rooms for rent or hire and which is actually occupied by the proprietor of such establishment as his residence . . .

It is admitted that the operation of the motel brings it within the provisions of 201 (a) of the Act and that appellant refused to provide lodging for transient Negroes because of their race or color and that it intends to continue that policy unless restrained. The sole question posed is, therefore, the constitutionality of the Civil Rights Act of 1964 as applied to these facts. The legislative history of the Act indicates that Congress based the Act on Section 5 and the Equal Protection Clause of the Fourteenth Amendment as well as its power to regulate interstate commerce under Art. I, [Sec.] 8, cl. 3, of the Constitution. . . .

In light of our ground for decision, it might be well at the outset to discuss the Civil Rights Cases, which declared provisions of the Civil Rights Act of 1875 unconstitutional. We think that decision inapposite, and without precedential value in determining the constitutionality of the present Act. Unlike Title II of the present legislation, the 1875 Act broadly proscribed discrimination in "inns, public conveyances on land or water, theaters, and other places of public amusement," without limiting the categories of affected businesses to those impinging upon interstate commerce. In contrast, the applicability of Title II is carefully limited to enterprises having a direct and substantial relation to the interstate flow of goods and people, except where state action is involved. Further, the fact that certain kinds of businesses may not in 1875 have been sufficiently involved in interstate commerce to warrant bringing them within the ambit of the commerce power is not necessarily dispositive of the same question today. Our populace had not reached its present mobility, nor were facilities, goods and services circulating as readily in interstate commerce as they are today. Although the principles which we apply today are those first formulated by Chief Justice Marshall in Gibbons v. Ogden (1824), the conditions of transportation and commerce have changed dramatically, and we must apply those principles to the present state of commerce. The sheer increase in volume of interstate traffic alone would give discriminatory practices which inhibit travel a far larger impact upon the Nation's commerce than such practices had on the economy of another day. . . .

Since the commerce power was not relied on by the Government and was without support in the record it is understandable that the Court narrowed its inquiry and excluded the Commerce Clause as a possible source of power. In any event, it is clear that such a limitation renders the opinion devoid of authority for the proposition that the Commerce Clause gives no power to Congress to regulate discriminatory practices now found substantially to affect interstate commerce. We, therefore, conclude that the Civil Rights Cases have no relevance to the basis of decision here where the Act explicitly relies upon the commerce power, and where the record is filled with testimony of obstructions and restraints resulting from the discriminations found to be existing. We now pass to that phase of the case.

While the Act as adopted carried no congressional findings the record of its passage through each house is replete with evidence of the burdens that discrimination by race or color places upon interstate commerce. This testimony included the fact that our people have become increasingly mobile with millions of people of all races traveling from State to State; that Negroes in particular have been the subject of discrimination in transient accommodations, having to travel great distances to secure the same; that often they have been unable to obtain accommodations and have had to call upon friends to put them up overnight; and that these conditions had become so acute as to require the listing of available lodging for Negroes in a special guidebook which was itself "dramatic testimony to the difficulties" Negroes encounter in travel. These exclusionary practices were found to be nationwide, the Under Secretary of Commerce testifying that there is "no question that this discrimination in the North still exists to a large degree" and in the West and Midwest as well. This testimony indicated a qualitative as well as quantitative effect on interstate travel by Negroes. The former was the obvious impairment of the Negro traveler's pleasure and convenience that resulted when he continually was uncertain of finding lodging. As for the latter, there was evidence that this uncertainty stemming from racial discrimination had the effect of discouraging travel on the part of a substantial portion of the Negro community. . . .

The power of Congress to deal with these obstructions depends on the meaning of the Commerce Clause. Its meaning was first enunciated 140 years ago by the great Chief Justice John Marshall in Gibbons v. Ogden (1824), in these words: The subject to be regulated is commerce; and . . . to ascertain the extent of the power, it becomes necessary to settle the meaning of the word. The counsel for the appellee would limit it to traffic, to buying and selling, or the interchange of commodities . . . but it is something more: it is intercourse . . . between nations, and parts of nations, in all its branches, and is regulated by prescribing rules for carrying on that intercourse. To what commerce does this power extend? The constitution informs us, to commerce "with foreign nations, and among the several States, and with the Indian tribes." It has, we believe, been universally admitted, that these words comprehend every species of commercial intercourse. . . . No sort of trade can be carried on . . . to which this power does not extend." . . .

In short, the determinative test of the exercise of power by the Congress under the Commerce Clause is simply whether the activity sought to be regulated is "commerce which concerns more States than one" and has a real and substantial relation to the national interest. Let us now turn to this facet of the problem. . . .

It is said that the operation of the motel here is of a purely local character. But, assuming this to be true, "[i]f it is interstate commerce that feels the pinch, it does not matter how local the operation which applies the squeeze.". . . Thus the power of Congress to promote interstate commerce also includes the power to regulate the local incidents thereof, including local activities in both the States of origin and destination, which might have a substantial and harmful effect upon that commerce. One need only examine the evidence which we have discussed above to see that Congress may—as it has—prohibit racial discrimination by motels serving travelers, however "local" their operations may appear. . . .

We, therefore, conclude that the action of the Congress in the adoption of the Act as applied here to a motel which concededly serves interstate travelers is within the power granted it by the Commerce Clause of the Constitution, as interpreted by this Court for 140 years. It may be argued that Congress could have pursued other methods to eliminate the obstructions it found in interstate commerce caused by racial discrimination. But this is a matter of policy that rests entirely with the Congress not with the courts. How obstructions in commerce may be removed—what means are to be employed—is within the sound and exclusive discretion of the Congress. It is subject only to one caveat—that the means chosen by it must be reasonably adapted to the end permitted by the Constitution. We cannot say that its choice here was not so adapted. The Constitution requires no more.

Affirmed.

MR. JUSTICE DOUGLAS, concurring.

Though I join the Court's opinions, I am somewhat reluctant here . . . to rest solely on the Commerce Clause. My reluctance is not due to any conviction that Congress lacks power to regulate commerce in the interests of human rights. It is rather my belief that the right of people to be free of state action that discriminates against them because of race, like the "right of persons to move freely from State to State . . . occupies a more protected position in our constitutional system than does the movement of cattle, fruit, steel and coal across state lines." Moreover, . . . the result reached by the Court is for me much more obvious as a protective measure under the Fourteenth Amendment than under the Commerce Clause. For the former deals with the constitutional status of the individual not with the impact on commerce of local activities or vice versa. Hence I would prefer to rest on the assertion of legislative power contained in Section 5 of the Fourteenth Amendment which states: "The Congress shall have power to enforce, by appropriate legislation, the provisions of this article"—a power which the Court concedes was exercised at least in part in this Act.

A decision based on the Fourteenth Amendment would have a more settling effect, making unnecessary litigation over whether a particular restaurant or inn is within the commerce definitions of the Act or whether a particular customer is an interstate traveler. Under my construction, the Act would apply to all customers in all the enumerated places of public accommodation. And that construction would put an end to all obstructionist strategies and finally close one door on a bitter chapter in American history. . . .

LOVING V. VIRGINIA
388 U.S. 1 (1967)

"The freedom to marry has long been recognized as one of the vital personal rights essential to the orderly pursuit of happiness by free men. . . . Under our Constitution, the freedom to marry, or not marry, a person of another race resides with the individual and cannot be infringed by the state."

The Question: Can a state enact a law that prohibits persons of different races from marrying, and subject them to criminal penalties for violating such a law?

The Arguments: PRO

The Virginia legislature, reflecting the views of a majority of the state's voters, decided in 1924 that miscegenation (the marriage of persons of different races) was a danger to the "racial purity" of the state's population. Marriage is an issue that has always been left to the states for regulation. State laws that set minimum ages for marriage, and that prohibit persons from marrying close relatives, have been upheld by the courts as within the states' "police powers" to protect the public welfare and morals. Striking down a miscegenation law would infringe on this important state power.

CON

The Equal Protection Clause of the Fourteenth Amendment was designed to prevent states from passing laws that discriminated on the basis of race or ethnicity. Marriage is one of the fundamental rights of every person, and laws that prevent persons of different races from marrying not only violate this constitutional provision but also are clearly designed to protect "white supremacy" and reflect the racial bias of the white majority in Virginia and other states with similar laws.

MR. CHIEF JUSTICE WARREN delivered the opinion of the Court.

This case presents a constitutional question never addressed by this Court: whether a statutory scheme adopted by the State of Virginia to prevent marriages between persons solely on the basis of racial classifications violates the Equal Protection and Due Process Clauses of the Fourteenth Amendment. For reasons which seem to us to reflect the central meaning of those constitutional commands, we conclude that these statutes cannot stand consistently with the Fourteenth Amendment.

In June 1958, two residents of Virginia, Mildred Jeter, a Negro woman, and Richard Loving, a white man, were married in the District of Columbia pursuant to its laws. Shortly after their marriage, the Lovings returned to Virginia and established their marital abode in Caroline County. At the October Term, 1958, of the Circuit Court of Caroline County, a grand jury issued an indictment charging the Lovings with violating Virginia's ban on interracial marriages. On January 6, 1959, the Lovings pleaded guilty to the charge and were sentenced to one year in jail; however, the trial judge suspended the sentence for a period of 25 years on the condition that the Lovings leave the State and not return to Virginia together for 25 years. He stated in an opinion that: "Almighty God created the races white, black, yellow, Malay and red, and he placed them on separate continents. And but for the interference with his arrangement there would be no cause for such marriages. The fact that he separated the races shows that he did not intend for the races to mix."

After their convictions, the Lovings took up residence in the District of Columbia. On November 6, 1963, they filed a motion in the state trial court to vacate the judgment and set aside the sentence on the ground that the statutes which they had violated were repugnant to the Fourteenth Amendment. The motion not having been decided by October 28, 1964, the Lovings instituted a class action in the United States District Court for the Eastern District of Virginia requesting that a three-judge court be convened to declare the Virginia anti-miscegenation statutes unconstitutional and to enjoin state officials from enforcing their convictions. On January 22, 1965, the state trial judge denied the motion to vacate the sentences, and the Lovings perfected an appeal to the Supreme Court of Appeals of Virginia. On February 11, 1965, the three-judge District Court continued the case to allow the Lovings to present their constitutional claims to the highest state court. The Supreme Court of Appeals upheld the constitutionality of the anti-miscegenation statutes and, after modifying the sentence, affirmed the convictions. The Lovings appealed this decision, and we noted probable jurisdiction. . . .

The two statutes under which appellants were convicted and sentenced are part of a comprehensive statutory scheme aimed at prohibiting and punishing interracial marriages. The Lovings were convicted of violating 20-58 of the Virginia Code: "Leaving State to evade law. If any white person and colored person shall go out of this State, for the purpose of being married, and with the intention of returning, and be married out of it, and afterwards return to and reside in it, cohabiting as man and wife, they shall be punished as provided in 20-59, and the marriage shall be governed by the same law as if it had been solemnized in this State. The fact of their cohabitation here as man and wife shall be evidence of their marriage." Section 20-59, which defines the penalty for miscegenation, provides: "Punishment for marriage. If any white person intermarry with a colored person, or any colored person intermarry with a white person, he shall be guilty of a felony and shall be punished by confinement in the penitentiary for not less than one nor more than five years." . . . The Lovings have never disputed in the course of this litigation that Mrs. Loving is a "colored person" or that Mr. Loving is a "white person" within the meanings given those terms by the Virginia statutes.

Virginia is now one of 16 States which prohibit and punish marriages on the basis of racial classifications. Penalties for miscegenation arose as an incident to slavery and have been common in Virginia since the colonial period. The present statutory scheme dates from the adoption of the Racial Integrity Act of 1924, passed during the period of extreme nativism which followed the end of the First World War. The central features of this Act, and current Virginia law, are the absolute prohibition of a "white person" marrying other than another "white person," prohibition against issuing marriage licenses until the issuing official is satisfied that the applicants' statements as to their race are correct, certificates of "racial composition" to be kept by both local and state registrars, and the carrying forward of earlier prohibitions against racial intermarriage.

In upholding the constitutionality of these provisions in the decision below, the Supreme Court of Appeals of Virginia referred to its 1955 decision in Naim v. Naim, as stating the reasons supporting the validity of these laws. In Naim, the state court concluded that the State's legitimate purposes were "to preserve the racial integrity of its citizens," and to prevent "the corruption of blood," "a mongrel breed of citizens," and "the obliteration of racial pride," obviously an endorsement of the doctrine of White Supremacy. The court also reasoned that marriage has traditionally been subject to state regulation without federal intervention, and, consequently, the regulation of marriage should be left to exclusive state control by the Tenth Amendment. While the state court is no doubt correct in asserting that marriage is a social relation subject to the State's police power, the State does not contend in its argument before this Court that its powers to regulate marriage are unlimited notwithstanding the commands of the Fourteenth Amendment. Nor could it do so in light of Meyer v. Nebraska (1923), and Skinner v. Oklahoma (1942). Instead, the State argues that the meaning of the Equal Protection Clause, as illuminated by the statements of the Framers, is only that state penal laws containing an interracial element as part of the definition of the offense must apply equally to whites and Negroes in the sense that members of each race are punished to the same degree. Thus, the State contends that, because its miscegenation statutes punish equally both the white and the Negro participants in an interracial marriage, these statutes, despite their reliance on racial classifications, do not constitute an invidious discrimination based upon race. The second argument advanced by the State assumes the validity of its equal application theory. The argument is that, if the Equal Protection Clause does not outlaw miscegenation statutes because of their reliance on racial classifications, the question of constitutionality would thus become whether there was any rational basis for a State to treat interracial marriages differently from other marriages. On this question, the State argues, the scientific evidence is substantially in doubt and, consequently, this Court should defer to the wisdom of the state legislature in adopting its policy of discouraging interracial marriages.

Because we reject the notion that the mere "equal application" of a statute containing racial classifications is enough to remove the classifications from the Fourteenth Amendment's proscription of all invidious racial discriminations, we do not accept the State's contention that these statutes should be upheld if there is any possible basis for concluding that they serve a rational purpose. The mere fact of equal application does not mean that our analysis of these statutes should follow the approach we have taken in cases involving no racial discrimination where the Equal Protection Clause has been arrayed against a statute discriminating between the kinds of advertising which may be displayed on trucks in New York City, or an exemption in Ohio's ad valorem tax for merchandise owned by a nonresident in a storage warehouse. In these cases, involving distinctions not drawn according to race, the Court has merely asked whether there is any rational foundation for the discriminations, and has deferred to the wisdom of the state legislatures. In the case at bar, however, we deal with statutes containing racial classifications, and the fact of equal application does not immunize the statute from the very heavy burden of justification which the Fourteenth Amendment has traditionally required of state statutes drawn according to race.

The State argues that statements in the Thirty-ninth Congress about the time of the passage of the Fourteenth Amendment indicate that the Framers did not intend the Amendment to make unconstitutional state miscegenation laws. Many of the statements alluded to by the State concern the debates over the Freedmen's Bureau Bill, which President Johnson vetoed, and the Civil Rights Act of 1866, enacted over his veto. While these statements have some relevance to the intention of Congress in submitting the Fourteenth Amendment, it must be understood that they pertained to the passage of specific statutes and not to the broader, organic purpose of a constitutional amendment. As for the various statements directly concerning the Fourteenth Amendment, we have said in connection with a related problem, that although these historical sources "cast some light" they are not sufficient to resolve the problem; "[a]t best, they are inconclusive. The most avid proponents of the post–War Amendments undoubtedly intended them to remove all legal distinctions among 'all persons born or naturalized in the United States.' Their opponents, just as certainly, were antagonistic to both the letter and the spirit of the Amendments and wished them to have the most limited effect." We have rejected the proposition that the debates in the Thirty-ninth Congress or in the state legislatures which ratified the Fourteenth Amendment supported the theory advanced by the State, that the requirement of equal protection of the laws is satisfied by penal laws defining offenses based on racial classifications so long as white and Negro participants in the offense were similarly punished. McLaughlin v. Florida, (1964). . . .

There can be no question but that Virginia's miscegenation statutes rest solely upon distinctions drawn according to race. The statutes proscribe generally accepted conduct if engaged in by members of different races. Over the years, this Court has consistently repudiated "[d]istinctions between citizens solely because of their ancestry" as being "odious to a free people whose institutions are founded upon the doctrine of equality." Hirabayashi v. United States (1943). At the very least, the Equal Protection Clause demands that racial classifications, especially suspect in criminal statutes, be subjected to the "most rigid scrutiny," Korematsu v. United States (1944), and, if they are ever to be upheld, they must be shown to be necessary to the accomplishment of some permissible state objective, independent of the racial discrimination which it was the object of the Fourteenth Amendment to eliminate. . . .

There is patently no legitimate overriding purpose independent of invidious racial discrimination which justifies this classification. The fact that Virginia prohibits only interracial marriages involving white persons demonstrates that the racial classifications must stand on their own justification, as measures designed to maintain White Supremacy. We have consistently denied the constitutionality of measures which restrict the rights of citizens on account of race. There can be no doubt that restricting the freedom to marry solely because of racial classifications violates the central meaning of the Equal Protection Clause.

These statutes also deprive the Lovings of liberty without due process of law in violation of the Due Process Clause of the Fourteenth Amendment. The freedom to marry has long been recognized as one of the vital personal rights essential to the orderly pursuit of happiness by free men. Marriage is one of the "basic civil rights of man," fundamental to our very existence and survival. Skinner v. Oklahoma (1942). To deny this fundamental freedom on so unsupportable a basis as the racial classifications embodied in these statutes, classifications so directly subversive of the principle of equality at the heart of the Fourteenth Amendment, is surely to deprive all the State's citizens of liberty without due process of law. The Fourteenth Amendment requires that the freedom of choice to marry not be restricted by invidious racial discriminations. Under our Constitution, the freedom to marry, or not marry, a person of another race resides with the individual and cannot be infringed by the State. These convictions must be reversed (Irons, 1988).

It is so ordered.

MEET MILDRED LOVING

On a warm night when she was a new bride of 17, Mildred Loving awoke in terror to a sheriff standing above her bed. He arrested her for the crime of being a black woman married to a white man. It was the beginning of a legal battle that led to the Supreme Court's rejection 25 years ago of all laws forbidding interracial marriage. "I believe that's why we were put here," Mrs. Loving said softly. "That's why we were married." But in 1958 Mildred Jeter and Richard Loving were simply a young couple in love who wanted to marry. "I didn't know it was against any law. We were just happy," she said.

Her husband may have known about Virginia's antimiscegenation or race mixing law. But she didn't ask why they traveled 80 miles from Caroline County to Washington, D.C., to marry. "We weren't out to change nothing," she said. But the marriage of the pretty, slim woman and the shy, gangly bricklayer changed everything. It put them in jail. It forced them to leave the hilly countryside near some of the storied battlefields of a war over race fought a century before. And, in 1967, it resulted in a ruling that overturned one of the last legal struts to racism and segregation in Virginia and 15 other states. "It was taken for granted before 1954," said Erwin Griswold, former US solicitor general. "It was all part of the Jim Crow pattern."

Mildred Loving is alone now—The marriage that entered her name in law school textbooks ended in 1975 when a drunken driver broadsided the couple's car and killed her husband. She lives quietly in the small cinderblock house Loving built for her and three children after the Supreme Court decision allowed them to return to Virginia. . . .

At 52, Mrs. Loving is hobbled by arthritis and rarely ventures more than a few miles from the tiny town where she and Loving grew up. She thinks of the case only rarely. "It's history. It's all different now." Then, the Lovings were the only black-white married couple they knew. There were about 231,000 such couples in the United States last year, according to Census data. Mrs. Loving knew her husband from childhood. No one voiced objections to their plans to marry. An anonymous enemy called authorities a month after the couple was married. Three officers came to the house and woke them at 2 a.m. "I was scared to death," she said. With a flashlight on their faces, the officers demanded that Richard Loving identify the woman beside him. "He didn't say anything. So I spoke up. I said I was his wife." They had broken a 1922 law that said: "If any white person intermarry with a colored person or any colored person intermarry with a white person, he shall be guilty of a felony."

Mildred and Richard Loving were sentenced to a year in prison. The judge suspended the sentence on condition the couple leave the state. He told them "Almighty God created the races white, black, yellow, Malay and red, and he placed them on separate continents. And but for the interference with his arrangement there would be no cause for such marriages. The Lovings spent several unhappy years in Washington, unable to travel to Virginia together. In 1964, Mildred Loving wrote to Attorney General Robert Kennedy, asking whether the just-passed Civil Rights Act would help them return home. No, Kennedy replied. But he urged her to contact the American Civil Liberties" Union. They did, and attorney Bernard Cohen said he took the case for free. The case bounced back and forth between state and federal courts for several years, before the Virginia Supreme Court ruled the law valid.

Before arguing the case to the U.S. Supreme Court, Cohen tried to explain the issues to Richard Loving. "He was very country, sort of rough. He just said. 'Tell them I don't understand why if a man loves a woman he can't marry her no matter what her color'" (Gearan, 1992).

CHAPTER 9

Schools: "Separate and Unequal"

INTRODUCTION

Writing for the Supreme Court in *Brown v. Board of Education,* Chief Justice Earl Warren called education "perhaps the most important function of state and local governments." To Warren, the overriding purpose of education was, not instruction in academic subjects, but providing children with "the very foundation of good citizenship." And the opportunity for education "is a right which must be made available to all on equal terms."

Warren wrote these words, of course, in the case that struck down the practice by seventeen Southern and border states of providing public school education on decidedly unequal terms, segregating black children from white students, segregation that was imposed by law. The education provided to black children in these states—and others, some in Northern states such as New Jersey and Ohio, in which schools were segregated by "custom" that had the force of law—was an integral part of the Jim Crow system that followed the abolition of slavery and was designed to keep blacks in their "place" as cheap labor and second-class citizens. No amount of "gloss" on the record of Jim Crow education, no listing of blacks who achieved some measure of wealth or prominence, can hide the degrading "stigma" that school segregation inflicted on many generations of black children. Even today, the debilitating effects of Jim Crow education can be seen in the persisting gap in test scores and academic performance between black and white children.

The cases in this chapter all deal with school segregation and efforts to remedy or overcome its effects. Before the Supreme Court opinions in these cases, however, it is instructive to examine the historical record of Jim Crow education.

The Civil War ended the legal institution of slavery, at the cost of six hundred thousand lives, most of them young men who fought neither to abolish nor defend slavery but simply to survive the carnage of the bloodiest war in American history. The ratification of the Fourteenth Amendment in 1868, three years after the Thirteenth Amendment abolished slavery, conferred state and national citizenship on the former slaves and promised a federal guarantee of "the equal protection of the laws." Firmly in the control of "Radical Republicans" whose Reconstruction policy imposed a military government on the former Confederacy, Congress granted the franchise to the former slaves, who flocked to the ballot boxes and elected delegates to conventions that rewrote the constitutions of the Southern states. Several of these constitutions provided for systems of free public education, and black children began attending school in large numbers. In Mississippi, for example, the legislature—controlled by black members and their white Republican allies—established a school system in 1870 that enrolled 127,000 black children the following year, 39 percent of the school-age black population. Even under Reconstruction and black rule, Mississippi's public schools were segregated, because white parents refused to pay taxes for integrated schools. Close to a century passed before the first black child in Mississippi attended school with whites.

The South Carolina constitution, written by black legislators, required that all schools be racially mixed, and black and white children attended classes together in many communities. The state also established an integrated teachers' college, which trained many black teachers. Other Southern states, however, experienced serious problems with public education, largely because many white voters refused to pay taxes to support black education. Even in states that funded black schools, the lack of qualified black teachers made it difficult to maintain academic standards.

Many of the schools for black children that did exist in the South during the Reconstruction period had been established by the Freedmen's Bureau, the federal agency created by Congress to provide aid and services to former slaves, to help them purchase land, farming equipment, and supplies, and to give them enough schooling to read, write, and keep books. Bureau agents set up classes for adults and also provided schools for children, largely staffed by white teachers from the North, most of whom were young women who had never been to the South and were treated with scorn and outright hostility by many whites. One female teacher in northern Virginia, just across the Potomac River from the nation's capital, abandoned her job after being shunned by every white person in the community. "If you are mean enough to teach niggers," one told her, "you may eat and sleep with them." Male teachers were a small minority, but they became targets for threats. One teacher in Alabama received this anonymous and barely literate warning: "You have set up a nigger school in the settlement which we will not allow you to teach if you was a full blooded negro we would have nothing to say but a white skin negro is more than we can stand you can dismiss the school imediately or prepar yourself to travail we will give you a chance to save yourself and you had better move instanter." Some white teachers faced greater dangers than threats. Captain James McCleery, the Freedmen's Bureau superintendent of education in Texas and northwestern Louisiana, barely escaped a band of night riders in Louisiana by hiding in a swamp all night. One of his teachers in Henderson County, Texas, was grabbed by a white mob, stripped naked, covered with tar and cotton, and given two minutes to run before he faced a volley of rifle fire.

Teachers who ignored the hostility and threats often lost their schools to violence. Black schools were burned and pillaged throughout the South. Seven schools were burned in Georgia in 1866; three schools were burned that year in Texas. A school at Orangeburg, South Carolina, was fired into; the black school in Hardinsburg, Kentucky, was blown up on Christmas Eve in 1867. Despite the efforts to drive them from the South, the vast majority of the Freedmen's Bureau teachers stuck with their schools and their black students. By 1870, more than nine thousand teachers were instructing some two hundred thousand black children, about 12 percent of the school-age population. Northern missionary groups also sent teachers into Southern states, and black churches set up schools for their children. All together, these public and private groups offered schooling to perhaps one of every five black children in the South, which meant that four out of five black children received no education at all during the Reconstruction period and remained illiterate, as their parents had during slavery.

The small minority of black children who did attend school during Reconstruction had an obvious zest for learning. One white teacher in Mississippi reported that when her students turned in their slates or copybooks, "my face was eagerly watched, to find therein approval or disapproval (they were quick to read the human countenance) and if a word of praise fell from my lips, a look of triumph would light up their sable faces as to make even them look beautiful." The condescending tone of this remark, however unintended, reflected the superior attitude and status of the white teacher. But even the most sensitive and understanding teachers encountered problems that stemmed from the reality of black life and culture in the rural South. The learning of black children was clearly hindered by the fact that virtually all came from families with illiterate parents, who could not help their children with lessons. Cut off from the written word, Southern blacks had retained the oral traditions of their African roots, which they adapted to their churches and communities, where everyone joins in calling out verses and children's rhymes. Most teachers in Reconstruction schools reported that students in the early grades were quick to learn the alphabet, numbers, spelling of simple words, and the rote memorization of short poems and Bible passages, a reflection of this oral culture. Even in crowded classrooms, children enjoyed chanting in unison as they went through letters, numbers, and verses. One teacher in Virginia wrote that "instruction is necessarily mostly oral, as much time would be lost if we trained pupils singly. The little things gave us almost undivided attention, and are much stimulated by recitations in concert."

Past the primary level, however, teachers expressed frustration at the inability of black children to master arithmetic and composition. Part of the problem lay in textbooks designed for Northern white students. A black child on a Mississippi farm was unlikely to associate a picture of Xerxes with the letter X or to know that a "newsboy" was an n word. One scholar of black education has noted this problem of Reconstruction schools: "In the world of the rural black schoolchild, very little of what was taught and of its presentation had much relationship to daily existence. The drudgery of manual labor, the lively conversations in the black people's cabins, and the generally non-literate nature of southern living for both races had almost nothing to do with what instructors talked about, once the concrete naming of things had passed."

The most difficult subject for black children was mathematics, which teachers in the nineteenth century approached from an abstract perspective. Children were not allowed to count on their fingers, or given problems that dealt with real objects like apples, chickens, or cotton bales. One critic of "mental" arithmetic wrote that teachers, most of them poorly trained in the subject, were often "completely nonplussed in any attempt to explain what they have done, or analyze the principles upon which it is performed." As a result, the "neglect of mathematics, the single most unmet need of black education, resulted in mass innumeracy, as tragic as illiteracy, a deficiency that has received more attention."

There were additional barriers to effective learning that came from outside the schoolhouse. The need for black children to plant, hoe, and harvest crops cut weeks and even months from already short school years; many children lived miles from school and could not walk on dirt roads when it rained; children got sick or injured and had no medical care; and because hostile whites sometimes ran teachers out of town or burned schools, even when children arrived at school, it was not always staffed or even standing. What is remarkable about the Reconstruction period is not that so few black children got so little good education, but that teachers and students alike persevered in the face of such enormous odds. It is also a testament to their faith in the liberating power of education that black parents—most of them illiterate themselves—worked hard to build schools, raise money for books and teachers, and give their children the desire to learn. One former slave, Charles White-side, was told by his master that he would remain in slavery "'cause you got no education, and education is what makes a man free." This remark spurred Whiteside's determination that each of his thirteen children would attend school, no matter how long and hard he would have to work. It was worth all the labor "to make them free," he said.

The modest spread of literacy and learning for the former slaves and their children ended with the return of whites to power in the South, twelve years after their surrender at Appomattox Court House. The official demise of Reconstruction came in 1877, the payoff of a political deal that Republican presidential candidate Rutherford Hayes had made with Southern Democrats to win the "Stolen Election" of 1876. Although Hayes had lost the popular vote to Democrat Samuel Tilden, he promised to look with "kind consideration" on Southern demands that Reconstruction end, and the sudden resignation of a pro-Tilden member of the commission set up to count the disputed electoral votes gave Hayes a one-vote victory.

With the end of Reconstruction, the white "Redeemers" who returned to power in the South had no desire to give black children an education that would equip them for more than menial labor as sharecroppers or household servants. The Freedmen's Bureau was abolished and its schools closed, and Northern churches withdrew their teachers from black schools. Black voters, who had gained representation in every Southern legislature, were systematically disenfranchised through a combination of harassment, ballot fraud, and outright violence. During the last two decades of the nineteenth century, the white lawmakers who controlled the South began the process of replacing slavery with segregation, installing the Jim Crow system that separated the races in every aspect of life.

The heart of the Jim Crow system, and the institution most central to its functioning, was the segregated public school system. The consignment of black children to separate schools kept them "in their place" and safely away from white children, especially girls, who might not realize that black males—even at the grade school level—might threaten the "purity" of the young "flowers of southern womanhood." The combined power of racial prejudice and sexual phobia should not be underestimated as a motivating factor in the Southern insistence on school segregation. But an equally important reason for maintaining separate schools was to make it simpler to provide a separate curriculum for black children, one that would provide the rudiments of literacy and training for manual labor and domestic service. There was no need to educate blacks in literature, foreign languages, or advanced mathematics, or to encourage them to aspire to higher education. White Southerners did recognize the need for "normal schools" to train black teachers, but these postsecondary schools were hardly "colleges" with a full curriculum in the liberal arts and sciences. The governor of Georgia expressed a common attitude toward the efforts of Northern philanthropists to establish black colleges: "We can attend to the education of the darkey in the South and give them the education they most need. I do not believe in the higher education of the darkey. He must be taught the trades. When he is taught the fine arts, he is educated above his caste, and it makes him unhappy."

Many blacks, even those with little or no education, were unhappy that their children were forced to attend segregated schools, many of them housed in churches or private homes, and most lacking desks and books for each student. The children sat on benches, crowded together, and shared tattered, hand-me-down books that had been discarded by white schools. These Jim Crow schools were "public" in name only, and often received so little funding from county school boards that hard-strapped parents had to "board" the teachers to supplement their meager salaries. One fact that is little known about black education is that most schools were segregated by law well before the Jim Crow system took hold in the late nineteenth century. Many states had imposed school segregation even before the Civil War, and only a handful of Southern states—notably Louisiana and South Carolina—had integrated their schools during the Reconstruction years. Another little-known fact is that Jim Crow schooling actually began in Massachusetts in 1820, and spread to several other northern and western states during the 1860s and '70s. And few people know that black parents in a dozen states mounted legal challenges to segregated public schools during the five decades that preceded the Supreme Court's approval in 1896 of "separate but equal" facilities in the *Plessy* case.

The first of these cases came from the capital of the anti-slavery crusade, Massachusetts, where Horace Mann had pioneered the system of free public schools as the state's commissioner of education. But the free schools had been segregated from the very beginning, even before Mann took his post in 1837. In 1820 the city of Boston had opened the Smith Grammar School for black children. The Boston school board later established two more primary schools for black children, and also adopted a regulation that all children attend the school "nearest their residences." These regulations created a conflict in 1849 for Benjamin Roberts, whose daughter Sarah was five. He first tried to enroll her in the white primary school nearest to her home, but she was "ejected from the school by the teacher, on the ground of her being a colored person." The Smith school was almost half a mile from Sarah's home, while there were five white schools that were closer.

This rebuff to his daughter spurred Benjamin Roberts to file a lawsuit against the city. Roberts enlisted Charles Sumner to argue the challenge to segregated schooling before the Massachusetts Supreme Judicial Court, headed by a renowned judge, Lemuel Shaw. Sumner's eloquent opposition to slavery later propelled him to the Senate, where he served from 1851 to 1874 and headed the abolitionist forces. His argument in *Roberts v. City of Boston* relied on provisions of the Massachusetts constitution that gave every citizen equal rights in civil and political affairs. Confining Boston's black children to segregated schools branded "a whole race with the stigma of inferiority and degradation," Sumner asserted. The city conceded that the Smith school was dilapidated and that its equipment "has been so shattered and neglected that it cannot be used until it has been thoroughly repaired." But Sumner did not base his argument on the physical inequality of the black and white primary schools in Boston. "Admitting that it is an equivalent," he said, "still the colored children cannot be compelled to take it. They have an equal right with the white children to the general public schools." Sumner used words that would be echoed, a century later, by Thurgood Marshall in the United States Supreme Court. "The separation of the schools," Sumner told the Massachusetts judges, "so far from being for the benefit of both races, is an injury to both. It tends to create a feeling of degradation in the blacks, and of prejudice and uncharitableness in the whites."

Chief Justice Shaw did not agree. "The great principle, advanced by the learned and eloquent advocate for the plaintiff," Shaw wrote of Sumner's argument, that "all persons without distinction of age or sex, birth or color, origin or condition, are equal before the law . . . is perfectly sound." But the principle of equal treatment, Shaw added, must yield to the "paternal consideration" of elected lawmakers, whose judgments should not be disturbed so long as their power is "reasonably exercised." The Boston school committee, Shaw wrote, had concluded after "great deliberation" that the interests of the city's children of both races "will best be promoted, by maintaining the separate primary schools for colored and for white children, and we can perceive no ground to doubt, that this is the honest result of their experience and judgment." Shaw noted Sumner's argument that "this maintenance of separate schools tends to deepen and perpetuate the odious distinction of caste, founded in a deep-rooted prejudice in public opinion," but he rejected any judicial responsibility to deal with the impact of white hostility toward blacks. "This prejudice, if it exists, is not created by law, and probably cannot be changed by law," Shaw proclaimed.

The *Roberts* decision, which gave elected officials the power to decide that the interests of black and white children "will best be promoted" by separate schools, became the standard for judges in other states, even after the Fourteenth Amendment—added to the Constitution in 1868—directed the states to guarantee every person "the equal protection of the laws."

Against this historical record of Jim Crow education, it should be noted that the Supreme Court's majority opinion in *Plessy v. Ferguson* drew its only support in precedent from the *Roberts* decision of the Massachusetts supreme court, handed down in 1849, and the judicial rulings in later challenges to school segregation—all of them rebuffed by the courts—that relied on *Roberts* for authority. Laws permitting or requiring the segregation of black children in schools, the Court noted in *Plessy*,

> have been generally, if not universally, recognized as within the competency of state legislatures in the exercise of their police power. The most common instance of this is connected with the establishment of separate schools for white and colored children, which has been held to be a valid exercise of the legislative power even by courts of States where the political rights of the colored race have been longest and most earnestly enforced.

The founding of the National Association for the Advancement of Colored People (NAACP) in 1909 marked the beginning of the protracted legal struggle to eradicate Jim Crow education. During the first three decades of the twentieth century, this campaign had no success, as state judges and the Supreme Court both relied on the "separate but equal" doctrine of *Plessy* to turn back the few challenges that were mounted against school segregation. However, during the 1930s and '40s, NAACP lawyers began a concerted effort, directed by the organization's brilliant and tenacious legal director, Thurgood Marshall. The following excerpts from *Jim Crow's Children* recount the first two decades of this campaign.

Thurgood Marshall, counsel for the NAACP Legal Defense and Education Fund, was the nation's leading black lawyer. Born in Baltimore in 1908, he applied to the University of Maryland's all-white law school after graduating from an all-black college. Turned down because of his race, Marshall studied law at Howard University, the "black Harvard" in Washington, D.C. He won his first civil rights case in 1936, forcing Maryland to admit Donald Murray to its law school. Because the state did not appeal to the Supreme Court, the *Murray* case did not establish any precedent on racial segregation outside Maryland.

Thurgood Marshall commanded a dedicated platoon of lawyers who fought segregation with a battle plan drafted in 1931 by Nathan Margold, a young Jewish lawyer and protégé of Felix Frankfurter, then a Harvard law professor. Hired by the NAACP to research Jim Crow laws and recommend a long-range litigation strategy against segregation in public education, Margold produced a 218-page document that became the "master plan" for Marshall's legal troops. Margold took the Supreme Court's "separate but equal" ruling in *Plessy v. Ferguson* as his starting point. After documenting the obvious fact that schools for blacks were rarely equal to those for whites, Margold considered two legal strategies. One would focus on lawsuits designed to force Southern officials to make black and white schools truly equal in quality. This approach had two advantages: it would avoid a frontal attack on *Plessy*, which stood firmly in the 1930s as precedent; and judicial rulings that ordered equal facilities would impose heavy financial burdens on local school boards. The second legal strategy would assert that separate schools could never be equal because segregation imposed a "badge of servitude" on black children. This approach had many risks, but one virtue: judges could not evade the Equal Protection Clause of the Fourteenth Amendment. Margold urged NAACP lawyers to rely for precedent on *Yick Wo v. Hopkins*, in which the Supreme Court ruled in 1888 that laws that public officials applied to racial minorities "with an evil eye and an unequal hand" violated the Constitution.

Margold advised NAACP leaders that "it would be a great mistake to fritter away our limited funds on sporadic attempts to force the making of equal divisions of school funds in the few instances where such attempts might be expected to succeed." This approach would force civil rights lawyers to file separate lawsuits in each Southern school district, to recruit plaintiffs in each district who had the courage and fortitude to face hostility from whites and delays in court, and to perform the laborious task of digging out the facts of school funding disparities in each case. Even if they succeeded, lawsuits to equalize facilities would require judges to act as school superintendents, checking the quality of textbooks, playgrounds, and lavatories. "And we should be leaving untouched the very essence of the existing evils" of segregation, Margold warned. "On the other hand," he wrote, "if we boldly challenge the constitutional validity of segregation if and when accompanied irremediably by discrimination, we can strike directly at the most prolific sources of discrimination."

* * *

The "Margold Report" became a bible for Thurgood Marshall and his legal staff. But they did not read it literally as commanding a frontal attack on elementary and secondary school segregation in the Deep South. Such an approach would have sent Marshall's troops on a suicide mission. The notion of little black boys rubbing knees with little white girls was unthinkable in the 1930s. Marshall decided instead to mount a flanking attack on the Old Confederacy, beginning with graduate education in border states. This campaign, if successful, would establish legal precedent for a final assault on the citadel of segregation, grade schools in the Deep South.

Marshall's strategy of encirclement won its first major victory in 1938 over the University of Missouri, which excluded blacks from its law school. Lloyd Gaines was denied admission because he was black, just as Thurgood Marshall had been turned away in Maryland. University officials agreed to pay his tuition if Gaines attended law school in another state, but he demanded admission in Missouri. The NAACP filed suit in state court against the university's registrar, whose last name was Canada; the Missouri supreme court ruled against Gaines, and the Supreme Court accepted his appeal.

Chief Justice Hughes wrote for the Court in *Gaines v. Canada,* holding that Missouri could not give whites a legal education in the state and deny blacks that right. Hughes cited *Yick Wo* for support on this issue, calling that decision "the pivot upon which the case turns." But he then let Missouri off the hook. Hughes cited *Plessy* in holding that states could provide black and white law students with "equal facilities in separate schools" without violating the Constitution. Missouri promptly established a black law school, but Lloyd Gaines never showed up for classes and his case ended with a Pyrrhic victory for NAACP lawyers.

World War II interrupted the NAACP campaign against segregated education, and ten years separated the *Gaines* decision from the next graduate school case. Ada Lois Sipuel graduated with honors from Oklahoma's State College for Negroes and applied in 1946 to the state's all-white law school. She was denied admission and promised that a black law school with "substantially equal" facilities would soon be established. Thurgood Marshall argued for Ada Sipuel in the Supreme Court on January 8, 1948. This was an easy case for the justices. Four days later, they unanimously ordered Oklahoma to provide her a legal education "as soon as it does for applicants of any other group." The Court's brief and unsigned opinion cited the *Gaines* decision as precedent. Missouri had opened a real law school for blacks, although it was certainly not equal to the all-white school. Oklahoma took a different tack, roping off a section of the state capitol and calling it a law school. This pretend school had no library and no faculty, and Ada Sipuel refused to be a pretend student.

Thurgood Marshall returned to the Supreme Court in *Sipuel v. Oklahoma Board of Regents* and argued, for the first time, that segregation was flatly unconstitutional. Even if states provided blacks with better schools than whites, he said, separating them by race imposed a "badge of inferiority" on blacks. But 1948 was a presidential election year and the Court shied away from this divisive issue. Over the dissents of Justices Frank Murphy and Wiley Rutledge, the Court sent the *Sipuel* case back to state court for hearings on whether Oklahoma's pretend law school was equal to its real, all-white school. Marshall called Dean Erwin Griswold of Harvard Law School as a witness, but the state judges covered their ears and ruled against Ada Sipuel. By 1949, after Harry Truman returned to the White House with a surprising upset of Thomas Dewey, Oklahoma officials wearied of legal battle and admitted Ada Sipuel to its real law school.

The NAACP victories in the *Gaines* and *Sipuel* cases did nothing to end public school segregation in the Deep South. They did not topple *Plessy* or destroy the "separate but equal" doctrine. They did not even force the admission of blacks into all-white schools; Oklahoma legislators, not the state's judges, ended segregation at the university level. But these cases gave civil rights lawyers a powerful weapon for the battles that lay head. The *Gaines* decision established, and *Sipuel* echoed, the principle that states must furnish blacks with educational facilities "substantially equal" in quality to those afforded whites. Given the vast disparity in funding between black and white schools, virtually no chance existed that separate schools would ever approach equality. In 1940, the average yearly expenditure in Southern states for black children was $21.40, less than half the $50.14 spent on whites. Bridging this gap would cost each state millions of dollars, and white lawmakers were not willing to spend that much on black children.

Between 1948 and 1950, civil rights lawyers and leaders debated their options in challenging segregation at the elementary and secondary level: they could file suits to equalize school expenditures, or mount an attack on segregation itself. During this time, two more graduate school cases—from Texas and Oklahoma—moved slowly through the lower courts. Thurgood Marshall viewed these cases as the last skirmishes before the final assault on public school segregation in the Deep South. He offered lawmakers in Texas and Oklahoma a last chance to make separate university facilities equal in every respect. This alternative to integration would impose a crushing financial burden on Southern states. In Texas, for example, the physical plant of the state's white universities was valued at $72 million, those for blacks at $4 million. Whites could choose from 106 fields of study, blacks from only forty-nine (including carpeting and mattress making). The white libraries owned 750,000 volumes, the black schools just 82,000. Complying with *Plessy* would cost the Jim Crow states hundreds of millions of dollars at the university level, and billions more for elementary and secondary schools. Hoping to evade the equally unpleasant choices of integration or bankruptcy, university officials in Texas and Oklahoma tried different approaches in the *Sweatt* and *McLaurin* cases.

Heman Marion Sweatt, a black postal worker, had applied to the University of Texas Law School in 1946 and was rejected on racial grounds. After NAACP lawyers filed suit against state officials, Texas judges gave the university six months to offer Sweatt a legal education "substantially equivalent" to that provided whites. Charles T. McCormick, dean of the all-white law school, quickly offered plans for an all-black school. It would occupy four basement rooms in an Austin office building, it would have no library, and it would employ three part-time instructors. McCormick would also serve as the new school's dean. Marshall promptly challenged these plans, and state judges ordered a second hearing, at which McCormick testified under oath that the two law schools were equal in quality. The Texas judges agreed that four rooms for blacks equaled the massive building in which 850 white students took classes. Marshall filed an appeal with the Supreme Court that invited the justices—including Tom Clark, an alumnus of the Austin law school—to look for themselves at the two schools and decide whether Dean McCormick had testified truthfully.

George McLaurin applied in 1948 to the University of Oklahoma's graduate education school. Then in his sixties, McLaurin had taught for decades in black public schools; he held a master's degree and now sought a doctorate. The Supreme Court had ruled in January 1948 that Oklahoma must offer Ada Sipuel a legal education "as soon at it does" for any white applicant. Rather than build a new school for blacks, officials in the Sooner State admitted her to the white law school. They also admitted George McLaurin to the white graduate school. But his "equal" education came with conditions. University officials decided to teach the longtime teacher a lesson. He could not sit in classrooms, but could listen to lectures from a hallway seat, next to a sign that read "Reserved for Colored." He could study at a "colored" desk on the library's mezzanine, but not in the reading room. He could eat at a "colored" table in the cafeteria, but only after white students finished their meals. NAACP lawyers challenged these demeaning conditions as "badges of slavery" imposed on McLaurin, but they lost the first two rounds in lower federal courts.

Their Supreme Court victories in the graduate and law school cases spurred NAACP lawyers to launch a frontal attack on Jim Crow schooling in primary and secondary schools, the citadels of segregation. Thurgood Marshall picked his targets with care, and between 1950 and 1952 five cases had been decided by lower courts and were ready for decision by the Supreme Court. The communities from which these five cases emerged had little in common except one thing: they all maintained segregated schools by law. The first to be filed came from a rural, overwhelmingly black county in the Deep South state of South Carolina; a second from another rural county in Virginia, in which the black and white residents were roughly equal in number; a third from the nation's capitol, Washington, D.C., where blacks made up one-third of the population; a fourth from the most northerly of Delaware's three counties, just below the Mason-Dixon line, with a 16-percent black population; and the fifth from Topeka, Kansas, a city in which just 8 percent of the residents were black and only four primary schools were segregated. Between them, these five communities spanned the range of the Jim Crow system, from the Deep South where segregation was deeply entrenched to the Midwest, where it was imposed in very few cities and towns.

It is simply a historical accident that the first school segregation case to reach the Supreme Court, *Briggs v. Elliott* from rural South Carolina, which was also first of the five in alphabetical order, did not lend its name to the Court's historic decision in 1954. If the justices had not sent the *Briggs* case back to the lower court for a few months for a totally useless hearing, we would today be reading the Supreme Court's historic opinion in *Briggs v. Elliott* rather than *Brown* and remember the name of Harry Briggs Jr., rather than Linda Carol Brown as the black child in whose name the suit was filed. Because it shows the Jim Crow system in its most damaging form, a brief account of the *Briggs* case, drawn from *A People's History of the Supreme Court*, is worth reading before the case excerpts that follow.

The long road to the Supreme Court for black children began in Clarendon County, South Carolina, on July 28, 1947. Their journey ended on May 17, 1954, with the momentous ruling in *Brown v. Board of Education of Topeka, Kansas* [(I)]. During this seven-year period, five cases that challenged racial segregation in public schools moved through the courts in four states and the District of Columbia. Oliver Brown, acting as "next friend" of his eight-year-old daughter Linda, was the first of twelve plaintiffs in the Topeka lawsuit that made his last name the best known in American constitutional history. But the *Brown* case was not the first that Thurgood Marshall and his staff of NAACP lawyers filed against school segregation. That distinction went to a suit against school officials in rural South Carolina; Harry Briggs, Sr., the "next friend" of his nine-year-old son Harry Jr., was the first of twenty plaintiffs in *Briggs v. Elliott*.

Only a handful of Americans recognize the name of Harry Briggs, Jr., yet students in every American school read about Linda Brown and the landmark case brought on her behalf. A quirk of court scheduling put the *Brown* case before *Briggs* on the Supreme Court docket when the five school cases were combined for argument and decision. This historical accident has no real significance, but it reminds us that history reflects many accidents of time and place. The deeper forces of social change, however, move with little regard to names and dates. It does not really matter which name—Oliver Brown or Harry Briggs—appears in the caption of the school cases. What matters is that both men challenged their children's segregation at a time when the Court was finally ready to confront the "separate but equal" doctrine of the *Plessy* decision.

Thurgood Marshall had several good reasons for picking Clarendon County as the first target in his final assault on school segregation. First, segregation in the Deep South was deeply rooted in the region's laws and customs; it stemmed from three centuries of slavery and Jim Crow discrimination. Second, NAACP lawyers could easily document the enormous disparities between Clarendon County's black and white schools to point up the utter hypocrisy of "separate but equal" and its defenders. Third, Marshall wanted to acknowledge the courage of black parents who stood up for their children in a citadel of segregation like South Carolina, where politicians like Governor Strom Thurmond pandered to racial bigots. These are also good reasons for looking more closely at Clarendon County than at Topeka in following the school cases to the Supreme Court.

Located on the flat plain between the swampy lowlands along the Atlantic coast and the rolling Piedmont hills in the west, Clarendon County in 1947 had some 32,000 residents, more than 70 percent of them black. All but a few black families lived on farms, but few owned their land. They raised cotton and worked as sharecroppers for white owners. More than two thirds of the black families earned less than a thousand dollars each year; more than a third of all blacks over ten could not read or write. Black children attended sixty-one ramshackle schools, most without plumbing or electricity. The county spent $179 for each white child in public school, but only $43 for each black child.

On the surface, blacks and whites got along well in Clarendon County. "We got a good bunch of nigras here," said David McClary, who owned the biggest feed and livestock business in the county. "Colored have made wonderful progress down here," echoed H. C. Carrigan, the twelve-term mayor of Summerton, a town of one thousand. "I have several farms, and they all have Negroes on them. I sharecrop with them, and they are all as happy as can be." But not all the county's blacks were happy. "Oh, there was a lot goin' on that we didn't like," said Joseph Richburg, a black teacher, "but everything was fine on the face of it, so long as we kept saying, 'Yes, sir' and 'No, sir' and tipping our hat."

One black man in Clarendon county did not tip his hat to whites. The Rev. J.A. DeLaine, pastor of the African Methodist Episcopal church in Summerton, also taught in a rural black school. His students walked to school along dirt roads, their clothes spattered with dust or mud by school buses that carried white children past them. The lack of buses for black children bothered DeLaine. During the summer of 1947, he attended a speech in Columbia, the state capital, by the Rev. James Hinton, president of the state's NAACP chapters. Hinton told his listeners that South Carolina's black schools were a disgrace and would improve only if they forced whites to make them better. Hinton suggested they start with buses. And he challenged his audience. "No teacher or preacher in South Carolina has the courage," he charged, "to find a plaintiff to challenge the legality of the discriminatory bus-transportation practices of this state."

J.A. DeLaine took the challenge. The first Sunday after returning to Summerton, he visited Levi Pearson, a black farmer with three children at the Scott's Branch high school, nine miles from their home. Pearson owned his farm and was known for standing up to whites. He listened to DeLaine and agreed to stand up for his kids. DeLaine then drove back to Columbia and visited Harold Boulware, the state's only black civil rights lawyer. He returned to Summerton with a two-page petition, which Levi Pearson signed. DeLaine then visited another preacher, the Rev. L. B. McCord, a Presbyterian pastor and the county's school superintendent. The two men knew each other well. "I was one of McCord's good niggers," DeLaine said. But not after their meeting on July 28. The black teacher handed the white superintendent Pearson's petition, demanding bus transportation "for use of the said children of your Petitioner and other Negro school children similarly situated." McCord read it and told DeLaine the county had no money for buses for black children.

After this rebuff, Harold Boulware wrote the school board that Levi Pearson had retained his legal services and asked for a hearing on his petition. He got no answer to this or subsequent letters. Finally, on March 16, 1948, Boulware filed suit in federal court, seeking an injunction to bar Clarendon County officials from making any "distinction on account of race or color" in busing children to school. But the case was dismissed in June 1948 because Pearson's farm straddled the line between two school districts; he paid property taxes in one and his children attended school in another.

Levi Pearson paid for his stand; every white-owned bank and store cut off his credit and no white farmer would rent him a harvester. His crops rotted in the field that fall. Whites told him to forget about buses and finally gave him credit for next year's crops. But he could not forget his children's inferior schools. The next spring, in March 1949, Harold Boulware summoned Pearson and DeLaine to Columbia to meet another civil rights lawyer. Thurgood Marshall had come from New York to South Carolina, looking for plaintiffs willing to ask for more than buses. Marshall proposed a new lawsuit, demanding equal treatment in every area: buildings, teachers, books, and buses. The NAACP lawyer told Pearson and DeLaine that he wanted at least twenty plaintiffs, to spread the risk of retaliation. And he wanted Clarendon County, to expose the myth of "separate but equal" in South Carolina's most unequal county.

It took Pearson and DeLaine eight months to find twenty black parents willing to challenge the county's white power structure. They got the last signature on November 11, 1949, and took the list to Boulware. He drafted a complaint and put names on the caption in alphabetical order. The first was Harry Briggs, a navy veteran with five children; his oldest boy was Harry Jr., whose name appeared first among the black children. Harry Sr. pumped gas and fixed cars at Mayor Carrigan's Sinclair station in Summerton, and his wife, Liza, worked as a motel chambermaid. The same day he got the twenty names, Boulware drove to the federal courthouse in Charleston and filed the complaint—listing himself and Thurgood Marshall as counsel—in *Briggs v. Elliott*; the first defendant was Roderick Elliott, the county school board chairman.

Word spread quickly in Clarendon County that "nigras" had sued the school board. Virtually every plaintiff paid a heavy price for joining the suit. Mayor Carrigan fired Harry Briggs, and the motel fired his wife. Bo Stukes lost his garage job; James Brown was fired by a trucking company; John McDonald, a combat veteran of Iwo Jima and Okinawa, lost his credit for farm equipment; and Lee Richardson had his farm mortgage foreclosed. Even Harry Briggs's cow got arrested for stepping on a headstone in a white cemetery. Whites laughed at that little comedy, but blacks in Clarendon County found no humor in the spiteful response to their lawsuit.

* * *

May 24, 1951, is one of those unremembered dates that marks a significant event. On that hot spring day in Clarendon County, Kenneth B. Clark visited the Scott's Branch school near Summerton and met with sixteen black children between six and nine years old. He came with a box of four dolls, each about a foot high and dressed in diapers. Two dolls were boys and two were girls. They differed in one other way: two were pink and two were brown. One by one, Clark sat down with the youngsters and gave them instructions: "Give me the white doll." "Give me the colored doll." "Give me the Negro doll." Clark then said, "Give me the doll you like to play with." "Give me the doll that is the nice doll." "Give me the doll that looks bad." "Give me the doll that is a nice color."

Clark made notes of each child's responses. When he tallied them, the results closely matched his findings in similar tests he had conducted in New York City, Philadelphia, Boston, and several Arkansas communities. All sixteen of the Clarendon County black children correctly identified both the white and brown dolls. But ten chose the white doll as the one they wanted to play with; eleven said the brown doll looked "bad" to them; and nine picked the white doll as the "nice" one.

What brought Kenneth Clark from New York to Scott's Branch? Thurgood Marshall had decided to use the *Briggs* case to attack school segregation at its roots: what made the enforced separation of black children from whites most damaging, he felt, was not tattered books and untrained teachers, but the stigma of inferiority that segregation inflicted on black children. School officials could buy newer books and hire better teachers for black children, but they could not erase feelings of inferiority from their minds. Marshall enlisted Clark as an expert witness, hoping that his testimony would make this point. His credentials were impressive. A social psychologist who taught at City College in New York, Clark and his wife, Mamie, also a psychologist, had devised the doll test to study the development of self-images in black children. "We were really disturbed by our findings," Clark later said of his initial studies. "What was surprising was the degree to which the children suffered from self-rejection. I don't think we had quite realized the extent of the cruelty of racism and how hard it hit." The Clarks published an article in 1940 titled "Segregation as a Factor in the Racial Identification of Negro Pre-School Children" and reported on a decade of follow-up studies at a White House conference in 1950. Thurgood Marshall hoped that federal judges would listen carefully to this eminent scholar.

The *Briggs* case was assigned to federal district judge J. Waties Waring, a scion of Charleston society. Marshall had tailored the case for Judge Waring, certain that he would get a favorable ruling. Born in 1880 into a family that had owned slaves, Waring had slowly turned against segregation. He joined the federal bench in 1941 and shocked fellow members of the upper-crust Charleston Light Dragoons with his judicial rulings. He jailed a white farmer for holding a black man in "peonage" against his will and ruled in 1945 that South Carolina must equalize the salaries of black and white teachers. He also presided in 1946 over the trial of the white police chief who had blinded Isaac Woodward, a black army veteran, with his billy club. "I was shocked by the hypocrisy of my government," Waring later said of the federal prosecutor's failure to call witnesses against the chief. And in 1948, Thurgood Marshall argued before Waring that South Carolina could not exclude blacks from its primary elections. "It is time for South Carolina to rejoin the Union," Waring wrote in ruling for Marshall. For this opinion, he endured burning crosses on his lawn, gunshots at his house, and a large chunk of concrete through his front window.

"Unfortunately, the judge was not hit," a rural newspaper lamented.

Unfortunately for Marshall, Waring shared the bench at the *Briggs* trial with two other federal judges. Putting the case before a three-judge panel had been Waring's decision. Marshall had originally sought only equal spending on Clarendon County's schools, but Waring had urged him to amend his complaint and attack South Carolina's segregation laws directly. Federal law then provided that constitutional challenges to state laws would come before three-judge panels. Marshall complied with Waring's initiative, although the outcome of the *Briggs* case was now doubtful. Judge George Timmerman, who sat with Waring on the South Carolina federal bench, was a rabid defender of white supremacy and a sure vote for segregation. The third judge, John Parker of the Fourth Circuit Court of Appeals, had been nominated to the Supreme Court in 1930 by President Hoover, but was rejected by the Senate, largely because he had spoken against black voting. However, Parker had gained the respect of blacks after his defeat and upheld their claims in two important cases Thurgood Marshall had argued before him. Everyone knew the *Briggs* case rested on Parker's vote.

* * *

The trial began on May 28, 1951, and opened with a surprise. The school board's lawyer, Robert Figg, admitted to the judges that "inequalities in the facilities, opportunities and curricula in the schools of this district do exist." Figg hoped his concession would "eliminate the necessity of taking a great deal of testimony." He also hoped, quite obviously, that his ploy would keep Marshall's expert witnesses off the stand. Marshall looked stunned, but quickly replied that since his complaint attacked segregation on constitutional grounds, "we must be able to show the inequalities as they actually exist." Fortunately, Judge Parker, who presided, allowed Marshall to continue. He first called L. B. McCord, Clarendon's school superintendent. Marshall asked why the county separated the white and black children. "You would have to ask the children why," McCord replied. "None of them have ever asked me to go to one school or the other." He had trouble with other questions as well, refusing to admit that the county spent less on black children than whites. Roderick Elliott, the first defendant and school board chairman for twenty-five years, could not even identify the district's boundaries or name any schools.

Marshall turned the podium over to Robert Carter, his young but experienced associate. He first called Matthew Whitehead, professor of education at Howard University, who had inspected both white and black schools in Clarendon, armed with Judge Waring's order. Whitehead's report had prompted Robert Figg to concede the obvious inequalities. The white schools all had lunchrooms; none of the black schools did. In one black school "there was not a single desk" for students; "there was a desk for every child" in the white schools. The white schools had indoor toilets; the black schools had outhouses.

Kenneth Clark spent just one hour on the witness stand in the *Briggs* trial. He had never before testified as an expert, but he spoke calmly and confidently. "I was just stating what I had learned over the years," he later recalled. Robert Carter led him through his background and credentials, and Clark outlined his prior research on the self-images of black children. The cumulative effects of discrimination, prejudice, and segregation "have definitely detrimental effects on the personality development of the Negro child," Clark stated. "The essence of this detrimental effect is a confusion in the child's concept of his own self[-]esteem—basic feelings of inferiority, conflict, confusion in his self-image, resentment, hostility towards himself, hostility towards whites," he continued.

Clark then described his "doll studies" at the Scott's Branch school. "The conclusion which I was forced to reach was that these children in Clarendon County, like other human beings who are subjected to an obviously inferior status in the society in which they live, have been definitely harmed in the development of their personalities," he concluded. Robert Figg hardly bothered with cross-examination; he expressed surprise that Clark had conducted his tests alone with each child. Once the judges knew "that his testimony was based on very few children, that there was no witnesses to the tests," Figg later said, "I didn't press the matter." His final comment showed how badly Figg misjudged Clark's testimony: "Nobody took it seriously."

Three years would pass before the American people learned how seriously the Supreme Court took Kenneth Clark's testimony. Meanwhile, the three judges who heard it met to decide the case. Robert Figg had conceded the inequality of Clarendon County's schools at the trial. Judge Parker had asked him what decree the court should issue "in the light of your admissions." Figg asked in return for "a reasonable time" to draw up plans to equalize the black and white schools. Judge Parker issued the panel's decision on June 23, 1951. Writing for himself and Judge Timmerman,

Parker gave the defendants six months to report back on progress toward that goal. He also denied the plaintiff's motion to declare school segregation unconstitutional. Parker did not consider the *Sweatt* and *McLaurin* decisions relevant to public schools, where "the thought of establishing professional contacts does not enter into the picture." He deferred to *Plessy* in declining to find that "segregation is violative of fundamental constitutional rights." Parker ended with an echo of Oliver Wendell Holmes's dissent in the *Lochner* case: "The members of the judiciary have no more right to read their ideas of sociology into the Constitution than their ideas of economics."

Judge Waring filed a lengthy dissent that focused on the connections of racial prejudice and segregation. "There is absolutely no reasonable explanation for racial prejudice," he wrote. "It is all caused by unreasoning emotional reactions and these are gained in early childhood." Waring considered *Sweatt* and *McLaurin* even more reason to rule for the *Briggs* plaintiffs: "If segregation is wrong, then the place to stop it is in the first grade and not in graduate colleges." He put his last words into italics: "*Segregation is per se inequality.*"

Much like Harry Briggs and the other Clarendon County plaintiffs, Judge Waring paid a price for his Briggs dissent. Social ostracism and death threats finally drove Waring from his ancestral home in Charleston. He resigned his judicial post and moved to New York, where he died in 1968 at eighty-eight. He returned in death to Charleston; only a handful of white people attended the services at Magnolia Cemetery, but two hundred black mourners came, many from Clarendon County. "He's dead," one black farmer said, "but living in the minds of the people here still" (Irons, 2002).

McLaurin v. Oklahoma State Regents
339 U.S. 667 (1950)

"The State, in administering the facilities it affords for professional and graduate study, sets McLaurin apart from the other students. . . . Such restrictions impair and inhibit his ability to study, to engage in discussions and exchange views with other students, and, in general, to learn his profession."

The Question: Can a state require a student admitted to graduate school in the state university, and who is black, to sit in a seat designated for "colored" in classrooms, to sit at a separate table in the library, and to sit at a separate table in the student cafeteria, as a condition of his admission?

The Arguments: PRO

The state of Oklahoma, in this case, has admitted George McLaurin, who is black, to the state university's graduate school of education. He is offered facilities in classrooms, the library, and the student cafeteria that are separate but equal in quality to those designated for white students. The state's constitution requires that all public facilities be operated on a racially segregated basis, and the Supreme Court has upheld in *Plessy v. Ferguson* the state's power to segregate its facilities, so long as they are equal in quality for both races. The decision remains the law that governs this case.

CON

The segregated facilities McLaurin has been forced to accept in this case are demeaning and humiliating, and constitute a "badge of servitude" that is forbidden by the Thirteenth Amendment. In addition, keeping him apart from other students in this manner hinders his ability to converse with white students and to learn his profession. These segregated facilities are inherently unequal because they tell other students that McLaurin is not accepted by the university as their equal, and that his skin color requires that he be kept apart from white students. He is not being accorded the "equal protection of the laws" that the Fourteenth Amendment commands.

MR. CHIEF JUSTICE VINSON delivered the opinion of the Court.

In this case, we are faced with the question whether a state may, after admitting a student to graduate instruction in its state university, afford him different treatment from other students solely because of his race. We decide only this issue.

Appellant is a Negro citizen of Oklahoma. Possessing a Master's Degree, he applied for admission to the University of Oklahoma in order to pursue studies and courses leading to a Doctorate in Education. At that time, his application was denied, solely because of his race. The school authorities were required to exclude him by the Oklahoma statutes, which made it a misdemeanor to maintain or operate, teach or attend a school at which both whites and Negroes are enrolled or taught. Appellant filed a complaint requesting injunctive relief, alleging that the action of the school authorities and the statutes upon which their action was based were unconstitutional and deprived him of the equal protection of the laws. Citing our decisions in Missouri ex rel. Gaines v. Canada (1938), and Sipuel v. Board of Regents (1948), a statutory three-judge District Court held that the State had a Constitutional duty to provide him with the education he sought as soon as it provided that education for applicants of any other group. It further held that to the extent the Oklahoma statutes denied him admission they were unconstitutional and void. . . .

Following this decision, the Oklahoma legislature amended these statutes to permit the admission of Negroes to institutions of higher learning attended by white students, in cases where such institutions offered courses not available in the Negro schools. The amendment provided, however, that in such cases the program of instruction "shall be given at such colleges or institutions of higher education upon a segregated basis." Appellant was thereupon admitted to the University of Oklahoma Graduate School. In apparent conformity with the amendment, his admission was made subject to "such rules and regulations as to segregation as the President of the University shall consider to afford to Mr. G. W. McLaurin substantially equal educational opportunities as are afforded to other persons seeking the same education in the Graduate College," a condition which does not appear to have been withdrawn. Thus he was required to sit apart at a designated desk in an anteroom adjoining the classroom; to sit at a designated desk on the mezzanine floor of the library, but not to use the desks in the regular reading room; and to sit at a designated table and to eat at a different time from the other students in the school cafeteria.

To remove these conditions, appellant filed a motion to modify the order and judgment of the District Court. That court held that such treatment did not violate the provisions of the Fourteenth Amendment and denied the motion. This appeal followed.

In the interval between the decision of the court below and the hearing in this Court, the treatment afforded appellant was altered. For some time, the section of the classroom in which appellant sat was surrounded by a rail on which there was a sign stating, "Reserved For Colored," but these have been removed. He is now assigned to a seat in the classroom in a row specified for colored students; he is assigned to a table in the library on the main floor; and he is permitted to eat at the same time in the cafeteria as other students, although here again he is assigned to a special table.

It is said that the separations imposed by the State in this case are in form merely nominal. McLaurin uses the same classroom, library and cafeteria as students of other races; there is no indication that the seats to which he is assigned in these rooms have any disadvantage of location. He may wait in line in the cafeteria and there stand and talk with his fellow students, but while he eats he must remain apart.

These restrictions were obviously imposed in order to comply, as nearly as could be, with the statutory requirements of Oklahoma. But they signify that the State, in administering the facilities it affords for professional and graduate study, sets McLaurin apart from the other students. The result is that appellant is handicapped in his pursuit of effective graduate instruction. Such restrictions impair and inhibit his ability to study, to engage in discussions and exchange views with other students, and, in general, to learn his profession.

Our society grows increasingly complex, and our need for trained leaders increases correspondingly. Appellant's case represents, perhaps, the epitome of that need, for he is attempting to obtain an advanced degree in education, to become, by definition, a leader and trainer of others. Those who will come under his guidance and influence must be directly affected by the education he receives. Their own education and development will necessarily suffer to the extent that his training is unequal to that of his classmates. State-imposed restrictions which produce such inequalities cannot be sustained.

It may be argued that appellant will be in no better position when these restrictions are removed, for he may still be set apart by his fellow students. This we think irrelevant. There is a vast difference—a Constitutional difference—between restrictions imposed by the state which prohibit the intellectual commingling of students, and the refusal of individuals to commingle where the state presents no such bar. Shelley v. Kraemer (1948). The removal of the state restrictions will not necessarily abate individual and group predilections, prejudices and choices. But at the very least, the state will not be depriving appellant of the opportunity to secure acceptance by his fellow students on his own merits.

We conclude that the conditions under which this appellant is required to receive his education deprive him of his personal and present right to the equal protection of the laws. We hold that under these circumstances the Fourteenth Amendment precludes differences in treatment by the state based upon race. Appellant, having been admitted to a state-supported graduate school, must receive the same treatment at the hands of the state as students of other races. The judgment is reversed.

BROWN V. BOARD OF EDUCATION OF TOPEKA, KANSAS [I]*
347 U.S. 483 (1954)

"To separate [children] from others of similar age and qualifications solely because of their race generates a feeling of inferiority as to their status in the community that may affect their hearts and minds in a way unlikely ever to be undone. . . . We conclude that in the field of public education the doctrine of "separate but equal" has no place. Separate educational facilities are inherently unequal."

The Question: Can a state permit a local school board to require that elementary schools in the district be segregated by race, and can states require that all public schools in the state be segregated by race?

The Arguments: PRO

Public education is a state and local responsibility, and the Constitution does not allow judicial interference in the educational decisions of state and local officials. In decisions going back to 1849, the courts in more than a dozen states, including the Northern states of Massachusetts, New York, and Ohio, have upheld the power of state and local officials to operate schools in which students are segregated by race. The Framers of the Fourteenth Amendment, in the same session of Congress in which it was adopted, also provided for segregated schools in the District of Columbia. Most importantly, the Court's decision in *Plessy v. Ferguson* remains the law in the area, and no good reason exists to overrule the "separate but equal" doctrine established in that case.

CON

Racial segregation in public schools violates the Equal Protection Clause of the Fourteenth Amendment, which bars all racial discrimination imposed by law. The *Plessy* decision applies to transportation, and it has no relevance to education, which is the most important function of most state and local governments. Separating students by race imposes a "stigma" on black children and is meant to convey the message that they are not fit to associate with white children. The Court's holding in *Dred Scott* that blacks are inherently inferior to whites was reversed and repudiated in the Fourteenth Amendment. If the *Plessy* decision does apply to these cases, it should be reversed.

BACKGROUND

In 1950, Oliver Brown and his family lived in a small house on First Street in Topeka, Kansas. Their neighborhood, close by the Kansas River, was on the city's north side and was racially diverse, with whites predominating but with black,

Indian, and Hispanic families added to the mixture. Brown was thirty-two, the father of three girls and a welder at the Santa Fe railroad shop, where he repaired boxcars. He also served as the part-time assistant pastor at St. John African Methodist Episcopal Church, the city's largest black church. His oldest daughter, Linda Carol, was eight years old and was scheduled to begin third grade at the Monroe School, located about a mile from her home. The previous two years, Linda had walked down the grassy strip between the train tracks that ran past her house, going six blocks to catch a school bus to Monroe, a trip of thirty or forty minutes if the bus was on time.

---

*Together with Briggs v. Elliott, on appeal from the United States District Court for the Eastern District of South Carolina; Davis v. County School Board of Prince Edward County, Virginia, on appeal from the United States District Court for the Eastern District of Virginia; and Gebhart v. Belton, on certiorari to the Supreme Court of Delaware.

Shortly before school began in the fall of 1950, Oliver Brown took Linda by the hand and walked with her to the Sumner School, about six blocks from her house. Linda waited outside the principal's office while her father went in to enroll her. Although he knew his daughter would be turned away from the white school closest to home, Linda recalled that her father was nonetheless "quite upset" by the rejection at Sumner, a school ironically named for a leading abolitionist during the crusade against slavery. After that humiliating experience, Oliver Brown agreed to join a lawsuit being prepared by NAACP lawyers and was selected to be the lead plaintiff in *Brown v. Board of Education of Topeka, Kansas*. Years later, Linda Brown recalled that her father's name appeared first on the complaint not because his last name was first in alphabetical order, but rather because he was the only man among the plaintiffs, and a minister to boot.

Located smack in the nation's heartland, the territory known as "Bleeding Kansas" had seen bloody warfare between John Brown and his abolitionist followers and the defenders of slavery before the Civil War began in earnest. It became a state in 1861 and remained a racial battleground during the decades that followed the Union victory. By the end of the nineteenth century, the lure of free land and the booming market for wheat and corn had drawn almost one and a half million people to Kansas. But the state's population was overwhelmingly white; fewer than fifty thousand blacks had settled there, most of them in the area just across the Missouri River from Kansas City. Many of these migrants from the South, known as "Exodusters," found work as laborers in railroad and housing construction, and the booming economy drew blacks to cities like Topeka and Wichita. The state's welcome mat stopped, however, at schoolhouse doors. When the first session of the Kansas legislature met in 1861, its members voted to segregate black and white students in all schools, although the power to establish separate schools later was limited to cities and towns with more than one thousand residents. For a brief period of three years, from 1876 to 1879, the Kansas legislature dropped from the state's laws any mention of segregation, and the public schools were opened to students of both races. The school superintendent in Wyandotte County, across from Missouri and the home of about a third of the blacks in Kansas, deplored the end of segregation: "There are a large number of colored pupils in this county," he reported in 1876, "and where they predominate, or attend schools in considerable numbers, these mixed schools are not a success," although he did not elaborate on the ways in which the schools, or their students, had failed.

When the state legislature voted in 1879 to end the short-lived period of school integration, it limited the power to resegregate to "first-class" cities with more than fifteen thousand residents, and only in their elementary schools, although Kansas City, Kansas, was permitted to open a high school for blacks. Of the state's "first-class" cities, only Topeka segregated its elementary students. William Reynolds, a black parent in Topeka, challenged the segregation law in 1903 in state court after his son was turned away from a white grade school. Upholding the segregation law in a unanimous opinion, the Kansas Supreme Court ruled in *Reynolds v. Board of Education of Topeka* that the state legisla-

ture had the power to separate grade-school children by race: "Whether, in view of the history of this state, the traditions of its people, the composition and quality of its citizenship, its political and social ideals, and the relations of the white and colored people of large cities to each other, such a law is wise or beneficent this court is forbidden to investigate." The *Reynolds* opinion consisted almost entirely of lengthy quotations from earlier state cases that upheld school segregation, stretching back to *Roberts v. City of Boston*, decided in 1849. The Kansas judges also quoted approvingly from the *Plessy* case, decided just seven years earlier, and dismissed the argument that Jim Crow schools violated the Equal Protection clause of the Fourteenth Amendment in one sentence: "Counsel for plaintiff cites no authority for this position, and none can be found."

Half a century after William Reynolds lost his suit against the Topeka school board, the capital of Kansas had grown to a city of almost eighty thousand residents, just 8 percent of whom were black. With grain elevators within sight of the green-domed capitol building in downtown Topeka, the city linked the state's farmers with its government and served as the hub and headquarters of the Atchison, Topeka, and Santa Fe railroad, which carried freight and passengers across the nation's vast western region. It was less a city than a large town, whose big white houses, wrapped with verandas, sat on spacious green plots along tree-shaded streets. Most of Topeka's six thousand black citizens lived on the city's east side, close to the Kansas River and the railroad yards, but this neighborhood was nothing like the ghettos of other northern cities, and small pockets of blacks lived in widely scattered parts of Topeka.

The elected school board reflected the racial attitudes of a white population that kept the city's blacks out of hotels, restaurants, movie theaters, and even the swimming pool in Gage Park, the site of a well-kept zoo and a well-tended rose garden. Black children were allowed to swim in the Gage pool just once a year, when the park directors invited Topeka's blacks to hold a picnic.

The whites who ran Topeka not only kept blacks out of the municipal pool, they kept them out of state government offices and the city's businesses. In 1950, almost a quarter of Topeka's white males worked in professional or managerial posts, while only 4 percent of black men held such jobs. Topeka had 425 white accountants in 1950, but just one black. There were no blacks among the city's 350 engineers, only 5 black lawyers out of 214, and 14 blacks among 315 doctors. The only occupational category in which black men outnumbered whites was that of "janitors and porters." Black women in Topeka faced a similar exclusion from good jobs. Fewer than 1 percent of the city's female clerical workers were black; just 47 out of 5,740 women in this category. More than half of the 998 black women holding jobs in Topeka were employed as "private household workers" in the homes of white people or as "service workers" in the city's hospitals and nursing homes. These occupational disparities reflected wide gaps between the educational levels of Topeka's residents, with blacks having three years less schooling than whites. In turn, these disparities in education created a wide income gap. The median income of Topeka's white workers in 1950 was $2,068, compared to $1,160 for blacks, a difference of almost two-to-one. Only 15 blacks in

Topeka had incomes of more than $5,000 in 1950, while more than 3,000 whites exceeded this level.

Not all of Topeka's black citizens endured the Jim Crow schools without complaint. In 1941, after the school board established an all-white junior high in violation of state law, which limited school segregation to the elementary grades, a group of black parents sued the school board. They won the case and Topeka's junior high wrestling and tennis teams were limited to whites, and black girls were advised not to take stenography and typing classes, since there were few jobs for black women in these fields. The advice was accurate, since only 16 of the 2,245 stenographers and typists in Topeka were black. Of course, black girls could hardly expect to get jobs for which they were not trained.

With only four elementary schools for Topeka's black children, the school board had drawn attendance district lines that forced many of them, as young as five or six, to travel many blocks to reach their schools. The board did provide buses for black students, but they were often late and children who did not live near a school bus stop had to walk, often across busy streets and railroad tracks. The black schools also lacked some of the facilities and programs in the eighteen grade schools for white children. Few of the black parents complained about the segregated and second-class schools, and those who did were reminded that junior high school integration had cost black teachers their jobs. Teachers and parents also confronted the intimidation of Harrison Caldwell, a hulking black teacher and administrator who enforced the internal segregation at Topeka High and ran the black grade schools under Superintendent McFarland. One black student at Topeka High during the 1940s recalled that Caldwell "would tell us not to rock the boat and how to be as little offensive to whites as possible—to be clean and study hard and accept the status quo—and things were getting better."

Things did not get better enough to satisfy the most outspoken black leader in Topeka, McKinley Burnett, who became president of the city's NAACP chapter in 1948. The son of a slave, he worked for the federal government in a supply depot that served Forbes Air Force Base, a job that protected him from retaliation for his civil rights activism. The NAACP chapter was small, because most black teachers and others who worked for the city or white-owned businesses either worried about being fired or had become comfortable with the racial status quo in Topeka. Burnett, however, began in 1948 to pressure the school board to end segregation in the city's grade schools. The board turned a deaf ear to his appeals, and some board members reacted with insults. One member got so angry when Burnett said that blacks paid taxes just like whites and were entitled to the same rights that he jumped from his seat and said, "Let's go outside and settle this matter right now." Burnett calmly replied, "I don't settle these matters that way. I settle them by legal means."

The NAACP leader did not rush to the courthouse after this rebuff. He continued to show up at school board meetings, repeating his appeals to send all grade-school children to the school nearest their home. But after two years of fruitless effort, Burnett finally lost his patience. In August 1950 he told the board the time had come to end the Jim Crow system in Topeka. One board member shouted at him, "Is that a request or is that an ultimatum?" Burnett responded by turning to legal means to settle the matter. He sent a letter to NAACP headquarters in New York, asking for help in preparing a lawsuit against the Topeka school board and venting his anger at the board's open hostility toward him. "Words will not express the humiliation and disrespect in this matter," he wrote.

Burnett's letter reached Thurgood Marshall, who assigned Robert Carter to help draft a complaint. Four of the five black lawyers in Topeka, all graduates of the local law school at Washburn University, a municipal institution of little distinction, agreed to help Burnett. Three of them belonged to one family. Elisha Scott, born in 1890, had graduated from Washburn's law school in 1916 and became Topeka's first black lawyer.

Three of Elisha Scott's sons had become lawyers, and two of them, John and Charles, joined their father's law practice after returning from military service in World War II. Both of the younger Scotts had chafed in the Jim Crow army, and they plunged into NAACP work in Topeka. Along with Charles Bledsoe, the fourth of Topeka's five black lawyers, the Scotts drafted a legal complaint against the city's Jim Crow schools and sent copies to Robert Carter in New York. Carter was shocked by the lack of legal expertise in the draft, particularly on constitutional issues, but he tactfully complimented the Topeka lawyers while he completely revised their work. McKinley Burnett looked for plaintiffs as the complaint took shape.

Most of the twenty plaintiffs recruited by Burnett were NAACP members, and all but one were women. Oliver Brown was not a member, although he had once given the opening prayer at an NAACP meeting. Mamie Williams had been one of Brown's teachers at the segregated Buchanan School, and recalled of her former student: "He was an average pupil and a good citizen—he was not a fighter in his manner." But he was willing to join the legal fight against the segregated grade schools his three daughters were forced to attend, leaving the leadership to McKinley Burnett and the NAACP lawyers. The case of *Brown v. Board of Education of Topeka, Kansas* was filed in the U.S. District Court in Topeka on February 28, 1951. The federal courthouse was about a mile from the all-black Monroe School that Linda Brown attended and a few blocks from the all-white Sumner School that had turned her away. Those were almost exactly the same distances from the Brown family's home to those schools. But this case was not really about which school was closer or farther from Linda's home, but about the reason she was forced to attend the Monroe School and whether that reason—the color of her skin—violated the Constitution's guarantee that every person will receive "the equal protection of the laws."

Thurgood Marshall sent Robert Carter and Jack Greenberg to Topeka for the *Brown* hearing, which began on June 22, 1951. . . . Lester Goodell, the school board's lawyer and a former county prosecutor, who sounded like Perry Mason in objecting to dozens of questions by the NAACP lawyers as "incompetent, irrelevant, and immaterial." Heading the panel of three federal judges who ruled on Goodell's objections was Walter Huxman, a former Kansas governor and a member of the United States Court of Appeals for the Tenth Circuit. Huxman had been elected governor as a Democrat, during the Great Depression, and had been placed on the bench by President Franklin Roosevelt.

Testimony in the *Brown* case began on June 25. No sooner had Robert Carter asked his first witness, a former school board member, why the board had not used its power to end segregation in Topeka, than Goodell jumped up: "Object to that as incompetent, irrelevant, and immaterial and invading the province of the court." Judge Huxman sustained the objection and firmly told Carter that the only issue in the case was whether the board was "furnishing adequate facilities" for black children in separate schools. "If they are doing that, then what they are thinking about is immaterial," Huxman admonished Carter.

Because the black grade schools in Topeka, although older and not as well equipped as most white schools, had "adequate facilities" and more experienced teachers, the NAACP lawyers hammered at the fact that most black children had to travel longer distances to school than white children. The fact that the board provided buses for black students, but not for whites, weakened the claim that the four black grade schools failed to meet the *Plessy* standard of "separate but equal" facilities. Nonetheless, the NAACP lawyers called several witnesses to testify about the burden on their children of spending up to two hours each day on school buses. Robert Carter had asked John Scott to examine the plaintiffs, and he first called Lena Mae Carper, whose ten-year-old daughter, Katherine, had to walk across two busy intersections to catch a bus that would take her twenty-four blocks to school. The bus was often late and overcrowded, Mrs. Carper said, adding that two grade schools for whites were closer to their home than Katherine's school. Scott then called Katherine to the stand, the only child among the plaintiffs to testify. He asked her about the buses. "It is loaded, and there is no place hardly to sit," she answered.

Oliver Brown took the stand after Katherine Carper stepped down, although his daughter, Linda, was not in the courtroom to hear her father testify in the case that bore his name. His nervousness showed in speaking so quietly that Judge Huxman asked him to raise his voice, and he stumbled over how many blocks his home was from the Monroe school. But he described how Linda had to walk through the railroad switching yards to the school bus stop, telling the judges the bus, which was due at eight in the morning, was often late and "many times she had to wait through the cold, the rain, and the snow until the bus got there." When the bus was on time, Linda would have to wait outside the school for thirty minutes until the doors were unlocked at nine. Charles Bledsoe, who examined Brown, asked if he would prefer having Linda attend the Sumner school. Goodell jumped up once again, and Judge Huxman again sustained his objection that the question was irrelevant to the case. Oliver Brown left the stand after thirty minutes, the third of ten plaintiffs to testify but the only one whose name is remembered.

Robert Carter and Jack Greenberg had recruited seven expert witnesses, three of them to document the physical and curricular differences between Topeka's black and white grade schools. This proved a difficult task, since some of the older white schools had no playground space and their classrooms were smaller. The lack of differences, in fact, added strength to the claim that the real harm of segregation was the lesson it gave black children that there was something bad about black skin, something wrong about letting them sit next to white children in school. Three of the NAACP's experts made this point, but the one whose testimony most powerfully affected the outcome of the *Brown* case—not before this panel of judges but in the Supreme Court—was Louisa Holt, an assistant professor of sociology at the University of Kansas in Lawrence, twenty-five miles east of Topeka. Holt was thirty-four and held three degrees from Radcliffe, the "separate and unequal" women's branch of Harvard University. Her main attraction as a witness was her connection with the prestigious Menninger Clinic in Topeka, where she taught part-time in the school of psychiatry. Holt also lived in Topeka and had two children in the public schools.

Robert Carter conducted the examination of Louisa Holt, and his first question went right to the heart of the case: "Does enforced legal separation have any adverse effect upon the personality development of the Negro child?"

"The fact that it is enforced, that it is legal," she replied, "has more importance than the mere fact of segregation by itself does because this gives legal and official sanction to a policy which is inevitably interpreted both by white people and by Negroes as denoting the inferiority of the Negro group. Were it not for the sense that one group is inferior to the other, there would be no basis—and I am not granting that this is a rational basis—for such segregation."

Carter next asked how segregation affected the "learning process" of black children. "A sense of inferiority must always affect one's motivation for learning since it affects the feeling one has of one's self as a person," Holt said. She went on, using the jargon of psychiatry, to assert that a person's "sense of ego-identity is built up on the basis of attitudes that are expressed toward a person by others who are important—first the parents and then teachers and other people in the community, whether they are older or one's peers." Holt continued her lecture to the judges, who leaned forward with attentive looks at the attractive witness." If these attitudes that are reflected back and then internalized or projected, are unfavorable ones, then one develops a sense of one's self as an inferior being," she said,

Lester Goodell excused Louisa Holt from the witness stand without questioning her testimony, which she based on studies by other social scientists. . . . Judge Huxman and his colleagues asked few questions from the bench, and seemed eager to end the hearing after Holt's testimony. Goodell cooperated by calling just a handful of witnesses to make the point that Topeka's black and white grade schools were equal in curriculum, teacher salaries, and facilities. The board's lawyer then called Superintendent Kenneth McFarland to the stand. Goodell asked McFarland if he believed the superintendent had any duty to shape the "social customs and usage in the community." McFarland disavowed any intention to "dictate the social customs of the people who support the public school system." Goodell then asked if "the separation of the schools that we have is in harmony with the public opinion, weight of public opinion, in this community." The departing superintendent replied in bureaucratic jargon: "We have no objective evidence that the majority sentiment of the public would desire a change in the fundamental structure" of Topeka's schools.

Five weeks after the hearing ended, the three-judge panel issued its opinion on August 3, 1951, upholding the power of the Topeka school board under Kansas law to separate children by race in the city's grade schools. Judge Huxman wrote for all three members in finding that "the physical facilities, the curricula, courses of study, qualification of and quality of teachers, as well as other educational facilities in the two sets of schools are comparable." In fact, Huxman noted, the NAACP lawyers did not give "great emphasis" to this issue, and "relied primarily upon the contention that segregation in and of itself without more violates" the Fourteenth Amendment. Huxman admitted that this claim "poses a question not free from difficulty." As did the judges in the other school segregation cases, he looked to the *Plessy* case for guidance. The Supreme Court had not discarded the "separate but equal" doctrine and *Plessy* still stood as "authority for the maintenance of a segregated school system in the lower grades." But the Supreme Court's recent decisions in the graduate and law school cases troubled Huxman. Looking at the *McLaurin* and *Sweatt* decisions, handed down the year before, he posed two questions: "If segregation within a school as in the *McLaurin* case is a denial of due process, it is difficult to see why segregation in separate schools would not result in the same denial. Or if the denial of the right to commingle with the majority group in higher institutions of learning in the *Sweatt* case and gain the educational advantages resulting therefrom, is a lack of due process, it is difficult to see why such denial would not result in the same lack of due process if practiced in the lower grades."

Judge Huxman clearly hoped the Supreme Court would answer his troubling questions in the *Brown* case. And he offered the justices some help in framing their answers, in the eighth of nine "Findings of Fact" that he appended to his opinion. Restating the testimony of Louisa Holt almost verbatim, Huxman wrote: "Segregation of white and colored children in public schools has a detrimental effect upon the colored children. The impact is greater when it has the sanction of the law; for the policy of separating the races is usually interpreted as denoting the inferiority of the Negro group. A sense of inferiority affects the motivation of a child to learn. Segregation with the sanction of law, therefore, has a tendency to retard the educational and mental development of Negro children and to deprive them of some of the benefits they would receive in a racially integrated school system."

Two decades after he wrote this opinion, upholding the law that allowed school segregation but also finding that segregation harmed black children, Judge Huxman looked back. "We weren't in sympathy with the decision we rendered," he said of the judicial panel he headed in 1951. "If it weren't for *Plessy v. Ferguson,* we surely would have found the law unconstitutional. But there was no way around it—the Supreme Court would have to overrule itself" (Irons, 2002).

MR. CHIEF JUSTICE WARREN delivered the opinion of the Court.

These cases come to us from the States of Kansas, South Carolina, Virginia, and Delaware. They are premised on different facts and different local conditions, but a common legal question justifies their consideration together in this consolidated opinion.

In each of the cases, minors of the Negro race, through their legal representatives, seek the aid of the courts in obtaining admission to the public schools of their community on a nonsegregated basis. In each instance, they had been denied admission to schools attended by white children under laws requiring or permitting segregation according to race. This segregation was alleged to deprive the plaintiffs of the equal protection of the laws under the Fourteenth Amendment. In each of the cases other than the Delaware case, a three-judge federal district court denied relief to the plaintiffs on the so-called "separate but equal" doctrine announced by this Court in Plessy v. Ferguson. Under that doctrine, equality of treatment is accorded when the races are provided substantially equal facilities, even though these facilities be separate. In the Delaware case, the Supreme Court of Delaware adhered to that doctrine, but ordered that the plaintiffs be admitted to the white schools because of their superiority to the Negro schools.

The plaintiffs contend that segregated public schools are not "equal" and cannot be made "equal," and that hence they are deprived of the equal protection of the laws. Because of the obvious importance of the question presented, the Court took jurisdiction. Argument was heard in the 1952 Term, and reargument was heard this Term on certain questions propounded by the Court.

Reargument was largely devoted to the circumstances surrounding the adoption of the Fourteenth Amendment in 1868. It covered exhaustively consideration of the Amendment in Congress, ratification by the states, then existing practices in racial segregation, and the views of proponents and opponents of the Amendment. This discussion and our own investigation convince us that, although these sources cast some light, it is not enough to resolve the problem with which we are faced. At best, they are inconclusive. The most avid proponents of the post–War Amendments undoubtedly intended them to remove all legal distinctions among "all persons born or naturalized in the United States." Their opponents, just as certainly, were antagonistic to both the letter and the spirit of the Amendments and wished them to have the most limited effect. What others in Congress and the state legislatures had in mind cannot be determined with any degree of certainty.

An additional reason for the inconclusive nature of the Amendment's history, with respect to segregated schools, is the status of public education at that time. In the South, the movement toward free common schools, supported by general taxation, had not yet taken hold. Education of white children was largely in the hands of private groups. Education of Negroes was almost nonexistent, and practically all of the race were illiterate. In fact, any education of Negroes was forbidden by law in some states. Today, in contrast, many Negroes have achieved outstanding success in the arts and sciences as well as in the business and professional world. It is true that public school education at the time of the Amendment had advanced further in the North, but the effect of the Amendment on Northern States was generally ignored in the congressional debates. Even in the North, the conditions of public education did not approximate those existing today. The curriculum was usually rudimentary; ungraded schools were common in rural areas; the school term was but three months a year in many states; and compulsory school attendance was virtually unknown. As a consequence, it is not surprising that there should be so little in the history of the Fourteenth Amendment relating to its intended effect on public education. . . .

In the first cases in this Court construing the Fourteenth Amendment, decided shortly after its adoption, the Court interpreted it as proscribing all state-imposed discriminations against the Negro race. The doctrine of "separate but equal" did not make its appearance in this Court until 1896 in the case of Plessy v. Ferguson, involving not education but transportation. American courts have since labored with the doctrine for over half a century. . . . In the instant cases . . . there are findings below that the Negro and white schools involved have been equalized, or are being equalized, with respect to buildings, curricula, qualifications and salaries of teachers, and other "tangible" factors. Our decision, therefore, cannot turn on merely a comparison of these tangible factors in the Negro and white schools involved in each of the cases. We must look instead to the effect of segregation itself on public education.

In approaching this problem, we cannot turn the clock back to 1868 when the Amendment was adopted, or even to 1896 when Plessy v. Ferguson was written. We must consider public education in the light of its full development and its present place in American life throughout the Nation. Only in this way can it be determined if segregation in public schools deprives these plaintiffs of the equal protection of the laws.

Today, education is perhaps the most important function of state and local governments. Compulsory school attendance laws and the great expenditures for education both demonstrate our recognition of the importance of education to our democratic society. It is required in the performance of our most basic public responsibilities, even service in the armed forces. It is the very foundation of good citizenship. Today it is a principal instrument in awakening the child to cultural values, in preparing him for later professional training, and in helping him to adjust normally to his environment. In these days, it is doubtful that any child may reasonably be expected to succeed in life if he is denied the opportunity of an education. Such an opportunity, where the state has undertaken to provide it, is a right which must be made available to all on equal terms.

We come then to the question presented: Does segregation of children in public schools solely on the basis of race, even though the physical facilities and other "tangible" factors may be equal, deprive the children of the minority group of equal educational opportunities? We believe that it does.

In Sweatt v. Painter, in finding that a segregated law school for Negroes could not provide them equal educational opportunities, this Court relied in large part on "those qualities which are incapable of objective measurement but which make for greatness in a law school." In McLaurin v. Oklahoma State Regents, the Court, in requiring that a Negro admitted to a white graduate school be treated like all other students, again resorted to intangible considerations: ". . . his ability to study, to engage in discussions and

exchange views with other students, and, in general, to learn his profession." Such considerations apply with added force to children in grade and high schools. To separate them from others of similar age and qualifications solely because of their race generates a feeling of inferiority as to their status in the community that may affect their hearts and minds in a way unlikely ever to be undone. The effect of this separation on their educational opportunities was well stated by a finding in the Kansas case by a court which nevertheless felt compelled to rule against the Negro plaintiffs:

> Segregation of white and colored children in public schools has a detrimental effect upon the colored children. The impact is greater when it has the sanction of the law; for the policy of separating the races is usually interpreted as denoting the inferiority of the negro group. A sense of inferiority affects the motivation of a child to learn. Segregation with the sanction of law, therefore, has a tendency to [retard] the educational and mental development of negro children and to deprive them of some of the benefits they would receive in a racial[ly] integrated school system.

Whatever may have been the extent of psychological knowledge at the time of Plessy v. Ferguson, this finding is amply supported by modern authority.* Any language in Plessy v. Ferguson contrary to this finding is rejected.

We conclude that in the field of public education the doctrine of "separate but equal" has no place. Separate educational facilities are inherently unequal. Therefore, we hold that the plaintiffs and others similarly situated for whom the actions have been brought are, by reason of the segregation complained of, deprived of the equal protection of the laws guaranteed by the Fourteenth Amendment. This disposition makes unnecessary any discussion whether such segregation also violates the Due Process Clause of the Fourteenth Amendment.

Because these are class actions, because of the wide applicability of this decision, and because of the great variety of local conditions, the formulation of decrees in these cases presents problems of considerable complexity. On reargument, the consideration of appropriate relief was necessarily subordinated to the primary question—the constitutionality of segregation in public education. We have now announced that such segregation is a denial of the equal protection of the laws. In order that we may have the full assistance of the parties in formulating decrees, the cases will be restored to the docket, and the parties are requested to present further argument on [implementation of the Court's decree]. . . .

---

*K[enneth] B. Clark, Effect of Prejudice and Discrimination on Personality Development (Midcentury White House Conference on Children and Youth, 1950); Witmer and Kotinsky, Personality in the Making (1952), c. VI; Deutscher and Chein, The Psychological Effects of Enforced Segregation: A Survey of Social Science Opinion, 26 J. Psychol. 259 (1948); Chein, What are the Psychological Effects of Segregation Under Conditions of Equal Facilities?, 3 Int. J. Opinion and Attitude Res. 229 (1949); Brameld, Educational Costs, in Discrimination and National Welfare (MacIver, ed., (1949), 44–48); Frazier, The Negro in the United States (1949), 674–681. And see generally Myrdal, An American Dilemma (1944).

Brown v. Board of Education of Topeka, Kansas [II]
349 U.S. 294 (1955)

"Full implementation of these constitutional principles may require solution of varied local school problems....
The cases are remanded to the District Courts to ... enter such orders ... as are necessary and proper to admit
to public schools on a racially nondiscriminatory basis with all deliberate speed the parties to these cases."

Mr. Chief Justice Warren delivered the opinion of the Court.

These cases were decided on May 17, 1954. The opinions of that date, declaring the fundamental principle that racial discrimination in public education is unconstitutional, are incorporated herein by reference. All provisions of federal, state, or local law requiring or permitting such discrimination must yield to this principle. There remains for consideration the manner in which relief is to be accorded. . . .

Full implementation of these constitutional principles may require solution of varied local school problems. School authorities have the primary responsibility for elucidating, assessing, and solving these problems; courts will have to consider whether the action of school authorities constitutes good faith implementation of the governing constitutional principles. Because of their proximity to local conditions and the possible need for further hearings, the courts which originally heard these cases can best perform this judicial appraisal. Accordingly, we believe it appropriate to remand the cases to those courts.

In fashioning and effectuating the decrees, the courts will be guided by equitable principles. Traditionally, equity has been characterized by a practical flexibility in shaping its remedies and by a facility for adjusting and reconciling public and private needs. These cases call for the exercise of these traditional attributes of equity power. At stake is the personal interest of the plaintiffs in admission to public schools as soon as practicable on a nondiscriminatory basis. To effectuate this interest may call for elimination of a variety of obstacles in making the transition to school systems operated in accordance with the constitutional principles set forth in our May 17, 1954, decision. Courts of equity may properly take into account the public interest in the elimination of such obstacles in a systematic and effective manner. But it should go without saying that the vitality of these constitutional principles cannot be allowed to yield simply because of disagreement with them.

While giving weight to these public and private considerations, the courts will require that the defendants make a prompt and reasonable start toward full compliance with our May 17, 1954, ruling. Once such a start has been made, the courts may find that additional time is necessary to carry out the ruling in an effective manner. The burden rests upon the defendants to establish that such time is necessary in the public interest and is consistent with good faith compliance at the earliest practicable date. To that end, the courts may consider problems related to administration, arising from the physical condition of the school plant, the school transportation system, personnel, revision of school districts and attendance areas into compact units to achieve a system of determining admission to the public schools on a nonracial basis, and revision of local laws and regulations which may be necessary in solving the foregoing problems. They will also consider the adequacy of any plans the defendants may propose to meet these problems and to effectuate a transition to a racially nondiscriminatory school system. During this period of transition, the courts will retain jurisdiction of these cases.

The judgments below ... are accordingly reversed, and the cases are remanded to the District Courts to take such proceedings and enter such orders and decrees consistent with this opinion as are necessary and proper to admit to public schools on a racially nondiscriminatory basis with all deliberate speed the parties to these cases. . . .

It is so ordered.

Cooper v. Aaron
358 U.S. 1 (1958)

"The constitutional rights of [black children] are not to be sacrificed or yielded to the violence and disorder
which have followed upon the actions of the Governor and Legislature.... Thus law and order here
are not to be preserved by depriving the Negro children of their constitutional rights.... No state
legislator or executive or judicial officer can war against the Constitution."

The Question:	Can a federal judge, on the ground that the integration of a public high school in Little Rock, Arkansas, will create further "chaos, bedlam, and turmoil" in the city's schools, suspend further integration for at least two years?
The Arguments:	PRO

The integration of Central High School in Little Rock, through a court order that nine black students be admitted in September 1957, caused an outbreak of disorder, both inside and outside the school, that resulted in the dispatch of federal troops to keep order and protect the black students. Nonetheless, the integration of Central High caused such "chaos, bedlam, and turmoil" that a federal judge made a reasonable decision to delay any further integration of Little Rock's schools for a period of two years. Without such delays, the public schools may well be destroyed for students of both races. The decisions of federal district judges, who are closest to the scene, should not be disturbed so long as their rulings have a basis in the evidence before the court.

CON

The "chaos, bedlam, and turmoil" at Central High were caused, not by the nine black students who have a constitutional right to attend that school, but by the defiant and inflammatory acts of the Arkansas legislature, Governor Orval Faubus, and the white segregationists who heeded their calls for resistance to federal court orders. These officials have violated their oaths to defend the Constitution and deserve the harshest condemnation. Upholding a judicial order to delay further integration simply because state officials and some whites refuse to obey the law would send a message to officials in other states and cities that they, too, can defy lawful judicial orders with impunity.

BACKGROUND

What good is the Constitution if government officials refuse to obey its commands? More to the point, what if they defy judicial orders to carry out these commands? The justices who served under Chief Justice Warren—including three who joined the Court after *Brown* was decided—faced that momentous question in 1958, a year after federal troops quelled an armed rebellion against the admission of nine black students to Central High School in Little Rock, Arkansas. The refusal of Arkansas officials to obey federal judicial orders produced a case, known as *Cooper v. Aaron*, that tested not only the Court's resolve but also the nation's commitment to the rule of law.

In a real sense, the greatest responsibility for the Little Rock insurrection in 1957 lay with President Eisenhower, who had pointedly declined in 1956 to support the *Brown* decision. "I think it makes no difference whether or not I endorse it," he told reporters. "It is difficult through law and through force to change a man's heart," he added. Statements like these created a vacuum of leadership, which demagogues quickly rushed to fill.

One Southern politician, however, did not immediately join the Dixiecrats who urged "massive resistance" to the *Brown* decision. Arkansas governor Orval Faubus, elected as a racial "moderate" in 1954, added black members to state boards and Democratic Party committees. The rural Arkansas town of Hoxie ended its separate school system in June 1955. Even before the Supreme Court issued its second *Brown* opinion, the Little Rock school board adopted a plan for "phased" integration, beginning with the admission of black students to prestigious Central High in September 1957. Integration of other high schools, then junior highs, and finally elementary schools would be

"phased in" over a ten-year period. The glacial pace of the Little Rock plan failed to satisfy the Arkansas NAACP, which filed suit against the board in February 1956. Six months later, federal judge John E. Miller endorsed the ten-year plan as a "good-faith" effort to "ultimately bring about a school system not based on color distinctions." The Eighth Circuit appellate court in St. Louis upheld Miller's decision and cleared a path for nine black students to enter Central High on September 3, 1957.

Although most whites in Little Rock supported the school board's "phased integration" plan, news reports of the judicial order to integrate Central High inflamed the city's racial bigots, who began waving Confederate battle flags and vowed to block the school's doors to black students. Holding his finger to political winds that had blown up to gale force, Governor Faubus shed his "moderate" mask and began railing against federal judges. The night before the "Little Rock Nine" were set to begin school, Faubus spoke to the state on television. Warning that "blood will run in the streets" if the black students entered Central High, Faubus announced that he had ordered National Guard troops to surround the school and keep them out. The next morning, eight of the nine gathered at the home of Daisy Bates, the young president of the state's NAACP chapters. They left in station wagons for the short drive to their new school. Fifteen-year-old Elizabeth Eckford did not show up at Daisy Bates's home. Walking alone, holding her head high, she tried to enter Central High and was turned away by soldiers with bayonets. A menacing crowd surrounded Elizabeth and began yelling, "Get her! Lynch her!" Someone hollered, "Get a rope and drag her over to this tree!" Protected by a white NAACP member, she finally escaped the mob on a city bus.

Americans across the country witnessed Elizabeth Eckford's dignity in the face of lynch-mob hysteria on their television screens. Many people had never seen the face of racism so clearly, and could not believe that "a man's heart" could hold so much hatred for anyone's child. The public also watched President Eisenhower playing golf in Newport, Rhode Island, unwilling to interrupt his vacation to deal with the most serious threat to federal authority since the Civil War. Pressure mounted on Eisenhower to intervene, but he took no action. National Guardsmen blocked Central High's doors to the Little Rock Nine until September 20, when a federal judge ordered Governor Faubus to remove the Guardsmen. Little Rock police then escorted the black students into the school, but an unruly mob stormed the building and the nine youngsters barely escaped with their lives. Facing the prospect of televised lynchings, Eisenhower finally ordered army airborne troops into Little Rock. The city's racists lacked the guts to battle paratroopers, and the Little Rock Nine finally began their classes. During the remainder of the school year, a band of white students harassed them unmercifully, while school officials turned their heads. On May 27, 1958, Ernest Green became the first black graduate of Central High; he later served as assistant labor secretary in Jimmy Carter's cabinet.

Also in May 1958, the Little Rock school board asked federal judge Harry Lemley to delay any further integration until January 1961. The board's lawyers argued that school integration "runs counter to the ingrained attitudes" of many Little Rock whites. They also pointed to Governor Faubus, who had persuaded the Arkansas legislature to pass laws authorizing him to take over local school boards that admitted any black students to white schools. Faubus had also issued statements that the *Brown* decisions had no force in Arkansas. Judge Lemley heard the board's witnesses—all white—testify about the "chaos, bedlam, and turmoil" at Central High. He did not ask who had caused the chaos, but he granted the board's petition on June 20, 1958. Lemley's move precipitated a legal storm, as NAACP lawyers rushed between St. Louis, Little Rock, and Washington. They sought and obtained a stay of Judge Lemley's order from the Eighth Circuit appellate court, which reversed his order after a hearing. But the appellate judges later changed their minds and reinstated Lemley's order. The NAACP lawyers then asked the Supreme Court to step in and end the legal chaos. Although the justices had scattered around the country during their summer recess, Chief Justice Warren summoned them back to Washington for a "special term" on August 28. Little Rock schools were scheduled to open on September 15, and Warren wanted to decide the case before the class bells rang.

William Cooper, the Little Rock school board president, and John Aaron, first in alphabetical order of the black plaintiffs, gave their names to *Cooper v. Aaron.* But the real parties were Orval Faubus and Earl Warren; this case was really a contest for supremacy between the defiant governor and the determined Chief Justice. All nine justices had answered Warren's call and returned to Washington for the oral arguments, which began with an appeal for delay by Richard Butler, the board's lawyer. "All we're asking," he said, "is for time to work this thing out in a climate of calm rather than in a climate of hysteria." Earl Warren listened politely to Butler's assurance that he was not speaking for the "law

defiers" in Little Rock. "I know you're not," Warren soothingly replied.

The Chief's soothing smile quickly faded when Butler spoke for the chief law defier in Arkansas. "The point I'm making is this," Butler said, "that if the governor of any state says that a United States Supreme Court decision is not the law of the land, the people of that state, until it is really resolved, have a doubt in their mind and a right to have a doubt." Warren exploded. "I have never heard such an argument made in a court of justice before," he shot back, "and I've tried many a case, over many a year. I never heard a lawyer say that the statement of a governor, as to what was legal or illegal, should control the action of any court." The former California governor now wore a black robe, and would not tolerate this challenge to his authority.

Russell Baker, covering the hearing for the *New York Times,* reported that Thurgood Marshall took the podium with "the hint of a scowl on his face, looking like Othello in a tan business suit." Marshall was just as angry as the Chief Justice, and his voice rose as he spoke for Little Rock's black children. "I think we need to think about these children and their parents," he said, "these Negro children that went through this every day, and their parents that stayed at home wondering what was happening to their children, listening to the radio about the bomb threats and all that business. I don't know how anybody under the sun could say, that after all those children and those families went through for a year to tell them: All you have done is gone. You fought for what you considered to be democracy and you lost. And you go back to the segregated school from which you came. I just don't believe it."

The justices did not believe it either, and they scolded Governor Faubus with a single voice. On September 12, the day after the Court heard a second round of arguments that largely rehashed the issues, the Court issued an unsigned order reversing Judge Lemley's two-year delay. Central High could now begin classes, with two thousand white and nine black students. On September 29, the Court handed down its written opinion in *Cooper v. Aaron.* Never before—or since—has every justice personally signed an opinion. Richard Butler had argued that Governor Faubus's claim that *Brown* had no effect in Arkansas left its citizens "in actual doubt as to what the law is." Warren proposed the collective opinion to remove any doubt.

The justices professed astonishment that Faubus and Arkansas lawmakers would claim "that they are not bound by our holding in the *Brown* case." The Court's opinion treated the defiant officials like schoolroom dunces. It was their "determination to resist this Court's decision in the *Brown* case" which had "brought about violent resistance to that decision in Arkansas," the justices stated. Had the Arkansas officials not read the Constitution? Article VI "makes the Constitution the 'supreme Law of the Land.'" Had they not all taken oaths "to support this Constitution?" The justices took out their rulers: "No state legislator or executive or judicial officer can war against the Constitution without violating his undertaking to support it." And who had the power to enforce the Constitution? "It follows that the interpretation of the Fourteenth Amendment enunciated in the *Brown* case is the supreme law of the land," the justices told the Arkansas officials. Looking beyond Little Rock, they demanded "the obedience of the States" to "the command of the Constitution" that federal court orders must be obeyed.

Despite this stern lecture, the Arkansas officials did not learn their lesson. Defying the Court once again, Governor Faubus and the state legislature closed down Little Rock's schools for an entire year. Going back to federal court, NAACP lawyers won a ruling in 1959 that reopened the schools. By spring 1960, Central High had fifteen hundred white students and just five blacks. Litigation dragged on for years, raising the question once again: What good is the Constitution if government officials refuse to obey its commands? What the Arkansas politicians finally obeyed was not the Supreme Court, but the commands of public opinion. Little Rock's voters finally tired of chaos and turmoil in their schools and voted in a new board that moved toward compliance with court orders (Irons, 1999).

Opinion of the Court by The Chief Justice, MR. JUSTICE BLACK, MR. JUSTICE FRANKFURTER, MR. JUSTICE DOUGLAS, MR. JUSTICE BURTON, MR. JUSTICE CLARK, MR. JUSTICE HARLAN, MR. JUSTICE BRENNAN, and MR. JUSTICE WHITTAKER.

As this case reaches us it raises questions of the highest importance to the maintenance of our federal system of government. It necessarily involves a claim by the Governor and Legislature of a State that there is no duty on state officials to obey federal court orders resting on this Court's considered interpretation of the United States Constitution. Specifically it involves actions by the Governor and Legislature of Arkansas upon the premise that they are not bound by our holding in Brown v. Board of Education. That holding was that the Fourteenth Amendment forbids States to use their governmental powers to bar children on racial grounds from attending schools where there is state participation through any arrangement, management, funds or property. We are urged to uphold a suspension of the Little Rock School Board's plan to do away with segregated public schools in Little Rock until state laws and efforts to upset and nullify our holding in Brown v. Board of Education have been further challenged and tested in the courts. We reject these contentions. . . .

The following are the facts and circumstances so far as necessary to show how the legal questions are presented. . . . On May 20, 1954, three days after the first Brown opinion, the Little Rock District School Board adopted, and on May 23, 1954, made public, a statement of policy entitled "Supreme Court Decision—Segregation in Public Schools." In this statement the Board recognized that "It is our responsibility to comply with Federal Constitutional Requirements and we intend to do so when the Supreme Court of the United States outlines the method to be followed." Thereafter the Board . . . instructed the Superintendent of Schools to prepare a plan for desegregation, and approved such a plan on May 24, 1955, seven days before the second Brown opinion. The plan provided for desegregation at the senior high school level (grades 10 through 12) as the first stage. Desegregation at the junior high and elementary levels was to follow. It was contemplated that desegregation at the high school level would commence in the fall of 1957, and the expectation was that complete desegregation of the school system would be accomplished by 1963. . . .

While the School Board was thus going forward with its preparation for desegregating the Little Rock school system, other state authorities, in contrast, were actively pursuing a program designed to perpetuate in Arkansas the system of racial segregation which this Court had held violated the Fourteenth Amendment. First came, in November 1956, an amendment to the State Constitution flatly commanding the Arkansas General Assembly to oppose "in every Constitutional manner the un-constitutional desegregation decisions . . . of the United States Supreme Court." . . . Pursuant to this state constitutional command, a law relieving school children from compulsory attendance at racially mixed schools [was enacted]. . . .

The School Board and the Superintendent of Schools nevertheless continued with preparations to carry out the first stage of the desegregation program. Nine Negro children were scheduled for admission in September 1957 to Central High School, which has more than two thousand students. Various administrative measures, designed to assure the smooth transition of this first stage of desegregation, were undertaken.

On September 2, 1957, the day before these Negro students were to enter Central High, the school authorities were met with drastic opposing action on the part of the Governor of Arkansas who dispatched units of the Arkansas National Guard to the Central High School grounds and placed the school "off limits" to colored students. . . . The Governor's action caused the School Board to request the Negro students on September 2 not to attend the high school "until the legal dilemma was solved." The next day, September 3, 1957, the Board petitioned the District Court for instructions, and the court, after a hearing, found that the Board's request of the Negro students to stay away from the high school had been made because of the stationing of the military guards by the state authorities. The court determined that this was not a reason for departing from the approved plan, and ordered the School Board and Superintendent to proceed with it.

On the morning of the next day, September 4, 1957, the Negro children attempted to enter the high school but, as the District Court later found, units of the Arkansas National Guard "acting pursuant to the Governor's order, stood shoulder to shoulder at the school grounds and thereby forcibly prevented the 9 Negro students . . . from entering," as they continued to do every school day during the following three weeks.

That same day, September 4, 1957, the United States Attorney for the Eastern District of Arkansas was requested by the District Court to begin an immediate investigation in order to fix responsibility for the interference with the orderly implementation of the District Court's direction to carry out the desegregation program. . . . [T]he Attorney General of the United States, at the District Court's request, entered the proceedings and filed a petition on behalf of the United States, as amicus curiae, to enjoin the Governor of Arkansas and officers of the Arkansas National Guard from further attempts to prevent obedience to the court's order. After hearings on the petition, the District Court . . . granted a preliminary injunction on September 20, 1957, enjoining the Governor and the officers of the Guard from preventing the attendance of Negro children at Central High

School, and from otherwise obstructing or interfering with the orders of the court in connection with the plan. The National Guard was then withdrawn from the school.

The next school day was Monday, September 23, 1957. The Negro children entered the high school that morning under the protection of the Little Rock Police Department and members of the Arkansas State Police. But the officers caused the children to be removed from the school during the morning because they had difficulty controlling a large and demonstrating crowd which had gathered at the high school. On September 25, however, the President of the United States dispatched federal troops to Central High School and admission of the Negro students to the school was thereby effected. Regular army troops continued at the high school until November 27, 1957. They were then replaced by federalized National Guardsmen who remained throughout the balance of the school year. Eight of the Negro students remained in attendance at the school throughout the school year.

We come now to the aspect of the proceedings presently before us. On February 20, 1958, the School Board and the Superintendent of Schools filed a petition in the District Court seeking a postponement of their program for desegregation. Their position in essence was that because of extreme public hostility, which they stated had been engendered largely by the official attitudes and actions of the Governor and the Legislature, the maintenance of a sound educational program at Central High School, with the Negro students in attendance, would be impossible. The Board therefore proposed that the Negro students already admitted to the school be withdrawn and sent to segregated schools, and that all further steps to carry out the Board's desegregation program be postponed for a period later suggested by the Board to be two and one-half years.

After a hearing the District Court granted the relief requested by the Board. Among other things the court found that the past year at Central High School had been attended by conditions of "chaos, bedlam and turmoil"; that there were "repeated incidents of more or less serious violence directed against the Negro students and their property"; . . . and that the situation was "intolerable." The District Court's judgment was dated June 20, 1958. The Negro respondents appealed to the Court of Appeals for the Eighth Circuit and also sought there a stay of the District Court's judgment. . . . The Court of Appeals . . . reversed the District Court [but] stayed its mandate to permit the School Board to petition this Court for certiorari. . . . Recognizing the vital importance of a decision of the issues in time to permit arrangements to be made for the 1958–1959 school year, we convened in Special Term [and heard oral argument on August 28 and September 11, 1958]. . . .

[T]he record before us [shows that the conditions depicted above] are directly traceable to the actions of legislators and executive officials of the State of Arkansas, taken in their official capacities, which reflect their own determination to resist this Court's decision in the Brown case and which have brought about violent resistance to that decision in Arkansas. In its petition for certiorari filed in this Court, the School Board itself describes the situation in this language: "The legislative, executive, and judicial departments of the state government opposed the desegregation of Little Rock schools by enacting laws, calling out troops, making statements vilifying federal law and federal courts, and failing to utilize state law enforcement agencies and judicial processes to maintain public peace."

One may well sympathize with the position of the Board in the face of the frustrating conditions which have confronted it, but, regardless of the Board's good faith, the actions of the other state agencies responsible for those conditions compel us to reject the Board's legal position. Had Central High School been under the direct management of the State itself, it could hardly be suggested that those immediately in charge of the school should be heard to assert their own good faith as a legal excuse for delay in implementing the constitutional rights of these respondents, when vindication of those rights was rendered difficult or impossible by the actions of other state officials. The situation here is in no different posture because the members of the School Board and the Superintendent of Schools are local officials; from the point of view of the Fourteenth Amendment, they stand in this litigation as the agents of the State.

The constitutional rights of respondents are not to be sacrificed or yielded to the violence and disorder which have followed upon the actions of the Governor and Legislature. . . . Thus law and order are not here to be preserved by depriving the Negro children of their constitutional rights. The record before us clearly establishes that the growth of the Board's difficulties to a magnitude beyond its unaided power to control is the product of state action. Those difficulties, as counsel for the Board forthrightly conceded on the oral argument in this Court, can also be brought under control by state action.

The controlling legal principles are plain. The command of the Fourteenth Amendment is that no "State" shall deny to any person within its jurisdiction the equal protection of the laws." . . . Thus the prohibitions of the Fourteenth Amendment extend to all action of the State denying equal protection of the laws; whatever the agency of the State taking the action, or whatever the guise in which it is taken. In short, the constitutional rights of children not to be discriminated against in school admission on grounds of race or color declared by this Court in the Brown case can neither be nullified openly and directly by state legislators or state executive or judicial officers, nor nullified indirectly by them through evasive schemes for segregation whether attempted "ingeniously or ingenuously." . . .

What has been said, in the light of the facts developed, is enough to dispose of the case. However, we should answer the premise of the actions of the Governor and Legislature that they are not bound by our holding in the Brown case. It is necessary only to recall some basic constitutional propositions which are settled doctrine.

Article VI of the Constitution makes the Constitution the "supreme Law of the Land." In 1803, Chief Justice Marshall, speaking for a unanimous Court, referring to the Constitution as "the fundamental and paramount law of the nation," declared in the notable case of Marbury v. Madison, that "It is emphatically the province and duty of the judicial department to say what the law is." This decision declared the basic principle that the federal judiciary is supreme in the exposition of the law of the Constitution, and that principle has ever since been respected by this Court and the Country as a permanent and indispensable feature of our constitutional system. It follows that the interpretation of the Fourteenth Amendment enunciated by this Court in the Brown case is the supreme law of the land, and Art. VI of the Constitution makes it of binding effect on the States "any Thing in the Constitution or Laws of any State to the Contrary notwithstanding." Every state legislator and executive and judicial officer is solemnly committed by oath . . . "to support this Constitution." . . .

No state legislator or executive or judicial officer can war against the Constitution without violating his undertaking to support it. Chief Justice Marshall spoke for a unanimous Court in saying that: "If the legislatures of the several states may, at will, annul the judgments of the courts of the United States, and destroy the rights acquired under those judgments, the constitution itself becomes a solemn mockery." United States v. Peters. A Governor who asserts a power to nullify a federal court order is similarly restrained. If he had such power, said Chief Justice Hughes, in 1932, also for a unanimous Court, "it is manifest that the fiat of a state Governor, and not the Constitution of the United States, would be the supreme law of the land; that the restrictions of the Federal Constitution upon the exercise of state power would be but impotent phrases. . . ."

It is, of course, quite true that the responsibility for public education is primarily the concern of the States, but it is equally true that such responsibilities, like all other state activity, must be exercised consistently with federal constitutional requirements as they apply to state action. The Constitution created a government dedicated to equal justice under law. The Fourteenth Amendment embodied and emphasized that ideal. State support of segregated schools through any arrangement, management, funds, or property cannot be squared with the Amendment's command that no State shall deny to any person within its jurisdiction the equal protection of the laws. The right of a student not to be segregated on racial grounds in schools so maintained is indeed so fundamental and pervasive that it is embraced in the concept of due process of law. The basic decision in Brown was unanimously reached by this Court only after the case had been briefed and twice argued and the issues had been given the most serious consideration. Since the first Brown opinion three new Justices have come to the Court. They are at one with the Justices still on the Court who participated in that basic decision as to its correctness, and that decision is now unanimously reaffirmed. The principles announced in that decision and the obedience of the States to them, according to the command of the Constitution, are indispensable for the protection of the freedoms guaranteed by our fundamental charter for all of us. Our constitutional ideal of equal justice under law is thus made a living truth.

SWANN V. BOARD OF EDUCATION OF CHARLOTTE-MECKLENBURG COUNTY, NORTH CAROLINA
402 U.S. 1 (1971)

"The importance of bus transportation as a normal and accepted tool of educational policy is readily discernible in this case. . . . We find no basis for holding that the local school authorities may not be required to employ bus transportation as one tool of school desegregation. Desegregation plans cannot be limited to the walk-in school."

The Question: Can a federal judge order the large-scale busing of students in a consolidated city-county school district as a means of creating a roughly equivalent racial balance of white and black students in each school?

The Arguments: PRO

The school district in this case, which had operated segregated schools until 1965, has a school population that is 71-percent white and 29-percent black. However, more than two-thirds of the black students attend schools that are either all black or more than 99-percent black. This racial imbalance reflects the residential segregation in the city of Charlotte. After considering several plans to reduce racial imbalance, a federal judge ordered a set of remedies, including the large-scale busing of students to achieve a mix of white and black students in each school that reflects the district balance. This remedy is within the powers of federal judges to fashion remedies that will end segregation "root and branch" in public schools.

CON

The federal judge in this case has devised a remedy that is drastic and will undoubtedly contribute to "white flight" from the public schools. Parents of both races are opposed to busing their children, especially those in elementary grades, long distances from their neighborhoods. The Constitution does not require a particular racial balance in each school, but merely that admission of students to any school not be based on race. Other remedies, such as majority-to-minority transfer plans and the creation of magnet schools, will achieve greater racial balance in the district's schools without the wholesale disruption of busing.

BACKGROUND

The case that made busing a heated national issue was filed in 1964 and was decided by the Supreme Court in 1971 under the caption of *Swann v. Charlotte-Mecklenburg Board of Education.* But it really began in September 1957, when a fifteen-year-old black girl named Dorothy Counts started classes at Harding High School in Charlotte, North Carolina. The state's largest city and its commercial hub, Charlotte is home to four-fifths of the residents of Mecklenburg County, which sits on the state's border with South Carolina. The county covers some five hundred square miles, and the suburban and rural areas that surround the city of Charlotte are virtually all white.

Dorothy Counts was one of four black students whose parents had decided to send them to formerly all-white schools, after Charlotte officials announced that students of either race could attend the school closest to their homes. Blacks made up about one-quarter of Charlotte's population in 1957, and most lived in the city's northeast section. Very few black students lived closer to an all-white school than to the black schools they formerly attended, and Dorothy's parents were among the few who took advantage of the "neighborhood school" policy to make their children pioneers in Charlotte's small first step toward integration. This new policy was initiated by Superintendent Elmer Garinger, who gathered his principals in the spring of 1957 and told them firmly that "desegregation is not only the law, it is also right."

Not all whites in Charlotte agreed with Garinger, and some four hundred of them—including many students at Harding High—clogged the street outside the school on the morning of September 4, 1957. Walking beside a family friend, Dorothy Counts was quickly surrounded by shouting protesters who spat on her and screamed racial epithets. Once she entered the school, Dorothy was pushed and baited by white students in the hallways and cafeteria. The next day, newspapers across the country and around the world carried photographs of Dorothy, in a black-and-white checkered dress with a long white bow and crinoline petticoats, looking straight ahead with grim determination as grinning whites, most of them boys in white T-shirts with their sleeves rolled up, swarmed around her.

After one week in Harding High, Dorothy gave up. Her locker had been ransacked, white teachers pointedly ignored her, racial slurs followed her down the hallways, a blackboard eraser hit her in the back, and several boys threw trash on her plate in the cafeteria. When her older brother came to pick Dorothy up, his windshield was shattered by a heavy mock orange, thrown at his car by a group of white boys who laughed and made obscene gestures. That night, after a

meeting at Dorothy's home with Charlotte's black leaders, her father said, "Dot, I really don't think it's worth it." The next day, Herman Counts, a philosophy professor at all-black Johnson C. Smith University in Charlotte, read a statement to a press conference: "It is with compassion for our native land and love for our daughter Dorothy that we withdraw her as a student at Harding High School. As long as we felt she could be protected from bodily injury and insults within the school's walls and upon the school premises, we were willing to grant her desire to study at Harding. . . . Contrary to this optimistic view, her experiences at school on Wednesday disillusioned our faith and left us no alternative."

One of the people who read about Dorothy's ordeal in 1957 and saw the photograph of the gauntlet she faced at Harding High was Darius Swann, a Presbyterian missionary in Allabahad, India. Those images made a lasting impression on Swann, who had studied under Herman Counts in college and greatly admired his former professor. Swann and his wife, Vera, returned to Charlotte in 1964 with their two young children. That fall, they took their six-year-old son, James, to the school nearest their home. Seversville Elementary had several black children in its first-grade classroom, and the Swanns were pleased that James would be attending an integrated school. But they discovered, through a note James brought home after his first day at Seversville, that he had been assigned to an all-black school, Biddleville Elementary. The Swanns learned that their home was located in an attendance district carved out to keep all but a few black children out of Seversville. Darius wrote a letter to the Charlotte-Mecklenburg board of education: "James attended Seversville briefly on August 31 and he liked the school and its atmosphere. We did also and feel that this is where we would like him to be." Swann reminded the board that white students were allowed to transfer out of integrated schools, but that black students could not transfer into these schools. "We hold that the law should be equally binding on both races," Swann wrote. "Otherwise the law is discriminatory."

After the school board rejected their request to transfer James back to the Seversville school, the Swanns contacted Julius Chambers, a young black lawyer who had come to Charlotte in 1964 after completing law school at the University of North Carolina.

Chambers began a practice in Charlotte and immediately began looking for plaintiffs to challenge the "minority-to-majority" transfer policy of the Charlotte-Mecklenburg school district. The city and the surrounding county had merged their districts in 1960, and the combined district in 1964 had more than a hundred schools that housed 84,000 students, about 24,000 of them black.

Julius Chambers filed a lawsuit in federal court in January 1965, claiming that the "minority-to-majority" transfer policy was designed to allow white students who lived closest to a formerly all-black school to escape from integration. The lead plaintiff in the suit was Darius Swann, who had been outraged by the ordeal suffered by Dorothy Counts when integration first began in Charlotte. The complaint that Chambers drafted noted that 88 of the district's 109 schools remained segregated after seven years of token integration—57 had only white students and 31 were all black. Only 6 of the 21 "integrated" schools had more than a dozen black students, and just 11 white children attended a largely black school.

The *Swann* case first came before District Judge Braxton Craven in 1965. Although most lawyers considered him thoughtful and fair, Craven displayed little interest in the case, and held just one brief hearing before he issued a ruling on July 14, the day after the school board's lawyer told the judge that the board was committed to the "ultimate" ending of segregation in the district's schools. Yet, the board had adopted a desegregation plan that retained neighborhood school zoning, and allowed "freedom of choice" transfers for parents who wanted their children out of schools in which their race was the minority. During the hearing, Julius Chambers noted that the board's plan left more than 90 percent of the district's black children in all-black schools. In his brief order, Judge Craven approved the board's plan without change, except for ordering a quicker pace for faculty and staff desegregation. "As a general proposition," Craven wrote, "it is undoubtedly true that one could sit down with the purpose in mind to change [district] lines in order to increase the mixing of the races and accomplish that with some degree of success. I know of no such duty upon either the school board or the district court." The board's plan, of course, did virtually nothing to "increase the mixing of the races" in schools that kept the Jim Crow system intact.

Julius Chambers filed an appeal from Judge Craven's decision, arguing that his decision was "patently erroneous." The Fourth Circuit Court of Appeals upheld the ruling in October 1966, and Chambers decided that a further appeal to the Supreme Court would be futile. Shortly after the Court struck down "freedom of choice" plans in the *Green v. New Kent County* case in 1968, however, Chambers went back to federal court and asked for "further relief" to bring about the "root and branch" elimination of segregation the Supreme Court had ordered in that case. Judge Craven had been elevated to the Fourth Circuit bench in 1968, and Chambers was encouraged that the revived *Swann* case was now before James McMillan, a Harvard Law School graduate who had voted against the exclusion of black lawyers from the North Carolina bar association and served on the board of the Charlotte legal aid society.

Judge McMillan took the case seriously and held extensive hearings in March 1969. His first opinion, issued on April 23, noted that segregation in the Charlotte-Mecklenburg schools had declined since Judge Craven's ruling in 1965, but "approximately 14,000 of the 24,000 Negro students still attend schools that are all black, or very nearly all black, and most of the 24,000 have no white teachers." The board's "neighborhood" zoning plan, McMillan wrote, "superimposed on an urban population where Negro residents have become concentrated almost entirely in one quadrant of a city of 270,000, is racially discriminatory." Most of Charlotte's black residents lived in the city's northeast section, and the school board had drawn its attendance zones precisely on the boundaries of the black residential area. McMillan ordered the board to submit a "positive plan" to integrate the schools, adding that it was "free to consider all known ways of desegregation, including busing." He pointedly noted that white parents had not objected when buses were used to maintain segregation. "There is no reason except emotion," he wrote, "why school buses can not be used by the Board to provide the flexibility and economy necessary to desegregate the schools."

Judge McMillan had underestimated the emotion his decision would unleash among whites in Charlotte. William E. Poe, the school board chairman, declared that he was "unequivocally" opposed to busing, and his speeches at civic-group meetings around the city spurred the listeners to organize the Concerned Parents Association, which plastered NO FORCED BUSING bumper stickers on thousands of cars and gathered 67,355 signatures on an antibusing petition that was delivered to the White House. Busing opponents picketed McMillan's home, and he received death threats over the phone and in the mail. Critics overlooked the fact that McMillan had not actually ordered any busing, pending the school board's submission of a plan to accomplish real integration. But the board, led by Poe, dragged its feet until McMillan appointed an expert, Dr. Robert Finger of Rhode Island College, to fashion an integration plan that would produce as closely as possible in each school the district-wide percentages of 79 white and 21 black students. The "Finger Plan" did not substantially change the board's revision of junior and senior high attendance zones, which put black and white students in every school, but kept the black enrollment below 40 percent in each one. An unspoken assumption behind this plan was that few white parents would send their children to a majority-black school, and that a "tipping point" of 40 percent black students became the upper limit of white tolerance.

The Finger Plan departed substantially from the board's proposal for integrating the district's seventy-six elementary schools, which largely retained neighborhood school zoning. His plan "grouped" inner-city black schools with outlying white schools, producing student bodies that ranged from 9 to 38 percent black. The district already bused 23,000 children, about a third of all students; under the Finger Plan, black students in grades one through four would be bused to outlying white schools, and white students in the fifth and sixth grades would ride buses to the inner-city black schools. The Finger Plan would put an additional 13,000 children, most from the grade schools, onto buses. Ruling on February 5, 1970, Judge McMillan rejected the board's neighborhood school proposal and adopted the Finger Plan. Citing the Supreme Court ruling in *Alexander v. Holmes County*, McMillan ordered the board to implement the Finger Plan by April 1, a deadline that sent shock waves through the white community. Leaders of the Concerned Parents Association stepped up their protests, and the board's lawyers filed an appeal with the Fourth Circuit Court of Appeals in Richmond. One of the NAACP lawyers received a blunt message from Judge Braxton Craven, who now sat on the appellate court but recused himself from further proceedings in the *Swann* case. Speaking for his fellow judges,

Craven said: "You guys have led your friend McMillan out on a limb. And we're about to cut it off behind him."

Craven was right. The Fourth Circuit issued a stay of McMillan's order, directing him to hold new hearings and apply a "test of reasonableness" to the busing of grade school children. McMillan conducted the hearings and allowed school board members to vent their hostility to busing, but he refused to budge from the Finger Plan and reinstated his original order on August 7, 1970, with a new deadline of September 9, when schools were scheduled to open in the Charlotte-Mecklenburg district. Reeling from shock, the board's lawyers flew to Washington and asked Chief Justice Warren Burger for a stay of McMillan's order. But he refused to intervene, setting the *Swann* case for argument on October 12. On the morning of September 9, some 525 school buses—including almost 200 that had been hurriedly borrowed from other districts across the state—began rolling along their new routes, carrying thousands of black and white children to new schools. At 8:10 that morning, a bomb scare forced the early dismissal of South Mecklenburg High School. It was the first of six that day, and the bomb scares continued for three months. The Concerned Parents Association had called for a boycott, and more than three thousand white children left the public schools for good, swelling the enrollment of private schools that had few, if any, black students. Community leaders appealed for calm, but tension remained high as lawyers on both sides prepared for a showdown in the Supreme Court.

He oral arguments in *Swann* began on a sour note for the school board's lawyer, William Waggoner, who told the justices he would discuss the issue of racial balance in the district's schools, leaving the question of busing to his colleague, Benjamin Horack. Justice Thurgood Marshall quickly knocked Waggoner off balance, demanding to know if Charlotte had bused "children of tender age" before the 1970 school year. Marshall explained to a puzzled Waggoner that he meant children in grade schools.

"They were busing children of tender age," Waggoner conceded.
"For the purpose of maintaining segregation?" Marshall continued.
"No, sir."
"For what other reason?" Marshall pressed.
"They were bused to get them to school," Waggoner answered, trying to duck the question.
"Did they ever pass a colored school on the way?" Marshall asked.
"We bused white children past black schools, and black children past white schools" Wagonner admitted. "This is incontrovertible."
Marshall landed the punch he had set up with his previous jabs. "So what is wrong with busing them for the purpose of integrating?"
Waggoner countered weakly. "Do two wrongs make a right?"
"Is that the only answer?" Marshall asked.
The board's lawyer could not find a better answer. "I think so, yes, sir," he concluded lamely.

In contrast to Waggoner, who seemed unnerved by Marshall's interrogation, Julius Chambers "was absolutely unflappable; brilliant," one reporter later wrote, "as if he had rehearsed his answers before he ever came in the room—which in fact he had." Chambers, facing the justices for the first time at the age of thirty-four, had endured two "woodshed" sessions before his argument, at both Howard and Columbia law schools. His major point was that the neighborhood school policy and "freedom of choice" plan that the school board adopted to keep black and white children in separate schools. "It would be a rejection of the faith that black children and parents have had in *Brown,* the hope of eventually obtaining a desegregated education, for this Court now to reverse the decision of the District Court and now adopt, sixteen years after *Brown,* a test that would sanction the continued operation of racially segregated schools."

The justices gathered in their conference room to discuss the *Swann* case on October 17, 1970. They all recognized that their decision might have the greatest impact on America's schools since *Brown,* largely because the connection between "state action" in creating and maintaining segregated residential patterns and the segregation that resulted from "neighborhood school" policies was not limited to Southern cities like Charlotte. All of the Court's earlier school cases had come from states in which schools had been segregated by law, known to lawyers as "de jure" segregation. But if the Court accepted the argument of Julius Chambers, Northern cities in which black ghettos had been created by "state action" in zoning, public housing placement, and urban renewal programs could be challenged for the "de facto" segregation of their schools. Cities like Chicago, Philadelphia, Detroit, and scores of smaller Northern cities might become targets for lawsuits and demands that students be bused to achieve the racial balance that Judge McMillan had ordered in Charlotte (Irons, 2002).

MR. CHIEF JUSTICE BURGER delivered the opinion of the Court.

We granted certiorari in this case to review important issues as to the duties of school authorities and the scope of powers of federal courts under this Court's mandates to eliminate racially separate public schools established and maintained by state action Brown v. Board of Education (Brown I).

This case and those argued with it arose in States having a long history of maintaining two sets of schools in a single school system deliberately operated to carry out a governmental policy to separate pupils in schools solely on the basis of race. That was what Brown v. Board of Education was all about. These cases present us with the problem of defining in more precise terms than heretofore the scope of the duty of school authorities and district courts in implementing Brown I and the mandate to eliminate dual systems and establish unitary systems at once. Meanwhile district courts and courts of appeals have struggled in hundreds of cases with a multitude and variety of problems under this Court's general directive. Understandably, in an area of evolving remedies, those courts had to improvise and experiment without detailed or specific guidelines. This Court, in Brown I, appropriately dealt with the large constitutional principles; other federal courts had to grapple with the flinty, intractable realities of day-to-day implementation of those constitutional commands. Their efforts, of necessity, embraced a process of "trial and error," and our effort to formulate guidelines must take into account their experience.

The Charlotte-Mecklenburg school system, the 43d largest in the Nation, encompasses the city of Charlotte and surrounding Mecklenburg County, North Carolina. The area is large—550 square miles—spanning roughly 22 miles east-west and 36 miles north-south. During the 1968–1969 school year the system served more than 84,000 pupils in 107 schools. Approximately 71% of the pupils were found to be white and 29% Negro. As of June 1969 there were approximately 24,000 Negro students in the system, of whom 21,000 attended schools within the city of Charlotte. Two-thirds of those 21,000—approximately 14,000 Negro students—attended 21 schools which were either totally Negro or more than 99% Negro.

This situation came about under a desegregation plan approved by the District Court at the commencement of the present litigation in 1965, based upon geographic zoning with a free-transfer provision. The present proceedings were initiated in September 1968 by petitioner Swann's motion for further relief based on Green v. County School Board (1968), and its companion cases. All parties now agree that in 1969 the system fell short of achieving the unitary school system that those cases require.

The District Court held numerous hearings and received voluminous evidence. In addition to finding certain actions of the school board to be discriminatory, the court also found that residential patterns in the city and county resulted in part from federal, state, and local government action other than school board decisions. School board action based on these patterns, for example, by locating schools in Negro residential areas and fixing the size of the schools to accommodate the needs of immediate neighborhoods, resulted in segregated education. . . . In December 1969 the District Court . . . appointed an expert in education administration, Dr. John Finger, to prepare a desegregation plan. . . . Thereafter in February 1970, the District Court was presented with two alternative pupil assignment plans—the finalized "board plan" and the "Finger plan." . . .

The board plan proposed substantial assignment of Negroes to nine of the system's 10 high schools, producing 17% to 36% Negro population in each. The projected Negro attendance at the 10th school, Independence, was 2%. . . . As for junior high schools, the board plan rezoned the 21 school areas so that in 20 the Negro attendance would range from 0% to 38%. The other school, located in the heart of the Negro residential area, was left with an enrollment of 90% Negro. The board plan with respect to elementary schools relied entirely upon gerrymandering of geographic zones. More than half of the Negro elementary pupils were left in nine schools that were 86% to 100% Negro; approximately half of the white elementary pupils were assigned to schools 86% to 100% white.

The Finger plan . . . adopted the school board zoning plan for senior high schools with one modification: it required that an additional 300 Negro students be transported from the Negro residential area of the city to the nearly all-white Independence High School. The Finger plan for the junior high schools employed much of the rezoning plan of the board, combined with the creation of nine "satellite" zones. Under the satellite plan, inner-city Negro students were assigned by attendance zones to nine outlying predominately white junior high schools, thereby substantially desegregating every junior high school in the system. The Finger plan departed from the board plan chiefly in its handling of the system's 76 elementary schools. Rather than relying solely upon geographic zoning, Dr. Finger proposed use of zoning, pairing, and grouping techniques, with the result that student bodies throughout the system would range from 9% to 38% Negro. . . . Under the Finger plan, nine inner-city Negro schools were grouped in this manner with 24 suburban white schools.

On February 5, 1970, the District Court adopted the board plan, as modified by Dr. Finger, for the junior and senior high schools. The court rejected the board elementary school plan and adopted the Finger plan as presented. . . . On appeal the Court of Appeals affirmed the District Court's order as to . . . the secondary school plans, but vacated the order respecting elementary schools. While agreeing that the District Court properly disapproved the board plan concerning these schools, the Court of Appeals feared that the pairing and grouping of elementary schools would place an unreasonable burden on the board and the system's pupils. The case was remanded to the District Court for reconsideration and submission of further plans . . . The District Court, by order dated August 7, 1970, directed that the Finger plan remain in effect. . . .

None of the parties before us questions the Court's 1955 holding in Brown II, that "School authorities have the primary responsibility for elucidating, assessing, and solving these problems; courts will have to consider whether the action of school authorities constitutes good faith implementation of the governing constitutional principles." . . . Over the 16 years since Brown II, many difficulties were encountered in implementation of the basic constitutional requirement that the State not discriminate between public school children on the basis of their race. Nothing in our national experience prior to 1955 prepared anyone for dealing with changes and adjustments of the magnitude and complexity encountered since then. Deliberate resistance of some to the Court's mandates has impeded the good-faith efforts of others to bring school systems into compliance. The detail and nature of these dilatory tactics have been noted frequently by this Court and other courts.

By the time the Court considered Green v. County School Board in 1968, very little progress had been made in many areas where dual school systems had historically been maintained by operation of state laws. In Green, the Court was confronted with a record of a freedom-of-choice program that the District Court had found to operate in fact to preserve a dual system more than a decade after Brown II. . . . The objective today remains to eliminate from the public schools all vestiges of state-imposed segregation. Segregation was the evil struck down by Brown I as contrary to the equal protection guarantees of the Constitution. That was the violation sought to be corrected by the remedial measures of Brown II. That was the basis for the holding in Green that school authorities are "clearly charged with the affirmative duty to take whatever steps might be necessary to convert to a unitary system in which racial discrimination would be eliminated root and branch."

If school authorities fail in their affirmative obligations under these holdings, judicial authority may be invoked. Once a right and a violation have been shown, the scope of a district court's equitable powers to remedy past wrongs is broad, for breadth and flexibility are inherent in equitable remedies. . . .

The central issue in this case is that of student assignment, and there are essentially four problem areas:

(1) to what extent racial balance or racial quotas may be used as an implement in a remedial order to correct a previously segregated system;

(2) whether every all-Negro and all-white school must be eliminated as an indispensable part of a remedial process of desegregation;

(3) what the limits are, if any, on the rearrangement of school districts and attendance zones, as a remedial measure; and

(4) what the limits are, if any, on the use of transportation facilities to correct state-enforced racial school segregation.

(1) Racial Balances or Racial Quotas.

The constant theme and thrust of every holding from Brown I to date is that state-enforced separation of races in public schools is discrimination that violates the Equal Protection Clause. The remedy commanded was to dismantle dual school systems. . . . Our objective in dealing with the issues presented by these cases is to see that school authorities exclude no pupil of a racial minority from any school, directly or indirectly, on account of race; it does not and cannot embrace all the problems of racial prejudice, even when those problems contribute to disproportionate racial concentrations in some schools. In this case . . . the District Court [directed] "that efforts should be made to reach a 71-29 ratio in the various schools so that there will be no basis for contending that one school is racially different from the others. . . ." . . . The District Judge went on to acknowledge that variation "from that norm may be unavoidable." This contains intimations that the "norm" is a fixed mathematical racial balance reflecting the pupil constituency of the system. If we were to read the holding of the District Court to require, as a matter of substantive constitutional right, any particular degree of racial balance or mixing, that approach would be disapproved and we would be obliged to reverse. The constitutional command to desegregate schools does not mean that every school in every community must always reflect the racial composition of the school system as a whole. . . .

(2) One-race Schools.

The record in this case reveals the familiar phenomenon that in metropolitan areas minority groups are often found concentrated in one part of the city. In some circumstances certain schools may remain all or largely of one race until new schools can be provided or neighborhood patterns change. Schools all or predominately of one race in a district of mixed population will require close scrutiny to determine that school assignments are not part of state-enforced segregation.

In light of the above, it should be clear that the existence of some small number of one-race, or virtually one-race, schools within a district is not in and of itself the mark of a system that still practices segregation by law. . . . Where the school authority's proposed plan for conversion from a dual to a unitary system contemplates the continued existence of some schools that are all or predominately of one race, they have the burden of showing that such school assignments are gen-

uinely nondiscriminatory. The court should scrutinize such schools, and the burden upon the school authorities will be to satisfy the court that their racial composition is not the result of present or past discriminatory action on their part. . . .

(3) Remedial Altering of Attendance Zones.

The maps submitted in these cases graphically demonstrate that one of the principal tools employed by school planners and by courts to break up the dual school system has been a frank—and sometimes drastic—gerrymandering of school districts and attendance zones. An additional step was pairing, "clustering," or "grouping" of schools with attendance assignments made deliberately to accomplish the transfer of Negro students out of formerly segregated Negro schools and transfer of white students to formerly all-Negro schools. More often than not, these zones are neither compact nor contiguous; indeed they may be on opposite ends of the city. As an interim corrective measure, this cannot be said to be beyond the broad remedial powers of a court.

Absent a constitutional violation there would be no basis for judicially ordering assignment of students on a racial basis. All things being equal, with no history of discrimination, it might well be desirable to assign pupils to schools nearest their homes. But all things are not equal in a system that has been deliberately constructed and maintained to enforce racial segregation. The remedy for such segregation may be administratively awkward, inconvenient, and even bizarre in some situations and may impose burdens on some; but all awkwardness and inconvenience cannot be avoided in the interim period when remedial adjustments are being made to eliminate the dual school systems. . . .

(4) Transportation of Students.

The scope of permissible transportation of students as an implement of a remedial decree has never been defined by this Court and by the very nature of the problem it cannot be defined with precision. No rigid guidelines as to student transportation can be given for application to the infinite variety of problems presented in thousands of situations. Bus transportation has been an integral part of the public education system for years, and was perhaps the single most important factor in the transition from the one-room schoolhouse to the consolidated school. Eighteen million of the Nation's public school children, approximately 39%, were transported to their schools by bus in 1969–1970 in all parts of the country.

The importance of bus transportation as a normal and accepted tool of educational policy is readily discernible in this case. The Charlotte school authorities did not purport to assign students on the basis of geographically drawn zones until 1965 and then they allowed almost unlimited transfer privileges. The District Court's conclusion that assignment of children to the school nearest their home serving their grade would not produce an effective dismantling of the dual system is supported by the record. Thus the remedial techniques used in the District Court's order were within that court's power to provide equitable relief; implementation of the decree is well within the capacity of the school authority.

The decree provided that the buses used to implement the plan would operate on direct routes. Students would be picked up at schools near their homes and transported to the schools they were to attend. The trips for elementary school pupils average about seven miles and the District Court found that they would take "not over 35 minutes at the most." This system compares favorably with the transportation plan previously operated in Charlotte under which each day 23,600 students on all grade levels were transported an average of 15 miles one way for an average trip requiring over an hour. In these circumstances, we find no basis for holding that the local school authorities may not be required to employ bus transportation as one tool of school desegregation. Desegregation plans cannot be limited to the walk-in school. . . .

On the facts of this case, we are unable to conclude that the order of the District Court is not reasonable, feasible and workable. However, in seeking to define the scope of remedial power or the limits on remedial power of courts in an area as sensitive as we deal with here, words are poor instruments to convey the sense of basic fairness inherent in equity. Substance, not semantics, must govern, and we have sought to suggest the nature of limitations without frustrating the appropriate scope of equity.

At some point, these school authorities and others like them should have achieved full compliance with this Court's decision in Brown I. The systems would then be "unitary" in the sense required by our decisions in Green and Alexander. It does not follow that the communities served by such systems will remain demographically stable, for in a growing, mobile society, few will do so. Neither school authorities nor district courts are constitutionally required to make year-by-year adjustments of the racial composition of student bodies once the affirmative duty to desegregate has been accomplished and racial discrimination through official action is eliminated from the system. This does not mean that federal courts are without power to deal with future problems; but in the absence of a showing that either the school authorities or some other agency of the State has deliberately attempted to fix or alter demographic patterns to affect the racial composition of the schools, further intervention by a district court should not be necessary.

For the reasons herein set forth, the judgment of the Court of Appeals is affirmed as to those parts in which it affirmed the judgment of the District Court. The order of the District Court, dated August 7, 1970, is also affirmed.

MILLIKEN V. BRADLEY*
418 U.S. 717 (1974)

"The notion that school district lines may be casually ignored or treated as a mere administrative convenience is contrary to the history of public education in our country. No single tradition in public education is more deeply rooted than local control over the operation of schools."

The Question: Can a federal judge order a "metropolitan remedy" for school segregation in Detroit, created in large part by state officials, under which public school students in 53 school districts in the Detroit suburbs would be bused into the city and students in Detroit be bused into the suburbs, although none of the suburban districts had contributed to Detroit's school segregation?

The Arguments: PRO

The remedial powers of federal judges are broad enough to support the "metropolitan remedy" in this case, as the only feasible means of reducing the segregation of Detroit's schools. School districts in Michigan are created by the state legislature, and their boundaries can be changed at will; they are not independent political entities. Having created the segregation in Detroit's schools by a long series of acts that had the effect of making those schools inferior in quality, the state is responsible for providing a remedy.

CON

There is nothing in the record to show that any of the suburban school districts engaged in any act of racial discrimination, or contributed to the segregation of Detroit's schools. It would be unfair to the parents and students in these districts to uproot them from their neighborhood schools and bus them long distances to remedy a problem they did not create.

---

*Together with No. 73–435, *Allen Park Public Schools et al. v. Bradley et al.*, and No. 73–436, *Grosse Pointe Public School System v. Bradley et al.*, also on certiorari to the same court.

BACKGROUND

The Supreme Court's approval of busing as a remedy for school segregation lit a fuse that led to protests—most of them noisy and some of them violent—in cities across the country. Resistance to busing by white parents had first emerged in medium-sized cities like Pontiac and Knoxville, Tennessee, in which black students were a minority in the school population. Whether the busing conflict would spread to big cities in which the schools were heavily black was a question that troubled many Americans, including civil rights activists who had not anticipated the explosive reaction in Pontiac. The Supreme Court's decision in the *Swann* case had not addressed the issue of whether federal district judges could order busing across school district lines, as the only feasible method of creating greater "racial balance" in the metropolitan areas around big cities. This was a question most likely to arise in a Northern city, in which the growth of black ghettos during the 1950s and '60s had created largely black school districts, surrounded by lily-white schools in the suburbs. The case that brought this question to the Supreme Court came from a city just twenty miles from a city with a long history of racial conflict and violence, just twenty miles from Pontiac.

Detroit, the "Motor City" and the hub of the nation's auto industry, had seen its black population grow rapidly as Henry Ford's sprawling factories, and those of his competitors, offered better jobs and bigger paychecks than most blacks could hope for in the rural South. Beginning in 1910, when blacks comprised just 1.2 percent of the city's population, the Great Migration from the South brought new black residents on every train and bus. By 1940, the black population in Detroit had grown to 9 percent, and that figure increased to 16 percent in 1950.

Even though blacks made up a relatively small minority of Detroit's population until the 1960s, the growth of the city's ghetto areas caused friction as blacks moved into previously all-white neighborhoods. Conflicts over housing had sparked a race riot in 1943, as blacks poured into the city to fill defense jobs during World War II. Bands of armed whites roamed the streets, beating and shooting blacks and burning their homes and shops. When the gunfire ended and the smoke cleared, the human toll was 34 dead and 675 seriously injured. Yet, despite the overt hostility that blacks encountered in many areas of Detroit, the lure of jobs swelled their numbers after the war. By 1960, the black population of Detroit reached 487,000, some 29 percent of the city's residents.

Not surprisingly, Detroit was not spared from the death and destruction that swept across the country, from Newark to Los Angeles, during the urban riots of the mid-60s. When that decade began, close to half of the nation's black citizens lived below the federal poverty line, and black unemployment more than doubled the white rate, with more than a third of all young black men jobless and idle in big-city ghettos. Angry and frustrated, urban blacks lashed out at the white police who pushed them off their stoops and street corners and goaded them with racial epithets. Between 1964 and 1967, more than twenty urban ghettos blew up and burned.

Detroit erupted in 1967 after the police raided an after-hours bar whose patrons were black; the rioting that followed culminated in forty-three deaths, $50 million in property damage, and the occupation of the city by seventeen thousand U.S. army and national guard troops. In the wake of the Detroit riot, white residents fled from the city in droves. By 1970, the city's black population of Detroit grew to 660,000, some 44 percent of the total. During the preceding decade, the white population within the city limits had declined by 350,000, while the suburban white population swelled by just that number. These were not all the same white people, of course, as some left the state and others moved directly into the suburbs, but the trend was clear: Detroit was becoming a black city surrounded by a ring—or noose—of white suburbs in the surrounding three counties. Most of these suburbs, including two of the largest, Dearborn and Warren, had just a handful of black residents in 1970. Just 13 of Dearborn's 104,000 residents were black, as were only 132 of Warren's population of 179,000. Hardly any blacks lived in such upper-income suburbs as Sterling Heights, Birmingham, and Madison Heights; in fact, just 71 of the 125,000 residents of these three cities were black. Some 86 percent of all blacks in the Detroit metropolitan area lived within the city in 1970, and most of the remainder lived in working-class suburbs like Inkster and Pontiac and labored in the auto plants in those towns.

The segregation of Detroit and its suburbs was even more pronounced in schools. Although blacks and whites lived within the city limits in roughly equal numbers in 1970, the city's neighborhoods were clearly separated by race. The vast majority of Detroit census tracts were more than 90 percent white or black, and the city's public schools mirrored this residential segregation. In 1970 more than 70 percent of the schools were virtually all-white or all-black, with more than 90 percent of their students in the majority race. The phenomenon of "white flight" had already begun in Detroit, as white families with school-age children either moved to the suburbs or sent their children to private and parochial schools. The steady flow of whites from the city to the suburbs became a virtual stampede after the 1967 riot.

Given the segregation in Detroit's schools, it was hardly surprising that NAACP lawyers filed a lawsuit in August 1970 on behalf of "all school children in the City of Detroit, Michigan, and all Detroit resident parents who have children of school age." Ronald and Verda Bradley were the black parents whose names appeared first on the caption, but some of the plaintiffs were sympathetic white parents who felt their children were being denied an integrated education. Michigan's Republican governor, William Milliken, headed the list of defendants, which included the Detroit and Michigan boards of education. The case—decided by the Supreme Court under the caption of *Milliken v. Bradley*—fell on the docket of District Judge Stephen J. Roth, who was born in Hungary in 1908 and whose parents had brought him to Detroit at the age of five. Roth had been a prosecuting attorney, state court judge, and attorney general of Michigan before his nomination to the federal bench in 1962 by President John F. Kennedy.

Judge Roth held several rounds of hearings in the *Milliken* case and considered desegregation plans from both sides before he ruled in June 1972 that Detroit officials had intentionally segregated the city's schools by building new schools well inside neighborhood boundaries, to keep black and white students in separate schools, rather than placing new schools in areas that would draw students of both races. Roth also found that school officials had allowed transfers from schools in racially "transitional" areas, allowing white students to escape from largely black schools. The judge's finding that Detroit had practiced de jure segregation did not surprise anyone, given the clear evidence in the testimony and records at the hearings. But one aspect of Roth's decision shocked the white residents of the white suburbs that ringed Detroit. He ordered a "multi-district" remedy that would include fifty-three suburban districts in a desegregation plan under which 310,000 students would be bused across district lines to new schools. White children would ride buses from their suburban homes into city schools, and black children would sit in suburban classrooms that had never had black students. Judge Roth made clear in his opinion that "no school, grade, or classroom" in the Detroit metropolitan area would have a racial balance "substantially disproportionate to the overall pupil racial composition" of the three-county area covered by his order.

Roth noted in his *Milliken* opinion that school district boundaries in Michigan—like those in most states—were drawn by the state legislature. "School district lines," he wrote, "are simply matters of political convenience and may not be used to deny constitutional rights." Roth found nothing sacrosanct about school district boundaries, pointing out that state lawmakers had often redrawn district lines to consolidate rural schools, and that several districts covered by his order included two or three towns. He placed the blame on state officials for allowing the Detroit school board to build schools and draw attendance zones in ways that produced the segregation he found to be an "official" policy.

Public reaction to Roth's decision flooded the area's newspapers and radio shows with outrage from whites. One parent objected to sending his children to school in "dirty, violent, undesirable Detroit." The fact that some three hundred thousand children in the three-county area were already bused to school did not change many minds. "No kid of mine is going to get on a bus," one white mother said. "I'd go to jail first." Some parents admitted they had joined the "white flight" to the suburbs because "my kids weren't going to go to that school down there" in Detroit, as one put it.

School officials in forty-four of the fifty-three suburban districts that had been included in Judge Roth's busing order filed appeals with the Sixth Circuit Court of Appeals, claiming there was no evidence they had done anything to segregate any school in their district, and that they bore no responsibility for the segregation in Detroit's schools. Lawyers for the suburban districts complained that they had not even been parties to the NAACP lawsuit until Roth dragged them in by judicial order. The appellate judges upheld his order in 1973, however, finding that the Michigan board of education had adopted policies that "fostered segregation throughout the Detroit Metropolitan area."

Oral argument in *Milliken v. Bradley* began on February 27, 1974. Frank Kelley, Michigan's Democratic attorney general, defended the state's Republican governor and other state officials. He quoted Judge Roth's comment at the initial hearings: "This lawsuit is limited to the city of Detroit and the

school system; so that we are only concerned with the city itself, and we are not talking about the metropolitan area." Months later, Kelley said, Roth had "candidly revealed" his real goal in the case: "The task that we are called upon to perform is a social one—which the society has been unable to accomplish—to attain a social goal through the education system by using law as a lever." Kelley urged the justices not to hold Governor Milliken responsible for the long-ago acts of the Detroit school board.

William Saxton, a partner in one of Detroit's most prestigious law firms, argued for the forty-four suburban districts that had appealed from Judge Roth's order. He did not contest Roth's findings that Detroit officials had deliberately segregated their schools, "aided and abetted by acts of certain officials of the state government." But the suburbs had done nothing to deserve judicial finger-pointing. "You will search this record in vain to find one whit, one jot, of evidentiary material that any suburban school district committed any de jure act of segregation, either by itself, in complicity with the state, or complicity with anyone else," Saxton claimed.

J. Harold Flannery, a partner in another of Detroit's leading firms and himself a suburban resident, followed Saxton to the podium to argue for the NAACP in the *Milliken* case. He stressed Judge Roth's findings that the acts of state and local officials had "caused housing segregation and school segregation to be mutually supportive, mutually interlocking devices, with the result that black families and black children were confined to a small portion of the tri-county area," unable to escape from Detroit's black ghetto. Flannery shared his time with Nathaniel Jones, the NAACP's general counsel and a future Sixth Circuit judge. Given the residential segregation in Detroit and its origins in official acts, Jones argued, any "Detroit-only" remedy for school segregation would result in "the perpetuation of a black school district surrounded by a ring of white schools." Judge Roth had ample grounds for including all three metropolitan counties in his remedial order, Jones added, since "they are bound together by economic interests, recreation interests, social concerns and interests, governmental interests of various sorts, and a transportation network."

Three years before the *Milliken* case reached the Supreme Court, Chief Justice Warren Burger had warned in his *Swann* opinion that only proof of a "constitutional violation" could justify remedies such as busing, even within a single district. Burger was upset that district judges like Stephen Roth had not heeded his warning, and he exercised his prerogative as Chief to assign the *Milliken* opinion to himself. But he did not write for a unanimous Court. For the first time since the *Brown* decision in 1954, the justices were split in a school case, voting by a five-to-four margin to reverse Judge Roth (Irons, 2002).

MR. CHIEF JUSTICE BURGER delivered the opinion of the Court.

We granted certiorari in these consolidated cases to determine whether a federal court may impose a multi-district, areawide remedy to a single-district de jure segregation problem absent any finding that the other included school districts have failed to operate unitary school systems within their districts, absent any claim or finding that the boundary lines of any affected school district were established with the purpose of fostering racial segregation in public schools, absent any finding that the included districts committed acts which effected segregation within the other districts, and absent a meaningful opportunity for the included neighboring school districts to present evidence or be heard on the propriety of a multidistrict remedy or on the question of constitutional violations by those neighboring districts.

I

The action was commenced in August 1970 by the respondents, the Detroit Branch of the National Association for the Advancement of Colored People and individual parents and students, on behalf of a class later defined by order of the United States District Court for the Eastern District of Michigan, dated February 16, 1971, to include "all school children in the City of Detroit, Michigan, and all Detroit resident parents who have children of school age." The named defendants in the District Court included the Governor of Michigan, the Attorney General, the State Board of Education, the State Superintendent of Public Instruction, the Board of Education of the city of Detroit, its members, and the city's former superintendent of schools. The State of Michigan as such is not a party to this litigation and references to the State must be read as references to the public officials, state and local, through whom the State is alleged to have acted. In their complaint respondents attacked the constitutionality of a statute of the State of Michigan known as Act 48 of the 1970 Legislature on the ground that it put the State of Michigan in the position of unconstitutionally interfering with the execution and operation of a voluntary plan of partial high school desegregation, known as the April 7, 1970 Plan, which had been adopted by the Detroit Board of Education to be effective beginning with the fall 1970 semester. The complaint also alleged that the Detroit Public School System was and is segregated on the basis of race as a result of the official policies and actions of the defendants and their predecessors in office, and called for the implementation of a plan that would eliminate "the racial identity of every school in the [Detroit] system and . . . maintain now and hereafter a unitary, nonracial school system." . . .

The District Court found that the Detroit Board of Education created and maintained optional attendance zones within Detroit neighborhoods undergoing racial transition and between high school attendance areas of opposite predominant racial compositions. These zones, the court found, had the "natural, probable, foreseeable and actual effect" of allowing white pupils to escape identifiably Negro schools. . . . Similarly, the District Court found that Detroit school attendance zones had been drawn along north-south boundary lines despite the Detroit Board's awareness that drawing boundary lines in an east-west direction would result in significantly greater desegregation. Again, the District Court concluded, the natural and actual effect of these acts was the creation and perpetuation of school segregation within Detroit.

The District Court found that in the operation of its school transportation program, which was designed to relieve overcrowding, the Detroit Board had admittedly bused Negro Detroit pupils to predominantly Negro schools which were beyond or away from closer white schools with available space. This practice was found to have continued in recent years despite the Detroit Board's avowed policy, adopted in 1967, of utilizing transportation to increase desegregation:

> With one exception (necessitated by the burning of a white school), defendant Board has never bused white children to predominantly black schools. The Board has not bused white pupils to black schools despite the enormous amount of space available in innercity schools. There were 22,961 vacant seats in schools 90% or more black. . . .

With respect to the Detroit Board of Education's practices in school construction, the District Court found that Detroit school construction generally tended to have a segregative effect with the great majority of schools being built in either overwhelmingly all-Negro or all-white neighborhoods so that the new schools opened as predominantly one-race schools. Thus, of the 14 schools which opened for use in 1970–1971, 11 opened over 90% Negro and one opened less than 10% Negro. . . .

II

Ever since Brown v. Board of Education, judicial consideration of school desegregation cases has begun with the standard:

> [I]n the field of public education the doctrine of "separate but equal" has no place. Separate educational facilities are inherently unequal. . . .

This has been reaffirmed time and again as the meaning of the Constitution and the controlling rule of law.

The target of the Brown holding was clear and forthright: the elimination of state-mandated or deliberately maintained dual school systems with certain schools for Negro pupils and others for white pupils. This duality and racial segregation were held to violate the Constitution in the cases subsequent to 1954, including particularly . . . Swann v. Charlotte-Mecklenburg Board of Education. . . .

The Swann case, of course, dealt

> with the problem of defining in more precise terms than heretofore the scope of the duty of school authorities and district courts in implementing Brown I and the mandate to eliminate dual systems and establish unitary systems at once. . . .

Proceeding from these basic principles, we first note that in the District Court the complainants sought a remedy aimed at the condition alleged to offend the Constitution—the segregation within the Detroit City School District. The court acted on this theory of the case and in its initial ruling on the "Desegregation Area" stated:

> The task before this court, therefore, is now, and . . . has always been, how to desegregate the Detroit public schools. . . .

Thereafter, however, the District Court abruptly rejected the proposed Detroit-only plans on the ground that "while [they] would provide a racial mix more in keeping with the Black-White proportions of the student population [they] would accentuate the racial identifiability of the [Detroit] district as a Black school system, and would not accomplish desegregation." . . . "[T]he racial composition of the student body is such," said the court, "that the plan's implementation would clearly make the entire Detroit public school system racially identifiable. . . . leav[ing] many of its schools 75 to 90 per cent Black." . . . Consequently, the court reasoned, it was imperative to "look beyond the limits of the Detroit school district for a solution to the problem of segregation in the Detroit public schools . . ." since "[s]chool district lines are simply matters of political convenience and may not be used to deny constitutional rights." . . . Accordingly, the District Court proceeded to redefine the relevant area to include areas of predominantly white pupil population in order to ensure that "upon implementation, no school, grade or classroom [would be] substantially disproportionate to the overall pupil racial composition" of the entire metropolitan area. . . . The metropolitan area was then defined as Detroit plus 53 of the outlying school districts.

Here the District Court's approach to what constituted "actual desegregation" raises the fundamental question, not presented in Swann, as to the circumstances in which a federal court may order desegregation relief that embraces more than a single school district. The court's analytical starting point was its conclusion that school district lines are no more than arbitrary lines on a map drawn "for political convenience." Boundary lines may be bridged where there has been a constitutional violation calling for interdistrict relief, but the notion that school district lines may be casually ignored or treated as a mere administrative convenience is contrary to the history of public education in our country. No single tradition in public education is more deeply rooted than local control over the operation of schools; local autonomy has long been thought essential both to the maintenance of community concern and support for public schools and to quality of the educational process. . . .

The Michigan educational structure involved in this case, in common with most States, provides for a large measure of local control, and a review of the scope and character of these local powers indicates the extent to which the interdistrict remedy approved by the two courts could disrupt and alter the structure of public education in Michigan. The metropolitan remedy would require, in effect, consolidation of 54 independent school districts historically administered as separate units into a vast new super school district. . . . Entirely apart from the logistical and other serious problems attending large-scale transportation of students, the consolidation would give rise to an array of other problems in financing and operating this new school system. Some of the more obvious questions would be: What would be the status and authority of the present popularly elected school boards? Would the children of Detroit be within the jurisdiction and operating control of a school board elected by the parents and residents of other districts? What board or boards would levy taxes for school operations in these 54 districts constituting the consolidated metropolitan area? What provisions could be made for assuring substantial equality in tax levies among the 54 districts, if this were deemed requisite? What provisions would be made for financing? Would the validity of long-term bonds be jeopardized unless approved by all of

the component districts as well as the State? What body would determine that portion of the curricula now left to the discretion of local school boards? Who would establish attendance zones, purchase school equipment, locate and construct new schools, and indeed attend to all the myriad day-to-day decisions that are necessary to school operations affecting potentially more than three-quarters of a million pupils? . . .

It may be suggested that all of these vital operational problems are yet to be resolved by the District Court, and that this is the purpose of the Court of Appeals' proposed remand. But it is obvious from the scope of the interdistrict remedy itself that absent a complete restructuring of the laws of Michigan relating to school districts the District Court will become first, a de facto "legislative authority" to resolve these complex questions, and then the "school superintendent" for the entire area. This is a task which few, if any, judges are qualified to perform and one which would deprive the people of control of schools through their elected representatives. . . .

The controlling principle consistently expounded in our holdings is that the scope of the remedy is determined by the nature and extent of the constitutional violation. . . . Before the boundaries of separate and autonomous school districts may be set aside by consolidating the separate units for remedial purposes or by imposing a cross-district remedy, it must first be shown that there has been a constitutional violation within one district that produces a significant segregative effect in another district. Specifically, it must be shown that racially discriminatory acts of the state or local school districts, or of a single school district have been a substantial cause of interdistrict segregation. Thus an interdistrict remedy might be in order where the racially discriminatory acts of one or more school districts caused racial segregation in an adjacent district, or where district lines have been deliberately drawn on the basis of race. In such circumstances an interdistrict remedy would be appropriate to eliminate the interdistrict segregation directly caused by the constitutional violation. Conversely, without an interdistrict violation and interdistrict effect, there is no constitutional wrong calling for an interdistrict remedy.

The record before us, voluminous as it is, contains evidence of de jure segregated conditions only in the Detroit schools; indeed, that was the theory on which the litigation was initially based and on which the District Court took evidence. . . . With no showing of significant violation by the 53 outlying school districts and no evidence of any interdistrict violation or effect, the court went beyond the original theory of the case as framed by the pleadings and mandated a metropolitan area remedy. To approve the remedy ordered by the court would impose on the outlying districts, not shown to have committed any constitutional violation, a wholly impermissible remedy based on a standard not hinted at in Brown I and II or any holding of this Court. . . .

We conclude that the relief ordered by the District Court and affirmed by the Court of Appeals was based upon an erroneous standard and was unsupported by record evidence that acts of the outlying districts effected the discrimination found to exist in the schools of Detroit. Accordingly, the judgment of the Court of Appeals is reversed and the case is remanded for further proceedings consistent with this opinion leading to prompt formulation of a decree directed to eliminating the segregation found to exist in Detroit city schools, a remedy which has been delayed since 1970.

Reversed and remanded.

MR. JUSTICE MARSHALL, with whom MR. JUSTICE DOUGLAS, MR. JUSTICE BRENNAN, and MR. JUSTICE WHITE join, dissenting.

In Brown v. Board of Education, this Court held that segregation of children in public schools on the basis of race deprives minority group children of equal educational opportunities and therefore denies them the equal protection of the laws under the Fourteenth Amendment. This Court recognized then that remedying decades of segregation in public education would not be an easy task. Subsequent events, unfortunately, have seen that prediction bear bitter fruit. But however imbedded old ways, however ingrained old prejudices, this Court has not been diverted from its appointed task of making "a living truth" of our constitutional ideal of equal justice under law. Cooper v. Aaron.

After 20 years of small, often difficult steps toward that great end, the Court today takes a giant step backwards. Notwithstanding a record showing widespread and pervasive racial segregation in the educational system provided by the State of Michigan for children in Detroit, this Court holds that the District Court was powerless to require the State to remedy its constitutional violation in any meaningful fashion. Ironically purporting to base its result on the principle that the scope of the remedy in a desegregation case should be determined by the nature and the extent of the constitutional violation, the Court's answer is to provide no remedy at all for the violation proved in this case, thereby guaranteeing that Negro children in Detroit will receive the same separate and inherently unequal education in the future as they have been unconstitutionally afforded in the past.

I cannot subscribe to this emasculation of our constitutional guarantee of equal protection of the laws and must respectfully dissent. Our precedents, in my view, firmly establish that where, as here, state-imposed segregation has been demonstrated, it becomes the duty of the State to eliminate root and branch all vestiges of racial discrimination and to achieve the greatest possible degree of actual desegregation. I agree with both the District Court and the Court of Appeals that, under the facts of this case, this duty cannot be fulfilled unless the State of Michigan involves outlying metropolitan area school districts in its desegregation remedy. Furthermore, I perceive no basis either in law or in the practicalities of the situation justifying the State's interposition of school district boundaries as absolute barriers to the implementation of an effective desegregation remedy. Under established and frequently used Michigan procedures, school district lines are both flexible and permeable for a wide variety of purposes, and there is no reason why they must now stand in the way of meaningful desegregation relief.

The rights at issue in this case are too fundamental to be abridged on grounds as superficial as those relied on by the majority today. We deal here with the right of all of our children, whatever their race, to an equal start in life and to an equal opportunity to reach their full potential as citizens. Those children who have been denied that right in the past deserve better than to see fences thrown up to deny them that right in the future. Our Nation, I fear, will be ill served by the Court's refusal to remedy separate and unequal education, for unless our children begin to learn together, there is little hope that our people will ever learn to live together.

I

The great irony of the Court's opinion and, in my view, its most serious analytical flaw may be gleaned from its concluding sentence, in which the Court remands for "prompt formulation of a decree directed to eliminating the segregation found to exist in Detroit city schools, a remedy which has been delayed since 1970." . . . The majority, however, seems to have forgotten the District Court's explicit finding that a Detroit-only decree, the only remedy permitted under today's decision, "would not accomplish desegregation."

Nowhere in the Court's opinion does the majority confront, let alone respond to, the District Court's conclusion that a remedy limited to the city of Detroit would not effectively desegregate the Detroit city schools. I, for one, find the District Court's conclusion well supported by the record and its analysis compelled by our prior cases. . . .

The District Court's consideration of this case began with its finding, which the majority accepts, that the State of Michigan, through its instrumentality, the Detroit Board of Education, engaged in widespread purposeful acts of racial segregation in the Detroit School District. Without belaboring the details, it is sufficient to note that the various techniques used in Detroit were typical of methods employed to segregate students by race in areas where no statutory dual system of education has existed. See, e.g., Keyes v. School District No. 1, Denver, Colorado, 413 U. S. 189 (1973). Exacerbating the effects of extensive residential segregation between Negroes and whites, the school board consciously drew attendance zones along lines which maximized the segregation of the races in schools as well. Optional attendance zones were created for neighborhoods undergoing racial transition so as to allow whites in these areas to escape integration. Negro students in areas with overcrowded schools were transported past or away from closer white schools with available space to more distant Negro schools. Grade structures and feeder-school patterns were created and maintained in a manner which had the foreseeable and actual effect of keeping Negro and white pupils in separate schools. Schools were also constructed in locations and in sizes which ensured that they would open with predominantly one-race student bodies. In sum, the evidence adduced below showed that Negro children had been intentionally confined to an expanding core of virtually all-Negro schools immediately surrounded by a receding band of all-white schools. . . .

Having found a de jure segregated public school system in operation in the city of Detroit, the District Court turned next to consider which officials and agencies should be assigned the affirmative obligation to cure the constitutional violation. The court concluded that responsibility for the segregation in the Detroit city schools rested not only with the Detroit Board of Education, but belonged to the State of Michigan itself and the state defendants in this case—that is, the Governor of Michigan, the Attorney General, the State Board of Education, and the State Superintendent of Public Instruction. While the validity of this conclusion will merit more extensive analysis below, suffice it for now to say that it was based on three considerations. First, the evidence at trial showed that the State itself had taken actions contributing to the segregation within the Detroit schools. Second, since the Detroit Board of Education was an agency of the State of Michigan, its acts of racial discrimination were acts of the State for purposes of the Fourteenth Amendment. Finally, the District Court found that under Michigan law and practice, the system of education was in fact a *state* school system, characterized by relatively little local control and a large degree of centralized state regulation, with respect to both educational policy and the structure and operation of school districts.

Having concluded, then, that the school system in the city of Detroit was a de jure segregated system and that the State of Michigan had the affirmative duty to remedy that condition of segregation, the District Court then turned to the difficult task of devising an effective remedy. It bears repeating that the District Court's focus at this stage of the litigation remained what it had been at the beginning—the condition of segregation within the Detroit city schools. . . .

Vesting responsibility with the State of Michigan for Detroit's segregated schools is particularly appropriate as Michigan, unlike some other States, operates a single statewide system of education rather than several separate and independent local school systems. The majority's emphasis on local governmental control and local autonomy of school districts in Michigan will come as a surprise to those with any familiarity with that State's system of education. School districts are not separate and distinct sovereign entities under Michigan law, but rather are "'auxiliaries of the State,'" subject to its "absolute power." . . . The courts of the State have repeatedly emphasized that education in Michigan is not a local governmental concern, but a state function. . . .

The State's control over education is reflected in the fact that, contrary to the Court's implication, there is little or no relationship between school districts and local political units. To take the 85 outlying local school districts in the Detroit metropolitan area as examples, 17 districts lie in two counties, two in three counties. One district serves five municipalities; other suburban municipalities are fragmented into as many as six school districts. Nor is there any apparent state policy with regard to the size of school districts, as they now range from 2,000 to 285,000 students. . . .

In sum, several factors in this case coalesce to support the District Court's ruling that it was the State of Michigan itself, not simply the Detroit Board of Education, which bore the obligation of curing the condition of segregation within the Detroit city schools. The actions of the State itself directly contributed to Detroit's segregation. Under the Fourteenth Amendment, the State is ultimately responsible for the actions of its local agencies. And, finally, given the structure of Michigan's educational system, Detroit's segregation cannot be viewed as the problem of an independent and separate entity. Michigan operates a single statewide system of education, a substantial part of which was shown to be segregated in this case . . .

Under a Detroit-only decree, Detroit's schools will clearly remain racially identifiable in comparison with neighboring schools in the metropolitan community. Schools with 65% and more Negro students will stand in sharp and obvious contrast to schools in neighboring districts with less than 2% Negro enrollment. Negro students will continue to perceive their schools as segregated educational facilities and this perception will only be increased when whites react to a Detroit-only decree by fleeing to the suburbs to avoid integration. School district lines, however innocently drawn, will surely be perceived as fences to separate the races when, under a Detroit-only decree, white parents withdraw their children from the Detroit city schools and move to the suburbs in order to continue them in all-white schools. The message of this action will not escape the Negro children in the city of Detroit. . . .

It will be of scant significance to Negro children who have for years been confined by de jure acts of segregation to a growing core of all-Negro schools surrounded by a ring of all-white schools that the new dividing line between the races is the school district boundary. . . .

Desegregation is not and was never expected to be an easy task. Racial attitudes ingrained in our Nation's childhood and adolescence are not quickly thrown aside in its middle years. But just as the inconvenience of some cannot be allowed to stand in the way of the rights of others, so public opposition, no matter how strident, cannot be permitted to divert this Court from the enforcement of the constitutional principles at issue in this case. Today's holding, I fear, is more a reflection of a perceived public mood that we have gone far enough in enforcing the Constitution's guarantee of equal justice than it is the product of neutral principles of law. In the short run, it may seem to be the easier course to allow our great metropolitan areas to be divided up each into two cities—one white, the other black—but it is a course, I predict, our people will ultimately regret.

I dissent.

BOARD OF EDUCATION OF OKLAHOMA CITY V. DOWELL
498 U.S. 237 (1991)

"Dissolving a desegregation decree after the local authorities have operated in compliance with it for a reasonable period of time properly recognizes that . . . a federal court's regulatory control of such systems not extend beyond the time required to remedy the effects of past intentional discrimination."

The Question: Can a federal judge rule that a school district that had been segregated by law and subject to a desegregation order be released from judicial supervision on a finding that it has achieved "unitary" status, even though many of its schools are more than 90 percent of one race?

The Arguments: PRO

The Supreme Court rulings in the Brown case and subsequent decisions did not envision that federal judges would continue supervision of desegregation plans for an indefinite period. The schools in Oklahoma City were found to be desegregated in 1977 and the court held that the district had achieved "unitary" status. The present racial imbalance is the result of residential housing patterns, over which school officials have no control, and does not justify further litigation and judicial oversight of schools that had satisfied all the provisions of earlier judicial orders.

CON

The record in this case, which began in 1961, clearly establishes that school segregation in Oklahoma City was fostered by residential segregation, and that both were caused by official acts. The problem of "resegregation" in American cities threatens to undo the advances made since the *Brown* decision. The practice of drawing school attendance boundaries to reflect the racial composition of neighborhoods is a factor that judges should take into account in framing remedial orders. A finding of "unitary" status should be subject to review and revision in cases like this one.

BACKGROUND

In the years after *Milliken*, dozens of federal judges had been asked by school officials to free them from desegregation orders that had been imposed fifteen or twenty years earlier. In most cases, the judges had refused to vacate those orders. The Supreme Court now faced, in 1990, the task of deciding whether districts that had achieved "unitary" status by eliminating the "vestiges" of segregation could run their schools without further judicial oversight. The question was complicated by the claims of lawyers for black parents and children that the "resegregation" of urban schools, which followed the return of the "neighborhood school" policy, required additional remedies to bring about greater racial balance in the schools. Many cities now had substantial numbers of "one-race" schools, a distressing return to the Jim Crow era. To many observers and activists, the very notion of school integration and the unfulfilled promise of the *Brown* decision hung on the Court's decisions in cases that asked for the lifting of desegregation orders.

The first of these cases, *Oklahoma City v. Dowell*, reached the Court in October 1990, four months after Justice Brennan's departure. His seat was still empty as the eight remaining justices entered the chamber for oral argument. The Oklahoma City case had begun in 1961 with a lawsuit to integrate the city's Jim Crow schools, which had been segregated by law since Oklahoma joined the Union in 1907 with a constitution that mandated segregation in the state's public schools. Robert L. Dowell and other black students and parents, represented by NAACP lawyers, sued the Oklahoma City school board and won a federal court ruling from Judge Luther L. Bohanon in 1963 that ordered school officials to dismantle their "dual" system. In 1965, Bohanon issued another order, based on his finding that the "neighborhood zoning" plan adopted by the board had not produced any real integration, because the city's residential segregation—which had once been imposed by law—had resulted in the perpetuation of one-race schools. While the city's black population was less than 20 percent, it was tightly clustered in the northeast quadrant. In 1972, still dissatisfied with the board's foot-dragging, Judge Bohanon adopted a plan drafted by Dr. John Finger of Rhode Island College, who had previously designed the integration plan imposed by judicial order in Charlotte, North Carolina. Under the "Finger Plan," black children in the first four grades would be bused to formerly white schools, white fifth-graders would be bused to black schools, and students in upper grades would be bused to schools around the city to achieve racial balance.

The Oklahoma City board asked Bohanon to close the case in 1977, and he complied with an "Order Terminating Case" in which he professed his confidence that "the present members and their successors on the Board will now and in the future continue to follow the constitutional desegregation requirements." Robert Dowell and the other black plaintiffs did not appeal this order. But in 1985, after the board adopted a Student Reassignment Plan that returned to the "neighborhood school" policy of the 1960s, the plaintiffs asked the court to reopen the case, charging that under the new plan, thirty-three of the city's sixty-four elementary schools would have more than 90 percent of their students from one race. The revived *Dowell* case bounced back and forth between the district and appellate courts until 1989, when the Tenth Circuit Court of Appeals, holding that Judge Bohanon had not specifically dissolved his 1972 order "terminating" the case, reinstated the original decree with instructions to require the Oklahoma City board to draft a new integration plan.

Oral argument on the Oklahoma City school board's appeal from the Tenth Circuit ruling took place on the first day of the Supreme Court's new term on October 2, 1990. Ronald L. Day, who represented the board, led off with the claim that Jim Crow schools in his city were history. "Today, in Oklahoma City, no child is compelled to attend school by virtue of his race," he stated. "The important thing today is that parents of all races have a choice." Day was referring to the board's "majority-to-minority" policy, allowing parents to transfer their children from neighborhood schools in which they were in the majority race to schools where they would be in the minority. Few parents of either race had chosen this option, and school attendance boundaries had not been revised to create more racially balanced schools.

Justice Thurgood Marshall had first visited Oklahoma City in 1941 as an NAACP lawyer, after local blacks begged him to defend an illiterate black man who was charged with killing a white couple and one of their children, and who had been savagely beaten by police to extract a confession. As soon as his train from New York pulled into the Oklahoma City station, the black men who met him pushed Marshall into the backseat of a car and sped away, fearful that Klansmen would try to kill him. Marshall was shuttled from one house to another every few hours, with armed blacks keeping watch. He lost the case, after a circus-atmosphere trial before an all-white jury, But he never lost his memories of Oklahoma City, and Marshall grilled Ronald Day in his gruff, raspy voice.

"How is the school board injured by being required to continue to operate the schools in conformity to the United States Constitution?" Marshall asked.

"They weren't harmed that much," Day replied, "not as much as the black schoolchildren, who the district court found were adversely affected by busing."

"What assurance is there that the school board will continue to comply with the Constitution absent a court order?" Marshall continued.

"The board must comply with the Constitution's Equal Protection requirements," Day answered.

"But you'll have to file a new suit to assure that," Marshall retorted.

Day focused his argument on Judge Bohanon's finding that the Oklahoma City schools had achieved "unitary" status after dismantling the "dual" system of segregated schools. He claimed the district had complied with the Court's demand in *Green v. New Kent County*, the Virginia case decided in 1968, that school officials eliminate "every vestige of segregation" before any judicial finding of "unitary" status. The "*Green* standard," defined in Justice William Brennan's opinion, had become the judicial test of compliance with desegregation orders. Justice Anthony Kennedy questioned Day on this issue, citing the number of "one-race" schools in Oklahoma City.

"Does the fact that some neighborhood schools remain black mean that the desegregation plan didn't work?" Kennedy asked.

"No, Your Honor." Day replied. "The fact that some neighborhood schools are not integrated is not under the school board's control."

"But didn't an early district court order find that residential segregation resulted in part from school segregation?" Kennedy inquired.

"That finding related only to segregated schools, not neighborhoods," Day responded.

Kennedy seemed satisfied by Day's answers. "You're operating in an environment in which any family, assuming economic ability, can move to any neighborhood," he concluded.

Julius Chambers, who had argued the *Swann* case that led to the Court's approval of busing, argued for the Oklahoma City black children who no longer rode buses to schools outside their all-black neighborhoods. The *Swann* decision, he said, "demands that where there is a segregated system as in Oklahoma City, the school board must take affirmative steps to desegregate." Those steps included busing students to eliminate "one-race" schools. Justice Scalia, the Court's most active and aggressive questioner, grilled Chambers about his claim that residential segregation was a "vestige" of segregated schools.

"You're using 'segregated' in an unusual way," Scalia began.

"Oklahoma City is a segregated community," Chambers replied. "No one expects whites to move to the black residential area."

"But 'segregated' means blacks aren't allowed to move to white areas," Scalia countered, noting that residential segregation was no longer imposed by law in Oklahoma City. Scalia's own definition of the term "segregated" seemed more unusual than Chambers's use of the word.

Chambers then faced a question from Justice O'Connor. "What if the same residential pattern exists one hundred years from now?" she asked. "Would the school board still be subject to the busing order?"

"The order should remain and must remain in force until all vestiges of discrimination have been eliminated," Chambers doggedly replied.

"So the answer is 'Yes,'" O'Connor said.

Along with Thurgood Marshall, Justice Byron White was the last remaining member of the Warren Court. White had vigorously enforced civil rights laws as a Justice Department official under President Kennedy, and had written a pointed dissent in the *Milliken* case, lamenting that "deliberate acts of segregation and their consequences will go unremedied" by the Court's rejection of busing across school district lines. He now posed a skeptical question to Chambers.

> "It is not against the law for blacks and whites to go to school anymore in Oklahoma City," White began. "You're saying that they're back to their same old tricks," he said of the school board. "That isn't so, is it?"
>
> "They have gone back to the same geographic zones," Chambers replied. "However unitariness is defined, it should not permit a city to reinstate the same pupil assignment practices that caused segregation in the past. The neighborhood school plan perpetuates black segregated schools in the same black residential area as before the district court's decree" (Irons, 2002).

CHIEF JUSTICE REHNQUIST delivered the opinion of the Court.

This school desegregation litigation began almost 30 years ago. In 1961, respondents, black students and their parents, sued the Board to end de jure segregation in the public schools. In 1963, the District Court found that Oklahoma City had intentionally segregated both schools and housing in the past, and that Oklahoma City was operating a "dual" school system—one that was intentionally segregated by race. In 1965, the District Court found that the Board's attempt to desegregate by using neighborhood zoning failed to remedy past segregation because residential segregation resulted in one-race schools. Residential segregation had once been state imposed, and it lingered due to discrimination by some realtors and financial institutions. The District Court found that school segregation had caused some housing segregation.

In 1972, finding that previous efforts had not been successful at eliminating state imposed segregation, the District Court ordered the Board to adopt the "Finger plan," under which kindergarteners would be assigned to neighborhood schools unless their parents opted otherwise; children in grades 1–4 would attend formerly all-white schools, and thus black children would be bused to those schools; children in grade five would attend formerly all black schools, and thus white children would be bused to those schools; students in the upper grades would be bused to various areas in order to maintain integrated schools; and in integrated neighborhoods there would be stand-alone schools for all grades.

In 1977, after complying with the desegregation decree for five years, the Board made a "Motion to Close Case." The District Court held in its "Order Terminating Case:" "The Court has concluded that [the Finger plan] worked, and that substantial compliance with the constitutional requirements has been achieved.... Jurisdiction in this case is terminated...." This unpublished order was not appealed.

In 1984, the Board faced demographic changes that led to greater burdens on young black children. As more and more neighborhoods became integrated, more stand-alone schools were established, and young black students had to be bused further from their inner-city homes to outlying white areas. In an effort to alleviate this burden and to increase parental involvement, the Board adopted the Student Reassignment Plan (SRP), which relied on neighborhood assignments for students in grades K–4 beginning in the 1985–1986 school year. Busing continued for students in grades 5–12. Any student could transfer from a school where he or she was in the majority to a school where he or she would be in the minority. Faculty and staff integration was retained, and an "equity officer" was appointed.

In 1985, respondents filed a "Motion to Reopen the Case," contending that the school district had not achieved "unitary" status and that the SRP was a return to segregation. Under the SRP, 11 of 64 elementary schools would be greater than 90% black, 22 would be greater than 90% white plus other minorities, and 31 would be racially mixed. The District Court refused to reopen the case, holding that its 1977 finding of unitariness was res judicata as to those who were then parties to the action, and that the district remained unitary.... Because unitariness had been achieved, the District Court concluded that court-ordered desegregation must end.

The Court of Appeals for the Tenth Circuit reversed. It held that, while the 1977 order finding the district unitary was binding on the parties, nothing in that order indicated that the 1972 injunction itself was terminated.... The case was remanded to determine whether the decree should be lifted or modified. On remand, the District Court found that demographic changes made the Finger plan unworkable, that the Board had done nothing for 25 years to promote residential segregation, and that the school district had bused students for more than a decade in good-faith compliance with the court's orders. The District Court found that present residential segregation was the result of private decision-making and economics, and that it was too attenuated to be a vestige of former school segregation. It also found that the district had maintained its unitary status, and that the neighborhood assignment plan was not designed with discriminatory intent. The court concluded that the previous injunctive decree should be vacated, and the school district returned to local control.

The Court of Appeals again reversed.... Given that a number of schools would return to being primarily one-race schools under the SRP, circumstances in Oklahoma City had not changed enough to justify modification of the decree. The Court of Appeals held that, despite the unitary finding, the Board had the "affirmative duty ... not to take any action that would impede the process of disestablishing the dual system and its effects." We granted the Board's petition for certiorari.... We now reverse the Court of Appeals....

The lower courts have been inconsistent in their use of the term "unitary." Some have used it to identify a school district that has completely remedied all vestiges of past discrimination. Under that interpretation of the word, a unitary school district is one that has met the mandate of Brown v. Board of Education [II], and Green v. New Kent County School Board. Other courts, however, have used "unitary" to describe any school district that has currently desegregated student assignments, whether or not that status is solely the result of a court-imposed desegregation plan. In other words, such a school district could be called unitary and nevertheless still contain vestiges of past discrimination....

We think it is a mistake to treat words such as "dual" and "unitary" as if they were actually found in the Constitution.... Courts have used the terms "dual" to denote a school system which has engaged in intentional segregation of students by race, and "unitary" to describe a school system which has been brought into compliance with the command of the Constitution. We are not sure how useful it is to define these terms more precisely, or to create subclasses within them. But there is no doubt that the differences in usage described above do exist. The District Court's 1977 order is unclear with respect to what it meant by unitary, and the necessary result of that finding. We therefore decline to overturn the conclusion of the Court of Appeals that, while the 1977 order of the District Court did bind the parties as to the unitary character of the district, it did not finally terminate the Oklahoma City school litigation. . . .

In the present case, a finding by the District Court that the Oklahoma City School District was being operated in compliance with the commands of the Equal Protection Clause of the Fourteenth Amendment, and that it was unlikely that the Board would return to its former ways, would be a finding that the purposes of the desegregation litigation had been fully achieved. . . . From the very first, federal supervision of local school systems was intended as a temporary measure to remedy past discrimination. Brown considered the "complexities arising from the transition to a system of public education freed of racial discrimination" in holding that the implementation of desegregation was to proceed "with all deliberate speed." Green also spoke of the "transition to a unitary, nonracial system of public education." . . .

The legal justification for displacement of local authority by an injunctive decree in a school desegregation case is a violation of the Constitution by the local authorities. Dissolving a desegregation decree after the local authorities have operated in compliance with it for a reasonable period of time properly recognizes that "necessary concern for the important values of local control of public school systems" dictates that a federal court's regulatory control of such systems not extend beyond the time required to remedy the effects of past intentional discrimination. . . .

A district court need not accept at face value the profession of a school board which has intentionally discriminated that it will cease to do so in the future. But in deciding whether to modify or dissolve a desegregation decree, a school board's compliance with previous court orders is obviously relevant. In this case, the original finding of de jure segregation was entered in 1963, the injunctive decree from which the Board seeks relief was entered in 1972, and the Board complied with the decree in good faith until 1985. Not only do the personnel of school boards change over time, but the same passage of time enables the district court to observe the good faith of the school board in complying with the decree. The test espoused by the Court of Appeals would condemn a school district, once governed by a board which intentionally discriminated, to judicial tutelage for the indefinite future. Neither the principles governing the entry and dissolution of injunctive decrees, nor the commands of the Equal Protection Clause of the Fourteenth Amendment require any such Draconian result.

Petitioners urge that we reinstate the decision of the District Court terminating the injunction, but we think that the preferable course is to remand the case to that court so that it may decide, in accordance with this opinion, whether the Board made a sufficient showing of constitutional compliance as of 1985, when the SRP was adopted, to allow the injunction to be dissolved. The District Court should address itself to whether the Board had complied in good faith with the desegregation decree since it was entered, and whether the vestiges of past discrimination had been eliminated to the extent practicable. In considering whether the vestiges of de jure segregation had been eliminated as far as practicable, the District Court should look not only at student assignments, but "to every facet of school operations—faculty, staff, transportation, extracurricular activities and facilities." After the District Court decides whether the Board was entitled to have the decree terminated, it should proceed to decide respondent's challenge to the SRP. A school district which has been released from an injunction imposing a desegregation plan no longer requires court authorization for the promulgation of policies and rules regulating matters such as assignment of students and the like, but it of course remains subject to the mandate of the Equal Protection Clause of the Fourteenth Amendment. If the Board was entitled to have the decree terminated as of 1985, the District Court should then evaluate the Board's decision to implement the SRP under appropriate equal protection principles. The judgment of the Court of Appeals is reversed, and the case is remanded to the District Court for further proceedings consistent with this opinion.

JUSTICE MARSHALL, with whom JUSTICE BLACKMUN and JUSTICE STEVENS join, dissenting.

Oklahoma gained statehood in 1907. For the next 65 years, the Oklahoma City School Board (Board) maintained segregated schools—initially relying on laws requiring dual school systems; thereafter, by exploiting residential segregation that had been created by legally enforced restrictive covenants. In 1972—18 years after this Court first found segregated schools unconstitutional—a federal court finally interrupted this cycle, enjoining the Board to implement a specific plan for achieving actual desegregation of its schools.

The practical question now before us is whether, 13 years after that injunction was imposed, the same Board should have been allowed to return many of its elementary schools to their former one-race status. The majority today suggests that 13 years of desegregation was enough. The Court remands the case for further evaluation of whether the purposes of the injunctive decree were achieved sufficient to justify the decree's dissolution. However, the inquiry it commends to the District Court fails to recognize explicitly the threatened reemergence of one-race schools as a relevant "vestige" of de jure segregation.

In my view, the standard for dissolution of a school desegregation decree must reflect the central aim of our school desegregation precedents. In Brown v. Board of Education, 1954 (Brown I), a unanimous Court declared that racially "[s]eparate educational facilities are inherently unequal." This holding rested on the Court's recognition that state-sponsored segregation conveys a message of "inferiority as to th[e] status [of Afro-American school children] in the community that may affect their hearts and minds in a way unlikely ever to be undone." Remedying this evil and preventing its recurrence were the motivations animating our requirement that formerly de jure segregated school districts take all feasible steps to eliminate racially identifiable schools.

I believe a desegregation decree cannot be lifted so long as conditions likely to inflict the stigmatic injury condemned in Brown I persist and there remain feasible methods of eliminating such conditions. Because the record here shows, and the Court of Appeals found, that feasible steps could be taken to avoid one-race schools, it is clear that the purposes of the decree have not yet been achieved, and the Court of Appeals' reinstatement of the decree should be affirmed.

I therefore dissent.

In order to assess the full consequence of lifting the decree at issue in this case, it is necessary to explore more fully than does the majority the history of racial segregation in the Oklahoma City schools. This history reveals nearly unflagging resistance by the Board to judicial efforts to dismantle the City's dual education system.

When Oklahoma was admitted to the Union in 1907, its Constitution mandated separation of Afro-American children from all other races in the public school system. In addition to laws enforcing segregation in the schools, racially restrictive covenants, supported by state and local law, established a segregated residential pattern in Oklahoma City. Petitioner Board exploited this residential segregation to enforce school segregation, locating "all-Negro" schools in the heart of the City's northeast quadrant, in which the majority of the City's Afro-American citizens resided.

Matters did not change in Oklahoma City after this Court's decision in Brown I and Brown v. Board of Education, 1955 (Brown II). Although new school boundaries were established at that time, the Board also adopted a resolution allowing children to continue in the schools in which they were placed or to submit transfer requests that would be considered on a case-by-case basis. Because it allowed thousands of white children each year to transfer to schools in which their race was the majority, this transfer policy undermined any potential desegregation.

Parents of Afro-American children relegated to schools in the northeast quadrant filed suit against the Board in 1961. Finding that the Board's special transfer policy was "designed to perpetuate and encourage segregation," the District Court struck down the policy as a violation of the Equal Protection Clause. Undeterred, the Board proceeded to adopt another special transfer policy which, as the District Court found in 1965, had virtually the same effect as the prior policy—"perpetuat[ion] [of] a segregated system." The District Court also noted that, by failing to adopt an affirmative policy of desegregation, the Board had reversed the desegregation process in certain respects. For example, eight of the nine new schools planned or under construction in 1965 were located to serve all-white or virtually all-white school zones. Rather than promote integration through new school locations, the District Court found that the Board destroyed some integrated neighborhoods and schools by adopting inflexible neighborhood school attendance zones that encouraged whites to migrate to all-white areas. Because the Board's pupil assignments coincided with residential segregation initiated by law in Oklahoma City, the Board also preserved and augmented existing residential segregation.

Thus, by 1972, 11 years after the plaintiffs had filed suit and 18 years after our decision in Brown I, the Board contin-

ued to resist integration and, in some respects, the Board had worsened the situation. Four years after this Court's admonition to formerly de jure segregated school districts to come forward with realistic plans for immediate relief, the Board still had offered no meaningful plan of its own. . . . Consequently, the District Court ordered the Board to implement the only available plan that exhibited the promise of achieving actual desegregation—the "Finger plan" offered by the plaintiffs. In 1975, after a mere three years of operating under the Finger Plan, the Board filed a "Motion to Close Case," arguing that it had "eliminated all vestiges of state imposed racial discrimination in its school system." . . . The Board continued to operate under the Finger Plan until 1985, when it implemented the Student Reassignment Plan (SRP). The SRP superimposed attendance zones over some residentially segregated areas. As a result, considerable racial imbalance reemerged in 33 of 64 elementary schools in the Oklahoma City system with student bodies either greater than 90% Afro-American or greater than 90% non–Afro-American. More specifically, 11 of the schools ranged from 96.9% to 99.7% Afro-American, and approximately 44% of all Afro-American children in grades K–4 were assigned to these virtually all–Afro-American schools.

In response to the SRP, the plaintiffs moved to reopen the case. Ultimately, the District Court dissolved the desegregation decree, finding that the school district had been "unitary" since 1977, and that the racial imbalances under the SRP were the consequence of residential segregation arising from "personal preferences." The Court of Appeals reversed, finding that the Board had not met its burden to establish that "the condition the [decree] sought to alleviate, a constitutional violation, has been eradicated."

I agree with the majority that the proper standard for determining whether a school desegregation decree should be dissolved is whether the purposes of the desegregation litigation, as incorporated in the decree, have been fully achieved. I strongly disagree with the majority, however, on what must be shown to demonstrate that a decree's purposes have been fully realized. In my view, a standard for dissolution of a desegregation decree must take into account the unique harm associated with a system of racially identifiable schools, and must expressly demand the elimination of such schools.

Our pointed focus in Brown I upon the stigmatic injury caused by segregated schools explains our unflagging insistence that formerly de jure segregated school districts extinguish all vestiges of school segregation. The concept of stigma also gives us guidance as to what conditions must be eliminated before a decree can be deemed to have served its purpose. In the decisions leading up to Brown I, the Court had attempted to curtail the ugly legacy of Plessy v. Ferguson, by insisting on a searching inquiry into whether "separate" Afro-American schools were genuinely "equal" to white schools in terms of physical facilities, curricula, quality of the faculty and certain "intangible" considerations. In Brown I, the Court finally liberated the Equal Protection Clause from the doctrinal tethers of Plessy, declaring that, "in the field of public education, the doctrine of 'separate but equal' has no place. Separate educational facilities are inherently unequal." The Court based this conclusion on its recognition of the particular social harm that racially segregated schools inflict on Afro-American children. . . .

Just as it is central to the standard for evaluating the formation of a desegregation decree, so should the stigmatic injury associated with segregated schools be central to the standard for dissolving a decree. The Court has indicated that "the ultimate end to be brought about" by a desegregation remedy is "a unitary, nonracial system of public education." We have suggested that this aim is realized once school officials have "eliminate[d] from the public schools all vestiges of state-imposed segregation." . . . Although the Court has never explicitly defined what constitutes a "vestige" of state-enforced segregation, the function that this concept has performed in our jurisprudence suggests that it extends to any condition that is likely to convey the message

of inferiority implicit in a policy of segregation. So long as such conditions persist, the purposes of the decree cannot be deemed to have been achieved.

Consistent with the mandate of Brown I, our cases have imposed on school districts an unconditional duty to eliminate any condition that perpetuates the message of racial inferiority inherent in the policy of state-sponsored segregation. The racial identifiability of a district's schools is such a condition. Whether this "vestige" of state-sponsored segregation will persist cannot simply be ignored at the point where a district court is contemplating the dissolution of a desegregation decree. In a district with a history of state-sponsored school segregation, racial separation, in my view, remains inherently unequal.

I dissent.

PLYLER V. DOE
457 U.S. 202 (1982)*

"A State may withhold its beneficence from those whose very presence in the United States is a product of their own unlawful conduct. . . . But the children of these illegal entrants are not comparably situated. . . . Denial of education to some isolated group of children poses an affront to one of the goals of the Equal Protection Clause: the abolition of governmental barriers presenting unreasonable obstacles to advancement on the basis of individual merit."

The Question: Can a state deny a free public education to children whose parents entered the United States illegally, by withholding state funds to school districts that admit such undocumented children?

The Arguments: PRO

This case, from the state of Texas, illustrates the problems caused by the massive influx of illegal aliens across our nation's southwestern borders. The education of children whose parents entered the country illegally has created a substantial drain on the state's budget, and these children have no lawful right to be in this country, let alone to attend its public schools. These children and their parents are subject to deportation and are, in fact, in a criminal status. The state legislature is free to determine that education funds should be spent on children who are citizens or lawfully in this country.

CON

There is no good reason to punish children for having parents who are undocumented, many of whom have lived in this country for years. Denying these children an education will create a large class of illiterates, who will be more likely to become unemployed and to turn to crime and alcohol and drug abuse. The Equal Protection Clause of the Constitution protects all persons, regardless of citizenship status, against deprivation of basic rights. Having established a system of free public schools, the state of Texas is not empowered to deny an education to any class of children for reasons over which they have no control.

---

*Together with No. 80-1934, Texas et al. v. Certain Named and Unnamed Undocumented Alien Children et al., also on appeal from the same court.

JUSTICE BRENNAN delivered the opinion of the Court.

The question presented by these cases is whether, consistent with the Equal Protection Clause of the Fourteenth Amendment, Texas may deny to undocumented school-age children the free public education that it provides to children who are citizens of the United States or legally admitted aliens. Since the late 19th century, the United States has restricted immigration into this country. Unsanctioned entry into the United States is a crime, and those who have entered unlawfully are subject to deportation. But despite the existence of these legal restrictions, a substantial number of persons have succeeded in unlawfully entering the United States, and now live within various States, including the State of Texas.

In May 1975, the Texas Legislature revised its education laws to withhold from local school districts any state funds for the education of children who were not "legally admitted" into the United States. The 1975 revision also authorized local school districts to deny enrollment in their public schools to children not "legally admitted" to the country. These cases involve constitutional challenges to those provisions.

Plyler v. Doe . . . is a class action, filed in the United States District Court for the Eastern District of Texas in September 1977, on behalf of certain school-age children of Mexican origin residing in Smith County, Tex., who could not establish that they had been legally admitted into the United States. The action complained of the exclusion of plaintiff children from the public schools of the Tyler Independent School District. The Superintendent and members of the Board of Trustees of the School District were named as defendants; the State of Texas intervened as a party-defendant. . . . The District Court held that illegal aliens were entitled to the protection of the Equal Protection Clause of the Fourteenth Amendment, and that [the Texas law] violated that Clause. . . . The Court of Appeals for the Fifth Circuit upheld the District Court's injunction. . . . We noted probable jurisdiction. . . .

The Fourteenth Amendment provides that "[n]o State shall . . . deprive any person of life, liberty, or property, without due process of law; nor deny to any person within its jurisdiction the equal protection of the laws." Appellants argue at the outset that undocumented aliens, because of their immigration status, are not "persons within the jurisdiction" of the State of Texas, and that they therefore have no right to the equal protection of Texas law. We reject this argument. Whatever his status under the immigration laws, an alien is surely a "person" in any ordinary sense of that term. Aliens, even aliens whose presence in this country is unlawful, have long been recognized as "persons" guaranteed due process of law by the Fifth and Fourteenth Amendments. Indeed, we have clearly held that the Fifth Amendment protects aliens whose presence in this country is unlawful from invidious discrimination by the Federal Government. . . .

Our conclusion that the illegal aliens who are plaintiffs in these cases may claim the benefit of the Fourteenth Amendment's guarantee of equal protection only begins the inquiry. The more difficult question is whether the Equal Protection Clause has been violated by the refusal of the State of Texas to reimburse local school boards for the education of children who cannot demonstrate that their presence within the United States is lawful, or by the imposition by those school boards of the burden of tuition on those children. It is to this question that we now turn.

The Equal Protection Clause directs that "all persons similarly circumstanced shall be treated alike." A legislature must have substantial latitude to establish classifications that roughly approximate the nature of the problem perceived, that accommodate competing concerns both public and private, and that account for limitations on the practical ability of the State to remedy every ill. In applying the Equal Protection Clause to most forms of state action, we thus seek only the assurance that the classification at issue bears some fair relationship to a legitimate public purpose. But we would not be faithful to our obligations under the Fourteenth Amendment if we applied so deferential a standard to every classification. The Equal Protection Clause was intended as a restriction on state legislative action inconsistent with elemental constitutional premises. Thus we have treated as presumptively invidious those classifications that disadvantage a "suspect class," or that impinge upon the exercise of a "fundamental right." With respect to such classifications, it is appropriate to enforce the mandate of equal protection by requiring the State to demonstrate that its classification has been precisely tailored to serve a compelling governmental interest. In addition, we have recognized that certain forms of legislative classification, while not facially invidious, nonetheless give rise to recurring constitutional difficulties; in these limited circumstances we have sought the assurance that the classification reflects a reasoned judgment consistent with the ideal of equal protection by inquiring whether it may fairly be viewed as furthering a substantial interest of the State. . . .

Sheer incapability or lax enforcement of the laws barring entry into this country, coupled with the failure to establish an effective bar to the employment of undocumented aliens, has resulted in the creation of a substantial "shadow population" of illegal migrants—numbering in the millions—within our borders. This situation raises the specter of a permanent caste of undocumented resident aliens, encouraged by some to remain here as a source of cheap labor, but nevertheless denied the benefits that our society makes available to citizens and lawful residents. The existence of such an underclass presents most difficult problems for a Nation that prides itself on adherence to principles of equality under law.

The children who are plaintiffs in these cases are special members of this underclass. Persuasive arguments support the view that a State may withhold its beneficence from those whose very presence within the United States is the product of their own unlawful conduct. These arguments do not apply with the same force to classifications imposing disabilities on the minor children of such illegal entrants. At the least, those who elect to enter our territory by stealth and in violation of our law should be prepared to bear the consequences, including, but not limited to, deportation. But the children of those illegal entrants are not comparably situated. Their "parents have the ability to conform their conduct to societal norms," and presumably the ability to remove themselves from the State's jurisdiction; but the children who are plaintiffs in these cases "can affect neither their parents' conduct nor their own status." Even if the State found it expedient to control the conduct of adults by acting against their children, legislation directing the onus of a parent's misconduct against his children does not comport with fundamental conceptions of justice. . . .

Public education is not a "right" granted to individuals by the Constitution. But neither is it merely some governmental "benefit" indistinguishable from other forms of social welfare legislation. Both the importance of education in maintaining our basic institutions, and the lasting impact of its deprivation on the life of the child, mark the distinction. . . . In addition, education provides the basic tools by which individuals might lead economically productive lives to the benefit of us all. In sum, education has a fundamental role in maintaining the fabric of our society. We cannot ignore the significant social costs borne by our Nation when select groups are denied the means to absorb the values and skills upon which our social order rests.

In addition to the pivotal role of education in sustaining our political and cultural heritage, denial of education to some isolated group of children poses an affront to one of the goals of the Equal Protection Clause: the abolition of governmental barriers presenting unreasonable obstacles to advancement on the basis of individual merit. Paradoxically, by depriving the children of any disfavored group of an education, we foreclose the means by which that group might raise the level of esteem in which it is held by the majority. But more directly, "education prepares individuals to be self-reliant and self-sufficient participants in society." Illiteracy is an enduring disability. The inability to read and write will handicap the individual deprived of a basic education each and every day of his life. The inestimable toll of that deprivation on the social, economic, intellectual, and psychological well-being of the individual, and the obstacle it poses to individual achievement, make it most difficult to reconcile the cost or the principle of a status-based denial of basic education with the framework of equality embodied in the Equal Protection Clause. . . .

If the State is to deny a discrete group of innocent children the free public education that it offers to other children residing within its borders, that denial must be justified by a showing that it furthers some substantial state interest. No such showing was made here. Accordingly, the judgment of the Court of Appeals in each of these cases is Affirmed.

CHIEF JUSTICE BURGER, with whom JUSTICE WHITE, JUSTICE REHNQUIST, and JUSTICE O'CONNOR join, dissenting.

Were it our business to set the Nation's social policy, I would agree without hesitation that it is senseless for an enlightened society to deprive any children—including illegal aliens—of an elementary education. I fully agree that it would be folly—and wrong—to tolerate creation of a segment of society made up of illiterate persons, many having a limited or no command of our language. However, the Constitution does not constitute us as "Platonic Guardians" nor does it vest in this Court the authority to strike down laws because they do not meet our standards of desirable social policy, "wisdom," or "common sense." . . . We trespass on the assigned function of the political branches under our structure of limited and separated powers when we assume a policymaking role as the Court does today.

The Court makes no attempt to disguise that it is acting to make up for Congress' lack of "effective leadership" in dealing with the serious national problems caused by the influx of uncountable millions of illegal aliens across our borders. . . . The failure of enforcement of the immigration laws over more than a decade and the inherent difficulty and expense of sealing our vast borders have combined to create a grave socioeconomic dilemma. It is a dilemma that has not yet even been fully assessed, let alone addressed. However, it is not the function of the Judiciary to provide "effective leadership" simply because the political branches of government fail to do so.

The Court's holding today manifests the justly criticized judicial tendency to attempt speedy and wholesale formulation of "remedies" for the failures—or simply the laggard pace—of the political processes of our system of government. The Court employs, and in my view abuses, the Fourteenth Amendment in an effort to become an omnipotent and omniscient problem solver. That the motives for doing so are noble and compassionate does not alter the fact that the Court distorts our constitutional function to make amends for the defaults of others.

In a sense, the Court's opinion rests on such a unique confluence of theories and rationales that it will likely stand for little beyond the results in these particular cases. Yet the extent to which the Court departs from principled constitutional adjudication is nonetheless disturbing.

I have no quarrel with the conclusion that the Equal Protection Clause of the Fourteenth Amendment *applies* to aliens who, after their illegal entry into this country, are indeed physically "within the jurisdiction" of a state. However, as the Court concedes, this "only begins the inquiry." . . .

The dispositive issue in these cases, simply put, is whether, for purposes of allocating its finite resources, a state has a legitimate reason to differentiate between persons who are lawfully within the state and those who are unlawfully there. The distinction the State of Texas has drawn—based not only upon its own legitimate interests but on classifications established by the Federal Government in its immigration laws and policies—is not unconstitutional. . . .

The Court acknowledges that, except in those cases when state classifications disadvantage a "suspect class" or impinge upon a "fundamental right," the Equal Protection Clause permits a state "substantial latitude" in distinguishing between different groups of persons. . . . Moreover, the Court expressly—and correctly—rejects any suggestion that illegal aliens are a suspect class, . . . that education is a fundamental right. . . . Yet by patching together bits and pieces of what might be termed quasi-suspect-class and quasi-fundamental-rights analysis, the Court spins out a theory custom-tailored to the facts of these cases.

In the end, we are told little more than that the level of scrutiny employed to strike down the Texas law applies only when illegal alien children are deprived of a public education. . . . If ever a court was guilty of an unabashedly result-oriented approach, this case is a prime example. . . .

The Court first suggests that these illegal alien children, although not a suspect class, are entitled to special solicitude under the Equal Protection Clause because they lack "control" over or "responsibility" for their unlawful entry into this country. . . . Similarly, the Court appears to take the position that $21.031 is presumptively "irrational" because it has the effect of imposing "penalties" on "innocent" children. . . . However, the Equal Protection Clause does not preclude legislators from classifying among persons on the basis of factors and characteristics over which individuals may be said to lack "control." Indeed, in some circumstances persons generally, and children in particular, may have little control over or responsibility for such things as their ill health, need for public assistance, or place of residence. Yet a state legislature is not barred from considering, for example, relevant differences between the mentally healthy and the mentally ill, or between the residents of different counties, simply because these may be factors unrelated to individual choice or to any "wrongdoing." The Equal Protection Clause protects against arbitrary and irrational classifications, and against invidious discrimination stemming from prejudice and hostility; it is not an all-encompassing "equalizer" designed to eradicate every distinction for which persons are not "responsible."

The Court does not presume to suggest that appellees' purported lack of culpability for their illegal status prevents them from being deported or otherwise "penalized" under federal law. Yet would deportation be any less a "penalty" than denial of privileges provided to legal residents? Illegality of presence in the United States does not—and need not—depend on some amorphous concept of "guilt" or "innocence" concerning an alien's entry. Similarly, a state's use of federal immigration status as a basis for legislative classification is not necessarily rendered suspect for its failure to take such factors into account. . . .

The second strand of the Court's analysis rests on the premise that, although public education is not a constitutionally guaranteed right, "neither is it merely some governmental 'benefit' indistinguishable from other forms of social welfare legislation.". . . Whatever meaning or relevance this opaque observation might have in some other context, it simply has no bearing on the issues at hand. Indeed, it is never made clear what the Court's opinion means on this score. . . .

The importance of education is beyond dispute. Yet we have held repeatedly that the importance of a governmental service does not elevate it to the status of a "fundamental right" for purposes of equal protection analysis. . . . Moreover, the Court points to no meaningful way to distinguish between education and other governmental benefits in this context. Is the Court suggesting that education is more "fundamental" than food, shelter, or medical care?

Once it is conceded—as the Court does—that illegal aliens are not a suspect class, and that education is not a fundamental right, our inquiry should focus on and be limited to whether the legislative classification at issue bears a rational relationship to a legitimate state purpose. . . .

The State contends primarily that $21.031 serves to prevent undue depletion of its limited revenues available for education, and to preserve the fiscal integrity of the State's school-financing system against an ever-increasing flood of illegal aliens—aliens over whose entry or continued presence it has no control. Of course such fiscal concerns alone could not justify discrimination against a suspect class or an arbitrary and irrational denial of benefits to a particular group of persons. Yet I assume no Member of this Court would argue that prudent conservation of finite state revenues is per se an illegitimate goal. Indeed, the numerous classifications this Court has sustained in social welfare legislation were invariably related to the limited amount of revenues available to spend on any given program or set of programs. . . .

Without laboring what will undoubtedly seem obvious to many, it simply is not "irrational" for a state to conclude that it does not have the same responsibility to provide benefits for persons whose very presence in the state and this country is illegal as it does to provide for persons lawfully present. By definition, illegal aliens have no right whatever to be here, and the state may reasonably, and constitutionally, elect not to provide them with governmental services at the expense of those who are lawfully in the state. . . .

Denying a free education to illegal alien children is not a choice I would make were I a legislator. Apart from compassionate considerations, the long-range costs of excluding any children from the public schools may well outweigh the costs of educating them. But that is not the issue; the fact that there are sound *policy* arguments against the Texas Legislature's choice does not render that choice an unconstitutional one. . . .

The Constitution does not provide a cure for every social ill, nor does it vest judges with a mandate to try to remedy every social problem. . . . Moreover, when this Court rushes in to remedy what it perceives to be the failings of the political processes, it deprives those processes of an opportunity to function. When the political institutions are not forced to exercise constitutionally allocated powers and responsibilities, those powers, like muscles not used, tend to atrophy. Today's cases, I regret to say, present yet another example of unwarranted judicial action which in the long run tends to contribute to the weakening of our political processes. . . .

While the "specter of a permanent caste" of illegal Mexican residents of the United States is indeed a disturbing one, . . . it is but one segment of a larger problem, which is for the political branches to solve. I find it difficult to believe that Congress would long tolerate such a self-destructive result—that it would fail to deport these illegal alien families or to provide for the education of their children. Yet instead of allowing the political processes to run their course—albeit with some delay—the Court seeks to do Congress' job for it, compensating for congressional inaction. It is not unreasonable to think that this encourages the political branches to pass their problems to the Judiciary.

The solution to this seemingly intractable problem is to defer to the political processes, unpalatable as that may be to some.

SAN ANTONIO INDEPENDENT SCHOOL DISTRICT V. RODRIGUEZ
411 U.S. 1 (1973)

"We must decide whether the Texas system of financing public education . . . impinges upon a fundamental right explicitly or implicitly protected by the Constitution. . . . Education . . . is not among the rights afforded explicit protection under our Federal Constitution. . . . At least where wealth is involved, the equal protection clause does not require absolute equality [in the funding of public school systems]."

The Question: Does a state system of funding public schools largely through property taxes violates the Constitution if schools in districts with large numbers of minority students receive fewer funds because property values are lower than in districts that are largely white and more affluent?

The Arguments: PRO

Basing public school funding on the value of property in each district has the effect of penalizing students who attend schools in largely minority districts and with lower property values. In many cities, such as San Antonio, Texas, schools in districts with large minority populations receive less than half the per-student funding than schools in more affluent districts receive. The property-tax system of funding education deprives minority students of their right to an equal education.

CON

Public education has historically been the responsibility of state and local governments. Basing a school funding program on property taxes has long been used in most states, and is a decision that each state's voters and lawmakers should be entitled to make. The fact that minority students are concentrated in districts with low property values does not raise a constitutional issue, because there is no state-imposed discrimination on the basis of race or ethnicity.

BACKGROUND

The name of Demetrio Rodriguez appeared first among those on the complaint filed in the federal court of San Antonio, Texas, on July 10, 1968. Six other parents of children in the Edgewood Independent School District, located in the sprawling Hispanic barrio on the West Side of San Antonio, added their names to the suit against a long list of school and state officials. The suit charged that Edgewood children, and those of all other poor families in Texas, suffered from inferior education because of the inequitable property-tax basis of the state's school financing system. The Edgewood parents asked the federal court to find the system in violation of the U.S. Constitution and to order the state to equalize the funding of all 1,000 school districts in Texas.

Demetrio Rodriguez was the logical choice to head the list of plaintiffs in the complaint. The forty-two-year-old Navy and Air Force veteran had worked more than fifteen years at Kelly Air Force Base, just south of his Edgewood home. Demetrio and his family lived in a neat white house on Sylvia Avenue, a street with no sidewalks or storm sewers. Roosters crowed in his neighbors' yards. Three of his four sons attended Edgewood Elementary School, just a block away across a dusty playing field. The school building was crumbling, classrooms lacked basic supplies, and almost half the teachers were not certified and worked on emergency permits. Demetrio feared that Edgewood schools would not

prepare his sons to compete for the good jobs that "Anglos" controlled in San Antonio. He became a grass-roots community activist and helped to organize the Edgewood District Concerned Parents Association.

The parents group met with frustration in asking Edgewood school officials to improve the district's twenty-five schools, which enrolled 22,000 students. Dr. Jose Cardenas, the district superintendent, explained sadly that he had no money to rebuild crumbling schools and hire more qualified teachers. Behind the gloomy financial figures lay ethnic statistics. More than 90 percent of Edgewood students were Hispanic, 6 percent were black, and fewer than one in twenty came from the Anglo community that dominated San Antonio's business and political leadership.

San Antonio was a booming Sun Belt city in 1968, brimming with confidence and eager to attract high-tech industries to balance the city's dependence on livestock production and military spending at its three air force bases. San Antonio won a national "Cleanest City" award in 1967, and bulldozers cleared a downtown slum area to make way for HemisFair '68, the exposition that city leaders hoped would bring millions of tourists and create thousands of jobs. Visitors would flock to see the historic Alamo, whose Anglo defenders fought and died in 1836 at the hands of Mexican troops; and the brand-new Tower of the Americas, soaring 750 feet above the city. The exposition did lure tourists to

San Antonio, but few of them visited the Hispanic barrio that housed more than a third of the city's half-million residents. Four miles from the Alamo, Edgewood parents fought to protect their children from Anglo legislators in the state capitol of Austin who refused to correct the imbalance in school funding.

Just before HemisFair opened in 1968, Demetrio Rodriguez led a group of Edgewood parents to Arthur Gochman's law office in downtown San Antonio. Well-known for defending civil rights, Gochman was also well-connected in the city's business and political elite. Born in 1931, he graduated from Trinity University in San Antonio and the University of Texas Law School. Gochman welcomed the Edgewood parents, who first raised charges of financial hanky-panky in the district's schools. After listening patiently to their complaints, Gochman explained that the real source of poor schools for poor families was unfair funding, not fiddling with the books. He had recently read a federal court decision which struck down funding disparities between schools in Washington, D.C. Although this decision was limited to schools within one district, Gochman felt that its holding could be expanded on a state-wide basis.

Gochman assured the Edgewood parents that he would help them challenge the state's property-tax system. Knowing that his new clients had little money, he hoped to enlist support for the suit from the Mexican American Legal Defense and Education Fund, which copied its name and purpose from the NAACP lawyers' group headed by Thurgood Marshall. Gochman sent MALDEF a legal memo on the Edgewood case, but internal political factors intervened and the group declined to participate. MALDEF was then a small organization and had decided to focus on individual cases of police brutality or job discrimination. Suits against the state of Texas, on behalf of millions of Mexican Americans, would have drained the group's limited resources. Gochman accepted the MALDEF decision and went ahead, funding the Rodriguez case from his own pocket.

Arthur Gochman prepared the complaint with great care. The case rested upon two major claims, neither of which had been accepted by any federal court. One was that the Fourteenth Amendment to the U.S. Constitution included education as a "fundamental right" which states must provide on an equal basis to all students. The other was that poor families constituted a "suspect class" which deserved special judicial protection against discrimination by state officials. Gochman added a third claim: Mexican Americans were a distinct racial and ethnic group and were included, like blacks, in the "suspect class" category. If the federal court accepted *any* of these claims, judicial precedent required that Texas officials present a "compelling" reason to justify the property-tax basis of school funding. Gochman knew that these claims rested on shaky legal foundations, but he supported each with a rock-solid factual argument.

Because the Rodriguez case challenged a state law on federal grounds, it came before a three-judge panel which would rule without a jury. There would be no courtroom dramatics in this case. Gochman knew that his strong suit would be statistical evidence, which by its nature was dry and dull, and he assembled a high-powered crew of six expert witnesses. Five came from San Antonio, including Dr. Cardenas, the Edgewood superintendent, and two

Trinity University professors. The sixth was Dr. Joel Berke, director of the Education Finance and Governance Program at Syracuse University, perhaps the nation's leading expert on school financing.

The case began slowly and wound through the court like a dry creekbed. Lawyers for the state asked the judges to dismiss the complaint, arguing that there was no legal basis for relief to the Edgewood parents. More than a year passed before the judges denied the motion on October 15, 1969. The state then argued that the Texas legislature, which would not convene until January 1971, had authorized a committee study of school financing and should be allowed to act on the study. The state's lawyers predicted that legislative reform would equalize funding among districts and provide relief to the parents. Aware that the legislature that convened in January 1969 had adjourned in May without acting on similar reform proposals, the judges reluctantly granted the state's go-slow motion, directing the defendants to advise the court every 90 days of progress by the committee.

Despite these assurances, the Texas legislators came to Austin in 1971 and left without acting on school finance reform. Judge Adrian Spears of the federal panel lectured the state's lawyers at a hearing in December 1971: "I think it is a little disconcerting to a court, when it abstains and does it on specific grounds that it wishes for the legislature to do something about it, and with education as important as it is to the citizenry of our state and our nation, for the legislature to completely ignore it. It makes you feel that it just does no good for a court to do anything other than, if it feels these laws are suspect, declare them unconstitutional." Judge Spears, a Democrat placed on the federal bench by President John F. Kennedy, lived in Alamo Heights, an independent city inside San Antonio's borders. Spears knew very well the disparities between schools in Edgewood and Alamo Heights.

Preparing for the long-delayed trial with his expert witnesses, Arthur Gochman decided to dramatize the issues by contrasting Edgewood, the poorest of the county's seven systems, with Alamo Heights, its most wealthy district. The names alone illustrated the division—the Hispanic district at the city's edge, and the Anglo district on its heights. Wealth looks down on poverty in most cities and, despite its modest hills, San Antonio is no exception to this rule. Lawyers, doctors, and bankers lived in Alamo Heights; 54 percent of its male workers held executive or professional positions in 1970, against just 4 percent in Edgewood. Three of every four Alamo Heights residents had completed high school. The Edgewood figure was less than one in ten.

Gochman drove home the disparities with simple charts, extracted from more than 100,000 pages of documents. School funding began with local property values: The 1970 figure for Edgewood was only $5,429 per student, while the Alamo Heights figure was $45,095. Even though Edgewood parents taxed themselves at the highest rate in the city, property taxes provided only $26 for each pupil. State funding added $222 and federal programs contributed $108, for a total of $356 for each Edgewood student. Parents in Alamo Heights, eight times as wealthy in property, taxed themselves at the city's lowest rate and still raised $333 for each student. The state program added even more for Alamo Heights than for Edgewood, $225 per student; and federal funding of $26 gave a total of $594. With almost twice as much to spend on each student, Alamo Heights could afford better teachers; 40 percent had masters degrees, as opposed to just 15 percent in Edgewood. Each school counselor in Edgewood had six times as many students to help as those in Alamo Heights.

Gochman put his case into a nutshell with this figure: Edgewood parents would have to tax themselves at twenty times the rate of those in Alamo Heights to match their revenues from property taxes. This would require a tax of almost $13 for each $100 of property value. But the state imposed a property tax ceiling of $1.50. "The Texas system makes it impossible for poor districts to provide quality education," Gochman concluded.

Two days before Christmas in 1971, more than three years after the Edgewood parents filed their suit, the three-judge panel, like the Wise Men of old, brightened their holiday with a ruling that the Texas school-finance system violated the "equal protection" guarantee of the Fourteenth Amendment. The judges held that "wealth" discrimination was "suspect" under the Constitution and that education was a "fundamental" right, as Gochman had argued. The panel also ruled that not only had Texas been "unable to demonstrate compelling state interests" in basing school funding on property values, but it had failed "even to establish a reasonable basis" for the existing system. This latter holding meant that the state had flunked even the most simple test for judging laws. But the brightly-wrapped Christmas package was empty: The judges granted the state two more years to reform the unlawful system (Irons, 1988).

Mr. Justice Powell delivered the opinion of the Court.

This suit attacking the Texas system of financing public education was initiated by Mexican-American parents whose children attend the elementary and secondary schools in the Edgewood Independent School District, an urban school district in San Antonio, Texas. They brought a class action on behalf of schoolchildren throughout the State who are members of minority groups or who are poor and reside in school districts having a low property tax base. Named as defendants were the State Board of Education, the Commissioner of Education, the State Attorney General, and the Bexar County (San Antonio) Board of Trustees. The complaint was filed in the summer of 1968 and a three-judge court was impaneled in January 1969. In December 1971 the panel rendered its judgment in a *per curiam* opinion holding the Texas school finance system unconstitutional under the equal protection clause of the Fourteenth Amendment. The State appealed, and we noted probable jurisdiction to consider the far-reaching constitutional questions presented. . . . For the reasons stated in this opinion, we reverse the decision of the District Court.

The first Texas State Constitution, promulgated upon Texas' entry into the Union in 1845, provided for the establishment of a system of free schools. Early in its history, Texas adopted a dual approach to the financing of its schools, relying on mutual participation by the local school districts and the State. . . .

Until recent times, Texas was a predominantly rural State and its population and property wealth were spread rela-

tively evenly across the State. Sizable differences in the value of assessable property between local school districts became increasingly evident as the State became more industrialized and as rural-to-urban population shifts became more pronounced. The location of commercial and industrial property began to play a significant role in determining the amount of tax resources available to each school district. These growing disparities in population and taxable property between districts were responsible in part for increasingly notable differences in levels of local expenditure for education.

. . . The District Court held that the Texas system discriminates on the basis of wealth in the manner in which education is provided for its people. . . . Finding that wealth is a "suspect" classification and that education is a "fundamental" interest, the District Court held that the Texas system could be sustained only if the State could show that it was premised upon some compelling state interest. . . . On this issue the court concluded that "[n]ot only are defendants unable to demonstrate compelling state interests . . . they fail even to establish a reasonable basis for these classifications."

Texas virtually concedes that its historically rooted dual system of financing education could not withstand the strict judicial scrutiny that this Court has found appropriate in reviewing legislative judgments that interfere with fundamental constitutional rights or that involve suspect classifications. . . .

This, then, establishes the framework for our analysis. We must decide whether the Texas system of financing public education operates to the disadvantage of some suspect class or impinges upon a fundamental right explicitly or implicitly protected by the Constitution, thereby requiring strict judicial scrutiny. . . .

We are unable to agree that this case, which in significant aspects is sui generis, may be so neatly fitted into the conventional mosaic of constitutional analysis under the Equal Protection Clause. Indeed, for the several reasons that follow, we find neither the suspect-classification nor the fundamental-interest analysis persuasive. . . .

The case comes to us with no definitive description of the classifying facts or delineation of the disfavored class. . . . The precedents of this Court provide the proper starting point. The individuals, or groups of individuals, who constituted the class discriminated against in our prior cases shared two distinguishing characteristics: because of their impecunity they were completely unable to pay for some desired benefit, and as a consequence, they sustained an absolute deprivation of a meaningful opportunity to enjoy that benefit. . . .

Only appellees' first possible basis for describing the class disadvantaged by the Texas school-financing system—discrimination against a class of definably "poor" persons—might arguably meet the criteria established in . . . prior cases. Even a cursory examination, however, demonstrates that neither of the two distinguishing characteristics of wealth classifications can be found here. First, in support of their charge that the system discriminates against the "poor," appellees have made no effort to demonstrate that it operates to the peculiar disadvantage of any class fairly definable as indigent, or as composed of persons whose incomes are beneath any designated poverty level. Indeed, there is reason to believe that the poorest families are not necessarily clustered in the poorest property districts....

Second, neither appellees nor the District Court addressed the fact that, unlike each of the foregoing cases, lack of personal resources has not occasioned an absolute deprivation of the desired benefit. The argument here is not that the children in districts having relatively low assessable property values are receiving no public education; rather, it is that they are receiving a poorer quality education than that available to children in districts having more assessable wealth. Apart from the unsettled and disputed question whether the quality of education may be determined by the amount of money expended for it, a sufficient answer to appellees' argument is that, at least where wealth is involved, the equal protection clause does not require absolute equality or precisely equal advantages....

We thus conclude that the Texas system does not operate to the peculiar disadvantage of any suspect class. But in recognition of the fact that this Court has never heretofore held that wealth discrimination alone provides an adequate basis for invoking strict scrutiny, appellees have not relied solely on this contention. They also assert that the State's system impermissibly interferes with the exercise of a "fundamental" right and that accordingly the prior decisions of this Court require the application of the strict standard of judicial review.... It is this question—whether education is a fundamental right, in the sense that it is among the rights and liberties protected by the Constitution—which has so consumed the attention of courts and commentators in recent years.

In *Brown v. Board of Education,* a unanimous Court recognized that "education is perhaps the most important function of state and local governments."...

Nothing this Court holds today in any way detracts from our historic dedication to public education. We are in complete agreement with the conclusion of the three-judge panel below that "the grave significance of education both to the individual and to our society" cannot be doubted. But the importance of a service performed by the State does not determine whether it must be regarded as fundamental for purposes of examination under the equal protection clause....

... It is not the province of this Court to create substantive constitutional rights in the name of guaranteeing equal protection of the laws. Thus, the key to discovering whether education is "fundamental" is not to be found in comparisons of the relative societal significance of education as opposed to subsistence or housing. Nor is it to be found by weighing whether education is as important as the right to travel. Rather the answer lies in assessing whether there is a right to education explicitly or implicitly guaranteed by the Constitution....

Education, of course, is not among the rights afforded explicit protection under our Federal Constitution. Nor do we find any basis for saying it is implicitly so protected.... It is appellees' contention, however, that education is distinguishable from other services and benefits provided by the State because it bears a peculiarly close relationship to other rights and liberties accorded protection under the constitution. Specifically, they insist that education is itself a funda-

mental personal right because it is essential to the effective exercise of First Amendment freedoms and to intelligent utilization of the right to vote. In asserting a nexus between speech and education, appellees urge that the right to speak is meaningless unless the speaker is capable of articulating his thoughts intelligently and persuasively. The "marketplace of ideas" is an empty forum for those lacking basic communicative tools. Likewise, they argue that the corollary right to receive information becomes little more than a hollow privilege when the recipient has not been taught to read, assimilate, and utilize available knowledge.

A similar line of reasoning is pursued with respect to the right to vote. Exercise of the franchise, it is contended, cannot be divorced from the educational foundation of the voter. The electoral process, if reality is to conform to the democratic ideal, depends on an informed electorate: a voter cannot cast his ballot intelligently unless his reading skills and thought processes have been adequately developed.

We need not dispute any of these propositions. The Court has long afforded zealous protection against unjustifiable governmental interference with the individual's rights to speak and to vote. Yet we have never presumed to possess either the ability or the authority to guarantee to the citizenry the most effective speech or the most informed electoral choice. That these may be desirable goals of a system of freedom of expression and of a representative form of government is not to be doubted. These are indeed goals to be pursued by a people whose thoughts and beliefs are freed from governmental interference. But they are not values to be implemented by judicial intrusion into otherwise legitimate state activities.

Even if it were conceded that some identifiable quantum of education is a constitutionally protected prerequisite to the meaningful exercise of either right, we have no indication that the present levels of educational expenditures in Texas provide an education that falls short.

... Furthermore, the logical limitations on appellees' nexus theory are difficult to perceive. How, for instance, is education to be distinguished from the significant personal interests in the basics of decent food and shelter? Empirical examination might well buttress an assumption that the ill-fed, ill-clothed, and ill-housed are among the most ineffective participants in the political process.

... We have carefully considered each of the arguments supportive of the District Court's finding that education is a fundamental right or liberty and have found those arguments unpersuasive....

The consideration and initiation of fundamental reforms with respect to state taxation and education are matters reserved for the legislative processes of the various States and we do no violence to the values of federalism and separation of powers by staying our hand. We hardly need add that this Court's action today is not to be viewed as placing its judicial imprimatur on the status quo. The need is apparent for reform in tax systems which may well have relied too long and too heavily on the local property tax. And certainly innovative thinking as to public education, its methods and its funding is necessary to assure both a higher level of quality and greater uniformity of opportunity. These matters merit the continued attention of the scholars who already have contributed much to their challenges. But the ultimate solutions must come from the lawmakers and from the democratic pressures of those who elect them.

Reversed.

MR. JUSTICE MARSHALL, with whom MR. JUSTICE DOUGLAS concurs, dissenting.

The Court today decides, in effect, that a State may constitutionally vary the quality of education which it offers its children in accordance with the amount of taxable wealth located in the school districts within which they reside. . . . More unfortunately . . . the majority's holding can only be seen as a retreat from our historic commitment to equality of educational opportunity and as unsupportable acquiescence in a system which deprives children in their earliest years of the chance to reach their full potential as citizens. . . .

In my judgment, the right of every American to an equal start in life, so far as the provision of a state service as important as education is concerned, is far too vital to permit state discrimination on grounds as tenuous as those presented by this record. Nor can I accept the notion that it is sufficient to remit these appellees to the vagaries of the political process which, contrary to the majority's suggestion, has proved singularly unsuited to the task of providing a remedy for this discrimination. I, for one, am unsatisfied with the hope of an ultimate "political" solution sometime in the indefinite future while, in the meantime, countless children unjustifiably receive inferior educations that "may affect their hearts and minds in a way unlikely ever to be undone." Brown v. Board of Education. I must therefore respectfully dissent. . . .

The appellants do not deny the disparities in educational funding caused by variations in taxable district property wealth. They do contend, however, that whatever the differences in per-pupil spending among Texas districts, there are no discriminatory consequences for the children of the disadvantaged districts. . . . In their view, there is simply no denial of equal educational opportunity to any Texas schoolchildren as a result of the widely varying per-pupil spending . . .

. . . We sit, however, not to resolve disputes over educational theory but to enforce our Constitution. It is an inescapable fact that if one district has more funds available per pupil than another district, the former will have greater choice in educational planning than will the latter. In this regard, I believe the question of discrimination in educational quality must be deemed to be an objective one that looks to what the State provides its children, not to what the children are able to do with what they receive. . . . Indeed, who can ever measure for a child the opportunities lost and the talents wasted for want of a broader, more enriched education? Discrimination in the opportunity to learn that is afforded a child must be our standard. . . .

In my view, then, it is inequality—not some notion of gross inadequacy—of educational opportunity that raises a question of denial of equal protection of the laws. I find any other approach to the issue unintelligible and without directing principle. Here, appellees have made a substantial showing of wide variations in educational funding and the resulting educational opportunity afforded to the schoolchildren of Texas. This discrimination is, in large measure, attributable to significant disparities in the taxable wealth of local Texas school districts. This is a sufficient showing to raise a substantial question of discriminatory state action in violation of the equal protection clause. . . . Texas has chosen to provide free public education for all its citizens, and it has embodied that decision in its constitution. Yet, having established public education for its citizens, the State, as a direct consequence of the variations in local property wealth endemic to Texas' financing scheme, has provided some Texas schoolchildren with substantially less resources for their education than others. Thus, while on its face the Texas scheme may merely discriminate between local districts, the impact of that discrimination falls directly upon the children whose educational opportunity is dependent upon where they happen to live. Consequently, the District Court correctly concluded that the Texas financing scheme discriminates from a constitutional perspective, between schoolchildren on the basis of the amount of taxable property located within their local districts. . . .

The Court seeks solace for its action today in the possibility of legislative reform. The Court's suggestions of legislative redress and experimentation will doubtless be of great comfort to the schoolchildren of Texas' disadvantaged districts, but considering the vested interests of wealthy school districts in the preservation of the status quo, they are worth little more. The possibility of legislative action is, in all events, no answer to this Court's duty under the Constitution to eliminate unjustified state discrimination. In this case we have been presented with an instance of such discrimination, in a particularly invidious form, against an individual interest of large constitutional and practical importance. To support the demonstrated discrimination in the provision of educational opportunity the State has offered a justification which, on analysis, takes on at best an ephemeral character. Thus, I believe that the wide disparities in taxable district property wealth inherent in the local property tax element of the Texas financing scheme render that scheme violative of the Equal Protection Clause.

I would therefore affirm the judgment of the District Court.

MEET DEMETRIO RODRIGUEZ

I was born in 1925 in a small town in Texas that doesn't exist anymore. The name of it is Valley Wells. It was between Cotulla and Carrizo Springs, down near Laredo in Dimmit County, near the Rio Grande. It was a farming town; mostly winter vegetables. My folks lived in Valley Wells, and from there they went to Crystal City, then they moved to Hondo and Uvalde. Most of my brothers are in Uvalde now. My great-grandfather was a born Texan, my father was a born Texan, but my mother came from Mexico. She met my father in Eagle Pass, down on the border.

My father was a migrant worker—he worked in the fields. He would settle in a town until there was no more work, and he'd move to another town. In the early years, when he was young, he used to clear land. They would go around in buggies and wagons and sleep out in the fields. He used to tell me that they'd go into a town, and they'd tell him, Mexican, don't let that sun set on you here! They had guys riding on a horse with a gun.

I came to San Antonio with my brother to go to school here in 1931, when I was about six years old. I had an uncle here, and he suggested to my father that maybe we could get a better education here in San Antonio, because where we were living then the school was segregated. They had one school and one teacher for the Mexican children. We had an Anglo teacher. She was a good teacher, trying to help us out, but it was hard for her, all by herself. I don't think she could speak Spanish.

When I came to San Antonio I spoke one time to my brother in Spanish and the teacher told me, No, don't speak like that! She told me, It's better that you speak English. But my teachers here in San Antonio were very understanding. The schools here were not segregated, but they had different groups in each grade, A and B. A was mostly Anglo kids and B was Mexican kids. At that time the blacks couldn't go to school with white people. Mostly all the Mexican kids were in the B class. When I passed to the second grade they put me with the advanced kids in the A class. I still remember this Anglo kid named Harold. He was the dumbest thing you could think of, but they put him in the A class even though he couldn't compete with us. That was the name of the game; we had to compete with the Anglo kids.

I went to about the tenth grade—then I was drafted into the Navy in 1944, when I was eighteen. My brother and I were the only two kids from that little town in the service. The Anglo kids stayed there because their fathers were farm owners and got them exemptions. I served in the Pacific, in the Marshall and Gilbert islands, in a carrier aircraft-service unit, like a maintenance squadron. I learned sheet-metal work in the Navy. I didn't even know what a plane *looked* like before that. To me the Navy was a good experience. It helped me quite a bit, and I learned how to eat like a gringo—like shit on a shingle. You know, chipped beef on toast. I came back after the Navy and started working for a company that manufactured toilets and wash basins.

I got married in 1951, and my first wife died. We had a boy in 1953, David. Then I got married again and we got divorced. Then I married my third wife. We had a son, Alex; then Carlos; then James; and Patricia, she's the youngest, she was born in 1971.

I served in the Air Force in 1951. I was in the reserves and they called me to active duty during the Korean War. After I came back from the Air Force I made an application for federal civil service, and they called me and told me I had passed the exam. I was an aircraft sheet–metal worker at Kelly Air Force Base here in San Antonio. We would manufacture parts for aircraft, mostly old B-52s. They were real old aircraft and the aluminum corrodes on them. The parts that were needed were no longer being manufactured. That was our job, to manufacture exact duplicates. Later on I advanced to quality control, where I was an inspector for the last five years that I was there. It was hard work, and I put in thirty-nine years, with my service time. I don't get much of a pension, but I make a living. My house is paid up. Of course, it isn't a mansion, it's in a poor district. But I can live on what I'm getting.

I moved into Edgewood in about 1957. This is the southwest part of San Antonio, near the Air Force base where I worked. Edgewood used to be mostly a Belgian area; they were farmers with gardens. When Mexican people started coming they sold them lots, very small, about forty by a hundred and fifty feet. They called it Las Colonias, The Colonies. That's funny. They didn't have any drainage, and the streets were dirt. We had a lot of problems in Edgewood; the schools were all shot. A lot of people realized their kids weren't getting a good education, like the kids on the north side of San Antonio were getting, where the Anglos lived. So they kind of rebelled against the schools. We blamed the problems on the superintendent. He was an Anglo who had been in Edgewood for many years.

The Edgewood elementary school was an old school, all beat up and falling down. It had a lot of bats, and they could only use the first floor. Sometimes bricks would fall down. We had a lot of problems in that school, teaching problems and disciplinary problems; they didn't care what the kids were doing. A lot of parents got together in 1968. We didn't know each other, but we got to know each other. We organized a group we named the Edgewood District Concerned Parents Association. The organizer was a very active lady named Mrs. Alberta Sneed; she was one of the plaintiffs in the case. From there we started having meetings and trying to organize the people to have some kind of dialogue with the school board, with the superintendent. They didn't want to listen to us, so we had a little demonstration, with people marching in front of the school. It got to where the media got caught up in it. I think the media has helped us a lot.

Willie Velazquez heard about it; he's director of Southwest Voter Registration. He got us together with a lawyer named Arthur Gochman. Arthur is a real down-to-earth man; he's got a lot of money but he doesn't show it. We started talking about why we had problems in Edgewood. Arthur told us, The problem's not your superintendent; your problem is the way the state finances your schools. It's a very complicated thing for a layman to understand. Even now there's a lot of things I don't understand. So I asked Arthur, What are we *doing* here? So he said, Well, I'm willing to file a suit against the state of Texas, but we need people, plaintiffs. All I need is for the people to support me, get me signatures from parents. And I said, If that's what you need, I'm willing to sign, to put my name there. What the heck, there's nothing they can do to *me!* So I was the first plaintiff to sign. I didn't know that I was going to be the lead-off plaintiff. I knew there was going to be a case filed: Arthur explained what a class-action suit was. He said, It's going to be all the citizens of Texas that are being discriminated against in school financing, not only the ones that sign; it's going to be everybody against the state of Texas. It was a good conversation. In my mind I thought, I ain't got nothing to lose; I think maybe we could do some good. I didn't envision that it was going to be something this big, that it would take *this* long!

Then I went around, trying to get more people. For a couple of weeks I walked the streets in Edgewood, trying to get people to sign. So we got about fifteen parents. Some of the people didn't want to sign. They said, We sign that thing and they'll just forget about it. I told them, Well, we can try—at least we're doing something. When it came out in the press, a lot of people found out at work that I filed a suit against the state of Texas and they said, You can't do that. You're a civil service employee; you're under the Hatch Act. I said, That's baloney. I can do anything as long as I take the route through the judicial system. A lot of the Anglo guys used to argue with me; they didn't like it. They thought I was a Communist. I told them, I'm no more Communist than you are. I'm using the judicial system and I don't care what you say. I told them, You know why I'm doing this? Because I've *been* the victim of discrimination.

I always thought about the discrimination that I've been through. When I was in the Navy I came back to visit my brother in Hondo. I was in my Navy uniform, very proud, with my Donald Duck cap. I went into a restaurant and they told me they couldn't serve me—I'd have to go back in the kitchen. I went to a theater in Hondo; they told me I couldn't sit there, I had to sit on the side for Mexicans or in the balcony with the blacks. When I was a boy, we went to pick cotton in West Texas and there was no restaurant you could go in. You could go order something at a little window in the back, but you couldn't eat in the restaurants. My boy says, Dad, I heard that story so many times and it's the same story you always tell. I said, It's the same story because I went *through* it, dammit! And I'll never forget it! I was a kid and I went through those things.

Edgewood hasn't changed too much since I moved here twenty years ago. We still don't have no sidewalks, no drainage. When the kids go to school they have to walk on the street and they get wet. Yesterday, when it was raining, the kids were coming out of the Kennedy High School and walking along McMullen, which has a lot of traffic coming in and out of Kelly. The streets are flooded and the cars come by and throw water on the kids. That kid ain't going to school, so then we don't get as much state aid, which is based on ADA, average daily attendance. But we developed a homeowners' association, and the last two years we started to work with the city councilman to bring us money for drainage. We got a bond passed; we're going to have $18.4 million for that area. We're going to get drainage, and sidewalks and streets resurfaced, over the next five years.

But it's still not that good. We still have a lot of obstacles thrown in front of us. Not only the blacks and Mexican Americans, but a lot of poor people are being put on the back burner, where nobody wants to think about it or do something about it. Like in the Appalachian mountains. It's a shame that we have such a rich country, that we're not sharing with a lot of these people. It's bringing this country down. If you don't educate your citizens, something's going to happen and it's not going to help this country. We talk about the Communist takeover from South America—they're going to cross over the Rio Grande and all that baloney. We don't *have* to have the Communists come over here! We are doing the harm to this country by not having equal education. That's the only thing you can give a poor people. Give them an education and they'll be better citizens; they will help this country more. The more education that you have, the better it's going to be for your country. We need intelligent people to work, especially now that you have computers.

This country has been growing, and we have a lot of problems. I think they can be solved, but it will take years to do it. I guess I'm going to die and not get to see this thing resolved, these problems that we have. The Establishment doesn't want to make any waves for the people that got the money, the districts with money. But one of these days we're going to solve it; maybe it will be another fifty years. I hope with all the actions we're taking in the courts, to bring up the schools and the college system, all these things will bring changes. And the outlook of the Mexican American people here is positive. I'm better off than my parents were, my kids are going to be better off than I am. Of course, you have to hustle, you have to be aggressive. I tell my kids, You have to be aggressive like a gringo! He's aggressive! If he doesn't get in there, he'll push himself in.

But things are getting better in this country for everybody. And I *like* San Antonio! This is my home town. This is where I made my living, where my sons and daughter were born. This city has been growing. We're going to get drainage in our area in five years; it's going to be better. I think we'll have better schools. I *know* it's going to be better (Irons, 1988).

CHAPTER 10

The Bill of Rights at War: The Wartime Internment of Japanese Americans

INTRODUCTION

The Japanese American wartime internment cases are in a separate chapter in this book because they deserve study and critical examination as an important episode in American legal and political history. The mass internment of more than 110,000 persons of Japanese ancestry from the West Coast during World War II, preceded by curfew and exclusion orders issued by military officials, produced the two closely related cases in this chapter, *Hirabayashi v. United States* and *Korematsu v. United States*. The Supreme Court decisions in these cases, handed down eighteen months apart in 1943 and 1944, have been condemned by virtually all legal scholars; writing in 1945, Yale law professor Eugene Rostow called the rulings a "constitutional disaster." Yet, although the criminal convictions in these cases were vacated by federal judges in the 1980s on the grounds of "governmental misconduct" during their prosecution in the 1940s, the *Hirabayashi* and *Korematsu* decisions have not been reversed or repudiated by the Supreme Court. As Justice Robert Jackson wrote in his *Korematsu* dissent, the Court's holding that American citizens can be placed in indefinite confinement during wartime without any charges against them "lies around like a loaded weapon ready for the hand of any authority that can bring forward a plausible claim."

Those who dismiss fears of this legal weapon being used against any other American citizens as unfounded need only look at the war on terrorism launched by the U.S. government after the attacks on the World Trade Center and Pentagon on September 11, 2001. American troops in Afghanistan detained several men thought to be members of the Al Qaeda terrorist network who were later discovered to be American citizens. Branded as "enemy combatants," they were held without being charged, without access to lawyers, and without any recourse to the courts. They were literally "men without a country," held incommunicado and threatened with possible lifetime imprisonment without ever going before a judge for a hearing on the legality of their detention. Justice Jackson's prophecy came true when the Justice Department filed briefs in the cases of other persons held without charges as "material witnesses" in the hunt for terrorists, citing the *Hirabayashi* and *Korematsu* cases as authority for the government's power to suspend constitutional guarantees during a period of "national emergency."

To place these two cases of historic importance and current relevance in perspective, the following discussion will provide a more complete understanding of the factors that led to the wartime internment. It will also illustrate the human dimension of these cases in brief accounts of the three young men who challenged the curfew and exclusion orders in 1942.

The justices who decided the *Barnette* case on Flag Day in 1943 were bitterly divided over the expulsion of young Witnesses from their schools for disloyalty. Just a week later, however, they agreed without dissent in a case that involved more than 100,000 Americans who were expelled from their communities for disloyalty. The mass evacuation of Japanese Americans from the West Coast during World War II and their confinement for three years in tar-paper barracks—fenced by barbed wire and guarded by armed soldiers—confronted the justices with their own test of loyalty. Does the Constitution protect "all classes of men, at all times, and under all circumstances, equally in war and in peace," as the justices stated without dissent in 1866? Or can "the clamor of an excited people" and the government's claims of "military necessity" allow the suspension of constitutional rights during wartime? The justices faced these momentous questions in deciding the challenges of three young Japanese

Americans—Gordon Hirabayashi, Minoru Yasui, and Fred Korematsu—to the army's evacuation and exclusion orders.

Taking a closer look at events we "know" through history books can be surprising. One surprise about the wartime treatment of Japanese Americans is that the initial reaction in the area most stricken with "Pearl Harbor panic" was one of tolerance and understanding. Most of the "thousands of Japanese here and in other coast cities," the *Los Angeles Times* editorialized on December 8, 1941, were "good Americans, born and educated as such." Published in the city with the largest number of Japanese Americans, this influential paper urged its readers that "there be no precipitation, no riots, no mob law." The *Times* editors tried to calm fears of a follow-up Japanese attack on West Coast targets. "Let's Not Get Rattled," they cautioned on December 10. It would be virtually impossible for Japanese aircraft carriers to "sneak up on this Coast undetected by our now aroused sky scouters," they assured a jittery public. Echoed by other prominent West Coast papers, such assurances helped to calm public fears and protected Japanese Americans from retaliation.

Some six weeks after Pearl Harbor, however, the tide of public opinion abruptly shifted. Both the press and public officials demanded the removal of all Japanese Americans from the West Coast. On January 16, 1942, Los Angeles congressman Leland Ford urged that "all Japanese, whether citizens or not, be placed in inland concentration camps." Two weeks later the *Los Angeles Times* reversed its editorial stance and argued that "the rigors of war demand proper detention of Japanese and their immediate removal from the most acute danger spots" along the coast. Walter Lippmann, the nation's most respected columnist, deplored "the unwillingness of Washington to adopt a policy of mass evacuation and mass internment" of Japanese Americans. "Nobody's constitutional rights include the right to reside and do business on a battlefield," he wrote like a judge. Westbrook Pegler issued another ruling in his widely read column: "The Japanese in California should be under armed guard to the last man and woman right now—and to hell with habeas corpus until the danger is over."

The growing force of demands like these hit Washington like a tidal wave. Officials in the War and Justice Departments ended their squabbling over legal niceties and sent a two-page document to the White House. On February 19, 1942, President Franklin Roosevelt signed Executive Order 9066, authorizing Secretary of War Henry L. Stimson and his subordinates to designate military zones "from which any or all persons may be excluded." General John L. DeWitt, the West Coast army commander, first imposed a nighttime curfew on "all persons of Japanese ancestry" and then issued "exclusion orders" that were backed by Congress with criminal penalties. By the end of 1942, all but a handful of the Japanese Americans who lived between Seattle and San Diego had been herded into ten "relocation centers," the government's euphemism for America's wartime concentration camps. Scattered from the California desert to Arkansas swamps, these camps imprisoned more than 110,000 people—most of them native-born American citizens—who were never charged with crimes or given a hearing.

Behind the initial appeals for tolerance after Pearl Harbor lay decades of intolerance toward Orientals of any nationality. The arrival of Chinese laborers in the 1850s to lay railroad track and pick vegetables produced resentment among Caucasian workers, many of them also recent immigrants. With congressional passage in 1882 of the Chinese Exclusion Act, nativist groups turned their demagoguery against the Japanese, who numbered only two thousand in 1890, almost all in California. But the flow increased until Congress shut off all further Japanese immigration in 1924, by which time more than 100,000 lived on the West Coast. Japanese natives were excluded from citizenship and barred in California from owning or leasing land.

Despite these legal barriers, Japanese Americans worked hard and prospered. Many found ways around the Alien Land Law and operated farms owned by friendly whites, or bought land in the names of their native-born children, granted citizenship at birth by the Fourteenth Amendment. By 1940, Japanese farmers produced close to half of California's vegetables. Leaders of the Grower-Shipper Vegetable Association, a powerful lobby of white farmers, took advantage of "Pearl Harbor panic" to cut down their competitors. "We're charged with wanting to get rid of the Japs for selfish reasons," the group's manager said. "We might as well be honest. We do."

Another group was less honest in its campaign to rid the coast of Japanese Americans. Military officials made claims of widespread "sabotage and espionage" in arguing for mass internment. But they had no evidence that any Japanese American had committed such crimes. They were not deterred by this fact. In the "Final Recommendation" he sent to Secretary Stimson, urging mass internment, General DeWitt blamed this lack of evidence against Japanese Americans on their sneaky nature: "The very fact that no sabotage has taken place to date is a disturbing and confirming indication that such action will be taken," he claimed. DeWitt's support for internment was really based on unvarnished racism. "The Japanese race is an enemy race," he stated, "and while many second and third generation Japanese born on United States soil, possessed of United States citizenship, have become 'Americanized,' the racial strains are undiluted." DeWitt used blunter language before a congressional panel: "A Jap's a Jap," he said; "it makes no difference whether he is an American citizen or not. I have no confidence in their loyalty whatsoever."

General Dewitt was hardly alone in basing his wartime decisions about Japanese Americans on racial stereotypes. DeWitt had no legal training, but many military and civilian officials who attended prestigious law schools showed little respect for the Constitution they had sworn to uphold as lawyers. One of the first and most influential advocates of mass internment was Colonel Karl Bendetsen, a Stanford Law School graduate who drafted General DeWitt's "Final Recommendation" for the evacuation of Japanese Americans. Admitting in February 1942 the army's inability to justify "the sheer military necessity for such action," Bendetsen nonetheless argued that "a substantial majority" of Japanese Americans "bear allegiance to Japan, are well controlled and disciplined by the enemy, and at the proper time will engage in organized sabotage" to aid the Japanese cause. He presented no evidence for this claim, simply asserting that the "racial affinities" of Japanese Americans predisposed them to disloyalty.

Even those officials with qualms about the constitutional basis for mass internment fell prey to racial stereotypes. During the internal debate that preceded President Roosevelt's executive order, even General DeWitt acknowledged the legal barriers to the military orders he later signed. "An American citizen, after all, is an American citizen," he reminded the army's chief lawyer. At the War Department's very top, Secretary Henry Stimson—a Harvard lawyer—knew the Constitution stood in Dewitt's way. "We cannot discriminate against our citizens on the ground of racial origin," he admitted before DeWitt's "Final Recommendation" reached his desk. But after reading its racist claims, Stimson agreed that "their racial characteristics are such that we cannot understand or trust even the citizen Japanese." He backed mass internment even though "it will make a tremendous hole in our constitutional system." Perhaps the most revealing—and cynical—remark came from John J. McCloy, another Harvard lawyer who served as Stimson's chief deputy. "To a Wall Street lawyer," he told an army official, "the Constitution is just a piece of paper."

Many civilian officials shared the racial views of their military counterparts. Attorney General Francis Biddle asked three young government lawyers to advise him on the internment question. All three—Benjamin Cohen, Oscar Cox, and Joseph Rauh—were trained at Harvard Law School. None had any training in anthropology, but this did not deter them. "Since the Occidental eye cannot readily distinguish one Japanese resident from another," they told Biddle, "effective surveillance of the movement of particular Japanese residents suspected of disloyalty is extremely difficult if not impossible." As Caucasians, Biddle's legal advisers considered it unnecessary "to bar the millions of persons of German or Italian stock from either seacoast area," since "the normal Caucasian countenances of such persons enable the average American to recognize particular individuals by distinguishing minor facial characteristics." None of these lawyers had ever met Gordon Hirabayashi, Min Yasui, or Fred Korematsu, whose faces were easily distinguishable to anyone with normal vision. Biddle's legal adviser recommended setting aside "special reservations" where Japanese Americans could "live under special restrictions."

Perhaps the most extreme version of the "racial characteristics" argument was presented in a brief submitted to a federal district judge by Charles Burdell, a special assistant to Attorney General Biddle. Urging the judge to dismiss a constitutional challenge to the army's internment orders, Burdell wrote that "Jap citizens are inevitably bound, by intangible ties, to the people of the Empire of Japan. They are alike, physically and psychologically." Burdell elaborated his genetic theory of loyalty. "Even now, though we have been separated from the English people for over 100 years, we still take pride in the exploits of the RAF over Berlin, and the courageous fighting of the Aussies in Northern Africa. Why? Because they are people like us. They are Anglo-Saxons." Burdell's theory equally fit the Japanese Americans. "Who can doubt that these Japs in this country, citizens as well as aliens, feel a sense of pride in the feats of the Jap Army—this feeling of pride is strong in some, weak in others, but the germ of it must be present in the mind of every one of them."

* * *

What feelings *did* go through the minds of the three young men whose challenges to General DeWitt's military orders reached the Supreme Court? Much like Dred Scott and Homer Plessy before them, these young Americans were viewed by the Supreme Court solely on the basis of their shared race and ancestry. But their stories, even briefly told, show us how members of the same group—supposedly identical in their physical and psychological characteristics—can differ in many ways.

Gordon Hirabayashi was born in 1918 in Auburn, a rural town near Seattle, where his father ran a roadside fruit market. His parents belonged to a Japanese pacifist sect, similar to the Society of Friends, better known as Quakers; both groups worshiped without ministers and rejected military service. During high school, Gordon became an Eagle Scout and served as president of the Auburn Christian Fellowship. When he entered the University of Washington in Seattle in 1937, he joined the University Quaker Meeting and registered with his local draft board as a conscientious objector. When General DeWitt imposed a nighttime curfew order on all Japanese Americans in March 1942, Gordon was living in the campus YMCA dormitory. He obeyed the curfew for more than a month, often running back to his dorm to beat the clock. He later recalled thinking, "Why the hell am I running back? Am I an American or not? Why am I running back and nobody else is?"

On the night of May 4, Gordon stopped running and stayed out past the curfew hour. He recorded his feeling in his diary: "Peculiar, but I received a lift—perhaps it is a release—when I consciously break the silly old curfew." The army's evacuation orders gave Japanese Americans one week to dispose of their property and report to "assembly centers" at racetracks and fairgrounds. Before the orders reached Seattle, Gordon worked with the Quakers in helping families store their household goods and move with suitcases to the Puyallup Fairgrounds near Seattle. "Gosh!—something seems wrong there; helping people to go behind barbed wires and flimsy shacks," he wrote. "What a mixed-up life this is—the American way."

When the evacuation orders reached Seattle on May 16, Gordon became a conscientious objector to internment. He went to the downtown FBI office and told Special Agent Francis Manion that he would not report to Puyallup. Manion recorded Gordon's statement that "it was the principle of the Society of Friends that each person should follow the will of God according to his own convictions and that he could not reconcile the will of God, a part of which was expressed in the Bill of Rights and the United States Constitution, with the order discriminating against Japanese aliens and American citizens of Japanese ancestry." Agent Manion arrested Gordon for violating both the curfew and evacuation orders and placed him in the county jail to await trial.

Minoru Yasui did not share Gordon Hirabayashi's pacifism. Born in 1916 in the apple-growing region of Hood River, Oregon, he entered the University of Oregon in 1933 and volunteered for the army's reserve officer training program. After receiving a second lieutenant's commission in 1937, Min attended the university's law school, graduating in 1939. His law dean later wrote that he held a "relatively high opinion" of Yasui as a student, "but on many occasions I detected a streak of blind stubbornness in him." Unable to find legal work in Oregon, Min landed a job with the Japanese consulate in Chicago. His work was mostly clerical, but he also gave speeches defending Japanese policies in Asia before Rotary Clubs and similar groups. As an American citizen, he duly registered with the State Department as a foreign agent.

The day after Pearl Harbor, Min received a telegram from his father: "Now that this country is at war and needs you, and since you are trained as an officer, I as your father urge you to enlist immediately." Responding to this patriotic appeal, he resigned his consular post and returned to Oregon. Min then received an army order to report for duty at Fort Vancouver, near Portland. But when he arrived in uniform, army officers told him he was unacceptable for service and ordered him off the base. This rebuff on racial grounds triggered a stubborn reaction; Min returned eight times to Fort Vancouver and was turned away each time.

Even before the evacuation orders reached Portland, Min decided to challenge the curfew, imposed by General DeWitt through Military Order Number 3 of the army's Western Defense Command. Min had no quarrel with a curfew applied to aliens. "But Military Order Number 3 applied to all persons of Japanese ancestry," he later said. "I said, 'There the general is wrong, because it makes distinctions between citizens on the basis of ancestry.' That order infringed my rights as a citizen." The night of March 28, 1942, Min approached a policeman in downtown Portland. "I pulled out this order that said all persons of Japanese ancestry must be in their place of abode, and I pulled out my birth certificate and said, 'Look, I'm a person of Japanese ancestry, arrest me.' And the policeman said, 'Run along home, you'll get in trouble.'" Min stubbornly persisted, finally convincing a sergeant at police headquarters to arrest him for curfew violation. He spent nine months in solitary confinement before his trial.

Fred Korematsu did not challenge the internment from religious conviction or legal training. Unlike Gordon Hirabayashi and Min Yasui, he did not court arrest. In fact, Fred tried to evade the evacuation orders by changing his name, altering his draft card, and undergoing plastic surgery on his eyelids and nose. But his effort to escape detection as a Japanese American failed. On the afternoon of May 30, 1942, police officers in San Leandro, California, got a tip and picked up a young man walking down the street with his girlfriend. The suspect claimed to be Clyde Sarah, of Spanish-Hawaiian origin. But his story quickly fell apart; he spoke no Spanish, and his draft card had been crudely altered with ink eradicator. The officers took him to police headquarters. "One of the girls who worked in the office seemed to recognize me," Fred recalled, "and so I finally said who I was."

Born in 1919 in Oakland, California, Korematsu finished high school in 1938 and dropped out of college after one month for financial reasons. He then attended welding school in Oakland and worked as a shipyard welder following this training. The navy turned him away in June 1941 because of gastric ulcers, and his union expelled its Japanese American members after Pearl Harbor. Fred took piano lessons from an Italian woman and fell in love with her daughter. After his arrest, he told an FBI agent what he did after his family reported to the Tanforan Racetrack for evacuation: "I stayed in Oakland to earn enough money to take my girl with me to the Middle West. Her name is Miss Ida Boitano. She is a different nationality—Italian. The operation was for the purpose of changing my appearance so that I would not be subjected to ostracism when my girl and I went East." Fred never saw Ida again; FBI agents reported that she answered Fred's letters from jail by "telling him not to write her anymore."

Fred Korematsu did not volunteer to challenge the evacuation orders, but he eagerly accepted legal help from Ernest Besig, the ACLU director in San Francisco. The city's newspapers had reported Fred's arrest, and Besig visited him in jail. He was pleased to find a willing client for a test case. Behind his personal reasons for evading the evacuation, Fred shared with Gordon Hirabayashi and Min Yasui an awareness of his constitutional rights. During a jailhouse visit, he gave Ernest Besig a handwritten statement arguing that Japanese Americans "should have been given a fair trial in order that they may defend their loyalty at court in a democratic way, but they were placed in imprisonment without a fair trial!" He posed this question to the government: "Is this a racial issue?" And he suggested a way to find the answer: "Fred Korematsu's Test Case may help."

*　*　*

Despite the differing motivations of the "test case" defendants, their criminal trials in federal district courts were uniformly brief and perfunctory. Judge Lloyd Black, who presided at Gordon Hirabayashi's trial in Seattle, rejected his lawyers' claims that General DeWitt's curfew and evacuation orders violated the Due Process Clause of the Fifth Amendment by singling out a racial group for "special restrictions" not imposed on others. Noting the proximity of aircraft plants and naval bases to Seattle, Black pointed to "the fact that the parachutists and saboteurs, as well as the soldiers, of Japan make diabolically clever use of infiltration tactics. They are shrewd masters of tricky concealment among any who resemble them. With the aid of any artifice or treachery they seek such human camouflage and with uncanny skill discover and take advantage of any disloyalty among their kind." Judge Black directed the jurors to convict Gordon, which they did after just ten minutes of deliberation.

Min Yasui's trial in Portland took a bit longer, largely because Judge Alger Fee took over the questioning from the government's lawyer, Charles Burdell, who had pressed the "genetic disloyalty" claim in his pretrial brief. Fee surprised Min, who had never been to Japan, with questions about Japanese customs and beliefs. "What is Shinto?" he abruptly asked. Min was clearly puzzled by the question. "Shinto? As I understand, Shinto is the national religion of Japan," he answered. "Do you give adherence to its precepts?" Fee asked. "My mother and father were Methodists in Japan," Min replied, "and I myself have been a Methodist in this country and I don't know the precepts of the Shinto religion." Fee pressed on doggedly: "Was not Shinto practiced in your household?" Min tried to conceal his irritation. "Both my mother and father are good, devout Methodists," he assured Fee. "They are really Christians." Fee heard the case without a jury, and pronounced Min guilty for his admitted curfew violation. Before passing sentence, Fee ruled in a written opinion that despite Min's American birth and citizenship, he considered him "a citizen of Japan and subject to the Emperor of Japan," a finding the judge based on "the nativity of his parents and the subtle nuances of traditional mores engrained in his race by centuries of social discipline." After linking Min to "the treacherous attack by the armed forces of

Japan" on Pearl Harbor, Judge Fee imposed the maximum penalty of one year in prison and a $5,000 fine.

Fred Korematsu came to trial in San Francisco before Judge Adolphus St. Sure, who differed from his Seattle and Portland colleagues in treating the defendant with respect. After an FBI agent testified about Fred's draft-card forgery and plastic surgery, the soft-spoken defendant took the stand to explain his actions. His description of Dr. Bennett Masten's bargain-rate surgery drew smiles in the courtroom. "I don't think he made any change in my appearance," he said, "for when I went to the Tanforan Assembly Center everyone knew me and my folks didn't know the difference." Fred told the judge that he had applied for military service before Pearl Harbor, but had been rejected on medical grounds. "As a citizen of the United States I am ready, willing, and able to bear arms for this country," he affirmed. This forthrightness impressed Judge St. Sure, but he nonetheless found Fred guilty and sentenced him to a five-year probationary sentence. When Fred's lawyer announced his intention to appeal the conviction, St. Sure obligingly set bail at $2,500. Fred was legally free to remain at liberty, but when he stepped outside the courthouse he was grabbed by a waiting military policeman, who pulled a pistol and took his prisoner to the army jail at General DeWitt's headquarters, from which Fred was shipped to the Tanforan Racetrack, where his parents were confined in horse stalls, awaiting transfer to an internment camp in the Utah desert.

All three test-case defendants appealed to the Supreme Court after circuit court judges upheld their convictions, but the Justices sent Fred Korematsu's case back to the circuit court for a ruling on Judge St. Sure's sentencing decision. Before it returned, the Court heard argument in the *Hirabayashi* and *Yasui* cases in April 1943. The briefs on both sides stuck closely to legal issues and included no evidence on the government's claim that Japanese Americans posed a danger of "espionage and sabotage" to West Coast defense facilities. There was, in fact, no evidence that *any* member of this racial group had committed these treasonous acts (Irons, 1988).

HIRABAYASHI V. UNITED STATES
320 U.S. 81 (1943)

"Because racial discriminations are in most circumstances irrelevant and therefore prohibited, it by no means follows that, in dealing with the perils of war, Congress and the Executive are wholly precluded from taking into account those facts and circumstances which . . . may in fact place citizens of one ancestry in a different category from others."

The Question: Can the Congress pass a law, based on a presidential executive order issued in February 1942, making it a federal crime for any person of Japanese ancestry, including native-born American citizens, to disobey military orders imposing curfews and requiring them to report to "assembly centers" for indefinite detention?

The Arguments: PRO

The nation faced a crisis after the Japanese attack on Pearl Harbor in December 1941, and military officials had a reasonable fear that persons of Japanese ancestry, some 110,000 in the West Coast states, posed a danger of espionage and sabotage to aid the Japanese war effort. The curfew and exclusion orders at issue in these cases were imposed after findings by military officials and congressional committees that it was impossible to distinguish between loyal and disloyal persons of Japanese ancestry. In time of national crisis, the powers of the federal government are broad enough to require that citizens relinquish some of the rights they have during peacetime.

CON

There is no constitutional basis for subjecting American citizens to a deprivation of their liberties solely on the basis of their ancestry. Citizens of German and Italian ancestry, for example, were not subjected to similar orders. The defendants in these cases, of Japanese ancestry, were singled out because of racial hostility toward them and unfounded stereotypes about their "sneaky" nature and attachments to Japan. No American citizen can be detained, either by a curfew or in an internment camp, without being charged with a crime and given a hearing that accords due process to him or her.

MR. CHIEF JUSTICE STONE delivered the opinion of the Court.

Appellant [Gordon Hirabayashi], an American citizen of Japanese ancestry, was convicted in the district court of violating the Act of Congress of March 21, 1942, which makes it a misdemeanor knowingly to disregard restrictions made applicable by a military commander to persons in a military area prescribed by him as such, all as authorized by an Executive Order of the President.

The questions for our decision are whether the particular restriction violated, namely that all persons of Japanese ancestry residing in such an area be within their place of residence daily between the hours of 8:00 p.m. and 6:00 a.m., was adopted by the military commander in the exercise of an unconstitutional delegation by Congress of its legislative power, and whether the restriction unconstitutionally discriminated between citizens of Japanese ancestry and those of other ancestries in violation of the Fifth Amendment.

The indictment . . . charges that appellant, being a person of Japanese ancestry, had on a specified date, contrary to a restriction promulgated by the military commander of the Western Defense Command, Fourth Army, failed to remain in his place of residence in the designated military area between the hours of 8:00 o'clock p.m. and 6:00 a.m. . . . [A]ppellant asserted that the indictment should be dismissed because he was an American citizen who had never been a subject of and had never borne allegiance to the Empire of Japan, and also because the Act of March 21, 1942, was an unconstitutional delegation of Congressional power. On the trial to a jury it appeared that appellant was born in Seattle in 1918, of Japanese parents who had come from Japan to the United States, and who had never afterward returned to Japan; that he was educated in the Washington public schools and at the time of his arrest was a senior in the University of Washington; that he had never been in Japan or had any association with Japanese residing there.

The evidence showed that appellant had failed to report to the Civil Control Station on May 11 or May 12, 1942, as directed, to register for evacuation from the military area. He admitted failure to do so, and stated it had at all times been his belief that he would be waiving his rights as an American citizen by so doing. The evidence also showed that for like reason he was away from his place of residence after 8:00 p.m. on May 9, 1942. The jury returned a verdict of guilty on both counts and appellant was sentenced to imprisonment for a term of three months on each, the sentences to run concurrently. . . .

The curfew order which appellant violated, and to which the sanction prescribed by the Act of Congress has been deemed to attach, purported to be issued pursuant to an Executive Order of the President. In passing upon the authority of the military commander to make and execute the order, it becomes necessary to consider in some detail the official action which preceded or accompanied the order and from which it derives its purported authority. On December 8, 1941, one day after the bombing of Pearl Harbor by a Japanese air force, Congress declared war against Japan. On February 19, 1942, the President promulgated Executive Order No. 9066. The Order recited that "the successful prosecution of the war requires every possible protection against espionage and against sabotage to national-defense material,

national-defense premises, and national-defense utilities." . . . By virtue of the authority vested in him as President and as Commander in Chief of the Army and Navy, the President purported to "authorize and direct the Secretary of War, and the Military Commanders whom he may from time to time designate, whenever he or any designated Commander deems such action necessary or desirable, to prescribe military areas in such places and of such extent as he or the appropriate Military Commander may determine, from which any or all persons may be excluded, and with respect to which, the right of any person to enter, remain in, or leave shall be subject to whatever restrictions the Secretary of War or the appropriate Military Commander may impose in his discretion."

On February 20, 1942, the Secretary of War designated Lt. General J. L. DeWitt as Military Commander of the Western Defense Command, comprising the Pacific Coast states and some others, to carry out there the duties prescribed by Executive Order No. 9066. On March 2, 1942, General DeWitt promulgated Public Proclamation No. 1. The proclamation recited that the entire Pacific Coast "by its geographical location is particularly subject to attack, to attempted invasion by the armed forces of nations with which the United States is now at war, and, in connection therewith, is subject to espionage and acts of sabotage, thereby requiring the adoption of military measures necessary to establish safeguards against such enemy operations." . . . [O]n March 24, 1942, General DeWitt issued Public Proclamation No. 3, [which required that] "all persons of Japanese ancestry residing or being within the geographical limits of Military Area No. 1 . . . shall be within their place of residence between the hours of 8:00 P.M. and 6:00 A.M."

Appellant does not deny that he knowingly failed to obey the curfew order as charged in the second count of the indictment, or that the order was authorized by the terms of Executive Order No. 9066, or that the challenged Act of Congress purports to punish with criminal penalties disobedience of such an order. His contentions are only that Congress unconstitutionally delegated its legislative power to the military commander by authorizing him to impose the challenged regulation, and that, even if the regulation were in other respects lawfully authorized, the Fifth Amendment prohibits the discrimination made between citizens of Japanese descent and those of other ancestry.

It will be evident from the legislative history that the Act of March 21, 1942, contemplated and authorized the curfew order which we have before us. . . . The proposed legislation provided criminal sanctions for violation of orders, in terms broad enough to include the curfew order now before us, and the legislative history demonstrates that Congress was advised that curfew orders were among those intended, and was advised also that regulation of citizen and alien Japanese alike was contemplated. The conclusion is inescapable that Congress, by the Act of March 21, 1942, ratified and confirmed Executive Order No. 9066. . . . And so far as it lawfully could, Congress authorized and implemented such curfew orders as the commanding officer should promulgate pursuant to the Executive Order of the President. The question then is not one of Congressional power to delegate to the President the promulgation of the Executive Order, but whether, acting in cooperation, Congress and the

Executive have constitutional authority to impose the curfew restriction here complained of. We must consider also whether, acting together, Congress and the Executive could leave it to the designated military commander to appraise the relevant conditions and on the basis of that appraisal to say whether, under the circumstances, the time and place were appropriate for the promulgation of the curfew order and whether the order itself was an appropriate means of carrying out the Executive Order for the "protection against espionage and against sabotage" to national defense materials, premises and utilities. For reasons presently to be stated, we conclude that it was within the constitutional power of Congress and the executive arm of the Government to prescribe this curfew order for the period under consideration and that its promulgation by the military commander involved no unlawful delegation of legislative power. . . .

We have no occasion to consider whether the President, acting alone, could lawfully have made the curfew order in question, or have authorized others to make it. For the President's action has the support of the Act of Congress, and we are immediately concerned with the question whether it is within the constitutional power of the national government, through the joint action of Congress and the Executive, to impose this restriction as an emergency war measure. . . . The war power of the national government is "the power to wage war successfully." It extends to every matter and activity so related to war as substantially to affect its conduct and progress. The power is not restricted to the winning of victories in the field and the repulse of enemy forces. It embraces every phase of the national defense, including the protection of war materials and the members of the armed forces from injury and from the dangers which attend the rise, prosecution and progress of war. . . . Where, as they did here, the conditions call for the exercise of judgment and discretion and for the choice of means by those branches of the Government on which the Constitution has placed the responsibility of warmaking, it is not for any court to sit in review of the wisdom of their action or substitute its judgment for theirs.

The actions taken must be appraised in the light of the conditions with which the President and Congress were confronted in the early months of 1942. . . . On December 7, 1941, the Japanese air forces had attacked the United States Naval Base at Pearl Harbor without warning, at the very hour when Japanese diplomatic representatives were conducting negotiations with our State Department ostensibly for the peaceful settlement of differences between the two countries. Simultaneously or nearly so, the Japanese attacked Malaysia, Hong Kong, the Philippines, and Wake and Midway Islands. . . . Although the results of the attack on Pearl Harbor were not fully disclosed until much later, it was known that the damage was extensive, and that the Japanese by their successes had gained a naval superiority over our forces in the Pacific which might enable them to seize Pearl Harbor, our largest naval base and the last stronghold of defense lying between Japan and the west coast. That reasonably prudent men charged with the responsibility of our national defense had ample ground for concluding that they must face the danger of invasion, take measures against it, and in making the choice of measures consider our internal situation, cannot be doubted.

The challenged orders were defense measures for the avowed purpose of safeguarding the military area in question, at a time of threatened air raids and invasion by the Japanese forces, from the danger of sabotage and espionage. As the curfew was made applicable to citizens residing in the area only if they were of Japanese ancestry, our inquiry must be whether in the light of all the facts and circumstances there was any substantial basis for the conclusion, in which Congress and the military commander united, that the curfew as applied was a protective measure necessary to meet the threat of sabotage and espionage which would substantially affect the war effort and which might reasonably be expected to aid a threatened enemy invasion. The alternative which appellant insists must be accepted is for the military authorities to impose the curfew on all citizens within the military area, or on none. In a case of threatened danger requiring prompt action, it is a choice between inflicting obviously needless hardship on the many, or sitting passive and unresisting in the presence of the threat. We think that constitutional government, in time of war, is not so powerless and does not compel so hard a choice if those charged with the responsibility of our national defense have reasonable ground for believing that the threat is real.

When the orders were promulgated there was a vast concentration, within Military Areas No. 1 and 2, of installations and facilities for the production of military equipment, especially ships and airplanes. Important Army and Navy bases were located in California and Washington. . . . In the critical days of March, 1942, the danger to our war production by sabotage and espionage in this area seems obvious. The German invasion of the Western European countries had given ample warning to the world of the menace of the "fifth column." Espionage by persons in sympathy with the Japanese Government had been found to have been particularly effective in the surprise attack on Pearl Harbor. At a time of threatened Japanese attack upon this country, the nature of our inhabitants' attachments to the Japanese enemy was consequently a matter of grave concern. Of the 126,000 persons of Japanese descent in the United States, citizens and non-citizens, approximately 112,000 resided in California, Oregon and Washington at the time of the adoption of the military regulations. Of these approximately two-thirds are citizens because [they were] born in the United States. Not only did the great majority of such persons reside within the Pacific Coast states but they were concentrated in or near three of the large cities, Seattle, Portland and Los Angeles, all in Military Area No. 1.

There is support for the view that social, economic and political conditions which have prevailed since the close of the last century, when the Japanese began to come to this country in substantial numbers, have intensified their solidarity and have in large measure prevented their assimilation as an integral part of the white population. . . . The large number of resident alien Japanese, approximately one-third of all Japanese inhabitants of the country, are of mature years and occupy positions of influence in Japanese communities. The association of influential Japanese residents with Japanese Consulates has been deemed a ready means for the dissemination of propaganda and for the maintenance of the influence of the Japanese Government with the Japanese population in this country.

As a result of all these conditions affecting the life of the Japanese, both aliens and citizens, in the Pacific Coast area, there has been relatively little social intercourse between them and the white population. The restrictions, both practical and legal, affecting the privileges and opportunities afforded to persons of Japanese extraction residing in the United States, have been sources of irritation and may well have tended to increase their isolation, and in many instances their attachments to Japan and its institutions.

Viewing these data in all their aspects, Congress and the Executive could reasonably have concluded that these conditions have encouraged the continued attachment of members of this group to Japan and Japanese institutions. These are only some of the many considerations which those charged with the responsibility for the national defense could take into account in determining the nature and extent of the danger of espionage and sabotage, in the event of invasion or air raid attack. The extent of that danger could be definitely known only after the event and after it was too late to meet it. Whatever views we may entertain regarding the loyalty to this country of the citizens of Japanese ancestry, we cannot reject as unfounded the judgment of the military authorities and of Congress that there were disloyal members of that population, whose number and strength could not be precisely and quickly ascertained. We cannot say that the war-making branches of the Government did not have ground for believing that in a critical hour such persons could not readily be isolated and separately dealt with, and constituted a menace to the national defense and safety, which demanded that prompt and adequate measures be taken to guard against it.

Appellant does not deny that, given the danger, a curfew was an appropriate measure against sabotage. It is an obvious protection against the perpetration of sabotage most readily committed during the hours of darkness. If it was an appropriate exercise of the war power its validity is not impaired because it has restricted the citizen's liberty. Like every military control of the population of a dangerous zone in wartime, it necessarily involves some infringement of individual liberty, just as does the police establishment of fire lines during a fire, or the confinement of people to their houses during an air raid alarm—neither of which could be thought to be an infringement of constitutional right. Like them, the validity of the restraints of the curfew order depends on all the conditions which obtain at the time the curfew is imposed and which support the order imposing it.

But appellant insists that the exercise of the power is inappropriate and unconstitutional because it discriminates against citizens of Japanese ancestry, in violation of the Fifth Amendment. . . . Distinctions between citizens solely because of their ancestry are by their very nature odious to a free people whose institutions are founded upon the doctrine of equality. For that reason, legislative classification or discrimination based on race alone has often been held to be a denial of equal protection. Yick Wo v. Hopkins. We may assume that these considerations would be controlling here were it not for the fact that the danger of espionage and sabotage, in time of war and of threatened invasion, calls upon the military authorities to scrutinize every relevant fact bearing on the loyalty of populations in the danger areas. Because racial discriminations are in most circumstances

irrelevant and therefore prohibited, it by no means follows that, in dealing with the perils of war, Congress and the Executive are wholly precluded from taking into account those facts and circumstances which are relevant to measures for our national defense and for the successful prosecution of the war, and which may in fact place citizens of one ancestry in a different category from others. The adoption by Government, in the crisis of war and of threatened invasion, of measures for the public safety, based upon the recognition of facts and circumstances which indicate that a group of one national extraction may menace that safety more than others, is not wholly beyond the limits of the Constitution and is not to be condemned merely because in other and in most circumstances racial distinctions are irrelevant.

Here the aim of Congress and the Executive was the protection against sabotage of war materials and utilities in areas thought to be in danger of Japanese invasion and air attack. We have stated in detail facts and circumstances with respect to the American citizens of Japanese ancestry residing on the Pacific Coast which support the judgment of the war-waging branches of the Government that some restrictive measure was urgent. We cannot say that these facts and circumstances, considered in the particular war setting, could afford no ground for differentiating citizens of Japanese ancestry from other groups in the United States. The fact alone that attack on our shores was threatened by Japan rather than another enemy power set these citizens apart from others who have no particular associations with Japan. . . .

Affirmed.

MR. JUSTICE MURPHY, concurring.

It is not to be doubted that the action taken by the military commander in pursuance of the authority conferred upon him was taken in complete good faith and in the firm conviction that it was required by considerations of public safety and military security. Neither is it doubted that the Congress and the Executive working together may generally employ such measures as are necessary and appropriate to provide for the common defense and to wage war "with all the force necessary to make it effective." This includes authority to exercise measures of control over persons and property which would not in all cases be permissible in normal times. It does not follow, however, that the broad guaranties of the Bill of Rights and other provisions of the Constitution protecting essential liberties are suspended by the mere existence of a state of war. . . .

Distinctions based on color and ancestry are utterly inconsistent with our traditions and ideals. They are at variance with the principles for which we are now waging war. We cannot close our eyes to the fact that for centuries the Old World has been torn by racial and religious conflicts and has suffered the worst kind of anguish because of inequality of treatment for different groups. There was one law for one and a different law for another. Nothing is written more firmly into our law than the compact of the Plymouth voyagers to have just and equal laws. To say that any group cannot be assimilated is to admit that the great American experiment has failed, that our way of life has failed when confronted with the normal attachment of certain groups to the lands of their forefathers. As a nation we embrace many groups, some of them among the oldest settlements in our midst, which have isolated themselves for religious and cultural reasons.

Today is the first time, so far as I am aware, that we have sustained a substantial restriction of the personal liberty of citizens of the United States based upon the accident of race or ancestry. Under the curfew order here challenged no less than 70,000 American citizens have been placed under a special ban and deprived of their liberty because of their particular racial inheritance. In this sense it bears a melancholy resemblance to the treatment accorded to members of the Jewish race in Germany and in other parts of Europe. The result is the creation in this country of two classes of citizens for the purposes of a critical and perilous hour—to sanction discrimination between groups of United States citizens on the basis of ancestry. In my opinion this goes to the very brink of constitutional power.

Except under conditions of great emergency a regulation of this kind applicable solely to citizens of a particular racial extraction would not be regarded as in accord with the requirement of due process of law contained in the Fifth Amendment. We have consistently held that attempts to apply regulatory action to particular groups solely on the basis of racial distinction or classification is not in accordance with due process of law as prescribed by the Fifth and Fourteenth Amendments. Yick Wo. v. Hopkins. In view, however, of the critical military situation which prevailed on the Pacific Coast area in the spring of 1942, and the urgent necessity of taking prompt and effective action to secure defense installations and military operations against the risk of sabotage and espionage, the military authorities should not be required to conform to standards of regulatory action appropriate to normal times. Because of the damage wrought by the Japanese at Pearl Harbor and the availability of new weapons and new techniques with greater capacity for speed and deception in offensive operations, the immediate possibility of an attempt at invasion somewhere along the Pacific Coast had to be reckoned with. However desirable such a procedure might have been, the military authorities could have reasonably concluded at the time that determinations as to the loyalty and dependability of individual members of the large and widely scattered group of persons of Japanese extraction on the West Coast could not be made without delay that might have had tragic consequences. Modern war does not always wait for the observance of procedural requirements that are considered essential and appropriate under normal conditions. Accordingly I think that the military arm, confronted with the peril of imminent enemy attack and acting under the authority conferred by the Congress, made an allowable judgment at the time the curfew restriction was imposed. Whether such a restriction is valid today is another matter.

MEET GORDON HIRABAYASHI

I was born in Seattle, Washington, on April 23, 1918. Both of my parents were born in Japan. My father came over to this country in 1907, when he was nineteen, and my mother came over in 1914, when she was also nineteen. They were married in this country, but their marriage was arranged in Japan by their families. I was the oldest of five kids in the family. My dad operated a fruit and vegetable store, more like a roadside stand, in Auburn, which was a rural farm community about twenty miles south of Seattle.

My parents had grown up in Buddhist homes in Japan, but they were both converted to Christianity when they were taking English lessons, preparatory to coming over to the United States. Although they took these lessons seven years apart, they both happened to have an English instructor who was a disciple of a unique Protestant movement which was known in Japan as Mukyokai. In English this would mean "Non-Church Movement." This was a small, unorthodox, nondenominational movement which had beliefs and values very much like the Quakers, with a strong emphasis on pacifism.

While I was a child, and through my teenage period, I often felt that our religious group was too rigid and restrictive. I also had to cope with the conflicts between Japanese and Western ideals and values. Growing up in a Japanese home created serious problems at school. The teacher would encourage me by saying, Speak up, Gordon! What do you think about that? Let's hear *your* view. The Japanese value system told me not to blurt out anything that was only half-baked, bringing shame to me and my family, and I frequently sat like a sphinx in school. But I was active in school activities and the Boy Scouts. I became a Life Scout and a senior patrol leader.

I entered the University of Washington in Seattle after I finished high school, and at first I was majoring in math. I wasn't very active politically at the university. I guess I still am not, in the formal political sense. But I was involved in a lot of issues. I belonged to the student YMCA, which was the main group around the so-called independents versus the Greek Row, with their "for white gentiles only" policy, which was legal at that time. So when issues came up, we'd get into debates over certain positions, and I got involved in that sort of thing. Debates within the Y, Student Christian Movement, and conferences. Whenever issues came up, I always found myself taking the extreme liberal side, arguing those positions.

My roommate and I had been visiting different church groups, not belonging to any. We went to the University temple because they had an excellent choir, and we'd go to the Unitarian church once in a while because we liked what the minister said, and we'd drop in at the Quakers. And we liked that setting. That kind of appealed to us and we found ourselves gravitating over there more frequently, and after awhile we weren't shopping around.

I remember that December 7, 1941 was a quiet Sunday morning in Seattle. We had just finished Meeting for Worship at the Friends Meeting and we drifted outside for visiting. Then, one of our members, who had stayed by the radio, broke the news. Japan has attacked Pearl Harbor in Hawaii! We are at war! It was unreal. The impact did not sink in for some time. My immediate worry was what would happen to my parents and their generation. Since they were legally ineligible for American citizenship, war with Japan instantly transformed them into "enemy aliens."

After the curfew order was announced, we knew there would be further orders to remove all persons of Japanese ancestry from the West Coast. When the exclusion orders specifying the deadline for forced removal from various districts of Seattle were posted on telephone poles, I was confronted with a dilemma: Do I stay out of trouble and succumb to the status of second-class citizen, or do I continue to live like other Americans and thus disobey the law?

When the curfew was imposed I obeyed for about a week. We had about twelve living in the Y dormitory, so it was a small group, and they all became my volunteer time-keepers. "Hey, Gordy, it's five minutes to eight!" And I'd have to dash back from the library or from the coffee shop. One of those times, I stopped and I thought, Why the hell am I running back? Am I an American? And if I am, why am I running back and nobody else is? I think if the order said *all* civilians must obey the curfew, if it was just a nonessential restrictive move, I might not have objected. But I felt it was unfair, just to be referred to as a "non-alien"—they never referred to me as a citizen. This was so pointedly, so obviously a violation of what the Constitution stood for, what citizenship meant. So I stopped and turned around and went back.

This shocked some of my friends. So I said, Well, *you're* here. What gives you any more right to stay here than me? And they couldn't answer that. After that, I just ignored the curfew. But nothing happened. And it became a kind of expression of freedom for me to make sure that I was out after eight. It wasn't hard in the University district; there were a lot of activities after eight.

I had no plans to bring a test case. Today, if I violate anything on the grounds of principle, I would spend some time thinking about the legal aspects, the court battles and so on. But at that time, I was just a student. I had read of World War I and constitutional cases, but I didn't give it very much thought. I did anticipate that I would be apprehended, but I didn't know very much about the legal procedures in these things. I just felt that something was going to happen to curtail my freedom.

I had met a lawyer named Arthur Barnett at the Friends Meeting. Bill and I met with Art and asked him some questions about the legal implications of the position we were contemplating. But there was no, Should we, or shouldn't we? Some people knew what I was thinking, but they didn't know what I was going to do.

Eventually, I wrote out a statement explaining the reasons I was refusing evacuation, and I planned to give it to the FBI when I turned myself in.

The day after the University district deadline for evacuation, Art took me to the FBI office to turn myself in. At first, I was only charged with violating the exclusion order. They threw in the curfew count afterward. One of the FBI agents who interrogated me regarding the exclusion order refusal stopped at one point and said, Well, gee, if you feel this way about it, what would you do about curfew? And I said, Well, what were *you* doing the past few nights? Were you out after eight o'clock? He said, Yeah. And I said, So was I. Other Americans were ignoring it, and so did I. When they confiscated my journal from my briefcase, I had some events listed of violating the curfew, and they picked one of those and added it to the counts against me.

My trial in October lasted just one day. It started in the morning and they took a noon recess and continued in the afternoon until my conviction. The government subpoenaed my parents and they put Dad on the stand. They only asked

him a couple of questions, like, Were you born in Japan? Are you a Japanese citizen? The only point was to impress on the jury that this man was Japanese and didn't speak English well and that this defendant is his son.

I really objected to the government putting my parents in jail for ten days before my trial. They were brought up from the Tule Lake Concentration Camp in California and my Dad was placed in the federal tank with me. Mother was put in the only tank for women, with street walkers, petty thieves, embezzlers. The tank was cockroachy and the food was greasy. On the day of my trial, we had to wait ten minutes for her to come down. Six of the women had been working on her hair and fingernails. She came out looking like a queen. She told me that whatever the women were charged with, she had never met such warmhearted people. But I'll *never* forgive the government for putting my parents in jail like that, just to prejudice the jury against me.

Judge Black's instructions to the jury before they retired were very succinct. You can forget all those legal arguments, he said. Here are the only questions that you must determine. I am instructing you that the curfew and exclusion orders of the Army are valid. You are to determine whether the defendant is of Japanese ancestry, and if he is, he's subject to this regulation. Then you are to determine whether he complied with it. Gee, there's no question! They go in and they were back in ten minutes. I was guilty on both counts. You could have a whole bunch of civil-liberties people on the jury and they are subject to the judge's instructions. They *had* to vote against me. It was cut and dried.

Judge Black sentenced me the next day. He said, Taking into consideration that you have already been five months in jail on a conviction with a maximum of twelve months, I'm going to sentence you to thirty days for the exclusion order conviction and thirty days for curfew order violation, to be served consecutively, or sixty days. Then he asked if the prisoner had anything to say, and I asked if he could add fifteen days to each count so that it would total ninety days. I'd been told by jailhouse friends that if my sentence was ninety days or longer, I could serve on a work camp and be outdoors instead of in jail behind bars. When Judge Black heard this he smiled and said, I could accommodate that. Why don't we make it three months on each count, to be served concurrently. Nobody saw any objection to that, and nobody realized that the Supreme Court would use that to avoid ruling on the exclusion order conviction.

After the Supreme Court decided my case in 1943, there was always a continuous hope and interest on my part that the case could be reviewed at some point. Not being a lawyer, I didn't know exactly what my options were. During the time I was overseas I didn't spend much time looking into that possibility, but during the latter part of the sixties and beginning of the seventies I had discussions with law professors at the University of California, but they couldn't find anything promising. And later I talked with a judge who suggested that I move to quash the charges in my case. The courts would have to look at that motion and in that process we might get a kind of hearing.

I shared that idea with a few others, but nothing came of it. I had certain feelings of finality about my case. You know, while I'm hoping as a layman that something can be done, well, the Supreme Court is the Supreme Court. That's the end, and when they have made a decision, there aren't many ways open to reverse it. It wasn't until Peter Irons called me from Boston in 1981, saying that he had discovered some documents that might present an opportunity under a rarely used legal device to petition for a rehearing, that I felt there was a chance. I said to him, I've been waiting over forty years for this kind of a phone call. So he arranged to fly out to Edmonton, and eventually we got a legal team organized that filed a petition in the federal court in Seattle to vacate my conviction.

My petition was filed in January 1983 and we had a two-week evidentiary hearing in June 1985. Judge Donald Voorhees, who presided over the case, impressed me as a very fair judge. He was obviously interested in the case and well-informed about the evidence. Naturally, I was delighted that he ruled that my exclusion order conviction had been tainted by government misconduct. But I was disap-

pointed that he upheld the curfew conviction, and we appealed that. The government also appealed on the exclusion order. We had arguments before the appellate judges in March 1987, and they handed down a unanimous opinion in September, upholding Judge Voorhees on the exclusion order and also striking down the curfew conviction. So I finally got the vindication that I had wanted for forty years, although I'm a little disappointed that the Supreme Court didn't have a chance to overrule the decision they made in 1943.

When my case was before the Supreme Court in 1943, I fully expected that as a citizen the Constitution would protect me. Surprisingly, even though I lost, I did not abandon my beliefs and values. And I never look at my case as just my own, or just as a Japanese American case. It is an *American* case, with principles that affect the fundamental human rights of all Americans (Irons, 1988).

KOREMATSU V. UNITED STATES
323 U.S. 214 (1944)

"Korematsu was not excluded from the Military Area because of hostility to him or his race. He was excluded because we are at war with the Japanese Empire, because the properly constituted military authorities . . . decided that the military urgency of the situation demanded that all citizens of Japanese ancestry be segregated from the West Coast temporarily."

Mr. Justice Black delivered the opinion of the Court.

The petitioner, an American citizen of Japanese descent, was convicted in a federal district court for remaining in San Leandro, California, a "Military Area," contrary to Civilian Exclusion Order No. 34 of the Commanding General of the Western Command, U.S. Army, which directed that after May 9, 1942, all persons of Japanese ancestry should be excluded from that area. No question was raised as to petitioner's loyalty to the United States. The Circuit Court of Appeals affirmed, and the importance of the constitutional question involved caused us to grant certiorari.

It should be noted, to begin with, that all legal restrictions which curtail the civil rights of a single racial group are immediately suspect. That is not to say that all such restrictions are unconstitutional. It is to say that courts must subject them to the most rigid scrutiny. Pressing public necessity may sometimes justify the existence of such restrictions; racial antagonism never can.

In the instant case prosecution of the petitioner was begun by information charging violation of an Act of Congress, of March 21, 1942, which provides that

... whoever shall enter, remain in, leave, or commit any act in any military area or military zone prescribed, under the authority of an Executive order of the President, by the Secretary of War, or by any military commander designated by the

Secretary of War, contrary to the restrictions applicable to any such area or zone or contrary to the order of the Secretary of War or any such military commander, shall, if it appears that he knew or should have known of the existence and extent of the restrictions or order and that his act was in violation thereof, be guilty of a misdemeanor and upon conviction shall be liable to a fine of not to exceed $5,000 or to imprisonment for not more than one year, or both, for each offense.

Exclusion Order No. 34, which the petitioner knowingly and admittedly violated was one of a number of military orders and proclamations, all of which were substantially based upon Executive Order No. 9066. That order, issued after we were at war with Japan, declared that "the successful prosecution of the war requires every possible protection against espionage and against sabotage to national-defense material, national-defense premises, and national-defense utilities. . . ."

One of the series of orders and proclamations, a curfew order, which like the exclusion order here was promulgated pursuant to Executive Order 9066, subjected all persons of Japanese ancestry in prescribed West Coast military areas to remain in their residences from 8 p.m. to 6 a.m. As is the case with the exclusion order here, that prior curfew order was designed as a "protection against espionage and against sabotage." In Hirabayashi v. United States, we sustained a conviction obtained for violation of the curfew order. The

Hirabayashi conviction and this one thus rest on the same 1942 Congressional Act and the same basic executive and military orders, all of which orders were aimed at the twin dangers of espionage and sabotage.

The 1942 Act was attacked in the Hirabayashi case as an unconstitutional delegation of power; it was contended that the curfew order and other orders on which it rested were beyond the war powers of the Congress, the military authorities and of the President, as Commander in Chief of the Army; and finally that to apply the curfew order against none but citizens of Japanese ancestry amounted to a constitutionally prohibited discrimination solely on account of race. To these questions, we gave the serious consideration which their importance justified. We upheld the curfew order as an exercise of the power of the government to take steps necessary to prevent espionage and sabotage in an area threatened by Japanese attack.

In the light of the principles we announced in the Hirabayashi case, we are unable to conclude that it was beyond the war power of Congress and the Executive to exclude those of Japanese ancestry from the West Coast war area at the time they did. True, exclusion from the area in which one's home is located is a far greater deprivation than constant confinement to the home from 8 p.m. to 6 a.m. Nothing short of apprehension by the proper military authorities of the gravest imminent danger to the public safety can constitutionally justify either. But exclusion from a threatened area, no less than curfew, has a definite and close relationship to the prevention of espionage and sabotage. The military authorities, charged with the primary responsibility of defending our shores, concluded that curfew provided inadequate protection and ordered exclusion. They did so, as pointed out in our Hirabayashi opinion, in accordance with Congressional authority to the military to say who should, and who should not, remain in the threatened areas. . . .

Like curfew, exclusion of those of Japanese origin was deemed necessary because of the presence of an unascertained number of disloyal members of the group, most of whom we have no doubt were loyal to this country. It was because we could not reject the finding of the military authorities that it was impossible to bring about an immediate segregation of the disloyal from the loyal that we sustained the validity of the curfew order as applying to the whole group. In the instant case, temporary exclusion of the entire group was rested by the military on the same ground. The judgment that exclusion of the whole group was for the same reason a military imperative answers the contention that the exclusion was in the nature of group punishment based on antagonism to those of Japanese origin. That there were members of the group who retained loyalties to Japan has been confirmed by investigations made subsequent to the exclusion. Approximately five thousand American citizens of Japanese ancestry refused to swear unqualified allegiance to the United States and to renounce allegiance to the Japanese Emperor, and several thousand evacuees requested repatriation to Japan.

We uphold the exclusion order as of the time it was made and when the petitioner violated it. In doing so, we are not unmindful of the hardships imposed by it upon a large group of American citizens. But hardships are part of war, and war is an aggregation of hardships. All citizens alike, both in and out of uniform, feel the impact of war in greater or lesser measure. Citizenship has its responsibilities as well as its privileges, and in time of war the burden is always heavier. Compulsory exclusion of large groups of citizens from their homes, except under circumstances of direst emergency and peril, is inconsistent with our basic governmental institutions. But when under conditions of modern warfare our shores are threatened by hostile forces, the power to protect must be commensurate with the threatened danger. . . .

It is said that we are dealing here with the case of imprisonment of a citizen in a concentration camp solely because of his ancestry, without evidence or inquiry concerning his loyalty and good disposition towards the United States. Our task would be simple, our duty clear, were this a case involving the imprisonment of a loyal citizen in a concentration camp because of racial prejudice. Regardless of the true nature of the assembly and relocation centers—and we deem it unjustifiable to call them concentration camps with all the ugly connotations that term implies—we are dealing specifically with nothing but an exclusion order. To cast this case into outlines of racial prejudice, without reference to the real military dangers which were presented, merely confuses the issue. Korematsu was not excluded from the Military Area because of hostility to him or his race. He was excluded because we are at war with the Japanese Empire, because the properly constituted military authorities feared an invasion of our West Coast and felt constrained to take proper security measures, because they decided that the military urgency of the situation demanded that all citizens of Japanese ancestry be segregated from the West Coast temporarily, and finally, because Congress, reposing its confidence in this time of war in our military leaders—as inevitably it must—determined that they should have the power to do just this. There was evidence of disloyalty on the part of some, the military authorities considered that the need for action was great, and time was short. We cannot—by availing ourselves of the calm perspective of hindsight—now say that at that time these actions were unjustified.

Affirmed.

MR. JUSTICE MURPHY, dissenting.

This exclusion of "all persons of Japanese ancestry, both alien and non-alien," from the Pacific Coast area on a plea of military necessity in the absence of martial law ought not to be approved. Such exclusion goes over "the very brink of constitutional power" and falls into the ugly abyss of racism.

In dealing with matters relating to the prosecution and progress of a war, we must accord great respect and consideration to the judgments of the military authorities who are on the scene and who have full knowledge of the military facts. The scope of their discretion must, as a matter of necessity and common sense, be wide. And their judgments ought not to be overruled lightly by those whose training and duties ill-equip them to deal intelligently with matters so vital to the physical security of the nation.

At the same time, however, it is essential that there be definite limits to military discretion, especially where martial law has not been declared. Individuals must not be left impoverished of their constitutional rights on a plea of military necessity that has neither substance nor support. Thus, like other claims conflicting with the asserted constitutional rights of the individual, the military claim must subject itself to the judicial process of having its reasonableness determined and its conflicts with other interests reconciled. The judicial test of whether the Government, on a plea of military necessity, can validly deprive an individual of any of his constitutional rights is whether the deprivation is reasonably related to a public danger that is so "immediate, imminent, and impending" as not to admit of delay and not to permit the intervention of ordinary constitutional processes to alleviate the danger. Civilian Exclusion Order No. 34, banishing from a prescribed area of the Pacific Coast "all persons of Japanese ancestry, both alien and non-alien," clearly does not meet that test. Being an obvious racial discrimination, the order deprives all those within its scope of the equal protection of the laws as guaranteed by the Fifth Amendment. It further deprives these individuals of their constitutional rights to live and work where they will, to establish a home where they choose and to move about freely. In excommunicating them without benefit of hearings, this order also deprives them of all their constitutional rights to procedural due process. Yet no reasonable relation to an "immediate, imminent, and impending" public danger is evident to support this racial restriction which is one of the most sweeping and complete deprivations of constitutional rights in the history of this nation in the absence of martial law.

It must be conceded that the military and naval situation in the spring of 1942 was such as to generate a very real fear of invasion of the Pacific Coast, accompanied by fears of sabotage and espionage in that area. The military command was therefore justified in adopting all reasonable means necessary to combat these dangers. In adjudging the military action taken in light of the then apparent dangers, we must not erect too high or too meticulous standards; it is necessary only that the action have some reasonable relation to the removal of the dangers of invasion, sabotage and espionage. But the exclusion, either temporarily or permanently, of all persons with Japanese blood in their veins has no such reasonable relation. And that relation is lacking because the exclusion order necessarily must rely for its reasonableness upon the assumption that all persons of Japanese ancestry may have a dangerous tendency to commit sabotage and espionage and to aid our Japanese enemy in other ways. It is difficult to believe that reason, logic or experience could be marshalled in support of such an assumption.

That this forced exclusion was the result in good measure of this erroneous assumption of racial guilt rather than bona fide military necessity is evidenced by the Commanding General's Final Report on the evacuation from the Pacific Coast area. In it he refers to all individuals of Japanese descent as "subversive," as belonging to "an enemy race" whose "racial strains are undiluted," and as constituting "over 112,000 potential enemies . . . at large today" along the Pacific Coast. In support of this blanket condemnation of all persons of Japanese descent, however, no reliable evidence is cited to show that such individuals were generally disloyal, or had generally so conducted themselves in this area as to constitute a special menace to defense installations or war

industries, or had otherwise by their behavior furnished reasonable ground for their exclusion as a group.

Justification for the exclusion is sought, instead, mainly upon questionable racial and sociological grounds not ordinarily within the realm of expert military judgment, supplemented by certain semi-military conclusions drawn from an unwarranted use of circumstantial evidence. Individuals of Japanese ancestry are condemned because they are said to be "a large, unassimilated, tightly knit racial group, bound to an enemy nation by strong ties of race, culture, custom and religion." They are claimed to be given to "emperor worshipping ceremonies" and to "dual citizenship." Japanese language schools and allegedly pro-Japanese organizations are cited as evidence of possible group disloyalty, together with facts as to certain persons being educated and residing at length in Japan. . . . The main reasons relied upon by those responsible for the forced evacuation, therefore, do not prove a reasonable relation between the group characteristics of Japanese Americans and the dangers of invasion, sabotage and espionage. The reasons appear, instead, to be largely an accumulation of much of the misinformation, half-truths and insinuations that for years have been directed against Japanese Americans by people with racial and economic prejudices—the same people who have been among the foremost advocates of the evacuation. A military judgment based upon such racial and sociological considerations is not entitled to the great weight ordinarily given the judgments based upon strictly military considerations. Especially is this so when every charge relative to race, religion, culture, geographical location, and legal and economic status has been substantially discredited by independent studies made by experts in these matters. . . .

I dissent, therefore, from this legalization of racism. Racial discrimination in any form and in any degree has no justifiable part whatever in our democratic way of life. It is unattractive in any setting but it is utterly revolting among a free people who have embraced the principles set forth in the Constitution of the United States. All residents of this nation are kin in some way by blood or culture to a foreign land. Yet they are primarily and necessarily a part of the new and distinct civilization of the United States. They must accordingly be treated at all times as the heirs of the American experiment and as entitled to all the rights and freedoms guaranteed by the Constitution.

MR. JUSTICE JACKSON, dissenting.

Korematsu was born on our soil, of parents born in Japan. The Constitution makes him a citizen of the United States by nativity and a citizen of California by residence. No claim is made that he is not loyal to this country. There is no suggestion that apart from the matter involved here he is not law-abiding and well disposed. Korematsu, however, has been convicted of an act not commonly a crime. It consists merely of being present in the state whereof he is a citizen, near the place where he was born, and where all his life he has lived. . . .

A citizen's presence in the locality, however, was made a crime only if his parents were of Japanese birth. Had Korematsu been one of four—the others being, say, a German alien enemy, an Italian alien enemy, and a citizen of American-born ancestors, convicted of treason but out on parole—only Korematsu's presence would have violated the order. The difference between their innocence and his crime would result, not from anything he did, said, or thought, different than they, but only in that he was born of different racial stock.

Now, if any fundamental assumption underlies our system, it is that guilt is personal and not inheritable. . . . But here is an attempt to make an otherwise innocent act a crime merely because this prisoner is the son of parents as to whom he had no choice, and belongs to a race from which there is no way to resign. If Congress in peace-time legislation should enact such a criminal law, I should suppose this Court would refuse to enforce it. . . .

I cannot say, from any evidence before me, that the orders of General DeWitt were not reasonably expedient military precautions, nor could I say that they were. But even if they were permissible military procedures, I deny that it follows that they are constitutional. If, as the Court holds, it does follow, then we may as well say that any military order will be constitutional and have done with it. . . .

Much is said of the danger to liberty from the Army program for deporting and detaining these citizens of Japanese extraction. But a judicial construction of the due process clause that will sustain this order is a far more subtle blow to liberty than the promulgation of the order itself. A military order, however unconstitutional, is not apt to last longer than the military emergency. Even during that period a succeeding commander may revoke it all. But once a judicial opinion rationalizes such an order to show that it conforms to the Constitution, or rather rationalizes the Constitution to show that the Constitution sanctions such an order, the Court for all time has validated the principle of racial discrimination in criminal procedure and of transplanting American citizens. The principle then lies about like a loaded weapon ready for the hand of any authority that can bring forward a plausible claim of an urgent need. Every repetition embeds that principle more deeply in our law and thinking and expands it to new purposes. . . .

I should hold that a civil court cannot be made to enforce an order which violates constitutional limitations even if it is a reasonable exercise of military authority. The courts can exercise only the judicial power, can apply only law, and must abide by the Constitution, or they cease to be civil courts and become instruments of military policy. Of course the existence of a military power resting on force, so vagrant, so centralized, so necessarily heedless of the individual, is an inherent threat to liberty. But I would not lead people to rely on this Court for a review that seems to me wholly delusive. The military reasonableness of these orders can only be determined by military superiors. If the people ever let command of the war power fall into irresponsible and unscrupulous hands, the courts wield no power equal to its restraint. The chief restraint upon those who command the physical forces of the country, in the future as in the past, must be their responsibility to the political judgments of their contemporaries and to the moral judgments of history.

My duties as a justice as I see them do not require me to make a military judgment as to whether General DeWitt's evacuation and detention program was a reasonable military necessity. I do not suggest that the courts should have attempted to interfere with the Army in carrying out its task. But I do not think they may be asked to execute a military expedient that has no place in law under the Constitution. I would reverse the judgment and discharge the prisoner.

POSTSCRIPT

The impact of Supreme Court decisions is often immediately apparent; the *Gobitis* ruling in 1940 provoked a wave of persecution against Jehovah's Witnesses. But that decision was reversed just three years later, after the Court realized the destructive consequences of its action. The impact on Japanese Americans of the *Hirabayashi* and *Korematsu* decisions, however, was not evident to many people for more than three decades after the Court upheld their exclusion from the West Coast. The former internees returned to their communities after the war and rebuilt their lives as hardworking, law-abiding citizens. But underneath their image as a "model minority" was pent-up anger at the injustice they endured for no reason but their race. Some of them, and many of their children, marched for civil rights and against the Vietnam War. During the 1970s, several groups of Japanese Americans began a grassroots lobbying campaign, asking Congress to make symbolic payments to Japanese Americans who had been forced into internment camps.

The first victory of the "redress movement" came in 1980 when Congress established a blue-ribbon Commission on Wartime Relocation and Internment of Civilians, charged with reviewing the mass internment and making recommendations for methods of redress. This nine-member body—which included former Supreme Court justice Arthur Goldberg—conducted hearings around the country at which more than 750 people testified, many speaking tearfully about their wartime hardships and lingering pain. In a 467-page report in 1983, the commissioners agreed unanimously that Japanese Americans had suffered a "grave injustice" that was produced by "race prejudice, war hysteria, and a failure of political leadership." All but one commissioner—Republican congressman Daniel Lungren of Caliornia—recommended that Congress provide compensation of $20,000 for each survivor of the internment camps.

The redress campaign included a legal effort to reverse the wartime convictions of Gordon Hirabayashi, Min Yasui, and Fred Korematsu. Normally, criminal defendants cannot ask judges to reopen their cases after appeals have been exhausted and sentences completed. The only exception to the "finality" rule stems from one of the "ancient writs" of English law, called the writ of error coram nobis. This term is legal Latin for "error before us," referring to the trial judges. This application for judicial relief is related to the better-known writ of habeas corpus, an order to "bring the body" of the defendant into court for a hearing on the legality of the detention. In coram nobis cases, the former defendant must show that "prosecutorial misconduct" during the original trial deprived him or her of a fair trial. There are two grounds for coram nobis relief: one requires proof that government lawyers deliberately withheld "exculpatory" evidence that would show the defendant's innocence; the other involves the government's introduction at trial of false evidence of the defendant's guilt. The burden of proof on defendants is high, and coram nobis relief is rarely sought and even more rarely granted.

The coram nobis effort in the wartime internment cases began in 1981, when Peter Irons (this book's author and also a lawyer) was conducting research for a book on the cases, hoping to explain why the Supreme Court—with so many "liberal" members—made decisions in these cases that scholars have agreed were judicial "disasters," as Yale law professor Eugene Rostow wrote in 1945. Using the Freedom of Information Act, Irons obtained the Justice Department's files in the *Hirabayashi, Yasui,* and *Korematsu* cases, and he discovered several astounding documents. The "loaded weapons" that Justice Jackson warned about in his *Korematsu* dissent were really "smoking guns" of legal misconduct.

Two memoranda by Edward Ennis, who headed the Justice Department's Alien Enemy Control Unit, shot out of these files. He sent the first to Solicitor General Fahy in April 1943, shortly before Fahy's Supreme Court argument in the *Hirabayashi* case. Ennis had obtained military intelligence reports to General DeWitt, informing him that no evidence existed to support claims of Japanese American disloyalty. Ennis reminded Fahy of his "duty to advise the Court of the existence" of these crucial reports. Failing to perform this duty "might approximate the suppression of evidence," he warned. But Fahy ignored the warning and assured the Court that DeWitt had evidence of disloyalty among Japanese Americans before he signed the internment orders in 1942. Chief Justice Stone based his *Hirabayashi* opinion in large part on Fahy's assurances, citing "the judgment of the military authorities" that "there were disloyal members" of the Japanese American community who constituted "a menace to the national defense and safety" on the West Coast.

Ennis sent another memorandum to Fahy in September 1944, during his preparation for the *Korematsu* argument. Suspicious of General Dewitt's claims to have evidence of "espionage and sabotage" by Japanese Americans, Ennis had found more intelligence reports that refuted the charges DeWitt made in his "Final Report" on the internment program. Excerpts of DeWitt's report were included in the *Korematsu* brief that Fahy was about to file with the Court. Ennis urged Fahy to disavow the report's claims that "overt acts of treason were being committed" by Japanese Americans. "Since this is not so," Ennis wrote, "it is highly unfair to this racial minority that these lies, put out in an official publication, go uncorrected." Again, Fahy ignored Ennis and assured the justices that he vouched for "every sentence, every line, and every word" in DeWitt's report. Again, the Court accepted Fahy's assurances in upholding Fred Korematsu's conviction; Justice Hugo Black cited DeWitt's report as providing sufficient "evidence of disloyalty" among Japanese Americans to justify their mass evacuation from the West Coast.

Armed with these "smoking guns" and other records of legal misconduct, Irons tracked down Gordon Hirabayashi, Min Yasui, and Fred Korematsu and showed them his findings. All three men, then in their sixties, agreed to join an effort to erase their criminal records. Irons then recruited a team of committed young lawyers, most of them the children of in-

ternment camp survivors, headed by San Francisco attorney Dale Minami. The coram nobis team prepared a 150-page petition, which was submitted in 1983 to federal district judges in San Francisco, Portland, and Seattle, the courts in which the "test case" defendants had been tried and convicted in 1942. Based entirely on evidence from government files, the petition urged the judges "to carefully weigh the complete record of governmental abuses" in the wartime cases and "do justice where it was denied forty years ago."

Fred Korematsu's petition came before federal judge Marilyn Hall Patel in November 1983, at a hearing crowded with internment survivors. After Dale Minami reviewed the evidence of legal misconduct, Fred made a brief statement to Judge Patel. "Your Honor, I still remember 40 years ago when I was handcuffed and arrested as a criminal," he began. Fred recalled his family's living quarters at the Tanforan Racetrack: "The horse stalls that we stayed in were made for horses, not human beings." Speaking for "all Japanese Americans who were escorted to concentration camps," he asked the government to "admit that they were wrong and do something about it so this will never happen again to any American citizen of any race, creed, or color." The government's lawyer, Victor Stone, denied that the Supreme Court's *Korematsu* decision still "lies around like a loaded gun" and asked Judge Patel to dismiss Korematsu's petition. Ruling from the bench, she found "substantial support" in the petition that "the government deliberately omitted relevant information and provided misleading information" to the Supreme Court in 1944. Judge Patel passed a posthumous verdict on Solicitor General Fahy. "The judicial process is seriously impaired when the government's law enforcement officers violate their ethical obligations to the court," she concluded. Patel ended by reminding her audience—which needed no reminder—that the *Korematsu* decision "remains on the pages of our legal and political history" as a "constant caution that in times of war or declared military necessity our institutions must be vigilant in protecting constitutional guarantees."

Federal judges in Portland and Seattle later vacated the wartime convictions of Min Yasui and Gordon Hirabayashi. Justice Department lawyers had withdrawn an earlier appeal of Judge Patel's ruling to the Ninth Circuit Court of Appeals, but they pursued an appeal in 1987 of the ruling of Judge Donald Voorhees that granted Hirabayashi's petition. Government lawyers never revealed their reasons, but members of the coram nobis legal team suspected that pressure from veterans' groups on the Reagan administration lay behind this legal about-face. During argument before the Ninth Circuit panel, Judge Mary Schroeder asked Victor Stone why the government had not acted on its own to vacate the convictions. "We didn't think there was anyone out there who cared," Stone replied, bringing gasps from the courtroom audience. Writing for the appellate panel, which unanimously reversed both of Hirabayashi's wartime convictions, Judge Schroeder showed that she cared: "A United States citizen who is convicted of a crime on account of race is lastingly aggrieved." Government lawyers did not appeal Schroeder's ruling, and the coram nobis campaign ended with total victory: all three wartime defendants had their records cleared after more than forty years. Gordon Hirabayashi spoke the last words on the steps of the Seattle courthouse in which he received final vindication of his wartime stand: "Ancestry is not a crime."

The nation finally showed that it cared as well. At a White House ceremony in January 1998, President Bill Clinton placed the Presidential Medal of Freedom around Fred Korematsu's neck. "A man of quiet bravery," the president said, "Fred Korematsu deserves our respect and thanks for his patient pursuit to preserve the civil liberties we hold dear." Fred pursued his constitutional rights for almost half a century, never losing his faith in American justice. But other Japanese Americans had lost faith, and more than sixty thousand camp survivors had died before Congress finally enacted a redress bill in 1988 and President Ronald Reagan signed the national apology that accompanied the redress checks of $20,000 to those who remained. For three years of their lives, imprisoned without charges in desolate camps and denied their rights and dignity, this was small compensation (Irons, 1999).

CHAPTER 11

Race, Gender, and Affirmative Action

INTRODUCTION

The principle of a "color-blind" constitution, stated in Justice John Marshall Harlan's dissent in the *Plessy* case in 1896, has retained its appeal for more than a century. There are compelling reasons why the Equal Protection Clause should protect every American from discrimination on the basis of race, ethnicity, or gender. But, as was noted in Chapter 8, Harlan prefaced his statement with the observation that members of the white majority constituted the "dominant race" in this country, "in prestige, in achievements, in education, in wealth, and in power." Harlan could not look a century or more ahead of his time, but his words still hold true. However, he wrote them in dissenting from the Supreme Court's approval of legalized racial segregation. Today segregation and discrimination imposed by law is no longer permitted; state and federal lawmakers have enacted scores of statutes, and established numerous enforcement agencies, to protect Americans of all races and both genders from discrimination in many areas of society, including education and employment.

Despite efforts over the past half-century to remove barriers to educational and job opportunities for members of racial minorities and women, substantial inequalities have persisted in schools and the workplace. A look at racial and gender disparities in employment will show the current effects of past discrimination. The following table gives the percentages of blacks and women in selected occupations and professions, both in 1983 and 2000.

This table is just a snapshot of the American workforce and leaves out the growing Hispanic population, which in 2000 made up 16 percent of the total workforce. Hispanic workers, in fact, now constitute the largest number of workers in textile sewing, farm work, and cleaning jobs. But the table does show that blacks and women, despite progress in many job categories, are still underrepresented in higher status (and higher income) occupations, and are overrepresented (except for black women in secretarial jobs) in lower status (and lower income) positions.

There is no need in this book to prove with statistics what everyone already knows and what most people will admit: that education is closely linked with occupational status, which in turn is closely linked with income. It is necessary, however, to point out what many people do not know: that until Congress passed the Civil Rights Act of 1964, racial and gender discrimination was not prohibited by federal law, and only a few states at that time had effective antidiscrimination laws. Title VI of the Civil Rights Act made it unlawful for recipients of federal funding (which include virtually every college and university in the country) to discriminate

Table 11.1 Percent of Workforce by Occupation

	Blacks		Women	
	1983	2000	1983	2000
Total workforce	9.3	11.3	43.7	46.5
Higher Status				
Engineers	2.7	5.7	5.8	9.9
Physicians	3.2	6.3	15.8	27.9
Lawyers	2.6	5.4	15.3	29.6
Natural scientists	2.6	5.4	20.5	33.5
Lower Status				
Secretaries	5.8	8.5	99.0	98.5
Maids and housemen	32.3	27.7	81.2	81.3
Nursing aides	27.3	35.2	88.7	89.9
Textile sewing	15.5	6.3	94.4	78.4

2001 *Statistical Abstract of the United States.*

on the basis of race or gender, and Title VII prohibited discrimination in private employment. Congress established the Equal Employment Opportunity Commission to enforce these laws in the workplace. The Office of Civil Rights in the Department of Education has a similar responsibility in the field of education.

Since 1964 the Supreme Court has decided many cases that have involved programs known as affirmative action, designed to increase the numbers of women and members of racial minorities in higher education and workplaces. Such programs came under increasing attack by members of the "dominant race" (most of them white males) just as affirmative action programs began to produce significant gains for women and minorities. In virtually every case that challenged such programs, the notion of a color-blind (and by analogy, a gender-blind) constitution was invoked. Two legal principles lie behind such challenges. First, as the Supreme Court has stated in many decisions, constitutional rights are individual rights; no person has any greater claim to protection by the Constitution than any other, regardless of race or gender. Flowing from this is a second principle, namely, that the courts can provide remedies for discrimination only to individuals whose rights have been violated, not to remedy what the Court labeled as "societal" discrimination against particular groups as a whole. Of course, the whole purpose of the Civil Rights Act was to protect members of groups that had suffered historic patterns of discrimination on the basis of their shared characteristic, whether race or gender.

The inherent conflict between these legal principles and legislative purpose gave rise to the five affirmative action cases in this chapter. In each case, a white person (or white-owned business) filed suit to challenge a governmental program that was designed to increase the numbers of racial minorities or women who received a "benefit" of education, employment, or public funds. The facts in each case are different, but each involved an affirmative action program that in effect prevented a white person or business owner from gaining a place in a school, receiving a job promotion, or being awarded a government contract.

These five cases also raise the conflict between "invidious" and "benign" discrimination. The Supreme Court has long ruled that invidious discrimination, designed to harm members of identifiable groups such as blacks or women, violates the Equal Protection Clause. However, if the law or policy gives a preference to, or otherwise benefits, members of these groups to rectify past discrimination against them, the fact that males or whites receive a smaller share of the preferences or benefits they previously enjoyed is allowable as a form of benign discrimination. Whether or not such benign discrimination violates the Equal Protection Clause has been a highly debated issue and has split the Supreme Court in many cases, including those in this chapter.

Affirmative action programs remain highly debatable, in both political rhetoric and judicial opinions. In the political sphere, conservatives such as Ward Connerly, a black member of the University of California regents, have mounted successful campaigns to abolish affirmative action programs in public education and government contracting. Defenders of such programs have disavowed reliance on racial and gender quotas in schools and workplaces, but continue to argue that "race-conscious" programs are still needed to raise the numbers of women and minorities to their fair share. On the Supreme Court, Justice Antonin Scalia has been a forceful advocate of a color-blind constitution, often quoting the following phrase from Justice Harlan's dissent in the *Plessy* case, while Justice Harry Blackmun countered in his opinion in the *Bakke* case: "In order to get beyond racism, we must take account of race. There is no other way." Blackmun's words apply just as well to gender discrimination, and underscore the persisting controversy between the two sides on this issue.

REGENTS OF THE UNIVERSITY OF CALIFORNIA V. BAKKE
438 U.S. 265 (1978)

"It is evident that the Davis special admissions program involves the use of an explicit racial classification never before countenanced by this Court. It tells applicants [to medical school] who are not Negro, Asian, or Chicano that they are totally excluded from a specific percentage of the seats in an entering class."

The Question: Can a state-funded medical school set aside 16 places out of 100 in each entering class for members of "disadvantaged minority groups," and can it consider applicants for these 16 places using academic standards that are lower than those required of applicants for the remaining 84 places?

The Arguments: PRO

The record in this case establishes beyond doubt that members of racial and ethnic minorities are greatly underrepresented in the medical profession. The only feasible way to increase those numbers, and to ensure diversity in medical school classes, is to give a preference to minority applicants. Setting aside 16 seats in each entering class is a reasonable means of achieving this goal. No student is excluded because of his or her race, and those who apply under the minority admissions program must meet the school's minimum academic standards for admission.

CON

In this case, a white medical school applicant, Allan Bakke, was twice rejected for admission. The record shows that he had significantly higher undergraduate grades and scores on all parts of the medical college admissions test than most, if not all, of the minority applicants who were admitted. In effect, Bakke was forced to compete for 1 of only 84 places in a class of 100. The Equal Protection Clause of the Fourteenth Amendment protects "any person" from official discrimination based on race, and Bakke's race was the determining factor in rejecting his applications. The medical school's goal of increasing the diversity of its classes can be achieved through means that do not require racial discrimination.

BACKGROUND

The road to the Supreme Court for white males began on August 3, 1973, when Allan Bakke met with Peter Storandt in the admissions office of the University of California's medical school at Davis, near the state capital of Sacramento. Bakke was thirty-three, an aerospace engineer at a NASA research center close to Stanford University. Storandt was assistant dean of student affairs at the UC Davis medical school. One of these white males wanted to become a doctor; the other wanted to help him get into medical school. Bakke had applied twice to UC Davis, in 1972 and 1973, and had been rejected both times. In fact, Bakke had been turned away by more than a dozen medical schools across the country; most had frankly told him that he was too old. Even UC Davis officials had cited "your present age" as a factor in Bakke's rejection. But he was convinced he had lost his medical school place to a minority applicant with lower grades and test scores. After his first rejection in 1972, he discovered that the UC Davis medical school had an "affirmative action" program that set aside sixteen places in an entering class of one hundred for members of "disadvantaged" minorities. These sixteen places were known as Task Force seats, filled through a separate admissions process.

Before his meeting with Bakke, Peter Storandt studied Bakke's file carefully. Bakke certainly had good grades and test scores. His undergraduate average at the University of Minnesota, where he majored in engineering, was 3.46. His scores on the science, verbal, and math sections of the Medical College Admission Test were in the 97th, 96th, and 94th percentiles. Bakke's grades were higher than those of half the students admitted to the eighty-four places not filled by Task Force students, and his MCAT scores were considerably higher than average. Compared to the Task Force students, Bakke had higher grades than all but one of those admitted in 1973: their undergraduate grades averaged 2.88, and their MCAT scores on the science, verbal, and math sections averaged in the 46th, 24th, and 35th percentiles.

Bakke's numbers were impressive. So what had kept him out of the UC Davis medical school? The major reason was that he had received lukewarm reviews on his admission interviews with medical school faculty and students. The sole interviewer in 1972 had reported that Bakke was "tall and strong and Teutonic in appearance," not surprising for a former Marine Corps officer of Norwegian descent. The interviewer also wrote that Bakke's "main handicap is the unavoidable fact that he is now 33 years of age." But he considered Bakke "a very desirable applicant to this medical school and I shall so recommend him." However, his interview score, added to his grade and test scores, left Bakke two points shy of admission. When he applied again in 1973, after hinting that he might sue the university for giving preference to minority applicants with lower scores, his interview scores plummeted. The dean of student affairs, who had received Bakke's first complaint, interviewed him personally and called him "a rather rigidly oriented young man" who was "certainly not an outstanding candidate for our school."

At their meeting in August 1973, Peter Storandt explained the Task Force program to Allan Bakke in detail and gave him several documents about it. He later wrote Bakke and encouraged him "to pursue your research into admissions policies based on quota-oriented minority recruiting." Storandt also included several legal references and a Washington State court opinion, directing the state's law school to admit a rejected white applicant, Marco DeFunis. Ruling in 1974, the Supreme Court declined to hear the state's appeal on the ground the case was "moot" because DeFunis was nearing graduation. Justice Willam Brennan predicted in dissent that reverse discrimination cases "will not disappear" from the Court's docket. "They must inevitably return to the federal courts and ultimately to the Court," Brennan wrote. Allan Bakke did not disappear, and he turned to federal court after drawing the obvious conclusion that Storandt thought he should sue the UC Davis medical school. Through the material Storandt gave him, Bakke found a San Franciso lawyer, Reynold Colvin, who agreed to take his case. Colvin filed suit against the University of California Regents (who govern all UC schools) in state court in June 1974, alleging in his complaint that Bakke had been rejected "on account of his race, to-wit, Caucasian and white, and not for reasons applicable to persons of every race." Bakke won his case in the trial court, and the California supreme court upheld the ruling, striking down the UC Davis minority admissions program and ordering Bakke's admission to the medical school. Unlike the Washington court in the DeFunis case, however, the state court issued a stay of its order while the Regents asked the Supreme Court to review the ruling. This avoided any "mootness" problem when the Court granted the Regents' petition for certiorari in 1977.

The case of *Regents v. Bakke* confronted the Supreme Court with a dilemma. The justices had ruled for racial minorities in virtually all the job and school discrimination cases filed under Title VI of the Civil Rights Act. Would they make a "color-blind" decision in Bakke's case? The factual evidence was clear: Bakke had higher grades and scores than almost every minority student admitted to the UC Davis medical school under the Task Force program.

Did the Regents have any defense? They could—and did—argue that increasing the number of minority physicians in California offered a "compelling state interest" that overrode Bakke's interest in becoming a doctor. The Regents had numbers on their side as well: fewer than 2 percent of California's doctors came from minority groups. The only way to raise that number was to increase the number of minority medical students. Because their elementary and high school educations had generally been inferior, in ghetto or rural schools, minority applicants to medical school were burdened with lower college grades and test scores than whites. But this did not mean they were unqualified; more than 90 percent of minority medical students graduated and passed their licensing exams, only a slightly smaller percentage than white students. Setting aside sixteen places in the UC Davis entering class was a reasonable way, school officials felt, to achieve the goal of educating more minority doctors. Allan Bakke was not the only disappointed applicant; he was just one of 2,464 who competed for one hundred places at UC Davis. Bakke's argument, however, was that the Task Force program forced him to compete for one of just eighty-four places, which reduced his chances for admission. He might have been admitted if all one hundred places had been open to all applicants.

* * *

The justices heard argument in *Regents v. Bakke* on October 12, 1977. The dozens of amicus briefs piled on the bench testified to the high stakes in this case. The groups on the university's side included the ACLU, the Association of American Medical Colleges, the NAACP, and the National Council of Churches of Christ. Siding with Bakke were the American Federation of Teachers, the American Jewish Committee, the Fraternal Order of Police, the Sons of Italy, and Young Americans for Freedom. The civil rights coalition of blacks and Jews, who marched together for twenty years after *Brown*, had split over *Bakke* amid charges of racism on both sides.

The arguments inside the Court did not mention the acrimony outside its chamber. Archibald Cox took the podium first. The University of California Regents had hired the noted Harvard law professor because their own lawyers, although they won the case in state court, lacked the Supreme Court experience that Cox, a former solicitor general under President Kennedy, had in abundance. Cox made a professorial appeal for the medical school's Task Force program. "There is no racially blind method of selection which will enroll today more than a trickle of minority students in the nation's colleges and professions," he asserted. But the Task Force quota of sixteen places raised judicial eyebrows. Justice Potter Stewart asked a skeptical question: "It did put a limit on the number of white people, didn't it?" Cox dodged the question, responding that "the designation of sixteen places was not a quota, at least as I would use that word." He preferred the word "goal." Justice John Paul Stevens,

the Burger Court's newest member, tried to pin Cox down. "The question is not whether the sixteen is a quota; the question is whether the eighty-four is a quota." Cox wriggled away. "I would say that neither is properly defined as a quota." He explained that since minority applicants could apply through the "regular" admission process, the Task Force program did not place "a limit on the number of minority students." Pressed to provide a "compelling" interest for the program, Cox argued that "the minority applicant may have qualities that are superior to those of his classmate who is not minority." A Chicano doctor "certainly will be more effective in bringing it home to the young Chicano that he too may become a doctor."

Archibald Cox mentioned Allan Bakke just once, conceding that he "would be ranked above the minority applicant" under the "conventional standards for admission" to UC Davis. When he took the podium, Reynold Colvin talked *only* about Allan Bakke. "I am Allan Bakke's lawyer and Allan Bakke is my client," he reminded the justices. Colvin addressed the justices as if they were members of the UC Davis admission committee. "Look at the record in the case," he urged. "You'll find it on page 13 of our brief." He rattled off Bakke's impressive grades and scores, noting how much he outshone the minority applicants.

Justice Lewis Powell finally grew tired of Colvin's figures. "You have devoted twenty minutes to laboring the facts, if I may say so," he said. "I would like help, I really would, on the constitutional issues." But the dogged Colvin preferred talking about quotas. "What is the appropriate quota for a medical school? Sixteen, eight, thirty-two, sixty-four, one hundred?" Justice William Rehnquist tried to interest Colvin in the Constitution. Cox had argued, Rehnquist said, that UC Davis "could take race into account, and that under the Fourteenth Amendment there was no barrier to doing that, because of the interests that were involved. Now, what's your response to that?" Colvin answered that "race is an improper classification in this situation." Justice Thurgood Marshall wanted to know if UC Davis could reserve just one place for a minority student. Colvin's negative answer provoked Marshall. "So numbers are just unimportant?" he asked. "The numbers are unimportant," Colvin replied. "It is the principle of keeping a man out because of his race that is important."

How would the Burger Court resolve this dilemma? During their conference after the arguments, the justices split into two factions, each unwilling to compromise. It would take a Solomon to decide the *Bakke* case, with compelling interests on both sides and no clear-cut answer in the Constitution. As it happened, the Court had a Solomon on the bench, willing to cut the baby in half. With four justices on either side, Lewis Powell proposed giving Bakke and UC Davis what each wanted. Bakke would get into medical school, and minorities would receive a "plus" in the admissions process. The Davis quota of sixteen places would be replaced by a "race-conscious" program that could even exceed that number in admitting minorities.

Lewis Powell assumed his Solomonic role only because William Douglas had grudgingly left the bench in November 1975 after thirty-six years, the longest service of any justice. Crippled by strokes, Douglas tried to hang on, even writing opinions after his resignation. He finally gave up trying to be the "tenth justice" after his embarrassed colleagues ignored his memos. Douglas would certainly have voted to uphold the UC Davis program, but his replacement took Bakke's side. John Paul Stevens, a former clerk to Justice Wiley Rutledge, had practiced antitrust law in Chicago before President Nixon named him to the federal appellate bench in 1970. A judicial "moderate" in the Potter Stewart mold, Stevens would not have joined the Court if Nixon, crippled by Watergate, had not resigned in August 1974 after trying to hang on as president in the face of certain impeachment. Ironically, Warren Burger, who had administered the oath in which Nixon swore to "protect and defend the Constitution," wrote the unanimous opinion that forced him to hand over the "smoking gun" Watergate tapes revealing Nixon's contempt for the Constitution. Nixon would certainly have replaced Douglas with a more conservative justice than Stevens, who became Gerald Ford's sole nominee in November 1975.

It took Lewis Powell eight months to draft an opinion—actually two opinions in one—stating "the judgement of the Court" in the *Bakke* case. The first section of Powell's opinion also spoke for Burger, Rehnquist, Stewart, and Stevens. These five justices struck down the UC Davis quota system, ruling that it established "a classification based on race and ethnic background." Powell cited the Japanese American internment cases, *Hirabayashi* and *Korematsu,* in writing that "racial and ethnic distinctions of any sort are inherently suspect and thus call for the most exacting judicial examination." After examining Allan Bakke's skin, Powell stated that "discrimination against members of the white 'majority'" could not pass the "strict scrutiny" test. Speaking of minority groups, Powell wrote that the Equal Protection Clause does not permit "the recognition of special wards entitled to a degree of protection greater than that accorded others." Consciously or not, Powell echoed the words of Justice Joseph Bradley in 1883, writing in the *Civil Rights Cases* that the Fourteenth Amendment did not make blacks "the special favorite of the law."

At this point in Powell's opinion, the four justices who had been riding with him got off the train. They had achieved their goal of striking down racial quotas and had no desire to travel with Powell into "race-conscious" territory. For the final leg of this trip, four justices—Brennan, Marshall, White, and Blackmun—joined the excursion. In the second part of Powell's opinion, he asserted that "race or ethnic background may be deemed a 'plus' in a particular applicant's file," to be counted along with grades and test scores. The "plus" factors could also include "exceptional personal talents, unique work or service experience, leadership potential, maturity, demonstrated compassion, a history of overcoming disadvantage, ability to communicate with the poor, or other qualifications deemed important" to making good doctors. Powell's formula allowed UC Davis and other schools to "take race into account" in choosing students, although that factor could not be "decisive" in admissions decisions.

Unlike Solomon, who never cut the disputed baby in half, Powell sliced the *Bakke* case down the middle and handed each party what it wanted. But this compromise did not satisfy the four justices who supported the UC Davis quota system. They produced a separate opinion—drafted by William Brennan—disputing claims that officials must be "color-blind" in choosing between applicants for jobs and schools. Brennan's opinion noted that "race has too often been used by those who would stigmatize and oppress minorities." The American people, he wrote, cannot "let color blindness become myopia which masks the reality that many 'created equal' have been treated within our lifetimes as inferior both by the law and by their fellow citizens."

The Court's only black member, Thurgood Marshall, felt compelled to remind his colleagues—and those few Americans who actually read the opinions—that "the Negro was dragged to this country in chains to be sold into slavery." Marshall cited books by John Hope Franklin and C. Vann Woodward in presenting a brief but graphic history of slavery and its legacy. "The system of slavery brutalized and dehumanized both master and slave," he wrote. Marshall recalled the "Great Compromise" at the Constitutional Convention in Philadelphia, where "the Framers made it plain that 'we the people,' for whose protection the Constitution was designed, did not include those whose skins were the wrong color." Marshall linked this history to the present. "The position of the Negro today in America is the tragic but inevitable consequence of centuries of unequal treatment," he continued. "Measured by any benchmark of comfort or achievement, meaningful equality remains a distant dream for the Negro."

The justices produced five opinions in the *Bakke* case, spread over 153 pages of the Court's reports. Harry Blackmun's came last, and he spoke a final word on race and the Constitution. "In order to get beyond racism," he wrote, "we must first take account of race. There is no other way. And in order to treat some persons equally, we must treat them differently. We cannot—we dare not—let the Fourteenth Amendment perpetuate racial supremacy."

Chief Justice Charles Evans Hughes once said that "the Constitution is what the judges say it is." But what *did* they say in *Bakke?* The inability of nine justices to agree on a clear statement of what the Fourteenth Amendment says to UC Davis admissions officials speaks volumes about the continuing racial chasm in American society. The Supreme Court refused in 1997 to hear a challenge to the new policy of the University of California Regents, who voted in 1995 to remove any "plus" factors based on race or ethnicity in admissions decisions. Under the university's "color-blind" policy, the number of black and Hispanic students entering the nation's largest public university system has dropped by more than half. The first-year class at the UC Davis medical school in 1998 included just five black and three Hispanic students. That same year, not a single black student entered the university's prestigious law school at Berkeley. Allan Bakke, meanwhile, received his medical degree from Davis in 1982 and returned to Minnesota, where he practices anesthesiology (Irons, 1999).

MR. JUSTICE POWELL announced the judgment of the Court.

This case presents a challenge to the special admissions program of the petitioner, the Medical School of the University of California at Davis, which is designed to assure the admission of a specified number of students from certain minority groups. The Superior Court of California sustained respondent's challenge, holding that petitioner's program violated the California Constitution, Title VI of the Civil Rights Act of 1964, . . . and the Equal Protection Clause of the Fourteenth Amendment. The court enjoined petitioner from considering respondent's race or the race of any other applicant in making admissions decisions. It refused, however, to order respondent's admission to the Medical School, holding that he had not carried his burden of proving that he would have been admitted but for the constitutional and statutory violations. The Supreme Court of California affirmed those portions of the trial court's judgment declaring the special admissions program unlawful and enjoining petitioner from considering the race of any applicant. It modified that portion of the judgment denying respondent's requested injunction and directed the trial court to order his admission.

For the reasons stated in the following opinion, I believe that so much of the judgment of the California court as holds petitioner's special admissions program unlawful and directs that respondent be admitted to the Medical School must be affirmed. For the reasons expressed in a separate opinion, my Brothers The Chief Justice, Mr. Justice Stewart, Mr. Justice Rehnquist, and Mr. Justice Stevens concur in this judgment.

I also conclude for the reasons stated in the following opinion that the portion of the court's judgment enjoining petitioner from according any consideration to race in its admissions process must be reversed. For reasons expressed in separate opinions, my Brothers Mr. Justice Brennan, Mr. Justice White, Mr. Justice Marshall, and Mr. Justice Blackmun concur in this judgment.

Affirmed in part and reversed in part.

* * *

The Medical School of the University of California at Davis opened in 1968 with an entering class of 50 students. In 1971, the size of the entering class was increased to 100 students, a level at which it remains. No admissions program for disadvantaged or minority students existed when the school opened, and the first class contained three Asians but no blacks, no Mexican-Americans, and no American Indians. Over the next two years, the faculty devised a special admissions program to increase the representation of "disadvantaged" students in each Medical School class. The special program consisted of a separate admissions system operating in coordination with the regular admissions process.

Under the regular admissions procedure, a candidate could submit his application to the Medical School beginning in July of the year preceding the academic year for which admission was sought. Because of the large number of applications, the admissions committee screened each one to select candidates for further consideration. The special admissions program operated with a separate committee, a majority of whom were members of minority groups. On the 1973 application form, candidates were asked to indicate whether they wished to be considered as "economically and/or educationally disadvantaged" applicants; on the 1974 form the question was whether they wished to be considered as members of a "minority group," which the Medical School apparently viewed as "Blacks," "Chicanos," "Asians," and "American Indians." If these questions were answered affirmatively, the application was forwarded to the special admissions committee. No formal definition of "disadvantaged" was ever produced, but the chairman of the special committee screened each application to see whether it reflected economic or educational deprivation. Having passed this initial hurdle, the applications then were rated by the special committee in a fashion similar to that used by the general admissions committee, except that special candidates did not have to meet the 2.5 grade point average cutoff applied to regular applicants. . . .

From the year of the increase in class size—1971—through 1974, the special program resulted in the admission of 21 black students, 30 Mexican-Americans, and 12 Asians, for a total of 63 minority students. Over the same period, the regular admissions program produced 1 black, 6 Mexican-Americans, and 37 Asians, for a total of 44 minority students. Although disadvantaged whites applied to the special program in large numbers, none received an offer of admission through that process. Indeed, in 1974, at least, the special committee explicitly considered only "disadvantaged" special applicants who were members of one of the designated minority groups.

Allan Bakke is a white male who applied to the Davis Medical School in both 1973 and 1974. In both years Bakke's application was considered under the general admissions program, and he received an interview. His 1973 interview was with Dr. Theodore C. West, who considered Bakke "a very desirable applicant to [the] medical school." Despite a strong benchmark score of 468 out of 500, Bakke was rejected. His application had come late in the year, and no applicants in the general admissions process with scores below 470 were accepted after Bakke's application was completed. There were four special admissions slots unfilled at that time, however, for which Bakke was not considered. After his 1973 rejection, Bakke wrote to Dr. George H. Lowrey, Associate Dean and Chairman of the Admissions Committee, protesting that the special admissions program operated as a racial and ethnic quota.

Bakke's 1974 application was completed early in the year. His student interviewer gave him an overall rating of 94, finding him "friendly, well tempered, conscientious and delightful to speak with." His faculty interviewer was, by coincidence, the same Dr. Lowrey to whom he had written in protest of the special admissions program. Dr. Lowrey found Bakke "rather limited in his approach" to the problems of the medical profession and found disturbing Bakke's "very definite opinions which were based more on his personal viewpoints than upon a study of the total problem." Dr. Lowrey gave Bakke the lowest of his six ratings, an 86; his total was 549 out of 600. Again, Bakke's application was rejected. In neither year did the chairman of the admissions committee, Dr. Lowrey, exercise his discretion to place Bakke on the waiting list. In both years, applicants were admitted under the special program with grade point averages, MCAT scores, and benchmark scores significantly lower than Bakke's. . . .

Petitioner does not deny that decisions based on race or ethnic origin by faculties and administrations of state universities are reviewable under the Fourteenth Amendment. For his part, respondent does not argue that all racial or ethnic classifications are per se invalid. The parties do disagree as to the level of judicial scrutiny to be applied to the special admissions program. Petitioner argues that the court below erred in applying strict scrutiny, as this inexact term has been applied in our cases. That level of review, petitioner asserts, should be reserved for classifications that disadvantage "discrete and insular minorities." See United States v. Carolene Products Co., n. 4 (1938). Respondent, on the other hand, contends that the California court correctly rejected the notion that the degree of judicial scrutiny accorded a particular racial or ethnic classification hinges upon membership in a discrete and insular minority and duly recognized that the "rights established [by the Fourteenth Amendment] are personal rights." Shelley v. Kraemer (1948).

En route to this crucial battle over the scope of judicial review, the parties fight a sharp preliminary action over the proper characterization of the special admissions program. Petitioner prefers to view it as establishing a "goal" of minority representation in the Medical School. Respondent, echoing the courts below, labels it a racial quota. This semantic distinction is beside the point: The special admissions program is undeniably a classification based on race and ethnic background. To the extent that there existed a pool of at least minimally qualified minority applicants to fill the 16 special admissions seats, white applicants could compete only for 84 seats in the entering class, rather than the 100 open to minority applicants. Whether this limitation is described as a quota or a goal, it is a line drawn on the basis of race and ethnic status.

The guarantees of the Fourteenth Amendment extend to all persons. Its language is explicit: "No State shall . . . deny to any person within its jurisdiction the equal protection of the laws." It is settled beyond question that the "rights created by the first section of the Fourteenth Amendment are, by its terms, guaranteed to the individual. The rights established are personal rights," Shelley v. Kraemer. The guarantee of equal protection cannot mean one thing when applied to one individual and something else when applied to a person of another color. If both are not accorded the same protection, then it is not equal.

Nevertheless, petitioner argues that the court below erred in applying strict scrutiny to the special admissions program because white males, such as respondent, are not a "discrete and insular minority" requiring extraordinary protection from the majoritarian political process. Carolene Products Co., n. 4. This rationale, however, has never been invoked in our decisions as a prerequisite to subjecting racial or ethnic distinctions to strict scrutiny. Nor has this Court held that discreteness and insularity constitute necessary preconditions to a holding that a particular classification is invidious. These characteristics may be relevant in deciding whether or not to add new types of classifications to the list of "suspect" categories or whether a particular classification survives close examination. Racial and ethnic classifications, however, are subject to stringent examination without regard to these additional characteristics. . . . Racial and ethnic distinctions of any sort are inherently suspect and thus call for the most exacting judicial examination. . . .

Over the past 30 years, this Court has embarked upon the crucial mission of interpreting the Equal Protection Clause with the view of assuring to all persons "the protection of equal laws," Yick Wo, in a Nation confronting a legacy of slavery and racial discrimination. Because the landmark decisions in this area arose in response to the continued exclusion of Negroes from the mainstream of American society, they could be characterized as involving discrimination by the "majority" white race against the Negro minority. But they need not be read as depending upon that characterization for their results. It suffices to say that "[o]ver the years, this Court has consistently repudiated '[d]istinctions between citizens solely because of their ancestry' as being 'odious to a free people whose institutions are founded upon the doctrine of equality.'"

Petitioner urges us to adopt for the first time a more restrictive view of the Equal Protection Clause and hold that discrimination against members of the white "majority" cannot be suspect if its purpose can be characterized as "benign." The clock of our liberties, however, cannot be turned back to 1868. It is far too late to argue that the guarantee of equal protection to all persons permits the recognition of special wards entitled to a degree of protection greater than that accorded others. . . .

If it is the individual who is entitled to judicial protection against classifications based upon his racial or ethnic background because such distinctions impinge upon personal rights, rather than the individual only because of his membership in a particular group, then constitutional standards may be applied consistently. Political judgments regarding the necessity for the particular classification may be weighed in the constitutional balance, Korematsu v. United States (1944), but the standard of justification will remain constant. This is as it should be, since those political judgments are the product of rough compromise struck by contending groups within the democratic process. When they touch upon an individual's race or ethnic background, he is entitled to a judicial determination that the burden he is asked to bear on that basis is precisely tailored to serve a compelling governmental interest. The Constitution guarantees that right to every person regardless of his background. . . . We have held that in "order to justify the use of a suspect classification, a State must show that its purpose or interest is both constitutionally permissible and substantial, and that its use of the classification is 'necessary . . . to the accomplishment' of its purpose or the safeguarding of its interest." . . . If petitioner's purpose is to assure within its student body some specified percentage of a particular group merely because of its race or ethnic origin, such a preferential purpose must be rejected not as insubstantial but as facially invalid. Preferring members of any one group for no reason other than race or ethnic origin is discrimination for its own sake. This the Constitution forbids. . . .

Ethnic diversity, however, is only one element in a range of factors a university properly may consider in attaining the goal of a heterogeneous student body. Although a university must have wide discretion in making the sensitive judgments as to who should be admitted, constitutional limitations protecting individual rights may not be disregarded. . . . It may be assumed that the reservation of a specified number of seats in each class for individuals from the preferred ethnic groups would contribute to the attainment of considerable ethnic diversity in the student body. But petitioner's argument that this is the only effective means of serving the interest of diversity is seriously flawed. In a most fundamental sense the argument misconceives the nature of the state interest that would justify consideration of race or ethnic background. It is not an interest in simple ethnic diversity, in which a specified percentage of the student body is in effect guaranteed to be members of selected ethnic groups, with the remaining percentage an undifferentiated aggregation of students. The diversity that furthers a compelling state interest encompasses a far broader array of qualifications and characteristics of which racial or ethnic origin is but a single though important element. Petitioner's special admissions program, focused solely on ethnic diversity, would hinder rather than further attainment of genuine diversity. . . .

The experience of other university admissions programs, which take race into account in achieving the educational diversity valued by the First Amendment, demonstrates that the assignment of a fixed number of places to a minority group is not a necessary means toward that end. An illuminating example is found in the Harvard College program: "In recent years Harvard College has expanded the concept of diversity to include students from disadvantaged economic, racial and ethnic groups. Harvard College now recruits not only Californians or Louisianans but also blacks and Chicanos and other minority students. . . . In practice, this new definition of diversity has meant that race has been a factor in some admission decisions. When the Committee on Admissions reviews the large middle group of applicants who are 'admissible' and deemed capable of doing good work in their courses, the race of an applicant may tip the balance in his favor just as geographic origin or a life spent on a farm may tip the balance in other candidates' cases. A farm boy from Idaho can bring something to Harvard College that a Bostonian cannot offer. Similarly, a black student can usually bring something that a white person cannot offer. . . .

This kind of program treats each applicant as an individual in the admissions process. The applicant who loses out on the last available seat to another candidate receiving a "plus" on the basis of ethnic background will not have been foreclosed from all consideration for that seat simply because he was not the right color or had the wrong surname. It would mean only that his combined qualifications, which may have included similar nonobjective factors, did not outweigh those of the other applicant. His qualifications would have been weighed fairly and competitively, and he would have no basis to complain of unequal treatment under the Fourteenth Amendment. . . .

In summary, it is evident that the Davis special admissions program involves the use of an explicit racial classification never before countenanced by this Court. It tells applicants who are not Negro, Asian, or Chicano that they are totally excluded from a specific percentage of the seats in an entering class. No matter how strong their qualifications, quantitative and extracurricular, including their own potential for contribution to educational diversity, they are never afforded the chance to compete with applicants from the preferred groups for the special admissions seats. At the same time, the preferred applicants have the opportunity to compete for every seat in the class.

The fatal flaw in petitioner's preferential program is its disregard of individual rights as guaranteed by the Fourteenth Amendment. Such rights are not absolute. But when a State's distribution of benefits or imposition of burdens hinges on ancestry or the color of a person's skin, that individual is entitled to a demonstration that the challenged classification is necessary to promote a substantial state interest. Petitioner has failed to carry this burden. For this reason, that portion of the California court's judgment holding petitioner's special admissions program invalid under the Fourteenth Amendment must be affirmed.

In enjoining petitioner from ever considering the race of any applicant, however, the courts below failed to recognize that the State has a substantial interest that legitimately may be served by a properly devised admissions program involving the competitive consideration of race and ethnic origin. For this reason, so much of the California court's judgment as enjoins petitioner from any consideration of the race of any applicant must be reversed.

With respect to respondent's entitlement to an injunction directing his admission to the Medical School, petitioner has conceded that it could not carry its burden of proving that, but for the existence of its unlawful special admissions program, respondent still would not have been admitted. Hence, respondent is entitled to the injunction, and that portion of the judgment must be affirmed.

Opinion of MR. JUSTICE BRENNAN, MR. JUSTICE WHITE, MR. JUSTICE MARSHALL, and MR. JUSTICE BLACKMUN, concurring in the judgment in part and dissenting in part.

The Court today, in reversing in part the judgment of the Supreme Court of California, affirms the constitutional power of Federal and State Governments to act affirmatively to achieve equal opportunity for all. The difficulty of the issue presented—whether government may use race-conscious programs to redress the continuing effects of past discrimination—and the mature consideration which each of our Brethren has brought to it have resulted in many opinions, no single one speaking for the Court. But this should not and must not mask the central meaning of today's opinions: Government may take race into account when it acts not to demean or insult any racial group, but to remedy disadvantages cast on minorities by past racial prejudice, at least when appropriate findings have been made by judicial, legislative, or administrative bodies with competence to act in this area. . . .

Our Nation was founded on the principle that "all men are created equal." Yet candor requires acknowledgment that the Framers of our Constitution, to forge the 13 Colonies into one Nation, openly compromised this principle of equality with its antithesis: slavery. The consequences of this compromise are well known and have aptly been called our "American Dilemma." Still, it is well to recount how recent the time has been, if it has yet come, when the promise of our principles has flowered into the actuality of equal opportunity for all regardless of race or color.

The Fourteenth Amendment, the embodiment in the Constitution of our abiding belief in human equality, has been the law of our land for only slightly more than half its 200 years. And for half of that half, the Equal Protection Clause of the Amendment was largely moribund so that, as late as 1927, Mr. Justice Holmes could sum up the importance of that Clause by remarking that it was the "last resort of constitutional arguments." Buck v. Bell (1927). Worse than desuetude, the Clause was early turned against those whom it was intended to set free, condemning them to a "separate but equal" status before the law, a status always separate but seldom equal. Not until 1954—only 24 years ago—was this odious doctrine interred by our decision in Brown v. Board of Education, which proclaimed that separate schools and public facilities of all sorts were inherently unequal and forbidden under our Constitution. . . .

Against this background, claims that law must be "colorblind" or that the datum of race is no longer relevant to public policy must be seen as aspiration rather than as description of reality. This is not to denigrate aspiration; for reality rebukes us that race has too often been used by those who would stigmatize and oppress minorities. Yet we cannot . . . let color blindness become myopia which masks the reality that many "created equal" have been treated within our lifetimes as inferior both by the law and by their fellow citizens. . . .

We turn [now] to our analysis of the Equal Protection Clause of the Fourteenth Amendment. . . . The assertion of human equality is closely associated with the proposition that differences in color or creed, birth or status, are neither significant nor relevant to the way in which persons should be treated. Nonetheless, the position that such factors must be "constitutionally an irrelevance," summed up by the shorthand phrase "[o]ur Constitution is color-blind," Plessy v. Ferguson (1896) (Harlan, J., dissenting), has never been adopted by this Court as the proper meaning of the Equal Protection Clause. Indeed, we have expressly rejected this proposition on a number of occasions.

Our cases have always implied that an "overriding statutory purpose," could be found that would justify racial classifications. See, e.g., Loving v. Virginia (1967); Korematsu v. United States (1944); Hirabayashi v. United States (1943). . . . We conclude, therefore, that racial classifications are not per se invalid under the Fourteenth Amendment. Accordingly, we turn to the problem of articulating what our role should be in reviewing state action that expressly classifies by race. Respondent argues that racial classifications are always suspect and, consequently, that this Court should weigh the importance of the objectives served by Davis' special admissions program to see if they are compelling. In addition, he asserts that this Court must inquire whether, in its judgment, there are alternatives to racial classifications which would suit Davis' purposes. Petitioner, on the other hand, states that our proper role is simply to accept petitioner's determination that the racial classifications used by its program are reasonably related to what it tells us are its benign purposes. We reject petitioner's view, but, because our prior cases are in many respects in apposite to that before us now, we find it necessary to define with precision the meaning of that inexact term, "strict scrutiny." . . .

. . . [A] number of considerations . . . lead us to conclude that racial classifications designed to further remedial purposes "must serve important governmental objectives and must be substantially related to achievement of those objectives." . . . Davis' articulated purpose of remedying the effects of past societal discrimination is, under our cases, sufficiently important to justify the use of race-conscious admissions programs where there is a sound basis for concluding that minority underrepresentation is substantial and

chronic, and that the handicap of past discrimination is impeding access of minorities to the Medical School. . . . If it was reasonable to conclude—as we hold that it was—that the failure of minorities to qualify for admission at Davis under regular procedures was due principally to the effects of past discrimination, then there is a reasonable likelihood that, but for pervasive racial discrimination, respondent would have failed to qualify for admission even in the absence of Davis' special admissions program. . . .

. . . [O]ur cases under Title VII of the Civil Rights Act have held that, in order to achieve minority participation in previously segregated areas of public life, Congress may require or authorize preferential treatment for those likely disadvantaged by societal racial discrimination. Such legislation has been sustained even without a requirement of findings of intentional racial discrimination by those required or authorized to accord preferential treatment, or a case-by-case determination that those to be benefited suffered from racial discrimination. These decisions compel the conclusion that States also may adopt race-conscious programs designed to overcome substantial, chronic minority under representation where there is reason to believe that the evil addressed is a product of past racial discrimination. . . .

Certainly, on the basis of the undisputed factual submissions before this Court, Davis had a sound basis for believing that the problem of under representation of minorities was substantial and chronic and that the problem was attributable to handicaps imposed on minority applicants by past and present racial discrimination. Until at least 1973, the practice of medicine in this country was, in fact, if not in law, largely the prerogative of whites. In 1950, for example, while Negroes constituted 10% of the total population, Negro physicians constituted only 2.2% of the total number of physicians. The overwhelming majority of these, moreover, were educated in two predominantly Negro medical schools, Howard and Meharry. By 1970, the gap between the proportion of Negroes in medicine and their proportion in the population had widened: The number of Negroes employed in medicine remained frozen at 2.2% while the Negro population had increased to 11.1%. The number of Negro admittees to predominantly white medical schools, moreover, had declined in absolute numbers during the years 1955 to 1964. . . . Davis clearly could conclude that the serious and persistent underrepresentation of minorities in medicine depicted by these statistics is the result of handicaps under which minority applicants labor as a consequence of a background of deliberate, purposeful discrimination against minorities in education and in society generally, as well as in the medical profession. . . .

The second prong of our test—whether the Davis program stigmatizes any discrete group or individual and whether race is reasonably used in light of the program's objectives—is clearly satisfied by the Davis program. It is not even claimed that Davis' program in any way operates to stigmatize or single out any discrete and insular, or even any identifiable, nonminority group. Nor will harm comparable to that imposed upon racial minorities by exclusion or separation on grounds of race be the likely result of the program. It does not, for example, establish an exclusive preserve for minority students apart from and exclusive of whites. Rather, its purpose is to overcome the effects of segregation by bringing the races together. True, whites are excluded from participation in the special admissions program, but this fact only operates to reduce the number of whites to be admitted in the regular admissions program in order to permit admission of a reasonable percentage—less than their proportion of the California population—of otherwise underrepresented qualified minority applicants.

Nor was Bakke in any sense stamped as inferior by the Medical School's rejection of him. Indeed, it is conceded by all that he satisfied those criteria regarded by the school as generally relevant to academic performance better than most of the minority members who were admitted. Moreover, there is absolutely no basis for concluding that Bakke's rejection as a result of Davis' use of racial preference will affect him throughout his life in the same way as the segregation of the Negro school children in Brown I would have affected them. Unlike discrimination against racial minorities, the use of racial preferences for remedial purposes does not inflict a pervasive injury upon individual whites in the sense that wherever they go or whatever they do there is a significant likelihood that they will be treated as second-class citizens because of their color. This distinction does not mean that the exclusion of a white resulting from the preferential use of race is not sufficiently serious to require justification; but it does mean that the injury inflicted by such a policy is not distinguishable from disadvantages caused by a wide range of government actions, none of which has ever been thought impermissible for that reason alone. . . .

Finally, Davis' special admissions program cannot be said to violate the Constitution simply because it has set aside a predetermined number of places for qualified minority applicants rather than using minority status as a positive factor to be considered in evaluating the applications of disadvantaged minority applicants. For purposes of constitutional adjudication, there is no difference between the two approaches. In any admissions program which accords special consideration to disadvantaged racial minorities, a determination of the degree of preference to be given is unavoidable, and any given preference that results in the exclusion of a white candidate is no more or less constitutionally acceptable than a program such as that at Davis. Furthermore, the extent of the preference inevitably depends on how many minority applicants the particular school is seeking to admit in any particular year so long as the number of qualified minority applicants exceeds that number. There is no sensible, and certainly no constitutional, distinction between, for example, adding a set number of points to the admissions rating of disadvantaged minority applicants as an expression of the preference with the expectation that this will result in the admission of an approximately determined number of qualified minority applicants and setting a fixed number of places for such applicants as was done here.

The "Harvard" program, as those employing it readily concede, openly and successfully employs a racial criterion for the purpose of ensuring that some of the scarce places in institutions of higher education are allocated to disadvantaged minority students. That the Harvard approach does not also make public the extent of the preference and the precise workings of the system while the Davis program employs a specific, openly stated number, does not condemn the latter plan for purposes of Fourteenth Amendment adjudication. It may be that the Harvard plan is more acceptable to the public than is the Davis "quota." If it is, any State, including California, is free to adopt it in preference to a less acceptable alternative, just as it is generally free, as far as the Constitution is concerned, to abjure granting any racial preferences in its admissions program. But there is no basis for preferring a particular preference program simply because in achieving the same goals that the Davis Medical School is pursuing, it proceeds in a manner that is not immediately apparent to the public.

Accordingly, we would reverse the judgment of the Supreme Court of California holding the Medical School's special admissions program unconstitutional and directing respondent's admission, as well as that portion of the judgment enjoining the Medical School from according any consideration to race in the admissions process.

COMMENTARY: "BAKKE"

The complexities of the Supreme Court ruling in the reverse-discrimination case of Allan Bakke will be years in the sorting out, yet its basic meaning is already apparent. In simplest terms, the ruling is a defeat for rigid quotas of any sort and a go-ahead to affirmative-action programs which would remedy a legacy of racial discrimination in this country through a balancing of factors that include consideration of race, but in a context of many categories and types of criteria. This narrow victory and guarded approval for affirmative action disappointed many who felt that the injustices of two hundred years should allow for the boldest interpretations of what is permissible under law, even to the extra-constitutional. Much as we sympathize with the point of view, we are persuaded that the Court ruled sagaciously and in manner that will ultimately expand rather than contract opportunities of every kind for the disadvantaged.

We must confess, however, that that wasn't our initial reaction to *Bakke*. On quick first reading we feared that the Court had paid lip-service to a principle—affirmative action—then, by citing the "illuminating" example of Harvard University, had put the principle out of reach so far as broad application was concerned. It was a worry easy enough to harbor. If specific numerical quotas were to be outlawed, and diversity to be achieved through the sophisticated means of a Harvard, then it was easy to picture affirmative action being effectively tied in knots by groups that had neither the imagination, nor the will, nor the interest in diversity that Harvard and similar educational institutions have, almost by reason of what they are, Diversity belongs to the nature of a university, or should; the same is not true in the trades or other fields.

Our concern, we are happy to say, was dispelled within days of *Bakke*, when the Court ruled in four less celebrated cases, all widening the implications of the Bakke decision and all in favor of affirmative action. The most important was a ruling upholding a 1973 consent decree that required AT&T to hire more blacks, ethnics, and women. The special significance here was the suggestion that the Court would continue to view affirmative action programs in employment in a different light from the universities. The AT&T decision, for instance, appeared to reinforce government's powers to use goals, timetables and other prods, short of course of fixed quotas, to end discriminatory practices in industry. Thus a double-track corrective to discrimination seems in the shaping, and maybe even more before the need for affirmative action is ended in the country. In this context it is interesting to note that the Court has agreed to hear next year the case of a woman who claims that her sex has kept her from being admitted to two Illinois medical colleges.

Bakke, accordingly, isn't the final word, but it is an historic first word to what the future will be in the United States. The Justices were deeply divided on the case; the pundits are grappling yet with the nuances of their narrow votes and the multiple concurring and dissenting opinions. But, as Justice Brennan stated in his opinion, none of this should mask the central meaning of what the Court ruled on June 28, 1978: "Government may take race into account when it acts not to demean or insult any racial group, but to remedy disadvantages cast on minorities by past racial prejudice, at least when appropriate findings have been made by judicial, legislative or administrative bodies with competence to act in this area."

In this sense, *Bakke* is the most important civil-rights pronouncement made by the Supreme Court since *Brown* vs. *Board of Education of Topeka*, the 1954 school desegregation decision. *Bakke* will not have the immediate impact of *Brown*, but it is likely to be no less important in the long range and as good for the soul of the nation and its people.

We applaud it (Commonweal Foundation, 1978).

COMMENTARY: BAKKE: ENDURING QUESTION

The ideal of a color-blind society has always posed difficulties. As long as there was the suspicion of color prejudice, the strain of ambiguity could be unbearable. The only way to prove color-blindness is to perform a color-conscious act: as by hiring a black. Thus Lyndon Johnson, who ushered in the Civil Rights Act of 1964, could denounce reverse discrimination—and then, with great fanfare, appoint the first black Supreme Court Justice. Thurgood Marshall, for all his objective qualifications as a lawyer, was indeed an early beneficiary of affirmative action.

The affirmative action principle need not scandalize: ethnic politics is nothing new, and Marshall's appointment, if not based solely on merit, is in the old American tradition of balancing the ticket. There have been Catholic and Jewish "seats" on the Court; the novelty of Marshall's appointment in 1967 was merely that blacks had "arrived" as a constituency.

Color-blindness was thus a fiction, partly noble, partly hypocritical. Race has always and everywhere been a matter of explosive potential. The 1964 Civil Rights Act tried to defuse the issue by banning public reference to it as a criterion of official and commercial relations among citizens. The Act had, really, two aims. One was the improvement of the Negro's lot. The other and broader one was the institutionalization of the meritocratic principle. These were assumed, by most of us, to be perfectly compatible. Once discriminatory "barriers" were removed, the Negro would naturally "take his place" in the American system.

Whether this would have happened is not established (though we think it is broadly true; obvious, even). What did

happen, all too soon, was that the American liberal decided that the meritocratic principle was "loaded" in favor of whites. Pending a public consensus on the empirical answers, or even on the criteria of answers, the question must remain metaphysical and ideological. And in the absence of such a consensus, the question can only be answered by power. Hence the bitter affirmative action struggle.

The answers given by the Court in *Bakke* are fairly lucid, taken separately; taken together, however, they are Delphic. The Stevens faction (of four) says simply that the Civil Rights Act bans discrimination, period benign discrimination is no more permitted by the pro-Negro purposes of the Act than mercy-killing is permitted by laws against murder. Even here, though, there lurks a problem: the Act itself deals with motives rather than deeds. You may refuse to hire a black, so long as the reason for the refusal isn't his blackness. Is the ban, then, on formal, explicit discrimination or on subjective hidden, even unconscious, bias? Is the implication that every applicant must be regarded solely as an individual rather than a group member? And does this implication have the force of law? The Stevens group construes the Act as banning *future* acts of discrimination, even, apparently, if this means accepting the remaining (and still to come) impact of *past* discrimination. It sustains the color-blind paradigm.

The Brennan faction (also of four) flatly rejects the paradigm except as a desideratum. It appeals to the purposes, as it understands them, of the Act and the Constitution, and virtually sweeps aside the letter and the common understanding of the Act (though without directly challenging either) for the sake of promoting racial justice. The Brennan group barely conceals its indignation with the majority, and takes the rare step of announcing the "central meaning" of the very decision it dissents from: that "Government may take race into account when it acts not to demean or insult any racial group, but to remedy disadvantages cast on minorities by past racial prejudice." This is a breathtaking piece of exegesis: the Court as a whole has often made bold statements of the real meaning of the Constitution, but seldom has a dissenting minority taken it upon itself to expound the real meaning of the majority it has dissented from.

Smack in the middle is Justice Powell, who finds all discrimination unconstitutional, but finds that the goal of ethnic diversity in a student body is implicit in the First Amendment as an aspect of academic freedom. He upholds the individualist principle, but maintains that for certain purposes race may be regarded as a component of the individual.

The legal accretions have now reached a point of perhaps irresolvable confusion. The *Bakke* rulings create no clear precedent and leave the status of the Civil Rights Act unclear. A few days after *Bakke* the Court let stand, by refusing to review, a government affirmative action program that requires AT&T to hire more blacks and women. All that is undisputed is that overt quotas are out, just as overt discrimination is out. And that there will be loads of litigation.

Most of the suits will be brought by white males, so the net effect of *Bakke* may be, if not to elucidate the law, at least to place the law's weight on the shoulders of aggressive governmental equalizers. It is one thing to approve a generalized affirmative action program in which race is "one of many factors"; another to tell the person who is palpably excluded because of his race that he is not a victim of discrimination. Private institutions that implement their own racial-balance programs will face few problems, so long as they avoid quotas. Private businesses convicted of discrimination will be forced to submit to government programs. But businesses and universities not so convicted may now have a powerful legal base from which to resist the doctrinaire leveling of Eleanor Holmes Norton and her associates, who contend that there is a positive duty to integrate color-consciously, even when no discrimination is proved. In short, the era of presumptive racial guilt may have come to an end: it may be necessary to convict before sentencing (National Review, 1978).

GRATZ V. BOLLINGER
(Decided June 23, 2003)

"Justice Powell's opinion in Bakke emphasized the importance of considering each particular applicant as an individual. [The University of Michigan's] policy, which automatically distributes . . . one-fifth of the points needed to guarantee admission, to every single "underrepresented minority" applicant solely because of race . . . does not provide such individualized consideration."

The Question: Can a state university promote the racial and ethnic diversity of its undergraduate student body by adopting a policy that awards extra points on the admissions scale to members of "underrepresented" minorities, without establishing any particular quote for members of these groups?

The Arguments: PRO

The Supreme Court has ruled that race and ethnicity can be used as "plus" factors in university admissions, as long as no quotas are established and members of minorities are not considered in a separate admissions process. There are recognized educational advantages to racial and ethnic diversity in universities, and awarding extra points to members of these minorities is no different from awarding extra points to athletes, children of alumni, and applicants with special talents (such as music). Without such an admissions policy, for fewer racial and ethnic minorities would be able to gain college degrees.

CON

It is just as much a violation of the Constitution to reward members of racial and ethnic minorities as it is to punish or penalize them. Every agency of government, including colleges and universities, should operate in a "color-blind" manner. Any program that gives preference to some persons on the basis of race or ethnicity has the effect of penalizing others for a fact that is irrelevant to their qualifications or character. Also, so-called affirmative action programs, however well intentioned, confer a stigma on all minority students, who are seen by others as gaining an unfair advantage.

CHIEF JUSTICE REHNQUIST delivered the opinion of the Court.

Petitioners Jennifer Gratz and Patrick Hamacher both applied for admission to the University of Michigan's (University) College of Literature, Science, and the Arts (LSA) as residents of the State of Michigan. Both petitioners are Caucasian. Gratz, who applied for admission for the fall of 1995, was notified in January of that year that a final decision regarding her admission had been delayed until April. This delay was based upon the University's determination that, although Gratz was "well qualified," she was "less competitive than the students who ha[d] been admitted on first review." Gratz was notified in April that the LSA was unable to offer her admission. She enrolled in the University of Michigan at Dearborn, from which she graduated in the spring of 1999.

Hamacher applied for admission to the LSA for the fall of 1997. A final decision as to his application was also postponed because, though his "academic credentials [were] in the qualified range, they [were] not at the level needed for first review admission." Hamacher's application was subsequently denied in April 1997, and he enrolled at Michigan State University.

In October 1997, Gratz and Hamacher filed a lawsuit in the United States District Court for the Eastern District of Michigan against the University of Michigan, the LSA,

James Duderstadt [president of the University when Gratz applied], and Lee Bollinger [president when Hamacher applied]. Petitioners' complaint was a class-action suit alleging "violations and threatened violations of the rights of the plaintiffs and the class they represent to equal protection of the laws under the Fourteenth Amendment, and for racial discrimination in violation of [federal civil rights laws]. . . . "

The University's Office of Undergraduate Admissions (OUA) oversees the LSA admissions process. In order to promote consistency in the review of the large number of applications received, the OUA uses written guidelines for each academic year. Admissions counselors make admissions decisions in accordance with these guidelines.

OUA considers a number of factors in making admissions decisions, including high school grades, standardized test scores, high school quality, curriculum strength, geography, alumni relationships, and leadership. OUA also considers race. During all periods relevant to this litigation, the University has considered African-Americans, Hispanics, and Native Americans to be "underrepresented minorities," and it is undisputed that the University admits "virtually every qualified . . . applicant" from these groups. . . .

Beginning with the 1998 academic year, the OUA [adopted] a "selection index," on which an applicant could score a maximum of 150 points. This index was divided linearly into ranges generally calling for admissions dispositions as follows: 100–150 (admit); 95–99 (admit or postpone); 90–94 (postpone or admit); 75–89 (delay or postpone); 74 and below (delay or reject).

Each application received points based on high school grade point average, standardized test scores, academic quality of an applicant's high school, strength or weakness of high school curriculum, in-state residency, alumni relationship, personal essay, and personal achievement or leadership. Of particular significance here, under a "miscellaneous" category, an applicant was entitled to 20 points based upon his or her membership in an underrepresented racial or ethnic minority group. The University explained that the "development of the selection index for admissions in 1998 changed only the mechanics, not the substance of how race and ethnicity were considered in admissions." . . .

Petitioners argue, first and foremost, that the University's use of race in undergraduate admissions violates the Fourteenth Amendment. Specifically, they contend that this Court has only sanctioned the use of racial classifications to remedy identified discrimination, a justification on which respondents have never relied. Petitioners further argue that "diversity as a basis for employing racial preferences is simply too open-ended, ill-defined, and indefinite to constitute a compelling interest capable of supporting narrowly-tailored means." But for the reasons set forth today in Grutter v. Bollinger, the Court has rejected these arguments of petitioners.

Petitioners alternatively argue that even if the University's interest in diversity can constitute a compelling state interest, the District Court erroneously concluded that the University's use of race in its current freshman admissions policy is narrowly tailored to achieve such an interest. Petitioners argue that the guidelines the University began using in 1999 do not "remotely resemble the kind of consideration of race and ethnicity that Justice Powell endorsed in Bakke."

Respondents reply that the University's current admissions program *is* narrowly tailored and avoids the problems of the Medical School of the University of California at Davis program (U. C. Davis) rejected by Justice Powell. They claim that their program "hews closely" to both the admissions program described by Justice Powell as well as the Harvard College admissions program that he endorsed. Specifically, respondents contend that the LSA's policy provides the individualized consideration that "Justice Powell considered a hallmark of a constitutionally appropriate admissions program." For the reasons set out below, we do not agree. . . . We find that the University's policy, which automatically distributes 20 points, or one-fifth of the points needed to guarantee admission, to every single "underrepresented minority" applicant solely because of race, is not narrowly tailored to achieve the interest in educational diversity that respondents claim justifies their program. . . .

Justice Powell's opinion in Bakke emphasized the importance of considering each particular applicant as an individual, assessing all of the qualities that individual possesses, and in turn, evaluating that individual's ability to contribute to the unique setting of higher education. . . . The current LSA policy does not provide such individualized consideration. The LSA's policy automatically distributes 20 points to every single applicant from an "underrepresented minority" group, as defined by the University. The only consideration that accompanies this distribution of points is a factual review of an application to determine whether an individual is a member of one of these minority groups. Moreover, unlike Justice Powell's example, where the race of a "particular black applicant" could be considered without being decisive, the LSA's automatic distribution of 20 points has the effect of making "the factor of race . . . decisive" for virtually every minimally qualified underrepresented minority applicant. . . . Nothing in Justice Powell's opinion in Bakke signaled that a university may employ whatever means it desires to achieve the stated goal of diversity without regard to the limits imposed by our strict scrutiny analysis. We conclude, therefore, that because the University's use of race in its current freshman admissions policy is not narrowly tailored to achieve respondents' asserted compelling interest in diversity, the admissions policy violates the Equal Protection Clause of the Fourteenth Amendment. . . . Accordingly, we reverse that portion of the District Court's decision granting respondents summary judgment with respect to liability and remand the case for proceedings consistent with this opinion.

It is so ordered.

Justice Ginsburg, with whom Justice Souter joins, dissenting.

Educational institutions, the Court acknowledges, are not barred from any and all consideration of race when making admissions decisions. But the Court once again maintains that the same standard of review controls judicial inspection of all official race classifications. This insistence on "consistency" would be fitting were our Nation free of the vestiges of rank discrimination long reinforced by law. But we are not far distant from an overtly discriminatory past, and the effects of centuries of law-sanctioned inequality remain painfully evident in our communities and schools.

In the wake "of a system of racial caste only recently ended," large disparities endure. Unemployment, poverty, and access to health care vary disproportionately by race. Neighborhoods and schools remain racially divided. African-American and Hispanic children are all too often educated in poverty-stricken and underperforming institutions. Adult African-Americans and Hispanics generally earn less than whites with equivalent levels of education. Equally credentialed job applicants receive different receptions depending on their race. Irrational prejudice is still encountered in real estate markets and consumer transactions. . . .

The Constitution instructs all who act for the government that they may not "deny to any person . . . the equal protection of the laws." In implementing this equality instruction, as I see it, government decision-makers may properly distinguish between policies of exclusion and inclusion. Actions designed to burden groups long denied full citizenship stature are not sensibly ranked with measures taken to hasten the day when entrenched discrimination and its after effects have been extirpated. . . .

Examining in this light the admissions policy employed by the University of Michigan's College of Literature, Science, and the Arts (College), I see no constitutional infirmity. Like other top-ranking institutions, the College has many more applicants for admission than it can accommodate in an entering class. Every applicant admitted under the current plan, petitioners do not here dispute, is qualified to attend the College. The racial and ethnic groups to which the College accords special consideration (African-Americans, Hispanics, and Native-Americans) historically have been relegated to inferior status by law and social practice; their members continue to experience class-based discrimination to this day. There is no suggestion that the College adopted its current policy in order to limit or decrease enrollment by any particular racial or ethnic group, and no seats are reserved on the basis of race. Nor has there been any demonstration that the College's program unduly constricts admissions opportunities for students who do not receive special consideration based on race.

The stain of generations of racial oppression is still visible in our society, and the determination to hasten its removal remains vital. One can reasonably anticipate, therefore, that colleges and universities will seek to maintain their minority enrollment—and the networks and opportunities thereby opened to minority graduates—whether or not they can do so in full candor through adoption of affirmative action plans of the kind here at issue. Without recourse to such plans, institutions of higher education may resort to camouflage. For example, schools may encourage applicants to write of their cultural traditions in the essays they submit, or to indicate whether English is their second language. Seeking to improve their chances for admission, applicants may highlight the minority group associations to which they belong, or the Hispanic surnames of their mothers or grandparents. In turn, teachers' recommendations may emphasize who a student is as much as what he or she has accomplished. If honesty is the best policy, surely Michigan's accurately described, fully disclosed College affirmative action program is preferable to achieving similar numbers through winks, nods, and disguises. For the reasons stated, I would affirm the judgment of the District Court.

GRUTTER V. BOLLINGER
(June 23, 2003)

"Universities cannot establish quotas for members of certain racial groups or put members of those groups on separate admissions tracks. Nor can universities insulate applicants who belong to certain racial or ethnic groups from the competition for admission. Universities can, however, consider race or ethnicity more flexibly as a "plus" factor in the context of individualized consideration of each and every applicant."

The Question: Can a state law school promote the racial and ethnic diversity of its student body by making a factor in admissions a "plus" membership in a minority, as long as no quotas are established and all applicants are given the same level of individualized consideration?

The Arguments: PRO

Although much progress has been achieved in increasing the number of lawyers who belong to racial and ethnic minorities, they are still underrepresented in law schools and the legal profession, largely because of inferior schools at lower levels and economic deprivation. Law schools need a "critical mass" of minority students to make classroom discussion more stimulating and relevant. The Supreme Court has ruled that making race and ethnicity a "plus" factor in admissions does not violate the Constitution, and this precedent should be affirmed and continued.

CON

Under the guise of making race and ethnicity a "plus" factor in law school admissions, many schools have in effect adopted an unstated quota system for minority applicants. Many of those admitted under such programs are objectively less qualified than many "majority" applicants who are rejected to make room for minority students. There is no basis for claiming that law school classes will be enriched by having a "critical mass" of minority students; this claim is based on the false assumption that all minority students share a similar perspective and have similar views on issues in legal education.

JUSTICE O'CONNOR delivered the opinion of the Court.

This case requires us to decide whether the use of race as a factor in student admissions by the University of Michigan Law School (Law School) is unlawful.

The Law School ranks among the Nation's top law schools. It receives more than 3,500 applications each year for a class of around 350 students. Seeking to "admit a group of students who individually and collectively are among the most capable," the Law School looks for individuals with "substantial promise for success in law school" and "a strong likelihood of succeeding in the practice of law and contributing in diverse ways to the well-being of others." More broadly, the Law School seeks "a mix of students with varying backgrounds and experiences who will respect and learn from each other." In 1992, the dean of the Law School charged a faculty committee with crafting a written admissions policy to implement these goals. In particular, the Law School sought to ensure that its efforts to achieve student body diversity complied with this Court's most recent ruling on the use of race in university admissions. See Regents of Univ. of Cal. v. Bakke (1978). Upon the unanimous adoption of the committee's report by the Law School faculty, it became the Law School's official admissions policy.

The hallmark of that policy is its focus on academic ability coupled with a flexible assessment of applicants' talents, experiences, and potential "to contribute to the learning of those around them." The policy requires admissions officials to evaluate each applicant based on all the information available in the file, including a personal statement, letters of recommendation, and an essay describing the ways in which the applicant will contribute to the life and diversity of the Law School. In reviewing an applicant's file, admissions officials must consider the applicant's undergraduate grade point average (GPA) and Law School Admissions Test (LSAT) score because they are important (if imperfect) predictors of academic success in law school. The policy stresses that "no applicant should be admitted unless we expect that applicant to do well enough to graduate with no serious academic problems."

The policy makes clear, however, that even the highest possible score does not guarantee admission to the Law School. Nor does a low score automatically disqualify an applicant. Rather, the policy requires admissions officials to look beyond grades and test scores to other criteria that are important to the Law School's educational objectives. So-called "'soft' variables" such as "the enthusiasm of recommenders, the quality of the undergraduate institution, the quality of the applicant's essay, and the areas and difficulty of undergraduate course selection" are all brought to bear in assessing an "applicant's likely contributions to the intellectual and social life of the institution."

The policy aspires to "achieve that diversity which has the potential to enrich everyone's education and thus make a law school class stronger than the sum of its parts." The policy does not restrict the types of diversity contributions eligible for "substantial weight" in the admissions process, but instead recognizes "many possible bases for diversity admissions." The policy does, however, reaffirm the Law School's long-standing commitment to "one particular type of diversity," that is, "racial and ethnic diversity with special reference to the inclusion of students from groups which have been historically discriminated against, like African-Americans, Hispanics and Native Americans, who without this commitment might not be represented in our student body in meaningful numbers." By enrolling a "'critical mass' of [underrepresented] minority students," the Law School seeks to "ensur[e] their ability to make unique contributions to the character of the Law School." . . .

Petitioner Barbara Grutter is a white Michigan resident who applied to the Law School in 1996 with a 3.8 grade point average and 161 LSAT score. The Law School initially placed petitioner on a waiting list, but subsequently rejected her application. In December 1997, petitioner filed suit in the United States District Court for the Eastern District of Michigan against the Law School, the Regents of the University of Michigan, [and] Lee Bollinger (Dean of the Law School from 1987 to 1994, and President of the University of Michigan from 1996 to 2002). Petitioner alleged that respondents discriminated against her on the basis of race in violation of the Fourteenth Amendment [and] Title VI of the Civil Rights Act of 1964. . . .

Petitioner further alleged that her application was rejected because the Law School uses race as a "predominant" factor, giving applicants who belong to certain minority groups "a significantly greater chance of admission than students with similar credentials from disfavored racial groups." Petitioner also alleged that respondents "had no compelling interest to justify their use of race in the admissions process." . . .

During the 15-day bench trial [before the district court], the parties introduced extensive evidence concerning the Law School's use of race in the admissions process. Dennis Shields, Director of Admissions when petitioner applied to the Law School, testified that he did not direct his staff to admit a particular percentage or number of minority students, but rather to consider an applicant's race along with all other factors. . . . This was done, Shields testified, to ensure that a critical mass of underrepresented minority students would be reached so as to realize the educational benefits of a diverse student body. Shields stressed, however, that he did not seek to admit any particular number or percentage of underrepresented minority students. . . .

In the end, the District Court concluded that the Law School's use of race as a factor in admissions decisions was unlawful. Applying strict scrutiny, the District Court determined that the Law School's asserted interest in assembling a diverse student body was not compelling because "the attainment of a racially diverse class . . . was not recognized as such by Bakke and is not a remedy for past discrimination." The District Court went on to hold that even if diversity were compelling, the Law School had not narrowly tailored its use of race to further that interest. The District Court granted petitioner's request for declaratory relief and enjoined the Law School from using race as a factor in its admissions decisions. . . .

Sitting en banc, the Court of Appeals reversed the District Court's judgment and vacated the injunction. The Court of Appeals first held that Justice Powell's opinion in Bakke was binding precedent establishing diversity as a compelling state interest. . . . The Court of Appeals also held that the Law School's use of race was narrowly tailored because race was merely a "potential 'plus' factor" and because the Law School's program was "virtually identical" to the Harvard admissions program described approvingly by Justice Powell and appended to his Bakke opinion. . . .

We granted certiorari to resolve . . . a question of national importance: Whether diversity is a compelling interest that can justify the narrowly tailored use of race in selecting applicants for admission to public universities.

We last addressed the use of race in public higher education over 25 years ago. In the landmark Bakke case, we reviewed a racial set-aside program that reserved 16 out of 100 seats in a medical school class for members of certain minority groups. The decision produced six separate opinions, none of which commanded a majority of the Court. Four Justices would have upheld the program against all attack on the ground that the government can use race to "remedy disadvantages cast on minorities by past racial prejudice." Four other Justices avoided the constitutional question altogether and struck down the program on statutory grounds. Justice Powell provided a fifth vote not only for invalidating the set-aside program, but also for reversing the state court's injunction against any use of race whatsoever. The only holding for the Court in Bakke was that a "State has a substantial interest that legitimately may be served by a properly devised admissions program involving the competitive consideration of race and ethnic origin." . . .

In Justice Powell's view, when governmental decisions "touch upon an individual's race or ethnic background, he is entitled to a judicial determination that the burden he is asked to bear on that basis is precisely tailored to serve a compelling governmental interest." . . . Under this exacting standard, only one of the interests asserted by the university survived Justice Powell's scrutiny.

Justice Powell was . . . careful to emphasize that in his view race "is only one element in a range of factors a university properly may consider in attaining the goal of a heterogeneous student body." . . . [F]or the reasons set out below, today we endorse Justice Powell's view that student body diversity is a compelling state interest that can justify the use of race in university admissions. . . .

With these principles in mind, we turn to the question whether the Law School's use of race is justified by a compelling state interest. Before this Court, as they have throughout this litigation, respondents assert only one justification for their use of race in the admissions process: obtaining "the educational benefits that flow from a diverse student body." In other words, the Law School asks us to recognize, in the context of higher education, a compelling state interest in student body diversity. . . . Today, we hold that the Law School has a compelling interest in attaining a diverse student body. The Law School's educational judgment that such diversity is essential to its educational mission is one to which we defer. . . .

The Law School's claim of a compelling interest is further bolstered by its amici, who point to the educational benefits that flow from student body diversity. . . . In addition to the expert studies and reports entered into evidence at trial, numerous studies show that student body diversity promotes learning outcomes, and "better prepares students for an increasingly diverse workforce and society, and better prepares them as professionals." These benefits are not theoretical but real, as major American businesses have made clear that the skills needed in today's increasingly global marketplace can only be developed through exposure to widely diverse people, cultures, ideas, and viewpoints. . . .

In order to cultivate a set of leaders with legitimacy in the eyes of the citizenry, it is necessary that the path to leadership be visibly open to talented and qualified individuals of every race and ethnicity. All members of our heterogeneous society must have confidence in the openness and integrity of the educational institutions that provide this training. As we have recognized, law schools "cannot be effective in isolation from the individuals and institutions with which the law interacts." Access to legal education (and thus the legal profession) must be inclusive of talented and qualified individuals of every race and ethnicity, so that all members of our heterogeneous society may participate in the educational institutions that provide the training and education necessary to succeed in America. . . . The Law School has determined, based on its experience and expertise, that a "critical mass" of under-represented minorities is necessary to further its compelling interest in securing the educational benefits of a diverse student body. Even in the limited circumstance when drawing racial distinctions is permissible to further a compelling state interest, government is still "constrained in how it may pursue that end: [T]he means chosen to accomplish the [government's] asserted purpose must be specifically and narrowly framed to accomplish that purpose." . . . To be narrowly tailored, a race-conscious admissions program cannot use a quota system—it cannot "insulat[e] each category of applicants with certain desired qualifications from competition with all other applicants." . . .

We find that the Law School's admissions program bears the hallmarks of a narrowly tailored plan. As Justice Powell made clear in Bakke, truly individualized consideration demands that race be used in a flexible, nonmechanical way. It follows from this mandate that universities cannot establish quotas for members of certain racial groups or put members of those groups on separate admissions tracks. Nor can universities insulate applicants who belong to certain racial or ethnic groups from the competition for admission. Universities can, however, consider race or ethnicity more flexibly as a "plus" factor in the context of individualized consideration of each and every applicant.

We are satisfied that the Law School's admissions program . . . does not operate as a quota. Properly understood, a "quota" is a program in which a certain fixed number or proportion of opportunities are "reserved exclusively for certain minority groups." . . .

The Law School's goal of attaining a critical mass of underrepresented minority students does not transform its program into a quota. . . .

That a race-conscious admissions program does not operate as a quota does not, by itself, satisfy the requirement of individualized consideration. When using race as a "plus" factor in university admissions, a university's admissions program must remain flexible enough to ensure that each applicant is evaluated as an individual and not in a way that makes an applicant's race or ethnicity the defining feature of his or her application. The importance of this individualized consideration in the context of a race-conscious admissions program is paramount. Here, the Law School engages in a highly individualized, holistic review of each applicant's file, giving serious consideration to all the ways an applicant might contribute to a diverse educational environment. The Law School affords this individualized consideration to applicants of all races. There is no policy, either de jure or de facto, of automatic acceptance or rejection based on any single "soft" variable. Unlike the program at issue in Gratz v. Bollinger, the Law School awards no mechanical, predetermined diversity "bonuses" based on race or ethnicity. . . .

We are mindful, however, that "[a] core purpose of the Fourteenth Amendment was to do away with all governmentally imposed discrimination based on race." Accordingly, race-conscious admissions policies must be limited in time. This requirement reflects that racial classifications, however compelling their goals, are potentially so dangerous that they may be employed no more broadly than the interest demands. Enshrining a permanent justification for racial preferences would offend this fundamental equal protection principle. We see no reason to exempt race-conscious admissions programs from the requirement that all governmental use of race must have a logical end point. . . . It has been 25 years since Justice Powell first approved the use of race to further an interest in student body diversity in the context of public higher education. Since that time, the number of minority applicants with high grades and test scores has indeed increased. We expect that 25 years from now, the use of racial preferences will no longer be necessary to further the interest approved today.

In summary, the Equal Protection Clause does not prohibit the Law School's narrowly tailored use of race in admissions decisions to further a compelling interest in obtaining the educational benefits that flow from a diverse student body. The judgment of the Court of Appeals for the Sixth Circuit, accordingly, is affirmed.

It is so ordered.

JUSTICE THOMAS, . . . concurring in part and dissenting in part.

. . . Because I wish to see all students succeed whatever their color, I share, in some respect, the sympathies of those who sponsor the type of discrimination advanced by the University of Michigan Law School. The Constitution does not, however, tolerate institutional devotion to the status quo in admissions policies when such devotion ripens into racial discrimination. Nor does the Constitution countenance the unprecedented deference the Court gives to the Law School, an approach inconsistent with the very concept of "strict scrutiny."

No one would argue that a university could set up a lower general admission standard and then impose heightened requirements only on black applicants. Similarly, a university may not maintain a high admission standard and grant exemptions to favored races. The Law School, of its own choosing, and for its own purposes, maintains an exclusionary admissions system that it knows produces racially disproportionate results. Racial discrimination is not a permissible solution to the self-inflicted wounds of this elitist admissions policy.

The majority upholds the Law School's racial discrimination not by interpreting the people's Constitution, but by responding to a faddish slogan of the cognoscenti. Nevertheless, I concur in part in the Court's opinion. First, I agree with the Court insofar as its decision, which approves of only one racial classification, confirms that further use of race in admissions remains unlawful. Second, I agree with the Court's holding that racial discrimination in higher education admissions will be illegal in 25 years. I respectfully dissent from the remainder of the Court's opinion and the judgment, however, because I believe that the Law School's current use of race violates the Equal Protection Clause and that the Constitution means the same thing today as it will in 300 months. . . .

The Constitution abhors classifications based on race, not only because those classifications can harm favored races or are based on illegitimate motives, but also because every time the government places citizens on racial registers and makes race relevant to the provision of burdens or benefits, it demeans us all. Unlike the majority, I seek to define with precision the interest being asserted by the Law School before determining whether that interest is so compelling as to justify racial discrimination. The Law School maintains that it wishes to obtain "educational benefits that flow from student body diversity." This statement must be evaluated carefully, because it implies that both "diversity" and "educational benefits" are components of the Law School's compelling state interest. . . . Undoubtedly there are other ways to "better" the education of law students aside from ensuring that the student body contains a "critical mass" of underrepresented minority students. Attaining "diversity," whatever it means, is the mechanism by which the Law School obtains educational benefits, not an end of itself. The Law School, however, apparently believes that only a racially mixed student body can lead to the educational benefits it seeks. How, then, is the Law School's interest in these allegedly unique educational "benefits" not simply the forbidden interest in "racial balancing," that the majority expressly rejects?

A distinction between these two ideas (unique educational benefits based on racial aesthetics and race for its own sake) is purely sophistic—so much so that the majority uses them interchangeably. The Law School's argument, as facile as it is, can only be understood in one way: Classroom aesthetics yields educational benefits, racially discriminatory admissions policies are required to achieve the right racial mix, and therefore the policies are required to achieve the educational benefits. It is the educational benefits that are the end, or allegedly compelling state interest, not "diversity." ... The Law School adamantly disclaims any race-neutral alternative that would reduce "academic selectivity," which would in turn "require the Law School to become a very different institution, and to sacrifice a core part of its educational mission." In other words, the Law School seeks to improve marginally the education it offers without sacrificing too much of its exclusivity and elite status. The proffered interest that the majority vindicates today, then, is not simply "diversity." Instead the Court upholds the use of racial discrimination as a tool to advance the Law School's interest in offering a marginally superior education while maintaining an elite institution....

A close reading of the Court's opinion reveals that all of its legal work is done through one conclusory statement: The Law School has a "compelling interest in securing the educational benefits of a diverse student body." No serious effort is made to explain how these benefits fit with the state interests the Court has recognized (or rejected) as compelling, or to place any theoretical constraints on an enterprising court's desire to discover still more justifications for racial discrimination. In the absence of any explanation, one might expect the Court to fall back on the judicial policy of stare decisis. But the Court eschews even this weak defense of its holding, shunning an analysis of the extent to which Justice Powell's opinion in Bakke is binding, in favor of an unfounded wholesale adoption of it.

Justice Powell's opinion in Bakke and the Court's decision today rest on the fundamentally flawed proposition that racial discrimination can be contextualized so that a goal, such as classroom aesthetics, can be compelling in one context but not in another. This "we know it when we see it" approach to evaluating state interests is not capable of judicial application. Today, the Court insists on radically expanding the range of permissible uses of race to something as trivial (by comparison) as the assembling of a law school class. I can only presume that the majority's failure to justify its decision by reference to any principle arises from the absence of any such principle.... The majority's broad deference to both the Law School's judgment that racial aesthetics leads to educational benefits and its stubborn refusal to alter the status quo in admissions methods finds no basis in the Constitution or decisions of this Court....

Putting aside the absence of any legal support for the majority's reflexive deference, there is much to be said for the view that the use of tests and other measures to "predict" academic performance is a poor substitute for a system that gives every applicant a chance to prove he can succeed in the study of law. The rallying cry that in the absence of racial discrimination in admissions there would be a true meritocracy ignores the fact that the entire process is poisoned by numerous exceptions to "merit." For example, in the national debate on racial discrimination in higher education admissions, much has been made of the fact that elite institutions utilize a so-called "legacy" preference to give the children of alumni an advantage in admissions. This, and other, exceptions to a "true" meritocracy give the lie to protestations that merit admissions are in fact the order of the day at the Nation's universities. The Equal Protection Clause does not, however, prohibit the use of unseemly legacy preferences or many other kinds of arbitrary admissions procedures. What the Equal Protection Clause does prohibit are classifications made on the basis of race. So while legacy preferences can stand under the Constitution, racial discrimination cannot. I will not twist the Constitution to invalidate legacy preferences or otherwise impose my vision of higher education admissions on the Nation. The majority should similarly stay its impulse to validate faddish racial discrimination the Constitution clearly forbids....

The absence of any articulated legal principle supporting the majority's principal holding suggests another rationale. I believe what lies beneath the Court's decision today are the benighted notions that one can tell when racial discrimination benefits (rather than hurts) minority groups, and that racial discrimination is necessary to remedy general societal ills. This Court's precedents supposedly settled both issues, but clearly the majority still cannot commit to the principle that racial classifications are per se harmful and that almost no amount of benefit in the eye of the beholder can justify such classifications....

The silence in this case is deafening to those of us who view higher education's purpose as imparting knowledge and skills to students, rather than a communal, rubber-stamp, credentialing process. The Law School is not looking for those students who, despite a lower LSAT score or undergraduate grade point average, will succeed in the study of law. The Law School seeks only a facade—it is sufficient that the class looks right, even if it does not perform right.

The Law School tantalizes unprepared students with the promise of a University of Michigan degree and all of the opportunities that it offers. These overmatched students take the bait, only to find that they cannot succeed in the cauldron of competition.... While these students may graduate with law degrees, there is no evidence that they have received a qualitatively better legal education (or become better lawyers) than if they had gone to a less "elite" law school for which they were better prepared. And the aestheticists will never address the real problems facing "underrepresented minorities," instead continuing their social experiments on other people's children....

CITY OF RICHMOND, VIRGINIA V. J. A. CROSON CO.
488 U.S. 469 (1989)

"While there is no doubt that the sorry history of both private and public discrimination in this country has contributed to a lack of opportunities for black entrepreneurs, this observation, standing alone, cannot justify a rigid racial quota in the awarding of public contracts. . . . An amorphous claim that there has been past discrimination in a particular industry cannot justify the use of an unyielding racial quota."

The Question: Can a city require prime contractors who bid on city-funded construction projects to subcontract at least 30 percent of the dollar amount of the contract to minority business enterprises, defined as those with 51 percent or more ownership by minority group members?

The Arguments: PRO

The record in this case shows that minority-owned construction firms have in the past received less than 1 percent of city-funded construction projects. The city itself is now more than 50-percent black in population. The construction industry in Richmond has always been dominated by whites, and blacks have been kept out of the industry by a pattern of discrimination, including exclusion from unions and apprenticeship programs, lack of start-up funding from backs and government agencies, and a complicated maze of regulations that require prior experience to bid on contracts while making such experience difficult to obtain. The figure of 30 percent for minority-owned firms is a reasonable response to many decades of discrimination.

CON

Although the Supreme Court has upheld minority "set-aside" programs in federal contracting, those plans did not exceed 10 percent of contract value and were based upon congressional findings that minority-owned firms had been deliberately excluded from bidding. In this case, the record reveals no evidence that any particular minority-owned firm has been excluded from bidding on city-funded projects in Richmond. Whatever barriers may have been erected in the past to minority participation in the construction industry, the existence of "societal discrimination" does not justify a law that in effect creates a racial preference for minority-owned firms.

JUSTICE O'CONNOR announced the judgment of the Court. . . .

In this case, we confront once again the tension between the Fourteenth Amendment's guarantee of equal treatment to all citizens, and the use of race-based measures to ameliorate the effects of past discrimination on the opportunities enjoyed by members of minority groups in our society. In Fullilove v. Klutznick (1980), we held that a congressional program requiring that 10% of certain federal construction grants be awarded to minority contractors did not violate the equal protection principles embodied in the Due Process Clause of the Fifth Amendment. Relying largely on our decision in Fullilove, some lower federal courts have applied a similar standard of review in assessing the constitutionality of state and local minority set-aside provisions under the Equal Protection Clause of the Fourteenth Amendment. Since our decision two Terms ago in Wygant v. Jackson Board of Education (1986), the lower federal courts have attempted to apply its standards in evaluating the constitutionality of state and local programs which allocate a portion of public contracting opportunities exclusively to minority-owned businesses. We noted probable jurisdiction in this case to consider the applicability of our decision in Wygant to a minority set-aside program adopted by the city of Richmond, Virginia.

On April 11, 1983, the Richmond City Council adopted the Minority Business Utilization Plan (the Plan). The Plan required prime contractors to whom the city awarded construction contracts to subcontract at least 30% of the dollar amount of the contract to one or more Minority Business Enterprises (MBE's). The 30% set-aside did not apply to city contracts awarded to minority-owned prime contractors. The Plan defined an MBE as "[a] business at least fifty-one (51) percent of which is owned and controlled . . . by minority group members." "Minority group members" were defined as "[c]itizens of the United States who are Blacks, Spanish-speaking, Orientals, Indians, Eskimos, or Aleuts." There was no geographic limit to the Plan; an otherwise qualified MBE from anywhere in the United States could avail itself of the 30% set-aside. The Plan declared that it was "remedial" in nature, and enacted "for the purpose of promoting wider participation by minority business enterprises in the construction of public projects." . . .

The Plan was adopted by the Richmond City Council after a public hearing. Seven members of the public spoke to the merits of the ordinance: five were in opposition, two in favor. Proponents of the set-aside provision relied on a study which indicated that, while the general population of Richmond was 50% black, only 0.67% of the city's prime construction contracts had been awarded to minority businesses in the 5-year period from 1978 to 1983. It was also established that a variety of contractors' associations, whose representatives appeared in opposition to the ordinance, had virtually no minority businesses within their membership. There was no direct evidence of race discrimination on the part of the city in letting contracts or any evidence that the city's prime contractors had discriminated against minority-owned subcontractors. . . .

On September 6, 1983, the city of Richmond issued an invitation to bid on a project for the provision and installation of certain plumbing fixtures at the city jail. On September 30, 1983, Eugene Bonn, the regional manager of J. A. Croson Company (Croson), a mechanical plumbing and heating contractor, received the bid forms. The project involved the installation of stainless steel urinals and water closets in the city jail. . . . Bonn determined that to meet the 30% set-aside requirement, a minority contractor would have to supply the fixtures. The provision of the fixtures amounted to 75% of the total contract price. . . . Melvin Brown, president of Continental Metal Hose (Continental), a local MBE, indicated that he wished to participate in the project. Brown subsequently contacted two sources of the specified fixtures in order to obtain a price quotation. One supplier . . . had already made a quotation directly to Croson, and refused to quote the same fixtures to Continental. Brown also contacted an agent of Bradley, one of the two manufacturers of the specified fixtures. The agent was not familiar with Brown or Continental, and indicated that a credit check was required which would take at least 30 days to complete. [Croson could not locate an MBE bidder and submitted a request to the City that it grant a waiver from the MBE requirement. The City declined to grant the waiver.] Shortly thereafter Croson brought this action under 42 U.S.C. 1983 in the Federal District Court for the Eastern District of Virginia, arguing that the Richmond ordinance was unconstitutional on its face and as applied in this case.

The District Court upheld the Plan in all respects. . . . [On appeal], a divided panel of the Court of Appeals struck down the Richmond set-aside program as violating both prongs of strict scrutiny under the Equal Protection Clause of the Fourteenth Amendment. The [majority held] that even if the city had demonstrated a compelling interest in the use of a race-based quota, the 30% set-aside was not narrowly tailored to accomplish a remedial purpose. The court found that the 30% figure was "chosen arbitrarily" and was not tied to the number of minority subcontractors in Richmond or to any other relevant number. We noted probable jurisdiction of the city's appeal, and we now affirm the judgment.

The parties and their supporting amici fight an initial battle over the scope of the city's power to adopt legislation designed to address the effects of past discrimination. Relying on our decision in Wygant, appellee argues that the city must limit any race-based remedial efforts to eradicating the effects of its own prior discrimination. This is essentially the position taken by the Court of Appeals below. Appellant argues that our decision in Fullilove is controlling, and that as a result the city of Richmond enjoys sweeping legislative power to define and attack the effects of prior discrimination in its local construction industry. We find that neither of these two rather stark alternatives can withstand analysis. . . .

What appellant ignores is that Congress, unlike any State or political subdivision, has a specific constitutional mandate to enforce the dictates of the Fourteenth Amendment. The power to "enforce" may at times also include the power to define situations which Congress determines threaten principles of equality and to adopt prophylactic rules to deal with those situations. . . . That Congress may identify and redress the effects of society-wide discrimination does not mean that, a fortiori, the States and their political subdivisions are free to decide that such remedies are appropriate. Section 1 of the Fourteenth Amendment is an explicit constraint on state power, and the States must undertake any remedial efforts in accordance with that provision. To hold otherwise would be to cede control over the content of the Equal Protection Clause to the 50 state legislatures and their myriad political subdivisions. The mere recitation of a benign or compensatory purpose for the use of a racial classification would essentially entitle the States to exercise the full power of Congress under Section 5 of the Fourteenth Amendment and insulate any racial classification from judicial scrutiny under Section 1. We believe that such a result would be contrary to the intentions of the Framers of the Fourteenth Amendment, who desired to place clear limits on the States' use of race as a criterion for legislative action, and to have the federal courts enforce those limitations. . . .

It would seem equally clear, however, that a state or local subdivision (if delegated the authority from the State) has the authority to eradicate the effects of private discrimination within its own legislative jurisdiction. This authority must, of course, be exercised within the constraints of Section 1 of the Fourteenth Amendment. Our decision in Wygant is not to the contrary. Wygant addressed the constitutionality of the use of racial quotas by local school authorities pursuant to an agreement reached with the local teachers' union. It was in the context of addressing the school board's power to adopt a race-based layoff program affecting its own work force that the Wygant plurality indicated that the Equal Protection Clause required "some showing of prior discrimination by the governmental unit involved." As a matter of state law, the city of Richmond has legislative authority over its procurement policies, and can use its spending powers to remedy private discrimination, if it identifies that discrimination with the particularity required by the Fourteenth Amendment. To this extent, on the question of the city's competence, the Court of Appeals erred in following Wygant by rote in a case involving a state entity which has state-law authority to address discriminatory practices within local commerce under its jurisdiction. . . . Thus, if the city could show that it had essentially become a "passive participant" in a system of racial exclusion practiced by elements of the local construction industry, we think it clear that the city could take affirmative steps to dismantle such a system. It is beyond dispute that any public entity, state or federal, has a compelling interest in assuring that public dollars, drawn from the tax contributions of all citizens, do not serve to finance the evil of private prejudice.

The Equal Protection Clause of the Fourteenth Amendment provides that "[n]o State shall . . . deny to any person within its jurisdiction the equal protection of the laws." As this Court has noted in the past, the "rights created by the first section of the Fourteenth Amendment are, by its terms, guaranteed to the individual. The rights established are personal rights." Shelley v. Kraemer (1948). The Richmond Plan denies certain citizens the opportunity to compete for a fixed percentage of public contracts based solely upon their race. To whatever racial group these citizens belong, their "personal rights" to be treated with equal dignity and respect are implicated by a rigid rule erecting race as the sole criterion in an aspect of public decisionmaking. Absent searching judicial inquiry into the justification for such race-based measures, there is simply no way of determining what classifications are "benign" or "remedial" and what classifications are in fact motivated by illegitimate notions of racial inferiority or simple racial politics. Indeed, the purpose of strict scrutiny is to "smoke out" illegitimate uses of race by assuring that the legislative body is pursuing a goal important enough to warrant use of a highly suspect tool. The test also ensures that the means chosen "fit" this compelling goal so closely that there is little or no possibility that the motive for the classification was illegitimate racial prejudice or stereotype.

Classification based on race carry a danger of stigmatic harm. Unless they are strictly reserved for remedial settings, they may in fact promote notions of racial inferiority and lead to a politics of racial hostility. We thus reaffirm the view expressed by the plurality in Wygant that the standard of review under the Equal Protection Clause is not dependent on the race of those burdened or benefited by a particular classification. . . .

While there is no doubt that the sorry history of both private and public discrimination in this country has contributed to a lack of opportunities for black entrepreneurs, this observation, standing alone, cannot justify a rigid racial quota in the awarding of public contracts in Richmond, Virginia. Like the claim that discrimination in primary and secondary schooling justifies a rigid racial preference in medical school admissions, an amorphous claim that there has been past discrimination in a particular industry cannot justify the use of an unyielding racial quota.

It is sheer speculation how many minority firms there would be in Richmond absent past societal discrimination, just as it was sheer speculation how many minority medical students would have been admitted to the medical school at Davis absent past discrimination in educational opportunities. Defining these sorts of injuries as "identified discrimination" would give local governments license to create a patchwork of racial preferences based on statistical generalizations about any particular field of endeavor. These defects are readily apparent in this case. The 30% quota cannot in any realistic sense be tied to any injury suffered by anyone. . . .

The city and the District Court . . . relied on evidence that MBE membership in local contractors' associations was extremely low. Again, standing alone this evidence is not probative of any discrimination in the local construction industry. There are numerous explanations for this dearth of minority participation, including past societal discrimination in education and economic opportunities as well as both black and white career and entrepreneurial choices. Blacks may be disproportionately attracted to industries other than construction. The mere fact that black membership in these trade organizations is low, standing alone, cannot establish a prima facie case of discrimination. . . .

In sum, none of the evidence presented by the city points to any identified discrimination in the Richmond construction industry. We, therefore, hold that the city has failed to demonstrate a compelling interest in apportioning public contracting opportunities on the basis of race. To accept Richmond's claim that past societal discrimination alone can serve as the basis for rigid racial preferences would be to open the door to competing claims for "remedial relief" for every disadvantaged group. The dream of a Nation of equal citizens in a society where race is irrelevant to personal opportunity and achievement would be lost in a mosaic of shifting preferences based on inherently unmeasurable claims of past wrongs. We think such a result would be contrary to both the letter and spirit of a constitutional provision whose central command is equality. . . .

Because the city of Richmond has failed to identify the need for remedial action in the awarding of its public construction contracts, its treatment of its citizens on a racial basis violates the dictates of the Equal Protection Clause. Accordingly, the judgment of the Court of Appeals for the Fourth Circuit is Affirmed.

JUSTICE MARSHALL, with whom JUSTICE BRENNAN and JUSTICE BLACKMUN join, dissenting.

It is a welcome symbol of racial progress when the former capital of the Confederacy acts forthrightly to confront the effects of racial discrimination in its midst. In my view, nothing in the Constitution can be construed to prevent Richmond, Virginia, from allocating a portion of its contracting dollars for businesses owned or controlled by members of minority groups. Indeed, Richmond's set-aside program is indistinguishable in all meaningful respects from—and in fact was patterned upon—the federal set-aside plan which this Court upheld in Fullilove v. Klutznick (1980).

A majority of this Court holds today, however, that the Equal Protection Clause of the Fourteenth Amendment blocks Richmond's initiative. The essence of the majority's position is that Richmond has failed to catalog adequate findings to prove that past discrimination has impeded minorities from joining or participating fully in Richmond's construction contracting industry. I find deep irony in second-guessing Richmond's judgment on this point. As much as any municipality in the United States, Richmond knows what racial discrimination is; a century of decisions by this and other federal courts has richly documented the city's disgraceful history of public and private racial discrimination. In any event, the Richmond City Council has supported its determination that minorities have been wrongly excluded from local construction contracting. Its proof includes statistics showing that minority-owned businesses have received virtually no city contracting dollars and rarely if ever belonged to area trade associations; testimony by municipal officials that discrimination has been widespread in the local construction industry; and the same exhaustive and widely publicized federal studies relied on in Fullilove, studies which showed that pervasive discrimination in the Nation's tight-knit construction industry had operated to exclude minorities from public contracting. These are precisely the types of statistical and testimonial evidence which, until today, this Court had credited in cases approving of race-conscious measures designed to remedy past discrimination.

More fundamentally, today's decision marks a deliberate and giant step backward in this Court's affirmative-action jurisprudence. Cynical of one municipality's attempt to redress the effects of past racial discrimination in a particular industry, the majority launches a grapeshot attack on race-conscious remedies in general. The majority's unnecessary pronouncements will inevitably discourage or prevent governmental entities, particularly States and localities, from acting to rectify the scourge of past discrimination. This is the harsh reality of the majority's decision, but it is not the Constitution's command.

As an initial matter, the majority takes an exceedingly myopic view of the factual predicate on which the Richmond City Council relied when it passed the Minority Business Utilization Plan. The majority analyzes Richmond's initiative as if it were based solely upon the facts about local construction and contracting practices adduced during the city council session at which the measure was enacted. In so doing, the majority downplays the fact that the city council had before it a rich trove of evidence that discrimination in the Nation's construction industry had seriously impaired the competitive position of businesses owned or controlled by members of minority groups. It is only against this backdrop of documented national discrimination, however, that the local evidence adduced by Richmond can be properly understood.

The majority's refusal to recognize that Richmond has proved itself no exception to the dismaying pattern of national exclusion which Congress so painstakingly identified infects its entire analysis of this case.... Congress further found that minorities seeking initial public contracting assignments often faced immense entry barriers which did not confront experienced nonminority contractors. A report submitted to Congress in 1975 by the United States Commission on Civil Rights, for example, described the way in which fledgling minority-owned businesses were hampered by "deficiencies in working capital, inability to meet bonding requirements, disabilities caused by an inadequate 'track record,' lack of awareness of bidding opportunities, unfamiliarity with bidding procedures, preselection before the formal advertising process, and the exercise of discretion by government procurement officers to disfavor minority businesses." ... The members of the Richmond City Council were well aware of these exhaustive congressional findings, a point the majority, tellingly, elides. The transcript of the session at which the council enacted the local set-aside initiative contains numerous references to the 6-year-old con-

gressional set-aside program, to the evidence of nationwide discrimination barriers described above, and to the Fullilove decision itself.

The city council's members also heard testimony that, although minority groups made up half of the city's population, only 0.67% of the $24.6 million which Richmond had dispensed in construction contracts during the five years ending in March 1983 had gone to minority-owned prime contractors. They heard testimony that the major Richmond area construction trade associations had virtually no minorities among their hundreds of members. Finally, they heard testimony from city officials as to the exclusionary history of the local construction industry. As the District Court noted, not a single person who testified before the city council denied that discrimination in Richmond's construction industry had been widespread. So long as one views Richmond's local evidence of discrimination against the backdrop of systematic nationwide racial discrimination which Congress had so painstakingly identified in this very industry, this case is readily resolved....

The majority is wrong to trivialize the continuing impact of government acceptance or use of private institutions or structures once wrought by discrimination. When government channels all its contracting funds to a white-dominated community of established contractors whose racial homogeneity is the product of private discrimination, it does more than place its imprimatur on the practices which forged and which continue to define that community. It also provides a measurable boost to those economic entities that have thrived within it, while denying important economic benefits to those entities which, but for prior discrimination, might well be better qualified to receive valuable government contracts. In my view, the interest in ensuring that the government does not reflect and reinforce prior private discrimination in dispensing public contracts is every bit as strong as the interest in eliminating private discrimination—an interest which this Court has repeatedly deemed compelling. The more government bestows its rewards on those persons or businesses that were positioned to thrive during a period of private racial discrimination, the tighter the deadhand grip of prior discrimination becomes on the present and future. Cities like Richmond may not be constitutionally-required to adopt set-aside plans. But there can be no doubt that when Richmond acted affirmatively to stem the perpetuation of patterns of discrimination through its own decisionmaking, it served an interest of the highest order....

The majority today sounds a full-scale retreat from the Court's longstanding solicitude to race-conscious remedial efforts "directed toward deliverance of the century-old promise of equality of economic opportunity." The new and restrictive tests it applies scuttle one city's effort to surmount its discriminatory past, and imperil those of dozens more localities. I, however, profoundly disagree with the cramped vision of the Equal Protection Clause which the majority offers today and with its application of that vision to Richmond, Virginia's, laudable set-aside plan. The battle against pernicious racial discrimination or its effects is nowhere near won.

I must dissent.

JOHNSON V. TRANSPORTATION AGENCY OF SANTA CLARA COUNTY, CALIFORNIA
480 U.S. 616 (1987)

"The Agency appropriately took into account as one factor the sex of Diane Joyce in determining that she should be promoted to the road dispatcher position. There is ample evidence that the Agency does not seek to . . . maintain a permanent racial and sexual balance [in its workforce]."

The Question: Can a county agency adopt an affirmative action plan that is applied to prefer women for promotion over men who have higher scores on qualifying tests, with no finding of past discrimination against women in employment and promotions?

The Arguments: PRO

The record in this case shows that the Transportation Agency of Santa Clara County had never had a woman employee in the "skilled craft worker" classification, which had 238 men at the time of this case, although women made up 76 percent of office and clerical workers. When the position of road dispatcher (also never held by a woman) opened up, the agency director had a choice of two applicants, a male and female, with equivalent seniority and qualifications, and with only a two-point difference in scores on interviews. Choosing the woman to advance the goals of affirmative action was a reasonable decision, and the male applicant had no greater claim to the job than the woman.

CON

The male applicant for the position was in fact more qualified than the female applicant, and scored higher on the interview. The record makes clear that the agency director chose the woman solely because he wanted to avoid criticism that the agency did not employ any women in several job categories traditionally filled by men. Congress made it an offense in the Civil Rights Act of 1964 to discriminate in employment on the basis of gender, and that is exactly what happened in this case. Because there was no finding that the agency had discriminated against women, using gender as a preferential factor is unlawful.

JUSTICE BRENNAN delivered the opinion of the Court.

Respondent, Transportation Agency of Santa Clara County, California, unilaterally promulgated an Affirmative Action Plan applicable, inter alia, to promotions of employees. In selecting applicants for the promotional position of road dispatcher, the Agency, pursuant to the Plan, passed over petitioner Paul Johnson, a male employee, and promoted a female employee applicant, Diane Joyce. The question for decision is whether in making the promotion the Agency impermissibly took into account the sex of the applicants in violation of Title VII of the Civil Rights Act of 1964. The District Court for the Northern District of California, in an action filed by petitioner following receipt of a right-to-sue letter from the Equal Employment Opportunity Commission (EEOC), held that respondent had violated Title VII. The Court of Appeals for the Ninth Circuit reversed. We granted certiorari. We affirm.

In December 1978, the Santa Clara County Transit District Board of Supervisors adopted an Affirmative Action Plan (Plan) for the County Transportation Agency. The Plan implemented a County Affirmative Action Plan, which had been adopted, declared the County, because "mere prohibi-tion of discriminatory practices is not enough to remedy the effects of past practices and to permit attainment of an equitable representation of minorities, women and handicapped persons." Relevant to this case, the Agency Plan provides that, in making promotions to positions within a traditionally segregated job classification in which women have been significantly underrepresented, the Agency is authorized to consider as one factor the sex of a qualified applicant.

In reviewing the composition of its work force, the Agency noted in its Plan that women were represented in numbers far less than their proportion of the County labor force in both the Agency as a whole and in five of seven job categories. Specifically, while women constituted 36.4% of the area labor market, they composed only 22.4% of Agency employees. Furthermore, women working at the Agency were concentrated largely in EEOC job categories traditionally held by women: women made up 76% of Office and Clerical Workers, but only 7.1% of Agency Officials and Administrators, 8.6% of Professionals, 9.7% of Technicians, and 22% of Service and Maintenance Workers. As for the job classification relevant to this case, none of the 238 Skilled Craft Worker positions was held by a woman. The Plan noted that this underrepresentation of women in part reflected the fact that women had not traditionally been employed in these positions, and that they had not been strongly motivated to seek training or employment in them "because of the limited opportunities that have existed in the past for them to work in such classifications." The Plan also observed that, while the proportion of ethnic minorities in the Agency as a whole exceeded the proportion of such minorities in the County work force, a smaller percentage of minority employees held management, professional, and technical positions.

The Agency stated that its Plan was intended to achieve "a statistically measurable yearly improvement in hiring, training and promotion of minorities and women through-out the Agency in all major job classifications where they are underrepresented." As a benchmark by which to evaluate progress, the Agency stated that its long-term goal was to attain a work force whose composition reflected the proportion of minorities and women in the area labor force. The Agency's Plan ... set aside no specific number of positions for minorities or women, but authorized the consideration of ethnicity or sex as a factor when evaluating qualified candidates for jobs in which members of such groups were poorly represented. One such job was the road dispatcher position that is the subject of the dispute in this case.

On December 12, 1979, the Agency announced a vacancy for the promotional position of road dispatcher in the Agency's Roads Division. Dispatchers assign road crews, equipment, and materials, and maintain records pertaining to road maintenance jobs. The position requires at minimum four years of dispatch or road maintenance work experience for Santa Clara County. The EEOC job classification scheme designates a road dispatcher as a Skilled Craft Worker. Twelve County employees applied for the promotion, including Joyce and Johnson.

Joyce had worked for the County since 1970, serving as an account clerk until 1975. She had applied for a road dispatcher position in 1974, but was deemed ineligible because she had not served as a road maintenance worker. In 1975, Joyce transferred from a senior account clerk position to a road maintenance worker position, becoming the first woman to fill such a job. During her four years in that position, she occasionally worked out of class as a road dispatcher.

Petitioner Johnson began with the County in 1967 as a road yard clerk, after private employment that included working as a supervisor and dispatcher. He had also unsuccessfully applied for the road dispatcher opening in 1974. In 1977, his clerical position was downgraded, and he sought and received a transfer to the position of road maintenance worker. He also occasionally worked out of class as a dispatcher while performing that job.

Nine of the applicants, including Joyce and Johnson, were deemed qualified for the job, and were interviewed by a two-person board. Seven of the applicants scored above 70 on this interview, which meant that they were certified as eligible for selection by the appointing authority. The scores awarded ranged from 70 to 80. Johnson was tied for second with a score of 75, while Joyce ranked next with a score of 73. A second interview was conducted by three Agency supervisors, who ultimately recommended that Johnson be promoted. Prior to the second interview, Joyce had contacted the County's Affirmative Action Office because she feared that her application might not receive disinterested review. The Office in turn contacted the Agency's Affirmative Action Coordinator, whom the Agency's Plan makes responsible for, inter alia, keeping the Director informed of opportunities for the Agency to accomplish its objectives under the Plan. At the time, the Agency employed no women in any Skilled Craft position, and had never employed a woman as a road dispatcher. The Coordinator recommended to the Director of the Agency, James Graebner, that Joyce be promoted.

Graebner, authorized to choose any of the seven persons deemed eligible, thus had the benefit of suggestions by the second interview panel and by the Agency Coordinator in arriving at his decision. After deliberation, Graebner concluded that the promotion should be given to Joyce. As he testified: "I tried to look at the whole picture, the combination of her qualifications and Mr. Johnson's qualifications, their test scores, their expertise, their background, affirmative action matters, things like that.... I believe it was a combination of all those."

The certification form naming Joyce as the person promoted to the dispatcher position stated that both she and Johnson were rated as well qualified for the job. The evaluation of Joyce read: "Well qualified by virtue of 18 years of past clerical experience including 3 1/2 years at West Yard plus almost 5 years as a [road maintenance worker]." App. 27. The evaluation of Johnson was as follows: "Well qualified applicant; two years of [road maintenance worker] experience plus 11 years of Road Yard Clerk. Has had previous outside Dispatch experience but was 13 years ago." Graebner testified that he did not regard as significant the fact that Johnson scored 75 and Joyce 73 when interviewed by the two-person board....

As a preliminary matter, we note that petitioner bears the burden of establishing the invalidity of the Agency's Plan. Only last Term, in Wygant v. Jackson Board of Education (1986), we held that "[t]he ultimate burden remains with the employees to demonstrate the unconstitutionality of an affirmative-action program," and we see no basis for a different rule regarding a plan's alleged violation of Title VII. This case also fits readily within the analytical framework set forth in McDonnell Douglas Corp. v. Green (1973). Once a plaintiff establishes a prima facie case that race or sex has been taken into account in an employer's employment decision, the burden shifts to the employer to articulate a nondiscriminatory rationale for its decision. The existence of an affirmative action plan provides such a rationale. If such a plan is articulated as the basis for the employer's decision, the burden shifts to the plaintiff to prove that the employer's justification is pretextual and the plan is invalid. As a practical matter, of course, an employer will generally seek to avoid a charge of pretext by presenting evidence in support of its plan. That does not mean, however, as petitioner suggests, that reliance on an affirmative action plan is to be treated as an affirmative defense requiring the employer to carry the burden of proving the validity of the plan. The burden of proving its invalidity remains on the plaintiff. ...

It is clear that the decision to hire Joyce was made pursuant to an Agency plan that directed that sex or race be taken into account for the purpose of remedying underrepresentation. The Agency Plan acknowledged the "limited opportunities that have existed in the past," for women to find employment in certain job classifications "where women have not been traditionally employed in significant numbers." As a result, observed the Plan, women were concentrated in traditionally female jobs in the Agency, and represented a lower percentage in other job classifications than would be expected if such traditional segregation had not occurred. Specifically, 9 of the 10 Para-Professionals and 110 of the 145 Office and Clerical Workers were women. By contrast, women were only 2 of the 28 Officials and Administrators, 5 of the 58 Professionals, 12 of the 124 Technicians, none of the Skilled Craft Workers, and 1—who was Joyce—of the 110 Road Maintenance Workers. The Plan sought to remedy these imbalances through "hiring, training and promotion of . . . women throughout the Agency in all major job classifications where they are underrepresented." . . .

As the Agency Plan recognized, women were most egregiously underrepresented in the Skilled Craft job category, since none of the 238 positions was occupied by a woman. . . . Given the obvious imbalance in the Skilled Craft category, and given the Agency's commitment to eliminating such imbalances, it was plainly not unreasonable for the Agency to determine that it was appropriate to consider as one factor the sex of Ms. Joyce in making its decision. . . . In addition, petitioner had no absolute entitlement to the road dispatcher position. Seven of the applicants were classified as qualified and eligible, and the Agency Director was authorized to promote any of the seven. Thus, denial of the promotion unsettled no legitimate, firmly rooted expectation on the part of petitioner. Furthermore, while petitioner in this case was denied a promotion, he retained his employment with the Agency, at the same salary and with the same seniority, and remained eligible for other promotions.

Finally, the Agency's Plan was intended to attain a balanced work force, not to maintain one. . . . The Agency acknowledged the difficulties that it would confront in remedying the imbalance in its work force, and it anticipated only gradual increases in the representation of minorities and women. . . . In this case, however, substantial evidence shows that the Agency has sought to take a moderate, gradual approach to eliminating the imbalance in its work force, one which establishes realistic guidance for employment decisions, and which visits minimal intrusion on the legitimate expectations of other employees. Given this fact, as well as the Agency's express commitment to "attain" a balanced work force, there is ample assurance that the Agency does not seek to use its Plan to maintain a permanent racial and sexual balance. . . .

We therefore hold that the Agency appropriately took into account as one factor the sex of Diane Joyce in determining that she should be promoted to the road dispatcher position. The decision to do so was made pursuant to an affirmative action plan that represents a moderate, flexible, case-by-case approach to effecting a gradual improvement in the representation of minorities and women in the Agency's work force. Such a plan is fully consistent with Title VII, for it embodies the contribution that voluntary employer action can make in eliminating the vestiges of discrimination in the workplace. Accordingly, the judgment of the Court of Appeals is Affirmed.

JUSTICE SCALIA, with whom THE CHIEF JUSTICE joins, and with whom JUSTICE WHITE joins in Parts I and II, dissenting.

With a clarity which, had it not proven so unavailing, one might well recommend as a model of statutory draftsmanship, Title VII of the Civil Rights Act of 1964 declares:

> It shall be an unlawful employment practice for an employer— (1) to fail or refuse to hire or to discharge any individual, or otherwise to discriminate against any individual with respect to his compensation, terms, conditions, or privileges of employment, because of such individual's race, color, religion, sex, or national origin. . . ."

The Court today completes the process of converting this from a guarantee that race or sex will not be the basis for employment determinations, to a guarantee that it often will. Ever so subtly, without even alluding to the last obstacles preserved by earlier opinions that we now push out of our path, we effectively replace the goal of a discrimination-free society with the quite incompatible goal of proportionate representation by race and by sex in the workplace. . . .

Several salient features of the [affirmative action] plan should be noted. Most importantly, the plan's purpose was assuredly not to remedy prior sex discrimination by the Agency. It could not have been, because there was no prior sex discrimination to remedy. The majority, in cataloging the Agency's alleged misdeeds, neglects to mention the District Court's finding that the Agency "has not discriminated in the past, and does not discriminate in the present against women in regard to employment opportunities in general and promotions in particular." This finding was not disturbed by the Ninth Circuit.

Not only was the plan not directed at the results of past sex discrimination by the Agency, but its objective was not to achieve the state of affairs that this Court has dubiously assumed would result from an absence of discrimination—an overall work force "more or less representative of the racial and ethnic composition of the population in the community." Rather, the oft-stated goal was to mirror the racial and sexual composition of the entire county labor force, not merely in the Agency work force as a whole, but in each and every individual job category at the Agency. In a discrimination-free world, it would obviously be a statistical oddity for every job category to match the racial and sexual composition of even that portion of the county work force qualified for that job; it would be utterly miraculous for each of them to match, as the plan expected, the composition of the entire work force. Quite obviously, the plan did not seek to replicate what a lack of discrimination would produce, but rather imposed racial and sexual tailoring that would, in defiance of normal expectations and laws of probability, give each protected racial and sexual group a governmentally determined "proper" proportion of each job category. . . .

Finally, the one message that the plan unmistakably communicated was that concrete results were expected, and supervisory personnel would be evaluated on the basis of the affirmative-action numbers they produced. The plan's implementation was expected to "result in a statistically measurable yearly improvement in the hiring, training and promotion of minorities, women and handicapped persons in the major job classifications utilized by the Agency where these groups are underrepresented." . . . [S]upervisors were reminded of the need to give attention to affirmative action in every employment decision, and to explain their reasons for failing to hire women and minorities whenever there was an opportunity to do so.

The petitioner in the present case, Paul E. Johnson, had been an employee of the Agency since 1967, coming there from a private company where he had been a road dispatcher for 17 years. He had first applied for the position of Road Dispatcher at the Agency in 1974, coming in second. . . . When the Road Dispatcher job next became vacant, in 1979, he was the leading candidate—and indeed was assigned to work out of class full time in the vacancy, from September 1979 until June 1980. There is no question why he did not get the job.

The fact of discrimination against Johnson is much clearer, and its degree more shocking, than the majority . . . would suggest. . . . Worth mentioning, for example, is the trier of fact's determination that, if the Affirmative Action Coordinator had not intervened, "the decision as to whom to promote . . . would have been made by [the Road Operations Division Director]," who had recommended that Johnson be appointed to the position. Likewise, the even more extraordinary findings that James Graebner, the Agency Director who made the appointment, "did not inspect the applications and related examination records of either [Paul Johnson] or Diane Joyce before making his decision," ibid., and indeed "did little or nothing to inquire into the results of the interview process and conclusions which [were] described as of critical importance to the selection process." In light of these determinations, it is impossible to believe (or to think that the District Court believed) Graebner's self-serving statements, such as the assertion that he "tried to look at the whole picture, the combination of [Joyce's] qualifications and Mr. Johnson's qualifications, their test scores, their expertise, their background, affirmative action matters, things like that." . . .

The most significant proposition of law established by today's decision is that racial or sexual discrimination is permitted under Title VII when it is intended to overcome the effect, not of the employer's own discrimination, but of societal attitudes that have limited the entry of certain races, or of a particular sex, into certain jobs. . . . In fact, however, today's decision goes well beyond merely allowing racial or sexual discrimination in order to eliminate the effects of prior societal discrimination. . . . It is absurd to think that the nationwide failure of road maintenance crews, for example, to achieve the Agency's ambition of 36.4% female representation is attributable primarily, if even substantially, to systematic exclusion of women eager to shoulder pick and shovel. It is a "traditionally segregated job category" . . . in the sense that, because of longstanding social attitudes, it has not been regarded by women themselves as desirable work. . . . There are, of course, those who believe that the social attitudes which cause women themselves to avoid certain jobs and to favor others are as nefarious as conscious, exclusionary discrimination. Whether or not that is so (and there is assuredly no consensus on the point equivalent to our national consensus against intentional discrimination), the two phenomena are certainly distinct. And it is the alteration of social attitudes, rather than the elimination of discrimination, which today's decision approves as justification for state-enforced discrimination. This is an enormous expansion, undertaken without the slightest justification or analysis. . . .

A statute designed to establish a color-blind and gender-blind workplace has thus been converted into a powerful engine of racism and sexism, not merely permitting intentional race- and sex-based discrimination, but often making it, through operation of the legal system, practically compelled. It is unlikely that today's result will be displeasing to politically elected officials, to whom it provides the means of quickly accommodating the demands of organized groups to achieve concrete, numerical improvement in the economic status of particular constituencies. . . . In fact, the only losers in the process are the Johnsons of the country, for whom Title VII has been not merely repealed but actually inverted. The irony is that these individuals—predominantly unknown, unaffluent, unorganized—suffer this injustice at the hands of a Court fond of thinking itself the champion of the politically impotent.

I dissent.

CHAPTER 12

Gender and the Constitution

INTRODUCTION

The Equal Protection Clause of the Fourteenth Amendment was adopted to protect the civil rights of an oppressed minority, the 4 million black Americans who had been held in slavery. Its application has long been considered as devoted to protecting blacks and members of other minority groups from discrimination. When Justice Harlan Fiske Stone announced in 1938 the Court's new test of "strict scrutiny" of legislation that was challenged as violating some provision of the Bill of Rights, in footnote 4 of his *Carolene Products* opinion, his list of groups deserving of special judicial protection included racial, religious, and ethnic minorities and other "discrete and insular minorities." The basic premise of Footnote Four was that members of minority groups had been historically subject to "prejudice" by the majority and barred from participation in American society on equal terms.

One group in our society, however, is both a numerical majority and has been the object of prejudice and stereotypes during the entire course of American history. This majority is made up of women; the 2000 census counted 140.6 million females and only 135.5 million males. In many respects, however, women have been a majority that is treated like a minority. Those men who speak of women as "the weaker sex" and who believe that "a woman's place is in the home" have lowered their voices in recent years, but such attitudes are still prevalent; years after women shed their aprons and moved into the workplace in numbers almost as great as men the income of women lags well behind that of men. These dismissive stereotypes and attitudes have persisted since the colonial era.

There was a "woman's movement" in this country long before the "feminist movement" emerged as a political force

in the 1960s and '70s, with Betty Friedan's book, *The Feminine Mystique,* as its manifesto and the National Organization for Women as its major lobbying and educational arm. The Seneca Falls Declaration of Sentiments, named after the New York town in which women gathered in 1848, deliberately adapted the wording of the Declaration of Independence: "We hold these truths to be self-evident; that all men and women are created equal." Among the demands of the Seneca Falls manifesto were the rights to vote and to own property in her own name. The women who adopted this statement also resolved "that such laws which prevent women from occupying such a station in society as her conscience shall dictate, or which place her in a position inferior to that of man, are contrary to the great precept of nature and therefore of no force or authority."

The Seneca Falls Declaration fell on deaf ears among the male population, the "dominant gender" in prestige, achievements, wealth, and power, to borrow the words of Justice Harlan about the dominant white race in his *Plessy* dissent. However, women did not give up their struggle for political and legal equality, and the Suffragist Movement of the early twentieth century finally achieved its primary goal, the right to vote, with ratification of the Nineteenth Amendment in 1920, which provided: "The right of citizens of the United States to vote shall not be denied or abridged by the United States or by any State on account of sex." Gaining the franchise, however, did not measurably improve the status of women in the fields of education or employment, or secure to them equal legal rights with men. The women's movement, in fact, suffered its greatest political defeat in the 1970s when the proposed Equal Rights Amendment to the Constitution, first submitted to Congress in 1923 and modeled on the Nineteenth Amendment, was adopted by substantial majorities in both houses of Congress in 1972 but failed of ratification by two states before its deadline expired a decade later in 1982. This amendment would have provided that "equality of rights under the law shall not be denied or abridged by the United States or by any state on account of sex." As was the case with the "white backlash" to affirmative action programs, the Equal Rights Amendment [ERA] fell victim to the "male backlash" to the vocal, and often strident, feminist movement. Many men, in fact, supported the amendment and the movement, and an equally vocal collection of women, most notably the Eagle Forum under the leadership of Phyllis Schafley, spearheaded the opposition to the ERA.

However, the defeat of the ERA was balanced by significant legal victories for the women's movement. Exactly one century before Congress sent the ERA to the states for ratification, the Supreme Court had ruled in *Bradwell v. Illinois* that states could deny women the right to practice law. In his concurring opinion in this case, Justice Joseph Bradley stated that "the civil law, as well as nature herself, has always recognized a wide difference in the respective spheres and destinies of man and woman." Bradley's relegation of women to the roles of "wife and mother" reflected the "romantic paternalism" of his times, as Justice William Brennan later wrote. The Court, however, did uphold in 1908 a state law that limited the working hours of women in *Muller v. Oregon.* But even in his *Muller* opinion, Justice David Brewer defended the maximum hours law as one designed to allow women more time for the "proper discharge of her maternal functions." What might seem a conflict between the *Bradwell* and *Muller* decisions is actually an agreement that women are best suited, even if they hold jobs, for their "maternal" role in society.

As late as 1948, the Supreme Court continued to uphold the exclusion of women from certain jobs. Justice Felix Frankfurter wrote in *Goesaert v. Cleary* that Michigan could ban women from working as bartenders unless they belonged to the owner's family. "The fact that women may now have achieved the virtues that men have long claimed as their prerogatives and now indulge in vices that men have long practiced," Frankfurter wrote "does not preclude the States from drawing a sharp line between the sexes, certainly in such matters as the regulation of the liquor traffic." Not until 1971 did the Court finally apply the Equal Protection Clause to strike down a law that singled out women for legal discrimination. The Court unanimously invalidated in *Reed v. Reed* an Idaho law that preferred men over women as administrators of the estates of deceased family members. Chief Justice Warren Burger concluded in his brief opinion that "by providing dissimilar treatment for men and women" who were "similarly situated" in their relation to the deceased person, the law "violates the Equal Protection Clause." Burger left unstated, however, the doctrinal basis of his opinion, although presumably he concluded that the

law failed the minimal "rational basis" test, since Idaho advanced no reasons at all to justify its discrimination against women. The lawyer for Sally Reed, who challenged the Idaho law, was an ACLU lawyer, Ruth Bader Ginsburg, who later joined the Supreme Court as its second female member and who wrote the opinion in the final case in this chapter, striking down Virginia's exclusion of women from its state-run military institute.

The three cases in this chapter that follow *Bradwell* and *Muller* raised questions of what level of scrutiny the Court should apply in gender discrimination cases. Although the *Reed* case had failed the "rational basis" test, applying "strict scrutiny" in this area would expand the limited category of "suspect classes" from true minorities such as blacks to an actual majority group. The Court's decision in *Frontiero v. Richardson,* which challenged an Air Force policy that favored men over women in allocating benefits for dependents of service members, struck down the regulation at issue in 1973. Justice William Brennan wrote an opinion that announced "the judgment of the Court" in the *Frontiero* case, holding that "classifications based upon sex, like classifications based upon race, alienage, or national origin, are inherently suspect, and must therefore be subjected to strict judicial scrutiny."

However, only three fellow justices joined Brennan's opinion. Justice Lewis Powell wrote a concurring opinion, joined by two other justices, finding a "compelling" reason for "deferring a general categorizing of sex classifications as invoking the strictest test of judicial scrutiny." Powell noted that the ERA, "which if adopted will resolve the substance of this precise question" had recently been adopted by Congress and sent to the states for ratification. He felt that "reaching out to pre-empt by judicial action a major political decision which is currently in process of resolution does not reflect appropriate respect for duly prescribed legislative processes." Adding women to the list of "suspect classes" under the "strict scrutiny" test fell one vote short in the Supreme Court.

Nonetheless, the Supreme Court has generally sided with women in gender discrimination cases since the *Frontiero* decision. The final two cases in this chapter, decided in 1984 and 1996, struck down the exclusion of women from the Jaycees, a national civic group, and from the Virginia Military Institute, a state-run college in Virginia. In neither case did the Court apply the "strict scrutiny" case, but in both it applied all but the phrase to accomplish the same end. Most of the gender discrimination cases that have come before the Court in recent years do not involve total exclusion of women from schools, jobs, and other programs, but raise challenges to "disparate treatment" of women who have been admitted or employed in them. Few of the Court's decisions in such cases have produced any rulings of doctrinal significance, but the number of such cases illustrates the fact that women are still a majority treated like a minority.

BRADWELL V. STATE OF ILLINOIS
83 U.S. 130 (1872)

"Man is, or should be, woman's protector and defender. The natural and proper timidity and delicacy which belongs to the female sex evidently unfits it for many of the occupations of civil life. . . . The paramount destiny and mission of woman are to fulfil the noble and benign offices of wife and mother. This is the law of the Creator."

The Question: Can a state exclude women from admission to the bar and the practice of law as a matter of state power to regulate the professions?

The Arguments: PRO

In the context of attitudes toward women in the nineteenth century, it is a reasonable exercise of state power to exclude women from the practice of law for several reasons. First, women are best suited by nature and biology for the roles of wives and mothers. Second, the practice of law requires characteristics and skills that few women possess, and excluding them as a group is designed to protect them from the rough-and-tumble of courtroom practice.

CON

Prejudice against women as lawyers, and in other professions as well, is based on nothing more than outmoded stereotypes. Women who are qualified to practice law, by education and training, are presumed to have all the skills necessary to practice law, particularly if they have passed the bar examination, as is true in this case. The Constitution prohibits discrimination based on race, and women deserve its protections as well.

BACKGROUND

Her primary goal was to be helpful to her husband at his law office. But seven men decreed that she could not. Because those seven were all members of the Illinois Supreme Court, Myra Bradwell was officially barred from the bar.

During the latter part of the nineteenth century, there were two avenues of entry into the legal profession. One could either take a formal course of study at a law school or serve as an apprentice at the office of a practicing lawyer. Many prospective lawyers chose the latter alternative. Among them was Myra Bradwell.

Myra's training began informally in 1852, the year of her marriage to James Bradwell, a struggling young law student who was financing his legal apprenticeship by working as a manual laborer. Given the absorptive qualities of Myra's mind, it is probable that much of her early learning took place through the process of osmosis. A few years later, however, after James had been admitted to the practice of law in both Tennessee and Illinois, Myra began a more intensive apprenticeship with her husband. It was then that she became "determined to read [law] in good earnest" so that she and James could "work side by side and think side by side." Her studies, however, were interrupted by several events: the birth of four children (two of whom died in early childhood) and countless civic activities organized all over the North to aid the sick and wounded soldiers of the Civil War.

Finally, on August 2, 1869, Myra Bradwell at the age of thirty-eight, amid predictions that she would "wreck [her]

family and break [her] hearthstone to smithereens," passed the Illinois bar exam with high honors and made a formal application to practice law in Illinois. That she chose this moment to do so was probably due to a confluence of three factors.

First, her two surviving children, aged thirteen and eleven no longer needed constant attention. Second, her husband had decided not to run for reelection as judge. He was returning to a busy practice and was in need of her assistance in doing research and preparing briefs. Third, prior to the summer of 1869, there was little hope that a woman would be permitted to practice law anywhere in the United States. However, on June 15 of that year, six weeks before Bradwell passed the bar exam in Illinois, another midwestern state, Iowa, quietly opened the gates of the legal profession to a young married woman, Arabella Mansfield. Mansfield was a teacher of English and history who had no intention of practicing law and who had no subsequent contact with the legal profession. Her admission to the bar was simply part of a plan devised by an Iowa judge, Francis Springer, who was dedicated to promoting the equality of women.

Myra, however, must have realized that others did not see it that way, for her application was accompanied not only by a document certifying that she had passed the bar examination, but also by a brief in which she stated: "The only question involved in this case is—Does being a woman disqualify [me] under the law of Illinois from receiving a license to practice law?"

The Illinois Supreme Court promptly denied her petition, a decision that probably came as no surprise to either Myra or other interested observers. What jolted many were the grounds upon which the court's denial rested. Myra Bradwell was rejected from the legal profession *not* on the grounds that she was a woman, but because she was a *married* woman. Exactly two months after her stellar performance on the bar examination, she received the following communication from the reporter for the Illinois Supreme Court:

Madam: The court instructs me to inform you that they are compelled to deny your application for a license to practice as an attorney-at-law in the courts of this State, upon the ground that you would not be bound by the [contractual] obligations necessary to be assumed where the relation of attorney and client shall exist, by reason of the DISABILITY IMPOSED BY YOUR MARRIED CONDITION—it being assumed that you are a married woman.... Until such DISABILITY shall be removed by legislation, the court regards itself as powerless to grant your application.

[Myra] quickly filed a counterassault. In a detailed and scholarly brief, she cited countless Illinois statutes and cases under which married women's legal disabilities had been removed. In addition to statutory and judicial precedents, she included reports of recent admissions of women to both law schools and medical schools. She also cited the state of Iowa's granting a license to practice law to Arabella Mansfield; and she discussed the recent opening to women of other trades and occupations from which they had previously been barred.

She concluded her brief with the following exhortation:

This honorable court can send me from its bar and prevent me from practicing as an attorney, and it is of small consequence; but if in so doing, [you base your decision on] ... the disability imposed by [my] married condition, you, in my judgment in striking *me* down, strike a blow at the right of every married woman in the great State of Illinois who is dependent on her labor for support, and say to her, you can not enter the smallest contract in relation to your earnings or separate property, that can be enforced against you in a court of law.

The Illinois Supreme Court must have known that it had been bested because it quickly issued a second opinion, once again unanimously denying her application for admission. This time, however, the court gave a different reason: the obstacle to Myra Bradwell's admission to the bar was not that she was a *married* woman, but simply that she was a woman.

The court began by noting that its previous holding, which had been based on married women's disabilities, had been "earnestly and ably" contested by Myra. Moreover, "of the qualifications of the applicant we have no doubt...." But, explained the court,

After further consultation in regard to this application, we find ourselves constrained to hold that the *sex of the applicant,* independently of coverture is, as our law now stands, a sufficient reason for not granting this license.

The court then buttressed its decision with a four-pronged rationale. First, the Illinois legislature had been silent on the issue of whether women could enter the profession. Therefore, concluded the court, the legislature must have intended that women should not be permitted to practice law.

The second reason given by the court was one which lawyers often call the "opening of the floodgates." The court reasoned that if it opened the doors of the legal profession to women then "every civil office in this state may be filled by women—that it . . . [would follow] that women should be made governors and sheriffs." The court stood aghast at its own speculation.

Third, the court was concerned that the "hot strifes of the bar" and the "momentous verdicts, the prizes of struggle [would] tend to destroy the deference and delicacy with which it is a matter of pride of our ruder sex to treat [women]. . . ."

Finally, echoing the anxieties of contemporary commentators, the court voiced concern over "what effect the presence of women as barristers in our courts would have upon the administration of justice."

Myra's response to the court's opinion was swift and curt:

What the decision of the Supreme Court of the United States in the Dred Scott case was to the rights of the negroes as citizens of the U.S., this decision is to the political rights of women in Illinois—*annihilation.*

Yet, Myra had the amazing ability to separate her professional and political goals from her relationships with the men who had attempted to "annihilate" those goals. For example, sitting on the Illinois Supreme Court, which had twice ruled unanimously against her, was Justice Sidney Breeze, a friend of Myra's with whom she frequently corresponded and socialized. Even in the wake of Breeze's adverse ruling in Myra's case, their friendship remained unscathed.

Although Myra continued to have cordial relations with members of the highest court of Illinois, she did not hesitate to appeal that court's decision to the United States Supreme Court, retaining as her attorney Senator Matthew H. Carpenter of Wisconsin, one of the country's ablest constitutional lawyers.

Matthew Carpenter was not only an outstanding constitutional lawyer, he was also a staunch advocate of equal rights for women. In 1870 he had publicly vowed to Elizabeth Cady Stanton that he would fight for women's suffrage in the Senate. Later, in 1874, he pleaded for the remission of a fine that had been slapped on Susan B. Anthony for her audacity in attempting to vote in the presidential election of 1872.

As Carpenter began to prepare his case, he immediately realized that the greatest *political* obstacle to a favorable judicial decision was the widespread fear that if women were declared constitutionally entitled to practice law, it might follow, as night to day, that they were also constitutionally entitled to vote, even in the absence of a woman's suffrage amendment to the U.S. Constitution.

Carpenter realized that the specter of nationwide woman's suffrage was far more terrifying to the populace than was the threat of women being admitted to the bar. The prospect of women casting the ballot, which was both a symbol and an instrument of independence, was troublesome to every man who feared his wife's (sister's, daughter's, etc.) partial freedom from male control. That idea was terrifying to many nineteenth-century women as well. The prospect of women practicing law, however, was a direct threat to only a select few, the gentlemen of the bar and those few men whose wives or female relatives might wish to enter the profession.

Carpenter thus took great pains to distinguish Myra's constitutional right to practice law from the "establishment of the right of female suffrage, which, it is assumed, would overthrow Christianity, defeat the ends of modern civilization, and upturn the world." He argued with force that women had no constitutional right to vote unless and until a suffrage amendment was passed. This position probably caused him great discomfort, as he had always advocated the cause of woman suffrage. But his first duty was to his client, and he must have believed that the only road to victory was to persuade the Court that a decision favorable to Myra would not, in any way, serve as a precedent requiring the Court to hold that women also had the constitutional right to vote.

The remainder of Carpenter's brief in *Bradwell* v. *Illinois* was based on the argument that the U.S. Constitution *did affirmatively* grant women the legal right to practice law. That assertion was based on the Fourteenth Amendment's "Privileges and Immunities Clause," which provides that "No State shall make or enforce any law which shall abridge the privileges or immunities of citizens of the United States. . . ." Carpenter contended that since Myra was a "citizen of the United States," she had the "privilege" to practice her chosen profession and that that privilege could not be "abridged" by the states. That was the main point to be established, but Carpenter addressed it almost as an afterthought. His argument was based on neither precedent nor logic, and at best can be characterized as a mere assertion:

> I maintain that the Fourteenth Amendment opens to every citizen of the U.S., male or female, black or white, married or single, the honorable professions as well as the servile employments of life; and no citizen can be excluded from any one of them. Intelligence, integrity, and honor are the only qualifications that can be prescribed as conditions.

In responding to the commonly held belief that most men would never retain the services of a female lawyer, Carpenter stated simply that that possibility should be governed by the marketplace, and not by governmental fiat:

> The inequalities of sex will undoubtedly have their influence, and be considered by every client desiring to employ counsel. . . . Of a bar composed of men and women of equal integrity and learning, women might be more or less frequently retained, as the taste or judgment of clients might dictate. But the broad shield of the Constitution is over them all, and protects each in that measure of success which his or her individual merits may secure.

Although Myra exclaimed that Carpenter's argument was "concise and unanswerable," the State of Illinois did not take the matter the least bit seriously. Indeed, the state did not even deign to send counsel to oppose Carpenter in the Supreme Court (Friedman, 1993).

MR. JUSTICE MILLER delivered the opinion of the court.

The record in this case is not very perfect, but it may be fairly taken that the plaintiff asserted her right to a license on the grounds, among others, that she was a citizen of the United States, and that having been a citizen of Vermont at one time, she was, in the State of Illinois, entitled to any right granted to citizens of the latter State. The court having overruled these claims of right founded on the clauses of the Federal Constitution before referred to, those propositions may be considered as properly before this court.

As regards the provision of the Constitution that citizens of each State shall be entitled to all the privileges and immunities of citizens in the several States, the plaintiff in her affidavit has stated very clearly a case to which it is inapplicable. The protection designed by that clause, as has been repeatedly held, has no application to a citizen of the State whose laws are complained of. If the plaintiff was a citizen of the State of Illinois, that provision of the Constitution gave her no protection against its courts or its legislation. The plaintiff seems to have seen this difficulty, and attempts to avoid it by stating that she was born in Vermont. While she remained in Vermont that circumstance made her a citizen of that State. But she states, at the same time, that she is a citizen of the United States, and that she is now, and has been for many years past, a resident of Chicago, in the State of Illinois.

The fourteenth amendment declares that citizens of the United States are citizens of the State within which they reside; therefore the plaintiff was, at the time of making her application, a citizen of the United States and a citizen of the State of Illinois.

We do not here mean to say that there may not be a temporary residence in one State, with intent to return to another, which will not create citizenship in the former. But the plaintiff states nothing to take her case out of the definition of citizenship of a State as defined by the first section of the fourteenth amendment.

In regard to that amendment counsel for the plaintiff in this court truly says that there are certain privileges and immunities which belong to a citizen of the United States as such; otherwise it would be nonsense for the fourteenth amendment to prohibit a State from abridging them, and he proceeds to argue that admission to the bar of a State of a person who possesses the requisite learning and character is one of those which a State may not deny. In this latter proposition we are not able to concur with counsel. We agree with him that there are privileges and immunities belonging to citizens of the United States, in that relation and character, and that it is these and these alone which a State is forbidden to abridge. But the right to admission to practice in the courts of a State is not one of them. This right in no sense depends on citizenship of the United States. It has not, as far as we know, ever been made in any State, or in any case, to depend on citizenship at all. Certainly many prominent and distinguished lawyers have been admitted to practice, both in the State and Federal courts, who were not citizens of the United States or of any State. But, on whatever basis this right may be placed, so far as it can have any relation to citizenship at all, it would seem that, as to the courts of a State, it would relate to citizenship of the State, and as to Federal courts, it would relate to citizenship of the United States.

The opinion just delivered in the Slaughter-House Cases renders elaborate argument in the present case unnecessary; for, unless we are wholly and radically mistaken in the principles on which those cases are decided, the right to control and regulate the granting of license to practice law in the courts of a State is one of those powers which are not transferred for its protection to the Federal government, and its exercise is in no manner governed or controlled by citizenship of the United States in the party seeking such license.

It is unnecessary to repeat the argument on which the judgment in those cases is founded. It is sufficient to say they are conclusive of the present case.

Judgment Affirmed.

MR. JUSTICE BRADLEY, concurring.

I concur in the judgment of the court in this case, by which the judgment of the Supreme Court of Illinois is affirmed, but not for the reasons specified in the opinion just read. The claim of the plaintiff, who is a married woman, to be admitted to practice as an attorney and counsellor-at-law, is based upon the supposed right of every person, man or woman, to engage in any lawful employment for a livelihood. The Supreme Court of Illinois denied the application on the ground that, by the common law, which is the basis of the laws of Illinois, only men were admitted to the bar, and the legislature had not made any change in this respect, but had simply provided that no person should be admitted to practice as attorney or counsellor without having previously obtained a license for that purpose from two justices of the Supreme Court, and that no person should receive a license without first obtaining a certificate from the court of some county of his good moral character. In other respects it was left to the discretion of the court to establish the rules by which admission to the profession should be determined. The court, however, regarded itself as bound by at least two limitations. One was that it should establish such terms of admission as would promote the proper administration of justice, and the other that it should not admit any persons, or class of persons, not intended by the legislature to be admitted, even though not expressly excluded by statute. In view of this latter limitation the court felt compelled to deny the application of females to be admitted as members of the bar. Being contrary to the rules of the common law and the usages of Westminster Hall from time immemorial, it could not be supposed that the legislature had intended to adopt any different rule.

The claim that, under the fourteenth amendment of the Constitution, which declares that no State shall make or enforce any law which shall abridge the privileges and immunities of citizens of the United States, the statute law of Illinois, or the common law prevailing in that State, can no longer be set up as a barrier against the right of females to pursue any lawful employment for a livelihood (the practice of law included), assumes that it is one of the privileges and immunities of women as citizens to engage in any and every profession, occupation, or employment in civil life. It certainly cannot be affirmed, as an historical fact, that this has ever been established as one of the fundamental privileges and immunities of the sex. On the contrary, the civil law, as well as nature herself, has always recognized a wide difference in the respective spheres and destinies of man and woman. Man is, or should be, woman's protector and defender. The natural and proper timidity and delicacy which belongs to the female sex evidently unfits it for many of the occupations of civil life. The constitution of the family organization, which is founded in the divine ordinance, as well as in the nature of things, indicates the domestic sphere as that which properly belongs to the domain and functions of womanhood. The harmony, not to say identity, of interest and views which belong, or should belong, to the family institution is repugnant to the idea of a woman adopting a distinct and independent career from that of her husband. So firmly fixed was this sentiment in the founders of the common law that it became a maxim of that system of jurisprudence that a woman had no legal existence separate from her husband, who was regarded as her head and representative in the social state; and, notwithstanding some recent modifications of this civil status, many of the special rules of law flowing from and dependent upon this cardinal principle still exist in full force in most States. One of these is, that a married woman is incapable, without her husband's consent, of making contracts which shall be binding on her or him. This very incapacity was one circumstance which the Supreme Court of Illinois deemed important in rendering a married woman incompetent fully to perform the duties and trusts that belong to the office of an attorney and counsellor.

It is true that many women are unmarried and not affected by any of the duties, complications, and incapacities arising out of the married state, but these are exceptions to the general rule. The paramount destiny and mission of woman are to fulfil the noble and benign offices of wife and mother. This is the law of the Creator. And the rules of civil society must be adapted to the general constitution of things, and cannot be based upon exceptional cases.

The humane movements of modern society, which have for their object the multiplication of avenues for woman's advancement, and of occupations adapted to her condition and sex, have my heartiest concurrence. But I am not prepared to say that it is one of her fundamental rights and privileges to be admitted into every office and position, including those which require highly special qualifications and demanding special responsibilities. In the nature of things it is not every citizen of every age, sex, and condition that is qualified for every calling and position. It is the prerogative of the legislator to prescribe regulations founded on nature, reason, and experience for the due admission of qualified persons to professions and callings demanding special skill and confidence. This fairly belongs to the police power of the State; and, in my opinion, in view of the peculiar characteristics, destiny, and mission of woman, it is within the province of the legislature to ordain what offices, positions, and callings shall be filled and discharged by men, and shall receive the benefit of those energies and responsibilities, and that decision and firmness which are presumed to predominate in the sterner sex.

For these reasons I think that the laws of Illinois now complained of are not obnoxious to the charge of abridging any of the privileges and immunities of citizens of the United States.

MR. JUSTICE SWAYNE and MR. JUSTICE FIELD concurred in the foregoing opinion of MR. JUSTICE BRADLEY.

THE CHIEF JUSTICE dissented from the judgment of the court, and from all the opinions.

MULLER V. OREGON
208 U.S. 412 (1908)

"History discloses . . . that woman has always been dependent upon man. . . . In the struggle for subsistence she is not an equal competitor with her brother. . . . She is properly placed in a class by herself, and legislation designed for her protection may be sustained, even when like legislation is not necessary for men."

The Question: Can a state pass a law that sets a maximum workday of ten hours for women who are employed in laundries?

The Arguments: PRO

States are free to use their police powers to protect women workers against conditions that might adversely affect their safety or health. Setting a maximum workday of ten hours for female laundry workers is a reasonable exercise of this power. Many studies have shown that working long hours in laundries, and thus being exposed to excessive heat and humidity, has a damaging effect on the health and well-being of women workers.

CON

The Due Process Clause of the Constitution forbids legislative interference with the right of employers and workers to freely bargain over wages, hours, and working conditions. The "right of contract" is essential if we are to avoid the interference and paternalism of government in this economic relationship. Women who do not wish to work longer than ten hours in laundries are free to find employment in other occupations.

MR. JUSTICE BREWER delivered the opinion of the court.

On February 19, 1903, the legislature of the state of Oregon passed an act (Session Laws 1903, p. 148) the first section of which is in these words:

> Sec. 1. That no female (shall) be employed in any mechanical establishment, or factory, or laundry in this state more than ten hours during any one day. The hours of work may be so arranged as to permit the employment of females at any time so that they shall not work more than ten hours during the twenty-four hours of any one day.

Sec. 3 made a violation of the provisions of the prior sections a misdemeanor subject to a fine of not less than $10 nor more than $25. On September 18, 1905, an information was filed in the circuit court of the state for the county of Multnomah, charging that the defendant "on the 4th day of September, A.D. 1905, in the county of Multnomah and state of Oregon, then and there being the owner of a laundry, known as the Grand Laundry, in the city of Portland, and the employer of females therein, did then and there unlawfully permit and suffer one Joe Haselbock, he, the said Joe Haselbock, then and there being an overseer, superintendent, and agent of said Curt Muller, in the said Grand Laundry, to require a female, to wit, one Mrs. E. Gotcher, to work more than ten hours in said laundry on said 4th day of September, A.D. 1905, contrary to the statutes in such cases made and provided, and against the peace and dignity of the state of Oregon."

A trial resulted in a verdict against the defendant, who was sentenced to pay a fine of $10. The supreme court of the state affirmed the conviction whereupon the case was brought here on writ of error.

The single question is the constitutionality of the statute under which the defendant was convicted, so far as it affects the work of a female in a laundry. That it does not conflict with any provisions of the state Constitution is settled by the decision of the supreme court of the state. The contentions of the defendant, now plaintiff in error, are thus stated in his brief:

> (1) Because the statute attempts to prevent persons sui juris from making their own contracts, and thus violates the provisions of the 14th Amendment, as follows:
> "No state shall make or enforce any law which shall abridge the privileges or immunities of citizens of the United States; nor shall any state deprive any person of life, liberty, or property, without due process of law; nor deny to any person within its jurisdiction the equal protection of the laws."
> (2) Because the statute does not apply equally to all persons similarly situated, and is class legislation.
> (3) The statute is not a valid exercise of the police power. The kinds of work prescribed are not unlawful, nor are they declared to be immoral or dangerous to the public health; nor can such a law be sustained on the ground that it is designed to protect women on account of their sex. There is no necessary or reasonable connection between the limitation prescribed by the act and the public health, safety, or welfare.

It is the law of Oregon that women, whether married or single, have equal contractual and personal rights with men.

As said by Chief Justice Wolverton, in First Nat. Bank v. Leonard, 36 Or. 390, after a review of the various statutes of the state upon the subject:

> We may therefore say with perfect confidence that, with these three sections upon the statute book, the wife can deal, not only with her separate property, acquired from whatever source, in the same manner as her husband can with property belonging to him, but that she may make contracts and incur liabilities, and the same may be enforced against her, the same as if she were a feme sole. There is now no residuum of civil disability resting upon her which is not recognized as existing against the husband. The current runs steadily and strongly in the direction of the emancipation of the wife, and the policy, as disclosed by all recent legislation upon the subject in this state, is to place her upon the same footing as if she were a feme sole, not only with respect to her separate property, but as it affects her right to make binding contracts; and the most natural corollary to the situation is that the remedies for the enforcement of liabilities incurred are made coextensive and coequal with such enlarged conditions.

It thus appears that, putting to one side the elective franchise, in the matter of personal and contractual rights they stand on the same plane as the other sex. Their rights in these respects can no more be infringed than the equal rights of their brothers. We held in Lochner v. New York, 198 U.S. 45, that a law providing that no laborer shall be required or permitted to work in bakeries more than sixty hours in a week or ten hours in a day was not as to men a legitimate exercise of the police power of the state, but an unreasonable, unnecessary, and arbitrary interference with the right and liberty of the individual to contract in relation to his labor, and as such was in conflict with, and void under, the Federal Constitution. That decision is invoked by plaintiff in error as decisive of the question before us. But this assumes that the difference between the sexes does not justify a different rule respecting a restriction of the hours of labor.

In patent cases counsel are apt to open the argument with a discussion of the state of the art. It may not be amiss, in the present case, before examining the constitutional question, to notice the course of legislation, as well as expressions of opinion from other than judicial sources. In the brief filed by Mr. Louis D. Brandeis for the defendant in error is a very copious collection of all these matters.

The legislation and opinions referred to in the margin may not be, technically speaking, authorities, and in them is little or no discussion of the constitutional question presented to us for determination, yet they are significant of a widespread belief that woman's physical structure, and the functions she performs in consequence thereof, justify special legislation restricting or qualifying the conditions under which she should be permitted to toil. Constitutional questions, it is true, are not settled by even a consensus of present public opinion, for it is the peculiar value of a written constitution that it places in unchanging form limitations upon legislative action, and thus gives a permanence and stability to popular government which otherwise would be lacking. At the same time, when a question of fact is debated and debatable, and the extent to which a special constitutional limitation goes is affected by the truth in respect to that fact, a widespread and longcontinued belief concerning it is worthy of consideration. We take judicial cognizance of all matters of general knowledge.

It is undoubtedly true, as more than once declared by this court, that the general right to contract in relation to one's business is part of the liberty of the individual, protected by the 14th Amendment to the Federal Constitution; yet it is equally well settled that this liberty is not absolute and extending to all contracts, and that a state may, without conflicting with the provisions of the 14th Amendment, restrict in many respects the individual's power of contract.

That woman's physical structure and the performance of maternal functions place her at a disadvantage in the struggle for subsistence is obvious. This is especially true when the burdens of motherhood are upon her. Even when they are not, by abundant testimony of the medical fraternity continuance for a long time on her feet at work, repeating this from day to day, tends to injurious effects upon the body, and, as healthy mothers are essential to vigorous offspring, the physical well-being of woman becomes an object of public interest and care in order to preserve the strength and vigor of the race.

Still again, history discloses the fact that woman has always been dependent upon man. He established his control at the outset by superior physical strength, may, without conflicting with the provisions and this control in various forms, with diminishing intensity, has continued to the present. As minors, thought not to the same extent, she has been looked upon in the courts as needing especial care that her rights may be preserved. Education was long denied her, and while now the doors of the schoolroom are opened and her opportunities for acquiring knowledge are great, yet even with that and the consequent increase of capacity for business affairs it is still true that in the struggle for subsistence she is not an equal competitor with her brother. Though limitations upon personal and contractual rights may be removed by legislation, there is that in her disposition and habits of life which will operate against a full assertion of those rights. She will still be where some legislation to protect her seems necessary to secure a real equality of right. Doubtless there are individual exceptions, and there are many respects in which she has an advantage over him; but looking at it from the viewpoint of the effort to maintain an independent position in life, she is not upon an equality. Differentiated by these matters from the other sex, she is properly placed in a class by herself, and legislation designed for her protection may be sustained, even when like legislation is not necessary for men, and could not be sustained. It is impossible to close one's eyes to the fact that she still looks to her brother and depends upon him. Even though all restrictions on political, personal, and contractual rights were taken away, and she stood, so far as statutes are concerned, upon an absolutely equal plane with him, it would still be true that she is so constituted that she will rest upon and look to him for protection; that her physical structure and a proper discharge of her maternal functions—having in view not merely her own health, but the well-being of the race—justify legislation to protect her from the greed as well as the passion of man. The limitations which this statute places upon her contractual powers, upon her right to agree with her employer as to the time she shall labor, are not imposed solely for her benefit, but also largely for the benefit of all. Many words cannot make this plainer. The two sexes differ in structure of body, in the functions to be performed by each, in the amount of physical strength, in the capacity for long continued labor, particularly when done standing, the influence of vigorous health upon the future well-being of the race, the self-reliance which enables one to assert full rights, and in the capacity to maintain the struggle for subsistence. This difference justifies a difference in legislation, and upholds that which is designed to compensate for some of the burdens which rest upon her.

We have not referred in this discussion to the denial of the elective franchise in the state of Oregon, for while that may disclose a lack of political equality in all things with her brother, that is not of itself decisive. The reason runs deeper, and rests in the inherent difference between the two sexes, and in the different functions in life which they perform.

For these reasons, and without questioning in any respect the decision in Lochner v. New York, we are of the opinion that it cannot be adjudged that the act in question is in conflict with the Federal Constitution, so far as it respects the work of a female in a laundry, and the judgment of the Supreme Court of Oregon is affirmed.

FRONTIERO V. RICHARDSON
411 U.S. 677 (1973)

"There can be no doubt that our Nation has had a long and unfortunate history of sex discrimination. Traditionally, such discrimination was rationalized by an attitude of "romantic paternalism" which, in practical effect, put women not on a pedestal but in a cage."

The Question: Can the Congress pass a law that permits a male member of the armed services to claim his wife as a "dependent" in order to obtain increased housing allowances and medical and dental benefits, whether or not she depends on him for any financial support, while a female service member may not claim her husband unless she provides more than half of his support?

The Arguments: PRO

In providing benefits to members of the military services, Congress has the power to create different classes of beneficiaries and different qualification rules for these benefits. As a general principle, promoting the ease of administration is a legitimate reason for establishing such different classes and procedures. Congress could have decided that requiring every applicant for benefits, most of whom are males, to provide evidence that his spouse depends on him for more than half of her support would increase the administrative burden. In addition, the husbands of female service members are less likely to depend on their wife for support, and requiring a showing of support is reasonable.

CON

There is simply no "rational basis" for a regulation that imposes greater burdens on women than on men, without any showing that women in fact are less likely to qualify for benefits than men. Laws that discriminate against women should be subject to the same "strict scrutiny" test as those directed against members of racial and religious minorities. The government cannot rely on an unsupported claim of "administrative ease" to justify a requirement that should apply equally to men or women.

MR. JUSTICE BRENNAN announced the judgment of the Court and an opinion in which MR. JUSTICE DOUGLAS, MR. JUSTICE WHITE, and MR. JUSTICE MARSHALL join.

The question before us concerns the right of a female member of the uniformed services to claim her spouse as a "dependent" for the purposes of obtaining increased quarters allowances and medical and dental benefits under [federal law], on an equal footing with male members. Under these statutes, a serviceman may claim his wife as a "dependent" without regard to whether she is in fact dependent upon him for any part of her support. A servicewoman, on the other hand, may not claim her husband as a "dependent" under these programs unless he is in fact dependent upon her for over one-half of his support. Thus, the question for decision is whether this difference in treatment constitutes an unconstitutional discrimination against servicewomen in violation of the Due Process Clause of the Fifth Amendment. A three-judge District Court for the Middle District of Alabama, one judge dissenting, rejected this contention and sustained the constitutionality of the provisions of the statutes making this distinction. We noted probable jurisdiction.

In an effort to attract career personnel through reenlistment, Congress established a scheme for the provision of fringe benefits to members of the uniformed services on a competitive basis with business and industry. Thus, a member of the uniformed services with dependents is entitled to an increased "basic allowance for quarters" and a member's dependents are provided comprehensive medical and dental care.

Appellant Sharron Frontiero, a lieutenant in the United States Air Force, sought increased quarters allowances, and housing and medical benefits for her husband, appellant Joseph Frontiero, on the ground that he was her "dependent." Although such benefits would automatically have been granted with respect to the wife of a male member of the uniformed services, appellant's application was denied because she failed to demonstrate that her husband was dependent on her for more than one-half of his support. Appellants then commenced this suit, contending that, by making this distinction, the statutes unreasonably discriminate on the basis of sex in violation of the Due Process Clause of the Fifth Amendment. In essence, appellants asserted that the discriminatory impact of the statutes is twofold: first, as a procedural matter, a female member is required to demonstrate her spouse's dependency, while no such burden is imposed upon male members; and, second, as a substantive matter, a male member who does not provide more than one-half of his wife's support receives benefits, while a similarly situated female member is denied such benefits. Appellants therefore sought a permanent injunction against the continued enforcement of these statutes and an order directing the appellees to provide Lieutenant Frontiero with the same housing and medical benefits that a similarly situated male member would receive. . . .

At the outset, appellants contend that classifications based upon sex, like classifications based upon race, alienage, and national origin, are inherently suspect and must therefore be subjected to close judicial scrutiny. We agree and, indeed, find at least implicit support for such an approach in our unanimous decision only last Term in Reed v. Reed (1971). In Reed, the Court considered the constitutionality of an Idaho statute providing that, when two individuals are otherwise equally entitled to appointment as administrator of an estate, the male applicant must be preferred to the female. Appellant, the mother of the deceased, and appellee, the father, filed competing petitions for appointment as administrator of their son's estate. Since the parties, as parents of the deceased, were members of the same entitlement class, the statutory preference was invoked and the father's petition was therefore granted. Appellant claimed that this statute, by giving a mandatory preference to males over females without regard to their individual qualifications, violated the Equal Protection Clause of the Fourteenth Amendment.

The Court noted that the Idaho statute "provides that different treatment be accorded to the applicants on the basis of their sex; it thus establishes a classification subject to scrutiny under the Equal Protection Clause." Under "traditional" equal protection analysis, a legislative classification must be sustained unless it is "patently arbitrary" and bears no rational relationship to a legitimate governmental interest. In an effort to meet this standard, appellee contended that the statutory scheme was a reasonable measure designed to reduce the workload on probate courts by eliminating one class of contests. Moreover, appellee argued that the mandatory preference for male applicants was in itself reasonable since "men [are] as a rule more conversant with business affairs than . . . women." Indeed, appellee maintained that "it is a matter of common knowledge, that women still are not engaged in politics, the professions, business or industry to the extent that men are." . . . Despite these contentions, however, the Court held the statutory preference for male applicants unconstitutional. In reaching this result, the Court implicitly rejected appellee's apparently rational explanation of the statutory scheme, and concluded that, by ignoring the individual qualifications of particular applicants, the challenged statute provided "dissimilar treatment for men and women who are . . . similarly situated." The Court therefore held that, even though the State's interest in achieving administrative efficiency "is not without some legitimacy," "[t]o give a mandatory preference to members of either sex over members of the other, merely to accomplish the elimination of hearings on the merits, is to make the very kind of arbitrary legislative choice forbidden by the [Constitution]. . . ." This departure from "traditional" rational-basis analysis with respect to sex-based classifications is clearly justified.

There can be no doubt that our Nation has had a long and unfortunate history of sex discrimination. Traditionally, such discrimination was rationalized by an attitude of "romantic paternalism" which, in practical effect, put women, not on a pedestal, but in a cage. Indeed, this paternalistic attitude became so firmly rooted in our national consciousness that, 100 years ago, a distinguished Member of this Court was able to proclaim: "Man is, or should be, woman's protector and defender. The natural and proper timidity and delicacy which belongs to the female sex evidently unfits it for many of the occupations of civil life. The constitution of the family organization, which is founded in the divine ordinance, as well as in the nature of things, indicates the domestic sphere as that which properly belongs to the domain and functions of womanhood. The harmony, not to say identity, of interests and views which belong, or should belong, to the family institution is repugnant to the idea of a woman adopting a distinct and independent career from that of her husband. . . . The paramount destiny and mission of woman are to fulfill the noble and benign offices of wife and mother. This is the law of the Creator." Bradwell v. State (1873) (Bradley, J., concurring).

As a result of notions such as these, our statute books gradually became laden with gross, stereotyped distinctions between the sexes and, indeed, throughout much of the 19th century the position of women in our society was, in many respects, comparable to that of blacks under the pre–Civil War slave codes. Neither slaves nor women could hold office, serve on juries, or bring suit in their own names, and married women traditionally were denied the legal capacity to hold or convey property or to serve as legal guardians of their own children. And although blacks were guaranteed the right to vote in 1870, women were denied even that right—which is itself "preservative of other basic civil and political rights"—until adoption of the Nineteenth Amendment half a century later.

It is true, of course, that the position of women in America has improved markedly in recent decades. Nevertheless, it can hardly be doubted that, in part because of the high visibility of the sex characteristic, women still face pervasive, although at times more subtle, discrimination in our educational institutions, in the job market and, perhaps most conspicuously, in the political arena. Moreover, since sex, like race and national origin, is an immutable characteristic determined solely by the accident of birth, the imposition of special disabilities upon the members of a particular sex because of their sex would seem to violate "the basic concept of our system that legal burdens should bear some relationship to individual responsibility. . . ." And what differentiates sex from such nonsuspect statuses as intelligence or physical disability, and aligns it with the recognized suspect criteria, is that the sex characteristic frequently bears no relation to ability to perform or contribute to society. As a result, statutory distinctions between the sexes often have the effect of invidiously relegating the entire class of females to inferior legal status without regard to the actual capabilities of its individual members.

We might also note that, over the past decade, Congress has itself manifested an increasing sensitivity to sex-based classifications. In Title VII of the Civil Rights Act of 1964, for example, Congress expressly declared that no employer, labor union, or other organization subject to the provisions of the Act shall discriminate against any individual on the basis of "race, color, religion, sex, or national origin." Similarly, the Equal Pay Act of 1963 provides that no employer covered by the Act "shall discriminate . . . between employees on the basis of sex." And the Equal Rights Amendment, passed by Congress on March 22, 1972, and submitted to the legislatures of the States for ratification, declares that "[e]quality of rights under the law shall not be denied or abridged by the United States or by any State on account of sex." Thus, Congress itself has concluded that classifications based upon sex are inherently invidious, and this conclusion of a coequal branch of Government is not without significance to the question presently under consideration.

With these considerations in mind, we can only conclude that classifications based upon sex, like classifications based upon race, alienage, or national origin, are inherently suspect, and must therefore be subjected to strict judicial scrutiny. Applying the analysis mandated by that stricter standard of review, it is clear that the statutory scheme now before us is constitutionally invalid.

The sole basis of the classification established in the challenged statutes is the sex of the individuals involved. Thus, a female member of the uniformed services seeking to obtain housing and medical benefits for her spouse must prove his dependency in fact, whereas no such burden is imposed upon male members. In addition, the statutes operate so as to deny benefits to a female member, such as appellant Sharron Frontiero, who provides less than one-half of her spouse's support, while at the same time granting such benefits to a male member who likewise provides less than one-half of his spouse's support. Thus, to this extent at least, it may fairly be said that these statutes command "dissimilar treatment for men and women who are . . . similarly situated." Reed v. Reed.

Moreover, the Government concedes that the differential treatment accorded men and women under these statutes serves no purpose other than mere "administrative convenience." In essence, the Government maintains that, as an empirical matter, wives in our society frequently are dependent upon their husbands, while husbands rarely are dependent upon their wives. Thus, the Government argues that Congress might reasonably have concluded that it would be both cheaper and easier simply conclusively to presume that wives of male members are financially dependent upon their husbands, while burdening female members with the task of establishing dependency in fact. The Government offers no concrete evidence, however, tending to support its view that such differential treatment in fact saves the Government any money. In order to satisfy the demands of strict judicial scrutiny, the Government must demonstrate, for example, that it is actually cheaper to grant increased benefits with respect to all male members, than it is to determine which male members are in fact entitled to such benefits and to grant increased benefits only to those members whose wives actually meet the dependency requirement. Here, however, there is substantial evidence that, if put to the test, many of the wives of male members would fail to qualify for benefits. And in light of the fact that the dependency determination with respect to the husbands of female members is presently made solely on the basis of affidavits, rather than through the more costly hearing process, the Government's explanation of the statutory scheme is, to say the least, questionable.

In any case, our prior decisions make clear that, although efficacious administration of governmental programs is not without some importance, "the Constitution recognizes higher values than speed and efficiency. And when we enter the realm of "strict judicial scrutiny," there can be no doubt that "administrative convenience" is not a shibboleth, the mere recitation of which dictates constitutionality. On the contrary, any statutory scheme which draws a sharp line between the sexes, solely for the purpose of achieving administrative convenience, necessarily commands "dissimilar treatment for men and women who are . . . similarly situated," and therefore involves the "very kind of arbitrary legislative choice forbidden by the [Constitution]. . . ." We therefore conclude that, by according differential treatment to male and female members of the uniformed services for the sole purpose of achieving administrative convenience, the challenged statutes violate the Due Process Clause of the Fifth Amendment insofar as they require a female member to prove the dependency of her husband.

Reversed.

MR. JUSTICE POWELL, with whom THE CHIEF JUSTICE and MR. JUSTICE BLACKMUN join, concurring in the judgment.

I agree that the challenged statutes constitute an unconstitutional discrimination against servicewomen in violation of the Due Process Clause of the Fifth Amendment, but I cannot join the opinion of Mr. Justice Brennan, which would hold that all classifications based upon sex, "like classifications based upon race, alienage, and national origin," are "inherently suspect and must therefore be subjected to close judicial scrutiny." It is unnecessary for the Court in this case to characterize sex as a suspect classification, with all of the far-reaching implications of such a holding. Reed v. Reed, which abundantly supports our decision today, did not add sex to the narrowly limited group of classifications which are inherently suspect. In my view, we can and should decide this case on the authority of Reed and reserve for the future any expansion of its rationale.

There is another, and I find compelling, reason for deferring a general categorizing of sex classifications as invoking the strictest test of judicial scrutiny. The Equal Rights Amendment, which if adopted will resolve the substance of this precise question, has been approved by the Congress and submitted for ratification by the States. If this Amendment is duly adopted, it will represent the will of the people accomplished in the manner prescribed by the Constitution. By acting prematurely and unnecessarily, as I view it, the Court has assumed a decisional responsibility at the very time when state legislatures, functioning within the traditional democratic process, are debating the proposed Amendment. It seems to me that this reaching out to preempt by judicial action a major political decision which is currently in process of resolution does not reflect appropriate respect for duly prescribed legislative processes.

There are times when this Court, under our system, cannot avoid a constitutional decision on issues which normally should be resolved by the elected representatives of the people. But democratic institutions are weakened, and confidence in the restraint of the Court is impaired, when we appear unnecessarily to decide sensitive issues of broad social and political importance at the very time they are under consideration within the prescribed constitutional processes.

ROBERTS V. UNITED STATES JAYCEES
468 U.S. 609 (1984)

"The undisputed facts reveal that the local chapters of the Jaycees are large and basically unselective groups. The Jaycees already invites women to share the group's views and philosophy and to participate in much of its training and community activities. . . . Any claim that admission of women as full voting members will impair a symbolic message conveyed by the fact that women are not permitted to vote is attenuated at best."

The Question: Can a state apply its antidiscrimination law to force a private organization to admit women as members, on the ground that the organization is a "place of public accommodation" and cannot discriminate on the basis of gender?

The Arguments: PRO

In this case, the Minneapolis and St. Paul chapters of the United States Jaycees (formerly the Junior Chamber of Commerce) began admitting women as full members, despite the national organization's rule that women could only join as associate members, without voting rights. The national group threatened the two chapters with expulsion if they did not change their policies. There are no qualifications for Jaycees membership except paying dues, and no reason that women cannot (as they do in these two chapters) fully participate and even hold office. Because membership is open, the Jaycees are a "place of public accommodation" and subject to the state's antidiscrimination law.

CON

Forcing private organizations that limit their membership to one gender, whether male or female, to admit members of both genders threatens the freedom of association that is protected by the Constitution. The fact that the Jaycees do not require applicants for membership to take qualifying tests or demonstrate special skills does not make its chapters "places of public accommodation" like hotels and restaurants. To illustrate the problem, would the state require the Girl Scouts to admit boys as full members and the Boy Scouts to admit girls? The Jaycees was founded to provide "young men" with business experience and fellowship, and has the right to continue that policy and tradition.

JUSTICE BRENNAN delivered the opinion of the Court.

This case requires us to address a conflict between a State's efforts to eliminate gender-based discrimination against its citizens and the constitutional freedom of association asserted by members of a private organization. In the decision under review, the Court of Appeals for the Eighth Circuit concluded that, by requiring the United States Jaycees to admit women as full voting members, the Minnesota Human Rights Act violates the First and Fourteenth Amendment rights of the organization's members. We noted probable jurisdiction, and now reverse.

The United States Jaycees (Jaycees), founded in 1920 as the Junior Chamber of Commerce, is a nonprofit membership corporation, incorporated in Missouri with national headquarters in Tulsa, Okla. The objective of the Jaycees, as set out in its bylaws, is to pursue "such educational and charitable purposes as will promote and foster the growth and development of young men's civic organizations in the United States [and] to provide them with opportunity for personal development and achievement and an avenue for intelligent participation by young men in the affairs of their community, state and nation, and to develop true friendship and understanding among young men of all nations."

The organization's bylaws establish seven classes of membership, including individual or regular members, associate individual members, and local chapters. Regular membership is limited to young men between the ages of 18 and 35, while associate membership is available to individuals or groups ineligible for regular membership, principally women and older men. An associate member, whose dues are somewhat lower than those charged regular members, may not vote, hold local or national office, or participate in certain leadership training and awards programs. The bylaws define a local chapter as "[a]ny young men's organization of good repute existing in any community within the United States, organized for purposes similar to and consistent with those" of the national organization. The ultimate policy-making authority of the Jaycees rests with an annual national convention, consisting of delegates from each local chapter, with a national president and board of directors. At the time of trial in August 1981, the Jaycees had approximately 295,000 members in 7,400 local chapters affiliated with 51 state organizations. There were at that time about 11,915 associate members. The national organization's executive vice president estimated at trial that women associate members make up about two percent of the Jaycees' total membership. . . .

In 1974 and 1975, respectively, the Minneapolis and St. Paul chapters of the Jaycees began admitting women as regular members. Currently, the memberships and boards of directors of both chapters include a substantial proportion of women. As a result, the two chapters have been in violation of the national organization's bylaws for about 10 years. The national organization has imposed a number of sanctions on the Minneapolis and St. Paul chapters for violating the bylaws, including denying their members eligibility for state or national office or awards programs, and refusing to count their membership in computing votes at national conventions.

In December 1978, the president of the national organization advised both chapters that a motion to revoke their charters would be considered at a forthcoming meeting of the national board of directors in Tulsa. Shortly after receiving this notification, members of both chapters filed charges of discrimination with the Minnesota Department of Human Rights. The complaints alleged that the exclusion of women from full membership required by the national organization's bylaws violated the Minnesota Human Rights Act, which provides in part: "It is an unfair discriminatory practice: "To deny any person the full and equal enjoyment of the goods, services, facilities, privileges, advantages, and accommodations of a place of public accommodation because of race, color, creed, religion, disability, national origin or sex." The term "place of public accommodation" is defined in the Act as "a business, accommodation, refreshment, entertainment, recreation, or transportation facility of any kind, whether licensed or not, whose goods, services, facilities, privileges, advantages or accommodations are extended, offered, sold, or otherwise made available to the public."

After an investigation, the Commissioner of the Minnesota Department of Human Rights found probable cause to believe that the sanctions imposed on the local chapters by the national organization violated the statute and ordered that an evidentiary hearing be held before a state hearing examiner. . . . The examiner concluded that the Jaycees organization is a "place of public accommodation" within the Act and that it had engaged in an unfair discriminatory practice by excluding women from regular membership. He ordered the national organization to cease and desist from discriminating against any member or applicant for membership on the basis of sex and from imposing sanctions on any Minnesota affiliate for admitting women. . . . With the record of the administrative hearing before it, the Minnesota Supreme Court . . . concluded that the Jaycees organization (a) is a "business" in that it sells goods and extends privileges in exchange for annual membership dues; (b) is a "public" business in that it solicits and recruits dues-paying members based on unselective criteria; and (c) is a public business "facility" in that it conducts its activities at fixed and mobile sites within the State of Minnesota. . . .

Our decisions have referred to constitutionally protected "freedom of association" in two distinct senses. In one line of decisions, the Court has concluded that choices to enter into and maintain certain intimate human relationships must be secured against undue intrusion by the State because of the role of such relationships in safeguarding the individual freedom that is central to our constitutional scheme. In this respect, freedom of association receives protection as a fundamental element of personal liberty. In another set of decisions, the Court has recognized a right to associate for the purpose of engaging in those activities protected by the First Amendment—speech, assembly, petition for the redress of grievances, and the exercise of religion. The Constitution guarantees freedom of association of this kind as an indispensable means of preserving other individual liberties.

The intrinsic and instrumental features of constitutionally protected association may, of course, coincide. In particular, when the State interferes with individuals' selection of those with whom they wish to join in a common endeavor, freedom of association in both of its forms may be implicated. The Jaycees contend that this is such a case. Still, the nature and degree of constitutional protection afforded freedom of association may vary depending on the extent to which one or the other aspect of the constitutionally protected liberty is at stake in a given case. We therefore find it useful to consider separately the effect of applying the Minnesota statute to the Jaycees on what could be called its members' freedom of intimate association and their freedom of expressive association.

The Court has long recognized that, because the Bill of Rights is designed to secure individual liberty, it must afford the formation and preservation of certain kinds of highly personal relationships a substantial measure of sanctuary from unjustified interference by the State. Without precisely identifying every consideration that may underlie this type of constitutional protection, we have noted that certain kinds of personal bonds have played a critical role in the culture and traditions of the Nation by cultivating and transmitting shared ideals and beliefs; they thereby foster diversity and act as critical buffers between the individual and the power of the State. Moreover, the constitutional shelter afforded such relationships reflects the realization that individuals draw much of their emotional enrichment from close ties with others. Protecting these relationships from unwarranted state interference therefore safeguards the ability independently to define one's identity that is central to any concept of liberty.

The personal affiliations that exemplify these considerations, and that therefore suggest some relevant limitations on the relationships that might be entitled to this sort of constitutional protection, are those that attend the creation and sustenance of a family—marriage, childbirth, the raising and education of children, and cohabitation with one's relatives. Family relationships, by their nature, involve deep attachments and commitments to the necessarily few other individuals with whom one shares not only a special community of thoughts, experiences, and beliefs but also distinctively personal aspects of one's life. Among other things, therefore, they are distinguished by such attributes as relative smallness, a high degree of selectivity in decisions to begin and maintain the affiliation, and seclusion from others in critical aspects of the relationship. As a general matter, only relationships with these sorts of qualities are likely to reflect the considerations that have led to an understanding of freedom of association as an intrinsic element of personal liberty. Conversely, an association lacking these qualities—such as a large business enterprise—seems remote from the concerns giving rise to this constitutional protection. Accordingly, the Constitution undoubtedly imposes constraints on the State's power to control the selection of one's spouse that would not apply to regulations affecting the choice of one's fellow employees.

Between these poles, of course, lies a broad range of human relationships that may make greater or lesser claims to constitutional protection from particular incursions by the State. Determining the limits of state authority over an individual's freedom to enter into a particular association therefore unavoidably entails a careful assessment of where that relationship's objective characteristics locate it on a spectrum from the most intimate to the most attenuated of personal attachments. We need not mark the potentially significant points on this terrain with any precision. We note only that factors that may be relevant include size, purpose, policies, selectivity, congeniality, and other characteristics that in a particular case may be pertinent. In this case, however, several features of the Jaycees clearly place the organization outside of the category of relationships worthy of this kind of constitutional protection.

The undisputed facts reveal that the local chapters of the Jaycees are large and basically unselective groups. At the time of the state administrative hearing, the Minneapolis chapter had approximately 430 members, while the St. Paul chapter had about 400. Apart from age and sex, neither the national organization nor the local chapters employ any criteria for judging applicants for membership, and new members are routinely recruited and admitted with no inquiry into their backgrounds. In fact, a local officer testified that he could recall no instance in which an applicant had been denied membership on any basis other than age or sex. Furthermore, despite their inability to vote, hold office, or receive certain awards, women affiliated with the Jaycees attend various meetings, participate in selected projects, and engage in many of the organization's social functions. Indeed, numerous nonmembers of both genders regularly participate in a substantial portion of activities central to the decision of many members to associate with one another, including many of the organization's various community programs, awards ceremonies, and recruitment meetings.

In short, the local chapters of the Jaycees are neither small nor selective. Moreover, much of the activity central to the formation and maintenance of the association involves the participation of strangers to that relationship. Accordingly, we conclude that the Jaycees chapters lack the distinctive characteristics that might afford constitutional protection to the decision of its members to exclude women. We turn therefore to consider the extent to which application of the Minnesota statute to compel the Jaycees to accept women infringes the group's freedom of expressive association.

An individual's freedom to speak, to worship, and to petition the government for the redress of grievances could not be vigorously protected from interference by the State unless a correlative freedom to engage in group effort toward those ends were not also guaranteed. According protection to collective effort on behalf of shared goals is especially important in preserving political and cultural diversity and in shielding dissident expression from suppression by the majority. Consequently, we have long understood as implicit in the right to engage in activities protected by the First Amendment a corresponding right to associate with others in pursuit of a wide variety of political, social, economic, educational, religious, and cultural ends. In view of the various protected activities in which the Jaycees engages, that right is plainly implicated in this case.

Government actions that may unconstitutionally infringe upon this freedom can take a number of forms. Among other things, government may seek to impose penalties or withhold benefits from individuals because of their membership in a disfavored group; it may attempt to require disclosure of the fact of membership in a group seeking anonymity; and it may try to interfere with the internal organization or affairs of the group. By requiring the Jaycees to admit women as full voting members, the Minnesota Act works an infringement of the last type. There can be no clearer example of an intrusion into the internal structure or affairs of an association than a regulation that forces the group to accept members it does not desire. Such a regulation may impair the ability of the original members to express only those views that brought them together. Freedom of association therefore plainly presupposes a freedom not to associate.

The right to associate for expressive purposes is not, however, absolute. Infringements on that right may be justified by regulations adopted to serve compelling state interests, unrelated to the suppression of ideas, that cannot be achieved through means significantly less restrictive of associational freedoms. We are persuaded that Minnesota's compelling interest in eradicating discrimination against its female citizens justifies the impact that application of the statute to the Jaycees may have on the male members' associational freedoms.

On its face, the Minnesota Act does not aim at the suppression of speech, does not distinguish between prohibited and permitted activity on the basis of viewpoint, and does not license enforcement authorities to administer the statute on the basis of such constitutionally impressible criteria. Nor does the Jaycees contend that the Act has been applied in this case for the purpose of hampering the organization's ability to express its views. Instead, as the Minnesota Supreme Court explained, the Act reflects the State's strong historical commitment to eliminating discrimination and assuring its citizens equal access to publicly available goods and services. That goal, which is unrelated to the suppression of expression, plainly serves compelling state interests of the highest order. . . .

By prohibiting gender discrimination in places of public accommodation, the Minnesota Act protects the State's citizenry from a number of serious social and personal harms. In the context of reviewing state actions under the Equal Protection Clause, this Court has frequently noted that discrimination based on archaic and overbroad assumptions about the relative needs and capacities of the sexes forces individuals to labor under stereotypical notions that often bear no relationship to their actual abilities. It thereby both deprives persons of their individual dignity and denies society the benefits of wide participation in political, economic, and cultural life. . . . Like many States and municipalities, Minnesota has adopted a functional definition of public accommodations that reaches various forms of public, quasi-commercial conduct. This expansive definition reflects a recognition of the changing nature of the American economy and of the importance, both to the individual and to society, of removing the barriers to economic advancement and political and social integration that have historically plagued certain disadvantaged groups, including women. . . .

In applying the Act to the Jaycees, the State has advanced those interests through the least restrictive means of achieving its ends. Indeed, the Jaycees has failed to demonstrate that the Act imposes any serious burdens on the male members' freedom of expressive association. . . . Over the years, the national and local levels of the organization have taken public positions on a number of diverse issues, and members of the Jaycees regularly engage in a variety of civic, charitable, lobbying, fundraising, and other activities worthy of constitutional protection under the First Amendment. There is, however, no basis in the record for concluding that admission of women as full voting members will impede the organization's ability to engage in these protected activities or to disseminate its preferred views. The Act requires no change in the Jaycees' creed of promoting the interests of young men, and it imposes no restrictions on the organization's ability to exclude individuals with ideologies or philosophies different from those of its existing members. Moreover, the Jaycees already invites women to share the group's views and philosophy and to participate in much of its training and community activities. Accordingly, any claim that admission of women as full voting members will impair a symbolic message conveyed by the very fact that women are not permitted to vote is attenuated at best. . . .

The judgment of the Court of Appeals is reversed.

UNITED STATES V. VIRGINIA
518 U.S. 515 (1996)

"[The Virginia Military Institute] is today the sole single-sex school among Virginia's 15 public institutions of higher learning. . . . VMI constantly endeavors to instill physical and mental discipline in its cadets and impart to them a strong moral code. . . . Neither the goal of producing citizen-soldiers nor VMI's implementing methodology is inherently unsuitable to women."

The Question: Can the state of Virginia deny admission to women at the Virginia Military Institute (VMI), a state-funded college, on the ground that women cannot adapt to VMI's "adversative" program of education?

The Arguments: PRO

VMI was established in 1839 to train "citizen-soldiers," and uses an "adversative" program of education that includes the "rat line" in which upperclassmen torment and harass first-year students as a means of instilling discipline and obedience, and promoting bonding between students. It is highly likely that women could not adapt to this stressful and physically demanding program. VMI is the only single-sex college among Virginia's 15 public institutions of higher learning, and there is no good reason to require that every state college be coeducational.

CON

The record in this case includes no evidence that women cannot successfully complete the VMI program of "adversative" education. A hard-and-fast rule that women cannot be admitted to VMI not only continues the sexual stereotypes of the school's nineteenth-century founders but also makes it impossible for women to challenge that stereotype by sharing a VMI education with male students. The state's claim that maintaining a single-sex public college fosters "diversity" in educational choices is unpersuasive, especially since there is no diversity of gender at VMI.

JUSTICE GINSBURG delivered the opinion of the Court.

Virginia's public institutions of higher learning include an incomparable military college, Virginia Military Institute (VMI). The United States maintains that the Constitution's equal protection guarantee precludes Virginia from reserving exclusively to men the unique educational opportunities VMI affords. We agree.

Founded in 1839, VMI is today the sole single-sex school among Virginia's 15 public institutions of higher learning. VMI's distinctive mission is to produce "citizen-soldiers," men prepared for leadership in civilian life and in military service. VMI pursues this mission through pervasive training of a kind not available anywhere else in Virginia. Assigning prime place to character development, VMI uses an "adversative method" modeled on English public schools and once characteristic of military instruction. VMI constantly endeavors to instill physical and mental discipline in its cadets and impart to them a strong moral code. The school's graduates leave VMI with heightened comprehension of their capacity to deal with duress and stress, and a large sense of accomplishment for completing the hazardous course. . . . Neither the goal of producing citizen-soldiers nor VMI's implementing methodology is inherently unsuitable to women. And the school's impressive record in producing leaders has made admission desirable to some women. Nevertheless, Virginia has elected to preserve exclusively for men the advantages and opportunities a VMI education affords. . . .

VMI today enrolls about 1,300 men as cadets. Its academic offerings in the liberal arts, sciences, and engineering are also available at other public colleges and universities in Virginia. But VMI's mission is special. It is the mission of the school "to produce educated and honorable men, prepared for the varied work of civil life, imbued with love of learning, confident in the functions and attitudes of leadership, possessing a high sense of public service, advocates of the American democracy and free enterprise system, and ready as citizen-soldiers to defend their country in time of national peril." . . . VMI cadets live in spartan barracks where surveillance is constant and privacy nonexistent; they wear uniforms, eat together in the mess hall, and regularly participate in drills. Entering students are incessantly exposed to the rat line, "an extreme form of the adversative model," comparable in intensity to Marine Corps boot camp. Tormenting and punishing, the rat line bonds new cadets to their fellow sufferers and, when they have completed the 7-month experience, to their former tormentors. . . .

In 1990, prompted by a complaint filed with the Attorney General by a female high-school student seeking admission to VMI, the United States sued the Commonwealth of Virginia and VMI, alleging that VMI's exclusively male admission policy violated the Equal Protection Clause of the Fourteenth Amendment. . . . In the two years preceding the lawsuit, the District Court noted, VMI had received inquiries from 347 women, but had responded to none of them. "[S]ome women, at least," the court said, "would want to attend the school if they had the opportunity." The court further recognized that, with recruitment, VMI could "achieve at least 10% female enrollment"—"a sufficient 'critical mass' to provide the female cadets with a positive educational experience." And it was also established that "some women are capable of all of the individual activities required of VMI cadets." In addition, experts agreed that if VMI admitted women, "the VMI ROTC experience would become a better training program from the perspective of the armed forces, because it would provide training in dealing with a mixed-gender army."

The District Court ruled in favor of VMI, however, and rejected the equal protection challenge pressed by the United States. . . . The District Court reasoned that education in "a single-gender environment, be it male or female," yields substantial benefits. VMI's school for men brought diversity to an otherwise coeducational Virginia system, and that diversity was "enhanced by VMI's unique method of instruction." If single-gender education for males ranks as an important governmental objective, it becomes obvious, the District Court concluded, that the only means of achieving the objective "is to exclude women from the all-male institution—VMI." . . . The Court of Appeals for the Fourth Circuit disagreed and vacated the District Court's judgment. The appellate court held: "The Commonwealth of Virginia has not . . . advanced any state policy by which it can justify its determination, under an announced policy of diversity, to afford VMI's unique type of program to men and not to women."

[T]his case presents two ultimate issues. First, does Virginia's exclusion of women from the educational opportunities provided by VMI—extraordinary opportunities for military training and civilian leadership development—deny to women "capable of all of the individual activities required of VMI cadets," the equal protection of the laws guaranteed by the Fourteenth Amendment? Second, if VMI's "unique" situation as Virginia's sole single-sex public institution of higher education offends the Constitution's equal protection principle, what is the remedial requirement? . . .

Parties who seek to defend gender-based government action must demonstrate an "exceedingly persuasive justification" for that action. Today's skeptical scrutiny of official action denying rights or opportunities based on sex responds to volumes of history. As a plurality of this Court acknowledged a generation ago, "our Nation has had a long and unfortunate history of sex discrimination." Frontiero v. Richardson (1973). Through a century plus three decades and more of that history, women did not count among voters composing "We the People"; not until 1920 did women gain a constitutional right to the franchise. And for a half century thereafter, it remained the prevailing doctrine that government, both federal and state, could withhold from women opportunities accorded men so long as any "basis in reason" could be conceived for the discrimination. . . .

In 1971, for the first time in our Nation's history, this Court ruled in favor of a woman who complained that her State had denied her the equal protection of its laws. Reed v. Reed (holding unconstitutional Idaho Code prescription that, among "several persons claiming and equally entitled to administer [a decedent's estate], males must be preferred to females"). Since Reed, the Court has repeatedly recognized that neither federal nor state government acts compatibly with the equal protection principle when a law or official policy denies to women, simply because they are women, full citizenship stature—equal opportunity to aspire, achieve, participate in and contribute to society based on their individual talents and capacities. . . . To summarize the Court's current directions for cases of official classification based on gender: Focusing on the differential treatment or denial of opportunity for which relief is sought, the reviewing court must determine whether the proffered justification is "exceedingly persuasive." The burden of justification is demanding and it rests entirely on the State. The State must show "at least that the [challenged] classification serves 'important governmental objectives and that the discriminatory means employed' are 'substantially related to the achievement of those objectives.'" The justification must be genuine, not hypothesized or invented post hoc in response to litigation. And it must not rely on overbroad generalizations about the different talents, capacities, or preferences of males and females.

The heightened review standard our precedent establishes does not make sex a proscribed classification. Supposed "inherent differences" are no longer accepted as a ground for race or national origin classifications. See Loving v. Virginia (1967). . . . "Inherent differences" between men and women, we have come to appreciate, remain cause for celebration, but not for denigration of the members of either sex or for artificial constraints on an individual's opportunity. Sex classifications may be used to compensate women "for particular economic disabilities [they have] suffered," to advance full development of the talent and capacities of our Nation's people. But such classifications may not be used, as they once were, to create or perpetuate the legal, social, and economic inferiority of women.

Measuring the record in this case against the review standard just described, we conclude that Virginia has shown no "exceedingly persuasive justification" for excluding all women from the citizen-soldier training afforded by VMI. . . . Virginia asserts two justifications in defense of VMI's exclusion of women. First, the Commonwealth contends, "single-sex education provides important educational benefits," and the option of single-sex education contributes to "diversity in educational approaches." Second, the Commonwealth argues, "the unique VMI method of character development and leadership training," the school's adversative approach, would have to be modified were VMI to admit women. We consider these two justifications in turn.

Single-sex education affords pedagogical benefits to at least some students, Virginia emphasizes, and that reality is uncontested in this litigation. Similarly, it is not disputed that diversity among public educational institutions can serve the public good. But Virginia has not shown that VMI was established, or has been maintained, with a view to diversifying, by its categorical exclusion of women, educational opportunities within the State. In cases of this genre, our precedent instructs that "benign" justifications proffered in defense of categorical exclusions will not be accepted automatically; a tenable justification must describe actual state purposes, not rationalizations for actions in fact differently grounded. . . .

Neither recent nor distant history bears out Virginia's alleged pursuit of diversity through single-sex educational options. In 1839, when the State established VMI, a range of educational opportunities for men and women was scarcely contemplated. Higher education at the time was considered dangerous for women; reflecting widely held views about women's proper place, the Nation's first universities and colleges—for example, Harvard in Massachusetts, William and Mary in Virginia—admitted only men. VMI was not at all novel in this respect: In admitting no women, VMI followed the lead of the State's flagship school, the University of Virginia, founded in 1819. . . . In 1879, the State Senate resolved to look into the possibility of higher education for women, recognizing that Virginia "has never, at any period of her history," provided for the higher education of her daughters, though she "has liberally provided for the higher education of her sons." Virginia eventually provided for several women's seminaries and colleges. . . . Debate concerning women's admission as undergraduates at the main university continued well past the century's midpoint. . . . Ultimately, in 1970, "the most prestigious institution of higher education in Virginia," the University of Virginia, introduced coeducation and, in 1972, began to admit women on an equal basis with men. Virginia describes the current absence of public single-sex higher education for women as "an historical anomaly." But the historical record indicates action more deliberate than anomalous: First, protection of women against higher education; next, schools for women far from equal in resources and stature to schools for men; finally, conversion of the separate schools to coeducation. . . .

In sum, we find no persuasive evidence in this record that VMI's male-only admission policy "is in furtherance of a state policy of 'diversity.'" No such policy can be discerned from the movement of all other public colleges and universities in Virginia away from single-sex education. A purpose genuinely to advance an array of educational options is not served by VMI's historic and constant plan—a plan to "affor[d] a unique educational benefit only to males." However "liberally" this plan serves the State's sons, it makes no provision whatever for her daughters. That is not equal protection.

Virginia next argues that VMI's adversative method of training provides educational benefits that cannot be made available, unmodified, to women. Alterations to accommodate women would necessarily be "radical," so "drastic," Virginia asserts, as to transform, indeed "destroy," VMI's program. Neither sex would be favored by the transformation, Virginia maintains: Men would be deprived of the unique opportunity currently available to them; women would not gain that opportunity because their participation would "eliminat[e] the very aspects of [the] program that distinguish [VMI] from . . . other institutions of higher education in Virginia." The District Court forecast from expert witness testimony that coeducation would materially affect "at least these three aspects of VMI's program— physical training, the absence of privacy, and the adversative approach." And it is uncontested that women's admission would require accommodations, primarily in arranging housing assignments and physical training programs for female cadets. It is also undisputed, however, that "the VMI methodology could be used to educate women." The District Court even allowed that some women may prefer it to the methodology a women's college might pursue. . . .

[S]ince this Court's turning point decision in Reed v. Reed, we have cautioned reviewing courts to take a "hard look" at generalizations or "tendencies" of the kind pressed by Virginia, and relied upon by the District Court. State actors controlling gates to opportunity, we have instructed, may not exclude qualified individuals based on "fixed notions concerning the roles and abilities of males and females." It may be assumed, for purposes of this decision, that most women would not choose VMI's adversative method. . . . Education, to be sure, is not a "one size fits all" business. The issue, however, is not whether "women—or men—should be forced to attend VMI"; rather, the question is whether the State can constitutionally deny to women who have the will and capacity, the training and attendant opportunities that VMI uniquely affords. The notion that admission of women would downgrade VMI's stature, destroy the adversative system and, with it, even the school, is a judgment hardly proved, a prediction hardly different from other "self-fulfilling prophec[ies]," once routinely used to deny rights or opportunities. . . . Women's successful entry into the federal military academies, and their participation in the Nation's military forces, indicate that Virginia's fears for the future of VMI may not be solidly grounded. The State's justification for excluding all women from "citizen-soldier" training for which some are qualified, in any event, cannot rank as "exceedingly persuasive," as we have explained and applied that standard. . . .

A prime part of the history of our Constitution, historian Richard Morris recounted, is the story of the extension of constitutional rights and protections to people once ignored or excluded. VMI's story continued as our comprehension of "We the People" expanded. There is no reason to believe that the admission of women capable of all the activities required of VMI cadets would destroy the Institute rather than enhance its capacity to serve the "more perfect Union." For the reasons stated, the case is remanded for further proceedings consistent with this opinion.

JUSTICE SCALIA, dissenting.

Today the Court shuts down an institution that has served the people of the Commonwealth of Virginia with pride and distinction for over a century and a half. To achieve that desired result, it rejects (contrary to our established practice) the factual findings of two courts below, sweeps aside the precedents of this Court, and ignores the history of our people. As to facts: it explicitly rejects the finding that there exist "gender-based developmental difference" supporting Virginia's restriction of the "adversative" method to only a

men's institution, and the finding that the all-male composition of the Virginia Military Institute (VMI) is essential to that institution's character. As to precedent: it drastically revises our established standards for reviewing sex-based classifications. And as to history: it counts for nothing the long tradition, enduring down to the present, of men's military colleges supported by both States and the Federal Government.

Much of the Court's opinion is devoted to deprecating the closed-mindedness of our forebears with regard to women's education, and even with regard to the treatment of women in areas that have nothing to do with education. Closed-minded they were—as every age is, including our own, with regard to matters it cannot guess, because it simply does not consider them debatable. The virtue of a democratic system with a First Amendment is that it readily enables the people, over time, to be persuaded that what they took for granted is not so, and to change their laws accordingly. That system is destroyed if the smug assurances of each age are removed from the democratic process and written into the Constitution. So to counterbalance the Court's criticism of our ancestors, let me say a word in their praise: they left us free to change. The same cannot be said of this most illiberal Court, which has embarked on a course of inscribing one after another of the current preferences of the society (and in some cases only the counter-majoritarian preferences of the society's law-trained elite) into our Basic Law. Today it enshrines the notion that no substantial educational value is to be served by an all-men's military academy—so that the decision by the people of Virginia to maintain such an institution denies equal protection to women who cannot attend that institution but can attend others. Since it is entirely clear that the Constitution of the United States—the old one—takes no sides in this educational debate, I dissent.

I shall devote most of my analysis to evaluating the Court's opinion on the basis of our current equal-protection jurisprudence, which regards this Court as free to evaluate everything under the sun by applying one of three tests: "rational basis" scrutiny, intermediate scrutiny, or strict scrutiny. These tests are no more scientific than their names suggest, and a further element of randomness is added by the fact that it is largely up to us which test will be applied in each case. Strict scrutiny, we have said, is reserved for state "classifications based on race or national origin and classifications affecting fundamental rights." . . . We have no established criterion fo "intermediate scrutiny" either, but essentially apply it when it seems like a good idea to load the dice. So far it has been applied to content-neutral restrictions that place an incidental burden on speech, to disabilities attendant to illegitimacy, and to discrimination on the basis of sex.

I have no problem with a system of abstract tests such as rational-basis, intermediate, and strict scrutiny (though I think we can do better than applying strict scrutiny and intermediate scrutiny whenever we feel like it). Such formulas are essential to evaluating whether the new restrictions that a changing society constantly imposes upon private conduct comport with that "equal protection" our society has always accorded in the past. But in my view the function of this Court is to preserve our society's values regarding (among other things) equal protection, not to revise them; to prevent backsliding from the degree of restriction the Constitution imposed upon democratic government, not to prescribe, on our own authority, progressively higher degrees. For that reason it is my view that, whatever abstract tests we may choose to devise, they cannot supersede—and indeed ought to be crafted so as to reflect—those constant and unbroken national traditions that embody the people's understanding of ambiguous constitutional texts. . . .

The all-male constitution of VMI comes squarely within such a governing tradition. Founded by the Commonwealth of Virginia in 1839 and continuously maintained by it since, VMI has always admitted only men. And in that regard it has not been unusual. For almost all of VMI's more than a century and a half of existence, its single-sex status reflected the uniform practice for government-supported military colleges. Another famous Southern institution, The Citadel, has existed as a state-funded school of South Carolina since 1842. And all the federal military colleges—West Point, the Naval Academy at Annapolis, and even the Air Force Academy, which was not established until 1954—admitted only males for most of their history. Their admission of women in 1976 (upon which the Court today relies), came not by court decree, but because the people, through their elected representatives, decreed a change. In other words, the tradition of having government-funded military schools for men is as well rooted in the traditions of this country as the tradition of sending only men into military combat. The people may decide to change the one tradition, like the other, through democratic processes; but the assertion that either tradition has been unconstitutional through the centuries is not law, but politics-smuggled-into-law. And the same applies, more broadly, to single-sex education in general, which, as I shall discuss, is threatened by today's decision with the cut-off of all state and federal support. Government-run nonmilitary educational institutions for the two sexes have until very recently also been part of our national tradition. These traditions may of course be changed by the democratic decisions of the people, as they largely have been.

Today, however, change is forced upon Virginia, and reversion to single-sex education is prohibited nationwide, not by democratic processes but by order of this Court. Even while bemoaning the sorry, bygone days of "fixed notions" concerning women's education, the Court favors current notions so fixedly that it is willing to write them into the Constitution of the United States by application of custom-built "tests." This is not the interpretation of a Constitution, but the creation of one. . . . Our task is to clarify the law—not to muddy the waters, and not to exact over-compliance by intimidation. The States and the Federal Government are entitled to know before they act the standard to which they will be held, rather than be compelled to guess about the outcome of Supreme Court peek-a-boo.

The Court's intimations are particularly out of place because it is perfectly clear that, if the question of the applicable standard of review for sex-based classifications were to be regarded as an appropriate subject for reconsideration, the stronger argument would be not for elevating the standard to strict scrutiny, but for reducing it to rational-basis review. The latter certainly has a firmer foundation in our past jurisprudence: Whereas no majority of the Court has ever applied strict scrutiny in a case involving sex-based classifi-

cations, we routinely applied rational-basis review until the 1970's. . . . With this explanation of how the Court has succeeded in making its analysis seem orthodox—and indeed, if intimations are to be believed, even overly generous to VMI—I now proceed to describe how the analysis should have been conducted. The question to be answered, I repeat, is whether the exclusion of women from VMI is "substantially related to an important governmental objective."

It is beyond question that Virginia has an important state interest in providing effective college education for its citizens. That single-sex instruction is an approach substantially related to that interest should be evident enough from the long and continuing history in this country of men's and women's colleges. . . . There can be no serious dispute that, as the District Court found, single-sex education and a distinctive educational method "represent legitimate contributions to diversity in the Virginia higher education system." . . . Virginia's election to fund one public all-male institution and one on the adversative model—and to concentrate its resources in a single entity that serves both these interests in diversity—is substantially related to the State's important educational interests. . . .

Under the constitutional principles announced and applied today, single-sex public education is unconstitutional. By going through the motions of applying a balancing test—asking whether the State has adduced an "exceedingly persuasive justification" for its sex-based classification—the Court creates the illusion that government officials in some future case will have a clear shot at justifying some sort of single-sex public education. . . . And the rationale of today's decision is sweeping: for sex-based classifications, a redefinition of intermediate scrutiny that makes it indistinguishable from strict scrutiny. Indeed, the Court indicates that if any program restricted to one sex is "uniqu[e]," it must be opened to members of the opposite sex "who have the will and capacity" to participate in it. I suggest that the single-sex program that will not be capable of being characterized as "unique" is not only unique but nonexistent.

In any event, regardless of whether the Court's rationale leaves some small amount of room for lawyers to argue, it ensures that single-sex public education is functionally dead. The costs of litigating the constitutionality of a single-sex education program, and the risks of ultimately losing that litigation, are simply too high to be embraced by public officials. Any person with standing to challenge any sex-based classification can haul the State into federal court and compel it to establish by evidence (presumably in the form of expert testimony) that there is an "exceedingly persuasive justification" for the classification. Should the courts happen to interpret that vacuous phrase as establishing a standard that is not utterly impossible of achievement, there is considerable risk that whether the standard has been met will not be determined on the basis of the record evidence—indeed, that will necessarily be the approach of any court that seeks to walk the path the Court has trod today. No state official in his right mind will buy such a high-cost, high-risk lawsuit by commencing a single-sex program. The enemies of single-sex education have won; by persuading only seven Justices (five would have been enough) that their view of the world is enshrined in the Constitution, they have effectively imposed that view on all 50 States. . . .

PART IV

The Right to Privacy and the Due Process Clause

CHAPTER 13

Sterilization, Contraception, and Abortion

INTRODUCTION

Writing for the Court in *Roe v. Wade* in 1973, Justice Harry Blackmun acknowledged "our awareness of the sensitive and emotional nature of the abortion controversy, of the vigorous opposing views, even among physicians, and of the seemingly absolute convictions that the subject inspires." Having made this frank acknowledgment, Blackmun added that the Court's task in deciding this difficult case "is to resolve the issue by constitutional measurement, free of emotion and of predilection." Was it possible, however, for any group of nine men—or, for that matter, any group of nine people in this country—to decide "free of emotion" whether pregnant women should be able to obtain an abortion and, if so, in what circumstances and with what procedures? No issue in American society has generated more emotion, on both sides, over the years since *Roe* was decided than abortion. The "seemingly absolute convictions" of those who call themselves "pro-choice" and those who adopt the label of "pro-life" have led to polite arguments and debate, loud confrontations on picket lines, and even to the murder of doctors who performed abortions. However much those on both sides of this divisive issue have deplored the violence that has followed the *Roe* decision, it is clear that no other ruling of the Supreme Court in the past century has provoked more controversy.

The *Roe* decision surprised many people who had not given much thought to the abortion question before the Court handed down its ruling in January 1973; it shocked those who had not anticipated the outcome. For most Americans, the constitutional reasoning behind the decision, carefully expressed in Justice Blackmun's opinion, was far less important than the result itself. Few people read Supreme Court opinions, even in cases that reach newspaper head-

lines or television reports. It is likely that few lawyers, most of whom practice in fields that rarely involve the kinds of constitutional issues that arose in the *Roe* case, have read the full text of the opinions in that case. Even books on constitutional law, like this one, include only excerpts of those opinions, some much briefer than the edited versions in this chapter. But it is essential that anyone who studies constitutional law, especially in the areas of civil rights and liberties, read the opinions in the *Roe* case, and the cases that preceded and followed that decision, with some exposure to the political and social context in which the abortion controversy is deeply embedded.

Each of the six cases in this chapter has a broader context than the dispute between the parties on both sides. That context goes back for centuries, as Justice Blackmun showed at length in his opinion, which devoted more pages to the historical record of the abortion issue than it did to the constitutional issues in the case. Efforts to prevent conception and to terminate pregnancies began in ancient times; the Greeks and Romans debated these questions long before the Constitution was adopted. Terms such as *quickening* became part of the legal discourse on this issue.

Most of the states adopted laws relating to abortion—generally imposing criminal penalties on those who performed abortions—in the nineteenth century, but few challenges to these laws reached the courts, and none came before the Supreme Court until the late 1960s. Given this fact, it is not surprising that Justice Blackmun's opinion in *Roe* looked in odd places for precedent to support the right to privacy that he found in the Constitution. Blackmun cited cases that dealt with negligence by railroad companies, wiretaps on telephone booths, "stop and frisk" searches by the police, and possession of pornographic films to buttress his argument. But this was understandable; Blackmun was looking for doctrine and principles, not for cases with similar facts to *Roe,* since no such cases were available.

There were, however, a few cases decided before *Roe* that dealt with issues of human reproduction, and that bear on the controversy over abortion. Two of these cases are included in this chapter, and both raise a question equally as difficult in moral and ethical terms: Does the state have the right to force a person to undergo sterilization as a means of preventing conception and possibly the birth of "unfit" children, or at least children of "unfit" parents? This is hardly a trivial question. It is one that raises difficult constitutional issues, which the Supreme Court has never directly answered. But it also raises deeper questions of the limits of state power over reproduction, and of the motives and methods of those who believed that preventing the "unfit" from having children was necessary for the "welfare" of society.

The social and political forces that produced the two sterilization cases in this chapter, *Buck v. Bell* and *Skinner v. Oklahoma,* had their roots in the early–twentieth-century nativist movement, whose leaders pressed for limiting the further immigration of "lower" classes—people from Italy, Poland, Russia, and other non-Aryan countries—into this country. The nativists persuaded Congress to enact the Immigration Restriction Act in 1924, sharply reducing the number of immigrants—most of them Catholics or Jews—who might taint the "purity" of the Anglo-Saxon majority. Another goal of the nativists was to persuade state legislatures to adopt "eugenic sterilization" laws that would prevent other "unfit" people—even those of Anglo-Saxon descent—from having children, "to prevent our being swamped with incompetence," as Justice Oliver Wendell Holmes wrote in *Buck v. Bell,* sustaining such laws in 1927. Leaders of the eugenics movement argued that such traits as "moral delinquency" were inherited and passed from one generation to the next, and that sterilization would break this chain. In upholding the power of Virginia to prevent Carrie Buck from becoming the "potential parent of socially inadequate offspring," Justice Holmes put the eugenics argument in these words: "Three generations of imbeciles are enough."

The eugenics movement was based on pseudoscience, and advances in genetics soon exposed its flaws. Another factor, the rise to power in the 1930s of the Nazis in Germany, also gave pause to supporters of sterilization as a eugenics measure. The most prominent "scientist" in this movement, Harry Laughlin, provided testimony that Carrie Buck was both a "low-grade moron" and "morally delinquent." He later received an honorary degree in the 1930s from Heidelberg University, now firmly controlled by Nazis, for his role in drafting the Hitler regime's "Race Hygiene" law, under which thousands of "unfit" Germans were sterilized. The adoption of eugenic sterilization by the Nazis, and exposure of its scientific fallacies, revolted many Americans. The Supreme Court responded in 1942 by striking down in *Skinner v. Oklahoma* a state law that allowed the sterilization of persons convicted three times of certain felonies; the offenses of the "habitual criminal" in this case, Jack Skinner, included chicken theft. However, the Supreme Court sidestepped in *Skinner* the claim that the law violated the Due Process Clause of the Fourteenth Amendment, which protects "liberty" against state deprivation, basing its ruling

on the Equal Protection Clause, since Oklahoma had exempted those who committed crimes such as embezzlement from the law's reach.

The eugenics movement also promoted contraception as a means of persuading the "lower classes" to limit their birth rate, which exceeded that of the "better" classes. Well after eugenics lost its public appeal, advocates of birth control such as Planned Parenthood set up clinics to distribute contraceptives, with low-income women a special target, although middle-class couples also obtained birth control devices at these clinics. A few states had adopted laws during the nineteenth century that banned the distribution of contraceptives, and a challenge to Connecticut's law reached the Supreme Court in 1965. By this time, the growing women's movement had replaced the discredited eugenicists in advocating legal access to contraception, and the Court was receptive to this claim during the heyday of the Warren Court, which gave an expansive reading to the "liberty" interest in the Due Process Clause. However, the Court's decision in *Griswold v. Connecticut* again sidestepped that clause and looked elsewhere in the Constitution for provisions that would create "zones of privacy" that would place marital bedrooms out of the state's reach. Justice William O. Douglas, who also wrote the *Skinner* opinion in 1942, based his *Griswold* opinion on "specific guarantees" of the First, Third, Fourth, Fifth, and Ninth Amendments, which collectively created an implied guarantee of protection against government intrusion into the "intimate relation of husband and wife and their physician's role in one aspect of that relation."

Fueled by their victory in the *Griswold* case, women's groups and other advocates of "reproductive rights" turned their attention to abortion, fashioning a strategy that included lobbying and litigation. They persuaded the New York legislature in 1971 to liberalize its abortion law, and looked for cases that might persuade judges to strike down the laws of other states that made most—or even all—abortions a criminal offense. The case that reached the Supreme Court in 1971, and was decided as *Roe v. Wade* in January 1973, began in Dallas, Texas, when a pregnant woman named Norma McCorvey (whose identity was shielded by the pseudonym of "Jane Roe") contacted two young lawyers, Sarah Weddington and Linda Coffee, for aid in obtaining an abortion. They filed suit against Dallas County District Attorney Henry Wade, asking a three-judge federal judicial panel to rule the state's abortion law, which permitted abortions only to save a pregnant woman's life, unconstitutional. The judges agreed, basing their ruling on the Ninth Amendment, which broadly provides that "the enumeration in the Constitution, of certain rights, shall not be construed to deny or disparage others retained by the people." Along with another case from Georgia, whose abortion law was more liberal than the almost total ban in Texas, the abortion cases confronted the Supreme Court with its most difficult and potentially divisive issue since it ruled in 1954 on school segregation in *Brown v. Board of Education.*

The political reaction to the *Roe* decision is widely known and needs little discussion here, except to note that members of Congress have proposed constitutional amendments to reverse that ruling in every session over the past three decades, none of them gaining the required two-thirds vote needed for passage and submission to state legislatures.

However, local, state, and federal lawmakers have passed dozens of laws designed to limit access to abortion in many ways, including bans on federal funding of abortions, requirements that pregnant teenagers notify or secure the approval of their parents before obtaining an abortion, and regulations of the medical procedures and facilities of hospitals and clinics that perform abortions. The Supreme Court has upheld many of these limiting statutes, most notably in *Webster v. Reproductive Health Services*, decided in 1989, while striking down others in cases that include *Akron v. Akron Center for Reproductive Health* in 1983. In deciding these cases, the Court has adopted the "undue burden" test, fashioned and refined by Justice Sandra Day O'Connor, whose votes in abortion cases is often critical to the outcome.

During the years that followed the *Roe* decision, from which only two justices dissented, partisans on both sides of the abortion issue have turned the judicial confirmation process in the Senate into a political battleground, hoping to keep off the Court, or to place on it, the crucial fifth vote that could overturn *Roe*. The defeat of Judge Robert Bork's nomination to the Court by President Ronald Reagan in 1987 was largely a result of his often-stated opposition to *Roe*. In five different abortion cases, lawyers in the administrations of presidents Reagan and George W. Bush had asked the Supreme Court to overturn the *Roe* decision. In 1992, shortly after Judge Clarence Thomas replaced Justice Thurgood Marshall on the Court's bench, abortion opponents thought they had finally gained the deciding fifth vote to reverse *Roe* in a Pennsylvania case that challenged several limits on access to abortion, *Planned Parenthood v. Casey*. "All lingering doubt has been erased," the *Wall Street Journal* assured its readers. "Conservatives have locked up control of the U.S. Supreme Court."

The optimism of the pro-life movement was shattered by the Court's decision in *Casey*. Three justices, Sandra Day O'Connor, Anthony Kennedy, and David Souter, all placed on the Court by Republican presidents whose party's platform called for reversing *Roe*, "announced the judgment of the Court" in an opinion that stated: "The essential holding of Roe v. Wade should be retained and once again reaffirmed." They based this holding on fears that the Court's "legitimacy" would be undermined by reversing *Roe* "without serious inequity to those who have relied upon it" over the past nineteen years. Justices Harry Blackmun and John Paul Stevens joined this part of the opinion, making a majority of five to spare the *Roe* decision from reversal. The three swing justices, however, voted with the Court's four *Roe* opponents to uphold all but one provision of the challenged provisions of the Pennsylvania law.

The *Casey* decision ended, for at least the following decade, the political battle to overturn *Roe*. Abortion opponents turned their efforts to persuading state and federal lawmakers to ban so-called partial-birth abortions, a rarely used procedure doctors call "dilation and extraction." In this procedure, a late-term fetus is aborted by inserting surgical instruments into the uterus, sucking out the brain and crushing the skull to facilitate removal of the fetus. A *Gallup* poll conducted in March 2000 showed that 66 percent of the public supported laws to ban partial-birth abortions, except to save a pregnant woman's life. Three months after this poll, however, the Supreme Court ruled by a five-to-four margin that a Nebraska law making the dilation-and-extraction procedure unlawful conflicted with *Roe* and placed an "undue burden" on pregnant women seeking late-term abortions. Justice Kennedy, who had voted to reaffirm the *Roe* decision in his *Casey* opinion in 1992, joined the three implacable abortion opponents—Chief Justice Rehnquist and Justices Scalia and Thomas—in the Nebraska case, *Stenberg v. Carhart*. Leaders of the pro-life movement and their congressional supporters reacted to this ruling with outrage, but the Supreme Court later struck down without argument or opinion several other state bans on partial-birth abortions.

The pubic reaction to the Supreme Court's decisions in abortion cases—from *Roe* in 1973 through *Stenberg* in 2000—reveal the emotional nature of this issue and the seemingly absolute convictions of those on both sides of the question. Attitudes toward abortion have hardly shifted over more than a decade of spirited debate: a *Gallup* poll in 1989 showed that 29 percent of the public supported a right to abortion "under any circumstances," a slight majority of 51 percent felt it should be legal in "certain circumstances," and 17 percent believed it should be illegal "in all circumstances." To date, the Supreme Court has rejected both extremes and has sided with those in the middle. The fact that a majority of justices and of the general public agree on this middle course does not mean, of course, that the Court should look at polls in deciding cases. Rather, it shows that—on this issue, at least—the Court's "legitimacy" remains intact in the minds of most Americans.

BUCK V. BELL
274 U.S. 200 (1927)

"It is better for all the world, if instead of waiting to execute degenerate offspring for crime, or to let them starve for their imbecility, society can prevent those who are manifestly unfit from continuing their kind. The principle that sustains compulsory vaccination is broad enough to cover cutting the Fallopian tubes."

The Question:	Can states pass laws allowing the eugenic sterilization of persons who are allegedly feebleminded or who have been convicted three times of certain felonies, in one case a female inmate of the Virginia State Colony for Epileptics and Feeble Minded and in the other case a male inmate of the Oklahoma penitentiary who had been convicted once of chicken theft as a juvenile and twice of armed robbery?
The Arguments:	PRO

To prevent the transmission of feeblemindedness and criminality, the state has a legitimate interest in reducing the social and economic cost of further generations of persons with these inherited traits. The Virginia law in question is designed to prevent the further propagation of feebleminded persons through a medical procedure that carries little risk and that allows inmates to leave the institution and lead normal lives. In this case, Carrie Buck was found to be the daughter of a feebleminded mother and the mother herself of a feebleminded daughter. The Oklahoma law was applied to Jack Skinner, who had three times been convicted of felonies involving moral turpitude.

CON

There is no more invasive and irreversible medical procedure than sterilization. The records in these cases do not show that either Carrie Buck or Jack Skinner has a genetically transmissible condition that poses any danger to their potential offspring or to society. The concept of eugenic sterilization can be used to eliminate entire groups of people who are considered "defective" or "dangerous" by preventing them from having children. And, the genetic evidence for the transmission of feeblemindedness and criminality, at the time of these cases, is far from conclusive.

BACKGROUND: THE SUPREME COURT BRIEF OF VIRGINIA IN *BUCK V. BELL*

THE FACTS

Commitment to the Colony

Carrie Buck, then seventeen years of age, but of a mental age of only nine years, and the mother of an illegitimate child, was under an inquisition duly held in Albemarle County, Virginia, committed to the State Colony for Epileptics and Feeble-Minded on January 23, 1924.

Carrie's child was afterwards found to give evidences of defective mentality, while Carrie's mother, Emma Buck, of a mental age of seven years, had previously been committed to the same Colony, as a feeble-minded person where with Carrie she remains in the custody of the State. Carrie's father is dead.

Previous to Carrie's commitment to the Colony she had for some years lived as a member of the household with a respectable family who had received her into their home when very young, taken good care of her in return for the simple services she might render despite her affliction and who would be glad to have her back again but for the risk they would have to run of her bearing other children.

Sterilization Petition

Dr. A. S. Priddy, an eminent physchiatrist and surgeon, Superintendent of the Colony, when Carrie was committed, after due observation confirmed the finding that she was a feeble-minded person, and after the passage of the sterilization statute being of opinion that Carrie was within its

provisions and that both her welfare and the welfare of society would be promoted by her sterilization so that she might properly be returned to the liberty of the good home still open to her in Albemarle County instead of being kept in confinement for at least the more than twenty years that still remained of her child-bearing period of life, presented to the Special Board of Directors of the Colony a petition under the act, praying authority to perform or to have performed upon her the operation of salpingectomy.

The Testimony of Witnesses

Dr. H. H. Laughlin, of Long Island, New York, Assistant Director of the Eugenics Record Office of the Carnegie Institution of Washington, Expert Eugenical Agent for the Committee on Immigration and Naturalization of the House of Representatives and Eugenics Associate of the Psychopathic Laboratory of the Municipal Court of Chicago and author of a 502-page volume on Eugenical Sterilization in the United States, gave in testimony by deposition an analysis of the hereditary nature of Carrie Buck (Rec., pp. 29–41.) After reciting Carrie's family and personal history, Dr. Laughlin finds: "All this is a typical picture of a low grade moron. . . . The family history record and the individual case histories, if true, demonstrate the hereditary nature of the feeble-mindedness and moral delinquency described in Carrie Buck. She is therefore a potential parent of socially inadequate or defective offspring."

Dr. Laughlin further testified: "Let me say, also, that in the archives of the Eugenics Record Office there are many hundreds of manuscript pedigrees of families with feeble-minded members. These pedigrees prove conclusively that both feeble-mindedness and other intelligence levels are, in most cases, accounted for by hereditary qualities," that the operation of "salpingectomy in the female has but little physiological effect other than sexual sterility." Modern eugenical sterilization is a force for the mitigation of race degeneracy which, if properly used, is safe and effective. I have come to this conclusion after a thorough study of the legal, biological and eugenical aspects, and the practical working out, of all of the sterilization laws which have been enacted by the several states up to the present time.... I believe the Virginia statute is, in the main, one of the best laws thus far enacted in that it has avoided the principal eugenical and legal defects of previous statutes, and has incorporated into it the most effective eugenical features and the soundest legal principles of previous laws."

Dr. A. S. Priddy, Superintendent of the Colony, with twenty-one years of experience in this and similar institutions, testified as to Carrie:

> I arrived at the conclusion that she was a highly proper case for the benefit of the Sterilization Act, by a study of her family history; personal examination of Carrie Buck, and subsequent observation since admission to the hospital covering the whole fields of inquiry connected with the feeble-minded.... She was eighteen years old on the second of last July, and according to the natural expectancy, if the purposes of the act chartering this institution are to be observed and carried out, that is to keep her under custody during her period of child-bearing, she would have some thirty years of strict custody and care, under which she would receive only her board and clothes; would be denied all of the blessings of outdoor life and liberty, and be a burden on the State of Virginia of about $200,00 a year for thirty years; whereas, if by the operation of sterilization, with the training she has got, she could go out, get a good home under supervision, earn good wages, and probably marry some man of her own level and do as many whom I have sterilized for diseases have done—be good wives—be producers, and lead happy and useful lives in their spheres.

> Q. Would you think her welfare would be promoted by such sterilization?
> A. I certainly do.
> Q. Why? And how?
> A. Well, every human being craves liberty; she would get that, under supervision. She would not have a feeling of dependence; she would be earning her own livelihood, and would get some pleasure out of life, which would be denied her in having to spend her life in custodial care in an institution.
> Q. Would you think the public welfare would be promoted by her sterilization?
> A. Unquestionably. You mean society in its full scope?
> Q. Yes, sir.
> A. Well, in the first place, she would cease to be a charge on society if sterilized; it would remove one potential source of the incalculable number of descendants who would be feeble-minded. She would contribute to the raising of the general mental average and standard.
> Q. Well, taking into consideration the years of experience you have had in dealing with the socially inadequate, and more particularly with the feeble-minded, what, in your judgment, would be the general effect, both upon patients and upon society at large, by the operation of this law?
> A. It would be a blessing.

> Q. To whom?
> A. To both society and to the individuals on whom the operation is performed.
> Q. Of course these people, being of limited intelligence, lack full judgment of what is best for them, but generally, so far as patients are concerned, do they object to this operation or not?
> A. They clamor for it.
> Q. Why?
> A. Because they know that it means the enjoyment of life and the peaceful pursuance of happiness, as they view it, on the outside of institution walls. Also they have the opportunity of marrying men of their mental levels and making good wives in many cases.

MR. JUSTICE HOLMES delivered the opinion of the Court.

This is a writ of error to review a judgment of the Supreme Court of Appeals of the State of Virginia, affirming a judgment of the Circuit Court of Amherst County, by which the defendant in error, the superintendent of the State Colony for Epileptics and Feeble Minded, was ordered to perform the operation of salpingectomy upon Carrie Buck, the plaintiff in error, for the purpose of making her sterile. The case comes here upon the contention that the statute authorizing the judgment is void under the Fourteenth Amendment as denying to the plaintiff in error due process of law and the equal protection of the laws.

Carrie Buck is a feeble-minded white woman who was committed to the State Colony above mentioned in due form. She is the daughter of a feeble-minded mother in the same institution, and the mother of an illegitimate feeble-minded child. She was eighteen years old at the time of the trial of her case in the Circuit Court in the latter part of 1924. An Act of Virginia approved March 20, 1924 recites that the health of the patient and the welfare of society may be promoted in certain cases by the sterilization of mental defectives, under careful safeguard, etc.; that the sterilization may be effected in males by vasectomy and in females by salpingectomy, without serious pain or substantial danger to life; that the Commonwealth is supporting in various institutions many defective persons who if now discharged would become a menace but if incapable of procreating might be discharged with safety and become self-supporting with benefit to themselves and to society; and that experience has shown that heredity plays an important part in the transmission of insanity, imbecility, etc. The statute then enacts that whenever the superintendent of certain institutions including the above-named State Colony shall be of opinion that it is for the best interest of the patients and of society that an inmate under his care should be sexually sterilized, he may have the operation performed upon any patient afflicted with hereditary forms of insanity, imbecility, etc., on complying with the very careful provisions by which the act protects the patients from possible abuse.

The superintendent first presents a petition to the special board of directors of his hospital or colony, stating the facts and the grounds for his opinion, verified by affidavit. Notice of the petition and of the time and place of the hearing in the institution is to be served upon the inmate, and also upon his guardian, and if there is no guardian the superintendent is to apply to the Circuit Court of the County to appoint one. If the inmate is a minor notice also is to be given to his parents, if any, with a copy of the petition. The board is to see to it that the inmate may attend the hearings if desired by him or his guardian.... There can be no doubt that so far as procedure is concerned the rights of the patient are most carefully considered, and as every step in this case was taken in scrupulous compliance with the statute and after months of observation, there is no doubt that in that respect the plaintiff in error has had due process at law.

The attack is not upon the procedure but upon the substantive law. It seems to be contended that in no circumstances could such an order be justified. It certainly is contended that the order cannot be justified upon the existing grounds. The judgment finds the facts that have been recited and that Carrie Buck "is the probable potential parent of socially inadequate offspring, likewise afflicted, that she may be sexually sterilized without detriment to her general health and that her welfare and that of society will be promoted by her sterilization," and thereupon makes the order. In view of the general declarations of the Legislature and the specific findings of the Court obviously we cannot say as matter of law that the grounds do not exist, and if they exist they justify the result. We have seen more than once that the public welfare may call upon the best citizens for their lives. It would be strange if it could not call upon those who already sap the strength of the State for these lesser sacrifices, often not felt to be such by those concerned, in order to prevent our being swamped with incompetence. It is better for all the world, if instead of waiting to execute degenerate offspring for crime, or to let them starve for their imbecility, society can prevent those who are manifestly unfit from continuing their kind. The principle that sustains compulsory vaccination is broad enough to cover cutting the Fallopian tubes. Jacobson v. Massachusetts (1905). Three generations of imbeciles are enough.

But, it is said, however it might be if this reasoning were applied generally, it fails when it is confined to the small number who are in the institutions named and is not applied to the multitudes outside. It is the usual last resort of constitutional arguments to point out shortcomings of this sort. But the answer is that the law does all that is needed when it does all that it can, indicates a policy, applies it to all within the lines, and seeks to bring within the lines all similarly situated so far and so fast as its means allow. Of course so far as the operations enable those who otherwise must be kept confined to be returned to the world, and thus open the asylum to others, the equality aimed at will be more nearly reached.

AFTERMATH OF THE *BUCK* CASE

It is inconceivable that the Supreme Court today, or anytime in the future, would uphold forced sterilization laws of the kind it endorsed in *Buck v. Bell*. Those laws reflected the pseudo-science of the "eugenics" movement, which has been thoroughly repudiated by every reputable scientist in the fields of genetics and biology. Surprisingly, however, the Court has never over-ruled the *Buck* decision. To borrow the words of Justice Robert Jackson in his *Korematsu* dissent in 1944, the principle of the *Buck* case "lies about like a loaded weapon" that could be fired in the future against those people who are considered "manifestly unfit from continuing their kind," as Justice Holmes wrote in upholding Carrie Buck's sterilization in 1927.

The "eugenics" movement was discredited not only by scientific advances, but also because it was adopted in the 1930s by the Nazi regime in Germany, which passed a "Race Hygiene" law under which hundreds of thousands of "unfit" people were sterilized. Revulsion at this early step toward the "Final Solution" of the Holocaust led most Americans to reject forced sterilization as a means of "race betterment." By the 1960s, most states with laws similar to the Virginia statute upheld in the *Buck* case had repealed them. But it was not until the late 1990s that state officials heard any voices calling for apologies to those who had been robbed of the chance to have children. There was, however, recent precedent for such official apologies. The Japanese American survivors of the World War Two internment camps had received apologies in 1988 from both Congress and President Ronald Reagan for having been robbed of their liberty.

In thinking about civil rights and liberties, we need to recognize that campaigns to repeal "unjust" laws and to challenge them in courts are not the only means to provide "redress" to their victims. The successful grass-roots efforts of Japanese Americans to secure an official apology from Congress were directed at Congress and the White House, and were national in scope and organization. In contrast, the campaigns to gain apologies for the victims of forced sterilization laws had no national coordination or leadership. Thus far, they have succeeded in only five of the more than thirty states that passed and enforced these laws. The following material focuses on California, the state with the largest number of sterilizations. The governors of four other states—Virginia, North Carolina, South Carolina, and Oregon—issued official apologies in 2002. In March 2003, a California state senate committee scheduled a hearing on the state's "eugenic sterilization" law, under which more than 20,000 state residents had been sterilized. The committee heard testimony from Professor Paul Lombardo of the University of Virginia, perhaps the nation's leading authority on the "eugenics" movement. Four hours after the hearing ended, both Governor Davis and California's attorney general issued formal apologies for the state's forced sterilizations. This material offers an object lesson in the broader context of civil rights and liberties.

California Senate Select Committee on Genetics, Genetic Technologies, and Public Safety—March 11, 2003, State Capitol, Sacramento, California:

SENATOR DEDE ALPERT: I want to welcome today's lecturer, Dr. Paul Lombardo, and I want to welcome all of you who have traveled here to the Capitol today to join us for this lecture.

Dr. Lombardo is Associate Professor and Director of the Program in Law and Medicine at the Center for Biomedical Ethics at the University of Virginia.

Dr. Paul A. Lombardo: Thank you, Senator Alpert.

The case which brings to international attention sterilization in America is this case of *Buck* vs. *Bell,* and I want to spend a few minutes talking about it.

It was a challenge, as Senator Alpert told us a little bit earlier, to a Virginia law written in 1924 that allowed for compulsory sterilization. At that time, there were probably 14 or 15 other states that already had laws, but Virginia's law was very carefully crafted, using a model that was developed by a man named Harry Laughlin.

The people who are featured in the cases, the principals are Dr. John Bell, the superintendent and director of the Virginia Colony for the Epileptic and the Feebleminded, an institution near Lynchburg, Virginia, which was founded in 1910 and expanded in 1916 to allow in people who were called "feebleminded." That characteristic covered not just cognitive disability but also, according to the eugenicists, an inability to control oneself—a moral weakness, a lack of inhibition—and, in many ways, this is all connected to sexual behavior. This is the model that was applied to Carrie Buck to say that she was actually a member of a family that had three generations of defect.

Emma Buck, who was Carrie's mother, also a resident there at the Colony for the Epileptic and the Feebleminded, had a series of relationships with men other than her husband, and those relationships generated a series of children, all of whom were marked with the mark of feeblemindedness; the "F" in the pedigree.

Carrie, herself, had a child, also an illegitimate child, with a young man named Clarence Garland, and the third generation Vivian Alice Elaine Buck is marked here also as feebleminded in 1924, at the time of the trial, having been tested at the age of seven months and showing what the witness called "backwardness." This case was decided in the courts of Virginia in favor of the Colony and endorsing the state law, saying that it was valid and constitutional. It went through the appellate process, thereon to the United States Supreme Court, where, in 1927, it reached a court that was very, very ready to embrace the theory of eugenics upon which it was based.

My own interest in this case began in the late 1970s and early 1980s when litigation was brought back in Virginia on behalf of people who had been sterilized. Carrie's picture and her story became public in a way that it never had been before. I was fortunate enough to meet her right after Christmas of that year, just before she died, and I learned what other people had learned, and that is that her so-called moral delinquency, the reason that she was sterilized, was because she was the mother of an illegitimate child supposedly carrying around the potential for feeblemindedness herself. In fact, she had no cognitive disabilities, and, in fact, she was not responsible even for the child that was born. She asserted that she had been raped by the young man that she'd been spending time with. He promised to marry her, and then he promptly disappeared. He was sent away to save the family shame because he was a relative of her foster parents. They then turned her over to the authorities to be sterilized, and she was sent down to the Colony there near Lynchburg.

Following up on the research on the Buck family after Carrie died, I discovered that Vivian, the baby, was also charged with characteristics which were inaccurate. This is her grade report showing her, in the second grade, on the Honor Roll. Clearly, some evidence that she was hardly feebleminded. At that time, her foster mother as well as her teachers would have asserted that she did just fine in the intellectual department. Unfortunately, she died soon after this. She got the measles and developed a secondary infection and died at the age of eight. So, she's not around to tell us her part of the story.

What does this add up to? Well, it adds up to fraud. The case, really, is an example of legal fraud. I don't say that lightly. I am a lawyer. There's a lot more of the case having to do with the way that the lawyers set it up, which was truly reprehensible. But at least it demonstrates to us that the foundation of the Supreme Court opinion is extraordinarily weak just on the factual side, let alone on the public policy side which is a whole other issue.

Here we have both Emma, Carrie, and Vivian, called "Three Generations of Imbeciles" with no real evidence that any of them suffered from the kinds of moral or cognitive deficits with which they were charged.

The usual question that people ask me when I talk about eugenics and sterilization is: Is there really a connection between all this stuff in America and what happened over there in the Holocaust? This sounds an awful lot like Hitler." Well, in fact, there is a very direct connection, and the connection has to do with the kind of propaganda that was generated in Germany very much paralleling the kind of propaganda that was generated in this country as part of the eugenics movement.

It was out of that sympathy with the people who supported public welfare that a law was generated in 1933. It's really the very first piece of legislation of any importance that the Hitler administration wrote, and that was an "Act for the Prevention of Hereditarily Diseased Offspring"—a sterilization law—modeled, in large part, on the law written by Harry Laughlin in 1914 which became the statute that Virginia sent through the courts and had endorsed in *Buck* vs. *Bell*. The German law was more extensive than anywhere else and certainly more harsh. It covered larger groups of people, and it was used more extensively as well. On the rate of something between 50 and 80 thousand people a year were sterilized for several years, generating a total approaching 400,000. Some people say many more than that, but the official records show something just short of 400,000.

So, what does that have to do with America? Well, as I said, Harry Laughlin was the person who wrote the Model Sterilization Act, focusing on all those people—the alcoholics, the mentally ill, the feebly inhibited, etc.—in his Model Sterilization Act. He was eventually rewarded by his colleagues, many of whom were at Hitler's elbow, the scientists who generated the Nuremberg laws on racial separation, the sterilization laws, and other laws that had a eugenic tinge to them.

So, the connection between Germany and America through people like Laughlin in palpable, made even more clear in 1936 when he is invited to come to the 550th anniversary of the University of Heidelberg's founding. The actual anniversary ceremony's presided over by Herman Goering and given great attention in the German press. Laughlin can't go. By then, he's out of favor in America. His employer has put him on a very short lease. Nevertheless, he goes downtown to the consulate in New York after a few months and picks up his diploma, which is given to him as an "Honorary Doctor of Medicine" for his work in the science of racial cleansing. He was given credit in the citation for that diploma for having engineered the Immigration Restriction Act in America, something which Hitler praised in his own book, *Mien Kampf,* for having been the architect of sterilization laws that were used worldwide and also for being a strong proponent and a theoretical advocate in the area of racial separation and anti-miscegenation laws.

And if that isn't enough evidence, go to the transcripts of the Nuremberg trials and see where, when German doctors were prosecuted for doing experiments in the camps—experiments that exposed people unwittingly, without telling them, to x-rays, to find out whether this x-ray would prevent them from having children, or given various injections of caustic chemicals to produce the same result—when they were prosecuted for that kind of torture and, in some cases, eventual death, their response was to say, "How dare you charge us with carrying out sterilization. How dare you. We just did the same thing you did," and they cited and quoted from *Buck* vs. *Bell* in the United State Supreme Court opinion. So, the German Nazi connection is not fanciful at all.

SKINNER V. OKLAHOMA
316 U.S. 535 (1942)

*"The power to sterilize, if exercised, may have subtle, far-reaching, and devastating effects.
In evil or reckless hands it can cause races or types which are inimical to the dominant
group to wither and disappear. There is no redemption for the individual whom
the law touches."*

The Question: Can a state pass a law that allows the sexual sterilization of persons who have been convicted three or more times of specified crimes?

The Arguments: PRO

There is evidence from eugenic studies that criminal traits are passed on from generation to generation. Sexual sterilization of persons who have shown a pattern of committing serious crimes is a reasonable exercise of the state's "police powers" to protect the public safety and welfare. This procedure will help to prevent future generations of criminals who might otherwise inherit these traits from their parent.

CON

There is no right more important than the right to have children. This is an essential part of the "liberty" of the individual that is protected by the Due Process Clause of the Fourteenth Amendment. In addition, there is no scientific evidence that the propensity to engage in criminal behavior is a "trait" that is inherited from parents. Finally, exempting from sterilization those inmates who have not been convicted of the specified crimes violates the Equal Protection Clause of the Fourteenth Amendment by setting up an arbitrary classification.

MR. JUSTICE DOUGLAS delivered the opinion of the Court.

This case touches a sensitive and important area of human rights. Oklahoma deprives certain individuals of a right which is basic to the perpetuation of a race—the right to have offspring. Oklahoma has decreed the enforcement of its law against petitioner, overruling his claim that it violated the Fourteenth Amendment. Because that decision raised grave and substantial constitutional questions, we granted the petition for certiorari.

The statute involved is Oklahoma's Habitual Criminal Sterilization Act. That Act defines an "habitual criminal" as a person who, having been convicted two or more times for crimes "amounting to felonies involving moral turpitude" either in an Oklahoma court or in a court of any other State, is thereafter convicted of such a felony in Oklahoma and is sentenced to a term of imprisonment in an Oklahoma penal institution. Machinery is provided for the institution by the Attorney General of a proceeding against such a person in the Oklahoma courts for a judgment that such person shall be rendered sexually sterile. Notice, an opportunity to be heard, and the right to a jury trial are provided. The issues triable in such a proceeding are narrow and confined. If the court or jury finds that the defendant is an "habitual criminal" and that he "may be rendered sexually sterile without detriment to his or her general health," then the court "shall render judgment to the effect that said defendant be rendered sexually sterile" by the operation of vasectomy in case of a male and of salpingectomy in case of a female. Only one other provision of the Act is material here and that provides that "offenses arising out of the violation of the prohibitory laws, revenue acts, embezzlement, or political offenses, shall not come or be considered within the terms of this Act."

Petitioner was convicted in 1926 of the crime of stealing chickens and was sentenced to the Oklahoma State Reformatory. In 1929 he was convicted of the crime of robbery with fire arms and was sentenced to the reformatory. In 1934 he was convicted again of robbery with firearms and was sentenced to the penitentiary. He was confined there in 1935 when the Act was passed. In 1936 the Attorney General instituted proceedings against him. Petitioner in his answer challenged the Act as unconstitutional by reason of the Fourteenth Amendment. A jury trial was had. The court instructed the jury that the crimes of which petitioner had been convicted were felonies involving moral turpitude and that the only question for the jury was whether the operation of vasectomy could be performed on petitioner without detriment to his general health. The jury found that it could be. A judgment directing that the operation of vasectomy be performed on petitioner was affirmed by the Supreme Court of Oklahoma by a five to four decision.

Several objections to the constitutionality of the Act have been pressed upon us. It is urged that the Act cannot be sustained as an exercise of the police power in view of the state of scientific authorities respecting inheritability of criminal traits. It is argued that due process is lacking because under this Act, unlike the act upheld in Buck v. Bell, the defendant is given no opportunity to be heard on the issue as to whether he is the probable potential parent of socially undesirable offspring. It is also suggested that the Act is penal in character and that the sterilization provided for is cruel and unusual punishment and violative of the Fourteenth Amendment. We pass those points without intimating an opinion on them, for there is a feature of the Act which clearly condemns it. That is its failure to meet the requirements of the equal protection clause of the Fourteenth Amendment.

We do not stop to point out all of the inequalities in this Act. A few examples will suffice. In Oklahoma grand larceny is a felony. Larceny is grand larceny when the property taken exceeds $20 in value. Embezzlement is punishable "in the manner prescribed for feloniously stealing property of the value of that embezzled." Hence he who embezzles property worth more than $20 is guilty of a felony. A clerk who appropriates over $20 from his employer's till and a stranger who steals the same amount are thus both guilty of felonies. If the latter repeats his act and is convicted three times, he may be sterilized. But the clerk is not subject to the pains and penalties of the Act no matter how large his embezzlements nor how frequent his convictions. A person who enters a chicken coop and steals chickens commits a felony; and he may be sterilized if he is thrice convicted. If, however, he is a bailee of the property and fraudulently appropriates it, he is an embezzler. Hence no matter how habitual his proclivities for embezzlement are and no matter how often his conviction, he may not be sterilized. Thus the nature of the two crimes is intrinsically the same and they are punishable in the same manner. . . .

It was stated in Buck v. Bell that the claim that state legislation violates the equal protection clause of the Fourteenth Amendment is "the usual last resort of constitutional arguments." Under our constitutional system the States in determining the reach and scope of particular legislation need not provide "abstract symmetry." They may mark and set apart the classes and types of problems according to the needs and as dictated or suggested by experience. . . . Thus, if we had here only a question as to a State's classification of crimes, such as embezzlement or larceny, no substantial federal question would be raised. For a State is not constrained in the exercise of its police power to ignore experience which marks a class of offenders or a family of offenses for special treatment. Nor is it prevented by the equal protection clause from confining "its restrictions to those classes of cases where the need is deemed to be clearest." But the instant legislation runs afoul of the equal protection clause, though we give Oklahoma that large deference which the rule of the foregoing cases requires.

We are dealing here with legislation which involves one of the basic civil rights of man. Marriage and procreation are fundamental to the very existence and survival of the race. The power to sterilize, if exercised, may have subtle, far-reaching and devastating effects. In evil or reckless hands it can cause races or types which are inimical to the dominant group to wither and disappear. There is no redemption for the individual whom the law touches. Any experiment which the State conducts is to his irreparable injury. He is forever deprived of a basic liberty. We mention these matters not to reexamine the scope of the police power of the States. We advert to them merely in emphasis of our view that strict scrutiny of the classification which a State makes in a sterilization law is essential, lest unwittingly or otherwise invidious discriminations are made against groups or types of individuals in violation of the constitutional guaranty of just and equal laws. The guaranty of "equal protection of the laws is a pledge of the protection of equal laws." Yick Wo v. Hopkins. When the law lays an unequal hand on those who have committed intrinsically the same quality of offense and sterilizes one and not the other, it has made as an invidious a discrimination as if it had selected a particular race or nationality for oppressive treatment. Sterilization of those who have thrice committed grand larceny with immunity for those who are embezzlers is a clear, pointed, unmistakable discrimination. Oklahoma makes no attempt to say that he who commits larceny by trespass or trick or fraud has biologically inheritable traits which he who commits embezzlement lacks. . . . We have not the slightest basis for inferring that that line has any significance in eugenics nor that the inheritability of criminal traits follows the neat legal distinctions which the law has marked between those two offenses. In terms of fines and imprisonment the crimes of larceny and embezzlement rate the same under the Oklahoma code. Only when it comes to sterilization are the pains and penalties of the law different. The equal protection clause would indeed be a formula of empty words if such conspicuously artificial lines could be drawn. . . .

Reversed.

Mr. Chief Justice Stone, concurring.

I concur in the result, but I am not persuaded that we are aided in reaching it by recourse to the equal protection clause. If Oklahoma may resort generally to the sterilization of criminals on the assumption that their propensities are transmissible to future generations by inheritance, I seriously doubt that the equal protection clause requires it to apply the measure to all criminals in the first instance, or to none. Moreover, if we must presume that the legislature knows—what science has been unable to ascertain—that the criminal tendencies of any class of habitual offenders are transmissible regardless of the varying mental characteristics of its individuals, I should suppose that we must likewise presume that the legislature, in its wisdom, knows that the criminal tendencies of some classes of offenders are more likely to be transmitted than those of others. And so I think the real question we have to consider is not one of equal protection, but whether the wholesale condemnation of a class to such an invasion of personal liberty, without opportunity to any individual to show that his is not the type of case which would justify resort to it, satisfies the demands of due process.

There are limits to the extent to which the presumption of constitutionality can be pressed, especially where the liberty of the person is concerned (see United States v. Carolene Products Co., n. 4) and where the presumption is resorted to only to dispense with a procedure which the ordinary dictates of prudence would seem to demand for the protection of the individual from arbitrary action. Although petitioner here was given a hearing to ascertain whether sterilization would be detrimental to his health, he was given none to discover whether his criminal tendencies are of an inheritable type. Undoubtedly a state may, after appropriate inquiry, constitutionally interfere with the personal liberty of the individual to prevent the transmission by inheritance of his socially injurious tendencies. Buck v. Bell. But until now we have not been called upon to say that it may do so without giving him a hearing and opportunity to challenge the existence as to him of the only facts which could justify so drastic a measure. Science has found and the law has recognized that there are certain types of mental deficiency associated with delinquency which are inheritable. But the State does not contend—nor can there be any pretense—that eithe[r]

common knowledge or experience, or scientific investigation has given assurance that the criminal tendencies of any class of habitual offenders are universally or even generally inheritable. In such circumstances, inquiry whether such is the fact in the case of any particular individual cannot rightly be dispensed with. Whether the procedure by which a statute carries its mandate into execution satisfies due process is a matter of judicial cognizance. A law which condemns, without hearing, all the individuals of a class to so harsh a measure as the present because some or even many merit condemnation, is lacking in the first principles of due process. And so, while the state may protect itself from the demonstrably inheritable tendencies of the individual which are injurious to society, the most elementary notions of due process would seem to require it to take appropriate steps to safeguard the liberty of the individual by affording him, before he is condemned to an irreparable injury in his person, some opportunity to show that he is without such inheritable tendencies. The state is called on to sacrifice no permissible end when it is required to reach its objective by a reasonable and just procedure adequate to safeguard rights of the individual which concededly the Constitution protects.

Mr. Justice Jackson, concurring.

I join the Chief Justice in holding that the hearings provided are too limited in the context of the present Act to afford due process of law. I also agree with the opinion of Mr. Justice Douglas that the scheme of classification set forth in the Act denies equal protection of the law. I disagree with the opinion of each in so far as it rejects or minimizes the grounds taken by the other.

Perhaps to employ a broad and loose scheme of classification would be permissible if accompanied by the individual hearings indicated by the Chief Justice. On the other hand, narrow classification with reference to the end to be accomplished by the Act might justify limiting individual hearings to the issue whether the individual belonged to a class so defined. Since this Act does not present these questions, I reserve judgment on them.

I also think the present plan to sterilize the individual in pursuit of a eugenic plan to eliminate from the race characteristics that are only vaguely identified and which in our present state of knowledge are uncertain as to transmissibility presents other constitutional questions of gravity. This Court has sustained such an experiment with respect to an imbecile, a person with definite and observable characteristics where the condition had persisted through three generations and afforded grounds for the belief that it was transmissible and would continue to manifest itself in generations to come. Buck v. Bell.

There are limits to the extent to which a legislatively represented majority may conduct biological experiments at the expense of the dignity and personality and natural powers of a minority—even those who have been guilty of what the majority define as crimes. But this Act falls down before reaching this problem, which I mention only to avoid the implication that such a question may not exist because [it is] not discussed. On it I would also reserve judgment.

GRISWOLD V. CONNECTICUT
381 U.S. 479 (1965)

"Would we allow the police to search the sacred precincts of marital bedrooms for telltale signs of the use of contraceptives? The very idea is repulsive to the notions of privacy surrounding the marriage relationship. We deal with a right of privacy older than the Bill of Rights."

The Question: Can a state pass a law that makes it a criminal offense for any person, including married couples and doctors, to use or to distribute contraceptive drugs or devices?

The Arguments: PRO

The state has a legitimate interest in making it more difficult for persons who might consider engaging in extramarital sex to avoid conception, and a legislative ban on the use or distribution of contraceptive devices is a reasonable means of furthering that goal. The Constitution does not prevent the states from passing measures that promote the public "health, safety, welfare, or morals," and the law in question, from the state of Connecticut, serves more than one of those interests. The courts should not interfere with the decisions of legislative bodies in areas that are reserved to the states, including the promotion of marital fidelity.

CON

The Connecticut law in question is a relic of Victorian morality and remains on the books only because succeeding generations of state legislators have feared the electoral wrath of religious groups, most importantly the Roman Catholic Church. If they voted to repeal this law, which the record discloses it has never been enforced until this suit was brought to challenge it. The right of married couples to use birth control methods is an aspect of the "liberty" protected by the Fourteenth Amendment, and physicians should not face prosecution for supplying contraceptive drugs and devices to their patients.

MR. JUSTICE DOUGLAS delivered the opinion of the Court.

Appellant Griswold is Executive Director of the Planned Parenthood League of Connecticut. Appellant Buxton is a licensed physician and a professor at the Yale Medical School who served as Medical Director for the League at its Center in New Haven—a center open and operating from November 1 to November 10, 1961, when appellants were arrested. They gave information, instruction, and medical advice to married persons as to the means of preventing conception. They examined the wife and prescribed the best contraceptive device or material for her use. Fees were usually charged, although some couples were serviced free.

The statutes whose constitutionality is involved in this appeal are 53-32 and 54-196 of the General Statutes of Connecticut. The former provides:

Any person who uses any drug, medicinal article or instrument for the purpose of preventing conception shall be fined not less than fifty dollars or imprisoned not less than sixty days nor more than one year or be both fined and imprisoned.

Section 54-196 provides:

Any person who assists, abets, counsels, causes, hires or commands another to commit any offense may be prosecuted and punished as if he were the principal offender.

The appellants were found guilty as accessories and fined $100 each, against the claim that the accessory statute as so applied violated the Fourteenth Amendment. The Appellate Division of the Circuit Court affirmed. The Supreme Court of Errors affirmed that judgment. We noted probable jurisdiction. . . .

Coming to the merits, we are met with a wide range of questions that implicate the Due Process Clause of the Fourteenth Amendment. Overtones of some arguments suggest that Lochner v. New York (1905) should be our guide. But we decline that invitation as we did in West Coast Hotel Co. v. Parrish (1937). . . . We do not sit as a super-legislature to determine the wisdom, need, and propriety of laws that touch economic problems, business affairs, or social conditions. This law, however, operates directly on an intimate relation of husband and wife and their physician's role in one aspect of that relation.

The association of people is not mentioned in the Constitution nor in the Bill of Rights. The right to educate a child in a school of the parents' choice—whether public or private or parochial—is also not mentioned. Nor is the right to study any particular subject or any foreign language. Yet the First Amendment has been construed to include certain of those rights.

By Pierce v. Society of Sisters, the right to educate one's children as one chooses is made applicable to the States by the force of the First and Fourteenth Amendments. By Meyer v. Nebraska, the same dignity is given the right to study the German language in a private school. In other words, the State may not, consistently with the spirit of the First Amendment, contract the spectrum of available knowledge. The right of freedom of speech and press includes not only the right to utter or to print, but the right to distribute, the right to receive, the right to read and freedom of inquiry, freedom of thought, and freedom to teach. . . . Without those peripheral rights the specific rights would be less secure. . . . In other words, the First Amendment has a penumbra where privacy is protected from governmental intrusion. . . .

The foregoing cases suggest that specific guarantees in the Bill of Rights have penumbras, formed by emanations from those guarantees that help give them life and substance. Various guarantees create zones of privacy. The right of association contained in the penumbra of the First Amendment is one, as we have seen. The Third Amendment in its prohibition against the quartering of soldiers "in any house" in time of peace without the consent of the owner is another facet of that privacy. The Fourth Amendment explicitly affirms the "right of the people to be secure in their persons, houses, papers, and effects, against unreasonable searches and seizures." The Fifth Amendment in its Self-Incrimination Clause enables the citizen to create a zone of privacy which government may not force him to surrender to his detriment. The Ninth Amendment provides: "The enumeration in the Constitution, of certain rights, shall not be construed to deny or disparage others retained by the people." . . .

The present case, then, concerns a relationship lying within the zone of privacy created by several fundamental constitutional guarantees. And it concerns a law which, in forbidding the use of contraceptives rather than regulating their manufacture or sale, seeks to achieve its goals by means having a maximum destructive impact upon that relationship. Such a law cannot stand in light of the familiar principle, so often applied by this Court, that a "governmental purpose to control or prevent activities constitutionally subject to state regulation may not be achieved by means which sweep unnecessarily broadly and thereby invade the area of protected freedoms." Would we allow the police to search the sacred precincts of marital bedrooms for telltale signs of the use of contraceptives? The very idea is repulsive to the notions of privacy surrounding the marriage relationship.

We deal with a right of privacy older than the Bill of Rights—older than our political parties, older than our school system. Marriage is a coming together for better or for worse, hopefully enduring, and intimate to the degree of being sacred. It is an association that promotes a way of life, not causes; a harmony in living, not political faiths; a bilateral loyalty, not commercial or social projects. Yet it is an association for as noble a purpose as any involved in our prior decisions.

Reversed.

Mr. Justice Goldberg, whom The Chief Justice and Mr. Justice Brennan join, concurring.

I agree with the Court that Connecticut's birth-control law unconstitutionally intrudes upon the right of marital privacy, and I join in its opinion and judgment. Although I have not accepted the view that "due process" as used in the Fourteenth Amendment incorporates all of the first eight amendments, I do agree that the concept of liberty protects those personal rights that are fundamental, and is not confined to the specific terms of the Bill of Rights. My conclusion that the concept of liberty is not so restricted and that it embraces the right of marital privacy though that right is not mentioned explicitly in the Constitution is supported both by numerous decisions of this Court, referred to in the Court's opinion, and by the language and history of the Ninth Amendment. In reaching the conclusion that the right of marital privacy is protected, as being within the protected penumbra of specific guarantees of the Bill of Rights, the Court refers to the Ninth Amendment. I add these words to emphasize the relevance of that Amendment to the Court's holding. . . .

This Court, in a series of decisions, has held that the Fourteenth Amendment absorbs and applies to the States those specifics of the first eight amendments which express fundamental personal rights. The language and history of the Ninth Amendment reveal that the Framers of the Constitution believed that there are additional fundamental rights, protected from governmental infringement, which exist alongside those fundamental rights specifically mentioned in the first eight constitutional amendments.

The Ninth Amendment reads, "The enumeration in the Constitution, of certain rights, shall not be construed to deny or disparage others retained by the people." The Amendment is almost entirely the work of James Madison. It was introduced in Congress by him and passed the House and Senate with little or no debate and virtually no change in language. It was proffered to quiet expressed fears that a bill of specifically enumerated rights could not be sufficiently broad to cover all essential rights and that the specific mention of certain rights would be interpreted as a denial that others were protected. . . .

While this Court has had little occasion to interpret the Ninth Amendment, "[i]t cannot be presumed that any clause in the constitution is intended to be without effect." Marbury v. Madison. In interpreting the Constitution, "real effect should be given to all the words it uses." The Ninth Amendment to the Constitution may be regarded by some as a recent discovery and may be forgotten by others, but since 1791 it has been a basic part of the Constitution which we are sworn to uphold. To hold that a right so basic and fundamental and so deep-rooted in our society as the right of privacy in marriage may be infringed because that right is not guaranteed in so many words by the first eight amendments to the Constitution is to ignore the Ninth Amendment and to give it no effect whatsoever. Moreover, a judicial construction that this fundamental right is not protected by the Constitution because it is not mentioned in explicit terms by one of the first eight amendments or elsewhere in the Constitution would violate the Ninth Amendment, which specifically states that "[t]he enumeration in the Constitution, of certain rights, shall not be construed to deny or disparage others retained by the people." . . .

As any student of this Court's opinions knows, this Court has held, often unanimously, that the Fifth and Fourteenth Amendments protect certain fundamental personal liberties from abridgment by the Federal Government or the States.

The Ninth Amendment simply shows the intent of the Constitution's authors that other fundamental personal rights should not be denied such protection or disparaged in any other way simply because they are not specifically listed in the first eight constitutional amendments. I do not see how this broadens the authority of the Court; rather it serves to support what this Court has been doing in protecting fundamental rights.

Nor am I turning somersaults with history in arguing that the Ninth Amendment is relevant in a case dealing with a State's infringement of a fundamental right. While the Ninth Amendment—and indeed the entire Bill of Rights—originally concerned restrictions upon federal power, the subsequently enacted Fourteenth Amendment prohibits the States as well from abridging fundamental personal liberties. And, the Ninth Amendment, in indicating that not all such liberties are specifically mentioned in the first eight amendments, is surely relevant in showing the existence of other fundamental personal rights, now protected from state, as well as federal, infringement. In sum, the Ninth Amendment simply lends strong support to the view that the "liberty" protected by the Fifth and Fourteenth Amendments from infringement by the Federal Government or the States is not restricted to rights specifically mentioned in the first eight amendments. . . .

I agree fully with the Court that . . . the right of privacy is a fundamental personal right, emanating "from the totality of the constitutional scheme under which we live." . . . The Connecticut statutes here involved deal with a particularly important and sensitive area of privacy—that of the marital relation and the marital home. . . . The entire fabric of the Constitution and the purposes that clearly underlie its specific guarantees demonstrate that the rights to marital privacy and to marry and raise a family are of similar order and magnitude as the fundamental rights specifically protected. Although the Constitution does not speak in so many words of the right of privacy in marriage, I cannot believe that it offers these fundamental rights no protection. The fact that no particular provision of the Constitution explicitly forbids the State from disrupting the traditional relation of the family—a relation as old and as fundamental as our entire civilization—surely does not show that the Government was meant to have the power to do so. Rather, as the Ninth Amendment expressly recognizes, there are fundamental personal rights such as this one, which are protected from abridgment by the Government though not specifically mentioned in the Constitution. . . .

In sum, I believe that the right of privacy in the marital relation is fundamental and basic—a personal right "retained by the people" within the meaning of the Ninth Amendment. Connecticut cannot constitutionally abridge this fundamental right, which is protected by the Fourteenth Amendment from infringement by the States. I agree with the Court that petitioners' convictions must therefore be reversed.

MR. JUSTICE BLACK, with whom MR. JUSTICE STEWART joins, dissenting.

. . . I do not to any extent whatever base my view that this Connecticut law is constitutional on a belief that the law is wise or that its policy is a good one. . . . There is no single one of the graphic and eloquent strictures and criticisms fired at the policy of this Connecticut law either by the Court's opinion or by those of my concurring Brethren to which I cannot subscribe—except their conclusion that the evil qualities they see in the law make it unconstitutional. . . .

The Court talks about a constitutional "right of privacy" as though there is some constitutional provision or provisions forbidding any law ever to be passed which might abridge the "privacy" of individuals. But there is not. There are, of course, guarantees in certain specific constitutional provisions which are designed in part to protect privacy at certain times and places with respect to certain activities. Such, for example, is the Fourth Amendment's guarantee against "unreasonable searches and seizures." But I think it belittles that Amendment to talk about it as though it protects nothing but "privacy." To treat it that way is to give it a niggardly interpretation, not the kind of liberal reading I think any Bill of Rights provision should be given. The average man would very likely not have his feelings soothed any more by having his property seized openly than by having it seized privately and by stealth. He simply wants his property left alone. And a person can be just as much, if not more, irritated, annoyed and injured by an unceremonious public arrest by a policeman as he is by a seizure in the privacy of his office or home.

One of the most effective ways of diluting or expanding a constitutionally guaranteed right is to substitute for the crucial word or words of a constitutional guarantee another word or words, more or less flexible and more or less restricted in meaning. This fact is well illustrated by the use of the term "right of privacy" as a comprehensive substitute for the Fourth Amendment's guarantee against "unreasonable searches and seizures." "Privacy" is a broad, abstract and ambiguous concept which can easily be shrunken in meaning but which can also, on the other hand, easily be interpreted as a constitutional ban against many things other than searches and seizures. I have expressed the view many times that First Amendment freedoms, for example, have suffered from a failure of the courts to stick to the simple language of the First Amendment in construing it, instead of invoking multitudes of words substituted for those the Framers used. For these reasons I get nowhere in this case by talk about a constitutional "right of privacy" as an emanation from one or more constitutional provisions. I like my privacy as well as the next one, but I am nevertheless compelled to admit that government has a right to invade it unless prohibited by some specific constitutional provision. For these reasons I cannot agree with the Court's judgment and the reasons it gives for holding this Connecticut law unconstitutional. . . .

I realize that many good and able men have eloquently spoken and written, sometimes in rhapsodical strains, about the duty of this Court to keep the Constitution in tune with the times. The idea is that the Constitution must be changed from time to time and that this Court is charged with a duty to make those changes. For myself, I must with all deference reject that philosophy. The Constitution makers knew the need for change and provided for it. Amendments suggested by the people's elected representatives can be submitted to the people or their selected agents for ratification. That method of change was good for our Fathers, and being somewhat old-fashioned I must add it is good enough for me. And so, I cannot rely on the Due Process Clause or the Ninth Amendment or any mysterious and uncertain natural law concept as a reason for striking down this state law. The Due Process Clause with an "arbitrary and capricious" or "shocking to the conscience" formula was liberally used by this Court to strike down economic legislation in the early decades of this century, threatening, many people thought, the tranquility and stability of the Nation. See, e.g., Lochner v. New York. That formula, based on subjective considerations of "natural justice," is no less dangerous when used to enforce this Court's views about personal rights than those about economic rights. I had thought that we had laid that formula, as a means for striking down state legislation, to rest once and for all in cases like West Coast Hotel Co. v. Parrish. . . .

So far as I am concerned, Connecticut's law as applied here is not forbidden by any provision of the Federal Constitution as that Constitution was written, and I would therefore affirm.

MR. JUSTICE STEWART, whom MR. JUSTICE BLACK joins, dissenting.

Since 1879 Connecticut has had on its books a law which forbids the use of contraceptives by anyone. I think this is an uncommonly silly law. As a practical matter, the law is obviously unenforceable, except in the oblique context of the present case. As a philosophical matter, I believe the use of contraceptives in the relationship of marriage should be left to personal and private choice, based upon each individual's moral, ethical, and religious beliefs. As a matter of social policy, I think professional counsel about methods of birth control should be available to all, so that each individual's choice can be meaningfully made. But we are not asked in this case to say whether we think this law is unwise, or even asinine. We are asked to hold that it violates the United States Constitution. And that I cannot do.

In the course of its opinion the Court refers to no less than six Amendments to the Constitution: the First, the Third, the Fourth, the Fifth, the Ninth, and the Fourteenth. But the Court does not say which of these Amendments, if any, it thinks is infringed by this Connecticut law. We are told that the Due Process Clause of the Fourteenth Amendment is not, as such, the "guide" in this case. With that much I agree. There is no claim that this law, duly enacted by the Connecticut Legislature is unconstitutionally vague. There is no claim that the appellants were denied any of the elements of procedural due process at their trial, so as to make their convictions constitutionally invalid. And, as the Court says, the day has long passed since the Due Process Clause was

regarded as a proper instrument for determining "the wisdom, need, and propriety" of state laws. . . .

As to the First, Third, Fourth, and Fifth Amendments, I can find nothing in any of them to invalidate this Connecticut law, even assuming that all those Amendments are fully applicable against the States. It has not even been argued that this is a law "respecting an establishment of religion, or prohibiting the free exercise thereof." And surely, unless the solemn process of constitutional adjudication is to descend to the level of a play on words, there is not involved here any abridgment of "the freedom of speech, or of the press; or the right of the people peaceably to assemble, and to petition the Government for a redress of grievances." No soldier has been quartered in any house. There has been no search, and no seizure. Nobody has been compelled to be a witness against himself.

The Court also quotes the Ninth Amendment, and my Brother Goldberg's concurring opinion relies heavily upon it. But to say that the Ninth Amendment has anything to do with this case is to turn somersaults with history. The Ninth Amendment, like its companion the Tenth, which this Court held "states but a truism that all is retained which has not been surrendered," was framed by James Madison and adopted by the States simply to make clear that the adoption of the Bill of Rights did not alter the plan that the Federal Government was to be a government of express and limited powers, and that all rights and powers not delegated to it were retained by the people and the individual States. Until today no member of this Court has ever suggested that the Ninth Amendment meant anything else, and the idea that a federal court could ever use the Ninth Amendment to annul a law passed by the elected representatives of the people of the State of Connecticut would have caused James Madison no little wonder.

What provision of the Constitution, then, does make this state law invalid? The Court says it is the right of privacy "created by several fundamental constitutional guarantees." With all deference, I can find no such general right of privacy in the Bill of Rights, in any other part of the Constitution, or in any case ever before decided by this Court. At the oral argument in this case we were told that the Connecticut law does not "conform to current community standards." But it is not the function of this Court to decide cases on the basis of community standards. We are here to decide cases "agreeably to the Constitution and laws of the United States." It is the essence of judicial duty to subordinate our own personal views, our own ideas of what legislation is wise and what is not. If, as I should surely hope, the law before us does not reflect the standards of the people of Connecticut, the people of Connecticut can freely exercise their true Ninth and Tenth Amendment rights to persuade their elected representatives to repeal it. That is the constitutional way to take this law off the books.

ROE V. WADE
410 U.S. 113 (1973)

"[The] right of privacy . . . is broad enough to encompass a woman's decision whether or not to terminate her pregnancy. The detriment that the State would impose upon the pregnant woman by denying this choice altogether is apparent."

The Question: Can a state pass a law that makes it a criminal offense for any person to "procure an abortion" or to attempt one, unless an abortion is necessary to save the pregnant woman's life?

The Arguments: PRO

The state has a legitimate interest in protecting potential life from destruction, and a fetus is a "person" under a construction of the United States and Texas constitutions that recognizes that human life is a continuum from conception through birth. There is nothing in the federal constitution that refers to abortion, and the courts should not stretch its provisions to create a right the Framers did not intend or contemplate. The question of abortion is one for legislative decision, and the people of each state should be allowed to make this decision for themselves.

CON

The Fourteenth Amendment provides that no state shall deprive any person of "liberty" without due process of law, and the state of Texas has not shown any compelling interest in preventing women and their doctors from making this highly personal choice for themselves. The Supreme Court has ruled in the *Griswold* case that states cannot limit access to contraception, and the "right of privacy" stated in that case should extend to the abortion decision as well. In addition, there are no cases that confer the status of a "person" with full legal rights on an unborn fetus, especially before the stage of fetal viability.

BACKGROUND

Texas lawmakers—all men and all white—had enacted a criminal abortion statute in 1854, providing that "any person" who performed an abortion "shall be confined in the penitentiary not less than two nor more than five years." Fifty years later, the state legislature amended the law to permit abortions that doctors considered necessary to save a woman's life. Was the Texas criminal abortion statute an unwise or asinine law? Even if it was, did the law violate the Constitution? If so, which provision did it offend? Between them, the Supreme Court justices wrote six opinions on both sides of the *Griswold* case in 1965. Five years later, this judicial cacophony presented three federal judges in Dallas with several choices in deciding these questions at a hearing on May 22, 1970.

This judicial panel had convened to hear arguments on three separate lawsuits filed against the Texas abortion law. The first suit had been filed two months earlier, on March 3, on behalf of "Jane Roe." This legal pseudonym shielded the identity of a young woman named Norma McCorvey, who had asked her lawyers to keep her name out of the newspapers; the public did not learn her true name until 1984, when she finally took off her legal mask. Norma was twenty-two years old and three months pregnant when she first tried to get an abortion in January 1970. She was not another Sherri Finkbine, happily married with four children and her own

television show. Norma Nelson McCorvey was a high school dropout from a broken home; she had been raped at an early age and spent much of her childhood in reform schools. She was sixteen and working as a carhop when she met "Woody" McCorvey, eight years older and twice divorced. They got married six weeks later and soon left Dallas for California, where Norma discovered she was pregnant. Woody flew into a rage, accusing his wife of sleeping around and punching her black and blue. She took a bus back to Dallas, got a job in a lesbian bar, and gave birth to Melissa in May 1965. Upset with Norma's bisexual lifestyle, her mother moved to Louisiana with Melissa and gained legal custody with her second husband.

Norma had a second daughter in 1967, the result of a brief affair, and willingly surrendered custody to the baby's father. She left Dallas in the fall of 1969 with a traveling circus, working as a ticket-taker. Sometime in October 1969, Norma discovered she was pregnant for the third time and returned home. She visited Dr. Frank Bradley, who had delivered her two daughters, and he confirmed her pregnancy; she later recalled that he was "absolutely appalled" when she told him she did not want another baby. Dr. Bradley would not give her any help, even the names of other doctors who might perform an abortion. Norma went to see an osteopath, Dr. Richard Lane, who said he could not help but referred her to a lawyer named Henry McCluskey. Time was running short for Norma to have an abortion, and she wanted help in arranging an adoption for her baby, which was due in July. McCluskey met with her in late January 1970 and agreed to help arrange an adoption with a good family who would pay her childbirth expenses. They talked about abortion, and Norma said that she wished it were legal in Texas. McCluskey had recently won a case before a federal judicial panel, challenging a Texas law under which a married couple had been prosecuted for committing acts of sodomy. Writing for the panel, district judge Sarah Hughes had cited *Griswold v. Connecticut* in holding that moral disapproval of sodomy "is not sufficient reason for the State to encroach upon the liberty of married persons in their private conduct." A young Dallas lawyer named Linda Coffee had helped McCluskey in this case, and had asked his help in finding a pregnant woman who might be willing to challenge the Texas abortion law.

After his meeting with Norma, McCluskey called Linda Coffee and said he might have found her a plaintiff. She was excited and asked him to arrange for her to meet with Norma. Coffee then called her friend Sarah Weddington, a law school classmate from the University of Texas who had set up practice in Austin after graduating in 1967. The two young lawyers had been working with a group of Dallas women at the First Unitarian Church, who were planning a public campaign to repeal the Texas abortion law. Coffee and Weddington thought a lawsuit might help the campaign and might even succeed in striking down the law in court.

Weddington agreed to come to Dallas for a meeting with Norma McCorvey, and the three women first met at Columbo's Pizza Parlor in late January. Norma had told another woman in Dr. Lane's waiting room that she wanted an abortion and was advised that doctors might be sympathetic if she told them she had been raped. This was not true, but she told the two lawyers that a group of men had gang-raped her in Florida while she walked late one night from the carnival to her motel room. Coffee and Weddington expressed sympathy, but the Texas abortion law did not include a rape-victim exception and they did not want to ask the courts to create one. They also did not want to help Norma obtain a late-term abortion before they filed suit; they needed a pregnant plaintiff who still wanted an abortion. Norma agreed, and they finished their pizza with an understanding that the suit would be filed without her name on the caption.

Linda Coffee did most of the work in February 1970 on the complaint for "Jane Roe." She and Sarah Weddington had decided it would be helpful to file another complaint on behalf of a married couple. They reasoned that judges might dismiss Jane Roe's case for "mootness" if she was no longer pregnant when the case was heard. Judge Hughes's decision in Henry McCluskey's sodomy case suggested that married couples might find more judicial sympathy than unmarried women. Giving the judges a choice of cases also increased the odds of getting a favorable decision in at least one. Linda Coffee knew a married couple, Marsha and David King, who agreed to become "John and Jane Doe." She filed the "Roe" and "Doe" complaints in federal court on March 3, 1970. They both asked for a "declaratory judgment" that the Texas abortion statute violated the First, Fourth, Fifth, Eighth, Ninth, and Fourteenth Amendments. Both also named Dallas County's district attorney, Henry Wade, as defendant and

sought an injunction barring him from enforcing the statute. Jane Roe's complaint alleged that the law infringed her "right to safe and adequate medical advice pertaining to the decision of whether to carry a given pregnancy to term" and also infringed "the fundamental right of all women to choose whether to bear children." The Does' complaint alleged that the abortion law intruded on their "right to marital privacy" and that fear of an unwanted pregnancy had "a detrimental effect upon Plaintiffs' marital happiness."

Coffee had talked with a *Dallas Times-Herald* reporter about the lawsuit, and the paper ran a front-page story the evening she filed the complaints. A follow-up article reported estimates of three thousand illegal abortions in Dallas each year. The paper's editors evenhandedly deplored both the Texas abortion law, which they called "badly in need of an intelligent overhaul," and the suits against it, for "tossing an extremely sensitive and complex moral issue into the laps of a mere handful of individuals—the judges who are to decide the case." Linda Coffee and Sarah Weddington drew a good panel of federal judges to decide the "sensitive and complex moral issue" of abortion. All three were elderly—their average age was sixty-six—but all had been appointed by Democratic presidents and were considered liberal by civil rights lawyers. Irving Goldberg, who presided at the hearing on May 22, 1970, was a native Texan with a Harvard law degree who had practiced in a powerhouse Dallas law firm before President Johnson named him to the Fifth Circuit Court of Appeals in 1966. District judge Sarah Hughes, born in Baltimore in 1896, had earned a law degree while she worked as a police officer in Washington, D.C. She moved to Dallas in 1922, was elected twice to the state legislature, and served as a state judge from 1935 to 1961, when President Kennedy named her to the federal bench. On November 23, 1963, Judge Hughes administered the presidential oath to Lyndon Johnson after Kennedy's assassination in Dallas. The third panel member, Judge William Taylor, had practiced law in Dallas from 1932 until President Johnson placed him on the bench in 1966.

Six lawyers sat at the counsel tables when Judge Goldberg opened the hearing. Linda Coffee and Sarah Weddington spoke for Jane Roe and the Does; John Tolle and Jay Floyd represented District Attorney Henry Wade and Texas attorney general Crawford Martin. Fred Brunner and Ray Merrill appeared for Dr. James Hallford, an "intervenor" who had been indicted for performing illegal abortions. Dr. Hallford's patients included rape and incest victims, and women who had contracted German measles, or rubella, during their pregnancies and faced great risks of having deformed babies. His complaint asked that the state criminal charges be dismissed because the Texas abortion law violated the federal Constitution.

Linda Coffee led off, moving from questions of federal jurisdiction into the constitutional issues raised in the complaint. She spoke confidently, certain that Judge Hughes—for whom she had clerked the year after law school—and Judge Goldberg were sympathetic. Coffee started running down the list of five constitutional amendments—from the First to Ninth—that she claimed the Texas abortion law violated. Judge Hughes cut her off at the First and directed her to the Ninth. The judge had obviously read Justice Arthur Goldberg's concurrence in *Griswold* and liked his Ninth

Amendment argument. Coffee agreed and sat down, sensing victory.

Sarah Weddington then stood up, nervous in her first court appearance. Judge Hughes "gave me a reassuring smile and a slight wink," she later recalled. More relaxed, Weddington addressed the question of the state's interests in limiting or preventing abortions; even a constitutional right can be overcome by a "compelling" state interest. Judge Goldberg interrupted, asking her to assume that the Ninth Amendment applied to abortion: Could Texas require that abortions be done in hospitals, or be limited to married women? Weddington's answers were superfluous; Goldberg and Hughes had already decided the case on Ninth Amendment grounds. The remaining lawyers went through the motions, but they also knew the inevitable outcome. Arguing for the state, Jay Floyd asked the judges to dismiss Jane Roe's complaint for lack of proof she was still pregnant. Judge Hughes was not impressed. "Apparently you don't think anybody has standing," she retorted. Floyd answered the question Judge Goldberg had asked Weddington by asserting that the state's "compelling" interest in banning abortion was to protect unborn fetuses. Asked for evidence that Texas lawmakers had ever asserted this interest, Floyd confessed he had none. The hearing ended with John Tolle's claim that "the right of the child to life is superior to that of a woman's right to privacy."

The panel's opinion came down on June 17, 1970, less than a month after the hearing. It was short and unsigned; all three judges agreed on the outcome. They dealt with the "sensitive and complex" issue of abortion in two words. Linda Coffee and Sarah Weddington, the judges wrote, claimed the Texas abortion laws "must be declared unconstitutional because they deprive single women and married couples of their right, secured by the Ninth Amendment, to choose whether to have children. We agree." The judges quoted Justice Goldberg's concurrence in *Griswold*, ignoring Justice Douglas's opinion for the Court. But they also declined to enjoin state officials from enforcing the abortion law, citing the "strong reluctance of federal courts to interfere with the process of state criminal procedure," a reference to the charges against Dr. Hallford. However, the judges had just declared unconstitutional the law under which he was prosecuted. This seemingly inconsistent ruling, giving both sides a partial victory, signaled the lawyers that either side could ask the Supreme Court to review the case. Just as Judge Hughes had winked at Sarah Weddington, both sides got the message and promptly sent petitions for certiorari to Washington (Irons, 1999).

MR. JUSTICE BLACKMUN delivered the opinion of the Court.

This Texas federal appeal and its Georgia companion, Doe v. Bolton, present constitutional challenges to state criminal abortion legislation. The Texas statutes under attack here are typical of those that have been in effect in many States for approximately a century. The Georgia statutes, in contrast, have a modern cast and are a legislative product that, to an extent at least, obviously reflects the influences of recent attitudinal change, of advancing medical knowledge and techniques, and of new thinking about an old issue.

We forthwith acknowledge our awareness of the sensitive and emotional nature of the abortion controversy, of the vigorous opposing views, even among physicians, and of the deep and seemingly absolute convictions that the subject inspires. One's philosophy, one's experiences, one's exposure to the raw edges of human existence, one's religious training, one's attitudes toward life and family and their values, and the moral standards one establishes and seeks to observe, are all likely to influence and to color one's thinking and conclusions about abortion. In addition, population growth, pollution, poverty, and racial overtones tend to complicate and not to simplify the problem.

Our task, of course, is to resolve the issue by constitutional measurement, free of emotion and of predilection. We seek earnestly to do this, and, because we do, we have inquired into, and in this opinion place some emphasis upon, medical and medical-legal history and what that history reveals about man's attitudes toward the abortion procedure over the centuries. We bear in mind, too, Mr. Justice Holmes' admonition in his now-vindicated dissent in Lochner v. New York (1905):

> [The Constitution] is made for people of fundamentally differing views, and the accident of our finding certain opinions natural and familiar or novel and even shocking ought not to conclude our judgment upon the question whether statutes embodying them conflict with the Constitution of the United States.

The Texas statutes that concern us here . . . make it a crime to "procure an abortion," or to attempt one, except with respect to "an abortion procured or attempted by medical advice for the purpose of saving the life of the mother." Similar statutes are in existence in a majority of the States. Texas first enacted a criminal abortion statute in 1854. This was soon modified into language that has remained substantially unchanged to the present time.

Jane Roe, a single woman who was residing in Dallas County, Texas, instituted this federal action in March 1970 against the District Attorney of the county. She sought a declaratory judgment that the Texas criminal abortion statutes were unconstitutional on their face, and an injunction restraining the defendant from enforcing the statutes. Roe alleged that she was unmarried and pregnant; that she wished to terminate her pregnancy by an abortion "performed by a competent, licensed physician, under safe, clinical conditions"; that she was unable to get a "legal" abortion in Texas because her life did not appear to be threatened by the continuation of her pregnancy; and that she could not afford to travel to another jurisdiction in order to secure a legal abortion under safe conditions. She claimed that the Texas statutes were unconstitutionally vague and that they abridged her right of personal privacy, protected by the First, Fourth, Fifth, Ninth, and Fourteenth Amendments. By an amendment to her complaint Roe purported to sue "on behalf of herself and all other women" similarly situated. . . .

On the merits, the District Court held that the "fundamental right of single women and married persons to choose whether to have children is protected by the Ninth Amendment, through the Fourteenth Amendment," and that the Texas criminal abortion statutes were void on their face because they were both unconstitutionally vague and constituted an overbroad infringement of the plaintiffs' Ninth Amendment rights. . . .

The principal thrust of appellant's attack on the Texas statutes is that they improperly invade a right, said to be possessed by the pregnant woman, to choose to terminate her pregnancy. Appellant would discover this right in the concept of personal "liberty" embodied in the Fourteenth Amendment's Due Process Clause; or in personal, marital, familial, and sexual privacy said to be protected by the Bill of Rights or its penumbras, see Griswold v. Connecticut (1965); or among those rights reserved to the people by the Ninth Amendment. Before addressing this claim, we feel it desirable briefly to survey, in several aspects, the history of abortion, for such insight as that history may afford us, and then to examine the state purposes and interests behind the criminal abortion laws.

It perhaps is not generally appreciated that the restrictive criminal abortion laws in effect in a majority of States today are of relatively recent vintage. Those laws, generally proscribing abortion or its attempt at any time during pregnancy except when necessary to preserve the pregnant woman's life, are not of ancient or even of common-law origin. Instead, they derive from statutory changes effected, for the most part, in the latter half of the 19th century. . . .

It is undisputed that at common law, abortion performed before "quickening"—the first recognizable movement of the fetus in utero, appearing usually from the 16th to the 18th week of pregnancy—was not an indictable offense. The absence of a common-law crime for pre-quickening abortion appears to have developed from a confluence of earlier philosophical, theological, and civil and canon law concepts of when life begins. These disciplines variously approached the question in terms of the point at which the embryo or fetus became "formed" or recognizably human, or in terms of when a "person" came into being, that is, infused with a "soul" or "animated." A loose consensus evolved in early English law that these events occurred at some point between conception and live birth. . . . The significance of quickening was echoed by later common-law scholars and found its way into the received common law in this country.

Whether abortion of a quick fetus was a felony at common law, or even a lesser crime, is still disputed. . . . A recent review of the common-law precedents argue . . . that even post-quickening abortion was never established as a common-law crime. . . . In this country, the law in effect in all but a few States until mid-19th century was the pre-existing English common law. . . . In 1828, New York enacted legislation 31 that, in two respects, was to serve as a model for early anti-abortion statutes. First, while barring destruction of an unquickened fetus as well as a quick fetus, it made the former only a misdemeanor, but the latter second-degree manslaughter. Second, it incorporated a concept of therapeutic abortion by providing that an abortion was excused if it "shall have been necessary to preserve the life of such mother, or shall have been advised by two physicians to be necessary for such purpose." . . . It is thus apparent that at common law, at the time of the adoption of our Constitution, and throughout the major portion of the 19th century, abortion was viewed with less disfavor than under most American statutes currently in effect. Phrasing it another way, a woman enjoyed a substantially broader right to terminate a pregnancy than she does in most States today. At least with respect to the early stage of pregnancy, and very possibly without such a limitation, the opportunity to make this choice was present in this country well into the 19th century. Even later, the law continued for some time to treat less punitively an abortion procured in early pregnancy. . . .

Three reasons have been advanced to explain historically the enactment of criminal abortion laws in the 19th century and to justify their continued existence. It has been argued occasionally that these laws were the product of a Victorian social concern to discourage illicit sexual conduct. Texas, however, does not advance this justification in the present case, and it appears that no court or commentator has taken the argument seriously. . . . A second reason is concerned with abortion as a medical procedure. When most criminal abortion laws were first enacted, the procedure was a hazardous one for the woman. This was particularly true prior to the development of antisepsis. . . . Modern medical techniques have altered this situation. Appellants and various amici refer to medical data indicating that abortion in early pregnancy, that is, prior to the end of the first trimester, although not without its risk, is now relatively safe. Mortality rates for women undergoing early abortions, where the procedure is legal, appear to be as low as or lower than the rates for normal childbirth. Consequently, any interest of the State in protecting the woman from an inherently hazardous procedure, except when it would be equally dangerous for her to forgo it, has largely disappeared. Of course, important state interests in the areas of health and medical standards do remain. The State has a legitimate interest in seeing to it that abortion, like any other medical procedure, is performed under circumstances that insure maximum safety for the patient. This interest obviously extends at least to the performing physician and his staff, to the facilities involved, to the availability of after-care, and to adequate provision for any complication or emergency that might arise. The prevalence of high mortality rates at illegal "abortion mills" strengthens, rather than weakens, the State's interest in regulating the conditions under which abortions are performed. Moreover, the risk to the woman increases as her pregnancy continues. Thus, the State retains a definite interest in protecting the woman's own health and safety when an abortion is proposed at a late stage of pregnancy.

The third reason is the State's interest—some phrase it in terms of duty—in protecting prenatal life. Some of the argument for this justification rests on the theory that a new human life is present from the moment of conception. The State's interest and general obligation to protect life then extends, it is argued, to prenatal life. Only when the life of the pregnant mother herself is at stake, balanced against the life she carries within her, should the interest of the embryo or fetus not prevail. Logically, of course, a legitimate state interest in this area need not stand or fall on acceptance of the belief that life begins at conception or at some other point prior to live birth. In assessing the State's interest, recognition may be given to the less rigid claim that as long as at least potential life is involved, the State may assert interests beyond the protection of the pregnant woman alone. . . . It is with these interests, and the weight to be attached to them, that this case is concerned.

The Constitution does not explicitly mention any right of privacy. In a line of decisions, however, going back perhaps as far as Union Pacific R. Co. v. Botsford (1891), the Court has recognized that a right of personal privacy, or a guarantee of certain areas or zones of privacy, does exist under the Constitution. In varying contexts, the Court or individual Justices have, indeed, found at least the roots of that right in the First Amendment, Stanley v. Georgia (1969); in the Fourth and Fifth Amendments, Terry v. Ohio (1968), Katz v. United States (1967), Boyd v. United States (1886), see Olmstead v. United States (1928) (Brandeis, J., dissenting); in the penumbras of the Bill of Rights, Griswold v. Connecticut; in the Ninth Amendment, or in the concept of liberty guaranteed by the first section of the Fourteenth Amendment, see Meyer v. Nebraska (1923). These decisions make it clear that only personal rights that can be deemed "fundamental" or "implicit in the concept of ordered liberty," Palko v. Connecticut (1937), are included in this guarantee of personal privacy. They also make it clear that the right has some extension to activities relating to marriage, Loving v. Virginia (1967); procreation, Skinner v. Oklahoma (1942); contraception, Eisenstadt v. Baird (1972); family relationships, Prince v. Massachusetts (1944); and child rearing and education, Pierce v. Society of Sisters (1925).

This right of privacy, whether it be founded in the Fourteenth Amendment's concept of personal liberty and restrictions upon state action, as we feel it is, or, as the District Court determined, in the Ninth Amendment's reservation of rights to the people, is broad enough to encompass a woman's decision whether or not to terminate her pregnancy. The detriment that the State would impose upon the pregnant woman by denying this choice altogether is apparent. Specific and direct harm medically diagnosable even in early pregnancy may be involved. Maternity, or additional offspring, may force upon the woman a distressful life and future. Psychological harm may be imminent. Mental and physical health may be taxed by child care. There is also the distress, for all concerned, associated with the unwanted child, and there is the problem of bringing a child into a family already unable, psychologically and otherwise, to care for it. In other cases, as in this one, the additional difficulties and continuing stigma of unwed motherhood may be involved. All these are factors the woman and her responsible physician necessarily will consider in consultation.

On the basis of elements such as these, appellant and some amici argue that the woman's right is absolute and that she is entitled to terminate her pregnancy at whatever time, in whatever way, and for whatever reason she alone chooses. With this we do not agree. Appellant's arguments that Texas either has no valid interest at all in regulating the abortion decision, or no interest strong enough to support any limitation upon the woman's sole determination, are unpersuasive. The Court's decisions recognizing a right of privacy also acknowledge that some state regulation in areas protected by that right is appropriate. As noted above, a State may properly assert important interests in safeguarding health, in maintaining medical standards, and in protecting potential life. At some point in pregnancy, these respective interests become sufficiently compelling to sustain regulation of the factors that govern the abortion decision. The privacy right involved, therefore, cannot be said to be absolute.... We, therefore, conclude that the right of personal privacy includes the abortion decision, but that this right is not unqualified and must be considered against important state interests in regulation....

The appellee and certain amici argue that the fetus is a "person" within the language and meaning of the Fourteenth Amendment. In support of this, they outline at length and in detail the well-known facts of fetal development. If this suggestion of personhood is established, the appellant's case, of course, collapses, for the fetus' right to life would then be guaranteed specifically by the Amendment. The appellant conceded as much on reargument. On the other hand, the appellee conceded on reargument that no case could be cited that holds that a fetus is a person within the meaning of the Fourteenth Amendment. The Constitution does not define "person" in so many words. Section 1 of the Fourteenth Amendment contains three references to "person." The first, in defining "citizens," speaks of "persons born or naturalized in the United States." The word also appears both in the Due Process Clause and in the Equal Protection Clause.... [T]he use of the word is such that it has application only postnatally. None indicates, with any assurance, that it has any possible pre-natal application. All this, together with our observation that throughout the major portion of the 19th century prevailing legal abortion practices were far freer than they are today, persuades us that the word "person," as used in the Fourteenth Amendment, does not include the unborn....

We repeat, however, that the State does have an important and legitimate interest in preserving and protecting the health of the pregnant woman, whether she be a resident of the State or a nonresident who seeks medical consultation and treatment there, and that it has still another important and legitimate interest in protecting the potentiality of human life. These interests are separate and distinct. Each grows in substantiality as the woman approaches term and, at a point during pregnancy, each becomes "compelling."

With respect to the State's important and legitimate interest in the health of the mother, the "compelling" point, in the light of present medical knowledge, is at approximately the end of the first trimester. This is so because of the now-established medical fact that until the end of the first trimester mortality in abortion may be less than mortality in normal childbirth. It follows that, from and after this point, a State may regulate the abortion procedure to the extent that the regulation reasonably relates to the preservation and protection of maternal health. Examples of permissible state regulation in this area are requirements as to the qualifications of the person who is to perform the abortion; as to the licensure of that person; as to the facility in which the procedure is to be performed, that is, whether it must be a hospital or may be a clinic or some other place of less-than-hospital status; as to the licensing of the facility; and the like.

This means, on the other hand, that, for the period of pregnancy prior to this "compelling" point, the attending physician, in consultation with his patient, is free to determine, without regulation by the State, that, in his medical judgment, the patient's pregnancy should be terminated. If that decision is reached, the judgment may be effectuated by an abortion free of interference by the State.

With respect to the State's important and legitimate interest in potential life, the "compelling" point is at viability.

This is so because the fetus then presumably has the capability of meaningful life outside the mother's womb. State regulation protective of fetal life after viability thus has both logical and biological justifications. If the State is interested in protecting fetal life after viability, it may go so far as to proscribe abortion during that period, except when it is necessary to preserve the life or health of the mother. Measured against these standards, the Texas Penal Code, in restricting legal abortions to those "procured or attempted by medical advice for the purpose of saving the life of the mother," sweeps too broadly. The statute makes no distinction between abortions performed early in pregnancy and those performed later, and it limits to a single reason, "saving" the mother's life, the legal justification for the procedure. The statute, therefore, cannot survive the constitutional attack made upon it here. . . .

To summarize and to repeat:

A state criminal abortion statute of the current Texas type, that excepts from criminality only a life-saving procedure on behalf of the mother, without regard to pregnancy stage and without recognition of the other interests involved, is violative of the Due Process Clause of the Fourteenth Amendment.

> (a) For the stage prior to approximately the end of the first trimester, the abortion decision and its effectuation must be left to the medical judgment of the pregnant woman's attending physician.
> (b) For the stage subsequent to approximately the end of the first trimester, the State, in promoting its interest in the health of the mother, may, if it chooses, regulate the abortion procedure in ways that are reasonably related to maternal health.
> (c) For the stage subsequent to viability, the State in promoting its interest in the potentiality of human life may, if it chooses, regulate, and even proscribe, abortion except where it is necessary, in appropriate medical judgment, for the preservation of the life or health of the mother. . . .

This holding, we feel, is consistent with the relative weights of the respective interests involved, with the lessons and examples of medical and legal history, with the lenity of the common law, and with the demands of the profound problems of the present day. The decision leaves the State free to place increasing restrictions on abortion as the period of pregnancy lengthens, so long as those restrictions are tailored to the recognized state interests. The decision vindicates the right of the physician to administer medical treatment according to his professional judgment up to the points where important state interests provide compelling justifications for intervention. Up to those points, the abortion decision in all its aspects is inherently, and primarily, a medical decision, and basic responsibility for it must rest with the physician. If an individual practitioner abuses the privilege of exercising proper medical judgment, the usual remedies, judicial and intra-professional, are available.

MR. JUSTICE REHNQUIST, dissenting.

The Court's opinion brings to the decision of this troubling question both extensive historical fact and a wealth of legal scholarship. While the opinion thus commands my respect, I find myself nonetheless in fundamental disagreement with those parts of it that invalidate the Texas statute in question, and therefore dissent. . . .

I have difficulty in concluding, as the Court does, that the right of "privacy" is involved in this case. Texas, by the statute here challenged, bars the performance of a medical abortion by a licensed physician on a plaintiff such as Roe. A transaction resulting in an operation such as this is not "private" in the ordinary usage of that word. Nor is the "privacy" that the Court finds here even a distant relative of the freedom from searches and seizures protected by the Fourth Amendment to the Constitution, which the Court has referred to as embodying a right to privacy. Katz v. United States (1967). If the Court means by the term "privacy" no more than that the claim of a person to be free from unwanted state regulation of consensual transactions may be a form of "liberty" protected by the Fourteenth Amendment, there is no doubt that similar claims have been upheld in our earlier decisions on the basis of that liberty. I agree . . . that the "liberty," against deprivation of which without due process the Fourteenth Amendment protects, embraces more than the rights found in the Bill of Rights. But that liberty is not guaranteed absolutely against deprivation, only against deprivation without due process of law. The test traditionally applied in the area of social and economic legislation is whether or not a law such as that challenged has a rational relation to a valid state objective. Williamson v. Lee Optical Co. (1955). The Due Process Clause of the Fourteenth Amendment undoubtedly does place a limit, albeit a broad one, on legislative power to enact laws such as this. If the Texas statute were to prohibit an abortion even where the mother's life is in jeopardy, I have little doubt that such a statute would lack a rational relation to a valid state objective under the test stated in Williamson. But the Court's sweeping invalidation of any restrictions on abortion during the first trimester is impossible to justify under that standard, and the conscious weighing of competing factors that the Court's opinion apparently substitutes for the established test is far more appropriate to a legislative judgment than to a judicial one. . . .

The fact that a majority of the States reflecting, after all, the majority sentiment in those States, have had restrictions on abortions for at least a century is a strong indication, it seems to me, that the asserted right to an abortion is not "so rooted in the traditions and conscience of our people as to be ranked as fundamental," Snyder v. Massachusetts (1934). Even today, when society's views on abortion are changing, the very existence of the debate is evidence that the "right" to an abortion is not so universally accepted as the appellant would have us believe.

To reach its result, the Court necessarily has had to find within the scope of the Fourteenth Amendment a right that was apparently completely unknown to the drafters of the Amendment. . . . There apparently was no question concerning the validity of this provision or of any of the other state statutes when the Fourteenth Amendment was adopted. The only conclusion possible from this history is that the drafters did not intend to have the Fourteenth Amendment withdraw from the States the power to legislate with respect to this matter. . . .

For all of the foregoing reasons, I respectfully dissent.

PLANNED PARENTHOOD OF SOUTHEASTERN PENNSYLVANIA V. CASEY
505 U.S. 833 (1992)

"After considering the fundamental constitutional questions resolved by Roe, principles of institutional integrity, and the rule of stare decisis, we are led to conclude . . . the essential holding of Roe v. Wade should be retained and once again reaffirmed."

The Question: Can a state pass an "Abortion Control Act" that its legislative sponsors admit is designed to discourage abortions, and that includes provisions requiring that (a) women indicate on official forms their consent to the abortion procedure, (b) women seeking abortions be provided with information on abortion risks at least 24 hours before the procedure is performed, (c) minors obtain the consent of a parent, with provision for a "judicial bypass" if the minor cannot or does not wish to obtain consent, (d) married women notify their husbands of their abortion decision, and (e) the forms required by this law be open for public inspection?

The Arguments: PRO

The provisions of the law in question, passed by the Pennsylvania legislature, do not prohibit any woman from obtaining an abortion and are designed to ensure that women seeking abortions make an informed choice and notify parents or spouses who have an interest in the decision. These are reasonable regulations and fall within the guidelines set by the Supreme Court in cases decided after *Roe v. Wade.*

CON

The Pennsylvania regulations, as their sponsors admit, are designed to discourage women from obtaining abortions. In fact, some women will likely forego an abortion rather than comply with these intrusive regulations, opening their private decision to public inspection. These regulations impose an "undue burden" on the exercise of the right to an abortion.

JUSTICE O'CONNOR, JUSTICE KENNEDY, and JUSTICE SOUTER announced the judgment of the Court. . . .

Liberty finds no refuge in a jurisprudence of doubt. Yet, 19 years after our holding that the Constitution protects a woman's right to terminate her pregnancy in its early stages, Roe v. Wade (1973), that definition of liberty is still questioned. Joining the respondents as amicus curiae, the United States, as it has done in five other cases in the last decade, again asks us to overrule Roe.

At issue in these cases are five provisions of the Pennsylvania Abortion Control Act of 1982, as amended in 1988 and 1989. The Act requires that a woman seeking an abortion give her informed consent prior to the abortion procedure, and specifies that she be provided with certain information at least 24 hours before the abortion is performed. For a minor to obtain an abortion, the Act requires the informed consent of one of her parents, but provides for a judicial bypass option if the minor does not wish to or cannot obtain a parent's consent. Another provision of the Act requires that, unless certain exceptions apply, a married woman seeking an abortion must sign a statement indicating that she has notified her husband of her intended abortion. The Act exempts compliance with these three requirements in the event of a "medical emergency," which is defined in 3203 of the Act. In addition to the above provisions regulating the

performance of abortions, the Act imposes certain reporting requirements on facilities that provide abortion services.

Before any of these provisions took effect, the petitioners, who are five abortion clinics and one physician representing himself as well as a class of physicians who provide abortion services, brought this suit seeking declaratory and injunctive relief. Each provision was challenged as unconstitutional on its face. The District Court entered a preliminary injunction against the enforcement of the regulations, and, after a 3-day bench trial, held all the provisions at issue here unconstitutional, entering a permanent injunction against Pennsylvania's enforcement of them. The Court of Appeals for the Third Circuit affirmed in part and reversed in part, upholding all of the regulations except for the husband notification requirement. We granted certiorari. . . .

After considering the fundamental constitutional questions resolved by Roe, principles of institutional integrity, and the rule of stare decisis, we are led to conclude this: the essential holding of Roe v. Wade should be retained and once again reaffirmed. It must be stated at the outset and with clarity that Roe's essential holding, the holding we reaffirm, has three parts. First is a recognition of the right of the woman to choose to have an abortion before viability and to obtain it without undue interference from the State. Before viability, the State's interests are not strong enough to support a prohibition of abortion or the imposition of a substantial obstacle to the woman's effective right to elect the procedure. Second is a confirmation of the State's power to restrict abortions after fetal viability if the law contains exceptions for pregnancies which endanger the woman's life or health. And third is the principle that the State has legitimate interests from the outset of the pregnancy in protecting the health of the woman and the life of the fetus that may become a child. These principles do not contradict one another; and we adhere to each. . . .

Men and women of good conscience can disagree, and we suppose some always shall disagree, about the profound moral and spiritual implications of terminating a pregnancy, even in its earliest stage. Some of us as individuals find abortion offensive to our most basic principles of morality, but that cannot control our decision. Our obligation is to define the liberty of all, not to mandate our own moral code. The underlying constitutional issue is whether the State can resolve these philosophic questions in such a definitive way that a woman lacks all choice in the matter, except perhaps in those rare circumstances in which the pregnancy is itself a danger to her own life or health, or is the result of rape or incest. . . .

While we appreciate the weight of the arguments made on behalf of the State in the cases before us, arguments which in their ultimate formulation conclude that Roe should be overruled, the reservations any of us may have in reaffirming the central holding of Roe are outweighed by the explication of individual liberty we have given, combined with the force of stare decisis. We turn now to that doctrine.

The obligation to follow precedent begins with necessity, and a contrary necessity marks its outer limit. . . . Indeed, the very concept of the rule of law underlying our own Constitution requires such continuity over time that a respect for precedent is, by definition, indispensable. At the other extreme, a different necessity would make itself felt if a prior judicial ruling should come to be seen so clearly as error that its enforcement was, for that very reason, doomed. Even when the decision to overrule a prior case is not, as in the rare, latter instance, virtually foreordained, it is common wisdom that the rule of stare decisis is not an "inexorable command," and certainly it is not such in every constitutional case Rather, when this Court reexamines a prior holding, its judgment is customarily informed by a series of prudential and pragmatic considerations designed to test the consistency of overruling a prior decision with the ideal of the rule of law, and to gauge the respective costs of reaffirming and overruling a prior case. Thus, for example, we may ask whether the rule has proven to be intolerable simply in defying practical workability, whether the rule is subject to a kind of reliance that would lend a special hardship to the consequences of overruling and add inequity to the cost of repudiation, whether related principles of law have so far developed as to have left the old rule no more than a remnant of abandoned doctrine, or whether facts have so changed, or come to be seen so differently, as to have robbed the old rule of significant application or justification.

So in this case, we may enquire whether Roe's central rule has been found unworkable; whether the rule's limitation on state power could be removed without serious inequity to those who have relied upon it or significant damage to the stability of the society governed by it; whether the law's growth in the intervening years has left Roe's central rule a doctrinal anachronism discounted by society; and whether Roe's premises of fact have so far changed in the ensuing two decades as to render its central holding somehow irrelevant or unjustifiable in dealing with the issue it addressed. . . .

Although Roe has engendered opposition, it has in no sense proven "unworkable," representing as it does a simple limitation beyond which a state law is unenforceable. While Roe has, of course, required judicial assessment of state laws affecting the exercise of the choice guaranteed against government infringement, and although the need for such review will remain as a consequence of today's decision, the required determinations fall within judicial competence.

The inquiry into reliance counts the cost of a rule's repudiation as it would fall on those who have relied reasonably on the rule's continued application. . . . The ability of women to participate equally in the economic and social life of the Nation has been facilitated by their ability to control their reproductive lives. The Constitution serves human values, and while the effect of reliance on Roe cannot be exactly measured, neither can the certain cost of overruling Roe for people who have ordered their thinking and living around that case be dismissed. No evolution of legal principle has left Roe's doctrinal footings weaker than they were in 1973. No development of constitutional law since the case was decided has implicitly or explicitly left Roe behind as a mere survivor of obsolete constitutional thinking. . . .

The sum of the precedential enquiry to this point shows Roe's underpinnings unweakened in any way affecting its central holding. While it has engendered disapproval, it has not been unworkable. An entire generation has come of age free to assume Roe's concept of liberty in defining the capacity of women to act in society, and to make reproductive decisions; no erosion of principle going to liberty or personal autonomy has left Roe's central holding a doctrinal remnant. Roe portends no developments at odds with other precedent for the analysis of personal liberty; and no changes of fact have rendered viability more or less appropriate as the point at which the balance of interests tips. Within the bounds of normal stare decisis analysis, then, and subject to the considerations on which it customarily turns, the stronger argument is for affirming Roe's central holding, with whatever degree of personal reluctance any of us may have, not for overruling it. . . .

Our analysis would not be complete, however, without explaining why overruling Roe's central holding would not only reach an unjustifiable result under principles of stare decisis, but would seriously weaken the Court's capacity to exercise the judicial power and to function as the Supreme Court of a Nation dedicated to the rule of law. To understand why this would be so, it is necessary to understand the source of this Court's authority, the conditions necessary for its preservation, and its relationship to the country's understanding of itself as a constitutional Republic.

The root of American governmental power is revealed most clearly in the instance of the power conferred by the Constitution upon the Judiciary of the United States, and specifically upon this Court. As Americans of each succeeding generation are rightly told, the Court cannot buy support for its decisions by spending money, and, except to a minor degree, it cannot independently coerce obedience to its decrees. The Court's power lies, rather, in its legitimacy, a product of substance and perception that shows itself in the people's acceptance of the Judiciary as fit to determine what the Nation's law means, and to declare what it demands.

The underlying substance of this legitimacy is of course the warrant for the Court's decisions in the Constitution and the lesser sources of legal principle on which the Court draws. That substance is expressed in the Court's opinions, and our contemporary understanding is such that a decision without principled justification would be no judicial act at all. But even when justification is furnished by apposite legal principle, something more is required. Because not every conscientious claim of principled justification will be accepted as such, the justification claimed must be beyond dispute. The Court must take care to speak and act in ways that allow people to accept its decisions on the terms the Court claims for them, as grounded truly in principle, not as compromises with social and political pressures having, as such, no bearing on the principled choices that the Court is obliged to make. Thus, the Court's legitimacy depends on making legally principled decisions under circumstances in which their principled character is sufficiently plausible to be accepted by the Nation.

The need for principled action to be perceived as such is implicated to some degree whenever this, or any other appellate court, overrules a prior case. This is not to say, of course, that this Court cannot give a perfectly satisfactory explanation in most cases. People understand that some of the Constitution's language is hard to fathom, and that the Court's Justices are sometimes able to perceive significant facts or to understand principles of law that eluded their predecessors and that justify departures from existing decisions. However upsetting it may be to those most directly affected when one judicially derived rule replaces another, the country can accept some correction of error without necessarily questioning the legitimacy of the Court.

In two circumstances, however, the Court would almost certainly fail to receive the benefit of the doubt in overruling prior cases. There is, first, a point beyond which frequent overruling would overtax the country's belief in the Court's good faith. Despite the variety of reasons that may inform and justify a decision to overrule, we cannot forget that such a decision is usually perceived (and perceived correctly) as, at the least, a statement that a prior decision was wrong. There is a limit to the amount of error that can plausibly be imputed to prior Courts. If that limit should be exceeded, disturbance of prior rulings would be taken as evidence that justifiable reexamination of principle had given way to drives for particular results in the short term. The legitimacy of the Court would fade with the frequency of its vacillation.

That first circumstance can be described as hypothetical; the second is to the point here and now. Where, in the performance of its judicial duties, the Court decides a case in such a way as to resolve the sort of intensely divisive controversy reflected in Roe and those rare, comparable cases, its decision has a dimension that the resolution of the normal case does not carry. It is the dimension present whenever the Court's interpretation of the Constitution calls the contending sides of a national controversy to end their national division by accepting a common mandate rooted in the Constitution. The Court is not asked to do this very often,

having thus addressed the Nation only twice in our lifetime, in the decisions of Brown and Roe. But when the Court does act in this way, its decision requires an equally rare precedential force to counter the inevitable efforts to overturn it and to thwart its implementation. Some of those efforts may be mere unprincipled emotional reactions; others may proceed from principles worthy of profound respect. But whatever the premises of opposition may be, only the most convincing justification under accepted standards of precedent could suffice to demonstrate that a later decision overruling the first was anything but a surrender to political pressure and an unjustified repudiation of the principle on which the Court staked its authority in the first instance. So to overrule under fire in the absence of the most compelling reason to reexamine a watershed decision would subvert the Court's legitimacy beyond any serious question.

The country's loss of confidence in the Judiciary would be underscored by an equally certain and equally reasonable condemnation for another failing in overruling unnecessarily and under pressure. Some cost will be paid by anyone who approves or implements a constitutional decision where it is unpopular, or who refuses to work to undermine the decision or to force its reversal. The price may be criticism or ostracism, or it may be violence. An extra price will be paid by those who themselves disapprove of the decision's results when viewed outside of constitutional terms, but who nevertheless struggle to accept it, because they respect the rule of law. To all those who will be so tested by following, the Court implicitly undertakes to remain steadfast, lest in the end a price be paid for nothing. . . . If the Court's legitimacy should be undermined, then, so would the country be in its very ability to see itself through its constitutional ideals. The Court's concern with legitimacy is not for the sake of the Court, but for the sake of the Nation to which it is responsible.

The Court's duty in the present case is clear. In 1973, it confronted the already-divisive issue of governmental power to limit personal choice to undergo abortion, for which it provided a new resolution based on the due process guaranteed by the Fourteenth Amendment. Whether or not a new social consensus is developing on that issue, its divisiveness is no less today than in 1973, and pressure to overrule the decision, like pressure to retain it, has grown only more intense. A decision to overrule Roe's essential holding under the existing circumstances would address error, if error there was, at the cost of both profound and unnecessary damage to the Court's legitimacy, and to the Nation's commitment to the rule of law. It is therefore imperative to adhere to the essence of Roe's original decision, and we do so today.

From what we have said so far, it follows that it is a constitutional liberty of the woman to have some freedom to terminate her pregnancy. We conclude that the basic decision in Roe was based on a constitutional analysis which we cannot now repudiate. The woman's liberty is not so unlimited, however, that, from the outset, the State cannot show its concern for the life of the unborn and, at a later point in fetal development, the State's interest in life has sufficient force so that the right of the woman to terminate the pregnancy can be restricted.

That brings us, of course, to the point where much criticism has been directed at Roe, a criticism that always inheres when the Court draws a specific rule from what in the

Constitution is but a general standard. We conclude, however, that the urgent claims of the woman to retain the ultimate control over her destiny and her body, claims implicit in the meaning of liberty, require us to perform that function. Liberty must not be extinguished for want of a line that is clear. And it falls to us to give some real substance to the woman's liberty to determine whether to carry her pregnancy to full term. We conclude the line should be drawn at viability, so that, before that time, the woman has a right to choose to terminate her pregnancy. We adhere to this principle for two reasons. First, as we have said, is the doctrine of stare decisis. Any judicial act of line-drawing may seem somewhat arbitrary, but Roe was a reasoned statement, elaborated with great care. . . . The woman's right to terminate her pregnancy before viability is the most central principle of Roe v. Wade. It is a rule of law and a component of liberty we cannot renounce. . . .

As our jurisprudence relating to all liberties save perhaps abortion has recognized, not every law which makes a right more difficult to exercise is, ipso facto, an infringement of that right. . . . Numerous forms of state regulation might have the incidental effect of increasing the cost or decreasing the availability of medical care, whether for abortion or any other medical procedure. The fact that a law which serves a valid purpose, one not designed to strike at the right itself, has the incidental effect of making it more difficult or more expensive to procure an abortion cannot be enough to invalidate it. Only where state regulation imposes an undue burden on a woman's ability to make this decision does the power of the State reach into the heart of the liberty protected by the Due Process Clause. . . .

Some guiding principles should emerge. What is at stake is the woman's right to make the ultimate decision, not a right to be insulated from all others in doing so. Regulations which do no more than create a structural mechanism by which the State, or the parent or guardian of a minor, may express profound respect for the life of the unborn are permitted, if they are not a substantial obstacle to the woman's exercise of the right to choose. Unless it has that effect on her right of choice, a state measure designed to persuade her to choose childbirth over abortion will be upheld if reasonably related to that goal. Regulations designed to foster the health of a woman seeking an abortion are valid if they do not constitute an undue burden. . . . Even when jurists reason from shared premises, some disagreement is inevitable. That is to be expected in the application of any legal standard which must accommodate life's complexity. We do not expect it to be otherwise with respect to the undue burden standard. We give this summary:

(a) To protect the central right recognized by Roe v. Wade while at the same time accommodating the State's profound interest in potential life, we will employ the undue burden analysis as explained in this opinion. An undue burden exists, and therefore a provision of law is invalid, if its purpose or effect is to place a substantial obstacle in the path of a woman seeking an abortion before the fetus attains viability.

(b) We reject the rigid trimester framework of Roe v. Wade. To promote the State's profound interest in potential life, throughout pregnancy, the State may take measures to ensure that the woman's choice is informed, and measures designed to advance this interest will not be invalidated as long as their purpose is to persuade the woman to choose childbirth over abortion. These measures must not be an undue burden on the right.

(c) As with any medical procedure, the State may enact regulations to further the health or safety of a woman seeking an abortion. Unnecessary health regulations that have the purpose or effect of presenting a substantial obstacle to a woman seeking an abortion impose an undue burden on the right.

(d) Our adoption of the undue burden analysis does not disturb the central holding of Roe v. Wade, and we reaffirm that holding. Regardless of whether exceptions are made for particular circumstances, a State may not prohibit any woman from making the ultimate decision to terminate her pregnancy before viability.

(e) We also reaffirm Roe's holding that, subsequent to viability, the State, in promoting its interest in the potentiality of human life, may, if it chooses, regulate, and even proscribe, abortion except where it is necessary, in appropriate medical judgment, for the preservation of the life or health of the mother.

These principles control our assessment of the Pennsylvania statute, and we now turn to the issue of the validity of its challenged provisions. . . . [After discussion of each provision, the Court upheld the constitutionality of all but the spousal notification requirement.]

JUSTICE BLACKMUN, concurring in part, concurring in the judgment in part, and dissenting in part.

Three years ago, in Webster v. Reproductive Health Service (1989), four Members of this Court appeared poised to "cas[t] into darkness the hopes and visions of every woman in this country" who had come to believe that the Constitution guaranteed her the right to reproductive choice. All that remained between the promise of Roe and the darkness of the plurality was a single, flickering flame. Decisions since Webster gave little reason to hope that this flame would cast much light. But now, just when so many expected the darkness to fall, the flame has grown bright.

I do not underestimate the significance of today's joint opinion. Yet I remain steadfast in my belief that the right to reproductive choice is entitled to the full protection afforded by this Court before Webster. And I fear for the darkness as four Justices anxiously await the single vote necessary to extinguish the light.

Make no mistake, the joint opinion of Justices O'Connor, Kennedy, and Souter is an act of personal courage and constitutional principle. . . . A fervent view of individual liberty and the force of stare decisis have led the Court to this conclusion. Today a majority reaffirms that the Due Process Clause of the Fourteenth Amendment establishes "a realm of personal liberty which the government may not enter,"—a realm whose outer limits cannot be determined by interpretations of the Constitution that focus only on the specific practices of States at the time the Fourteenth Amendment was adopted. Included within this realm of liberty is "the right of the individual, married or single, to be free from unwarranted governmental intrusion into matters so fundamentally affecting a person as the decision whether to bear or beget a child." These matters, involving the most intimate and personal choices a person may make in a lifetime, choices central to personal dignity and autonomy, are central to the liberty protected by the Fourteenth Amendment. Finally, the Court today recognizes that, in the case of abortion, the liberty of the woman is at stake in a sense unique to the human condition and so unique to the law. The mother who carries a child to full term is subject to anxieties, to physical constraints, to pain that only she must bear. . . .

At long last, The Chief Justice and those who have joined him admit it. Gone are the contentions that the issue need not be (or has not been) considered. There, on the first page, for all to see, is what was expected: We believe that Roe was wrongly decided, and that it can and should be overruled consistently with our traditional approach to stare decisis in constitutional cases. If there is much reason to applaud the advances made by the joint opinion today, there is far more to fear from The Chief Justice's opinion. The Chief Justice's criticism of Roe follows from his stunted conception of individual liberty. While recognizing that the Due Process Clause protects more than simple physical liberty, he then goes on to construe this Court's personal liberty cases as establishing only a laundry list of particular rights, rather than a principled account of how these particular rights are grounded in a more general right of privacy. . . . Even more shocking than The Chief Justice's cramped notion of individual liberty is his complete omission of any discussion of the effects that compelled childbirth and motherhood have on women's lives. The only expression of concern with women's health is purely instrumental—for The Chief Justice, only women's psychological health is a concern, and only to the extent that he assumes that every woman who decides to have an abortion does so without serious consideration of the moral implications of their decision. In short, The Chief Justice's view of the State's compelling interest in maternal health has less to do with health than it does with compelling women to be maternal. . . .

In one sense, the Court's approach is worlds apart from that of The Chief Justice and Justice Scalia. And yet, in another sense, the distance between the two approaches is short—the distance is but a single vote. I am 83 years old. I cannot remain on this Court forever, and when I do step down, the confirmation process for my successor well may focus on the issue before us today. That, I regret, may be exactly where the choice between the two worlds will be made.

CHIEF JUSTICE REHNQUIST, with whom JUSTICE WHITE, JUSTICE SCALIA, and JUSTICE THOMAS join, concurring in the judgment in part and dissenting in part.

The joint opinion, following its newly minted variation on stare decisis, retains the outer shell of Roe v. Wade, but beats a wholesale retreat from the substance of that case. We believe that Roe was wrongly decided, and that it can and should be overruled consistently with our traditional approach to stare decisis in constitutional cases. We would adopt the approach of the plurality in Webster v. Reproductive Health Services (1989), and uphold the challenged provisions of the Pennsylvania statute in their entirety. . . .

The joint opinion of Justices O'Connor, Kennedy, and Souter cannot bring itself to say that Roe was correct as an original matter, but the authors are of the view that the immediate question is not the soundness of Roe's resolution of the issue, but the precedential force that must be accorded to its holding. Instead of claiming that Roe was correct as a matter of original constitutional interpretation, the opinion therefore contains an elaborate discussion of stare decisis. This discussion of the principle of stare decisis appears to be almost entirely dicta, because the joint opinion does not apply that principle in dealing with Roe. Roe decided that a woman had a fundamental right to an abortion. The joint opinion rejects that view. Roe decided that abortion regulations were to be subjected to "strict scrutiny," and could be justified only in the light of "compelling state interests." The joint opinion rejects that view. Roe analyzed abortion regulation under a rigid trimester framework, a framework which has guided this Court's decisionmaking for 19 years. The joint opinion rejects that framework. Stare decisis is defined in Black's Law Dictionary as meaning "to abide by, or adhere to, decided cases." Whatever the "central holding" of Roe that is left after the joint opinion finishes dissecting it is surely not the result of that principle. While purporting to adhere to precedent, the joint opinion instead revises it. Roe continues to exist, but only in the way a storefront on a western movie set exists: a mere facade to give the illusion of reality. . . .

In our view, authentic principles of stare decisis do not require that any portion of the reasoning in Roe be kept intact. . . . The joint opinion discusses several stare decisis factors which, it asserts, point toward retaining a portion of Roe. Two of these factors are that the main "factual underpinning" of Roe has remained the same, and that its doctrinal foundation is no weaker now than it was in 1973. Of course, what might be called the basic facts which gave rise to Roe have remained the same—women become pregnant, there is a point somewhere, depending on medical technology, where a fetus becomes viable, and women give birth to children. But this is only to say that the same facts which gave rise to Roe will continue to give rise to similar cases. It is not a reason, in and of itself, why those cases must be decided in the same incorrect manner as was the first case to deal with the question. And surely there is no requirement, in considering whether to depart from stare decisis in a constitutional case, that a decision be more wrong now than it was at the time it was rendered. If that were true, the most outlandish constitutional decision could survive forever, based simply on the fact that it was no more outlandish later than it was when originally rendered.

Nor does the joint opinion faithfully follow this alleged requirement. The opinion frankly concludes that Roe and its progeny were wrong in failing to recognize that the State's interests in maternal health and in the protection of unborn human life exist throughout pregnancy. But there is no indication that these components of Roe are any more incorrect at this juncture than they were at its inception.

The joint opinion also points to the reliance interests involved in this context in its effort to explain why precedent must be followed for precedent's sake. Certainly it is true that, where reliance is truly at issue, as in the case of judicial decisions that have formed the basis for private decisions, "[c]onsiderations in favor of stare decisis are at their acme." But, as the joint opinion apparently agrees, any traditional notion of reliance is not applicable here. The Court today cuts back on the protection afforded by Roe, and no one claims that this action defeats any reliance interest in the disavowed trimester framework. Similarly, reliance interests would not be diminished were the Court to go further and acknowledge the full error of Roe, as "reproductive planning could take virtually immediate account of" this action.

The joint opinion thus turns to what can only be described as an unconventional—and unconvincing—notion of reliance, a view based on the surmise that the availability of abortion since Roe has led to "two decades of economic and social developments" that would be undercut if the error of Roe were recognized. . . . In the end, having failed to put forth any evidence to prove any true reliance, the joint opinion's argument is based solely on generalized assertions about the national psyche, on a belief that the people of this country have grown accustomed to the Roe decision over the last 19 years and have "ordered their thinking and living around" it. As an initial matter, one might inquire how the joint opinion can view the "central holding" of Roe as so deeply rooted in our constitutional culture when it so casually uproots and disposes of that same decision's trimester framework. . . .

Apparently realizing that conventional stare decisis principles do not support its position, the joint opinion advances a belief that retaining a portion of Roe is necessary to protect the "legitimacy" of this Court. Because the Court must take care to render decisions "grounded truly in principle," and not simply as political and social compromises, the joint opinion properly declares it to be this Court's duty to ignore the public criticism and protest that may arise as a result of a decision. Few would quarrel with this statement, although it may be doubted that Members of this Court, holding their tenure as they do during constitutional "good behavior," are at all likely to be intimidated by such public protests.

But the joint opinion goes on to state that, when the Court "resolve[s] the sort of intensely divisive controversy reflected in Roe and those rare, comparable cases," its decision is exempt from reconsideration under established principles of stare decisis in constitutional cases. This is so, the joint opinion contends, because, in those "intensely divisive" cases, the Court has call[ed] the contending sides of a national controversy to end their national division by accepting a common mandate rooted in the Constitution, and must therefore take special care not to be perceived as "surrender[ing] to political pressure" and continued opposition. This is a truly novel principle, one which is contrary to both the Court's historical practice and to the Court's traditional willingness to tolerate criticism of its opinions. Under this principle, when the Court has ruled on a divisive issue, it is apparently prevented from overruling that decision for the sole reason that it was incorrect, unless opposition to the original decision has died away.

The first difficulty with this principle lies in its assumption that cases that are "intensely divisive" can be readily distinguished from those that are not. The question of whether a particular issue is "intensely divisive" enough to qualify for special protection is entirely subjective and dependent on the individual assumptions of the Members of this Court. In addition, because the Court's duty is to ignore public opinion and criticism on issues that come before it, its Members are in perhaps the worst position to judge whether a decision divides the Nation deeply enough to justify such uncommon protection. Although many of the Court's decisions divide the populace to a large degree, we have not previously on that account shied away from applying normal rules of stare decisis when urged to reconsider earlier decisions. Over the past 21 years, for example, the Court has overruled in whole or in part 34 of its previous constitutional decisions. . . .

The end result of the joint opinion's paeans of praise for legitimacy is the enunciation of a brand new standard for evaluating state regulation of a woman's right to abortion—the "undue burden" standard. As indicated above, Roe v. Wade adopted a "fundamental right" standard under which state regulations could survive only if they met the requirement of "strict scrutiny." While we disagree with that standard, it at least had a recognized basis in constitutional law at the time Roe was decided. The same cannot be said for the "undue burden" standard, which is created largely out of whole cloth by the authors of the joint opinion. It is a standard which even today does not command the support of a majority of this Court. And it will not, we believe, result in the sort of "simple limitation," easily applied, which the joint opinion anticipates. In sum, it is a standard which is not built to last. . . .

[W]e . . . would hold that each of the challenged provisions of the Pennsylvania statute is consistent with the Constitution. It bears emphasis that our conclusion in this regard does not carry with it any necessary approval of these regulations. Our task is, as always, to decide only whether the challenged provisions of a law comport with the United States Constitution. If, as we believe, these do, their wisdom as a matter of public policy is for the people of Pennsylvania to decide.

STENBERG V. CARHART
530 U.S. 914 (2000)

"By no means must a State grant physicians "unfettered discretion" in their selection of abortion method. But where substantial medical authority supports the proposition that banning a particular abortion procedure could endanger women's health, Casey requires the statute to include a health exception when the procedure is 'necessary, in appropriate medical judgment, for the preservation of the life or health of the mother.'"

The Question: Can a state pass a law that imposes criminal penalties and loss of medical licenses on physicians who perform partial-birth abortion, with no exception for protecting the health of a woman seeking an abortion with this procedure?

The Arguments: PRO

The Supreme Court, in "reaffirming" the basic right to abortion in its *Casey* decision in 1992, made clear that states were free to regulate abortion procedures in the latter stages of pregnancy, prior to fetal viability. The Nebraska law at issue in this case, similar to those in 29 other states, reflects the belief of the state's voters and lawmakers that partial-birth abortion is such a gruesome procedure, involving the deliberate killing of a partially delivered baby, that it is a form of infanticide. Banning this procedure does not prevent physicians from using other methods of terminating late-term pregnancies.

CON

The opponents of partial-birth abortion, properly known as "dilation and extraction," have inflamed public opinion by equating this procedure with infanticide. However, it is not and cannot be used after a fetus becomes viable. The procedure is rarely employed, in less than 1 percent of all abortions, and is often the only safe method of performing an abortion when the fetus is seriously malformed or otherwise unlikely to survive a live birth. States do not have the power to interfere with a physician's professional judgment as to the best medical procedure to employ.

JUSTICE BREYER delivered the opinion of the Court.

We again consider the right to an abortion. We understand the controversial nature of the problem. Millions of Americans believe that life begins at conception and consequently that an abortion is akin to causing the death of an innocent child; they recoil at the thought of a law that would permit it. Other millions fear that a law that forbids abortion would condemn many American women to lives that lack dignity, depriving them of equal liberty and leading those with least resources to undergo illegal abortions with the attendant risks of death and suffering. Taking account of these virtually irreconcilable points of view, aware that constitutional law must govern a society whose different members sincerely hold directly opposing views, and considering the matter in light of the Constitution's guarantees of fundamental individual liberty, this Court, in the course of a generation, has determined and then redetermined that the Constitution offers basic protection to the woman's right to choose. Roe v. Wade (1973); Planned Parenthood of Southeastern Pa. v. Casey (1992). We shall not revisit those legal principles. Rather, we apply them to the circumstances of this case.

Three established principles determine the issue before us. We shall set them forth in the language of the joint opinion in Casey. First, before "viability . . . the woman has a right to choose to terminate her pregnancy." Second, "a law designed to further the State's interest in fetal life which imposes an undue burden on the woman's decision before fetal viability" is unconstitutional. An "undue burden is . . . shorthand for the conclusion that a state regulation has the purpose or effect of placing a substantial obstacle in the path of a woman seeking an abortion of a nonviable fetus." Third, "subsequent to viability, the State in promoting its interest in the potentiality of human life may, if it chooses, regulate, and even proscribe, abortion except where it is necessary, in appropriate medical judgment, for the preservation of the life or health of the mother."

We apply these principles to a Nebraska law banning "partial birth abortion." The statute reads as follows: "No partial birth abortion shall be performed in this state, unless such procedure is necessary to save the life of the mother

whose life is endangered by a physical disorder, physical illness, or physical injury, including a life-endangering physical condition caused by or arising from the pregnancy itself."

The statute defines "partial birth abortion" as: "an abortion procedure in which the person performing the abortion partially delivers vaginally a living unborn child before killing the unborn child and completing the delivery." It further defines "partially delivers vaginally a living unborn child before killing the unborn child" to mean "deliberately and intentionally delivering into the vagina a living unborn child, or a substantial portion thereof, for the purpose of performing a procedure that the person performing such procedure knows will kill the unborn child and does kill the unborn child." The law classifies violation of the statute as a "Class III felony" carrying a prison term of up to 20 years, and a fine of up to $25,000. It also provides for the automatic revocation of a doctor's license to practice medicine in Nebraska.

We hold that this statute violates the Constitution.

Dr. Leroy Carhart is a Nebraska physician who performs abortions in a clinical setting. He brought this lawsuit in Federal District Court seeking a declaration that the Nebraska statute violates the Federal Constitution, and asking for an injunction forbidding its enforcement. After a trial on the merits, during which both sides presented several expert witnesses, the District Court held the statute unconstitutional. On appeal, the Eighth Circuit affirmed. We granted certiorari to consider the matter.

Because Nebraska law seeks to ban one method of aborting a pregnancy, we must describe and then discuss several different abortion procedures. Considering the fact that those procedures seek to terminate a potential human life, our discussion may seem clinically cold or callous to some, perhaps horrifying to others. There is no alternative way, however, to acquaint the reader with the technical distinctions among different abortion methods and related factual matters, upon which the outcome of this case depends. For that reason, drawing upon the findings of the trial court, underlying testimony, and related medical texts, we shall describe the relevant methods of performing abortions in technical detail.

The evidence before the trial court, as supported or supplemented in the literature, indicates the following:

1. About 90% of all abortions performed in the United States take place during the first trimester of pregnancy, before 12 weeks of gestational age. During the first trimester, the predominant abortion method is "vacuum aspiration," which involves insertion of a vacuum tube (cannula) into the uterus to evacuate the contents. Such an abortion is typically performed on an outpatient basis under local anesthesia. Vacuum aspiration is considered particularly safe. The procedure's mortality rates for first trimester abortion are, for example, 5 to 10 times lower than those associated with carrying the fetus to term. Complication rates are also low. As the fetus grows in size, however, the vacuum aspiration method becomes increasingly difficult to use.

2. Approximately 10% of all abortions are performed during the second trimester of pregnancy (12 to 24 weeks). In the early 1970's, inducing labor through the injection of saline into the uterus was the predominant method of second trimester abortion. Today, however, the medical profession has switched from medical induction of labor to surgical procedures for most second trimester abortions. The most commonly used procedure is called "dilation and evacuation" (D&E). That procedure (together with a modified form of vacuum aspiration used in the early second trimester) accounts for about 95% of all abortions performed from 12 to 20 weeks of gestational age.

3. D&E "refers generically to transcervical procedures performed at 13 weeks gestation or later." American Medical Association, Report of Board of Trustees on Late-Term Abortion. The AMA Report, adopted by the District Court, describes the process as follows. Between 13 and 15 weeks of gestation: "D&E is similar to vacuum aspiration except that the cervix must be dilated more widely because surgical instruments are used to remove larger pieces of tissue. Osmotic dilators are usually used. Intravenous fluids and an analgesic or sedative may be administered. A local anesthetic such as a paracervical block may be administered, dilating agents, if used, are removed and instruments are inserted through the cervix into the uterus to removal fetal and placental tissue. Because fetal tissue is friable and easily broken, the fetus may not be removed intact. The walls of the uterus are scraped with a curette to ensure that no tissue remains." After 15 weeks: "Because the fetus is larger at this stage of gestation (particularly the head), and because bones are more rigid, dismemberment or other destructive procedures are more likely to be required than at earlier gestational ages to remove fetal and placental tissue." After 20 weeks: "Some physicians use intrafetal potassium chloride or digoxin to induce fetal demise prior to a late D&E (after 20 weeks), to facilitate evacuation."

There are variations in D&E operative strategy. However, the common points are that D&E involves (1) dilation of the cervix; (2) removal of at least some fetal tissue using nonvacuum instruments; and (3) (after the 15th week) the potential need for instrumental disarticulation or dismemberment of the fetus or the collapse of fetal parts to facilitate evacuation from the uterus. . . . The D&E procedure carries certain risks. The use of instruments within the uterus creates a danger of accidental perforation and damage to neighboring organs. Sharp fetal bone fragments create similar dangers. And fetal tissue accidentally left behind can cause infection and various other complications. Nonetheless studies show that the risks of mortality and complication that accompany the D&E procedure between the 12th and 20th weeks of gestation are significantly lower than those accompanying induced labor procedures (the next safest midsecond trimester procedures).

At trial, Dr. Carhart . . . described a variation of the D&E procedure, . . . referred to as an "intact D&E." Like other versions of the D&E technique, it begins with induced dilation of the cervix. The procedure then involves removing the fetus from the uterus through the cervix "intact," i.e., in one pass, rather than in several passes. It is used after 16 weeks at the earliest, as vacuum aspiration becomes ineffective and the fetal skull becomes too large to pass through the cervix. The intact D&E proceeds in one of two ways, depending on the presentation of the fetus. If the fetus presents head first (a vertex presentation), the doctor collapses the skull; and the doctor then extracts the entire fetus through the cervix. If the fetus presents feet first (a breech presentation), the doctor pulls the fetal body through the cervix, collapses the skull, and extracts the fetus through the cervix. The breech extraction version of the intact D&E is also known commonly as "dilation and extraction," or D&X. . . . There are no reliable data on the number of D&X abortions performed annually. Estimates have ranged between 640 and 5,000 per year.

The question before us is whether Nebraska's statute, making criminal the performance of a "partial birth abortion," violates the Federal Constitution, as interpreted in Planned Parenthood of Southeastern Pa. v. Casey and Roe v. Wade. We conclude that it does for at least two independent reasons. First, the law lacks any exception "for the preservation of the . . . health of the mother." Second, it "imposes an undue burden on a woman's ability" to choose a D&E abortion, thereby unduly burdening the right to choose abortion itself. We shall discuss each of these reasons in turn.

The Casey joint opinion reiterated what the Court held in Roe; that "subsequent to viability, the State in promoting its interest in the potentiality of human life may, if it chooses, regulate, and even proscribe, abortion except where it is necessary, in appropriate medical judgment, for the preservation of the life or health of the mother." The fact that Nebraska's law applies both pre- and postviability aggravates the constitutional problem presented. The State's interest in regulating abortion previability is considerably weaker than postviability. Since the law requires a health exception in order to validate even a postviability abortion regulation, it at a minimum requires the same in respect to previability regulation. The quoted standard also depends on the state regulations "promoting [the State's] interest in the potentiality of human life." The Nebraska law, of course, does not directly further an interest "in the potentiality of human life" by saving the fetus in question from destruction, as it regulates only a method of performing abortion. Nebraska describes its interests differently. It says the law "show[s] concern for the life of the unborn," "prevent[s] cruelty to partially born children," and "preserve[s] the integrity of the medical profession." But we cannot see how the interest-related differences could make any difference to the question at hand, namely, the application of the "health" requirement. Consequently, the governing standard requires an exception "where it is necessary, in appropriate medical judgment for the preservation of the life or health of the mother," for this Court has made clear that a State may promote but not endanger a woman's health when it regulates the methods of abortion.

Justice Thomas says [in his dissent] that . . . this principle [is limited] to situations where the pregnancy itself creates a threat to health. He is wrong. . . . [A] state cannot subject women's health to significant risks both in that context, and also where state regulations force women to use riskier methods of abortion. Our cases have repeatedly invalidated statutes that in the process of regulating the methods of abortion, imposed significant health risks. They make clear that a risk to a women's health is the same whether it happens to arise from regulating a particular method of abortion, or from barring abortion entirely. Our holding does not go beyond those cases, as ratified in Casey.

Nebraska responds that the law does not require a health exception unless there is a need for such an exception. And here there is no such need, it says. It argues that "safe alternatives remain available" and "a ban on partial-birth abortion/D&X would create no risk to the health of women." The problem for Nebraska is that the parties strongly contested this factual question in the trial court below; and the findings and evidence support Dr. Carhart. The State fails to demonstrate that banning D&X without a health exception may not create significant health risks for women, because the record shows that significant medical authority supports the proposition that in some circumstances, D&X would be the safest procedure. . . .

In sum, Nebraska has not convinced us that a health exception is "never necessary to preserve the health of women." Rather, a statute that altogether forbids D&X creates a significant health risk. The statute consequently must contain a health exception. This is not to say . . . that a State is prohibited from proscribing an abortion procedure whenever a particular physician deems the procedure preferable. By no means must a State grant physicians "unfettered discretion" in their selection of abortion methods. But where substantial medical authority supports the proposition that banning a particular abortion procedure could endanger women's health, Casey requires the statute to include a health exception when the procedure is "necessary, in appropriate medical judgment, for the preservation of the life or health of the mother." Requiring such an exception in this case is no departure from Casey, but simply a straightforward application of its holding.

The Eighth Circuit found the Nebraska statute unconstitutional because, in Casey's words, it has the "effect of placing a substantial obstacle in the path of a woman seeking an abortion of a nonviable fetus." It thereby places an "undue burden" upon a woman's right to terminate her pregnancy before viability. Nebraska does not deny that the statute imposes an "undue burden" if it applies to the more commonly used D&E procedure as well as to D&X. And we agree with the Eighth Circuit that it does so apply.

Our earlier discussion of the D&E procedure shows that it falls within the statutory prohibition. The statute forbids "deliberately and intentionally delivering into the vagina a living unborn child, or a substantial portion thereof, for the purpose of performing a procedure that the person performing such procedure knows will kill the unborn child." We do not understand how one could distinguish, using this language, between D&E (where a foot or arm is drawn through the cervix) and D&X (where the body up to the head is drawn through the cervix). Evidence before the trial court makes clear that

D&E will often involve a physician pulling a "substantial portion" of a still living fetus, say, an arm or leg, into the vagina prior to the death of the fetus. . . . Even if the statute's basic aim is to ban D&X, its language makes clear that it also covers a much broader category of procedures. The language does not track the medical differences between D&E and D&X—though it would have been a simple matter, for example, to provide an exception for the performance of D&E and other abortion procedures. Nor does the statute anywhere suggest that its application turns on whether a portion of the fetus' body is drawn into the vagina as part of a process to extract an intact fetus after collapsing the head as opposed to a process that would dismember the fetus. Thus, the dissenters' argument that the law was generally intended to bar D&X can be both correct and irrelevant. The relevant question is not whether the legislature wanted to ban D&X; it is whether the law was intended to apply only to D&X. The plain language covers both procedures. . . .

The judgment of the Court of Appeals is Affirmed.

JUSTICE KENNEDY, with whom THE CHIEF JUSTICE joins, dissenting.

For close to two decades after Roe v. Wade, the Court gave but slight weight to the interests of the separate States when their legislatures sought to address persisting concerns raised by the existence of a woman's right to elect an abortion in defined circumstances. When the Court reaffirmed the essential holding of Roe, a central premise was that the States retain a critical and legitimate role in legislating on the subject of abortion, as limited by the woman's right the Court restated and again guaranteed. Planned Parenthood of Southeastern Pa. v. Casey (1992). The political processes of the State are not to be foreclosed from enacting laws to promote the life of the unborn and to ensure respect for all human life and its potential. The State's constitutional authority is a vital means for citizens to address these grave and serious issues, as they must if we are to progress in knowledge and understanding and in the attainment of some degree of consensus.

The Court's decision today, in my submission, repudiates this understanding by invalidating a statute advancing critical state interests, even though the law denies no woman the right to choose an abortion and places no undue burden upon the right. The legislation is well within the State's competence to enact. . . .

The Court's failure to accord any weight to Nebraska's interest in prohibiting partial-birth abortion is erroneous and undermines its discussion and holding. The Court's approach in this regard is revealed by its description of the abortion methods at issue, which the Court is correct to describe as "clinically cold or callous." The majority views the procedures from the perspective of the abortionist, rather than from the perspective of a society shocked when confronted with a new method of ending human life. . . .

As described by Dr. Carhart, the D&E procedure requires the abortionist to use instruments to grasp a portion (such as a foot or hand) of a developed and living fetus and drag the grasped portion out of the uterus into the vagina. Dr. Carhart uses the traction created by the opening between the uterus and vagina to dismember the fetus, tearing the grasped portion away from the remainder of the body. . . . The fetus, in many cases, dies just as a human adult or child would: It bleeds to death as it is torn from limb to limb. The fetus can be alive at the beginning of the dismemberment process and can survive for a time while its limbs are being torn off. Dr. Carhart agreed that "[w]hen you pull out a piece of the fetus, let's say, an arm or a leg and remove that, at the time just prior to removal of the portion of the fetus, . . . the fetus [is] alive." . . . At the conclusion of a D&E abortion no intact fetus remains. In Dr. Carhart's words, the abortionist is left with "a tray full of pieces."

The other procedure implicated today is called "partial-birth abortion" or the D&X. The D&X can be used, as a general matter, after 19 weeks gestation because the fetus has become so developed that it may survive intact partial delivery from the uterus into the vagina. In the D&X, the abortionist initiates the woman's natural delivery process by causing the cervix of the woman to be dilated, sometimes over a sequence of days. The fetus' arms and legs are delivered outside the uterus while the fetus is alive; witnesses to the procedure report seeing the body of the fetus moving outside the woman's body. At this point, the abortion procedure has the appearance of a live birth. As stated by one group of physicians, "[a]s the physician manually performs breech extraction of the body of a live fetus, excepting the head, she continues in the apparent role of an obstetrician delivering a child." With only the head of the fetus remaining in utero, the abortionist tears open the skull. . . . Witnesses report observing the portion of the fetus outside the woman react to the skull penetration. The abortionist then inserts a suction tube and vacuums out the developing brain and other matter found within the skull. . . . Brain death does not occur until after the skull invasion, and, according to Dr. Carhart, the heart of the fetus may continue to beat for minutes after the contents of the skull are vacuumed out. The abortionist next completes the delivery of a dead fetus, intact except for the damage to the head and the missing contents of the skull.

Of the two described procedures, Nebraska seeks only to ban the D&X. In light of the description of the D&X procedure, it should go without saying that Nebraska's ban on partial-birth abortion furthers purposes States are entitled to pursue. . . . The Court, as I read its opinion . . . misunderstand[s] Casey and the authorities it confirmed.

Casey is premised on the States having an important constitutional role in defining their interests in the abortion debate. It is only with this principle in mind that Nebraska's interests can be given proper weight. The State's brief describes its interests as including concern for the life of the unborn and "for the partially-born," in preserving the integrity of the medical profession, and in "erecting a barrier to infanticide." A review of Casey demonstrates the legitimacy of these policies. The Court should say so. States may take sides in the abortion debate and come down on the side of life, even life in the unborn. . . .

States also have an interest in forbidding medical procedures which, in the State's reasonable determination, might cause the medical profession or society as a whole to become insensitive, even disdainful, to life, including life in the human fetus. Abortion, Casey held, has consequences beyond the woman and her fetus. The States' interests in

regulating are of concomitant extension. Casey recognized that abortion is, "fraught with consequences for . . . the persons who perform and assist in the procedure [and for] society which must confront the knowledge that these procedures exist, procedures some deem nothing short of an act of violence against innocent human life." A State may take measures to ensure the medical profession and its members are viewed as healers, sustained by a compassionate and rigorous ethic and cognizant of the dignity and value of human life, even life which cannot survive without the assistance of others. Casey demonstrates that the interests asserted by the State are legitimate and recognized by law. It is argued, however, that a ban on the D&X does not further these interests. This is because, the reasoning continues, the D&E method, which Nebraska claims to be beyond its intent to regulate, can still be used to abort a fetus and is no less dehumanizing than the D&X method. . . . The Court's refusal to recognize Nebraska's right to declare a moral difference between the procedure is a dispiriting disclosure of the illogic and illegitimacy of the Court's approach to the entire case.

Nebraska was entitled to find the existence of a consequential moral difference between the procedures. We are referred to substantial medical authority that D&X perverts the natural birth process to a greater degree than D&E, commandeering the live birth process until the skull is pierced. . . . D&X's stronger resemblance to infanticide means Nebraska could conclude the procedure presents a greater risk of disrespect for life and a consequent greater risk to the profession and society, which depend for their sustenance upon reciprocal recognition of dignity and respect. The Court is without authority to second-guess this conclusion.

Those who oppose abortion would agree, indeed would insist, that both procedures are subject to the most severe moral condemnation, condemnation reserved for the most repulsive human conduct. This is not inconsistent, however, with the further proposition that as an ethical and moral matter D&X is distinct from D&E and is a more serious concern for medical ethics and the morality of the larger society the medical profession must serve. Nebraska must obey the legal regime which has declared the right of the woman to have an abortion before viability. Yet it retains its power to adopt regulations which do not impose an undue burden on the woman's right. By its regulation, Nebraska instructs all participants in the abortion process, including the mother, of its moral judgment that all life, including the life of the unborn, is to be respected. The participants, Nebraska has determined, cannot be indifferent to the procedure used and must refrain from using the natural delivery process to kill the fetus. The differentiation between the procedures is itself a moral statement, serving to promote respect for human life; and if the woman and her physician in contemplating the moral consequences of the prohibited procedure conclude that grave moral consequences pertain to the permitted abortion process as well, the choice to elect or not to elect abortion is more informed; and the policy of promoting respect for life is advanced.

It ill-serves the Court, its institutional position, and the constitutional sources it seeks to invoke to refuse to issue a forthright affirmation of Nebraska's right to declare that critical moral differences exist between the two procedures. The natural birth process has been appropriated; yet the Court refuses to hear the State's voice in defining its interests in its law. The Court's holding contradicts Casey's assurance that the State's constitutional position in the realm of promoting respect for life is more than marginal. . . .

Ignoring substantial medical and ethical opinion, the Court substitutes its own judgment for the judgment of Nebraska and some 30 other States and sweeps the law away. The Court's holding stems from misunderstanding the record, misinterpretation of Casey, outright refusal to respect the law of a State, and statutory construction in conflict with settled rules. The decision nullifies a law expressing the will of the people of Nebraska that medical procedures must be governed by moral principles having their foundation in the intrinsic value of human life, including life of the unborn. Through their law the people of Nebraska were forthright in confronting an issue of immense moral consequence. The State chose to forbid a procedure many decent and civilized people find so abhorrent as to be among the most serious of crimes against human life, while the State still protected the woman's autonomous right of choice as reaffirmed in Casey. The Court closes its eyes to these profound concerns.

From the decision, the reasoning, and the judgment, I dissent.

JUSTICE THOMAS, with whom THE CHIEF JUSTICE and JUSTICE SCALIA join, dissenting.

Abortion is a unique act, in which a woman's exercise of control over her own body ends, depending on one's view, human life or potential human life. Nothing in our Federal Constitution deprives the people of this country of the right to determine whether the consequences of abortion to the fetus and to society outweigh the burden of an unwanted pregnancy on the mother. Although a State may permit abortion, nothing in the Constitution dictates that a State must do so. . . .

My views on the merits of the Casey joint opinion have been fully articulated by others. I will not restate those views here, except to note that the Casey joint opinion was constructed by its authors out of whole cloth. The standard set forth in the Casey joint opinion has no historical or doctrinal pedigree. The standard is a product of its authors' own philosophical views about abortion, and it should go without saying that it has no origins in or relationship to the Constitution and is, consequently, as illegitimate as the standard it purported to replace. Even assuming, however, as I will for the remainder of this dissent, that Casey's fabricated undue-burden standard merits adherence (which it does not), today's decision is extraordinary. Today, the Court inexplicably holds that the States cannot constitutionally prohibit a method of abortion that millions find hard to distinguish from infanticide and that the Court hesitates even to describe. This holding cannot be reconciled with Casey's undueburden standard, as that standard was explained to us by the authors of the joint opinion, and the majority hardly pretends otherwise. In striking down this statute—which expresses a profound and legitimate respect for fetal life and which leaves unimpeded several other safe forms of abortion—the majority opinion gives the lie to the promise of Casey that regulations that do no more than "express profound respect for the life of the unborn are permitted, if they are not a substantial obstacle to the woman's exercise of the right to choose" whether or not to have an abortion. Today's decision is so obviously irreconcilable with Casey's explication of what its undue-burden standard requires, let alone the Constitution, that it should be seen for what it is, a reinstitution of the . . . abortion-on-demand era in which the mere invocation of "abortion rights" trumps any contrary societal interest. If this statute is unconstitutional under Casey, then Casey meant nothing at all, and the Court should candidly admit it.

To reach its decision, the majority must take a series of indefensible steps. The majority must first disregard the principles that this Court follows in every context but abortion: We interpret statutes according to their plain meaning and we do not strike down statutes susceptible of a narrowing construction. The majority also must disregard the very constitutional standard it purports to employ, and then displace the considered judgment of the people of Nebraska and 29 other States. The majority's decision is lamentable, because of the result the majority reaches, the illogical steps the majority takes to reach it, and because it portends a return to an era I had thought we had at last abandoned. . . .

In the almost 30 years since Roe, this Court has never described the various methods of aborting a second- or thirdtrimester fetus. From reading the majority's sanitized description, one would think that this case involves state regulation of a widely accepted routine medical procedure. Nothing could be further from the truth. The most widely used method of abortion during this stage of pregnancy is so gruesome that its use can be traumatic even for the physicians and medical staff who perform it. And the particular procedure at issue in this case, "partial birth abortion," so closely borders on infanticide that 30 States have attempted to ban it. . . .

Nebraska, along with 29 other States, has attempted to ban the partial birth abortion procedure. Although the Nebraska statute purports to prohibit only "partial birth abortion," a phrase which is commonly used, as I mentioned, to refer to the breech extraction version of intact D&E, the majority concludes that this statute could also be read in some future case to prohibit ordinary D&E, the first procedure described above. According to the majority, such an application would pose a substantial obstacle to some women seeking abortions and, therefore, the statute is unconstitutional. The majority errs with its very first step. I think it is clear that the Nebraska statute does not prohibit the D&E procedure. . . . "Partial birth abortion" is a term that has been used by a majority of state legislatures, the United States Congress, medical journals, physicians, reporters, even judges, and has never, as far as I am aware, been used to refer to the D&E procedure. . . .

There is no question that the State of Nebraska has a valid interest—one not designed to strike at the right itself—in prohibiting partial birth abortion. Casey itself noted that States may "express profound respect for the life of the unborn." Ibid. States may, without a doubt, express this profound respect by prohibiting a procedure that approaches infanticide, and thereby dehumanizes the fetus and trivializes human life. . . .

CHAPTER 14

The Rights of Gays and Lesbians

INTRODUCTION

Among the wide range of groups in American society, one in particular has historically faced prejudice and discrimination, often reflected in laws that have made this group's private behavior a criminal offense. This group is made up of homosexuals, both male and female. (For convenience, we'll refer to them collectively as "gays," including lesbians in this label.) The sexual practices of gays, which do not include heterosexual intercourse, are limited to acts known as "sodomy," defined as sexual contact between the genitals of one person and the mouth or anus of another. Sodomy is not limited to gays, of course. Heterosexual couples can and do engage in sodomy, most often through sexual acts known as "fellatio" or "cunnilingus." Studies have reported that more than 80 percent of heterosexuals have engaged in sodomy, and many do so on a regular basis. But the practice of sodomy by gays has long made them a target of those who believe that such behavior is immoral and should be punished by law.

Many of those who have supported the criminalization of homosexual sodomy base their beliefs on religious grounds. They cite verses in the Old Testament, such as Leviticus 20:13, which reads: "If a man also lie with mankind, as he lieth with a woman, both of them have committed an abomination; they shall surely be put to death; their blood shall be upon them." Today, very few supporters of anti-sodomy laws favor capital punishment for this practice, although leaders of a small group known as Christian Reconstructionists, who advocate a government based on Old Testament laws, have advocated the death penalty for sodomy. But we should keep in mind that sodomy (both heterosexual and homosexual) was a capital crime in seventeenth-century England, and the Puritan colonists who settled in Massachusetts Bay provided the death penalty for sodomy in their first legal code, the Body of Laws. These colonial laws were published with citations to Old Testament verses in the margin, an indication of the theocratic nature of colonial government. There is no record of any heterosexuals being executed for sodomy in Massachusetts or other colonies, but a small number of homosexuals (probably no more than a dozen) were hung for this crime.

For more than three centuries since the Puritan settlement, gays faced both legal sanctions and social hostility. All thirteen colonies made sodomy a crime, although only Massachusetts allowed the death penalty. And these colonial laws were incorporated in the legal codes of the thirteen states that formed the United States after the Revolution. As late as 1961, all of the fifty states made sodomy a crime. This history forms a backdrop for the cases in this chapter, as it illuminates the deep roots of legal sanctions against gays, and the barriers they faced in challenging anti-sodomy laws and discrimination against them in employment, housing, access to public accommodations, and other areas of life.

Writing for the Supreme Court in 1938, in his famous Footnote Four of the *Carolene Products* case, Justice Harlan Fiske Stone proposed a "more searching judicial inquiry" into laws that discriminated against members of racial, religious, and national minorities. But Stone also said that courts should apply what is now called "strict scrutiny" to laws that disadvantage members of other "discrete and insular" minorities, without naming any such groups. There is little question that gays fall within this undefined category. Over the past several decades, studies and polls have reported that somewhere between 3 and 10 percent of the American population is gay or lesbian, although they differ on definitions of homosexual behavior and orientation. But the true figure is most likely within this range.

If gays belong to a "discrete and insular" minority, do they qualify for "strict scrutiny" of laws that make sodomy a crime or that otherwise discriminate against them? The Supreme Court did not address this question until 1986, in the case of *Bowers v. Hardwick.* This was more than three decades after the Court ruled in *Brown v. Board of Education* that legal discrimination against African Americans violated both the Due Process and Equal Protection Clauses of the Constitution. But there are political and social factors that help to explain why it took the Court so long to decide the first gay-rights case. Most importantly, gays did not emerge as an organized group, with a political and legal agenda, until long after the black community began its crusade against school segregation and other forms of discrimination. That campaign began in the late 1930s, under the leadership of Thurgood Marshall, the general counsel of the NAACP. It took Marshall and his fellow civil rights lawyers almost two decades to bring the *Brown* case to the Supreme Court. Until they felt that public opinion was beginning to swing against school segregation (outside the Deep South), the justices were reluctant to confront this issue.

It is also significant that gays, as a group, did not come "out of the closet" and begin a similar legal crusade against anti-sodomy laws until they saw the effect of the black community's campaign and absorbed its lessons. The gay-rights movement did not emerge as an organized and militant force until a single incident in 1969 outraged and mobilized gays and their "straight" supporters. Before then, gays had largely endured without protest the police harassment of gay bars and other gathering places. In many cities, the police invaded gay bars with impunity, closing them down on any pretext and shoving their patrons into the streets. But the example of civil rights and antiwar protesters inspired many gays who were fed up with this harassment.

On the hot summer night of June 29, 1969, New York police made a serious mistake when they raided the Stonewall Inn, a popular gay bar in Greenwich Village. Refusing to leave the bar when the police ordered them out, gays fought back in bloody battles that spilled into the streets and lasted for three nights. Out of the Stonewall Riots came the Gay Liberation Movement, which soon moved its agitation from the streets to council chambers and courtrooms. Civil liberties groups like the American Civil Liberties Union and Lambda, a gay legal defense organization, began to challenge anti-sodomy laws and other forms of discrimination against gays. By 1975, lobbying and litigation had succeeded in repealing or invalidating anti-sodomy laws in 25 states. But none of these states was below the Mason-Dixon line, where gays faced particular hostility and frequent prosecution.

Just as civil rights lawyers had confronted the Supreme Court's "separate but equal" ruling in the *Plessy* case as precedent, lawyers who represented gays charged with sodomy faced a similar hostile precedent. In 1975, the Supreme Court refused to hear an appeal from a federal appellate court in Virginia, in the case of *Doe v. Commonwealth's Attorney.* The appellate panel had turned back a challenge to Virginia's anti-sodomy law, ruling that homosexual sodomy was not protected by the Constitution because it "is obviously no portion of marriage, home, or family life," and that laws against sodomy had "ancestry going back to Judaic and Christian law." In other words, the Old Testament legal code still prevailed in this area, and the *Doe* ruling stood as legal precedent.

In 1986, however, the Supreme Court faced a ruling of another federal appellate court in Georgia, dismissing *Doe* as precedent and holding that "private consensual sexual behavior among adults" was protected by the Constitution against punishment. Because this appellate ruling would have struck down the anti-sodomy laws of several Deep South states, the Court agreed to review this decision in the case of *Bowers v. Hardwick.*

The story of the *Bowers* case, which involved a challenge to Georgia's anti-sodomy law by a gay bartender named Michael Hardwick, is told in this chapter. But it's worth noting here that the Court's five-to-four decision, upholding the Georgia law, reflected public opinion on this issue. A 1986 *Gallup* poll showed that only 33 percent of the public agreed that "homosexual relations between consenting adults should be legal," while 54 percent disagreed and 13 percent expressed no opinion.

As we will see in the last case in this chapter, *Lawrence v. Texas,* the Supreme Court shifted its position and overruled the *Bowers* case in June 2003. Again, it's worth noting the shift in public opinion on the question of anti-sodomy laws. Just before this ruling, in May 2003, the *Gallup* poll showed that a majority—60 percent—of the public agreed that homosexual relations should be legal, while 35 percent disagreed and 5 percent had no opinion. And by the time of the *Lawrence* ruling, only thirteen states still had laws making sodomy illegal for both heterosexual and gay couples, while just four, including Texas, retained laws that singled out gays for sodomy prosecutions.

However, this major swing in public acceptance of gay sexual practices has significant limits. Writing for the Court in the *Lawrence* case, Justice Anthony Kennedy took an expansive view of "liberty" in matters of sex. "When sexuality finds overt expression in intimate conduct with another person, the conduct can be but one element in a personal bond that is more enduring," Kennedy wrote. One relationship that is meant to be enduring, of course, is marriage. And Kennedy's broad language provoked a heated response from those who saw in it a forecast of judicial recognition of same-sex marriages. In his *Lawrence* dissent, Justice Antonin Scalia warned that Kennedy's opinion "dismantles the structure of constitutional law that has been permitted a distinction to be made between heterosexual and homosexual unions, insofar as formal recognition in marriage is concerned."

The gay-rights campaign, both for supporters and opponents, has shifted to the issue of same-sex marriage. At the time of the *Lawrence* ruling, no state recognized these marriages, although Vermont had adopted a "civil union" law that extended to gay couples most of the legal benefits of marriage, without the name. But the *Lawrence* decision not only energized the gay community to press for legal recognition of same-sex marriages, it also spurred a backlash among supporters of "traditional" marriage, limited to male and female couples. Two national polls conducted in July 2003, a month after the *Lawrence* ruling, showed that a majority of the public (53 percent in one poll and 55 percent in the other) opposed any legal recognition of same-sex marriages, while about 40 percent approved. But there were striking demographic differences among the public: Republicans, evangelical Christians, and older people were overwhelmingly opposed to same-sex marriage, while

Democrats, members of "mainline" Protestant churches, and younger people were supportive.

Justice Scalia's warning that the Court had "taken sides in the culture war" over gay rights and had adopted the "homosexual agenda" indicates that this "war" has not ended, as the battleground shifts to the issue of same-sex marriage. Much as the Court's opinions in the *Gobitis* and *Barnette* cases in the 1940s, over the issue of compulsory flag salutes, revealed two conflicting judicial views of the balance between majority rule and minority rights, the opinions in *Bowers* and *Lawrence* illustrate a more contemporary judicial conflict over this same balance on a very different issue. It is worth going back to the flag-salute decisions in Chapter 4, and reading them again, along with those in the sodomy cases.

This chapter includes opinions in two other cases that involved gay rights. Ruling in 1996 in *Romer v. Evans*, the Court struck down an amendment to the Colorado Constitution, adopted by a majority of voters in an election referendum that withdrew legal protection for gays under state and local antidiscrimination laws. The significance of the *Romer* decision stems from the Court's rejection of public hostility toward gays as a justification for legislation that singles them out for exclusion from legal protections enjoyed by other minorities. However, in 2000 the Court ruled in *Boy Scouts of American v. Dale* that the Scouts were not subject to New Jersey's antidiscrimination laws as a private organization, and could exclude gays from membership and leadership positions. Strictly speaking, the *Dale* decision more aptly fits with free speech and freedom of association cases as a First Amendment case. State and federal courts had earlier upheld the right of the Scouts to exclude atheists and agnostics from membership on First Amendment grounds, and the *Dale* ruling followed that position. But it also affected gay rights in allowing "private" groups like the Scouts to base their exclusion of gays on "moral" objections to homosexuality. This judicial recognition of the religious basis of opposition to homosexuality seems at odds with the Court's rejection in *Lawrence* of "morality" as a justification for laws that single out gays for punishment for sexual conduct that is legal for heterosexuals. Whether we view *Dale* as a First Amendment or a gay-rights case, it illustrates the Court's difficulty in dealing with "moral" issues in the law.

BOWERS V. HARDWICK
478 U.S. 186 (1986)

"[Michael Hardwick] would have us announce a fundamental right to engage in homosexual sodomy. This we are quite unwilling to do. . . . The law . . . is constantly based on notions of morality, and if all laws representing essentially moral choices are to be invalidated under the Due Process Clause, the courts will be very busy indeed."

The Question: Can a state pass a law that imposes criminal penalties, up to 20 years of imprisonment, on any person, heterosexual or homosexual, who engages in the sexual act of sodomy, defined as any contact between the genitals of one person and the mouth or anus of another person?

The Arguments: PRO

The law in question, passed by the Georgia legislature in 1816, expresses the state's legitimate concern with morality. Proscriptions against sodomy go back hundreds of years, and are within the state's power to prohibit and punish sexual behavior that its citizens find abhorrent. This case has nothing to do with the areas of procreation, child rearing, education, and decisions about whether or not to have children that the Supreme Court has recognized in earlier decisions. Sodomy is a practice that has been condemned by legislatures in most of the states and many other countries, and it does not deserve constitutional protection.

CON

The state of Georgia admits that its law providing criminal penalties for sodomy cannot be enforced against heterosexual couples under the Supreme Court ruling in the *Griswold* case. Enforcing the law only against homosexuals is a clear statement of prejudice against a disfavored group, and the law should be subject to the "strict scrutiny" test, requiring the state to show a "compelling" reason for this official discrimination. In addition, the "right of privacy" is not limited to the areas of procreation and decisions about having and raising children.

BACKGROUND

Early in the morning of August 3, 1982, Officer K.R. Torick entered Michael Hardwick's house in the Virginia Highland neighborhood of Atlanta, Georgia. Torick carried a warrant for Hardwick's arrest on a charge of failing to appear in court for drinking in public. Several weeks earlier, Torick had ticketed Michael outside the bar where he worked, for carrying an open beer bottle. Torick later claimed in his official report that when he arrived to serve the arrest warrant, one of Michael's housemates answered the door and admitted the officer. "The roommate told me he didn't know if Hardwick was home but said I could come in to look for him. While walking down the hallway inside the house, I saw a bedroom door partially open." Torick entered the bedroom and promptly arrested Michael and his male companion for violating the Georgia sodomy statute.

While Michael and his friend were dressing, Officer Torick searched the room and discovered a small amount of marijuana, which he confiscated. Handcuffing his prisoners, Torick drove them to the central police station, where they were booked, photographed, and fingerprinted. Officers then tossed Michael and his friend into the holding tank, informing both guards and prisoners in graphic terms of the charges against the two gay men. They spent most of the day behind bars before friends were permitted to post bail for their release. Torick never served the arrest warrant. Three weeks earlier, Michael had appeared in court and paid a $50 fine for the public-drinking ticket, which wiped out the warrant.

Shortly after his sodomy arrest, Michael accepted an offer by the Georgia affiliate of the American Civil Liberties Union to begin a test-case challenge of the law. Michael understood the risks in this effort. Conviction for sodomy carried a maximum prison term of twenty years. Too, a college-educated gay artist like Michael would be torn apart by the human pit bulls in Georgia's prisons. Michael also risked the unwelcome glare of publicity—his lawyers could not guarantee they could keep his face off television screens and his name out of newspapers. After his first encounter with Officer Torick, Michael was attacked and badly beaten by assailants who knew his name. Wider publicity might expose him—and other Atlanta gays—to vigilante violence. Michael's greatest risk was legal defeat; his most formidable opponent was the U.S. Supreme Court. Despite the Court's approval of "privacy" rights for married couples, unmarried heterosexuals, and pregnant women, the justices adamantly refused to hear appeals by homosexuals for similar protection against state prosecution for their intimate activities. . . .

Michael listened as his volunteer ACLU lawyers, John Sweet and Louis Levenson, described these risks and stressed that the case might take years to reach final decision. Although he had not been a gay activist, Michael worked in gay bars and knew the constant fear of harassment, arrest, and prison that pervaded Atlanta's gay community. After a few days of solitary reflection, Michael decided to go ahead. The ACLU lawyers first disposed of the marijuana charge with a misdemeanor guilty plea in Atlanta Municipal Court. As a felony charge, the sodomy case went before the Fulton County Superior Court after an initial municipal court hearing.

Sweet and Levenson actually hoped for a guilty finding against Michael. Without an adverse judgment, they could not begin the appellate route that led through state courts to the U.S. Supreme Court. Before the case reached trial, Fulton County District Attorney Lewis Slaton pulled the case from the court's docket by refusing to present the charges to a grand jury for indictment. Slaton, a sixty-year-old, no-nonsense prosecutor, declined to discuss his reasons for keeping the case out of court. Most likely, he did not want to arouse the Atlanta gay community and its enemies, who obeyed an uneasy truce in the Virginia Highland area and in Piedmont Park, where gays congregated and competed in softball leagues, complete with uniforms, raunchy team names, and cheerleaders. Slaton undoubtedly knew that Officer Torick's expired warrant, his earlier arrest of Michael, and disputes over how he gained entrance to Michael's house might embarrass the police and prosecutors.

Unlike many prosecutors who defended entrapment tactics and police sweeps of parks and gay bars, Slaton kept a relatively tight rein on his troops. Most of the gays arrested in public places like Piedmont Park, even if the police witnessed acts of sodomy, were simply charged with the misdemeanor offense of "public indecency." Slaton later explained his views to an Atlanta reporter: "Consensual sodomy should be a misdemeanor, not a felony," he said, "but nobody has the courage to push it that way." But the law remained on the books as a felony, and Michael Hardwick had been arrested for sodomy. Slaton's refusal to prosecute did not protect Michael from indictment at some time before the four-year statute of limitations expired.

Frustrated at the state level, ACLU lawyers shifted their attack to the federal courts. Kathleen Wilde, a twenty-eight-year-old graduate of Yale Law School, volunteered to take the case before District Judge Robert H. Hall. She decided to broaden the attack on the sodomy law, which subjected heterosexuals as well as homosexuals to prosecution and prison. Wilde recruited a married couple as additional plaintiffs and drafted a complaint which claimed that the law deprived Michael Hardwick and "John and Mary Doe" of their constitutional rights of "privacy, due process, and freedom of expression and association." She filed the complaint with Judge Hall under a statute which allowed federal judges to declare that state laws violated the U.S. Constitution and could not be enforced.

The Georgia law that Kathleen Wilde asked Judge Hall to strike down had been enacted in 1816. It provided that "a person commits the offense of sodomy when he performs or submits to any sexual act involving the sex organs of one person and the mouth or anus of another." Unlike the abortion laws the Supreme Court struck down in 1973, sodomy laws had deep roots in social bedrock. Abortion had not been a "common law" crime in England, and most American states did not outlaw abortion until late in the nineteenth century. But "the detestable and abominable crime against nature," as common-law judges described oral and anal sex, had been proscribed and punished for centuries. Hostility toward homosexuals had not, however, been universal or eternal. Many cultures tolerated or even encouraged homosexual behavior, and ancient Greeks gave their name to acts of sodomy. Until the thirteenth century, the Catholic church had no official policy of persecution; St. Thomas Aquinas first castigated homosexual conduct as "unnatural" and cast those who practiced sodomy into hell's fiery furnace. Criminal law followed church law, and the sin of sodomy became a crime.

All the original thirteen states had made sodomy a criminal offense when the Bill of Rights became part of the Constitution in 1791. As late as 1961, all fifty states had outlawed sodomy. Pressure to liberalize these laws first came from medical, social-welfare, and legal groups. The American Law Institute, an impeccably conservative group of establishment lawyers, urged state legislatures in the late 1950s to enact a Model Penal Code which decriminalized adult, consensual, private sexual conduct. Illinois became the first state, in 1961, to adopt the ALI code.

Homosexual organizations played a quiet role in the initial lobbying to repeal sodomy laws. Founded in 1951, the Mattachine Society represented gays for more than a decade. Its leaders first adopted a low profile, fearful of public hostility, but the black civil-rights movement of the 1960s stirred gays toward militance and activism. Franklin Kameny, a Mattachine maverick, argued in 1964 that gays should examine "the case of the Negro," whose gains in the ninety years after Emancipation "were nothing compared to those of the past ten years, when he tried a vigorous civil-liberties, social-action approach" to legal oppression.

Kameny's rhetorical spark did not ignite the gay movement until the hot summer night of June 27, 1969, when New York poilce raided the Stonewall Inn on Christopher Street in Greenwich Village. Beaten and abused, gays fought back in bloody battles which lasted for three nights. Out of the "Stonewall riots" came the Gay Liberation Movement, which soon moved its agitation from the streets to council chambers and courtrooms. Lobbying and litigation paid off: By 1975, more than half the states had repealed or invalidated their sodomy laws. But none of those states was below the Mason–Dixon line, where hostility toward gays fed on the "good ol' boy" Southern syndrome of exaggerated masculinity.

Kathleen Wilde filed her complaint against three Georgia officials: Attorney General Michael Bowers, a forty-two-year-old West Point graduate; Lewis Slaton, the Fulton County district attorney who refused to prosecute Michael Hardwick; and George Napier, Atlanta's police commissioner. Judge Robert Hall, who first ruled on the complaint, had been a Georgia official for many years. The sixty-two-year-old judge served in the state attorney general's office and on Georgia courts before President Jimmy Carter, a long-time friend, placed Hall on the federal bench in 1979.

Judge Hall had no desire to rule on the Georgia sodomy law. He looked for an easy out, and found one in the 1975 decision of a federal judicial panel which upheld Virginia's almost identical sodomy law. In a case called *Doe v. Commonwealth's Attorney*, the panel's majority denied that homosexuals shared the "privacy" rights of their straight neighbors. Supreme Court precedent, the majority held, provided these rights only to marital or familial relationships which states had legally approved. Because homosexual conduct "is obviously no portion of marriage, home or family life," Virginia could punish sodomy "in the promotion of morality and decency," the panel ruled. The two-judge majority added that "the longevity of the Virginia statute does testify to the State's interest and its legitimacy." Punishment of sodomy "is not an upstart notion; it has ancestry going back to Judaic and Christian law."

District Judge Robert Merhige dissented from the *Doe* ruling. He viewed the Supreme Court cases cited by his colleagues "as standing for the principle that every individual has a right to be free from unwarranted governmental intrusion into one's decisions on private matters of intimate concern." Judge Merhige would extend privacy rights to all consenting adults, regardless of gender: "A mature individual's choice of an adult sexual partner," he wrote, "would appear to me to be a decision of the utmost private and intimate concern." Merhige suggested that the sodomy issue "centers not around morality or decency, but the constitutional right of privacy."

Judge Merhige had pinpointed the conflict over sodomy laws, with claims of "morality and decency" posed against the "right of privacy." The Supreme Court had refused to hear an appeal from the *Doe* ruling, and Judge Hall looked no farther for guidance. "The Virginia statute challenged in that case is quite similar to the Georgia legislation in question," he ruled on April 18, 1983, "and all the constitutional arguments made by Hardwick here were rejected in *Doe*." Dismissing Hardwick's complaint Judge Hall also denied the challenge of "John and Mary Doe" to the sodomy law. Because District Attorney Slaton had not threatened them with prosecution, the Does faced no "immediate danger of sustaining some direct injury as a result of the statute's enforcement."

Kathleen Wilde took Michael's challenge to the federal appellate court in Atlanta, and they waited more than two years for the next decision. The result was worth the long wait. Writing for a two-judge majority, Judge Frank M. Johnson rejected the *Doe* case and declared that Michael had a privacy right that began in his bedroom. Appointed to the federal bench by President Dwight Eisenhower, Johnson had endured the hostility of fellow Alabamans for ruling that black children had the right to attend public schools with white children. Placed on the appellate bench by President Jimmy Carter in 1979, Johnson continued on his liberal course. He wrote for the panel that subsequent Supreme Court decisions had left the *Doe* ruling "an open question." Citing a 1977 Supreme Court opinion which struck down state restrictions on contraceptive sales, Johnson held that "private consensual sexual behavior among adults" was protected from punishment. Covered by the "privacy" blanket, Johnson wrote, were all kinds of "intimate associations" based on consent and caring. "For some," he added, "the sexual activity in question here serves the same purpose as the intimacy of marriage" (Irons, 1988).

JUSTICE WHITE delivered the opinion of the Court.

In August 1982, respondent Hardwick (hereafter respondent) was charged with violating the Georgia statute criminalizing sodomy by committing that act with another adult male in the bedroom of respondent's home. [Georgia Code Ann. 16-6-2 (1984) provides, in pertinent part, as follows: "(a) A person commits the offense of sodomy when he performs or submits to any sexual act involving the sex one person and the mouth or anus of another. . . . person convicted of the offense of sodomy shall be punished by imprisonment for not less than one nor more than 20 years. . . ."]

After a preliminary hearing, the District Attorney decided not to present the matter to the grand jury unless further evidence developed. Respondent then brought suit in the Federal District Court, challenging the constitutionality of the statute insofar as it criminalized consensual sodomy. He asserted that he was a practicing homosexual, that the Georgia sodomy statute, as administered by the defendants, placed him in imminent danger of arrest, and that the statute for several reasons violates the Federal Constitution. The District Court granted the defendants' motion to dismiss for failure to state a claim. . . . A divided panel of the Court of Appeals for the Eleventh Circuit reversed. The court [held] that the Georgia statute violated respondent's fundamental rights because his homosexual activity is a private and intimate association that is beyond the reach of state regulation by reason of the Ninth Amendment and the Due Process Clause of the Fourteenth Amendment. . . . Because other Courts of Appeals have arrived at judgments contrary to that of the Eleventh Circuit in this case, we granted the Attorney General's petition for certiorari questioning the holding that the sodomy statute violates the fundamental rights of homosexuals. We agree with petitioner that the Court of Appeals erred, and hence reverse its judgment.

This case does not require a judgment on whether laws against sodomy between consenting adults in general, or between homosexuals in particular, are wise or desirable. It raises no question about the right or propriety of state legislative decisions to repeal their laws that criminalize homosexual sodomy, or of state-court decisions invalidating those laws on state constitutional grounds. The issue presented is whether the Federal Constitution confers a fundamental right upon homosexuals to engage in sodomy and hence invalidates the laws of the many States that still make such conduct illegal and have done so for a very long time. The case also calls for some judgment about the limits of the Court's role in carrying out its constitutional mandate.

We first register our disagreement with the Court of Appeals and with respondent that the Court's prior cases have construed the Constitution to confer a right of privacy that extends to homosexual sodomy and for all intents and purposes have decided this case. . . . Pierce v. Society of Sisters and Meyer v. Nebraska were described as dealing with child rearing and education; Prince v. Massachusetts with family relationships; Skinner v. Oklahoma with procreation; Loving v. Virginia with marriage; Griswold v. Connecticut and Eisenstadt v. Baird with contraception; and Roe v. Wade with abortion. The latter three cases were interpreted as construing the Due Process Clause of the Fourteenth Amendment to confer a fundamental individual right to decide whether or not to beget or bear a child. Accepting the decisions in these cases . . . , we think it evident that none of the rights announced in those cases bears any resemblance to the claimed constitutional right of homosexuals to engage in acts of sodomy that is asserted in this case. No connection between family, marriage, or procreation on the one hand and homosexual activity on the other has been demonstrated, either by the Court of Appeals or by respondent. Moreover, any claim

that these cases nevertheless stand for the proposition that any kind of private sexual conduct between consenting adults is constitutionally insulated from state proscription is unsupportable. . . .

Precedent aside, however, respondent would have us announce, as the Court of Appeals did, a fundamental right to engage in homosexual sodomy. This we are quite unwilling to do. It is true that despite the language of the Due Process Clauses of the Fifth and Fourteenth Amendments, which appears to focus only on the processes by which life, liberty, or property is taken, the cases are legion in which those Clauses have been interpreted to have substantive content, subsuming rights that to a great extent are immune from federal or state regulation or proscription. Among such cases are those recognizing rights that have little or no textual support in the constitutional language. Meyer, Prince, and Pierce fall in this category, as do the privacy cases from Griswold to Carey.

Striving to assure itself and the public that announcing rights not readily identifiable in the Constitution's text involves much more than the imposition of the Justices' own choice of values on the States and the Federal Government, the Court has sought to identify the nature of the rights qualifying for heightened judicial protection. In Palko v. Connecticut (1937), it was said that this category includes those fundamental liberties that are "implicit in the concept of ordered liberty," such that "neither liberty nor justice would exist if [they] were sacrificed." A different description of fundamental liberties appeared in Moore v. East Cleveland (1977), where they are characterized as those liberties that are "deeply rooted in this Nation's history and tradition."

It is obvious to us that neither of these formulations would extend a fundamental right to homosexuals to engage in acts of consensual sodomy. Proscriptions against that conduct have ancient roots. Sodomy was a criminal offense at common law and was forbidden by the laws of the original 13 States when they ratified the Bill of Rights. In 1868, when the Fourteenth Amendment was ratified, all but 5 of the 37 States in the Union had criminal sodomy laws. In fact, until 1961, all 50 States outlawed sodomy, and today, 24 States and the District of Columbia continue to provide criminal penalties for sodomy performed in private and between consenting adults. Against this background, to claim that a right to engage in such conduct is "deeply rooted in this Nation's history and tradition" or "implicit in the concept of ordered liberty" is, at best, facetious.

Nor are we inclined to take a more expansive view of our authority to discover new fundamental rights imbedded in the Due Process Clause. The Court is most vulnerable and comes nearest to illegitimacy when it deals with judge-made constitutional law having little or no cognizable roots in the language or design of the Constitution. That this is so was painfully demonstrated by the face-off between the Executive and the Court in the 1930's, which resulted in the repudiation of much of the substantive gloss that the Court had placed on the Due Process Clauses of the Fifth and Fourteenth Amendments. There should be, therefore, great resistance to expand the substantive reach of those Clauses, particularly if it requires redefining the category of rights deemed to be fundamental. Otherwise, the Judiciary necessarily takes to itself further authority to govern the country

to recognize that the threat to national cohesion posed by a refusal to salute the flag was vastly outweighed by the threat to those same values posed by compelling such a salute. See West Virginia Board of Education v. Barnette (1943). I can only hope that here, too, the Court soon will reconsider its analysis and conclude that depriving individuals of the right to choose for themselves how to conduct their intimate relationships poses a far greater threat to the values most deeply rooted in our Nation's history than tolerance of nonconformity could ever do. Because I think the Court today betrays those values,

I dissent.

MEET MICHAEL HARDWICK

I was born in Miami in 1954 and raised in Miami. My mother is a very wonderful and intelligent and sensitive woman. My father was a very intelligent and crafty-type man. He was a fireman and worked during the Cuban missile crisis with fallout shelters and radiation. My parents divorced when I was twelve years old and I lived with my mom until I was seventeen. I went to high school here and it was pretty normal, just like high school anywhere.

I have two sisters and a brother that are all older than me. My older sister is forty and she is a lesbian. She has a daughter who is sixteen and she's been a strong influence on me all my life. I have an older brother who is straight and married and has children.

I wanted to be a landscape architect, and I went to school in botany and horticulture at Florida State University in Gainesville. I spent three years up there, pretty much as a spiritual recluse. I was seriously considering becoming a Buddhist monk, and I was into a very spiritual frame, as far as Karma and all of that. My family was all Catholic, so they were rather disturbed about this. They were actually relieved when I told them I was coming out instead. Their attitude was, Thank God!

From Gainesville I went up to Atlanta and met this man that I fell in love with. When I met this guy it seemed like a perfectly normal thing and that was that. Things didn't work out between me and this man in Atlanta. He had a lover, which I didn't know, so I left and went to Knoxville, Tennessee. I went there because I had a girlfriend I had originally gone up to see in Atlanta, who was also gay, and she and her girlfriend were moving to Knoxville. They were telling me, You've got to do something; you're a mess. So they brought me up there and nursed me back to mental health. I was totally devastated for about six months. All I did was listen to Billy Holliday and have The Blues. When I got my balance I went to Gatlinburg, up in the Smoky Mountains, and I really loved it there. It was good for me inside, soul-searching and putting things back into perspective. I really liked the place.

Then I left and went back down to Miami and told my mother and my sister I was gay, and they were very supportive. I was twenty-one years old at the time. And I've been out since then. My mother was very accepting. She has become very independent for the first time in her life. She's now living all by herself on fourteen acres of land up in Gainesville, and she's loving it. She's been great all along.

I started working in Miami, and I opened a business called Growth Concept Environmental Design. Because I had bar-tended in a private gay restaurant, very elite, I knew all these top designers. So when I opened my business I immediately had an excellent clientele. I worked for about a year and a half and I finally decided I needed more time by myself. I had questions that I really hadn't worked out. So I sold my business to my junior partner and I moved back to Gatlinburg because I was so taken with the Smoky Mountains. I opened a health-food store and I hiked about forty miles a week. I was there for two years and I lost my ass in the health-food store, but at the same time I gained a lot of knowledge of myself and became a friend to myself, which is what I was really seeking to do.

This girlfriend that had pulled me out four years earlier was living in Atlanta, so I went down there to visit her, which is how this whole case started. I had been working for about a year, in a gay bar that was getting ready to open up a discothèque. I was there one night until seven o'clock in the morning, helping them put in insulation. When I left, I went up to the bar and they gave me a beer. I was kind of debating whether I wanted to leave, because I was pretty exhausted, or stay and finish the beer. I decided to leave, and I opened the door and threw the beer bottle into this trash can by the front door of the bar. I wasn't really in the mood for the beer.

Just as I did that I saw a cop drive by. I walked about a block, and he turned around and came back and asked me where the beer was. I told him I had thrown it in the trash can in front of the bar. He insisted I had thrown the beer bottle right as he pulled up. He made me get in the car and asked me what I was doing. I told him that I worked there, which immediately identified me as a homosexual, because he knew it was a homosexual bar. He was enjoying *his* position as opposed to *my* position.

After about twenty minutes of bickering he drove me back so I could show him where the beer bottle was. There was no way of getting out of the back of a cop car. I told him it was in the trash can and he said he couldn't see it from the car. I said fine, just give me a ticket for drinking in public. He was just busting my chops because he knew I was gay.

Anyway, the ticket had a court date on the top and a date in the center and they didn't coincide; they were one day apart. Tuesday was the court date, and the officer had written Wednesday on top of the ticket. So Tuesday, two hours after my court date, he was at my house with a warrant for my arrest. This was Officer Torick. This was unheard of, because it takes forty-eight hours to process a warrant. What I didn't realize, and didn't find out until later, was that he had personally processed a warrant for the first time in ten years. So I think there is reason to believe that he had it out for me.

I wasn't there when he came with the warrant. I got home that afternoon and my roommate said there was a cop here with a warrant. I said, That's impossible; my court date isn't until tomorrow. I went and got my ticket and realized the court date was Tuesday, not Wednesday. I asked my roommate if he'd seen the warrant and he said he hadn't. So I went down to the county clerk and showed him the discrepancy on the ticket. He brought it before the judge, and he fined me $50. I told the county clerk the cop had already been at my house with a warrant and he said that was impossible. He said it takes forty-eight hours to process a warrant. He wrote me a receipt just in case I had any problems with it further down the road. That was that, and I thought I had taken care of it and everything was finished, and I didn't give it much thought.

Three weeks went by, and my mom had come up to visit me. I came home one morning after work at 6:30 and there were three guys standing in front of my house. I cannot say for *sure* that they had anything to do with this, but they were very straight, middle thirties, civilian clothes. I got out of the car, turned around, and they said "Michael" and I said yes, and they proceeded to beat the hell out of me. Tore all the cartilage out of my nose, kicked me in the face, cracked about six of my ribs. I passed out. I don't know how long I was unconscious. When I came to, all I could think of was, God, I don't want my *mom* to see me like this!

I managed to crawl up the stairs into the house, into the back bedroom. What I didn't realize was that I'd left a trail of blood all the way back. My mom woke up, found this trail of blood, found me passed out, and just freaked out. I assured her that everything was okay, that it was like a fluke accident, these guys were drunk or whatever. They weren't drunk, they weren't ruffians, and they knew who I was. I convinced her everything was okay and she left to go visit a friend in Pennsylvania.

I had a friend come in a few days later who was from out of town, in Atlanta to apply for a government job. He waited for me to get off work, we went home, and then my roommate left for work. That night at work, another friend of mine had gotten really drunk, and I took his car keys, put him in a cab, and sent him to my house, so he was passed out on the couch in the living room. He did not hear me and my friend come in. I retired with my friend. He had left the front door open, and Officer Torick came into my house about 8:30 in the morning. He had a warrant that had not been valid for three weeks and that he didn't bother to call in and check on. Officer Torick came in and woke up the guy who was passed out on my couch, who didn't know I was there and had a friend with me.

Officer Torick then came to my bedroom. The door was cracked, and the door opened up and I looked up and there was nobody there. I just blew it off as the wind and went back to what I was involved in, which was mutual oral sex. About thirty-five seconds went by and I heard another noise and I looked up, and this officer is standing in my bedroom. He identified himself when he realized I had seen him. He said, My name is Officer Torick. Michael Hardwick, you are under arrest. I said, For what? What are you doing in my bedroom? He said, I have a warrant for your arrest. I told him the warrant isn't any good. He said, it doesn't matter, because I was acting under good faith.

I asked Torick if he would leave the room so we could get dressed and he said, There's no reason for that, because I have already seen you in your most intimate aspect. He stood there and watched us get dressed, and then he brought us over to a substation. We waited in the car for about twenty-five minutes, handcuffed to the back floor. Then he brought us downtown; brought us in and made sure everyone in the holding cells and guards and people who were processing us knew I was in there for "cocksucking" and that I should be able to get what I was looking for. The guards were having a *real* good time with that.

There was somebody there to get me out of jail within an hour, but it took them twelve hours to get me out. In the meantime, after they processed me and kept me in a holding cell for about four hours, they brought me up to the third floor, where there was convicted criminals. I had no business being up there. They again told all the people in the cells what I was in there for. It was not a pleasant experience. My friend was freaking out, and when I got out of jail I came back within an hour and got him out. He decided because of his government position he could not go on with the case.

I was contacted about three days later by a man named Clint Sumrall who was working in and out of the ACLU. For the last five years, he would go to the courts every day and find sodomy cases and try to get a test case. By this time, my mom had come back into town and found out what had happened. We had a typical mother conversation—she was saying, I *knew* I shouldn't have left! So she went with me to meet with Sumrall and this team of ten lawyers. I asked them what was the worst that could happen, what was the best that could happen? They explained to me that the judge could make an example out of me and give me twenty years in jail. My mom was saying, Do you realize I'll be *dead* before I see you again? So they said, Just think about it for two or three days.

I realized that if there was anything I could do, even if it was just laying the foundation to change this horrendous law, that I would feel pretty bad about myself if I just walked away from it. One thing that influenced me was that they'd been trying for five years to get a perfect case. Most of the arrests that are made for sodomy in Atlanta are of people who are having sex outside in public; or an adult and a minor; or two consenting adults, but their families don't know they are gay; or they went through seven years of college to teach and they'd be jeopardizing their teaching position. There's a lot of different reasons why people would not want to go on with it. I was fortunate enough to have a supportive family who knew I was gay. I'm a bartender, so I can always work in a gay bar. And I was arrested in my own house. So I was a perfect test case.

* * *

I was at work when I heard about the [Supreme Court] decision. I cater a complimentary buffet for about a hundred people a day, so I go into work about four or five hours before anyone else gets there to do all my prep work. On this particular morning I could not sleep, and I got to work about nine o'clock. A friend of mine had been watching cable news and had seen it and knew where to find me and came over. When I opened the door he was crying and saying that he was sorry, and I didn't know what the hell he was talking about. Finally I calmed him down and he told me what had happened: that I had lost by a five-to-four vote.

I was totally stunned. My friend took off and I was there for about four hours by myself and that's when it really sunk in. I just cried—not so much because I had failed but because to me it was frightening to think that in the year of 1986 our Supreme Court, next to God, could make a decision that was more suitable to the mentality of the Spanish Inquisition. It was frightening and it stunned me. I was scared. I had been fighting this case for five years and everyone had seemed so confident that I was really *not* expecting this decision the way that they handed it down.

Gays are just a step up from drug addicts in the way society treats us. We're second-class citizens. I would fight to my dying day to defend my rights as a homosexual. I am a perfectly well-adjusted person. I am very productive, I am very talented. I refuse to be suppressed, I refuse to be treated as a second-class citizen. There's no *way* the Supreme Court can say that I can't have sex with a consenting adult in the privacy of my own bedroom (Irons, 1988).

COMMENTARY: THE PURPOSE OF PRIVACY

Free speech is right there in the Constitution. Sodomy is not. Nevertheless, in the Supreme Court term that just ended, liberals cheered the Court for allowing the government to ban certain kinds of advertising, and booed the Court for allowing the government to ban homosexual sodomy. Meanwhile Justice Byron White, whose decision in the sodomy case incorporates a sermonette about the danger of activist judges overturning government policies with "ancient roots," also wrote the decision authorizing judges to overturn extreme partisan gerrymandering—a practice with equally ancient roots in our republic.

Then there's the Reagan administration, which usually can be heard carrying on about federalism and getting the government off people's backs, but now is heard fretting about the Court's repeated refusal to interfere with private and local government affirmative action plans. Finally, on the last day of the term, we have four justices who had joined White's plea against activism in the sodomy case (led by Chief Justice Warren Burger, in his swan song) voting to toss out the most important piece of legislation of the past year, the Gramm-Rudman budget act, because of a never-used technicality in a 65-year-old law about who can fire the comptroller general.

The point isn't that everyone's a hypocrite when it comes to the Constitution, though that's pretty close to being true. The point is that the purpose of having a Constitution in a democracy is to use it from time to time, and using it means judges thwarting the will of the majority. If a majority already supports something, invoking the Constitution is redundant.

A "restrainer" can win the first round of almost any constitutional argument by saying, "show me where it says anything about 'x'"—sodomy, gerrymandering, advertising— "in the Constitution." But this gets tiresome. Even the basic principle of judicial review—the power of judges to throw out laws they find unconstitutional—is not obvious from the plain words of the document itself. It was an initial bold act of interpretation by John Marshall in 1803 that has since evolved into a tradition and an institution, in a process that conservatives especially should feel comfortable with. This isn't a license for judges to do whatever they want under the Constitution. It's simply a recognition that they must do *something*.

Given the need for some amount of literary exegesis in interpreting the Constitution, it's not so farfetched to find a protection of sexual privacy in the Fifth Amendment's magisterial invocation of "liberty," combined with the Fourth Amendment's quite specific assertion of a "right of the people to be secure in their persons [and] houses . . . against unreasonable searches and seizures." On the other hand, it may not be impossibly stinting to see these grand phrases as applying only to political freedoms and criminal procedures.

What *is* logically impossible is the law as the Court now leaves it, under which the Constitution protects people's right to practice birth control, miscegenation, abortion, and even perhaps (according to a footnote in the most recent case) heterosexual sodomy, but not homosexual sodomy. Justice White quotes some pretty flowery phrases about why the Constitution applies to one thing and not another. But I would love to hear his explanation of how heterosexual sodomy is "implicit in the concept of ordered liberty such that neither liberty nor justice would exist if [it] were sacrificed," whereas homosexual sodomy is not.

Of course you have to draw the line somewhere. But in extending the reach of constitutionally protected sexual privacy, this is a very bad line to draw. Just as in the area of free speech, you don't need the Constitution to protect what's conventional and popular. You need it to protect what's unconventional and unpopular. A constitutional protection that only applies to opinions or sexual practices that aren't offensive to the majority is worthless.

This ruling makes the Court's notorious 1973 abortion decision look even more bizarre. (Maybe that's the idea.) Unlike abortion, sodomy between consenting adults in private involves no even arguable harm to any third party. Justice White doesn't even attempt to explain what legitimate, let alone compelling, interest the state might have in preventing it. The abortion decision plunged the Court into a morass of regulatory detail involving pregnancy trimesters and questions of fetal movement—implausible matters to find in the Constitution. A plain declaration that private sexual practices are no one else's business, by contrast, would have the classic constitutional virtues of clarity and simplicity. Finally, the abortion decision actually did run roughshod over the policies of many states. Sodomy laws, by contrast, are virtually unenforced. Ironically, for all of White's talk about "deeply rooted" taboos, our society has already made its decision about private consensual sodomy.

In his eloquent dissent, Justice Blackmun quotes a famous dissent by Justice Brandeis. This case is not about a right to commit sodomy, he says, but rather about "the right most valued by civilized men, the right to be left alone." That's pretty good. But I think the Court came closer to the real issue in its 1967 decision invalidating state laws against miscegenation (also widespread and "deeply rooted" at the time), when it invoked an even more famous phrase: "the pursuit of happiness." During the Liberty Weekend hoo-ha, I heard two conservative commentators on TV invoking this beautiful phrase as a justification for some of the celebratory excesses. But if the right to pursue happiness only extends as far as celebrating liberty too hard on the Fourth of July, what we're celebrating isn't very meaningful.

The right to pursue happiness is held to be "self-evident." Equally self-evident—as every member of the Supreme Court surely knows from personal experience—is that the pursuit of happiness is not an easy one. It's hard to be happy. That's why if a person, or two people, or three people and a billy goat find a way to be happy that strikes most other people as peculiar, or even revolting, that's hardly reason enough for the government to thwart them. They're only trying to find an answer to the question we're all trying to answer in our own ways (Kinsley, 1986).

COMMENTARY: GOD SAVE THIS VULNERABLE COURT

Put aside for the moment the question of whether there should be state laws against sodomy. Dr. Jerry Falwell is surely wrong when he says the Supreme Court "has issued a clear statement that perverted moral behavior is not accepted practice in this country." Among millions of Americans the culture of buggery is not only accepted but championed. What the Court said is that the text and structure of the Constitution do not establish the practice of sodomy as a "fundamental right."

The Court said other things that needed saying. In upholding the Georgia sodomy law, it said that in this Republic the people have a fundamental right to make their own laws, within the limits specified by the Constitution. In making such laws, the Court further said, the people may properly be influenced by tradition, custom, and religious belief. When judges try to override this democratic process by imposing their own values, they are themselves acting unconstitutionally. In the words of the majority opinion by Justice Byron White: "The Court is most vulnerable and comes nearest to illegitimacy when it deals with judge-made constitutional law having little or no cognizable roots in the language or design of the Constitution."

Divorce Proceedings

Whether or not there should be a law against sodomy is for the representatives of the people to debate and decide. Either way, it is a question of moral judgment. As Justice White says, "The law . . . is constantly based on notions of morality, and if all laws representing essentially moral choices are to be invalidated . . . , the courts will be very busy indeed." Furthermore, the courts would be busily putting themselves out of business, for a democratic people would not long countenance a legal system that formally divorced law from moral judgment. Admittedly, law and moral judgment have too frequently been separated in recent decades. But a final divorce decree has not come through, and now, at long last, the Court may be favoring a reconciliation.

Justice Harry Blackmun, in bitter dissent, unfurled the tattered banner of unbridled individualism. Two centuries of American jurisprudence may be described as a descent from Providence to privacy, but Justice Blackmun thinks it's progress all the way. With remarkable candor Blackmun argues that the Court's only reason for interest in questions of marriage, family, childhood, and sexuality is that they bear upon the freedom of the individual. Seldom has the classical concern for the "common good" been rejected so explicitly. Blackmun writes: "We protect [such] rights not because they contribute, in some direct and material way,

to the general public welfare, but because they form so central a part of an individual life." It is a revealing glimpse into the mind of the author of the *Roe* v. *Wade* decision on abortion.

Consistent with his libertarian premise, Blackmun would employ judicial coercion to liberate the individual by destroying the bonds of community and tradition, even when such bonds are legitimated by democratic consent. He cites the infamous statement of Justice Holmes: "It is revolting to have no better reason for a rule of law than that so it was laid down in the time of Henry IV. It is still more revolting if the grounds upon which it was laid down have vanished long since, and the rule simply persists from blind imitation of the past." Yet more revolting is the hubris of judges who declare the people's wise affirmation to be blind imitation, and who conform the law to "current values" as defined, of course, by themselves.

But the full force of Blackmun's animus is saved for religion. I do not know whether he is against religion as such, but he is certainly against religion that is so impertinent as to impinge upon the *res publica*. In the present case he detects religion breaking out from the sphere of privacy to which it is properly consigned. Blackmun says he is not impressed by the "invocation" of Leviticus, Romans, and St. Thomas Aquinas to the effect that sodomy is gravely wrong. "The legitimacy of secular legislation," he argues, "depends . . . on whether the state can advance some justification for its law beyond its conformity to religious doctrine." Surely he is right in that. However, he overlooks the fact that Georgia and other states do advance justifications beyond religious doctrine. Such justifications have to do with the common good, but we have seen what Justice Blackmun thinks of the common good.

Public Nuisance

Blackmun, it is to be feared, does not want justifications "beyond" religion; he wants justifications that *exclude* religion. In this view, the inclusion of religion or religiously based morality lethally taints the law. Says Blackmun, "A state can no more punish private behavior because of religious intolerance than it can punish such behavior because of racial animus." Religion, when it impinges upon the public arena, is by definition religious intolerance. Legal historians note that in the last four decades there has been scarcely a Supreme Court reference to public religion that is not strongly pejorative. Providence is protected by the privacy doctrine, so long as it doesn't make a nuisance of itself in public. Such is the perversity of mind that has made the Court so vulnerable to challenge by democratic theory and practice. That is the most important perversity addressed by Justice White's majority opinion (Neuhaus, 1986).

ROMER V. EVANS
517 U.S. 620 (1996)

*"Amendment 2 [of the Colorado Constitution] . . . , in making a general pronouncement that gays and lesbians
shall not have any particular protections from the law, inflicts on them immediate, continuing, and
real injuries that outrun and belie any legitimate justifications that may be claimed for it. . . .
This Colorado cannot do. A State cannot so deem a class of persons a stranger to its laws."*

The Question: Can the voters of a state, by majority vote, amend the state's constitution to nullify state and local laws that ban discrimination against homosexuals in housing, employment, access to public accommodations, and other areas?

The Arguments: PRO

Homosexuals are not among the groups that are protected from discrimination under the Equal Protection Clause of the Fourteenth Amendment, such as racial and religious minorities. A majority of a state's voters should have the power to amend the state's constitution, as long as such amendments do not violate the federal Constitution, which does not include homosexuals among the protected groups. Homosexuals and their supporters are free to use the democratic process to repeal such amendments, but the courts should not interfere in this process.

CON

The Supreme Court has ruled that state laws or constitutional provisions that are designed to harm an unpopular group, of whatever kind, violate the Constitution. There is no doubt that Amendment 2 of the Colorado Constitution was motivated by hostility toward homosexuals, and was designed to withdraw from them protections against discrimination that members of other groups have been accorded by state and local laws.

JUSTICE KENNEDY delivered the opinion of the Court.

One century ago, the first Justice Harlan admonished this Court that the Constitution "neither knows nor tolerates classes among citizens." Plessy v. Ferguson (1896) (dissenting opinion). Unheeded then, those words now are understood to state a commitment to the law's neutrality where the rights of persons are at stake. The Equal Protection Clause enforces this principle and today requires us to hold invalid a provision of Colorado's Constitution.

The enactment challenged in this case is an amendment to the Constitution of the State of Colorado, adopted in a 1992 statewide referendum. The parties and the state courts refer to it as "Amendment 2," its designation when submitted to the voters. The impetus for the amendment and the contentious campaign that preceded its adoption came in large part from ordinances that had been passed in various Colorado municipalities. For example, the cities of Aspen and Boulder and the City and County of Denver each had enacted ordinances which banned discrimination in many transactions and activities, including housing, employment, education, public accommodations, and health and welfare services. What gave rise to the statewide controversy was the protection the ordinances afforded to persons discriminated against by reason of their sexual orientation. Amendment 2 repeals these ordinances to the extent they prohibit

discrimination on the basis of "homosexual, lesbian or bisexual orientation, conduct, practices or relationships." Yet Amendment 2, in explicit terms, does more than repeal or rescind these provisions. It prohibits all legislative, executive or judicial action at any level of state or local government designed to protect the named class, a class we shall refer to as homosexual persons or gays and lesbians. The amendment reads: "No Protected Status Based on Homosexual, Lesbian, or Bisexual Orientation. Neither the State of Colorado, through any of its branches or departments, nor any of its agencies, political subdivisions, municipalities or school districts, shall enact, adopt or enforce any statute, regulation, ordinance or policy whereby homosexual, lesbian or bisexual orientation, conduct, practices or relationships shall constitute or otherwise be the basis of or entitle any person or class of persons to have or claim any minority status, quota preferences, protected status or claim of discrimination. This Section of the Constitution shall be in all respects self-executing."

Soon after Amendment 2 was adopted, this litigation to declare its invalidity and enjoin its enforcement was commenced in the District Court for the City and County of Denver. Among the plaintiffs (respondents here) were homosexual persons, some of them government employees. They alleged that enforcement of Amendment 2 would subject them to immediate and substantial risk of discrimination on the basis of their sexual orientation. Other plaintiffs (also respondents here) included the three municipalities whose ordinances we have cited and certain other governmental entities which had acted earlier to protect homosexuals from discrimination but would be prevented by Amendment 2 from continuing to do so. Although Governor Romer had been on record opposing the adoption of Amendment 2, he was named in his official capacity as a defendant, together with the Colorado Attorney General and the State of Colorado.

The trial court granted a preliminary injunction to stay enforcement of Amendment 2, and an appeal was taken to the Supreme Court of Colorado. Sustaining the interim injunction and remanding the case for further proceedings, the State Supreme Court held that Amendment 2 was subject to strict scrutiny under the Fourteenth Amendment because it infringed the fundamental right of gays and lesbians to participate in the political process. To reach this conclusion, the state court relied on our voting rights cases, e.g., Reynolds v. Sims (1964); and on our precedents involving discriminatory restructuring of governmental decision-making. We granted certiorari and now affirm the judgment, but on a rationale different from that adopted by the State Supreme Court.

The State's principal argument in defense of Amendment 2 is that it puts gays and lesbians in the same position as all other persons. So, the State says, the measure does no more than deny homosexuals special rights. This reading of the amendment's language is implausible.... Sweeping and comprehensive is the change in legal status effected by this law. So much is evident from the ordinances that the Colorado Supreme Court declared would be void by operation of Amendment 2. Homosexuals, by state decree, are put in a solitary class with respect to transactions and relations in both the private and governmental spheres. The amendment withdraws from homosexuals, but no others, specific legal protection from the injuries caused by discrimination, and it forbids reinstatement of these laws and policies.

The change that Amendment 2 works in the legal status of gays and lesbians in the private sphere is far-reaching, both on its own terms and when considered in light of the structure and operation of modern anti-discrimination laws. That structure is well illustrated by contemporary statutes and ordinances prohibiting discrimination by providers of public accommodations.... Amendment 2 bars homosexuals from securing protection against the injuries that ... public-accommodations laws address. That in itself is a severe consequence, but there is more. Amendment 2, in addition, nullifies specific legal protections for this targeted class in all transactions in housing, sale of real estate, insurance, health and welfare services, private education, and employment.

Not confined to the private sphere, Amendment 2 also operates to repeal and forbid all laws or policies providing specific protection for gays or lesbians from discrimination by every level of Colorado government.... Amendment 2's reach may not be limited to specific laws passed for the benefit of gays and lesbians. It is a fair, if not necessary, inference from the broad language of the amendment that it deprives gays and lesbians even of the protection of general laws and policies that prohibit arbitrary discrimination in governmental and private settings. At some point in the systematic administration of these laws, an official must determine whether homosexuality is an arbitrary and thus forbidden basis for decision. Yet a decision to that effect would itself amount to a policy prohibiting discrimination on the basis of homosexuality, and so would appear to be no more valid under Amendment 2 than the specific prohibitions against discrimination the state court held invalid....

In any event, even if, as we doubt, homosexuals could find some safe harbor in laws of general application, we cannot accept the view that Amendment 2's prohibition on specific legal protections does no more than deprive homosexuals of special rights. To the contrary, the amendment imposes a special disability upon those persons alone. Homosexuals are forbidden the safeguards that others enjoy or may seek without constraint. They can obtain specific protection against discrimination only by enlisting the citizenry of Colorado to amend the state constitution or perhaps, on the State's view, by trying to pass helpful laws of general applicability. This is so no matter how local or discrete the harm, no matter how public and widespread the injury. We find nothing special in the protections Amendment 2 withholds. These are protections taken for granted by most people either because they already have them or do not need them; these are protections against exclusion from an almost limitless number of transactions and endeavors that constitute ordinary civic life in a free society.

The Fourteenth Amendment's promise that no person shall be denied the equal protection of the laws must co-exist with the practical necessity that most legislation classifies for one purpose or another, with resulting disadvantage to various groups or persons. We have attempted to reconcile the principle with the reality by stating that, if a law neither burdens a fundamental right nor targets a suspect class, we will uphold the legislative classification so long as it bears a rational relation to some legitimate end. Amendment 2 fails, indeed defies, even this conventional inquiry. First, the amendment has the peculiar property of imposing a broad and undifferentiated disability on a single named group, an exceptional and, as we shall explain, invalid form of legislation. Second, its sheer breadth is so discontinuous with the reasons offered for it that the amendment seems inexplicable by anything but animus toward the class that it affects; it lacks a rational relationship to legitimate state interests....

It is not within our constitutional tradition to enact laws of this sort. Central both to the idea of the rule of law and to our own Constitution's guarantee of equal protection is the principle that government and each of its parts remain open on impartial terms to all who seek its assistance. Respect for this principle explains why laws singling out a certain class of citizens for disfavored legal status or general hardships are rare. A law declaring that in general it shall be more difficult for one group of citizens than for all others to seek aid from the government is itself a denial of equal protection of the laws in the most literal sense....

[L]aws of the kind now before us raise the inevitable inference that the disadvantage imposed is born of animosity toward the class of persons affected. Even laws enacted for broad and ambitious purposes often can be explained by reference to legitimate public policies which justify the incidental disadvantages they impose on certain persons. Amendment 2, however, in making a general announcement that gays and lesbians shall not have any particular protections from the law, inflicts on them immediate, continuing, and real injuries that outrun and belie any legitimate justifications that may be claimed for it. We conclude that, in addition to the far-reaching deficiencies of Amendment 2 that we have noted, the principles it offends, in another sense, are conventional and venerable; a law must bear a rational relationship to a legitimate governmental purpose, and Amendment 2 does not. . . . We must conclude that Amendment 2 classifies homosexuals not to further a proper legislative end but to make them unequal to everyone else. This Colorado cannot do. A State cannot so deem a class of persons a stranger to its laws. Amendment 2 violates the Equal Protection Clause, and the judgment of the Supreme Court of Colorado is affirmed.

It is so ordered.

JUSTICE SCALIA, with whom THE CHIEF JUSTICE and JUSTICE THOMAS join, dissenting.

The Court has mistaken a Kulturkampf for a fit of spite. The constitutional amendment before us here is not the manifestation of a "bare . . . desire to harm" homosexuals, but is rather a modest attempt by seemingly tolerant Coloradans to preserve traditional sexual mores against the efforts of a politically powerful minority to revise those mores through use of the laws. That objective, and the means chosen to achieve it, are not only unimpeachable under any constitutional doctrine hitherto pronounced (hence the opinion's heavy reliance upon principles of righteousness rather than judicial holdings); they have been specifically approved by the Congress of the United States and by this Court.

In holding that homosexuality cannot be singled out for disfavorable treatment, the Court contradicts a decision, unchallenged here, pronounced only 10 years ago, see Bowers v. Hardwick (1986), and places the prestige of this institution behind the proposition that opposition to homosexuality is as reprehensible as racial or religious bias. . . . Since the Constitution of the United States says nothing about this subject, it is left to be resolved by normal democratic means, including the democratic adoption of provisions in state constitutions. This Court has no business imposing upon all Americans the resolution favored by the elite class from which the Members of this institution are selected, pronouncing that "animosity" toward homosexuality is evil. I vigorously dissent. . . .

Despite all of its hand-wringing about the potential effect of Amendment 2 on general antidiscrimination laws, the Court's opinion ultimately does not dispute all this, but assumes it to be true. The only denial of equal treatment it contends homosexuals have suffered is this: They may not obtain preferential treatment without amending the state constitution. That is to say, the principle underlying the Court's opinion is that one who is accorded equal treatment under the laws, but cannot as readily as others obtain preferential treatment under the laws, has been denied equal protection of the laws. If merely stating this alleged "equal protection" violation does not suffice to refute it, our constitutional jurisprudence has achieved terminal silliness.

The central thesis of the Court's reasoning is that any group is denied equal protection when, to obtain advantage (or, presumably, to avoid disadvantage), it must have recourse to a more general and hence more difficult level of political decision-making than others. The world has never heard of such a principle, which is why the Court's opinion is so long on emotive utterance and so short on relevant legal citation. And it seems to me most unlikely that any multilevel democracy can function under such a principle. For whenever a disadvantage is imposed, or conferral of a benefit is prohibited, at one of the higher levels of democratic decision-making (i.e., by the state legislature rather than local government, or by the people at large in the state constitution rather than the legislature), the affected group has (under this theory) been denied equal protection. . . .

I turn next to whether there was a legitimate rational basis for the substance of the constitutional amendment—for the prohibition of special protection for homosexuals. It is unsurprising that the Court avoids discussion of this question, since the answer is so obviously yes. The case most relevant to the issue before us today is not even mentioned in the Court's opinion: In Bowers v. Hardwick (1986), we held that the Constitution does not prohibit what virtually all States had done from the founding of the Republic until very recent years—making homosexual conduct a crime. That holding is unassailable, except by those who think that the Constitution changes to suit current fashions. . . . If it is constitutionally permissible for a State to make homosexual conduct criminal, surely it is constitutionally permissible for a State to enact other laws merely disfavoring homosexual conduct. . . .

But assuming that, in Amendment 2, a person of homosexual "orientation" is someone who does not engage in homosexual conduct but merely has a tendency or desire to do so, Bowers still suffices to establish a rational basis for the provision. If it is rational to criminalize the conduct, surely it is rational to deny special favor and protection to those with a self-avowed tendency or desire to engage in the conduct. Indeed, where criminal sanctions are not involved, homosexual "orientation" is an acceptable stand-in for homosexual conduct. . . .

The foregoing suffices to establish what the Court's failure to cite any case remotely in point would lead one to suspect: No principle set forth in the Constitution, nor even any imagined by this Court in the past 200 years, prohibits what Colorado has done here. But the case for Colorado is much stronger than that. What it has done is not only unprohibited, but eminently reasonable, with close, congressionally approved precedent in earlier constitutional practice.

First, as to its eminent reasonableness. The Court's opinion contains grim, disapproving hints that Coloradans have been guilty of "animus" or "animosity" toward homosexuality, as though that has been established as Un-[A]merican. Of course it is our moral heritage that one should not hate any human being or class of human beings. But I had thought that one could consider certain conduct reprehensible— murder, for example, or polygamy, or cruelty to animals— and could exhibit even "animus" toward such conduct. Surely that is the only sort of "animus" at issue here: moral disapproval of homosexual conduct, the same sort of moral disapproval that produced the centuries-old criminal laws that we held constitutional in Bowers. The Colorado amendment does not, to speak entirely precisely, prohibit giving favored status to people who are homosexuals; they can be favored for many reasons—for example, because they are senior citizens or members of racial minorities. But it prohibits giving them favored status because of their homosexual conduct—that is, it prohibits favored status for homosexuality. . . .

Today's opinion has no foundation in American constitutional law, and barely pretends to. The people of Colorado have adopted an entirely reasonable provision which does not even disfavor homosexuals in any substantive sense, but merely denies them preferential treatment. Amendment 2 is designed to prevent piecemeal deterioration of the sexual morality favored by a majority of Coloradans, and is not only an appropriate means to that legitimate end, but a means that Americans have employed before. Striking it down is an act, not of judicial judgment, but of political will.

I dissent.

BOY SCOUTS OF AMERICA V. DALE
530 U.S. 640 (2000)

"The forced inclusion of an unwanted person in a group infringes the group's freedom of expressive association if the presence of that person affects in a significant way the group's ability to advocate public or private viewpoints. . . . We are not, as we must not be, guided by our views of whether the Boy Scouts' teachings with respect to homosexual conduct are right or wrong."

The Question: Can a state apply its public accommodations law to require the Boy Scouts of America to rescind its revocation of the membership of a former Eagle Scout after he publicly identified himself as a homosexual?

The Arguments: PRO

The Supreme Court has ruled that organizations such as the Jaycees are "places of public accommodation" and cannot refuse to admit women as members. The same reasoning applies to this case, in which the Boy Scouts revoked the adult membership of a former Eagle Scout after he told a newspaper reporter he was gay. The New Jersey public accommodations law, like those in several other states, bars discrimination on the basis of sexual orientation. The record in this case shows no evidence that gays in general, or the Scout in this case, James Dale, would in any way undermine the Boy Scouts program.

CON

Unlike the Jaycees, whose members are all adults and which does not promote a set of moral values, the Boy Scouts has a special mission of teaching boys and young men to lead "morally straight" lives and practice "clean" behavior. The Boys Scouts interprets these terms to exclude homosexual behavior and should not be forced to include homosexuals in its membership. In this case James Dale has publicly stated his homosexuality and is an officer of a gay-rights group at Rutgers University. His continued membership would undermine the Boy Scouts program of teaching moral values as it interprets them.

CHIEF JUSTICE REHNQUIST delivered the opinion of the Court.

Petitioners are the Boy Scouts of America and the Monmouth Council, a division of the Boy Scouts of America (collectively, Boy Scouts). The Boy Scouts is a private, not-for-profit organization engaged in instilling its system of values in young people. The Boy Scouts asserts that homosexual conduct is inconsistent with the values it seeks to instill. Respondent is James Dale, a former Eagle Scout whose adult membership in the Boy Scouts was revoked when the Boy Scouts learned that he is an avowed homosexual and gay rights activist. The New Jersey Supreme Court held that New Jersey's public accommodations law requires that the Boy Scouts admit

Dale. This case presents the question whether applying New Jersey's public accommodations law in this way violates the Boy Scouts' First Amendment right of expressive association. We hold that it does.

James Dale entered scouting in 1978 at the age of eight by joining Monmouth Council's Cub Scout Pack 142. Dale became a Boy Scout in 1981 and remained a Scout until he turned 18. By all accounts, Dale was an exemplary Scout. In 1988, he achieved the rank of Eagle Scout, one of Scouting's highest honors. Dale applied for adult membership in the Boy Scouts in 1989. The Boy Scouts approved his application for the position of assistant scoutmaster of Troop 73. Around the same time, Dale left home to attend Rutgers University. After arriving at Rutgers, Dale first acknowledged to himself and others that he is gay. He quickly became involved with, and eventually became the co-president of, the Rutgers University Lesbian/Gay Alliance. In 1990, Dale attended a seminar addressing the psychological and health needs of lesbian and gay teenagers. A newspaper covering the event interviewed Dale about his advocacy of homosexual teenagers' need for gay role models. In early July 1990, the newspaper published the interview and Dale's photograph over a caption identifying him as the co-president of the Lesbian/Gay Alliance. Later that month, Dale received a letter from Monmouth Council Executive James Kay revoking his adult membership. Dale wrote to Kay requesting the reason for Monmouth Council's decision. Kay responded by letter that the Boy Scouts "specifically forbid membership to homosexuals."

In 1992, Dale filed a complaint against the Boy Scouts in the New Jersey Superior Court. The complaint alleged that the Boy Scouts had violated New Jersey's public accommodations statute and its common law by revoking Dale's membership based solely on his sexual orientation. New Jersey's public accommodations statute prohibits, among other things, discrimination on the basis of sexual orientation in places of public accommodation. The New Jersey Superior Court's Chancery Division granted summary judgment in favor of the Boy Scouts. . . . The New Jersey Superior Court's Appellate Division . . . held that New Jersey's public accommodations law applied to the Boy Scouts and that the Boy Scouts violated it. The Appellate Division rejected the Boy Scouts' federal constitutional claims. The New Jersey Supreme Court affirmed the judgment of the Appellate Division. It held that the Boy Scouts was a place of public accommodation subject to the public accommodations law, that the organization was not exempt from the law under any of its express exceptions, and that the Boy Scouts violated the law by revoking Dale's membership based on his avowed homosexuality. . . . We granted the Boy Scouts' petition for certiorari to determine whether the application of New Jersey's public accommodations law violated the First Amendment.

In Roberts v. United States Jaycees (1984), we observed that "implicit in the right to engage in activities protected by the First Amendment" is "a corresponding right to associate with others in pursuit of a wide variety of political, social, economic, educational, religious, and cultural ends." This right is crucial in preventing the majority from imposing its views on groups that would rather express other, perhaps unpopular, ideas. Government actions that may unconstitutionally burden this freedom may take many forms, one of which is "intrusion into the internal structure or affairs of an association" like a "regulation that forces the group to accept members it does not desire." Forcing a group to accept certain members may impair the ability of the group to express those views, and only those views, that it intends to express. Thus, "[f]reedom of association . . . plainly presupposes a freedom not to associate."

The forced inclusion of an unwanted person in a group infringes the group's freedom of expressive association if the presence of that person affects in a significant way the group's ability to advocate public or private viewpoints. But the freedom of expressive association, like many freedoms, is not absolute. We have held that the freedom could be overridden "by regulations adopted to serve compelling state interests, unrelated to the suppression of ideas, that cannot be achieved through means significantly less restrictive of associational freedoms." To determine whether a group is protected by the First Amendment's expressive associational right, we must determine whether the group engages in "expressive association." The First Amendment's protection of expressive association is not reserved for advocacy groups. But to come within its ambit, a group must engage in some form of expression, whether it be public or private. . . .

The Boy Scouts is a private, nonprofit organization. According to its mission statement: "It is the mission of the Boy Scouts of America to serve others by helping to instill values in young people and, in other ways, to prepare them to make ethical choices over their lifetime in achieving their full potential. The values we strive to instill are based on those found in the Scout Oath and Law:

> Scout Oath: On my honor I will do my best, to do my duty to God and my country, and to obey the Scout Law; to help other people at all times; to keep myself physically strong, mentally awake, and morally straight.
> Scout Law: A Scout is: Trustworthy, Obedient, Loyal, Cheerful, Helpful, Thrifty, Friendly, Brave, Courteous, Clean, Kind, Reverent.

Thus, the general mission of the Boy Scouts is clear: "[T]o instill values in young people." The Boy Scouts seeks to instill these values by having its adult leaders spend time with the youth members, instructing and engaging them in activities like camping, archery, and fishing. During the time spent with the youth members, the scoutmasters and assistant scoutmasters inculcate them with the Boy Scouts' values—both expressly and by example. It seems indisputable that an association that seeks to transmit such a system of values engages in expressive activity. Given that the Boy Scouts engages in expressive activity, we must determine whether the forced inclusion of Dale as an assistant scoutmaster would significantly affect the Boy Scouts' ability to advocate public or private viewpoints. This inquiry necessarily requires us first to explore, to a limited extent, the nature of the Boy Scouts' view of homosexuality.

The Boy Scouts asserts that homosexual conduct is inconsistent with the values embodied in the Scout Oath and Law, particularly with the values represented by the terms "morally straight" and "clean." Obviously, the Scout Oath and Law do not expressly mention sexuality or sexual orientation. And the terms "morally straight" and "clean" are by no means self-defining. Different people would attribute to those terms very different meanings. For example, some people may believe that engaging in homosexual conduct is not at odds with being "morally straight" and "clean." And others may believe that engaging in homosexual conduct is contrary to being "morally straight" and "clean." The Boy Scouts says it falls within the latter category. . . . The Boy Scouts asserts that it "teach[es] that homosexual conduct is not morally straight," and that it does "not want to promote homosexual conduct as a legitimate form of behavior." We accept the Boy Scouts' assertion. We need not inquire further to determine the nature of the Boy Scouts' expression with respect to homosexuality. . . .

We must then determine whether Dale's presence as an assistant scoutmaster would significantly burden the Boy

Scouts' desire to not "promote homosexual conduct as a legitimate form of behavior." As we give deference to an association's assertions regarding the nature of its expression, we must also give deference to an association's view of what would impair its expression. That is not to say that an expressive association can erect a shield against anti-discrimination laws simply by asserting that mere acceptance of a member from a particular group would impair its message. But here Dale, by his own admission, is one of a group of gay Scouts who have "become leaders in their community and are open and honest about their sexual orientation." Dale was the co-president of a gay and lesbian organization at college and remains a gay rights activist. Dale's presence in the Boy Scouts would, at the very least, force the organization to send a message, both to the youth members and the world, that the Boy Scouts accepts homosexual conduct as a legitimate form of behavior. . . .

Dale makes much of the claim that the Boy Scouts does not revoke the membership of heterosexual Scout leaders that openly disagree with the Boy Scouts' policy on sexual orientation. But if this is true, it is irrelevant. The presence of an avowed homosexual and gay rights activist in an assistant scoutmaster's uniform sends a distinctly different message from the presence of a heterosexual assistant scoutmaster who is on record as disagreeing with Boy Scouts policy. The Boy Scouts has a First Amendment right to choose to send one message but not the other. The fact that the organization does not trumpet its views from the housetops, or that it tolerates dissent within its ranks, does not mean that its views receive no First Amendment protection. . . .

We are not, as we must not be, guided by our views of whether the Boy Scouts' teachings with respect to homosexual conduct are right or wrong; public or judicial disapproval of a tenet of an organization's expression does not justify the State's effort to compel the organization to accept members where such acceptance would derogate from the organization's expressive message. The judgment of the New Jersey Supreme Court is reversed. . . .

JUSTICE STEVENS, with whom JUSTICE SOUTER, JUSTICE GINSBURG and JUSTICE BREYER join, dissenting.

New Jersey "prides itself on judging each individual by his or her merits" and on being "in the vanguard in the fight to eradicate the cancer of unlawful discrimination of all types from our society." Since 1945, it has had a law against discrimination. The law broadly protects the opportunity of all persons to obtain the advantages and privileges "of any place of public accommodation." And as amended in 1991, the law prohibits discrimination on the basis of nine different traits including an individual's "sexual orientation." The question in this case is whether that expansive construction trenches on the federal constitutional rights of the Boy Scouts of America (BSA). . . .

In this case, Boy Scouts of America contends that it teaches the young boys who are Scouts that homosexuality is immoral. Consequently, it argues, it would violate its right to associate to force it to admit homosexuals as members, as doing so would be at odds with its own shared goals and values. This contention, quite plainly, requires us to look at what, exactly, are the values that BSA actually teaches. . . .

To bolster its claim that its shared goals include teaching that homosexuality is wrong, BSA directs our attention to two terms appearing in the Scout Oath and Law. The first is the phrase "morally straight," which appears in the Oath ("On my honor I will do my best . . . To keep myself . . . morally straight"); the second term is the word "clean," which appears in a list of 12 characteristics together comprising the Scout Law. The Boy Scout Handbook defines "morally straight" as such: "To be a person of strong character, guide your life with honesty, purity, and justice. Respect and defend the rights of all people. Your relationships with others should be honest and open. Be clean in your speech and actions, and faithful in your religious beliefs. The values you follow as a Scout will help you become virtuous and self-reliant." The Scoutmaster Handbook emphasizes these points about being "morally straight": "In any consideration of moral fitness, a key word has to be 'courage.' A boy's courage to do what his head and his heart tell him is right. And the courage to refuse to do what his heart and his head say is wrong. Moral fitness, like emotional fitness, will clearly present opportunities for wise guidance by an alert Scoutmaster." As for the term "clean," the Boy Scout Handbook offers the following: "A Scout is CLEAN. A Scout keeps his body and mind fit and clean. He chooses the company of those who live by these same ideals. He helps keep his home and community clean. You never need to be ashamed of dirt that will wash off. If you play hard and work hard you can't help getting dirty. But when the game is over or the work is done, that kind of dirt disappears with soap and water. There's another kind of dirt that won't come off by washing. It is the kind that shows up in foul language and harmful thoughts. Swear words, profanity, and dirty stories are weapons that ridicule other people and hurt their feelings. The same is true of racial slurs and jokes making fun of ethnic groups or people with physical or mental limitations. A Scout knows there is no kindness or honor in such mean-spirited behavior. He avoids it in his own words and deeds. He defends those who are targets of insults."

It is plain as the light of day that neither one of these principles—"morally straight" and "clean"—says the slightest thing about homosexuality. Indeed, neither term in the Boy Scouts' Law and Oath expresses any position whatsoever on sexual matters. BSA's published guidance on that topic underscores this point. Scouts, for example, are directed to receive their sex education at home or in school, but not from the organization: "Your parents or guardian or a sex education teacher should give you the facts about sex that you must know." To be sure, Scouts are not forbidden from asking their Scoutmaster about issues of a sexual nature, but Scoutmasters are, literally, the last person Scouts are encouraged to ask: "If you have questions about growing up, about relationships, sex, or making good decisions, ask. Talk with your parents, religious leaders, teachers, or Scoutmaster." Moreover, Scoutmasters are specifically directed to steer curious adolescents to other sources of information: "If Scouts ask for information regarding . . . sexual activity, answer honestly and factually, but stay within your realm of expertise and comfort. If a Scout has serious concerns that you cannot answer, refer him to his family, religious leader, doctor, or other professional." . . .

In light of BSA's self-proclaimed ecumenism, furthermore, it is even more difficult to discern any shared goals or common moral stance on homosexuality. Insofar as religious matters are concerned, BSA's bylaws state that it is "absolutely nonsectarian in its attitude toward . . . religious training." In fact, many diverse religious organizations sponsor local Boy Scout troops. Because a number of religious groups do not view homosexuality as immoral or wrong and reject discrimination against homosexuals, it is exceedingly difficult to believe that BSA nonetheless adopts a single particular religious or moral philosophy when it comes to sexual orientation. This is especially so in light of the fact that Scouts are advised to seek guidance on sexual matters from their religious leaders (and Scoutmasters are told to refer Scouts to them); BSA surely is aware that some religions do not teach that homosexuality is wrong. . . .

The evidence before this Court makes it exceptionally clear that BSA has, at most, simply adopted an exclusionary membership policy and has no shared goal of disapproving of homosexuality. BSA's mission statement and federal charter say nothing on the matter; its official membership policy is silent; its Scout Oath and Law—and accompanying definitions—are devoid of any view on the topic; its guidance for Scouts and Scoutmasters on sexuality declare that such matters are "not construed to be Scouting's proper area," but are the province of a Scout's parents and pastor; and BSA's posture respecting religion tolerates a wide variety of views on the issue of homosexuality. Moreover, there is simply no evidence that BSA otherwise teaches anything in this area, or that it instructs Scouts on matters involving homosexuality in ways not conveyed in the Boy Scout or Scoutmaster Handbooks. In short, Boy Scouts of America is simply silent on homosexuality. There is no shared goal or collective effort to foster a belief about homosexuality at all—let alone one that is significantly burdened by admitting homosexuals. . . .

An organization can adopt the message of its choice, and it is not this Court's place to disagree with it. But we must inquire whether the group is, in fact, expressing a message (whatever it may be) and whether that message (if one is expressed) is significantly affected by a State's anti-discrimination law. More critically, that inquiry requires our independent analysis, rather than deference to a group's litigating posture. Reflection on the subject dictates that such an inquiry is required. Surely there are instances in which an organization that truly aims to foster a belief at odds with the purposes of a State's anti-discrimination laws will have a First Amendment right to association that precludes forced compliance with those laws. But that right is not a freedom to discriminate at will, nor is it a right to maintain an exclusionary membership policy simply out of fear of what the public reaction would be if the group's membership were opened up. It is an implicit right designed to protect the enumerated rights of the First Amendment, not a license to act on any discriminatory impulse. To prevail in asserting a right of expressive association as a defense to a charge of violating an anti-discrimination law, the organization must at least show it has adopted and advocated an unequivocal position inconsistent with a position advocated or epitomized by the person whom the organization seeks to exclude. . . .

Even if BSA's right to associate argument fails, it nonetheless might have a First Amendment right to refrain from including debate and dialogue about homosexuality as part of its mission to instill values in Scouts. It can, for example, advise Scouts who are entering adulthood and have questions about sex to talk "with your parents, religious leaders, teachers, or Scoutmaster," and in turn, it can direct Scoutmasters who are asked such questions, "not [to] undertake to instruct Scouts, in any formalized manner, in the subject of sex and family life" because "it is not construed to be Scouting's proper area." Dale's right to advocate certain beliefs in a public forum or in a private debate does not include a right to advocate these ideas when he is working as a Scoutmaster. And BSA cannot be compelled to include a message about homosexuality among the values it actually chooses to teach its Scouts, if it would prefer to remain silent on that subject. . . .

In its briefs, BSA implies, even if it does not directly argue, that Dale would use his Scoutmaster position as a "bully pulpit" to convey immoral messages to his troop, and therefore his inclusion in the group would compel BSA to include a message it does not want to impart. . . . BSA has not contended, nor does the record support, that Dale had ever advocated a view on homosexuality to his troop before his membership was revoked. Accordingly, BSA's revocation could only have been based on an assumption that he would do so in the future. . . . The Scoutmaster Handbook instructs Dale, like all Scoutmasters, that sexual issues are not their "proper area," and there is no evidence that Dale had any intention of violating this rule. Indeed, from all accounts Dale was a model Boy Scout and Assistant Scoutmaster up until the day his membership was revoked, and there is no reason to believe that he would suddenly disobey the directives of BSA. . . .

The only apparent explanation for the majority's holding, then, is that homosexuals are simply so different from the rest of society that their presence alone—unlike any other individual's—should be singled out for special First Amendment treatment. Under the majority's reasoning, an openly gay male is irreversibly affixed with the label "homosexual." That label, even though unseen, communicates a message that permits his exclusion wherever he goes. His openness is the sole and sufficient justification for his ostracism. Though unintended, reliance on such a justification is tantamount to a constitutionally prescribed symbol of inferiority. . . .

Unfavorable opinions about homosexuals "have ancient roots." Bowers v. Hardwick (1986). Like equally atavistic opinions about certain racial groups, those roots have been nourished by sectarian doctrine. Over the years, however, interaction with real people, rather than mere adherence to traditional ways of thinking about members of unfamiliar classes, have modified those opinions. . . . That such prejudices are still prevalent and that they have caused serious and tangible harm to countless members of the class New Jersey seeks to protect are established matters of fact that neither the Boy Scouts nor the Court disputes. That harm can only be aggravated by the creation of a constitutional shield for a policy that is itself the product of a habitual way of thinking about strangers. As Justice Brandeis so wisely advised, "we must be ever on our guard, lest we erect our prejudices into legal principles." If we would guide by the light of reason, we must let our minds be bold.

I respectfully dissent.

MEET JAMES DALE

Sitting across from James Dale you can't help feeling you are in the presence of an archetypal Boy Scout. Earnest, polite, handsome, charismatic, and well-spoken are all words that immediately spring to mind. And, indeed, the 27-year-old Dale spent 12 years of his life tirelessly serving the Boy Scouts of America, eventually rising to the rank of assistant scoutmaster until the organization expelled him in 1990 after learning he was gay. For the past eight years, Dale has turned the same moral righteousness that he learned from the Scouts against the group in court.

Initially Dale lost his case to a judge who called him a "sodomite." But on March 2 [1998] a split three-judge appeals-court panel in New Jersey ruled that the restriction was illegal and that Dale should be allowed to serve as a scoutmaster. According to Evan Wolfson, who represented Dale on a pro bono basis for the Lambda Legal Defense and Education Fund, the gay legal group that is fighting a similar case in California, it was the first time "any court has ruled in our favor against the discriminatory policy of the Boy Scouts of America." The court said the Scouts cannot discriminate on the basis of sexual orientation. The opinion read, "There is absolutely no evidence before us supporting a conclusion that a gay scoutmaster, solely because he is a homosexual, does not possess the strength of character necessary to properly care for or impart BSA humanitarian ideals to the young boys in his charge." The judges went further, praising Dale's moral character and issuing a scathing rebuke to the first judge for his homophobic remarks. Maintaining that it has the right to set its own membership criteria, the BSA has vowed to appeal the decision to the state supreme court. In an interview with The Advocate, Dale, who now lives in New York City and works as a publicist and events coordinator for Poz magazine, talks about his long battle to set the Scouts straight.

What did the Boy Scouts mean to you?

I think what the scouting program teaches is self-reliance and leadership. Giving your best to society. Leaving things better than you found them. Standing up for what's right. That's one of the tragic ironies of this whole story—that when they found out that I was gay, suddenly I wasn't good enough anymore.

Growing up, did you find the Scouts to be a homophobic environment?

If anything, I think it was much less homophobic than the norm of society. I think the Boy Scouts allows for the human factor a lot more than other organizations. It was a more supportive environment. This policy really goes against everything this program taught me.

When did you come out?

I came out when I was 19. Going to Rutgers University and meeting other gay people, I was seeing positive role models who were gay. After that the whole idea of being gay wasn't so alien to me. The summer between my first and second years of college, I met a guy who was gay. He told me about the gay community. That gave me the self-respect and pride I needed so that when I went back to Rutgers in my sophomore year, I had no problem telling other people. I immediately started going to the lesbian and gay organization at Rutgers. About three months later there was a vacancy in the presidency position. I was elected by the lesbian and gay alliance to take that position. I was always taught that if there's a need, you pick up the slack.

How did the Scouts find out you were gay?

It was the summer between my sophomore and junior years that I was speaking at a conference for social workers. Shortly thereafter a newspaper article ran. About a week later I got a letter from the Boy Scouts that said I no longer met its standards for leadership. I didn't even know what it was about. So I sent them a letter, and then I got a second letter back from them, and that said avowed homosexuals are not permitted in the Boy Scouts of America. When I heard that I felt really devastated and betrayed. This is a program that I spent my weekends and time after school focusing on, helping out at nursing homes and cleaning parks. I had given so much to the program so freely and so happily.

When did you decide to fight back?

A month later, after I had talked it over with some friends, I knew what they had done was wrong and that this wrong must be undone. I found Lambda, which took my case in 1990. But it wasn't a very strong case at first. Even though it appeared to be illegal, it wasn't. New Jersey didn't have a nondiscrimination law inclusive of sexual orientation. But shortly thereafter New Jersey enacted a nondiscrimination law that included gays. Then the first judge, who was very, very antigay, ruled against me and even mentioned brimstone and fire in his decision.

How did your family deal with the publicity associated with your court fight?

Not every parent has to deal with the fact of their child's being gay becoming public. They take it personally too. My mother was a den leader when I was a Cub Scout. It's not just what they did to me; it's what they did to us. My mother was recently at a seminar, and one of the people there said some antigay stuff. And my mother stood up and said, "That's my son you're talking about. You don't know what you are talking about. You're ignorant." My father is in the military, and he goes and raises money for the Gay Men's Health Crisis's walkathon.

How do you feel about your victory? [The New Jersey Supreme Court ruled in Dale's favor in 1998, and the Boy Scouts appealed to the Supreme Court.]

It was a wonderfully worded opinion. They went the exact opposite way that the first judge did. It has taken eight years, but I'd wait another eight years to get this decision. It's a shame so much money is being wasted on this bigotry and discrimination. When I think about all the money I spent on uniforms, camps, and merit badges, I get really upset. There are often these drives for kids to go to camp who can't afford it. If they stopped suing people for being gay, they could afford to send a lot more people to camp.

What would you say to a young scout today who wanted to come out?

I don't want to ever advise somebody not to come out of the closet, because it was the most wonderful thing I ever did. But a gay scout called me up a few years ago when my lawsuit was first announced. Against my better judgment, I had to tell him that they'll kick him out of the program if he comes out.

Do you think there is hope for change at the Boy Scouts?

There's a 13-year-old kid who's made it his own personal issue for his Eagle Scout project to generate a million signa-tures to overturn this policy I'm fighting. His father and one of his assistant scoutmasters are behind an organization called Scouting for All. They are all straight. It's one thing to say homophobia is wrong. It's another to put your money where your mouth is, to make this his own personal strug-gle. This boy is my hero (Meers, 1999).

LAWRENCE V. TEXAS
Decided June 26, 2003

"When sexuality finds overt expression in intimate conduct with another person, the conduct can be but one element in a personal bond that is more enduring. The liberty protected by the Constitution allows homo-sexual persons the right to make this choice. . . . Bowers v. Hardwick should be and now is overruled."

The Question:	Does a state law that makes it a crime for two persons of the same sex to engage in acts of sodomy, while not imposing penalties on persons of opposite sexes, violates the Due Process or Equal Protection Clauses of the Constitution?
The Arguments:	PRO

Until recently the state of Texas made it unlawful for both heterosexual and homo-sexual couples to engage in sodomy. That law was repealed and replaced with one that limited criminal punishment for sodomy to homosexuals. This law clearly re-flects hostility toward gays and lesbians, who are singled out for unequal treatment. There is no "rational basis" for this law, since the moral disapproval of homosexu-als by Texas voters and lawmakers does not constitute a legitimate state interest.

CON

The Supreme Court has ruled that state laws may reflect the moral views of voters and lawmakers on the issue of homosexual sodomy. The Court has also ruled that the Constitution does not include a "fundamental right" to engage in such con-duct, and that homosexuals do not constitute a "suspect class." Laws do not vio-late the Due Process or Equal Protection Clauses if they do not restrict a funda-mental right or discriminate against a suspect class. Therefore, Texas has a right to pass a law that prohibits homosexual sodomy.

JUSTICE KENNEDY delivered the opinion of the Court.

Liberty protects the person from unwarranted government intrusions into a dwelling or other private places. In our tra-dition the State is not omnipresent in the home. And there are other spheres of our lives and existence, outside the home, where the State should not be a dominant presence. Freedom extends beyond spatial bounds. Liberty presumes an autonomy of self that includes freedom of thought, belief, expression, and certain intimate conduct. The instant case in-volves liberty of the person both in its spatial and more tran-scendent dimensions.

The question before the Court is the validity of a Texas statute making it a crime for two persons of the same sex to engage in certain intimate sexual conduct. In Houston, Texas, officers of the Harris County Police Department were dispatched to a private residence in response to a reported weapons disturbance. They entered an apartment where one of the petitioners, John Geddes Lawrence, resided. The right of the police to enter does not seem to have been questioned. The officers observed Lawrence and another man, Tyron Garner, engaging in a sexual act. The two petitioners were arrested, held in custody overnight, and charged and con-victed before a Justice of the Peace.

The complaints described their crime as "deviate sexual intercourse, namely anal sex, with a member of the same sex (man)." The applicable state law is Tex. Penal Code Ann. §21.06(a) (2003). It provides: "A person commits an offense if he engages in deviate sexual intercourse with another individual of the same sex." The statute defines "[d]eviate sexual intercourse" as follows:

(A) any contact between any part of the genitals of one person and the mouth or anus of another person; or
(B) the penetration of the genitals or the anus of another person with an object.

The petitioners exercised their right to a trial de novo in Harris County Criminal Court. They challenged the statute as a violation of the Equal Protection Clause of the Fourteenth Amendment and of a like provision of the Texas Constitution. Those contentions were rejected. The petitioners, having entered a plea of nolo contendere, were each fined $200 and assessed court costs of $141.25.

The Court of Appeals for the Texas Fourteenth District considered the petitioners' federal constitutional arguments under both the Equal Protection and Due Process Clauses of the Fourteenth Amendment. After hearing the case en banc the court, in a divided opinion, rejected the constitutional arguments and affirmed the convictions. The majority opinion indicates that the Court of Appeals considered our decision in Bowers v. Hardwick (1986), to be controlling on the federal due process aspect of the case. Bowers then being authoritative, this was proper.

We granted certiorari to consider three questions:

1. Whether Petitioners' criminal convictions under the Texas "Homosexual Conduct" law—which criminalizes sexual intimacy by same-sex couples, but not identical behavior by different-sex couples—violate the Fourteenth Amendment guarantee of equal protection of laws?

2. Whether Petitioners' criminal convictions for adult consensual sexual intimacy in the home violate their vital interests in liberty and privacy protected by the Due Process Clause of the Fourteenth Amendment?

3. Whether Bowers v. Hardwick should be overruled?

The petitioners were adults at the time of the alleged offense. Their conduct was in private and consensual.

We conclude the case should be resolved by determining whether the petitioners were free as adults to engage in the private conduct in the exercise of their liberty under the Due Process Clause of the Fourteenth Amendment to the Constitution. For this inquiry we deem it necessary to reconsider the Court's holding in Bowers . . . .

The facts in Bowers had some similarities to the instant case. A police officer, whose right to enter seems not to have been in question, observed Hardwick, in his own bedroom, engaging in intimate sexual conduct with another adult male. The conduct was in violation of a Georgia statute making it a criminal offense to engage in sodomy. One difference between the two cases is that the Georgia statute prohibited the conduct whether or not the participants were of the same sex, while the Texas statute, as we have seen, applies only to participants of the same sex. Hardwick was not prosecuted, but he brought an action in federal court to declare the state statute invalid. He alleged he was a practicing homosexual and that the criminal prohibition violated rights guaranteed to him by the Constitution. The Court, in an opinion by Justice White, sustained the Georgia law. Chief Justice Burger and Justice Powell joined the opinion of the Court and filed separate, concurring opinions. Four Justices dissented.

The Court began its substantive discussion in Bowers as follows: "The issue presented is whether the Federal Constitution confers a fundamental right upon homosexuals to engage in sodomy and hence invalidates the laws of the many States that still make such conduct illegal and have done so for a very long time." That statement, we now conclude, discloses the Court's own failure to appreciate the extent of the liberty at stake. To say that the issue in Bowers was simply the right to engage in certain sexual conduct demeans the claim the individual put forward, just as it would demean a married couple were it to be said marriage is simply about the right to have sexual intercourse. The laws involved in Bowers and here are, to be sure, statutes that purport to do no more than prohibit a particular sexual act. Their penalties and purposes, though, have more far-reaching consequences, touching upon the most private human conduct, sexual behavior, and in the most private of places, the home. The statutes do seek to control a personal relationship that, whether or not entitled to formal recognition in the law, is within the liberty of persons to choose without being punished as criminals.

This, as a general rule, should counsel against attempts by the State, or a court, to define the meaning of the relationship or to set its boundaries absent injury to a person or abuse of an institution the law protects. It suffices for us to acknowledge that adults may choose to enter upon this relationship in the confines of their homes and their own private lives and still retain their dignity as free persons. When sexuality finds overt expression in intimate conduct with another person, the conduct can be but one element in a personal bond that is more enduring. The liberty protected by the Constitution allows homosexual persons the right to make this choice.

Having misapprehended the claim of liberty there presented to it, and thus stating the claim to be whether there is a fundamental right to engage in consensual sodomy, the Bowers Court said: "Proscriptions against that conduct have ancient roots." . . . At the outset it should be noted that there is no long-standing history in this country of laws directed at homosexual conduct as a distinct matter. Beginning in colonial times there were prohibitions of sodomy derived from the English criminal laws passed in the first instance by the Reformation Parliament of 1533. The English prohibition was understood to include relations between men and women as well as relations between men and men. . . . The absence of legal prohibitions focusing on homosexual conduct may be explained in part by noting that according to some scholars the concept of the homosexual as a distinct category of person did not emerge until the late 19th century. . . . Thus early American sodomy laws were not directed at homosexuals as such but instead sought to prohibit non-procreative sexual activity more generally. This does not suggest approval of homosexual conduct. It does tend to show that this particular form of conduct was not thought of as a separate category from like conduct between heterosexual persons. . . .

But far from possessing "ancient roots," American laws targeting same-sex couples did not develop until the last third of the 20th century. The reported decisions concerning the prosecution of consensual, homosexual sodomy between adults for the years 1880–1995 are not always clear in the details, but a significant number involved conduct in a public place. It was not until the 1970's that any State singled out same-sex relations for criminal prosecution, and only nine States have done so. Post-Bowers even some of these States did not adhere to the policy of suppressing homosexual conduct. Over the course of the last decades, States with same-sex prohibitions have moved toward abolishing them. In summary, the historical grounds relied upon in Bowers are more complex than the majority opinion and the concurring opinion by Chief Justice Burger indicate. Their historical premises are not without doubt and, at the very least, are overstated.

It must be acknowledged, of course, that the Court in Bowers was making the broader point that for centuries there have been powerful voices to condemn homosexual conduct as immoral. The condemnation has been shaped by religious beliefs, conceptions of right and acceptable behavior, and respect for the traditional family. For many persons these are not trivial concerns but profound and deep convictions accepted as ethical and moral principles to which they aspire and which thus determine the course of their lives. These considerations do not answer the question before us, however. The issue is whether the majority may use the power of the State to enforce these views on the whole society through operation of the criminal law. "Our obligation is to define the liberty of all, not to mandate our own moral code." Planned Parenthood of Southeastern Pa. v. Casey (1992). . . .

Two principal cases decided after Bowers cast its holding into even more doubt. In Casey, the Court reaffirmed the substantive force of the liberty protected by the Due Process Clause. The Casey decision again confirmed that our laws and tradition afford constitutional protection to personal decisions relating to marriage, procreation, contraception, family relationships, child rearing, and education. . . . The second post-Bowers case of principal relevance is Romer v. Evans (1996). There the Court struck down class-based legislation directed at homosexuals as a violation of the Equal Protection Clause. Romer invalidated an amendment to Colorado's constitution which named as a solitary class persons who were homosexuals, lesbians, or bisexual either by "orientation, conduct, practices or relationships," and deprived them of protection under state antidiscrimination laws. We concluded that the provision was "born of animosity toward the class of persons affected" and further that it had no rational relation to a legitimate governmental purpose. . . . Equality of treatment and the due process right to demand respect for conduct protected by the substantive guarantee of liberty are linked in important respects, and a decision on the latter point advances both interests. If protected conduct is made criminal and the law which does so remains unexamined for its substantive validity, its stigma might remain even if it were not enforceable as drawn for equal protection reasons. When homosexual conduct is made criminal by the law of the State, that declaration in and of itself is an invitation to subject homosexual persons to discrimination both in the public and in the private spheres. The central holding of Bowers has been brought in question by this case, and it should be addressed. Its continuance as precedent demeans the lives of homosexual persons. . . .

The foundations of Bowers have sustained serious erosion from our recent decisions in Casey and Romer. When our precedent has been thus weakened, criticism from other sources is of greater significance. In the United States criticism of Bowers has been substantial and continuing, disapproving of its reasoning in all respects, not just as to its historical assumptions. . . . To the extent Bowers relied on values we share with a wider civilization, it should be noted that the reasoning and holding in Bowers have been rejected elsewhere. The European Court of Human Rights has followed not Bowers but its own decision in Dudgeon v. United Kingdom (2001). Other nations, too, have taken action consistent with an affirmation of the protected right of homosexual adults to engage in intimate, consensual conduct. The right the petitioners seek in this case has been accepted as an integral part of human freedom in many other countries. There has been no showing that in this country the governmental interest in circumscribing personal choice is somehow more legitimate or urgent.

The doctrine of stare decisis is essential to the respect accorded to the judgments of the Court and to the stability of the law. It is not, however, an inexorable command. In Casey we noted that when a Court is asked to overrule a precedent recognizing a constitutional liberty interest, individual or societal reliance on the existence of that liberty cautions with particular strength against reversing course. The holding in Bowers, however, has not induced detrimental reliance comparable to some instances where recognized individual rights are involved. Indeed, there has been no individual or societal reliance on Bowers of the sort that could counsel against overturning its holding once there are compelling reasons to do so. Bowers itself causes uncertainty, for the precedents before and after its issuance contradict its central holding. The rationale of Bowers does not withstand careful analysis. . . . Bowers was not correct when it was decided, and it is not correct today. It ought not to remain binding precedent. Bowers v. Hardwick should be and now is overruled.

The present case does not involve minors. It does not involve persons who might be injured or coerced or who are situated in relationships where consent might not easily be refused. It does not involve public conduct or prostitution. It does not involve whether the government must give formal recognition to any relationship that homosexual persons seek to enter. The case does involve two adults who, with full and mutual consent from each other, engaged in sexual practices common to a homosexual lifestyle. The petitioners are entitled to respect for their private lives. The State cannot demean their existence or control their destiny by making their private sexual conduct a crime. Their right to liberty under the Due Process Clause gives them the full right to engage in their conduct without intervention of the government. The Texas statute furthers no legitimate state interest which can justify its intrusion into the personal and private life of the individual.

Had those who drew and ratified the Due Process Clauses of the Fifth Amendment or the Fourteenth Amendment known the components of liberty in its manifold possibilities, they might have been more specific. They did not presume to have this insight. They knew times can blind us to certain truths and later generations can see that laws once thought necessary and proper in fact serve only to oppress. As the Constitution endures, persons in every generation can invoke its principles in their own search for greater freedom.

The judgment of the Court of Appeals for the Texas Fourteenth District is reversed, and the case is remanded for further proceedings not inconsistent with this opinion.

JUSTICE O'CONNOR, concurring in the judgment.

The Court today overrules Bowers v. Hardwick. I joined Bowers, and do not join the Court in overruling it. Nevertheless, I agree with the Court that Texas' statute banning same-sex sodomy is unconstitutional. Rather than relying on the substantive component of the Fourteenth Amendment's Due Process Clause, as the Court does, I base my conclusion on the Fourteenth Amendment's Equal Protection Clause. . . . Laws such as economic or tax legislation that are scrutinized under rational basis review normally pass constitutional muster, since "the Constitution presumes that even improvident decisions will eventually be rectified by the democratic processes." We have consistently held, however, that some objectives, such as "a bare . . . desire to harm a politically unpopular group," are not legitimate state interests. When a law exhibits such a desire to harm a politically unpopular group, we have applied a more searching form of rational basis review to strike down such laws under the Equal Protection Clause.

We have been most likely to apply rational basis review to hold a law unconstitutional under the Equal Protection Clause where, as here, the challenged legislation inhibits personal relationships. . . . Texas attempts to justify its law, and the effects of the law, by arguing that the statute satisfies rational basis review because it furthers the legitimate governmental interest of the promotion of morality. In Bowers, we held that a state law criminalizing sodomy as applied to homosexual couples did not violate substantive due process. We rejected the argument that no rational basis existed to justify the law, pointing to the government's interest in promoting morality. The only question in front of the Court in Bowers was whether the substantive component of the Due Process Clause protected a right to engage in homosexual sodomy. Bowers did not hold that moral disapproval of a group is a rational basis under the Equal Protection Clause to criminalize homosexual sodomy when heterosexual sodomy is not punished.

This case raises a different issue than Bowers: whether, under the Equal Protection Clause, moral disapproval is a legitimate state interest to justify by itself a statute that bans homosexual sodomy, but not heterosexual sodomy. It is not. Moral disapproval of this group, like a bare desire to harm the group, is an interest that is insufficient to satisfy rational basis review under the Equal Protection Clause. Indeed, we have never held that moral disapproval, without any other asserted state interest, is a sufficient rationale under the Equal Protection Clause to justify a law that discriminates among groups of persons.

Moral disapproval of a group cannot be a legitimate governmental interest under the Equal Protection Clause because legal classifications must not be "drawn for the purpose of disadvantaging the group burdened by the law." Texas' invocation of moral disapproval as a legitimate state interest proves nothing more than Texas' desire to criminalize homosexual sodomy. But the Equal Protection Clause prevents a State from creating "a classification of persons undertaken for its own sake." And because Texas so rarely enforces its sodomy law as applied to private, consensual acts, the law serves more as a statement of dislike and disapproval against homosexuals than as a tool to stop criminal behavior. . . . A State can of course assign certain consequences to a violation of its criminal law. But the State cannot single out one identifiable class of citizens for punishment that does not apply to everyone else, with moral disapproval as the only asserted state interest for the law. . . .

That this law as applied to private, consensual conduct is unconstitutional under the Equal Protection Clause does not mean that other laws distinguishing between heterosexuals and homosexuals would similarly fail under rational basis review. Texas cannot assert any legitimate state interest here, such as national security or preserving the traditional institution of marriage. Unlike the moral disapproval of same-sex relations—the asserted state interest in this case—other reasons exist to promote the institution of marriage beyond mere moral disapproval of an excluded group. A law branding one class of persons as criminal solely based on the State's moral disapproval of that class and the conduct associated with that class runs contrary to the values of the Constitution and the Equal Protection Clause, under any standard of review. I therefore concur in the Court's judgment that Texas' sodomy law banning "deviate sexual intercourse" between consenting adults of the same sex, but not between consenting adults of different sexes, is unconstitutional.

JUSTICE SCALIA, with whom THE CHIEF JUSTICE and JUSTICE THOMAS join, dissenting.

. . . I begin with the Court's surprising readiness to reconsider a decision rendered a mere 17 years ago in Bowers v. Hardwick. I do not myself believe in rigid adherence to stare decisis in constitutional cases; but I do believe that we should be consistent rather than manipulative in invoking the doctrine. Today's opinions in support of reversal do not bother to distinguish—or indeed, even bother to mention—the paean to stare decisis coauthored by three members of today's majority in Planned Parenthood v. Casey. There, when stare decisis meant preservation of judicially invented abortion rights, the widespread criticism of Roe was strong reason to reaffirm it:

> Where, in the performance of its judicial duties, the Court decides a case in such a way as to resolve the sort of intensely divisive controversy reflected in Roe[,] . . . its decision has a dimension that the resolution of the normal case does not carry. . . . [T]o over-rule under fire in the absence of the most compelling reason . . . would subvert the Court's legitimacy beyond any serious question.

Today, however, the widespread opposition to Bowers, a decision resolving an issue as "intensely divisive" as the issue in Roe, is offered as a reason in favor of overruling it. . . .

It seems to me that the "societal reliance" on the principles confirmed in Bowers and discarded today has been overwhelming. Countless judicial decisions and legislative enactments have relied on the ancient proposition that a governing majority's belief that certain sexual behavior is "immoral and unacceptable" constitutes a rational basis for regulation. We ourselves relied extensively on Bowers when we concluded, in Barnes v. Glen Theatre, Inc. (1991), that Indiana's public indecency statute furthered "a substantial government interest in protecting order and morality." State laws against bigamy, same-sex marriage, adult incest, prostitution, masturbation, adultery, fornication, bestiality, and obscenity are likewise sustainable only in light of Bowers' validation of laws based on moral choices. Every single one of these laws is called into question by today's decision; the Court makes no effort to cabin the scope of its decision to exclude them from its holding. The impossibility of distinguishing homosexuality from other traditional "morals" offenses is precisely why Bowers rejected the rational-basis challenge. "The law," it said, "is constantly based on notions of morality, and if all laws representing essentially moral choices are to be invalidated under the Due Process Clause, the courts will be very busy indeed."

What a massive disruption of the current social order, therefore, the overruling of Bowers entails. . . . To tell the truth, it does not surprise me, and should surprise no one, that the Court has chosen today to revise the standards of stare decisis set forth in Casey. It has thereby exposed Casey's extraordinary deference to precedent for the result-oriented expedient that it is. . . .

I turn now to the ground on which the Court squarely rests its holding: the contention that there is no rational basis for the law here under attack. This proposition is so out of accord with our jurisprudence—indeed, with the jurisprudence of any society we know—that it requires little discussion.

The Texas statute undeniably seeks to further the belief of its citizens that certain forms of sexual behavior are "immoral and unacceptable," the same interest furthered by criminal laws against fornication, bigamy, adultery, adult incest, bestiality, and obscenity. Bowers held that this was a legitimate state interest. The Court today reaches the opposite conclusion. . . . This effectively decrees the end of all morals legislation. If, as the Court asserts, the promotion of majoritarian sexual morality is not even a legitimate state interest, none of the above-mentioned laws can survive rational-basis review. . . .

Today's opinion is the product of a Court, which is the product of a law-profession culture, that has largely signed on to the so-called homosexual agenda, by which I mean the agenda promoted by some homosexual activists directed at eliminating the moral opprobrium that has traditionally attached to homosexual conduct. . . . One of the most revealing statements in today's opinion is the Court's grim warning that the criminalization of homosexual conduct is "an invitation to subject homosexual persons to discrimination both in the public and in the private spheres." It is clear from this that the Court has taken sides in the culture war, departing from its role of assuring, as neutral observer, that the democratic rules of engagement are observed. Many Americans do not want persons who openly engage in homosexual conduct as partners in their business, as scoutmasters for their children, as teachers in their children's schools, or as boarders in their home. They view this as protecting themselves and their families from a lifestyle that they believe to be immoral and destructive. The Court views it as "discrimination" which it is the function of our judgments to deter. . . .

Let me be clear that I have nothing against homosexuals, or any other group, promoting their agenda through normal democratic means. Social perceptions of sexual and other morality change over time, and every group has the right to persuade its fellow citizens that its view of such matters is the best. That homosexuals have achieved some success in that enterprise is attested to by the fact that Texas is one of the few remaining States that criminalize private, consensual homosexual acts. But persuading one's fellow citizens is one thing, and imposing one's views in absence of democratic

majority will is something else. I would no more require a State to criminalize homosexual acts—or, for that matter, display any moral disapprobation of them—than I would forbid it to do so. What Texas has chosen to do is well within the range of traditional democratic action, and its hand should not be stayed through the invention of a brand-new "constitutional right" by a Court that is impatient of democratic change. It is indeed true that "later generations can see that laws once thought necessary and proper in fact serve only to oppress," and when that happens, later generations can repeal those laws. But it is the premise of our system that those judgments are to be made by the people, and not imposed by a governing caste that knows best.

One of the benefits of leaving regulation of this matter to the people rather than to the courts is that the people, unlike judges, need not carry things to their logical conclusion. The people may feel that their disapproval of homosexual conduct is strong enough to disallow homosexual marriage, but not strong enough to criminalize private homosexual acts—and may legislate accordingly. The Court today pretends that it possesses a similar freedom of action, so that we need not fear judicial imposition of homosexual marriage. . . . Do not believe it. More illuminating than this bald, unreasoned disclaimer is the progression of thought displayed by an earlier passage in the Court's opinion, which notes the constitutional protections afforded to "personal decisions relating to marriage, procreation, contraception, family relationships, child rearing, and education," and then declares that "[p]ersons in a homosexual relationship may seek autonomy for these purposes, just as heterosexual persons do." Today's opinion dismantles the structure of constitutional law that has permitted a distinction to be made between heterosexual and homosexual unions, insofar as formal recognition in marriage is concerned. If moral disapproval of homosexual conduct is "no legitimate state interest" for purposes of proscribing that conduct, and if, as the Court coos (casting aside all pretense of neutrality), "[w]hen sexuality finds overt expression in intimate conduct with another person, the conduct can be but one element in a personal bond that is more enduring," what justification could there possibly be for denying the benefits of marriage to homosexual couples exercising "[t]he liberty protected by the Constitution"? Surely not the encouragement of procreation, since the sterile and the elderly are allowed to marry. This case "does not involve" the issue of homosexual marriage only if one entertains the belief that principle and logic have nothing to do with the decisions of this Court. Many will hope that, as the Court comfortingly assures us, this is so.

The matters appropriate for this Court's resolution are only three: Texas's prohibition of sodomy neither infringes a "fundamental right" (which the Court does not dispute), nor is unsupported by a rational relation to what the Constitution considers a legitimate state interest, nor denies the equal protection of the laws.

I dissent.

COMMENTARY: "THE MARRIAGE BATTLE BEGINS"

Profamily activists fear that the Supreme Court's June 26 [2003] *Lawrence and Garner v. Texas* decision, which struck down state laws prohibiting homosexual sodomy, also jeopardizes the marriage laws of all 50 states. "Laws defining marriage as between a man and a woman are in the gun sights of the courts," said Matt Daniels, founder of the Alliance for Marriage in Springfield, Virginia. "The Lawrence case has everything to do with the legal status of marriage." . . .

Paul M. Smith of the gay-rights organization Lambda Legal Defense and Education Fund argued before the Court in March that Texas's statute violates the 14th Amendment's Equal Protection Clause. "The petitioners are entitled to respect for their private lives," wrote Justice Anthony Kennedy for the majority. "The State cannot demean their existence or control their destiny by making their private sexual conduct a crime." After the Court announced its verdict, Lambda officials said they would use Lawrence as a tool in future lawsuits concerning marriage.

Daniels said the Lawrence ruling, coupled with an expected pro-homosexual marriage decision by the Massachusetts Supreme Judicial Court in Goodridge v. Massachusetts Department of Public Health, would have immediate national implications. Because of the Full Faith and Credit Clause in Article 4 of the U.S. Constitution, the Goodridge verdict could invalidate the Defense of Marriage Act. Congress overwhelmingly passed DOMA, which President Clinton signed, only seven years ago. DOMA defines marriage as a union between one man and one woman. Recent appeals court decisions in Ontario, British Columbia, and Quebec overturning traditional marriage laws could spark further judicial activism in the United States, Daniels said. "Canada is an example of where we're headed unless we put this in the hands of the American people." Daniels said a constitutional amendment is the solution. He believes it is feasible, considering that 37 states already have passed DOMA laws—including, most recently, Texas. For a proposed amendment to become part of the Constitution, three-fourths of the states (38) must ratify it. The amendment is succinct: "Marriage in the United States shall consist only of a man and a woman. Neither this Constitution nor the constitution of any state under state or federal law shall be construed to require that marital status or legal incidents thereof be conferred upon unmarried couples or groups." It says nothing about domestic partnerships and civil unions, which would be left to the states. First-term U.S. Rep. Marilyn Musgrave secured 75 House cosponsors of the amendment within weeks of the Lawrence ruling. In 2000 she successfully championed defense of marriage legislation as a Republican state senator in Colorado.

Public opinion is less comforting to conservatives than it used to be. As recently as 1960, every state had anti-sodomy laws. In 1986, at the time of Bowers, only 26 did. Before Lawrence, Texas was one of only four states to outlaw sodomy only between homosexual partners. A May [2003] Gallup poll indicated that a record 60 percent of Americans say that homosexual relations between consenting adults should be legal and that homosexuality is an acceptable way of life. However, a July Gallup poll found that support had slipped to 48 percent in the wake of the ruling. That compares to only 32 percent at the time of Bowers.

Randy Thomas, ministry manager for Exodus International, an Orlando-based ministry helping people leave homosexuality, said Lawrence will shape public policy. "This ruling gives validity to the gay community," Thomas said. "In addition to potentially redefining the family, it further solidifies their position as a political and social force." . . . Senate Majority Leader Bill Frist (R.-Tenn.) endorsed a constitutional amendment . . . immediately after the decision, but he has been largely silent on the matter since then.

Homosexual activists are seeking a social revolution that replicates the judicial fait accompli following Roe v. Wade on abortion, Daniels said. Musgrave said Christians must take a stand. "In this cultural war," she said, "we cannot lose this one" (Kennedy, 2003)

COMMENTARY: "THE CONSEQUENCES OF LAWRENCE V. TEXAS"

Recently, and famously, in Lawrence v. Texas, the Supreme Court invalidated Texas' anti-homosexual-sodomy law. It did so by invoking the constitutional right to privacy. But it also indicated that constitutional equal protection doctrines would have provided another reason to invalidate the statute, which targeted only same-sex sodomy. The decision extended long-overdue recognition of the rights of gays and lesbians. In doing so, it also overturned a notoriously hateful precedent, Bowers v. Hardwick.

Justice Antonin Scalia wrote an angry dissent to Lawrence. Among other points, Scalia warned that the Court's decision means that state criminal laws against fornication, bigamy, adultery, adult incest, bestiality, and obscenity cannot survive. Is he right? The answer is surprisingly unclear from the Lawrence opinion. Accordingly, the status of these other laws will remain fodder for lower court challenges.

The Right of Privacy: The Pre-Lawrence Decisions

Prior to Lawrence, the Supreme Court had developed a well-known and sometimes controversial line of cases recognizing a right of privacy surrounding decision-making about marriage, family, and procreation. As it evolved, this constitutional right of privacy became tethered to the Due Process Clause of the Fourteenth Amendment—and, specifically, to the liberty interest it protects. The thrust of the right is that individuals have the right to make certain decisions, and engage in certain forms of conduct, without interference from the state.

Claims that the constitutional right of privacy has been infringed are traditionally analyzed in two steps. First, the Court asks whether the decision or conduct is a fundamental right. In deciding this issue, the Court applies some rather nebulous standards. Is the right "implicit in the concept of ordered liberty"? Is it "deeply rooted in this Nation's history and tradition"? It is helpful if an asserted right is similar to rights that have already been declared fundamental in the past. Pursuant to Court precedents, fundamental rights include the rights to marry, to use contraceptives, to make decisions about the rearing and education of children, to live with individuals of one's choice, and the right to terminate a pregnancy. (The right, famously established by Roe v. Wade, was reaffirmed, albeit under a slightly different analytic framework, in 1992 in Planned Parenthood v. Casey.)

If the right at issue is indeed fundamental, then the Court applies strict scrutiny to the law. Most laws fail this analysis. For the law to survive, the state must prove both that it had a compelling interest at stake and that the law at issue was narrowly tailored to achieve that interest. On the other hand, if the right at issue is not fundamental, the Court simply applies rational basis review. If the state had a legitimate interest in regulating the conduct, and the law at issue was a rational means of achieving that interest, then the law stands.

Bowers v. Hardwick: The Court's Prior Anti-Sodomy Law Precedent

In 1986, against this backdrop, the Court decided *Bowers v. Hardwick.* In that case, a man was arrested, in his bedroom, for engaging in sexual conduct with another male. He was convicted under a Georgia statute that prohibited sodomy, regardless of the gender of the persons engaging in it. When he challenged his conviction, the Court first confronted the issue of whether the right he asserted was fundamental. The majority formulated the question this way: "whether the Federal Constitution confers a fundamental right upon homosexuals to engage in sodomy. . . ." But of course, it might have also been phrased in other ways—as a fundamental right to consensual sexual conduct between adults in a private context. The Court refused to recognize sodomy as a fundamental right, based on its review of history. Indeed, it deemed the claim that there was such a right "at best, facetious." Finding no fundamental right, the Court applied only the rational basis standard of review. In doing so, the Court found the law valid as an expression of the state's "sentiments about the morality of homosexuality." In other words, the state's belief that homosexual conduct was immoral was a sufficiently "rational" basis to support the law.

The Majority Opinion in *Lawrence v. Texas:* Strong But Strange

That brings us to the recent *Lawrence* opinion—in which *Bowers* was explicitly overruled. In this case, two men were arrested after the police—dispatched on a report of a weapons disturbance—encountered them in their apartment engaged in a sexual act. They were convicted under a Texas law criminalizing "deviate sexual intercourse with another individual of the same sex." By a 6-3 majority, the Court, in a majority opinion authored by Justice Anthony Kennedy, invalidated the law—and all anti-sodomy laws, even those that apply to both same-sex and opposite-sex couples. That much is clear. Much else is not.

Oddly, the Court never expressly labeled the conduct at issue a "fundamental" right. It did, however, say that the Texas law sought to "control a personal relationship that . . . is within the liberty of persons to choose without being punished." And it also said that adults have the right to "choose to enter upon this relationship in the confines of their homes and their own private lives and still retain their dignity as free persons." Homosexuals, the Court wrote, also share in this "liberty protected by the Constitution." All of these statements sound like those used to describe a fundamental right. Thus, one would expect that strict scrutiny would follow. Did it?

All the Court said with respect to the standard of review was that the "Texas statute furthers no legitimate state interest which can justify its intrusion into the personal and private life of the individual." That sounds like rational basis review, not strict scrutiny. So what's going on? It apparently was plain to the Court that the statute would not even survive the lax rational basis standard—let alone strict scrutiny. So the same Court that had avoided the easier equal protection argument, to invoke the right of privacy instead, also eschewed the easier application of the more lethal strict scrutiny test, to reach for the rational basis test instead. . . . In invalidating the Texas law even under the rational basis law, the Court sent this message: "This law is so deeply flawed and reprehensible, we can strike it down with one hand tied behind our backs." Of course, one could also take an almost diametrically opposite view of the opinion—seeing it as intentionally narrow, not intentionally far-reaching. On this view, the six majority Justices—perhaps because they disagreed among themselves on these points—intentionally withheld two important rulings. First, they declined explicitly to hold that private sexual conduct, including sodomy, is a fundamental right. Second, they declined explicitly to hold that strict scrutiny applies when this right is infringed. Therefore, on this view, these holdings are not law. But no one who has read the majority opinion as a whole can plausibly endorse this latter interpretation of the Court's opinion. It is too strong an embrace of rights, and a proclamation of freedom for gays and lesbians, for that interpretation to be sustainable. . . .

What *Lawrence* Means for Other "Morals" Laws: Its Possibilities and Limits

But how far does this embrace extend? The key to developing the privacy line of cases in the past has been analogy—how much does a newly asserted right look like those the Court has already recognized? That will undoubtedly hold true with *Lawrence* as courts are asked to reconsider the validity of other laws regulating similar conduct. When laws that regulate analogous conduct are examined, morality justifications alone plainly will not be enough to save them. In *Lawrence,* the Court explicitly adopted the following language from Justice Stevens's *Bowers* dissent: "the fact that the governing majority in a State has traditionally viewed a particular practice as immoral is not a sufficient reason for upholding a law prohibiting the practice."

But which kinds of conduct, exactly, will be deemed similar to the conduct at issue in *Lawrence?* At one point, *Lawrence* refers to an "emerging awareness that liberty gives substantial protection to adult persons in deciding how to conduct their private lives in matters pertaining to sex." Later, however, the opinion also makes plain that not all statutes regulating sex will be vulnerable to constitutional attack. Indeed, the Court tries to hem in its holding by listing the factors not implicated by the Texas anti-sodomy law: minors, coercion, public conduct, prostitution, and public or governmental recognition of the relationship. It also points out what is involved here: two adults, mutual consent, and sexual acts common to their lifestyle. This analysis spells doom for the few remaining anti-fornication laws on the books. Like homosexual sodomy, fornication is a private, consensual, sexual act, and the laws forbidding it have no conceivable justification other than morality. But what about the other laws Justice Scalia lists in his dissent as now being vulnerable?

Laws That May or May Not Be Vulnerable Under *Lawrence*

Justice Scalia predicts that, besides anti-fornication laws, laws regulating or prohibiting same-sex marriage, prostitution, adultery, bigamy, incest, and bestiality will also come under fire, and be invalidated, after *Lawrence*. Will they really? Laws against prostitution and bestiality are the easiest cases. After *Lawrence*, anti-prostitution laws can still be justified based on concerns about coercion, exploitation of women, and the public health. And bestiality laws plainly can be upheld on a "cruelty to animals" justification, or, in the age of SARS, maybe a public health one. A legislature entirely unconcerned about the morality of either practice could still seek to prohibit both. . . . To some extent, incest prohibitions can be justified based on a state's desire to avoid genetically disadvantaged offspring. To some extent, they can be justified based on the desire to avoid corruption of parent-child relationships; without such laws, such relationships could be tainted by the possibility that an older relative may be grooming a minor relative for intimate partnership later in life. But some applications of incest laws may reach too far—beyond either of these concerns—and be struck down. A law that prohibited cousins from marrying might be one example. So might a law prohibiting an adopted sibling from marrying a close-in-age "natural" sibling who shared no genes. Or one that prohibited the marriage of blood relatives who did not know each other as minors.

Adultery and bigamy laws are somewhat harder. They can probably be justified by a state's desire to preserve a monogamous tradition, protect spouses from harm visited by the other spouse (a longstanding feature of state criminal, marriage, and divorce law), maintain an orderly system for assigning the benefits and burdens associated with marriage, and so on. On the other hand, though, it seems hard to deny that morality concerns are the main motivating force behind such laws: Adultery and bigamy are prohibited not so much for their consequences, but because society sees them as morally wrong. But unlike private sexual conduct, like sodomy, neither adultery nor bigamy has ever been protected by our society—to the contrary both have always been illegal, and a basis for marital dissolution. And unlike the history of sodomy laws detailed in *Lawrence*, there is a long history of these laws being enforced. So to the extent that the due process inquiry is based in tradition, the rights to commit adultery or bigamy look very unlike the right at issue in *Lawrence* (and thus would not generate heightened scrutiny at all).

Laws Banning Same-Sex Marriage Are Indeed Vulnerable After *Lawrence*

What about laws banning same-sex marriage? The Court in *Lawrence* seemed to limit its holding so as not to decide this question, noting that it was not considering the issue of public or governmental recognition of a relationship. But, importantly, its reasoning may well extend to invalidate such laws anyway. In *Lawrence*, the Court dispensed with tradition as the sole determinant of a privacy right, emphasizing the role of autonomy and personhood in assessing what rights are too important to be toyed with. Same-sex marriage has not traditionally been seen as a right, but neither has same-sex sodomy—or sodomy in general—and *Lawrence* found a right to these latter practices.

Certainly, individuals desiring to marry a person of the same sex have at least as strong an interest in having that freedom, as individuals choosing to engage in sexual conduct with a person of the same sex have in the freedom they are exercising. If not, the Court will, at the same time, have given its protection to all forms of non-marital sexual relationships—including wild one-night stands—while deterring the kind of permanent, legally sanctioned relationships on which society has been built. Indeed, one would think that, putting tradition aside, the right to marry the person of your choice should be one of the most fundamental of all. If it isn't, the Court will be hard put to say why. Once a right to same-sex marriage is recognized, any law banning it—or regulating it differently from the way opposite-sex marriage is regulated—will predictably be struck down. Such laws have no valid justification; they are based either on pure animus against homosexual persons, or on so-called "morality" considerations that *Lawrence* and *Romer* have made clear cannot alone support a liberty- or equality-infringing law. In sum, *Lawrence* is itself a monumental development in Constitutional law, but the future may be even more interesting. After *Lawrence*, challenges to laws banning same-sex marriage are the logical next step (Grossman, 2003).

CHAPTER 15

The Right to Die

INTRODUCTION

It seems fitting to end this book with cases that involve the ending of life. Every human life, of course, will end at some point. Some of these endings are abrupt and unexpected, through accidents, homicide, or sudden events like strokes and heart attacks. Other lives end after many years (even more than a century) by so-called natural causes, as human bodies wear out and can no longer function. But the lives of most people today end in hospitals or hospices, after an illness that has been diagnosed and treated by doctors and other medical professionals. An increasing number of people who become terminally ill and most likely will die within weeks or months decide to spend their final days in their own homes or in those of family members. More and more people are facing the prospect that their lives will end within months, as their illnesses progress and their chances of recovery fade. And some of these terminally ill or permanently disabled people—a relatively small minority—consider the option of suicide as a way to avoid unbearable pain or a life of disability and dependence on others.

As the life span of Americans becomes longer, questions about the "quality of life" of those who are terminally ill or permanently disabled have moved into public discourse and debate. The "graying" of the American population has helped to fuel the debate over this issue. Since 1900 the percentage of people over the age of 65 has more than tripled, from 4 percent to 13 percent in 2003, more than one in eight in the entire population. Life expectancy has reached record levels, 74 years for men and almost 80 for women in 2003. A century ago, men could expect to live only 48 years, with a 51-year life span for women. But these older Americans, although living longer, are not all healthy. Some 80 percent of those over the age of 65 suffer from at least one serious medical condition, such as heart disease or diabetes, and 55 percent have two or more

serious conditions. Many of these people will face diagnoses of terminal illness, and the likelihood of death within months. In recent years, groups such as the Hemlock Society and Death With Dignity have campaigned for laws that will allow people in these situations to commit suicide with the aid of a physician, and to die at a time and place of their own choice. In 1997 Oregon became the first (and thus far the only) state to allow physician-assisted suicide, under very strict conditions. To qualify for a prescription for lethal medication under this law, a person must be diagnosed by two physicians as likely to die within six months, must request lethal medication at least three times, and must wait at least fifteen days between receiving the medication and using it. By 2002, after five years of legal, physician-assisted suicide in Oregon, only 159 people had ended their lives in this manner, less than 0.3 percent of all the Oregonians who died from the same illnesses of those who chose suicide.

Despite the small number of people in Oregon who have chosen physician-assisted suicide, the issue remains a topic of passionate, and often heated, debate. Campaigns for laws similar to that of Oregon have been waged in several states, although none has thus far succeeded. Despite losses in states like Maine, where a referendum that would allow physician-assisted suicide was defeated by a narrow 51-percent margin, advocates of what they call "death with dignity" have counted on shifts in public opinion to prevail in future electoral campaigns.

The most important point in this discussion is that the Supreme Court has emphatically rejected arguments that the Constitution protects a right to choose physician-assisted suicide. Ruling in 1997, the Court unanimously dismissed this claim in two cases, from Washington State and New York. The justices turned the debate over this issue to the public forum. "Throughout the Nation," wrote Chief Justice

William Rehnquist in *Washington v. Glucksberg*, "Americans are engaged in an earnest, profound debate about the morality, legality, and practicality of physician-assisted suicide. Our holding permits this debate to continue, as it should in a democratic society."

On the surface, Chief Justice Rehnquist's statement seems quite reasonable. After all, our constitutional system is based on the premise that the American people (at least those who take part in the democratic process by voting) *should* make the decisions on matters of public policy, and that electoral majorities should prevail. But the same constitutional system guarantees, in the Bill of Rights, that some matters are "beyond the reach of majorities," as Justice Robert Jackson wrote in his *Barnette* opinion in 1943. Those matters include the prohibition in the Fifth Amendment of governmental deprivation of "liberty" without due process of law. The scope of that liberty, and its application in particular cases, has evolved and expanded over the past eight decades, as the Court has confronted issues such as the "liberty" of parents to educate their children in private schools, of people to live with their relatives, of women to obtain abortions, and of gays and lesbians to engage in intimate relations. Each of these "liberties" is rooted in the notion that personal decisions in these areas are beyond the reach of electoral majorities and beyond the power of governmental prohibition.

Given these constitutional rulings, Chief Justice Rehnquist's statement in his *Glucksberg* opinion that the decision to end one's life with a physician's assistance must yield to electoral decisions to prohibit this practice raises important questions. For one, Rehnquist himself wrote in his *Cruzan* opinion in 1990 that "we assume that the United States Constitution would grant a competent person a constitutionally protected right to refuse lifesaving hydration and nutrition." The *Cruzan* case did not involve a competent person, but rather a young woman, Nancy Cruzan, who had been left in a "persistent vegetative state" after an automobile accident. But the justices unanimously agreed in *Cruzan* that competent adults have the right to starve themselves to death; in other words, to commit suicide. Given that holding, can a person who is competent but who lacks either the physical or psychological ability to end their life obtain a physician's assistance in doing what other people with those abilities can do? The Court said no in its *Glucksberg* opinion. But its reasoning in that opinion relied more on "history" and "tradition" than on a well-reasoned distinction between the two forms of suicide, one by the person's own hand and the other with a physician's assistance. Chief Justice Rehnquist restated his *Cruzan* holding in *Glucksberg*, writing that "the Due Process Clause protects the traditional right to refuse unwanted lifesaving medical treatment." This would constitute a "fundamental right" under the Court's long-standing doctrines, and thus be protected from legislative prohibition. But the Court rejected the claim that this fundamental right included the decision to end one's life with a physician's assistance, because of the "consistent and almost universal tradition that has long rejected the asserted right" of physician-assisted suicide.

However, as we saw in the previous chapter, the Court has acknowledged a "fundamental right" of gays and lesbians to engage in sodomy despite a long history of social opposition and legal prohibition. Perhaps the distinction between the *Lawrence* decision on homosexual sodomy and the *Glucksberg* ruling on physician-assisted suicide rests on the fact, as Justice Anthony Kennedy noted in his *Lawrence* opinion, that "states with same-sex prohibitions [of homosexual sodomy] have moved toward abolishing them" over the past several decades. But only one state, Oregon, has thus far abolished its prohibition on physician-assisted suicide. In other words, "history" and "tradition" lose their force as constitutional guidelines when the tides of public opinion have shifted, as reflected in legislative repeal of laws that embodied the "tradition" of public disapproval of practices such as homosexual sodomy.

Public opinion has shifted in recent years on the issue of physician-assisted suicide. A national poll in 2001 showed that 65 percent of those questioned agreed that "the law should allow doctors to comply with the wishes of a dying patient in severe distress who asks to have his or her life ended," while only 29 percent disagreed. In the same poll, 63 percent disagreed with the polling question "that individuals do not have a constitutional right to doctor-assisted suicide," and thus with the Court's ruling in the *Glucksberg* case.

The Court's decisions on the question of physician-assisted suicide, and the ongoing debate over legislative proposals to end legal prohibitions of this practice, illustrate the fundamental conflict the justices have faced in the cases we have read and discussed: the conflict between majority rule and minority rights. Debates on this and other controversial issues, such as same-sex marriage, will continue to present both citizens and the courts with difficult choices. And we will continue to confront the task, as Justice Felix Frankfurter put it in his *Gobitis* opinion in 1940, of how best "to reconcile the conflicting claims of liberty and authority."

CRUZAN V. DIRECTOR, MISSOURI DEPARTMENT OF HEALTH
497 U.S. 261 (1990)

"Close family members may have a strong feeling—a feeling not at all ignoble or unworthy—that they do not wish to witness the continuation of the life of a loved one which they regard as hopeless, meaningless, and even degrading. But there is no automatic assurance that the view of close family members will necessarily be the same as the patient's would have been had she been confronted with the prospect of her situation while competent."

The Question:	Can a state court refuse to grant a request by the parents of a young woman who has been in a coma since her injuries in an automobile crash to withdraw her artificial nutrition and hydration, on the ground there was no "clear and convincing evidence" that the young woman had expressed a desire before her accident that life support be withdrawn in such a situation?

The Arguments:

PRO

The state's requirement that "clear and convincing evidence" be shown of a person's desire that life support be withdrawn if he or she later enters a "persistent vegetative state" and cannot communicate such a desire is designed to protect those who may wish to continue to live, even in this state. However difficult it may be for parents to see their children in such a helpless condition, the state cannot presume that parents or other surrogates will make a decision the comatose person would have made. Because there is no constitutional "right to die," requiring convincing evidence of a person's wishes is a reasonable legislative choice.

CON

As a general principle, competent adults should be able to make decisions about whether life support should be withdrawn if they become irreversibly comatose. In this case, the parents of Nancy Beth Cruzan are in the best position to make this decision for her, since she will never be able to make an informed decision herself. Courts should not make it impossible for life support to be withdrawn in situations where the comatose person has not made a clear statement of her wishes before becoming unable to make that decision.

BACKGROUND

Nancy Cruzan, an attractive and vivacious twenty-five-year-old, probably fell asleep while driving home from work at the cheese factory near her home in Carterville, Missouri. She lost control of her 1963 Nash Rambler on lonely Elm Road and was thrown out of the car as it crashed. Nancy lay face down in a roadside ditch for about fifteen minutes without breathing or having a heartbeat before a state highway patrolman and paramedics discovered her and began resuscitation. Her lungs and heart began to work again, but since permanent brain damage begins after about six minutes without oxygen, Nancy was in a coma and soon descended into a permanent unconscious vegetative state. Not brain dead, her body performed respiration, circulation, and digestion without medical devices, but she would never regain consciousness or become aware of her surroundings.

Shortly after the crash, which occurred in January 1983, her then husband, hoping that she might awaken and recover, agreed to have a feeding tube implanted in Nancy's stomach. Later her parents, Lester "Joe" and Joyce Cruzan, brought her home from the Missouri Rehabilitation Center forty miles east at Mt. Vernon, hoping that familiar surroundings would stimulate her, but nothing worked. Years passed, and Nancy lay in a tightly contracted fetal position with her muscles and tendons irreversibly damaged, spinal fluid gradually replacing destroyed brain tissue. There was no hope whatever that Nancy Cruzan would change for the better, although with food and water administered artificially through the stomach feeding tube, she could have lived for several decades. Her care cost $130,000 per year, paid by the state of Missouri. Social Security contributions for medical care had long been exhausted.

Four years after her accident and with no change in her condition, Nancy's parents tried to reverse the early approval of the artificial feeding tube so that Nancy could be, in her father's words, "turned loose" and allowed to die. Medical personnel refused, however, and the Cruzans asked the Missouri chapter of the American Civil Liberties Union for help. In turn, the ACLU obtained the free services of a young and vigorous attorney from a large, prestigious Kansas City law firm. Again, the rehabilitation center refused, and the only remaining path was a lawsuit to persuade a local judge to order the feeding tube removed.

A trial began in March 1988 with the Cruzan's lawyer presenting medical testimony from several neurologists, who confirmed that Nancy was in a persistent vegetative state, and from her family and friends, who testified that Nancy had clearly told them that she would not want to be kept alive in her condition. The state rehabilitation center, represented by an assistant state attorney general, countered with doctors and nurses who said Nancy sometimes exhibited awakelike reactions, such as crying, grimaces, and eye movements, that seemed to indicate awareness. Nurses also testified that they did not want to see Nancy's treatment stopped. But the doctors admitted that Nancy's reactions, including tearing, were common in a vegetative state and did not indicate that Nancy was interacting with her environment. A few months after the trial began, Judge Charles Teel Jr., ruled that a patient has a state and federal constitutional right to refuse medical treatment and that Joe and Joyce Cruzan, acting as Nancy's guardians, had the right to act in her best interests and to order the withdrawal of treatment, including the artificial feeding and hydration.

But the dispute did not end. The state appealed to the Missouri Supreme Court, and Nancy Cruzan's plight quickly changed from a personal tragedy to a state and national issue. Seven medical, right-to-die, and right-to-life organizations and advocates for the retarded and disabled filed friend of the court (amicus curiae) briefs on both sides of the issue.

In November 1988, in a four–three split decision, the court reversed the trial judge (*Cruzan v. Harmon*). It concluded that there is no right to privacy that allows a person to refuse medical treatment in all circumstances and that removal of the feeding tube would result in death by starvation; it found that Nancy's wishes expressed to a friend were unreliable and denied that Nancy's parents had the power to act on her behalf. The court also ruled that, although Nancy had not executed a living will and was not terminally ill, Missouri's living will statute indicated the legislature's intended policy in such cases; the statute has a prolife preamble, and the law prohibits the withdrawal of food and hydration from terminally ill patients. Also, to the court majority, Nancy was alive and the treatment was not a burden to her. Therefore, the state had a legitimate interest in preserving her life.

The Cruzans' lawyers quickly filed a petition for certiorari with the U.S. Supreme Court. In the past the Court had declined to hear right-to-die cases, but this time it granted the request. The Bush administration filed an amicus brief in support of Missouri's appeal. On June 25, 1990, the U.S. Supreme Court upheld Missouri in a five–four decision (*Cruzan v. Director, Missouri Department of Health*). Writing for the majority, Chief Justice William Rehnquist agreed that Missouri had the right to require clear and convincing evidence of Nancy's wishes not to be kept alive if she were in a vegetative state, and that the state may guard against potential abuses by a patient's surrogate or guardian.

The majority also indicated that oral agreements and instructions were generally suspect in legal transactions but that written instructions concerning medical treatment left by a competent patient would be binding. But, unlike Missouri, the Court did not distinguish between food and hydration and other medical treatment, indicating that both could be withdrawn if a patient had requested. In a concurring opinion, Justice Sandra Day O'Connor urged adults to use living wills or the durable power of attorney to convey in writing their advance wishes concerning final medical care. The dissenters argued that the Cruzans should be permitted to order the withdrawal of Nancy's artificial feeding.

Nancy Cruzan's case continued. Her court-appointed guardian and her lawyer returned in November to the Missouri trial court where the case had begun with three newly discovered former friends who testified that Nancy Cruzan had told them she would not wish to be kept alive if she were in a vegetative state. This time the state of Missouri did not contest the renewed request to disconnect the feeding tube, and within a few weeks Judge Teel ordered its removal so that Nancy could die.

The Society for the Right to Die praised the Cruzans and the decision while right to life protesters denounced what they termed the frenzy to kill Nancy Cruzan. Right-to-life organizations filed several unsuccessful petitions in state and federal courts to overturn Judge Teel's ruling, and twenty-five protesters were blocked and arrested as they tried to get to Nancy Cruzan's hospital room to force the reconnection of the feeding tube. The day after Christmas 1990—twelve days after the feeding tube had been withdrawn, nearly seven years after her automobile accident, and almost three years after the first court hearing—Nancy Cruzan died (Glick, 1992).

CHIEF JUSTICE REHNQUIST delivered the opinion of the Court.

Petitioner Nancy Beth Cruzan was rendered incompetent as a result of severe injuries sustained during an automobile accident. Copetitioners Lester and Joyce Cruzan, Nancy's parents and coguardians, sought a court order directing the withdrawal of their daughter's artificial feeding and hydration equipment after it became apparent that she had virtually no chance of recovering her cognitive faculties. The Supreme Court of Missouri held that, because there was no clear and convincing evidence of Nancy's desire to have life-sustaining treatment withdrawn under such circumstances, her parents lacked authority to effectuate such a request. We granted certiorari, and now affirm.

On the night of January 11, 1983, Nancy Cruzan lost control of her car as she traveled down Elm Road in Jasper County, Missouri. The vehicle overturned, and Cruzan was discovered lying face down in a ditch without detectable respiratory or cardiac function. Paramedics were able to restore her breathing and heartbeat at the accident site, and she was transported to a hospital in an unconscious state. An attending neurosurgeon diagnosed her as having sustained probable cerebral contusions compounded by significant anoxia (lack of oxygen). The Missouri trial court in this case found that permanent brain damage generally results after 6 minutes in an anoxic state; it was estimated that Cruzan was deprived of oxygen from 12 to 14 minutes. She remained in a coma for approximately three weeks, and then progressed to an unconscious state in which she was able to orally ingest some nutrition. In order to ease feeding and further the recovery, surgeons implanted a gastrostomy feeding and hydration tube in Cruzan with the consent of her then husband. Subsequent rehabilitative efforts proved unavailing. She now lies in a Missouri state hospital in what is commonly referred to as a persistent vegetative state: generally, a condition in which a person exhibits motor reflexes but evinces no indications of significant cognitive function. The State of Missouri is bearing the cost of her care.

After it had become apparent that Nancy Cruzan had virtually no chance of regaining her mental faculties, her parents asked hospital employees to terminate the artificial nutrition and hydration procedures. All agree that such a removal would cause her death. The employees refused to honor the request without court approval. The parents then sought and received authorization from the state trial court for termination. The court found that a person in Nancy's condition had a fundamental right under the State and Federal Constitutions to refuse or direct the withdrawal of "death prolonging procedures." The court also found that Nancy's "expressed thoughts at age twenty-five in somewhat serious conversation with a housemate friend that, if sick or injured, she would not wish to continue her life unless she could live at least halfway normally suggests that, given her present condition, she would not wish to continue on with her nutrition and hydration."

The Supreme Court of Missouri reversed by a divided vote. The court recognized a right to refuse treatment embodied in the common law doctrine of informed consent, but expressed skepticism about the application of that doctrine in the circumstances of this case. The court also declined to read a broad right of privacy into the State Constitution which would "support the right of a person to refuse medical treatment in every circumstance," and expressed doubt as to whether such a right existed under the United States Constitution. It then decided that the Missouri Living Will statute embodied a state policy strongly favoring the preservation of life. The court found that Cruzan's statements to her roommate regarding her desire to live or die under certain conditions were "unreliable for the purpose of determining her intent . . . and thus insufficient to support the coguardians['] claim to exercise substituted judgment on Nancy's behalf." It rejected the argument that Cruzan's parents were entitled to order the termination of her medical treatment, concluding that "no person can assume that choice for an incompetent in the absence of the formalities required under Missouri's Living Will statutes or the clear and convincing, inherently reliable evidence absent here." The court also expressed its view that "[b]road policy questions bearing on life and death are more properly addressed by representative assemblies" than judicial bodies. We granted certiorari to consider the question of whether Cruzan has a right under the United States Constitution which would require the hospital to withdraw life-sustaining treatment from her under these circumstances.

This is the first case in which we have been squarely presented with the issue of whether the United States Constitution grants what is in common parlance referred to as a "right to die." . . . The Fourteenth Amendment provides that no State shall "deprive any person of life, liberty, or property, without due process of law." The principle that a competent person has a constitutionally protected liberty interest in refusing unwanted medical treatment may be inferred from our prior decisions. In Jacobson v. Massachusetts (1905), for instance, the Court balanced an individual's liberty interest in declining an unwanted smallpox vaccine against the State's interest in preventing disease. . . .

But determining that a person has a "liberty interest" under the Due Process Clause does not end the inquiry; "whether respondent's constitutional rights have been violated must be determined by balancing his liberty interests against the relevant state interests." Petitioners insist that, under the general holdings of our cases, the forced administration of life-sustaining medical treatment, and even of artificially-delivered food and water essential to life, would implicate a competent person's liberty interest. Although we think the logic of the cases discussed above would embrace such a liberty interest, the dramatic consequences involved in refusal of such treatment would inform the inquiry as to whether the deprivation of that interest is constitutionally permissible. But for purposes of this case, we assume that the United States Constitution would grant a competent person a constitutionally protected right to refuse lifesaving hydration and nutrition.

Petitioners go on to assert that an incompetent person should possess the same right in this respect as is possessed by a competent person. . . . The difficulty with petitioners' claim is that, in a sense, it begs the question: an incompetent person is not able to make an informed and voluntary choice to exercise a hypothetical right to refuse treatment or any other right. Such a "right" must be exercised for her, if at all, by some sort of surrogate. Here, Missouri has in effect recognized that, under certain circumstances, a surrogate may act

for the patient in electing to have hydration and nutrition withdrawn in such a way as to cause death, but it has established a procedural safeguard to assure that the action of the surrogate conforms as best it may to the wishes expressed by the patient while competent. Missouri requires that evidence of the incompetent's wishes as to the withdrawal of treatment be proved by clear and convincing evidence. The question, then, is whether the United States Constitution forbids the establishment of this procedural requirement by the State. We hold that it does not.

Whether or not Missouri's clear and convincing evidence requirement comports with the United States Constitution depends in part on what interests the State may properly seek to protect in this situation. Missouri relies on its interest in the protection and preservation of human life, and there can be no gainsaying this interest. As a general matter, the States—indeed, all civilized nations—demonstrate their commitment to life by treating homicide as serious crime. Moreover, the majority of States in this country have laws imposing criminal penalties on one who assists another to commit suicide. We do not think a State is required to remain neutral in the face of an informed and voluntary decision by a physically able adult to starve to death. But in the context presented here, a State has more particular interests at stake. The choice between life and death is a deeply personal decision of obvious and overwhelming finality. We believe Missouri may legitimately seek to safeguard the personal element of this choice through the imposition of heightened evidentiary requirements. . . .

In our view, Missouri has permissibly sought to advance these interests through the adoption of a "clear and convincing" standard of proof to govern such proceedings. . . . We think it self-evident that the interests at stake in the instant proceedings are more substantial, both on an individual and societal level, than those involved in a run-of-the-mine civil dispute. But not only does the standard of proof reflect the importance of a particular adjudication, it also serves as "a societal judgment about how the risk of error should be distributed between the litigants." The more stringent the burden of proof a party must bear, the more that party bears the risk of an erroneous decision. We believe that Missouri may permissibly place an increased risk of an erroneous decision on those seeking to terminate an incompetent individual's life-sustaining treatment. An erroneous decision not to terminate results in a maintenance of the status quo; the possibility of subsequent developments such as advancements in medical science, the discovery of new evidence regarding the patient's intent, changes in the law, or simply the unexpected death of the patient despite the administration of life-sustaining treatment, at least create the potential that a wrong decision will eventually be corrected or its impac[t] mitigated. An erroneous decision to withdraw life-sustaining treatment, however, is not susceptible of correction. . . .

In sum, we conclude that a State may apply a clear and convincing evidence standard in proceedings where a guardian seeks to discontinue nutrition and hydration of a person diagnosed to be in a persistent vegetative state. We note that many courts which have adopted some sort of substituted judgment procedure in situations like this, whether they limit consideration of evidence to the prior expressed wishes of the incompetent individual, or whether they allow more general proof of what the individual's decision would have been, require a clear and convincing standard of proof for such evidence. . . . The testimony adduced at trial consisted primarily of Nancy Cruzan's statements, made to a housemate about a year before her accident, that she would not want to live should she face life as a "vegetable," and other observations to the same effect. The observations did not deal in terms with withdrawal of medical treatment or of hydration and nutrition. We cannot say that the Supreme Court of Missouri committed constitutional error in reaching the conclusion that it did. . . .

No doubt is engendered by anything in this record but that Nancy Cruzan's mother and father are loving and caring parents. If the State were required by the United States Constitution to repose a right of "substituted judgment" with anyone, the Cruzans would surely qualify. But we do not think the Due Process Clause requires the State to repose judgment on these matters with anyone but the patient herself. Close family members may have a strong feeling—a feeling not at all ignoble or unworthy, but not entirely disinterested, either—that they do not wish to witness the continuation of the life of a loved one which they regard as hopeless, meaningless, and even degrading. But there is no automatic assurance that the view of close family members will necessarily be the same as the patient's would have been had she been confronted with the prospect of her situation while competent. All of the reasons previously discussed for allowing Missouri to require clear and convincing evidence of the patient's wishes lead us to conclude that the State may choose to defer only to those wishes, rather than confide the decision to close family members. The judgment of the Supreme Court of Missouri is Affirmed.

JUSTICE STEVENS, dissenting.

Our Constitution is born of the proposition that all legitimate governments must secure the equal right of every person to "Life, Liberty, and the pursuit of Happiness." In the ordinary case, we quite naturally assume that these three ends are compatible, mutually enhancing, and perhaps even coincident.

The Court would make an exception here. It permits the State's abstract, undifferentiated interest in the preservation of life to overwhelm the best interests of Nancy Beth Cruzan, interests which would, according to an undisputed finding, be served by allowing her guardians to exercise her constitutional right to discontinue medical treatment. Ironically, the Court reaches this conclusion despite endorsing three significant propositions which should save it from any such dilemma. First, a competent individual's decision to refuse life-sustaining medical procedures is an aspect of liberty protected by the Due Process Clause of the Fourteenth Amendment. Second, upon a proper evidentiary showing, a qualified guardian may make that decision on behalf of an incompetent ward. Third, in answering the important question presented by this tragic case, it is wise "not to attempt by any general statement, to cover every possible phase of the subject." Together, these considerations suggest that Nancy Cruzan's liberty to be free from medical treatment must be understood in light of the facts and circumstances particular to her. I would so hold: in my view, the Constitution requires the State to care for Nancy Cruzan's life in a way that gives appropriate respect to her own best interests.

This case is the first in which we consider whether, and how, the Constitution protects the liberty of seriously ill patients to be free from life-sustaining medical treatment. So put, the question is both general and profound. We need not, however, resolve the question in the abstract. Our responsibility as judges both enables and compels us to treat the problem as it is illuminated by the facts of the controversy before us. The most important of those facts are these: "Clear and convincing evidence" established that Nancy Cruzan is "oblivious to her environment except for reflexive responses to sound and perhaps to painful stimuli"; that "she has no cognitive or reflexive ability to swallow food or water"; that "she will never recover" these abilities; and that her "cerebral cortical atrophy is irreversible, permanent, progressive and ongoing." Recovery and consciousness are impossible; the highest cognitive brain function that can be hoped for is a grimace in "recognition of ordinarily painful stimuli" or an "apparent response to sound." . . .

The portion of this Court's opinion that considers the merits of this case is . . . unsatisfactory. It . . . fails to respect the best interests of the patient. It . . . relies on what is tantamount to a waiver rationale: the dying patient's best interests are put to one side, and the entire inquiry is focused on her prior expressions of intent. An innocent person's constitutional right to be free from unwanted medical treatment is thereby categorically limited to those patients who had the foresight to make an unambiguous statement of their wishes while competent. The Court's decision affords no protection to children, to young people who are victims of unexpected accidents or illnesses, or to the countless thousands of elderly persons who either fail to decide, or fail to explain, how they want to be treated if they should experience a similar fate. Because Nancy Beth Cruzan did not have the foresight to preserve her constitutional right in a living will, or some comparable "clear and convincing" alternative, her right is gone forever, and her fate is in the hands of the state legislature instead of in those of her family, her independent neutral guardian ad litem, and an impartial judge—all of whom agree on the course of action that is in her best interests. The Court's willingness to find a waiver of this constitutional right reveals a distressing misunderstanding of the importance of individual liberty.

It is perhaps predictable that courts might undervalue the liberty at stake here. Because death is so profoundly personal, public reflection upon it is unusual. As this sad case shows, however, such reflection must become more common if we are to deal responsibly with the modern circumstances of death. Medical advances have altered the physiological conditions of death in ways that may be alarming: Highly invasive treatment may perpetuate human existence through a merger of body and machine that some might reasonably regard as an insult to life, rather than as its continuation. But those same advances, and the reorganization of medical care accompanying the new science and technology, have also transformed the political and social conditions of death: people are less likely to die at home, and more likely to die in relatively public places such as hospitals or nursing homes. Ultimate questions that might once have been dealt with in intimacy by a family and its physician have now become the concern of institutions. When the institution is a state hospital, as it is in this case, the government itself becomes involved. . . .

Choices about death touch the core of liberty. Our duty, and the concomitant freedom, to come to terms with the conditions of our own mortality are undoubtedly "so rooted in the traditions and conscience of our people as to be ranked as fundamental," and indeed are essential incidents of the unalienable rights to life and liberty endowed us by our Creator. The more precise constitutional significance of death is difficult to describe; not much may be said with confidence about death unless it is said from faith, and that alone is reason enough to protect the freedom to conform choices about death to individual conscience. We may also, however, justly assume that death is not life's simple opposite, or its necessary terminus, but rather its completion. Our ethical tradition has long regarded an appreciation of mortality as essential to understanding life's significance. It may, in fact, be impossible to live for anything without being prepared to die for something. . . . These considerations cast into stark relief the injustice, and unconstitutionality, of Missouri's treatment of Nancy Beth Cruzan. Nancy Cruzan's death, when it comes, cannot be an historic act of heroism; it will inevitably be the consequence of her tragic accident. But Nancy Cruzan's interest in life, no less than that of any other person, includes an interest in how she will be thought of after her death by those whose opinions mattered to her. There can be no doubt that her life made her dear to her family, and to others. How she dies will affect how that life is remembered. The trial court's order authorizing Nancy's parents to cease their daughter's treatment would have permitted the family that cares for Nancy to bring to a close her tragedy and her death. Missouri's objection to that order subordinates Nancy's body, her family, and the lasting significance of her life to the State's own interests. The decision we review thereby interferes with constitutional interests of the highest order. . . .

Nancy Cruzan, it must be remembered, is not now simply incompetent. She is in a persistent vegetative state, and has been so for seven years. The trial court found, and no party contested, that Nancy has no possibility of recovery, and no consciousness. It seems to me that the Court errs insofar as it characterizes this case as involving "judgments about the 'quality' of life that a particular individual may enjoy." Nancy Cruzan is obviously "alive" in a physiological sense. But for patients like Nancy Cruzan, who have no consciousness and no chance of recovery, there is a serious question as to whether the mere persistence of their bodies is "life" as that word is commonly understood, or as it is used in both the Constitution and the Declaration of Independence. The State's unflagging determination to perpetuate Nancy Cruzan's physical existence is comprehensible only as an effort to define life's meaning, not as an attempt to preserve its sanctity. . . .

In short, there is no reasonable ground for believing that Nancy Beth Cruzan has any personal interest in the perpetuation of what the State has decided is her life. As I have already suggested, it would be possible to hypothesize such

an interest on the basis of theological or philosophical conjecture. But even to posit such a basis for the State's action is to condemn it. It is not within the province of secular government to circumscribe the liberties of the people by regulations designed wholly for the purpose of establishing a sectarian definition of life. My disagreement with the Court is thus unrelated to its endorsement of the clear and convincing standard of proof for cases of this kind. Indeed, I agree that the controlling facts must be established with unmistakable clarity. The critical question, however, is not how to prove the controlling facts but rather what proven facts should be controlling. In my view, the constitutional answer is clear: the best interests of the individual, especially when buttressed by the interests of all related third parties, must prevail over any general state policy that simply ignores those interests. Indeed, the only apparent secular basis for the State's interest in life is the policy's persuasive impact upon people other than Nancy and her family. Yet, "[a]lthough the State may properly perform a teaching function," and although that teaching may foster respect for the sanctity of life, the State may not pursue its project by infringing constitutionally protected interests for "symbolic effect." The failure of Missouri's policy to heed the interests of a dying individual with respect to matters so private is ample evidence of the policy's illegitimacy. . . .

Only because Missouri has arrogated to itself the power to define life, and only because the Court permits this usurpation, are Nancy Cruzan's life and liberty put into disquieting conflict. If Nancy Cruzan's life were defined by reference to her own interests, so that her life expired when her biological existence ceased serving any of her own interests, then her constitutionally protected interest in freedom from unwanted treatment would not come into conflict with her constitutionally protected interest in life. Conversely, if there were any evidence that Nancy Cruzan herself defined life to encompass every form of biological persistence by a human being, so that the continuation of treatment would serve Nancy's own liberty, then once again there would be no conflict between life and liberty. The opposition of life and liberty in this case are thus not the result of Nancy Cruzan's tragic accident, but are instead the artificial consequence of Missouri's effort and this Court's willingness, to abstract Nancy Cruzan's life from Nancy Cruzan's person. . . .

The Cruzan family's continuing concern provides a concrete reminder that Nancy Cruzan's interests did not disappear with her vitality or her consciousness. However commendable may be the State's interest in human life, it cannot pursue that interest by appropriating Nancy Cruzan's life as a symbol for its own purposes. Lives do not exist in abstraction from persons, and to pretend otherwise is not to honor but to desecrate the State's responsibility for protecting life. A State that seeks to demonstrate its commitment to life may do so by aiding those who are actively struggling for life and health. In this endeavor, unfortunately, no State can lack for opportunities: there can be no need to make an example of tragic cases like that of Nancy Cruzan.

I respectfully dissent.

*"In almost every State—indeed, in almost every western democracy—it is a crime to assist a suicide.
The States' assisted suicide bans are not innovations. Rather, they are long-standing expressions
of the States' commitment to the protection and preservation of all human life."*

The Question: Does a state law that makes it a crime for a physician to assist a terminally ill patient in committing suicide, by providing lethal medication, violates the Constitution's protection of "liberty" from deprivation?

The Arguments: PRO

The Supreme Court has upheld a broad "liberty" right that includes important personal decisions, such as contraception and abortion. The Court has also upheld the right of competent adults to end their lives by refusing medical treatment or nutrition. These rights should extend to those terminally ill persons who wish to end their lives but need a physician's assistance to do so. Forcing people to continue their suffering, from unbearable pain or loss of bodily control, deprives them of a choice they should be able to make for themselves.

CON

Every state but one makes it a crime to assist another person in committing suicide. This indicates a broad consensus that such a practice is wrong. Physicians take an oath and have a duty to refrain from ending their patients' lives, either directly or indirectly. Medical advances in pain relief, and treatment for depression, can help many people regain their will to live. Physician-assisted suicide could easily lead to euthanasia of people who are burdens on their families or who require costly medical treatment and care.

BACKGROUND

On January 29, 1994, three terminally ill patients, five doctors whose practice included the treatment of such patients, and a nonprofit organization called Compassion in Dying filed suit in the federal district court in Seattle. The suit challenged a Washington statute that held "a person is guilty of promoting a suicide attempt when he knowingly causes or aids another person to attempt suicide." Promoting a suicide constituted a class C felony, punishable by imprisonment for up to five years and a fine of up to ten thousand dollars. The Washington law had been on the books in one form or another since 1854, but had rarely been enforced. Even Compassion in Dying, while seemingly operating in violation of the statute, had never been threatened with prosecution. The state, it should be noted, had no law prohibiting suicide or attempted suicide.

The three patients, who all used pseudonyms, were each suffering from a terminal illness when the suit was originally filed. "Jane Roe," a 69-year-old retired pediatrician, had been almost completely bedridden and in constant pain since June 1993, as cancer had metastasized throughout her skeleton. "John Doe," a 44-year-old artist, had been diagnosed with AIDS in 1991, and his physical condition had deteriorated consistently since that time. He had also been the primary caregiver for his long-term companion, who had died

of AIDS in June 1991. Both of these patients died before the case came to trial. The third patient, 69-year-old "James Poe," suffered from emphysema, which caused him a constant sensation of suffocating, and he had to take morphine on a regular basis to calm the panic reaction. All three patients were mentally competent, and all wished to commit suicide by taking physician-prescribed drugs.

The five physicians regularly treated terminally ill patients. Harold Glucksberg was an assistant professor of oncology at the University of Washington School of Medicine. In his declaration to the court, Glucksberg had written:

> Pain management at this stage often requires the patient to choose between enduring unrelenting pain or surrendering an alert mental state because the dose of drugs adequate to alleviate the pain will impair consciousness. Many patients will choose one or the other of these options; however, some patients do not want to end their days racked with pain or in a drug-induced stupor. For some patients pain cannot be managed even with aggressive use of drugs.

*   *   *

The plaintiffs all challenged the Washington law, but on somewhat differing grounds. The patients alleged that they had a constitutionally protected liberty interest under the Fourteenth Amendment's Due Process Clause to secure physician assistance for suicide without undue governmental interference. They also attacked the statute on equal protection grounds. The physicians claimed that the Fourteenth Amendment protected their right to practice medicine consistent with their best professional judgment, including the right to assist competent terminally ill patients end their lives. Compassion in Dying feared that in carrying out its mission of assisting terminally ill patients in committing suicide, it could be criminally prosecuted for its activities "in assisting dying persons as they exercise their alleged constitutional right to hasten their own deaths."

Chief Judge Barbara Rothstein began her legal analysis, handed down on May 3, 1994, by granting the plaintiffs' claim of a liberty interest. The Supreme Court, she noted, had established "through a long line of cases that personal decisions relating to marriage, procreation, contraception, family relationships, child rearing and education are constitutionally protected." She cited the Court's decision in *Planned Parenthood v. Casey* (1992) that matters "involving the most intimate and personal choices a person may make in a lifetime, choices central to personal dignity and autonomy, are central to the liberty protected by the Fourteenth Amendment." Although *Casey* dealt with abortion, Rothstein found the decision of a terminally ill person to end his or her own life to be of the same category of "the most intimate and personal choices" and "central to personal dignity and autonomy."

Similarly, the Supreme Court in *Casey* had spoken of the suffering of the pregnant woman, which "is too intimate and personal for the State to insist, without more, upon its own vision of the woman's role, however dominant that vision has been in the course of our history and our culture." The district court therefore concluded "that the suffering of a terminally ill person cannot be deemed any less intimate or personal, or any less deserving of protection from unwarranted governmental interference, than that of a pregnant woman."

The court also found a liberty interest under the *Cruzan* decision, in which Chief Justice Rehnquist had held "that the United States Constitution would grant a competent person a constitutionally protected right to refuse lifesaving hydration and nutrition." The court then asked whether a constitutional difference could be drawn between "refusal or withdrawal of medical treatment which results in death, and the situation in this case involving competent, terminally ill individuals who wish to hasten death by self-administering drugs prescribed by a physician." "From a constitutional perspective," Rothstein concluded, "the court does not believe that a distinction can be drawn between refusing life-sustaining medical treatment and physician-assisted suicide by an uncoerced, mentally competent, terminally ill adult."

* * *

Having found that the state did impose an undue burden on the exercise of a liberty interest protected by the Fourteenth Amendment, Judge Rothstein then turned to the most interesting part of her analysis, equal protection. The Fourteenth Amendment's Equal Protection Clause, she noted, "is essentially a direction that all persons similarly situated should be treated alike." In equal protection analysis, a higher standard of review, that of strict scrutiny, is used, as opposed to the undue-burden standard of a liberty interest. The plaintiffs had claimed that Washington State law unconstitutionally distinguished between two groups of similarly situated people, those on life support or under medical treatment whose withdrawal would mean death and those who were likewise terminally ill, but not on life-sustaining equipment or treatment. The Washington Natural Death Act clearly stated that "adult persons have the fundamental right to control the decisions relating to the rendering of their own health care, including the decision to have the life sustaining treatment withheld or withdrawn, in instances of a terminal condition or permanent unconscious condition."

The court agreed, finding that no significant difference existed between adult, mentally competent, terminally ill patients on life support, who could decide to end their suffering by turning off the equipment, and adult, mentally competent, terminally ill patients who wished to end their suffering by committing suicide. By making such a distinction, Washington "creates a situation in which the fundamental rights of one group are burdened while those of a similarly situated group are not." The state's law, therefore, also violated the Fourteenth Amendment's Equal Protection Clause.

* * *

The State of Washington appealed Judge Rothstein's decision, and a panel of the Court of Appeals for the Ninth Circuit, consisting of Eugene A. Wright, John T. Noonan Jr., and Diarmuid F. O'Scannlain, heard arguments on December 7, 1994. By a vote of 2 to 1, the panel reversed the district court. In an opinion written by Judge Noonan, the majority held that the district court's conclusion that the Washington statute deprived plaintiffs of both a liberty interest protected by the Fourteenth Amendment and equal protection could not be sustained.

* * *

Losing parties in the courts of appeal often ask for a rehearing *en banc*, that is, by the full circuit court rather than by a three-judge panel, although such requests are rarely granted. But in this case, the Ninth Circuit agreed on August 1, 1995, and heard oral argument before a panel of eleven judges on October 26, 1995. By a vote of 8 to 3, the court reversed Noonan's decision and found that the Washington State statute violated the Due Process Clause of the Fourteenth Amendment.

Judge Stephen Reinhardt, in a lengthy forty-six-page opinion for the majority, described as "extremely thoughtful" Judge Rothstein's lower court opinion. . . .

The important thing about the Ninth Circuit's opinion is that Judge Reinhardt decided to focus his opinion entirely on the Due Process Clause and therefore did not feel it necessary to deal with the equal protection analysis. Although he fleshed out his argument with copious references, Reinhardt made it clear from the start that he believed the Constitution protected a right to die, and he then phrased the question as whether "prohibiting physicians from prescribing life-ending medication for use by terminally ill patients who wish to die violates the patients' due process rights." . . .

The key to the panel's analysis is that Judge Reinhardt at all times focused on what he considered the larger liberty interest, namely, the right to die, which had already been articulated by the Supreme Court in *Cruzan*. Judge Noonan, by defining the alleged liberty interest only as a right to assisted death, could ignore the larger issue, and in doing so could dismiss much of the district court's analysis. Reinhardt's approach was more encompassing. "We do not ask simply whether there is a liberty interest in receiving 'aid in killing oneself' because such a narrow interest could not exist in the absence of a broader and more important underlying interest—the right to die. In short, it is the end and not the means that defines the liberty interest."

*　*　*

On the East Coast, Dr. Timothy Quill, the doctor who had leaped into national prominence with his admission that he had helped one of his patients commit suicide, launched a legal attack against the law under which local prosecutors had tried to indict him. In July 1994 Quill, along with two other doctors, Samuel C. Klagsbrun and Howard A. Grossman, brought suit in the Southern District of New York to have New York's ban on assisted suicide declared unconstitutional. Three terminally ill patients had originally joined the suit, but all of them had died before the case went to trial, leaving only the physicians. . . .

The state asserted that no actual case or controversy existed, and therefore the suit should be dismissed as nonjusticiable. Although Chief Judge Thomas P. Griesa held that the action did in fact provide a justiciable controversy, he went on to rule that patients did not have any fundamental right to physician-assisted suicide and that the state laws criminalizing assisted suicide did not violate the Equal Protection Clause.

*　*　*

The New York decision came down seven months after Judge Rothstein had decided the Washington decision and only a week after the latter case had been argued before the three-judge panel of the Ninth Circuit. Yet the New York case did not draw as much attention as the Washington case, and the decision mentioned no *amici* briefs filed on either side. This situation had changed dramatically when the Second Circuit heard argument on the case at the beginning of September 1995, and a significant number of groups, many of whom had also filed in the Ninth Circuit, now joined the fray on the East Coast. The case came before a panel of Roger J. Miner, Guido Calabresi, and Milton Pollack, a senior district judge from the Southern District of New York sitting by designation. Miner wrote the unanimous opinion. . . .

Like the lower court, the Second Circuit rejected the state's claim that no justiciable issue existed. . . . The court then began its inquiry into whether assisted suicide could qualify as a fundamental liberty interest. "Rights that have no textual support in the language of the Constitution but qualify for heightened judicial protection include fundamental liberties so 'implicit in the concept of ordered liberty' that 'neither liberty nor justice would exist if they were sacrificed.'" While the Supreme Court had counted privacy as among the rights protected by due process, it had been reluctant to expand the meaning of privacy and had given lower courts tenuous guidelines on how they could proceed. That line, "albeit a shaky one," could be found in *Bowers v. Hardwick* (1986), where the high court had found no fundamental right to engage in consensual sodomy, since the statutes proscribing such conduct had "ancient roots." Taking its cue from that case, the appellate court declined to define physician-assisted suicide as a right implicit in the concept of ordered liberty. . . .

Such restraint, however, seemed to evaporate as the court turned to the plaintiffs' other argument, that a denial of physician-assisted suicide violated the Equal Protection Clause. Seeking an appropriate level of review, the court reviewed those types of legislation that called for rational basis (matters of social welfare and economics), intermediate scrutiny (matters of gender and illegitimacy), and strict scrutiny (matters involving suspect classes). It then concluded that the prohibition against physician-assisted suicide fell into the class of social welfare and could be examined under a rational basis test. . . .

After reviewing the Supreme Court's holding in *Cruzan*, Judge Miner concluded that "it seems clear that New York does not treat similarly circumstanced people alike: those in the final stages of terminal illness who are on life-support systems are allowed to hasten their deaths by directing the removal of such systems, but those who are similarly situated, except for the previous attachment of life-sustaining equipment, are not allowed to hasten death by self-administering prescribed drugs." The court could see little difference between assisted suicide and the withholding or withdrawal of treatment.

Having found unequal treatment, the court then had to determine whether a rational basis existed for establishing such inequality. At oral argument, the state had argued that its "principal interest is in preserving the life of all its citizens at all times and under all conditions," to which Miner responded:

> But what interest can the state possibly have in requiring the prolongation of a life that is all but ended? Surely, the state's interest lessens as the potential for life diminishes. And what business is it of the state to require the continuation of agony when the result is imminent and inevitable? What concern prompts the state to interfere with a mentally competent patient's "right to define [his] own concept of existence, of meaning, of the universe, and of the mystery of human life," when the patient seeks to have drugs prescribed to end life during the final stages of a terminal illness? The greatly reduced interest of the state in preserving life compels the answer to these questions: "None."

In conclusion, the court found that New York statutes criminalizing assisted suicide violated the Equal Protection Clause, insofar as preventing a doctor from prescribing drugs to a mentally competent patient bore no rational relationship to any legitimate state interest (Urofsky, 2000).

CHIEF JUSTICE REHNQUIST delivered the opinion of the Court.

The question presented in this case is whether Washington's prohibition against "caus[ing]" or "aid[ing]" a suicide offends the Fourteenth Amendment to the United States Constitution. We hold that it does not.

It has always been a crime to assist a suicide in the State of Washington. In 1854, Washington's first Territorial Legislature outlawed "assisting another in the commission of self murder." Today, Washington law provides: "A person is guilty of promoting a suicide attempt when he knowingly causes or aids another person to attempt suicide." "Promoting a suicide attempt" is a felony, punishable by up to five years' imprisonment and up to a $10,000 fine. At the same time, Washington's Natural Death Act, enacted in 1979, states that the "withholding or withdrawal of life sustaining treatment" at a patient's direction "shall not, for any purpose, constitute a suicide."

Petitioners in this case are the State of Washington and its Attorney General. Respondents Harold Glucksberg, M.D., Abigail Halperin, M.D., Thomas A. Preston, M.D., and Peter Shalit, M.D., are physicians who practice in Washington. These doctors occasionally treat terminally ill, suffering patients, and declare that they would assist these patients in ending their lives if not for Washington's assisted suicide ban. In January 1994, respondents, along with three gravely ill, pseudonymous plaintiffs who have since died and Compassion in Dying, a nonprofit organization that counsels people considering physician assisted suicide, sued in the United States District Court, seeking a declaration that [the Washington ban on assisted suicide] is, on its face, unconstitutional. The plaintiffs asserted "the existence of a liberty interest protected by the Fourteenth Amendment which extends to a personal choice by a mentally competent, terminally ill adult to commit physician assisted suicide." Relying primarily on Planned Parenthood v. Casey (1992), and Cruzan v. Director, Missouri Dept. of Health (1990), the District Court agreed, and concluded that Washington's assisted suicide ban is unconstitutional because it "places an undue burden on the exercise of [that] constitutionally protected liberty interest." The District Court also decided that the Washington statute violated the Equal Protection Clause's requirement that "all persons similarly situated . . . be treated alike."

A panel of the Court of Appeals for the Ninth Circuit reversed, emphasizing that "[i]n the two hundred and five years of our existence no constitutional right to aid in killing oneself has ever been asserted and upheld by a court of final jurisdiction." The Ninth Circuit reheard the case en banc, reversed the panel's decision, and affirmed the District Court. Like the District Court, the en banc Court of Appeals emphasized our Casey and Cruzan decisions. The court also discussed what it described as "historical" and "current societal attitudes" toward suicide and assisted suicide, and concluded that "the Constitution encompasses a due process liberty interest in controlling the time and manner of one's death—that there is, in short, a constitutionally recognized 'right to die.'" After "[w]eighing and then balancing" this interest against Washington's various interests, the court held that the State's assisted suicide ban was unconstitutional "as applied to terminally ill competent adults who wish to hasten their deaths with medication prescribed by their physicians." The court did not reach the District Court's equal protection holding. We granted certiorari, and now reverse.

We begin, as we do in all due process cases, by examining our Nation's history, legal traditions, and practices. In almost every State—indeed, in almost every western democracy—it is a crime to assist a suicide. The States' assisted suicide bans are not innovations. Rather, they are longstanding expressions of the States' commitment to the protection and preservation of all human life. . . . Indeed, opposition to and condemnation of suicide—and, therefore, of assisting suicide—are consistent and enduring themes of our philosophical, legal, and cultural heritages. More specifically, for over 700 years, the Anglo American common law tradition has punished or otherwise disapproved of both suicide and assisting suicide. . . . Though deeply rooted, the States' assisted suicide bans have in recent years been reexamined and, generally, reaffirmed. Because of advances in medicine and technology, Americans today are increasingly likely to die in institutions, from chronic illnesses. Public concern and democratic action are therefore sharply focused on how best to protect dignity and independence at the end of life, with the result that there have been many significant changes in state laws and in the attitudes these laws reflect. Many States, for example, now permit "living wills," surrogate health care decision-making, and the withdrawal or refusal of life sustaining medical treatment. At the same time, however, voters and legislators continue for the most part to reaffirm their States' prohibitions on assisting suicide. . . . Despite changes in medical technology and notwithstanding an increased emphasis on the importance of end of life decision-making, we have not retreated from this prohibition. Against this backdrop of history, tradition, and practice, we now turn to respondents' constitutional claim.

The Due Process Clause guarantees more than fair process, and the "liberty" it protects includes more than the absence of physical restraint. In a long line of cases, we have held that, in addition to the specific freedoms protected by the Bill of Rights, the "liberty" specially protected by the Due Process Clause includes the rights to marry, Loving v. Virginia (1967); to have children, Skinner v. Oklahoma (1942); to direct the education and upbringing of one's children, Meyer v. Nebraska (1923) [and] Pierce v. Society of Sisters (1925); to marital privacy, Griswold v. Connecticut (1965); . . . and to abortion, Casey. We have also assumed, and strongly suggested, that the Due Process Clause protects the traditional right to refuse unwanted lifesaving medical treatment. Cruzan. But we "ha[ve] always been reluctant to expand the concept of substantive due process because guideposts for responsible decision-making in this uncharted area are scarce and open ended." By extending constitutional protection to an asserted right or liberty interest, we, to a great extent, place the matter outside the arena of public debate and legislative action. We must therefore "exercise the utmost care whenever we are asked to break new ground in this field," lest the liberty protected by the Due Process Clause be subtly transformed into the policy preferences of the members of this Court.

Our established method of substantive due process analysis has two primary features: First, we have regularly observed that the Due Process Clause specially protects those fundamental rights and liberties which are, objectively, "deeply rooted in this Nation's history and tradition," and "implicit in the concept of ordered liberty," such that "neither liberty nor justice would exist if they were sacrificed," Palko v. Connecticut (1937). Second, we have required in substantive due process cases a "careful description" of the asserted fundamental liberty interest. Our Nation's history, legal traditions, and practices thus provide the crucial "guideposts for responsible decisionmaking," that direct and restrain our exposition of the Due Process Clause. . . . In our view, however, the development of this Court's substantive due process jurisprudence has been a process whereby the outlines of the "liberty" specially protected by the Fourteenth Amendment—never fully clarified, to be sure, and perhaps not capable of being fully clarified—have at least been carefully refined by concrete examples involving fundamental rights found to be deeply rooted in our legal tradition. This approach tends to rein in the subjective elements that are necessarily present in due process judicial review. In addition, by establishing a threshold requirement—that a challenged state action implicate a fundamental right—before requiring more than a reasonable relation to a legitimate state interest to justify the action, it avoids the need for complex balancing of competing interests in every case.

Turning to the claim at issue here, . . . [w]e now inquire whether this asserted right has any place in our Nation's traditions. Here, we are confronted with a consistent and almost universal tradition that has long rejected the asserted right, and continues explicitly to reject it today, even for terminally ill, mentally competent adults. To hold for respondents, we would have to reverse centuries of legal doctrine and practice, and strike down the considered policy choice of almost every State.

Respondents contend, however, that the liberty interest they assert is consistent with this Court's substantive due process line of cases, if not with this Nation's history and practice. . . . According to respondents, our liberty jurisprudence, and the broad, individualistic principles it reflects, protects the "liberty of competent, terminally ill adults to make end of life decisions free of undue government interference." The question presented in this case, however, is whether the protections of the Due Process Clause include a right to commit suicide with another's assistance. . . . The history of the law's treatment of assisted suicide in this country has been and continues to be one of the rejection of nearly all efforts to permit it. That being the case, our decisions lead us to conclude that the asserted "right" to assistance in committing suicide is not a fundamental liberty interest protected by the Due Process Clause. The Constitution also requires, however, that Washington's assisted suicide ban be rationally related to legitimate government interests. This requirement is unquestionably met here. . . .

First, Washington has an "unqualified interest in the preservation of human life." The State's prohibition on assisted suicide, like all homicide laws, both reflects and advances its commitment to this interest. . . . The State also has an interest in protecting the integrity and ethics of the medical profession. . . . [T]he American Medical Association, like many other medical and physicians' groups, has concluded that "[p]hysician assisted suicide is fundamentally incompatible with the physician's role as healer." And physician assisted suicide could, it is argued, undermine the trust that is essential to the doctor patient relationship by blurring the time honored line between healing and harming. Next, the State has an interest in protecting vulnerable groups—including the poor, the elderly, and disabled persons—from abuse, neglect, and mistakes. . . . If physician assisted suicide were permitted, many might resort to it to spare their families the substantial financial burden of end of life health care costs. . . . The State's interest here goes beyond protecting the vulnerable from coercion; it extends to protecting disabled and terminally ill people from prejudice, negative and inaccurate stereotypes, and "societal indifference." The State's assisted suicide ban reflects and reinforces its policy that the lives of terminally ill, disabled, and elderly people must be no less valued than the lives of the young and healthy, and that a seriously disabled person's suicidal impulses should be interpreted and treated the same way as anyone else's.

Finally, the State may fear that permitting assisted suicide will start it down the path to voluntary and perhaps even involuntary euthanasia. . . . This concern is further supported by evidence about the practice of euthanasia in the Netherlands. The Dutch government's own study revealed that in 1990, there were 2,300 cases of voluntary euthanasia (defined as "the deliberate termination of another's life at his request"), 400 cases of assisted suicide, and more than 1,000 cases of euthanasia without an explicit request. In addition to these latter 1,000 cases, the study found an additional 4,941 cases where physicians administered lethal morphine overdoses without the patients' explicit consent. This study suggests that, despite the existence of various reporting procedures, euthanasia in the Netherlands has not been limited to competent, terminally ill adults who are enduring physical suffering, and that regulation of the practice may not have prevented abuses in cases involving vulnerable persons, including severely disabled neonates and elderly persons suffering from dementia. . . . Washington, like most other States, reasonably ensures against this risk by banning, rather than regulating, assisting suicide.

We need not weigh exactly the relative strengths of these various interests. They are unquestionably important and legitimate, and Washington's ban on assisted suicide is at least reasonably related to their promotion and protection. We therefore hold that [the challenged law] does not violate the Fourteenth Amendment, either on its face or "as applied to competent, terminally ill adults who wish to hasten their deaths by obtaining medication prescribed by their doctors."

Throughout the Nation, Americans are engaged in an earnest and profound debate about the morality, legality, and practicality of physician-assisted suicide. Our holding permits this debate to continue, as it should in a democratic society. The decision of the en banc Court of Appeals is reversed, and the case is remanded for further proceedings consistent with this opinion.

It is so ordered.

VACCO V. QUILL
521 U.S. 793 (1997)

CHIEF JUSTICE REHNQUIST delivered the opinion of the Court.

In New York, as in most States, it is a crime to aid another to commit or attempt suicide, but patients may refuse even life-saving medical treatment. The question presented by this case is whether New York's prohibition on assisting suicide therefore violates the Equal Protection Clause of the Fourteenth Amendment. We hold that it does not.

Petitioners are various New York public officials. Respondents Timothy E. Quill, Samuel C. Klagsbrun, and Howard A. Grossman are physicians who practice in New York. They assert that although it would be "consistent with the standards of [their] medical practice[s]" to prescribe lethal medication for "mentally competent, terminally ill patients" who are suffering great pain and desire a doctor's help in taking their own lives, they are deterred from doing so by New York's ban on assisting suicide. Respondents, and three gravely ill patients who have since died, sued the State's Attorney General in the United States District Court. They urged that because New York permits a competent person to refuse life sustaining medical treatment, and because the refusal of such treatment is "essentially the same thing" as physician assisted suicide, New York's assisted suicide ban violates the Equal Protection Clause.

The District Court disagreed: "[I]t is hardly unreasonable or irrational for the State to recognize a difference between allowing nature to take its course, even in the most severe situations, and intentionally using an artificial death producing device." The court noted New York's "obvious legitimate interests in preserving life, and in protecting vulnerable persons," and concluded that "[u]nder the United States Constitution and the federal system it establishes, the resolution of this issue is left to the normal democratic processes within the State."

The Court of Appeals for the Second Circuit reversed. The court determined that, despite the assisted suicide ban's apparent general applicability, "New York law does not treat equally all competent persons who are in the final stages of fatal illness and wish to hasten their deaths," because "those in the final stages of terminal illness who are on life support systems are allowed to hasten their deaths by directing the removal of such systems; but those who are similarly situated, except for the previous attachment of life sustaining equipment, are not allowed to hasten death by self administering prescribed drugs. . . . The Court of Appeals then examined whether this supposed unequal treatment was rationally related to any legitimate state interests, and concluded that "to the extent that [New York's statutes] prohibit a physician from prescribing medications to be self administered by a mentally competent, terminally ill person in the final stages of his terminal illness, they are not rationally related to any legitimate state interest." We granted certiorari, and now reverse. . . .

On their faces, neither New York's ban on assisting suicide nor its statutes permitting patients to refuse medical treatment treat anyone differently than anyone else or draw any distinctions between persons. Everyone, regardless of physical condition, is entitled, if competent, to refuse unwanted lifesaving medical treatment; no one is permitted to assist a suicide. Generally speaking, laws that apply evenhandedly to all "unquestionably comply" with the Equal Protection Clause.

The Court of Appeals, however, concluded that some terminally ill people—those who are on life support systems—are treated differently than those who are not, in that the former may "hasten death" by ending treatment, but the latter may not "hasten death" through physician assisted suicide. This conclusion depends on the submission that ending or refusing lifesaving medical treatment "is nothing more nor less than assisted suicide." Unlike the Court of Appeals, we think the distinction between assisting suicide and withdrawing life sustaining treatment, a distinction widely recognized and endorsed in the medical profession and in our legal traditions, is both important and logical; it is certainly rational. The distinction comports with fundamental legal principles of causation and intent. First, when a patient refuses life sustaining medical treatment, he dies from an underlying fatal disease or pathology; but if a patient ingests lethal medication prescribed by a physician, he is killed by that medication. Furthermore, a physician who withdraws, or honors a patient's refusal to begin, life sustaining medical treatment purposefully intends, or may so intend, only to respect his patient's wishes and "to cease doing useless and futile or degrading things to the patient when [the patient] no longer stands to benefit from them." The same is true when a doctor provides aggressive palliative care; in some cases, painkilling drugs may hasten a patient's death, but the physician's purpose and intent is, or may be, only to ease his patient's pain. A doctor who assists a suicide, however, "must, necessarily and indubitably, intend primarily that the patient be made dead." Similarly, a patient who commits suicide with a doctor's aid necessarily has the specific intent to end his or her own life, while a patient who refuses or discontinues treatment might not. . . .

Given these general principles, it is not surprising that many courts, including New York courts, have carefully distinguished refusing life sustaining treatment from suicide. . . . Similarly, the overwhelming majority of state legislatures have drawn a clear line between assisting suicide and withdrawing or permitting the refusal of unwanted lifesaving medical treatment by prohibiting the former and permitting the latter. Thus, even as the States move to protect and promote patients' dignity at the end of life, they remain opposed to physician assisted suicide. . . . Logic and contemporary practice support New York's judgment that the two acts are different, and New York may therefore, consistent with the

Constitution, treat them differently. By permitting everyone to refuse unwanted medical treatment while prohibiting anyone from assisting a suicide, New York law follows a longstanding and rational distinction. . . . The judgment of the Court of Appeals is reversed.

COMMENTARY: "THE CASE FOR VOLUNTARY PHYSICIAN-ASSISTED SUICIDE"

Modern medicine has been enormously successful in saving and extending lives. No one can reasonably regret this, but it exacerbates a problem which has always been with us, namely, how to treat those who are alive, but are not living lives they think worthwhile, and have no prospects for anything better. Under current law, terminal patients who want to die can either commit suicide, or, if they are competent, refuse all treatment necessary for life. But patients do not always have the ability and opportunity to do the former, and the latter does not always bring about a gentle and easy death for either them or their loved ones. The question thus arises as to whether we should make legal provision for voluntary physician-assisted suicide and provide the means for it.

There is a strong case for allowing persons who are facing intractable pain, or indignities in the final stages of their life, to determine for themselves when life is no longer worth living and, where necessary, receive assistance in ending their life. This case is constructed from the principles of liberty, autonomy, and equality; from the value of preventing unnecessary suffering and preserving the dignity of the individual; and from the inconsistency between legally allowing suicide while denying legal space to voluntary physician-assisted suicide. If we are to continue to legally bar these practices, there must be a compelling reason for doing so.

None of the reasons that have been put forward for continuing the current absolute ban on voluntary physician-assisted suicide is compelling. These arguments include: the sanctity of life and the moral wrongness of killing; the possibility of an incorrect diagnosis or a miracle cure; the alleged inability to know that voluntary informed consent has been obtained; the "slippery slope" argument; and the ability of modern medicine to control pain. Since none of these arguments against prohibiting voluntary physician-assisted suicide is compelling, the case for the legalization of these practices is great.

The logic of the debate is this: there is admittedly a case for legalizing voluntary physician-assisted suicide; however, there is a long list of objections to doing so. If all the objections can be answered satisfactorily, the pro-legalization case will be left in sole possession of the field, and the legal system should act accordingly. On the other hand, if any of the objections are valid, that case will be cancelled and the judicial system should keep the legal door to the practices in question shut. Nevertheless, none of the objections are valid.

There are five arguments designed to provide a case for voluntary euthanasia:

1. Liberty   The first and simplest argument appeals to the value of liberty. Freedom is good. Restraint of freedom is tyranny. This forms the basis of the common view that individuals can do as they want unless there are weighty reasons that dictate otherwise. Restrictions on liberty are certainly sometimes justifiable, but the onus of justification always lies on their defenders. Thus, given that prohibiting voluntary physician-assisted suicide are restrictions on liberty—patients are prevented from getting what they want, and physicians from providing it—there is a standing case for legalizing those practices, and it is up to opponents of such practices to show why they should be forbidden.

2. Prevention of Suffering and the Dignity of the Individual   Appealing to two other equally uncontroversial values can strengthen this case: the prevention of suffering and the dignity of the individual. Patients sometimes are in medical conditions for which there is no relief, and awaiting them is a future filled with suffering, or the indignity of the disintegration of their bodily and mental functions, or both. They often want to avoid these evils and shield loved ones from their sight. It is also sometimes the case that the only way to do this is to die, and the only way to do that within a desired time is to receive some assistance in the form of help in committing voluntary physician-assisted suicide. If we now grant, as we surely must, that people have a right to preserve their dignity and minimize their suffering and that of others, we again get a strong presumption in favor of making some kind of legal allowance for voluntary euthanasia.

3. The Principle of Equality   The principle of equality supports a further argument. Prohibition against voluntary physician-assisted suicide creates an inequality since it prevents persons physically unable to end their lives unassisted from choosing suicide, when that option is open to others. Although the blanket prohibition on voluntary physician-assisted suicide appears to treat all persons equally, its actual effect is to deprive people who are unable to end their suffering the ability to do so in any way that is lawful.

4. Consistency with Legal Passive Voluntary Euthanasia   Finally, we turn to a pair of arguments which proceed by alleging there is an inconsistency between what the law permits and prohibits, and since it is right to permit what it does, the prohibition should be removed. The first of these begins with the fact that passive voluntary euthanasia is allowed by the law: a competent and fully informed person may, for whatever reason, appropriately refuse any treatment necessary for life. Thus, if active voluntary euthanasia is to be legally proscribed, there must be some relevant difference between killing and letting die. It is, however, not clear that there is a difference. If both the intention—to bring about a death—and the certainty of outcome—death coming about—are the same in each situation, it is hard to see how there could be any morally relevant difference between killing patients and letting them die. It does not follow that we can appropriately aid persons in securing their death by refusing treatment, for even when they refuse treatment for bad reasons, and while there may be nothing immoral or properly preventable about them harming themselves, there is something wrong in our assisting them in doing so. However, it does follow that if they have a good reason for refusing treatment—if, say, their future is brief and only holds pain and indignity—there is a presumption that there is nothing wrong with our assisting them while they are refusing treatment, and the law should not stand in our way either to help them end their suffering or to euthanize them on their authority.

5. Consistency with Legal Suicide   Our second argument runs along exactly similar lines, and begins with the fact that suicide is not a criminal offense. This does not mean we should not prevent suicide when we can. In all cases we certainly should because most of those who wish to commit suicide typically have very bad reasons for wanting to die, and they need our help. But suicide cannot be prevented in all cases. If some people have a good reason for wanting to die—if, for instance, they are elderly and terminal and suffering—it

would be unspeakably meddlesome to interfere. But if we do interfere, we get the presumption that in just those circumstances in which we should not prevent some people from bringing about their own death, we can appropriately help them do so by voluntary physician-assisted suicide. If some people do have a good reason to die, and do not have the means to end their suffering, they should be legally allowed to request and receive those means from those willing to provide them, and if they are too weak to swallow a pill or inject themselves, to authorize others to deliver the fatal dose. Thus, under certain conditions, the right to suicide entails the right to voluntary physician-assisted suicide—even though suicide is morally unjustifiable and voluntary euthanasia is not. This completes the case for the legalization of voluntary euthanasia. Insofar as we value liberty, the prevention of suffering, and dignity, and admit that sometimes people have a good reason for wanting to die and need help to do so—all surely uncontroversial claims—there is no avoiding the conclusion that the burden of proof lies on those who wish to oppose legalizing the practices in question (Williams, 2004).

COMMENTARY: "WHAT'S WRONG WITH MAKING ASSISTING SUICIDE LEGAL?"

Many argue that a decision to kill oneself is a private choice about which society has no right to be concerned. This position assumes that suicide results from competent people making autonomous, rational decisions to die, and then claims that society has no business "interfering" with a freely chosen life or death decision that harms no one other than the suicidal individual. But according to experts who have studied suicide, the basic assumption is wrong. A careful 1974 British study, which involved extensive interviews and examination of medical records, found that 93 percent of those studied who committed suicide were mentally ill at the time. A similar St. Louis study, published in 1984, found a mental disorder in 94 percent of those who committed suicide. There is a great body of psychological evidence that those who attempt suicide are normally ambivalent, that they usually attempt suicide for reasons other than a settled desire to die, and that they are predominantly the victims of mental disorder.

Still, shouldn't it be the person's own choice?

Almost all of those who attempt suicide do so as a subconscious cry for help, not after a carefully calculated judgment that death would be better than life. A suicide attempt powerfully calls attention to one's plight. The humane response is to mobilize psychiatric and social service resources to address the problems that led the would-be suicide to such an extremity. Typically, this counseling and assistance is successful. One study of 886 people who were rescued from attempted suicides found that five years later only 3.84 percent had gone on to kill themselves. A Swedish study with a 36-year follow-up found only 10.9 percent later killed themselves. Paradoxically, the prospects for a happy life are often greater for those who attempt suicide, but are stopped and helped, than for those with similar problems who never attempt suicide. In the words of academic psychiatrist Dr. Erwin Stengel, "The suicidal attempt is a highly effective though hazardous way of influencing others and its effects are as a rule . . . lasting." In short, suicidal people should be helped with their problems, not helped to die.

But shouldn't we distinguish between those who are emotionally unbalanced and those who are making a rational, competent decision?

Psychologist Joseph Richman, writing in the Journal of Suicide and Life-Threatening Behavior, notes, "[A]s a clinical suicidologist, and therapist who has interviewed or treated over 800 suicidal persons and their families, I have been impressed [that those] who are suicidal are more like each other than different, including . . . those who choose 'rational suicide.'" . . . [A]ll suicides, including the "rational," can be an avoidance of or substitute for dealing with basic life-and-death issues. The suicidal person and significant others usually do not know the reasons for the decision to commit suicide, but they give themselves reasons. That is why rational suicide is more often rationalized, based upon reasons that are unknown, unconscious, and a part of social and family system dynamics. . . . The proponents of rational suicide are often guilty of tunnel vision, defined as the absence of perceived alternatives to suicides.

What about those who are terminally ill?

Contrary to the assumptions of many in the public, a scientific study of people with terminal illness published in the American Journal of Psychiatry found that fewer than one in four expressed a wish to die, and all of those who did had clinically diagnosable depression. As Richman points out, "[E]ffective psychotherapeutic treatment is possible with the terminally ill, and only irrational prejudices prevent the greater resort to such measures." And suicidologist Dr. David C. Clark observes that depressive episodes in the seriously ill "are not less responsive to medication" than depression in others. Indeed, the suicide rate in persons with terminal illness is only between 2 percent and 4 percent. Compassionate counseling and assistance, such as that provided in many hospices, together with medical and psychological care, provide a positive alternative to euthanasia among those who have terminal illness.

What about those in uncontrollable pain?

They are not getting adequate medical care and should be provided up-to-date means of pain control, not killed. Even Dr. Pieter Admiraal, a leader of the successful movement to legalize direct killing in the Netherlands, has publicly observed that pain is never an adequate justification for euthanasia in light of current medical techniques that can manage pain in virtually all circumstances. Why, then, are there so many personal stories of people in hospitals and nursing homes having to cope with unbearable pain? Tragically, pain control techniques that have been perfected at the frontiers of medicine have not become universally known at the clinical level. What we need is better training in those techniques for health care personnel—not the legalization of physician-aided death.

What about those with severe disabilities?

What would it say about our attitude as a society were we to tell those who have neither terminal illness nor a disability, "You say you want to be killed, but what you really need is counseling and assistance," but, at the same time, we were to tell those with disabilities, "We understand why you want to be killed, and we'll let a doctor kill you"? It would certainly not mean that we were respecting the "choice" of the person with the disability. Instead, we would be discriminatorily denying suicide counseling on the basis of disability. We'd be saying to the nondisabled person, "We care too much about you to let you throw your life away," but to the person with the disability, "We agree that life with a disability is not worth living." True respect for the rights of people with disabilities would dictate action to remove those obstacles—not "help" in committing suicide. Most people with disabilities will tell you that it is not so much their physical or mental impairment itself that makes their lives difficult as it is the conduct of the nondisabled majority toward them. Denial of access, discrimination in employment, and an attitude of aversion or pity instead of respect are what make life intolerable. True respect for the rights of people with disabilities would dictate action to remove those obstacles—not "help" in committing suicide.

Opponents of legalizing assisting suicide say it will lead to nonvoluntary euthanasia. Aren't these overblown scare tactics?

Absolutely not. As attorney Walter Weber has written in the Journal of Suicide and Life-Threatening Behavior, "Under the equal-protection clause of the Fourteenth Amendment to the U.S Constitution, legislative classifications that restrict constitutional rights are subject to strict scrutiny and will be struck down unless narrowly tailored to further a compelling governmental interest. . . . A right to choose death for oneself would also probably extend to incompetent individuals. . . . [A] number of lower courts have held that an incompetent patient does not lose his or her right to consent to termination of life-supporting care by virtue of his or her incompetency. . . . [T]he ["substituted judgment"] doctrine authorizes . . . indeed, requires—a substitute decision maker, whether the court or a designated third party, to decide what the incompetent person would choose, if that person were competent. . . . Therefore infants, those with mental illness, retarded people, confused or senile elderly individuals, and other incompetent people would be entitled to have someone else enforce their right to die. Thus, if direct killing is legalized on request of a competent person, under court precedents that have already been set, someone who is not competent could be killed at the direction of that person's guardian even though the incompetent patient had never expressed a desire to be killed (Balch).

COMMENTARY: OREGON DEPARTMENT OF HUMAN SERVICES: FIFTH ANNUAL REPORT ON OREGON'S DEATH WITH DIGNITY ACT

Physician-assisted suicide (PAS) has been legal in Oregon since November 1997, when the Death with Dignity Act was approved by Oregon voters for the second time. In this fifth annual report, we characterize the 38 Oregonians who ingested legally-prescribed lethal medications during 1998–2002, and look at whether the numbers and characteristics of these patients differ from those who used PAS in prior years. Patients choosing PAS were identified through mandated physician and pharmacy reporting. Our information comes from these reports, physician interviews, and death certificates. We also compare the demographic characteristics of patients participating during 2002 with other Oregonians who died of the same underlying causes.

Mandated reporting of prescriptions written for lethal medication provides the Department of Human Services (DHS) with a unique opportunity to describe terminally ill patients choosing legal PAS. Both the number of prescriptions written and the number of Oregonians using PAS have increased over the five years that PAS has been legal in Oregon. In 2002, a total of 58 prescriptions of lethal doses of medication were written by 33 physicians. The number of prescriptions written has increased over the five years since legalization: 44 prescriptions were written in 2001, 39 prescriptions were written in 2000, 33 in 1999, and 24 in 1998. Thirty-six of the fifth-year prescription recipients died after ingesting the medication, 16 died from their illness, and six were alive on December 31, 2002. In addition, two patients who received prescriptions during 2001 died in 2002 after ingesting their medication for a total of 38 PAS deaths during 2002. The number of patients ingesting lethal medication has also increased over the five years since legalization. The 38 PAS deaths in 2002 compares to 21 in 2001, 27 in 2000, 27 in 1999, and 16 in 1998. The 38 patients who ingested lethal medications in 2002 represent an estimated 13/10,000 total deaths, compared with 6/10,000 in 1998 and 9/10,000 in both 1999 and 2000, and 7/10,000 in 2001. As in previous years, the majority of participants in 2002 were older (median age 69 years), well educated (50% had had some college), and had cancer (84%).

During the past five years, the 129 patients who took lethal medications differed in some ways from the 42,274 Oregonians dying from the same underlying diseases; rates of participation in PAS decreased with age, but were higher among those who were divorced, those with more years of education, and those with terminal cancer or amyotrophic lateral sclerosis. Physicians indicated that patient requests for lethal medications stemmed from multiple concerns related to autonomy and control at the end of life. The three most commonly mentioned end-of-life concerns during 2002 were: loss of autonomy, a decreasing ability to participate in activities that made life enjoyable, and losing control of bodily functions. . . . The median interval between ingestion and death varied by medication and dose: 30 minutes when 9 grams of secobarbital were prescribed, 60 minutes when 9 grams of pentobarbital were prescribed, 15 minutes when 10 grams of pentobarbital were prescribed. . . . One-half of patients became unconscious within five minutes and died within 20 minutes. The range of time from ingestion to death was five minutes to 14 hours. Emergency medical services were not called for any patient.

Although the number of Oregonians ingesting legally prescribed lethal medications has increased, the overall number of terminally ill patients ingesting lethal medication has remained small with fewer than 1/8 of 1 percent of Oregonians dying by physician-assisted suicide.

Appendix A

United States Constitution

We the People of the United States, in Order to form a more perfect Union, establish Justice, insure domestic Tranquility, provide for the common defence, promote the general Welfare, and secure the Blessings of Liberty to ourselves and our Posterity, do ordain and establish this Constitution for the United States of America.

Article I

Section 1. All legislative Powers herein granted shall be vested in a Congress of the United States, which shall consist of a Senate and House of Representatives.

Section 2. The House of Representatives shall be composed of Members chosen every second Year by the People of the several States, and the Electors in each State shall have the Qualifications requisite for Electors of the most numerous Branch of the State Legislature.

No Person shall be a Representative who shall not have attained to the age of twenty five Years, and been seven Years a Citizen of the United States, and who shall not, when elected, be an Inhabitant of that State in which he shall be chosen.

[Representatives and direct Taxes shall be apportioned among the several States which may be included within this Union, according to their respective Numbers, which shall be determined by adding to the whole Number of free Persons, including those bound to Service for a Term of Years, and excluding Indians not taxed, three fifths of all other Persons.][1] The actual Enumeration shall be made within three Years after the first Meeting of the Congress of the United States, and within every subsequent Term of ten Years, in such Manner as they shall by Law direct. The Number of Representatives shall not exceed one for every thirty Thousand, but each State shall have at Least one Representative; and until such enumeration shall be made, the State of New Hampshire shall be entitled to chuse three, Massachusetts eight, Rhode-Island and Providence Plantations one, Connecticut five, New York six, New Jersey four, Pennsylvania eight, Delaware one, Maryland six, Virginia ten, North Carolina five, South Carolina five, and Georgia three.

When vacancies happen in the Representation from any State, the Executive Authority thereof shall issue Writs of Election to fill such Vacancies.

The House of Representatives shall chuse their Speaker and other Officers; and shall have the sole Power of Impeachment.

Section 3. The Senate of the United States shall be composed of two Senators from each State, [chosen by the Legislature thereof,][2] for six Years; and each Senator shall have one Vote.

Immediately after they shall be assembled in Consequence of the first Election, they shall be divided as equally as may be into three Classes. The Seats of the Senators of the first Class shall be vacated at the Expiration of the second Year, of the second Class at the Expiration of the fourth Year, and of the third Class at the Expiration of the sixth Year, so that one third may be chosen every second Year; [and if Vacancies happen by Resignation, or otherwise, during the Recess of the Legislature of any State, the Executive thereof may make temporary Appointments until the

---

[1]The part in brackets was changed by Section 2 of the Fourteenth Amendment.

[2]The part in brackets was changed by the first paragraph of the Seventeenth Amendment.

next Meeting of the Legislature, which shall then fill such Vacancies].[3]

No Person shall be a Senator who shall not have attained to the Age of thirty Years, and been nine Years a Citizen of the United States, and who shall not, when elected, be an Inhabitant of that State for which he shall be chosen.

The Vice President of the United States shall be President of the Senate, but shall have no Vote, unless they be equally divided.

The Senate shall chuse their other Officers, and also a President pro tempore, in the Absence of the Vice President, or when he shall exercise the Office of President of the United States.

The Senate shall have the sole Power to try all Impeachments. When sitting for that Purpose, they shall be on Oath or Affirmation. When the President of the United States is tried, the Chief Justice shall preside: And no Person shall be convicted without the Concurrence of two thirds of the Members present.

Judgment in Cases of Impeachment shall not extend further than to removal from Office, and disqualification to hold and enjoy any Office of honor, Trust or Profit under the United States: but the Party convicted shall nevertheless be liable and subject to Indictment, Trial, Judgment and Punishment, according to Law.

Section 4. The Times, Places and Manner of holding Elections for Senators and Representatives, shall be prescribed in each State by the Legislature thereof; but the Congress may at any time by Law make or alter such Regulations, except as to the Places of chusing Senators.

The Congress shall assemble at least once in every Year, and such Meeting shall [be on the first Monday in December],[4] unless they shall by Law appoint a different day.

Section 5. Each House shall be the Judge of the Elections, Returns and Qualifications of its own Members, and a Majority of each shall constitute a Quorum to do Business; but a smaller Number may adjourn from day to day, and may be authorized to compel the Attendance of absent Members, in such Manner, and under such Penalties as each House may provide.

Each House may determine the Rules of its Proceedings, punish its Members for disorderly Behaviour, and, with the Concurrence of two thirds, expel a Member.

Each House shall keep a Journal of its Proceedings, and from time to time publish the same, excepting such Parts as may in their Judgment require Secrecy; and the Yeas and Nays of the Members of either House on any question shall, at the Desire of one fifth of those Present, be entered on the Journal.

Neither House, during the Session of Congress, shall, without the Consent of the other, adjourn for more than three days, nor to any other Place than that in which the two Houses shall be sitting.

Section 6. The Senators and Representatives shall receive a Compensation for their Services, to be ascertained by Law, and paid out of the Treasury of the United States. They shall in all Cases, except Treason, Felony and Breach of the Peace,

be privileged from Arrest during their Attendance at the Session of their respective Houses, and in going to and returning from the same; and for any Speech or Debate in either House, they shall not be questioned in any other Place.

No Senator or Representative shall, during the Time for which he was elected, be appointed to any civil Office under the Authority of the United States, which shall have been created, or the Emoluments whereof shall have been encreased during such time; and no Person holding any Office under the United States, shall be a Member of either House during his Continuance in Office.

Section 7. All Bills for raising Revenue shall originate in the House of Representatives; but the Senate may propose or concur with Amendments as on other Bills.

Every Bill which shall have passed the House of Representatives and the Senate, shall, before it become a Law, be presented to the President of the United States; If he approve he shall sign it, but if not he shall return it, with his Objections to that House in which it shall have originated, who shall enter the Objections at large on their Journal, and proceed to reconsider it. If after such Reconsideration two thirds of that House shall agree to pass the Bill, it shall be sent, together with the Objections, to the other House, by which it shall likewise be reconsidered, and if approved by two thirds of that House, it shall become a Law. But in all such Cases the Votes of both Houses shall be determined by yeas and Nays, and the Names of the Persons voting for and against the Bill shall be entered on the Journal of each House respectively. If any Bill shall not be returned by the President within ten Days (Sundays excepted) after it shall have been presented to him, the Same shall be a Law, in like Manner as if he had signed it, unless the Congress by their Adjournment prevent its Return, in which Case it shall not be a Law.

Every Order, Resolution, or Vote to which the Concurrence of the Senate and House of Representatives may be necessary (except on a question of Adjournment) shall be presented to the President of the United States; and before the Same shall take Effect, shall be approved by him, or being disapproved by him, shall be repassed by two thirds of the Senate and House of Representatives, according to the Rules and Limitations prescribed in the Case of a Bill.

Section 8. The Congress shall have Power To lay and collect Taxes, Duties, Imposts and Excises, to pay the Debts and provide for the common Defence and general Welfare of the United States; but all Duties, Imposts and Excises shall be uniform throughout the United States;

To borrow Money on the credit of the United States;

To regulate Commerce with foreign Nations, and among the several States, and with the Indian Tribes;

To establish an uniform Rule of Naturalization, and uniform Laws on the subject of Bankruptcies throughout the United States;

To coin Money, regulate the Value thereof, and of foreign Coin, and fix the Standard of Weights and Measures;

To provide for the Punishment of counterfeiting the Securities and current Coin of the United States;

To establish Post Offices and post Roads;

To promote the Progress of Science and useful Arts, by securing for limited Times to Authors and Inventors the exclusive Right to their respective Writings and Discoveries;

---

[3]The part in brackets was changed by the second paragraph of the Seventeenth Amendment.

[4]The part in brackets was changed by Section 2 of the Twentieth Amendment.

To constitute Tribunals inferior to the supreme Court;

To define and punish Piracies and Felonies committed on the high Seas, and Offences against the Law of Nations;

To declare War, grant Letters of Marque and Reprisal, and make Rules concerning Captures on Land and Water;

To raise and support Armies, but no Appropriation of Money to that Use shall be for a longer Term than two Years;

To provide and maintain a Navy;

To make Rules for the Government and Regulation of the land and naval Forces;

To provide for calling forth the Militia to execute the Laws of the Union, suppress Insurrections and repel Invasions;

To provide for organizing, arming, and disciplining, the Militia, and for governing such Part of them as may be employed in the Service of the United States, reserving to the States respectively, the Appointment of the Officers, and the Authority of training the Militia according to the discipline prescribed by Congress;

To exercise exclusive Legislation in all Cases whatsoever, over such District (not exceeding ten Miles square) as may, by Cession of particular States, and the Acceptance of Congress, become the Seat of the Government of the United States, and to exercise like Authority over all Places purchased by the Consent of the Legislature of the State in which the Same shall be, for the Erection of Forts, Magazines, Arsenals, dock-Yards, and other needful Buildings;—And

To make all Laws which shall be necessary and proper for carrying into Execution the foregoing Powers, and all other Powers vested by this Constitution in the Government of the United States, or in any Department or Officer thereof.

Section 9. The Migration or Importation of such Persons as any of the States now existing shall think proper to admit, shall not be prohibited by the Congress prior to the Year one thousand eight hundred and eight, but a Tax or duty may be imposed on such Importation, not exceeding ten dollars for each Person.

The Privilege of the Writ of Habeas Corpus shall not be suspended, unless when in Cases of Rebellion or Invasion the public Safety may require it.

No Bill of Attainder or ex post facto Law shall be passed.

No Capitation, or other direct, Tax shall be laid, unless in Proportion to the Census or Enumeration herein before directed to be taken.[5]

No Tax or Duty shall be laid on Articles exported from any State.

No Preference shall be given by any Regulation of Commerce or Revenue to the Ports of one State over those of another; nor shall Vessels bound to, or from, one State, be obliged to enter, clear, or pay Duties in another.

No Money shall be drawn from the Treasury, but in Consequence of Appropriations made by Law; and a regular Statement and Account of the Receipts and Expenditures of all public Money shall be published from time to time.

No Title of Nobility shall be granted by the United States: And no Person holding any Office of Profit or Trust under them, shall, without the Consent of the Congress, accept of any present, Emolument, Office, or Title, of any kind whatever, from any King, Prince, or foreign State.

Section 10. No State shall enter into any Treaty, Alliance, or Confederation; grant Letters of Marque and Reprisal; coin Money; emit Bills of Credit; make any Thing but gold and silver Coin a Tender in Payment of Debts; pass any Bill of Attainder, ex post facto Law, or Law impairing the Obligation of Contracts, or grant any Title of Nobility.

No State shall, without the Consent of the Congress, lay any Imposts or Duties on Imports or Exports, except what may be absolutely necessary for executing its inspection Laws; and the net Produce of all Duties and Imposts, laid by any State on Imports or Exports, shall be for the Use of the Treasury of the United States; and all such Laws shall be subject to the Revision and Controul of the Congress.

No State shall, without the Consent of Congress, lay any Duty of Tonnage, keep Troops, or Ships of War in time of Peace, enter into any Agreement or Compact with another State, or with a foreign Power, or engage in War, unless actually invaded, or in such imminent Danger as will not admit of delay.

Article II

Section 1. The executive Power shall be vested in a President of the United States of America. He shall hold his Office during the Term of four Years, and, together with the Vice President, chosen for the same Term, be elected, as follows

Each State shall appoint, in such Manner as the Legislature thereof may direct, a Number of Electors, equal to the whole Number of Senators and Representatives to which the State may be entitled in the Congress: but no Senator or Representative, or Person holding an Office of Trust or Profit under the United States, shall be appointed an Elector.

[The Electors shall meet in their respective States, and vote by Ballot for two Persons, of whom one at least shall not be an Inhabitant of the same State with themselves. And they shall make a List of all the Persons voted for, and of the Number of Votes for each; which List they shall sign and certify, and transmit sealed to the Seat of the Government of the United States, directed to the President of the Senate. The President of the Senate shall, in the Presence of the Senate and House of Representatives, open all the Certificates, and the Votes shall then be counted. The Person having the greatest Number of Votes shall be the President, if such Number be a Majority of the whole Number of Electors appointed; and if there be more than one who have such Majority, and have an equal Number of Votes, then the House of Representatives shall immediately chuse by Ballot one of them for President; and if no Person have a Majority, then from the five highest on the list the said House shall in like Manner chuse the President. But in chusing the President, the Votes shall be taken by States, the Representation from each State having one Vote; A quorum for this Purpose shall consist of a Member or Members from two thirds of the States, and a Majority of all the States shall be necessary to a Choice. In every Case, after the Choice of the President, the Person having the greatest Number of Votes of the Electors shall be the Vice President. But if there should remain two or more who have equal Votes, the Senate shall chuse from them by Ballot the Vice President.][6]

---

[5]The Sixteenth Amendment gave Congress the power to tax incomes.

[6]The material in brackets has been superseded by the Twelfth Amendment.

The Congress may determine the Time of chusing the Electors, and the Day on which they shall give their Votes; which Day shall be the same throughout the United States.

No Person except a natural born Citizen, or a Citizen of the United States, at time of the Adoption of this Constitution, shall be eligible to the Office of President; neither shall any Person be eligible to that Office who shall not have attained to the Age of thirty five Years, and been fourteen Years a Resident within the United States.

In Case of the Removal of the President from Office, or of his Death, Resignation, or Inability to discharge the Powers and Duties of the said Office,[7] the Same shall devolve on the Vice President, and the Congress may by Law provide for the Case of Removal, Death, Resignation or Inability, both of the President and Vice President, declaring what Officer shall then act as President, and such Officer shall act accordingly, until the Disability be removed, or a President shall be elected.

The President shall, at stated Times, receive for his Services, a Compensation, which shall neither be encreased nor diminished during the Period for which he shall have been elected, and he shall not receive within that Period any other Emolument from the United States, or any of them.

Before he enter on the Execution of his Office, he shall take the following Oath or Affirmation:—"I do solemnly swear (or affirm) that I will faithfully execute the Office of President of the United States, and will to the best of my Ability, preserve, protect and defend the Constitution of the United States."

Section 2. The President shall be Commander in Chief of the Army and Navy of the United States, and of the Militia of the several States, when called into the actual Service of the United States; he may require his Opinion, in writing, of the principal Officer in each of the executive Departments, upon any Subject relating to the Duties of their respective Offices, and he shall have Power to grant Reprieves and Pardons for Offences against the United States, except in Cases of Impeachment.

He shall have Power, by and with the Advice and Consent of the Senate, to make Treaties, provided two thirds of the Senators present concur; and he shall nominate, and by and with the Advice and Consent of the Senate, shall appoint Ambassadors, other public Ministers and Consuls, Judges of the supreme Court, and all other Officers of the United States, whose Appointments are not herein otherwise provided for, and which shall be established by Law: but the Congress may by Law vest the Appointment of such inferior Officers, as they think proper, in the President alone, in the Courts of Law, or in the Heads of Departments.

The President shall have Power to fill up all Vacancies that may happen during the Recess of the Senate, by granting Commissions which shall expire at the End of their next Session.

Section 3: He shall from time to time give to the Congress Information of the State of the Union, and recommend to their Consideration such Measures as he shall judge necessary and expedient; he may, on extraordinary Occasions, convene both Houses, or either of them, and in Case of Disagreement between them, with Respect to the Time of Adjournment, he may adjourn them to such Times he shall think proper; he shall receive Ambassadors and other public Ministers; he shall take Care that the Laws be faithfully executed, and shall Commission all the Officers of the United States.

Section 4. The President, Vice President and all civil Officers of the United States, shall be removed from Office on Impeachment for, and Conviction of, Treason, Bribery, or other high Crimes and Misdemeanors.

Article III

Section 1. The judicial Power of the United States, shall be vested in one supreme Court, and in such inferior Courts as the Congress may from time to time ordain and establish. The Judges, both of the supreme and inferior Courts, shall hold their Offices during good Behaviour, and shall, at stated Times, receive for their Services, a Compensation, which shall not be diminished during their Continuance in Office.

Section 2. The judicial Power shall extend to all Cases, in Law and Equity, arising under this Constitution, the Laws of the United States, and Treaties made, or which shall be made, under their Authority;—to all Cases affecting Ambassadors, other public Ministers and Consuls;—to all Cases of admiralty and maritime Jurisdiction;—to Controversies to which the United States shall be a Party;—to Controversies between two or more States;—between a State and Citizens of another State;[7]—between Citizens of different States;—between Citizens of the same State claiming Lands under Grants of different States, and between a State, or the Citizens thereof, and foreign States, Citizens, and Subjects.[8]

In all Cases affecting Ambassadors, other public Ministers and Consuls, and those in which a State shall be Party, the supreme Court shall have original Jurisdiction. In all the other Cases before mentioned, the supreme Court shall have appellate Jurisdiction, both as to Law and Fact, with such Exceptions, and under such Regulations as the Congress shall make.

The Trial of all Crimes, except in Cases of Impeachment, shall be by Jury; and such Trial shall be held in the State where the said Crimes shall have been committed; but when not committed within any State, the Trial shall be at such Place or Places as the Congress may by Law have directed.

Section 3. Treason against the United States, shall consist only in levying War against them, or in adhering to their Enemies, giving them Aid and Comfort. No Person shall be convicted of Treason unless on the Testimony of two Witnesses to the same overt Act, or on Confession in open Court.

The Congress shall have Power to declare the Punishment of Treason, but no Attainder of Treason shall work Corruption of Blood, or Forfeiture except during the Life of the Person attainted.

Article IV

Section 1. Full Faith and Credit shall be given in each State to the public Acts, Records, and judicial Proceedings of every other State. And the Congress may by general Laws prescribe the Manner in which such Acts, Records and Proceedings shall be proved, and the Effect thereof.

---

[7]These clauses were affected by the Eleventh Amendment.

[8]This provision has been affected by the Twenty-fifth Amendment.

Section 2. The Citizens of each State shall be entitled to all Privileges and Immunities of Citizens in the several States.

A Person charged in any State with Treason, Felony, or other Crime, who shall flee from Justice, and be found in another State, shall on Demand of the executive Authority of the State from which he fled, be delivered up, to be removed to the State having Jurisdiction of the Crime.

[No Person held to Service or Labour in one State, under the Laws thereof, escaping into another, shall, in Consequence of any Law or Regulation therein, be discharged from such Service or Labour, but shall be delivered up on Claim of the Party to whom such Service or Labour may be due.][9]

Section 3. New States may be admitted by the Congress into this Union; but no new State shall be formed or erected within the Jurisdiction of any other State; nor any State be formed by the Junction of two or more States, or Parts of States, without the Consent of the Legislatures of the States concerned as well as of the Congress.

The Congress shall have Power to dispose of and make all needful Rules and Regulations respecting the Territory or other-Property belonging to the United States; and nothing in this Constitution shall be so construed as to Prejudice any Claims of the United States, or of any particular State.

Section 4. The United States shall guarantee to every State in this Union a Republican Form of Government, and shall protect each of them against Invasion; and on Application of the Legislature, or of the Executive (when the Legislature cannot be convened) against domestic Violence.

Article V

The Congress, whenever two thirds of both Houses shall deem it necessary, shall propose Amendments to this Constitution, or, on the Application of the Legislatures of two thirds of the several States, shall call a Convention for proposing Amendments, which, in either Case, shall be valid to all Intents and Purposes, as Part of this Constitution, when ratified by the Legislatures of three fourths of the several States, or by Conventions in three fourths thereof, as the one or the other Mode of Ratification may be proposed by the Congress; Provided [that no Amendment which may be made prior to the Year One thousand eight hundred and eight shall in any Manner affect the first and fourth Clauses in the Ninth Section of the first Article; and][10] that no State, without its Consent, shall be deprived of its equal Suffrage in the Senate.

Article VI

All Debts contracted and Engagements entered into, before the Adoption of this Constitution, shall be as valid against the United States under this Constitution, as under the Confederation.

This Constitution, and the Laws of the United States which shall be made in Pursuance thereof; and all Treaties made, or which shall be made, under the Authority of the United States, shall be the supreme Law of the Land; and the judges in every State shall be bound thereby, any Thing in the Constitution or Laws of any State to the Contrary notwithstanding.

The Senators and Representatives before mentioned, and the Members of the several State Legislatures, and all executive and judicial Officers, both of the United States and of the several States, shall be bound by Oath or Affirmation, to support this Constitution; but no religious Test shall ever be required as a Qualification to any Office or public Trust under the United States.

Article VII

The Ratification of the Conventions of nine States, shall be sufficient for the Establishment of this Constitution between the States so ratifying the Same.

Done in Convention by the Unanimous Consent of the States present the Seventeenth Day of September in the Year of our Lord one thousand seven hundred and Eighty seven and of the Independence of the United States of America the Twelfth. IN WITNESS whereof We have hereunto subscribed our Names,

George Washington,
President and deputy from Virginia.

New Hampshire:	John Langdon, Nicholas Gilman.
Massachusetts:	Nathaniel Gorham, Rufus King.
Connecticut:	William Samuel Johnson, Roger Sherman.
New York:	Alexander Hamilton.
New Jersey:	William Livingston, David Brearley, William Paterson, Jonathan Dayton.
Pennsylvania:	Benjamin Franklin, Thomas Mifflin, Robert Morris, George Clymer, Thomas FitzSimons, Jared Ingersoll, James Wilson, Gouverneur Morris.
Delaware:	George Read, Gunning Bedford Jr., John Dickinson, Richard Bassett, Jacob Broom.
Maryland:	James McHenry, Daniel of St. Thomas Jenifer, Daniel Carroll.
Virginia:	John Blair, James Madison Jr.
North Carolina:	William Blount, Richard Dobbs Spaight, Hugh Williamson.
South Carolina:	John Rutledge, Charles Cotesworth Pinckney, Charles Pinckney, Pierce Butler.
Georgia:	William Few, Abraham Baldwin.

---

[9]This paragraph has been superseded by the Thirteenth Amendment.

[10]Obsolete.

[The language of the original Constitution, not including the amendments, was adopted by a convention of the states on September 17, 1787, and was subsequently ratified by the states on the following dates: Delaware, December 7, 1787; Pennsylvania, December 12, 1787; New Jersey, December 18, 1787; Georgia, January 2, 1788; Connecticut, January 9, 1788; Massachusetts, February 6, 1788; Maryland, April 28, 1788; South Carolina, May 23, 1788; New Hampshire, June 21, 1788.

Ratification was completed on June 21, 1788.

The Constitution subsequently was ratified by Virginia, June 25, 1788; New York, July 26, 1788; North Carolina, November 21, 1789; Rhode Island, May 29, 1790; and Vermont, January 10, 1791.]

AMENDMENTS

Amendment I

(First ten amendments ratified December 15, 1791)

Congress shall make no law respecting an establishment of religion, or prohibiting the free exercise thereof; or abridging the freedom of speech, or of the press; or the right of the people peaceably to assemble, and to petition the Government for a redress of grievances.

Amendment II

A well regulated Militia, being necessary to the security of a free State, the right of the people to keep and bear Arms, shall not be infringed.

Amendment III

No Soldier shall, in time of peace be quartered in any house, without the consent of the Owner, nor in time of war, but in a manner to be prescribed by law.

Amendment IV

The right of the people to be secure in their persons, houses, papers, and effects, against unreasonable searches and seizures, shall not be violated, and no Warrants shall issue, but upon probable cause, supported by Oath or affirmation, and particularly describing the place to be searched, and the persons or things to be seized.

Amendment V

No person shall be held to answer for a capital, or otherwise infamous crime, unless on a presentment or indictment of a Grand Jury, except in cases arising in the land or naval forces, or in the Militia, when in actual service in time of War or public danger; nor shall any person be subject for the same offence to be twice put in jeopardy of life or limb; nor shall be compelled in any criminal case to be a witness against himself, nor be deprived of life, liberty, or property, without due process of law; nor shall private property be taken for public use, without just compensation.

Amendment VI

In all criminal prosecutions, the accused shall enjoy the right to a speedy and public trial, by an impartial jury of the State and district wherein the crime shall have been committed, which district shall have been previously ascertained by law, and to be informed of the nature and cause of the accusation; to be confronted with the witnesses against him; to have compulsory process for obtaining witnesses in his favor; and to have the Assistance of Counsel for his defence.

Amendment VII

In Suits at common law, where the value in controversy shall exceed twenty dollars, the right of trial by jury shall be preserved, and no fact tried by a jury, shall be otherwise reexamined in any Court of the United States, than according to the rules of the common law.

Amendment VIII

Excessive bail shall not be required, nor excessive fines imposed, nor cruel and unusual punishments inflicted.

Amendment IX

The enumeration in the Constitution, of certain rights, shall not be construed to deny or disparage others retained by the people.

Amendment X

The powers not delegated to the United States by the Constitution, nor prohibited by it to the States, are reserved to the States respectively, or to the people.

Amendment XI

(Ratified February 7, 1795)

The Judicial power of the United States shall not be construed to extend to any suit in law or equity, commenced or prosecuted against one of the United States by Citizens of another State, or by Citizens or Subjects of any Foreign State.

Amendment XII

(Ratified June 15, 1804)

The Electors shall meet in their respective states and vote by ballot for President and Vice-President, one of whom, at least, shall not be an inhabitant of the same state with themselves; they shall name in their ballots the person voted for as President, and in distinct ballots the person voted for as Vice-President, and they shall make distinct lists of all persons voted for as President, and of all persons voted for as Vice-President, and of the number of votes for each, which lists they shall sign and certify, and transmit sealed to the seat of the government of the United States, directed to the President of the Senate;—The President of the Senate shall, in the presence of the Senate and House of Representatives, open all the certificates and the votes shall then be counted;—The person having the greatest number of votes for President, shall be the President, if such number be a majority of the whole number of Electors appointed; and if no person have such majority, then from the persons having the highest numbers not exceeding three on the list of those voted for as President, the House of Representative shall choose immediately, by ballot, the President. But in choosing the President, the votes shall be taken by states, the representation from each state having one vote; a quorum for this purpose shall consist of a member or members from two-thirds of the states, and a majority of all the states shall be necessary to a choice. [And if the House of Representatives shall not choose a President whenever the right of choice shall devolve upon them, before the fourth day of March next following, then the Vice-President shall act as President, as in the case of the death or other constitutional disability of the President.—][11] The person having the greatest number of votes as Vice-President, shall be the Vice-President, if such number be a majority of the whole number of Electors appointed, and if no person have a majority, then from the two highest numbers on the list, the Senate shall choose the Vice-President; a quorum for the purpose shall consist of two-thirds of the whole number of Senators, and a majority of the whole number shall be necessary to a choice. But no person constitutionally ineligible to the office of President shall be eligible to that of Vice-President of the United States.

Amendment XIII

(Ratified December 6, 1865)

Section 1. Neither slavery nor involuntary servitude, except as a punishment for crime whereof the party shall have been duly convicted, shall exist within the United States, or any place subject to their jurisdiction.

Section 2. Congress shall have power to enforce this article by appropriate legislation.

Amendment XIV

(Ratified July 9, 1868)

Section 1. All persons born or naturalized in the United States, and subject to the jurisdiction thereof, are citizens of the United States and of the State wherein they reside. No State shall make or enforce any law which shall abridge the privileges or immunities of citizens of the United States; nor shall any State deprive any person of life, liberty, or property, without due process of law; nor deny to any person within its jurisdiction the equal protection of the laws.

Section 2. Representatives shall be apportioned among the several States according to their respective numbers, counting the whole number of persons in each State, excluding Indians not taxed. But when the right to vote at any election for the choice of electors for President and Vice President of the United States, Representatives in Congress, the Executive and Judicial officers of a State, or the members of the Legislature thereof, is denied to any of the male inhabitants of such State, being twenty-one years of age,[12] and citizens of the United States, or in any way abridged, except for participation in rebellion, or other crime, the basis of representation therein shall be reduced in the proportion which the number of such male citizens shall bear to the whole number of male citizens twenty-one years of age in such State.

Section 3. No person shall be a Senator or Representative in Congress, or elector of President and Vice President, or hold any office, civil or military, under the United States, or under any State, who, having previously taken an oath, as a member of Congress, or as an officer of the United States, or as a member of any State legislature, or as an executive or judicial officer of any State, to support the Constitution of the United States, shall have engaged in insurrection or rebellion against the same, or given aid or comfort to the enemies thereof. But Congress may by a vote of two-thirds of each House, remove such disability.

Section 4. The validity of the public debt of the United States, authorized by law, including debts incurred for payment of pensions and bounties for services in suppressing insurrection or rebellion, shall not be questioned. But neither the United States nor any State shall assume or pay any debt or obligation incurred in aid of insurrection or rebellion against the United States, or any claim for the loss of emancipation of any slave; but all such debts, obligations and claims shall be held illegal and void.

Section 5. The Congress shall have power to enforce, by appropriate legislation, the provisions of this article.

Amendment XV

(Ratified February 3, 1870)

Section 1. The right of citizens of the United States to vote shall not be denied or abridged by the United States or by any State on account of race, color, or previous condition of servitude.

Section 2. The Congress shall have power to enforce this article by appropriate legislation.

Amendment XVI

(Ratified February 3, 1913)

The Congress shall have power to lay and collect taxes on incomes, from whatever source derived, without apportionment among the several States, and without regard to any census or enumeration.

Amendment XVII

(Ratified April 8, 1913)

The Senate of the United States shall be composed of two Senators from each State, elected by the people thereof, for six years; and each Senator shall have one vote. The electors in each State shall have the qualifications requisite for electors of the most numerous branch of the State legislatures.

When vacancies happen in the representation of any State in the Senate, the executive authority of such State shall issue writs of election to fill such vacancies: *Provided,* That the legislature of any State may empower the executive thereof to make temporary appointments until the people fill the vacancies by election as the legislature may direct.

This amendment shall not be so construed as to affect the election or term of any Senator chosen before it becomes valid as part of the Constitution.

Amendment XVIII

(Ratified January 16, 1919)[13]

Section 1. After one year from the ratification of this article the manufacture, sale, or transportation of intoxicating liquors within, the importation thereof into, or the exportation thereof

---

[11]The part in brackets has been superseded by Section 3 of the Twentieth Amendment.

[12]See the Nineteenth and Twenty-sixth Amendments.

---

[13]This Amendment was repealed by Section 1 of the Twenty-first Amendment.

from the United States and all territory subject to the jurisdiction thereof for beverage purposes is hereby prohibited.

Section 2. The Congress and the several States shall have concurrent power to enforce this article by appropriate legislation.

Section 3. This article shall be inoperative unless it shall have been ratified as an amendment to the Constitution by the legislatures of the several States, as provided in the Constitution, within seven years from the date of the submission hereof to the States by the Congress.

Amendment XIX

(Ratified August 18, 1920)

The right of citizens of the United States to vote shall not be denied or abridged by the United States or by any State on account of sex.

Congress shall have power to enforce this article by appropriate legislation.

Amendment XX

(Ratified January 23, 1933)

Section 1. The terms of the President and Vice President shall end at noon on the 20th day of January, and the terms of Senators and Representatives at noon on the 3d day of January, of the years in which such terms would have ended if this article had not been ratified; and the terms of their successors shall then begin.

Section 2. The Congress shall assemble at least once in every year, and such meeting shall begin at noon on the 3d day of January, unless they shall by law appoint a different day.

Section 3.[14] If, at the time fixed for the beginning of the term of the President, the President elect shall have died, the Vice President elect shall become President. If a President shall not have been chosen before the time fixed for the beginning of his term, or if the President elect shall have failed to qualify, then the Vice President elect shall act as President until a President shall have qualified; and the Congress may by law provide for the case wherein neither a President elect nor a Vice President elect shall have qualified, declaring who shall then act as President, or the manner in which one who is to act shall be selected, and such person shall act accordingly until a President or Vice President shall have qualified.

Section 4. The Congress may by law provide for the case of the death of any of the persons from whom the House of Representatives may choose a President whenever the right of choice shall have devolved upon them, and for the case of the death of any of the persons from whom the Senate may choose a Vice President whenever the right of choice shall have devolved upon them.

Section 5. Sections 1 and 2 shall take effect on the 15th day of October following the ratification of this article.

Section 6. This article shall be inoperative unless it shall have been ratified as an amendment to the Constitution by the legislatures of three-fourths of the several States within seven years from the date of its submission.

---

[14]See the Twenty-fifth Amendment.

Amendment XXI

(Ratified December 5, 1933)

Section 1. The eighteenth article of amendment to the Constitution of the United States is hereby repealed.

Section 2. The transportation or importation into any State, Territory, or possession of the United States for delivery or use therein of intoxicating liquors, in violation of the laws thereof, is hereby prohibited.

Section 3. This article shall be inoperative unless it shall have been ratified as an amendment to the Constitution by conventions in the several States, as provided in the Constitution, within seven years from the date of the submission hereof to the States by the Congress.

Amendment XXII

(Ratified February 27, 1951)

Section 1. No person shall be elected to the office of the President more than twice, and no person who has held the office of President, or acted as President, for more than two years of a term to which some other person was elected President shall be elected to the office of the President more than once. But this Article shall not apply to any person holding the office of President when this Article was proposed by the Congress, and shall not prevent any person who may be holding the office of President, or acting as President, during the term within which this Article become operative from holding the office of President or acting as President during the remainder of such term.

Section 2. This article shall be inoperative unless it shall have been ratified as an amendment to the Constitution by the legislatures of three-fourths of the several States within seven years from the date of its submission to the States by the Congress.

Amendment XXIII

(Ratified March 29, 1961)

Section 1. The District constituting the seat of Government of the United States shall appoint in such manner as the Congress may direct:

A number of electors of President and Vice President equal to the whole number of Senators and Representatives in Congress to which the District would be entitled if it were a State, but in no event more than the least populous State; they shall be in addition to those appointed by the States, but they shall be considered, for the purposes of the election of President and Vice President, to be electors appointed by a State; and they shall meet in the District and perform such duties as provided by the twelfth article of amendment.

Section 2. The Congress shall have power to enforce this article by appropriate legislation.

Amendment XXIV

(Ratified January 23, 1964)

Section 1. The right of citizens of the United States to vote in any primary or other election for President or Vice President, for electors for President or Vice President, or for Senator or Representative in Congress, shall not be denied or abridged by the United States or any State by reason of failure to pay any poll tax or other tax.

Section 2. The Congress shall have power to enforce this article by appropriate legislation.

Amendment XXV

(Ratified February 10, 1967)

Section 1. In case of the removal of the President from office or of his death or resignation, the Vice President shall become President.

Section 2. Whenever there is a vacancy in the office of the Vice President, the President shall nominate a Vice President who shall take office upon confirmation by a majority vote of both Houses of Congress.

Section 3. Whenever the President transmits to the President pro tempore of the Senate and the Speaker of the House of Representatives his written declaration that he is unable to discharge the powers and duties of his office, and until he transmits to them a written declaration to the contrary, such powers and duties shall be discharged by the Vice President as Acting President.

Section 4. Whenever the Vice President and a majority of either the principal officers of the executive departments or of such other body as Congress may by law provide, transmit to the President pro tempore of the Senate and the Speaker of the House of Representatives their written declaration that the President is unable to discharge the powers and duties of his office, the Vice President shall immediately assume the powers and duties of the office as Acting President.

Thereafter, when the President transmits to the President pro tempore of the Senate and the Speaker of the House of Representatives his written declaration that no inability exists, he shall resume the powers and duties of his office unless the Vice President and a majority of either the principal officers of the executive department or of such other body as Congress may by law provide, transmit within four days to the President pro tempore of the Senate and the Speaker of the House of Representatives their written declaration that the President is unable to discharge the powers and duties of his office. Thereupon Congress shall decide the issue, assembling within forty-eight hours for that purpose if not in session. If the Congress, within twenty-one days after receipt of the latter written declaration, or, if Congress is not in session, within twenty-one days after Congress is required to assemble, determines by two-thirds vote of both Houses that the President is unable to discharge the powers and duties of his office, the Vice President shall continue to discharge the same as Acting President; otherwise, the President shall resume the powers and duties of his office.

Amendment XXVI

(Ratified July 1, 1971)

Section 1. The right of citizens of the United States, who are eighteen years of age or older, to vote shall not be denied or abridged by the United States or by any State on account of age.

Section 2. The Congress shall have power to enforce this article by appropriate legislation.

Amendment XXVII

(Ratified May 7, 1992)

No law varying the compensation for the services of the Senators and Representatives shall take effect, until an election of Representatives shall have intervened.

APPENDIX B

Justices of the Supreme Court

Appointment Number/Justice[a]	Position	Appointing President	Years of Service[b]
1. John Jay	Chief justice	Washington	1789–1795
2. John Rutledge[c]	Associate justice	Washington	1789–1791
3. William Cushing	Associate justice	Washington	1789–1810
4. James Wilson	Associate justice	Washington	1789–1798
5. John Blair Jr.	Associate justice	Washington	1789–1796
6. James Iredell	Associate justice	Washington	1790–1799
7. Thomas Johnson	Associate justice	Washington	1791–1793
8. William Paterson	Associate justice	Washington	1793–1806
9. John Rutledge[d]	Chief justice	Washington	1795
10. Samuel Chase	Associate justice	Washington	1796–1811
11. Oliver Ellsworth	Chief justice	Washington	1796–1800
12. Bushrod Washington	Associate justice	J. Adams	1798–1829
13. Alfred Moore	Associate justice	J. Adams	1799–1804
14. John Marshall	Chief justice	J. Adams	1801–1835
15. William Johnson	Associate justice	Jefferson	1804–1834
16. Henry Brockholst Livingston	Associate justice	Jefferson	1806–1823
17. Thomas Todd	Associate justice	Jefferson	1807–1826
18. Gabriel Duvall	Associate justice	Madison	1811–1835
19. Joseph Story	Associate justice	Madison	1811–1845
20. Smith Thompson	Associate justice	Monroe	1823–1843
21. Robert Trimble	Associate justice	J. Q. Adams	1826–1828
22. John McLean	Associate justice	Jackson	1829–1861
23. Henry Baldwin	Associate justice	Jackson	1830–1844
24. James Moore Wayne	Associate justice	Jackson	1835–1867
25. Roger Brooke Taney	Chief justice	Jackson	1836–1864
26. Philip Pendleton Barbour	Associate justice	Jackson	1836–1841
27. John Catron	Associate justice	Jackson	1837–1865
28. John McKinley	Associate justice	Van Buren	1837–1852
29. Peter Vivian Daniel	Associate justice	Van Buren	1841–1860

(contd.)

| --- | --- | --- | --- |
30. Samuel Nelson	Associate justice	Tyler	1845–1872
31. Levi Woodbury	Associate justice	Polk	1846–1851
32. Robert Cooper Grier	Associate justice	Polk	1846–1870
33. Benjamin Robbins Curtis	Associate justice	Fillmore	1851–1857
34. John Archibald Campbell	Associate justice	Pierce	1853–1861
35. Nathan Clifford	Associate justice	Buchanan	1858–1881
36. Noah Haynes Swayne	Associate justice	Lincoln	1862–1881
37. Samuel Freeman Miller	Associate justice	Lincoln	1862–1890
38. David Davis	Associate justice	Lincoln	1862–1877
39. Stephen Johnson Field	Associate justice	Lincoln	1863–1897
40. Salmon Portland Chase	Chief justice	Lincoln	1864–1873
41. William Strong	Associate justice	Grant	1870–1880
42. Joseph P. Bradley	Associate justice	Grant	1870–1892
43. Ward Hunt	Associate justice	Grant	1872–1882
44. Morrison Remick Waite	Chief justice	Grant	1874–1888
45. John Marshall Harlan	Associate justice	Hayes	1877–1911
46. William Burnham Woods	Associate justice	Hayes	1880–1887
47. Stanley Matthews	Associate justice	Garfield	1881–1889
48. Horace Gray	Associate justice	Arthur	1881–1902
49. Samuel Blatchford	Associate justice	Arthur	1882–1893
50. Lucius Quintus Cincinnatus Lamar	Associate justice	Cleveland	1888–1893
51. Melville Weston Fuller	Chief justice	Cleveland	1888–1910
52. David Josiah Brewer	Associate justice	Harrison	1889–1910
53. Henry Billings Brown	Associate justice	Harrison	1890–1906
54. George Shiras Jr.	Associate justice	Harrison	1892–1903
55. Howell Edmunds Jackson	Associate justice	Harrison	1893–1895
56. Edward Douglass White[c]	Associate justice	Cleveland	1894–1910
57. Rufus Wheeler Peckham	Associate justice	Cleveland	1895–1909
58. Joseph McKenna	Associate justice	McKinley	1898–1925
59. Oliver Wendell Holmes Jr.	Associate justice	T. Roosevelt	1902–1932
60. William Rufus Day	Associate justice	T. Roosevelt	1903–1922
61. William Henry Moody	Associate justice	T. Roosevelt	1906–1910
62. Horace Harmon Lurton	Associate justice	Taft	1909–1914
63. Charles Evans Hughes[c]	Associate justice	Taft	1910–1916
64. Edward Douglass White[d]	Chief justice	Taft	1910–1921
65. Willis Van Devanter	Associate justice	Taft	1910–1937
66. Joseph Rucker Lamar	Associate justice	Taft	1910–1916
67. Mahlon Pitney	Associate justice	Taft	1912–1922
68. James Clark McReynolds	Associate justice	Wilson	1914–1941
69. Louis Dembitz Brandeis	Associate justice	Wilson	1916–1939
70. John Hessin Clarke	Associate justice	Wilson	1916–1922
71. William Howard Taft	Chief justice	Harding	1921–1930
72. George Sutherland	Associate justice	Harding	1922–1938
73. Pierce Butler	Associate justice	Harding	1922–1939
74. Edward Terry Sanford	Associate justice	Harding	1923–1930
75. Harlan Fiske Stone[c]	Associate justice	Coolidge	1925–1941
76. Charles Evans Hughes[d]	Chief justice	Hoover	1930–1941
77. Owen Josephus Roberts	Associate justice	Hoover	1930–1945
78. Benjamin Nathan Cardozo	Associate justice	Hoover	1932–1938
79. Hugo Lafayette Black	Associate justice	F. Roosevelt	1937–1971
80. Stanley Forman Reed	Associate justice	F. Roosevelt	1938–1957
81. Felix Frankfurter	Associate justice	F. Roosevelt	1939–1962
82. William Orville Douglas	Associate justice	F. Roosevelt	1939–1975

(contd.)

Appointment Number/Justice[a]	Position	Appointing President	Years of Service[b]
83. Francis William (Frank) Murphy	Associate justice	F. Roosevelt	1940–1949
84. Harlan Fiske Stone[d]	Chief justice	F. Roosevelt	1941–1946
85. James Francis Byrnes	Associate justice	F. Roosevelt	1941–1942
86. Robert Houghwout Jackson	Associate justice	F. Roosevelt	1941–1954
87. Wiley Blount Rutledge	Associate justice	F. Roosevelt	1943–1949
88. Harold Hitz Burton	Associate justice	Truman	1945–1958
89. Fred Moore Vinson	Chief justice	Truman	1946–1953
90. Tom Campbell Clark	Associate justice	Truman	1949–1967
91. Sherman Minton	Associate justice	Truman	1949–1956
92. Earl Warren	Chief justice	Eisenhower	1953–1969
93. John Marshall Harlan	Associate justice	Eisenhower	1955–1971
94. William Joseph Brennan Jr.	Associate justice	Eisenhower	1956–1990
95. Charles Evans Whittaker	Associate justice	Eisenhower	1957–1962
96. Potter Stewart	Associate justice	Eisenhower	1958–1981
97. Byron Raymond White	Associate justice	Kennedy	1962–1993
98. Arthur Joseph Goldberg	Associate justice	Kennedy	1962–1965
99. Abe Fortas	Associate justice	Johnson	1965–1969
100. Thurgood Marshall	Associate justice	Johnson	1967–1991
101. Warren Earl Burger	Chief justice	Nixon	1969–1986
102. Harry Andrew Blackmun	Associate justice	Nixon	1970–1994
103. Lewis Franklin Powell Jr.	Associate justice	Nixon	1971–1987
104. William Hubbs Rehnquist[c]	Associate justice	Nixon	1971–1986
105. John Paul Stevens	Associate justice	Ford	1975–
106. Sandra Day O'Connor	Associate justice	Reagan	1981–
107. William Hubbs Rehnquist[d]	Chief justice	Reagan	1986–
108. Antonin Scalia	Associate justice	Reagan	1986–
109. Anthony McLeod Kennedy	Associate justice	Reagan	1988–
110. David H. Souter	Associate justice	Bush	1990–
111. Clarence Thomas	Associate justice	Bush	1991–
112. Ruth Bader Ginsburg	Associate justice	Clinton	1993–
113. Stephen G. Breyer	Associate justice	Clinton	1994–

[a]Ordered according to date of appointment.

[b]Begin with date of Senate confirmation or date of recess appointment (whichever occurred first); end with date of service termination.

[c]Served subsequently as chief justice.

[d]Served previously as associate justice.

Credits